Pronunciation Key

The pronunciation key shows a letter, a letter with a diacritical mark, a combination of letters, or a symbol for each sound. Next to these pronunciation guides are familiar words. These words show what sound is being described.

a sand, fat
ā ate, tame
â bare, chair
ä father, car

b box, rub
ch cheese, itch
d do, rod

e sent, bed
ē me, easy
ėr fern, curb

f foot, off
g gas, egg
h he, heart

i fit, sip
ī bike, mile

j jump
k oak

l love, fill
m me, rim

n in, new
ng long, song

o pot, bond
ō rope, sew, so
ô fort, call
oi noise, boy
ou sound, mouse

p push, cap
r red, tar

s sit, miss
sh shine, dash

t toe, mat
th thick
th those, feather

u run, bump
u̇ pull
ü rule, cool
ū cute, music

v visit, cover
w wax, away
y yes

z zipper, zoo
zh treasure

ə sounds like:
a in agree, husband
e in waken, caper
i in animal, magical
o in seldom, bacon
u in minus, industry

DICTIONARY
of basic words

Based on the
Wolfe High Correlation Word List
Compiled Under the Direction of
Dr. Josephine B. Wolfe
Director of Language Arts Research
Chestnut Hill College

Day A. Perry, Editor
M. Hughes Miller, Project Coordinator

 CHILDRENS PRESS, CHICAGO

Library of Congress Catalog Card Number: 73-86343

10 11 12 13 14 15 16 17 18 19 20 21 22 23 24 25 R 75

PREFACE

The DICTIONARY OF BASIC WORDS is a practical reference work designed to meet the requirements of those who need an intermediate dictionary with a limited number of words. Thus the 21,000 words in the DICTIONARY OF BASIC WORDS have been carefully selected for their direct relationship to the basic vocabulary needs of those who have outgrown a beginning dictionary but do not want or cannot use the usual intermediate dictionary containing 40,000 or more words.

The final word list for the DICTIONARY OF BASIC WORDS is based on the Wolfe High Correlation Word List compiled by Dr. Josephine B. Wolfe, Director of Language Arts Research at Chestnut Hill College, Philadelphia, Pennsylvania. Dr. Wolfe, an internationally known linguist and language arts teacher, is also the senior editor of *English: Your Language,* grades 1-9, published by Allyn and Bacon, and former Director of Language Arts in the graduate school at the University of Scranton.

In compiling the Wolfe High Correlation Word List, Dr. Wolfe and her staff conducted extensive research on the words used in 38 textbook series for grades 1-6. The subject areas included reading, spelling, mathematics, science, social studies, health, and language arts. In addition, a large number of juvenile trade books were also analyzed. Statistical correlations were made, and those words showing a high frequency of use formed the basic list. These words were then checked against other outstanding word lists, such as the Dale List of 3000 Familiar Words, the Dolch List of Primary Words, Gates' Reading Vocabulary for the Primary Grades, and Rinsland's Basic Vocabulary of Elementary School Children. A final check was carried out by grouping related words in a variety of ways to see if any important words had somehow been left out.

The definitions and sample sentences for the DICTIONARY OF BASIC WORDS were created by a staff of experienced dictionary writers under the direction of the editor, Day A. Perry. All definitions are written in simple and concise language, and are supported by sample sentences which enable the reader to further understand the meaning by seeing the word used in context.

Finally, more than 2000 full-color illustrations add to the effectiveness of the DICTIONARY OF BASIC WORDS as a modern intermediate dictionary designed for today's students.

HOW TO USE THE DICTIONARY

The DICTIONARY OF BASIC WORDS shows how words are spelled, how they are pronounced, what they mean, and how they are used in sentences. This information has been arranged carefully to help you learn about words.

ALPHABETICAL ORDER

The words in dictionaries are arranged in *alphabetical order,* from A through Z. All words beginning with the same letter of the alphabet are grouped together. In each letter group, the words are again listed in alphabetical order. For example, words beginning with **ad** are listed before those beginning with **al.** To look up **alarm,** first turn to the **A** section of the dictionary. Then look for the words beginning with **al.** Near the beginning of the **al** words you will find the word—**alarm.**

This alphabetical order continues throughout the dictionary. Each word in the dictionary is listed alphabetically according to its first letter, its second letter, its third letter, and so on. For example, **about** comes before **alarm** because **ab** comes before **al.** In words like **barrel** and **base,** you look at the third letter to find the order. In words like **carpenter** and **carpet,** you must look at the sixth letter to find where the word is placed, because the first five letters of these two words are identical.

There are *no* exceptions to this alphabetical order. The arrangement is not altered by a word that begins with a capital letter (**America**), or one that has a hyphen (**old-fashioned**), or one that has an apostrophe (**can't**). These words, as well as word combinations (**ice cream, alarm clock**), are listed according to their letter-by-letter alphabetical order.

GUIDE WORDS

To help you quickly find the word you want in the dictionary, there are *guide words* set in boldface type at the top of each page. These guide words are the *first* and *last* words on that page. For example, the guide words for page 41, shown below, are **barn** and **baseball.**

Barn is a guide word because it is the first entry on the page. **Baseball** is a guide word because it is the last entry. Words such as **barnyard, barrel, barrette,** and **base** are on this page because they fall in alphabetical order between the guide words.

Below is a section of page 106, showing the guide words at the top of the page and the entries for these words on the page. (The middle of the page has been removed to save space.)

finding fault. *The landlord turned up the heat because of the tenant's complaints about his cold apartment.* 2. a legal charge against someone. *The man swore out a complaint against the boys who trampled on his flowers.* 3. illness; something causing pain. *She had to go to the doctor with her stomach complaint.* **com plaints.**
com plete (kəm plēt′), *v.* 1. to finish. *The new*

com pound (kom′pound for 1–3, kompound′ for 4), *n.* 1. a chemical substance formed by the combination of two or more elements. *Water is a compound of hydrogen and oxygen.* 2. a mixture of two or more things. *His feeling about going to Europe was a compound of happiness and sadness.* **com pounds.**
adj. 3. formed of two or more parts. *In English*

the way the parts of a thing are put together. *In general science we study the composition of substances.* **com po si tions.**

is concerned in the Drama Club. 2. worried. *The mayor is concerned by the traffic problem.*
con cern ing (kən sėr′ning), *prep.* having to do

You can see that the guide words for page 106 are **complete** and **concerning. Complete** is the first entry word on the page, or the first entry in the left-hand column. **Concerning** is the last entry word on the page, or the last entry in the right-hand column. All the words which fall in alphabetical order between **complete** and **concerning** will be found on this page.

If the word you are looking for comes in alphabetical order before the first guide word, turn the pages back to find it. If the word you are looking for comes in alphabetical order after the second guide word, turn the pages forward to find it.

Look at the section of page 106 again. In the material above **complete** the word *complaints* appears in boldface type. Because *complaints* is part of the entry for **complaint** which begins on the preceding page, it cannot be a guide word. Remember, guide words are the first and last entry words on a page.

THE PARTS OF AN ENTRY

Below is a sample entry. It has been enlarged to make it easier to study. The parts used in every entry in the DICTIONARY OF BASIC WORDS are identified by name and are located by the red lines.

1. The **entry word,** in boldface type, is the word being defined. The **entry word** shows how to spell the word and how to divide the word.
2. The **pronunciation,** enclosed in parentheses, shows how to pronounce the entry word correctly.
3. The **part of speech,** abbreviated and shown in italics, tells how the entry word is used in sentences.
4. The **definition** explains the meaning or meanings of the entry word. Each different meaning is numbered.
5. The **example sentences,** in italics, show how the entry word is used in a sentence. There is at least one example sentence for each definition.
6. The **inflectional forms,** in boldface type, show how the meaning of the entry word may be changed by adding different endings.

Each part of an entry is explained in detail on the following pages.

1. Entry word

2. Pronunciation

3. Part of speech

4. Definition

alarm (ə lärm′), *n.* 1. a warning that danger is near. *The alarm went from farmer to farmer that bad weather was coming.* 2. a thing that gives an alarm. *The firemen ran to their truck when they heard the fire alarm.* 3. a sudden fear. *The birds flew away in alarm when they saw the cat.* **alarms.** *v.* 4. to warn of danger. *The smoke in the house alarmed me, especially when I remembered I forgot to turn off the stove.* 5. to fill with anxiety and fear of danger. *The man crossing the desert was alarmed because he had no more water.* **alarms, alarmed, alarm ing.**

5. Example sentence

6. Inflectional forms

1. ENTRY WORD

The entry word is the word being defined. It appears in boldface type and is always set to the left of the other lines in the entry. In the example, the entry word is **alarm.**

> **alarm** (ə lärm′), *n.* 1. a warning that danger is near. *The alarm went from farmer to farmer that bad weather was coming.* 2. a thing that gives an

Most of the entries in this dictionary are one-word entries. Sometimes, however, two or more words go together to make a familiar word combination. When that happens, the word combination is treated as a *single* entry word. Some of the word combinations found in the DICTIONARY OF BASIC WORDS are: **alarm clock, frying pan, post office,** and **United States.**

Variant Spellings

Besides showing the word being defined, the entry word shows the correct spelling of that word. There are some words that have more than one correct spelling. These second spellings are called variant forms or spellings. The DICTIONARY OF BASIC WORDS shows all variant spellings. The spelling listed first is the preferred spelling, the one used most often.

Look at the entry for **fiber.** The entry word reads **fi ber** or **fi bre.** Both spellings are correct, but the first one, **fi ber,** is the preferred spelling.

> **fi ber** or **fi bre** (fī′bər), *n.* 1. a part that is like a thread. *Muscles are made up of many fibers. The fibers of cotton are made into yarn.* 2. the

How to Divide a Word

When an entry word has more than one vowel sound in it, it appears in the DICTIONARY OF BASIC WORDS with spaces between groups of letters. These spaces break the entry word into *syllables.* A *syllable* is a part of a word which consists of a single vowel sound. Knowing the syllables in a word helps you to:

1. Pronounce the word correctly
2. Spell the word correctly
3. Divide the word correctly at the end of a line

Suppose you were writing this sentence on a short line: *The band has a new arrangement of this song.* You might have to divide **arrangement** and put part of it on the next line. How would you divide it? The entry for **arrangement** on page 24 of the DICTIONARY OF BASIC WORDS shows you how to do it.

> **ar range ment** (ə rānj′mənt), *n.* 1. an establishment of order; a fixing of position. *The arrangement of furniture in our living room is still not settled. A flower arrangement was in the middle of the table.* 2. the order in which things appear. *The arrangement of words in your diction-*

Arrangement can be divided either **ar-rangement** or **arrange-ment.** Your sentence could be written:

The band has a new arrange-ment of this song.   or   *The band has a new ar-rangement of this song.*

Single Letter Syllables

Sometimes the beginning or ending of a word has a syllable consisting of only a single letter. These single letter syllables *should not* stand alone at the end or the beginning of a line. For this reason, in the DICTIONARY OF BASIC WORDS there is no space between a single letter syllable and the following or preceding syllable. For example, the word **about** has two distinct sounds and, therefore, two syllables. However, the first syllable, **a,** is a single letter and should not be separated at the end of a line in writing. Thus, the entry word appears as **about,** not as **a bout.**

The word **dictionary** has four distinct sounds and four syllables. Because the last syllable, **y,** consists of a single letter, the entry appears as **dic tion ary.** The last syllable, **y,** should not be separated from the preceding syllable, **ar.**

Different Meanings

Some entry words have two or more very different meanings. These words have a small number printed after them, to show that there is another entry word spelled the same way. Look at the entry for **arm.**

> **arm**[1] (ärm), *n.* 1. the part of the body which is between the shoulder and the hand. *To raise your hand, you must lift your arm.* 2. anything shaped like an arm or used like an arm. *Rest your elbows on the arms of that chair.* **arms.**
> **arm**[2] (ärm), *n.* 1. a weapon used in fighting. *Guns, knives, and clubs are arms. The soldiers prepared their arms for the battle.* 2. *pl.* symbols used on a coat of arms to represent a person, a family, a city, a government, etc. *Long ago, soldiers and kings displayed their arms on a coat worn over their armor.* **arms.**
> *v.* 3. to supply with weapons. *The Indians were armed with tomahawks and with bows and arrows.* 4. to prepare for battle by obtaining weapons. *The pirates armed themselves for the attack.* **arms, armed, arm ing.**

There are two entries for **arm.** By reading the definitions for each entry you can see that although the words are spelled the same, they have two completely different meanings. The first entry, **arm**[1], means a part of the body between the shoulder and the hand. The second entry, **arm**[2], means a weapon used in fighting. When you see a small number after an entry word, be sure to look at the other numbered entries for that word until you find the correct definition.

2. PRONUNCIATION

The pronunciation of the entry word appears immediately after the entry word on the first line of each entry. The pronunciation, enclosed in parentheses, uses symbols and letters to show how to pronounce the entry word correctly.

To understand the pronunciation symbols and letters, use either the full pronunciation key (shown below and on the inside front cover of the DICTIONARY OF BASIC WORDS) or the short pronunciation key (at the bottom of most of the right-hand pages of the dictionary).

Full Pronunciation Key

Because there are many more sounds in the English language than there are letters a special code has been developed to show these sounds. The full pronunciation key shows a letter, a letter with a diacritical mark, a combination of letters, or a symbol for each sound. Next to these pronunciation guides are familiar words. These words show what sound is being described. For example, when you see **â** in the pronunciation of an entry word, you know that the **â** in that entry word is pronounced like the **â** in **bare** or **chair**.

a sand, fat	**l** love, fill	**u** run, bump
ā ate, tame	**m** me, rim	**u̇** pull
â bare, chair		**ü** rule, cool
ä father, car	**n** in, new	**ū** cute, music
	ng long, song	
b box, rub		
ch cheese, itch		**v** visit, cover
d do, rod	**o** pot, bond	**w** wax, away
	ō rope, sew, sc	**y** yes
e sent, bed	**ô** fort, call	
ē me, easy	**oi** noise, boy	
ėr fern, curb	**ou** sound, mouse	
		z zipper, zoo
		zh treasure
f foot, off	**p** push, cap	
g gas, egg	**r** red, tar	
h he, heart		
	s sit, miss	**ə** sounds like:
i fit, sip	**sh** shine, dash	a in agree, husband
ī bike, mile		e in waken, caper
	t toe, mat	i in animal, magical
j jump	**th** thick	o in seldom, bacon
k oak	~~th~~ those, feather	u in minus, industry

Short Pronunciation Key

The short pronunciation key, shown below, lists the important vowel symbols and the difficult consonant sounds used in the pronunciations.

sand, āte, bâre, fäther; sent, mē, fėrn; fit, bīke; pot, rōpe, fôrt; run, pùll, rüle, cūte; noise, sounɑ; ch, cheese; ng, long; th, thick; ᵗʰ, those; zh, treasure; ə = a in about, e in waken, i in animal, o in seldom, and u in minus.

In the short pronunciation key only sample words are given. Within these words, the key symbols appear in boldface type. An unmarked **a** has the same sound as the **a** in **sand.** The long **ā** has the same pronunciation as the **a** in **āte.** The pronunciation for **th** is the same as the **th** in **thick.**

Most of the time you can use the short form to find the pronunciation you need to know. However, this short form does not list all of the symbols. If you cannot find the symbol you need, use the full pronunciation key on the inside front cover.

Diacritical Marks

The marks over certain letters in the pronunciation key are diacritical marks. These show special vowel sounds. Some of these are the umlaut (¨), the circumflex (ˆ), and the long vowel sound (‾). A symbol called the schwa, written **ə**, is also used to show a special sound. The schwa can represent any vowel, and is used to signify that a vowel is not stressed. Examples of the use of the schwa are given below.

ə—a, in **a**gree; e, in wak**e**n; i, in per**i**l; o, in bac**o**n; u, in min**u**s

Accent Marks

Accent marks are used in the pronunciation to show how strongly each syllable in the entry word is pronounced. Two kinds of accent marks are used. The accent in heavy type (′) is a primary accent. The syllable followed by a heavy accent mark is stressed or pronounced more strongly than the other syllable or syllables in the entry word. For example, **ad vise** (əd vīz′) is a two syllable entry. It has a primary accent mark to show that the second syllable, **vīz′,** is stressed. **Dan ger ous** (dān′ jər əs) is a three syllable entry. The syllable with the primary accent mark, **dān′,** is stressed, and the other two syllables are not stressed.

Some words with three or more syllables have two stressed syllables. Usually only one of the syllables has a primary accent mark (′). The other stressed syllable is marked with a secondary accent mark (′). This secondary accent is used to show syllables that are not stressed as strongly as the syllable marked with the primary accent. The secondary accent mark is written in lighter type (′). For example, **day time** (dā′tīm′) is a two syllable entry. **Dā′** receives the primary accent, and **tīm′,** the secondary accent. If you say daytime to yourself, you will be able to see the difference between primary and secondary accents.

Many words have unaccented syllables as well as accented syllables. These unaccented syllables are pronounced with the least amount of stress. For example, **ag ri cul ture** (ag′rə kùl′chər) is a four syllable entry. The first syllable, **ag′,** has a primary accent and receives the greater stress. The second syllable, **rə,** is unstressed. The third syllable, **kul',** receives the lighter stress, and the last syllable, **chər,** is unstressed. Say the word to yourself, and you will hear the difference between stressed and unstressed syllables.

Entry words of one syllable never have accent marks. For example, **add (ad)** is a one syllable entry and does not have an accent mark.

Pronouncing a Word

To pronounce a word correctly simply substitute sounds for the symbols given. Look at the pronunciation for **alarm.**

> **alarm** (ə lärm**/**), *n*. 1. a warning that danger is

The pronunciation for **alarm** is (**ə lärm'**). By looking at the pronunciation key you can see what sounds to use. The first symbol **ə** has the same sound as the **a** in **about.** The second letter **l** sounds like **l** in **love.** The third, **ä,** sounds like the **a** in **father.** The fourth sound is **r,** as in **red,** and the last sound is **m** as in **me.** Note that the primary accent is on the second syllable. Put all the sounds together, stressing the second syllable, and you can correctly pronounce **alarm.**

Pronunciation symbols may be confusing and difficult at first. But if you remember that each symbol stands for only one sound, you will find that the symbols are easy to understand and help you to pronounce unfamiliar words correctly.

Variant Pronunciations

For most entry words, only one pronunciation is given. However, there are some words that have more than one correct pronunciation. These additional pronunciations are given in the dictionary. For example, **adult** has two pronunciations. Look at the entry, shown below.

> **adult** (ə dult**/**, ad**/**ult), *adj*. 1. having full size
> and strength. *He is an adult dog, weighing more*

Adult may be pronounced as **ə dult'** with the accent on the second syllable, or it may be pronounced **ad'ult** with the accent on the first syllable. Either pronunciation is correct, though the first is preferred.

Sometimes a word is pronounced one way when it is used as one part of speech and a different way when it is used as another part of speech. The word **absent** is an example of this. Look at the entry.

> **ab sent** (ab**/**snt for 1 and 2, ab sent**/** for 3),
> *adj*. 1. away; not here. *That boy always seems*
> *to be absent on days when there is a ball game.*
> 2. not existing. *Feelings of happiness were absent*
> *after he finished making his radio, and it didn't*
> *work.* **ab sent ly,** *adv*.
> *v*. 3. to stay away on purpose. *You cannot absent*
> *yourself from class without a note from the principal.*
> **ab sents, ab sent ed, ab sent ing.**

When **absent** is an adjective, as in definitions 1 and 2, it is pronounced **ab'snt.** The accent is on the first syllable. But, when **absent** is used as a verb as in definition number 3, it is pronounced **ab sent′**. The second syllable is accented.

Occasionally, an entry word will list three pronunciations. The first pronunciation is correct no matter what part of speech the entry word is. The remaining pronunciations show the variant pronunciations for the different parts of speech. For example, look at the entry for **address.**

> **ad dress** (ə dres′, ad′res for 1–3, ə dres′ for 4–6), *n.* 1. a speech or writing. *Abraham Lincoln's Gettysburg Address has been remembered for more than one hundred years.* 2. the place where a person lives or works and where mail may be sent. *The package was sent to his business address.* 3. a direction on a piece of mail which tells where it is to be sent and to whom. *A zip code is included in most addresses today.* **ad dress-es.**
> *v.* 4. to put on a piece of mail where it should go. *Be sure that you address the envelope correctly.* 5. to speak to; write to. *The speaker addressed us on the reasons why we should try to be better students.* 6. to direct the energies of (oneself). *By addressing himself seriously to his work, the boy got good grades.* **ad dress es, ad dressed, ad-dress ing.**

Three pronunciations are given for **ad dress, (ə dres′, ad′res for 1-3, ə dres′ for 4-6).** The first one, set off by a comma, shows you that the pronunciation **ə dres′** may be used for all the meanings of the word. However, if you wish, you may use **ad′res** for the noun definitions 1, 2, and 3, and **ə dres′** for the verb definitions 4, 5, and 6.

You may choose to pronounce words of this type the same way all the time, or to vary your pronunciation. Both pronunciations are correct. However, the first pronunciation is the preferred one.

3. PART OF SPEECH

Following the pronunciation of the entry word is an abbreviation which shows the part of speech of the entry word. The part of speech tells how the word should be used in a sentence. The abbreviations used in the DICTIONARY OF BASIC WORDS to represent the parts of speech are:

n.	noun	*adv.*	adverb
pron.	pronoun	*prep.*	preposition
v.	verb	*conj.*	conjunction
adj.	adjective	*inter.*	interjection

indefinite article
definite article

Parts of Speech and Their Definitions

Study the definitions on the following page. They show how each part of speech can be identified.

A noun is the name of a person, place, thing, or idea.

magazine (mag′ ə zēn′, mag′ ə zēn), *n.*

The magazine was printed in England.

A pronoun is used in place of a noun. It can stand for a person, place, thing, or idea.

we (wē, wi), *pron.*

We are very happy to see you.

A verb is a word that shows action, makes a statement, or expresses being.

amuse (ə muz′), *v.*

Toys amuse young children.

An adjective is a word used to modify a noun or a pronoun. It is used to describe. It answers questions such as: What kind? Which one? How many?

mathematical (math ə mat′ a kl), *adj.*

He has a mathematical mind.

An adverb is used to modify a verb, adjective, or other adverb. It tells the following: Where? When? How often? To what extent?

above (ə buv′), *adv.*

Her class scored above ours in language skills.

A conjunction is used to connect words or groups of words.

and (and, ənd, an), *conj.*

He came home and cooked dinner.

An interjection is used to show strong and sudden feeling. It is separated from the rest of a sentence by a comma or an exclamation point.

welcome (wel′kəm), *inter.*

Welcome, we have been waiting for you.

An article is used as an adjective. **A** and **an** are indefinite articles. **The** is a definite article.

an (ən, an), *indefinite article.*

He ate an apple after dinner.

Many words can be only one part of speech. However, some are considered to be more than one part of speech, depending upon how they are used in a sentence. Within each entry in the DICTIONARY OF BASIC WORDS the definitions are arranged according to the part of speech. For example, all of a word's noun meanings are grouped together. Then all of its adjective meanings are similarly arranged.

Look at the entry below. The *n.* after the pronunciation tells you that **answer** is a noun.

an swer (an′sər), *n.* 1. a reply. *Send my answer to his letter quickly.* 2. a solution. *I had the answer to that problem in arithmetic.* **an swers.**
v. 3. to reply to. *He always answers letters on the same day he gets them.* 4. to act in response to. *Will someone please answer that telephone?* 5. to respond or reply. *He answered with a shake of his head. When we ask a question, our teacher always answers.* **an swers, an swered, an-swer ing.**

Now look at the fourth line of the entry. Here you see a *v.* This shows that **answer** is also used as a verb. Whether **answer** is a noun or a verb depends upon how it is used in a sentence.

Answer is a noun when it tells the name of something. It is a verb when it tells of some action. In the example sentence for definition 2, *I had the answer to that problem in arithmetic,* answer tells you what the speaker had. Answer acts as a noun. In the sentence for definition 5, *He answered with a shake of his head,* answer is a verb. It tells of some action. What did he do? He answered.

Most words are used as only one part of speech and will have only one group of definitions. However, when you are looking up an unfamiliar word in the dictionary be sure to see how the word is used in the sentence. This will help you know which part of speech the word is and which part of the entry to look at.

4. DEFINITION

In the DICTIONARY OF BASIC WORDS, the definition follows the part of speech in each entry. The definition tells you the meaning or meanings of the entry word. When there is more than one meaning of a word, each meaning is numbered. If the entry word has only one meaning, no number appears before the definition. Look at the entries below.

air port (âr′pôrt′), *n.* a landing place for airplanes. *The new airport has a control tower that tells planes when to take off; places to store planes; repair shops; ticket counters; lunch counters; and a drug store.* **air ports.**

rad ish (rad′ish), *n.* the root of a garden plant, usually red or white. *Radishes have a sharp taste and are often eaten in salads.* **rad ish es.**

The definitions for **airport** and **radish** are not numbered because each has only one meaning. In an entry with two or more definitions, the definitions are numbered in order from the beginning of the entry to the end. When an entry word has more than one definition, the most widely used meaning is listed first and the least common meaning is last.

When the entry word can be two or more different parts of speech (see page xiv), the definitions are grouped by the part of speech to which they apply. The definitions for the commonest part of speech are listed first and the least common listed last. This grouping by part of speech, however, does not change the numbering.

Look at the entry for **aim.**

aim (ām), *n.* 1. pointing. *His aim was so good that he never missed the target.* 2. a purpose; intention that one hopes will succeed. *His aim was to be a doctor.* **aims.**
v. 3. to point at some kind of object. *The hunter aimed his gun at the lion, fired, and missed.* 4. to direct. *The principal aimed his speech at the pupils who broke the rules.* 5. to try. *"We aim to please" said the big sign in the store.* **aims, aimed, aim ing.**

Aim has five definitions, numbered in order from 1 through 5. The noun **aim** is defined in definitions 1 and 2. The verb **aim** is explained in definitions 3, 4, and 5.

Finding the Correct Meaning

In order to understand the meaning of an unfamiliar word, you should read all of the definitions given for that word. This way you will find the meaning you need to know.

Read this sentence. *The guide stopped and pointed over the plain.* **Guide** is the word you are going to look up.

> **guide** (gīd), *v.* 1. to lead; to point out the way to someone. *The boy guided us through the narrow streets to the house we wanted to see.* 2. to instruct. *My father guided me in my study of the stars and planets.* **guides, guid ed, guid ing.**
> *n.* 3. a person who is hired to guide. *We needed a guide to take us down the river on our canoe trip.* 4. a book that includes directions and information for travelers. *I arrived in London with nothing but a guide to the city and a little money.* **guides.**

Now read all of the definitions given for **guide.** Which definition best explains the meaning of the word *guide* as it appears in your sentence? As you can see, definition 3, a person who is hired to guide, is the one you want.

Using Substitution to Find the Correct Meaning

Another way to make sure you understand a word is to use the definition in place of the new word. This is called *substitution.* Try using substitution in this sentence: *Our club has biennial elections.* **Biennial** is the unfamiliar word. The definition for **biennial** in the dictionary is: "coming once every two years; happening every other year."

If you substitute the definition of biennial for the word biennial the sentence reads: *Our club has every-other-year elections.* The meaning is clear, but the sentence is awkward. To make the sentence read smoothly you will change the words slightly to read: *Our club has elections every two years,* or *Our club has elections every other year.* Now the sentence reads smoothly and makes sense. You know what biennial means.

Substitution is one way to make sure you have selected the correct definition. If you have the correct meaning the sentence will be clear. If you have chosen incorrectly, the sentence will not make sense. If you should select a definition that does not fit the sentence, try another definition.

Special Definitions

Sometimes a definition in the DICTIONARY OF BASIC WORDS will be made up of only one word. Usually this means that the entry word is less common or less accurate than the word used to define it. The definition of **flu,** for example, is given as **influenza.** This is because **influenza** is the correct term for this illness. For a more complete definition of **flu,** look under the **influenza** entry.

Word Variations

Some words are variations of other words. To find the definitions for these words you must look at the most commonly accepted form.

Look at the entry below.

grey (grā), var. of **gray.**

The entry tells you that the word **grey** is a variation of the word **gray.** To find the definition you must look at **gray,** shown below.

gray (grā), *n.* 1. a color obtained by blending black and white. *Gray has always been used to paint battleships.* **grays.**

Usually in the DICTIONARY OF BASIC WORDS the root form (infinitive) of a verb is listed as an entry word. The inflectional forms of the verb are given at the end of the entry. Some inflectional forms, however, are widely used. These words are listed as entries, but they are not defined. Look at the entry for **arose.**

arose (ə rōz′), past tense of **arise.**

The entry tells you to look at the root word, printed in boldface type, for the definition. **Arose** is the past tense of the verb **arise.** To find its definition you must look at the root word, **arise.**

Synonyms

Synonyms are frequently used to define or explain the meaning of unfamiliar words. A synonym is a word that means the same or almost the same as another word. *Late* and *tardy, rapid* and *swift,* and *neat* and *tidy* are synonyms. An example of a synonym being used in a definition can be found in the definition for **additional.**

ad di tion al (ə dish′ən l), *adj.* extra; more. *After a heavy snowstorm, additional trucks and drivers are needed to clean the streets.* **ad di tion- al ly,** *adv.*

This definition uses more familiar words—*extra, more.* These synonyms make it easier for you to understand the unfamiliar word.

Some entry words are explained by words that mean the opposite or almost the opposite. *Good* and *bad, high* and *low,* and *fast* and *slow* have opposite meanings, and are called antonyms. If someone said he had a false friend, what would he mean? Look at the definition of **false.** **False** can mean *not true, lying,* or *not loyal.*

false (fôls), *adj.* 1. not true. *It is false to say that two plus two is equal to five.* 2. lying. *The robber gave false answers to the policeman who arrested him.* 3. not loyal. *People who only pretend to be friendly are false friends.* 4. not real or genuine. *The man wore a false beard.* 5. not based on true ideas; pretended. *His false pride kept him from accepting help from his friends.* **fals er, fals est; false ly,** *adv.*

If you know what a loyal friend is you now know that a false friend is just the opposite. The use of words that mean the same or the opposite for the entry word helps you to understand the meanings of many unfamiliar words.

Idioms

An idiom is a group of words that has a special meaning when used together, but a different meaning when each word is used separately. Idioms, in boldface type, are defined near the end of an entry. Look at the entry for **account.**

> **ac count** (ə kount′), *n.* 1. a statement of money received and spent. *He keeps a written account of all the money he receives.* 2. an explanation of some event. *She gave a good account of her trip.* **ac counts.**
>
> *v.* 3. **to account for,** to tell what has been done with. *Can you account for the ten dollars that seems to be missing?* 4. **to take into account,** to allow for. *You must take into account the heavy rain which may delay the train.* **ac counts, ac count ed, ac count ing.**

This entry shows two idioms—**to account for** and **to take into account.** Each idiom is defined. The definition applies to the entire phrase, not just to the word **account.** Because **account** is the most important word in each of these phrases, the phrases have been listed in the entry for **account.** Since the phrases are used as verbs, they are listed in the entry as verbs. When you use an idiom, you must use the whole phrase. Otherwise, you will change the meaning of your sentence.

Some words have so many idioms that a special listing is added to the entry. This list tells you that the entry "also has the following special meanings." The idioms appear in boldface type before their definitions. Look at the entry below.

> **run** (run), *n.* 1. the act of running. *He was*
>
> 〜〜〜〜〜〜〜〜〜〜
>
> *store?* 30. to develop a small tear or hole in. *She ran her stocking when she caught it on a chair.* 31. to go about with no control or governing force. *The soldiers were permitted to run the streets until dark.* **runs, ran, run, run ning.**
> **Run** also has the following special meanings:
> **run across,** to meet by surprise or by chance. *Last year I ran across a fellow I went to school with.* **run down,** (a) to stop working or operating. *My watch has run down.* (b) to speak against; to say evil things about a person. *He spent most of his time running down his boss instead of working.* **run into,** to meet by chance. *I ran into my Uncle Bill at a movie this evening.*

Idioms, like individual words, can have more than one meaning. The different meanings are shown as (a), (b), (c), and so on, instead of as 1, 2, and 3. Look at the definition for the idiom **run down.**

The first definition (a) is to stop working or operating. The second definition (b) is to speak against; to say evil things about a person.

There are many idioms in the DICTIONARY OF BASIC WORDS. They have been defined according to their present usage. Remember, the definitions apply to the entire phrase, not just to the entry word.

5. EXAMPLE SENTENCE

The example sentence shows how the entry word is used in a sentence. Every definition in the DICTIONARY OF BASIC WORDS has one or more example sentences. These are placed immediately after each definition and are printed in italics. These sentences help you understand the meaning of the entry word and frequently contain additional information not found in the definition. Look at the entry for **armor** shown below.

> **ar mor** (är′mər), *n.* 1. clothing made of metal which formerly covered the head and entire body to protect men in battle. *Since his armor was so heavy, the knight had to be lifted onto his horse.* 2. any device which is worn or carried for protection in battle. *Steel helmets and bullet-proof vests are examples of a modern soldier's armor. The Roman soldier's armor consisted of a helmet and a shield.* 3. metal plates used to protect a ship or airplane. *The armor on the sides and bottom of this ship is one foot thick.*

You will notice that the example sentence for the first definition tells you that the knight's **armor** was very heavy. The sentences for the second definition describe the **armor** commonly worn by modern soldiers and that worn by Roman soldiers. In the third definition the sentence tells you the **armor** protecting the side of a ship can be one foot thick.

Read the definitions carefully and see how the entry word is used in the example sentences.

6. INFLECTIONAL FORMS

The inflectional forms of the entry word show how the meaning of the entry word may be changed by adding different endings. They are listed in boldface type at the end of each group of definitions to which they apply. *All* of the inflectional forms are given, not just those which might be difficult to spell. The inflectional forms, like the entry word, are divided into syllables. This makes it easier for you to pronounce, spell, and divide these special forms.

Inflectional forms are made up of the root word (entry word) and an ending such as *s, es, ing, ed, er, est,* and *ly.* When one of these endings is added to a word, the meaning of the word changes. Five parts of speech are inflected: *nouns, pronouns, verbs, adjectives,* and *adverbs.*

Nouns

Most nouns have a plural form. This form is given after the noun definitions.

lamp (lamp), *n.* a device for giving light. *Before Edison invented the electric light bulb, people burned oil in their lamps. Early man made lamps by burning animal fat. Modern lamps come in different sizes and shapes; some stand on the floor, and others sit on tables.* **lamps.**

Some nouns have no plural forms or plural forms that are rarely, if ever, used. **Acropolis** or **New Jersey** have no plural forms because there was only one Acropolis and there is only one New Jersey.

Other nouns have more than one plural form that is correct. In these entries both plural forms are listed. The plural for **albatross** can be **albatross** or **albatrosses.** The plural for **fish** can be **fish** or **fishes.**

In some entries the plural form of a noun is the main entry word, because these nouns are plural. Look at the entry for **algae.**

al gae (al′jē), *n. pl.* water plants. *Algae are plants which do not have real roots, stems, and leaves like the plants that grow on land.*

Verbs

The inflectional forms for all verbs are listed in boldface type after the verb definitions. The inflectional forms given are: third person singular, past tense, past participle, and present participle. For example, the special forms listed after the verb definitions of **go** are: **goes, went, gone, going.**

go (gō), *v.* 1. to move; travel. *We passed an old car that was going very slowly. They are going to Canada.* 2. to pass. *A year goes by quickly.* 3. to be used up. *Where has my money gone?* 4. to cross. *The road goes over the river.* 5. to pass from one place or person to another. *He goes home from school. First prize goes to George.* 6. to pass from one condition to another. *He goes from bad to worse in his work. He has gone to sleep.* **goes, went, gone, go ing.**

When the past tense and past participle are the same, the verb form is only given once. The verb forms for **pitch** are: **pitches, pitched,** and **pitching. Pitched** is used as both the past tense and the past participle.

pitch[1] (pich), *v.* 1. to throw; to toss. *The newsboy pitches the paper on our porch.* 2. to put up. *The campers pitched their tent for the night.* 3. to move with the front end rising and falling. *The ship pitched in the big waves.* 4. in baseball, to throw the ball to the person at bat, who tries to hit it. *Tom wants to pitch in this game.* 5. to set at a certain level or degree. *Can you pitch the tone of the song a little lower?* 6. to slope down. *The church steeple pitches sharply.* **pitch es, pitched, pitch ing.**

Some verbs have more than one form for past tense and past participle. In these entries both forms are listed. Look at the entry for **leap.**

leap (lēp), *v.* 1. to jump. *The horse leaped over the fence. The wild animals are leaping away from the hunters.* 2. to jump across. *The deer leaped the stream to get away.* **leaps, leaped** (lēpt) or **leapt** (lept), **leap ing.**

The past tense and past participle for **leap** can be **leaped** or **leapt.** Both are correct. In the DICTIONARY OF BASIC WORDS all forms are given at the end of each verb entry.

Adjectives

Some adjectives show degree by adding an ending or suffix. *Er* and *est* are the suffixes which are added to some adjectives to show how much. If an adjective takes these forms, the forms are listed after the adjective definitions. Look at the entry below.

> **kind**[1] (kīnd), *adj.* 1. gentle and caring. *They are always very kind to animals.* 2. friendly; good; thoughtful of others. *She is a very kind person. He always has a kind word to say to everyone.* **kind er, kind est; kind ly,** *adv.*

A person may be **kind,** another may be **kinder,** and another may be the **kindest** of all.

Other adjectives show degree by placing the word *more* or *most* before the adjective in a sentence. If no special forms are shown after an adjective entry, you know that degree can only be shown by using the words *more* and *most* in front of the word.

> **beau ti ful** (bū′tə fəl), *adj.* having beauty; pleasing to the eye, ear, or mind; lovely. *She is a beautiful girl. That is a beautiful painting.* **beau ti ful ly,** *adv.*

A woman may be **beautiful,** her sister may be **more beautiful,** and their mother may be the **most beautiful** of the three.

Some adjectives cannot be used to show how much. A **male** chorus cannot be *more male* or *most male* or *maler* or *malest.* It is simply **male.** Your understanding of the meaning of the entry word, and careful attention to the way the entry word is used in the example sentence, will help you to recognize these adjectives and avoid errors.

Adverbs

Adverbs are often formed from adjectives by adding the suffix *ly* to the root word. In the DICTIONARY OF BASIC WORDS the adverbial form is listed after adjectives and is identified as an adverb.

Look back at the entries for **kind** and **beautiful.** The form given at the end of each entry is the adverbial form. The adverb for **kind** is **kindly,** and the adverb for **beautiful** is **beautifully.**

These six parts make up every entry in the DICTIONARY OF BASIC WORDS:
    ENTRY WORD
    PRONUNCIATION
    PART OF SPEECH
    DEFINITION
    EXAMPLE SENTENCE
    INFLECTIONAL FORMS

ILLUSTRATIONS

Approximately two thousand full-color illustrations have been used in the DICTIONARY OF BASIC WORDS. The illustrations are used to extend your understanding of a word. The comprehensive captions often give additional information.

The following entries are from the dictionary. Read each of the definitions carefully. Then look at the illustrations and captions.

The illustration of the entry, **beech,** shows you the beech branch with its nut, the beech tree, and what beech wood looks like.

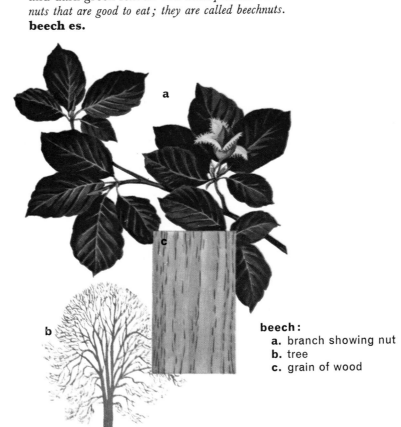

beech (bēch), *n.* a tree with smooth, gray bark and dark green leaves. *The beech produces sweet nuts that are good to eat; they are called beechnuts.* **beech es.**

beech:
a. branch showing nut
b. tree
c. grain of wood

Often an entry will have more than one definition. In such an instance, the illustration shows examples of the various things defined.

Look at the entry and illustration for **compass.**

Pictured here are three different types of compasses. Illustrations **a** and **b** are magnetic compasses used to find direction, as explained in the first definition. Illustration **c** shows a drawing compass used to draw circles, as explained in the second definition.

com pass (kum′pəs), *n.* 1. an instrument for finding direction. *When we go on a hike, we always carry a compass so we won't get lost.* 2. an instrument for drawing circles. *A compass has a sharp point which holds it down as the pen circles around it, creating a circle.* 3. a boundary. *He never left the compass of the town.* **com pass es.**

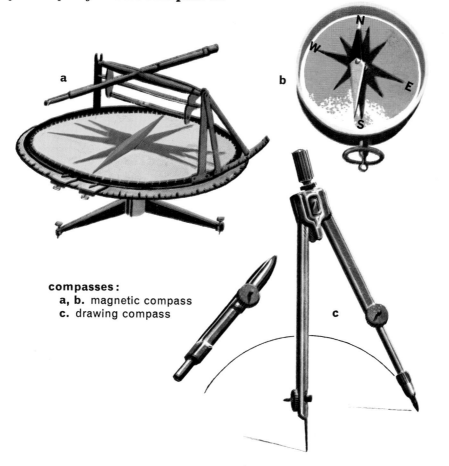

compasses:
   a, b. magnetic compass
   c. drawing compass

Whenever possible, illustrations have been placed on the same page as the entry word and definitions. However, some illustrations appear on the opposite page, and a few appear on the page following the entry. If the latter occurs, a note at the end of the entry directs you to "See illustration on the following page."

Be sure to look at the illustrations carefully. They were designed to add information and to clarify the meanings of the definitions found in the DICTIONARY OF BASIC WORDS.

CONCLUSION

If you are familiar with all of the kinds of information included in the dictionary, you will have no difficulty in using it to learn about words. You may want to review this section from time to time to refresh your memory and to make certain that you are getting from the DICTIONARY OF BASIC WORDS all of the help it offers.

A or **a** (ā), the first letter of the alphabet.

a (ə, ā), *indefinite article.* one; any; each; every. *The boy was paid ten dollars a week.* See **an.**

ab a cus (ab′ə kəs), *n.* a board with beads or balls that slide on wires, used in doing arithmetic problems. *The girl used an abacus to help her solve arithmetic problems.*

aban don (ə ban′dən), *v.* 1. to give up completely. *Sailors abandon their ship when it is wrecked.* 2. to leave for good. *The family abandoned their old house when they moved.* **aban dons, aban doned, aban don ing.**

ab bre vi ate (ə brē′vē āt′), *v.* to shorten. *Please abbreviate the names of the states.* **ab bre vi ates, ab bre vi at ed, ab bre vi at ing.**

ab bre vi a tion (ə brē′vē ā′shən), *n.* a shortened form; a syllable, letter, or letters standing for a word or words. *The abbreviation for noun is* n. **ab bre vi a tions.**

ab do men (ab′də mən or ab dō′mən), *n.* 1. the part of the body which contains the stomach and other organs for digestion. *He had a pain in his lower abdomen.* 2. the rear section of an insect. *A wasp's stinger is located at the tip of his abdomen.*

abacus

abil i ty (ə bil′ə tē), *n.* power to do something well. *A pilot has the ability to fly his plane through a storm.* **abil i ties.**

able (ā′bl), *adj.* having power, skill, or talent. *Most boys and girls are able to read well by the third grade.* **abler, ablest; ably,** *adv.*

ab nor mal (ab nôr′məl), *adj.* not normal; unusual; different from the average. *Freezing weather in June is abnormal.* **ab nor mal ly,** *adv.*

aboard (ə bôrd′), *adv.* on or in a ship, train, bus, or airplane. *The conductor says "All aboard!" when a train is ready to go.*

about (ə bout′), *prep.* 1. of; having to do with. *The girls spent all afternoon talking about new dresses.* 2. concerning. *Let me tell you something about baseball.* 3. on every side of; around. *Look about you and tell me what you see.* 4. with. *Many people prefer not to carry much cash about them, so they have a check-book.* 5. planning; ready. *We were about to go, and then I couldn't find the tickets.* 6. here and there; in or on; around. *It is fun to walk about the old castle grounds, thinking of kings and queens.*
adv. 7. somewhere near. *He had no watch, but he guessed it was about seven o'clock.* 8. nearby. *The child couldn't have gone far; he must be somewhere about.* 9. nearly; almost. *It's about time our team won a game, isn't it?* 10. here and there. *The man traveled about, searching for a place to settle.*

above (ə buv′), *adv.* 1. in a higher place. *The plane was flying far above.* 2. earlier in a book. *Writers say, "See the paragraph above," meaning "See the paragraph that appears somewhere earlier."* *prep.* 3. higher than; over. *A principal is above a teacher. The plane went above the clouds.* 4. more than. *There are above one thousand pupils in my school.* 5. beyond; past. *He lives in the first house above that bridge.* 6. superior to in any way. *The hero in the movie was above fighting unfairly.*

abroad (ə brôd′), *adv.* 1. outside one's own country. *We saw photographs of his trip abroad in France and England.* 2. going around. *The story is abroad that our class will win the trophy.*

ab sence (ab′sns), *n.* 1. being away. *During the president's absence, the vice-president ran the meetings of our club.* 2. not having; lack. *There was an absence of interest in the new movie, so they didn't go.* **ab senc es.**

ab sent (ab′snt for 1 and 2, ab sent′ for 3), *adj.* 1. away; not here. *That boy always seems to be absent on days when there is a ball game.* 2. not existing. *Feelings of happiness were absent after he finished making his radio, and it didn't work.* **ab sent ly,** *adv.*
v. 3. to stay away on purpose. *You cannot absent yourself from class without a note from the principal.* **ab sents, ab sent ed, ab sent ing.**

ab so lute (ab′sə lüt′), *adj.* 1. perfect; whole; complete. *The teacher gave absolute freedom to the class to choose their class project.* 2. having no limits. *The general said that he was now in*

sand, āte, bâre, fäther; sent, mē, fėrn; fit, bĭke; pot, rōpe, fôrt; run, pùll, rüle, cūte; noise, sound; ch, cheese; ng, long; th, thick; ~~th,~~ those; zh, treasure; ə = a in about, e in waken, i in animal, o in seldom, and u in minus.

absolute command, and he didn't have to listen to other officers. **ab so lute ly,** *adv.*

ab so lute ly (ab′sə lüt′lē), *adv.* 1. completely. *If you dive into a swimming pool, you will get absolutely soaked.* 2. positively. *I am absolutely sure the sun will rise tomorrow.*

ab sorb (əb sorb′), *v.* 1. to suck up or take in water and other liquids. *Dry earth absorbs the rain, but paved streets do not.* 2. to interest completely. *Some inventors get so absorbed in their work that they do not bother to eat or sleep.* **ab sorbs, ab sorbed, ab sorb ing.**

ab sorp tion (əb sorp′shən), *n.* 1. an absorbing; taking in. *You can watch the fast absorption of water by dry soil.* 2. taking up all attention (in work or play). *At World Series time, the whole United States seems to have an absorption in baseball.*

ab stract (ab′strakt for 1, ab strakt′ for 2), *adj.* 1. thought of without regard for a certain real object or particular thing. *"Happiness" and "love" are abstract words.*

v. 2. to take away; to get out. *Iron is abstracted from iron ore, which is found on the surface of the earth.* **ab stracts, ab stract ed, ab stract ing.**

abun dant (ə bun′dənt), *adj.* plenty; more than enough. *The store has an abundant supply of toys for Christmas time.* **abun dant ly,** *adv.*

abuse (ə būz′ for 1 and 2, ə būs′ for 3 and 4), *v.* 1. to put to a bad or wrong use. *You abuse a friendship when you break a promise to a friend.* 2. to treat badly; to injure. *The child abused the cat by dropping him.* **abus es, abused, abus ing.**

n. 3. bad or wrong use. *Because of the baseball player's abuse of the manager's rules, he was taken off the team.* 4. bad treatment. *There is no excuse for the abuse of our parks by messy people.* **abus es.**

ac cent (ak′sent for 1–3, ak′sent, ak sent′ for 4), *n.* 1. a stronger tone of voice given to certain syllables of words. *When you read this poem, put an accent on the syllables that the teacher has underlined.* 2. an unusual method of pronouncing heard in certain parts of a country. *In this class there are girls with New England accents, Southern accents, and Western accents.* 3. a

peculiar way of speaking a language not your own. *The French usually speak English with a French accent—and Americans usually speak French with an American–English accent.* **ac cents.**

v. 4. to pronounce or to write with an accent. *If you do not always accent the proper syllables, you may be misunderstood.* **ac cents, ac cent ed, ac cent ing.**

ac cept (ak sept′), *v.* 1. to take something given or offered. *You should accept gifts with a smile and a polite "thank you."* 2. to agree to; to consent to. *Mother accepted the idea of a party on Sunday because Joe will be ten years old that day.* 3. to believe. *Even today a few people accept the idea that the sun goes around the earth.* **ac cepts, ac cept ed, ac cept ing.**

ac cept a ble (ak sep′tə bl), *adj.* 1. worth accepting; satisfactory. *He had an acceptable excuse for being late.* 2. pleasing and agreeable; welcome. *Pictures of football players are always an acceptable gift to a young boy who is ill.* **ac cept a bly,** *adv.*

ac cept ance (ak sep′təns), *n.* 1. the taking of something that has been given or offered. *Father's acceptance of our birthday present made us very happy.* 2. approval of something. *We needed mother's acceptance of our plan to go camping.*

ac cept ed (ak sep′təd), *adj.* generally believed in or approved. *The idea that the world is round is an accepted fact.*

ac ci dent (ak′sə dənt), *n.* 1. a harmful or unlucky event. *Thousands of people are killed in automobile accidents every year.* 2. something that occurs without being planned or arranged for. *Inventors know that some important discoveries result from lucky accidents.* 3. chance. *I saw him by accident in the big crowd.* **ac ci dents.**

ac com mo date (ə kom′ə dāt′), *v.* 1. to adjust. *Your eyes will accommodate themselves to the dim light.* 2. to help out. *The bank will accommodate you by cashing your check.* 3. to make fit; have room for. *Our new school library accommodates one hundred pupils.* **ac com mo dates, ac com mo dat ed, ac com mo dat ing.**

ac com mo da tion (ə kom′ə dā′shən), *n.* 1. a room or place to stay, sometimes including food and other conveniences. *Their accommo-*

automobile **accident**

accordion

dations at the summer resort included air conditioning, television, and free breakfasts. That hotel has accommodations for two hundred people. 2. a help; convenience. It will be an accommodation to me if you will return my book. **ac com mo da tions.**

ac com pa ny (ə kum′pə nē), v. 1. to go along with. The little dog likes to accompany me when I take a walk. 2. to send or give along with. The doctor accompanied his letter with a bill. 3. to play or sing along with. Most singers have a pianist who accompanies them. **ac com pa nies, ac com pa nied, ac com pa ny ing.**

ac com plish (ə kom′plish), v. to do; carry out; complete. He works and works, but he never seems to accomplish anything. **ac com plish es, ac com plished, ac com plish ing.**

ac com plished (ə kom′plisht), adj. 1. excellent; expert. A good writer is an accomplished user of words and phrases. 2. expert in the manners of polite society. An accomplished gentleman has good manners and dances well. 3. done; carried out; finished. The accomplished work was done in the correct way.

ac cord (ə kôrd′), v. 1. to agree. My answer to this arithmetic problem accords with yours. **ac cords, ac cord ed, ac cord ing.** n. 2. **of one's own accord,** without being asked by anyone else. Finally, he began to do his homework of his own accord, without anyone telling him.

ac cord ance (ə kôrd′ns), n. agreement. In accordance with your wishes, I am returning your pencil.

ac cord ing ly (ə kôr′ding lē), adv. 1. in agreement with something said. We were told the school's rules of conduct, and we will act accordingly. 2. therefore. The doctor said to stay in bed; accordingly, I stayed in bed.

ac cord ing to (ə kôrd′ing tü), prep. 1. in agreement with. I enclose payment of three dollars, according to our contract. 2. as said by. According to him the plane will be on time. In Sunday school we are reading " The Gospel According to St. Mark."

ac cor di on (ə kôr′dē ən), n. a musical instrument with a keyboard, bellows, and reeds, or thin pieces of wood or metal. The player of the accordion forces air through the reeds by pumping the bellows with one arm and playing the keyboard with the other. **ac cor di ons.**

ac count (ə kount′), n. 1. a statement of money received and spent. He keeps a written account of all the money he receives. 2. an explanation of some event. She gave a good account of her trip. **ac counts.** v. 3. **to account for,** to tell what has been done with. Can you account for the ten dollars that seems to be missing? 4. **to take into account,** to allow for. You must take into account the heavy rain which may delay the train. **ac counts, ac count ed, ac count ing.**

ac count ing (ə kount′ing), n. keeping and explaining records of a business. Accounting requires the use of mathematics.

ac cu rate (ak′yə rət), adj. correct; true. My watch is always accurate, except when I forget to wind it. **ac cu rate ly,** adv.

ac cuse (ə kūz′), v. to bring a charge against; to blame for doing wrong. The police accused him of speeding and driving without a license. **ac cus es, ac cused, ac cus ing.**

ac cus tom (ə kus′təm), v. to make familiar by experience; to get used to something. Accustom yourself to finishing any job you start. **ac cus toms, ac cus tomed, ac cus tom ing.**

ac cus tomed (ə kus′təmd), adj. usual. The polar bear likes his accustomed home in the cold.

ache (āk), n. a pain that continues. The ache in the boy's back lasted for two days, in spite of the medicine he took. **aches.** v. to have a pain. His tooth began to ache. **aches, ached, ach ing.**

a chieve (ə chēv′), v. 1. to carry out; to accomplish. If you wish to achieve success, you must be willing to work hard. 2. to reach something by one's own efforts. During his short life, the author achieved fame. **a chieves, a chieved, a chiev ing.**

achieve ment (ə chēv′mənt), n. something done very well. The first space flights by our astronauts were a wonderful achievement. **achieve ments.**

ac id (as′əd), adj. 1. sour. Lemons are an acid fruit. He has an acid disposition. n. 2. a chemical compound. You learn about acids in your science classes. **ac ids.**

ac knowl edge (ak nol′ij), v. 1. to admit the truth of. A sensible person acknowledges his mistakes. 2. to give or send an expression of thanks for. It takes a bride a long time to acknowledge every wedding present. **ac knowl edg es, ac knowl edged, ac knowl edg ing.**

ac knowl edg ment (ak nol′ij mənt), n. 1. an admission of the truth. I liked his honest acknowledgment that he was wrong about what he said. 2. something given to show that an item has been received. The landlord gave an acknowledgment on a piece of scratch paper for the payment of this month's rent. **ac knowl edg ments.**

sand, āte, bâre, fäther; sent, mē, fėrn; fit, bīke; pot, rōpe, fôrt; run, pùll, rüle, cūte; noise, sound; ch, cheese; ng, long; th, thick; ~~th~~, those; zh, treasure; ə = a in about, e in waken, i in animal, o in seldom, and u in minus.

acorn:
  a. fruit
  b. shell
  c. branch with fruit

acorn (ā′kôrn, ā′kərn), *n.* the seed, or nut, that grows on an oak tree. *My little sister thinks that acorns look like small bells, because of their shape.* **acorns.**

ac quaint (ə kwānt′), *v.* to make familiar. *Your teacher will acquaint you with facts about science.* **ac quaints, ac quaint ed, ac quaint ing.**

ac quaint ance (ə kwānt′ns), *n.* a person whom you know, but who is not a friend. *You have many acquaintances in the schoolroom and in your neighborhood, but you become real friends with only a few persons.* **ac quaint anc es.**

ac quire (ə kwīr′), *v.* to get. *It took her twenty years attending classes part time, but my grandmother finally acquired a college degree.* **ac quires, ac quired, ac quir ing.**

acre (ā′kər), *n.* a piece of land that is 43,560 square feet. *The farmer owns 105 acres of land.* **acres.**

ac ro bat (ak′rə bat′), *n.* a person who performs physical stunts that require skill, speed, and body control. *At the circus we saw acrobats walk a tightrope and swing on bars high above the crowds.* **ac ro bats.**

Acrop o lis (ə krop′ə lis), *n.* the fortified hill in Athens on which the famous Parthenon was built. See the picture, which shows how the Acropolis once must have appeared, with the Parthenon at the right. *Seeing the Acropolis was one of the events of the student's trip to Greece.*

across (ə krôs′), *adv.* 1. from side to side. *The United States is three thousand miles across.*
prep. 2. to the other side of. *The bridge goes across the river.*

act (akt), *n.* 1. anything done; doing; deed. *Feeding the birds in wintertime is a kind act.* 2. a division of a play. *Most plays today have three acts.* **acts.**
v. 3. to perform. *Many girls would like to be actresses and act in the movies.* **acts, act ed, act ing.**

act ing (ak′ting), *adj.* taking another's place and doing his work. *When the principal was sick, my English teacher was acting principal of the school.*

ac tion (ak′shən), *n.* 1. being active; acting. *Quick action gets pupils out of the school fast in a fire drill.* 2. a battle. *The soldiers were in action for three days.* 3. way of working or behaving. *The newest jet planes have quiet actions. See that your actions always fit the time and place; don't whistle in church, for example.* **ac tions.**

ac tive (ak′tiv), *adj.* 1. busy. *Teachers are nearly always active with all the work they have.* 2. doing actions quickly. *A coach of a football team likes active players, not players who move slowly.*

ac tiv i ty (ak tiv′ə tē), *n.* 1. action; being active. *He shows a lot of activity for a boy just recovering from an illness.* 2. liveliness; prompt action. *A successful athlete or businessman is nearly always a man of activity.* 3. organized things to do. *Our school has many music, science, and art activities.* **ac tiv i ties.**

Acropolis

acrobats

ac tor (ak′tər), *n.* 1. a person who acts on the stage, in motion pictures, on radio, or on television. *A good actor can make people laugh or cry.* 2. a person or animal who acts or does something. *The general was the main actor in the plot against the king.* **ac tors.**

ac tu al (ak′chù əl), *adj.* real. *Don't guess—tell me the actual number of books you read last year.* **ac tu al ly,** *adv.*

ac tu al ly (ak′chù əl ē), *adv.* really; in fact. *Does he actually want to be a doctor, knowing he will have to spend ten years studying?*

adapt (ə dapt′), *v.* to make suitable. *All human beings adapt themselves to the places where they live. Many movies are adapted from books.* **adapts, adapt ed, adapt ing.**

add (ad), *v.* 1. to join or combine to get a total; to unite by addition. *If you add 3 and 2, you get 5.* 2. to join or unite to make something larger. *Add another log to the pile.* **adds, add ed, add ing.**

ad dend (ad′end), *n.* a number to be added to another number. *In the example 50 + 25 = 75 the number 25 is the addend.* **ad dends.**

ad dict (ad′ikt), *n.* 1. a person who has given in to a habit. *A drug addict usually finds that he cannot be cured because his body has become used to the drug.* **ad dicts.**

v. 2. to give in completely to something. *He*

is addicted to smoking. **ad dicts, ad dict ed, ad dic ting.**

ad dic tion (ə dik′shən), *n.* the condition of being given up or devoted to a habit; being a slave to a habit. *Some people have an addiction for tobacco, and they smoke continually.* **ad dic tions.**

ad di tion (ə dish′ən), *n.* 1. the adding of one number to another number to get the total. *A simple addition is 2 + 2 = 4.* 2. something added. *The new addition to the house is a playroom.* **ad di tions.**

ad di tion al (ə dish′ən l), *adj.* extra; more. *After a heavy snowstorm, additional trucks and drivers are needed to clean the streets.* **ad di tion al ly,** *adv.*

ad dress (ə dres′, ad′res for 1–3, ə dres′ for 4–6), *n.* 1. a speech or writing. *Abraham Lincoln's Gettysburg Address has been remembered for more than one hundred years.* 2. the place where a person lives or works and where mail may be sent. *The package was sent to his business address.* 3. a direction on a piece of mail which tells where it is to be sent and to whom. *A zip code is included in most addresses today.* **ad dress es.**

v. 4. to put on a piece of mail where it should go. *Be sure that you address the envelope correctly.* 5. to speak to; write to. *The speaker addressed us on the reasons why we should try to be better students.* 6. to direct the energies of (oneself). *By addressing himself seriously to his work, the boy got good grades.* **ad dress es, ad dressed, ad dress ing.**

ad e quate (ad′ə kwit), *adj.* enough; suitable. *My dad says that no matter how much money he earns, it never seems to be adequate for our family.* **ad e quate ly,** *adv.*

ad ja cent (ə jā′snt), *adj.* next to one another; nearby; close. *Tom and I became friends when we lived in adjacent houses. His house is adjacent to the highway.* **ad ja cent ly,** *adv.*

ad journ (ə jėrn′), *v.* to put off until later. *The judge said, " This court is adjourned until Tuesday at 10 A.M."* **ad journs, ad journed, ad journ ing.**

ad just (ə just′), *v.* 1. to put in order; change to make fit. *The store manager saw that our bill was too high, so he will adjust it.* 2. to become accustomed; to get used to something. *When boys and girls change schools, they must adjust to their new classes.* **ad justs, ad just ed, ad just ing.**

ad just ment (ə just′mənt), *n.* 1. a settlement. *The adjustment of our insurance claim was handled promptly.* 2. changing to make right. *The engine in our car always seems to need some kind of adjustment.* 3. the act of becoming accustomed; getting used to something. *The adjustment to a new classroom means getting to know the teacher and the pupils.* **ad just ments.**

ad min is tra tion (əd min′ə strā′shən), *n.* 1.

managing of a business, office, school, etc. *The clerks in a store may be good, but the store can still lose money because of poor administration.* 2. the time that a certain man and his political party take charge of a nation. *What war was fought during Abraham Lincoln's administration?* 3. the people managing a business, school, etc. *Your school's administration is made up of the principal, his assistant, and the teachers.* **ad min is- tra tions.**

ad mi ra tion (ad′mə rā′shən), *n.* high regard; approval; very favorable opinion. *We were filled with admiration for the man who wrote such beautiful music. A famous movie star gets used to the admiration of the public. I feel admiration for carpenters because I am so clumsy with my hands!*

ad mire (əd mīr′), *v.* 1. to look at or listen to with wonder, affection, and approval. *I admire the music played by a great orchestra; I also admire the musicians for their ability to play so beautifully.* 2. to like; feel enjoyment from something. *The visitors to New York City admired the tall buildings.* **ad mires, ad mired, ad mir ing.**

ad mis sion (əd mish′ən), *n.* 1. being admitted; permission to enter. *The Congress voted for the admission of Hawaii and Alaska to the United States.* 2. price paid to get in. *Admission to the movie was two dollars for adults, one dollar for children.* 3. confession; telling the truth about one's guilt. *Our poor dog was blamed for eating the cake—then we got an admission from the twins that they had eaten it!* **ad mis sions.**

ad mit (əd mit′), *v.* 1. to let in. *They will admit us to the show because we have tickets.* 2. to acknowledge; confess. *He admitted that he was late for school, but he said his father's car broke down.* **ad mits, ad mit ted, ad mit ting.**

adopt (ə dopt′), *v.* 1. to take into one's family and treat as one's own. *Many people adopt children who do not have parents of their own.* 2. to take for one's self. *I have adopted her idea of doing homework in the morning instead of at night, and I like it.* **adopts, adopt ed, adopt ing.**

ador a ble (ə dôr′ə bl), *adj.* attractive; sweet. *Whenever I take my baby sister outside, the women neighbors say, "My, isn't she adorable!"*

adore (ə dôr′), *v.* 1. to feel deep love and respect for. *That father adores his new baby.* 2. to admire; like very much. *The teen-ager says she just adores that singer.* 3. to worship. *We are taught in Sunday School to adore God.* **adores, adored, ador ing.**

adorn (ə dôrn′), *v.* to make attractive; put decorations on. *Every year we adorn the Christmas tree with lights and ornaments.* **adorns, adorned, adorn ing.**

adult (ə dult′, ad′ult), *adj.* 1. having full size and strength. *He is an adult dog, weighing more than one hundred pounds, so he looks funny when he chases around like a puppy, banging into furniture!* *n.* 2. a grown person. *Act like an adult, not like a child.* **adults.**

ad vance (əd vans′), *n.* 1. any forward movement; progress. *Doctors have made great advances in curing diseases.* **ad vanc es.**
v. 2. to go forward. *The crowd advanced closer to the speaker's platform to hear better.* 3. to offer; tell about. *He advanced three ideas for a Christmas party, and the club members chose one.* 4. to pay beforehand. *We advanced the store twenty dollars as part payment on the TV set we wanted.* 5. to raise; put up. *The price of a new car seems to advance every year.* **ad vanc es, ad vanced, ad vanc ing.**

ad vanced (əd vanst′), *adj.* 1. ahead of most others. *He takes an advanced course in mathematics.* 2. old. *Twenty years is an advanced age for a dog.*

ad van tage (əd van′tij), *n.* 1. anything that helps in being successful. *That basketball player has the advantage of being almost seven feet tall.* 2. any help, benefit, or gain. *A person who finishes school has an advantage over a dropout when it comes to getting a job.* 3. **take advantage of,** to be unfair to. *He takes advantage of the little boy by paying him less than he should for mowing the lawn.* **ad van tag es.**

adorning the Christmas tree

ad ven ture (əd ven′chər), *n.* 1. a bold and dangerous trip. *Christopher Columbus went on an adventure. Our astronauts go on an adventure each time they leave the earth.* 2. an unusual, exciting experience. *Going to the park is an adventure for young children.* **ad ven tures.**
v. 3. to venture; attempt. *He adventured to go outdoors after his illness.* **ad ven tures, ad ven tured, ad ven tur ing.**

ad ver tise (ad′vər tīz′), *v.* 1. to inform the public about; give public notice of. *Businessmen advertise things they want to sell in newspapers, on television, on radio, and on billboards. The store advertised a sale by sending out circulars.* 2. to ask (for) by advertisement. *A housewife will advertise in a newspaper for a cook, a maid, or a cleaning lady.* **ad ver tis es, ad ver tised, ad ver tis ing.**

ad ver tise ment (ad′vər tīz′mənt, əd vėr′tis-mənt), *n.* a printed or spoken notice for the public. *Advertisements of things for sale appear in magazines, on television, on radio, and on big signs or posters. Most advertisements today are prepared by advertising agencies.* **ad ver tise ments.**

ad vice (əd vīs′), *n.* an opinion about the way something should be done. *A person who doesn't take his doctor's advice is only hurting himself.* **ad vic es.**

ad vis a ble (əd vīz′ə bl), *adj.* suitable; wise; correct thing to be done or followed. *It is advisable to do what your parents and your teacher tell you to do.*

ad vise (əd vīz′), *v.* 1. to give information or advice to. *I advise you to take the bus and not the train to get to the city where I live.* 2. to inform. *The old camper advised the new men on the best ways to live in the jungle.* **ad vis es, ad vised, ad vis ing.**

aer i al (âr′ē əl), *n.* wires attached together for receiving or sending programs on television and radio. *Our television picture went blank, and we found that the heavy wind had blown down the aerial on the roof.* **aer i als.**

afar (ə fär′), *adv.* to or from a distance. *He was climbing the mountain, and we could see him from afar, looking like an ant crawling on a basketball.*

af fair (ə fâr′), *n.* 1. business of any kind; thing that is to be done. *My uncle travels around the country to take care of all his business affairs.* 2. any matter, concern, or thing. *The birthday party was a happy affair for Susan and for all her guests.* **af fairs.**

af fect (ə fekt′), *v.* 1. to produce a change upon; influence. *The sunshine affects snow by melting it.* 2. to move or touch by exciting the feelings. *Sad movies so affect some people that they cry.* 3. to make a show of. *She affects all the latest styles.* 4. to pretend. *I affected that I didn't know her, but she came over and said hello.* 5. to choose usually; do all the time. *Some boys and girls affect haircuts and clothes that make them look kind of silly—at least to me.* **af fects, af fect ed, af fect ing.**

af fect ed (ə fek′təd), *adj.* 1. not natural; pretended. *My friend wore an affected hairdo, so I didn't recognize her.* 2. injured or diseased. *His lungs were affected by the smog in the city.*

af fec tion (ə fek′shən), *n.* love; a friendly feeling. *Most people feel a warm affection for dogs.* **af fec tions.**

af fec tion ate (ə fek′shə nət), *adj.* having great love or affection; fond. *Members of a family should be affectionate toward each other.* **af fec tion ate ly,** *adv.*

af fi da vit (af′fə dā′vət), *n.* a signed statement in writing, giving facts about something that occurred. *An affidavit is usually made in the presence of an authorized official.* **af fi da vits.**

af ford (ə fôrd′), *v.* 1. to have enough money to buy or sell. *The family could not afford a new automobile, so they bought a good used car.* 2. to have enough time or strength. *He finished his work early, so he could afford to watch television.* **af fords, af ford ed, af ford ing.**

afraid (ə frād′), *adj.* frightened; filled with fear. *Some people are afraid of falling when they are high up in a tall building.*

af ter (af′tər), *prep.* 1. in search or pursuit of. *The man ran after the train, but he finally gave up and waited for the next one.* 2. behind. *Don't forget —you come after me in the parade!* 3. in view of; in consequence of. *After all your doctor's advice, why do you keep on eating too much candy? After failing the last two tests, he decided to spend more time studying.* 4. following; later in time than. *After lunch let's go on with the game.*
adv. 5. afterward; behind. *I arrived first, then the rest of the girls came shortly after.*
adj. 6. following; later in time. *The after results of the high windstorm were water in the streets, overturned automobiles, and broken windows.*
conj. 7. following the time that. *After the sun went down, the children went home.*

af ter noon (af′tər nün′), *n.* the part of the day that follows noon and lasts until evening. *Little children often take naps in the afternoon.*

af ter ward or **af ter wards** (af′tər wərd, af′tər wərdz), *adv.* later. *When I come home from school, I wash my hands and face; afterward we have dinner.*

again (ə gen′), *adv.* 1. once more. *When no one answered the door, the mailman rang the bell again.* 2. on the other hand. *The weatherman may be wrong but, again, he may be correct about the storm.*

against (ə genst′), *prep.* 1. in opposition to. *I like to watch the Bears play football against the Giants. When the wind is against it, an airplane slows down. There were twenty votes for him, and only two against him.* 2. upon. *We could hear the rain beating against the roof.* 3. next to. *The distant houses were dark against the red sunset.* 4. in contact with; on. *I left the ladder leaning against the house. He was so tired that he leaned against me for support.* 5. in preparation for. *Squirrels store nuts against the winter.*

---

sand, āte, bâre, fäther; sent, mē, fėrn; fit, bīke; pot, rōpe, fôrt; run, pùll, rüle, cūte; noise, sound; ch, cheese; ng, long; th, thick; ŧħ, those; zh, treasure; ə = a in about, e in waken, i in animal, o in seldom, and u in minus.

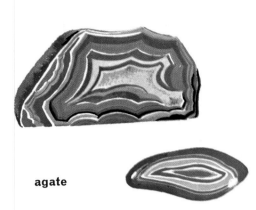

agate

ag ate (ag′ət), *n.* 1. a very hard stone with colored stripes. *When polished, an agate is beautiful.* 2. a playing marble used in a boy's game. *An agate is made either of agate or of colored glass that looks like agate.* **ag ates.**

age (āj), *n.* 1. number of years old. *The baby's age is now two years. Some giant turtles live to the age of two hundred years.* 2. a period of time. *The age of knights in armor is past. Cavemen lived in the Stone Age.* **ages.**
v. 3. to grow old. *My grandfather is so lively that he never seems to age.* **ages, aged, ag ing** or **age ing.**

aged (ā′jəd for 1, ājd for 2), *adj.* 1. old; having lived long. *My great-uncle is an aged man.* 2. having a certain age. *A child aged four should pick up his own toys.*

agen cy (ā′jən sē), *n.* 1. business of a company or person that is paid to help with the business of another person or company. *An advertising agency writes advertisements for companies making everything from toothpaste to foods.* 2. an active power or cause. *Clouds are the agency of rainfall.* **agen cies.**

agent (ā′jənt), *n.* 1. a person or company whose business is to help with the business of another person or company. *While my uncle is away, his lawyer is his agent, taking the place of my uncle.* 2. a body or substance that causes a certain action to begin. *The airplane is an agent of travel.* 3. a salesman. *This dictionary was prepared in an office by editors, and an agent sold it to your school.* **agents.**

ago (ə gō′), *adj.* past; gone. *We first met about two years ago. I like to see movies about the times long ago when knights, and even their horses, wore heavy armor.*

agree (ə grē′), *v.* 1. to have the same opinion. *Enough people agreed that Mr. Jones was the best man for mayor, so he was elected.* 2. to consent. *The carpenter agreed to do the work, so he will fix the chair next Saturday.* 3. **agree with,** to be good for. *Sunshine and fresh air agree with me; they make me feel healthy.* **agrees, agreed, agree ing.**

agree a ble (ə grē′ə bl), *adj.* 1. pleasing. *That girl has agreeable manners.* 2. ready to give consent or agree. *My employer is agreeable to a small increase in my salary.*

agree ment (ə grē′mənt), *n.* 1. an understanding; a mutual arrangement. *The two brothers made an agreement about watching their favorite TV programs. Can all of you come to an agreement as to where the party should be held?* 2. harmony; correspondence. *The United Nations tries to help nations get along in agreement. See if there is agreement between your answer and John's answer.* **agree ments.**

ag ri cul tur al (ag′rə kul′chə rəl), *adj.* having to do with agriculture or farming. *The agricultural production of the United States is very large.*

ag ri cul ture (ag′rə kul′chər), *n.* farming; raising food and farm animals for sale. *Years ago most young men chose agriculture as a way of life; today most of them choose factory work in the big cities.*

ah (ä), *interj.* a sound that can show pain, surprise, pity, dislike, joy, and many other feelings. *Ah, this is the last payment on the television set!*

ahead (ə hed′), *adv.* 1. in advance; in front; toward the front. *The army sent a scout ahead to look for Indians. You should always plan ahead. Let the smallest children walk ahead.*
prep. 2. **ahead of,** in advance of; in front of; before. *He finished his test ahead of the other students. Our airplane arrived ahead of time. He walked ahead of the others. The forest was ahead of us, so we camped for the night.*

ahoy (ə hoi′), *interj.* a word used mostly at sea by sailors in calling to another ship or boat. *Sailors shout "Ship ahoy!" when they see another ship at sea.*

aid (ād), *v.* 1. to help. *The doctor aided him promptly, and the pain stopped.* **aids, aid ed, aid ing.**
n. 2. a helper. *My sister is a fine aid when I clean the house.* 3. assistance. *Send aid at once to the men lost in the cave.* 4. **first aid,** quick help for the injured. *Boy Scouts learn first aid.* **aids.**

aim (ām), *n.* 1. pointing. *His aim was so good that he never missed the target.* 2. a purpose; intention that one hopes will succeed. *His aim was to be a doctor.* **aims.**
v. 3. to point at some kind of object. *The hunter aimed his gun at the lion, fired, and missed.* 4. to direct. *The principal aimed his speech at the pupils who broke the rules.* 5. to try. *"We aim to please" said the big sign in the store.* **aims, aimed, aim ing.**

air (âr), *n.* 1. the mixture of gases surrounding the earth. *All people breathe air. We put air in our tires.* 2. the space above the earth. *Birds and airplanes fly in the air.* 3. manner; look; appearance. *An air of happiness and love surrounded the little family.* 4. a song; tune. *Whenever my mother is happy, she hums an old Irish air.* 5. manners and

sand, āte, bâre, fäther; sent, mē, fėrn; fit, bīke; pot, rōpe, fôrt; run, pùll, rüle, cūte; noise, sound; ch, cheese; ng, long; th, thick; ŧh, those; zh, treasure; ə = a in about, e in waken, i in animal, o in seldom, and u in minus.

appearance used to show off. *After the girl came back from France, she put on airs to show how much more she traveled than we did.* **airs.**

v. 6. to let air into. *Every morning mother airs the house.* 7. to let everyone know. *The new father aired his happiness by giving out cigars.* **airs, aired, air ing.**

air craft (âr′kraft′), *n.* 1. airplanes, balloons, helicopters, and gliders. *Our Air Force has many aircraft.* 2. any airplane, balloon, helicopter, or glider. *Here comes the aircraft you will ride in.*

aircraft carrier, *n.* a large ship that carries airplanes and is used as their landing field. *The aircraft carrier is an important ship in the navy.* **aircraft carriers.**

air field (âr′fēld′), *n.* a place where airplanes can land and take off. *The plane flew around the airfield until the pilot was told by radio to land. An airfield is part of an airport.* **air fields.**

air line (âr′līn′), *n.* a business that makes money by carrying passengers and freight on airplanes. *There are many airlines in the United States.* **air lines.**

air lin er (âr′lī′nər), *n.* a large passenger airplane. *An airliner can carry more than a hundred people.* **air lin ers.**

AIRPLANES

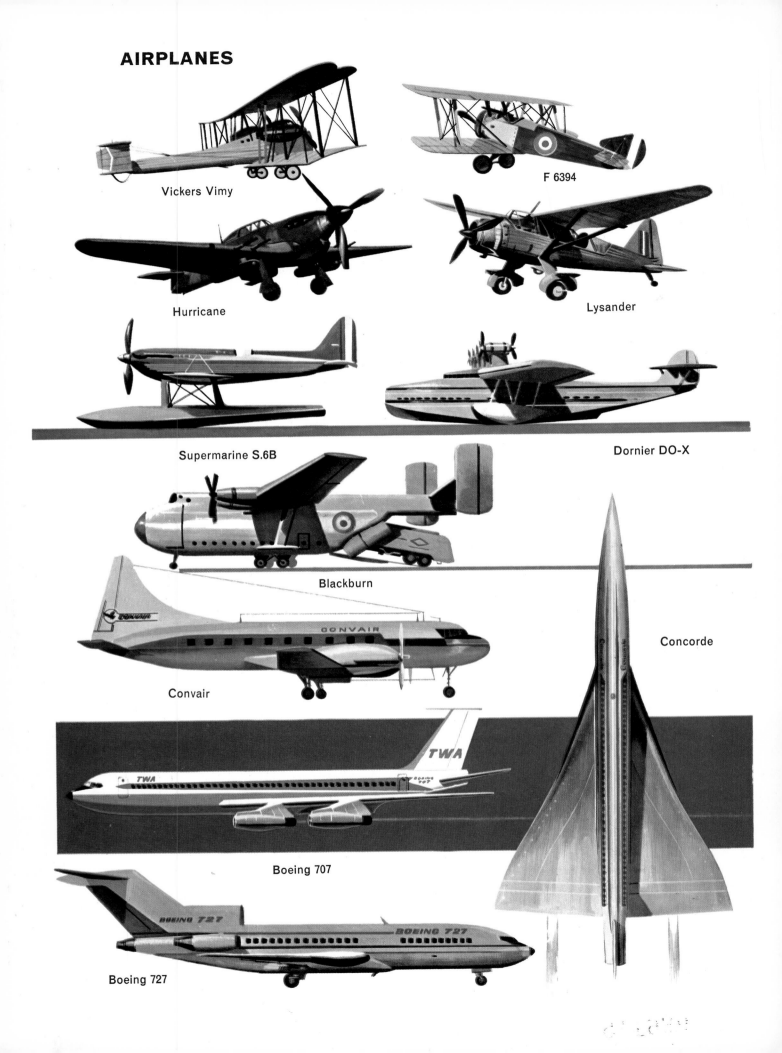

Vickers Vimy

F 6394

Hurricane

Lysander

Supermarine S.6B

Dornier DO-X

Blackburn

Convair

Concorde

Boeing 707

Boeing 727

airship

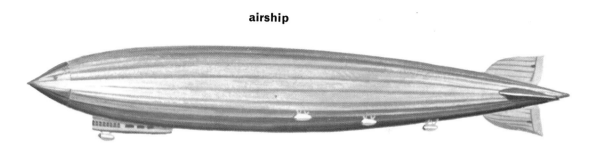

air mail (âr′māl′), *n.* mail carried by airplanes. *People send letters by airmail from New York to California in one day.*

air plane (âr′plān′), *n.* a machine for flying that has a motor, wings, and tail. *An airplane is different from other aircraft. An airship is a bag filled with gas; a helicopter has no wings; and a glider has no motor, but is towed into the air and rides on air currents.* **air planes.**

air port (âr′pôrt′), *n.* a landing place for airplanes. *The new airport has a control tower that tells planes when to take off; places to store planes; repair shops; ticket counters; lunch counters; and a drug store.* **air ports.**

air ship (âr′ship′), *n.* a long balloon with engines. *Airships are lighter than air because they are filled with a very light gas called helium.* **airships.**

airy (âr′ē), *adj.* 1. of the air; in the air. *Poets write of "airy voices."* 2. breezy. *This is a cool, airy place.* 3. graceful; delicate. *There is an airy appearance about the new house, in spite of its size.* 4. merry; light-hearted. *The airy laughter of the small children floated into my room.* **air i er, air i est; air i ly,** *adv.*

aisle (īl), *n.* a passage between rows of seats. *The teacher walks up and down the aisles while we are doing the problems. When my aunt was married, she walked down the aisle of the church in her white wedding gown.* **aisles.**

Al a ba ma (al′ə bam′ə), *n.* a Southern state of the United States. *Alabama is a good farming state because it has a long growing season and much rainfall.*

alarm (ə lärm′), *n.* 1. a warning that danger is near. *The alarm went from farmer to farmer that bad weather was coming.* 2. a thing that gives an alarm. *The firemen ran to their truck when they heard the fire alarm.* 3. a sudden fear. *The birds flew away in alarm when they saw the cat.* **alarms.** *v.* 4. to warn of danger. *The smoke in the house alarmed me, especially when I remembered I forgot to turn off the stove.* 5. to fill with anxiety and fear of danger. *The man crossing the desert was alarmed because he had no more water.* **alarms, alarmed, alarm ing.**

alarm clock, *n.* a clock that can be set to ring or buzz at a certain time. *My alarm clock wakes me up at eight o'clock every morning.* **alarm clocks.**

alas (ə las′), *interj.* a word showing sorrow, grief, pity, worry, or fear. *The princess said, "Alas, I cannot marry the man I love!"*

Alas ka (ə las′kə), *n.* a state of the United States. *Alaska is our largest state.*

al ba tross (al′bə trôs′), *n.* a large seabird with a white body, darker wings and tail, and a long, powerful bill. *The albatross has powerful wings; he just glides over the water for hours.* **al ba tross es** or **al ba tross.**

al co hol (al′kə hôl′), *n.* a liquid that is used in wine, beer, whiskey, etc., in medicines, and as a fuel. *Whiskey contains much alcohol.*

al fal fa (al fal′fə), *n.* a plant grown as a food for horses and cattle. *When dried, alfalfa is one kind of hay which animals eat.*

al gae (al′jē), *n. pl.* water plants. *Algae are plants which do not have real roots, stems, and leaves like the plants that grow on land.*

alike (ə līk′), *adj.* 1. similar; without a difference. *The twin sisters look alike—they have the same kind of eyes, hair, and smile.* *adv.* 2. in the same way. *You can't treat all children alike, because each child is different in background and in the things he wants to do.* 3. equally. *All of you are interested alike in reading, so all of you should join the book club.*

alive (ə līv′), *adj.* 1. living; not dead. *It's great to be alive!* 2. active; brisk. *That puppy racing*

alarm clock

albatross

around is certainly alive. 3. filled. *The room was alive with talking before the teacher came in; then everyone was quiet. The streets were alive with people.*

all (ôl), *adj.* 1. every one of. *All men are created equal. All the students arrived on time.*
adv. 2. wholly; completely; entirely. *The book is all yours; I have finished reading it. Someone had better go to the store; our milk is all gone.* 3. **above all,** before anything else; most important. *"Above all, be honest with me," said John's father to him.*
pron. 4. everyone. *All of us plan to attend the meeting.*

al ley (al′ē), *n.* a narrow passage in a city or town, built behind the houses on a street. *Our city is now putting lights in the alleys, so that people can see better at night to go to their garages.* **al leys.**

al li ga tor (al′ə gāt′ər), *n.* a large animal with a narrow body, short legs for crawling, long tail, and thick skin. *Alligators live in the warm, watery parts of North America. Last Christmas my dad got a beautiful wallet made of the hide of an alligator.* **al li ga tors.**

al low (ə lou′), *v.* 1. to let. *Her mother won't allow Mary out of the house until she does her homework.* 2. to give. *The store allows me ten extra days to pay my bill.* 3. to set apart. *Allow a certain amount of money every day for expenses like lunch, carfare, pencils, paper, and books.* **al lows, al lowed, al low ing.**

al low ance (ə lou′əns), *n.* 1. a definite amount of money given regularly for spending. *Mary's dad gives her an allowance of one dollar a week, which she can spend or save as she wishes.* 2. a certain sum granted. *That store gives you an allowance of seventy-five dollars on your old television set if you buy a new one.* 3. **to make allowance for,** to take into consideration. *You must make allowance for the extra time you will need for traveling in the snow.* **al low anc es.**

all right (ôl rīt), *adj.* 1. correct. *The teacher said that most of our answers were all right.* 2. safe; well. *Do you feel all right?* 3. suitable; proper. *That television program is all right for children.*
adv. 1. yes; very well. *All right, it's a deal. All right, I'll come home early.* 2. satisfactorily. *If it's all right with you, we will leave at eight o'clock.*

al mond (ä′mənd, am′ənd), *n.* 1. the nut or seed of a fruit that grows on a tree that looks like a peach tree. *Almonds are used in chocolate candy bars.* 2. the tree on which the almond grows. *The almond is a small tree that has pink blossoms.* **al monds.**

al most (ôl′mōst), *adv.* nearly. *That bus is almost on time; it is only two minutes late.*

alone (ə lōn′), *adv.* 1. apart from other people or things. *That dog likes to sit alone, sniffing the wind.* 2. without anyone else. *I can lift this box alone; you don't have to help me.* 3. without anything else. *Gifts alone are not enough for a child, because he needs love.*

along (ə lông′), *prep.* 1. in a line with the length. *Houses stretched along the river for miles.*
adv. 2. onward. *Move along! Don't block the entrance.* 3. in company; together. *The little boy said to his father, "Let me go along with you."* 4. with one. *Bring some money along.*

aloud (ə loud′), *adv.* with the natural voice; loudly, not quietly. *Reading aloud to the class, my teacher speaks clearly, and everyone understands her.*

al pha bet (al′fə bet′), *n.* the letters of a language arranged in order. *The letters of the English alphabet are a, b, c, d, e, f, g, h, i, j, k, l, m, n, o, p, q, r, s, t, u, v, w, x, y, z.* **al pha bets.**

al pha bet i cal (al′fə bet′ə kl), *adj.* arranged by letters in the order of the alphabet, from a to z. *All the words in this dictionary are in alphabetical order.* **al pha bet i cal ly,** *adv.*

al pha bet ize (al′fə bə tīz′), *v.* to arrange in alphabetical order. *A teacher usually alphabetizes the last names of the pupils in her class.* **al pha bet iz es,   al pha bet ized,   al pha bet iz ing.**

al read y (ôl red′ē), *adv.* before this time; by this time. *Let's go! We are already ten minutes late.*

al so (ôl′sō), *adv.* too; in addition; likewise. *My cousin sings in the church choir; he also sings in our school's music festival each year.*

al tar (ôl′tər), *n.* 1. a kind of platform on which sacrifices and offerings were made to a god. *Ancient altars were used to sacrifice an animal to the glory of a god.* 2. a table, usually at the front of a church, used during religious services. *The minister turned to the altar to say a prayer.* **al tars.**

al ter (ôl′tər), *v.* 1. to make some change in. *It seems that every time my mother buys a dress, she asks the store to alter it by making it longer or*

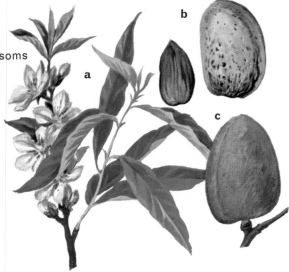

almond:
  a. branch with blossoms
  b. nut and shell
  c. green fruit

ABCDEFGHIJKLM NOPQRSTUVXYZ

Latin **alphabet**

АБВГДЕЖЗИКЛМ НОПРСТПУФХЦЧ ШЩЪЫЬѢЭЮЯѲѴ

Russian **alphabet**

Arabic **alphabet**

shorter or wider. 2. to become different in some way. *Since my brother left for college, his opinion on many things seems to have altered.* **al ters, al tered, al ter ing.**

al ter nate (ôl′tər nāt′ for 1, ôl′tər nət for 2 and 3), *v.* 1. to follow one another in turn. *My friend and I alternate in the job of washing the car.* **al ter nates, al ter nat ed, al ter nat ing.**
adj. 2. every other. *During a dry summer, our village requires that we water our lawns on alternate days.*
n. 3. a substitute. *When a jury is chosen, an extra member, called an alternate, is also chosen.* **al ter nates.**

al though (ôl thō′), *conj.* though. *I went to the beach, although there were clouds in the sky.*

al ti tude (al′tə tüd′, al′tə tūd′), *n.* height above sea level. *Airplanes fly at about 30,000 feet altitude; this means they are above the storms and clouds near the earth's surface.* **al ti tudes.**

al to geth er (ôl′tə geth′ər), *adv.* 1. wholly; entirely; completely. *The movie was altogether entertaining in my opinion.* 2. taking everything into consideration; on the whole. *Altogether, our winter this year was not too cold.*

alu mi num (ə lü′mə nəm), *n.* a silver-white metal that does not weigh much. *Aluminum is used for making pots and pans, airplanes, sides of houses, and many other products that require a metal that is strong, does not weigh too much, and does not rust. Housewives use aluminum foil to wrap up leftovers from meals.*

al ways (ôl′wāz, ôl′wiz), *adv.* all the time; constantly. *At the North Pole, it is always cold.*

am (am), *v.* one form of the verb *to be*, used with I. *I am here.*

am bas sa dor (am bas′ə dər), *n.* a high-ranking official representing his country in another country. *The United States has one ambassador in each important country in the world, and each of those countries has an ambassador in Washington, D.C.* **am bas sa dors.**

am big u ous (am big′ū əs), *adj.* 1. having more than one possible meaning. *This sentence is ambiguous: "The brothers and their dog walk to school every day; they are in the same grade."* 2. not clear. *His views on many subjects are*

altar

ambiguous, because he won't definitely say "yes" or "no." **am big u ous ly,** *adv.*

am bi tion (am bish′ən), *n.* 1. an eager desire for honor, power, fame, or money. *His ambition of twenty years came true when he was elected president of the bank.* 2. the thing that is wanted. *Winning the batting championship of the American League was his ambition.* **am bi tions.**

amend (əmend′), *v.* 1. to change; to improve. *I will amend my ways and stop talking in class.* 2. to change something formally. *The Constitution had to be amended before women could vote in America.* **amends, amended, amend ing.**

amend ment (ə mend′mənt), *n.* 1. a change in a law or bill; a correction. *The first ten amendments of our Constitution are called The Bill of Rights.* 2. changing for the better in any way. *When a textbook is four years old, it is time to make amendments in it to cover recent events.* **amend ments.**

Amer i ca (ə mer′ə kə), *n.* 1. the United States of America. *Although the name of our country is the United States of America, people usually shorten it to America.* 2. North America. *Canada and the United States are in North America.* 3. South America. *South America is the fourth largest continent in the world.* 4. North America and South America; the continents of the Western Hemisphere. *The Americas work together for the good of their people.* **Amer i cas.**

Amer i can (ə mer′ə kən), *n.* 1. a person born or living in the United States. *A citizen of the United States is an American.* 2. a person living in North America or South America. *Canadians are Americans.* **Amer i cans.** *adj.* 3. of or pertaining to the United States. *The American flag is red, white, and blue.*

among (ə mung′), *prep.* 1. in the midst of; surrounded by. *They are among that crowd.* 2. to each of. *These gifts should be divided among all the orphans.* 3. in the number of. *He is one among a thousand.* 4. with all or most of. *Our class president is very popular among the students.*

amount (ə mount′), *v.* 1. to add up; be equal. *The total cost of the storm amounts to one hundred dollars for repairs to our house.* 2. **amount to,** to be the same thing as. *His silence amounts to "No."* **amounts, amount ed, amount ing.** *n.* 3. the total of two or more particular sums. *The amount of the total cost was one hundred dollars.* 4. the full effect. *The amount of damage done by the tornado won't be known for weeks.* **amounts.**

am pere (am′pir), *n.* the unit used in measuring the strength of an electric current. *The ampere was named in honor of the French scientist André Marie Ampère, who studied electric current.* **am peres.**

am phi the a ter (am′fə thē′ə tər), *n.* a round building with rows of seats going up from the open space in the center. *Amphitheaters were first used by the ancient Greeks and Romans. Many amphitheaters are still standing.* **am phi the a ters.**

am ple (am′pl), *adj.* 1. large. *Alaska is a state of ample size; it is larger than any of the other forty-nine states.* 2. enough. *There was an ample supply of cake and ice cream for the party; if the guests said, "More, please," they got more.* 3. plentiful. *We have an ample supply of potatoes for a week, especially since mother is on a diet.* **am ply,** *adv.*

am pli fi er (am′plə fī′ər), *n.* a device that increases the strength of electric waves or impulses. *Amplifiers are used in radio and television sets.* **am pli fi ers.**

amuse (ə mūz′), *v.* 1. to entertain. *Parents amuse their children by reading funny or exciting stories to them.* 2. to cause to laugh or smile. *That boy in the third row amuses all of us when he makes funny faces.* **amus es, amused, amus ing.**

amuse ment (ə mūz′mənt), *n.* 1. being amused. *The child's amusement with the new toy was fun to watch.* 2. entertainment; sport; pastime. *My favorite amusements are sailing and reading.* **amuse ments.**

amus ing (ə mūz′ing), *adj.* 1. causing laughter or smiles. *A little child is amusing when he tries to walk and all of a sudden falls down.* 2. entertain-

amphitheater

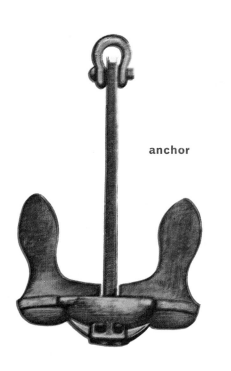

anchor

anchor being pulled up

ing. *My uncle is an amusing man; it is wonderful to listen to his jokes.* **a mus ing ly,** *adv.*

an (ən, an), *indefinite article.* 1. one; any. *Mother gave us an orange when we came home from school.* 2. each; every. *I can walk three miles an hour.* We use *an* before words beginning with vowel sounds: *an airplane, an American.* The vowels are *a, e, i, o,* and *u.* See **a.**

an al y sis (ə nal′ə səs), *n.* 1. the separation of a chemical into its parts. *By making an analysis of water, scientists discovered that it was made up of two parts of hydrogen and one part of oxygen.* 2. an examination or method of study which breaks down a whole into its parts. *By making an analysis of the problem, we were able to come up with a solution.* **an al y ses** (ə nal′ə sēz′).

an a lyze (′an l īz), *v.* to study the nature and relationships of parts. *Let's try to analyze the world situation.* **an a lyz es, an a lyzed, an a lyz ing.**

an chor (ang′kər), *n.* 1. a piece of heavy iron attached to a rope or chain, used for holding a ship steady. *The ship's anchor dug into the ocean floor.* 2. something we depend on that makes us feel safe and secure. *The minister's faith in God was his anchor while he was held prisoner by the enemy.* 3. **at anchor,** anchored. *The ships were not moving; all were at anchor in the harbor.* 4. **weigh anchor,** to pull up the anchor; get ready to move. *The ships weighed anchor and left the harbor.* **an chors.** *v.* 5. to drop anchor. *The ships anchored a mile from shore.* 6. to secure or fasten in place by anchor. *We anchored the boat and swam ashore.* **an chors, an chored, an chor ing.**

an cho vy (an′chō vē, an′chə vē), *n.* a very small fish living in the ocean around the south of Europe. *Anchovies are used for eating after they have been pickled or made into a kind of paste to spread on crackers.* **an cho vies.**

an cient (ān′shənt), *adj.* 1. belonging to times long ago. *There are many ancient temples in Greece, Italy, and Egypt. Some ancient buildings are six thousand years old.* 2. of or about times that are very old. *We study ancient history.*

and (and, ənd, ən), *conj.* 1. with; along with; together with; as well as; besides. *I use salt and pepper on my eggs. He likes to sing and dance.* 2. added to. *In arithmetic, 4 and 5 are 9.* 3. to. *Try and catch me!*

an e mom e ter (an′ə mom′ə tər), *n.* an instrument that shows the speed of the wind. It has small cups which are pushed around by the wind. *An anemometer is used by the weatherman.* **an e mom e ters.**

an gel (ān′jəl), *n.* 1. a spiritual being used by God. *The Bible tells how angels carried messages from God to His people.* 2. a woman who is like an angel in her goodness and helpfulness. *To a sick person, the nurse is an angel bringing comfort and relief from pain.* **an gels.**

an ger (ang′gər), *n.* 1. a feeling a person has when something or someone hurts him, cheats him, destroys his property, or behaves badly. *The boy was filled with anger when two strangers knocked down the snowman which had taken him all morning to build.* *v.* 2. to excite to anger. *The governor's speech angered the man, so the man voted for another candidate.* **an gers, an gered, an ger ing.**

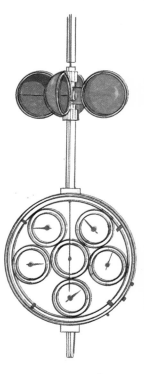

anemometer

sand, āte, bâre, fäther; sent, mē, fèrn; fit, bīke; pot, rōpe, fôrt; run, pùll, rüle, cūte; noise, sound; ch, cheese; ng, long; th, thick; ~~th~~, those; zh, treasure; ə = a in about, e in waken, i in animal, o in seldom, and u in minus.

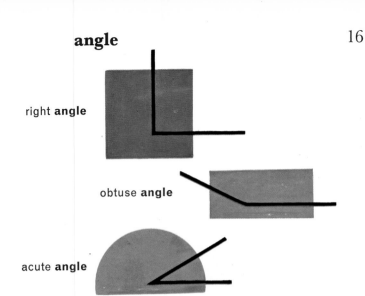

right **angle**

obtuse **angle**

acute **angle**

an gle (ang′gl), *n.* 1. the space between two lines which come together in a point. *On the math test, the class had to measure the size of four angles.* 2. the figure formed by two such lines. *The teacher drew an angle on the chalkboard.* **an gles.**

an gry (ang′grē), *adj.* 1. feeling or showing anger; filled with anger. *His father made an angry reply to his request for more money. He became so angry when he spilled ink on his homework that he tore the paper apart.* 2. stormy. *The angry sea has roaring waves.* 3. red; sore. *The cut on your arm is not much better; it still looks angry.* **an gri er, an gri est; an gri ly,** *adv.*

an i mal (an′ə ml), *n.* 1. a living being that is not a plant. *Most animals can move, and most plants cannot. Dogs, worms, elephants, and snakes are all animals.* **an i mals.**
adj. 2. of or pertaining to animals. *The animal world contains hundreds of thousands of kinds of animals.*

an kle (ang′kl), *n.* the joint connecting the foot with the leg. *It is very difficult to walk when you have a sore ankle.* **an kles.**

ant:
a. red ant; **b.** queen; **c.** worker;
d. anthill; **e.** eggs; **f.** larvae; **g.** pupae

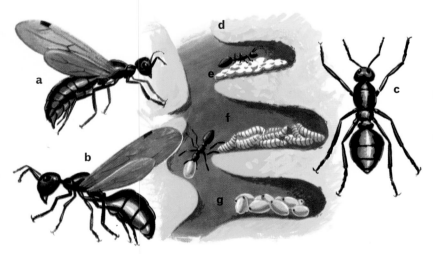

an ni ver sa ry (an′ə vẽr′sə rē), *n.* 1. the yearly return of some date. *My birthday is December 2, and every year we celebrate this anniversary with cake and ice cream.* 2. a celebration on the return of a special date. *Their wedding anniversary is next Sunday.* **an ni ver sa ries.**
adj. 3. having to do with an anniversary. *We will have a big anniversary dinner on his birthday.*

an nounce (ə nouns′), *v.* 1. to tell; make known; give notice. *At one o'clock we will announce that the school is closing because of the heavy snowfall.* 2. to make known to everybody. *Newspapers announce new movies and the dates of baseball games, auto races, and lectures.* **an nounc es, an nounced, an nounc ing.**

an nounce ment (ə nouns′mənt), *n.* a public or formal notice announcing something. *Every day the newspapers have announcements of births, deaths, weddings, plays, and lectures. We send to friends a card that contains the announcement of a marriage or a graduation.* **an nounce ments.**

an nu al (an′ū əl), *adj.* 1. coming once a year; occurring once a year. *Christmas is an annual holiday. Most workers get an annual vacation of two weeks.* 2. lasting one year. *Vegetables like beans and corn are annual plants; they must be planted every year.* **an nu al ly,** *adv.*
n. 3. a flower that lives only one season. *The marigold is a popular annual.* 4. a book published and printed only once a year. *Most high schools publish an annual, with pictures of all the graduates of the year.* **an nu als.**

an other (ə nuth′ər), *adj.* 1. one more. *Let me read another story to keep the boys quiet.* 2. any other; a different. *I am going to another part of the country since I've always lived in Texas.*
pron. 3. a different one. *We walked from one exhibit to another at the zoo. If you don't like that one, ask for another.* 4. one more; an additional one. *She drank one glass of milk, and then asked for another.*

an swer (an′sər), *n.* 1. a reply. *Send my answer to his letter quickly.* 2. a solution. *I had the answer to that problem in arithmetic.* **an swers.**
v. 3. to reply to. *He always answers letters on the same day he gets them.* 4. to act in response to. *Will someone please answer that telephone?* 5. to respond or reply. *He answered with a shake of his head. When we ask a question, our teacher always answers.* **an swers, an swered, an swer ing.**

ant (ant), *n.* a small insect that lives in the ground or in wood. *Ants live together in groups called colonies.* **ants.**

ant arc tic (ant ärk′tik, ant är′tik), *adj.* 1. around or near the South Pole. *There have been many antarctic explorations.*
n. 2. **the Antarctic,** the land and the water around the South Pole. *The Antarctic includes the continent of Antarctica and the Antarctic Ocean.*

ant eat er (ant′ēt′ər), *n.* an animal of Central and South America that eats ants, using its

sand, āte, bâre, fäther; sent, mē, fẽrn; fit, bīke; pot, rōpe, fôrt; run, pùll, rüle, cūte; noise, sound; ch, cheese; ng, long; th, thick; t̶h̶, those; zh, treasure; ə = a in about, e in waken, i in animal, o in seldom, and u in minus.

ANIMALS

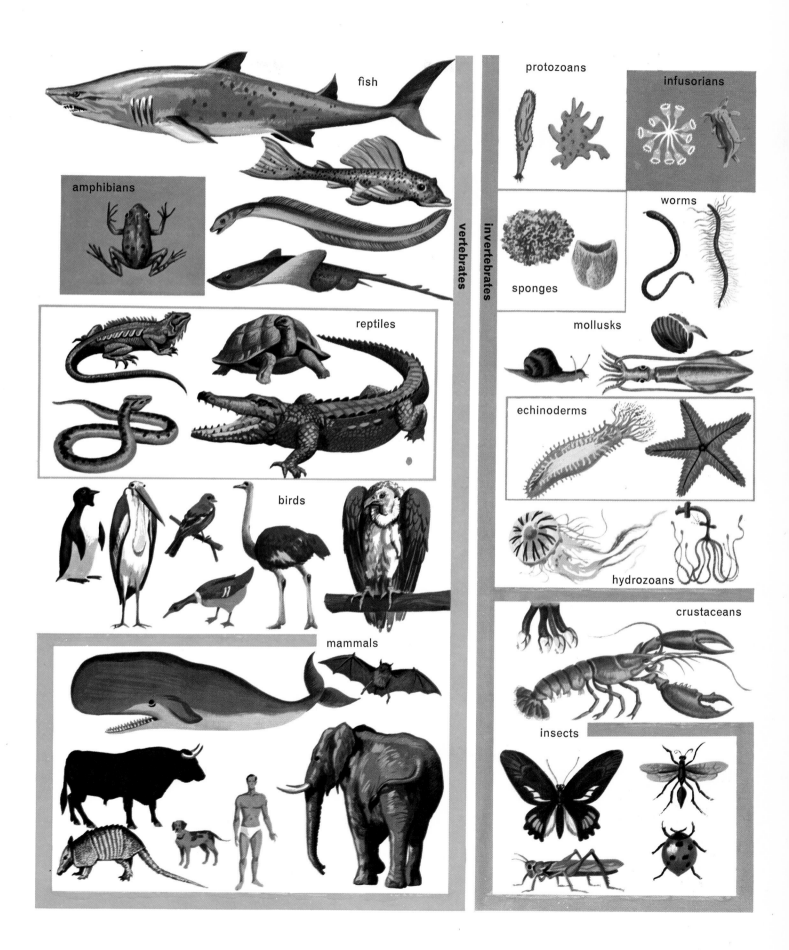

fish

amphibians

reptiles

birds

mammals

vertebrates

invertebrates

protozoans

infusorians

worms

sponges

mollusks

echinoderms

hydrozoans

crustaceans

insects

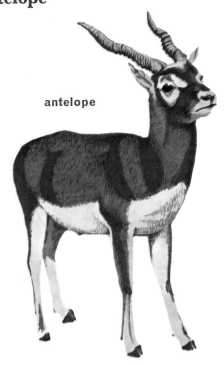

antelope

long, sticky tongue to reach out and grab them. *An anteater lives in the damp forests of warm areas.* **ant eaters.**

an te lope (an′tə lōp′), *n.* a swift animal that is somewhat like a deer. *Antelopes have horns.* **an te lopes.**

an ti-air craft (an′ti âr′kraft′), *adj.* used in defense against enemy airplanes. *The anti-aircraft guns were kept ready.*

an ti bi o tic (an′ti bī ot′ik), *n.* a germ-killing substance made from certain bacteria. *Doctors use antibiotics in the treatment of patients. Antibiotics can cure diseases in animals and plants.* **an ti bi o tics.**

an ti body (an′ti bod′ē), *n.* a substance in the blood that destroys or weakens bacteria. *When a doctor gives you vaccine for smallpox or polio, antibodies which fight the disease develop in your body.* **an ti bod ies.**

an tic i pate (an tis′ə pāt′), *v.* 1. to expect; look forward to. *We anticipate a hard-fought game with the state champions in baseball. The children were anticipating the arrival of their grandmother from out of town.* 2. to think of ahead of time. *The airplane and automobile were anticipated almost five hundred years ago by the famous Italian Leonardo da Vinci, who even drew plans of how to make them.* 3. to deal with ahead of time. *We anticipated the snow storm and bought a snow shovel.* **an tic i-pates, an tic i pat ed, an tic i pat ing.**

an tic i pa tion (an tis′ə pā′shən), *n.* expectation. *In anticipation of a heavy thunderstorm, mother asked us to shut all the windows before we left the house.*

an to nym (an′tə nim), *n.* word that means the opposite of another word. *"Hot" is an antonym of "cold"; "fast" is an antonym of "slow"; "beautiful" is an antonym of "ugly".* **an tonyms.**

an vil (an′vil), *n.* a block of iron or steel on which heated metal is hammered into a certain shape. *Blacksmiths use anvils to make iron shoes for horses.* **an vils.**

anx i e ty (ang zī′ə tē), *n.* 1. worry and distress about the bad things that could happen. *The passengers in the airliner felt anxiety when the heavy winds hit the plane, but it landed safely. The day before report cards came out, the pupils were filled with anxiety.* 2. intense eagerness. *He has an anxiety to be a scientist, so he takes extra science courses.* **anx i e ties.**

anx ious (angk′shəs), *adj.* 1. troubled and worried. *Mothers often feel anxious about their children when they are not home on time, or when they are not warmly dressed.* 2. eager; wanting very much. *I am anxious to see the final game of the World Series.*

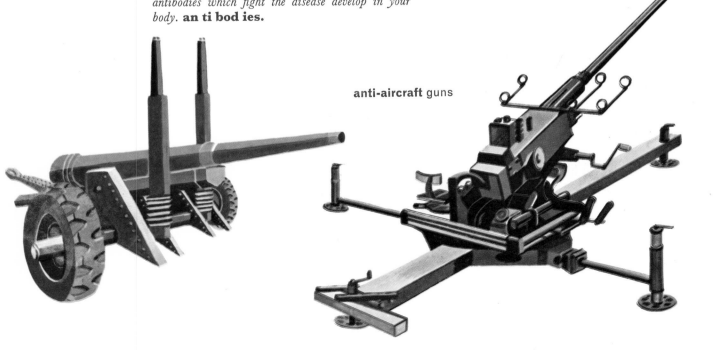

anti-aircraft guns

anvil

any (en′ē), *adj.* 1. one no matter which. *Take any piece of candy; I don't care which you choose.* 2. some. *I'm sorry, but I don't have any money to lend you—not even a dime.* 3. every. *Any dog's nose is so sensitive that he can just about smell his way home!*
adv. 4. at all; to some extent. *Since I've been away, has the town grown any?*

an y body (en′ē bud′ē, en′ē bod′ē), *pron.* any person. *Did you see anybody that I know at the meeting?*

an y how (en′ē hou′), *adv.* 1. in any case; regardless. *Well, anyhow, we'll meet downtown even if I can't tell you the exact place.* 2. in any manner. *Anyhow you look at it, education is always worthwhile.*

an y more (en′ē môr′), *adv.* from a certain time on. *Farmers don't use horses anymore; they use tractors and other machines. You don't see steam locomotives anymore; all trains are pulled by diesel engines.*

an y one (en′ē wun′), *pron.* anybody; any person, not anybody in particular. *This public beach is open to all, and anyone can go swimming here.*

an y thing (en′ē thing′), *pron.* 1. any thing; something. *We shopped at a dozen stores, and we couldn't find anything grandma might want for her birthday.* 2. at all. *Is your dog anything like mine, wanting to eat all the time?*

an y way (en′ē wā′), *adv.* anyhow; no matter what may happen. *It may rain tomorrow, but we are going to have the picnic anyway.*

an y where (en′ē hwâr′), *adv.* any place. *Mr. Cooper, the salesman, goes anywhere he is sent; one week he's in Chicago, the next week he's in New York.*

aor ta (ā ôr′tə), *n.* the main artery of the body. *The many branches of the aorta carry blood to all parts of the body.*

apart (ə pärt′), *adv.* 1. to pieces. *All soldiers are taught how to take a rifle apart and put it together again.* 2. away from others. *Most of the seats were taken, so he had to sit apart from his friends.* 3. one from the other. *The twin girls have always looked and dressed alike so that no one can tell them apart.*

apart ment (ə pärt′mənt), *n.* 1. a group of rooms to live in, usually in a larger building called an apartment house. *Some apartments contain twelve rooms; most are four, five, or six rooms.* 2. a single room. *They made each bedroom in the house into a separate apartment.* **apartments.**

ape (āp), *n.* 1. a long-armed monkey with no tail. *An ape can stand almost straight and can walk on his two feet.* **apes.**
v. 2. to act like; imitate. *Little children often ape the actions of persons they see.* **apes, aped, ap ing.**

apiece (ə pēs′), *adv.* each; for each item. *The new shirts cost a dollar apiece.*

apol o gy (ə pol′ə jē), *n.* words saying one is sorry for doing the wrong thing; asking pardon. *Please accept my apology for coming so late; I was delayed by heavy traffic.* **apol o gies.**

apos tro phe (ə pos′trə fē), *n.* a mark like this (') used (1) to show that a letter or letters are purposely left out of a word: *it'll* for *it will; you've* for *you have;* (2) to show that something belongs to someone, as in *Jim's friend; the boys' team;* (3) in forming certain plurals, as in *the three r's. The apostrophe looks like a misplaced comma.* **apos tro phes.**

ap par ent (ə par′ənt), *adj.* 1. clearly seen; easily understood; obvious. *It is apparent that he is growing; this is the third pair of larger shoes we bought for him in two years.* 2. appearing to be. *At the end of the first inning, our team was the apparent loser, 8–0; but we battled back and finally won, 9–8.* **ap par ent ly,** *adv.*

ap peal (ə pēl′), *n.* 1. a request made very seriously. *The lawyer said he would file an appeal for another trial for his client. The class sent an appeal to the principal for permission to decorate their room at Christmas.* 2. an attractive quality; interest. *A job in a summer resort has an appeal for many college students. Sailing has a great appeal for most Americans, and millions of them now own boats of various kinds.* **ap peals.**
v. 3. to make a serious request. *The teacher appealed for helpers for the school clean-up campaign.* 4. to be attractive; to be interesting. *Traveling by automobile appeals to many Americans, who spend their vacations going thousands of miles.* **ap peals, ap pealed, ap peal ing.**

ap pear (ə pir′), *v.* 1. to show up; be seen. *The New York Symphony Orchestra will appear at our next music festival. He appeared for breakfast promptly at seven o'clock.* 2. to seem; look; give an appearance. *A year ago the bank hired a man who appeared to have all the qualities of a good banker; yesterday he was made a vice-president.* **ap pears, ap peared, ap pear ing.**

ap pear ance (ə pir′əns), *n.* 1. coming into view. *The appearance of the President's car excited the people who shouted, waved, and cheered as it slowly drove past them.* 2. being seen by the public. *The girls are all excited because the television star is making a personal appearance today.* 3. the looks of a place or person. *The edge of this city has a lonely, deserted appearance.* **ap pear anc es.**

apple:
a. blossoms
b. fruit

ap pe tite (ap′ə tīt′), *n.* 1. a desire for food. *I always have an appetite after swimming.* 2. any desire. *He has such a big appetite for reading that you never see him without a book.* **ap pe tites.**

ap ple (ap′l), *n.* a fruit for eating, usually round, that grows on a tree. *Apples are red or green or yellow, depending on the kind they are. Green apples are often used in pies.* **ap ples.**

ap pli cant (ap′lə kənt), *n.* a person who is applying for a job or position. *There were ten applicants for the job, but Jim thinks he will get it.* **ap pli cants.**

ap pli ca tion (ap′lə kā′shən), *n.* 1. an applying; putting on. *The application of salve healed the burn.* 2. a request. *Jack sent in an application for the job.* 3. putting to use. *The application of something you learned in seventh grade can sometimes help in college work or in business.* 4. close attention; constant effort. *Application to your studying may be difficult, but it is worth the energy.* **ap pli ca tions.**

ap plied (ə plīd′), *adj.* put to practical use. *Applied science and applied mathematics deal with real, everyday problems; pure science and mathematics deal with theories.*

ap ply (ə plī′), *v.* 1. to put on. *The painter will apply three coats of paint to the house.* 2. to make a request. *I filled out three forms to apply for the job.* 3. to put to use. *Going to school is of more use if you apply the knowledge you get.* 4. to give the attention of (oneself); set (oneself). *If you apply*

yourself to the task, you will finish faster. 5. to refer; pertain. *The law applies to all persons.* **ap plies, ap plied, ap ply ing.**

ap point (ə point′), *v.* 1. to select; choose; assign. *The mayor of our village is going to appoint a new head for our Boys' Baseball League.* 2. to decide on or determine. *What time did the principal appoint for the assembly?* **ap points, ap point ed, ap point ing.**

ap point ment (ə point′mənt), *n.* 1. an arrangement to meet someone at a certain time. *I have an appointment with my dentist Saturday afternoon at two o'clock.* 2. the selecting or choosing of a person for a position. *The appointment of the Secretary of State was made by the President.* 3. position; office. *The former ambassador received the appointment of Treasurer.* **ap point-ments.**

ap pre ci ate (ə prē′shē āt′), *v.* 1. to see the value or good of something. *After working hard all day, I appreciate a quiet evening at home.* 2. to value; think good of. *The longer I look at that painting, the more I appreciate it. The child's mother appreciated his handmade valentine, which said, "I love you."* **ap pre ci ates, ap pre ci-at ed, ap pre ci at ing.**

ap pre ci a tion (ə prē′shē ā′shən), *n.* 1. thanks; gratitude. *You should show appreciation for the things your parents and friends do for you.* 2. under-standing and enjoyment. *The older you become, the more appreciation you will have for good music and books.*

ap proach (ə prōch′), *n.* 1. a way to reach a person or place. *The approach to the castle was an old wooden bridge over a river. The approaches to large cities today are big expressways.* **ap proach-es.**

v. 2. to come near or nearer. *I think a storm is approaching because of all those black clouds in the southwest. The car approached the intersection just as the traffic light turned green.* **ap proach es, ap proached, ap proach ing.**

ap prov al (ə prüv′l), *n.* 1. approving; speaking or thinking in favor of something. *Your idea is a good one, and it has my approval.* 2. consent; agreement. *Our teacher gave her approval to our plans for a graduation party.* **ap prov als.**

ap prove (ə prüv′), *v.* 1. to speak or think favor-ably. *Everybody approves of the plans for a new school building.* 2. to have a good opinion of someone or something. *Do you approve of the pictures in this book?* 3. to be in favor of. *The legislature approved the bill for a new dam.* **ap proves, ap proved, ap prov ing.**

ap prox i mate (ə prok′sə mət for 1 and 2, ə prok′sə māt′ for 3 and 4), *adj.* 1. nearly right; almost correct. *I can draw an approximate picture of the house.* 2. very much alike. *A good artist can make an approximate copy of a famous painting, but experts can always tell the difference.* **ap prox i mate ly,** *adv.*

v. 3. to come close to. *The number of people who*

apricot:
　a. branch with blossoms
　b. fruit

aquamarine

apron

the front part of one's clothing to cover and protect the clothes. *Women wear aprons in the kitchen.* **aprons.**

aq ua ma rine (ak′wə mə rēn′), *n.* 1. a clear mineral with a pale blue color. *Aquamarines are used in rings and other jewelry.* 2. a pale blue-green color. *This morning the ocean was aquamarine.* **aq ua ma rines.**

aquar i um (ə kwâr′ē əm), *n.* 1. a glass tank to hold live fish for display. *Johnny has a small aquarium with three goldfish in it.* 2. building used for showing large collections of living fish. *I never knew there were so many kinds of fish until I visited the aquarium.* **aquar i ums.**

arc (ärk), *n.* a curved line; a line that is part of a circle. *When the moon is new, it looks like an arc of light in the sky.* **arcs.**

arch (ärch), *n.* a structure curved like part of a circle. *Arches are built of wood, stone, brick, or any other building material. In the picture, the arches support one of the old Roman aqueducts, which were*

attended the fair approximated two thousand. 4. to have a likeness or similarity to. *His way of thinking approximates mine.* **ap prox i mates, ap prox i mat ed, ap prox i mat ing.**

apri cot (ā′pri kot′, ap′ri kot′), *n.* a small, round, orange-colored fruit. *The apricot has fuzz on it like a peach.* **apri cots.**

April (ā′prəl), *n.* the fourth month of the year. *April has thirty days.*

apron (ā′prən), *n.* a piece of cloth worn over

aquarium

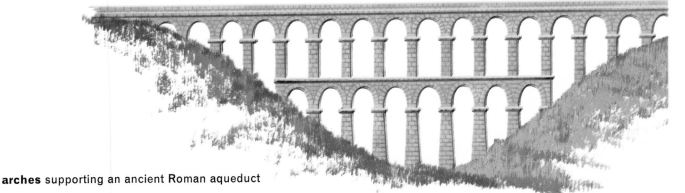

arches supporting an ancient Roman aqueduct

stone channels to carry the water supply to Rome. **arch es.**

ar chi tect (är′kə tekt), *n.* someone who designs buildings and who watches over the building's construction. *My father is the architect who designed the new school building.* **ar chi tects.**

ar chi tec ture (är′kə tek′chər), *n.* 1. the art of planning buildings. *Architecture is a profession that requires much schooling.* 2. a style or special kind of building. *Modern architecture uses more straight lines than many earlier kinds of architecture did.*

arc tic (ärk′tik, är′tik), *n.* 1. the region around or near the North Pole. *Men have learned about the arctic by traveling on the ice or by going under it in submarines.*
adj. 2. near the North Pole; of the region around the North Pole. *The arctic temperature sometimes is sixty degrees below zero.*

are (är), *v.* one form of the verb *to be*, used with *you*, *we*, and *they*. *You are first. We are next. They are last.*

ar ea (âr′ē ə), *n.* 1. an amount of space or surface. *My house is built on an area of half an acre. Ranches and big farms sometimes contain an area of 100,000 acres.* 2. extent; range. *Our city has made progress in the area of transportation; but we still need new kinds of trains and new highways.* **ar e as.**

aren't (ärnt), are not. *You aren't going to the party. We aren't invited. They aren't going either.*

ar gue (är′gū), *v.* to talk with someone who doesn't agree; give reasons for or against something. *The two friends would argue all night about baseball. The delegates in the United Nations argued about disarming their countries.* **ar gues, ar gued, ar gu ing.**

ar gu ment (är′gū mənt), *n.* 1. a discussion by

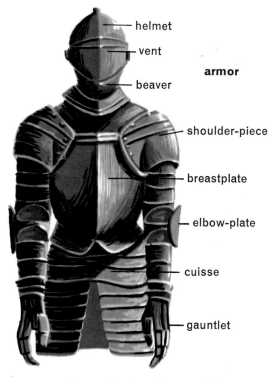

armor

- helmet
- vent
- beaver
- shoulder-piece
- breastplate
- elbow-plate
- cuisse
- gauntlet

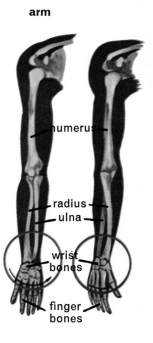

arm

- humerus
- radius
- ulna
- wrist bones
- finger bones

Ar kan sas (är′kən sô′), *n.* a state in the central southern part of the United States. *Farming and mining are the major industries of Arkansas.*

arm[1] (ärm), *n.* 1. the part of the body which is between the shoulder and the hand. *To raise your hand, you must lift your arm.* 2. anything shaped like an arm or used like an arm. *Rest your elbows on the arms of that chair.* **arms.**

arm[2] (ärm), *n.* 1. a weapon used in fighting. *Guns, knives, and clubs are arms. The soldiers prepared their arms for the battle.* 2. *pl.* symbols used on a coat of arms to represent a person, a family, a city, a government, etc. *Long ago, soldiers and kings displayed their arms on a coat worn over their armor.* **arms.**
v. 3. to supply with weapons. *The Indians were armed with tomahawks and with bows and arrows.* 4. to prepare for battle by obtaining weapons. *The pirates armed themselves for the attack.* **arms, armed, arm ing.**

arm ful (ärm′fül′), *n.* as much as can be held in one arm or in both arms. *I'm sorry I can't help you, but I have an armful of books.* **arm fuls.**

ar mor (är′mər), *n.* 1. clothing made of metal which formerly covered the head and entire body to protect men in battle. *Since his armor was so heavy, the knight had to be lifted onto his horse.* 2. any device which is worn or carried for protection in battle. *Steel helmets and bullet-proof vests are examples of a modern soldier's armor.*

two or more people who disagree. *The arguments in the United States Senate sometimes last for days. Sisters sometimes have an argument about who will help clean the house on Saturday.* 2. a statement that is supposed to prove a point. *One by one all his arguments were knocked down by the rest of the pupils.* **ar gu ments.**

arise (ə rīz′), *v.* 1. to get up. *A farmer arises early in the morning.* 2. to appear; begin. *If any quarrel arises between my brother and me, my dad settles it.* **aris es, arose, aris en, aris ing.**

arith me tic (ə rith′mə tik), *n.* the study and use of numbers. *Arithmetic includes addition, subtraction, multiplication, and division. We use arithmetic in many ways every day: at the grocery store, in keeping scores in games, in telling time, and in school.*

Ar i zo na (ar′ə zō′nə), *n.* a state in the southwestern part of the United States. *Arizona is called the Grand Canyon State.*

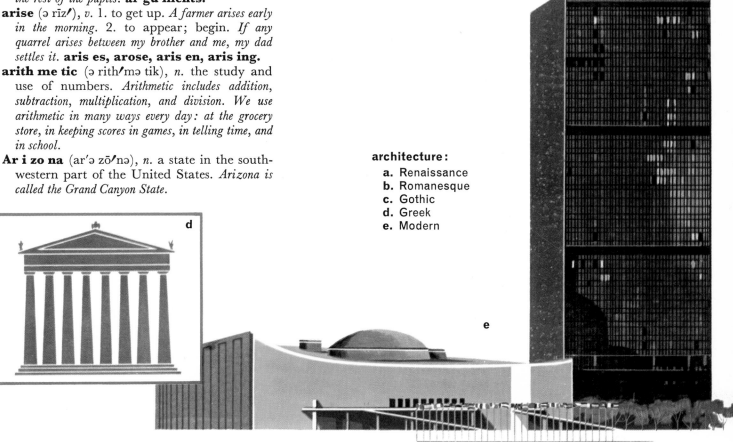

architecture:
- **a.** Renaissance
- **b.** Romanesque
- **c.** Gothic
- **d.** Greek
- **e.** Modern

sand, āte, bâre, fäther; sent, mē, fėrn; fit, bĭke; pot, rōpe, fôrt; run, pùll, rüle, cūte; noise, sound; ch, cheese; ng, long; th, thick; ᵺ, those; zh, treasure; ə = a in about, e in waken, i in animal, o in seldom, and u in minus.

The Roman soldier's armor consisted of a helmet and a shield. 3. metal plates used to protect a ship or airplane. *The armor on the sides and bottom of this ship is one foot thick.*

ar my (är′mē), *n.* 1. a large group of men who are organized and trained to serve as soldiers. *The army of the United States fought in Europe and in the Far East during World War II.* 2. any group of people who are organized for a purpose. *The Salvation Army is a religious organization.* 3. a large group; a great number. *An army of children gathered in the playground on the first day of school.* **ar mies.**

arose (ə rōz′), past tense of **arise.**

around (ə round′), *prep.* 1. in a circular path; about. *We rode around the block on our bikes.* 2. on; covering. *He wore a scarf around his neck.* 3. on every side of. *There was nothing but water around us.* 4. near to; close by. *Stay around the school until your brother comes.*
adv. 5. in a circular path. *The merry-go-round went around.* 6. in one place and another; from place to place. *We walked around in the museum for several hours.* 7. in every place; everywhere. *The toys from the toy box lay around.* 8. nearby; close; at a place. *I waited around for him but he didn't come.*

ar range (ə rānj′), *v.* 1. to organize; put in order. *Everything is arranged for the party.* 2. to decide beforehand; prepare. *I can arrange my schedule so that I can go tonight.* 3. to make music suitable for singing or playing by voices or instruments. *The music teacher has arranged several new songs for our class.* **ar rang es, ar ranged, ar rang ing.**

ar range ment (ə rānj′mənt), *n.* 1. an establishment of order; a fixing of position. *The arrangement of furniture in our living room is still not settled. A flower arrangement was in the middle of the table.* 2. the order in which things appear. *The arrangement of words in your dictionary is alphabetical.* 3. preparation. *What arrangements have been made for seating the audience?* 4. a piece of arranged music. *With this new arrangement, the band will play while the chorus sings.* **ar range ments.**

ar ray (ə rā′), *n.* 1. a neat or regular arrangement; order. *The men were grouped in battle array.* 2. an elaborate display. *The array of talent on the new show was surprising.* 3. beautiful clothes; finery. *The woman was dressed in her finest array.* 4. a group of numbers arranged in rows and columns. **ar rays.**
v. 5. to arrange in order. *The men were arrayed in battle formation.* 6. to dress in beautiful clothes. *The bride was arrayed in a white silk dress.* **ar rays, ar rayed, ar ray ing.**

ar rest (ə rest′), *v.* 1. to stop and hold by legal authority. *When the robber was arrested, the police found stolen goods in his car.* 2. to stop; to hold back; prevent from continuing. *The rising waters of the river were arrested by the dike.* 3. to catch and hold. *The beauty of the sunset arrested our interest for a moment.* **ar rests, ar rest ed, ar rest ing.**
n. 4. stopping and holding by legal authority. *The arrest of the criminal was made early this morning.* **ar rests.**

ar ri val (ə rīv′l), *n.* 1. reaching a destination; coming to a place. *The plane's arrival was delayed for several hours.* 2. a person or thing that has come to a place. *The early arrivals were asked to wait for the others.* **ar ri vals.**

ar rive (ə rīv′), *v.* 1. to come to a particular place; reach a destination. *When will your brother arrive at the airport?* 2. to come. *The day of our graduation has finally arrived.* **ar rives, ar rived, ar riv ing.**

ar row (ar′ō), *n.* 1. a thin, straight, wooden rod, having feathers at one end and usually coming to a point at the other, which is shot from a bow. *The feathers on an arrow maintain its direction in flight.* 2. anything that resembles an arrow. *An arrow of sunlight went through the darkness of the room.* 3. a symbol shaped like an arrow which indicates direction. *You must wait for the green arrow before you turn.* **ar rows.**

art (ärt), *n.* 1. writing, painting, music, etc., which can be enjoyed both through the senses and in the mind. *I enjoy looking at modern art even though I don't always understand it.* 2. a knowledge of the way in which something is done. *If you wish to meet many interesting people, you should begin to master the art of conversation.* 3. an occupation or task which requires skill and ability. *After many years, he mastered the art of playing the piano.* 4. use of tricks. *We were completely fooled by the magician's art.* 5. **the arts,** the field of knowledge that includes history, language, philosophy, etc. *My father is no baseball fan, but he loves the arts. In America there are a great number of writers, historians, musicians, and other men who have devoted their lives to the arts.* **arts.**

ar tery (är′tə ri), *n.* 1. any of the vessels in the body which carry blood from the heart to all parts of the body. *Which artery carries blood to the brain?* 2. any important path by which a thing is carried, especially a major road. *The major arteries in the city were blocked by rush-hour traffic.* **ar ter ies.**

ar ti choke (är′tə chōk′), *n.* 1. a plant that grows about three feet tall and has a flowering head that is eaten as a vegetable. *The artichoke looks like a thistle.* 2. the vegetable itself. *Fresh artichoke has to be cooked in boiling water before it can be eaten.* **ar ti chokes.**

ar ti cle (är′tə kl), *n.* 1. an essay or other piece of writing that is included in a book, newspaper, or magazine. *The plans for the new school building were discussed in an article in yesterday's newspaper.* 2. a separate, usually numbered section of a constitution, contract, treaty, or other formal agreement. *There are seven articles*

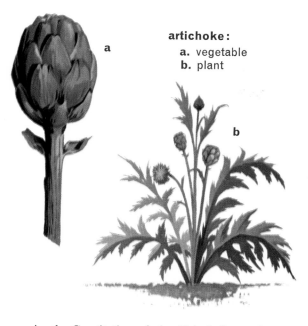

artichoke:
a. vegetable
b. plant

in the Constitution of the United States. 3. an object; thing. *Several articles of clothing were lying around the room.* 4. one of the words *a, an,* or *the,* used before nouns. *We went for a walk. I ate an apple. Did you like the movie?* **ar ti cles.**

ar ti fi cial (är′tə fish′əl), *adj.* 1. man-made; not occurring in nature; not produced in nature. *Nylon and plastic are artificial products.* 2. not sincere; not natural; not genuine. *When he tries hard to get people to like him, he sounds artificial.* **ar ti fi cial ly,** *adv.*

ar til lery (är til′ə rē), *n.* large guns so heavy they must be hauled. *Artillery is used for firing heavy cannon balls or explosives.* (See illustration on following page.)

ar tist (ärt′əst), *n.* 1. a painter or sculptor. *The exhibit at the museum contained works by many of our greatest artists.* 2. a writer, musician, or any other person skilled in one of the fine arts. *Several artists were guests of honor at the dance.* 3. any person who does his work extremely well. *Babe Ruth and Ted Williams were batting artists of rare ability.* **ar tists.**

as (az), *adv.* 1. to the same degree; to an equal extent. *Tom can run at least as quickly as his brother.* 2. for instance; for example. *Many natural products, as rubber, coal, and oil, are helpful in making our lives easier and more comfortable. Fruits, such as oranges, apples, and grapefruit, provide us with many of the vitamins we need.*
conj. 3. at the same time that; when. *They were leaving as we arrived.* 4. in the same manner that; in the way that. *Do unto others as you would have them do unto you.* 5. for the reason that; since; because. *As I was sick, I was unable to finish my work.*
prep. 6. in the dress, manner, or role of. *Sarah came to the party as Little Bo Peep. If you stay as quiet as mice, I will read a story to you.*
pron. 7. that. *He works in the same store as my*

father. 8. a fact that. *He is not coming, as you know.*

as cend (ə send′), *v.* 1. to go to a higher place; move upward; rise. *The big balloon ascended and disappeared into the clouds.* 2. to climb; to go up. *Slowly we ascended the stairs to the dark attic.* **as cends, as cend ed, as cend ing.**

as cer tain (as′ər tān′), *v.* to make certain of; to find out for sure; to determine. *How can we ascertain the correct time without a clock?* **as cer tains, as cer tained, as cer tain ing.**

ash[1] (ash), *n.* a common shade tree. *The wood of the ash is used for such things as furniture, tool handles, and baseball bats. The seeds of the ash are winged and spin to the ground in the fall.* **ash es.**

ash[2] (ash), *n.* the remains of a thing that has been burned. *The thick smoke was filled with bits of ash.* **ash es.**

ashamed (ə shāmd′), *adj.* 1. feeling shame because of doing something wrong or foolish. *He was ashamed because he forgot his part in the play.* 2. unwilling or fearful to act because of shame. *When she failed to recognize him, he was too ashamed to talk to her.*

aside (ə sīd′), *adv.* on or to one side. *If we move the dishes aside, we can use the table for our game of checkers.*

ask (ask), *v.* 1. to try to find out by questioning. *If you don't understand the problem, please ask me about it.* 2. to try to find information; to inquire. *Do not ask about tomorrow's test.* 3. to inquire of. *Ask him if he goes to your school.* 4. to request of. *He asked me for a pencil and a sheet of paper.* 5. to expect to receive; demand. *They are asking four dollars for that football.* 6. to request to come; invite. *Have you been asked to the party?* **asks, asked, ask ing.**

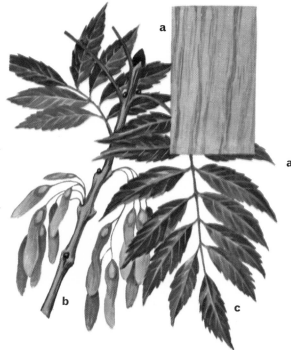

ash:
a. grain of wood
b. seeds
c. leaves

sand, āte, bâre, fäther; sent, mē, fėrn; fit, bīke; pot, rōpe, fôrt; run, pùll, rüle, cūte; noise, sound; ch, cheese; ng, long; th, thick; ~~th,~~ those; zh, treasure; ə = a in about, e in waken, i in animal, o in seldom, and u in minus.

ARTILLERY OVER THE YEARS

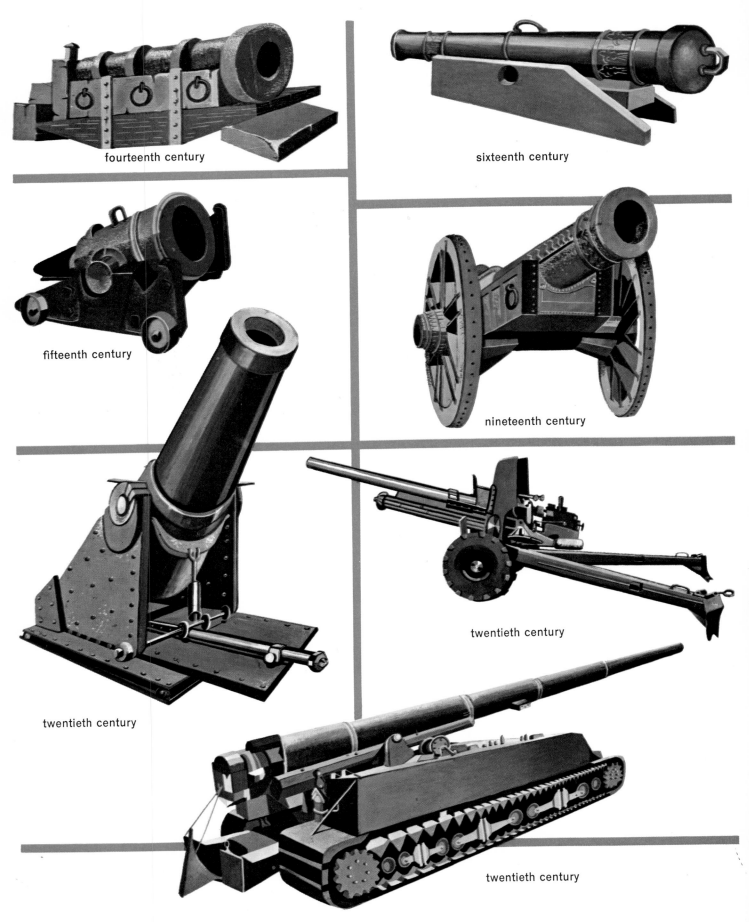

fourteenth century

sixteenth century

fifteenth century

nineteenth century

twentieth century

twentieth century

twentieth century

asleep (ə slēp′), *adj.* 1. not awake; sleeping. *The dog is asleep after a long walk.* 2. numb. *My hand is asleep, and I can't feel anything with it.* *adv.* 3. into a state of sleep. *He fell asleep during the movie.*

as par a gus (ə spar′ə gəs), *n.* a plant with small leaves like scales. *The upper part of the asparagus is cooked and eaten as a vegetable.*

as pect (as′pekt), *n.* 1. a point of view; way of looking at a subject. *You must examine all of the aspects of the problem before you try to solve it.* 2. expression; appearance; look. *The jolly aspect of Santa Claus made the children very happy.* **as pects.**

as pen (as′pən), *n.* a tree whose leaves have long, thin stems, so that they flutter in every light breeze. *The aspen has light green leaves and greenish-white bark, which fades to gray with age.* **as pens.**

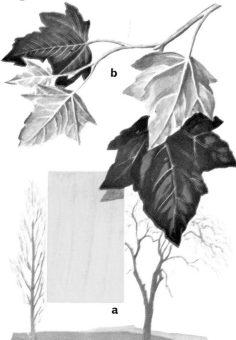

aspen:
  a. grain of wood
  b. branch with leaves

as pi rin (as′pə rən), *n.* a mild medicine in the form of a pill, used to relieve headaches, toothaches, and other minor pains and to reduce fever. *As soon as she began coughing and sneezing, her mother gave her two aspirins made especially for children.* **as pi rins.**

ass (as), *n.* 1. a donkey. *The old man bought three asses, loaded all of his belongings on their backs, and went out in the desert to live.* 2. a foolish person; stupid person. *Sometimes he acts like an ass.* **ass es.**

as sem ble (ə sem′bl), *v.* 1. to come together as a group; gather; meet. *The entire school will assemble in front of the building for the flag-raising ceremony.* 2. to put the parts of something

ass

together; make something by putting its parts together. *Have you ever assembled a jigsaw puzzle? Many boys enjoy assembling model airplanes and cars.* **as sem bles, as sem bled, as sembling.**

as sem bly (ə sem′blē), *n.* 1. a number of people gathered together for a common purpose; meeting. *The principal spoke at the assembly in the auditorium this morning.* 2. a meeting of the legislative body of a particular state, country, etc. *The General Assembly of the United Nations passed three resolutions last week.* 3. a putting together of the parts of a thing. *The assembly of a rocket and space capsule may take several years to complete.* **as sem blies.**

as sign (ə sīn′), *v.* 1. to give out; distribute. *The hotel rooms are assigned by the clerk at the desk in the lobby.* 2. to name a task and request that it be done. *Every time mother assigns the housework, Sally does the dishes, Tom mops the floors, and I clean the windows.* 3. to appoint to a position; to name for a task. *He was assigned to act as chairman for our first meeting.* 4. to establish for a particular purpose; to set; to fix. *The last Monday in May was assigned as the day of our picnic.* **as signs, as signed, as sign ing.**

as sign ment (ə sīn′mənt), *n.* 1. a thing assigned. *It took me three hours to complete my homework assignments.* 2. the act of naming or appointing; an assigning. *The class eagerly awaited the assignments of parts in the play.* **as sign ments.**

as sist (ə sist′), *v.* to help; aid. *Bob assisted me with my paper route yesterday.* **as sists, as sisted, as sist ing.**

as sist ance (ə sis′təns), *n.* help; aid. *I will be glad to offer my assistance when you paint your house.*

asparagus

as sist ant (ə sis′tənt), *n.* 1. a person who assists another; helper. *We need four more assistants to move this piano.* 2. a person who works under another person. *He is an assistant to the vice-president of the bank.* **as sist ants.**

as so ci ate (ə sō′shē āt′ for 1–3, ə sō′shē ət, ə sō′shē āt′ for 4 and 5), *v.* 1. to connect in the mind; to think of as related; to join in thought. *It is common to associate tears with sadness, but many people cry when they are very happy.* 2. to join as a friend or companion. *I usually associate with George because he is entertaining.* 3. to unite; to join as a partner for a particular task. *Several years ago I was associated with Mr. Williams in writing a book.* **as so ci ates, as so ci at ed, as so ci at ing.**
adj. 4. belonging to a group or organization but not having all of the rights and privileges of membership. *The associate members of the country club were not permitted to enter the golf tournament.*
n. 5. a friend, companion, fellow worker, or partner. *My associates and I will prepare a full report for the next meeting.* **as so ci ates.**

as so ci a tion (ə sō′sē ā′shən), *n.* 1. a number of persons joined together for the same purpose; organization. *The parents' association at our school bought uniforms for the baseball team.* 2. a joining together for a purpose; an associating. *I have enjoyed our association because you have been so easy to work with.* 3. something connected in the mind; a combining of ideas, feelings, memories, etc. in the mind. *The smell of burning logs always brings happy associations to my mind.* **as so ci a tions.**

as sort ed (ə sôrt′əd), *adj.* 1. divided and arranged in groups. *A group of boys of assorted heights marched in the parade.* 2. chosen and arranged to include a variety. *We gave Mother a box of assorted chocolates for her birthday.*

as sort ment (ə sôrt′mənt), *n.* 1. the division and arrangement of things in groups. *The assortment of these coins took us several hours to complete.* 2. a group of things chosen and arranged to include a variety. *You may select your shoes from the assortment on this table.* **as sort ments.**

as sume (ə süm′), *v.* 1. to accept as true without proof; take for granted. *We have to assume that the weather will be pleasant on the day of our picnic.* 2. to accept a responsibility or a position; take upon oneself. *Next week Harry will assume the office of president in our club. Betty assumed the responsibility of decorating the room for the party.* 3. to put on a false appearance; to pretend. *He assumed a confident attitude, even though he knew he would not succeed. The man assumed a pained expression when the little boy jabbed at his arm in fun.* **as sumes, as sumed, as sum ing.**

as sur ance (ə shùr′əns), *n.* 1. a statement intended to fill a person with confidence. *The manager of the store was given every assurance that the bill would be paid.* 2. a feeling of sureness; confidence. *We were filled with assurance that the store would still be open.* 3. confidence in one's own ability; self-confidence. *His assurance while answering questions convinced us that he was telling the truth.* **as sur anc es.**

as sure (ə shùr′), *v.* 1. to make certain; to make sure. *One more home run will assure the victory.* 2. to tell or inform positively. *The pilot assured us that the plane would land in an hour.* 3. to convince; to make someone sure. *My teacher assured me that I was doing well in school.* **as sures, as sured, as sur ing.**

as sured (ə shùrd′), *adj.* 1. sure of oneself; confident in one's ability. *Even though this was his first part in a play, Don was calm and assured on the stage.* 2. made certain; made sure. *Our victory was assured early in the game when we scored twelve runs in the first inning.*

as ton ish (ə ston′ish), *v.* to surprise unexpectedly; to amaze. *When he began to sing, we were astonished at the beauty of his voice.* **as ton ish es, as ton ished, as ton ish ing.**

as tro naut (as′trə nôt′), *n.* 1. a person who is being trained to travel in outer space in a spaceship. *All of the astronauts in the space program were in Washington for a meeting.* 2. a person who travels in outer space in a spaceship. *Because of trouble with one of the rockets, the astronauts were ordered to return to earth and give up their attempt to reach Mars.* **as tro nauts.**

as tron o my (ə stron′ə mē), *n.* 1. the study of the sun, moon, planets, stars, and other bodies found in outer space. *In astronomy, the distance, size, and movement of heavenly bodies are studied.* 2. a book on this subject. *There are several interesting astronomies in our school library.*

at (at), *prep.* 1. in or on a place or thing. *Ralph is at school. I was standing at the bottom of the ladder when you called.* 2. on a time; during a time. *School begins at nine o'clock.* 3. in a direction; toward. *Looking at the sun for long periods of time is not good for your eyes.* 4. in a state of; engaged in. *The sergeant told us to stand at ease. The children were at play when the bell rang.* 5. for the price of. *I was able to get these marbles at a penny apiece.*

ate (āt), past tense of **eat.**

ath lete (ath′lēt), *n.* 1. a person who is able to perform exercises or to play in games that require speed, strength, and skill. *Many of the greatest athletes in the world practice every day.* 2. any person who takes an active part in a sport or other contest requiring physical ability. *At our school the athletes play baseball, football, and basketball.* **ath letes.**

ath let ic (ath let′ik), *adj.* 1. able to perform as an athlete; having strength and ability. *He is athletic, and he keeps in shape by exercising.* 2. like an athlete in appearance or manner. *Bob's broad shoulders and strong legs make him look athletic.* 3. of or for an athlete or athletics. *She*

athlete

sand, āte, bâre, fäther; sent, mē, fern; fit, bīke; pot, rōpe, fôrt; run, pull, rüle, cūte; noise, sound; ch, cheese; ng, long; th, thick; ~~th,~~ those; zh, treasure; ə = a in about, e in waken, i in animal, o in seldom, and u in minus.

was given an athletic scholarship to college because she is an excellent swimmer. **ath let i cal ly,** *adv.*

ath let ics (ath let′iks), *n.* 1. sports, games, etc. requiring skill, speed, and strength. *Mike enjoys athletics so much that he is always taking part in some sport.* 2. the exercises and drills that build speed, skill, and strength. *Athletics is an important part of our school's health program.*

at las (at′ləs), *n.* a book of maps. *We have an atlas that has maps of all of the major highways and streets in the United States.* **at las es.**

at mos phere (at′məs fir′), *n.* 1. the air around the earth; air. *The atmosphere of the earth includes all of the gases that are held by the earth's gravity.* 2. the air in a single place. *The atmosphere of the mountain park was fresh and clean.* 3. the feeling one gets from a place; the mood in a place. *The quiet atmosphere of the library helps people to read and think.* **at mos pheres.**

at om (at′əm), *n.* 1. the smallest particle into which a chemical element can be divided. *Everything around us is made up of atoms.* 2. anything which is extremely small; a particle. *He hasn't an atom of envy in his nature.* **at oms.**

at tach (ə tach′), *v.* 1. to connect with something; fasten; join. *She used a paper clip to attach the note to the book.* 2. to include in; to add. *A table of contents was attached to the book.* 3. to connect, hold, or join by affection. *Terry is strongly attached to his dog.* 4. to belong. *Certain duties attach to this job.* **at tach es, at tached, at tach ing.**

at tack (ə tak′), *v.* 1. to begin to fight against with force or with weapons. *Hundreds of Indians attacked the fort at sunrise.* 2. to begin a task with force and energy; to work on with energy. *Tom attacked the fence with his brush in one hand and a bucket of paint in the other.* 3. to criticize sharply; to use strong words against. *The clean-up campaign attacked those people who are careless with wastepaper.* 4. to make an attack; to begin fighting. *The army attacked at night when the enemy was asleep.* **at tacks, at tacked, at tack-ing.**

n. 5. an attacking; a setting upon. *We knew that the attack had succeeded when we saw our flag raised over the fort.* **at tacks.**

at tain (ə tān), *v.* 1. to succeed in doing through hard work; to achieve. *When everyone in the class decided to help us, we knew that we could attain our goal in a short time.* 2. to arrive at; to reach. *When I attained the age of seven, I was only three feet tall.* **at tains, at tained, at tain ing.**

at tempt (ə tempt′), *v.* 1. to try; to make an effort. *We all attempted to be friends with the new students.* **at tempts, at tempt ed, at-tempt ing.**

n. 2. a try; an effort. *He made an attempt at playing baseball.* **at tempts.**

at tend (ə tend′), *v.* 1. to go to; to be present at. *Did you attend the last meeting of the club?* 2. to work at; to apply oneself. *You must attend to your homework before you go to bed.* 3. to go along with; to stay with. *Special policemen attend the*

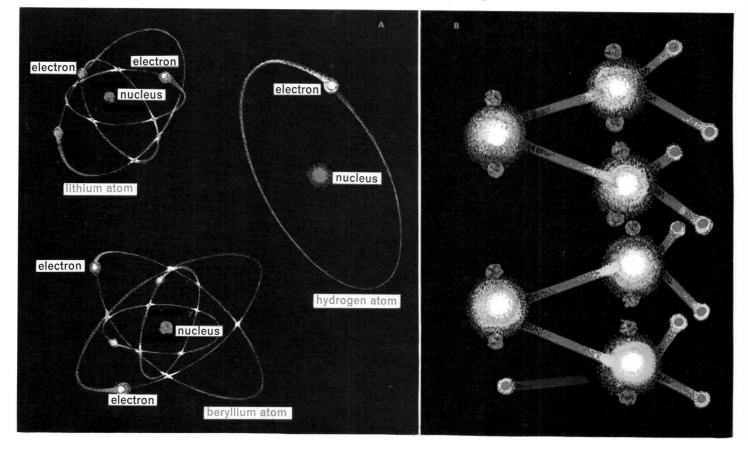

atom: a. atomic structures;   **b.** chain reaction; the nucleus of the atom breaks down into protons (shown in green) and neutrons (shown in red)

President whenever he is in public places. 4. to take care of as a servant; to wait on. *Four waiters attended us at dinner.* 5. to follow as a result. *Laughter often attends happiness.* **at tends, at tend ed, at tend ing.**

at tend ance (ə ten′dəns), *n.* 1. an attending; a being present. *His attendance at school has been perfect all year.* 2. all of the persons present; the number of persons who have attended. *The attendance at our meetings is growing.*

at tend ant (ə ten′dənt), *n.* 1. a person who serves or waits on others. *There are always four attendants working at this gas station.* 2. a person who is in attendance; one who is present. *Mary was one of the attendants at the play.* **at tend ants.**
adj. 3. serving another; waiting on another. *She was the attendant nurse who took care of my father when he was sick.* 4. coming with as a result; accompanying. *There is always some attendant fear when one is learning to drive.*

at ten tion (ə ten′shən), *n.* 1. an attending closely with the mind; a staying alert to what is happening. *Will you please pay attention to what I am saying.* 2. the power or ability of attending closely with the mind. *The cat's attention was distracted for a moment, and the mouse escaped.* 3. thoughtfulness; consideration. *His love for the dog could be seen in the attention he gave it.* 4. an act of kindness or courtesy. *My grandfather always receives many attentions when he comes to our house.* 5. in the army, a firm and straight position held by a soldier as he waits for an order. *The men stood at attention as they waited for the parade to begin.* **at ten tions.**

at ti tude (at′ə tüd′, at′ə tūd′), *n.* 1. a way of looking at a subject, thinking about something, or acting. *His attitude toward his job makes him a good worker.* 2. a position of the body or a manner of acting that shows a person's feeling. *She was resting her chin on her arm in a sleepy attitude when the teacher called on her.* **at ti tudes.**

at tor ney (ə tėr′nē), *n.* 1. a person who practices law; a lawyer. *The attorney won the case by proving that the man who was accused of the crime was asleep when the crime was committed.* 2. a person who has the power of doing business for another. *If you are sure that you can sell my house, I will name you as my attorney.* **at tor neys.**

at tract (ə′trakt), *v.* to pull or draw something to oneself. *Pretty girls attract a lot of attention.* **at tracts, at tracted, at tract ing.**

at trac tive (ə trak′tiv), *adj.* 1. pleasing; likable; appealing. *The colors in that picture make it very attractive.* 2. having the power to attract; attracting. *The attractive force of a magnet draws bits of iron to it.* **at trac tive ly,** *adv.*

au di ence (ô′dē əns), *n.* 1. a number of people who come together to see or hear something. *A large audience had gathered to see the new movie.* 2. all of the persons who can see or hear something. *More than half of the total television audience was watching the baseball game.* 3. a personal meeting with an important person; an interview. *During our audience with the king, he told us of his plans for the country.* **au di enc es.**

au dio (ô′dē ō′), *adj.* 1. of hearing; of sound. *The audio level of the phonograph was so low that we could not hear it.* 2. designed to be heard rather than viewed. *A phonograph record is an audio device.*

au di tion (ô dish′ən), *n.* 1. a hearing in which an actor or other performer who is trying out for a particular role shows his ability and skill. *Auditions for the school play were held this morning.* 2. the power of hearing; ability to hear. *Persons with poor audition may have to wear hearing aids.* **au di tions.**
v. 3. to try out for a role by showing one's skill and ability. *Several students auditioned for the leading part in the play.* **au di tions, au di tioned, au di tion ing.**

au di tor i um (ô′də tôr′ē əm), *n.* 1. a room in which an audience sits. *The auditorium was filled with people who had come to see the play.* 2. a building or a part of a building used to hold an audience. *The meeting will be held in the auditorium on Main Street.* **au di tor i ums.**

Au gust (ô′gəst), *n.* the eighth month of the year. *August has thirty-one days.*

aunt (ant, ont), *n.* 1. the sister of a person's father or mother. *Grandmother is Aunt Mary's mother and my father's mother.* 2. the wife of a person's uncle. *Uncle Larry and Aunt Sarah come to our house every Sunday.* **aunts.**

au ro ra bo re al is (ə rôr′ə bōr′e al′əs), *n.* bright light sometimes seen at night in the sky far north; northern lights. *The most common color of the aurora borealis is green, although red can be seen when the lights are strong.*

au thor (ô′thər), *n.* 1. the writer of a book, story, article, etc.; a writer. *The author sent us a copy of his book.* 2. a person who begins or starts a plan, program, idea, etc. *Who was the author of the cleanup campaign?* **au thors.**

au thor i ty (ə thôr′ə tē), *n.* 1. the right or power to control, command, or force. *A teacher must have complete authority in the classroom.* 2. an expert; a person who is skilled in a kind of work or who knows a great deal about a subject. *He is an authority on baseball; he knows all of the batting averages and records of the players.* 3. any source of correct information. *The encyclopedia is an authority on many different subjects.* 4. **authorities,** public officials who have the power to control the people and enforce the law. *If you see a crime taking place, you should report it to the authorities.* **au thor i ties.**

au thor ize (ô′thə rīz′), *v.* 1. to give authority to; to give power or right to. *The coach authorized the captain to speak for the team.* 2. to approve by law; to give official and legal permission

aurora borealis, or northern lights

for. *The governor of the state authorized an extra holiday from school.* 3. to show to be right; to give good reason for; to justify. *Wearing new spring clothes on Easter has been authorized by the practice of many people for many years.* **au thor iz es, au thor ized, au thor iz ing.**

au to (ô′tō), *n.* an automobile. *An old auto got stuck in the snow in the middle of the street.* **au tos.**

au to bi og ra phy (ô′tō bī og′rə fē), *n.* a person's life story told or written by himself. *The autobiography of a seven-year-old child would probably be much shorter than the autobiography of a ninety-year-old man.* **au to bi og ra phies.**

au to graph (ô′tə graf′), *n.* 1. anything written in a person's own handwriting, especially his name. *I have collected the autographs of all the students in my class.* **au to graphs.**

v. 2. to sign one's name in or on something. *All the players on the team autographed the ball for me.* **au to graphs, au to graphed, au to graphing.**

au to mat ic (ô′tə mat′ik), *adj.* 1. operating, running, or working by itself. *An automatic pencil sharpener can sharpen a pencil in only a few seconds.* 2. done by habit; acting without thought. *Holding out your arms to protect yourself when falling is an automatic reaction. The heart is an automatic organ in the body.* **au to mat ic al ly,** *adv.*

n. 3. a gun which fires more than one shot when the trigger is pulled and held. *An automatic will continue firing until all of the bullets are gone or until the trigger is released.* **au to mat ics.**

au to mo bile (ô′tə mə bēl′), *n.* 1. a vehicle which contains an engine that runs it and has space in which the driver and usually passengers may ride, used for traveling on streets, roads, and highways; an auto; a car. *There were so many automobiles on the highway that we had to drive very slowly.* **au to mo biles.**

adj. 2. made for an automobile; used on an automobile. *You can't put automobile tires on your bicycle!* (See illustration on following page.)

au tumn (ô′təm), *n.* 1. the season of the year that comes after summer and before winter; fall. *In the autumn, the leaves on the trees have many beautiful colors.* **au tumns.**

adj. 2. happening in autumn; of autumn. *When the autumn winds begin to blow, the trees begin to lose their leaves.*

avail (ə vāl′), *v.* 1. to be useful to; to have value for; to help. *When writing papers, most college students avail themselves of the books in the public library.* **avails, availed, avail ing.**

n. 2. usefulness; value; help. *A car is of no avail unless someone knows how to drive it.*

avail a ble (ə vāl′ə bl), *adj.* 1. able to be used; usable. *Every bit of available equipment was being used to fight the fire.* 2. able to be obtained; on hand. *Tickets to the concert are now available.*

---

sand, āte, bâre, fäther; sent, mē, férn; fit, bīke; pot, rōpe, fôrt; run, pùll, rüle, cūte; noise, sound; ch, cheese; ng, long; th, thick; ~~th,~~ those; zh, treasure; ə = a in about, e in waken, i in animal, o in seldom, and u in minus.

AUTOMOBILES

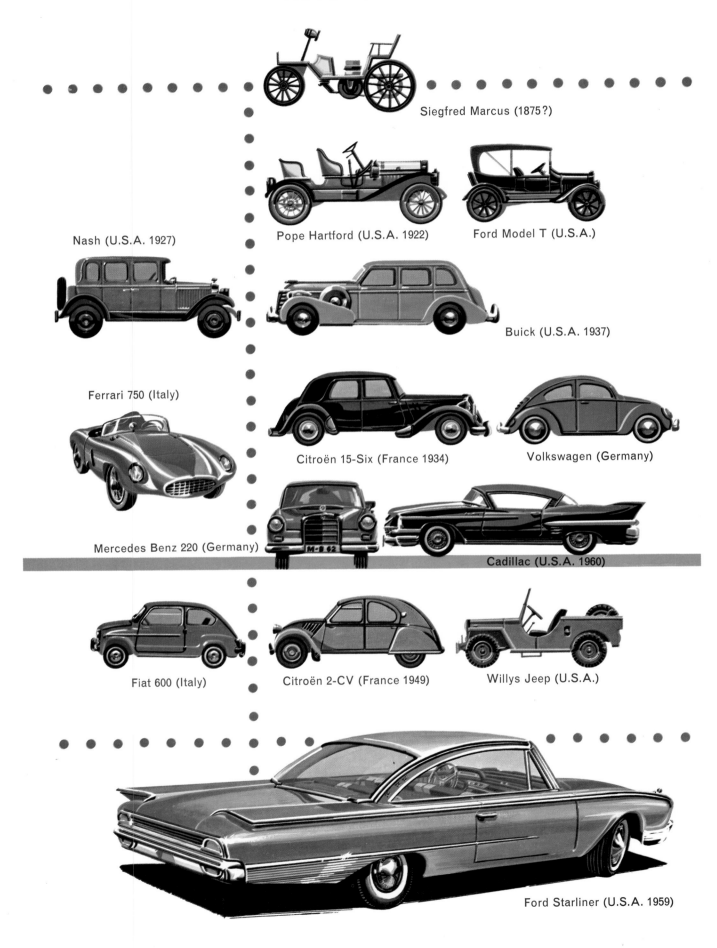

Siegfred Marcus (1875?)

Pope Hartford (U.S.A. 1922)

Ford Model T (U.S.A.)

Nash (U.S.A. 1927)

Buick (U.S.A. 1937)

Ferrari 750 (Italy)

Citroën 15-Six (France 1934)

Volkswagen (Germany)

Mercedes Benz 220 (Germany)

Cadillac (U.S.A. 1960)

Fiat 600 (Italy)

Citroën 2-CV (France 1949)

Willys Jeep (U.S.A.)

Ford Starliner (U.S.A. 1959)

av a lanche (av′ə lanch′), *n.* 1. a large mass of snow, sliding swiftly down a mountain. *The avalanche buried trees and houses as it came.* 2. anything that comes on suddenly. *The store had an avalanche of orders on Saturday.* **av a lanch es.**

av e nue (av′ə nü, av′ə nū), *n.* 1. any wide street or road. *Tom was on the other side of the avenue and didn't hear me call.* 2. a street or road which is lined with trees. *The shop was located on one side of a shady avenue.* 3. a way of approaching, entering, or leaving. *Going to school was the only avenue to success open to me.* **av e nues.**

av er age (av′ər ij), *n.* 1. the result obtained when the sum of two or more figures is divided by the total number of figures. *The average of 10, 4, 7, and 3 is 6.* 2. the ordinary kind; the usual amount. *The temperature and rainfall averages for every day in the year are listed on this chart.* **av er ag es.**
adj. 3. determined by averaging. *The average score on the test was 75.* 4. common; ordinary; usual. *It was an average day; nothing unusual happened.*
v. 5. to figure the average of. *If you average 6, 12, 2, and 8, you should obtain 7 as your result.* 6. to have or show on the average; to do or get on an average. *Ben averages eight hours of sleep a night.* **av er ag es, av er aged, av er ag ing.**

avi a tion (ā′vē ā′shən), *n.* 1. the study of airplanes and of what makes them fly. *A person who flies an airplane has to know a great deal about aviation.* 2. airplanes and flying in airplanes. *Aviation has made traveling from place to place much easier for people.*

avi a tor (ā′vē ā′tər), *n.* a person who flies an airplane. *Charles Lindbergh was the first aviator to fly across the Atlantic Ocean alone.* **avi a tors.**

avoid (ə void′), *v.* to stay away from; to keep from meeting. *I avoided him when he had the measles.* **avoids, avoid ed, avoid ing.**

await (ə wāt′), *v.* 1. to wait for; to expect. *We eagerly awaited the coming of summer.* 2. to be ready and waiting for. *A wonderful trip awaits you if you decide to come with us.* **awaits, await ed, await ing.**

awake (ə wāk′), *v.* 1. to wake up. *I will awake you at eight o'clock tomorrow morning.* **awakes, awoke** or **awaked, awak ing.**
adj. 2. not asleep. *The dog was awake and barking all night.* 3. **awake to,** alert to; aware of. *We surprised the enemy because they were not awake to the danger of their position.*

award (ə wôrd′), *v.* 1. to give after much careful thought. *Medals were awarded to the best speakers on the debating team.* 2. to give as a result of a legal decision. *The man was awarded one thousand dollars to pay for the damage to his car.* **awards, award ed, award ing.**
n. 3. something given after much careful thought. *The awards were given to the best students in each class.* 4. an amount given in a legal decision. *He used the award to pay for the fender that was dented in the accident.* **awards.**

aware (ə wâr′), *adj.* alert to; knowing; conscious of. *Are you aware that you are late to school?*

away (ə wā′), *adv.* 1. from a place; to a different place. *Our dog ran away last week.* 2. far; by a distance. *The event took place away back in history.* 3. out of one's possession; to someone else. *Try to give that extra ticket away.* 4. endlessly;

avalanche

on and on without stopping. *All night long he worked away at his report.* 5. out of existence, sight, hearing, notice, etc. *The last rays of the sun had faded away by the time we arrived.*
adj. 6. absent. *I was away from home during the weekend.*

aw ful (ô′fəl), *adj.* 1. filling with fear; frightening; dreadful. *The lightning bolt struck the tree with an awful sound.* 2. very bad; very ugly; unpleasant. *That was an awful movie.* **aw ful ly,** *adv.*

aw ful ly (ô′fəl ē), *adv.* 1. terribly; horribly. *The desert is awfully hot during the day.* 2. very; greatly; extremely. *She told me that she was awfully sorry for stepping on my toe.*

awhile (ə hwīl′), *adv.* for a short time; for a while. *Let's rest awhile before we run again.*

awoke (ə wōk′), past tense of **awake.**

ax or **axe** (aks), *n.* a tool having a handle attached to a heavy metal head with one or two sharp edges, used for chopping or splitting wood. *The wood was too thick to burn and had to be split with an ax.* **ax es.**

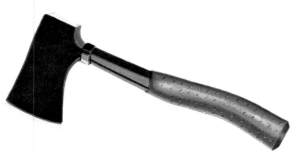

ax

wagon **axle**

ax i om (ak′sē əm), *n.* an established rule; a law; a truth. *An axiom of arithmetic tells us that if 2 plus 2 equals 4, and 3 plus 1 equals 4, then 2 plus 2 must equal 3 plus 1.* **ax i oms.**

ax is (ak′səs), *n.* a line that passes through the center of an object and around which the object turns. *The axis of the earth is an imaginary line that runs through the earth between the North Pole and the South Pole.* **ax es** (ak′sēz).

ax le (ak′sl), *n.* 1. the bar on which a wheel turns. *The chain on a bicycle is connected to the rear axle.* 2. a long rod which connects two wheels. *The rear axle on my wagon was bent from holding too much weight.* **ax les.**

ay or **aye** (ī), *adv.* 1. yes. *"Aye,"* the sailor said, *"I'll be there on time, Captain."*
n. 2. a vote in favor of something or a voter who votes in favor of something. *The ayes outnumber the nays, so the motion is passed.* **ayes.**

b

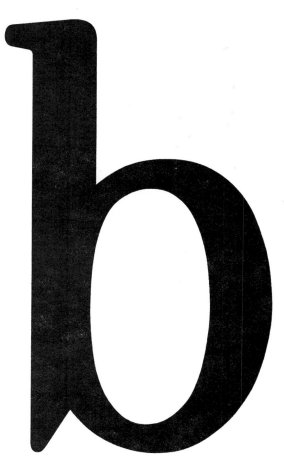

B or **b** (bē), the second letter of the alphabet.

baa (bä, ba), *n.* 1. the cry made by a sheep. *The barking of the sheep dog could be heard above the baas of the flock.* **baas.**
v. 2. to make such a cry. *The lost lamb baaed for its mother.* **baas, baaed, baa ing.**

babe (bāb), *n.* a baby; a very young child. *The mother held her newly born babe in her arms.* **babes.**

ba boon (ba bün′), *n.* a kind of large monkey that lives on the ground. *Baboons have large heads.* **ba boons.**

baboon

ba by (bā′bē), *n.* 1. an infant; a very young child. *A baby cannot walk or talk and must be taken care of by its mother.* 2. the youngest person in a group. *The baby of our family is now seven years old.* 3. anyone who acts like a very young child. *He is a big baby because he starts to cry every time he is asked to do something.* **ba bies.**
v. 4. to treat like a baby. *His mother babied him by keeping him out of school whenever it rained.* **ba bies, ba bied, ba by ing.**
adj. 5. made for a baby; used by a baby; belonging to a baby. *The doll was wearing baby clothes.* 6. small; young. *We saw a baby elephant at the zoo.*

ba by-sit (ba′be sit′), *v.* to take care of a child while its parents are away. *I often baby-sit for my sister's children.* **ba by-sits, ba by-sat, ba by-sit ting.**

ba by-sit ter (ba′bē sit′ər), *n.* one who baby-sits. *Before she went to the party, John's mother called a baby-sitter for him.* **ba by-sit ters.**

back (bak), *n.* 1. that part of the human body which is between the neck and the lower end of the backbone; the upper part of the body of an animal which does not have a backbone. *My back is stiff from shoveling the snow off the driveway. The turtle was turned over on its back.* 2. the rear part of anything; the part of a thing that is away from the front. *We were seated in the back of the auditorium.* 3. the part of a piece of furniture that supports the back of a person who is sitting. *Tom fell to the floor when the back of his chair broke.* **backs.**
v. 4. to be in favor of; help; support. *All of the girls in the class backed Mary when she ran for class president.* 5. to cause to move backward; to move backwards. *The woman backed her car into the parking space. As I backed out, I bumped into the door.* **backs, backed, back ing.**
adj. 6. at the back; in the rear. *You'll have to come in the back way because the front porch was just painted.* 7. not paid on time; overdue. *When he quit his job, he was given the two weeks' back pay that was coming to him.*
adv. 8. to the rear; away from something. *Everyone moved back when the policeman said there was danger of an explosion.* 9. to the person, form, or place from which something came. *Give the ball back to John. Steam turns back into water when it is cooled. Put that back.* 10. **in back of,** behind. *The cat was sleeping in back of the stove.*

back bone (bak′bōn′), *n.* 1. the small bones that run down the center of the back, from the neck to the lower end of the back; vertebrae. *The backbone encloses and protects a thick band of nerves.* 2. courage; determination; moral strength. *Only a man of great backbone would risk his life to save another.* **back bones.**

back ground (bak′ground′), *n.* 1. the parts of a picture or scene which are more distant than the main part; part toward the rear. *A*

backbone

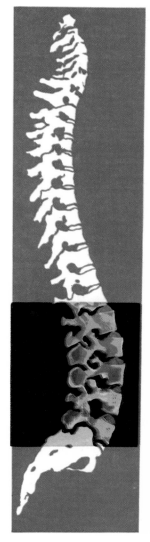

sand, āte, bâre, fäther; sent, mē, férn; fit, bĭke; pot, rōpe, fôrt; run, pùll, rüle, cūte; noise, sound; **ch, cheese;**
ng, long; th, thick; t̶h̶, those; **zh,** treasure; ə = a in about, e in waken, i in animal, o in seldom, and u in minus.

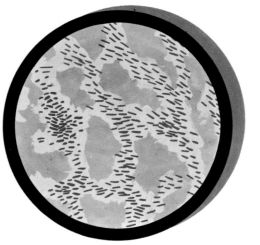

bacteria seen through
a microscope

vast desert and distant mountains formed the background of the painting. 2. the part behind a pattern or design. *A zebra has black stripes on a white background.* 3. the past experience, education, training, etc. of a person. *His background is limited by the fact that he has never traveled away from the city where he was born.* 4. **in the background,** out of sight or notice; not easily seen; attracting little attention. *Bob was in the background while the baseball teams were chosen because he had injured his ankle.* **backgrounds.**

back ward or **back wards** (bak′wərd bak′wərdz), *adv.* 1. toward the rear; in a direction away from the front. *Drive the car backward into the garage.* 2. on one's back; with the back first. *He stepped on a roller skate and fell backward.* 3. back in time; to the past. *By looking backward you can begin to know some of the great men of history.* 4. opposite to the usual or expected way. *He reads mysteries backward, learning the solution before reading the story.* 5. to a worse condition. *She is going backward in her piano playing because she doesn't practice.*
adj. 6. aimed at the rear or to the rear. *He left the room without so much as a backward glance.* 7. slow; behind in development. *In many backward countries primitive tools are used for farming.* 8. shy and uncertain; easily frightened. *Few children are backward about asking for a second serving of ice cream.*

ba con (bā′kən), *n.* salted and smoked or dried meat from the sides and back of a pig. *We had bacon and eggs for breakfast.*

bags:
a. bag for carrying game
b. feed bag for horses

a   b

bac te ria (bak tir′ē ə), *n., pl.* very tiny plants which are so small that they can be seen only through a microscope. *Some bacteria cause meat to spoil and milk to sour; some bacteria cause disease; and some bacteria are very useful to man.*

bad (bad), *adj.* 1. evil; wicked. *Only a very bad person would be mean to children.* 2. not good, right, healthy, polite, etc. *Always being late is a bad habit. That was a very bad guess. Eating too much candy is bad for you.* 3. not correct; not proper. *Bad table manners should be corrected.* 4. unpleasant; disagreeable. *The soup left a bad taste in my mouth.* 5. causing injury or sickness; harmful. *Shoveling snow is bad for a weak heart.* 6. serious; severe. *We had a very bad winter this year.* 7. rotten; spoiled; decayed. *Those potatoes were bad when we bought them at the store.* 8. sick. *I have a headache, my stomach is upset, and I have a fever; I just feel bad.* 9. sorry. *We felt bad about losing the game.* **worse, worst; bad ly,** *adv.*

badge (baj), *n.* 1. something worn to show that a person is a member of a group, organization, etc., or that he does a certain kind of work. *Our club's badge shows a handshake against a red and white background. Firemen and policemen wear badges.* 2. anything which shows something about a person, an occupation, etc. *Rough, hard hands are the carpenter's badge. An armful of books is the student's badge.* **badg es.**

badg er (baj′ər), *n.* 1. an animal with thick fur and short legs. *Badgers dig their homes in holes in the ground by using their sharp claws.* 2. the fur of this animal. *She wore her new jacket of badger to the party.* **badg ers.**

bag (bag), *n.* 1. a sack made of paper, cloth, etc. that is used to hold something and can usually be closed at the top. *Each of us carried two full bags of groceries home from the store.* 2. a purse. *Mother left the car keys in her other bag.* 3. a suitcase. *The boy carried my bag to my room in the hotel.* **bags.**
v. 4. to place in a bag. *Would you bag these groceries, please?* 5. to droop or hang loosely. *My new sweater will soon bag at the elbows and waist.* 6. to trap, catch, or kill in hunting. *The hunters saw many ducks during the day but failed to bag any.* **bags, bagged, bag ging.**

badger

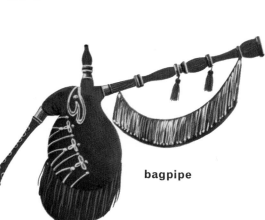

bagpipe

bag pipe (bag′pīp′), *n.* a musical instrument with a leather bag into which the player blows air. The air then goes through special tubes to make the music. *Bagpipes are now played mainly in Scotland.* **bag pipes.**

bait (bāt), *n.* 1. anything used to attract fish or other animals so that they may be caught or trapped. *Worms and minnows are common fishing bait.* 2. anything used to make a person want to do something. *Secret code rings, games, and puzzles are often used as bait for selling breakfast foods.* **baits.**
v. 3. to put bait on a hook or in a trap to attract fish or other animals. *The little girl was afraid of worms, so her father had to bait the hook for her.* 4. to tease in an unkind manner. *The woman baited the child by offering him candy and then taking it away from him.* **baits, bait ed, bait ing.**

bake (bāk), *v.* 1. to cook without applying fire directly; to cook in an oven. *Bacon is fried and bread is baked.* 2. to dry or harden by applying heat. *Clay becomes very hard when it is baked.* **bakes, baked, bak ing.**

bak er (bā′kər), *n.* 1. a person who makes and sells bread, cakes, cookies, etc. *We ordered a special birthday cake from the baker.* 2. **baker's dozen,** thirteen. *In a baker's dozen the thirteenth item is given free.* **bak ers.**

bak ery (bā′kə rē), *n.* a place that makes or sells bread, pastry, and cake. *I bought some fresh bread at the bakery.* **bak er ies.**

bak ing (bā′king), *n.* 1. cooking without applying fire directly; cooking in an oven. *Many women enjoy baking more than other kinds of cooking because it gives them time to do other things at the same time.* 2. the amount baked at one time. *Mother makes several loaves of bread in each baking.*

bal ance (bal′əns), *n.* 1. an instrument with two pans hung from the ends of a bar which is set on a central support, used for determining weight; a scale. The material to be weighed is placed in one pan and known amounts of weight are placed in the other pan. *A balance is a very delicate instrument and can*
provide exact weights of the lightest objects. 2. an equality in weight, amount, number, etc. *Our class has a perfect balance: there are thirteen boys and thirteen girls.* 3. a steady position; a being steady. *I tripped on the rug and lost my balance.* 4. a steady mental condition. *Don't let your home run throw you off balance for the rest of the ball game!* 5. anything left over; the part remaining. *We will spend the balance of the week reviewing what we have learned.* **bal anc es.**
v. 6. to determine the weight of something on a balance. *While the miner waited, the agent balanced his gold.* 7. to compare one thing with another. *He balanced the choices available to him, and then made his decision.* 8. to keep steady; to hold in a firm position. *The juggler balanced a broom on his chin while he juggled three cups.* 9. to make equal; to keep in proportion. *The bookkeeper was unable to balance the budget because more money was spent than was earned.* **bal anc es, bal anced, bal anc ing.**

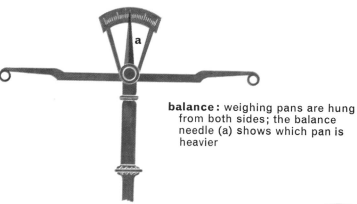

balance: weighing pans are hung from both sides; the balance needle (a) shows which pan is heavier

ball[1] (bôl), *n.* 1. a round, or nearly round, object. *He rolled his paper into a ball and threw it into the wastebasket.* 2. a round or oval object used in a game. *My father promised me a ball for my birthday, but I don't know if it will be a baseball, a football, or a basketball.* 3. any game played with a ball, especially baseball. *Bring your bat so we can play ball.* 4. in baseball, a ball not swung at because it is pitched too high, too low, or not over home plate. *The umpire called, "Ball four!" and the batter walked to first base.* 5. a bullet or a round piece of metal shot from a gun. *The cannon ball crushed the gate and allowed the enemy to enter the city.* 6. anything that is rounded like a ball. *I stood on the balls of my feet so that I could reach the top shelf.* **balls.**

ball[2] (bôl), *n.* a large, usually formal, dance. *I was dressed as The Headless Horseman at the Halloween ball.* **balls.**

soccer **ball**

basket**ball**

golf **ball**   tennis **ball**

balloons:
a. airship
b. toy

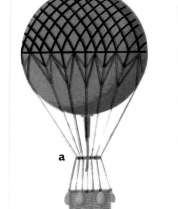

bal loon (bə lün′), *n.* 1. an airtight bag which rises and floats above the ground when it is filled with a gas that is lighter than air. *Some balloons are large enough to lift a basket or cabin in which people may travel from place to place.* 2. a child's toy, made of rubber, which can be filled with air or a gas. *Every child who entered the store was given a balloon on a string.* **bal loons.** *v.* 3. to swell out like a balloon. *The sails ballooned as the breeze drove the boat across the water.* **bal loons, bal looned, bal loon ing.**

ba nana (bə nan′ə), *n.* 1. a large plant with long leaves that bears bunches of fruit which have soft, sweet flesh within a yellow or red skin. *The banana grows best in regions where the weather is always warm.* 2. the curved fruit of this plant. *Bananas are green while they are growing and red or yellow when they are ripe.* **ba nan as.**

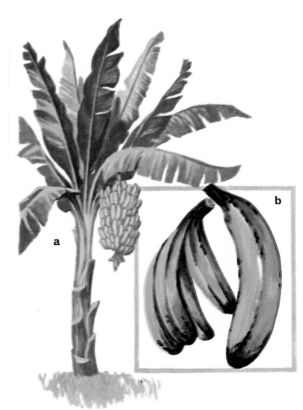

banana:
a. tree
b. fruit

band (band), *n.* 1. a group of persons or animals acting together or united for a purpose. *A band of wolves circled our campfire, waiting for darkness.* 2. a number of persons who play musical instruments together. *He plays the drums in a band.* 3. any flat strip of material used for holding something together. *The bundle of hay was tied with a metal band. Put a rubber band around each newspaper before delivering it.* 4. a strip of material placed around something as a decoration or for strength; a stripe. *She tied a blue band around her hair to match her dress. I painted a red band on each of the baseball bats so that we wouldn't lose any of them.* **bands.**
v. 5. to join in a group; to form a group. *We are going to band together against the bullies in the neighborhood.* 6. to hold with a band; to mark with a band. *We banded the papers together and handed them to the teacher.* **bands, band ed, band ing.**

band age (ban′dij), *n.* 1. a strip of cloth used to bind up or cover a wound or other injury. *His mother put a bandage over the cut on his finger.* **band ag es.**
v. 2. to bind up or cover a wound or other injury with a bandage. *We had to bandage his wounds with strips torn from our shirts because nothing else was available.* **band ag es, band aged, band ag ing.**

bang (bang), *n.* 1. a sudden, sharp noise. *When we heard the bang of the car door slamming, we went to see who was coming.* 2. a noisy blow. *The baby gave the table a bang with her spoon.* **bangs.**
v. 3. to make a sudden, sharp noise. *Firecrackers banged from early in the morning until late at night.* 4. to strike with noisy blows. *Will you please stop banging those pots and pans?* 5. to close noisily; to slam. *Bob tried to be quiet and not bang the door as he came in.* **bangs, banged, bang ing.**

ban jo (ban′jō), *n.* a musical instrument with either four or five strings, played by stroking or picking the strings with the fingers or a small piece of metal, plastic, or wood. *Anyone can make sounds with a banjo; it takes skill and practice to make music with one.* **ban jos** or **ban joes.**

bank[1] (bangk), *n.* 1. a mound or long pile of something. *The car was buried under a bank of snow.* 2. the ground at the edge of a lake, river, or stream. *After swimming for what seemed hours, we reached the opposite bank.* 3. a shallow place in a body of water, caused by a pile of earth or sand on the bottom. *About fifty yards from shore we came upon a bank of sand where the water was only three feet deep.* **banks.**
v. 4. to make a mound or long pile by heaping up earth, sand, etc. *The men banked the sides of the river with bags of sand to keep the flood from the city.* 5. to build up; pile up. *The wind banked the sand against the trees near the*

beach. **6.** to lean to one side while turning. *Suddenly the airplane banked to the right, and we began to turn sharply.* **7.** to cause a fire to burn slowly by covering it with ashes. *At nine o'clock we banked the campfire and went to sleep for the night.* **banks, banked, bank ing.**

bank² (bangk), *n.* **1.** a bench on which men sat while rowing a large ship which could be driven by both oars and sail. *In the Middle Ages slaves were forced to sit on banks and row huge ships until they were too sick or too old to work.* **2.** any arrangement of things in rows or lines. *An extra bank of seats was set up for the people who came late to see the game. An organ has several banks of keys.* **banks.**

bank³ (bangk), *n.* **1.** a place of business in which people may keep money or from which they can borrow money. Banks also exchange money and, in some cases, issue money. *Most people feel that large sums of money should be kept in a bank rather than at home.* **2.** a small holder in which money may be kept. *I have $4.37 in my piggy bank.* **3.** any place where an extra supply is kept; an extra supply of anything. *A hospital gets the blood it needs from the blood bank. The soil bank is not a place where dirt is kept; it consists of all of the unused farmland in the country.* **banks.**

v. **4.** to put in a bank. *He banks his check on his way home from work every week.* **5.** to do business at a bank. *Do you bank in your neighborhood or downtown?* **banks, banked, banking.**

bank er (bangk/ər), *n.* a person who works for a bank, especially one who runs a bank. *The banker was working in his office long after the bank was closed.* **bank ers.**

bank ing (bangk/ing), *n.* the business of operating or working in a bank. *He plans to study banking in college.*

bank rupt (bangk/rupt), *n.* **1.** a person who is unable to pay money that he owes, especially a person whose property is taken by a court to be divided among the people to whom he owes money. *The man was declared a bankrupt when his business failed.* **bank rupts.**

adj. **2.** unable to pay money that is owed. *Ten years ago he was bankrupt, but today he is successful and wealthy.*

v. **3.** to make bankrupt. *The loss of his store in the fire bankrupted him.* **bank rupts, bankrupt ed, bank rupt ing.**

bank rupt cy (bangk/rupt sē), *n.* the condition of being bankrupt. *When all of his plans to make money failed, he was forced into bankruptcy.* **bank rupt cies.**

ban ner (ban/ər), *n.* **1.** a flag. *Our national anthem, "The Star-Spangled Banner," is a song about the American flag.* **2.** a piece of cloth with a picture, design, writing, etc. on it. *A huge banner welcoming the heroes home was hung across the street.* **ban ners.**

adj. **3.** very good; outstanding. *This was a banner year for the farmers.*

ban quet (bang/kwət), *n.* **1.** a rich meal with a great deal of food of many kinds. *On Thanksgiving we were served a delicious banquet in the late afternoon.* **2.** a formal dinner at which speeches are given. *The Men's Club banquet was held in a hotel this year.* **ban quets.**

bar (bär), *n.* **1.** a long, evenly shaped piece of something solid. *I went to the store for a candy bar and two bars of soap.* **2.** a long, slender metal rod used to fasten or block a door, window, etc. *We had to put a bar on the gate, so that the dog could be locked in the yard.* **3.** anything that blocks the way; an obstacle. *You may find the inability to speak a foreign language a major bar to travel abroad.* **4.** a ridge of sand, earth, etc. in a lake, river, etc. *The steamboat was stuck on a sand bar in the middle of the river.* **5.** a strip or band of color. *There are seven red bars and six white bars on that flag.* **6.** a measure of music; the line that separates each measure in written music. *We decided not to sing the last four bars of the song.* **7.** lawyers; the law profession. *If he passes the examination, he can become a member of the bar.* **8.** a court of law. *He was brought before the bar for stealing two chickens.* **9.** a place where drinks and sometimes food are served; a long counter in such a place. *They lunched at the sandwich bar in the department store.* **bars.**

v. **10.** to fasten. *We barred the door so that no one else could enter.* **11.** to block the way of. *A pile of rocks barred the entrance to the cave.* **12.** to prevent from entering or joining. *Women are barred by that club.* **bars, barred, bar ring.**

bar bar i an (bär bâr/ē ən), *n.* a person who is not governed by laws and is ignorant of the ways of civilization. *The barbarians of several hundred years ago were hunters and soldiers who took pleasure in stealing and destroying property.* **barbar i ans.** (See illustration on following page.)

bar be cue (bär/bə kū), *n.* **1.** a meal cooked before or over an open fire, especially outdoors. *Hamburgers and steaks make a very delicious barbecue.* **2.** a picnic or other outdoor gathering at which an animal is roasted whole. *Last year we went to a barbecue at which a pig was cooked.* **3.** an open stove or fireplace used for outdoor cooking. *Charcoal is a good fuel to use in a barbecue because it burns slowly and gives off great heat.* **bar be cues.**

v. **4.** to cook outdoors before or over an open fire. *Dan burned the steaks while he was barbecuing them.* **5.** to cook in a seasoned sauce; to flavor with this sauce. *Please don't barbecue my hamburger; I'd like to have it plain.* **bar be cues, bar be cued, bar be cu ing.**

bar ber (bär/bər), *n.* a person whose business is giving haircuts, shaves, etc. *I had my hair cut only last week, and I already have to go back to the barber.* **bar bers.**

bare (bâr), *adj.* **1.** not wearing clothes; not

barbarian

covered; naked. *Should you be walking outside in your bare feet? The bark had been stripped back, leaving the trunk of the tree bare.* 2. without a covering. *The floor is bare because the rug is being cleaned.* 3. empty; without the usual furnishings, contents, etc. *The shelves in the store were bare at the end of the day.* 4. plain; not fancy or adorned. *His room was bare but comfortable.* 5. just enough and with nothing more than; mere. *He wants only the bare necessities of life.* **bar er, bar est; bare ly,** *adv.*

v. 6. to show. *The cat bared her teeth when she saw the mouse.* **bares, bared, bar ing.**

bare foot (bâr′fůt′), *adj.* 1. with the feet bare; wearing neither shoes nor socks. *A barefoot boy stood near the road as we drove by.*
adv. 2. with the feet bare; wearing neither shoes nor socks. *We walked barefoot across the hot sand.*

bare ly (bâr′lē), *adv.* 1. hardly; scarcely; not quite clearly or easily. *We could barely see the other cars because of the fog.* 2. with scarcely enough; poorly. *Their home is barely furnished, but they don't want more furniture.*

bar gain (bär′gən), *n.* 1. an agreement on what is to be given or done for something in return. *We struck a bargain when I said that I would wash the dishes if she would cook the meal. The bargain was that he would drive me to work and I would pay*

for the gas. 2. something bought or offered for sale at a low price. *My new bike was a great bargain.* **bar gains.**

v. 3. to try to agree on the terms of a deal. *I wanted to bargain with him for his car, but he refused to sell it.* 4. to try to get something at a low price. *When my father buys a new car, he tries to bargain with the salesman so that he can save a few hundred dollars.* **bar gains, bar gained, bar gain ing.**

bark[1] (bärk), *n.* 1. the outer covering of the trunk and branches of a tree. *Birch trees have smooth bark.* **barks.**

v. 2. to take the bark off. *The men barked the log before it was cut into planks.* 3. to scrape skin from. *He barked his elbow when he fell in the street.* **barks, barked, bark ing.**

bark[2] (bärk), *n.* 1. the sharp sound a dog makes. *I thought I heard a bark, but I couldn't see any dogs.* **barks.**

v. 2. to make this sound. *Whose dog was barking outside all night?* 3. to speak sharply and roughly. *When the captain is angry, he barks at everyone.* **barks, barked, bark ing.**

bark[3] (bärk), *n.* 1. a ship having three masts. *Columbus sailed to America in a bark.* 2. any boat or ship. *The harbor was filled with every kind of bark: modern submarines, pleasure boats, and even an old steamboat.* **barks.**

bar ley (bär′lē), *n.* 1. the seed or grain of a grasslike plant. *Barley is used for making soups, drinks, and cereals.* 2. the plant this grain grows on. *Barley grows rapidly in cool climates, and it is similar in appearance to wheat.*

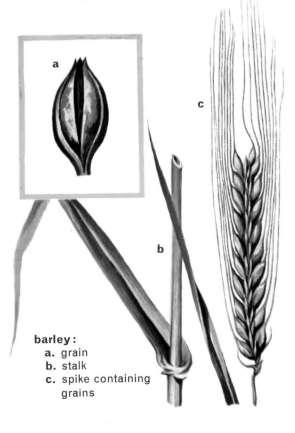

barley:
  a. grain
  b. stalk
  c. spike containing
    grains

barn (bärn), *n.* a farm building in which cows and horses may be kept and in which grain and hay are stored. *In many barns hay is stored on the second floor and animals are kept in stalls on the first floor.* **barns.**

barn yard (bärn′yärd′), *n.* the area of ground around a barn. *Make sure the cows are in the pasture before you bring the chickens into the barnyard.* **barn yards.**

bar o graph (bâr′ə graf′), *n.* a barometer that keeps a record of changes in air pressure. The barograph has a rotating cylinder on which air pressure changes are traced with a pen. *Yesterday's report from the barograph showed that there was a sudden drop in air pressure just before the storm.* **bar o graphs.**

ba rom e ter (bə rom′ə tər), *n.* 1. an instrument which measures air pressure. Barometers are used in telling what the weather will be, in determining height above sea level, and in determining the height at which an airplane is flying. *Even a slight change in the reading of a barometer can indicate a great change in the weather.* 2. anything that indicates changing conditions. *We will use ticket sales as a barometer in determining the success of the show.* **ba rom e ters.**

ba roque (bə rōk′), *adj.* having many ornaments and designs. *Baroque architecture is very different from the simple designs of modern architecture.*

bar rel (bar′əl), *n.* 1. a vessel for holding objects or liquids that is longer than it is wide and has slightly curved sides and round, flat ends. Barrels are usually made of thin pieces of wood bound by metal strips. *Mother keeps some of our old clothes in a barrel in the attic.* 2. the amount which a barrel contains; 31½ gallons. *How many barrels a day does that oil well produce?* 3. the hollow tube on a gun through which a bullet is fired. *The attack had lasted for so long that the men were burning their fingers on their gun barrels.* **bar rels.**
v. 4. to put in a barrel. *After cider is barreled, it turns into vinegar.* **bar rels, bar reled, bar rel ing.**

bar rette (bə ret′, bär et′), *n.* a pin with a clasp for holding a girl's or woman's hair in place. *She wore a red barrette to match her dress.* **bar rettes.**

Baroque design

barrette: a. front view;   **b.** rear view

base[1] (bās), *n.* 1. the part on which something stands or rests; bottom. *The vase was placed on a marble base.* 2. the major part of something; the main ingredient in a mixture. *This paste has a flour base.* 3. a starting place or headquarters, especially a place where supplies are kept. *The men established a base at the foot of the mountain, and then began their climb to the top.* 4. in baseball, one of the four stations which a runner must touch. *To score, the runner must touch all of the bases in order.* 5. in chemistry, any substance that forms a salt when it is combined with an acid. *A base has a salty, harsh, unpleasant taste.* **bas es.**
v. 6. to establish. *The verdict of the jury was based on the evidence they had heard.* **bas es, based, bas ing.**

base[2] (bās), *adj.* 1. of little or no value; worthless when compared to other things. *Many people have tried to make gold from base metals.* 2. mean; low; without honor, courage, etc. *How could anyone be so base as to tie tin cans to a dog's tail?* **bas er, bas est; base ly,** *adv.*

base ball (bās′bôl′), *n.* 1. a game played by two teams of nine players each, in which points or runs are scored by hitting a ball

barometer

baseball game

basketball game

with a bat and running around four bases. *Little League programs have made it possible for many young children to play baseball.* 2. the ball used in this game. *Robert was given a baseball and a bat for his birthday.* **base balls.**

base ment (bās′mənt), *n.* the story of a building which is below the main floor, partly or completely below ground level; cellar. *My father built a laundry room in our basement.* **base ments.**

ba sic (bā′sik), *adj.* of or having to do with base or foundation of a thing. *The basic outline for the house was laid out with string.* **ba si cal ly,** *adv.*

ba sis (bā′səs), *n.* 1. the foundation or reason for a decision, story, idea, etc. *What is the basis of your argument?* 2. the main part or ingredient of anything. *Honesty is the basis of good business. The basis of this soup is beef.* **ba ses** (bā′sēz).

bas ket (bas′kət), *n.* 1. a holder made by weaving together straw, metal, strips of wood, etc. *I have a wire basket on my bicycle.* 2. the amount held by a basket. *We bought three baskets of apples from the farmer.* 3. anything like a basket in use or appearance. *We have two metal waste baskets in our classroom.* 4. in basketball, an open net attached to a hoop, through which the ball is thrown. *There is a basket at each end of a basketball court.* 5. a score made in basketball by throwing the ball through this net. *We won the game by two baskets.* **bas kets.**

bas ket ball (bas′kət bôl′), *n.* 1. a game played by two teams of five players each, in which points are scored by throwing a ball through a basket. *Basketball is usually played indoors in a gymnasium.* 2. the large, round, inflated ball used in this game. *Our basketball had lost so much air that we couldn't even bounce it.* **bas ket balls.**

bass[1] (bās), *n.* 1. in music, the part that is lower in tone than any of the other parts. *A piano* *player plays the bass with his left hand and the higher parts with his right hand.* 2. the male singing voice which sings the lowest part. *When my voice was changing, it would shift unexpectedly to bass.* 3. a person who sings the lowest part; an instrument that plays the lowest part. *We have only three basses in our choir.* **bass es.**

adj. 4. low and deep in sound. *Do you have a bass voice?*

bass² (bas), *n.* a fresh-water or ocean fish used for food. *When we went fishing, we caught three trout and two bass.* **bass** or **bass es.**

bas si net (bas'ə net'), *n.* a baby's bed. *Some bassinets are on rockers, and others are on wheels.* **bas si nets.**

bass viol

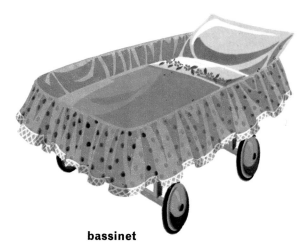

bassinet

bas soon (ba sün', bə sün'), *n.* a wooden musical instrument with a low tone. *The bassoon has double wooden tubes and a curved metal piece through which air is blown.* **bas soons.**

bass vi ol (bās' vī'əl), *n.* a musical instrument having strings that looks like a large violin. *A bass viol is about as tall as a man; the player rests it on the floor and plays it while he is standing.* **bass vi ols.**

bat¹ (bat), *n.* 1. any heavy stick or club. *The natives hunted for food with bats and spears.* 2. a wooden stick, broader at one end than at the other, used to hit a ball. *He held the bat very awkwardly, but managed to hit a home run anyway.* 3. in baseball, a turn at batting. *Tom was at bat when the game was stopped because of darkness.* **bats.**

v. 4. to hit; to hit with a bat. *The bully tried to bat him on the ear. He wanted to bat the ball out of the park for a home run.* 5. in baseball, to take a turn at batting. *The pitcher usually bats last.* **bats, bat ted, bat ting.**

bat² (bat), *n.* a small, flying animal that looks like a mouse but has long wings covered with skin. *Bats usually fly at night and sleep during the day.* **bats.**

batch (bach), *n.* 1. the quantity of anything

made at one time. *Mother baked a batch of bread this morning. We'll make one more batch of fudge for the party.* 2. any quantity of things taken together. *He held a batch of papers in his hand.* **batch es.**

bath (bath), *n.* 1. a washing of the entire body. *After I give my dog his bath, I usually have to take one too.* 2. the water, soap, towels, etc. used in taking a bath. *Will you have my bath ready when I return?* 3. a building, room, or tub used for bathing. *Some large cities still have public baths.* 4. any liquid into which objects are dipped. *The frame of a car is dipped into a bath which keeps it from rusting.* **baths.**

bathe (bāth), *v.* 1. to take a bath; to give a bath to; to wash. *Did you bathe today? I am bathing the baby.* 2. to wet with a liquid; to soak in a liquid. *You must bathe that wound before you bandage it. I always bathe my feet in hot water after a long hike.* 3. to go into a lake, river, etc. for enjoyment; to go swimming. *During our vacation we bathed in a different lake every day.* 4. to cover with a liquid or as if with a liquid. *The*

bassoon

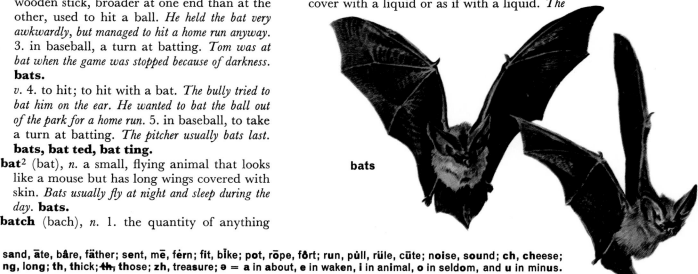

bats

sand, āte, bâre, fäther; sent, mē, fèrn; fit, bīke; pot, rōpe, fôrt; run, pull, rüle, cūte; noise, sound; **ch**, cheese; **ng**, long; **th**, thick; ~~th~~, those; **zh**, treasure; ə = **a** in about, **e** in waken, **i** in animal, **o** in seldom, and **u** in minus.

porch was bathed in moonlight. **bathes, bathed, bath ing.**

bath room (bath′rüm′), *n.* a room containing a shower, bathtub, washstand, and usually a toilet. *Father was shaving in the bathroom when I awoke.* **bath rooms.**

bath tub (bath′tub′), *n.* a large hollow vessel in which a person bathes. *Modern bathtubs are connected to pipes so that they may be filled and drained easily.* **bath tubs.**

bat tery (bat′ər ē), *n.* 1. a connected group of similar objects used for the same purpose. *We were given a battery of tests last year.* 2. an electric cell or a series of electric cells used to produce a current. *My radio operates on batteries.* 3. a number of large guns or cannons used together. *We began firing all of our batteries on the enemy as the attack began.* 4. in baseball, the pitcher and catcher, taken as a unit. *The battery of today's game is Smith pitching and Wilson catching.* **bat ter ies.**

bat ting (bat′ing), *n.* 1. in baseball, hitting the ball with a bat or taking a turn at bat. *My batting will improve as I get more practice. Baseball players must follow a certain order in batting.* 2. sheets of cotton or wool used as stuffing in quilts, etc. *The batting used in bandages is cotton.* **bat tings.**

bat tle (bat′l), *n.* 1. a fight between armies, navies, etc. during a war. *That battle was the turning point of the war.* 2. war or armed conflict in general. *He was wounded in battle.* 3. any fight or conflict. *That boxing match was the battle of the century. The two speakers were involved in a battle of wits.* **bat tles.**
v. 4. to fight. *We battled on to win the game even though we had been losing.* **bat tles, bat tled, bat tling.**

bat tle ship (bat′l ship′), *n.* a very large warship with thick armor and powerful guns. *Two battleships were used to protect the supply ship.* **bat tle ships.**

bawl (bôl), *v.* 1. to call out noisily; to shout. *"Wait for the light to change!" the policeman*

bawled. 2. to weep noisily. *The baby was bawling at the top of his lungs.* **bawls, bawled, bawling.**
n. 3. a loud cry; a noisy shout. *The baby's bawls filled the house.* **bawls.**

bay[1] (bā), *n.* a part of a large body of water which extends into the land, forming a curved shelter. *Several small boats came into the bay to escape the storm.* **bays.**

bay[2] (bā), *n.* 1. the long, deep, howling sound made by a dog. *The bay of the dogs could be heard through most of the night.* 2. the position of an animal or person who is forced to fight the persons or animals that are chasing him when escape is impossible. *The badger was brought to bay at the end of the tunnel.* 3. the position of persons or animals who are held off by a cornered animal or person. *The angry bear kept us at bay until her cubs were safe.* **bays.**
v. 4. to bark with long, deep, howling sounds. *The dogs bayed at the cat in the tree.* **bays, bayed, bay ing.**

bay[3] (bā), *n.* a small evergreen tree that has smooth, sweet-smelling leaves. *Bay leaves are used to flavor foods.* **bays.**

bay[4] (bā), *n.* 1. a reddish-brown horse. *There were three bays at the ranch.* **bays.**
adj. 2. having a reddish-brown color. *Only one of the horses was bay, the other was gray.*

be (bē), *v.* *Be* and its forms (*am, are, is, was, were, been, being*) are used as helping verbs in addition to having the following meanings: 1. to have the identity of; to equal. *He might be my cousin. This is good music.* 2. to belong to the class of. *She will be a teacher. Ants are insects.* 3. to have a particular quality; to have a specified appearance or character. *The sand is hot. He tried to be very careful. Their house is always neat.* 4. to happen; to take place. *When is the game? There will be school tomorrow.* 5. to live; to exist. *Just to be is an exciting adventure for most people.* 6. to continue as before. *Do not touch them; let them be.* **am, are, is, was, were, been, be ing.**

bay at Rio de Janeiro, Brazil

beach

beach (bēch), *n.* 1. the shore of a lake, sea, etc., usually of sand or small stones, that is washed by waves. *During the summer we go to the beach where it is cool.* **beach es.**
v. 2. to drive a boat onto a sandy shore; to pull a boat onto shore. *When the storm came, we beached the boat and ran for shelter.* **beach es, beached, beach ing.**

bead (bēd), *n.* 1. a small, usually round piece of glass, wood, plastic, etc., with a hole through its center so it can be strung on a thread. *When mother's necklace broke, the beads rolled off in all directions.* 2. any small, round body or drop. *Beads of dew sparkled on the grass.* 3. the small piece of raised metal at the end of a gun barrel, used in taking aim. *He drew a bead on the target and fired.* **beads.**
v. 4. to put beads on. *Have you finished beading that necklace?* **beads, bead ed, bead ing.**

beak (bēk), *n.* 1. the bill of a bird, especially a strong, curved bill. *The bird picked the bread crumb up in its beak.* 2. anything shaped like a beak. *Tom bent the front of his cap into a beak.* **beaks.**

beam (bēm), *n.* 1. a long, heavy piece of wood or metal used in building. *The frame of that building was made with steel beams.* 2. such a piece of wood or metal used as a support in a building or a ship. *The main beam runs across the center of the house.* 3. any long bar used as a support. *The beam on this balance is two feet long.* 4. the broadest part of a ship. *The boat was fifty feet across at its beam.* 5. a single ray of light. *A beam of moonlight shone through the trees.* 6. a happy expression; a bright smile. *A beam of happiness spread across his face.* 7. a steady radio signal sent out in a certain direction to guide ships or aircraft. *In spite of the fact that we couldn't see anything, we were able to fly in on the beam and land at the airport.* **beams.**
v. 8. to give off light; to shine. *The lighthouse beamed in the distance.* 9. to smile broadly; to have a happy expression. *Barbara beamed when she was told that she had won the contest.* 10. to send out a radio signal; to transmit. *This program is beamed to London.* **beams, beamed, beam ing.**

bean (bēn), *n.* 1. a plant that bears long, green or yellow tubes containing seeds. *We are growing beans in our garden.* 2. the tubes or the seeds

beaks

eagle   hummingbird   crow   crossbill   heron

toucan   carpenter bird   duck   flamingo   spoonbill

within the tubes, eaten as vegetables. *We eat the tubes and seeds of green beans; we eat only the seeds of lima beans.* 3. any seed that is shaped like a bean. *Chocolate is made from beans that are ground into cocoa.* **beans.**

bear[1] (bâr), *v.* 1. to hold up; support; carry. *That ice is too thin to bear your weight.* 2. to put up with patiently; to stand. *I can't bear this toothache any longer.* 3. to have an effect or bearing; to relate. *All of your ideas are interesting, but do any of them bear on our problems?* 4. to have or show. *He bears the name of a very famous family. She bears a definite likeness to the picture of her grandmother.* 5. to produce or bring forth as the result of growth. *That tree bears good fruit.* 6. to give birth to. *She was happy that she was to bear a child.* 7. to press; to push. *When he bears down on his pencil, he breaks its point. You will have to bear down on your studies if you expect to do well in school.* **bears, bore, borne** or **born, bear ing.**

bear[2] (bâr), *n.* 1. a large, heavy animal with long, coarse fur, short legs, and a very short tail. *When the bear stood on his hind legs, he was almost eight feet tall.* 2. a rude, grumpy person. *He is a bear every morning until he is fully awake.* **bears.**

beard (bird), *n.* 1. the hair that grows on the chin and cheeks of a man. *Most men have to shave their beards every day.* 2. a growth of hair on an animal's face or chin. *The goat wagged his beard slowly as he chewed.* 3. a number of hairlike threads on the heads of some plants. *Beards can be seen growing on the heads of oats and barley.* **beards.**
v. 4. to stand up to; to set oneself against, as if to pull the beard of. *Don't be afraid to beard that bully, even in his own neighborhood.* **beards, beard ed, beard ing.**

bear ing (bâr′ing), *n.* 1. the way in which a person stands, walks, etc. *The old man still had the bearing of a soldier.* 2. reference; connection. *This discussion has no bearing on the problems we are facing.* 3. sense of direction. *Once I had gotten my bearings, I had no trouble finding my friend's home.* 4. a part in a machine or device on which other parts can turn smoothly. *A* **roller bearing** *permits parts to slide in one direction or the other. A* **ball bearing** *permits parts to turn in any direction. Before every race he carefully checked the wheel bearings on his bicycle.* **bear ings.**

bearings:
a. ball bearing
b. roller bearing

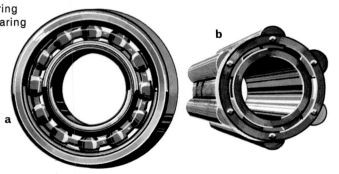

bean: a. seed pods; **b.** plant

beast (bēst), *n.* 1. any animal except man, especially a large, four-footed animal. *Horses, donkeys, and oxen are often called beasts of burden because they can pull or carry heavy loads.* 2. a coarse, dirty, or mean person. *What a beast he was, speaking as he did!* **beasts.**

beat (bēt), *v.* 1. to hit again and again. *I took the rug outside to beat it. Who would like to beat the drum in the parade?* 2. to throb. *His heart beat fast in his excitement.* 3. to mix by stirring; to stir rapidly. *Beat the eggs until they are fluffy.* 4. to flap; to move up and down again and again. *The bird beat its wings against the door of the cage.* 5. to make a sound by striking or as if by striking. *All night long footsteps beat past my door. If you are having trouble keeping up with the rest of the band, you can beat time with your foot.* 6. to defeat. *We beat them by four runs. Larry beat Don in the election.* **beats, beat, beat en, beat ing.**
n. 7. a blow or the sound of a blow made again and again. *Listen to the beat of the drum.* 8. a unit of time in music. *This song has four beats to the measure.* 9. a regular route or course taken by a policeman or watchman. *The policeman was on one end of his beat when the robbery took place on the other.* **beats.**

beat en (bēt′n), *adj.* 1. worn smooth by repeated walking or use. *We followed a beaten path through the woods.* 2. defeated, especially made sad by defeat. *The beaten army of General Lee was allowed to keep its horses and return home. He had a beaten look.* 3. made flat or shaped by repeated

beaver

hammering. *A vase of beaten silver was placed on the table.*

beat ing (bēt′ing), *n.* 1. a whipping; a spanking. *My father won more from us through love than he would have won through a beating.* 2. a defeat. *Our baseball team took a real beating today.* **beat ings.**

beau ti ful (bū′tə fəl), *adj.* having beauty; pleasing to the eye, ear, or mind; lovely. *She is a beautiful girl. That is a beautiful painting.* **beau ti ful ly,** *adv.*

beau ty (bū′tē), *n.* 1. the quality that makes a person or thing pleasing to the senses; a lovely quality. *The beauty of the music made us forget everything else.* 2. a beautiful woman. *The winner of the contest was a striking beauty.* **beau ties.**

bea ver[1] (bē′vər), *n.* 1. a small, fur-bearing animal with strong, sharp teeth, a broad, flat tail, and hind feet which have webs between the toes. *Beavers live both on land and in water and are noted for building dams.* 2. the brown fur of this animal. *She was wearing a beaver coat.* **bea vers.**

bea ver[2] (bē′vər), *n.* on a suit of armor, a metal section that moves up and down and protects the mouth and chin. *The beaver on this helmet was probably damaged during a long-ago battle for some fair lady.* **bea vers.**

be came (bi kām′), past tense of **become.**

be cause (bi kôz′), *conj.* 1. for the reason that. *I study because I want to learn.* 2. **because of,** on account of; as a result of. *Because of the icy roads we decided not to drive but to stay at a hotel.*

be come (bi kum′), *v.* 1. to develop into; to come or grow to be. *He became a doctor. A caterpillar may become a butterfly or a moth.* 2. to suit; to look attractive on. *Her new hat becomes her.* 3. **become of,** to happen to. *What became of your plans for visiting your grandmother?* **be comes, be came, be come, be com ing.**

be com ing (bi kum′ing), *adj.* suitable; attractive. *She wore a very becoming red dress to the party.* **be com ing ly,** *adv.*

bed (bed), *n.* 1. a large, flat piece of furniture on which a person lies to sleep or rest. *She liked the bed in her mother's room better than her own.* 2. anything on which a person or animal

sleeps. *The sky is my roof, and the ground is my bed.* 3. a piece of ground where plants, especially flowers, are grown. *We planted a bed of tulips along the fence.* 4. the bottom of a body of water. *The sunken ship rested on the bed of the river.* 5. the base on which something rests or stands. *The flagpole was standing in a bed of gravel.* 6. a layer of rock. *This well was drilled through several beds of limestone before water was found.* **beds.**

v. 7. to put in bed; to go to bed. *Are the animals bedded down for the night?* 8. to plant. *All of those flowers were bedded in black dirt.* **beds, bed ded, bed ding.**

bed rock (bed′rok′), *n.* the solid rock that lies under the soil and broken rocks. *The foundation of this building rests on bedrock.*

bed room (bed′rüm′), *n.* 1. a room with a bed, used for sleeping. *I can't sleep with a light on in my bedroom.* **bed rooms.**

bed time (bed′tīm′), *n.* the time at which a person goes to bed. *Everyone in our family has a different bedtime.* **bed times.**

bee (bē), *n.* 1. a small insect that gathers pollen from plants and lives in a colony with many other bees. *Honey and wax are made and stored by bees.* 2. any gathering of people for a contest, work, amusement, etc. *Mother goes to a sewing bee every week. We had a spelling bee in school today.* **bees.** (See illustration on following page.)

beech (bēch), *n.* a tree with smooth, gray bark and dark green leaves. *The beech produces sweet nuts that are good to eat; they are called beechnuts.* **beech es.**

beech:
a. branch showing nut
b. tree
c. grain of wood

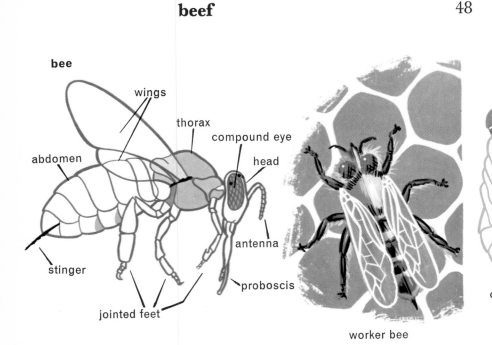

bee

wings

thorax

compound eye

head

abdomen

antenna

stinger

proboscis

jointed feet

worker bee

chrysalis

queen bee

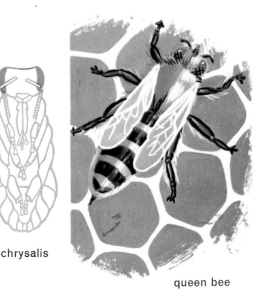

beehive

beef (bēf), *n.* 1. the meat of a steer, cow, ox, or bull, used as food. *We had beef sandwiches for lunch.* 2. a bull, cow, steer, or ox, especially one that is raised for its meat. *The rancher sent five hundred beefs to market.* **beefs** or **beeves.**

bee hive (bē'hīv'), *n.* a house in which bees live and make honey. *Beehives vary in size, but are usually dome shaped.* **bee hives.**

bee keep er (bē'kēp'ər), *n.* a person who raises bees. *Beekeepers usually wear special clothing when they gather honey from the hives.* **bee keep ers.**

been (bin), past participle of **be.**

beer (bir), *n.* 1. a somewhat bitter alcoholic drink made from barley, malt, and hops. *My father enjoys a glass of cold beer on a hot day.* 2. a sweet soft drink made from roots or plants. *I put a scoop of ice cream in my glass of root beer.* **beers.**

bees wax (bēz'waks'), *n.* the wax made by bees. *Beeswax is used for making candles. Bees build their honeycombs with beeswax.*

beet (bēt), *n.* 1. a plant which is grown for its juicy root. *The root of the red beet is eaten as a vegetable, and the root of the white beet is used in making sugar.* 2. the root of this plant used as a vegetable. *I went to the store for a jar of red beets.* **beets.**

bee tle (bēt'l), *n.* an insect that has four wings, the outer two of which form a hard, shiny, covering that protects it. *The outer wings of a beetle are not used for flying.* **bee tles.**

be fore (bi fôr'), *prep.* 1. ahead of; in front of. *A long road lay before us. A new teacher stood before the class.* 2. at an earlier time than. *I have to be home before six o'clock.*

adv. 3. at an earlier time; at a previous time. *Have you heard this story before?* 4. earlier; sooner. *You may go out when you have finished your work, not before.* 5. ahead; in front; in advance. *I'll walk before; the path is quite narrow.*

conj. 6. instead of; rather than. *I'll stay home before I'll ride in that car.* 7. earlier than the time when; previous to the time that. *Before you cross the street, look both ways.*

beg (beg), *v.* 1. to ask for something as a gift or as charity. *He came to beg money and clothes for the victims of the flood.* 2. to ask for or of with deep feeling. *We laughed so hard at his stories*

beekeeper

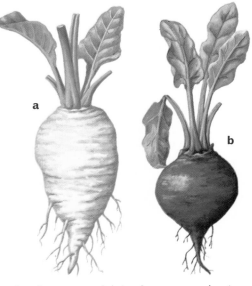

a

b

beet: a. sugar beet; **b.** common beet

that we had to beg him to stop. 3. to request politely; to ask humbly. *I beg your pardon.* **begs, begged, beg ging.**

be gan (bi gan′), past tense of **begin.**

beg gar (beg′ər), *n.* 1. a person who begs, especially a person who makes his living by begging. *Though he was poor, he was not a beggar; he worked hard for his living.* 2. a person who is very poor. *The flood swept away everything he owned and left him a beggar.* **beg gars.**

be gin (bi gin′), *v.* 1. to start; to do the first part of something. *I began collecting stamps when I was seven years old. We will begin our school day with the arithmetic lesson.* 2. to cause to be; to come into being. *We began this club as a way of raising money.* **be gins, be gan, be gun, be gin ning.**

be gin ning (bi gin′ing), *n.* 1. a start; the act of starting. *The beginning of the game was delayed by rain.* 2. the time when something starts; the place where something starts. *In the beginning I wasn't very interested in school, but as time went by I began to enjoy it. We are now at the beginning of the longest street in the world.* 3. the first part of anything. *The beginning of the book was the best part.* **be gin nings.**

be go nia (bi gō′nyə), *n.* a plant with red or green leaves and flowers that feel like wax. *Begonias produce flowers of different colors: red, white, or yellow.* **be go nias.**

be gun (bi gun′), past participle of **begin.**

be half (bi haf′), *n.* 1. interest; favor; name. *The gift was given in our behalf.* 2. **in behalf of,** in support of; in the interest of; in the name

of. *In behalf of the team I wish to thank you for your support.*

be have (bi hāv′), *v.* 1. to act properly; to do the right things. *If you don't behave, you will not be invited to come again.* 2. to act; to conduct oneself. *How did he behave at the party?* **be haves, be haved, be hav ing.**

be hav ior (bi hāv′yər), *n.* 1. the way a person acts; conduct. *His behavior is always very good in school.* 2. the way a thing acts. *The behavior of a compass needle when it is placed near a magnet helps us to understand more about magnetic force.* **be hav iors.**

be hind (bi hīnd′), *prep.* 1. in back of; at the rear of. *We are hiding behind the curtains. Stand behind the house until I call you.* 2. not as good as; below the general level of. *His running time is behind that of the other boys on his team.* 3. later than; slower than. *We were behind schedule before we even started our trip.*
adv. 4. to the rear; in the rear. *Don't look behind. We left him behind.* 5. below the general level. *He is behind in his reading.*

be hold (bi hōld′), *v.* 1. to see; to look at; to observe. *All of us went to the window to behold the sunset.* **be holds, be held, be hold ing.**
interj. 2. look! *Behold! Now that I have made the handkerchief disappear, I will bring it back!*

be ing (bē′ing), *v.* 1. present participle of **be.**
n. 2. a person; any living creature. *How can any human being be so evil?* 3. existence. *Horses were a major means of transportation until the automobile came into being.* **be ings.**

bel fry (bel′frē), *n.* a part of a building, usually high up, in which a bell is hung. *Every night we heard the bell ring out from the church belfry.* **bel fries.**

be lief (bi lēf′), *n.* 1. acceptance of something as true or real. *My brother destroyed my belief in Santa Claus.* 2. something believed to be true or real. *Every religion has its own beliefs.* 3. confidence; faith. *You must have belief in your own ability.* 4. something that is believed; an opinion. *It is my firm belief that most people want to work for their living.* **be liefs.**

be lieve (bi lēv′), *v.* 1. to accept something as true or real. *Do you believe that cats have nine lives?* 2. to have religious faith in something. *We believe that God helps us when we are in trouble.* 3. to accept what someone says as true. *I wanted to believe him, but his story was ridiculous.* 4. to think; to have an opinion. *I believe we have already met.* **be lieves, be lieved, be liev ing.**

bell (bel), *n.* 1. a hollow metal device, usually shaped like a cup, that makes a ringing sound when it is struck. *The bell in the tower is rung every hour.* 2. the ringing sound made by a bell when it is struck. *The entire class left the room at the bell. The downed boxer was saved by the bell.* 3. anything shaped like a bell. *Scientists explore the ocean floor in a diving bell.* **bells.**

belfry

begonia

---

sand, āte, bâre, fäther; sent, mē, fėrn; fit, bīke; pot, rōpe, fôrt; run, pùll, rüle, cūte; noise, sound; ch, cheese; ng, long; th, thick; ~~th~~, those; zh, treasure; ə = a in about, e in waken, i in animal, o in seldom, and u in minus.

v. 4. to put a bell on. *We belled the goat so that we could find him at night.* **bells, belled, bell ing.**

bel lows (bel/ōz), *n.* a device for blowing air out when its sides are pushed together. By pushing the handles tight, a strong gust of air comes from the little end. *A bellows is used to make a fire burn.*

bellows

be long (bi lông/), *v.* 1. to have a proper place. *Pots and pans belong in the kitchen, not in the dining room.* 2. to be suitable; to be attractive on a person or in a place. *That couch belongs in my living room. The clerk in the store said this hat looks like it belongs on me.* 3. **belong to,** (a) to be the property of someone. *The bike belongs to Larry.* (b) to be a member of something; to be a part of something. *We belong to the school band.* **be longs, be longed, be long ing.**

be long ings (bi long/ings), *n. pl.* a person's property or possessions. *All our belongings were lost in the fire.*

be lov ed (bi luv/əd, bi luvd/), *adj.* 1. greatly loved; very dear. *These are my beloved children.* *n.* 2. one who is greatly loved. *The prince wrote a letter to his beloved.*

be low (bi lō/), *adv.* 1. beneath; in a lower place. *Far below, we could see the bottom of the pit.* 2. on or to a lower floor, deck, level, etc. *When the storm began, the captain ordered all of the passengers to go below.*
prep. 3. in a lower place than; to a lower place than. *He felt a sharp pain below his heart. We swam below the boat.* 4. lower than in degree, price, rank, etc. *A lieutenant is below a captain in rank. The temperature was five degrees below zero.*

belt (belt), *n.* 1. a strip or band of leather, cloth, etc. worn around the body to support or hold in clothing, to hold tools or a weapon, or as an ornament. *When his belt broke, he used rope to hold up his pants.* 2. a wide strip or band of anything. *A belt of trees grew along the road. What is the major crop of the wheat belt?* 3. a band that connects and turns a series of pulleys or wheels in a machine. *When the belt broke, all of the wheels but one stopped turning.* **belts.**
v. 4. to place a belt on or around. *I sometimes belt this dress even though it can be worn without one.* 5. to attach with a belt. *The sheriff belted on his gun.* 6. to strike with a belt or as if with a belt. *The policeman will belt any dog that attacks him.* **belts, belt ed, belt ing.**

bench (bench), *n.* 1. a long, low, wooden or stone seat that sometimes has a back. *George fell asleep on a bench in the park.* 2. a strong table or platform on which work with tools or machines is done. *Put this hammer back on the tool bench in the basement.* 3. a judge or judges in a court. *The prisoner was asked to approach the bench to receive his sentence.* **bench es.**

bend (bend), *v.* 1. to curve something by force; to change the shape of something from straight to curved. *We were unable to bend the strip of wood without breaking it.* 2. to be curved; to become curved. *The tree bent under the weight of the fruit on its branches.* 3. to turn in a direction. *The road bent sharply to the right.* 4. to stoop over; to lean over. *He bent to the ground and picked up a dollar.* 5. to make a person give in; to give in under force. *If you do not bend to my wishes, you will not go on the trip with me.* **bends, bent** or **bend ed, bend ing.**
n. 6. a part that is curved; a bent part. *There is a service station at the next bend in the road.* **bends.**

be neath (bi nēth/), *adv.* 1. in a lower place. *The water fell to the rocks beneath.*
prep. 2. under; lower than in place, rank, position, etc. *I sat beneath a tree and took a nap. A captain is beneath a colonel.* 3. not worthy of. *Your actions are beneath my notice.*

ben e fit (ben/ə fit), *n.* 1. anything helpful to a person or a thing; advantage. *I am telling this story for your benefit, Mary.* 2. a public event held as a means of raising money for a good cause. *The benefit this year will be held for the children's hospital.* **ben e fits.**
v. 3. to be good for; to help. *A long vacation in a warm place will benefit you more than medicine, Mr. Williams.* 4. to gain; to profit. *Did you benefit from your experience?* **ben e fits, ben e fit ed, ben e fit ing.**

bent (bent), *v.* 1. past tense of **bend.**
adj. 2. curved, not straight. *You can use a bent branch as a cane.* 3. determined to do something. *He is bent on winning the race.*
n. 4. a strong liking or tendency because of ability or skill. *He has a natural bent for music.* **bents.**

ber ry (ber/ē), *n.* 1. a small, juicy fruit with soft flesh and many seeds. *We had berries and ice cream for dessert.* 2. the dry seed of certain plants. *The seed used in making coffee is a berry.* **ber ries.**

be side (bi sīd/), *prep.* 1. at the side of; near to. *The child walked beside his father.* 2. when compared with. *Beside her, anyone would seem dull.* 3. besides; in addition to. *There was no one in the room beside me.* 4. **beside the point,** not on the subject; away from the topic. *Your question is good but it is beside the point.* 5. **beside oneself,** very excited or upset because of worry, fear, anger, etc. *When the child failed to return home after school, his mother was beside herself with worry.*

be sides (bi sīdz/), *adv.* 1. in addition; also; furthermore. *We had coffee cake, and pancakes besides. I don't know the answer; besides, I didn't come here to answer questions.*
prep. 2. in addition to; other than; as well as. *Did you see anything besides cartoons at the show?*

best (best), *adj.* 1. better than all others; most excellent. *That dinner was the best meal I've had in a long time.* 2. largest; most. *You will spend the best part of your life going to school and working.*

n. 3. the finest of anything; the most excellent of its type. *We serve only the best in this restaurant.* 4. as much as a person can do; a person's finest effort, work, etc. *Try your best. Unless you can give your best at all times, you cannot be on the team.*

v. 5. to do better than; to defeat. *The boys in our class bested the girls in the last spelling contest.* **bests, best ed, best ing.**

be stow (bi stō′), *v.* to give as a gift, honor, etc. *They bestowed a collection of books on our library. The honor of carrying the flag in the parade was bestowed on Bill.* **be stows, be stowed, be stow ing.**

bet (bet), *n.* 1. an agreement between two or more persons to pay money to or to do something for the one who is proved right. *I made a dime bet with him that it would be sunny today.* 2. the money to be paid or the thing to be done as the result of a bet. *The bet was only a nickel, so I could easily pay it.* 3. something on which a bet is made. *He was a poor bet to win the race.* **bets.**

v. 4. to make a bet. *I'll bet you a quarter we win the game. He bet that the home team would lose.* 5. to be sure enough of something to risk a bet; to be certain. *I'll bet he asks us where we've been.* **bets, bet or bet ted, bet ting.**

be tray (bi trā′), *v.* 1. to aid the enemy; to give information, supplies, etc. to the enemy, putting one's own side, country, etc. at a disadvantage. *The captured soldiers betrayed the army in return for food.* 2. to be false to; to fail to keep promises, etc. *Don't betray us by not coming.* 3. to reveal without intending to; to show. *Tom's sneezing betrayed our position to the others. The expression on his face betrayed his anger.* **be trays, be trayed, be tray ing.**

bet ter (bet′ər), *adj.* 1. higher in quality; more excellent; finer. *She is a better student than her brother. Does anyone have a better plan?* 2. a larger part; more than half. *It took us the better part of an hour to change the flat tire.* 3. not as sick as before; improved in health. *When you are better, you can get out of bed.*

n. 4. anyone or anything which is better than another. *That car is the better of the two.* **bet ters.**

v. 5. to make better; to improve. *If you practice, you will soon better your ability.* **bet ters, bet tered, bet ter ing.**

be tween (bi twēn′), *prep.* 1. in the space that separates two things. *There were four people between me and the door.* 2. in a stated time period; during the time which separates two stated points of time. *I'll meet you between nine and ten o'clock. Spring comes between winter and summer.* 3. from one place, person, etc. to another. *Telephone cables lie between the United States and Europe.* 4. more than one and less than the other. *This ball costs between three and four dollars.* 5. involving two sides, countries, etc.; having to do with. *The Civil War is also*

called the *War Between the States.* 6. by the combined effort or action of. *Between them both they managed to get the job done quickly.* 7. of either one or the other of. *The choice between war and peace is easy to make.*

be yond (bi yond′), *prep.* 1. in a place farther away than. *The grocery store is just beyond the park.* 2. unable to be helped or affected by. *He is beyond punishment.* 3. unable to be understood by. *My vocabulary is beyond him. Why he has to go to that movie is beyond me.* 4. far more than; over and above. *The price of the ticket was beyond what I could afford. She is beautiful beyond words.*

adv. 5. in a place farther away. *We've looked everywhere for him; I even searched those woods beyond.*

bi an nu al (bī an′ū əl), *adj.* coming twice a year; happening twice a year. *Our biannual meetings are always held in January and in July.* **bi an nu al ly,** *adv.*

bib (bib), *n.* 1. a piece of cloth tied under a baby's chin to keep his clothing clean and dry. *After dinner the baby's face, hands, and bib were covered with food.* 2. the part of an apron that covers the chest and stomach. *The carpenter kept a pencil and nails in his bib.* **bibs.**

Bi ble (bī′bl), *n.* 1. the book of sacred writings of the Christian religions, containing the Old Testament and the New Testament. *Christians believe that the writings in the Bible were inspired by God.* 2. the sacred writings of any religion. *The Bible of the Jewish religion is called the Talmud.* **Bi bles.**

bib li og ra phy (bib′lē og′rə fē), *n.* a list of books, articles, etc. on a particular subject, person, etc. *There is a bibliography at the end of the history book.* **bib li og ra phies.**

bi cy cle (bī′sik′əl), *n.* 1. a vehicle having two wheels mounted on a light metal frame with a seat for the rider, a bar for steering, and levers turned by the feet for moving it. *The rider of a bicycle must learn to balance himself so that he will not fall.* **bi cy cles.**

v. 2. to ride a bicycle. *When the weather is good, he bicycles to school.* **bi cy cles, bi cy cled, bi cy cling.**

bicycle

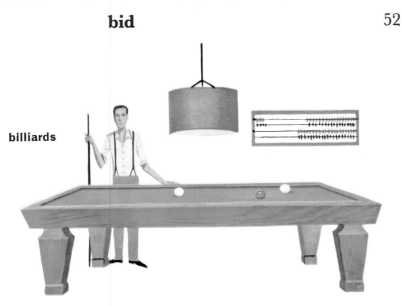

billiards

bid (bid), *v.* 1. to order to do something. *The fire chief bade the crowd to stand back from the blaze.* 2. to invite. *We were bidden to stay for dinner.* 3. to say or express a greeting or farewell to. *The mayor met the visitors at the airport to bid them welcome to the city.* 4. to offer to pay a certain amount of money for something. *The lady bid two dollars for the antique lamp, but someone else bid four dollars.* **bids, bade** or **bid, bid den** or **bid, bid ding.**
n. 5. an offer to pay a certain amount of money for something; the amount offered. *The final bid on the painting was thirty dollars.* **bids.**

bi en ni al (bī en′ē əl), *adj.* coming once every two years; happening every other year. *Since the officers of the club serve for two years, we have biennial elections.* **bi en ni al ly,** *adv.*

big (big), *adj.* 1. large in number or size. *They live in a big house that has sixteen rooms.* 2. very interesting or important. *The big story in the newspaper today is about the presidential election.* 3. fully grown; grown up. *When he gets big, he wants to be a jet pilot.* **big ger, big gest.**

bike (bīk), *n.* a bicycle. *Did your friend Jim get a new bike for Christmas?* **bikes.**

bile (bīl), *n.* a yellow or green liquid produced by the liver to aid in digesting foods. *Bile digests fats and keeps food moving through the system of digestion.*

bill¹ (bil), *n.* 1. a listing of how much money is owed for a purchase or service. *At the end of the month we received a bill from the milkman for all of the milk we had bought.* 2. a piece of paper money. *The prize for winning the race was a five-dollar bill.* 3. a plan for a new law which is offered to a legislative body for a vote. *Many bills are suggested each year, but not all of them become laws.* 4. a printed notice of a coming event; an advertisement. *Circus bills appeared all over town a month before the circus arrived.* **bills.**
v. 5. to send a bill to; to request payment from. *Dr. Stevens bills his patients at the end of each month.* **bills, billed, bill ing.**

bill² (bil), *n.* the beak of a bird. *Ducks have wide, flat bills.* **bills.**

bill board (bil′bôrd′), *n.* a large board, usually outdoors, on which are pasted advertisements or notices. *Some billboards along the highway advertise places to eat or sleep in the next town.* **bill boards.**

bill iards (bil′yərdz), *n. pl.* a game played with a long stick called a cue and solid balls on a felt-covered table with cushioned sides. *My father likes to play billiards with his friends.*

bin (bin), *n.* an enclosed space for storing something. *Mother keeps fresh vegetables in a bin in the bottom of the refrigerator.* **bins.**

bi na ry (bī′nə rē), *adj.* made up of two of something. *Binary numbers have two numerals, like the 2 and 4 in 24.*

bind (bīnd), *v.* 1. to fasten together. *The clerk bound the two boxes with heavy string.* 2. to cover with a bandage. *The doctor bound the wounds of the injured man.* 3. to require. *The rules of the club bind all of its members to pay dues every month.* 4. to fasten pages together and put them in a cover. *The pages of a book may be bound by gluing, by fastening with wire, or by sewing.* **binds, bound, bind ing.**

bi o sphere (bī′ə sfir′), *n.* the entire portion of the earth, including the land, sea, and air, on which plants and animals can live. *Scientists explore the biosphere to discover different forms of plant and animal life.*

birch (bėrch), *n.* 1. a tree with smooth bark and hard wood. *Birches grow in North America and in Europe.* 2. the wood of this tree. *Much furniture is made of birch.* **birch es.**

bird (bėrd), *n.* a warm-blooded, egg-laying animal, having feathers and wings. *Almost all birds can fly.* **birds.**

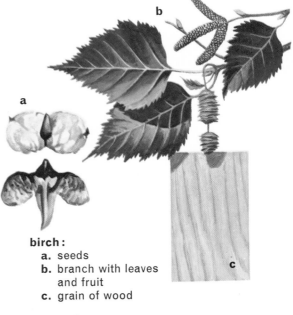

birch:
a. seeds
b. branch with leaves and fruit
c. grain of wood

BIRDS

owl

BIRDS OF PREY

vulture

sparrow hawk

SONGBIRDS   sparrow   nightingale   thrush   GAME BIRDS   quail

toucan

EXOTIC BIRDS   macaw   WADING BIRDS

SEABIRDS

sea gull

flamingo

marabou stork

birth (bėrth), *n*. 1. a coming into life as a living creature. *The entire family was very happy with the birth of the new baby.* 2. a beginning of anything. *Before the birth of the automobile, horses were widely used for transportation.* 3. family. *He is of royal birth because he is the son of the queen.* **births.**

birth day (bėrth/dā'), *n*. 1. the day of one's birth. *George Washington's birthday was in 1732.* 2. the yearly anniversary of one's birth. *We celebrate George Washington's birthday on February 22.* 3. the day when something started. *The birthday of the United States was July 4, 1776.* **birth days.**

bis cuit (bis/kət), *n*. 1. bread baked in small, usually round, pieces. *Biscuits rise when they are baked.* 2. a small, hard cracker. *Dog biscuits are often shaped like bones.* **bis cuits.**

bish op (bish/əp), *n*. 1. a high-ranking minister of a church. *A bishop is at the head of a large church district.* 2. one of two pieces in the game of chess. *At the beginning of a game of chess, one bishop stands to the right of the queen, another to the left of the king.* **bish ops.**

bit[1] (bit), *n*. 1. the part of a harness that fits into a horse's mouth. *The bit is made of smooth, heavy metal and is used to control the horse without injuring him.* 2. a tool with a sharp point, used for boring and drilling holes. *The carpenter put a larger bit in his drill to bore a larger hole.* **bits.**

bit[2] (bit), *n*. 1. a very small piece of something. *The dog ate every bit of his supper.* 2. a short period of time. *We watched a fire for a bit on our way home from school.* 3. a little; somewhat. *I was feeling a bit like a hero until I found that what I was saving from drowning was a toy balloon.* **bits.**

bit[3] (bit), past tense of **bite.**

bite (bīt), *v*. 1. to grab, hold, or cut with the teeth, or anything like teeth. *If any animal bites you hard enough to break the skin, have a doctor look at the wound.* 2. to sting. *The mosquitoes were biting everyone in the tent last night.* 3. to swallow bait. *Every fish in the lake was biting, and we caught a dozen trout quickly.* **bites, bit, bit ten** or **bit, bit ing.**
n. 4. any act of biting. *Mosquito bites cause your skin to itch.* 5. an amount bitten off, especially as food taken into the mouth. *Don't take too big a bite of cheese.* **bites.**

bit ing (bīt/ing), *adj*. 1. bitter; sharp. *The biting cold forced us back indoors.* 2. bitter in manner; intended to hurt the feelings. *Ann made a biting comment about friends who borrow things and never return them.* **bit ing ly,** *adv*.

bit ter (bit/ər), *adj*. 1. tasting sharp and unpleasant. *The medicine was very bitter, but it soon helped my cold.* 2. difficult to accept. *The injury to our team's best player was a bitter blow.* 3. unhappy; sorrowful. *There were bitter cries of disappointment from the audience when it was announced that the play would not be presented.* 4. biting; harsh. *A bitter wind blew across the frozen lake.* **bit ter ly,** *adv*.

black (blak), *n*. 1. the color of these words. *The type in this book is printed in black.* **blacks.**
adj. 2. having this color. *You will be cooler in summer if you don't wear black clothing.* 3. unhappy, angry, or sad. *The man wore a black look when we told him that we had broken his window.* 4. dirty. *The baby's knees were black from crawling on the floor.* **black er, black est; black ly,** *adv*.
v. 5. to make black. *He blacked and polished his shoes.* 6. **black out,** to become no longer conscious. *After standing in the sun for a while, Joe felt faint and soon blacked out.* **blacks, blacked, black ing.**

black ber ry (blak/ber'ē), *n*. 1. a bush or vine that bears black or purple berries. *Blackberries grow wild in many parts of the country.* 2. this berry used as food. *We picked several buckets of blackberries in the woods.* **black ber ries.**

blackberry:
 a. fruit
 b. flowers
 c. leaves

black board (blak/bôrd'), *n*. a smooth black surface for writing on with chalk. *The teacher wrote a sentence on the blackboard.* **black boards.**

black ness (blak/nəs), *n*. a black color or condition. *The blackness of the clouds warned us of the storm.*

black smith (blak/smith'), *n*. a man who makes or shapes objects out of iron. *The blacksmith used to shoe horses and repair farm tools.* **black smiths.**

blad der (blad/ər), *n*. 1. a small, baglike organ in the body that holds liquid wastes from the kidneys. *The bladder holds waste fluids until they* *can be discharged.* 2. a thin bag that can be filled with air or other gases. *The bladder in a football holds air under pressure and is protected by an outer covering of leather.* **blad ders.**

blade (blād), *n.* 1. the cutting edge of any metal object, especially a knife. *A bread knife usually has a broad, flat blade.* 2. a sword. *The knight drew his blade and prepared to duel.* 3. a flat leaf, especially of grass. *The cut blades of grass blew over the sidewalk.* 4. anything that is broad and flat. *He dipped the blade of his oar into the water and began to row the boat across the lake.* **blades.**

blame (blām), *v.* 1. to put the responsibility for something bad or unpleasant on a person or thing. *The police blamed the accident on the man who was driving too fast.* 2. to criticize; to find fault with. *Nobody can be blamed for wishing that winter were over.* 3. **be to blame,** to be the person who is at fault. *Who was to blame for the failure of our team in the tournament?* **blames, blamed, blam ing.**

n. 4. the responsibility for something bad or unpleasant. *Since Bill was driving too fast, the blame for the accident was his.* 5. finding fault. *Neither praise nor blame could make Don take any interest in his schoolwork.*

blank (blangk), *adj.* 1. without any writing or printing. *The art teacher gave each of us a blank sheet of paper to draw on.* 2. with spaces to be filled in. *He gave me a blank application form, and told me to put my name and address on it.* 3. without life or interest; as if half asleep. *After his long drive, the man walked into a hotel with a weary, blank expression.* **blank er, blank est; blank-ly,** *adv.*

n. 4. a paper or form with spaces to be filled in. *He filled out an application blank to work at the grocery store.* 5. a space on such a form. *Write an answer in the blank after each of the questions.* **blanks.**

blan ket (blang′kət), *n.* 1. a heavy woven piece of cloth used to keep one warm. *When the outside temperature drops below freezing, I put an extra blanket on my bed.* 2. anything that covers like a blanket. *There was a blanket of snow on the ground.* **blan kets.**

v. 3. to cover like a blanket. *The harbor was blanketed with fog.* **blan kets, blan ket ed, blan ket ing.**

blast (blast), *n.* 1. a strong gust of wind or air. *A blast of wind blew Bob's hat into the street.* 2. the sound made by a whistle, horn, etc. *We went home for lunch when we heard the blast of the factory whistle at noon.* 3. an explosion. *The dynamite blast tore a huge hole in the side of the mountain.* **blasts.**

v. 4. to blow up with explosives. *In order to build highways over or through mountains, huge amounts of solid rock must be blasted.* 5. to destroy; to cause to ruin. *The crops were blasted by a frost in late spring.* **blasts, blast ed, blast ing.**

blaze[1] (blāz), *n.* 1. a bright flame. *The blaze of*

the fire lit up the dark sky. 2. any bright shining light. *The blaze of the street lights made the business district as bright as day.* 3. a sudden violent emotion. *His blaze of temper surprised us since nothing had happened to make him angry.* 4. a bright display. *A blaze of color greeted us as we entered the garden.* **blazes.**

v. 5. to shine brightly. *The sun blazed down on us as we drove through the desert.* 6. to glow with light. *As we drove toward the city, we could see the neon signs blazing in the distance.* **blaz es, blazed, blaz ing.**

blaze[2] (blāz), *n.* 1. a light spot made on a tree by stripping off a piece of bark. *The hikers marked the trail by making blazes on the trees.* **blaz es.**

v. 2. to mark a tree or a trail with blazes. *The hunter blazed a new trail through the forest.* **blaz es, blazed, blaz ing.**

bled (bled), past tense of **bleed.**

bleed (blēd), *v.* 1. to lose blood. *His knee began to bleed after he scraped it on the sidewalk.* 2. to take blood from. *Many years ago doctors bled sick patients in an effort to remove poisons from the body.* 3. to lose sap through a cut or gash in the bark of a tree. *The tree bled where the boy carved his initials.* **bleeds, bled, bleed ing.**

blend (blend), *v.* 1. to mix thoroughly, so that the parts cannot be identified. *Mother blended the ingredients of the cake before she put it into the oven.* 2. to mix together; to come together in harmony. *The voices of the chorus blended perfectly in the beautiful song. The color of her blouse blends with the color of her skirt.* **blends, blend ed, blend ing.**

n. 3. a mixture of several different things. *Good coffee is often a blend of different types of coffee.* **blends.**

bless (bles), *v.* 1. to make holy. *The new church was blessed by the pastor.* 2. to make happy; to make successful. *Some people are blessed with a talent for music or art.* 3. to praise. *In church the minister said, "Bless the Lord!"* **bless es, blessed** or **blest, bless ing.**

bless ed (bles′əd or blest), *adj.* 1. holy; sacred. *This blessed ground is dedicated to God.* 2. happy; lucky. *The birth of the new baby was a blessed event.* **bless ed ly,** *adv.*

bless ing (bles′ing), *n.* 1. a prayer of thanks before a meal. *Our family listens quietly to the blessing given by Father at dinner.* 2. something that brings joy or happiness. *The heavy rain was a blessing since it ended the hot weather.* 3. a prayer asking for God's favor. *The minister gave a blessing to the new members of the church.* 4. good wishes; approval. *We finally got Dad to give his blessing to our trip up the mountain.* **bless ings.**

blew (blü), past tense of **blow**[1].

blind (blīnd), *adj.* 1. not able to see. *Charles was blind, but he was one of the best students in the whole state.* 2. unwilling to notice; unable to

judge. *Most people are blind to their own faults.*
3. having no way out. *We live on a blind street; it ends at the park.* 4. operating by instruments only. *A pilot takes a course in blind flying so that in bad weather he doesn't have to see where he is going.* **blind ly,** *adv.*

v. 5. to make unable to see. *The strong light blinded him for a minute.* 6. to take away the power to understand or to judge. *Harry's love for his brother blinds him to the boy's faults.* **blinds, blind ed, blind ing.**

n. 7. a window shade. *The blinds kept the inside of the house in darkness, even on a sunny day.* 8. a hiding place for a hunter. *From his blind, the hunter shot six ducks.* **blinds.**

blind fold (blīnd′fōld′), *n.* 1. a cover for the eyes. *For this game, we all wear blindfolds so that we cannot see.* **blind folds.**

v. 2. to cover the eyes of. *We blindfolded the spy with his own handkerchief before taking him to our camp.* **blind folds, blind fold ed, blind- fold ing.**

blis ter (blis′tər), *n.* 1. a soft, raised place on the skin that is filled with watery matter. *Wearing tight shoes can cause blisters on the feet. A burn can cause a blister.* 2. a swelling like a blister. *The paint on the wall near the radiator formed blisters from the heat.* **blis ters.**

v. 3. to make blisters on. *The hot sun blistered my bare shoulders.* 4. to form blisters. *The old paint on the house blistered.* **blis ters, blis tered, blis ter ing.**

bliz zard (bliz′ərd), *n.* a storm with snow and strong winds. *The blizzard piled snow up so high that automobiles couldn't move.* **bliz zards.**

block (blok), *n.* 1. a solid piece of wood, stone, metal, etc. *Children play with blocks. Some buildings are formed of big blocks of stone.* 2. a part of a city surrounded by four streets. *The new shopping center covers a city block.* 3. the distance from one street corner to the next. *Walk two*

blocks

blocks east, and you will come to the lake. 4. something that gets in the way; an obstacle; a stopping. *The repairs to the street were a block to traffic. Not doing any work is a big block to success.* **blocks.**

v. 5. to be in the way of. *The chair blocked the door. The blizzard blocked our plans to leave yesterday because no airliners could take off.* **blocks, blocked, block ing.**

blood (blud), *n.* 1. the red liquid that flows through the body of people and animals. *Blood carries food and oxygen and carries away waste products. I got blood on my shirt from the cut on my finger.* 2. family; birth. *They are related by blood.* 3. **in cold blood,** on purpose; without emotion. *The crime was committed in cold blood.*

blood stream, blood flowing through the body. *If disease germs get into the blood stream, you may become ill.*

bloody (blud′ē), *adj.* 1. bleeding. *Little Brian was proud of his bloody nose because he thought it proved he was a real fighter.* 2. with killing and wounding. *The bloody battle was over.* **blood i- er, blood i est.**

bloom (blüm), *n.* 1. the flower of a plant. *The rose is a fragrant, red bloom.* 2. the time for having blossoms. *Violets are in bloom in the spring.* 3. the time of beauty, growth, and health. *The bloom of youth is a joy to see.* **blooms.**

v. 4. to have flowers. *Fruit trees bloom in April and May.* 5. to be healthy; to be at one's best. *The boys and girls bloomed when they played outdoors during summer.* **blooms, bloomed, bloom ing.**

bloom er (blüm′ər), *n.* 1. a person who begins to bloom; person who is at a high point of ability. 2. **late bloomer,** a person who develops somewhat later than the average in knowledge and scholarship. *Some children who are late bloomers don't have an interest in a subject until they are about sixteen or seventeen.* **bloom ers.**

bloom ers (blüm′ərz), *n. pl.* 1. short, loose pants, fitting closely at the knees. *Years ago, girls in physical education classes wore bloomers.* 2. an undergarment that is like those formerly worn by women. *Bloomers were often trimmed with lace.*

blos som (blos′əm), *n.* 1. the flower of a plant or tree. *The orange blossoms smell sweet.* 2. a time for blooming. *The fruit trees in Michigan are in blossom in late spring.* **blos soms.**

v. 3. to bloom; to produce flowers. *The trees blossomed early because of the warm weather.* **blos soms, blos somed, blos som ing.**

blot (blot), *n.* 1. a spot; a stain. *The spilled cocoa left a big blot on the newspaper.* 2. something that hurts a reputation or record. *His one absence was the only blot on his perfect attendance.* **blots.**

v. 3. to make a spot or stain on. *That melting candy blotted half the page of the book.* 4. to dry up with a blotter. *Blot the ink before it smears.*

blunderbuss

5. **blot out,** (a) to hide completely. *His mind blotted out all memory of the accident.* (b) to destroy completely. *The town was blotted out by the hurricane.* **blots, blot ted, blot ting.**

blot ter (blot′ər), *n.* a soft paper which can soak up water, ink, or any spilled liquid. *Use a blotter on that writing before putting the letter in the envelope.* **blot ters.**

blouse (blous), *n.* 1. a shirt worn by women and children. *A skirt and blouse are often worn by girls.* 2. the upper part of a uniform. *The soldiers wear blouses over their shirts.* **blous es.**

blow[1] (blō), *v.* 1. to move rapidly. *We could hear the wind blow through the old house.* 2. to be moved or stirred by the wind. *The falling leaves are blowing out of the yard.* 3. to cause to make a sound by forcing air through. *The leader blew a whistle, and we all lined up. Scott blows a trumpet in the school band.* 4. to make a shrill sound. *The factory whistle blows at noon as a signal for lunch hour.* 5. **blow up,** (a) to explode. *The engineers blew up the old building to make room for the new highway.* (b) to fill with air. *The small boy blew up his balloon.* **blows, blew** or **blown, blow ing.**
n. 6. a strong blowing of wind. *The sailors in the ship suddenly ran into a blow.* **blows.**

blow[2] (blō), *n.* 1. a hard hit. *He gave the ball a mighty blow with his bat, and it sailed over the fence for a home run.* 2. a sudden shock; a happening that a person is not expecting. *Her kitten's death was a blow to the little girl. The bad news from my family was a blow to me.* **blows.**

blown (blōn), *v.* 1. past tense of **blow.**

blow torch (blō′tôrch′), *n.* a torch which sends out a flame hot enough to melt metal and to burn away old paint. *Many blowtorches use gas for fuel.* **blow torch es.**

blue (blü), *adj.* 1. having the color of the clear sky. *Irene's blue eyes attract attention.* 2. sad; unhappy. *Don is blue because he cannot go to the circus.* **blu er, blu est.**
n. 3. the color of the clear sky. *My favorite color is blue.* 4. anything colored blue. *Connie had her choice of dresses, so she chose the blue.* 5. **out of the blue,** without being expected. *The money sent by grandfather came out of the blue.* **blues.**

blue ber ry (blü′ber′ē), *n.* a small, blue, sweet fruit. *Blueberries taste good, especially in a dish with cream poured over them.* **blue ber ries.**

blue bird (blü′bėrd′), *n.* a bird with a blue back and blue wings. *The bluebird is smaller than the robin.* **blue birds.**

blue jay (blü′jā′), *n.* a bird having a blue back with black markings. *The bluejay is a noisy bird that screams rather than sings.* **blue jays.**

bluff[1] (bluf), *n.* 1. a high, steep bank or cliff. *Bluffs are usually found along a shore and are difficult to climb.* **bluffs.**
adj. 2. having a front that slopes steeply. *There is interesting scenery along the bluff, rocky coast of Maine.* 3. rough, but honest and friendly. *Howard's bluff manner scared away people until they got to know him.* **bluff ly,** *adv.*

bluff[2] (bluf), *v.* 1. to try to give the impression of something that is not so. *Edward was bluffing when he said he could play the piano.* **bluffs, bluffed, bluff ing.**
n. 2. a bluffing; a pretending; showing confidence that is not real. *His big talk is only a bluff, so don't be fooled.* 3. a person who bluffs. *Ed is such a bluff that you hardly know when to believe him.* **bluffs.**

blun der buss (blun′dər bus′), *n.* an old-style gun with a bell-shaped front end. *Blunderbusses were used for hunting and for protection about 1650.* **blun der bus ses.**

blush (blush), *v.* 1. to become red in the face because of being modest or ashamed. *Betty blushed when the principal praised her, and everyone looked at her.* **blush es, blushed, blush ing.**
n. 2. a turning red of the face because of being modest or ashamed. *A blush appeared on Joan's face when the teacher pointed out the mistakes she had made.* 3. a rosy color. *Just before the sun came up, we saw the blush in the eastern sky.* **blush es.**

boa con stric tor (bō′ə kən strik′tər), *n.* a kind of large snake that kills its victims by crushing them. *The boa constrictor lives in South America and Central America and is about ten feet long.* **boa con stric tors.**

blowtorch

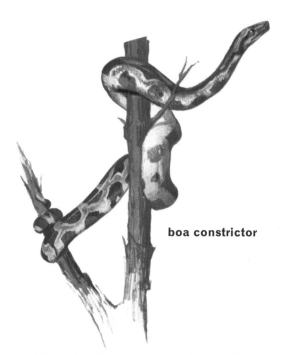

boa constrictor

board (bôrd), *n.* 1. a long, flat piece of sawed wood. *Boards are used in building the wooden parts of houses.* 2. a flat piece of wood or other material used for a special purpose. *Checkers is played on a board. There is a bulletin board in school near the office. An artist uses a drawing board.* 3. meals that one pays for. *We pay for our room and board in the little hotel.* 4. a group of persons which advises or directs. *The school board helps the superintendent of schools by giving him advice.* **boards.**
v. 5. to cover up with boards. *Before the big storm, Father boarded the front window so that it wouldn't be broken by the wind.* 6. to live and eat in another's house for pay. *George boarded with his aunt while going to college.* 7. to get on a plane, train, ship, or bus. *One hundred passengers waited to board the airliner.* **boards, board ed, board ing.**

boast (bōst), *v.* 1. to brag; to talk too much about oneself and about what one can do. *Joe is always boasting about his travels and about his family's new cars.* 2. to be proud of having. *Our village boasts a new park.* **boasts, boast ed, boast ing.**
n. 3. bragging talk. *His boast was that he had always paid his debts on time.* 4. something to be proud of. *Our college is the boast of our city.* **boasts.**

boat (bōt), *n.* 1. a small vessel for traveling on water. *Some boats are moved by oars (rowboats), and some boats move by wind blowing on sails (sailboats).* 2. a ship. *A big ship is sometimes called a boat, but all large vessels should be called ships.* **boats.**
v. 3. to travel in a boat. *On our vacation we swam and boated.* **boats, boat ed, boat ing.**

boat house (bōt′hous′), *n.* a building next to the water in which boats are kept. *A boathouse is used for boats as a garage is used for automobiles.* **boat hous es.**

bob (bob), *v.* 1. to move with short, jerking motions; to move up and down or from one side to the other. *The little toy boat bobbed on the waves.* 2. to cut the hair short. *This summer Marjorie will get her hair bobbed.* 3. to appear or arise suddenly. *The diver's head bobbed up from the water at the side of the boat.* **bobs, bobbed, bob bing.**
n. 4. a quick up-and-down motion. *Father gave a bob of his head when I asked him if I could go out.*

boat powered by a motor

5. a short haircut for women and children. *Mother's bob looks attractive.* **bobs.**

bob white (bob′hwīt′), *n.* a bird of North America, having a reddish back and white on its throat. *The bobwhite's call is a whistle that sounds as if it were saying, "Bob White!"*

body (bod′ē), *n.* 1. the physical part of a human being or animal. *People wear clothing to protect their bodies.* 2. the main part of something. *The branches of the big oak tree were burned, but its body is still in good shape.* 3. a group of persons; a group of things. *A large body of people watched the fireworks. We have a body of facts that seem to prove you are correct.* 4. a mass of matter. *The ocean is a large body of water. Stars and planets are called heavenly bodies.* **bod ies.**

boil[1] (boil), *v.* 1. to bubble and send out steam. *When water is heated enough, it boils.* 2. to heat a liquid until bubbles rise. *She boiled the milk.* 3. to cook in boiling water. *My mother boiled eggs for breakfast this morning.* 4. to be angry; to get excited. *Jack boiled when his own mistake lost the game.* **boils, boiled, boil ing.**
n. 5. the condition of something that is boiling. *The water is at a boil.* **boils.**

boil[2] (boil), *n.* a painful, hard swelling under the skin. *Boils are caused by infection.* **boils.**

boil er (boil′ər), *n.* 1. a large, strong metal holder that produces steam to heat a building or make an engine go. *The old steam locomotive had a boiler in the engine.* 2. any holder in which water is boiled. *Put the eggs in a boiler.* 3. a tank that holds hot water. *The boiler supplies us with heated water in the bathroom and kitchen.* **boil ers.**

bold (bōld), *adj.* 1. not afraid to face danger; having courage. *Bold men first traveled west in our country.* 2. showing bad manners. *The bold child interrupted the visitor's talk with his mother.* 3. clearly seen; sharp in detail. *The buildings of the city stood in bold outline against the clear sky.* 4. daring. *Scientists have some bold ideas about the beginning of the universe.* **bold er, bold est; bold ly,** *adv.*

bolt (bōlt), *n.* 1. a small metal bar that slides into a slot. *Bolts keep doors shut.* 2. a metal rod like a nail, but with threads on which a nut fits. *A nut and bolt are used to fasten parts of machinery together.* 3. the part of a lock that is moved by a key. *Only the correct key will move the bolt.* 4. a flash of lightning. *That bolt came very close to us.* 5. a roll of cloth. *My mother bought a bolt of red cotton to make a dress for me.* **bolts.**
v. 6. to fasten with a bolt or bolts. *The parts of a bicycle are bolted together. Be sure to bolt the door at night.* 7. to run away suddenly. *The horse was frightened by the noise of the firecracker and bolted across the field.* 8. to swallow rapidly, without much chewing. *The hungry dog bolted his food.* **bolts, bolt ed, bolt ing.**

bond (bond), *n.* 1. anything that binds, fastens, or holds. *Their bond of friendship lasted for all their lives. The prisoners were tied with heavy bonds.* 2. a written agreement to pay back the money that is borrowed. *A holder of a bond usually gets interest.* 3. a written agreement in which a person says he will pay money if he doesn't do what he is supposed to do. *A bond is issued to make sure a person appears in court.* **bonds.** *v.* 4. to fasten. *The boards were bonded together.* **bonds, bond ed, bond ing.**

bone (bōn), *n.* 1. the hard material that the skeleton is made of. *Bill has a little scar where he once cut his finger to the bone.* 2. one of the pieces that make up a skeleton. *The dog gnawed on the bone left over from our steak.* **bones.** *v.* 3. to take the bones out of. *Before I eat this fish, will you please bone it?* **bones, boned, bon ing.**

bon fire (bon′fīr′), *n.* a fire built outdoors. *We roasted marshmallows over the bonfire.* **bon fires.**

bon net (bon′ət), *n.* 1. a hat usually worn by children that ties under the chin. *A bonnet protects the head and ears, and will not blow off easily.* 2. any covering for the head. *American Indians wore bonnets made of feathers.* **bon nets.**

bo nus (bō′nəs), *n.* something extra given to a person. *In addition to his salary, at Christmas David was given a bonus amounting to two-week's salary.* **bo nus es.**

boo (bü), *interj., n.* 1. an exclamation used to frighten. *Bill jumped from the closet and said, "Boo!" to his little sister.* 2. a long sound made to show disapproval or dislike. *The actor's appearance was greeted with both applause and boos.* **boos.** *v.* 3. to shout "boo" at in order to show dislike. *The audience booed the actor.* **boos, booed, boo ing.**

book (bùk), *n.* 1. written or printed sheets of paper put together inside a cover. *Books are kept in a library.* 2. a long piece of writing. *Histories, novels, and biographies are books. A collection of short stories or poems is a book.* 3. blank pages of paper put together between covers. *The written records will be kept in this book.* **books.** *v.* 4. to reserve. *The airline booked a seat for me.* **books, booked, book ing.**

book case (bùk′kās′), *n.* shelves or a cabinet to hold books. *Some bookcases have glass doors.* **book cas es.**

book keep er (bùk′kēp′ər), *n.* a person whose job it is to keep accounts for a business. *A bookkeeper must know mathematics so that his work is accurate.* **book keep ers.**

book keep ing (bùk′kē′ping), *n.* keeping accounts for a business. *Bookkeeping includes records of money earned and money spent.*

book let (bùk′lət), *n.* a little book, usually with paper covers. *This booklet has only twenty-four pages.* **book lets.**

book mo bile (bùk′mə bēl′), *n.* a truck fitted out like a library. *Bookmobiles go to places that do not have local libraries.* **book mo biles.**

boom[1] (büm), *v.* 1. to make a deep, hollow sound like thunder or like a big drum. *The cannons boomed to celebrate July 4.* 2. to increase swiftly. *The town's population boomed with the arrival of summer visitors.* **booms, boomed, boom ing.** *n.* 3. a deep, loud, hollow noise. *Sometimes we can hear the boom of the high waves against the rocks.* 4. a time when business makes much money. *In 1849 there was a boom in the towns near the newly found gold mines.* **booms.**

boom[2] (büm), *n.* 1. a long pole to which is attached the bottom edge of a sail. *The boom keeps the sail stretched out.* 2. the long pole or beam that comes out from a derrick. *A boom is used for lifting a heavy load.* **booms.**

boot (büt), *n.* 1. a cover for the foot and leg, usually of rubber or leather, worn for protection against cold or wet. *The man put on his boots and waded into the stream.* **boots.** *v.* 2. to kick. *Tom had booted the football over the goalpost.* **boots, boot ed, boot ing.**

booth (büth), *n.* 1. a covered stand where something is sold at a fair or market. *Our class ran a candy booth at the school carnival.* 2. an enclosed place giving one person privacy. *The man called from a telephone booth at the airport.* 3. a table between two backed benches usually found in restaurants. *I think eating lunch in a booth is very comfortable.* **booths.**

bor der (bôr′dər), *n.* 1. an outer edge. *The cabin was built on the border of the forest.* 2. the imaginary line that divides one country from another. *We crossed the border when we visited Canada for our usual summer vacation.* **bor ders.** *v.* 3. to be next to; touch. *Mrs. Kell's backyard borders ours.* 4. to put something around the edge of. *My father has bordered our new swimming pool with beautiful green and blue tiles.* **bor ders, bor dered, bor der ing.**

bore[1] (bôr), *v.* 1. to make (a hole) by drilling. *The engineers bored a tunnel through the mountain.* 2. to make tired; to make weary. *That boy bores me with his silly jokes and his talk about his rich uncle.* **bores, bored, bor ing.** *n.* 3. the hollow part inside a pipe, a tube, or a gun barrel. *The bore of a gun should be clean.* 4. a person or thing that is dull or not interesting. *Many pupils think that certain kinds of music are a bore.* **bores.**

bore[2] (bôr), past tense of **bear.**

born (bôrn), *adj.* 1. natural. *That boy is a born athlete.* 2. brought into life. *The family next door has a newly born baby.*

bor row (bor′ō, bôr′ō), *v.* to get something to use for a while before returning or repaying it. *May we borrow a cup of milk until tomorrow?* **bor rows, bor rowed, bor row ing.**

bos om (bùz′əm), *n.* 1. the upper front part of a human body; breast. *The mother held the baby*

boots

to her bosom. 2. the part of clothing which covers the front part of the body. *The bosom of the dress is blue.* 3. the inside; the central part. *In the bosom of your family, your ideas can be freely expressed.* **bos oms.**

adj. 4. very close; very dear. *He is a bosom friend; we can trust each other completely.*

boss (bôs), *n.* a person who has other people working for him; manager. *A good boss knows how to get along with people.* **boss es.**

v. 2. to give orders to; tell what to do. *Every time we begin a job, Bill starts to boss us.* **boss es, bossed, boss ing.**

both (bōth), *adj.* the two. *Tell me both ways that can be used in solving the problem.*

pron. 2. the two together; the one as well as the other. *I can't choose between these two hats; both are attractive.*

conj. 3. alike; equally. *Both men and women can vote in the United States.*

adv. 4. alike; equally. *The new housekeeper both cooks and cleans.*

both er (both′ər), *n.* 1. something that troubles or worries. *Mosquitoes are a bother during the summer.* **both ers.**

v. 2. to give trouble to. *Take these children away; they bother me while I'm writing.* 3. to take the time and trouble. *Don't bother to help with the dishes; we can manage all right.* **both ers, both ered, both er ing.**

bot tle (bot′l), *n.* 1. a holder for liquids. *Instead of glass bottles, many companies now use cans for holding soft drinks.* 2. the amount any bottle holds. *He drank a bottle of milk.* **bot tles.**

v. 3. to put into bottles. *Milk must be bottled under very clean conditions.* **bot tles, bot tled, bot tl ing.**

bot tom (bot′əm), *n.* 1. the lowest part. *The sled flew fast on the snow to the bottom of the hill.* 2. the under part. *Water cannot come through the patch we made in the bottom of the rowboat.* 3. the ground underneath a body of water. *The wrecked ship sank to the bottom of the sea.* 4. important part; beginning. *The only way to solve our problem is first to get to the bottom of it.* 5. **the bottoms,** low land lying on each side of a river. *The bottoms of the river get flooded when the river rises.* **bot toms.**

adj. 6. lowest. *Look on the bottom shelf for your book.*

bow of a ship

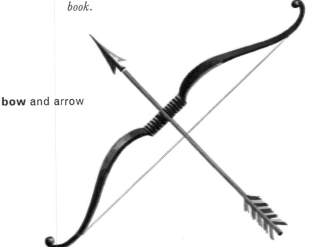

bow and arrow

bough (bou), *n.* a branch of a tree. *The boys built a tree house, using two of the largest boughs to support the floor.* **boughs.**

bought (bôt), past tense of **buy.**

boul der (bōl′dər), *n.* a large rock. *A boulder is round and smooth because of the action of wind and water on it.* **boul ders.**

bounce (bouns), *v.* 1. to hit against a surface and spring back. *The rubber ball bounced several times before it rolled to a stop.* 2. to jump; move suddenly. *Harry bounces out of bed the minute the alarm clock rings.* **bounc es, bounced, bouncing.**

n. 3. a backward or upward spring. *The ball took a high bounce over the third baseman's head, and a run scored.* 4. ability to spring back. *This old tennis ball has no bounce left.* **bounc es.**

bound[1] (bound), *v.* 1. past tense of **bind.**

adj. 2. obliged; required. *A soldier is bound by his oath to obey his officers.* 3. certain; sure. *You're bound to tire yourself with all that running.*

bound[2] (bound), *v.* 1. to move lightly; leap. *The deer bounded swiftly across the meadow.* 2. to bounce. *You can't tell which way a football will bound when it hits the ground.* **bounds, bounded, bound ing.**

n. 3. a leap or jump. *The frightened deer jumped across the stream in one bound.* **bounds.**

bound[3] (bound), *adj.* ready to go; going; on the way. *We are bound for our vacation.*

bound[4] (bound), *v.* 1. to form the boundary of. *The river bounds our town on the south.* **bounds, bound ed, bound ing.**

n. 2. a boundary; a limit. *If you hit the ball out of bounds, you must get it yourself.* **bounds.**

bound a ry (boun′də rē, boun′drē), *n.* the ending line or edge of one thing and the beginning edge or line of another. *The boundary between Iowa and Illinois is the Mississippi River. That fence marks the boundary of my property; the land on the other side belongs to my neighbor.* **bound a ries.**

bou quet (bō kā′ or bü kā′ for 1, bü kā′ for

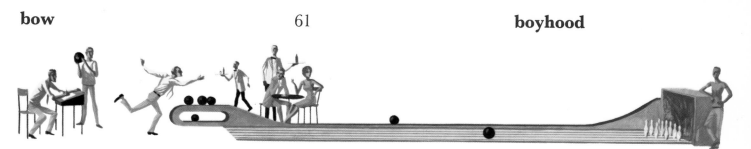

bowling

2), *n.* 1. a bunch of flowers. *The children gave their grandmother a bouquet of red roses on her fiftieth wedding anniversary.* 2. a pleasant smell. *Her perfume has a light and delicate bouquet.* **bou quets.**

bow[1] (bō), *n.* 1. a weapon used for shooting arrows. *A bow is a piece of wood bent by a cord stretched between the two ends.* 2. a piece of wood with horsehairs stretched on it. *When a bow is drawn across the strings of a violin, music is heard.* 3. a knot with open loops. *A hair ribbon is tied in a bow; so are shoelaces.* **bows.**

bow[2] (bou), *v.* 1. to bend the head or body in respect, greeting, thanks, or worship. *"Let us bow our heads in prayer," said the minister.* 2. to give in. *The pupils bowed to the wishes of the teacher.* **bows, bowed, bow ing.**
n. 3. a bend of the head or body. *The singer came back for three bows when the audience applauded.* **bows.**

bow[3] (bou), *n.* the front part of a ship or boat. *The ship headed her bow into the waves.* **bows.**

bowl[1] (bōl), *n.* 1. a round, deep dish. *Soup is usually served in a bowl.* 2. a thing shaped like a bowl. *Around New Year's Day, important football games are played in stadiums called the Cotton Bowl, the Orange Bowl, the Rose Bowl, and the Sugar Bowl.* **bowls.**

bowl[2] (bōl), *v.* to play the game of bowling by rolling a large ball down a smooth, wooden lane. *When you bowl, the object is to knock down as many of the ten wooden pins as possible.* **bowls, bowled, bowl ing.**

bowl ing (bō′ling), *n.* game in which a heavy ball is rolled along a wooden lane to try to knock down ten wooden pins at the end. *The picture shows just one bowling lane; usually there are from ten to fifty in a building.*

bow-wow (bou′wou′), *v.* 1. to make a sound like a dog barking. *The dog bow-wowed as the children ran by the yard.* **bow-wows, bow-wowed, bow-wow ing.**
n. 2. the sound of a dog barking. *The dog's "bow-wow" could be heard all over the block.* **bow-wows.**

box[1] (boks), *n.* 1. a case for holding things. *We used many boxes when we moved. Boxes are made of stiff paper or of wood.* 2. as much as a box holds. *The dog ate the whole box of candy!* 3. a special section for sitting. *One year we had a box at the opera. I like to sit in a box at the ball park.* **box es.**
v. 4. to put into a box. *We boxed all of our books for the mover.* **box es, boxed, box ing.**

box[2] (boks), *v.* 1. to fight with the fists enclosed in padded leather gloves. *The two men boxed to get exercise.* **box es, boxed, box ing.**
n. 2. a slap; a blow, especially on the ear. *He received a painful box on the ear.* **box es.**

box car (boks′kär′), *n.* a railroad freight car with sides and a roof. *Boxcars carry all kinds of goods.* **box cars.**

box er[1] (bok′sər), *n.* a man or boy who boxes. *My friends watched a young boxer who was the college champion for three years.* **box ers.**

boxer[2] (bok′sər), *n.* a short-haired dog, originally a German breed. *Our new dog is a boxer.* **boxers.**

box ing (bok′sing), *n.* the sport of hitting with gloved fists. *The aim of boxing is to get in one's own punches and avoid the punches of the other man, rather than to hurt one another.*

boy (boi), *n.* a male child. *A boy is legally considered to be a man when he is twenty-one.* **boys.**

boy hood (boi′hud), *n.* the time of being a boy. *The man looked back on his boyhood with happiness.*

boxing

sand, āte, bâre, fäther; sent, mē, fėrn; fit, bīke; pot, rōpe, fôrt; run, pull, rüle, cūte; noise, sound; ch, cheese; ng, long; th, thick; ŧħ, those; zh, treasure; ə = a in about, e in waken, i in animal, o in seldom, and u in minus.

bracelets:
  a. ancient Roman
  b. fifteenth century Venetian

brace (brās), *n.* 1. a thing that holds parts together or keeps them in place. *Many boys and girls wear braces on their teeth to make their teeth straight. A house sometimes needs a brace to support a weak part. Braces can be worn to support the back and the legs.* 2. a handle for a tool used for holding and turning a bit, or drill. *By using his brace, he was able to drill a hole in the board.* 3. two of something. *The hunters brought back a brace of ducks for dinner.* **brac es.**
v. 4. to make strong; support. *We braced the table by nailing a board across its weak side.* 5. to get ready for a crash; to prepare oneself. *The pilot braced himself as the plane headed for a landing with one engine not working.* 6. to give extra energy to. *This mountain air will brace you if you take deep breaths.* **brac es, braced, brac ing.**

brace let (brās′lət), *n.* a band or chain worn around the wrist as an ornament. *Bracelets are made of beads, gold, silver, or various other materials.* **brace lets.**

brack et (brak′ət), *n.* 1. a piece of metal or wood, shaped like an L, used to hold up a shelf. *The shelf lies across two or more brackets that stick out from a wall.* 2. **brackets,** the two marks like this [ ] used in writing and typing to set off or separate certain words from the text, as in this sentence: *It is difficult [impossible is more like it] to enjoy all foods.* **brack ets.**
v. 3. to support or hold up with brackets. *Please bracket this weak shelf for me.* 4. to put between brackets. *Your comments in the sentences should be bracketed.* **brack ets, brack et ed, brack et ing.**

brag (brag), *v.* to boast; talk too much about how good you are or how much you have. *Charles brags too much about his new dog.* **brags, bragged, brag ging.**

brain (brān), *n.* 1. the soft mass of nerve tissue in the skull, or head, of persons and animals. *The brain is the main part of the nervous system, and controls our thinking and the movement of our bodies.* 2. mind. *He has a fine brain.* 3. **brains,** intelligence; thinking. *He used his brains to find the answer.* **brains.**
v. 4. to hit hard on the head. *The football player brained himself against the goal post.* **brains, brained, brain ing.**

brake (brāk), *n.* 1. a thing that slows down or stops a car, a machine, a bicycle, etc. *The driver pressed on the brake when the traffic light turned red.* **brakes.**
v. 2. to slow down or stop by using a brake. *The driver braked the car as he approached the stop sign.* **brakes, braked, brak ing.**

bran (bran), *n.* the outer covering of grains, like wheat and rye, separated from the inner part which is made into flour. *Bran is used as a food.*

branch (branch), *n.* 1. a limb of a tree, growing from the trunk or from another limb. *Children climb the branches of large trees.* 2. a division of a large thing. *This small stream is a branch of the*

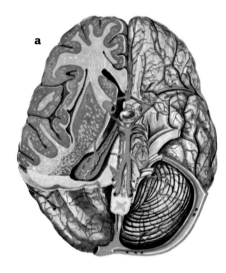

brain:
  a. cross section
      seen from below
  b. location
      in the head

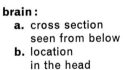

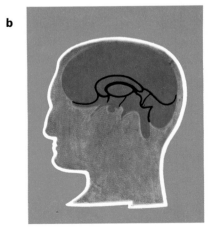

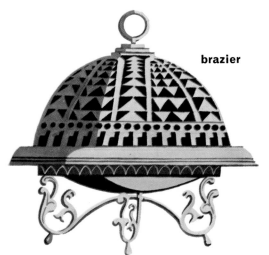

brazier

main river three miles away. *My uncle is in charge of the Iowa branch of his company.* **branch es.**

v. 3. to divide; to go in different directions. *The road branched at the town, but the driver knew which road would get us home.* **branch es, branched, branch ing.**

brand (brand), *n.* 1. a particular kind or make of product. *Every year a new brand of cookies or cereal is put on the market.* 2. a mark or drawing put on by burning with a hot iron. *A ranch owner puts his brand on all of his cattle so they won't be claimed by someone else.* 3. a piece of burning wood. *Put out all the brands in a campfire.* **brands.**

v. 4. to mark by burning the skin with a hot iron. *It is time to brand the cattle.* **brands, brand ed, brand ing.**

brass (bras), *n.* a yellow metal made by melting two metals together. *Brass is used to make candlesticks, bells, dishes, and doorknobs. Many of the instruments in a band are made of brass.* **brass es.**

brat (brat), *n.* a child who doesn't behave; a spoiled and naughty child. *Some of the little children at the birthday party behaved like brats.* **brats.**

brave[1] (brāv), *adj.* 1. not afraid; ready to face danger. *The brave father ran back into the burning building to carry out his young son.* **brav er, brav est; brave ly,** *adv.*

v. 2. to face or meet with courage. *The pilot braved the storm to carry the medicine that would save the man's life.* **braves, braved, brav ing.**

n. 3. an Indian warrior. *The braves of the tribe went through a long period of training.* **braves.**

brav er y (brāv'ərē), *n.* 1. being brave; an act of courage. *The policeman received a medal for his bravery in rescuing the child.* 2. fine clothes; colorful dress. *Many people in their native bravery marched in the parade.* **brav er ies.**

bra zier (brā'zhər), *n.* a heavy pan for holding burning coals or charcoal. *Braziers are used in some places for heating rooms.* **bra ziers.**

bread (bred), *n.* 1. a food baked from dough made with flour or meal. *Sandwiches are made with bread.* 2. food; living. *He earns his bread by hard work.* **breads.**

break (brāk), *v.* 1. to come apart; separate into pieces. *The dish broke when it fell to the floor.* 2. to fail to keep or carry out. *The convicts in jail have broken the law.* 3. to force one's way. *The dog broke loose from the chain. The prisoner broke away from the men guarding him.* 4. to cut open the surface of. *Our church held a ceremony when the minister broke ground for a new building.* 5. to appear; show up. *The storm broke suddenly, and we all ran for shelter.* 6. to make known. *Who will break the bad news to Betty about her sick kitten? Television stations broke the news of the old general's death.* 7. to train to obey; tame. *The cowboy spent six months in breaking the wild horse.* 8. to go beyond; to do better than. *He broke a city record while winning the mile run.* **breaks, broke, bro ken, break ing.**

n. 9. a crack or broken place. *There is a break in the fence that has to be fixed.* 10. a short time away from work; a rest. *The musicians have a ten-minute break from playing.* 11. the beginning. *We listen to the birds' songs at break of day.* 12. any breaking open or apart. *The new chick came through the break in the egg.* **breaks.**

break fast (brek'fəst), *n.* 1. the first meal of the day. *Jim ate a good breakfast of orange juice, cereal, toast, and milk.* **break fasts.**

v. 2. to eat breakfast. *We breakfasted early, at six o'clock.* **break fasts, break fast ed, break fast ing.**

break wa ter (brāk'wôt'ər), *n.* a wall built to break the force of waves. *A breakwater often forms a harbor for boats.* **break wa ters.**

bread

breakwater

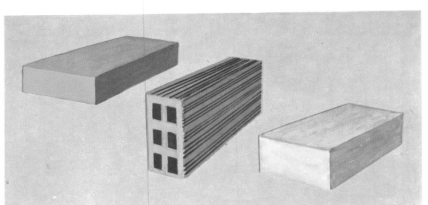

bricks

breast (brest), *n.* 1. the chest; upper part of the front of the body. *The baby was held to its mother's breast.* **breasts.**
v. 2. to struggle with; advance against. *He breasted the big waves as he swam.* **breasts, breast ed, breast ing.**

breath (breth), *n.* 1. air breathed into the lungs and then let out. *We all take breaths without thinking about it. Doctors sometimes say, " Take a deep breath" when they examine you.* 2. a slight breeze. *Just before the big storm, the sky grew dark, and there wasn't a breath of air.* **breaths.**

breathe (brēᵗħ), *v.* 1. to take air into the lungs, and then let it out. *Most people breathe about sixteen times a minute.* 2. to speak quietly. *"Careful," breathed Tom. "Don't wake up the little baby."* 3. to stop for breath; rest. *The cowboys stopped every ten miles to breathe their horses.* **breathes, breathed, breath ing.**

breeze (brēz), *n.* a light, gentle wind. *The flag barely moved in the breeze.* **breez es.**

breve (brēv), *n.* 1. a curved mark (˘) that is sometimes put over a vowel to show that it is short. *The teacher demonstrated on the chalkboard the use of the breve.* 2. in music, a note equal to two whole notes. *A breve is often called a double whole note.* **breves.**

brick (brik), *n.* 1. a block of clay baked by the sun or in an oven, used to pave streets and to build houses, walls, etc. *Many houses and apartments are built with bricks.* **bricks.**
adj. 2. built of bricks. *The old brick road was paved over with asphalt.*

bride (brīd), *n.* a woman who has just been married or is about to be married. *Mary was a beautiful bride in her long white wedding dress.* **brides.**

bridge (brij), *n.* 1. something built over a river or a valley for people, trains, automobiles, etc. to cross on. *Thousands of cars a day cross the Mississippi River on bridges.* 2. on a ship, the platform from which the captain or other officers can see what goes on. *The steering wheel is usually on the bridge in modern ships.* 3. a kind of card game for four players. *In bridge, the players are divided into two teams, and partners sit opposite each other.* 4. the upper bony part of the nose. *The boy broke the bridge of his nose when he fell.* 5. a device that holds false teeth in place next to real teeth. *Bob's front teeth were knocked out and he went to the dentist for a bridge.* **bridg es.**
v. 6. to make or be a bridge over; to span. *The railroad bridges the river. The soldiers used logs to bridge the stream.* 7. to get over (a time that is difficult). *She bridged the change from one school to another.* **bridg es, bridged, bridg ing.**

brief (brēf), *adj.* 1. short. *Our good-bye was brief.* **brief er, brief est; brief ly,** *adv.*
n. 2. a short statement. *The lawyer filed his brief of the case with the judge.* **briefs.**

bright (brīt), *adj.* 1. shining; giving light; reflecting light. *The moon on the snow was bright. See how bright the car is when it is polished.* 2. having a sharp, quick mind. *Steve is a bright child, as you can tell when you talk with him.* 3. full of hope; cheerful; happy. *He has a bright outlook*

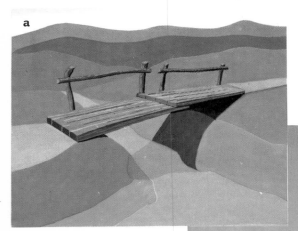

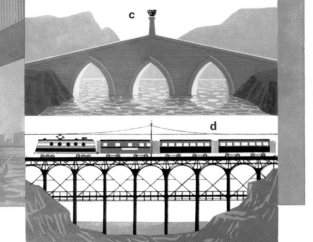

bridges:
  a. footbridge
  b. modern suspension bridge
  c. old stone bridge
  d. modern steel bridge

on life. 4. clear; brilliant. *She wore a bright red dress.* **bright er, bright est; bright ly,** *adv.*

bright ness (brīt′nəs), *n.* being bright; clearness; intelligence. *The brightness of the sun blinded me for a moment. His brightness for his age amazed all.*

bril liant (bril′yənt), *adj.* 1. bright; glittering; flashing with light. *The brilliant reflection on the water forced him to put on sunglasses.* 2. splendid; magnificent. *The president of the club gave a brilliant party for famous American writers and musicians.* 3. clever or smart; having great ability. *That new author seems to be a brilliant young man.* **bril liant ly,** *adv.*
n. 4. a diamond or other gem cut in a way that makes it flash with light. *The jeweler showed us a case of brilliants, all reflecting the light in many colors.* **bril liants.**

bring (bring), *v.* 1. to come with something or someone from somewhere else. *When you return, bring my book with you.* 2. to cause to come. *All this rain will be sure to bring a flood.* 3. to sell for. *I don't think my uncle's old car will bring a high price.* 4. **bring up,** to care for; educate. *The adopted boy was brought up in a fine family.* 5. **bring about,** to cause to happen. *The new principal will bring about many changes in the school.* **brings, brought, bring ing.**

Brit ish (brit′ish), *adj.* of England or its people. *British woolens are famous for their fine quality and workmanship.*

broad (brôd), *adj.* 1. wide; large from side to side. *The expressways are broad enough for three lanes of traffic to go each way. The West contains broad stretches of prairies and forests.* 2. clear and open. *It was broad daylight when he got up.* 3. plain; easy to understand. *We made several broad hints that we wanted the people to leave, and they finally did.* 4. of wide range; not small. *My father has a broad view of life.* 5. main; general. *Surely you know the broad points of the Constitution of the United States.* **broad er, broad est; broad ly,** *adv.*

broad cast (brôd′kast′), *v.* 1. to send through the air by radio or television. *The meeting of the United Nations will be broadcast today.* 2. to scatter or spread. *A farmer broadcasts seed.* **broad casts, broad cast** or **broad cast ed, broad cast ing.**
n. 3. a radio or television program. *We watch the six o'clock news broadcast every night.* 4. a scattering; spreading. *The broadcast of the seed was finished.* **broad casts.**

broke (brōk), past tense of **break.**

bro ken (brō′kən), *v.* 1. past participle of **break.**
adj. 2. split in two or more pieces; shattered. *Look at that broken window. He has a broken leg.* 3. not kept or carried out. *He has a long record of broken promises.* 4. weak; sick. *The old man has courage, but his spirit is broken.* 5. not spoken correctly. *The Mexican boy uses broken English*

now, *but after another year of study he will speak English well.* **bro ken ly,** *adv.*

bron co or **bron cho** (brong′kō), *n.* a small, partly wild horse used in western North America. *It is exciting to watch a cowboy try to stay seated on a bronco in action.* **bron cos** or **bron chos.**

brook (bruk), *n.* a small stream of water. *The children waded in the brook.* **brooks.**

broom (brüm), *n.* a brush with a long handle, used for sweeping. *We have a broom that we use for sweeping the basement, garage, and walks.* **brooms.**

broth er (bruŧħ′ər), *n.* 1. a boy or man having the same parents as another person. *There were three boys and one girl in the family, so the girl had three brothers.* 2. an unusually close friend. *I've known Alfred for years, and now he is like a brother to me.* 3. a member of the same club or church. *My uncle says he is going to visit a sick brother whenever a member of his club is ill.* **broth ers.**

brought (brôt), past tense of **bring.**

brown (broun), *n.* 1. the color of chocolate or coffee; a mixture of red, yellow, and black. *The dying leaves first turned red and gold, and then brown.* **browns.**
adj. 2. having this color. *The girl has beautiful brown eyes.*
v. 3. to become brown. *The girls on the beach were browning themselves beneath the hot summer sun.* **browns, browned, brown ing.**

brush (brush), *n.* 1. stiff hairs, straw, wire, etc. set in a stiff back or attached to a handle. *Brushes are used for scrubbing, for smoothing hair, for cleaning, for sweeping, and for painting.* 2. a short quick fight. *Our troops had several brushes with the enemy on their way forward.* 3. shrubs and bushes growing wild. *The rabbit hid in the brush.* 4. branches broken from trees. *Brush covered the lawn after the windstorm.*
v. 5. to remove; take away. *The girl brushed the dust off her clothes.* 6. to smooth or clean with a brush. *Brush your teeth after eating.* **brush es, brushed, brush ing.**

bub ble (bub′l), *n.* 1. a thin film of liquid that forms a ball around a gas or air. *It is fun to blow soap bubbles, and watch them float away.* 2. a tiny ball of air that rises to the surface in water or other liquid. *When water boils, it contains many bubbles which come to the top and break.* **bub bles.**
v. 3. to make bubbles; rise in bubbles. *When a bottle of root beer is opened, it bubbles.* 4. to make sounds like water boiling; gurgle. *The cool water from the spring bubbled up between the rocks.* **bub bles, bub bled, bub bling.**

buck et (buk′ət), *n.* 1. a pail made of wood or metal with a handle. *Buckets are used to carry water, or coal, or many other things.* 2. the amount that a bucket can carry. *We picked two buckets of strawberries.* **buck ets.**

---

sand, āte, bâre, fäther; sent, mē, fėrn; fit, bīke; pot, rōpe, fôrt; run, pùll, rüle, cūte; noise, sound; ch, cheese; ng, long; th, thick; ŧħ, those; zh, treasure; ə = a in about, e in waken, i in animal, o in seldom, and u in minus.

buckles

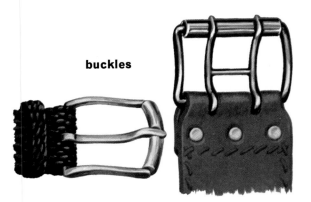

buds

bulb

buck le (buk′l), *n.* 1. a device that connects the two loose ends of a belt. *Jan's belt fastens in front with a pretty silver buckle.* **buck les.**
v. 2. to fasten with a buckle. *You must buckle your seat belt in a plane before it takes off.* 3. to bend. *The shelf buckled when the heavy boxes were placed on it.* **buck les, buck led, buck ling.**

bud (bud), *n.* 1. the small beginning of a flower or leaf. *Soon all the buds on that rosebush will be in full flower.* 2. **in bud,** the first stage of growth of a branch, leaf, or flower. *All our cherry trees are in bud; soon they will be covered with white blossoms.* **buds.**
v. 3. to form buds. *The trees and bushes are budding late this year because of the cold.* **buds, bud ded, bud ding.**

budg et (buj′ət), *n.* 1. a plan showing how much money will be used and for what purposes. *You will be better off if you live within a budget that you make out yourself.* **budg ets.**
v. 2. to make a plan for spending so much money and so much time on certain things. *Budget your time as well as your expenses.* **budgets, budg et ed, budg et ing.**

buf fa lo (buf′ə lō′), *n.* 1. any of several kinds of wild ox. *The water buffalo in India is used as a farm animal to pull carts.* 2. in America, a large animal with a hump on its back and a large head. *A hundred years ago there were millions of buffaloes, but most of them were killed by hunters; now the buffalo is protected by the United States government.* **buf fa lo** or **buf fa loes.**

bug (bug), *n.* a crawling insect. *Suzy is afraid of bugs.* **bugs.**

bug gy (bug′ē), *n.* 1. a small carriage seating two people and pulled by a horse. *Before the automobile, most people traveled in buggies.* 2. a carriage used for a baby. *On sunny afternoons, you can see dozens of baby buggies in the park.* **bug gies.**

build (bild), *v.* 1. to make; put together. *A bird builds a nest. Men build skyscrapers and airplanes.* **builds, built, build ing.**
n. 2. the way in which the body is put together. *The football player has a large, heavy build.* **builds.**

build er (bil′dər), *n.* a person whose business is putting up houses, schools, stores, and other buildings. *My uncle is a builder for a large housing project.* **build ers.**

build ing (bil′ding), *n.* a structure such as a house, school, factory, etc. *Our new school building is much larger than the old one.* **build ings.**

built (bilt), past tense of **build.**

bulb (bulb), *n.* 1. the round, underground stem of certain plants. *The onion, tulip, and lily are a few plants that grow from bulbs and not from seeds.* 2. a rounded glass globe that gives off electric light. *Put a new bulb in the lamp; the other one doesn't work.* 3. the bottom part of a thermometer which is shaped like a bulb. *I broke our thermometer and the mercury spilled out of the bulb.* **bulbs.**

bull (bul), *n.* 1. a male animal, especially of the ox or cow family. *A milk cow is a female; a bull is a male of the same animal.* 2. the male of the elephant, whale, and other large animals. *Female elephants are usually smaller and weigh less than the bulls.* **bulls.**

bull do zer (bul′dōz′ər), *n.* a large tractor with a metal blade on the front, used to clear land by moving earth, stones, trees, and other things. *Bulldozers are so powerful that they can be used for clearing paths through thick jungles.* **bull do zers.**

herd of **buffalo**

bulldozer

bul let (bůl′ət), *n.* a small piece of metal to be fired from a rifle, pistol, or machine gun. *The bullet from my gun hit exactly in the middle of the target.* **bul lets.**

bul le tin (bůl′ət n), *n.* 1. a short news report. *The television program was interrupted for a bulletin about the storm.* 2. a small magazine or newspaper. *My mother's women's club puts out a bulletin twice a month.* **bul le tins.**

bum ble bee (bum′bl bē′), *n.* a large kind of bee. *Bumblebees are black and yellow and make loud buzzing sounds.* **bum ble bees.**

bump (bump), *v.* 1. to knock or hit against something. *The baseball player bumped into the wall, trying to catch the ball.* **bumps, bumped, bump ing.**
n. 2. a blow or knock. *The boat got a lot of bumps from the high waves.* 3. a swelling or lump. *The baby had a bump on his forehead, caused by falling down the stairs.* 4. a raised place. *This road has a lot of bumps in it.* **bumps.**

bump er (bump′ər), *n.* 1. a strong bar across the front and the rear of a car, truck, or bus. *Bumpers are helpful in protecting fenders and front and rear lights.* **bump ers.**
adj. 2. unusually large. *Last year there was a bumper crop of wheat.*

bun (bun), *n.* a kind of sweet roll or biscuit. *I like the buns that have raisins in them.* **buns.**

bunch (bunch), *n.* 1. a group of things of the same kind, growing together. *Bananas and grapes are picked in bunches.* 2. a number of things put together. *We took a bunch of flowers to Edward who was in the hospital.* **bunch es.**
v. 3. to gather into a bunch. *The animals bunched together as the snow fell.* **bunch es, bunched, bunch ing.**

bun dle (bun′dl), *n.* 1. a number of things tied or bound together. *Every year our Cub Scout troop collects bundles of old magazines and newspapers to sell.* 2. a package or parcel. *At Christmas, the shoppers are loaded with bundles.* **bun dles.**
v. 3. to wrap; bind together. *We are going to bundle these clothes neatly and give them to the Salvation Army.* 4. **bundle off,** to send away. *The children were bundled off to bed.* **bun dles, bun dled, bun dling.**

bunk (bunk), *n.* 1. a plain, narrow bed fixed to a wall like a large shelf. *The army privates sleep in bunks.* 2. a narrow bed. *More bunks can be placed in a room than regular-sized beds.* **bunks.**
v. 3. to sleep in a bunk. *The sailors bunked in a large room while in training.* 4. to sleep almost anywhere. *You can bunk on this old bed in the basement.* **bunks, bunked, bunk ing.**

bun ny (bun′ē), *n.* a pet rabbit. *Joan is very fond of her little bunnies.* **bun nies.**

bunt (bunt), *v.* 1. to gently tap a pitched baseball so that it rolls slowly. *He bunted the ball down the third-base line and got to first base before the throw.* 2. to push with the head or horns. *The goat bunted my legs.* **bunts, bunt ed, bunt ing.**
n. 3. an act of bunting. *The player's bunt scored a run.* **bunts.**

bur (bėr), var. of **burr.**

bur den (bėrd′n), *n.* 1. a load; something that is carried. *The little man's burden was so heavy that he fell down.* 2. a job that must be done. *My dad carries the burden of seeing that the family has a home and food and good schooling.* **bur dens.**
v. 3. to fill with worry; weigh down. *I have a neighbor who burdens me with all her problems.* **bur dens, bur dened, bur den ing.**

bu reau (būr′ō), *n.* 1. a chest of drawers, often with a mirror, for holding clothing. *Father bought a small bureau for Frank to use.* 2. office for a special kind of business. *The Better Business Bureau gives information about stores and businesses when asked.* 3. a department of the government. *The Weather Bureau keeps records of the weather.* **bu reaus.**

bur ied (ber′ēd), past tense of **bury.**

burn (bėrn), *v.* 1. to be on fire. *We watched the logs burning in the fireplace.* 2. to set fuel on fire to get heat. *We burn oil in our furnace to heat our house.* 3. to destroy by heat or fire. *The city gets rid of all garbage by burning it.* 4. to damage or hurt by fire, heat, acid, electricity, sun, wind, etc. *The sun burned her arms. He spilled acid on his hand, burning it badly.* 5. to make by fire, heat, acid, etc. *A spark from the fire in the fireplace burned a small hole in the rug.* 6. to damage by too much heat. *Please don't let the steak burn.* 7. to feel hot. *I could feel my face burning with shame for using the wrong name.* **burns, burned** or **burnt, burn ing.**

automobile **bumper**

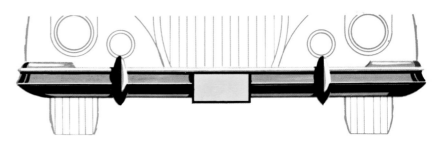

n. 8. an injury or sore made by something very hot. *He had a burn on his finger from touching the hot stove.* **burns.**

burnt (bėrnt), past tense of **burn.**

burr (bėr), *n.* 1. a rough case with sharp points, around the seeds of certain plants. *A burr clings to clothing. The dog came home with burrs sticking all over him.* 2. a plant or weed that grows burrs. *Keep out of that field with the burrs.* **burrs.**

bur row (bėr′ō), *n.* 1. a hole or tunnel made in the ground by an animal. *Rabbits live in burrows.* **bur rows.**

v. 2. to dig a burrow. *The animal burrowed under the shed in our back yard.* 3. to hide. *Our cat was burrowing under the carpet.* **bur rows, bur-rowed, bur row ing.**

burst (bėrst), *v.* 1. to break open suddenly. *If you blow too much air into a balloon, it will burst.* 2. to rush quickly and suddenly. *The boy burst into the room, excited and happy.* 3. to be full. *The girl's closet was bursting with her collection of games and dolls.* **bursts, burst, burst ing.**

n. 4. an exploding. *A burst of cheers followed the President's speech.* **bursts.**

bury (ber′ē), *v.* 1. to put into a grave. *They will bury the soldier with full military honors.* 2. to cover up. *We found Dad's wallet buried in the sand at the beach.* **bur ies, bur ied, bur y ing.**

bus (bus), *n.* 1. a large motor vehicle that can carry many passengers. *We take a bus to school.* **bus es** or **bus ses.**

v. 2. to ride in a bus; to send by bus. *About twenty pupils are bussed to school every day.* **bus es** or **bus ses, bused** or **bussed, bus ing** or **bus sing.**

bush (bush), *n.* 1. a plant smaller than a tree, with many branches growing near the ground; a shrub. *Roses grow on bushes.* 2. open forest or wild land. *Explorers and hunters look for animals in the bush.* **bush es.**

bush el (bush′əl), *n.* a measure of dry things, such as grain, fruit, and vegetables. *A bushel is equal to thirty-two quarts or four pecks. We bought a bushel of potatoes.* **bush els.**

bushy (bush′ē), *adj.* 1. thick and spreading. *A squirrel has a bushy tail.* 2. covered with bushes. *We found a bushy vacant lot, cleaned it up, and used it for a baseball field.* **bush i er, bush i est.**

busi ness (biz′nəs), *n.* 1. the work a person does to earn a living; occupation. *Both an editor and a reporter are in the newspaper business.* 2. volume of trade; amount of buying and selling. *Large grocery stores usually do a bigger business than the small food stores.* **busi ness es.**

bus man (bus′mən), *n.* the driver or conductor of a bus. *All the children were friends of the bus-man who drove them to school.* **bus men.**

buss (bus), *v.* to kiss. *Mark bussed his mother on the cheek when he came home from school.* **buss es, bussed, buss ing.**

bus tle (bus′l), *v.* 1. to hurry in a noisy, excited way. *The women bustled about the kitchen pre-paring the big Thanksgiving dinner.* **bus tles, bus tled, bus tling.**

n. 2. excited activity. *The stores were filled with the bustle of Saturday afternoon shopping.* **bus tles.**

bus tling (bus′ling), *adj.* 1. hurrying noisily and excitedly. *The bustling children settled down quickly as soon as the bell rang.*

n. 2. excited activity. *There is always a bustling at the end of the school day as the pupils get ready to leave.* **bus tlings.**

busy (biz′ē), *adj.* 1. at work; active. *We will be busy until dark, cleaning up the back yard.* 2. full of work or activity. *The first day of school is a busy one. He is such a busy man that he never gets home before nine o'clock at night.* **bus i er, bus i est; bus i ly,** *adv.*

v. 3. to make busy; keep busy. *My brother busied himself with cleaning his car.* **bus ies, bus ied, bus y ing.**

but (but), *conj.* 1. yet; however. *He knocked and knocked, but no one came to the door.* 2. except. *We looked for you everywhere but here.* 3. other than; more than. *We can do nothing now but hope.* 4. that. *I don't doubt but you are six feet tall.*

prep. 5. except. *We go to school every month but July and August.*

adv. 6. only; merely. *Don't forget he is but a pup and has to be trained to obey.*

butch er (buch′ər), *n.* 1. a man who runs a meat market. *The butcher sells many turkeys at Thanks-giving.* 2. a man who kills animals for food. *The butchers prepared the meat for the meat market.* **butch ers.**

v. 3. to kill for food. *Thousands of animals are butchered every day.* 4. to mess up; do a poor job on. *She butchered her part of the job.* **butch ers, butch ered, butch er ing.**

butt[1] (but), *v.* 1. to hit with the head lowered. *The goat butted the gate and knocked it open.* **butts, butt ed, butt ing.**

n. 2. a hit or push with the head lowered. *The little calf gave a harmless butt.* **butts.**

butt[2] (but), *n.* 1. the thick, heavy part of any-thing. 2. the remaining part of anything after most of it has been broken off or used up. *The butt of the branch scratched her arm as she walked by.* 3. something or someone that people make fun of. *Our bumpy road is the butt of our visitors' jokes.* **butts.**

but ter (but′ər), *n.* 1. the solid yellow fat that is made from cream or milk by churning or beating it. *Butter is used on bread and in cooking.* 2. any spread that goes on bread. *I like apple butter, peanut butter, and whipped butter.* **but ters.**

v. 3. to put butter on. *Butter your bread before you put jelly on it.* **but ters, but tered, but-ter ing.**

but ter cup (but′ər kup′), *n.* a common plant with bright yellow flowers shaped like cups and with large leaves. *Buttercups grow in woods and fields.* **but ter cups.**

---

sand, āte, bâre, fäther; sent, mē, fėrn; fit, bīke; pot, rōpe, fôrt; run, pull, rüle, cūte; noise, sound; ch, cheese; ng, long; th, thick; t̶h̶, those; zh, treasure; ə = a in about, e in waken, i in animal, o in seldom, and u in minus.

BUTTERFLIES

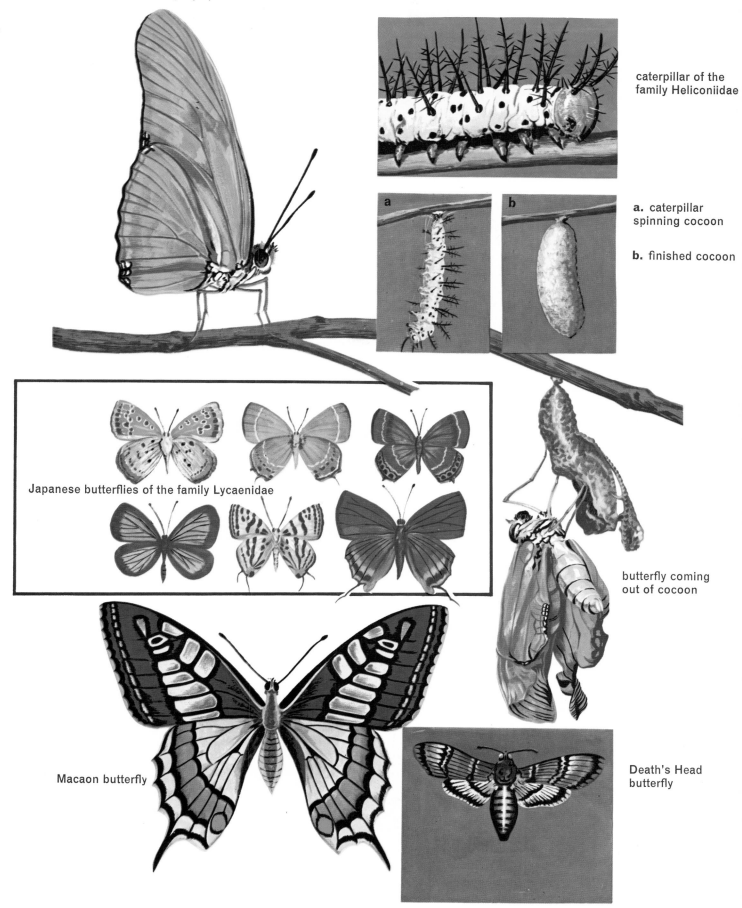

butterfly of the family Nymphalidae

caterpillar of the family Heliconiidae

a

b

a. caterpillar spinning cocoon

b. finished cocoon

Japanese butterflies of the family Lycaenidae

butterfly coming out of cocoon

Macaon butterfly

Death's Head butterfly

but ter fly (but′ər flī′), *n.* an insect with four brightly colored wings, two feelers, and a long slender tube that is used as a mouth. *The meadow was filled with hundreds of butterflies flying from flower to flower.* **but ter flies.** (See illustration on preceding page.)

but ter milk (but′ər milk′), *n.* a sour liquid left after butter has been taken from the churned or beaten milk. *Buttermilk is a favorite drink of many people.*

but ter scotch (but′ər skoch′), *n.* 1. a kind of hard, sticky candy made mostly of melted butter, brown sugar, and vanilla. *Brian likes lollipops made of butterscotch.* **but ter scotch es.** *adj.* 2. having the flavor of butterscotch. *After the show I had a butterscotch sundae.*

but ton (but′n), *n.* 1. a small, flat, round piece or knob used to fasten by slipping through a slit. *A button can be made of bone, wood, glass, or plastic.* 2. a small round device that is pushed to make a machine work. *Press the button for the elevator.* **but tons.**
v. 3. to fasten with a button. *You will have to button the child's clothes for me because I am busy.* **but tons, but toned, but ton ing.**

but ton hole (but′n hōl′), *n.* a hole or slit in clothing for a button to pass through. *If a button is too small for a buttonhole, the button slides out again.* **but ton holes.**

buy (bī), *v.* to get by paying money; purchase. *Sam said he will buy a new pair of shoes this week.* **buys, bought, buy ing.**

buy er (bī′ər), *n.* 1. a person who buys. *Mrs. Keefe is a very fussy buyer, so it takes a long time for her to make up her mind.* 2. a person whose work is buying things for a store. *The buyers for the toy department spend all summer picking out the new items for the Christmas sales.* **buy ers.**

buzz (buz), *n.* 1. the humming sound made by bees and mosquitoes. *The country air was still except for the buzz of the bees among the flowers.* 2. any humming sound. *From their bedroom, the boys heard the buzz of conversation downstairs.* **buzz es.**
v. 3. to make a buzz. *The bees buzzed among the flowers.* 4. to fly a plane too close to something. *If a pilot buzzes a building, the government punishes him.* **buzz es, buzzed, buzz ing.**

by (bī), *prep.* 1. near. *Stay by him.* 2. along. *We came home by this old road.* 3. through the use of; by means of. *We are getting there by the expressway. He is traveling by plane.* 4. through the effort of; by the act of. *The project was completed by the sixth-grade class. The door was opened by force.* 5. not later than. *The movie should be over by ten o'clock.* 6. during. *To cross the hot desert, they rested by day and traveled by night.* 7. according to. *You can tell he has played football by the way he throws the ball. The team played by the new rules.* 8. for the period or extent of. *He is paid by the day, not by the week.*
adv. 9. past. *We sat near the tracks and watched the trains go by.* 10. away; aside. *He put his usual three dollars by once a week.*

C

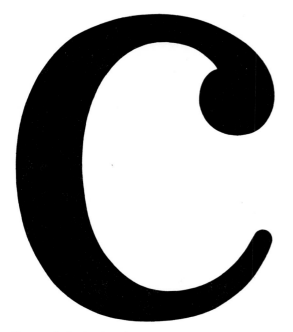

C or **c** (sē), 1. the third letter of the alphabet. 2. the Roman numeral 100.

cab (kab), *n.* 1. a taxi; automobile that can be hired for a fare that is paid to the driver. *Let's take a cab from the railroad station to the hotel.* 2. a carriage for hire pulled by one horse. *Old-fashioned cabs can still be seen in a few large cities where they are used for amusement.* 3. a place in a truck or train where the driver or engineer sits. *The truck driver can see all around him from his cab.* **cabs.**

cab bage (kab′ij), *n.* a vegetable with thick leaves growing tightly together in a round head. *Cabbage can be eaten raw or cooked.* **cab bag es.**

cab in (kab′ən), *n.* 1. a small house built of logs. *Abraham Lincoln lived in a cabin.* 2. the part of an airplane where the passengers sit. *Bob and I had seats next to the windows in the airplane's cabin.* 3. a room on a ship for a passenger. *There are many kinds of cabins on a ship to choose from; the bigger ones cost more.* **cab ins.**

cab i net (kab′ə nit), *n.* 1. a piece of furniture in which things are stored on shelves or in drawers. *We have a medicine cabinet in the bathroom.* 2. **Cabinet,** a group of men helping to run our government, chosen by the President. *The members of the Cabinet resign every time a new President takes office, and a new Cabinet is chosen.* **cab i nets.**

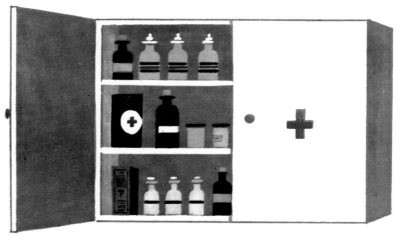

medicine **cabinet**

cabbage

ca ble (kā′bl), *n.* 1. a heavy metal rope, made of wires wound together. *Cables hold up bridges. Cables hold a ship at anchor.* 2. a rope of wires that can carry electric current. *Telephone and telegraph cables are laid on the floor of the ocean.* 3. a message sent by telegraph wires laid under the sea. *We received a cable from my aunt in England.* **ca bles.**
v. 4. to send by cable. *Reporters for the American newspapers cable their information from foreign countries.* **ca bles, ca bled, ca bling.**

ca boose (kə büs′), *n.* a small car on a freight train used by the trainmen for resting or sleeping. *The caboose is usually at the end of a long freight train.* **ca boos es.**

ca cao (kə kā′ō, kə kä′ō), *n.* 1. the seed of a tree that grows in tropical climates, from which cocoa and chocolate are made. *Chocolate comes from cacao seeds.* 2. the tree that the seeds grow on. *Cacao trees grow in South America.* **ca ca os.**

cack le (kak′l), *n.* 1. the sound a hen makes after laying an egg. *We heard the shrill, broken cackle the hen was making, and we started to hunt for the egg.* **cack les.**
v. 2. to make this sound. *A hen cackles.* 3. to laugh or talk in a shrill, chattering way. *The old woman cackled with amusement at the funny story.* **cack les, cack led, cack ling.**

sand, āte, bâre, fäther; sent, mē, fėrn; fit, bīke; pot, rōpe, fôrt; run, pùll, rüle, cūte; noise, sound; ch, cheese; ng, long; th, thick; th, those; zh, treasure; ə = a in about, e in waken, i in animal, o in seldom, and u in minus.

cac tus (kak′təs), *n.* a plant covered with sharp spines, but having no leaves. *Cactus grows in hot, dry places, such as deserts.* **cac tus es** or **cac ti** (kak′tī).

ca fé or **ca fe** (ka fā), *n.* a place where food and drinks are served; a restaurant, bar, or nightclub. *Last night our family had dinner in a French café.* **ca fés** or **ca fes.**

caf e te ria (kaf′ə tir′ē ə), *n.* a restaurant where people get their own food from a counter. *Jim saw so much good food at the cafeteria that he didn't know what to choose.* **caf e te rias.**

caf feine or **caf fein** (kaf′ēn, ka fēn′), *n.* a substance found in coffee and tea. *Doctors sometimes prescribe medicines that contain caffeine. My mother says that when she drinks coffee at night, the caffeine in it keeps her awake.*

cage (kāj), *n.* 1. a space or box with wires or bars on the sides in which to keep birds or other animals. *In the zoo the cages of the lions and tigers are made with heavy iron bars.* 2. anything like a cage. *The inside of an elevator in a building is a cage.* **cag es.**
v. 3. to shut up in a cage. *The hunters caged the animals to send to the zoo.* **cag es, caged, cag ing.**

cake (kāk), *n.* 1. a food made of a mixture of flour, eggs, milk, flavoring, and other things, and then baked in an oven. *The new frozen*

cake

cakes have already been mixed and baked, so all the cook does is heat them in the oven. 2. a small flat piece of dough that is baked or fried. *I like syrup and butter on my hot cakes.* 3. a flat mass in a definite shape. *A wet cake of soap is slippery to hold.* **cakes.**
v. 4. to become hard or solid. *Unless you clean that muddy jacket right now, the mud will cake.* **cakes, caked, cak ing.**

cal ci um (kal′sē əm), *n.* a substance found in combination with other substances, such as mineral chalk and limestone. *You need to eat foods that contain calcium in order to have good teeth and strong bones. Calcium is found in such foods as milk, fish, and cereal.*

cactuses or **cacti**

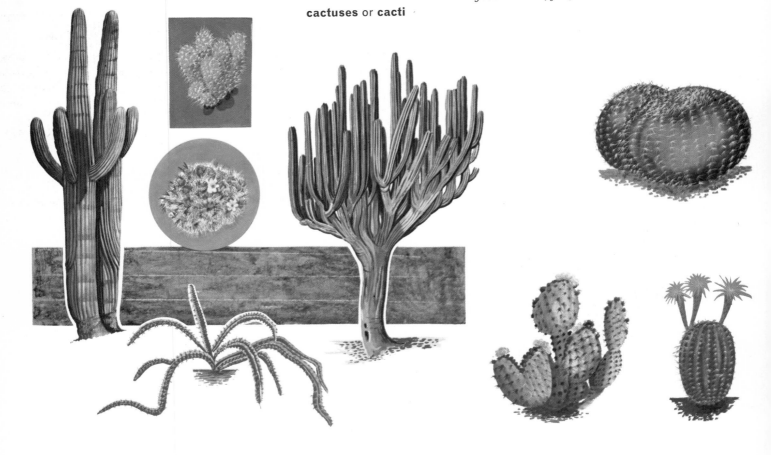

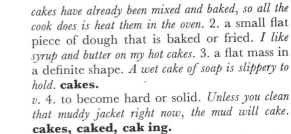

cal en dar (kal′ən dər), *n.* 1. a table or chart showing the months of the year, the weeks, the days of the month, and the number of days in each month. *A calendar will quickly show on what day of the week your birthday will fall this year.* 2. a list or schedule of things to be done. *Churches, courts, and clubs issue calendars of events.* **cal en dars.**

calf[1] (kaf), *n.* 1. a young cow. *The calf was only three days old, so he stayed close to his mother.* 2. a young whale, elephant, or moose. *The elephant and her calf walked through the jungle.* 3. the leather made from the skin of a calf. *Many wallets are made of calf.* **calves.**

calf[2] (kaf), *n.* the thick part of the back of the leg between the knee and the ankle. *The cramp in his left calf kept John from playing in the basketball tournament.* **calves.**

Cal i for nia (kal′ə fôrn′yə), *n.* a state in the southwestern part of the United States. *California borders on the Pacific Ocean; its capital is Sacramento.*

call (kôl), *v.* 1. to shout; cry out. *Bob called me from outside, so I left the house.* 2. to name. *What shall we call the new pup?* 3. to send for; ask to come. *The principal called me to his office to ask me to assist in stamping envelopes.* 4. to telephone. *I called three times, but there was no answer.* 5. to put off; stop. *The umpire called the game at the end of six innings because of rain.* 6. to visit. *The club members called, but stayed only five minutes.* **calls, called, call ing.**
n. 7. a cry; a voice. *We hear the bird calls early in the morning.* 8. a shout. *They heard a call for help coming from the woods.* 9. a visit. *The doctor is too busy to make calls, so he asks you to come to his office.* 10. a message. *Mother received a call to come at once to her sister's home.* **calls.**

call er (kôl′ər), *n.* 1. a person who calls on the telephone. *Can't you remember the name of the caller?* 2. a person who pays a call in person; visitor. *The new family in the neighborhood had four callers on the first day to welcome them.* **call ers.**

call ing (kôl′ing), *n.* a profession; occupation. *His calling is aviation, and it has been ever since he graduated from college.* **call ings.**

calm (käm), *adj.* 1. quiet; not excited; not disturbed. *The night was calm; not even the leaves moved. He is always calm even in times of trouble.* **calm er, calm est; calm ly,** *adv.*
v. 2. to make or become calm. *The nurse calmed the frightened girl by talking quietly to her.* **calms, calmed, calm ing.**
n. 3. a peacefulness; lack of noise. *A calm came over the class as the teacher began to read the story.* **calms.**

calves (kavz), *n.* more than one calf. See **calf.** *The calves have broken through the fence.*

came (kām), past tense of **come.**

cam el (kam′l), *n.* a large animal with one or two humps on its back. *Camels are used for*

camel

carrying loads in the desert because they can go without drinking water for many days. **cam els.**

ca mel lia (kə mēl′yə), *n.* a plant with glossy evergreen leaves and white or pink flowers which look somewhat like roses. *To grow well, camellias need rich soil and much water.* **ca mel lias.**

cam era (kam′ər ə), *n.* a machine for taking photographs or motion pictures. *We always take our camera on trips, so we have pictures to remind us of the fun.* **cam eras.**

camp (kamp), *n.* 1. a place in the country where people live in tents or in very simple buildings. *My brother has gone to camp every summer for five years.* 2. a place with tents or barracks where soldiers and sailors live. *The new soldier was sent to camp for six weeks of training.* **camps.**
v. 3. to live outdoors for a time, especially in a tent. *On our trip we camped out every night instead of staying in hotels.* **camps, camped, camping.** (See illustration on following page.)

cam paign (kam pān′), *n.* 1. a drive or plan to get money or to get something done. *We have a "clean-up" campaign every spring. The campaign for the building of the new school was a success.* 2. a series of battles in a war. *A campaign was planned by the generals to capture the enemy's largest city.* **cam paigns.**
v. 3. to work for a purpose, according to a plan. *My uncle is campaigning for the reelection of the governor, who is a friend of his.* **campaigns, cam paigned, cam paign ing.**

camp er (kamp′ər), *n.* 1. a person who lives outdoors, usually in a tent. *The campers always pitched their tents next to a stream.* 2. a person who goes to a camp. *He is one of the best Boy Scout campers.* **camp ers.**

camp fire (kamp′fīr′), *n.* a fire in a camp for keeping warm or for cooking. *It is fun to sit around a campfire at night and sing songs.* **camp fires.**

camp site (kamp′sīt′), *n.* the place where a

camellia

camping

camp is. *We chose a beautiful campsite near a waterfall.* **camp sites.**

camp stool (kamp′stül′), *n.* a light seat with no back or arms. *A campstool is easy to carry because it can be folded into a small shape.* **campstools.**

cam pus (kam′pəs), *n.* the grounds of a school, college, or university. *The college had an attractive campus—many trees, much grass, and beautiful flowers.* **cam pus es.**

can¹ (kan), *v.* 1. to know how to. *He can play the piano.* 2. to be able to. *John can swim two miles.* 3. to have the right to. *You can make a left turn at the next corner.* 4. to be allowed to. *Dad says I can stay until ten o'clock.* **can, could.**

can² (kan), *n.* 1. a metal container. *Cans come in all sizes, from a small can of sardines to a large can of paint. Our garbage cans are emptied twice a week.* **cans.**

canary

v. 2. to place food in airtight metal or glass containers to use later. *People don't can their own foods as much as they used to; today it is easier to buy canned and frozen foods.* **cans, canned, can ning.**

Can a da (kan′ə də), *n.* the country north of the United States. *Canada is larger than the United States, but it has fewer people.*

ca nal (kə nal′), *n.* a waterway dug across land. *Canals look like rivers, but they are made by men and machines. A big canal is used for boats; small canals are used to carry water to farmlands that need more water for crops.* **ca nals.**

ca nary (kə nâr′ē), *n.* a songbird with bright yellow feathers. *My grandmother has two canaries that sing all day.* **ca nar ies.**

can cel (kan′səl), *v.* 1. to cross out; to mark with lines. *The post office cancels letters by putting markings on the envelopes and stamps.* 2. to stop something that was going to happen; call off. *The ball game was canceled because of rain. Most stores will let you cancel an order. The ten o'clock flight was canceled because of fog.* **can cels, can celed, can cel ing.**

can cel la tion (kan′sə lā′shən), *n.* 1. a canceling. *The cancellation of the flight made me late.* 2. the marks that are used to cancel a stamp. *I could tell the stamp had already been used because of the cancellations on it.* **can cel la tions.**

cancellation on a Spanish stamp

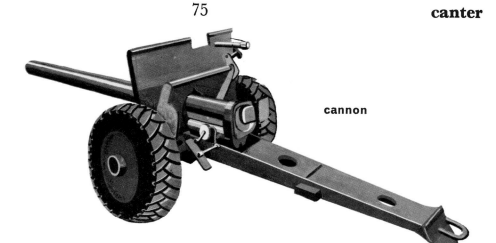

cannon

can cer (kan′sər), *n.* a very harmful, often fatal, growth. *Cancer can grow on the body or inside it.* **can cers.**

can di date (kan′də dāt′), *n.* a person who is running for office. *Mr. Smith is the Republican candidate for governor.* **can di dates.**

can dle (kan′dl), *n.* a stick of wax with a string, or wick, in it, burned to give light. *My mother keeps candles in case the lights go out during a storm.* **can dles.**

can dle stick (kan′dl stik′), *n.* a holder for a candle that makes it stand straight up. *Candlesticks are of many sizes; some of them are small and plain, others are large and fancy.* **can dle sticks.**

can dy (kan′dē), *n.* 1. a sweet food made from sugar or syrup combined with flavoring and coloring. *I gave my aunt a box of chocolate candy for her birthday.* **can dies.**
v. 2. to cook in syrup or sugar. *I candied the sweet potatoes.* **can dies, can died, can dy ing.**

cane (kān), *n.* 1. a stick used to help in walking. *I used a cane for a few days after I sprained my ankle.* 2. the long, hollow, jointed stem of certain plants. *Sugar is obtained from sugarcane. Some furniture is made from certain canes.* **canes.**
v. 3. to hit with a cane. *When the snake attacked the man, he caned it.* 4. to make or work with cane. *Today I will cane a chair.* **canes, caned, can ing.**

canned (kand), *adj.* preserved in a can or jar. *I like the taste of canned peas better than the taste of fresh or frozen peas.*

can ning (kan′ing), *n.* the sealing of food in cans or jars so it can be eaten later. *Canning was invented in the early 1800's as a way to keep food from spoiling.*

can non (kan′ən), *n.* a big gun. *Some cannons are so big that they have to be pulled by powerful tractors.* **can nons** or **can non.**

can not (kan ot′, kan′ot), can not. *My friend cannot go to the movie tomorrow because he will be playing in a baseball game.*

ca noe (kə nü′), *n.* 1. a light, narrow boat, pointed at both ends. *American Indians used canoes for travel.* **ca noes.**
v. 2. to travel in a canoe. *Many city people spend their vacations canoeing down the forest rivers.* **ca noes, ca noed, ca noe ing.**

can't (kant), can not. *Mother can't bake her pie until I bring the apples.*

can teen (kan tēn′), *n.* 1. a small container used for carrying water. *A boy scout carries a canteen of water with him on a long hike.* 2. a place in a city or town where entertainment, games, and food are supplied to military men who are below the rank of officer. *The canteen in our city is jammed every Saturday night with sailors.* 3. a store at a military camp for selling personal goods to the members of the army. *A soldier can buy small gifts and other things at very low prices at the canteen.* **can teens.**

can ter (kan′tər), *v.* 1. to gallop gently. *The horse cantered back to the stable after an afternoon of running.* **can ters, can tered, can ter ing.**
n. 2. an easy and gentle gallop. *That horse has a graceful canter when his rider slows him down.* **can ters.**

candle

candlestick
holding candle

canoe

sand, āte, bâre, fäther; sent, mē, férn; fit, bīke; pot, rōpe, fôrt; run, pull, rüle, cūte; noise, sound; **ch**, **cheese**;
ng, **long**; **th**, **thick**; ~~th~~, **those**; **zh**, **treasure**; ə = a in about, e in waken, i in animal, o in seldom, and u in minus.

caps

can vas (kan′vəs), *n.* a strong cloth. *A circus gives its performance under a canvas. The sails of a boat are made of canvas. Many pictures are painted on special canvas.* **can vas es.**

can vass (kan′vəs), *v.* 1. to go through thoroughly; ask everybody. *The boys canvassed the neighborhood, trying to sell subscriptions to magazines.* 2. to examine carefully. *We canvassed the paper every day, hoping that Jim's name would be mentioned as a scholarship winner.* **can vass es, can vassed, can vass ing.**

can yon (kan′yən), *n.* a deep valley with steep sides. *The Grand Canyon in Arizona is about one mile deep in solid rock, and at the bottom is the Colorado River.* **can yons.**

cap (kap), *n.* 1. a small hat that fits closely on the head. *Many men wear caps that keep the sun out of their eyes when they play golf.* 2. special head covering that shows the occupation of the wearer. *Nurses, sailors, and chefs wear special caps.* 3. something like a cap. *A soft drink bottle has a cap on it.* 4. a piece of paper with a small explosive inside. *Caps are put in a toy gun called a cap gun, and they make a popping noise when the trigger is pulled.* **caps.**

v. 5. to put a cap on. *As part of the graduation exercise, each nurse is capped. After the bottles are filled, the dairy caps them.* **caps, capped, cap ping.**

ca pa ble (kā′pə bl), *adj.* able; having the skill to do a good job. *Mary can be trusted with any child because she is a capable baby-sitter. He is capable of winning the scholarship because he studies hard.* **ca pa bly,** *adv.*

ca pac i ty (kə pas′ə tē), *n.* 1. the amount that can be held. *The capacity of that bottle is one quart.* 2. the position; relation. *I know him only in the capacity of a friend.* **ca pac i ties.**

cape (kāp), *n.* 1. an outer garment that has no sleeves, fastened around the neck so that it hangs from the shoulders. *Men used to wear capes instead of light topcoats.* 2. a piece of land that extends into the water. *A cape is surrounded by water on three sides.* **capes.**

cap il lary (kap′ə ler′ē), *n.* a tiny blood vessel, connecting an artery with a vein. *The capillary system forms a network in the human body.* **cap il lar ies.**

cap i tal (kap′ə tl), *n.* 1. the city or town where the government of a country or state is located. *Washington, D.C., is the capital of the United States. Sacramento is the capital of California.* 2. a large letter in writing or printing. *You begin a sentence with a capital. The first letter of your name is a capital.* 3. the money or property used in business. *The big automobile companies have a capital of many millions of dollars.* 4. the top of a pillar or column. *The capital of the column was very fancy, but the shaft was very simple.* **cap i tals.**

adj. 5. by putting to death. *Capital punishment for murder is the law in some states.* 6. the large letters in the alphabet; A,B,C. *All sentences begin with a capital letter.* 7. important; chief. *London is the capital city of England.*

cap i tol (kap′ə tl), *n.* a building in which the representatives and senators of a state or country meet. *The senators and representatives met in the capitol to discuss the tax plan.* 2. **Capitol,** the building in Washington, D.C., where Congress meets. *Much of the important business of our country is discussed in the Capitol.* **cap i tols.**

cap sule (kap′sl), *n.* a small container that holds a dose of medicine. *You can easily swallow a capsule and not taste the medicine.* **cap sules.**

cap tain (kap′tən), *n.* 1. the man who commands a ship. *The captain is responsible for the safety of all those aboard his ship.* 2. a person who is chosen to lead. *In high school, Charles was*

capitals: **a.** Egyptian lotiform;   **b.** Egyptian dactiliform;   **c.** Ionic;   **d.** Corinthian;   **e.** Gothic

captain of the football team and the track team. 3. an officer in the army who ranks above a lieutenant and below a major. *The captain received his orders from the major, and then the captain gave the orders to the lieutenants and privates.* 4. a navy officer above a commander. *The captain was very proud of the men he commanded.* **cap tains.**

cap tion (kap′shən), *n.* a short description in words, usually explaining a picture. *Some of the pictures in this dictionary have captions.* **cap tions.**

cap ture (kap′chər), *v.* to take, to seize; to get by strength or by a trick. *The robber was captured when he answered a help-wanted ad purposely placed by the police.* **cap tures, cap- tured, cap tur ing.**

car (kär), *n.* 1. an automobile. *Let Jim drive the car; I'll walk.* 2. anything using wheels for moving and carrying people or goods. *We counted ninety-nine freight cars on that train.* **cars.**

car a vel (kar′ə vel′), *n.* a kind of small ship. *Caravels were used by Columbus when he discovered America.* **car a vels.**

playing **cards**

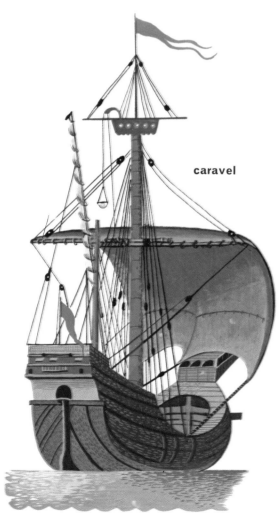

caravel

car bon (kär′bən), *n.* 1. a chemical element. *Diamonds are pure carbon, but carbon is also present in coal, coke, graphite, and charcoal.* 2. a copy made with carbon paper. *Business offices keep carbons of all letters that are written.* **car bons.**

card (kärd), *n.* 1. a small piece of stiff paper. *We sent you a post card when we took our vacation.* 2. **cards,** any game played with a deck of cards. *Bridge is a very popular game of cards.* **cards.**

card board (kärd′bôrd′), *n.* a kind of stiff, heavy paper used in making boxes, posters, tickets, and cards. *We advertised our school play on large pieces of cardboard and tacked them on the bulletin boards.* **card boards.**

care (kâr), *n.* 1. protection; a watching out for. *A mother's loving care is necessary for the health and comfort of a baby.* 2. close attention; caution. *The workers take great care in fixing an airplane's engine.* 3. anxiety; concern; worry. *The president has many cares about protecting our nation.* **cares.**

v. 4. to feel anxiety, interest, or worry. *My sister doesn't care who wins the football game.* 5. to love or like someone. *The children cared deeply for their aunt and uncle.* 6. **care for,** to watch over; provide for. *Our family cares for our dog.* **cares, cared, car ing.**

ca reer (kə rir′), *n.* work; a profession; an occupation. *That doctor chose medical science as a career when he was still in high school. My uncle has had a successful career driving a tractor.* **ca reers.**

care ful (kâr′fəl), *adj.* 1. watchful; cautious; full of care for something. *Children should be taught to be careful when they cross streets. Boys and girls in driving classes in high school are taught to be careful drivers.* 2. done exactly; done correctly. *He always hands in careful pieces of work.* **care ful ly,** *adv.*

care less (kâr′ləs), *adj.* 1. not paying attention; not watchful; not cautious. *He was careless*

sand, āte, bâre, fäther; sent, mē, fėrn; fit, bīke; pot, rōpe, fôrt; run, pull, rüle, cūte; noise, sound; ch, cheese; ng, long; th, thick; <s>th,</s> those; zh, treasure; ə = a in about, e in waken, i in animal, o in seldom, and u in minus.

about shutting the windows, so the rain poured in. *You can't afford to be careless with matches.* 2. not accurate; done or made without enough attention or hard work. *That painting is a sloppy, careless piece of work. A railroad company will not hire careless workers to inspect tracks.* **care less ly,** *adv.*

care less ness (kâr′ləs nəs), *n.* being without care or concern. *His carelessness about hanging up his clothes bothered his mother.*

car go (kär′gō), *n.* a load of goods carried on a ship. *The ship carried a cargo of trucks and farm machinery for South America.* **car goes** or **car gos.**

car i bou (kar′ə bü′), *n.* a North American reindeer. *The caribou stands about as high as a man's shoulder.* **car i bous** or **car i bou.**

car load (kär′lōd′), *n.* the amount carried by a freight car. *Every day about 150 carloads of new television sets leave the factory.* **car loads.**

car ni val (kär′nə vl), *n.* 1. an outdoor amusement show with games, rides, and refreshments. *Every year the men's club sponsors a carnival, operated by professional show people.* 2. a period of having a good time, often with people in costume. *The most famous carnival in this country is held in New Orleans every year.* **car ni vals.**

car ni vore (kär′nə vōr′), *n.* a flesh-eating animal. *A carnivore is the opposite of a herbivore, which is an animal that eats plants.* **car ni vores.**

car niv o rous (kär niv′ə rəs), *adj.* flesh-eating. *Dogs, cats, lions, and tigers are carnivorous animals.* **car niv o rous ly,** *adv.*

car ol (kar′əl), *n.* 1. a song of joy or praise. *"Silent Night, Holy Night" is a famous Christmas carol.* **car ols.**
v. 2. to sing carols. *Every year groups of singers go caroling through the town at Christmas time.* **car ols, car oled, car ol ing.**

carp[1] (kärp), *v.* to find fault; complain. *He was always carping about the weather; it was either too hot or too cold.* **carps, carped, carp ing.**

carp

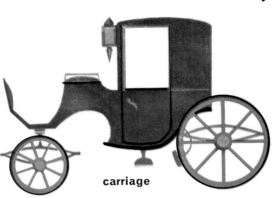

carriage

carp[2] (kärp), *n.* a freshwater fish that lives in streams and ponds. *Carp are good to eat.* **carp** or **carps.**

car pen ter (kär′pən tər), *n.* a person who can make things from wood, or repair them. *We hired a carpenter to make a cabinet for our kitchen. The carpenter is repairing our garage.* **car pen ters.**

car pet (kär′pət), *n.* 1. a thick, heavy fabric for covering a floor. *Mother told the boys to see that their shoes were clean before they walked on the new living room carpet.* **car pets.**
v. 2. to cover with a carpet. *This year we carpeted the bedrooms.* **car pets, car pet ed, car pet ing.**

car port (kär′pôrt′), *n.* a kind of garage, but with only a roof and no walls, attached to a house. *Carports are used in warm areas, where automobiles do not need much shelter from snow and cold.* **car ports.**

car riage (kar′ij), *n.* 1. a vehicle moving on wheels, pulled by horses, and used for carrying people. *Carriages were very popular in America until the car was invented.* 2. a small, wheeled vehicle that can be pushed. *The parents bought a baby carriage.* 3. a way of holding the head and body. *A soldier has a military carriage—head up and chest out.* **car riag es.**

car ri er (kar′ē ər), *n.* 1. a person or thing that carries. *The mail carrier in our neighborhood is a friend of all the children and their dogs. An aircraft carrier is a sort of floating airport for navy planes.* 2. a company whose business is transporting passengers and goods. *Railroad companies and bus companies are known as "common carriers."* **car ri ers.**

car rot (kar′ət), *n.* a plant with a long, orange-red root that is eaten as a vegetable. *I like to eat cooked carrots and also raw carrots.* **car rots.**

car ry (kar′ē), *v.* 1. to take from one place to another. *The busy expressways carry hundreds of cars an hour. Will you carry this package home for me, please?* 2. to hold up; support; bear. *This heavy, thick log carries the whole weight of the roof of the cabin.* 3. to pass or adopt a motion or bill. *The government's bill to build a new dam was carried by a vote of forty-three to one.* 4. to hold the head or body in a certain way. *The little boy carried himself like a soldier's son; he didn't slouch or drag his feet.* 5. **carry on,** to go on as before; continue. *The doctor's son will carry on his father's lifetime work.* 6. **carry out,** to get done. *I was glad to carry out my dad's requests.* **car ries, car ried, car ry ing.**

cart (kärt), *n.* 1. a two-wheeled vehicle used to carry heavy loads. *A cart is pulled by a horse.* 2. a two-wheeled wagon that can be pushed or pulled by a man. *The vegetable-and-fruit man walks by our house every day with his goods in his cart.* **carts.**
v. 3. to carry in a cart; to move something. *All our baggage was carted from the train to our car by the porter.* **carts, cart ed, cart ing.**

car toon (kär tün′), *n.* 1. a drawing in a newspaper or magazine that usually makes fun of a person or event. *Men in political life must get used to seeing cartoons of themselves that are sometimes unfair.* 2. a comic strip or humorous drawing in a newspaper or magazine. *Small children like to have someone read the Sunday cartoons to them.* **car toons.**

carve (kärv), *v.* 1. to cut into pieces or slices. *At Thanksgiving and at Christmas we always ask Uncle Roscoe to carve the turkey.* 2. to make by cutting. *Sculptors carve statues out of stone, wood, metal, or other materials. The store sold little people, houses, and animals carved out of wood.* 3. to cut a design on. *The boy carved his initials on his sled.* **carves, carved, carv ing.**

car y at id (kar′ē at′id), *n.* a statue of a woman used as a column. *Six caryatids hold up the roof of the Greek temple.* **car y at ids** or **car y at i-des** (kar′ē at′ə dēz′).

case[1] (kās), *n.* 1. an actual condition; real situation. *If this is the case, then we will have to take the bus instead of the train.* 2. a group of facts having to do with a certain thing. *The police are working on the case of the jewel robbery that happened yesterday.* 3. a matter or problem to be settled in a court of law. *The store owner, whose windows were broken by boys throwing stones,*

caryatids

took the case to court. 4. a person having a disease. *The doctor is taking care of ten cases of chicken pox.* 5. **in case of,** if there should be. *In case of fire, walk to the nearest exit.* 6. **in any case,** regardless; anyhow. *It may rain during the ball game, but in any case I am going.* **cas es.**

case[2] (kās), *n.* 1. a holder; container. *I have a small case for my glasses. A violinist carries his violin in a case.* 2. the amount that a box or carton will hold. *I bought a case of root beer to take on the picnic. We had twelve cases of books that had to be moved.* **cas es.**

cash (kash), *n.* 1. money in coins and bills. *I have a check for five dollars, and I have two dollars in cash.* 2. money paid when something is bought. *I pay by check or in cash when I make a purchase, but many people use charge accounts.*
v. 3. to exchange a check for money. *I need some money; can you cash a check for ten dollars?* **cash es, cashed, cash ing.**

cash ier (ka shir′), *n.* 1. a person in a store, hotel, or restaurant who handles money. *The waiter told us to pay the cashier for our dinner.* 2. a person in a bank in charge of taking in money and paying it out. *You can talk to the head cashier about opening an account at the bank.* **cash iers.**

cast (kast), *v.* 1. to throw. *The boy cast a stone into the water and watched the waves that were made. A fisherman casts his line into the water.* 2. to shape melted metal by pouring into a mold for hardening. *Parts of an automobile that are cast from metal include the fenders and the doors.* 3. to give a role or part in a play. *I was cast as a slave in the play, and my friend was cast as the king!* 4. **cast one's vote,** to vote. *Did you cast your vote for president yet?* **casts, cast, cast ing.**
n. 5. the actors in a play. *The movie had an impressive cast of actors.* 6. a plaster that is placed around a part of the body to help bones heal. *After Jerry broke his leg, it was in a plaster cast for six weeks.* 7. something formed in a mold by casting. *That store sells little metal casts of the city's famous buildings.* **casts.**

cas tle (kas′l), *n.* 1. a large building, in the days of kings and knights, that was built with high walls, towers, and sometimes a moat to keep out the enemy. *Nobles and friends of the king lived in castles.* 2. any large and solidly built house, particularly one with many rooms. *Many of the castles of England are open to the public, like museums.* **cas tles.** (See illustration on following page.)

cas u al (kazh′ù əl), *adj.* 1. without plan; happening by chance. *He paid a casual visit to his old neighborhood as he passed through that part of town.* 2. not worried; having an easy appearance. *Instead of being upset, she was very casual about losing her ring.* **cas u al ly,** *adv.*

cat (kat), *n.* 1. a small, carnivorous animal kept as a house pet or to catch mice. *We couldn't decide whether to buy the black cat or the white one with long hair.* 2. any larger animal that is also a

sand, āte, bâre, fäther; sent, mē, fèrn; fit, bīke; pot, rōpe, fôrt; run, pùll, rüle, cūte; noise, sound; ch, cheese; ng, long; th, thick; th, those; zh, treasure; ə = a in about, e in waken, i in animal, o in seldom, and u in minus.

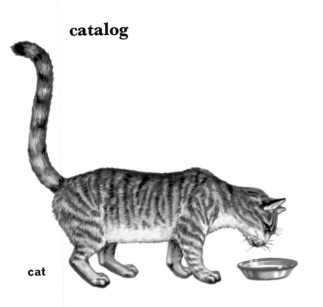

cat

part of the cat family. *A lion, a tiger, and a leopard are cats.* **cats.**

cat a log or **cat a logue** (kat′l ôg′), *n.* 1. a list of names, things, or books arranged in alphabetical order. *A mail-order company publishes a big catalog of its goods, with prices. A library has a catalog of all the books in it. A telephone book is a catalog.* **cat a logs** or **cat a logues.**
v. 2. to place in an orderly list. *Every year he catalogs the firm's merchandise, taking out old items and adding new ones.* **cat a logs** or **cat a logues, cat a loged** or **cat a logued, cat a log ing** or **cat a logu ing.**

castle

cat bird (kat′bėrd′), *n.* a gray American songbird whose call sounds like the mewing of a cat. *The catbird likes to eat worms.* **cat birds.**

catch (kach), *v.* 1. to get; take and hold on to; seize. *Watch that young boy catch the ball! The police caught the thief ten minutes after he left the store. The cat caught a mouse.* 2. to get to in time. *I ran all the way and caught the bus just as it was starting. John never can catch Joe in a fifty-yard dash.* 3. to discover by surprise; find out. *I caught the cat just as he put his paw between the bars of the canary's cage.* 4. to get from another. *I think I'm catching a cold from you.* 5. to be held by something. *I always catch my coat on that nail.* **catch es, caught, catch ing.**
n. 6. taking hold of; seizing. *The fans all cheered the catch made by the fielder when he jumped high in the air and grabbed the ball.* 7. something taken or captured. *The fisherman went home with a good catch of fish.* 8. a thing that fastens or holds. *The screen door kept banging in the wind because the catch didn't hold it shut. The catch on her dress was broken.* **catch es.**

catch er (kach′ər), *n.* in baseball, the player behind home plate who receives every pitch from the pitcher, except when the man at bat hits the ball. *The catcher can give a sign to his pitcher telling him the kind of pitch to throw—fast ball or curve ball, for example.* **catch ers.**

cat er pil lar (kat′ər pil′ər or kat′ə pil ər), *n.* 1. the wormlike form, or larva, of a moth or butterfly. *The caterpillar spins a cocoon and later comes out of it as a moth or butterfly.* 2. **Caterpillar tractor** (a trademark), a vehicle that moves on two continuous metal roller belts. *The Caterpillar tractor is used for heavy work in farming and building.* **cat er pil lars.**

cat fish (kat′fish′), *n.* a fish without scales, having feelers around the mouth that are supposed to look like a cat's whiskers. *Catfish use their feelers to find food in the muddy bottoms where they live.* **cat fish** or **cat fish es.**

ca the dral (kə thē′drəl), *n.* 1. the official church of a bishop. *Important services are held in the cathedral.* 2. any large, important church. *The most beautiful church in our city is the cathedral.* **ca the drals.**

cat sup (kech′əp, kat′səp), *n.* ketchup, a sauce made of tomatoes and spices. *I like catsup on my hamburger.*

cat tle (kat′l), *n.* cows, bulls, or oxen. *Herds of cattle can be seen on ranches in Texas.*

caught (kôt), past tense of **catch.**

cause (kôz), *n.* 1. a person or thing that makes something happen. *A leaking gas pipe was the cause of the big fire.* 2. an activity or idea which interests many people who support it. *We have joined a group that works for the cause of better education.* **caus es.**
v. 3. to make something happen. *The first prize of a bicycle caused dozens of students to enter the essay contest.* **caus es, caused, caus ing.**

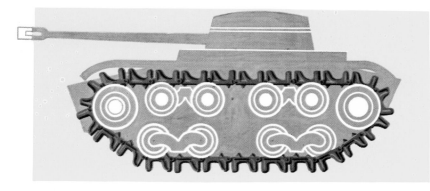

Caterpillar tank

Caterpillar truck

caterpillar (larva)

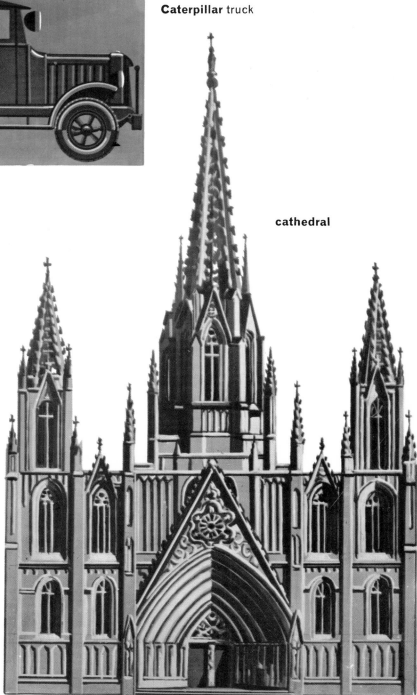

cathedral

cau tion (kô′shən), *n.* 1. being careful; taking care. *Small children should be taught to cross streets with caution. The settlers were told to use caution in passing through Indian territory.* 2. a warning. *His low marks were a caution to him to spend more time studying.* **cau tions.**
v. 3. to warn. *The mother cautioned her children to come home before dark.* **cau tions, cau tioned, cau tion ing.**

cau tious (kô′shəs), *adj.* careful; keeping away from danger. *He is a cautious driver, especially in heavy traffic.* **cau tious ly,** *adv.*

cave (kāv), *n.* 1. a hollow space inside the earth. *The guide led us through the cave and pointed out the beautiful kinds of rocks.* **caves.**
v. 2. **cave in,** to fall in. *The mine caved in, burying three men who later were dug out unharmed.* **caves, caved, cav ing.**

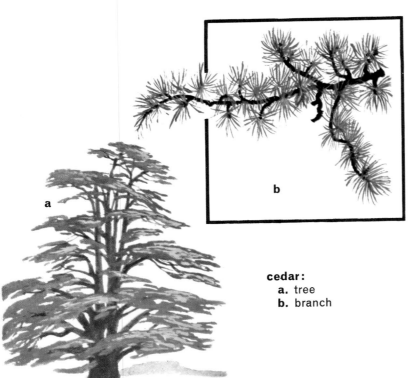

cedar:
  a. tree
  b. branch

celery

cave man (kāv′ man′), *n.* the kind of man who lived in caves thousands of years ago. *Cavemen had no tools, no wagons, and only crude weapons.* **cave men.**

cav i ty (kav′ə tē), *n.* a small hollow caused by decay in a tooth. *Children who don't have many cavities usually go to the dentist often and brush their teeth properly.* **cav i ties.**

caw (kô), *n.* 1. the cry of a crow. *We could hear the caws of the crows flying overhead.* **caws.**
v. 2. to make the sound of a crow. *The crows cawed all morning in the cornfield.* **caws, cawed, caw ing.**

cease (sēs), *v.* to stop; bring or come to an end. *Just be patient; this rain will have to cease sometime.* **ceas es, ceased, ceas ing.**

ce dar (sē′dər), *n.* 1. an evergreen tree with wide branches and durable, fragrant wood. *A fire of cedar logs smells sweet.* 2. the wood of this tree. *Because of its pleasant odor, cedar is used for making pencils, small boxes, and storage chests for clothes.* **ce dars.**

ceil ing (sēl′ing), *n.* 1. the top of a room. *In most rooms there is an overhead light attached to the ceiling.* 2. the highest an airplane can go and have the ground still visible. *When fog is very thick, the ceiling is said to be zero.* **ceil ings.**

cel e brate (sel′ə brāt′), *v.* 1. to honor a special time or event. *We celebrate Independence Day (July 4) by firework displays and patriotic speeches; we celebrate Easter by going to church.* 2. to perform a religious ceremony. *A priest celebrates Mass in a church. The Jewish people celebrate the Passover.* **cel e brates, cel e brat ed, cel e brat ing.**

cel e brat ed (sel′ə brāt′əd), *adj.* famous; well-known. *The celebrated London Symphony Orchestra will give a concert Thursday night, and the seats are already sold out for the performance.*

cel ery (sel′ər ē), *n.* a plant with firm, long stalks which are eaten either raw or cooked. *I like soup made from celery.*

cell (sel), *n.* 1. a small room in a prison or jail. *Some convicts in the prison get out of the cells to work in the laundry or in the furniture shop.* 2. one of the tiny parts of living matter of which all animals and plants are made. *Some animals and plants are made up of only one cell, but man is made up of billions of cells which may differ in size and shape.* 3. a small enclosed space. *Look at a honeycomb; it is made up of cells of honey. The walls of the cells are made of a kind of wax also produced by the honeybee.* 4. a container holding chemical substances that can produce electricity. *A car battery is made up of cells.* **cells.**

cel lar (sel′ər), *n.* the underground rooms beneath a building, usually used for storing things. *The family next door fixed up their cellar as a playroom for their children.* **cel lars.**

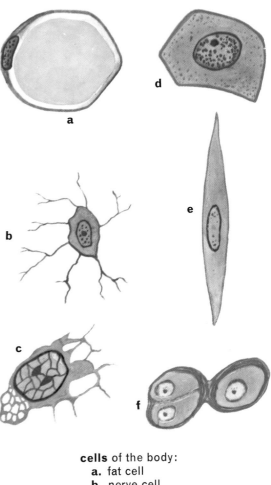

cells of the body:
  a. fat cell
  b. nerve cell
  c. bone cell
  d. skin cell
  e. muscle cell
  f. cartilage cell

sand, āte, bâre, fäther; sent, mē, fėrn; fit, bīke; pot, rōpe, fôrt; run, pùll, rüle, cūte; noise, sound; ch, cheese; ng, long; th, thick; ~~th~~, those; zh, treasure; ə = a in about, e in waken, i in animal, o in seldom, and u in minus.

ce ment (sə ment′), *n.* 1. a powder made by burning clay and limestone. When this powder is mixed with sand and water, it is used for making sidewalks, walls, basement floors, and roads. It dries out soon and becomes very hard. *Cement is usually used for sidewalks because it is hard and strong.* 2. anything causing things to stick together. *We used rubber cement instead of paste to attach two pieces of paper to each other.* **ce ments.**
v. 3. to fasten with cement. *Our kitchen tile is cemented to the wooden floor.* 4. to pave with cement. *The old dirt road was cemented last week, so now we will have no more dust blowing around during heavy winds.* **ce ments, ce ment ed, ce ment ing.**

cem e tery (sem′ə ter′ē), *n.* a place where dead people are buried. *This cemetery has beautiful grounds.* **cem e ter ies.**

cent (sent), *n.* a coin of the United States and Canada. *One hundred cents make one dollar. Five cents make a nickel. Ten cents make a dime. Twenty-five cents make a quarter. Fifty cents make a half dollar.* **cents.**

cen taur (sen′tôr), *n.* in Greek mythology, a monster with a man's head, trunk, and arms, and a horse's body and legs. *Centaurs were thought of as being wild creatures.* **cen taurs.**

cen ter (sen′tər), *n.* 1. a point in the middle. *The center of a circle is the point that is the same distance from all points in the circumference.* 2. a main area or place where people gather. *A new shopping center was opened in town. The center of attention at the auto show was the display that had a new electric car.* 3. the middle. *We watched the men paint a white line down the center of the road.* **cen ters.**
v. 4. to put in the center. *I want this table exactly centered in the room.* 5. to collect in one place. *The main part of the crowd will center near the speaker's stand.* 6. to settle; fix. *Center your attention on one problem at a time.* **cen ters, cen tered, cen ter ing.**

cen ti grade (sen′tə grād), *adj.* of or according to the centigrade scale for measuring temperature where the freezing point of water is 0 degrees and the boiling point of water is 100 degrees. *Centigrade thermometers are usually used in scientific experiments.*

cen ti pede (sen′tə pēd′), *n.* a small wormlike animal with many pairs of legs. *Centipedes destroy harmful insects.* **cen ti pedes.**

cen tral (sen′trəl), *adj.* 1. in or at the middle; near the center. *The biggest stores are in the central part of the city, but the shopping centers at the edge of town do a lot of business also.* 2. main; leading; chief. *What is the central idea that the*

centaur

author is trying to get across to us? **cen tral ly,** *adv.*

cen trif u gal (sen trif′yə gəl or sen trif′ə gl), *adj.* 1. moving away from the center. *A merry-go-round is an example of a ride with centrifugal movement.* **cen trif u gal ly,** *adv.*

centrifugal force (sen trif′yə gəl fōrs), *n.* the force that pulls a thing outward when it is moving around a center. *The centrifugal force caused the car to go to the outside of the curve in the road.*

cen tu ry (sen′chə rē), *n.* 1. one hundred years. *From 1875 to 1975 is a century.* 2. each 100 years, counting from a special occasion, like the birth of Christ. *The first century is from 1 to 100. The twentieth century, in which we live, lasts from 1901 to 2000. The year 2001 will be the first year of the twenty-first century.* **cen tu ries.**

ce re al (sir′ē əl), *n.* 1. a food made from grain, such as barley, rice, oats, wheat, corn, and rye. *For breakfast my favorite cereal is oatmeal with milk and sugar on it.* 2. the grass that the grain comes from. *Grains from some cereals are used in making flour for bread.* **ce re als.**
adj. 3. of or pertaining to grains. *Babies should have a lot of cereal food.*

cer e mo ny (ser′ə mō′nē), *n.* 1. a special set of acts done in a certain way. *The principal told all the girls to wear white dresses for the*

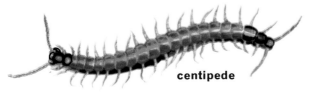

centipede

graduation ceremony. 2. behavior that follows certain rules; very polite behavior. *The distinguished visitors to the city were greeted with ceremony.* **cer e mon ies.**

cer tain (sėrt′n), *adj.* 1. without doubt; sure; positive. *I am certain that all my answers are correct.* 2. sure to happen. *The news of their dad's new job will bring certain happiness to the children.* 3. not mentioned by name, although known. *There are certain people in this group who have given generously to the library's building fund, but they don't want their names to be told.* **cer tain ly,** *adv.*

n. 4. **for certain,** surely; as a fact. *I know for certain that the sun rises and the sun sets.*

cer tif i cate (sər tif′i kət), *n.* a written or printed statement declaring that something is a fact or has taken place. *You must show a birth certificate to get a passport.* **cer tif i cates.**

cer ti fied (sėr′tə fīd′), *adj.* 1. guaranteed to meet certain standards. *We buy only certified grade A milk for the baby.* 2. having the correct certificate. *My sister is a certified teacher in New York.*

cer ti fy (sėr′tə fī′), *v.* to say that something is true by giving a written statement. *Every time a cold prevents me from going to school, the doctor certifies that illness kept me home.* **cer ti fies, cer ti fied, cer ti fy ing.**

chalice

a **challenge** to a duel

chain (chān), *n.* 1. a number of links or rings fastened together. *The dog was kept in the back yard by a chain.* 2. anything that holds or binds. *Prisoners in jail were bound in iron chains in olden days.* 3. series of things that are connected or joined. *The Rocky Mountains are a chain of mountains.* **chains.**

v. 4. to fasten with a chain. *The lamp in our living room is chained to the ceiling.* **chains, chained, chain ing.**

chair (châr), *n.* 1. a piece of furniture with legs and a back that holds one seated person. *Let Grandfather sit in the rocking chair; we'll use these armchairs.* 2. an official position. *He has the chair of English at that college.* 3. a chairman. *The chair will now call the meeting to order.* **chairs.**

chair man (châr′mən), *n.* the person who is in charge of a meeting, a committee, or a similar group. *The chairman sent us a notice of the meeting.* **chair men.**

chal ice (chal′is), *n.* a cup; especially the cup used in a church service. *The chalice used in our church is made of gold.* **chal ic es.**

chalk (chôk), *n.* 1. white, soft limestone, made up mostly of tiny sea shells. *Chalk is white, gray, or yellowish in color.* 2. a material like chalk, used for writing on chalkboards or blackboards. *Charles used white and blue chalk to draw his picture on the board.* **chalks.**

v. 3. to mark, draw, or write with chalk. *Some children chalk their names on sidewalks.* **chalks, chalked, chalk ing.**

chalk board (chôk′bôrd′), *n.* a hard, smooth surface, usually green or black, on which one writes with chalk. *You can easily erase the marks on a chalkboard in order to write something else.* **chalk boards.**

chal lenge (chal′ənj), *v.* 1. to doubt; disagree with the truth of something; question. *I challenge that remark of yours, and I would like to know where you got your information.* 2. to dare; invite to take part in a contest. *In ancient times one noble challenged another to a duel by throwing a glove in his face.* 3. to refuse entry to until a certain sign is made or produced. *The guard challenged the lieutenant when he started to enter the camp.* **chal leng es, chal lenged, chal leng ing.**

cham ber (chām′bər), *n.* 1. a bedroom. *The princess slept late in her chamber.* 2. a room or auditorium where lawmakers meet. *The chamber was crowded with spectators seated above the floor in a balcony.* 3. a group of lawmakers. *The Congress of the United States consists of two chambers: the House of Representatives and the Senate.* 4. the part of the gun that holds the bullet. *When the chamber was empty, the hunter's gun was useless to him.* 5. the room where a judge works when out of court. *The judge called the two lawyers into his chamber to settle a point of law among themselves.* **cham bers.**

cha me le on (kə mē′lē ən), *n.* a small lizard that can change the color of its skin. *If a*

chameleon

chameleon is placed on a green leaf, its skin slowly changes to green; if it is placed on wood, it becomes brownish. **cha me le ons.**

cham pi on (cham′pē ən), *n.* 1. the winner; the person or group that finishes first or has the best record. *Our school's football team was champion of the Suburban League. Mary Lou is the spelling champion of the fourth grade.* 2. a person who fights for other people or for a cause. *Abraham Lincoln was a champion of the Union.* **cham pi ons.**
adj. 3. winning over others; being the best. *One member of the champion swimming team raises champion dogs as a hobby.*
v. 4. to fight for; defend. *We must champion the right of all our citizens to obtain any jobs they can do well.* **cham pi ons, cham pi oned, cham pi on ing.**

cham pi on ship (cham′pē ən ship′), *n.* position of the winner; having the place of champion; being first. *Our team finally won the basketball championship.* **cham pi on ships.**

chance (chans), *n.* 1. luck; an unexpected happening of events. *Just by chance he bought fifty shares of that stock.* 2. a possibility; probability. *There is a chance that the girl may be elected.* 3. an opportunity; a time to take advantage. *The baseball player saw his chance and stole home to win the game.* **chanc es.**
adj. 4. happening by chance; not planned for. *It was a chance meeting between us.*
v. 5. to happen by chance. *We chanced to be leaving at the same time, so we walked home together.* 6. to leave to chance; risk. *With only two seconds left in the game, the basketball player chanced everything on a long shot.* **chanc es, chanced, chanc ing.**

chan de lier (shan′də lir′), *n.* a hanging light fixture with several sockets for lights. *Because chandeliers are so fancy, they add beauty to a room besides lighting it.* **chan de liers.**

change (chānj), *v.* 1. to make or become different. *She changed her appearance by dyeing her light hair a dark red.* 2. to give or take one thing for another. *Change that old, worn suit for this*

one that has just been cleaned and pressed. *Can you change this dollar bill for ten dimes?* **chang es, changed, chang ing.**
n. 3. making or becoming different. *Watch for a change in the weather tomorrow; it is going to be cooler.* 4. something put in place of something else. *There will be a change in the program tonight because one of the actors is ill.* 5. small coins. *John has a pocketful of change; it jingles when he walks.* 6. money returned to a person when he gives an amount larger than the price. *The book cost three dollars; I gave the clerk a five-dollar bill; my change was two dollars.* **chang es.**

chan nel (chan′l), *n.* 1. the bed of a river or stream. *The channel of a river is often dredged to keep it deep enough for ships.* 2. the deepest part of a river, bay, harbor, etc. *The channel is marked by lights so ships can sail in it at night.* 3. a body of water connecting two larger bodies of water. *The English Channel lies between the Atlantic Ocean and the North Sea.* 4. any tube or passage through which a liquid can pass. *The workmen dug a channel to remove water before they began digging the foundation of the house.* 5. the way by which something moves or passes. *Newspapers and magazines are channels of information.* 6. a radio frequency band, used for radio and television. *We watch Channel 7 every night.* **chan nels.**
v. 7. to make a channel in. *They are channeling the river again because it has gotten too shallow.* 8. to send through a channel. *Please channel this letter to someone higher up.* **chan nels, chan neled, chan nel ing.**

chant (chant), *n.* 1. a song in which a number of words are sung in the same tone. *Chants are heard in some church services.* **chants.**
v. 2. to sing or say in a chant. *The congregation was quiet as they heard the choir chant the prayer.* 3. to keep talking about; say or tell over and over. *All the kingdom chanted the praises of the king.* **chants, chant ed, chant ing.**

chap (chap), *n.* 1. a man or boy. *Tom is a good chap.* **chaps.**
v. 2. to crack open; make or become rough. *His hands chapped from the rain and cold.* **chaps, chapped, chap ping.**

chap el (chap′l), *n.* 1. a place of Christian worship. *A chapel is smaller than a church.* 2. a small room in a church. *The little chapel has its own altar.* 3. a room or building holding religious services in a college, army camp, hospital, or other building. *There is a beautiful little chapel in the United Nations Building.* **chap els.**

chap ter (chap′tər), *n.* 1. a part or main section of a book. *At the end of a chapter in a textbook you will usually find problems and questions.* 2. a local group that is part of a larger organization. *My mother belongs to our town's chapter of the Red Cross.* **chap ters.**

char ac ter (kar′ək tər), *n.* 1. a person in a play

chandelier

or book. *The character of Pinocchio, the little boy with the long pointed nose, appeals to children.* 2. a way of behaving, thinking, feeling, acting, and speaking. *His character changed when he became a success; he was no longer the person we once knew.* 3. the qualities of being sincere, honest, reliable, etc. *He is a man who has character, and I think he should be the head of our company.* 4. the things that give a person or place a certain identity. *The old city has its own character.* 5. an odd person; unusual man or woman. *That Charlie is a real character; he never wears a hat, even in the winter.* 6. a letter; a sign. *Chinese and Japanese writing and printing have characters completely different from ours.* **char ac ters.**

char ac ter is tic (kar′ək tər is′tik), *n.* 1. something that makes a person or thing different from others; a special feature. *The laugh of a hyena and the howl of a wolf are characteristics of those animals.* **char ac ter is tics.**
adj. 2. belonging to a certain person or thing. *She offered to help with her characteristic cheerfulness.* **char ac ter is ti cal ly,** *adv.*

char coal (chär′kōl′), *n.* a black substance made by partly burning wood in a closed container, without air. *Charcoal is used for making crayons for drawing. Many people cook their food outdoors in the summer, using charcoal as fuel.* **char coals.**

charge (chärj), *v.* 1. to load; fill. *The gun was ready to fire after it was charged with powder and shot. You ought to charge your battery before you go on that long automobile trip.* 2. to give a duty or job. *I am going to charge him with keeping the lawn mowed.* 3. to give an order. *The teacher charged us to keep quiet.* 4. to accuse. *The truck driver was charged with carrying an overweight load.* 5. to ask as a price or payment. *The store charges ten cents for notebooks.* 6. to put on a bill to be paid later. *I am going to charge a new dress, and pay for it at the end of the month.* 7. to rush at; attack. *The Indians charged the wagon train.* **charg es, charged, charg ing.**
n. 8 the amount used to fill a gun for firing.

chariot

The charge is in the gun, so it is ready to fire. 9. a task; duty; job. *Caring for babies was the charge of the nurse.* 10. care. *Our dog is in your charge until we return.* 11. a person under the care of someone. *The children in the classroom are the charges of the teacher.* 12. an order; command. *A judge gives a charge to a jury when he gives them final instructions before they leave to decide the case.* 13. a claim that one was wrong. *He admitted the charge and paid a fine.* 14. the price asked for something. *There is no charge for gift wrapping at Christmas.* 15. a rushing at; attacking. *The soldiers stopped the first charge.* **charg es.**

char i ot (char′ē ət), *n.* a two-wheeled vehicle pulled by horses in which the rider stands. *The ancient Greeks and Romans used chariots in battles and in races.* **char i ots.**

char i ty (char′ə tē), *n.* 1. the money or help given to poor people, sick people, or to anyone in some kind of trouble. *A person who is ill and cannot work sometimes has to depend on charity until he gets well.* 2. an organization, fund, or institution for giving help to the poor or sick. *My aunt works one day a week for her favorite charity.* 3. kindness; willingness to overlook faults. "*With charity toward all, with malice toward none,*" *said Abraham Lincoln, in speaking of the way a former enemy should be treated.* 4. love. *All religions teach the need for charity.* **char i ties.**

charm (chärm), *n.* 1. an attraction. *Life in the country holds a great charm for me.* 2. a quality or feature of a person that gives pleasure. *Tom's voice is his greatest charm, while Dorothy's charm is her lovely laugh.* 3. any small object worn as a decoration. *My mother bought some charms to put on my bracelet.* **charms.**
v. 4. to delight; please. *The beautiful old house charmed all who saw it.* 5. to act on as if by magic. *The music charmed her.* **charms, charmed, charm ing.**

chart (chärt), *n.* 1. a map used by sailors, showing depths of waters, the coastline, the flow of the currents, etc. *With a good chart the captain found the harbor in the night.* 2. information given in the form of diagrams, maps, and tables. *Newspapers often print weather charts. A hospital keeps a temperature chart for each patient.* **charts.**
v. 3. to make a map of. *The captain charted the route his ship would take.* **charts, chart ed, chart ing.**

chase (chās), *v.* 1. to run after, trying to catch. *The hounds chased the fox over fields and farms.* 2. to drive away. *She chased the cat away from the bird's nest.* **chas es, chased, chas ing.**
n. 3. a chasing. *It was a fine chase, but the fox got away.* 4. the hunting of game for sport. *He enjoys the chase.* 5. a hunted animal. *They often got near the chase, but each time the animal fooled them.* **chas es.**

chas sis (shas′ē, chas′ē), *n.* the body frame-work that supports an automobile or truck. *The chassis was bent, but the motor in the old car was still in good shape.* **chas sis** (shas′ēz).

chat (chat), *v.* 1. to talk in a friendly way. *The two women chatted whenever they met at the store.* **chats, chat ted, chat ting.**
n. 2. a friendly talk. *The women have many chats while relaxing and drinking coffee.* **chats.**

chat ter (chat′ər), *v.* 1. to talk fast without say-ing much. *Goodness, how that woman can chatter about her garden!* 2. to make quick, light noises. *Squirrels and birds were chattering in the back yard.* 3. to hit together. *It is so cold that my teeth are chattering.* **chat ters, chat tered, chat ter ing.**
n. 4. foolish talk. *Her chatter was annoying to all those sitting near her.* **chat ters.**

cheap (chēp), *adj.* 1. costing only a little money. *Oranges are cheap in the spring, when there are plenty on the market.* 2. of poor quality. *Those are cheap tires that will wear out quickly.* 3. easily got; obtained without much work, skill, or trouble. *They won a cheap victory when a dog ran on the baseball field and made our fielder take his eye off the ball.* 4. not worth having respect for. *A girl who talks loud, chews gum in class, and uses too much perfume is cheap.* **cheap er, cheap est; cheap ly,** *adv.*

cheat (chēt), *n.* 1. a person who is not honest. *A student who copies answers from another is a cheat.* **cheats.**
v. 2. to be unfair or dishonest in order to get something. *Our teacher told us that if we cheat to get good marks, we will not learn anything.* **cheats, cheat ed, cheat ing.**

check (chek), *v.* 1. to stop. *It is never too late to check a bad habit.* 2. to make sure of the correct-ness of. *Be sure to check your test before you hand it in.* 3. to make a mark (√) showing some-thing has been looked over. *Check each name on this list as I read them to you.* 4. to leave something in the care of another. *You check your overcoat before being seated in many restaurants.* 5. to hold back; control. *Check your temper or you'll have to stay after school.* **checks, checked, check ing.**
n. 6. a sudden stop. *The bell at the end of recess gave a check to the children's game.* 7. a mark (√) meaning something is satisfactory. *I make a check on my shopping list after each thing I buy.* 8. a ticket or receipt to get back something. *I lost my coat check, but I finally got the coat back.* 9. a bill in a restaurant. *The check for our dinners was three dollars.* 10. a written order from a bank to pay money to a certain person or place. *Please make out a check for twenty dollars for the church's building fund.* 11. one of the squares in a pattern of squares. *My new suit has checks of blue and white.* **checks.**

check er board (chek′ər bôrd′), *n.* a board having sixty-four squares of two different

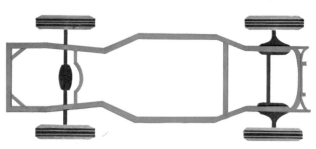
automobile **chassis**

colors. *A checkerboard is used in the games of checkers and chess.* **check er boards.**

check ers (chek′ərz), *n. pl.* a game played by two people on a checkerboard. Each player tries to capture the opponent's twelve pieces in a series of alternate moves. *Checkers is a game that takes a lot of thinking.*

cheek (chēk), *n.* 1. the side of the face below the eyes. *His cheeks were tanned by the sun.* 2. bold talk or action that is in poor taste. *Carl was punished for the cheek he showed when he interrupted the principal's speech.* **cheeks.**

cheer (chir), *n.* 1. a shout of joy, welcome, or approval. *As the President's car moved through the streets, cheers came from the crowds.* 2. comfort; joy; hope. *The return of their son from the army brought cheer to the parents.* **cheers.**
v. 3. to shout words of approval; to encourage by giving yells. *When the team appeared on the field, the crowd cheered each player.* 4. to encourage; to comfort. *A red dress cheers me on a gray day.* **cheers, cheered, cheer ing.**

cheer ful (chir′fəl), *adj.* 1. happy; joyful. *At last came the cheerful news—our school was picked as the best in the state.* 2. bright and pleasant. *It was a sunny, cheerful morning in spring.* 3. eager to help. *Cheerful workers are usually better workers.* **cheer ful ly,** *adv.*

cheese (chēz), *n.* a food made from the thick part of milk. *I like sandwiches made with cheese.* **chees es.**

chef (shef), *n.* 1. a head cook. *The hotel has a famous Frenchman as its chef.* 2. any kind of cook. *Tonight let's name Fred as our chef to cook the hamburgers.* **chefs.**

chem i cal (kem′ə kl), *n.* 1. any substance used in chemistry or made by chemistry. *Scientists have discovered a new chemical.* **chem i cals.**
adj. 2. having to do with chemistry. *A chemical experiment should be performed very carefully.* **chem i cal ly,** *adv.*

chem is try (kem′əs trē), *n.* the study of ele-ments or simple substances and the changes which take place when they combine to make other substances. *Chemistry tries to find out how elements and substances combine and act under various conditions.*

cher ry (cher′ē), *n.* 1. a small, round, red or white fruit with a stone or seed in the center. *Some cherries taste sweet, and some taste sour.* 2. the tree this fruit grows on. *Cherries are covered with*

sand, āte, bâre, fäther; sent, mē, fẽrn; fit, bīke; pot, rōpe, fôrt; run, pùll, rüle, cūte; noise, sound; ch, cheese; ng, long; th, thick; th, those; zh, treasure; ə = a in about, e in waken, i in animal, o in seldom, and u in minus.

chick

beautiful white blossoms in spring. 3. red. *The color she likes best is cherry.* **cher ries.**

chess (ches), *n.* a game played by two people, each having sixteen pieces. *Chess is played on a checkerboard.*

chest (chest), *n.* 1. a piece of furniture having drawers; a bureau. *Chests are generally used for holding clothing or linens.* 2. a large box with a lid on it. *The young child is taught to keep all of his toys in his toy chest.* 3. the upper front part of the body. *I have a cold in my chest.* **chests.**

chest nut (ches′nut′, ches′nət), *n.* 1. a dark-brown nut with a smooth, thin shell. *Chestnuts are usually roasted or cooked before they are eaten.* 2. the tree it grows on. *Chestnuts make fine shade trees.* 3. the wood of the tree. *Chestnut is used to make furniture.* **chest nuts.**
adj. 4. dark reddish-brown. *She brushes her chestnut hair every day.*

chew (chü), *v.* to bite and grind with the teeth. *Doctors say that food should be chewed into tiny pieces before swallowing it.* **chews, chewed, chew ing.**

chick (chik), *n.* 1. a young chicken. *Chicks peck their way out of their eggs when they are ready to hatch.* 2. a baby bird. *The robin has two chicks still in the nest with her.* **chicks.**

chick en (chik′ən), *n.* 1. a bird raised for its meat and its eggs; hen or rooster. *Most chickens are especially raised and fed so that their meat will taste good.* 2. the meat of a chicken *We usually eat chicken on Sunday.* **chick ens.**

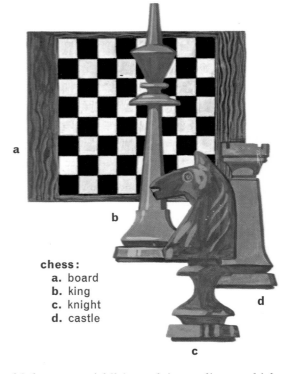

chess:
  a. board
  b. king
  c. knight
  d. castle

chick en pox (chik′ən poks), *n.* a disease which causes the skin to break out in red spots. *When Carl had chicken pox, it was hard for him to keep from scratching.*

chief (chēf), *n.* 1. a leader; a head of a tribe or group. *The pioneers made an agreement with the Indian chief that there would be no more fighting.* 2. a person who is in charge. *The police chief took charge personally of the case.* **chiefs.**
adj. 3. main; most important. *Hal's chief aim was a good education.*

chief ly (chēf′lē), *adv.* especially; mostly; mainly. *The pilot of an airliner is interested chiefly in safety, not in speed.*

child (chīld), *n.* 1. a baby. *The child is just learning to stand up.* 2. a young boy or girl. *That little twelve-year-old girl is a lovely child.* 3. a son or daughter. *I met Mrs. Keefe and her child in the store.* **chil dren.**

child hood (chīld′hùd), *n.* the time of being a child. *Tom's family often moved during his childhood, so he went to many different schools.* **child hoods.**

child ish (chīl′dish), *adj.* 1. of a child; like a child. *The two-year-old speaks with a cute childish voice.* 2. silly; foolish; not proper for an adult. *Why does that big man have the childish desire to show off?* **child ish ly,** *adv.*

chil dren (chil′drən), *n. pl.* more than one child. *The school yard is filled with children.*

chill (chil), *n.* 1. a coldness. *This morning was warm, but tonight there is a chill in the air.* 2. a feeling of coldness that makes the body shiver. *Even though the air was hot, he had a chill and wrapped himself in blankets.* **chills.**
v. 3. to make cold. *The dog was chilled from staying outside all night.* 4. to become cold.

cherry:
  a. fruit
  b. branch with blossoms

chest

Older people chill more easily than young people. **chills, chilled, chill ing.**

chilly (chil′ē), *adj.* 1. cool; somewhat cold. *In the fall of the year, the mornings are usually chilly.* 2. not very friendly. *The brush salesman got a chilly reception from the housewife.* **chill i er, chill i est; chill i ly,** *adv.*

chim ney (chim′nē), *n.* 1. an outside opening for smoke from a fireplace, stove, or furnace. *In homes burning oil or gas instead of coal, no heavy smoke comes from the chimney.* 2. the glass tube around the flame of an oil lamp. *The lamp's chimney keeps the little flame from being blown out by the wind.* **chim neys.**

chim pan zee (chim′pan zē′, chim pan′zē), *n.* an ape that lives in Africa. *Chimpanzees are very intelligent and can be trained to do tricks.* **chim-pan zees.**

chestnuts

chin (chin), *n.* 1. the part of the face beneath the bottom lip. *You move your chin when you chew.* **chins.**
v. 2. to pull oneself up while grasping a bar until one's chin is even with the bar. *Chinning is good for the muscles of the arms.* **chins, chinned, chin ning.**

chi na (chī′nə), *n.* 1. a fine white material made of clay baked in a special way. *This material is called china because it was invented in China; it is used for making dishes.* 2. dishes made of china. *Some china has delicately colored designs on it.*

chin chil la (chin chil′ə), *n.* 1. a small animal that lives in South America. *The fur of the chinchilla is valuable.* 2. the fur of the chinchilla, which is soft and whitish-gray. *The coat was made of chinchilla.* 3. a wool fabric used in making overcoats. *Chinchilla is especially warm and durable.* **chin chil las.**

Chi nese (chī nēz′), *adj.* 1. of or relating to China, its people or their language. *Our city's art museum has ancient Chinese art.*
n. 2. a person who lives in China. *The average Chinese earns his living by farming.* 3. the language of China. *Chinese is one of the oldest languages spoken in the world today.* **Chinese.**

chintz (chints), *n.* a cotton cloth with a somewhat hard, shiny surface. *Chintz usually is decorated with colors and designs.*

chip (chip), *n.* 1. a small piece broken or cut off something. *Start a fire with those chips of wood. We have three boxes of potato chips.* 2. an empty place where a small piece has been broken off. *Three of the dishes have chips on the edges.* 3. a small, flat, round piece of metal or plastic used in games instead of money. *We always play cards with chips.* **chips.**
v. 4. to break off small parts from. *You can't chip these heavy platters. Can you chip some ice for our lemonade?* **chips, chipped, chip ping.**

chip munk (chip′mungk), *n.* a small squirrel with stripes on its back. *Chipmunks live in holes in the ground.* **chip munks.**

chirp (chėrp), *n.* 1. a short, sharp sound made by some insects and animals. *The chirp of the crickets was the only sound in the quiet night.* **chirps.**
v. 2. to make this sound. *Crickets chirp. Sparrows chirp.* **chirps, chirped, chirp ing.**

chis el (chiz′l), *n.* 1. a tool with a strong sharp blade. *A chisel is used for cutting or making designs on wood, stone, or metal.* **chis els.**
v. 2. to cut or shape with a chisel. *The artist chiseled a statue out of the huge block of marble.* **chis els, chis eled, chis el ing.**

chiv al ry (shiv′l rē), *n.* 1. the way the ideal knight was supposed to act. *Kindness, honesty and bravery are marks of chivalry.* 2. the way of life followed by the knights and their kings. *We can use chivalry today; boys can be more courteous and helpful.*

chimpanzee

chisel

sand, āte, bâre, fäther; sent, mē, fėrn; fit, bīke; pot, rōpe, fôrt; run, pùll, rüle, cūte; noise, sound; ch, cheese; ng, long; th, thick; ₮ẖ, those; zh, treasure; ə = a in about, e in waken, i in animal, o in seldom, and u in minus.

chlo ro phyll or **chlo ro phyl** (klôr′ə fil), *n.* the green coloring matter of leaves and plants. *Sunlight helps chlorophyll make sugar and starch.*

choc o late (chôk′lət, chôk′ə lət), *n.* 1. a food made by roasting and grinding the beans of a cacao tree. *Bitter chocolate is used in cooking.* 2. a drink made from chocolate. *Mother made some hot chocolate when we came home from ice-skating.* 3. a candy made from chocolate. *My uncle always brings a large box of chocolates when he visits us.* 4. a dark brown. *The chair is chocolate in color.* **choc o lates.**
adj. 5. made or flavored with chocolate. *Chocolate ice cream tastes good.*

choice (chois), *n.* 1. a choosing; picking out; selection. *For dinner we will go to a restaurant of your choice.* 2. the power or right to choose. *If I have a choice of fruit, I'll take an apple.* 3. the thing or person chosen. *My choice for class president is Sidney.* 4. a group of things from which to choose. *You have a choice of sixty colors for painting the dining room.* **choic es.**
adj. 5. fine; select. *Our grocery store sells only choice vegetables, fruits, and meats.* **choic er, choic est.**

choir (kwīr), *n.* 1. a group of people who sing together, usually in a church. *Next Sunday the church choir will give a special afternoon concert.* 2. the part of a church in which the choir sings. *Workmen are repairing the choir.* 3. any group of singers. *The band has recently added a choir.* **choirs.**

choke (chōk), *v.* 1. to stop the breathing by blocking the air coming through the wind-pipe. *He took such a large bite of food that it choked him.* 2. to block up; fill up. *Our small river was choked with mud, leaves, and junk that people threw in it.* 3. to keep from growing. *Unless you take care of your garden, the weeds will choke your flowers.* **chokes, choked, chok ing.**

n. 4. a valve in an engine that controls the mixture of air and gasoline. *On many automobiles the choke is automatic.* **chokes.**

choose (chüz), *v.* 1. to pick out. *Choose the kind of candy you want.* 2. to prefer. *I do not choose to tell you my age.* **choos es, chose, chos en, choos ing.**

chop (chop), *v.* 1. to cut by hitting with a sharp tool like an ax. *The lumber company is chopping down the forest.* 2. to cut into tiny pieces. *You may chop the nuts to put over your ice cream.* **chops, chopped, chop ping.**
n. 3. a cut of meat. *I like pork chops.* 4. a short, cutting hit. *We heard the chop of the ax.* **chops.**

chops (chops), *n. pl.* 1. jaws. 2. the fleshy part about the mouth. *The dog licked his chops after eating.*

chore (chôr), *n.* an odd job; a task around the home. *One of my chores is mowing the lawn.* **chores.**

cho rus (kôr′əs), *n.* 1. a group of people singing together. *The chorus gave a concert.* 2. a number of voices speaking together. *There was a chorus of "yes" when the teacher asked the class if they wanted to go on a picnic.* 3. the part of a song that is repeated. *Most songs have verses before the chorus, which is the melody we remember.* **cho rus es.**
v. 4. to say together. *"Good morning," chorused the class.* **cho rus es, cho rused, cho rus ing.**

chose (chōz), past tense of **choose.**

cho sen (chō′zn), *adj.* picked out by choice. *A chosen group of Eagle Scouts guarded the flag.*

Christ (krīst), *n.* Jesus, regarded by Christians as being the Son of God. *The title "Christ" is from the Greek word meaning "Messiah."*

chris ten (kris′n), *v.* to give a name to at the time of admission into the Christian church. *The baby was chistened "Stephen."* **chris tens, chris tened, chris ten ing.**

Chris tian (kris′chən), *n.* 1. a person who

cicada

chorus

chrysanthemum

circle

believes in the teachings of Jesus Christ. *A Christian is a member of the largest religious group in the world.* **Chris tians.**

adj. 2. having to do with Christ or his teachings. *He has the Christian ideals of love and mercy.* 3. belonging to the religion based on the teachings of Jesus Christ. *Christian missionaries can be found in most parts of the world.* 4. having the qualities of a real Christian, such as love of one's fellow man, a desire to help others, etc. *Although he belongs to no church, he has a Christian philosophy of life.*

Christ mas (kris′məs), *n.* December 25, celebrated as the day of Christ's birth. *Christmas is the most joyous Christian holiday of the year.* **Christ mas es.**

chry san the mum (kri san′thə məm), *n.* a plant with round flowers that bloom in fall. *The blossoms of the chrysanthemum vary in size and range in color from white or yellow to pink or red.* **chry san the mums.**

chuck le (chuk′l), *v.* 1. to laugh quietly; laugh to oneself. *I chuckled as I read the book.* **chuck-les, chuck led, chuck ling.**

n. 2. a quiet laugh. *His humorous speech caused chuckles in the audience.* **chuck les.**

chum (chum), *n.* a close friend. *Years ago we were chums, doing everything together.* **chums.**

chunk (chungk), *n.* a thick, solid piece. *The dog ate a chunk of meat.* **chunks.**

church (chėrch), *n.* 1. a building in which Christians worship. *Our church has many activities for young people.* 2. an organized Christian group. *She attends the Presbyterian church.* 3. a religious service. *Church begins at ten o'clock.* **church es.**

adj. 4. of or relating to a church. *I love church music.*

churn (chėrn), *n.* 1. a container for shaking or

stirring milk so that it makes butter. *In pioneer days, most farm families owned churns.* **churns.**

v. 2. to shake or stir milk rapidly in a churn. *Churning milk by hand requires strength.* 3. to stir up; to shake. *The ship's propeller churned the water.* **churns, churned, churn ing.**

ci ca da (sə kā′də), *n.* a large insect with transparent wings. *The male cicada makes a loud sound.* **ci ca das.**

cig a rette also **cig a ret** (sig′ə ret′, sig′ə ret′), *n.* tobacco enclosed in a thin tube of paper for smoking. *Smoking cigarettes may cause serious illness.* **cig a rettes** also **cig a rets.**

cinch (sinch), *n.* 1. a strap that holds the saddle or a pack on a horse or other animal. *Fasten the cinch to make sure the saddle is firmly in place.* **cinch es.**

v. 2. to bind or fasten with a cinch; to fix firmly. *Our troop leader told us to cinch the packs on our backs before we began the hike.* **cinch es, cinched, cinch ing.**

cin der (sin′dər), *n.* 1. a piece of coal or wood that has been only partly burned. *We spread cinders on the sidewalk on icy days so that people won't slip.* 2. a coal that is still burning but not flaming. *Pour water over the cinders before we leave camp.* 3. **cinders,** ashes. *If coal or wood is completely burned, only cinders remain.* **cin ders.**

cir cle (sėr′kl), *n.* 1. a closed curve, forming a perfectly round figure. *Every part of a circle is the same distance from the center.* 2. the figure made by this kind of line. *A ring and a coin are circles.* 3. a group of people that have interests in common. *My circle of friends gets larger as I grow older. The family circle is still most important to me.* **cir cles.**

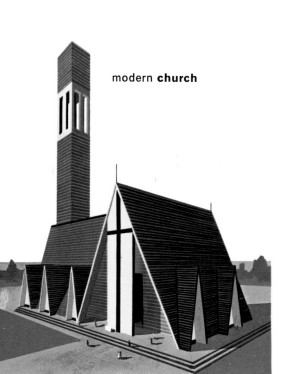

modern **church**

v. 4. to move in a circle around. *The pilot circled the landing field three times before he came down.* 5. to surround. *The police circled the building where the President was speaking.* **cir cles, cir cled, cir cling.**

cir cuit (sẻr′kət), *n.* 1. a going around. *The moon's circuit of the earth takes twenty-eight days. Every year the earth makes a circuit of the sun.* 2. the path of an electric current. *If a circuit is broken, it is called a "short circuit," and lights go out.* 3. a trip made regularly to perform certain duties. *The judge made a circuit of the county to conduct trials in small towns.* 4. a line or distance around an area or space. *You can make a long circuit around this ranch on horseback.* 5. a group of theaters managed by the same people. *Years ago, performers traveled the circuit.* **cir cuits.**

cir cu lar (sẻr′kyə lər), *adj.* 1. round; having the shape of a circle. *A lighthouse is usually a circular building.* 2. moving in a circle. *A merry-go-round is a circular ride.* **cir cu lar ly,** *adv.* *n.* 3. a printed advertisement sent or given to many people. *Every day the mail brings us at least two circulars announcing a big sale.* **cir cu lars.**

cir cu late (sẻr′kyə lāt′), *v.* 1. to move in a regular path back to a starting point. *The blood, pumped from the heart, circulates throughout the body and returns to the heart.* 2. to pass around; send out. *The free tickets to the ball game were circulated by mail.* **cir cu lates, cir cu lat ed, cir cu lat ing.**

cir cu la tion (sẻr′kyə lā′shən), *n.* 1. the movement of the blood in the body. *People get tired easily if their circulation is slow.* 2. a moving around; going from one to another. *Statements that are false seem to get quick circulation.* 3. the number of copies a magazine or newspaper sells. *The circulation of the newspaper went up when it added a new comic strip.* **cir cu la tions.**

cir cum fer ence (sər kum′fər əns), *n.* the dis-tance around a circle. *You can measure the circumference of a tree trunk by putting a tape measure around it.* **cir cum fer enc es.**

cir cum stance (sẻr′kəm stans′), *n.* 1. a fact; event. *It was a lucky circumstance that my neighbor happened to arrive just as I got a flat tire.* 2. **circumstances,** (a) the facts; events concerning a situation. *Now, please tell the judge the circumstances that brought you here.* (b) a state or condition in which one lives. *If a man is wealthy, he is said to be in good circumstances.* **cir cum stan ces.**

cir cus (sẻr′kəs), *n.* 1. a show featuring animal acts, clowns, men and women on trapezes, and acrobats. *A circus may be held under a tent or—especially in cities—in a large auditorium.* 2. a place in ancient Rome where games and races were held. *Romans held chariot races in the circus.* **cir cus es.**

cit i zen (sit′ə zn), *n.* a member of a nation who has rights, such as voting, and who also has the duty of being loyal to the nation. *A person born in this country is a citizen. People from other countries may become citizens of the United States.* **cit i zens.**

cit rus (sit′rəs), *n.* 1. a tree on which grow lemons, limes, oranges, or grapefruit. *The citrus fruit grows best in rather warm climates where there is not much wind or frost.* *adj.* 2. (also spelled **citrous**) of these trees and these fruits. *He is a citrus dealer.*

city (sit′ē), *n.* a large and important town. *The largest cities in the United States are New York, Chicago, Los Angeles, Philadelphia, and Detroit.* **cit ies.**

civ ic (siv′ik), *adj.* 1. of a city. *The mayor announced plans for an enormous new civic development, including new apartments, highways, and office buildings.* 2. of citizens. *Voting is a civic duty.*

civ il (siv′l), *adj.* 1. having to do with a citizen or citizens. *The United States Constitution guarantees the civil rights of all citizens, regardless of race, religion, or sex.* 2. not military or religious. *They asked for a civil marriage by a judge. The soldier was glad to return to civil life.* 3. polite; courteous. *The boy gave us a civil answer.*

civ i li za tion (siv′ə lə zā′shən), *n.* 1. an advanced stage in the way of life of a people. *The discovery that man could grow plants and tame animals was one of the first steps toward civilization.* 2. the way of life of a nation at a certain time. *The early Egyptian civilization produced great works in mathematics and in art.* 3. the countries and people who have a way of life beyond that of primitive tribes. *The missionary returned to civilization after three years in the jungle.* **civ i li za tions.**

claim (klām), *v.* 1. to ask for the return of something that one owns. *George claimed his suitcase at the baggage department in the train*

circus

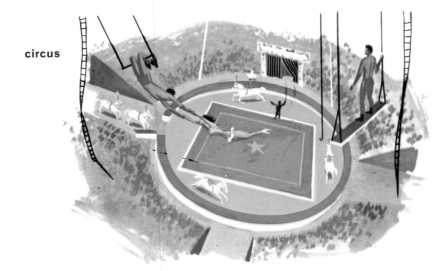

station. 2. to require; need. *The study of science claims all my attention.* 3. to say; state the facts. *Bill claims that the store charged him too much.* **claims, claimed, claim ing.**

n. 4. a demand for something as a right. *When I found out that the land actually belonged to someone else, I withdrew my claim on it.* 5. something that is claimed. *The prospector filed his claim in court for the mine he thought had gold in it.* 6. something said as a fact. *Charles claims his dog can count to ten.* **claims.**

clam (klam), *n.* 1. an oyster-like shellfish that can be eaten raw or cooked. *Clams live in sand along the ocean coasts.* **clams.**

v. 2. to dig for clams. *She goes clamming every day during the season.* **clams, clammed, clam ming.**

clang (klang), *n.* 1. a loud, ringing sound of pieces of metal being hit together. *We heard the clang of the big fire engine's bell.* **clangs.**

v. 2. to make this sound. *The bell in the town hall steeple clangs whenever there is a fire in our town.* **clangs, clanged, clang ing.**

clap (klap), *v.* 1. to strike the insides of the hands together. *The audience clapped after his speech to show their admiration.* 2. to hit with the palm of the hand to show friendship or offer congratulations. *When I graduated, mother kissed me, and dad clapped me on the shoulder.* **claps, clapped, clap ping.**

n. 3. a sudden loud noise or crash. *First came the flash of lightning and then the clap of thunder.* **claps.**

clar i net (klar′ə net′), *n.* a woodwind musical instrument. *Clarinets are played in orchestras and bands.* **clar i nets.**

class (klas), *n.* 1. a group of students meeting regularly with a teacher. *My English class is the first class of the day.* 2. a group of students in the same year at school. *My aunt went to the thirty-fifth reunion of her graduation class.* 3. persons, animals, or things thought of as a group because they are alike. *Dogs belong to the class of mammals. The truck driver is a member of the working class. A diamond is of the mineral class.* **class es.**

v. 4. to put in a class or group. *The library classes books according to subject matter.* **class es, classed, class ing.**

class mate (klas′māt′), *n.* a person who is in the same class at school. *You make many friends among your classmates.* **class mates.**

class room (klas′rüm′), *n.* a room in a school or college where classes meet. *The children in kindergarten decorate their classroom at Christmas, Thanksgiving, and Halloween.* **class rooms.**

clav i chord (klav′ə kôrd′), *n.* an old-fashioned musical instrument. *The clavichord was gradually changed by different inventions until the modern piano was produced.* **clav i chords.**

claw (klô), *n.* 1. one of the sharp, curved nails on the foot of an animal or bird. *Cats can use*

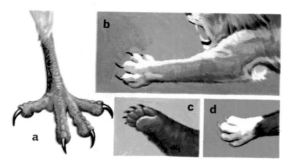

claws: **a.** bird of prey; **b.** lion; **c.** bear; **d.** cat

their claws to protect themselves, to catch food, and to climb trees. 2. the firm holding part on the front legs of a lobster or crab. *Claws are used for grasping other animals.* 3. something that is like a claw. *The claw of a hammer takes out nails.* **claws.**

v. 4. to scratch or tear with the claws. *We watched the lion claw his meat at feeding time.* **claws, clawed, claw ing.**

clay (klā), *n.* soft, sticky earth, which can be molded into different forms and then hardened in ovens. *Bricks, pottery, and tile are made of clay.* **clays.**

clean (klēn), *adj.* 1. not dirty. *Put on clean clothes to go visiting.* 2. with no evil thoughts of bad deeds. *He has led a clean life.* 3. skillful. *The swimmer made a clean dive into the water. This barber gives a clean shave.* 4. complete. *The family made a clean break from the town by moving away.* **clean er, clean est.**

adv. 5. wholly; completely. *He drove clean out of his way to get me the newspaper.* 6. in a fair way. *Always fight clean.*

v. 7. to make clean. *I cleaned my room before I went out to play.* **cleans, cleaned, clean ing, clean ly,** *adv.*

clean er (klēn′ər), *n.* 1. a person whose job is cleaning. *Take your dirty clothes to the cleaner.* 2. something used to take out dirt. *We bought a new cleaner for the windows.* **clean ers.**

clear (klir), *adj.* 1. having no clouds; bright. *The sun shone in the clear sky.* 2. distinct; not fuzzy or dim. *You get a clear view across the*

clarinet

clavichord

lake from this tower. 3. easy to understand. *He has a clear voice.* 4. easy to see through; transparent. *Through the clear water we could see the fish swimming.* 5. having no marks or flaws. *The girl has a clear skin.* 6. able to think well; not confused. *He has a mind that is clear and quick.* 7. not feeling guilty; innocent. *He had nothing to worry about; he had a clear conscience about the trouble at school.* 8. without any obstacles; having nothing in the way. *Follow this clear path through the woods to reach the road.* **clear er, clear est.**

adv. 9. in a clear manner. *The shouts came across the river loud and clear.*

v. 10. to make or become clear. *The sky soon cleared after the rain.* 11. to remove; take away. *Clear the garage of all those empty cans.* 12. to jump over without touching. *The horse cleared the bar by six inches.* 13. to make a profit of. *The Girl Scout troop cleared over thirty dollars on its cookie sale.* **clears, cleared, clear ing; clear ly,** *adv.*

clear ing (klir′ing), *n.* a piece of land with trees removed from it. *The pioneers first made a clearing, then built their houses.* **clear ings.**

clef (klef), *n.* a sign in music that shows the pitch of the notes. *Notes in the treble clef are usually above middle C, and the notes in the bass clef are mainly below it.* **clefs.**

clerk (klėrk), *n.* 1. a person who works in an office typing letters, filing orders, and keeping records. *A city clerk or county clerk is in charge of all records for the city or county.* 2. a person who sells things in a store. *My sister has a summer job as a clerk in a drugstore.* **clerks.**

v. 3. to hold a job as a clerk. *He goes to school in the day, and clerks at night.* **clerks, clerked, clerk ing.**

clev er (klev′ər), *adj.* 1. fast in thinking; smart. *You have to be clever to be a good television comic.* 2. skillful. *My neighbor is clever at making his own*

furniture in his workshop. 3. quick to catch on. *My dog is not very clever at learning tricks; in fact, he acts kind of stupid!* **clev er er, clev er est; clev er ly,** *adv.*

click (klik), *n.* 1. a short, sharp sound. *The camera made a click as I pressed the button to take the picture.* **clicks.**

v. 2. to make this sound. *The lady clicked her purse shut and quickly got off the bus.* 3. to become a success. *The singer clicked in his very first appearance.* **clicks, clicked, click ing.**

cliff (klif), *n.* a high, steep rock with a side that goes almost straight up. *Cliffs are difficult to climb.* **cliffs.**

cli mate (kli′mət), *n.* the average weather conditions of a place. *The Arctic has a cold climate; the jungles have a warm or hot climate.* **cli mates.**

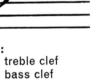

clef:
a. treble clef
b. bass clef

climbing a **cliff**

steep **cliff** in a mountain range

cli max (klī′maks), *n.* the most exciting part; the final, highest point of interest. *The climax of the story came when the girl learned that the bank robber was her father.* **cli max es.**

climb (klīm), *v.* 1. to go up or down. *The men climbed the mountain. The baby climbed the stairs.* 2. to grow up. *The ivy climbed the side of the building.* 3. to get to have a more important job. *He climbed from errand boy to vice-president.* **climbs, climbed, climb ing.**
n. 4. the act of climbing; a going up. *That last climb wore me out completely.* **climbs.**

clip[1] (klip), *v.* 1. to cut off; trim. *A poodle's hair must be clipped every six weeks. The barber clipped Bob's hair very short.* **clips, clipped, clip ping.**
n. 2. something that has been cut off. *Please sweep up those hair clippings.* **clips.**

clip[2] (klip), *v.* 1. to hold or grip tightly. *Clip all these papers together.* **clips, clipped, clip ping.**
n. 2. something used to hold things together. *You will need a strong paper clip for all these papers.* **clips.**

clip ping (klip′ing), *n.* an article or picture cut from a newspaper or magazine. *She tacked clippings of the popular singers on her bedroom walls.* **clip pings.**

cloak (klōk), *n.* 1. a loose outer garment. *Years ago men wore cloaks instead of overcoats.* 2. something that covers or hides. *His nice words were a cloak for the bad things he did.* **cloaks.**
v. 3. to cover or hide with a cloak. *Fog cloaks the city. He cloaked a sentimental heart with a sharp, tough attitude.* **cloaks, cloaked, cloak ing.**

clock[1] (klok), *n.* 1. a device made to tell the time. *A clock is not made to be carried or worn as a watch is.* **clocks.** (See illustration on following page.)
v. 2. to time with a watch. *The runner was clocked at only four minutes for the mile.* **clocks, clocked, clock ing.**

clock[2] (klok), *n.* a design or ornament on the side of a sock or stocking. *My aunt knitted a pair of gray socks with black clocks on them for my birthday.* **clocks.**

clock wise (klok′wīz′), *adv.* 1. in the direction in which the hands of a clock turn. *The plane circled clockwise in the sky.*
adj. 2. moving or directed clockwise. *Traffic moved clockwise around the village square.*

clois ter (klois′tər), *n.* 1. a covered walk built around a courtyard. *Cloisters can be seen in colleges, churches, and monasteries.* 2. monastery; convent. *Monks live in cloisters called monasteries; nuns live in cloisters called convents.* **clois ters.**

close (klōz for 1–5, klōs for 6–13), *v.* 1. to shut. *Close the door when you leave.* 2. to come to an end. *School closes on June 14.* 3. to bring or come together. *The child's eyelids slowly closed, and she was asleep.* 4. to fill up; stop up. *The workmen closed the big hole in the street.* **clos es, closed, clos ing, close ly,** *adv.*
n. 5. a finish; an ending. *At the close of the*

cloister

candidate's speech, the audience stood up and cheered. **clos es.**
adj. 6. near. *We planted the tree close to the house. It is close to lunchtime.* 7. stuffy; without fresh air. *The room is close, so open the windows.* 8. almost equal or even. *It was a close game, but they won.* 9. familiar; very dear. *The two girls have been close friends all through school.* 10. stingy. *He is close with his money, even though he is well-off.* 11. with not much space. *Three can fit in that seat, but it will be close.* 12. **close quarters,** crowded space. *We lived in close quarters last summer when we had five house guests.* **clos er, clos est.**
adv. 13. near. *We will follow close behind.*

clos et (kloz′it), *n.* 1. a small room for storing things. *We keep blankets and sheets in the hall linen closet. Each bedroom has a closet for hanging dresses and suits.* **clos ets.**
v. 2. to shut up in a room for private talk. *The leaders of the two nations closeted themselves for a talk about a peace treaty.* **clos ets, clos et ed, clos et ing.**

cloth (klôth), *n.* 1. a material made by weaving threads of cotton, wool, silk, nylon, etc. *Most of our clothes are made of cloth.* 2. a special piece of cloth. *Where are the polishing cloths I use for the car?* **cloths.**

clothe (klōth), *v.* 1. to dress; put clothes on. *He clothed himself warmly on this winter day.* 2. to supply with clothes. *A husband's task is to feed and clothe his family.* 3. to cover. *The buildings were clothed in snow.* **clothes, clothed** or **clad, cloth ing.**

clothes (klōz), *n. pl.* garments; articles of dress; things worn for covering the body. *Clothes can be bought or made.*

cloth ing (klōth′ing, klō′thing), *n.* clothes; things worn to cover the body. *People of different climates wear different clothing.*

cloud (kloud), *n.* 1. a large gray or white mass of tiny water drops floating in the sky. *Names have been given by scientists to different kinds of clouds.* 2. a mass of smoke, dust, or steam floating in the air. *A cloud of dust followed the car as it sped down the dry country road.* 3. many things moving together. *A cloud of mosquitoes ruined our*

CLOCKS THROUGH THE AGES

fourteenth century hourglass

seventeenth century standing wall clock

alarm clock

eighteenth century console wall clock

cuckoo clock

twentieth century lady's wristwatch

nineteenth century man's pocket watch

sixteenth century gilded bronze clock

twentieth century man's wristwatch

evening outdoors. 4. something that will cause trouble or unhappiness. *The adopted boy lived under a cloud of fear that he would be sent back to the orphan's home.* **clouds.**

v. 5. to grow or become cloudy. *The sky clouded.* 6. to become gloomy or sad. *The boys' face clouded when he struck out at bat.* **clouds, cloud ed, cloud ing.**

cloudy (kloud′ē), *adj.* 1. covered with clouds. *The cloudy sky was followed by rain.* 2. muddy; not clear. *The drinking water was cloudy. The speaker's ideas seemed cloudy to me.* **cloud i er, cloud i est; cloud i ly,** *adv.*

clo ver (klō′vər), *n.* a sweet-smelling plant with leaves growing in three parts. *White clover is grown in pastures and is often seen in lawns; red clover is used for food for cows and horses when it dries.* **clo vers.**

clo ver leaf (klō′vər lēf′), *n.* a place where highways meet, with one going under the other. *The entrances and exits of a cloverleaf allow cars to avoid cross-traffic turns.* **clo ver leaves.**

clown (kloun), *n.* 1. a man who acts funny, and dresses up in strange costumes. *Clowns appear in circuses and on television shows for children.* **clowns.**

v. 2. to act like a clown; be funny. *There's always a boy in class who likes to clown.* **clowns, clowned, clown ing.** (See illustration on following page.)

club (klub), *n.* 1. a heavy wooden stick used as a weapon. *Cavemen carried clubs for protection.* 2. a stick of wood or metal used for playing golf. *Golfers usually play with eight or nine clubs, each made to hit the ball a certain way.* 3. a group of people meeting for a common purpose. *Mother belongs to a bridge club and to the Women's Club; Dad is a member of a businessmen's club.*

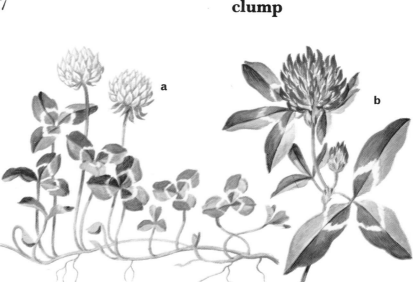

clover: **a.** white clover;   **b.** red clover

4. a place where a group of people can meet. *The dinner will be held at the country club.* **clubs.**

v. 5. to beat with a club. *She clubbed the poisonous snake to death.* **clubs, clubbed, club bing.**

cluck (kluk), *n.* 1. a sound made by a hen. *When a hen calls her chickens, it sounds like "cluck, cluck."* **clucks.**

v. 2. to make this sound. *We could hear the hens clucking in the barnyard.* **clucks, clucked, cluck ing.**

clump (klump), *n.* 1. a group of things together; a cluster. *The fox was hidden in a clump of trees.* 2. a chunk; a lump. *Don't bring any clumps of dirt into the house.* 3. a heavy sound of footsteps. *We heard the clump of the soldiers passing in front of our house.* **clumps.**

v. 4. to walk clumsily and noisily. *The tired old*

four **cloud** formations: **a.** stratocumulus;   **b.** cirrus;   **c.** cumulus;   **d.** altocumulus

clowns

horse clumped down the street. **clumps, clumped, clump ing.**

clum sy (klum′zē), *adj.* 1. without skill or grace. *I am a clumsy dancer.* 2. badly made. *The boy's model airplane was a clumsy piece of work, but he liked it.* **clum si er, clum si est; clum si ly,** *adv.*

clus ter (klus′tər), *n.* 1. a group of things growing or gathered together. *The girl picked a cluster of flowers.* **clus ters.**
v. 2. to gather together. *The people clustered in the hall to keep out of the rain.* **clus ters, clus tered, clus ter ing.**

clutch (kluch), *v.* 1. to grasp; to hold tightly. *The small boy clutched his big brother's hand.* 2. to seize with the hands or claws; to grab. *The hawk quickly clutched the hen in its claws.* **clutch es, clutched, clutch ing.**
n. 3. a tight hold; a firm grasp. *Timmy kept a tight clutch on the fireman's neck as they came down the ladder.* 4. a device in a machine that puts parts into gear and out of gear, helping the machine to run or to stop running. *He pressed down quickly on the clutch to keep the gears from grinding.* 5. power; control. *The magician had the princess in his clutches.* **clutch es.**

clut ter (klut′ər), *n.* 1. a group of various things piled or scattered about in an untidy way. *The baby left a clutter of toys in the living room.* **clut ters.**
v. 2. to place or leave things in an untidy way. *The girl cluttered her room with clothes, books, pictures, and old shoes.* **clut ters, clut tered, clut ter ing.**

coach (kōch), *n.* 1. a closed carriage drawn by horses. *Before railroads, people used to travel between cities and towns by coach.* 2. a passenger car on a train. *The train I was on had ten coaches and only one dining car.* 3. a person who trains athletes; person who teaches. *The football coach is always happy when the team wins. Mary's singing coach said she had a chance to go on the stage.* **coach es.**
v. 4. to teach; to train; to tutor in a special subject. *This summer a college student is coaching Sam in arithmetic.* **coach es, coached, coach ing.**

coal (kōl), *n.* 1. a black, hard substance found underground, used as a fuel for heating and for power. *Coal is gradually being replaced by oil and gas in homes and in industry.* 2. a piece of wood or charcoal that is still red-hot. *Campers bake potatoes in the coals of an outdoor fire.* **coals.**
v. 3. to take in a supply of coal. *The ship was stopping only for coaling.* **coals, coaled, coaling.**

coarse (kôrs), *adj.* 1. composed of large particles. *Our driveway is made of coarse gravel.* 2. not polite; crude. *He tells coarse jokes to everybody, including people he meets for the first time.* 3. of poor quality. *The prisoners were fed coarse food, and were given coarse clothing to wear.* **coars er, coars est; coarse ly,** *adv.*

coast (kōst), *n.* 1. the seashore; land along the sea or ocean. *The coasts of our country have many ports where ships from other lands unload goods.* 2. a slide downhill. *Let me have one more coast on your sled.* **coasts.**
v. 3. to sail along a seacoast. *The ship coasted from port to port. I would like to coast along the Pacific shore in a sailboat.* 4. to slide downhill on a sled. *In the winter we go coasting on King hill.* 5. to ride without using effort. *A boy can coast on his bicycle without moving the pedals.* **coasts, coast ed, coast ing.**

coast al (kōs′tl), *adj.* along a coast; near the seashore. *Coastal waters are often warmer than those far out at sea.*

coat (kōt), *n.* 1. an outer garment with sleeves. *In winter I wear a heavy coat over my other clothes.* 2. the hair or fur of an animal. *She brushes her cat's coat to keep it smooth.* 3. a covering. *I think this room will need two coats of paint. He has a deep coat of tan from being in the sun.* **coats.**
v. 4. to cover with a coat or layer. *Deep snow coated the roads.* **coats, coat ed, coat ing.**

coat of arms, 1. a special design which represents the history of a family, country, etc. *Long ago, many noble families in England had flags displaying their coats of arms.* 2. a shield or similar shape used to represent a government, a city, and sometimes a business. *Because of its many interesting details, Canada's coat of arms is very colorful.* **coats of arms.**

coax (kōks), *v.* to ask for something in a nice way; to keep on asking pleasantly. *Ellen coaxed*

COATS OF ARMS

shapes of the field according to country

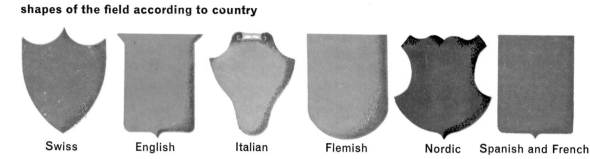

Swiss   English   Italian   Flemish   Nordic   Spanish and French

representation of colors, furs, crosses, and divisions of the field

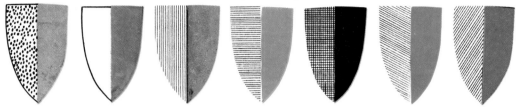

The patterns on the left of the coats of arms represent the colors on the right.

Symbols representing furs   **Symbols representing crosses**

Different ways in which coats of arms are divided

Examples of figures used on coats of arms

cobra

coffeepot

cockroach

her mother into letting her go to the movie. **coax es, coaxed, coax ing.**

cob (kob), *n.* 1. the hard part of an ear of corn on which the kernels grow. *After his family ate corn, the farmer threw the cobs to the hogs.* 2. a strong horse with short legs. *The cob pulled the big wagon easily.* **cobs.**

cob bler (kob′lər), *n.* 1. a person who mends shoes. *The cobbler put new heels on my old shoes.* 2. a fruit pie with a crust only on top. *We are having apple cobbler for dessert.* **cob blers.**

co bra (kō′brə), *n.* a poisonous snake that can widen the skin of its neck like a hood. *Cobras live mostly in India and in Africa.* **co bras.**

coch lea (kok′lē ə), *n.* a division, spiral in shape, of the internal ear. *The doctor diagnosed her earache as an infection in the cochlea.* **coch le ae** (kok′ lē ē′).

cock[1] (kok), *n.* 1. a rooster. *When the cock crows at dawn, let's get up.* 2. any male bird. *The people of Mexico enjoy watching the cocks fight, and often bet on the outcome.* 3. a faucet or valve that regulates the flow of water or gas. *The plumber shut off the cock to stop the flow of water.* 4. the hammer of a gun. *The hunter drew back the cock of the gun as the lion came into sight.* 5. the position of the hammer of a gun when ready for firing. *The gun was at half cock.* **cocks.**
v. 6. to pull back the hammer of a gun. *The sheriff cocked his gun and shot at the target.* **cocks, cocked, cock ing.**

cock[2] (kok), *v.* 1. to tilt; tip to one side. *He cocked his hat on the back of his head.* 2. to turn toward something. *The dog cocked his ear at the sudden noise.* **cocks, cocked, cock ing.**

cock[3] (kok), *n.* 1. a pile. *There were cocks of hay in the meadow after harvesting.* **cocks.**
v. 2. to pile. *Jerry helped Uncle Frank cock the hay.* **cocks, cocked, cock ing.**

cock pit (kok′pit′), *n.* the space where the pilot and passengers sit in a small airplane. *They could watch the pilot as he worked the controls in the cockpit.* **cock pits.**

cock roach (kok′rōch′), *n.* an insect pest, with a black or brown body and long feelers, found in kitchens and other places where there is food or moisture. *Cockroaches run around mostly at night.* **cock roach es.**

co coa (kō′kō), *n.* 1. a powder made of chocolate. *Put two teaspoons of cocoa into a cup of hot milk for a delicious drink.* 2. the drink made from this powder. *A cup of hot cocoa just before bedtime sometimes helps you to sleep better.*

co co nut or **co coa nut** (kō′kə nut′), *n.* the large, hard-shelled fruit of the coconut palm tree. *Coconuts have an inside white layer that is good to eat; the center contains a clear liquid, called milk, that is good to drink.* **co co nuts** or **co coa nuts.**

co coon (kə kün′), *n.* the silk covering made by a caterpillar to live in. *When the cocoon opens, the caterpillar comes out as a butterfly or as a moth.* **co coons.**

cod (kod), *n.* a large fish used for food. *Cod are caught in the cold waters of the North Atlantic Ocean.* **cod** or **cods.**

code (kōd), *n.* 1. a group of laws or rules by which people live. *Our village has a building code. States have criminal codes.* 2. a set of rules for conducting oneself. *My mother has a strict moral code: no lying, no cheating, or doing anything wrong; I hope I can be like her.* 3. a set of secret signals for sending messages. *The plans for the surprise attack were sent by code.* 4. any system used for sending messages. *The navy uses several codes: flags, lights, and radio.* **codes.**
v. 5. to put into a code. *The captain coded his message before sending it to the general.* **codes, cod ed, cod ing.**

cod fish (kod′fish′), *n.* cod. *My father's favorite dinner is codfish, baked potatoes, and salad.* **cod fish es** or **cod fish.**

cof fee (kôf′ē), *n.* 1. a drink made from the beans of the coffee plant. *The beans must be ground before coffee is made.* 2. the beans or seeds of the coffee plant. *The United States buys much of its coffee from Brazil.*

cof fee pot (kof′ē pot′), *n.* a pot in which coffee is made. *We bought an electric coffeepot to replace the one that had to be heated on the stove.* **cof fee pots.**

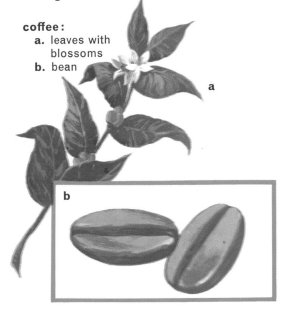

coffee:
a. leaves with blossoms
b. bean

co he sion (kō hē′zhən), *n.* 1. a sticking together. *Sharing many interests has given our friendship cohesion.* 2. the process by which the particles of a substance are bound together; attraction between molecules of the same kind. *Drops of liquid result from cohesion.*

coil (koil), *v.* 1. to wind in circles; wind around and around. *The garden hose was coiled, and then was hung on the wall. Vines were coiled around the fence posts.* **coils, coiled, coil ing.**
n. 2. anything wound in circles. *A telephone repairman carries coils of wires in his truck.* **coils.**

coin (koin), *n.* 1. a piece of metal money. *Pennies, nickels, dimes, and quarters are coins.* 2. metal money in general. *Governments make coins by stamping metals.* **coins.**
v. 3. to make metal into coins. *The United States has two mints where it coins money; one is in Philadelphia, the other in Denver.* 4. to make up or invent. *The English language has many words that have been coined recently.* **coins, coined, coin ing.**

coke (kōk), *n.* coal that has had much of its gases removed by heating. *Coke gives off very little smoke when it is burned.*

col an der (kul′ən dər, kol′ən dər), *n.* a sieve-like bowl-shaped container with holes in the side and bottom, used to drain water from vegetables and fruits. *The cook always used a colander for washing vegetables.* **col an ders.**

cold (kōld), *adj.* 1. having a low temperature; not warm; chilly. *January is usually our coldest month. The night is cold.* 2. feeling chilled. *She was cold, so she put on her coat.* 3. not friendly. *He was cold to me at our first meeting.* **cold er, cold est; cold ly,** *adv.*
n. 4. a lack of heat; lowness of temperature. *The terrible cold forced John to go inside and get warm.* 5. a common illness causing coughing, sneezing, and sore throat. *The best thing to do for a cold is stay in bed.* **colds.**

col lar (kol′ər), *n.* 1. the part of a shirt or coat that fits around the neck. *His collar was tight so he unbuttoned the neck of his shirt.* 2. a decorative band or chain of lace, cloth, or jewelry to go around the neck. *The old lady's collar of gold sparkled in the sunlight.* 3. a neckband for a dog. *I attach a leash to my dog's collar.* 4. a metal ring to hold two parts together. *A collar is used to attach a charm to a charm bracelet.* **col lars.**
v. 5. to put a collar on. *All dogs must be collared, according to our village law.* 6. to grab by the collar; take hold of. *The policeman collared the man wanted for robbery.* **col lars, col lared, col lar ing.**

col lat er al (kə lat′ər əl), *adj.* 1. aside from the main part. *The witness gave only collateral evidence.*
n. 2. the stocks, bonds, insurance policies, etc. given to a lender of money to guarantee he will be repaid. *The collateral belongs to the lender if he doesn't get back his loan.* **co lat er als.**

col lect (kə lekt′), *v.* 1. to gather; bring or come together. *A crowd collected around the burning house. Jane collected the tests from the class.* 2. to gather and keep as a hobby. *Bob collects stamps.* 3. to get money that is owed. *The landlord collected the rent.* **col lects, col lect ed, col lect ing.**

col lect ed (kə lek′tid), *adj.* calm; not disturbed or excited. *Throughout the excitement he remained collected.*

col lec tion (kə lek′shən), *n.* 1. things brought together to show or to study. *The professor has a collection of rare old books. Bob's stamp collection won a prize at the hobby show.* 2. a sum of money from many people. *When Joan was ill, the class took up a collection for flowers.* 3. any collecting or gathering together. *The deserted garden had a collection of weeds.* **col lec tions.**

col lege (kol′ij), *n.* 1. a school that is more advanced than a high school. *Many boys and girls go to college after graduation from high school.* 2. any school teaching a special subject. *A business college teaches the methods of working in a business office.* **col leg es.**

colo nel (kėr′nl), *n.* an army officer who ranks just below a general. *A colonel wears a silver eagle on the shoulder of his uniform.* **colo nels.**

col on nade (kol′ə nād′), *n.* a row of columns set the same distance apart. *Some colonnades form a court; some form a circle.* **col on nades.**

colander

colonnade:
a. enclosing a court
b. enclosing a circle

col o ny (kol′ə nē), *n.* 1. a group of people who leave their own country to live together in another land. *The early colonies in this country remained under the rule of the country from which they came.* 2. a group of people living in the same area in a city. *The artists' colony in New York holds a show of paintings every year.* 3. a group of insects, animals, or plants that live together. *A colony of ants lives in our yard.* **col o nies.**

col or (kul′ər), *n.* 1. the effect of light rays on the eyes. *All colors are combinations of red, yellow, and blue.* 2. the tint of the skin. *She has a healthy color.* 3. **the colors,** the flag. *The soldiers saluted the colors.* **col ors.**
v. 4. to change the color. *The children like to color Easter eggs.* 5. to blush. *His face colored with shame.* 6. to represent incorrectly. *Some newspapers color the news by stressing certain facts and leaving out others.* **col ors, col ored, col or ing.**

Col o ra do (kol′ə rad′ō, kol′ə rä′dō), *n.* a state in the western part of the United States. *Colorado is in the heart of the Rocky Mountains.*

col ored (kul′ərd), *adj.* belonging to a race other than the white.

col or ing (kul′ər ing), *n.* 1. something that is used to produce a color. *Coloring sometimes is put on oranges to make them look more appealing.* 2. the appearance of a person, animal, or thing in regard to color. *Some birds have a bright red coloring.* **col or ings.**

colt (kōlt), *n.* a young horse. *The newborn colt stood on its weak legs.* **colts.**

columns:
a. Egyptian
b. Greek
c. combination of the two styles

col umn (kol′əm), *n.* 1. a support or pillar for a building. *Columns are also decorative and appear in many shapes and forms.* 2. anything shaped like a pillar. *We saw a column of smoke.* 3. a straight row that goes up and down. *This book has two columns of definitions on each page.* 4. articles appearing regularly and written by one author. *He is the author of the travel-and-vacation column in the magazine.* 5. a long straight row. *A column of boys and girls marched down the football field.* **col umns.**

comb (kōm), *n.* 1. a strip of hard rubber, metal, plastic, or wood with teeth, used to smooth the hair. *Most people carry pocket combs.* 2. a tool with teeth used to make wool straight after it has been cut from the sheep. *A comb for wool is strong.* 3. the red top on the head of some birds. *Roosters have combs.* 4. the cluster of six-

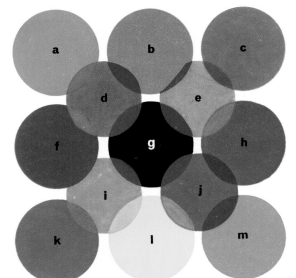

colors:
a. green
b. red
c. blue
d. purple
e. ocher
f. violet
g. black
h. brown
i. orange
j. magenta
k. sepia
l. yellow
m. cerulean blue

sided wax cells made by bees to hold their honey. *Honey is removed from combs and placed in jars for eating.* **combs.**

v. 5. to smooth with a comb. *Comb your hair before you meet the new teacher.* 6. to look through thoroughly. *The police combed the neighborhood to find the lost child.* **combs, combed, comb ing.**

com bi na tion (kom′bə nā′shən), *n.* 1. a combining or joining together. *The candy was a delicious combination of chocolate, honey, and peanuts.* 2. a thing made by combining. *Concrete is a combination of cement, sand, gravel, and water.* **com bi na tions.**

com bine[1] (kəm bīn′), *v.* 1. to join; work together. *Uncle Charlie combines his vacation trip with work.* 2. to mix. *Hydrogen and oxygen combine to make water. I combine powdered chocolate with milk to make cocoa.* **com bines, com bined, combin ing.**

com bine[2] (kom′bīn′), *n.* a big machine used on large farms to harvest grain and thresh it at the same time. *Combines are used in the wheat fields of Kansas.* **com bines.**

com bus tion (kəm bus′chən), *n.* a process of burning. *The combustion of logs in the fire produces heat.* **com bus tions.**

come (kum), *v.* 1. to move toward. *The dark clouds are coming this way.* 2. to happen; take place. *Your birthday comes once a year.* 3. to add up; amount. *The bill came to three dollars.* 4. to arrive. *What time does the bus come?* 5. to descend from. *The dog comes from a famous line of prize winners.* 6. **come about,** to happen. *How did the fire in that old building come about?* 7. **come across,** to meet without planning; to find by luck. *They came across an old friend as they walked through the town.* 8. **come out,** to be ready for sale. *The book came out in January.* 9. **come up,** to be mentioned. *The question of bringing in new members will come up at the next club meeting.* **comes, came, come, com ing.**

com e dy (kom′ə dē), *n.* 1. a funny movie or play. *The audience laughed at the comedy.* 2. any funny happening. *It was a comedy of errors.* **com e dies.**

com et (kom′it), *n.* a heavenly body that looks like a star, but has a tail of light. *A comet moves in orbit around the sun.* **com ets.**

com fort (kum′fərt), *v.* 1. to cheer up; ease grief or pain. *The little boy fell down and his mother comforted him.* **com forts, com fort ed, com fort ing.**

n. 2. a person or thing that helps to give hope or strength. *His friends were a comfort to him in his loneliness. The television set is a comfort to a hospital patient.* 3. ease; cheer; satisfaction. *A famous racehorse lives a life of comfort, with good food and plenty of space in which to run around.* **com forts.**

com fort a ble (kum′fər tə bl, kumf′tər bl), *adj.* 1. giving comfort; giving rest and peace. *We*

a rooster's **comb**

always give Grandfather the most comfortable chair.* 2. feeling comfort or ease. *This weather makes me feel comfortable—not too warm or too cold.* **com fort a bly,** *adv.*

com ic (kom′ik), *adj.* 1. funny. *The comic actions of the clown make me laugh.* 2. having to do with comedy. *The only thing he reads in the papers is the comic strips.* **com i cal,** *adj.*

n. 3. a person who does or says funny things to make people laugh. *The man in the baggy pants is a well-known comic.* 4. **comics,** funny pictures; cartoons. *Some Sunday papers have the comics in color.* **com ics.**

com ing (kum′ing), *n.* 1. an arrival; approach. *The coming of the new principal had everyone talking.* **com ings.**

adj. 2. approaching; next. *The concert will be given this coming Saturday.*

com ma (kom′ə), *n.* a punctuation mark [,] used to show a separation of words or ideas in a sentence. *You will learn about commas in your English or grammar classes.* **com mas.**

com mand (kə mand′), *v.* 1. to tell what to do; give an order to. *The general commanded the soldiers to remain and fight.* 2. to have control over. *The captain commands a ship, and all his orders should be obeyed.* **com mands, com mand ed, com mand ing.**

n. 3. an order; a direction. *Follow the commands of the policeman directing traffic.* 4. control; charge. *A captain is in command of a ship.* **com mands.**

com man der (kə man′dər), *n.* 1. a person who commands. *The superintendent of police in the city is the commander of the police force.* 2. a navy officer ranking next below a captain. *A commander wears three gold stripes on the sleeves of his uniform.* **com man ders.**

com mand ment (kə mand′mənt), *n.* a law; an order. *The Ten Commandments were given to Moses by God.* **com mand ments.**

---

sand, āte, bâre, fäther; sent, mē, fėrn; fit, bīke; pot, rōpe, fôrt; run, pùll, rüle, cūte; noise, sound; ch, cheese;
ng, long; th, thick; ~~th~~, those; zh, treasure; ə = a in about, e in waken, i in animal, o in seldom, and u in minus.

com mence (kə mens′), *v.* to begin. *The show will commence at eight o'clock.* **com menc es, com menced, com menc ing.**

com mence ment (kə mens′mənt), *n.* 1. a beginning or start. *The commencement of the show was eagerly awaited.* 2. the ceremonies during which persons receive degrees or diplomas from schools and colleges. *Commencement is an important day in a student's life.* **com mence ments.**

com mend (kə mend′), *v.* 1. to praise. *The teacher commended John for his neat work.* 2. to put into someone's care. *He commended his dog to his neighbor while he was away on vacation.* **com mends, com mend ed, com mending.**

com men da tion (kom′ən dā′shən), *n.* praise; approval. *The boy's work earned the commendation of his employer. The sailor received a commendation for his quick thinking in the battle.* **com men da tions.**

com ment (kom′ent), *n.* 1. a remark. *The teacher wrote comments on John's paper. Many people made comments about the play they just saw.* 2. talk; gossip. *We heard a lot of comment about the other team's ability and strength.* **com ments.** *v.* 3. to give views; make remarks. *The governor refused to comment about his running for president.* **com ments, com ment ed, com ment ing.**

com merce (kom′ərs), *n.* the buying and selling of goods. *Foreign commerce concerns trade between one country and another; domestic commerce is trade or business between sections of one country.*

com mer cial (kə mėr′shəl), *adj.* 1. having to do with trade or commerce. *Commercial businesses are run to make a profit.* **com mercial ly,** *adv.*
n. 2. an advertising message on a television or radio program. *Commercials usually urge people to buy a product or a service.* **com mer cials.**

com mis sion (kə mish′ən), *n.* 1. an order giving the right or duty to carry out certain activities. *All officers in the army receive a written commission from the president.* 2. a group of people appointed to get something done. *The mayor appointed a commission of businessmen and professors to study the traffic problem.* 3. the act of doing. *He was accused of the commission of a crime.* 4. money paid to a salesman. *Our company pays its salesmen a good commission for each hundred dollar sale they make.* 5. **in commission,** in working order. *After the mechanic finished working on my car, it was in commission again.* 6. **out of commission,** not in working order. *We won't be able to drive you home because our car is out of commission.* **com mis sions.**
v. 7. to give a commission to. *Doctors are commissioned when they enter the military service.* 8. to put a ship into service. *Today they commission the new submarine.* 9. to give the right or duty to do something. *My father commissioned an*

accountant to make out his income tax. **com missions, com mis sioned, com mis sion ing.**

com mis sion er (kə mish′ən ər), *n.* 1. a person who is a member of a commission. *The report is to be given by the man chosen by the commissioners.* 2. a person in charge of a government department. *The health commissioner and the water commissioner worked overtime to see that the water supply was pure.* **com mis sion ers.**

com mit (kə mit′), *v.* 1. to send to a mental hospital or to prison. *The two boys were committed to the House of Correction for six months for stealing.* 2. to do something wrong. *Charles committed an error in the fifth inning that let two runs score.* 3. to promise to do something. *I committed myself to help clean up after the party.* **com mits, com mit ted, com mit ting.**

com mit tee (kə mit′ē), *n.* a group of people named to do certain things for a larger group. *I was on the decorating committee for the class party.* **com mit tees.**

com mon (kom′ən), *adj.* 1. frequent; usual. *Temperatures of ninety degrees are common in the summer.* 2. seen or heard often. *Robins are common in this neighborhood. A common saying is "Haste makes waste."* 3. belonging to more than one person or company. *The city parks are common property, belonging to all the people. England and the United States share a common language.* 4. **in common,** shared equally by two or more. *Kate and I have one thing in common—we like the movies.* **com mon ly,** *adv.*

com mu ni cate (kə mū′nə kāt′), *v.* 1. to give ideas; exchange information. *We communicate with our western office by telephone every day.* 2. to pass along; transfer. *A stove communicates heat to the room. You can easily communicate your cold to other people.* 3. to connect. *The dining room in our house communicates with the kitchen.* **com mu ni cates, com mu ni cat ed, com mu ni cat ing.**

com mu ni ca tion (kə mū′nə kā′shən), *n.* 1. information given. *This communication just arrived by telegraph.* 2. a way or method of sending messages. *Communication among all countries is getting better as new ideas are worked out.* 3. a message; letter. *I received your communication.* **com mu ni ca tions.**

com mu ni ty (kə mū′nə tē), *n.* 1. all the people who live in one area; the residents of a town. *This town's activities are designed for the community, from the small children to the senior citizens.* 2. a group of people who live together and who are interested in the same things. *A community of artists is located on the south side of the city.* **com mu ni ties.**

com mute (kə mūt′), *v.* 1. to travel every day by train from a suburb to the city. *Some people commute sixty miles a day to go to work.* 2. to lighten a punishment already given. *The Governor commuted the convict's prison term.* **com mutes, com mut ed, com mut ing.**

com pan ion (kəm pan′yən), *n.* 1. a friend; a comrade. *I will miss Fred when we graduate, since we have been companions all through our school days.* 2. anything that matches another in kind or size or color. *We must buy a companion to that book end.* **com pan ions.**

com pa ny (kum′pə nē), *n.* 1. a group of people. *A large company gathered to see him leave.* 2. a group of people joined together for a common purpose. *A business company produces goods. A theater company puts on plays.* 3. friendship; society; association. *We enjoy each other's company.* 4. a group of soldiers, usually commanded by a captain. *In a daring attack, the company took the hill from the enemy.* 5. guests. *We are having company over for dinner, so I won't leave the house tonight.* **com pa nies.**

com par a tive (kəm par′ə tiv), *adj.* 1. done by comparing. *The agriculture department made a comparative study of the effects of the drug on cows and horses.* 2. measured by comparison with something else. *The part of the country we live in has comparative freedom from tornadoes. When we looked at last year's sales, we saw that the effort to sell tickets this year was a comparative success.* **com par a tive ly,** *adv.* *n.* 3. the second degree of comparison of an adjective or adverb. *The comparatives of large, rosy, and good are larger, rosier, and better.* **com par a tives.**

com pare (kəm pâr′), *v.* 1. to examine things to see how much alike or different they are. *The girls compared their new hairdos.* 2. to describe as being alike. *The poet compared his sweetheart to a summer day.* 3. to equal or come close to. *His story of what happened compares with the one you told me. That tree can't compare in size with the one in our yard.* **com pares, com pared, com par ing.**

com par i son (kəm par′ə sn), *n.* a comparing; being compared. *A comparison between a cat and a lion will show that both have similar habits.* 2. **no comparison,** no reason to compare because of great differences. *I think there is no comparison between those brands of ice cream; one is so much better than the other.* **com par i sons.**

com part ment (kəm pärt′mənt), *n.* any of the separate parts which divide an enclosed space. *Submarines have watertight compartments; each is locked in an emergency.* **com part ments.**

com pass (kum′pəs), *n.* 1. an instrument for finding direction. *When we go on a hike, we always carry a compass so we won't get lost.* 2. an instrument for drawing circles. *A compass has a sharp point which holds it down as the pen circles around it, creating a circle.* 3. a boundary. *He never left the compass of the town.* **com pass es.** *v.* 4. to move around; form a circle around. *The cowboys compassed the Indian village.* 5. to accomplish; achieve. *He finally compassed his aim of four A's in one semester.* **com pass es, com passed, com pass ing.**

com pel (kəm pel′), *v.* 1. to force. *The law compels automobile drivers to stop at red lights.* 2. to make do something. *The robber compelled his victims to turn over their jewels.* **com pels, com pelled, com pel ling.**

com pen sa tion (kom′pən sā′shən), *n.* 1. something that makes up for a loss. *The child's father gave her a new doll as a compensation for the one her brother accidentally broke.* 2. pay. *In most states, a worker who cannot get a job is entitled to workmen's compensation for six months.* **com pen sa tions.**

com pete (kəm pēt′), *v.* 1. to take part in a contest. *More than one hundred swimmers have signed up to compete in the state swimming meet.* 2. to be rivals. *Joan and Marjorie, although very good friends, will compete in the scholarship examination.* **com petes, com pet ed, com pet ing.**

com pe tent (kom′pə tənt), *adj.* having ability to do what is necessary; skillful; capable. *A competent person can be depended upon to do the right thing.* **com pe tent ly,** *adv.*

com pe ti tion (kom′pə tish′ən), *n.* a contest; an act of competing. *Every year the competition gets stronger in the battle for first place in the football league.* **com pe ti tions.**

com plain (kəm plān′), *v.* 1. to find fault. *People who are always complaining make me tired.* 2. to report something bad. *The neighbors complained to the police about the noisy motorcycle in the driveway across the street.* **com plains, com plained, com plain ing.**

com plaint (kəm plānt′), *n.* 1. a complaining;

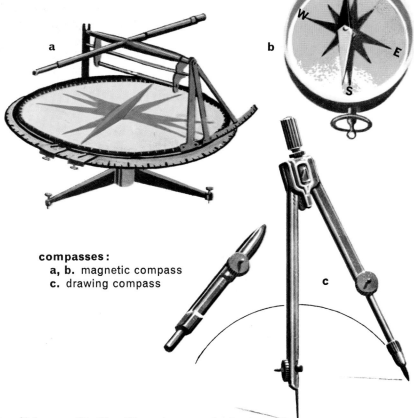

compasses :
   a, b. magnetic compass
   c. drawing compass

finding fault. *The landlord turned up the heat because of the tenant's complaints about his cold apartment.* 2. a legal charge against someone. *The man swore out a complaint against the boys who trampled on his flowers.* 3. illness; something causing pain. *She had to go to the doctor with her stomach complaint.* **com plaints.**

com plete (kəm plēt′), *v.* 1. to finish. *The new building was completed in June.* **com pletes, com plet ed, com plet ing.**
adj. 2. having no parts lacking; full. *He owns a complete set of Mark Twain's books.* 3. ended; finished. *The report by the committee will be complete tomorrow.* 4. thorough; perfect. *The gift was a complete surprise to her.* **com plete ly,** *adv.*

com ple tion (kəm plē′shən), *n.* a making or being completed or full; finishing. *The completion of a good job gives one a feeling of accomplishment.*

com pli ance (kəm plī′əns), *n.* 1. doing as requested or demanded. *His compliance to an official order was prompt.* 2. a tendency to give in to others. *His eager compliance to all our suggestions made us suspect he had no faith in his own ideas.*

com pli ment (kom′plə mənt for 1 and 2, kom′plə ment′ for 3), *n.* 1. a statement of praise or admiration. *A great musician is used to compliments about his musical ability.* 2. **compliments,** *n. pl.* greetings; respects. *I send my compliments to you on your birthday.* **com pli ments.**
v. 3. to give a compliment to; praise. *The principal complimented Bob on his record of no absences.* **com pli ments, com pli ment ed, com pli ment ing.**

com ply (kəm plī′), *v.* to do what is asked; to act according to a rule or to the law. *Most people comply with the signs stating the speed limits.* **com plies, com plied, com ply ing.**

com pose (kəm pōz′), *v.* 1. to make by putting different things together. *Concrete is composed of cement, sand, gravel, and water.* 2. to make up; to create; to write. *The words of "The Star-Spangled Banner" were composed by Francis Scott Key.* 3. to make calm; control. *Because of his nervousness, Jack had to compose himself before he made his speech.* **com pos es, com posed, com pos ing.**

com posed (kəm pōzd′), *adj.* calm; quiet. *The speaker had a composed attitude as he faced the press.* **com pos ed ly,** *adv.*

com po si tion (kom′pə zish′ən), *n.* 1. something made up and written down. *The first composition assigned by the teacher was to be called "What I Did This Summer."* 2. the work of composing. *The composition of the opera took two years.* 3. a piece of music. *The music teacher gave Betty another composition to practice.* 4. a mixture; the way the parts of a thing are put together. *In general science we study the composition of substances.* **com po si tions.**

com pound (kom′pound for 1–3, kompound′ for 4), *n.* 1. a chemical substance formed by the combination of two or more elements. *Water is a compound of hydrogen and oxygen.* 2. a mixture of two or more things. *His feeling about going to Europe was a compound of happiness and sadness.* **com pounds.**
adj. 3. formed of two or more parts. *In English you study compound sentences.*
v. 4. to make by mixing. *The drugstore will compound the medicine that the doctor prescribed.* **com pounds, com pounded, com pounding.**

com rade (kom′rad), *n.* a friend. *The two girls were comrades and were always together.* **comrades.**

con ceal (kən sēl′), *v.* to hide. *We concealed all my brother's birthday presents in the closet until the birthday party.* **con ceals, con cealed, conceal ing.**

con ceive (kən sēv′), *v.* 1. to think of; imagine. *Can you conceive that little dog scaring away a burglar?* 2. to form in the mind. *The first scientist to conceive the idea of using the energy of the atom was Albert Einstein.* 3. to understand. *Many people still can't conceive how an airplane is able to fly.* **con ceives, con ceived, conceiv ing.**

con cen trate (kon′sn trāt′), *v.* 1. to bring or come together at the same place. *Before the parade the marchers concentrated in the park.* 2. to put all attention on one thing or problem. *You will have to concentrate on this problem; it is hard!* 3. to make thicker; to make stronger. *Frozen orange juice is concentrated by removing most of the water from it.* **con cen trates, con cen trat ed, con cen trat ing.**
n. 4. something that has been concentrated. *This grape juice concentrate is good when water is added to it.* **con cen trates.**

con cept (kän sept), *n.* an idea; a thought. *The concept that all men should have an equal chance is very important to Americans.* **con cepts.**

con cep tion (kən sep′shən), *n.* an idea; a thought. *I haven't the slightest conception of how to put that puzzle together.* **con cep tions.**

con cern (kən sėrn′), *v.* 1. to relate to; to have an effect on. *The problem of world peace concerns all of us—boys, girls, men, women.* 2. to make anxious; make unhappy. *His low grade in arithmetic concerned his parents.* **con cerns, con cerned, con cern ing.**
n. 3. a worry; anxiety. *A great concern of parents is the health of their children.* 4. something that is related to one's own affairs. *My work is my own concern, not yours.* 5. a business or company. *Many concerns are moving from the city to the suburbs.* **con cerns.**

con cerned (kən sėrnd′), *adj.* 1. interested. *She is concerned in the Drama Club.* 2. worried. *The mayor is concerned by the traffic problem.*

con cern ing (kən sėr′ning), *prep.* having to do

with; about. *Concerning state politics, the governor said nothing.*

con cert (kon′sėrt), *n.* a program of music in which a number of players perform together. *Our school orchestra gives a concert every spring.* **con certs.**

con clude (kən klüd′), *v.* 1. to end; to finish. *He concluded his speech and sat down.* 2. to settle; to arrange after talking together. *The village council concluded the plans for a new parking lot.* 3. to decide; to resolve. *I concluded to do nothing about my neighbor's noisy dog.* **con cludes, con clud ed, con clud ing.**

con clu sion (kən klü′zhən), *n.* 1. the end. *We left in a hurry at the conclusion of the dinner.* 2. an opinion arrived at by thinking carefully. *The judge's conclusion was that Mr. Smith was innocent.* 3. settlement; arrangement. *The conclusion of the discussion was that Park Avenue would be a one-way street.* **con clu sions.**

con crete (kon′krēt, kon krēt′), *n.* 1. a hard substance made of cement, sand, gravel, and water. *Concrete is used for building roads.* *adj.* 2. made of concrete. *Many roads are concrete highways.* 3. actual; real; specific. *We need some worthwhile, concrete ideas for our program.*

con demn (kən dem′), *v.* 1. to say that a person or thing is wrong or bad. *The school condemns cheating.* 2. to say that something is not safe for use. *The fire department condemned the old building, so it was torn down.* 3. to sentence. *The judge condemned him to three months in prison for reckless driving.* **condemns, con demned, con demn ing.**

con den sa tion (kon′den sā′shən), *n.* 1. the change from a gas or vapor to a liquid. *Rain results from condensation of water vapor.* 2. reducing volume of a liquid by taking away water. *The condensation of orange juice results in a smaller amount to put in the container.* 3. using fewer words. *I read a condensation of the play before I saw it.* **con den sa tions.**

con dense (kən dens′), *v.* 1. to change from a gas or vapor to a liquid. *Steam condenses into water.* 2. to remove water from. *They now condense fresh grapefruit juice.* 3. to say in fewer words. *Condense your story, it is too long.* **con dens es, con densed, con dens ing.**

con di tion (kən dish′ən), *n.* 1. something that is needed before something else can be obtained. *Hard work is usually one of the conditions of being successful.* 2. the state in which a person or thing is. *The condition of his health worried us all. The weather conditions were good for flying. The summer camp is in poor condition; the storms last winter almost wrecked it.* **con di tions.** *v.* 3. to put in good shape. *Athletes condition themselves all year long.* 4. to form a habit in; get used to. *I conditioned my dog to bark once when he is hungry. He was conditioned to sleeping with noise all around him.* **con di tions, con di tioned, con di tion ing.**

condor

con dor (kon′dər), *n.* a large bird with black feathers and a bare neck. *Condors live in the high mountains of South America and California.* **con dors.**

con duct (kon′dukt for 1, kən dukt′ for 2–4), *n.* 1. behavior; way of acting. *The boy's conduct in class was good.* *v.* 2. to guide; to lead. *The student conducted the visitor through the new building.* 3. to manage; direct; be the leader of. *Today is my day to conduct the meeting of our home room.* 4. to carry; be a path for. *Copper conducts electricity. Pipes conduct water into our houses.* **con ducts, con duct ed, con duct ing.**

con duc tor (kən duk′tər), *n.* 1. a material that transmits electricity, heat, or sound. *Aluminum is a good conductor of heat.* 2. a director; leader. *All the orchestra watched the conductor as he held up his hands, ready to begin the concert.* 3. the person in charge of passengers on a train. *The conductor walked down the aisles of the train, collecting tickets.* **con duct ors.**

cone (kōn), *n.* 1. a solid object that is flat and round at one end but is pointed at the other end. *Cones are studied in geometry.* 2. anything shaped like a cone. *We eat ice-cream cones.* 3. the seed pod of an evergreen tree. *Pine cones are often used as Christmas decorations.* **cones.**

cone

con fed er a tion (kən fed′ə rā′shən), *n.* 1. a league; a union; a joining together. *A group of chiefs decided to form a confederation for mutual protection.* 2. **the Confederation,** the union of the thirteen colonies from 1781 to 1789. *The Confederation was replaced by the United States of America.* **con fed er a tions.**

---

sand, āte, bâre, fäther; sent, mē, fėrn; fit, bīke; pot, rōpe, fôrt; run, pùll, rüle, cūte; noise, sound; ch, cheese; ng, long; th, thick; ~~th,~~ those; zh, treasure; ə = a in about, e in waken, i in animal, o in seldom, and u in minus.

con fer ence (kon′fər əns), *n.* a meeting of people to discuss something. *Our teachers have a conference once a week. There will be a governors' conference in October.* **con fer enc es.**

con fess (kən fes′), *v.* 1. to admit. *Harry confessed that he was the boy who started the fight.* 2. to tell one's sins to God or a priest. *I went to church and confessed.* **con fess es, con fessed, con fess ing.**

con fi dence (kon′fə dəns), *n.* 1. a feeling of faith in oneself. *The captain's confidence made the passengers on the ship feel safe.* 2. trust; belief. *The small boy had confidence that his older brother would find the way home.* 3. a secret. *The boy and his friend shared many confidences.* 4. **in confidence,** with the belief that it will stay a secret. *He told me the whole story in confidence, so I will not repeat it.* **con fi denc es.**

con fi dent (kon′fə dənt), *adj.* sure; certain; having no doubts. *He was confident of winning the scholarship.* **con fi dent ly,** *adv.*

con fi den tial (kon′fə den′shəl), *adj.* 1. secret; private; not for public knowledge. *The ambassador sent a confidential letter to the president.* 2. allowed to handle private matters. *For years she was the confidential secretary to the company's president.* **con fi den tial ly,** *adv.*

con fine (kən fīn′ for 1 and 2, kon′fīn for 3), *v.* 1. to keep within limits. *Please confine your remarks to the subject.* 2. to keep in; to shut in. *He was confined to bed by a bad cold. The prisoner will be confined in the penitentiary.* **con fines, con fined, con fin ing.**
n. pl. 3. **confines,** a limit or boundary. *They trained the dog not to go any farther than the confines of the yard.* **con fines.**

con firm (kən fèrm′), *v.* 1. to make certain or sure. *The sound of thunder in the distance confirmed my suspicion that it would probably rain.* 2. to approve. *The principal will have to confirm your statement about leaving early.* 3. to make a person a member of a church. *Mary was confirmed last Sunday after months of study.* **con firms, con firmed, con firm ing.**

con fir ma tion (kon′fər mā′shən), *n.* 1. the act of confirming or making sure; proof. *We need confirmation of all reports from overseas. All scientific theories must have actual confirmation.* 2. a ceremony admitting a person to church membership. *My whole family attended the confirmation of my cousin.* **con fir ma tions.**

con flict (kon′flikt for 1 and 2, kən flikt′ for 3), *n.* 1. a battle; a fight. *The army is prepared for any conflict.* 2. a difference of ideas; inability to be in agreement. *There was a sharp conflict between my opinion of the accident and the other driver's opinion.* **con flicts.**
v. 3. to be against. *My idea about what game to play conflicted with his idea.* **con flicts, con flict ed, con flict ing.**

con fuse (kən fūz′), *v.* 1. to mix up in the mind; throw into disorder. *The child is getting confused with all the advice from so many people.* 2. to mistake one thing for another. *I had my dates confused in the history test.* **con fus es, con fused, con fus ing.**

con fu sion (kən fū′zhən), *n.* 1. a condition of being mixed up or being in disorder. *His room is always in confusion, with books and magazines scattered around. Poor directions caused confusion in his mind as he took the test.* 2. a mistaking of one thing for another. *There is often confusion of my name and her's because they are so much alike.*

con grat u late (kən grach′ə lāt), *v.* to give someone good wishes for some nice thing that has happened; give praise to. *All her relatives congratulated Sue when she was graduated from college.* **con grat u lates, con grat u lat ed, con grat u lat ing.**

con grat u la tion (kən grach′ə lā′shən), *n.* a good wish or praise given someone. *Please accept my congratulations on your victory in the election.* **con grat u la tions.**

con gre ga tion (kong′grə gā′shən), *n.* a group of people gathered together especially for church service. *The congregation was very quiet as the minister talked.* **con gre ga tions.**

con gress (kong′gris), *n.* 1. a meeting or getting together to make plans. *The next youth congress will meet in Cleveland.* 2. **Congress,** the national lawmaking body of the United States, consisting of the Senate and of the House of Representatives, each of which is composed of members elected by the citizens of each state. *Congress meets in the Capitol building in Washington, D.C., which is the capital of the United States.* **con gress es.**

con gru ent (kong′grü ənt, kən grü′ənt), *adj.* having exactly the same size and shape as another figure. *Two figures are congruent if all of their sides match exactly when one is placed upon the other.* **con gru ent ly,** *adv.*

con nect (kə nekt′), *v.* 1. to join two or more things together; to link one thing to another. *Before you turn on the water, connect the hose to the faucet. Airplanes connect every major city in the world.* 2. to join two ideas, events, etc. in the mind. *I connect cotton candy with the circus.* **con nects, con nect ed, con nect ing.**

Con nect i cut (kə net′ə kət), *n.* a state in the northeastern part of the United States. *Connecticut, a New England state, was one of the original Thirteen Colonies which formed the United States.*

con nec tion (kə nek′shən), *n.* 1. the connecting of one thing to another; the act of joining together. *The connection of the wires took only a few minutes.* 2. the union made by joining one thing to another; a part that joins two things together. *We had better repair the pipe line before any of the other connections break.* 3. a relation; the condition of being joined together. *Is there any connection between rainfall and temperature?* 4. a person joined to others in work, business, etc. *He has several business connections in Chicago.* 5. a person who is related, especially by marriage. *They are connections on my father's side of the family.* 6. a meeting of forms of transportation where travelers can transfer quickly from one to another. *Father had such poor connections that he was three hours late.* **con nec tions.**

con quer (kong′kər), *v.* 1. to overcome in war; to defeat by fighting. *The smaller army conquered the enemy because of better weapons and more ability. The police are always trying to conquer crime in the city.* 2. to overcome by effort in the mind. *You must conquer your bad habits.* **con quers, con quered, con quer ing.**

con science (kon′shəns), *n.* the feeling in the mind that helps a person to know right from wrong; the sense that tells a person to do what is right and not to do what is wrong. *The prisoner had committed so many crimes that he was no longer bothered by his conscience.* **con scienc es.**

con scious (kon′shəs), *adj.* 1. alert to; aware. *Are you conscious of the weight of your clothes on your body? I was not conscious of her until she called my name.* 2. awake; aware of things with the mind and the senses. *An hour after the accident he became conscious again.* **con scious ly,** *adv.*

con sent (kən sent′), *v.* 1. to agree; to permit. *Our teacher consented to our plans for a class party.* **con sents, con sent ed, con sent ing.** *n.* 2. an agreement with what is suggested or done; approval; permission. *The farmer gave his consent when we asked him if we could wait in the barn until the rain stopped.* **con sents.**

con se quence (kon′sə kwens′), *n.* 1. the result of one's actions. *If you broke the window, you must accept the consequences.* 2. importance. *The damage is of no consequence as long as no one was hurt.* **con se quenc es.**

con se quent (kon′sə kwənt′), *adj.* as a consequence; resulting; coming as a result. *The accident and consequent damage to the car made him very unhappy.*

con se quent ly (kon′sə kwent′lē), *adv.* as a result. *It rained all night and all morning; consequently, the game was canceled.*

con sid er (kən sid′ər), *v.* 1. to think carefully before doing something. *Have you considered what will happen to you if you are caught?* 2. to think of someone or something as; to regard as. *I consider that a compliment.* 3. to be kind and thoughtful to others. *He always considers the feelings of his playmates.* **con sid ers, con sid ered, con sid er ing.**

con sid er a ble (kən sid′ər ə bl), *adj.* 1. worthy of careful thought; of importance. *He made some considerable suggestions for solving our problem.* 2. a great deal of; a fairly large amount of. *You are demanding considerable payment for only a little work.* **con sid er a bly,** *adv.*

con sid er a tion (kən sid′ə rā′shən), *n.* 1. careful thinking. *Most of our time was spent in consideration of how to use the money.* 2. regard for the feelings of others; thoughtfulness for other people. *Selfish people have no consideration for the people they meet.* 3. anything taken as a reason for doing something. *Rain and cold weather were the considerations that forced us to call off the picnic.* 4. money given as payment for something; anything used as a payment or reward. *We will mow your lawn all summer for a fair consideration.* **con sid er a tions.**

con sid er ing (kən sid′ər ing), *prep.* in view of; taking into account. *He did very well in the race, considering the fact that he couldn't sleep last night.*

con sign (kən sīn′), *v.* 1. to hand over formally. *The prisoner was consigned to the guards and led from the room.* 2. to send goods; deliver something. *The books were consigned to you yesterday.* **con signs, con signed, con sign ing.**

con sist (kən sist′), *v.* to be composed of; to be made up of. *A giraffe's diet consists mainly of leaves.* **con sists, con sist ed, con sist ing.**

con sist ent (kən sis′tənt), *adj.* 1. not changing; continuing unchanged. *He could be a great ballplayer if he were consistent instead of being great one day and poor the next.* 2. in agreement with what is known or has been said. *Your story is not consistent with the facts.* **con sist ent ly,** *adv.*

con stant (kon′stənt), *adj.* 1. loyal; faithful. *Only a few constant friends offered to help him in his need.* 2. never changing or stopping; happening again and again. *The constant beat of the rain on the windows put us to sleep. The constant hum in the classroom began to annoy the teacher.* **con stant ly,** *adv.*

con stel la tion (kon′stə lā′shən), *n.* a group of stars with a name. *The ancients named certain constellations after the animals they seemed to form in the sky, such as Taurus, the Bull, and Cygnus, the Swan.* **con stel la tions.** (See illustration on following page.)

con sti tu tion (kon′stə tü′shən, kon′stə tū′shən), *n.* 1. the way in which a person's body is made up and operates. *He has a strong constitution and never gets ill.* 2. the way in which anything is made up. *The scientists tried to discover the constitution of the strange metal.* 3. the rules, laws, and principles by which a nation, state, club, etc. is governed. *The constitution of our club states that we must have a new president every year.* 4. **The Constitution,** the rules, laws, and principles by which the United States is governed. *The Constitution states that a person may not be elected President more than twice.* **con sti tu tions.**

con struct (kən strukt′), *v.* to make or form by putting various parts together; to build. *That building was constructed in two years.* **con structs, con struct ed, con struct ing.**

con struc tion (kən struk′shən), *n.* 1. a putting together of parts to make something. *The con-*

struction of the house was stopped when we ran out of material. 2. the manner in which something is built. *That ladder is of very solid construction.* 3. something constructed; a thing built. *The workers lived in wooden constructions while they were working on the new road.* 4. the way in which words are organized in a sentence. *A sentence having no verb is an ungrammatical construction.* 5. meaning; explanation. *He twisted my words so that they had a different construction than I intended.* **con struc tions.**

con sult (kən sult′), *v.* 1. to seek information, advice, or an opinion from. *If you want to be sure, consult an expert in the field. Consult your dictionary whenever you are not sure of the meaning, pronunciation, or spelling of a word.* 2. to have regard for something or someone when making plans. *You should consult the rights and interests of the others before you ask them to do something.* 3. to engage in a conference; to talk together and exchange ideas. *Several doctors have consulted on your case, and they say you are completely cured.* **con sults, con sult ed, con sult ing.**

con sume (kən süm′), *v.* 1. to use up time; to spend time doing something. *We consumed the entire evening in talking about the movie.* 2. to eat or drink. *She consumed the candy bar in a single bite.* 3. to destroy, especially by fire. *The fire consumed all of his important papers and books.* **con sumes, con sumed, con sum ing.**

con tact (kon′takt), *n.* 1. a joining of things together; a touching of things. *When the contact between the two wires was made, the radio started to play. My fingers came into contact with a cold, soft material.* 2. a connection, especially of people. *Without a few good business contacts, you won't be able to sell very much.* **con tacts.**
v. 3. to get in touch with; to reach by tele-

phone, mail, radio, etc. *We contacted the lost airplane by radio just after it crashed.* **con tacts, con tact ed, con tact ing.**

con tain (kən tān′), *v.* 1. to hold or carry; to enclose as contents. *This is the box that contains your groceries.* 2. to have as a capacity; to be able to hold. *A quart contains thirty-two ounces.* 3. to have as a part of its total contents. *Some dog foods contain a great deal of water and cereal and only a little meat.* 4. to hold in check; to control; to restrain. *He could hardly contain his excitement when he was chosen to play on the first team.* **con tains, con tained, con tain ing.**

con tain er (kən tān′ər), *n.* a thing that holds something. *Boxes, cans, barrels, bottles, and jugs are containers.* **con tain ers.**

con tem plate (kon′təm plāt′), *v.* 1. to look at something carefully or think about something carefully. *He contemplated the question for a few moments before answering. The policeman contemplated the scene of the accident as we told him what had happened.* 2. to plan to do; to intend. *I don't contemplate moving to a new neighborhood.* 3. to expect; to look forward to. *I don't contemplate having any problems with the homework.* **con tem plates, con tem plat ed, con tem plat ing.**

con tent[1] (kon′tent), *n.* 1. what is contained; what a thing holds or encloses. *The contents of the package were listed on the label.* 2. the ideas expressed in a book, article, or speech; the topic of a book, article, or speech. *The speech was varied in content and well delivered.* 3. the amount that can be contained. *The content of this truck is five tons.* **con tents.**

con tent[2] (kən tent′), *adj.* 1. satisfied; pleased. *We were content to win the game by only one point.* **con tent ed ly,** *adv.*
v. 2. to satisfy; to make pleased. *I am not*

a   b   c

 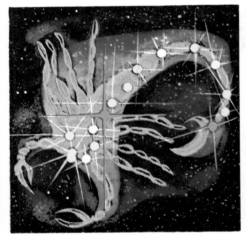 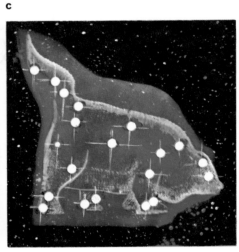

constellations:
  a. Pisces, the fish; **b.** Scorpio, the scorpion;
  c. Ursa Major, the great bear

The brightest stars are shown in red, the second brightest are white, and the third brightest are yellow.

constructing a building

contented with this hot weather. **con tents, con tent ed, con tent ing.**

n. 3. satisfaction; peace of mind. *We lay on the bank of the river, fishing and sleeping, in peaceful content.*

con test (kon′test for 1, kən test′ for 2 and 3), *n.* 1. a test, struggle, game, etc. to determine a winner. *There are many different contests in a rodeo. Who won the prize in the art contest?* **con tests.**

v. 2. to dispute; to argue against; to demand proof, evidence, etc. for something. *The prince contested his brother's claim to the throne.* 3. to

struggle for; to fight over. *Every step was contested in the tug of war.* **con tests, con test ed, con test ing.**

con tin ent (kon′tə nənt), *n.* 1. one of the seven main masses of land in the world: Africa, Antarctica, Asia, Australia, Europe, North America, and South America. *We live on the North American continent.* 2. **the Continent,** all of Europe except its island countries. *We left Great Britain in June to spend a month on the Continent.* **con tin ents.**

con tin u al (kən tin′ū əl), *adj.* 1. going on without stopping. *The continual sound of the* *rain soon put us to sleep.* 2. happening again and again; repeated often. *He made continual efforts to play the song on his guitar.* **con tin u al ly,** *adv.*

con tin ue (kən tin′ū), *v.* 1. to go on without stopping. *We continued walking until we arrived at the camp. The noise in the room continued until the teacher returned.* 2. to go on again after stopping; to resume after an interruption. *When the audience had stopped laughing, we continued the play. The story will be continued next week.* 3. to remain in the same place; to go on in the same position. *We continued at summer camp until the end of August. We decided to let Bob continue as president.* 4. to cause to remain or go on in a position. *The president was continued in office for another term.* **con tin ues, con tin ued, con tin u ing.**

con tin u ous (kən tin′ū əs), *adj.* going on without stopping; unbroken; connected. *A continuous line of people passed the window. A continuous line of cars blocked the street for miles.* **con tin u ous ly,** *adv.*

con tract (kon′trakt for 1–3, kən trakt′ for 4–6), *n.* 1. a legal agreement. *The Ace Steel Company is under contract to provide materials for the new building.* 2. a written statement of the terms of an agreement. *The baseball player would not sign his contract until his salary was increased.* **con tracts.**

v. 3. to make a legal agreement. *We contracted to mow their lawn for two dollars a week.* 4. to become smaller by shrinking. *Most things expand in warm weather and contract in cold weather.* 5. to draw together by tightening the muscles. *His mouth was contracted in an angry expression.* 6. to become infected by; to catch. *After becoming soaked by the rain, he contracted a cold.* **con tracts, con tract ed, con tract ing.**

con trac tion (kən trak′shən), *n.* 1. a drawing together; shrinking. *The contraction of metal in the winter and its expansion in the summer creates problems for builders of roads and buildings.* 2. a shortened form. *The word "can't" is a contraction of "cannot."* **con trac tions.**

con trary (kon′trer ē), *adj.* 1. completely different; opposite. *My plan is contrary to his. We have contrary opinions.* 2. opposed to; working against each other. *Contrary winds, if they are very strong, can cause a tornado.* 3. stubborn; opposed to everything. *He'll never agree with you when he's being contrary.* **con trar i ly,** *adv.* *n.* 4. something contrary; the exact opposite. *We believe the contrary of what you believe.* 5. **on the contrary,** on the opposite side; on the other hand. *On the contrary, more people watch television than go to the movies.* **con trar ies.**

con trast (kon′trast for 1 and 2, kən trast′ for 3 and 4), *n.* 1. a difference between things; a lack of resemblance between things when they are compared. *The contrast of good and evil*

should be clear to everyone. 2. something that produces a difference in appearance between things. *Those red and yellow roses make a nice contrast with the white fence.* **con trasts.**

v. 3. to compare in a way that shows differences. *At the zoo we were able to contrast the many different types of apes that exist.* 4. to produce or demonstrate a difference by placing things together. *The whiteness of the sand contrasted sharply with the dark blue of the water.* **con trasts, con trast ed, con trast ing.**

con trib ute (kən trib′ūt), *v.* 1. to give money, aid, etc. to an organization, church, etc. *Our class decided to contribute money to help some of the poor families in town.* 2. to write stories, articles, poems, etc. to be published in a newspaper or magazine. *My sister contributed two stories to the school paper.* 3. **contribute to,** to help; to have a part in. *The presence of several honeybees contributed to our discomfort in swimming in the cold water.* **con trib utes, con trib ut ed, con trib ut ing.**

con trol (kən trōl′), *v.* 1. to rule; to have power over; to manage. *The treasurer will control the spending of our dues. The driver could not control the car.* 2. to hold down; keep in check. *Try to control your tongue. Control your anger!* **con trols, con trolled, con trol ling.**

n. 3. the power or authority to rule. *The President has control over the armed forces.* 4. a holding down; a keeping in check; a restraining. *Price controls were enforced to prevent costs from rising too rapidly. The umpire kept the game under control.* 5. anything that controls or regulates a machine. *The pilot checked to make sure the controls were working before he took off.* **con trols.**

con tro ver sy (kon′trə vėr′sē), *n.* an argument, debate, or dispute over something. *The controversy over the new gym resulted in a decision to delay building it for a while.* **con tro ver sies.**

con ven ience (kən vēn′yəns), *n.* 1. anything used to provide comfort, ease, or help in doing something. *In mountainous country, a horse may be more of a convenience than a car.* 2. comfort or ease of a person. *The portable steps used on trains and airplanes are provided for the convenience of passengers.* 3. a being suitable, easy to use, or handy. *The convenience of public transportation makes this house very valuable.* 4. **at one's convenience,** at a suitable time; whenever it is best or easiest for a person. *You may make another appointment with the doctor at your convenience.* **con ven ienc es.**

con ven ient (kən vēn′yənt), *adj.* 1. causing no problems. *Can we find a more convenient time for our meetings?* 2. easy to use; suitable for use. *This is a very convenient reference book. A can opener is a convenient device.* 3. **convenient to,** within easy reach of; near. *Their house is convenient to the shopping center. Arrange your tools so that they are convenient to you while you are working.* **con ven ient ly,** *adv.*

con vent (kon′vent), *n.* a group of religious women who live together, or the place where they live. *A convent often trains teachers.* **con vents.**

con ven tion (kən ven′shən), *n.* 1. a meeting held for a special purpose. *Every four years, political parties hold conventions to choose candidates for President.* 2. all of the persons at such a meeting. *The convention was unanimous in its selection of candidates.* 3. the usual way of doing something; an accepted way of doing something; custom. *The teacher established the convention of starting the school day with a song.* 4. an agreement between persons, nations, etc. to do something. *Certain actions are forbidden by the conventions of war.* **con ven tions.**

con ver sa tion (kon′vər sā′shən), *n.* a discussion or talk between people. *We had an interesting conversation about popular music.* **con ver sa tions.**

con ver sa tion al (kon′vər sā′shən l), *adj.* of, or like a conversation; informal. *He delivered his speech in a conversational tone of voice.* **con ver sa tion al ly,** *adv.*

con verse (kən vėrs′), *v.* to talk; to engage in conversation. *We conversed on many subjects while we waited for the train to arrive.* **con vers es, con versed, con vers ing.**

con vey (kən vā′), *v.* 1. to take from one place to another; transport. *The new cars were conveyed from the factory to the dealer by truck.* 2. to be the means by which something is moved from one place to another. *This moving belt conveys the finished machines to another part of the factory.* 3. to communicate; to make known. *Did that movie convey any meaning to you?* 4. to transfer something from one person to another.

The will stated that the property was to be conveyed to the oldest son. **con veys, con veyed, con vey ing.**

con vict (kən vikt′ for 1, kon′vikt for 2 and 3), *v.* 1. to find or prove a person guilty of something, especially a crime. *The prisoner was convicted of setting fire to the store.* **con victs, con vict ed, con vict ing.**
n. 2. a person who is found guilty of a crime. *The convict was led from the court after his trial had ended.* 3. a person who is kept in a prison because of a crime he has committed. *During the day, the convicts were expected to work in the prison.* **con victs.**

con vic tion (kən vik′shən), *n.* 1. a proving that a person is guilty of something, especially a crime. *The case was closed when a conviction was returned by the jury.* 2. the state of being found guilty. *His conviction was reversed when another person confessed to the crime.* 3. a strong belief or opinion. *Christopher Columbus had a firm conviction that the earth was round.* **con vic tions.**

con vince (kən vins′), *v.* to make a person certain that something is true; to persuade to believe. *I wasn't able to convince him that it was raining until I took him to the window. He convinced me that the plan would work.* **con vinc es, con vinced, con vinc ing.**

con voy (kon′voi), *n.* 1. a group of ships sailing together, or a group of vehicles traveling together, usually with an armed guard. *During wartime, destroyers and other warships often guard convoys carrying goods across the ocean.* **con voys.**
v. 2. to sail with ships to guide and protect them. *Three destroyers convoyed the supply ships.* **con voys, con voyed, con voy ing.**

coo (kü), *n.* 1. the sound made by doves and pigeons. *All around the park, the coos of pigeons could be heard.* **coos.**
v. 2. to make this sound. *The dove cooed softly when it returned to its cage.* 3. to speak in a soft, murmuring voice. *Some people coo when they want a favor from you.* **coos, cooed, coo ing.**

cook (kůk), *v.* 1. to prepare food for eating by baking, roasting, frying, etc. *It will take two hours to cook this meat.* 2. to become ready for eating through cooking. *You didn't let the*

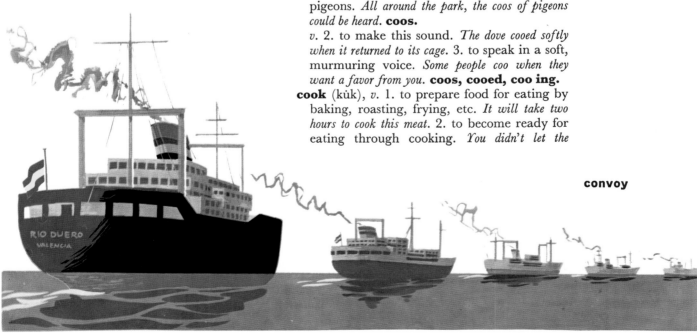

convoy

copper:
a. copper mine
b. copper ore

b

corn

potatoes cook long enough. **cooks, cooked, cook ing.**

n. 3. a person who prepares food for eating by cooking it. *The cook is in the kitchen getting our dessert ready.* **cooks.**

cook book (kŭk′bŭk′), *n.* a book which contains directions for cooking many foods. *It has been so long since I last baked bread that I had to use my cookbook for the recipe.* **cook books.**

cook ie or **cooky** (kŭk′ē), *n.* a small, usually flat, sweet cake. *Tim brought three dozen chocolate chip cookies to the school party.* **cook ies.**

cool (kül), *adj.* 1. not hot; not very cold. *We were hoping for a cool day for the game.* 2. not holding heat or letting heat in. *She was wearing a cool cotton dress.* 3. calm; unexcited; in control of one's emotions. *When the accident happened, the driver of the bus remained cool and helped us to safety.* 4. indifferent; uninterested; unfriendly. *His manner was cool and distant toward me.* **cool er, cool est; cool ly,** *adv.*

v. 5. to make cool; to become cool. *The city was cooled by a breeze from the lake. In a short time the root beer will cool.* **cools, cooled, cool ing.**

n. 6. a cool part or time. *The cows grazed in the shady cool of the pasture. We waited for the cool of the night before lighting the fire.* **cools.**

cool er (kül′ər), *n.* a container or room which cools foods or liquids or keeps them cool. *When we go on a picnic, we keep the meat in a cooler until we are ready to cook it.* **cool ers.**

coop (küp), *n.* 1. a cage or enclosed place for birds or other small animals. *The chickens were kept in a coop.* **coops.**

v. 2. to shut up in a coop or other enclosed place. *We were cooped in by the rain.* **coops, cooped, coop ing.**

co op er ate (kō op′ər āt′), *v.* to work together to get something done. *If everyone cooperates, we will soon finish.* **co op er ates, co op er at ed, co op er at ing.**

co op er a tion (kōop′ər a′shən), *n.* working together. *With everyone's cooperation, we soon cleaned the yard.*

cop per (kop′ər), *n.* 1. a soft, easily worked, reddish-brown metal. *Copper mines are on the surface of the earth. Copper is used to make electric wire and to make pennies.* **cop pers.**

adj. 2. made of copper. *Mary had several shiny copper pots in her kitchen.* 3. reddish-brown. *The girl has copper hair.*

copy (kop′ē), *n.* 1. anything made to be or look exactly like something else. *The painting was not genuine, but it was a good copy.* 2. something used as a model. *The small piece of sculpture was a good copy to imitate.* 3. one of many books, magazines, etc. that are just alike. *That was such a popular article that no more copies of the magazine are available.* 4. typewriting that is to be set in type for printing. *Newspaper reporters send in copy to their newspapers.* **cop ies.**

v. 5. to make like something else. *Copy this handwriting.* 6. to imitate; to act the same as. *The small boy copies his father.* **cop ies, cop ied, cop y ing.**

cord (kôrd), *n.* 1. a heavy string. *The big package was tied with cord.* 2. anything that looks like a cord. *When the weight lifter raised the heavy weight over his head, the cords in his neck stuck out.* 3. wires covered with rubber or other insulation that carry electricity from a plug or outlet to a lamp, an electric fan, etc. *A worn cord can be the cause of a fire.* 4. an amount of cut wood equal to a pile that is four feet high, four feet wide, and eight feet long. *Dad ordered several cords of wood for our fireplace.* **cords.**

cor dial ly (kôr′jə lē), *adv.* in a friendly way. *The owner of a store always greets his customers cordially.*

cork (kôrk), *n.* 1. the light bark of an oak tree that grows in Spain and Portugal. *Cork is used in life preservers because it is light in weight, and* *it floats in water.* 2. a piece of cork used to stop up the open end of a bottle. *The bottle of grape juice has a cork in the opening.* 3. anything used to stop up the open end of a bottle. *Rubber corks are used today.* **corks.**

v. 4. to put a cork or other stopper in a bottle. *Cork the bottle, and put it away.* **corks, corked, cork ing.**

cork screw (kôrk′skrü′), *n.* a pointed metal tool, usually shaped like a spiral, for pulling corks from bottles. *Corkscrews were often used when all drinks were in corked bottles.* **corkscrews.**

corn[1] (kôrn), *n.* 1. a grain that grows in kernels or seeds on large ears. *Corn is also called " Indian corn." Most corn grown in this country is fed to cattle, but people eat sweet corn that has small, tender, sweet kernels.* 2. the plant that corn grows on. *In states like Illinois and Iowa corn grows in huge fields to a height of more than ten feet.* *v.* 3. to preserve meat with salt or salt water. *Before the use of refrigerators, people corned meat for eating later.* **corns, corned, corn ing.**

corn[2] (kôrn), *n.* a painful thickening of the skin on the foot. *Shoes that are too small press or rub often causing corns.* **corns.**

corn bread, bread baked from ground corn instead of from wheat or rye flour. *Corn bread is coarse and crumbles easily.*

cor nea (kôr′nē ə), *n.* the transparent outside layer of the eyeball. *The cornea covers the iris and the pupil of the eye.* **cor neas.**

cor ner (kôr′nər), *n.* 1. the place where two lines, edges, or sides of something come together. *The dog sleeps in a corner of the room.* 2. the place where two or more streets come together. *The bus stops at the corner of Sixth and Main.* 3. any far away place. *The old sailor had been to every corner of the earth.* 4. a difficult place. *This job has to be done so fast that I am in a corner.* **cor ners.**

v. 5. to put or force into a corner. *The men from the circus cornered the runaway animal.* **cor ners, cor nered, cor ner ing.**

adj. 6. on or at a corner. *Jerry's best friend lives in the corner house at the end of this block.* 7. of or for a corner. *The corner chest was dark wood and highly polished.*

cor o na tion (kôr′ə nā′shən), *n.* the crowning of a king or queen. *Only the royal family was permitted to attend the coronation of the new queen.* **cor o na tions.**

cor po ra tion (kôr′pə rā′shən), *n.* a group of people, having certain legal rights that are similar to those of a single person. *A corporation can act legally as a single person, thereby simplifying many business problems. Businesses, colleges, and cities can be corporations.* **cor po ra tions.**

cor ral (kə ral′), *n.* 1. a place that is fenced in for horses, cattle, or other livestock. *Cattle are herded into a corral and counted before they are sent to market.* **cor rals.**

cork:
  a. bark from the cork tree
  b. the tree with bark removed

v. 2. to drive horses or cattle into a corral. *The cattle were corralled yesterday, and will be shipped today.* 3. to capture. *A few stray sheep had to be corralled in the north valley last week.* **cor rals, cor ralled, cor ral ling.**

cor rect (kə rekt′), *adj.* 1. having no mistakes; right. *Gary was sure he had the correct answer to the problem.* 2. agreeing with accepted standards or habits. *Visitors at the school are expected to observe correct behavior.* **cor rect ly,** *adv.*

v. 3. to remove errors from; to make right. *Please correct the spelling on your papers.* 4. to mark or point out the mistakes. *The teacher will return our tests after she corrects them.* 5. to speak sharply to. *When we give talks in English class, the teacher corrects our grammar. The child's mother corrected him for playing in the street.* **cor rects, cor rect ed, cor rect ing.**

corkscrews

cor rect ion (kə rek′shən), *n.* 1. the act of correcting; the pointing out of errors and mistakes. *Teachers spend many hours on the correction of pupils' papers.* 2. something put in place of a mistake or error. *The author made a correction in his story.* 3. punishment. *Mother's correction of the girl was severe, but later the girl was grateful for it.* **cor rect ions.**

cor re spond (kôr′ə spond′), *v.* 1. to be in agreement with something; be like. *Sam's idea of a vacation did not correspond with his wife's idea.* 2. to be the same as; to be similar to something else. *The coach of a team corresponds to the teacher of a class.* 3. to write letters back and forth. *Ann was away last summer, but we corresponded every week.* **cor re sponds, cor re spond ed, cor re spond ing.**

cor re spond ence (kôr′ə spon′dəns), *n.* 1. agreement. *There is no correspondence between Joan's and Mary's opinions of the new boy.* 2. writing letters back and forth. *We kept up our correspondence for several years after they moved away.* 3. letters, especially business letters. *All of the correspondence from our other office has been filed.* **cor re spond enc es.**

cor re spond ent (kôr′ə spon′dənt), *n.* 1. a person one writes letters to and receives letters from. *Good friends who live in different places are usually good correspondents.* 2. a person who writes articles for a newspaper or magazine from a distant place. *Foreign correspondents send stories from other countries.* **cor re spond ents.**

cor ri dor (kor′ə dər, kor′ə dôr′), *n.* a hall. *We do not run in the corridors of the school.* **cor ri dors.**

cor ru gat ed (kôr′ə gā′tid), *adj.* shaped in ridges or rounded folds for extra strength. *Corrugated cardboard is used for packaging because it protects the contents.*

cost (kôst), *v.* 1. to be for sale for; be worth. *The candy bar costs ten cents.* 2. to require the giving up of. *It costs nothing to be polite.* **costs, cost, cost ing.**
n. 3. price that is to be paid for. *The cost of meals in restaurants is going up.* 4. a loss or sacrifice. *He became a success in business at the cost of his health.* **costs.**

cos tume (kos′tüm, kos′tūm), *n.* 1. clothes. *People around the world wear different costumes.* 2. the particular clothing worn in imitation of another time or place. *He wore the costume of an Eskimo to the Halloween party.* **cos tumes.**
v. 3. to dress; to provide costumes for. *Marge was in charge of costuming the people in the play.* **cos tumes, cos tumed, cos tum ing.**

cot[1] (kot), *n.* a light, narrow bed that can be folded up and carried. *Most cots are made of canvas stretched over a frame of aluminum or wood.* **cots.**

cot[2] (kot), *n.* a small cottage. *The man lived in his humble cot.* **cots.**

cotton flowers and bolls

cot tage (kot′ij), *n.* 1. a small house. *The cottage is surrounded by big houses.* 2. a house at a summer resort. *The cottage we rented last August was right on the lakefront.* **cot tag es.**

cot ton (kot′n), *n.* 1. the soft white fibers that surround the tiny seeds of *certain plants. Cotton is one of the chief fiber crops of the world and is grown mainly to make cloth for clothing.* 2. the cotton plant. *Cotton is grown in the South.* 3. the thread or cloth made of cotton fibers. *Cotton is spun on large machines in mills in many Southern cities.* **cot tons.**
adj. 4. made of cotton. *Cotton shirts are not as warm as wool shirts.*

couch (kouch), *n.* 1. a piece of furniture that can seat several people; a sofa. *Whenever we have an overnight guest, we have him sleep on the couch.* 2. any comfortable place for sleeping or resting. *During a long walk in the woods, the boy lay briefly on a couch of dry leaves.* **couch es.**
v. 3. to put into words; phrase. *When Ed tries to get a point across, he couches his ideas in simple language.* **couch es, couched, couch ing.**

cough (kôf), *v.* 1. to force air quickly and noisily outward from the lungs. *The baby coughed several times during the night, waking his parents each time.* 2. to clear from the throat by coughing. *A little piece of popcorn stuck in Ray's throat, but he coughed, and it came out.* **coughs, coughed, cough ing.**
n. 3. the act or sound of coughing. *During the pause between scenes of the play, several coughs came from the audience.* 4. the condition of coughing often. *Bill's cold was over, but his cough lasted several more days.* **coughs.**

could (kud), past tense of **can.**

could n't (kud′nt), could not. *We couldn't get to school last Friday because of the deep snow.*

coun cil (koun′sl), *n.* 1. a group of people who meet to decide on plans or a course of action or to give advice. *The school council will make a* recommendation to the principal about the traffic problem. 2. a small group of people elected by the citizens to decide on the laws and general management of a town or city. *The city council meets once a month, and the public is invited to attend.* **coun cils.**

coun sel (koun′sl), *n.* 1. a talking together to exchange opinions or ideas. *Tom took counsel with friends before making a decision.* 2. advice. *He listens to counsel from people he likes.* 3. a lawyer or lawyers who are handling a case. *The counsel for the defense asked for a delay in the trial.* **coun sels.**
v. 4. to give counsel or advice to. *The minister counseled the people when they came to him with questions.* 5. to suggest or recommend. *The lawyer counseled them about their rights as citizens.* **coun sels, coun seled, coun sel ing.**

count[1] (kount), *v.* 1. to name the numbers in their regular order. *Charles could count from one to ten when he was four.* 2. to add together to find the total. *He counted the quarters in his bank.* 3. to include. *Counting me, we had fourteen members present last night.* 4. to consider; to regard. *We counted ourselves lucky to win the game with Central High.* 5. to have confidence in; depend. *We counted on Uncle Fred to help us prepare for the test.* 6. to be important or valuable. *Every day of practice will count toward making us a better team.* **counts, count ed, count ing.**
n. 7. a counting to find the number of. *The count showed that two fish were missing from the tank.* 8. a figure reached by counting. *The actual count was 10,486.* **counts.**

count[2] (kount), *n.* a man who is a member of a noble family. *Years ago counts were more important than they are now.* **counts.**

count down (kount′doun′), *n.* the final period of time just before the launching of a rocket or missile. *The countdown is given backward from some number to zero to show how much time remains before zero, or the actual time of launching.* **count downs.**

coun te nance (koun′tə nəns), *n.* 1. the face. *His countenance resembles that of his father.* 2. the appearance of the face that sometimes shows the character or emotions. *The doctor has a serious but gentle countenance.* 3. approval; consent. *Our teacher said she wouldn't give countenance to our plans.* **coun te nanc es.**
v. 4. to approve or give support to. *The United Nations does not countenance war.* **coun te nanc es, coun te nanced, coun te nanc ing.**

count er[1] (koun′tər), *n.* 1. a long table usually with stools, at which customers are served in a restaurant. *I like to eat at the counter, not at a table.* 2. a flat surface behind which a clerk stands in a store. *You will find the candy near the cashier's counter.* 3. a small piece of metal, wood, or plastic used in keeping score in games. *He had twenty counters; I had nineteen.* **count ers.**

coun ter[2] (koun′tər), *adv.* 1. in the opposite way; contrary. *I caught this cold because I acted counter to your advice and neglected to wear my boots.*
adj. 2. acting in the opposite way; opposed. *My counter suggestion to yours is that we buy some ice cream instead of popcorn.*
v. 3. to act or do in opposition to. *He countered all my plans with schemes of his own.* **coun ters, coun tered, coun ter ing.**

coun ter clock wise (koun′tər klok′wīz′), *adv.* 1. in a direction opposite from the way the hands of a clock move. *Hold a clock before a mirror, and the hands will move counterclockwise in the image.*
adj. 2. moving counterclockwise. *The counterclockwise traffic on the cloverleaf was delayed by an accident.*

coun try (kun′trē), *n.* 1. an area of land; region. *The country around here is actually a desert.* 2. the land occupied by a nation. *Switzerland is a small country; the United States is a large country.* 3. the land to which one belongs; land of one's birth or choice. *The United States is my country.* 4. the land outside the city; rural area of small towns and farms. *Every summer we go to the country for a vacation.* **coun tries.**
adj. 5. of the country; rural. *I like country life more than city life.*

coun ty (koun′tē), *n.* 1. a part of a state in the United States. *A county has its own elected officials to handle local affairs. In Louisiana a county is called a parish.* **coun ties.**
adj. 2. of a county. *The county elections will be held Tuesday.*

cou ple (kup′l), *n.* 1. two of anything; a pair. *All he had was a couple of dollars.* 2. a man and woman together. *Mary and Jack make an attractive couple.* 3. a husband and wife. *Our church has a club for couples only.* **cou ples.**
v. 4. to join; put together; connect. *Couple the trailer to the car, and we'll be on our way.* **cou ples, cou pled, cou pling.**

cou pon (kü′pon, kū′pon), *n.* 1. a printed card or paper that states the holder is supposed to get something. *In each carton of soapflakes was a coupon that could be exchanged for a bath towel.* 2. a printed order to be filled out. *Magazines sometimes contain coupons to simplify the ordering of an article or product by mail.* **cou pons.**

cour age (kėr′ij), *n.* the quality of facing danger or a difficult task without fear. *The fireman had courage to go back into the burning building to save the baby.*

cou ra geous (kə rā′jəs), *adj.* being without fear; brave; having courage. *After their historic flight around the earth, the three courageous astronauts stepped out of their small spacecraft.* **cou ra geous ly,** *adv.*

course (kôrs), *n.* 1. a route; a way; a path. *The plane went off its course to avoid the sudden storm.* 2. a way of proceeding or acting. *Your only* *course is to go to summer school to get the extra credit.* 3. a part of a meal. *The third course was roast beef.* 4. a series of lessons or classes. *Many adults take an art course in the evening classes at the high school.* 5. land used for a sport. *The golf course is ready for play.* 6. **of course,** naturally; without doubt. *Of course, I'll go with you.* **cours es.**

v. 7. to run; flow. *The river coursed swiftly under the bridge.* **cours es, coursed, cours ing.**

court (kôrt), *n.* 1. an open place enclosed by buildings or walls. *The children in the big apartment building have only the court to play in safely.* 2. a space marked off for a game. *Tennis is usually played outdoors on a court of grass or pavement.* 3. the place where a king or queen lives; a palace. *The king greeted his subjects at the court.* 4. the people who live in the palace or who are there every day. *The poor people of the country complained about the expenses of the court.* 5. a place for holding trials. *A court is presided over by a judge.* 6. a judge. *The court found him guilty.* **courts.**

v. 7. to try to get a woman to be one's wife. *Mr. Taylor courted Miss Higgins for four years before they were married.* 8. to try to get; invite. *Some men court fame and money. A tightrope walker courts injury or death while doing his act.* **courts, court ed, court ing.**

cour te ous (kėr′tē əs), *adj.* polite; kind. *Her courteous behavior made her popular.* **cour te ous ly,** *adv.*

cour te sy (kėr′tə sē), *n.* 1. polite behavior; respect for the feelings of others. *Thank you for your courtesy in driving me home.* 2. special attention; kindness. *Through the courtesy of Carol's father, the class visited a candy manufacturer.* **cour te sies.**

court house (kôrt′hous′), *n.* 1. a building where a court carries on its duties. *Trials are held in courthouses.* 2. a building in which the business of a county is taken care of. *A county sheriff has his office in the courthouse.* **court hous es.**

cous in (kuz′n), *n.* a son or daughter of an aunt or uncle. *I have seven cousins.* **cous ins.**

cove (kōv), *n.* a small bay or inlet that is set apart from a main body of water. *The man sailed his boat into a cove when he saw the storm coming across the lake.* **coves.**

cove

COW

cov er (kuv′ər), *n.* 1. the outside of a book; the binding. *Books have paper covers, cloth covers, or leather covers.* 2. a lid or top. *Put the cover on the pot when you boil corn.* 3. a blanket for a bed. *It was so hot we didn't need any cover to sleep.* 4. anything that hides. *Darkness was a good cover for his escape.* 5. anything put on to protect, keep warm, etc. *A sock is a cover for the foot.* **cov ers.**

v. 6. to put something on or over a person or thing to protect, keep warm, etc; to place a cover over. *Cover the sleeping baby with your coat. She covered the furniture to keep the dust off.* 7. to hide. *You can seldom cover a bad mistake. The hunter covered his tracks by smoothing snow over his footprints.* 8. to include; take in; deal with. *The movie covered the major events of the year.* 9. to extend or lie over. *Snow covered the sidewalks.* 10. to travel over. *We covered more than five miles on our hike through the woods.* **cov ers, cov ered, cov er ing.**

cov er ing (kuv′ər ing), *n.* something that covers. *A hat is a covering for the head. Shoes are coverings for the feet.* **cov er ings.**

cow[1] (kou), *n.* 1. a large farm animal that is raised to give milk. *Milk from cows is sometimes made into a powder, which can be turned into a liquid again by adding water.* 2. the female elephant, seal, whale, moose, etc. *The elephant cow watched her baby carefully.* **cows.**

cow[2] (kou), *v.* to make afraid. *The loud voice of the principal cowed the boy.* **cows, cowed, cow ing.**

cow ard (kou′ərd), *n.* a person who cannot control or hide his fear; a person who won't face danger. *Being a coward is sometimes not the fault of the person at all.* **cow ards.**

cow ard ly (kou′ərd lē), *adj.* 1. having no courage. *He is a cowardly person.* 2. of a coward. *Not admitting your mistake was a cowardly act.* **cow ard ly,** *adv.*

cow boy (kou′boi′), *n.* a person who takes care of cattle on a ranch. *The Mexican cowboy has the same job as our Western cowboy.* **cow boys.**

cow hide (kou′hīd′), *n.* 1. the raw or tanned skin of a cow. *At the tanning plant, we saw thousands of cowhides being dried.* 2. leather made from this skin. *The cowboy wore a jacket made of cowhide.* **cow hides.**

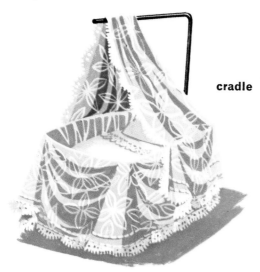

cradle

Mexican **cowboy**

coy (coi), *adj.* 1. shy; timid. *The coy child was hiding behind his mother.* 2. pretending to be shy. *The children at the birthday party were very coy until the cake was served.* **coy ly,** *adv.*

coy o te (kī′ōt, kī ō′tē), *n.* a small, wild wolf that lives in western North America. *A single coyote howled at the moon.* **coy o tes** or **coy o te.**

co zy (kō′zē), *adj.* comfortable; snug. *At the hotel, we had a cozy room with a fireplace.* **co zi er, co zi est; co zi ly,** *adv.*

crab (krab), *n.* a shellfish with a broad, flat body, eight legs, and two claws. *We ate fresh ocean crabs for supper.* **crabs.**

crack (krak), *v.* 1. to break or split without snapping apart. *The batter cracked the bat when he hit the ball.* 2. to make a sudden, loud, snapping noise with something. *The driver cracked his whip over the heads of the animals.* 3. to break, often with a loud noise. *We heard the ice on the pond cracking as we ran across it.* 4. to break suddenly. *In the middle of the song, his voice cracked, and he could not continue.* 5. to relate in a funny way; to tell something with humor. *Bill is never serious; he's always cracking jokes.* **cracks, cracked, crack ing.**

n. 6. a split or slight opening in something. *This egg has a crack in it.* 7. a sudden, loud snapping noise. *The crack of the thunder woke the dog.* 8. a sharp, loud blow. *I got a severe crack on the head when I bumped into the door.* **cracks.**

crack er (krak′ər), *n.* 1. a very thin bread product which has been baked until it is dry and crisp. *We ate cheese and crackers as we watched television.* 2. a small paper holder used as a party favor, containing an explosive, which pops when both ends are pulled. *Crackers usually have candy inside them.* **crack ers.**

cra dle (krā′dl), *n.* 1. a small bed, usually with rockers, used for a baby. *We took turns rocking the baby to sleep in his cradle.* 2. the place where anything starts; a place of origin. *Many people think of Italy as the cradle of art.* 3. a structure or frame that holds something or resembles a cradle. *Put the telephone receiver back on its cradle.* **cra dles.**

v. 4. to hold in a cradle or as if in a cradle. *The boy cradled the new puppy in his arms.*

coyote

5. to provide for in infancy; to raise or care for in youth. *Those children were cradled by their grandparents.* **cra dles, cra dled, cra dling.**

cramp (kramp), *n.* 1. a sudden, painful tightening of a muscle, often as a result of strain. *The swimmer got a cramp in his leg and had to stop.* **cramps.**

v. 2. to restrain; to confine; to hem in tightly. *The cattle were cramped in the corral.* **cramps, cramped, cramp ing.**

cran ber ry (kran′ber′ē), *n.* 1. a red berry that grows on low shrubs in very wet ground. *Cranberries are used for jelly and juice.* 2. the shrub on which the berry grows. *The cranberry is an evergreen.* **cran ber ries.**

crane (krān), *n.* 1. a large, wading bird with long legs and a long neck. *We saw three cranes at the zoo.* 2. a machine for lifting and moving heavy loads. *Three cranes were being used on the new fifty-story building.* **cranes.**

v. 3. to stretch the neck like a crane to see better. *Because of the large crowd, we craned our necks to watch the parade.* **cranes, craned, cran ing.**

crank (krangk), *n.* 1. a handle or part that is turned to start or operate a machine. *The handle that is used to raise and lower the window*

in a car is a crank. 2. a person who has strange ideas or fears; a person who has only one interest or thought. *Policemen are constantly bothered by cranks who imagine that someone is breaking into their houses.* **cranks.**

v. 3. to start or operate with a crank. *We had to crank the old car to start it.* **cranks, cranked, crank ing.**

cranky (krangk′ē), *adj.* easily angered. *The cranky man chased us out of his yard.* **crank i er, crank i est; crank i ly,** *adv.*

crash (krash), *n.* 1. a very loud noise; the noise made by something that falls and breaks. *Shortly after dinner we heard a crash of dishes from the kitchen.* 2. a forceful striking together of two or more solid things. *Many people were injured in the train crash.* 3. a sudden falling to earth of an airplane. *There have been no crashes at this airport in forty years.* 4. a sudden failure of business or severe decrease in buying. *Thousands of people lost all of their money in the stock market crash.* **crash es.**

v. 5. to make a very loud noise. *Thunder crashed throughout the night.* 6. to strike forcefully; to break. *The automobiles crashed at the intersection. The ball crashed through the window.* 7. to fall to earth suddenly; to strike the earth violently when making a landing. *The airplane*

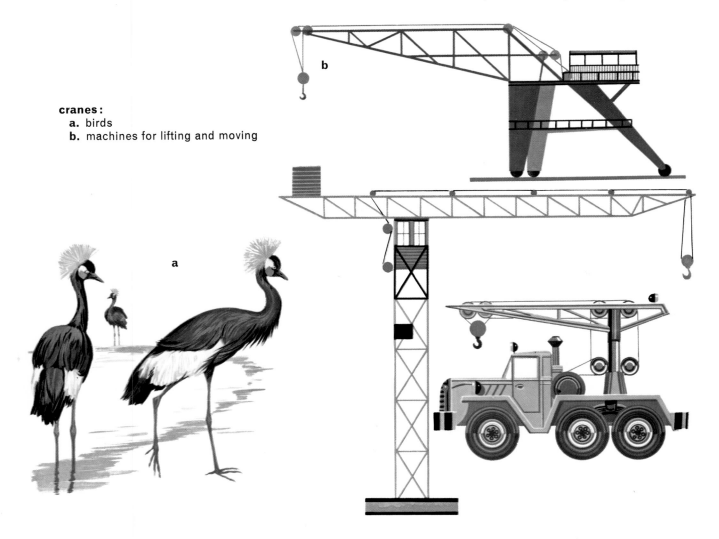

cranes:
 a. birds
 b. machines for lifting and moving

crashed in the thick fog. **crash es, crashed, crash ing.**

crawl (krôl), *v.* 1. to move slowly along the ground by pulling the body. *Worms and caterpillars crawl.* 2. to move on hands and knees. *Babies crawl before they walk.* 3. to move slowly. *The heavy traffic crawled along the crowded highway.* 4. to have many crawling things. *The picnic area was crawling with ants.* 5. to feel as if insects were creeping on one's body. *My skin crawls when I see the snakes in the zoo.* **crawls, crawled, crawl ing.**
n. 6. a crawling movement; slow, creeping progress. *Traffic was slowed to a crawl at the scene of the fire.* 7. a kind of stroke used in swimming, head underwater and legs kicking. *I learned the crawl at summer camp.*

cray on (krā/ən, krā/on), *n.* a kind of pencil made of colored wax or chalk. *Children draw on paper with wax crayons. The teacher writes on the chalkboard with a chalk crayon.* **cray ons.**

cra zy (krā/zē), *adj.* 1. insane; very sick in the mind. *A crazy person doesn't know why he does certain things.* 2. unsound; not making much sense. *Some new fashions are crazy.* 3. wild with enthusiasm. *Teen-agers go crazy when some singers appear on the stage.* **cra zi er, cra zi est; cra zi ly,** *adv.*

cream (krēm), *n.* 1. the thick, yellowish part of milk that rises to the top. *People use cream in coffee and for pouring on desserts.* 2. a food or candy made of cream. *Ice cream is a favorite dessert.* 3. the best part. *Charles always gets the cream of everything because he is the youngest.* 4. yellowish-white. *My uncle has a goat the color of cream.* 5. a greasy substance for the skin. *I put cream on my hands to keep the skin soft.* **creams.**
v. 6. to make a smooth mixture by beating. *Butter, sugar, milk, and chocolate are creamed together to put on the top of a cake.* **creams, creamed, cream ing.**

creamy (krēm/ē), *adj.* of, like, or full of cream; rich and smooth. *The soup is creamy.* **cream i er, cream i est.**

cre ate (krē āt/), *v.* 1. to make a thing which has not been made before; form. *The artist created a painting. Scientists created a spaceship.* 2. to cause. *It takes only one loud person to create a disturbance. Congress created a new committee.* **cre ates, cre at ed, cre at ing.**

crea ture (krē/chər), *n.* any living animal or human being. *All creatures need food.* **creatures.**

cred it (kred/it), *n.* 1. recognition; favorable regard. *He deserves credit for saving the life of the small pup.* 2. a reputation for paying bills on time. *Your credit is good at this store.* 3. a person or thing that improves a reputation; someone who brings praise. *That good player would be a credit to any ball team in the country.* 4. an amount paid on a debt. *I have a credit of fifty*

dollars on the seventy-five dollars I once owed; so now I only owe twenty-five dollars. 5. a unit of schoolwork. *He has three credits in history.* **cred its.**
v. 6. to believe in; to trust. *You can't credit anything he says.* 7. to add to a bank account. *The cashier credited my account with the five dollars I brought in.* **cred its, cred it ed, cred it ing.**

creek (krēk), *n.* a small stream or river. *The children waded in the creek.* **creeks.**

creep (krēp), *v.* 1. to move along with the body close to the ground; crawl. *The baby now creeps from one side of the room to the other.* 2. to move slowly; to go forward carefully. *The hunters had to creep up on the animal. Sometimes cars creep along in heavy traffic.* 3. to feel as if something were crawling on one's body. *The man's flesh crept as he heard the howl of the wolf in the moonlight.* 4. to grow along the ground, taking root at different places. *The vines are creeping over the garden.* **creeps, crept, creep ing.**

crept (krept), past tense of **creep.**

crew (krü), *n.* 1. the persons who run a boat, ship, train, or airplane. *A crew takes orders from a captain or other officer.* 2. any group of people working together on the same project. *The snow-removal crew has been on this street.* 3. a rowing team. *Jack made the crew at college.* **crews.**

crib (krib), *n.* 1. a small bed for a baby. *A crib usually has high sides to keep the baby from falling out.* 2. a kind of box holding food for animals. *The horse's food is in the crib.* 3. a box or building for storing grain, salt, or corn. *A crib is built with open spaces in it to let air in.* **cribs.**

crick et[1] (krik/ət), *n.* a small hopping insect somewhat like a grasshopper. *A male cricket makes a chirping sound by rubbing its wings together.* **crick ets.**

crick et[2] (krik/ət), *n.* an outdoor game played with bats and a ball. *Cricket is an English game, which is played by two teams of eleven players each.*

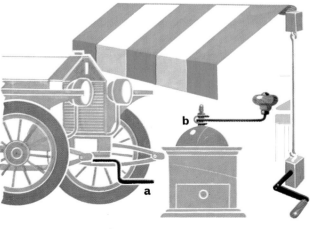

cranks:
  a. automobile crank
  b. hand mill to grind coffee
  c. crank to raise or lower awnings

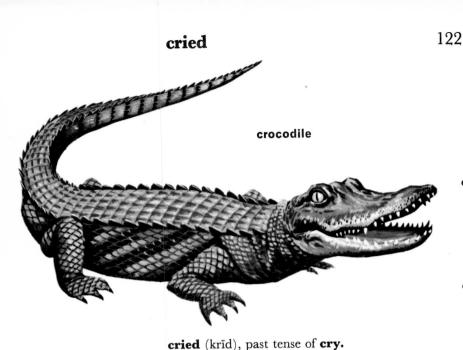

crocodile

cried (krīd), past tense of **cry.**

crime (krīm), *n.* 1. a bad act that is against the law. *Murder, burglary, and robbery are crimes that are punished by prison terms.* 2. a foolish action; a useless act. *His family thinks it's a crime for him to buy all those new records.* **crimes.**

crim i nal (krim′ə nl), *n.* 1. a person who has committed a crime. *Criminals go to prison.* **crim i nals.**
adj. 2. having to do with crime. *That prisoner has a long criminal record. The professor is an expert in criminal law.* **crim i nal ly,** *adv.*

cri sis (krī′səs), *n.* 1. an important turning point. *Once a very sick person reaches the crisis, he will either recover or die.* 2. a historical turning point. *The crisis came when the two armies faced each other across the boundary line.* 3. a time of struggle and difficulty. *The competition of buses and airplanes has created a crisis for passenger trains.* **cri ses** (krī′sēz).

crisp (krisp), *adj.* 1. easily broken. *Fried bacon is crisp. The little rabbit ran across the crisp snow.* 2. fresh and cool. *The crisp days in winter are good for your health.* 3. sharp and clear. *He speaks in a crisp way so that you always hear him. This is a crisp photograph.* **crisp ly,** *adv.*

crit ic (krit ik), *n.* 1. a person who gives his opinion of the good or bad points of something. *He is the movie critic for the newspaper.* 2. a person who finds fault or states disapproval. *My mother is my most important critic.* **crit ics.**

crit i cal (krit i kəl), *adj.* 1. to judge or evaluate something especially unfavorably. *The teacher was very critical of my paper.* 2. something involving critics or criticism. *All critical reports were gathered and put into one book.* 3. relating to a crises or turning point of something. *The critical point of the battle was reached when we broke through the enemy lines.* **crit i cal ly,** *adv.*

crit i cism (krit′ə siz′əm), *n.* 1. an opinion about the good points or bad points of something. *The reviewer's criticism was that the play was good, but that the acting was poor.* 2. disapproval; finding fault; unfavorable remarks. *Men holding public office must get used to criticism of their work.* **crit i cisms.**

crit i cize (krit ə sīz), *v.* 1. to evaluate or judge as a critic. *Mary was asked to criticize the poem John wrote.* 2. to judge unfavorably. *Mother criticized me for not keeping my room clean.* **crit i ciz es, crit i cized, crit i ciz ing.**

croak (krōk), *v.* 1. to make a low, harsh noise with the throat. *Frogs croak, and in a group can be very noisy.* 2. to speak in a deep voice that is rough. *"Let's go!" croaked the coach, still suffering from his cold.* **croaks, croaked, croak ing.**
n. 3. a low, harsh sound. *We listened to the croak of the frogs all night.* **croaks.**

croc o dile (krok′ə dīl′), *n.* a large animal with a narrow body, short legs for crawling, a long tail, and a thick skin. *Crocodiles live near the warm rivers of Africa, Asia, Australia, and America.* **croc o diles.**

crook (kruk), *n.* 1. a curved or hooked part of a thing. *The handle of an umbrella usually has a crook at the bottom.* 2. the staff a shepherd uses. *The shepherd uses his crook to hold sheep by the neck.* 3. a person who is not honest. *The crook climbed in the window and stole the money.* **crooks.**
v. 4. to bend; to curve. *He crooked his head to see the stage better.* **crooks, crooked, crook ing.**

crook ed (kruk′əd), *adj.* 1. bent, curved, or twisted. *We followed the crooked path to his hut.* 2. not honest. *The crooked salesman was selling land that was worthless.* **crook ed ly,** *adv.*

crop (krop), *n.* 1. food plants that are grown and harvested. *The farmer plants crops in the spring. There is a large fruit crop this year.* 2. people or things thought of as being grown and harvested. *We have a fine crop of pupils this year.* 3. a short whip. *The man on the horse hit the animal gently with his crop to get it to go faster.* 4. a close haircut. *He asked the barber to crop his hair short.* **crops.**
v. 5. to cut or bite off the top of. *They never mow their lawn; a herd of goats crops it.* 6. to cut short. *Some dogs' tails are cropped when they are puppies.* **crops, cropped, crop ping.**

cro quet (krō kā′), *n.* a game played by hitting wooden balls through wire arches to a stake at the end. *Croquet is played on a smooth, grass surface.*

croquet

cross (krôs), *n.* 1. a post with a bar across it, near the top. *In ancient Rome a criminal might be nailed to a cross.* 2. any trouble or burden a person must bear; suffering. *For years her sick brother has been her cross, since he needs constant attention.* 3. a mark (× or +) made by drawing one straight line across another. *Put a cross after each wrong answer.* 4. **the Cross,** the cross upon which Jesus Christ was put to death. *The Cross is a symbol of Christianity.* **cross es.**
v. 5. to make the sign of the cross as an act of religion or prayer. *Many people cross themselves as they enter church.* 6. to draw a line across. *Careful writers cross the letter "t" properly.* 7. to go from one side to the other. *Look at the traffic, and then cross the street.* 8. to pass while going in opposite directions. *Their letters crossed in the mail.* 9. to go against; to oppose. *Don't cross my father when he is angry.* **cross es, crossed, cross ing.**
adj. 10. in a bad temper; cranky. *Some people get cross when they lose a game.* 11. passing across. *This is a dangerous cross street because of speeding cars.* **cross ly,** *adv.*

cross-eyed (krôs′īd′), *adj.* having eyes which look toward the nose instead of forward. *A cross-eyed person can go to an eyedoctor for correction or special treatment.*

cross ing (krôs′ing), *n.* 1. a special place where a street may be crossed. *Many streets have crossings for school children.* 2. any place where a street should be crossed by people. *Don't run out in the middle of the street; wait until the next crossing.* **cross ings.**

cross-ref er ence (krôs ref′ər əns), *n.* a statement in a book to look in another place in the book for more information. *A good encyclopedia has many cross-references.* **cross-ref er enc es.**

crow[1] (krō), *n.* a large black bird with a harsh cry. *Crows sometimes eat most of the corn in a cornfield.* **crows.**

crow[2] (krō), *v.* 1. to make the cry of a rooster. *The rooster crows every morning.* 2. to make sounds of delight, frequently bragging. *"We won! We won!" crowed the team.* **crows, crowed, crow ing.**
n. 3. the sound of a rooster. *The crow of the rooster woke me up.* **crows.**

crowd (kroud), *n.* 1. a group of people gathered together. *A crowd of 100,000 saw the Michigan-Notre Dame game.* 2. people thought of in general; the average people. *This book is too deep for the crowd.* 3. a group or set. *Her crowd won't even speak to us.* **crowds.**
v. 4. to push or squeeze together. *The people crowded into the small room.* 5. to fill too full. *The beaches were crowded every hot Sunday in summer.* **crowds, crowd ed, crowd ing.**

crown (kroun), *n.* 1. a decorated covering for the head, worn by kings, queens, and others. *The king wears his crown only on very special occasions.* 2. the king or queen; the royal power of a king or queen. *The man was put into prison for his crimes against the crown.* 3. a band for the head, given as an award, honor, etc. *The girl who won the beauty contest was given a crown of flowers to wear.* 4. the top of anything. *He has a bare spot on the crown of his head. We could barely see the crown of the mountain through the fog.* 5. the head of a person. *Jack fell down and broke his crown.* **crowns.**
v. 6. to make someone a king or queen by putting on a crown. *He is a prince no longer; he was crowned this morning.* 7. to be on or at the top of something; to occupy the highest part of something. *A tall steeple crowned the little church.* 8. to reward or honor. *The determination of the team was crowned with victory.* **crowns, crowned, crown ing.**

crude (krüd), *adj.* 1. in its natural state. *Oil as it comes from the ground is crude oil.* 2. rough; clumsy. *The child drew a crude picture of me. Many people have crude manners at the dinner table. All his ideas were crude and not well thought out.* **crud er, crud est; crude ly,** *adv.*

cru el (krü′əl), *adj.* 1. wanting to make others suffer or cause them pain. *The cruel children threw stones at the birds.* 2. causing suffering; producing pain. *He was in agony from the cruel wound he had received.* 3. showing willingness to cause pain; mean and evil. *They played a cruel trick on the old man.* **cru el er, cru el est; cru el ly,** *adv.*

crumb (krum), *n.* 1. a small piece of something larger, especially a small piece of bread or cake. *We fed crumbs to the birds during the winter.* 2. a very small amount of anything. *He hasn't a crumb of envy in him.* **crumbs.**
v. 3. to break into small pieces. *The bread crumbed as I spread butter on it.* **crumbs, crumbed, crumb ing.**

crum ble (krum′bl), *v.* 1. to break apart into crumbs. *The cake began to crumble as soon as it was cut.* 2. to fall apart; to break into bits. *Over a long period of time the old building slowly crumbled.* **crum bles, crum bled, crum bling.**

crush (krush), *v.* 1. to press together tightly so as to break or bend out of the original shape. *The front of the car was crushed by the falling tree.* 2. to crumble something by squeezing it; to break into pieces. *The road roller crushed the stone into small bits.* 3. to overcome completely; to conquer. *The army crushed the enemy.* **crush es, crushed, crush ing.**
n. 4. a crushing together; pressure. *The roof finally gave way under the crush of snow.* 5. a large crowd of people. *The stores were jammed with a crush of shoppers.* **crush es.**

crust (krust), *n.* 1. the outer surface of a loaf of bread. *The crust on most loaves of bread is hard and crisp.* 2. a piece of this outer surface, or any piece of dry bread. *The birds were given crusts to eat during the snowstorm.* 3. the outer

crowns:
a. king
b. queen
c. prince
d. duke
e. marquis
f. count
g. baron

CRUSTACEANS

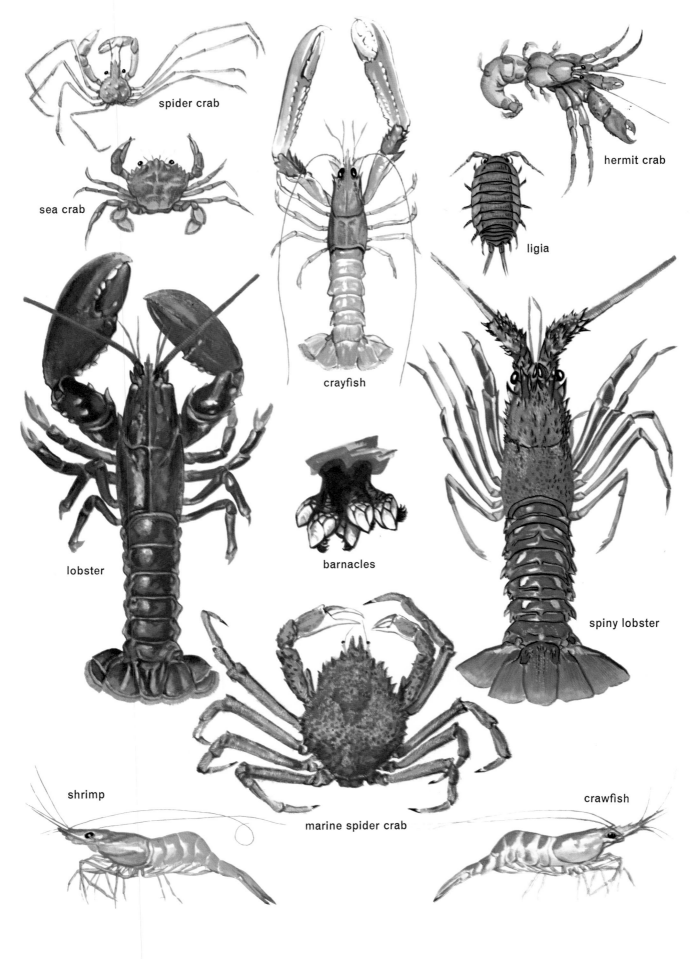

spider crab

sea crab

hermit crab

ligia

crayfish

lobster

barnacles

spiny lobster

shrimp

marine spider crab

crawfish

covering of a pie, which is on top of the filling. *The crust on her apple pie is light and flaky.* 4. any hard outer surface. *The crust of the earth is about twenty-five miles deep. A crust of ice had formed on the pond.* **crusts.**

v. 5. to cover or become covered with a crust; to form a crust on. *A thin layer of ice crusted the grass during the night.* **crusts, crust ed, crust ing.**

crus ta cean (krus tā′shən), *n.* any member of a class of animals which have hard outer shells. *Most crustaceans live in or near water.* **crus ta ceans.**

cry (krī), *v.* 1. to weep; to shed tears and make sounds of sadness and pain. *The baby cried all night, and kept us awake.* 2. to shout loudly. *"Look out!" she cried. "We're going to crash!"* 3. to sell something by shouting about it. *The peanut man cried "peanuts" all during the ball game.* **cries, cried, cry ing.**

n. 4. a sound of pain, unhappiness, etc. *When Father struck his thumb with the hammer, his cry of anger startled us all.* 5. a loud shout. *We heard his cries for help above the sound of the storm.* 6. a long period of weeping. *Sometimes a person feels better after having a good cry.* 7. the call made by someone who is selling something. *The cries of the salesman stopped suddenly as each item was sold.* 8. the sound made by an animal. *We woke up at dawn to the cries of the birds.* **cries.**

crys tal (kris′tl), *n.* 1 a solid body, formed from a liquid, with flat, regularly arranged surfaces. *Crystals of ice formed on the inside of the window.* 2. a clear, hard mineral that looks like ice or glass. *We found lovely crystals in the cave.* 3. a piece of this mineral used as an ornament. *Is that jewel a diamond or a crystal?* 4. very fine glass. *They always use their best crystal when they have guests for dinner.* 5. the transparent cover over the dial of a watch. *The crystal keeps dust and dirt out of the watch.* **crys tals.**

adj. 6. made of crystal or very fine glass. *She was wearing crystal earrings.* 7. like crystal; very clear. *We walked along the crystal lake in the early morning.*

cub (kub), *n.* 1. the young offspring of a bear, lion, wolf, etc. *A lion cub is a great pet until it becomes too large to be played with safely.* 2. **cub scout,** a member of a division of the Boy Scouts of America for boys eight to ten years old. *He was a cub scout for two years before he became a boy scout.* **cubs.**

cubism

cubist painting

cube (kūb), *n.* 1. a solid body which has six equal square sides. *The building blocks that many children have are cubes.* 2. the product obtained by multiplying a number by itself twice. *Since $4 \times 4 \times 4 = 64$, the cube of 4 is 64.* **cubes.**

v. to cut or form into a cube. *Sugar is cubed to make it easier to use in coffee and tea.* **cubes, cubed, cub ing.**

cub ism (kū′biz əm), *n.* a kind of painting that does not show objects in the way we usually see them. *Cubism, introduced in the early 1900's, uses cubes and other figures in geometry to show the feelings of the artist.*

cuck oo (kuk′ü), *n.* 1. a bird whose call sounds somewhat like "cuckoo." *The European cuckoo lays its eggs in nests built by other birds, and the other birds take care of the cuckoo eggs until they hatch.* 2. the sound made by the cuckoo. *The bird's cuckoo attracted our attention.* **cuck oos.**

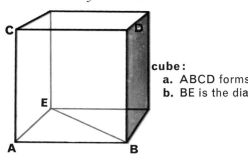

cube:
a. ABCD forms one side
b. BE is the diagonal of the base

cuckoo

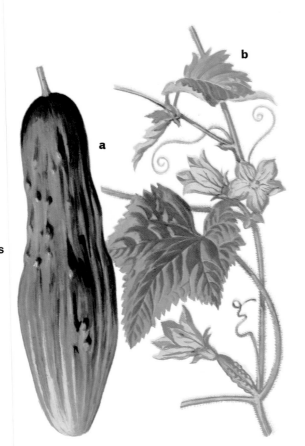

cucumber:
a. vegetable
b. vine with leaves and flowers

cu cum ber (kū′kəm bər), *n.* a long, green vegetable with a white inner part. *Cucumbers are eaten raw in salads, and are also made into pickles.* **cu cum bers.**

cuff[1] (kuf), *n.* the fold of material turned over at the end of a sleeve or turned up at the bottom of a trouser leg. *We looked for hours for the missing coin without success until I happened to look in the cuff of my pants.* **cuffs.**

cuff[2] (kuf), *v.* 1. to strike with the open hand; to slap. *The robbers cuffed the owner of the store until he told them where the money was hidden.* **cuffs, cuffed, cuff ing.**
n. 2. a slap; a hit made with the open hand. *He gave me a cuff on the ear for being late.* **cuffs.**

cul ti vate (kul′tə vāt′), *v.* 1. to make soil ready for the planting and raising of crops. *All of the farmer's fields were cultivated by the end of April.* 2. to assist the growth of plants by working and taking care of them. *When we cultivated the roses in our garden, we had to spray them regularly and keep the ground free of weeds.* 3. to break up the soil around plants. *If you cultivate the ground around your tulips, you will get bigger flowers.* 4. to improve the mind; develop mental abilities. *In first grade, he cultivated an interest in prehistoric animals.* 5. to develop the friendship of someone; to seek the company of someone. *He cultivated the best student in our class to help him with his homework.* **cul ti vates, cul ti vat ed, cul ti vat ing.**

cul tur al (kəl′chə rəl), *adj.* of or relating to

culture. *Schools are interested in the cultural development of their students.* **cul tur al ly,** *adv.*

cul ture (kəl′chər), *n.* 1. The growing or development of something by effort or careful attention. *The wheat culture developed by the scientists increased the farmer's crop.* 2. a civilization of a particular kind at a certain time or stage of being. *The Roman culture borrowed much of its art from the Greek.* **cul tures.**

cul tured (kəl′chərd), *adj.* made under artificial conditions; cultivated. *These are the cultured pearls I bought in Japan.*

cun ning (kun′ing), *adj.* 1. sly; clever; able to deceive easily. *The cunning robbers escaped with all of the jewels.* 2. expert at some art etc.; skillful. *The cunning hands of the magician amazed us all.* 3. pretty; attractive; charming. *Everyone was drawn to the cunning little child.* **cun ning ly,** *adv.*
n. 4. slyness; cleverness. *The cunning of the fox enabled him to escape from the hunters.*

cup (kup), *n.* 1. a small, hollow container, often having a handle, used for drinking. *Pour some tea into my cup, please.* 2. the amount that a cup can hold; cupful. *I'll have a cup of coffee. This recipe calls for one cup of sugar.* 3. anything shaped like a cup or used like a cup. *The winners were awarded gold cups as prizes.* **cups.**
v. 4. to form something into a shape like a cup. *The boy cupped his hands to hold his marbles.* **cups, cupped, cup ping.**

cup board (kub′ərd), *n.* a cabinet with shelves, used for storing food, dishes, etc. *When we had the kitchen remodeled, we had more cupboards installed.* **cup boards.**

cup ful (kup′fül′), *n.* the amount that a cup can hold; a half pint. *Don't forget to add an extra cupful of milk to the pancake mix.* **cup fuls.**

curb (kėrb), *n.* 1. a chain or strap on a horse's bit which pulls against his lower jaw. *The curb is used to control the horse's movements.* 2. a ridge or border of concrete, cement, etc. along the edge of a street, walk, etc. *The car pulled to the curb and stopped.* 3. anything which restrains or holds in check. *A slice of bread before dinner can be a curb to your appetite.* **curbs.**
v. 4. to restrain; to control; to check. *You must curb your dog by keeping him on a leash.* **curbs, curbed, curb ing.**

cure (kūr), *v.* 1. to restore to good health; to heal. *The doctor used special medicines to cure him of the measles.* 2. to free or get rid of something bad. *He finally was cured of the habit of shouting at everyone.* 3. to treat leather, meat, etc.; keep from spoiling. *Ham is cured by soaking it in salt water.* **cures, cured, cur ing.**
n. 4. a remedy; anything which brings back health or overcomes disease. *What cure do you use for a cold?* 5. the act of returning to good health. *His cure was rapid and complete.* **cures.**

cur few (kėr′fū), *n.* the time that children or young people should be off the streets and at home. *Many big cities have a curfew around ten o'clock at night.* **cur fews.**

cu ri os i ty (kūr′ē os′ə tē), *n.* 1. an eager interest in knowing things or learning about things. *His curiosity about electricity led him to many shocking discoveries.* 2. anything that is unusual or strange. *A two-headed dog is a real curiosity.* **cu ri os i ties.**

cu ri ous (kūr′ē əs), *adj.* 1. eager and interested in knowing about or learning things. *I was curious about how the police discovered the identity of the thief.* 2. unusual; strange; odd. *He has a curious habit of scratching his ear while he speaks.* **cu ri ous ly,** *adv.*

curl (kėrl), *v.* 1. to twist or turn into rings or spirals. *She curls her hair every night.* 2. to form into rings. *Smoke curled upward from the fire.* 3. to coil. *The cowboy's lasso was curled around the saddle.* **curls, curled, curl ing.**
n. 4. a lock of hair forming a ring. *Her head was covered with curls.* 5. anything shaped like a ring or spiral. *A curl of white smoke rose from the chimney.* **curls.**

curly (kėr′lē), *adj.* 1. having curls. *All of their boys have curly hair.* 2. shaped like a curl; curled. *Pigs have curly tails.* **curl i er, curl i est.**

cur rant (kėr′ənt), *n.* 1. a small, seedless raisin used in cooking and baking. *My mother puts currants in rice pudding.* 2. a small, sour red or black berry that grows in groups on a bush. *These currants taste best after they have been cooked with sugar and made into jelly.* 3. the bush on which these berries grow. *We saw currants growing wild along the side of the road.* **cur rants.**

cur rent (kėr′ənt), *n.* 1. the movement of water or air in a definite direction; a flow. *The canoe tipped over because of the strong current.* 2. the movement or flow of electricity in a wire. *The current was cut off when the fuse blew.* 3. the general movement or drift of opinions, ideas, etc. *No one can be sure of the next shift in the current of public opinion.* **cur rents.**
adj. 4. belonging to the present. *What is the current price of milk?* 5. passing from one person to another; in common use. *That was a current joke twenty years ago.* **cur rent ly,** *adv.*

cur sive (kėr′siv), *adj.* written with the letters joined together; not printed. *After children have mastered the alphabet and printing, they begin to learn cursive writing.*

cur tain (kėrt′n), *n.* 1. a hanging piece of cloth used to decorate a door or window, to separate the audience from the stage in a theater, to conceal something, etc. *Mother hung new curtains at the bedroom window. Theaters are required to have fireproof curtains on the stage.* 2. anything that looks like a curtain or is used like a curtain. *A curtain of rain made it impossible for us to see where we were going.* **cur tains.**
v. 3. to provide with curtains. *We curtained the windows in the tree house with old sheets.* **cur tains, cur tained, cur tain ing.**

curt sy (kėrt′sē), *n.* 1. a bow in which the body is lowered and the knees are bent, made by girls and women to show respect. *Her first curtsy was stiff, but she soon learned to do it smoothly.* **curt sies.**
v. 2. to make such a bow. *All of the women in the room curtsied when the queen entered.* **curt sies, curt sied, curt sy ing.**

curve (kėrv), *n.* 1. a bending line that has no angles and no straight sections. *Any arc of a circle is a curve. A rainbow is a curve.* 2. a bending in something. *Just ahead of us was a sharp curve in the road.* **curves.**
v. 3. to bend something so that it has no angles and no straight sections. *The street curved right and then left.* **curves, curved, curv ing.**

cush ion (kush′ən), *n.* 1. a soft pad or pillow used to sit, kneel, or lie on. *His father propped a cushion against a tree before sitting down.* 2. anything that looks like such a pad or can be used like one. *I took a nap on a cushion of fresh hay.* **cush ions.**
v. 3. to provide with a cushion; to act as a cushion for. *A huge pile of leaves cushioned his fall from the tree.* **cush ions, cush ioned, cush ion ing.**

cus tard (kus′tərd), *n.* a cooked mixture of sugar, eggs, and milk. *Tom had two dishes of vanilla custard for dessert.* **cus tards.**

cus to di an (kus tō′dē ən), *n.* 1. a person who is the guardian of something; person who is in charge. *The custodian of the zoo requested us not to feed the animals.* 2. janitor. *The custodian of the building kept the sidewalks free of snow during the winter.* **cus to di ans.**

cus tom (kus′təm), *n.* 1. a usual practice; the ordinary, accepted way of doing something. *Rising when a woman enters the room is a courteous custom practiced by men.* 2. the regular business given to a store or business by a customer. *I have been giving that store my custom for several years.* 3. **customs,** (a) taxes or duty paid on things brought into a country from a foreign country. *The customs on most goods are fairly reasonable.* (b) the department of the government that collects these taxes; any office used by this division. *We had to go through customs when we returned from France.* **cus toms.**
adj. 4. made for a particular person; made to order. *I ordered a custom suit from the tailor.* 5. doing only work that is made to order. *His father goes to a custom tailor for his shirts.*

cus tom er (kus′tə mər), *n.* any person who buys something, especially a person who buys regularly at the same place. *There were four other customers in the store when I went in.* **cus tom ers.**

cut (kut), *v.* 1. to pierce, separate, remove, or open with a sharp object. *I had to cut the grass before I went to the ball game.* 2. to make something by piercing, opening, etc. with a sharp object. *He cut a hole in his paper with a scissors.* 3. to pierce one's skin; to wound. *She cut her finger while peeling the potatoes.* 4. to make less; to reduce. *That store will have to cut its prices if it expects customers to return.* 5. to pass through and across; to cross. *The driver of an automobile must be alert for traffic that cuts across the highway.* 6. to go by a shorter route; to follow a more direct path. *The boys next door cut through our yard on their way to school.* 7. to sting by hitting sharply. *The freezing rain cut my face and hands.* 8. to hurt by an unkind or cruel remark, action, etc. *He was deeply cut by the constant teasing of his classmates.* 9. to refuse to accept someone socially or as a friend. *The other girls cut her by not inviting her to their party.* **cuts, cut, cut ting.**

n. 10. a piercing, opening, etc. made with a sharp object. *Sap oozed out through the cut in the tree.* 11. a wound. *The cut on his foot is almost healed.* 12. a reduction; a making less. *A cut in our expenses will enable us to make a profit.* 13. a piece of something that has been cut off. *We got a very nice cut of meat from the butcher.* 14. a path or passage made by something that passes through or across. *The river made a deep cut through the rocks. We followed a short cut through the woods.* 15. a remark or action that hurts one's feelings. *That cut about my brother's honesty made me angry.* 16. a block or plate used for printing; what is printed by such a plate. *The cuts in this book are colorful and clear.* 17. the way in which something is shaped or styled. *I like the cut of your new coat.* **cuts.**

cute (kūt), *adj.* 1. pretty; attractive. *We saw a cute little puppy at the pet shop.* 2. clever; shrewd. *That was a cute trick; can you do it again?* **cut er, cut est; cute ly,** *adv.*

cut lass (kut′ləs), *n.* a short, curved sword. *The pirates rushed onto the deck of the captured ship, waving their cutlasses.* **cut lass es.**

cut ter (kut′ər), *n.* 1. any person, tool, machine, etc. that cuts. *A butcher is a meat cutter. Use the paper cutter to trim those pages.* 2. a small sled having two runners in which people may ride. *We took a ride through the snow-filled woods on a horse-drawn cutter.* 3. a small, single-sailed boat. *Because of the waves the cutters were ordered to leave the lake, but the larger boats were allowed to sail.* 4. a small, armed boat used to watch the coast. *When our fishing boat overturned, we were rescued by a Coast Guard cutter.* 5. a small boat used to carry supplies, people, etc. between a warship and the shore. *The sailors had to wait for the cutter to return so that they could leave the ship.* **cut ters.**

cut ting (kut′ing), *n.* 1. a stem or branch cut from a plant and grown as a new plant. *Many*

cylinder

cymbals

cutlass

cypress:
a. branch
b. tree

a

b

of our friends have used cuttings from our rose bush to grow their own roses. **cut tings.**

adj. 2. having the ability to cut; used for cutting. *The cutting edge of this knife is very dull.* 3. intended to hurt the feelings. *His cutting remarks made us uncomfortable.* **cut ting ly,** *adv.*

cy cle (sī′kəl), *n.* 1. a complete series of events or conditions that occur over and over again in the same order. *The hours of the day and the seasons of the year form cycles.* 2. the period of time during which such a series takes place. *People perform certain regular functions during a twenty-four hour cycle.* 3. a complete series of poems or stories about a person or an event. *Have you read any of the stories in the King Arthur cycle?* 4. a long period of time; an age. *During one cycle, much of the United States was covered by ice.* **cy cles.**

v. 5. to ride a bicycle, tricycle, etc. *We cycled through the city on a bicycle built for two.* **cy cles, cy cled, cy cling.**

cy clone (sī′klōn), *n.* 1. a severe storm with high-speed winds blowing around a relatively calm center. *A cyclone may be as large as a thousand miles across the center.* 2. any violent windstorm. *A hurricane or a tornado may be called a cyclone even though it is smaller and occurs only in certain sections of the world.* **cy clones.**

cyl in der (sil′ən dər), *n.* a round body, either hollow or solid, with straight sides and flat ends. *A new piece of round chalk is a cylinder.* **cyl in ders.**

cym bal (sim′bəl), *n.* one of two metal musical instruments shaped like plates. *The cymbals clanged together as the band came to the exciting part of the music.* **cym bals.**

cy press (sī′prəs), *n.* a kind of evergreen tree. *The cypress is narrow and has fairly dark leaves.* **cy press es.**

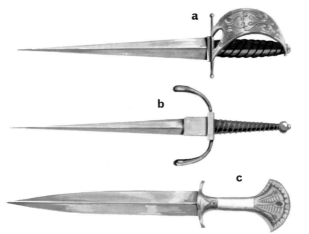

daggers:
a. Spanish
b. Italian
c. Sumerian

D or **d** (dē), 1. the fourth letter of the alphabet. 2. the Roman numeral 500.

dab (dab), *v.* 1. to tap or pat lightly; to touch gently. *The woman dabbed her nose with a handkerchief.* 2. to apply with light strokes. *The artist dabbed paint on the canvas.* **dabs, dabbed, dab bing.**
n. 3. a light touch; a tap. *The lion made a dab at the meat before he ate it.* 4. a small amount of something. *She gave me a dab of potatoes with my supper. Each of us had two dabs of butter.* **dabs.**

dad (dad), *n.* a father. *My dad took us to the movies.* **dads.**

dad dy (dad′ē), *n.* a father. *The first word the baby could say was "Daddy."* **dad dies.**

dag ger (dag′ər), *n.* a short, pointed knife used as a weapon. *In the days before guns, some soldiers used daggers.* **dag gers.**

dahl ia (dal′yə), *n.* a tall plant with large, showy flowers. *Dahlias grow from bulbs.* **dahl ias.**

dai ly (dā′lē), *adj.* 1. appearing, done, or occurring every day. *He takes a daily walk in the park. He delivers a daily newspaper.*
adv. 2. each day; every day. *He delivers newspapers daily.*
n. 3. a newspaper that is published every day. *There are four large dailies in our city.* **dai lies.**

dair y (dâr′ē), *n.* 1. a farm on which milk, cream, and other milk products are produced.

That herd of cows is part of the largest dairy in this area. 2. a company or store that sells or delivers milk and milk products. *This dairy buys milk from over one hundred farms.* 3. a building or a part of a building in which milk is stored or processed. *The farmers bring their milk to the dairy every morning.* **dair ies.** (See illustration on following page.)

dai sy (dā′zē), *n.* a common flower which has white, pink, or yellow petals around a brown or yellow center. *Daisies grow wild in many parts of the world.* **dai sies.** (See illustration on following page.)

dam[1] (dam), *n.* 1. a structure of earth, concrete, etc. which holds back water in a river or a stream and controls its flow. *Dams are used to produce electricity and to supply water for irrigation.* **dams.** (See illustration on page 131.)
v. 2. to hold back (the flow of water in a river or stream) with a dam. *A fallen tree had dammed the river.* **dams, dammed, dam ming.**

dam[2] (dam), *n.* the mother of a four-footed animal, especially a sheep or deer. *The dam guarded her young from the hunters.* **dams.**

dahlia

sand, āte, bâre, fäther; sent, mē, fėrn; fit, bīke; pot, rōpe, fôrt; run, pùll, rüle, cūte; noise, sound; ch, cheese; ng, long; th, thick; ~~th~~, those; zh, treasure; ə = a in about, e in waken, i in animal, o in seldom, and u in minus.

dairy farm

dam age (dam′ij), *n.* 1. an injury, harm, or break which lowers the worth or usefulness of something. *Severe damage was done to the house by the storm.* 2. **damages,** money paid or requested as a result of an injury, harm, or break. *The insurance company had to pay millions of dollars in damages to the people whose homes were struck by the storm.* **dam ag es.**
v. 3. to break, injure, or harm something. *He damaged the front of his car in the accident.* **dam ag es, dam aged, dam ag ing.**

dame (dām), *n.* 1. a British title given to a woman of position, rank, or authority. *Dame Sybil visited the queen this afternoon for tea.* 2. an old woman. *Several white-haired dames sat in the front row of the theater.* **dames.**

damp (damp), *adj.* 1. somewhat wet; moist. *The clothes were still damp when we took them out of the drier.* **damp er, damp est; damp ly,** *adv.*

daisy

v. 2. to hold back; check; extinguish. *The campers damped the fire before they went to sleep.* **damps, damped, damp ing.**
n. 3. a wetness; moisture. *We shivered in the damp of the forest.* 4. a poisonous gas mixture sometimes found in coal mines. *Several miners were burned by exploding damp.* **damps.**

damp en (dam′pən), *v.* 1. to hold back; check. *Her accident dampened our fun.* 2. make or become moist or wet. *Always dampen the clothes before ironing, and you will get better results.* **damp ens, damp ened, damp en ing.**

dance (dans), *v.* 1. to move, walk, step, etc. in time to music. *Can you dance to this song?* 2. to move through a particular series of steps in time to music. *Everyone at the party tried to dance to the waltz.* 3. to move or jump up and down and around. *The boxer danced lightly about the ring. Moonlight danced on the water.* **danc es, danced, danc ing.**
n. 4. a motion in time to music. *He did a little dance to the music on the radio.* 5. a particular series of steps done in time to music. *Can you do that new dance?* 6. a party or gathering of people for dancing. *There will be a dance in the gymnasium on Friday night.* 7. a set or round of dancing. *May I have this dance?* **danc es.**

danc er (dan′sər), *n.* 1. any person who dances. *The dancers stood on the floor, waiting for the music to begin.* 2. a person whose profession or work is dancing. *A good dancer must practice every day.* **danc ers.**

dan de li on (dan′də lī′ən), *n.* a common weed with large leaves and yellow flowers. *Dandelions appear on our lawn every spring.* **dan de li ons.**

dan dy (dan′dē), *n.* 1. a person who is too concerned about his clothes and appearance. *He is such a dandy, he spends two hours getting ready to go to school.* **dan dies.**
adj. 2. excellent; very good. *We saw a dandy football game on television.* **dan di er, dan di est.**

dan ger (dān′jər), *n.* 1. peril; risk; chance of

injury or harm. *The danger of his work does not bother a trapeze artist.* 2. anything that may cause damage, injury, or harm. *The current in the river is a danger to swimmers.* **dan gers.**

dan ger ous (dān′jər əs), *adj.* 1. perilous; risky; full of danger. *Mountain climbing is a dangerous sport.* 2. likely to cause injury, harm, or damage. *A dangerous criminal escaped from the prison.* **dan ger ous ly,** *adv.*

dare (dâr), *v.* 1. to have the courage to do something. *You wouldn't dare jump from that bridge.* 2. to have the courage to face something; to be bold enough to try something. *The swimmer dared the icy waters of the lake.* 3. to demand that someone do something as proof of courage; to challenge. *I dare you to say that again. They dared me to jump from the high diving board.* **dares, dared, dar ing.**
n. 4. a challenge. *I took the dare and jumped.* **dares.**

dar ing (dâr′ing), *adj.* bold; willing to take chances. *His daring adventure led him into the heart of the jungle.* **dar ing ly,** *adv.*

dark (därk), *adj.* 1. not light; having little or no light. *The dark street was deserted.* 2. almost black; not light in color. *Don't you have a dark suit to wear?* 3. gloomy. *A dark look crossed his face.* 4. mysterious; hidden; secret. *He refused to reveal the dark details of his past.* **dark er, dark est; dark ly,** *adv.*
n. 5. a darkness; nightfall. *You must return before dark.* 6. a blackness; a dark color. *There is a striking contrast of light and dark in that painting.* 7. **in the dark,** in ignorance; without knowledge of something. *We were in the dark about what he was saying.* **darks.**

dark en (där′kən), *v.* 1. to make dark. *He darkened the room by turning off the light.* 2. to become dark. *The sky darkened as the storm approached.* **dark ens, dark ened, dark en ing.**

dark ness (därk′nis), *n.* being without light; dark in color or shade. *The darkness of the room was a relief from the bright sun.* **dark ness es.**

ballet **dancers**

dar ling (där′ling), *n.* 1. a person who is greatly loved. *The baby was the darling of his parents.* **dar lings.**
adj. 2. greatly loved; dear. *What have you done, my darling child?*

darn (därn), *v.* 1. to repair a torn fabric by weaving thread back and forth across the hole or tear. *Mother darns my socks when they are torn.* **darns, darned, darn ing.**
n. 2. a place that has been mended by darning. *Some of my socks have two or three darns.* **darns.**

dart (därt), *n.* 1. a short, narrow, pointed weapon that is thrown by hand or blown through a gun. *The boy hit the target with his first dart.* 2. a sudden, quick movement. *The boy made a dart for the door.* 3. **darts,** a game in which darts are thrown at a target. *I have never been able to beat my father at darts.* **darts.**

dam

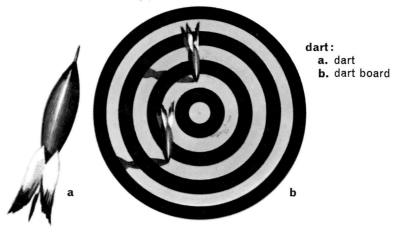

dart:
a. dart
b. dart board

v. 4. to move quickly and suddenly. *The child darted into the street.* 5. to send out or throw suddenly. *As I reached for the candy, mother darted an angry look at me.* **darts, dart ed, dart ing.**

dash (dash), *v.* 1. to rush quickly. *We dashed to the store, but it had closed.* 2. to throw or splash. *We dashed water in his face to wake him up.* 3. to throw down and break. *The baby dashed his bottle against the wall.* 4. to ruin; destroy. *Our plans were dashed when we were unable to raise any money.* 5. **dash off,** to do or make in a hurry. *The artist dashed off a sketch of his latest work.* **dash es, dashed, dash ing.**
n. 6. a very small amount; a little bit. *Add a dash of pepper to this recipe.* 7. a short race run at full speed. *He can do the hundred-yard dash in less than ten seconds.* 8. a punctuation mark (—) used to show a break in thought or the fact that something has been left out. *A dash can be used to show that a sentence is incomplete or that a sharp contrast is being used in the sentence.* **dash es.**

da ta (dāt′ə, dat′ə), *n. pl.* information; details, facts, and figures about something. *Scientists collect all kinds of data in their experiments.*

date¹ (dāt), *n.* 1. the day, month, or year in which something occurred or occurs. *The date of that battle was 1066. What is the date of your birth?* 2. a statement of the day, month, or year when a newspaper, book, coin, etc. was issued. *The date on this coin is 1911.* 3. a period of time to which a thing, fact, etc. belongs. *Before that date, books were copied by hand.* 4. an appointment to meet someone at a certain time and in a certain place. *I have a date to go to the movies with them.* **dates.**
v. 5. to mark a date on something. *The newspaper was dated April 14, 1865.* 6. to determine the time when something occurred. *Scientists have dated the fossils by their bone structure.* 7. to belong to the time of. *These costumes date from the early 1800's.* **dates, dat ed, dat ing.**

date² (dāt), *n.* 1. a kind of palm tree that bears a sweet fruit. *A number of dates grew around the edge of the oasis.* 2. the fruit of this tree. *She used dried dates in making these cookies.* **dates.**

daugh ter (dô′tər), *n.* 1. a girl or woman as she is related to her parents; a female child. *That man has seven daughters and seven granddaughters.* 2. a girl or woman as she is related to a group, country, etc. *She is one of America's most beautiful daughters.* **daugh ters.**

dawn (dôn), *n.* 1. the first appearance of light in the morning. *Dawn came at six o'clock this morning.* 2. the beginning of anything. *The invention of the automobile marked the dawn of a new age in transportation.* **dawns.**
v. 3. to grow light in the east in the morning. *We were on the trail as the day dawned.* 4. to begin; to start. *A new age dawned with the invention of the radio.* 5. to begin to be recog-

date:
a. date palm
b. bunch of dates

nized or understood. *It never dawned on me that he was asking a question.* **dawns, dawned, dawn ing.**

day (dā), *n.* 1. the time between sunrise and sunset; the period when there is light. *We traveled during the day and slept at night.* 2. the period of twenty-four hours that begins at midnight. *It takes the earth approximately one day to make a complete rotation on its axis.* 3. any certain period of time. *Many people went to the West during the days of the Gold Rush.* 4. the period of time set aside for working, going to school, etc. *Father had a hard day at the office today.* **days.**

day break (dā′brāk′), *n.* the time of the first appearance of light in the morning; dawn. *At daybreak the farmer rose and fed the horses and cows.*

day dream (dā′drēm′), *n.* 1. pleasant, dreamy thoughts. *She has daydreams about being a beautiful movie star.* **day dreams.**
v. 2. to have pleasant, dreamy thoughts. *I was daydreaming when the teacher called on me.* **day dreams, day dreamed, day dream ing.**

day light (dā′līt′), *n.* 1. the light of the sun; the light of day. *When I raised the shades, daylight streamed into the room.* 2. the time between sunrise and sunset when there is light. *Since there are no lights for the field, the game will be played during daylight.* 3. the dawn; daybreak. *The rooster crowed an hour before daylight.*

---

sand, āte, bâre, fäther; sent, mē, fėrn; fit, bīke; pot, rōpe, fôrt; run, pùll, rüle, cūte; noise, sound; ch, cheese; ng, long; th, thick; ŧħ, those; zh, treasure; ə = a in about, e in waken, i in animal, o in seldom, and u in minus.

day time (dā′tīm′), *n.* the time between sunrise and sunset when there is light. *We are allowed to play outside during the daytime.*

dead (ded), *adj.* 1. no longer alive. *The dead tree fell over and crashed in our driveway.* 2. not alive; without life. *Stones are dead objects.* 3. not active; uneventful and uninteresting. *We went to a dead party last night.* 4. lacking force, motion, power, etc.; not working. *The motor was dead and couldn't be started.* 5. lacking feeling; numb. *His fingers had fallen asleep and lay dead on the keyboard.* 6. no longer used. *Wearing spats and using pocket watches are dead customs.* 7. certain; sure. *He is a dead shot with a rifle.* 8. dull; not bright or shiny. *The house was painted a dead-green color.* 9. complete. *In spite of our efforts to sell tickets, the play was a dead loss.*
adv. 10. entirely; completely. *The teacher was dead right in his reply. She was dead tired from doing so much work.* 11. in a straight line; directly. *If you walk dead ahead, you will find the school.*
n. 12. **the dead:** (a) all of those persons who have died. *People in our society place the dead in cemeteries.* (b) the quietest time; the time when practically no one is awake. *We arrived home in the dead of night.*

dead ly (ded′lē), *adj.* 1. something that could cause death. *A gun is a deadly weapon.* 2. extremely accurate. *His deadly aim with a gun was known throughout the West.* 3. marked or extreme determination. *With deadly seriousness she approached the stage.*
adv. 4. a deathlike appearance. *Her appearance was deadly.* 5. extremely. *The party was deadly boring.*

deaf (def), *adj.* 1. unable to hear. *The deaf man had learned to read lips, and could talk with everyone.* 2. unable to hear well; hard of hearing. *You'll have to speak louder because I'm deaf.* 3. unwilling to listen; not giving attention to. *The teachers were deaf to our requests.*

deal (dēl), *v.* 1. to have to do with; to treat of; to be concerned with. *This book deals with the history of America.* 2. to act. *That store always deals fairly with its customers.* 3. to do business in; to buy or offer for sale. *In our stores we deal only in the finest merchandise.* 4. to do business with; to buy from. *Do you deal with that department store?* 5. to deliver; to give. *The horse dealt a hard kick to the side of the barn.* 6. to hand out; distribute. *Whose turn is it to deal the cards?* **deals, dealt, deal ing.**
n. 7. a good price on something; a bargain. *He got a real deal on his new car.* 8. a distribution; a giving out. *Be sure to hand out all of the cards on the next deal.* 9. a certain amount; a portion. *We spent a great deal of time practicing.* **deals.**

deal er (dēl′ər), *n.* 1. a buyer and seller of goods. *His uncle is a furniture dealer.* 2. the person who distributes cards in a card game. *The dealer gave each of us five cards.* **deal ers.**

deal ing (dēl′ing), *n.* 1. a manner of doing business or acting towards others. *He is known for his completely honest dealings.* 2. a business transaction. *You have to be careful when having dealings with him.* **deal ings.**

dear (dir), *adj.* 1. greatly loved. *He gave the book to a dear friend.* 2. expensive; high priced. *That car is too dear for me to buy.* **dear er, dear est; dear ly,** *adv.*
n. 3. darling; dearest. *"Let's go home, dear,"* he said to his wife. **dears.**

death (deth), *n.* 1. a dying; the ending of life. *His death was a great shock to us.* 2. the ending of anything. *The death of our plan came when the president of the club vetoed it.* 3. the fact or state of being dead. *His death was a shock to all his friends.* 4. something that causes death. *His decision meant the death of our hopes.* **deaths.**

de bate (di bāt′), *n.* 1. a formal discussion on a particular subject. *We heard a debate on methods of teaching reading last night.* 2. any discussion. *There was a great deal of debate about which play our class would present.* **de bates.**
v. 3. to discuss a subject according to formal rules. *Some of the students in our school will debate the importance of sports with students from other schools.* 4. to discuss any topic. *I don't wish to debate my opinions with you.* 5. to think about the reasons for and against something. *I debated about buying a new tennis racket, and decided against it.* **de bates, de bat ed, de bat ing.**

debt (det), *n.* 1. something owed to another person, usually money. *I owe him a debt of sixteen dollars.* 2. **in debt,** owing more than can be paid at once. *He is in debt for his house and his car.* **debts.**

debt or (det′ər), *n.* a person who owes money or something else to another person. *I will be your debtor forever because you saved my life.* **debt ors.**

dec ade (dek′ād), *n.* a ten-year period. *Great scientific advances were made in the decade between 1950 and 1960.* **dec ades.**

dec a gon (dek′ə gon), *n.* a closed, flat figure having ten sides and ten angles. *The sides of a regular decagon are all equal.* **dec a gons.**

Dec a logue (dek′ə log), *n.* the Ten Commandments. *The Bible says that Moses carved the Decalogue into a rock, as God told him.*

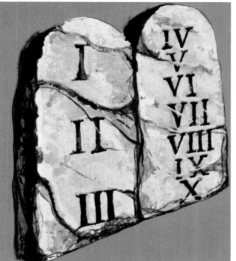

Decalogue

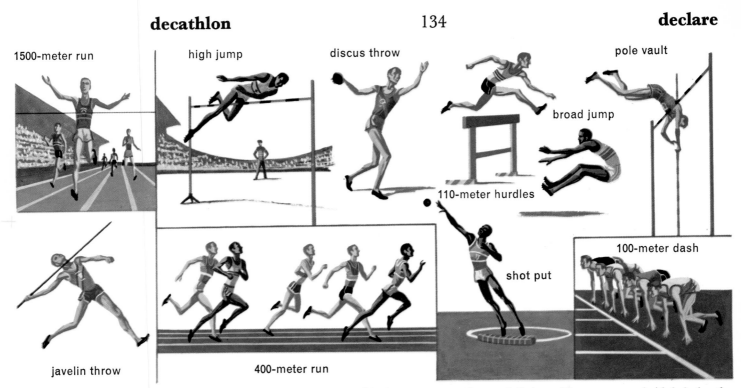

1500-meter run · high jump · discus throw · pole vault · broad jump · 110-meter hurdles · shot put · 100-meter dash · javelin throw · 400-meter run

decathlon

de cath lon (di kath′lon′), *n.* an athletic contest that tests ability in ten events. *The decathlon includes running, throwing heavy objects, and jumping.* **de cath lons.**

de cay (di kā′), *v.* 1. to rot; to become rotten. *Most fruits will decay if they are not kept in a cool, dry place.* 2. to become weaker, less strong, etc. gradually. *The house was so old that it was decaying and about to fall down.* **de cays, de cayed, de cay ing.**
n. 3. a gradual rotting or loss of strength, beauty, etc. *The decay of the fruit had gone too far for us to save any of it. The decay of the Roman Empire finally resulted in its complete destruction.*

de ceive (di sēv′), *v.* 1. to make a person believe something that is not true. *He deceived us into believing that he could make rain.* 2. to lie to; to cheat. *His brother deceived us when he told us that the bicycle was new.* **de ceives, de ceived, de ceiv ing.**

De cem ber (di sem′bər), *n.* the twelfth and final month of the year. *There are thirty-one days in December.*

de cent (dē′snt), *adj.* 1. suitable; fitting and proper. *He always uses decent language. I don't have a decent suit to wear to church.* 2. not very good but not very bad; fair. *He has a decent batting average, but he'll never be a star.* 3. kind; fair; thoughtful. *It was very decent of him to offer me a job for the summer.* **de cent ly,** *adv.*

de cide (di sīd′), *v.* 1. to settle a question. *We decided on where to go by taking a vote.* 2. to make a decision; to render a judgment. *The court decided in our favor and awarded us damages.* 3. to reach a decision; to make up one's mind. *I decided to tell them the whole story.* **de cides, de cid ed, de cid ing.**

de cid ed (di sīd′əd), *adj.* 1. unmistakable; clear; definite. *There was a decided lack of interest in my plan.* 2. firm; determined; not hesitating. *He has very decided attitudes toward everything.* **de cid ed ly,** *adv.*

dec i mal (des′ə ml), *n.* 1. a fraction of ten or any number that can be divided evenly by ten. *The numbers .4, .04, and .004 are decimals which are equal to $\frac{4}{10}$, $\frac{4}{100}$, and $\frac{4}{1000}$, respectively.* 2. any number that contains such a fraction. *The number 87.75 is a decimal.* **dec i mals.**
adj. 3. based on ten; counted by tens. *Units of money in the United States are determined according to a decimal system.*

de ci sion (di sizh′ən), *n.* 1. a deciding; something decided. *My decision to skip my homework last night was a very poor one.* 2. determination. *The head of a company must be a man of decision.* **de ci sions.**

deck (dek), *n.* 1. one of the floors on a ship or boat. *We went to the upper deck to lie in the sun.* 2. any platform which is like a deck on a ship. *There is a sun deck on the roof of the hotel.* 3. a complete pack of playing cards. *When it was my turn to deal, I shuffled the deck and passed out the cards.* **decks.**
v. 4. to dress; decorate; adorn. *She was decked out in her finest clothes.* **decks, decked, deck ing.**

dec la ra tion (dek′lə rā′shən), *n.* 1. a formal statement for the public; a proclaiming. *The declaration of war was made immediately after the attack.* 2. **Declaration of Independence,** the formal statement which declared that the American colonies were no longer under the rule of Great Britain. *The Declaration of Independence was signed on July 4, 1776.* **dec la ra tions.**

de clare (di klâr′), *v.* 1. to announce publicly

and formally; to make known to others. *The politician declared himself as a candidate for mayor. Only Congress can declare war.* 2. to say positively and surely; to state openly. *"You're going to bed and that's final!" declared the boy's mother.* 3. to reveal any goods on which tax must be paid as they are brought into the country. *We declared the jewelry and perfume we had bought in Europe to the customs officer.* **de clares, de clared, de clar ing.**

de cline (di klīn′ for 1-4, dē′klīn, di klīn′ for 5-7), *v.* 1. to refuse to do something. *I offered the job to him, but he declined.* 2. to refuse in a courteous way. *We had to decline their invitation because we had made other plans.* 3. to slope downward. *The road declines to the water's edge.* 4. to lose strength and power gradually; to become worse. *The sick man has been declining.* **de clines, de clined, de clining.**
n. 5. a downward slope. *When we got to the bottom of the decline, we saw that it had become an incline.* 6. a weakening or decrease in anything. *The sick man's decline stopped suddenly, and he began to get well. A decline in prices encouraged us to buy a washing machine.* 7. the end of something; the last part. *The decline of day is marked by the sunset.* **de clines.**

de com pose (dē′kəm pōz′), *v.* 1. to decay; to rot. *The apples began to decompose long before they reached the market.* 2. to divide something into its separate parts. *Water can be decomposed into hydrogen and oxygen.* **de com pos es, de com posed, de com pos ing.**

dec o rate (dek′ə rāt), *v.* 1. to add something which increases beauty; to add beauty to; to adorn. *We decorated the room with flowers before the party.* 2. to give an award, such as a ribbon or a medal, to someone. *The soldier was decorated for his courage during the battle.* **dec o rates, dec o rat ed, dec o rat ing.**

dec o ra tion (dek′ə rā′shən), *n.* 1. anything used to decorate or make something beautiful; ornament; adornment. *We used colored paper and balloons as decorations for the dance.* 2. the act of decorating something. *We worked on the decoration of the Christmas tree for several hours.* 3. a medal or ribbon given as an award. *He received three decorations while he was in the army.* **dec o ra tions.**

dec o ra tive (dek′ə rā′tiv, dek′rə tiv), *adj.* serving to decorate; helping to make attractive. *The pillows placed about the room were very decorative.* **dec o ra tive ly, adv.**

de coy (dē′koi, di koi′ for 1 and 2, di koi′ for 3), *n.* 1. a wooden bird used by hunters to fool other birds into thinking they have found a safe place to land. *As soon as the ducks got near his decoy, the hunter fired.* 2. a person or thing used to get someone else into a trap. *The police caught the car thief after they purposely left the keys in the car as a decoy.* **de coys.**
v. 3. to fool; to get into a trap. *They decoyed him*

into coming to the scene of the crime so they could arrest him. **de coys, de coyed, de coy ing.**

de crease (di krēs′ for 1 and 2, dē′krēs, di krēs′ for 3 and 4), *v.* 1. to become less; diminish. *The noise decreased sharply when the window was closed.* 2. to cause to become less; to cause to diminish. *He decreased the volume on the radio.* **de creas es, de creased, de creas ing.**
n. 3. a growing less; a decline; reduction. *There was a sharp decrease in interest after we lost seven games in a row.* 4. the amount anything decreases. *The decrease in cost was ten dollars.* **de creas es.**

de duct (di dukt′), *v.* to subtract an amount from the total. *We will deduct ten per cent of the cost as a discount.* **de ducts, de duct ed, de duct ing.**

de duc tion (di duk′shən), *n.* 1. a subtracting of an amount from the total. *We don't make any deductions on these prices.* 2. the amount subtracted. *We have already given you a generous deduction in the price.* 3. a conclusion reached by examining evidence and information. *The detective's deduction was that the crime had been committed by a tall man with no hair.* **de duc tions.**

deed (dēd), *n.* 1. an act; an action; a thing which is done. *The police are searching for the person who committed this evil deed.* 2. a written document which shows the legal owner of land or other property. *They keep the deed to their house in a fireproof box.* **deeds.**

deem (dēm), *v.* to think; to judge; to believe. *Our Scout leader deemed it unwise to go hiking without a compass.* **deems, deemed, deem ing.**

deep (dēp), *adj.* 1. going far down; reaching far below the surface. *The fish were swimming in the deep water away from the shore.* 2. going far back; reaching far back from the front. *The children were lost in a deep forest.* 3. low in pitch or tone. *He has a deep voice. The foghorn blasted deep sounds through the darkness.* 4. difficult to understand; requiring a great deal of thought. *He was lost in deep thought when the teacher called on him.* 5. sincere; earnest. *We gave deep thanks to the men who saved us.* 6. heavy; sound. *I fell into a deep sleep as soon as I got into bed.* 7. dark and rich in color. *The sky was painted a deep red by the setting sun.* **deep er, deep est; deep ly, adv.**
adv. 8. far down; far back; far below. *We dived deep into the clear water. The car was buried deep in the snow.*
n. 9. a very deep place. *There are many deeps on the ocean floor.* 10. **the deep,** the ocean or sea. *The old sailor had sailed the deep for fifty years.* **deeps.**

deep en (dē′pən), *v.* to make or become deeper. *The workers deepened the river so that boats would not become stuck on the bottom.* **deep ens, deep ened, deep en ing.**

a

b

decoys:
  a. unpainted duck decoy
  b. painted decoy

deer

deer (dir), *n.* a graceful animal with hooves that runs very swiftly, the male of which has branched horns that fall off every year. *The deer, like the cow, has two stomachs and brings food back from the first of these for a second chewing.* **deer.**

deer skin (dir′skin′), *n.* 1. the hide of a deer used to make a kind of leather. *We hung the deerskin in a hot place so that it would dry thoroughly.* 2. the clothing made from deerskin leather. *Daniel Boone wore a jacket of deerskin.* **deer skins.**

de feat (di fēt′), *v.* 1. to conquer; to win over; to beat. *Our team was defeated by a large score.* 2. to cause to fail; to produce failure. *Our plans for a parade were defeated when we couldn't get a permit.* **de feats, de feat ed, de feat ing.** *n.* 3. an overcoming; a conquering. *The defeat of the army brought an end to the war.* 4. a being overcome; a being conquered. *His defeat in the election convinced him that he should give up politics.* **de feats.**

de fect (dē′fekt for 1, di fekt′ for 2), *n.* 1. not made perfect; having a fault. *This car has a serious defect.* **de fects.** *v.* 2. to desert a country, cause, or belief for another. *The soldier defected to another country.* **de fects, de fect ed, de fect ing.**

de fec tive (di fek′tiv), *adj.* not made properly; imperfect; faulty. *This toaster must be defective because it always burns the bread. The fire was blamed on defective wiring.* **de fec tive ly,** *adv.*

de fec tor (dē′fekt ər), *n.* a person who deserts a country, cause, or belief for another. *That man is a defector from Russia.* **de fec tors.**

de fend (di fend′), *v.* 1. to protect from harm, danger, attack, etc.; to guard. *The soldiers continued to defend the fort. The lioness defends her cubs against enemies.* 2. to act or speak in defense of something; to uphold. *Congress defended the President's decision.* 3. to act as counsel in a court for a person accused of a crime. *The judge assigned a lawyer to defend the prisoner.* **de fends, de fend ed, de fend ing.**

de fense (di fens′), *n.* 1. a defending against something; resistance. *Our defense of the plan was completed just before the vote was to be taken.* 2. something that defends. *Warm clothing and good food are the best defense against catching colds.* 3. the defending team or side in a contest, trial, etc. *The defense held them to one touchdown for the entire game. The judge ordered the defense to present its case to the court.* **de fens es.**

de file (di fīl′), *n.* a narrow, steep pass in a mountain. *The mountain climbers made their way slowly through the defile.* **de files.**

de fine (di fīn′), *v.* 1. to describe the meaning of; to explain the use of. *The dictionary defines words.* 2. to establish by telling in detail. *The office of treasurer of the club is clearly defined in the constitution.* 3. to establish clearly the limits or boundaries of something. *The actual border between those countries has never been defined.* **de fines, de fined, de fin ing.**

def i nite (def′ə nət), *adj.* 1. clear; unmistakable; exact. *Please give a definite answer to my question.* 2. having clearly defined limits. *You will have a definite amount of time to take the test.* **def i nite ly,** *adv.*

def i ni tion (def′ə nish′ən), *n.* 1. a defining or describing of something. *His definition of my duties confused me more than it helped.* 2. a description of the meaning of a word. *There are three meanings given in this definition.* 3. the clearness of something as it is seen against a background. *This is not a good photograph because there is poor definition between the bear and the forest.* **def i ni tions.**

de gree (di grē′), *n.* 1. a level, step, or stage in a process or series. *He worked his way up to the management of the company by degrees.* 2. a unit used to measure temperature. *The symbol ° is used to express degrees of temperature. Water freezes at thirty-two degrees Fahrenheit and zero degrees centigrade.* 3. a unit used to measure the arc of a circle and the size of an angle.

defile

The symbol ° is also used to express these measurements. *A circle contains 360 degrees.* 4. social position; rank. *The chairman of the women's club is a lady of high degree.* 5. a title given by a college or university as an honor or for completing a certain course of study. *He received his Master of Arts degree last year.* 6. amount. *What degree of skill do you have in playing the piano?* 7. one of the three forms of an adjective or adverb. *The positive degree is "good"; the comparative degree is "better"; and the superlative degree is "best."* **de grees.**

Del a ware (Del′ə wâr), *n.* a state in the eastern United States, on the Atlantic Coast. *Delaware was the first state to approve the United States Constitution.*

de lay (di lā′), *v.* 1. to postpone until a later time; to put off. *We will have to delay the trip until he gets better.* 2. to keep something from going on; to hinder. *The game was delayed for an hour by the storm.* 3. to move or go slowly. *If you want to arrive at school on time, don't delay along the way.* **de lays, de layed, de lay ing.** *n.* 4. a postponement; a putting off. *We lost too much time in a delay caused by car trouble.* 5. the time of waiting because of a delay. *During the delay the teams practiced on the sidelines.* **de lays.**

del e gate (del′i gət for 1, del′i gāt for 2 and 3), *n.* 1. a person who represents a group at a meeting, convention, legislature, etc. *Barbara was chosen as our class delegate to the student government.* **del e gates.** *v.* 2. to name a person to act as a delegate. *Who was delegated to attend the meeting?* 3. to assign a duty, responsibility, etc. *Mother delegates a job for each of us to do on Saturdays.* **del e gates, del e gat ed, del e gat ing.**

del i cate (del′i kət), *adj.* 1. light and pleasing to the senses. *A delicate odor of perfume filled the room. The room was painted a delicate shade of pink.* 2. carefully and expertly done; requiring careful workmanship. *The spider spun a delicate web in the doorway. The doctor performed a delicate operation this morning.* 3. fragile; easily broken or hurt. *The roses were placed in a delicate vase.* 4. sensitive to very slight changes or differences. *This is a very delicate scale. Tuning a guitar requires a delicate ear.* 5. frail; sickly; inclined to become sick. *He must remain warm at all times because of his delicate condition.* **del i cate ly,** *adv.*

de li cious (di lish′əs), *adj.* pleasing in taste or smell; tasting good; delightful. *We were given a delicious meal at the restaurant.* **de li cious ly,** *adv.*

de light (di līt′), *v.* 1. to give pleasure to; to please. *Mother delighted us with the cake she baked.* 2. to find pleasure in; to take pleasure from; to be pleased by. *He delights in playing jokes on his friends.* **de lights, de light ed, de light ing.** *n.* 3. enjoyment; pleasure; joy; something delightful. *It is a delight to talk with him because of his sense of humor.* 4. anything which delights or pleases. *Watching his daughter dance in the show was a great delight to him.* **de lights.**

de light ful (di līt′fəl), *adj.* greatly pleasing; causing joy; causing delight. *We saw a delightful movie last night.* **de light ful ly,** *adv.*

de liv er (di liv′ər), *v.* 1. to carry something and give it to a particular person or place. *The groceries were delivered before we returned home from the store.* 2. to give a message to a person. *Since Mr. Rhodes was out when I called, I asked his secretary to deliver a message to him.* 3. to speak; to express in words. *After dinner several people delivered long speeches.* 4. to hit; to aim at and strike. *The fighter delivered a solid punch on the chin to his opponent. Robin Hood delivered an arrow to the center of the target.* 5. to release; to rescue; to set free. *The slaves were delivered from slavery by Abraham Lincoln.* **de liv ers, de liv ered, de liv er ing.**

de liv ery (di liv′ər ē), *n.* 1. a carrying and distributing of something; a delivering. *There will be no delivery of mail today.* 2. the way in which a speech is given. *His delivery was good, even though he was nervous throughout the speech.* 3. a setting free. *The delivery of the prisoners followed the end of the war.* 4. the way in which a pitcher throws the ball in baseball. *He has a tricky delivery because the batter doesn't see the ball until it is released.* **de liv er ies.**

del ta (del′tə), *n.* a deposit of mud and sand at the mouth of a river. *Deltas are formed when the river slows down and drops the materials that are carried by the current.* **del tas.**

de mand (di mand′), *v.* 1. to request forcefully; to ask for something you are entitled to receive. *The woman demanded to see her son. The loser in the election demanded that the votes be counted again.* 2. to ask for with authority; to request as a command. *The judge demanded the release of the prisoner.* 3. to require; to need. *This wound demands the attention of a doctor.* **de mands, de mand ed, de mand ing.** *n.* 4. a forceful request; something demanded. *The owners of the company granted the workers' demands for higher wages.* 5. a requirement; a need. *The demands of taking care of six dogs are too much for him.* 6. a desire or need to have something. *Every year there is a great demand for the new cars.* **de mands.**

de moc ra cy (di mok′rə sē), *n.* 1. a form of government in which the people rule either directly, by enacting laws in public meetings, or indirectly, by electing representatives to operate the government. *In a democracy, every adult has an equal voice in the government.* 2. a country which has such a form of government. *The United States is a democracy.* 3. fairness in dealing with others; a belief that all people are equal. *The judge was praised for his democracy*

---

sand, āte, bâre, fäther; sent, mē, férn; fit, bīke; pot, rōpe, fôrt; run, pùll, rüle, cūte; noise, sound; ch, cheese; ng, long; th, thick; <s>th,</s> those; zh, treasure; ə = a in about, e in waken, i in animal, o in seldom, and u in minus.

in solving problems among people. **de moc-ra cies.**

dem o crat (dem′ə krat), *n.* 1. a person who believes in democracy as a form of government. *The signers of the Declaration of Independence were democrats.* 2. a person who believes in democracy in dealing with other people. *A democrat will not stand back and watch others being deprived of their rights.* 3. **Democrat,** a member of the Democratic Party, one of the major political parties in the United States. *In the last election a Democrat was elected as mayor of the city.* **dem o crats.**

dem o crat ic (dem′ə krat′ik), *adj.* 1. having to do with or supporting democracy as a form of government. *The old democratic government was overthrown by a dictatorship.* 2. practicing or favoring democracy in dealing with people. *In spite of everything, the senator stood firm in his democratic beliefs.* 3. **the Democratic Party,** a major political party in the United States. *The Democratic Party supports a group of candidates for office in every election.* **dem o-crat i cal ly,** *adv.*

dem on strate (dem′ən strāt), *v.* 1. to show; make clear. *You must demonstrate a willingness to learn in school.* 2. to prove through an experiment or by using logical thinking. *The teacher demonstrated the force of gravity by dropping several objects to the floor.* 3. to show or prove through the use of examples. *The many sentences in your dictionary demonstrate the ways in which words can be used.* 4. to show the qualities of something by using it. *The salesman demonstrated the new soap by washing our floor with it.* 5. to reveal or make known one's feelings or attitudes in a public display, march, etc. *Many people who are in favor of higher pay for teachers demonstrated at the City Hall today.* **dem on strates, dem on-strat ed, dem on strat ing.**

dem on stra tion (dem′ən strā′shən), *n.* 1. a clear show of feelings, etc. *His demonstration of interest in the class surprised his teacher.* 2. a proof; a proving. *The demonstration of the force of gravity helped us to understand many things.* 3. a showing of the qualities of a product, device, etc. *The salesman gave us a demonstration of the car by taking us for a drive.* 4. a public display of the feelings, attitudes, etc., of people. *The street was blocked off to allow the marchers in the demonstration to pass.* **dem on stra tions.**

den (den), *n.* 1. the lair or home of a wild animal. *The lion kept other animals from entering his den.* 2. the hiding place, meeting place, etc. of criminals. *All but one of the robbers returned to their den after holding up the bank.* 3. any very dirty room. *The boy's room was a den of papers, dust, and broken toys.* 4. a small room where one can read, relax, work, etc. *Father is watching television in the den.* **dens.**

de nom i na tor (di nom′ə nā′tər), *n.* the number below the line in a fraction, showing the

dentist

number of parts into which the whole has been divided. *In the fraction $\frac{7}{8}$, the denominator is 8 and the numerator is 7.* **de nom i na tors.**

dent (dent), *n.* 1. a bend or hollow place made in something by striking it or putting pressure on it. *The heavy rocks made several dents in my wagon.* **dents.**
v. 2. to make a dent in. *He dented the fender on his car when he bumped into the wall.* 3. to become dented. *The old cars didn't seem to dent as easily as modern cars do.* **dents, dent ed, dent ing.**

den tist (den′tist), *n.* a doctor who takes care of the teeth by filling, removing, and straightening them, and by supplying artificial teeth when they are needed. *The dentist told me that I had no cavities.* **den tists.**

de ny (di nī′), *v.* 1. to state that something is untrue or incorrect. *The prisoner denied that he had robbed the store.* 2. to refuse to give or allow. *The court denied his request for a new trial.* 3. to refuse to recognize or acknowledge. *The scientist denied that the earth revolved around the sun.* **de nies, de nied, de ny ing.**

de part (di pärt′), *v.* 1. to leave; to go away. *When did the doctor depart? The plane departed at noon.* 2. to change from; to turn aside from. *We will depart from our usual order of business to show the movie at the meeting.* 3. to die. *Grandfather departed after a long illness.* **de parts, de part ed, de part ing.**

de part ment (di pärt′mənt), *n.* 1. a section or part of something; a division of an organization, government, etc. *He works for the police department. You'll find what you are looking for in the sporting-goods department.* 2. **department**

store, a store that sells a wide variety of goods in various departments. *We bought a refrigerator, a basketball, and a pair of shoes at the department store.* **de part ments.**

de par ture (di pär′chər), *n.* 1. the act of departing; a leaving. *He delayed his departure until everyone else had gone.* 2. a setting out on something new and different. *When the television set broke, I began reading books in the evening, which was a departure from an old habit for me.* 3. a changing from the usual; a turning aside from. *There were so many departures from the usual order of business that the meeting took over three hours.* **de par tures.**

de pend (di pend′), *v.* 1. to rely on for assistance. *I'm depending on you to help me with this problem.* 2. to be governed or controlled by; to achieve as a result of something. *The smooth operation of the government depends on tax moneys.* 3. to trust; to believe in; to count on. *He is depending on me to deliver the message.* **de pends, de pend ed, de pend ing.**

de pos it (di poz′it), *v.* 1. to set down. *Please deposit those books on this table.* 2. to lay down and leave. *The soil that makes the delta was deposited by the river over many hundreds of years.* 3. to put away for safety; to put money in a bank. *He deposited one hundred dollars in his account.* 4. to give as part of a payment or as a promise to do something. *We had to deposit ten percent of the cost of the house to make sure the house would not be sold to someone else.* **de pos its, de pos it ed, de pos it ing.**
n. 5. something put down and left behind. *It took several days to clean up the muddy deposit of the river after the flood.* 6. money put in a bank; something put away for safety. *There was no record of my deposit at the bank.* 7. money paid as a promise to do something. *You will get the deposit back when you return the bottles.* **de pos its.**

de pot (dē′pō for 1, dep′ō for 2 and 3), *n.* 1. a station for trains or buses. *We went down to the depot to meet his train.* 2. a storage house or area for military supplies. *Pick up some more bullets at the supply depot.* 3. any storehouse. *A new shipment from the book depot arrived at the school.* **de pots.**

de pre ci ate (di prē′shē āt), *v.* 1. to lower the value of something. *The accident sharply depreciated the value of the car.* 2. to become less valuable. *Most things depreciate as they get older.* 3. to make something seem less important;

to make little of. *Don't depreciate your importance to the team.* **de pre ci ates, de pre ci at ed, de pre ci at ing.**

de pre ci a tion (di prē′shē ā′shən), *n.* a falling or reduction in the value of something. *The depreciation on a new car is several hundred dollars for the first year.*

de press (di pres′), *v.* 1. to push or press down. *The keys of a piano are depressed to produce sound.* 2. to make sad and unhappy. *Dark, rainy weather depresses many people.* **de press es, de pressed, de press ing.**

de prive (di prīv′), *v.* 1. to take away the right, power, or authority of. *The law deprives criminals of their right to vote.* 2. to prevent from having. *The explosion deprived us of our sleep.* **de prives, de prived, de priv ing.**

depth (depth), *n.* 1. a distance from the top, front, or surface of anything. *We were skin diving at a depth of twenty-five feet. I need a carton with a depth of at least two feet.* 2. the middle or innermost part of something. *We were lost in the depths of the jungle.* 3. a deepness of feelings, knowledge, etc. *He spoke out of the depth of his joy.* **depths.**

de rail (dē rāl′), *v.* to cause to go off the tracks. *Bobby's toy train was derailed by his sister.* **de rails, de railed, de rail ing.**

der rick (der′ik), *n.* 1. a machine with a long beam to which pulleys, cables, ropes, etc. are attached, used for moving or lifting very heavy objects or loads. *A derrick was unloading automobiles from the hold of the ship.* 2. the structure above an oil well to which drilling and pumping equipment is attached. *When the gusher was struck, the entire derrick was hidden by a spouting stream of oil.* **der ricks.**

de scend (di send′), *v.* 1. to move to a lower place; to go downwards. *A huge waterfall descended from the top of the cliff. We descended to the cellar down a narrow flight of stairs.* 2. to decrease in number, tone, etc. *The street numbers descended as we approached the center of the city.* 3. to come from a certain family or group of people in history. *He descends from a family that came to America on the* Mayflower. 4. to pass to an heir. *The millionaire's fortune descended to his son.* 5. **descend on,** to attack suddenly. *The invaders descended on the city.* **de scends, de scend ed, de scend ing.**

de scribe (di skrīb′), *v.* 1. to tell about in some detail with words or pictures. *He described the*

derailed toy train

desert

movie so completely that I didn't even want to see it. 2. to draw or form the outline of something. *His hands described a square in the air.* **de scribes, de scribed, de scrib ing.**

de scrip tion (di skrip′shən), *n.* 1. a telling about something with words or pictures; the person, thing, etc. described. *The police have an accurate description of the criminal.* 2. a kind; sort. *Animals of every description can be seen at the zoo.* **de scrip tions.**

de scrip tive (di skrip′tiv), *adj.* telling about something; describing. *He has written a descriptive account of the basketball game.* **de scrip tive ly,** *adv.*

des ert[1] (dez′ərt), *n.* 1. a dry, sandy region on which little or nothing grows. *Camels are the only large animals that can get along in the desert.* **des erts.**
adj. 2. like a desert; living in or belonging to a desert. *The shipwrecked sailors made their way to a desert island. Most desert animals come out only at night.*

de sert[2] (di zərt′), *v.* 1. to abandon; to go away from and leave behind. *The children were deserted by their friends in their time of need.* 2. to leave a military post without permission and without the intention of returning. *The soldier who deserted was being sought by the military police.* **de serts, de sert ed, de sert ing.**

de sert[3] (di zərt′), *n.* a reward or punishment that is suitable to and deserved by a person. *Criminals get their just deserts.* **de serts.**

de serve (di zərv′), *v.* to be worthy of; to have earned as a reward, punishment, right, etc. *Your suggestion deserves further consideration. The boy deserved a medal for capturing the crook.* **de serves, de served, de serv ing.**

de sign (di zīn′), *v.* 1. to draw or sketch something to be done; to plan the details of something. *The builder designed a new shopping center.* 2. to plan in the mind; to decide mentally to do something. *He designed this scheme for raising money.* **de signs, de signed, de sign ing.**
n. 3. a drawing or plan to be followed in building or making something. *The design for the building called for an elevator.* 4. a plan made in the mind. *It was his design to become a doctor.* 5. a pattern or arrangement of colors, materials, etc. *There was an intricate design woven into the blanket.* **de signs.**

de sir a ble (di zīr′ə bl), *adj.* 1. worth having. *This little bat is desirable as a souvenir of the ball game.* 2. pleasant; satisfying. *Warm weather is desirable for the beach party.* **de sir a bly,** *adv.*

de sire (di zīr′), *v.* 1. to wish; to want. *Find out what she really desires for her birthday.* 2. to ask for; request. *The hotel manager desires every guest to sign his name in the register.* **de sires, de sired, de sir ing.**
n. 3. the thing that one wishes for. *To see her mother come home from the hospital is Susan's greatest desire.* 4. a wish that is strong. *Many people have a desire for money.* **de sires.**

de sir ous (di zīr′əs), *adj.* desiring; wishing; eager. *I am desirous of visiting Europe some day.*

desk (desk), *n.* a piece of furniture somewhat like a table, having a flat top for writing, and usually having drawers. *Office workers, teachers, and pupils have desks.* **desks.**

de spair (di spâr′), *n.* 1. a feeling that hope is gone. *Greg was in despair because his dog Topper had been lost for five days.*
v. 2. to give up; lose hope. *After ten losses in a row, the coach despaired of our winning a game.* **de spairs, de spaired, de spair ing.**

des per ate (des′pər ət), *adj.* 1. not caring what happens because one is without hope. *A desperate criminal will do almost anything because he knows he will be caught and punished. The desperate girl jumped from the third floor of the burning building.* 2. not having much chance for a fast cure; dangerous. *The doctor told us*

---

sand, āte, bâre, fäther; sent, mē, fèrn; fit, bīke; pot, rōpe, fôrt; run, pùll, rüle, cūte; noise, sound; ch, cheese; ng, long; th, thick; ~~th~~, those; zh, treasure; ə = a in about, e in waken, i in animal, o in seldom, and u in minus.

the baby had a desperate illness, but he would do all he could. **des per ate ly,** *adv.*

de spise (di spīz′), *v.* to dislike intensely; look down on. *I despise those who purposely do not want to tell the truth.* **de spis es, de spised, de spis ing.**

des sert (di zėrt′), *n.* a sweet food, fruit, or cheese served at the end of a meal. *After lunch I had an apple for dessert.* **des serts.**

des ti na tion (des′tə nā′shən), *n.* the place where a person or thing is going. *The boys on the plane said their destination was Denver, where they live.* **des ti na tions.**

de stroy (di stroi′), *v.* to put an end to; ruin; tear down; wreck completely. *The fire destroyed the beautiful cathedral. Insects can destroy crops. His hopes were destroyed.* **de stroys, de stroyed, de stroy ing.**

de stroy er (di stroi′ər), *n.* a swift, light, heavily-armed warship. *Destroyers are used to chase submarines.* **de stroy ers.**

de struc tion (di struk′shən), *n.* a destroying or being destroyed; damage; a wrecking. *The destruction caused by the tornado included more than twelve houses.*

de tail (dē′tāl, di tāl′), *n.* 1. a small part of something. *All the details of the house carried out the brown color scheme. Mrs. Jones needs help in some of the details of the birthday party, such as decorations, favors, and serving the food.* 2. **in detail,** item by item. *She told us about her trip in great detail.* **de tails.**
v. 3. to give all the particulars of. *The captain of the submarine detailed to us how the ship works.* **de tails, de tailed, de tail ing.**

de ter mi na tion (di tėr′mə nā′shən), *n.* 1. a determining; a deciding. *The determination of the judges was that the race ended in a tie.* 2. firmness in thinking and acting; fixed intention. *His determination to do well in school made him study every day.* **de ter mi na tions.**

de ter mine (di tėr′mən), *v.* 1. to decide firmly. *Tom has determined to go to college, so he is saving his money.* 2. to find out exactly. *The insurance company determined the cost of the repairs to the car.* 3. to be the cause for; to be a deciding fact. *The weather tomorrow will determine whether we go or stay. His love for animals probably determined that he would be an animal doctor.* 4. to decide upon. *The teacher says he hasn't yet*

determined the date of the test. **de ter mines, de ter mined, de ter min ing.**

de ter mined (di tėr′mənd), *adj.* 1. resolved; decided. *He is determined now to get better grades, so he studies hard and doesn't waste his time.* 2. firm; not changing. *The tired actor kept a determined smile throughout his performance.* **de ter mined ly,** *adv.*

de vel op (di vel′əp), *v.* 1. to grow; come into being. *The bud developed into a blossom. Reading helps to develop your mind. Richard's interest in playing the piano developed at the early age of six.* 2. to build up; to put to use. *Travel to outer space has developed rapidly since 1957. The teacher wants us to develop some ideas for a school newspaper.* 3. to bring out a picture on a film or plate. *The photographer developed the film by treating it with chemicals.* **de vel ops, de vel oped, de vel op ing.**

de vel op ment (di vel′əp mənt), *n.* 1. the act of developing; growth. *That child's development is a surprise to me, since I always remember him as being tiny. The development of the use of machines has changed many business operations.* 2. results; news. *What are the latest developments in the plans for a picnic? Call the doctor if there are any developments in your brother's condition.* 3. a section of land on which new or improved houses have just been built. *Suburbs have many housing developments, each containing a number of new houses. The apartments are large in the new housing development in the city.* **de vel op ments.**

de vice (di vīs′), *n.* 1. a tool or a machine having some special use. *A corkscrew is a device for removing a cork from the neck of a bottle. A thermometer is a device for recording temperature.* 2. a trick or scheme. *We can always wake up the dog by the device of meowing like a cat.* 3. **leave to one's own devices,** to leave to one's own ideas. *If those children were left to their own devices, I think they would wreck the furniture!* **de vic es.**

dev il (dev′l), *n.* 1. an evil spirit who is supposed to want people to be wicked. *In former days people claimed to see and talk with devils.* 2. a cruel person; person with evil ideas. *That man is a devil to his harmless dog.* 3. person who is lively and full of fun. *My brothers were devils when they were younger.* 4. **the Devil,** Satan, or the enemy of goodness. *The Devil is often*

destroyer

represented in works of art as having a forked tail and hooves. **dev ils.**

de vote (di vōt′), *v.* to give up to some ideal, activity, or person. *She has devoted her life to taking care of her mother.* **de votes, de vot ed, de vot ing.**

de vot ed (di vōt′əd), *adj.* loyal and loving; given up to some person or ideal. *Doctors are devoted men of science. The Indian chief and his devoted followers came to the fort for friendly talks.* **de vot ed ly,** *adv.*

de vo tion (di vō′shən), *n.* 1. a devoting or being devoted. *His devotion to his son made the boy into a fine man.* 2. prayers. *The religious man said his devotions each morning.* **de vo tions.**

dew (dü, dū), *n.* little drops of water that form at night on cool surfaces. *Early in the morning you will see dew on the leaves of bushes and trees.*

di ag o nal (dī ag′ə nl), *n.* 1. a line joining the opposite corners of a rectangle. *A diagonal is the longest line you can draw in a rectangle.* **di ag o nals.**

adj. 2. slanting. *She always takes a diagonal path across the park.* **di ag o nal ly,** *adv.*

di a gram (dī′ə gram), *n.* 1. a drawing showing the parts of something and how they are put together. *A diagram is like a map, not like a photograph. You can make a diagram of your schoolroom by drawing little squares for each desk.* **di a grams.**

v. 2. to make a diagram of. *John diagramed the location of the apartment house he lived in by drawing lines for streets, little squares for certain stores, and a big square for the park.* **di a grams, di a- gramed, di a gram ing.**

di al (dī′əl), *n.* 1. the face of a watch, a clock, or a compass. *The dial of a watch or clock shows the time, and the dial of a compass shows the directions.* 2. the part of a telephone that is turned to certain numbers when making a call. *Some telephone dials have a soft light so that the numbers can be seen in darkness.* **di als.**

v. 3. to call on a telephone by using the dial.

diamond

Dial the drugstore for me, will you? **di als, di aled, di al ing.**

di a logue (dī′ə log), *n.* 1. a conversation; a talking together. *The dialogue at the party last night was interesting.* 2. the talk between people in a play or book. *The acting in the play was good, but the dialogue was not lifelike.* **di a logues.**

di am e ter (dī am′ə tər), *n.* 1. a straight line which passes through the center of a circle and extends from one side of the circle to the other side. *Since he already knew the diameter of the circle, it was very easy for him to find the radius.* 2. the length of such a line through any circular object. *The diameter of our garden hose is exactly one inch.* **di am e ters.**

di a mond (dī′mənd, dī′ə mənd), *n.* 1. a bright and brilliant precious stone used in rings, pins, and other jewels. *The girls were excited by the diamond engagement ring worn by Betty.* 2. a four-sided figure that looks like a certain cut diamond. *We made diamond-shaped ornaments for our tree.* 3. a baseball field. *We can't get Jack away from that diamond once the season starts.* **di a monds.**

di a ry (dī′ə rē), *n.* a written record of the things that the writer has done or thought day by day. *Mary keeps a diary which she locks and hides so no one can read it.* **di a ries.**

dic tate (dik′tāt), *v.* 1. to say or read words to another person who writes them down. *When she wants to write a letter, the old woman dictates it to her grandson.* 2. to give a command that must be obeyed. *The judge dictated a strong punishment to the prisoner.* **dic tates, dic ta ted, dic tat ing.**

n. 3. an order or direction to be carried out. *That girl carefully follows the dictates of her mother.* **dic tates.**

dic ta tor (dik′tā tər), *n.* 1. a person who rules with absolute authority; often a person who seizes control of a government. *Although he ruled as a dictator, the king brought peace to his country.* 2. a person who dictates to another person or a machine. *Mr. Jones is a terrible dictator.* **dic ta tors.**

dic ta tor ship (dik′tā tər ship′), *n.* a system of government in which one person has complete power and control over all of the people. *There are no free elections in a dictatorship.* **dic ta tor ships.**

dic tion ary (dik′shən er′ē), *n.* a book which explains the words used in a language. *A good dictionary uses simple definitions and has useful pictures.* **dic tion ar ies.**

did (did), past tense of **do.**

did n't (did′nt), did not. *Jim didn't come to work on time this morning because of heavy traffic.*

die[1] (dī), *v.* 1. to stop living. *Those flowers will die unless you put them in water.* 2. to lose force; come to an end. *The car's engine died in the middle of traffic. The sound of the band died away as the parade passed us.* **dies, died, dy ing.**

die² (dī), *n.* a tool or device that can give a form to some object. *A die is used to stamp a design on a book cover, to stamp the lettering on a coin, or to make designs on leather goods.* **dies.**

di et (dī′ət), *n.* 1. the food usually eaten by a person or an animal. *The boy's diet contains too many sweet things. The diet of a bear is mostly berries.* 2. a special choice of food eaten, usually for purposes of improving the health. *Every year Mr. Collins goes on a diet to lose fifteen pounds.* **di ets.**
v. 3. to eat certain kinds of foods and avoid others for the purpose of losing weight. *I am dieting, so I can't eat the candy.* **di ets, di et ed, di et ing.**

dif fer (dif′ər), *v.* 1. to be unlike. *The two nations differ in their languages and in their customs.* 2. to disagree; to have unlike ideas or opinions. *People differ on many things: they differ in religions and customs.* **dif fers, dif fered, dif fer ing.**

dif fer ence (dif′rəns, dif′ər əns), *n.* 1. a way in which people or things are not alike. *There is a big difference in size between a mouse and an elephant.* 2. the amount by which one number, measure, etc. is greater than another. *The difference between ten and twelve is two.* 3. a quarrel. *We have our differences, but we like each other.* **dif fer enc es.**

dif fer ent (dif′rənt, dif′ər ənt), *adj.* 1. not alike. *Summer is different from winter. His answer to the question was different from mine.* 2. not the same; separate. *The boys both went to Wood High School, but they now go to different colleges.* 3. unusual; unlike many others. *Their room is really different.* **dif fer ent ly,** *adv.*

dif fi cult (dif′ə kult′, dif′ə kəlt), *adj.* 1. hard; not easy to do or understand. *Learning to play a musical instrument is difficult, but practice every day helps. It is difficult to climb a high mountain.* 2. hard to get along with. *The manager had a reputation for being difficult; no matter what his employees did, he found something wrong.* **dif fi cult ly,** *adv.*

dif fi cul ty (dif′ə kul′tē, dif′ə kəl tē), *n.* 1. trouble; hard work. *Some children have difficulty in doing arithmetic problems.* 2. something that is hard to do or understand. *The difficulties of traveling during the rainy season kept the Indians from starting out.* 3. a cause of trouble. *The difficulty of that road is that it has so many deep holes.* **dif fi cul ties.**

dig (dig), *v.* 1. to make a hole in the ground; break up the soil. *Dogs dig holes with their front paws. I used a spade to dig the soil before planting the flowers.* 2. to make a way through. *They dug the tunnel beneath the water. I found my old report cards after digging through the trunk containing letters, newspapers, and books.* 3. to get something out by turning up the ground. *We dug some worms for our fishing trip.* 4. to seek; look for. *After digging into the facts carefully, the man was able to make his report.* 5. to poke. *He dug his elbow into my ribs as he told his story.* **digs, dug, dig ging.**
n. 6. a poke. *He gave my arm a dig.* **digs.**

di gest (də jest′, dī′jest for 1 and 2, dī′jest for 3), *v.* 1. to change food in the stomach into a form that the body can use. *Your food will digest more quickly if you chew it well.* 2. to think over in order to understand. *He read the instructions and digested them thoroughly.* **di gests, di gest ed, di gest ing.**
n. 3. a short form of a longer article or story. *Some digests are better than the original long story.* **di gests.**

di ges tion (də jes′chən), *n.* 1. turning food in the stomach into a form that the body can use. *Your digestion will be better if you eat slowly and chew your food.* 2. the ability to digest food. *Digestion is often more difficult if you eat when you are excited or nervous.*

dig it (dij′it), *n.* 1. the numeral for any number from 1 to 9 and usually the numeral for 0. *We use digits when we write numerals like 150.* 2. a finger or toe. *You have a total of twenty digits.* **dig its.**

dig ni ty (dig′nə tē), *n.* 1. being worthy; a quality of character which is admired by others. *No matter what his occupation, every person can have dignity.* 2. a calm and serious manner. *Even though the rain soaked them, the prizewinning dogs stood with dignity until called for.* 3. any high rank or office that should be treated with honor. *The dignity of the President of the United States should be respected.*

di graph (dī′graf), *n.* a pair of letters representing a single speech sound. *The "ea" in "neat" is a digraph.* **di graphs.**

dike (dīk), *n.* 1. a wall or dam built to keep the sea or river from flooding the land. *Many dikes are made simply of earth piled high.* **dikes.**
v. 2. to protect with a dike. *Years ago the Dutch people diked their low lands to keep out the sea.* **dikes, diked, dik ing.**

dim (dim), *adj.* 1. not bright and clear; faint. *Most highway accidents occur during the dim twilight.* 2. not seeing clearly; not understanding. *The old man has dim eyesight, and a mind growing dim with age.* 3. not clear to the hearing. *The dim sounds were missed.* **dim mer, dim mest; dim ly,** *adv.*
v. 4. to make or become less bright. *Dim your lights when a car is coming.* **dims, dimmed, dim ming.**

dime (dīm), *n.* a silver coin used as money by the United States and by Canada. *A dime is worth ten cents, or one tenth of a dollar.* **dimes.**

di men sion (di men′shən), *n.* 1. a measurement of the length, width, or height of something. *The dimensions of the package are three feet in length, two feet in width, and one foot in height.* 2. **dimensions,** size; extent. *I don't think you really understand the dimensions of our new plan.* **di men sions.**

---

sand, āte, bâre, fäther; sent, mē, fėrn; fit, bīke; pot, rōpe, fôrt; run, pu̇ll, rüle, cūte; noise, sound; ch, cheese; ng, long; th, thick; ~~th~~, those; zh, treasure; ə = a in about, e in waken, i in animal, o in seldom, and u in minus.

di min ish (di min′ish), v. to make or become less; to decrease in size, amount, or importance. *We waited in a dry place for the rain to diminish.* **di min ish es, di min ished, di min ish-ing.**

dine (dīn), v. 1. to eat dinner. *We dine at seven o'clock, so be on time.* 2. to give a dinner for. *The school principal dined all the teachers at the end of the term.* **dines, dined, din ing.**

ding-dong (ding′dông′, ding′dong′), n. the sound of a bell ringing for a long time. *The ding-dong of the church bell finally woke me.* **ding-dongs.**

din ner (din′ər), n. 1. the main meal of the day. *Some people have dinner at noon, and other people have dinner in the evening.* 2. a banquet. *The dinner was given in honor of the new president of the company.* **din ners.**

di no saur (dī′nə sôr), n. any of a group of reptiles that lived a million years ago. *Some dinosaurs were the largest land animals that have ever lived—nearly one hundred feet long and weighing about fifty tons.* **di no saurs.**

di o ra ma (dī ə ram′ə, dī ə rä′mə), n. a scene made of modeled figures and objects placed in front of a background which is painted and lighted in natural colors. *The dioramas in the museum showed animals in the jungle and in the Arctic snows.* **di o ram as.**

dip (dip), v. 1. to put into a liquid and pull out again. *An artist dips his brush into paint. The boy dipped his toe into the lake to see how cold the water was. The cook dipped a spoon into the soup and tasted it to see if the soup had the right taste.* 2. to lower and raise again. *The flag was dipped by the warship as it sailed past the President's yacht.* 3. to slope downward. *The road dips suddenly after the next curve.* 4. **dip into,** to read or study something for a while. *He dips into a book in every spare moment.* **dips, dipped, dip ping.** n. 5. a dipping; a plunge. *Every morning they took a dip in the swimming pool.* 6. a downward slope; a low place. *Look out for the dips in the road.* **dips.**

di plo ma (di plō′mə), n. a document or certificate that is given to a student when he graduates from grammar school, high school, or college. *Our doctor has a diploma from his medical school that shows that he was given the*

degree of M.D. (*Doctor of Medicine*). **di plo-mas.**

di rect (də rekt′, dī rekt′), v. 1. to point out the way to a place. *The road map directed us correctly to the town. The usher directed us to our seats in the church.* 2. to be in charge of; manage. *A policeman directs traffic. Teachers direct their classes.* 3. to order; command. *The doctor directed William to eat less candy and more fresh fruit.* 4. to aim; point. *Direct all your attention to getting your homework finished.* **di rects, di rect ed, di rect ing.** adj. 5. straight; not round about. *Airliners usually fly the direct route to Europe.* 6. honest; frank. *John always gives direct answers to questions, rather than trying to avoid the truth.* **di rect,** adv. 7. without stopping. *The young man was told to go direct to the store.*

di rec tion (də rek′shən, dī rek′shən), n. 1. managing; control. *The school play will be presented under the direction of Miss Hayes, an English teacher.* 2. a point of the compass. *North, south, east, and west are directions.* 3. a point toward which one can face. *The crowd was going in the direction of the church.* 4. **directions,** an explanation of how to get somewhere or do something. *Her directions were clear, so we arrived at her house on time. The directions on how to put together the Christmas toy were too hard to follow.* **di rec tions.**

di rect ly (də rekt′lē, dī rekt′lē), adv. 1. in a direct line; straight. *The city is directly north of us. Tell your story directly to the boss.* 2. right away. *You come home directly.*

di rec tor (də rek′tər), n. 1. a person who directs or manages the work done by other people. *The director of a play is in charge of the actors. An orchestra needs a director who knows music.* 2. a person who directs a business. *The board of directors of a company is chosen by the owners of the business.* **dir ec tors.**

di rec to ry (də rek′tə rē), n. a book of names, addresses, and numbers. *A telephone directory lists the names of all the people who have telephones.* **di rec to ries.**

dir i gi ble (dir′ə jə bl), n. a large, long balloon that can be steered. *A dirigible has engines that make it go.* **dir i gi bles.**

dirt (dėrt), n. 1. mud, dust, soot, or any other

dinosaur

thing which can soil skin, clothes, and furniture. *The dirt from the factory smoke covered the table.* 2. earth; soil. *We put some dirt into the flowerpot.*

dirt y (dėrt′ē), *adj.* 1. not clean; containing dirt. *Put all the dirty clothes into the washing machine.* 2. not clear in color. *His painting has some dirty yellow in it.* 3. stormy. *The ship ran into some dirty weather two days ago.* **dirt i er, dirt i est.**
   v. 4. to make dirty; soil. *The little boy dirtied his new suit shortly after he put it on.* **dirt ies, dirt ied, dirt y ing.**

dis a gree (dis′ə grē′), *v.* 1. to not agree; to differ in opinion. *The children disagreed about the rules of the game.* 2. to not bring a good feeling or effect. *The hot weather disagrees with me.* **dis a grees, dis a greed, dis a gree ing.**

dis a gree a ble (dis′ə grē′ə bl), *adj.* 1. unpleasant. *The garbage had a disagreeable odor.* 2. cross; not in a good mood. *Harry was disagreeable for a week after he lost his job.* **dis a gree a bly,** *adv.*

dis ap pear (dis′ə pir′), *v.* 1. to go out of sight; to vanish. *The dog disappeared in the distance.* 2. to cease to be; to exist no more. *Some animals disappeared from earth a million years ago.* **dis ap pears, dis ap peared, dis ap pear ing.**

dis ap point (dis′ ə point′), *v.* 1. to fail to keep a promise to do something. *He disappointed us by arriving so late that our camping trip was spoiled.* 2. to fail to satisfy the wish or hope of. *The movie disappointed me; I thought it would be much better.* **dis ap points, dis ap point ed, dis ap point ing.**

dis ap point ment (dis′ə point′mənt), *n.* 1. a disappointing; being disappointed. *His disappointment was deep when he found out he received only a C in the course.* 2. a person or thing that disappoints. *That large dog is a big disappointment; all he does is sleep.* **dis ap point ments.**

dis arm (dis ärm′), *v.* 1. to take weapons away from. *The sheriff disarmed the robber.* 2. to get rid of unfriendliness. *The boy's innocent face disarmed people.* 3. to reduce the size of armed forces or of weapons. *Nations should think in terms of agreement and disarming rather than producing more war materials.* **dis arms, dis armed, dis arm ing.**

dis as ter (di zas′tər), *n.* something that happens which causes damage and brings suffering or sorrow to people. *The tornado was a disaster to the town.* **dis as ters.**

dis charge (dis chärj′ for 1–5, dis′chärj′, dis chärj′ for 6 and 7), *v.* 1. to let go; release. *He was discharged from the hospital, completely cured.* 2. to get rid of; to fire. *The lazy boy was discharged from his job.* 3. to remove; unload. *The plane discharged its passengers at New York.* 4. to perform. *He discharged his duties carefully.* 5. to let out. *The extra water is discharged through*

disarming a gunman

this pipe. *The cut discharged blood.* **dis charg es, dis charged, dis charg ing.**
   n. 6. a paper from one of the armed services releasing a man from serving. *Brian received an honorable discharge.* 7. a performance; carrying out. *In the discharge of his duties, he made many friends.* **dis charg es.**

dis ci pline (dis′ə plin), *n.* 1. training that stresses obedience and control of behavior. *The army has strict discipline to show a soldier that he must obey orders.* 2. self-control; keeping order. *When the fire drill was held, the pupils showed good discipline.* 3. a punishment given to train a person or animal. *That noisy boy needs some discipline.* **dis ci plines.**
   v. 4. to train in self-control and in order. *A man must discipline himself to do a job without help.* 5. to punish to train a person or animal. *The horses in the circus are disciplined when they forget a trick.* **dis ci plines, dis ci plined, dis ci plin ing.**

dis con tin ue (dis′kən tin′ū), *v.* to stop; give up. *When the rain came, he had to discontinue*

dirigible

painting the house for the day. **dis con tin ues, dis con tin ued, dis con tin u ing.**

dis count (dis′kount′ for 1, dis kount′, dis′kount′ for 2 and 3), *n.* 1. a reduction; an amount taken off a price. *Mary got a discount of five dollars on the hat she bought.* **dis counts.** *v.* 2. to take off an amount from a price. *The grocery store discounted all prices during the special sale.* 3. to believe only a part; to take away. *You have to discount about half of what Jerry says he did.* **dis counts, dis count ed, dis count ing.**

dis cov er (dis kuv′ər), *v.* 1. to be the first to find or learn about. *Columbus discovered America.* 2. to find out. *You can discover the meanings of words in a dictionary. I discovered the soup was too hot when the first spoonful burned my tongue.* **dis cov ers, dis cov ered, dis cov er ing.**

dis cov er y (dis kuv′ər ē), *n.* 1. finding out about something for the first time. *The discovery of gold in California caused many people to go there.* 2. something that is found out. *The discovery of new medicines has saved thousands of lives.* **dis cov er ies.**

dis cuss (dis kus′), *v.* to talk about seriously. *The class discussed their plans for Parents' Night.* **dis cuss es, dis cussed, dis cuss ing.**

dis cuss ion (dis kush′ən), *n.* a serious talk by two or more people. *The teachers' discussion lasted for more than two hours before everyone agreed on the days for final tests.* **dis cuss ions.**

dis ease (di zēz′), *n.* a sickness; illness. *Most common diseases, such as measles, can be prevented or cured these days.* **dis eas es.**

dis grace (dis grās′), *n.* 1. shame; loss of honor

disguise

or good reputation. *Cheating on an examination is a disgrace.* 2. a person or thing that brings shame. *The big city's streets were a disgrace; then the mayor and the citizens spent money to fix them all.* **dis grac es.** *v.* 3. to bring shame to. *The boy disgraced his mother by behaving badly at the party, but he later made an apology.* **dis grac es, dis graced, dis grac ing.**

dis guise (dis gīz′), *v.* 1. to change one's real appearance so that one will not be recognized. *In the school circus one boy was a clown, and two boys were disguised as a horse.* 2. to hide; mask; cover up. *He disguised his anger by being friendly.* **dis guis es, dis guised, dis guis ing.** *n.* 3. a costume used to hide one's real identity. *What disguise will you wear?* **dis guis es.**

dis gust (dis gust′), *n.* 1. a strong dislike; a severe loathing. *Most people feel disgust at the smell of burning garbage. Bob's behavior at the party filled Joan with disgust because she knew he really had good manners.* **dis gusts.** *v.* 2. to cause a strong feeling of dislike. *Bad table manners disgust us.* **dis gusts, dis gust ed, dis gust ing.**

dis gust ed (dis gust′əd), *adj.* filled with a feeling of disgust or strong dislike. *He was disgusted with himself for not getting a better grade.* **dis gust ed ly,** *adv.*

dish (dish), *n.* 1. a container used to hold food or used at meals; plates, cups, saucers, bowls, and platters. *When we have guests for dinner, we use our best dishes.* 2. food. *Oatmeal is my favorite dish for breakfast.* 3. the amount of food that a dish holds. *We each had two dishes of strawberries.* **dish es.** *v.* 4. to put in a dish; serve. *Mother is dishing the ice cream.* **dish es, dished, dish ing.**

dis hon est (dis on′əst), *adj.* not honest; not fair; lying or cheating. *The dishonest boy cheated on his mathematics test.* **dis hon est ly,** *adv.*

dis joint (dis joint′), *v.* to separate at the joints. *Usually we disjoint a roasted chicken before it is served.* **dis joints, dis joint ed, dis joint ing.**

dis like (dis līk′), *v.* 1. to have a feeling against; to not like. *At first I disliked him, but now we are friends.* **dis likes, dis liked, dis lik ing.** *n.* 2. a feeling against; a feeling of not liking. *Many people have a dislike for snakes.* **dis likes.**

dis miss (dis mis′), *v.* 1. to send away; let go. *The class was dismissed early on the day of graduation.* 2. to discharge; to fire; to remove from a job. *The man was dismissed from his job, but he got a better one the next week.* 3. to stop thinking about. *I can dismiss all my worries when I listen to beautiful music.* **dis miss es, dis missed, dis miss ing.**

dis patch (dis pach′), *v.* 1. to send out right away. *The telephone company dispatched a man to repair a break in the wire. Please dispatch these*

notices to all teachers. 2. to end quickly. *We will dispatch our meeting in ten minutes.* 3. to kill. *The hunter dispatched the wolf with only one shot.* **dis patch es, dis patched, dis patch ing.**
n. 4. a message. *The special messenger carried dispatches from the President.* 5. fast action. *An experienced person does his work with dispatch.* 6. a news report. *Dispatches from the hospital say that the patients are doing well.* **dis patch es.**

dis play (dis plā′), *v.* 1. to show; exhibit. *The prize winning drawings in the art show were displayed in the school corridors. The small boy displayed a good voice when he sang.* **dis plays, dis played, dis play ing.**
n. 2. a showing. *The display of old automobiles included one that was run by steam. A display of courage is expected of a football player.* 3. a showing that is not real or genuine. *His display of happiness was just an act.* **dis plays.**

dis pose (dis pōz′), *v.* 1. to place in a certain order or position. *He disposed his flowers in a large square around the yard.* 2. **dispose of,** (a) to get rid of. *We disposed of all the old clothes by giving them away.* (b) to settle; end. *Give me five minutes, and I will dispose of his arguments.* **dis pos es, dis posed, dis pos ing.**

dis posed (dis pōzd′), *adj.* inclined; feeling favorable toward. *I am disposed to go to the school concert tonight. The principal was disposed to believe Jack because Jack always tells the truth.*

dis po si tion (dis′pǝ zish′ǝn), *n.* 1. a person's all-round attitude or way of thinking; a way in which a person feels toward others. *Mary has a cheerful disposition and never gets angry.* 2. a disposing; an arrangement. *The disposition of the furniture in a room should be done carefully.* 3. a preference or liking. *I have a disposition for reading.* 4. the power to use as one wishes. *When he is thirty-one he will have $10,000 at his disposition.* **dis po si tions.**

dis pute (dis pūt′), *v.* 1. to argue; debate; have a different opinion about. *Our class disputed over the best date for the picnic.* 2. to say that something is not correct. *People disputed Columbus' idea that he could reach India by going in a western direction. Baseball players soon learn that you cannot dispute an umpire's decision.* **dis putes, dis put ed, dis put ing.**
n. 3. a disputing; argument; debate; quarrel. *After twenty years the dispute between the countries over ownership of the river was finally settled.* **dis putes.**

dis solve (di zolv′), *v.* 1. to break up and disappear; to make or become liquid. *When the snow dissolved suddenly, the streets looked like lakes. Sugar dissolves in cocoa.* 2. to finish; bring or come to an end. *Because it had no more money, the company was forced to dissolve. A friendship can be dissolved by the careless action of one of the friends.* 3. to go away. *His fears dissolved when he won first prize in the scholarship contest.* **dissolves, dis solved, dis solv ing.**

dis tance (dis′tǝns), *n.* 1. the space between two points or places. *I live a short distance from school. The distance from the earth to the sun is about 93,000,000 miles.* 2. **in the distance,** far away. *The airplane appeared as a speck in the distance.* **dis tanc es.**
v. 3. to pass; leave behind. *He distanced the rest of us by hard work, and we are happy he won the prize.* 4. **keep one's distance,** to be unfriendly. *Since our dispute, he has kept his distance.* **dis tanc es, dis tanced, dis tanc ing.**

dis tant (dis′tǝnt), *adj.* 1. far away. *The speaker had traveled in distant lands. An enormous sheet of ice, or glacier, covered all of the Midwest in the distant past.* 2. away. *The library is one mile distant from us.* 3. not easy to talk with; keeping to oneself. *The new boy seems distant only because he is a stranger; he is very pleasant when you know him.* 4. not friendly. *For a week after the argument, Carol was distant to Betty, then they made up.* 5. not closely related. *We only see our distant relatives, such as second or third cousins, at Christmas or Thanksgiving.* **dis tant ly,** *adv.*

dis tinct (dis tinkt′), *adj.* 1. not the same; not alike; different. *Every snowflake, seen under a magnifying glass, has a pattern distinct from those of the millions of other snowflakes.* 2. separate. *There are many distinct kinds of insects.* 3. plain; clear. *Speak with a distinct pronunciation; don't run your words together.* 4. definite; easily seen. *Your tests show that there is a distinct improvement in your work.* **dis tinct ly,** *adv.*

dis tinc tion (dis tink′shǝn), *n.* 1. a difference; being different. *One of the distinctions between man and animal is that man can think.* 2. great merit; honor. *The prize went to a writer of distinction. Many men served with distinction in the army.* **dis tinc tions.**

dis tinct ly (dis tinkt′lē), *adv.* 1. clearly; exactly. *A good speaker pronounces his words distinctly.* 2. definitely; easily noticed. *The brown horse is a distinctly faster runner than the black horse.*

dis tin guish (dis ting′gwish), *v.* 1. to notice a difference between or among. *I can distinguish a robin from a sparrow. An expert on birds can distinguish more than one hundred kinds.* 2. to see clearly; recognize by odor or taste. *We could distinguish the smell of roses in the room. In a fog you cannot distinguish objects easily.* **dis tin guish es, dis tin guished, dis tin guish ing.**

dis tin guished (dis ting′gwisht), *adj.* 1. famous; very well known. *This book was written by a distinguished man, and it tells how he became successful.* 2. showing distinction; having the appearance of a great person. *His white hair, tanned face, and clear blue eyes gave the old man a distinguished look.*

dis tract (dis trakt′), *v.* 1. to turn away thoughts or attention. *The noisy children distracted the man who was writing a letter. I like music because it distracts me from my worries.* 2. to confuse; make upset; disturb. *The relatives gave so much advice to the boy that he was distracted. Don't distract me; give me one direction at a time.* **dis tracts, dis tract ed, dis tract ing.**

dis tress (dis tres′), *n.* 1. pain; sorrow; trouble. *The torn dress caused her much distress, but when it was repaired she was happy again.* 2. misery; poverty. *The floods caused distress in the foreign city, but the United States gave quick relief and money.* 3. danger. *The ship in distress sent a radio message to four other ships, which came at once.* *v.* 4. to cause pain, sorrow, or trouble. *The news of the accident distressed her.* **dis tress es, dis tressed, dis tress ing.**

dis trib ute (dis trib′yŭt), *v.* 1. to give out. *Every year our room distributes toys among the children at the hospital.* 2. to spread around. *The boy distributed the advertisements in the neighborhood. The wind distributes the fallen leaves.* 3. to arrange; put into groups for easier handling. *The office boy distributed the morning's mail into ten piles: one for each person in the office.* **dis trib utes, dis trib ut ed, dis trib ut ing.**

dis trib u tion (dis′trə bū′shən), *n.* 1. a distributing; giving out. *The distribution of the textbooks took all morning.* 2. a spreading out. *There was a strange distribution of paint on his house; some parts were darker than others.* 3. the way something is distributed. *The distribution of the world's population is not even; some parts of the world are crowded, others are not.* **dis trib u tions.**

dis trict (dis′trikt), *n.* 1. a part of a country, state, town or county which has certain duties or functions. *We have school districts and voting districts.* 2. any region or part of a country. *Some people live in farming districts.* **dis tricts.**

District of Co lum bia (kə lum′bē ə), *n.* a district occupied by Washington, the capital of the United States. It lies near the Potomac River between Maryland and Virginia. *There are many beautiful buildings in Washington, the national capital; Washington covers the same area as the District of Columbia.*

dis turb (dis tėrb′), *v.* 1 to bother; interrupt. *Don't disturb the dog while he is eating. You are welcome any time, so never think that you are disturbing me.* 2. to upset; worry. *It disturbed us when we heard Harold was in the hospital, but he is already home and feeling fine.* 3. to put into disorder; mess up. *Don't disturb anything in my room.* **dis turbs, dis turbed, dis turb ing.**

ditch (dich), *n.* 1. a long, narrow horizontal hole in the ground. *The rain flows into the ditch, which leads to the river.* **ditch es.** *v.* 2. to dig a long hole. *We will ditch our garden so that it won't flood when the rain falls.* **ditch es, ditched, ditch ing.**

dive (dīv), *v.* 1. to plunge headfirst into water. *The boys raced to the pool and dived in with a splash.* 2. to plunge the body, head, or mind into anything. *He dived into the new book. The fireman dived into the burning room and came out carrying a small child.* 3. to make a steep plunge downward, nose first. *The airplane suddenly dived to avoid the thunderclouds.* **dives, dived** or **dove** (dōv), **div ing.** *n.* 4. the act of diving into water. *The swimming captain made a beautiful dive and won first place.* 5. a plunge or drop. *The bird suddenly made a dive to pick up the insect from the water.* **dives.**

div er (dīv′ər), *n.* 1. a person or animal that dives. *I am not good as a diver because I haven't practiced enough.* 2. a person who works under water, wearing special diving equipment. *Some divers wear diving suits with helmets and breathe through an air hose connected to a surface supply; others wear containers of air connected to a face mask.* **div ers.**

di vide (di vīd′), *v.* 1. to separate; keep apart. *The expressway has a high wire fence that divides northbound traffic from southbound.* 2. to separate into equal parts by using arithmetic. *The four boys divided their twenty cents, and each got five cents.* 3. to separate into parts; to share. *The family divided the cake. The men in the desert divided all of their water.* 4. to group; to organize. *All the books in the library are divided into the broad fields of knowledge, such as social science, chemistry, and geometry.* **di vides, di vid ed, di vid ing.** *n.* 5. a ridge between two river systems which flow in opposite directions. *From the Continental*

diver

Divide in the Rocky Mountains, the water on the west side flows into the Pacific Ocean, and that on the east side flows into the Gulf of Mexico or the Atlantic Ocean. **di vides.**

div i dend (div′ə dend), *n.* 1. the number into which another number is divided. *In 60 ÷ 2 = 30, the number 60 is the dividend.* 2. money from its profits which a company divides among people who own its stock. *Many people make a living just from dividends paid by successful corporations.* **div i dends.**

di vine (də vīn′), *adj.* 1. of or pertaining to God; holy. *In Sunday School we study the divine will of God.* 2. like a god; very unusual. *He has a divine gift for music.* **di vine ly,** *adv.* *n.* 3. a minister or priest. *From boyhood he wanted to be a divine.* **di vines.** *v.* 4. to guess; assume. *She looked so happy and gay that we all divined she had been elected class president.* **di vines, di vined, di vin ing.**

di vis i ble (də viz′ə bl), *adj.* capable of being divided. *The number 100 is evenly divisible by 2, 4, 5, 10, 20, 25, and 50.*

di vi sion (də vizh′ən), *n.* 1. a dividing; being divided. *The division between the two towns is clearly marked by signs. The book has three divisions, or chapters.* 2. a part; department. *The sales division of the company can use two more salesmen. The Wisconsin division of the railroad carries the most passengers.* 3. the method of finding out how many times one number is contained in another. *Addition, multiplication, subtraction, and division are all parts of mathematics.* 4. a difference of opinion or feeling; failure to agree. *The division between the two brothers was settled by their father.* 5. a part or section of the army, usually having about 15,000 men. *The 69th Division was known as " The Fighting 69th."* **di vis ions.**

di vi sor (də vī′zər), *n.* a number by which another number is divided. *In 60 ÷ 3 = 20, the number 3 is the divisor.* **di vi sors.**

diz zy (diz′ē), *adj.* 1. having a feeling of spinning around and almost falling; not steady. *Bob was a little dizzy after he was hit in the football game, so the coach told him to sit quietly for ten minutes.* 2. causing a feeling of whirling. *The office building rises to a dizzy height.* **diz zi er, diz zi est; diz zi ly,** *adv.*

do¹ (dü), *v.* 1. to perform; carry out a piece of work. *Always do your job as well as possible. The policeman did his duty. The class will do a play next Friday.* 2. to cause; bring about. *She does much good at the hospital.* 3. to get along; progress. *Don is doing well in school. The patient is doing well in the hospital.* 4. to take care of; attend to. *Someone will have to do the dishes. Susan is doing her hair.* 5. to be right for the job; be good enough. *Your clothes will do for this visit. Will this wallpaper do?* 6. to cover; go to. *This car can do one hundred miles an hour. She is doing Europe this year.* 7. to give. *His city will do honor to the scientist. Do me a favor, please.*

8. to work on; get in order. *Ask the hotel maid to do this room. Has the laundry been done?* 9. **Do** is used (a) to give force to a statement. *I do have a right to be here.* (b) to take the place of a verb already used. *He drives as well as I do.* (c) to ask a question. *Do you want to come?* 10. **do away with,** to get rid of. *He is doing away with his bad habits of speech.* 11. **do up,** to wrap. *Do up the birthday presents, please.* **does** (duz), **did, done, do ing.**

do² (dō), *n.* the first and last notes of a musical scale. *The names of the notes of the scale are do, re, mi, fa, sol, la, ti, do.*

dock¹ (dok), *n.* 1. a platform built out from the shore, used for loading and unloading ships; a wharf. *There are many docks in cities on the seacoast, such as New York and San Francisco.* **docks.** *v.* 2. to bring to a dock; arrive at a dock. *Powerful tugs help to dock big ships. The ship docked an hour early.* **docks, docked, dock ing.**

dock² (dok), *n.* 1. the solid part of an animal's tail. *The dock is the part of the tail close to the body.* **docks.** *v.* 2. to cut off the end of. *Many dogs have their tails docked.* 3. to take away part of. *The company docked his pay because of his absence.* **docks, docked, dock ing.**

dock³ (dok), *n.* the place in a courtroom where a prisoner sits or stands during his trial. *Three days of questioning in the dock made him tired.* **docks.**

dock yard (dok′yärd′), *n.* a place where ships are built and repaired. *A dockyard has docks, repair shops, warehouses, and building equipment.* **dock yards.** (See illustration on following page.)

doc tor (dok′tər), *n.* 1. a person trained to heal diseases and treat the sick (an M.D., Doctor of Medicine). *See a doctor when in doubt about the illness you may have.* 2. a person who has received the highest degree given by a university. *Years of study are required before one gets a Ph.D. (Doctor of Philosophy) degree, or a LL.D (Doctor of Laws) degree.* **doc tors.** *v.* 3. to try to heal. *Don't doctor yourself.* 4. to change or improve. *His written speech was so dull that he asked me to doctor it.* **doc tors, doc tored, doc tor ing.**

doc trine (dok′trən), *n.* something taught as the belief of a religion, a nation, or a group of persons. *A doctrine of the American way of life is that all persons are entitled to an education.* **doc trines.**

doc u ment (dok′yə mənt), *n.* 1. an official paper; any written or printed record used as evidence for some fact. *Your birth certificate is an important document.* **doc u ments.** *v.* 2. to furnish with documents. *"Document your statements with written evidence,"* said the judge. **doc u ments, doc u ment ed, doc u ment ing.**

sand, āte, bâre, fäther; sent, mē, fėrn; fit, bīke; pot, rōpe, fôrt; run, púll, rüle, cūte; noise, sound; **ch, cheese;** **ng, long; th, thick;** ~~th~~, those; **zh,** treasure; ə = a in about, e in waken, i in animal, o in seldom, and u in minus.

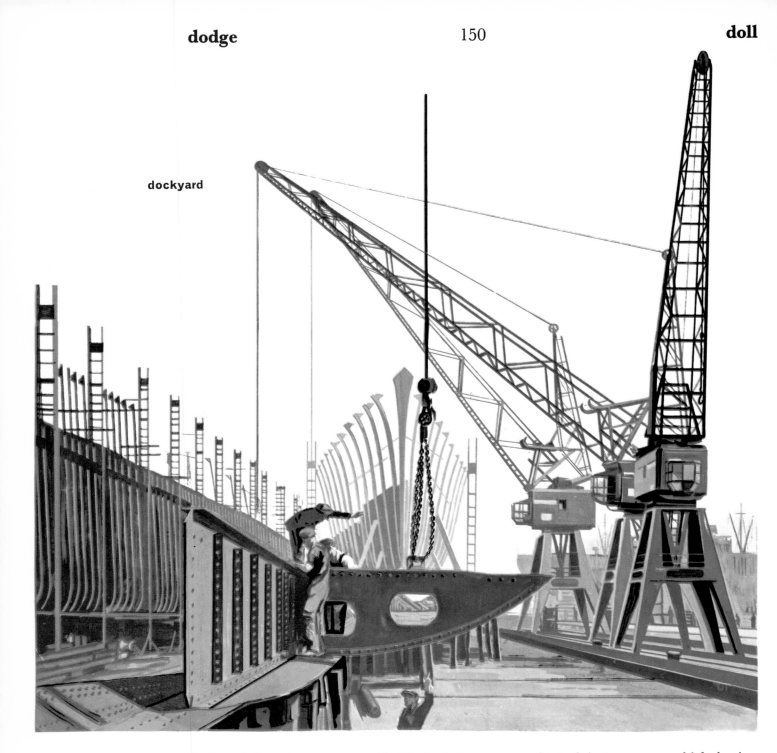

dockyard

dodge (doj), *v.* 1. to try to avoid. *The baseball runner dodged the batted ball by ducking his head.* 2. to avoid by tricks or by being clever. *The witness dodged every question until the judge told him to answer.* **dodg es, dodged, dodg ing.** *n.* 3. a sudden move to one side. *The rabbit's dodge caused the dog to bump into a tree, and the rabbit got away.* 4. a trick. *He knew all the dodges of the salesman.* **dodg es.**

does n't (duz′nt), does not. *She doesn't have a bit of trouble with homework; studying has always been easy for her.*

dog (dog), *n.* 1. a carnivorous animal very popular as a pet. *There are many kinds of dogs: some*

are used to tend sheep; some are useful for hunting; and one kind, the Saint Bernard, is trained to rescue travelers in the mountains.* **dogs.**
v. 2. to follow closely. *The police dogged the path of the thief.* **dogs, dogged, dog ging.**

dog wood (dog′wŭd′), *n.* a tree having white or pink flowers in the spring. *The dogwood produces red berries in the fall.* **dog woods.**

do ings (dü′ingz), *n. pl.* things that a person or people do; events. *There were great doings at the gym, and everyone had a good time.*

doll (dol), *n.* a toy that looks like a person. *Children like to play with dolls, and pretend they are real people.* **dolls.**

sand, āte, bâre, fäther; sent, mē, fėrn; fit, bĭke; pot, rōpe, fôrt; run, pùll, rüle, cūte; noise, sound; ch, cheese; ng, long; th, thick; ~~th~~, those; zh, treasure; ə = a in about, e in waken, i in animal, o in seldom, and u in minus.

DOGS

German shepherd

Saint Bernard

Collie

Irish Setter

Dachshund

Great Dane

English Bulldog

Springer Spaniel

Beagle

Newfoundland

Dalmatian

Boxer

Pointer

Cocker Spaniel

Pekingese

Poodle

Brussels Griffon

Greyhound

dol lar (dol′ər), *n.* a silver coin or piece of paper money worth one hundred cents, or ten dimes, or twenty nickels. *Other countries besides the United States use dollars—Canada and Ethiopia, for example. When we write $1.00, we mean "one dollar."* **dol lars.**

dol ly (dol′ē), *n.* 1. a low truck having small wheels, used in factories, warehouses, etc. for moving loads too heavy to be carried by a person. *A dolly can be pushed or pulled.* 2. a doll. *The little girl said, "I want my dolly."* **dol lies.**

dol phin (dol′fən), *n.* a water animal somewhat like a whale, but smaller. *Dolphins like to leap in and out of the water.* **dol phins.**

do mes tic (də mes′tik), *adj.* 1. having to do with the home or family. *Cleaning the apartment, washing dishes, and doing the laundry are domestic jobs.* 2. of or produced in one's own country. *I like domestic olives better than the olives grown in foreign countries.* 3. tame. *Dogs and cats are domestic animals that like to live with people.* 4. fond of home and household tasks. *Louise is a domestic girl who helps her mother in every task.* **do mes ti cal ly,** *adv.*
n. 5. a house servant, such as a maid, cook, or butler. *The rich family has four domestics.* **do mes tics.**

dom i no (dom′ə nō), *n.* one of twenty-eight small, flat pieces used in playing the game of dominoes. *A domino has on it from one to six dots, which each player tries to match from his supply of dominoes.* **dom i noes.**

done (dun), *v.* 1. past participle of **do.**
adj. 2. cooked. *The meat is done.* 3. completed; finished. *The job is done.*

don key (dong′kē, dung′kē), *n.* an animal somewhat like a horse, but having long ears. *A donkey is a strong work animal, but often he is stubborn and will just stand still if he wants to.* 2. a stubborn person; a stupid person. *At first I thought Jack was a donkey, then I saw that he knew what he was doing.* **don keys.**

dolphin

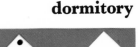

dominoes

don't (dōnt), do not. *I don't know her.*

door (dôr), *n.* a movable barrier that can be opened and closed, used as an entrance to a house, room, apartment building, cupboard, etc. *You open a door by pulling it, pushing it, or sliding it sideways. Open the door and go inside. Close the kitchen door before the rain blows in! The door of the cabinet is stuck.* **doors.**

door bell (dôr′bel′), *n.* a bell inside a house or apartment which rings when a visitor on the outside presses a button. *Ring the doorbell again; I am sure he is home.* **door bells.**

door knob (dôr′nob′), *n.* the handle for opening a door. *Turn the doorknob, pull, and the door will open.* **door knobs.**

door man (dôr′man′, dôr′mən), *n.* a man who stands at the outer door of an apartment, hotel, or nightclub to open doors and help people as is necessary. *The doorman will call a taxi for us.* **door men.**

door step (dôr′step), *n.* the step in front of an outside door. *The delivery boy leaves the groceries on our doorstep if we are not home.* **door steps.**

door way (dôr′wā′), *n.* the entrance to a building or room in which a door may be placed. *This is the doorway to the bedroom.* **door ways.**

dope (dōp), *n.* 1. a drug used as a narcotic. *People who start taking dope can seldom stop.* 2. a thick liquid used on cloth to make it waterproof or stronger. *They brushed some dope on the old tent, and now it is like new.* 3. information. *What's the latest dope?* 4. a stupid person. *Sometimes that smart boy acts like a dope.* **dopes.**
v. 5. to give a drug to. *The doctor doped the lion so he could treat his paw.* **dopes, doped, dop ing.**

Dor ic (dôr ik), *adj.* pertaining to the oldest and plainest type of column used in ancient Greece. *Doric columns have simple decorations.*

dor mi to ry (dôr′mə tôr′ē), *n.* 1. a building having many rooms for sleeping. *Most students in a university live in dormitories.* 2. a large room with many beds. *My four brothers sleep in a dormitory in our house.* **dor mi to ries.**

doorman

dose (dōs), *n.* 1. the amount of medicine that is to be taken at one time. *He takes a dose of cough medicine twice a day.* **dos es.**
v. 2. to give medicine to. *Betty dosed her cat three times a day when it was sick.* **dos es, dosed, dos ing.**

dot (dot), *n.* 1. a small round spot. *In printing and writing, a dot is placed above "i" and "j," except when they are used as capital letters. Some neckties have a design made of dots.* **dots.**
v. 2. to mark with a small round spot. *Be sure to dot your "i's."* 3. to cover, as with dots. *The large lake was dotted with sailing boats.* **dots, dot ted, dot ting.**

dou ble (dub′l), *adj.* 1. twice as much, as large, as fast, as heavy, etc. *When I'm hungry, I like a double helping of food. You will get double pay for working on Sunday.* 2. made of two parts that are alike. *The double doors lead to the garden.* 3. having more than the usual number of petals. *A double rose is larger than the usual rose.* 4. made for two. *You can put two cars in a double garage.* **dou bly,** *adv.*
n. 5. an amount twice as great. *My salary is the double of his.* 6. a person or thing that looks like another. *I saw your double today. My house is the double of his.* 7. a two-base hit in baseball. *Jones leads the league in the number of doubles.* 8. **doubles,** a game of tennis, handball, etc. with two players on each side. *He was much better at doubles than at singles.* **dou bles.**
adv. 9. two at one time. *To ride double on a bicycle is dangerous.*

v. 10. to make or become twice as big, as strong, as great, etc. *He doubled his money by buying stocks, and he now has $1000 instead of $500. The population of the school doubled in four years.* 11. to fold over. *Double your test paper, and sign your name on the blank side. He doubled his fist in anger, but he didn't lose his temper.* 12. to serve more than one purpose. *The living room couch doubles as a bed at night.* 13. to turn and go back. *A hunted animal will double back to escape pursuit.* 14. to turn around; reverse. *The ship doubled back and picked up supplies.* 15. **double up,** (a) to bend over. *He doubled up with laughter.* (b) to share a room with someone. *Harry and Russell will double up, so Aunt Harriet can have a room to herself.* **dou bles, dou bled, dou bling.**

doubt (dout), *v.* 1. to be not sure; to question; to be uncertain. *I doubt that the Smiths are home from their vacation. I doubt that his experience will help us.* **doubts, doubt ed, doubt ing.**
n. 2. being uncertain; being not sure. *I have my doubts that we have enough gasoline in the car.* 3. **no doubt,** surely. *He will, no doubt, be here in ten minutes.* **doubts.**

doubt ful (dout′fəl), *adj.* not sure; not certain. *I am doubtful that we can finish the game in this rain.* **doubt ful ly,** *adv.*

doubt less (dout′ləs), *adv.* no doubt; surely. *The dogs will doubtless bark as soon as the doorbell rings.*

dough (dō), *n.* a soft mixture of flour, milk or water, salt, and other things. *Bread, cake, and rolls are made from dough which is baked.*

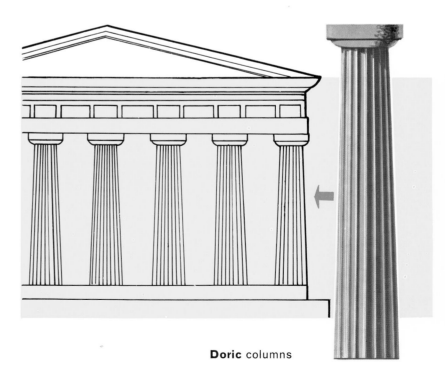

Doric columns

sand, āte, bâre, fäther; sent, mē, fėrn; fit, bīke; pot, rōpe, fôrt; run, pùll, rüle, cūte; noise, sound; ch, cheese; ng, long; th, thick; ᵗℎ, those; zh, treasure; ə = a in about, e in waken, i in animal, o in seldom, and u in minus.

dove[1] (dōv), past tense of **dive**.

dove[2] (duv), *n.* a kind of pigeon. *Bob's uncle raises doves, and has a house for them on the roof of his apartment.* **doves.**

down[1] (doun), *adv.* 1. from a place that is high to a place that is low. *The acrobat jumped down from the tall swing. The airplane came down for a landing. The sun goes down at eight o'clock this time of year.* 2. from a time in the past to today. *This old clock has been handed down from my great-grandfather.* 3. to a size or amount that is smaller. *Joan's weight has gone down from 120 pounds to 110 pounds. All prices are marked down during the sale.* 4. in money paid now. *Pay five dollars down and five dollars a month.* 5. to a state of quiet and seriousness. *You had better settle down to work.*
adj. 6. sad; worried. *Father seems down today.* 7. sick; ill. *Mother is down with a sore back. Half the class is down with colds.*
prep. 8. along. *The cars speed down the highway.*
v. 9. to knock down; put down. *The movie hero downed the thief with one punch. Drink water slowly; don't down it in one swallow.* **downs, downed, down ing.**

down[2] (doun), *n.* 1. soft feathers. *The down of birds is used to stuff pillows.* 2. soft fuzz or hair. *A small baby has down on his head.*

down stairs (doun′stârz′), *adv.* 1. to a lower floor. *I am going downstairs to finish the laundry.*
adj. 2. on the lower floor. *The boys sleep in a downstairs bedroom.*

down town (doun′toun′), *adv.* 1. toward the main business part of a city. *We all went downtown to shop.*
adj. 2. in the main business part. *The downtown stores have a bigger selection of items than the suburban stores.*

down ward or **down wards** (doun′wərd, doun′wərdz), *adv.* 1. toward a lower place. *The car at the top of the hill rolled downward.*
adj. 2. going toward a lower place. *This downward path leads to the house.*

doze (dōz), *v.* 1. to sleep lightly; to take a nap. *After lunch I want to doze for ten minutes.* **doz es, dozed, doz ing.**
n. 2. a short sleep or nap. *The dog was taking his afternoon doze.*

doz en (duz′n), *n.* twelve. *She bought a dozen bottles of root beer.* **doz ens** or **doz en.**

draft (draft), *n.* 1. a plan or design of work to be done. *The draft of the new house showed where all the rooms will be. The writer spent a long time writing the first draft of his new book.* 2. a movement of air. *A cold draft came from the open window.* 3. the selection of young men to serve in the army. *Since Bob was nineteen and in good health, he was sure the draft would take him soon.* 4. a drink. *A draft of cold water tastes fine on a hot day.* 5. the depth of water needed to float a loaded ship. *The freighter has a draft of twenty feet.* **drafts.**

adj. 6. for pulling loads. *A draft horse is a strong animal.*
v. 7. to prepare the outline or design of. *The builder drafted a plan for a building. The writer drafted the first chapters of his book.* 8. to choose men to serve in the army. *Instead of waiting to be drafted, Ed asked to enter the army.* **drafts, draft ed, draft ing.**

drag (drag), *v.* 1. to pull slowly; haul. *They dragged the sled loaded with five children to the top of the hill.* 2. to move or go slowly. *The afternoon dragged on as the children waited for the rain to stop. The music wasn't lively; it dragged.* 3. to try to find at the bottom of water. *The men will drag the lake for the sunken boat.* **drags, dragged, drag ging.**
n. 4. anything that slows down or holds back. *He's a drag on the rest of us because we always have to wait for him.* **drags.**

drag on (drag′ən), *n.* an imaginary, fire-breathing monster which was supposed to have the body of a snake and the wings of a bird, told about in old stories. *The brave knight killed the dragon.* **drag ons.**

drag on fly (drag′ən flī′), *n.* a large insect with a slender body and four wings. *Dragonflies live on small flying insects and are often found near water.* **drag on flies.**

drain (drān), *v.* 1. to draw off or take away slowly. *We used a pump to drain the water from the flooded basement.* 2. to remove water or any liquid from; to empty of liquid. *Drain the tub after your bath.* 3. to flow off or away. *The city's sewers drain into a river.* 4. to become dry by the drawing off of liquid. *Don't put the dishes away until they drain.* 5. to use slowly and completely;

dragonfly

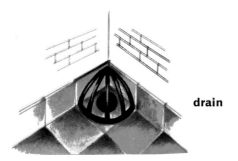

drain

to exhaust. *The warm and humid weather drained my strength.* **drains, drained, drain ing.**

n. 6. a pipe, sewer, etc. through which water or waste liquids flow. *The drain in the basement has a heavy iron cover.* 7. anything which uses up a supply. *Taking his friends to the movies was a drain on his allowance.* **drains.**

dra ma (drä′mə, dram′ə), *n.* 1. a story which is acted on a stage; a play. *The senior class presented a drama about safety.* 2. the writing, producing, or performing of plays. *She is planning for a career in drama.* 3. anything which has the adventure and excitement of a play. *The drama of the swimmers rescue was described in the newspaper.* **dra mas.**

dra mat ic (drə mat′ik), *adj.* 1. having to do with plays or the theater. *An actor is a dramatic artist.* 2. exciting and full of adventure. *The young men made a dramatic attempt to reach the top of the mountain.* **dra mat i cal ly,** *adv.*

n. pl. 3. **dramatics,** the art or study of producing or performing in plays. *There will be a class in dramatics at our school next year.*

dram a tize (dram′ə tīz′), *v.* 1. to write, produce, or perform something as a play. *The story of Alice in Wonderland has been dramatized in plays and movies.* 2. to present in an exciting manner. *The teacher dramatized the force of gravity by dropping a ball on the floor.* **dram a tiz es, dram a tized, dram a tiz ing.**

drank (drangk), past tense of **drink.**

draw (drô), *v.* 1. to pull or drag behind; to pull towards one; haul. *The sled was drawn by two white horses. I drew the table closer to me.* 2. to remove by pulling up or hauling out. *We drew our drinking water from a nearby well.* 3. to withdraw money from a bank. *He drew fifty dollars from his account.* 4. to attract the attention of. *The ball game drew a very large crowd of people.* 5. to move or come gradually. *Winter is drawing near. As we drew away from the city, it began to rain.* 6. to make a design, picture, etc. *The artist drew an outline before he painted the picture.* 7. to write out. *He drew a money order for ten dollars. The lawyer drew up a contract.* 8. to require a certain depth of water to

float; to sink to a certain level when floating. *A small boat may draw less than one foot of water, while a large ship may draw as much as thirty feet.* 9. to breathe in. *The runner drew a deep breath as the race began.* 10. to carry off smoke in a current of air. *Something must be blocking the chimney to make it draw so poorly.* **draws, drew, drawn, draw ing.**

n. 11. the result of a game or contest in which neither side wins because the score is even; a tie. *The judges called the match a draw because neither fighter was better than the other.* 12. a shallow valley. *The cowboy decided to camp for the night in a draw.* **draws.**

draw er (drô′ər for 1, drôr for 2), *n.* 1. any person or thing that draws. *He sometimes paints scenes, but he is mainly a drawer of animals.* 2. a sliding box in a desk, cabinet, chest, etc. *Put your socks in the top drawer of your dresser.* **draw ers.**

draw ing (drô′ing), *n.* 1. a design, picture, etc. which is drawn. *The drawing of a covered bridge won first prize in the art contest.* 2. the making of such a design, picture, etc. *He has a great deal of ability for drawing.* 3. a contest in which prizes are awarded to some of the persons who have bought chances. *They won a new car in the drawing.* **draw ings.**

dread (dred), *v.* 1. to fear; to look forward to something with great fear. *He dreaded going to class without his homework.* **dreads, dread ed, dread ing.**

n. 2. a great fear. *His dread of falling prevented him from using the fire escape.* **dreads.**

adj. 3. dreadful; unpleasant; feared. *Polio was a dread disease before a vaccine was discovered.*

dread ful (dred′fəl), *adj.* 1. causing great fear; awful; terrible. *We heard a dreadful roar in the forest.* 2. very bad; very unpleasant. *I have a dreadful toothache.* **dread ful ly,** *adv.*

dream (drēm), *n.* 1. the thoughts, feelings, and pictures that occur in a person's mind as he sleeps. *His dream was about flying in an airplane.* 2. something imagined while awake; a daydream. *Do you have dreams of being a major-league baseball player?* **dreams.**

v. 3. to have a dream while sleeping. *He dreamed about food because he was hungry.* 4. to have a daydream; to imagine. *He was looking out of the window and dreaming when the bell rang.* 5. to suppose or imagine that a thing could happen. *We never dreamed that we'd win all our games.* **dreams, dreamed** or **dreamt, dream ing.**

dreamy (drēm′ē), *adj.* 1. given to imagining things; given to having daydreams; impractical. *The dreamy boy developed into an inventor.* 2. like a dream; vague. *He had only a dreamy idea of what he was going to do.* 3. filled with dreams. *I spent a dreamy afternoon gazing at the sky.* **dream i ly,** *adv.*

dredge (drej), *n.* 1. a machine mounted on a

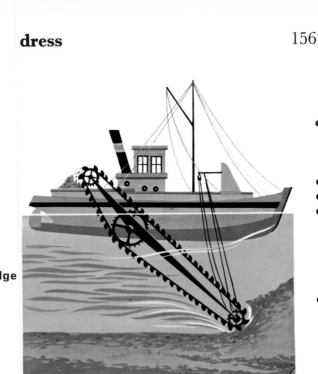

dredge

float that is used for cleaning out or deepening a harbor or river. *Dredges are used in preparing foundations for bridges.* **dredg es.**
v. 2. to clean out or deepen with a dredge. *Bigger boats can use the river now that it has been dredged.* **dredg es, dredged, dredg ing.**

dress (dres), *n.* 1. an outer garment worn by a woman or a girl. *She wore a long, white dress for the wedding.* 2. any clothing. *The soldiers were in battle dress.* **dress es.**
v. 3. to clothe; to put clothes on. *Mother dressed the baby after his nap. Are you dressed already?* 4. to wear clothes. *She dresses better than anyone else in the class.* 5. to wear formal clothing. *We were asked to dress for the dance.* 6. to prepare for cooking; to prepare for use. *She had to dress the turkey before putting it in the oven.* 7. to take care of a wound by applying medicine, putting on a bandage, etc. *The doctor dressed the cut on his arm.* 8. to decorate; to arrange in a pleasant way. *The store windows were dressed with holiday decorations.* 9. to set in a straight line. *The soldiers dressed their ranks for inspection.* **dress es, dressed, dress ing.**

dress er[1] (dres′ər), *n.* 1. a person who dresses something or someone. *She is interested in decorating and plans to be a window dresser.* 2. a person who wears a certain kind of clothing. *The banker is a very sensible dresser. His brother is a flashy dresser.* **dress ers.**

dress er[2] (dres′ər), *n.* a cabinet with drawers and often a mirror, used for storing clothes. *She has two dressers in her bedroom.* **dress ers.**

dress ing (dres′ing), *n.* 1. a liquid sauce poured on salads. *Would you like French or Italian dressing on your lettuce?* 2. a mixture of bread and spices cooked inside a chicken or turkey. *The*

turkey dressing was moist and tasty. 3. the medicine and bandages put on a wound. *The doctor will change the dressing every three days until the wound is healed.* **dress ings.**

dress mak er (dres′māk′ər), *n.* a person whose occupation is making clothes for women and girls. *She will have to go back to the dressmaker for a fitting.* **dress mak ers.**

drew (drü), past tense of **draw.**

dried (drīd), past tense of **dry.**

dri er or **dry er** (drī′ər), *n.* a machine that dries things by blowing air through them. *After Mother washed the clothes, she put them in the drier. Girls sometimes use a small drier to get the water out of their hair after washing it.* **dri ers** or **dry ers.**

drift (drift), *v.* 1. to be moved along by a current of air or water. *When its motor died, the boat drifted out towards the middle of the lake.* 2. to move through life with no direction; to be directed by circumstances or events rather than by exercising choice. *The man drifted from job to job and place to place, never staying anywhere very long.* 3. to pile up in large mounds. *The snow had drifted against the door of the cabin.* **drifts, drift ed, drift ing.**
n. 4. the movement caused by a current of air or water. *In steering a large boat, the captain must consider the drift of the ship as well as its forward motion.* 5. the direction of such movement. *The northeast drift of the waves carried us far off our course.* 6. the general idea of a statement, discussion, etc. *No one seemed able to catch the drift of his remarks.* 7. a large mound of something piled up by the wind, water, etc. *In some places the drifts of snow were ten feet deep.* **drifts.**

drill[1] (dril), *n.* 1. a machine or tool which bores holes in anything. *The workers dug up the street with automatic drills and shovels. The dentist used his drill to clean out the cavity before filling it.* 2. the practice of a skill or an exercise over and over again to learn it well. *The football team spends two hours in drill every afternoon. We were supposed to do our spelling drills for homework.* 3. the training of a soldier in marching, using a weapon, and other military skills. *The new soldiers lined up for drill.* **drills.**
v. 4. to make holes with a boring tool. *He had to drill a hole in the door to install the lock.* 5. to teach something by having it done over and over again. *The teacher drilled the class in handwriting.* 6. to undergo training in military skills. *The soldiers continued to drill long after it was dark.* **drills, drilled, drill ing.**

drill[2] (dril), *n.* a machine which plants seeds in rows. *The farmer used a drill to plant the corn.* **drills.**

drink (dringk), *v.* 1. to take a liquid into the mouth and swallow it. *He drank a glass of milk in a single gulp.* 2. to take in a liquid; to absorb. *Some plants drink up more water than others.* 3. to take in anything. *Their eyes drank in every detail of the toy display.* 4. to drink liquor, beer, or wine. *He doesn't drink when he is going to drive.* **drinks, drank, drunk, drink ing.**

n. 5. anything which is drunk. *May I have a drink of water?* 6. any liquor, beer, or wine. *The man poured a drink for his guest.* **drinks.**

drip (drip), *v.* 1. to fall or let fall in drops. *Water dripped from the melting icicle.* **drips, dripped, drip ping.**

n. 2. a falling in drops. *The steady drip of water from the leaky faucet kept us awake.* **drips.**

drive (drīv), *v.* 1. to cause to go; to make something move. *We drove the cows into the barn for milking.* 2. to force something in a direction by striking it. *I drove a nail into the wall.* 3. to direct and control the movement of a vehicle, working animals, etc. *Who drove the car to the railroad station? The farmer drove a team of horses through the fields.* 4. to go somewhere or carry something or someone in an automobile, carriage, etc. *My father drove me to school this morning.* 5. to achieve a result through force, cleverness, etc. *The salesman finally drove a bargain with the customer.* 6. to force or compel someone to do work. *The boss drives the men to produce more and more each day.* 7. to force into a certain state or condition. *His constant arguing drove us to dislike him very much.* **drives, drove, driv en, driv ing.**

n. 8. a trip taken in an automobile. *We took a drive into the country last Sunday.* 9. a road on which vehicles travel. *They built a drive from the street to the garage.* 10. an organized attempt to achieve some purpose. *The school sponsored a food drive at Thanksgiving.* **drives.**

driv en (driv/ən), past participle of **drive.**

driv er (drīv/ər), *n.* 1. any person who drives a vehicle or an animal. *The bus driver collected our fares when we got on.* 2. a person who forces people to work very hard. *His boss acts like a slave driver if work piles up.* **driv ers.**

drive way (drīv/wā/), *n.* a path for automobiles which goes from the street to a garage or house. *Sometimes we park our car in our driveway.* **drive ways.**

drom e dary (drom/ə der/ē), *n.* a camel with one hump. *A dromedary is used for fast riding rather than for carrying goods.* **drom e dar ies.**

drone (drōn), *n.* 1. a male bee. *Drones do no work, produce no honey, and have no sting.* 2. a person who does no work; a lazy person. *Drones have a hard time holding jobs because employers expect their employees to work.* 3. a steady hum; a monotonous sound. *The drone of the engines faded as the cars passed us.* **drones.**

v. 4. to make a steady, monotonous sound. *Mosquitoes and bees drone as they fly.* 5. to use a dull, monotonous tone when speaking. *The speaker droned on long after everyone had stopped listening to him.* **drones, droned, dron ing.**

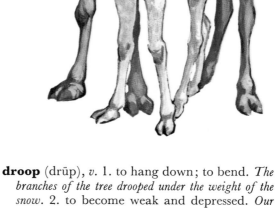

 dromedary and its young

droop (drüp), *v.* 1. to hang down; to bend. *The branches of the tree drooped under the weight of the snow.* 2. to become weak and depressed. *Our spirits drooped as the rain began.* **droops, drooped, droop ing.**

n. 3. a hanging down; a drooping. *The droop of his shoulders told us he had lost.* **droops.**

drop (drop), *n.* 1. a small amount of liquid formed in a rounded mass. *A single drop of water was on the leaf.* 2. anything having this shape. *We ate several chocolate drops after dinner.* 3. a small amount of anything. *Would you like a drop of cream in your coffee? There wasn't a drop of evidence to support his story.* 4. a sudden fall. *After the fire, there was a sharp drop in the value of the house.* 5. the distance of a fall; the distance one may fall. *There was a drop of seventy feet from the edge of the cliff.* 6. something into which a thing may fall. *There was a letter drop in the door.* **drops.**

v. 7. to fall or let fall in drops. *Perspiration dropped from his forehead.* 8. to fall or let fall. *I dropped a dish as I was drying it.* 9. to stop dealing with something; to let go. *Let us drop the subject before anyone gets too angry.* 10. to cause to fall down; to knock down. *The fighter dropped his opponent with a hard blow to the chin.* 11. to send; to give to someone. *He dropped a line to me last week. I dropped a hint about the heat, but the manager of the theater refused to turn up the thermostat.* 12. to cause to become lower or quieter. *Please drop your voice before the others hear you.* 13. to become lower. *The price of food has not dropped for several years.* 14. **drop in,** to arrive unexpectedly; to visit informally. *Some friends from out of town dropped in to see us last Sunday.* **drops, dropped, drop ping.**

drop let (drop′lət), *n.* a very small drop. *Droplets of dew had formed on the grass.* **drop lets.**

drought (drout), *n.* 1. a period of time during which there is no rain. *The crops were ruined by a two-month drought last summer.* 2. a lack of water. *The cattle were thirsty because of drought.* **droughts.**

drove (drōv), past tense of **drive.**

drown (droun), *v.* 1. to die while underwater or in another liquid because of being unable to breathe. *A lifeguard saves people from drowning.* 2. to kill someone or something by keeping its head underwater and not permitting it to breathe. *The cruel children tried to drown the baby squirrel.* 3. to be louder or stronger than. *The music drowned out the voices of the singers.* **drowns, drowned, drown ing.**

drow sy (drou′zē), *adj.* 1. sleepy; half sleeping. *Many people get drowsy while watching television.* 2. causing one to become sleepy. *The weather was hot and humid, and there was nothing to do on such a drowsy day.* **drow si er, drow si est; drow si ly,** *adv.*

drug (drug), *n.* 1. a medicine or any substance used in making medicines. *He was given a drug which cured his illness.* 2. a medicine which is used to reduce pain or induce sleep. *The patient was given drugs because he was in terrible pain.* **drugs.**
v. 3. to treat an illness or a disease with drugs or medicine. *The man was drugged with antibiotics in an effort to reduce his fever.* 4. to make sleepy or less alert with drugs. *The man was drugged and carried off by kidnappers.* 5. to place drugs in food or drink. *The evil witch drugged the apple before giving it to the princess.* **drugs, drugged, drug ging.**

drum (drum), *n.* 1. a musical instrument which consists of a hollow cylinder with a skin or fabric stretched taut over one or both ends. *The marchers kept time to the beat of a drum.* 2. something shaped like a drum. *An empty oil drum was floating in the water.* **drums.**
v. 3. to beat a drum. *As the music grew louder, he drummed faster and faster.* 4. to strike the fingers or feet against something with regular strokes. *Long before we saw the soldiers, we heard their feet drumming on the pavement.* 5. to teach something forcefully by repeating it over and over again. *The lines for the play were finally drummed into my head.* **drums, drummed, drum ming.**

drum mer (drum′ər), *n.* 1. a person who beats a drum. *There are eleven drummers in the marching band.* 2. a salesman, especially a traveling salesman. *A drummer of pots and pans tried to sell his wares to my mother.* **drum mers.**

drunk (drungk), *v.* 1. past participle of **drink.** *adj.* 2. in a dulled or dazed condition as a result of drinking alcoholic beverages; intoxicated. *Many automobile accidents are caused by drunk drivers.* **drunk er, drunk est.**

dry (drī), *adj.* 1. free of moisture; not wet. *The ground was dry and dusty before the rain began.* 2. receiving little or no rainfall. *The desert has a very dry climate.* 3. not covered by water. *The pitcher's mound was the only piece of dry land on the flooded baseball field.* 4. empty of its normal supply of liquid. *The creek is dry during the hot weather.* 5. no longer giving milk. *When we brought the cow in for milking, we found she was dry.* 6. thirsty. *We were dry after playing ball all afternoon.* 7. quiet but clever and shrewd. *He never smiled, but his dry humor kept us laughing.* 8. dull; boring; uninteresting. *We listened to a dry speech on the need for better roads.* 9. rough; harsh. *The child had a sore throat and a dry cough.* 10. of solid substances rather than liquids. *A dry measure of sixteen ounces equals one pound; a liquid measure of sixteen ounces equals one pint.* **dri er, dri est; dry ly,** *adv.*

drums: a. African tribal drums; **b.** field drum; **c.** snare drum

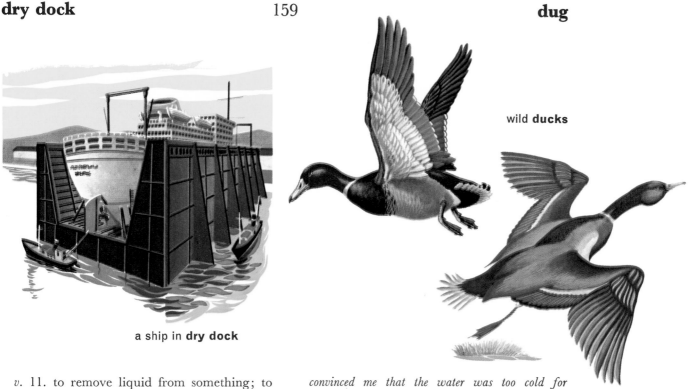

wild **ducks**

a ship in **dry dock**

v. 11. to remove liquid from something; to become dry. *We dried the dishes with a towel. Mother hung the wash on the clothesline to dry.* **dries, dried, dry ing.**

dry dock (drī dok), *n.* a floating hollow structure which can be lowered by allowing water to enter its sides. A ship then enters the structure, the water is pumped out, and the ship is ready for repairs. *A ship can be examined in the ocean if a dry dock is used.* **dry docks.**

duck[1] (duk), *n.* 1. a swimming bird having webbed feet, a short neck, and a flat bill. *A huge flock of ducks flew overhead on their way south for the winter.* 2. a female duck. *The duck waddled toward the water with her babies following in a row.* **ducks.**

duck[2] (duk), *v.* 1. to move the head or bend the body to avoid being struck by something. *He ducked just as the ball was thrown, but it hit him anyway.* 2. to go under water for a moment and come up quickly. *I ducked under the water to find the lost key.* 3. to push or pull someone under water for a moment. *The boys were ducking each other in the shallow end of the pool.* **ducks, ducked, duck ing.**

n. 4. a sudden movement of the head or bending of the body to avoid being struck. *His duck was too late, and the blow landed on his ear.* 5. a quick dive below the water. *One duck*

convinced me that the water was too cold for swimming. **ducks.**

duck[3] (duk), *n.* a strong fabric of cotton or linen. *Duck is used for clothing, sails, and umbrellas.* **ducks.**

due (dü, dū), *adj.* 1. owed; payable as a debt. *The rent is due on the first of the month.* 2. proper; suitable; something owed to a person as a right. *They always show due respect to their parents.* 3. expected; scheduled to arrive. *The bus is not due for another two hours.*

prep. 4. **due to,** because of; as a result of; owing to. *Due to the rainy weather, the picnic was canceled.*

n. 5. something owed to a person. *To give him his due, he played an outstanding game.* 6. **dues,** *pl.* a fee or regular charge, as for membership in a club or group. *The members of our club pay one dollar in dues each month.* **dues.**

adv. 7. in a straight line; directly. *We drove due west out of the city.*

du el (dü′əl, dū′əl), *n.* 1. a private fight according to strict rules between two men using guns or swords, and watched by witnesses for each man. *The object of the duel was to satisfy the honor of one of the men.* **duels.**

v. 2. to fight a duel. *They dueled at dawn.* **du els, du eled, du el ing.**

dug (dug), past tense of **dig.**

duel

duke (dük, dūk), *n.* a nobleman with a rank next below that of a prince. *All of the dukes in the kingdom attended the coronation of the king.* **dukes.**

dull (dul), *adj.* 1. not sharp; not pointed; blunt. *We couldn't chop the wood because the ax was dull.* 2. slow in learning or understanding. *Some students are brilliant in one subject and dull in another.* 3. uninteresting; boring. *It was such a dull book that I fell asleep reading it.* 4. inactive; slow. *The snow-shovel business is dull until the first snowfall of the season.* 5. dim; not bright; vague. *The sky is dull and cloudy today. The children gave the teacher dull looks when she asked about the book they hadn't read.* **dull er, dull est; dul ly,** *adv.*
v. 6. to cause something to become dull. *He dulled the blade of his knife by cutting very hard wood.* 7. to become dull. *Our excitement dulled when it became clear that we could not win the game.* **dulls, dulled, dull ing.**

du ly (dü′lē, dū′lē), *adv.* in a proper or due manner; suitably. *He was duly rewarded for his work.*

dumb (dum), *adj.* 1. not having the ability to speak. *The deaf and dumb man used sign language to express himself.* 2. not having the power of speech. *Animals are dumb creatures.* 3. unintelligent; stupid. *He is dumb only because he refuses to read anything.* **dumb er, dumb est; dumb ly,** *adv.*

dump (dump), *v.* 1. to empty a container or vehicle by letting its contents fall out. *The truck dumped a load of gravel on the edge of the road.* **dumps, dumped, dump ing.**
n. 2. a place where anything, especially trash, may be dumped. *All of our trash is taken to the city dump, where it is burned.* 3. a place where supplies, especially military supplies, are stored. *The enemy tried to blow up one of our ammunition dumps last night.* **dumps.**

dune (dün, dūn), *n.* a rounded hill of sand piled up by the wind. *Dunes are formed in many deserts and along sandy shores.* **dunes.**

dune

du pli cate (dü′plə kit, dū′plə kit for 1 and 2, dü′plə kāt′, dū′plə kāt for 3), *adj.* 1. exactly like another thing. *I have duplicate copies of this book.*
n. 2. anything that is exactly like another thing. *The copy of the painting was so good that we couldn't tell the duplicate from the original.* **du pli cates.**
v. 3. to make an exact copy or duplicate of something. *I duplicated the letter and sent a copy to my brother.* **du pli cates, du pli cat ed, du pli cat ing.**

du ra ble (dur′ə bl, dyur′ə bl), *adj.* lasting a long time. *These shoes are durable; I've worn them for five years.* **du ra bly,** *adv.*

dur ing (dur′ing, dyur′ing), *prep.* 1. throughout the entire time of. *The boys went to a camp during the summer.* 2. at the time of; in the time of. *I received a telephone call during dinner.*

dusk (dusk), *n.* 1. the time between sunset and darkness. *The lights in the house were turned on at dusk.* 2. partial darkness; shade. *The dusk of the cave was a little frightening.* **dusks.**

dust (dust), *n.* 1. a light, dry powder, especially of earth. *A thin layer of dust covered the furniture in the room.* 2. the ground; the earth. *The officer ordered his men to hit the dust when they were attacked.* **dusts.**
v. 3. to remove dust from something by brushing or wiping it away. *He dusted the books as he took them from the shelf.* 4. to put dust or powder on. *Mother dusts the baby with powder after his bath.* **dusts, dust ed, dust ing.**

dust y (dus′tē), *adj.* 1. full of dust; having a covering of dust. *The rooms in the old house were hot and dusty.* 2. similar to dust; powdery. *A dusty layer of dandelion seeds covered the lawn.* **dust i er, dust i est; dust i ly,** *adv.*

Dutch (duch), *n.* 1. the people of the Netherlands. *The Dutch have produced some of the world's greatest works of art.* 2. the language spoken by these people. *Dutch is similar to German in its sounds and in many of its words.*
adj. 3. of the Netherlands, its people, or their language. *We read a story about a Dutch boy who prevented a dike from breaking.*

du ty (dü′tē, dū′tē), *n.* 1. a thing that a person ought to do. *He felt that it was his duty to tell the policeman about the thief's hiding place.* 2. a sense of responsibility towards one's parents, country, etc.; respect. *He regarded serving in the army as a duty to his country.* 3. a task performed as an occupation or as part of an occupation. *His duties included taking orders over the telephone and delivering merchandise.* 4. a tax paid on goods when they are brought into a country. *The duty is added to the cost of the purchases.* **du ties.**

dwarf (dwôrf), *n.* 1. a person, animal, or plant that is much smaller than normal size. *Snow White lived with seven dwarfs.* 2. such a person in fairy tales who has evil or magical powers.

The dwarf changed the straw into gold for the princess. **dwarfs.**

v. 3. to prevent a thing from growing to its normal size. *A lack of proper minerals in the soil dwarfed the trees.* 4. to cause to appear to be smaller than normal. *I was dwarfed by the tall men standing around me.* **dwarfs, dwarfed, dwarf ing.**

dwell (dwel), *v.* 1. to live in or at a place; to have one's home in a place. *The king in the story dwells in a far-off land.* 2. **dwell on,** to talk or write about a subject at great length. *Everyone in the room seemed to dwell on the details of the school fire.* **dwells, dwelt** or **dwelled, dwell ing.**

dwelt (dwelt), past tense of **dwell.**

dye (dī), *v.* 1. to give color to something or change its color. *Mother dyed the shirt blue.* **dyes, dyed, dye ing.**
n. 2. coloring matter used in dyeing. *You can use either red or blue dye on this fabric.* 3. the color produced by dyeing. *The dye in the shirt faded after it was washed.* **dyes.**

dy ing (dī′ing), *v.* 1. present participle of **die.**
adj. 2. occurring at the time of death or at the end of anything. *The rays of the dying sun could be seen on the western horizon. His dying wish was for another chance at life.*

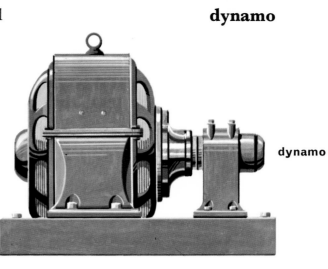

dynamo

dy na mite (dī′nə mīt), *n.* 1. an explosive used for blasting rocks, earth, etc. *We used a stick of dynamite to blow up the tree stump.*
v. 2. to blast something with dynamite. *The road builders dynamited a tunnel through the mountain.* **dy na mites, dy na mit ed, dy na mit ing.**

dy na mo (dī′nə mō), *n.* a machine for changing mechanical energy into electricity. *Some dynamos are as tall as a two-story building, and a group of them can supply electricity for a city.* **dy na mos.**

E or **e** (ē), the fifth letter of the alphabet.

each (ēch), *adj.* 1. every individual or thing considered as a unit in a larger group. *Each child was given a prize at the birthday party.* *pron.* 2. every individual; each one. *Each of us tried to answer the question.* *adv.* 3. for each one; apiece. *The tickets are one dollar each.*

ea ger (ē′gər), *adj.* full of desire; anxiously wanting something. *We were eager for school to begin in September.* **ea ger ly,** *adv.*

ea gle (ē′gl), *n.* a very large bird with sharp eyesight, strong wings, powerful legs and claws, and a hooked beak. *An eagle is the symbol of the United States.* **ea gles.**

earring

eagle

ear[1] (ir), *n.* 1. the organ by which animals and man hear. *The ear consists of three major parts, only one of which can be easily seen.* 2. the sense of hearing, especially the sense of determining the quality of something or its correctness by listening to it. *Tom never took piano lessons; he plays the piano by ear. He has a fine ear for music, and can always tell when someone is singing off key.* 3. attention by listening. *The soldiers gave ear to the orders of the general.* 4. anything which is shaped like an ear. *The handle of a pitcher or cup is an ear.* **ears.**

ear[2] (ir), *n.* the seed-bearing part of certain grains, such as corn, rice, barley, etc. *Mother boiled six ears of corn for dinner.* **ears.**

ear drum (ir′drum′), *n.* the thin, skinlike membrane that covers the opening between the outer ear and the middle ear. *A heavy blow may break the eardrum by forcing air into the ear canal.* **ear drums.**

ear ly (ėr′lē), *adv.* 1. at or near the beginning of something. *I became tired very early in the race.* 2. sooner than usual; before the usual time. *I will have to get up early to go fishing tomorrow.* *adj.* 3. coming or happening at the beginning of something. *The early election returns indicated that Thompson would win by a large margin.* **ear li er, ear li est.**

earn (ėrn), *v.* 1. to receive in return for performing a service, doing work, etc. *I earned four dollars today for mowing grass.* 2. to deserve as a result of performing a service, doing work, etc. *She paid him for washing her windows even though he didn't earn the money.* **earns, earned, earn ing.**

ear nest (ėr′nəst), *adj.* 1. sincere; serious. *His earnest efforts in school made him an excellent student.* **ear nest ly,** *adv.* *n.* 2. **in earnest,** serious; eager and determined to do something well. *Are you in earnest about your offer to help me? He was in earnest about learning to play the violin, so he practiced every day.*

ear ring (ir′ring′), *n.* an ornament fastened to the bottom part of the ear. *Earrings are worn by many women.* **ear rings.**

earth (ėrth), *n.* 1. the third planet from the sun; the planet on which we live. *The earth revolves around the sun.* 2. the portion of our planet which is not covered by water. *During the last ice age, more than half of the earth was covered by ice.* 3. ground; soil. *Plant these seeds in black earth, and they will soon sprout.* **earths.**

earth worm (ėrth′wėrm′), *n.* a common worm that burrows in the ground; an angleworm. *We found many earthworms while digging in the garden.* **earth worms.**

ease (ēz), *n.* 1. freedom from pain, trouble, or unhappiness. *The painter lived a life of ease on a faraway island.* 2. freedom from shame or nervousness. *He spoke confidently and with ease.* *v.* 3. to relieve pain or discomfort. *This new medicine will ease your headache.* 4. to make less

sand, āte, bâre, fäther; sent, mē, fėrn; fit, bīke; pot, rōpe, fôrt; run, pull, rüle, cūte; noise, sound; ch, cheese; ng, long; th, thick; <u>th</u>, those; zh, treasure; ə = a in about, e in waken, i in animal, o in seldom, and u in minus.

tight; to loosen. *The man eased his belt after finishing a huge dinner.* 5. to move gently and carefully. *The doctors eased the patient into the bed.* **eas es, eased, eas ing.**

ea sel (ē′zl), *n.* a stand or frame used to hold a picture. *An artist uses an easel to hold his canvas while he paints on it.* **ea sels.**

eas i ly (ē′zə lē), *adv.* 1. with little or no difficulty; with ease. *He performed the difficult operation easily.* 2. comfortable; with no discomfort. *The patient slept easily all night.* 3. with no question or doubt; certainly. *She is easily the most beautiful girl in the class.*

east (ēst), *n.* 1. the direction to your right as you face north; the direction from which the sun rises. *We saw a glow of light in the east before dawn.* 2. the eastern part of a country or region. *His parents were born in the east of Ireland.* 3. **the East,** (a) the eastern part of the United States; the part of the United States that is east of the Mississippi River. *Many of the famous cowboys of the Old West were born and raised in the East.* (b) the Orient; the countries of Asia. *Japan and Korea are countries in the East.* *adv.* 4. to the east; in the direction of east. *We walked east until we came to the hotel.* *adj.* 5. from the east. *An east wind brought rain and colder temperatures.* **east er ly.**

East er (ēs′tər), *n.* the annual Christian festival day celebrating Christ's rising from the dead. *Easter is celebrated in spring on the first Sunday that follows a full moon.* **East ers.**

east ern (ēs′tərn), *adj.* 1. in the east; toward the east. *The eastern coast of the country was lined with mountains.* 2. from the east. *An eastern wind drove the ship against the rocks.* 3. **Eastern,** of the East; in the East. *Many Eastern customs have been adopted by people in other parts of the world.*

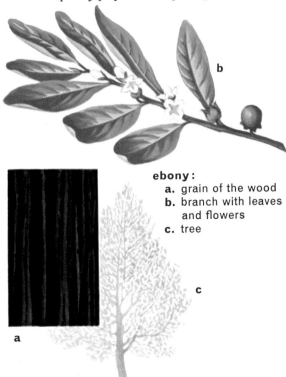

ebony:
a. grain of the wood
b. branch with leaves and flowers
c. tree

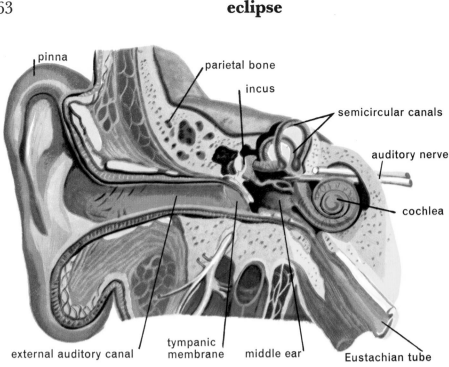

human **ear**

eas y (ēz′ē), *adj.* 1. not hard to understand, learn, etc.; not difficult to obtain, do, etc. *Spelling is an easy subject for some people. It is easy to find a good book in the library.* 2. without worry, discomfort, pain, or trouble. *The baby enjoys an easy sleep every night.* 3. comfortable; providing rest. *Father sat in an easy chair, reading the newspaper.* 4. pleasant; happy; not forced or made up. *He has an easy smile.* 5. not strict; not difficult to get along with or to carry out. *She is an easy teacher. You can pay for this in ten easy payments.* **eas i er, eas i est; eas i ly.**

eat (ēt), *v.* 1. to take food into the mouth, chew it, and swallow it. *We ate eggs and toast for breakfast.* 2. to have a meal. *Did you eat yet?* 3. to destroy by wearing away, using up, etc. *Much of the soil was eaten away by the heavy rains. That car eats a lot of gas.* **eats, ate, eat en, eat ing.**

eb ony (eb′ə nē), *n.* 1. the black, hard wood of a tree that grows in the tropical parts of Asia and Africa. *Ebony is used for making cabinets, piano keys, and decorative ornaments.* **eb on ies.** *adj.* 2. dark or black. *The farmer dug his hands into the ebony soil.*

ech o (ek′ō), *n.* 1. the repetition of a sound, caused by sound waves bouncing off a surface. *When we shouted into the cave, we heard an echo.* **ech oes.** *v.* 2. to be repeated; to be sent back as an echo. *Every sound was echoed by the walls of the huge room.* 3. to repeat what someone else says or does. *The children echoed the lines of the poem as the teacher read them.* **ech oes, ech oed, ech o ing.**

eclipse (i klips′), *n.* 1. a complete or partial darkening of the moon by the shadow of the earth. *An eclipse occurs only during a full moon.*

easel

2. a complete or partial darkening of the sun caused by the moon's passing between it and the earth. *Look at an eclipse of the sun only through very dark glasses.* **eclips es.**

v. 3. to throw into the shade. *Bill's acting in the play eclipsed John's acting.* **eclips es, eclipsed, eclips ing.**

eco nom ic (ē′kə nom′ik, ek′ə nom′ik), *adj.* having to do with the production, distribution, and use of money, goods, and services. *That company is losing money because its economic development has not kept up with its increase in production.*

ec o nom i cal (ē kə nom′i kəl), *adj.* spending and saving money without waste. *She is a very economical person.* **ec o nom i cal ly,** *adv.*

eco nom ics (ē′kə nom′iks, ek′ə nom′iks), *n. pl.* the study of the production, distribution, and use of money, goods, and services. *A successful businessman applies the rules of economics to his work.*

econ o mize (i kän′ə mīz), *v.* to be economical; to spend or save money wisely. *We will have to economize if we want to buy a new car.* **e con o-miz es, e con o mized, e con o miz ing.**

econ o my (i kon′ə mē), *n.* 1. a wise use of one's money to avoid waste and to save money; thrift. *Through economy, he was able to save enough money to buy a bicycle.* 2. the use and management of money, goods, and services in a home, business, country, etc. *The success of a country's economy depends on producing only the goods that can be used or sold.* **econ o mies.**

edge (ej), *n.* 1. the side of a blade that cuts. *The tall man sharpened the edge of his ax.* 2. the outer part of anything; the line where anything ends. *The glass was resting on the edge of the table. I found a quarter on the edge of the sidewalk.* **edg es.**

v. 3. to put an edge or border on something. *He edged the garden with small, bright flowers.*

4. to move sideways. *The owner of the store edged his way through the crowd at the door.* 5. to move slowly and carefully. *The mountain climber edged along a narrow ledge of rock.* **edg es, edged, edg ing.**

ed it (ed ət), *v.* to check, correct, prepare, and arrange materials for publication. *My mother edits children's books.* **ed its, ed it ed, ed it ing.**

edi tion (i dish′ən), *n.* 1. the form in which a book is published. *He read a short edition of "Gulliver's Travels."* 2. all of the copies of a book, magazine, etc. that are published at the same time. *The fifth edition of the book has more chapters and more illustrations than the fourth edition.* **edi tions.**

ed i tor (ed′ə tər), *n.* 1. a person who prepares another person's writings for publication by checking for correct facts, proper English, correct spelling, etc. *The editor of a dictionary must check every detail of every definition before the book can be published.* 2. a person who is in charge of the publication of a newspaper or magazine. *Tom was named as editor of the school paper.* 3. a person who writes editorials. *Harry is one of twelve editors who write for that newspaper.* **ed i tors.**

ed i to ri al (ed′ə tôr′e əl), *n.* 1. an article in a newspaper or magazine or a statement on a radio or television station that gives the attitudes or opinions of the editor, publisher, or owner on a matter of public interest. *The owner of the paper wrote an editorial, backing the highway plan.* **ed i to ri als.**

adj. 2. having to do with an editor. *He does editorial work for a scientific journal. That newspaper has an unpopular editorial policy and is losing readers because of it.* **ed i to ri al ly,** *adv.*

ed u cate (ej ə kāt′), *v.* to school or train; to develop mental skills by teaching. *Public schools educate all children between the ages of six and sixteen.* **ed u cates, ed u cat ed, ed u-cat ing.**

ed u ca tion (ej′ù kā′shən), *n.* 1. the teaching or training of people; schooling. *Everyone in the United States is entitled to a free, public education.* 2. the art or study of teaching people. *He studied education in college.* 3. all of the things one learns through training or schooling. *He has not forgotten the education he received in mathematics.*

ed u ca tion al (ej′ù kā′shən l), *adj.* 1. having to do with education. *Most teachers belong to educational organizations.* 2. presenting information; giving knowledge. *We watched a program about electricity on the educational television station.* **ed u ca tion al ly,** *adv.*

ed u ca tor (ej′ù kā′tər), *n.* 1. a teacher. *A good educator tries to help each student.* 2. a person who trains other people to be teachers. *Professor Evans is an educator who teaches college courses in classroom behavior.* **ed u ca tors.**

eel (ēl), *n.* a fish whose long, slippery body

eclipse:
a. eclipse of the moon
b. eclipse of the sun

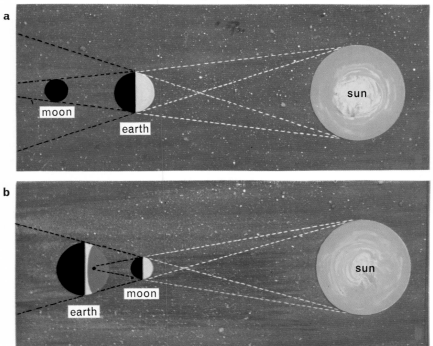

a

b

makes it look like a snake. *Some kinds of eels are good to eat.* **eels.**

ef fect (i fekt/), *n.* 1. something caused by another thing; result. *A flood was the effect of the heavy rain.* 2. influence. *Our talk had a good effect on Don's behavior.* 3. the impression produced in the mind. *The colors in the room created a cheerful effect.* 4. **effects,** *n. pl.* personal property or belongings. *He kept his effects in his room.* 5. **in effect,** in force. *Curfew is in effect at ten o'clock.* 6. **take effect,** to begin to be active. *The aspirin took effect quickly, and soon my headache was gone.* **ef fects.**
v. 7. to bring about; cause to happen. *The new principal effected changes in the rules of the school.* **ef fects, ef fect ed, ef fect ing.**

ef fec tive (i fek/tiv), *adj.* 1. having the effect that is wanted. *The pills the doctor gave me were effective in stopping my cough.* 2. making an impression on the mind; impressive. *Ken is an effective speaker because he talks naturally and knows the subject.* 3. in operation; in effect. *The new bus schedules become effective Monday.* **ef fec tive ly,** *adv.*

ef fi cien cy (i fish/ən sē), *n.* the ability to do things without wasting time or money. *Sue shows efficiency in her job as secretary of the club.* **ef fi cien cies.**

ef fi cient (i fish/ənt), *adj.* able to do things without waste of time or money. *An efficient worker does his job well and on time.* **ef fi cient ly,** *adv.*

ef fort (ef/ərt), *n.* 1. using one's strength or power. *To ride a bicycle uphill requires effort.* 2. to do something. *Ron is making an effort to get on the honor roll.* **ef forts.**

egg[1] (eg), *n.* 1. the round, or somewhat round, hard-shelled body that is laid by the female of many animals. *Baby chickens grow from eggs. Baby fish grow from eggs.* 2. **egg cell,** a living cell produced by a female within the body. *Female animals have egg cells within their bodies.* **eggs.**

egg[2] (eg), *v.* to urge to do something; to encourage. *Roy didn't really want to jump down from the high tree, but the other boys egged him on.* **eggs, egged, egg ing.**

eh (ā), *interj.* a sound that expresses surprise or doubt. *"Eh? You mean he really did a good job?"*

eight (āt), *n.* the next number after seven; seven plus one; 8. *The sum of three eights is twenty-four.* **eights.**

eight een (ā/tēn/), *n.* the next number after seventeen; ten plus eight; 18. *The sum of two nines is eighteen.* **eight eens.**

eighth (ātth), *adj.* 1. coming next after the seventh. *The eighth float in the parade won first prize.*
n. 2. the one after the seventh. *As the gym class lined up according to height, Larry was the eighth from the end.* 3. a single one of eight equal parts. *Pies are often cut into eighths.* **eighths.**

eight y (ā/tē), *n.* the next number after seventy-nine; eight times ten; 80. *Eighty plus twenty equals one hundred.* **eight ies.**

ei ther (ē/thər, ī/thər), *adj.* 1. one or the other of the two. *I couldn't beat either twin in running.* 2. each of two. *Boxers wear a glove on either hand.*
pron. 3. one or the other of two. *Either of the girls may erase the work on the chalkboard.*
conj. 4. one or the other. *Your report card has to be signed by either your mother or your father.*
adv. 5. also; any more than the other. *I don't like pickles, and my sister doesn't either.*

elab o rate (i lab/ə rit for 1, i lab/ə rāt/ for 2 and 3), *adj.* 1. carefully made or worked out; done in great detail. *Jerry has an elaborate plan for the surprise party.* **elab o rate ly,** *adv.*
v. 2. to make or work out very carefully; do with great attention to detail. *The boys elaborated their plan to improve the school's playground.* 3. to give more details of something already spoken or written. *The speaker elaborated on his general idea by giving examples.* **elab o rates, elab o rat ed, elab o rat ing.**

elapse (i laps/), *v.* to go by; pass. *Several minutes elapsed before the applause stopped.* **elaps es, elapsed, elaps ing.**

el bow (el/bō), *n.* 1. the joint in the arm between wrist and shoulder. *Keep your elbows off the table at dinner.* 2. something like an elbow. *The elbow of a water pipe is curved.* **el bows.**
v. 3. to shove rudely with the elbows. *The man elbowed three people while hurrying to catch his bus.* **el bows, el bowed, el bow ing.**

eld er (el/dər), *adj.* 1. older. *Steve has an elder brother and three younger sisters.*
n. 2. an older person than oneself. *Children are often told to respect their elders.* 3. an officer in some churches. *The minister met with the elders of the church to ask for their advice.* **el ders.**

eld est (el/dəst), *adj.* oldest. *The eldest child in the family is fourteen.*

elect (i lekt/), *v.* 1. to choose or select for an office by voting. *We will elect our class president soon.* 2. to choose or decide. *Dan elected to save his summer earnings instead of spending the money.* **elects, elect ed, elect ing.**
adj. 3. chosen or elected, but not yet serving in office. *The president-elect will take office on Tuesday.*

elec tion (i lek/shən), *n.* 1. the choosing or selecting by voting. *In the United States there is a presidential election every four years.* 2. the day for voting. *The election is next Tuesday.* **elec tions.**

elec tric (i lek/trik), *adj.* 1. having to do with electricity. *Our lighting depends upon an electric*

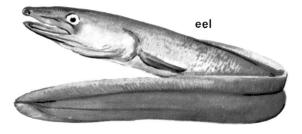

eel

electromagnet

elevator

current. 2. worked by electricity. *We have an electric clock in our schoolroom.* 3. producing electricity. *Electric generators light all the houses in the city.* 4. causing a thrill; exciting. *The game was filled with electric moments.*

elec tri cal (i lek′trə kl), *adj.* 1. electric. *Since the lights had gone out twice, Dad wanted the man to look at the whole electrical system in our house.* 2. of electricity. *Electrical engineers design equipment to produce electricity.* **elec tri cal ly,** *adv.*

elec tric i ty (i lek′tris′ə tē), *n.* a kind of energy most often carried by wires, used to produce light and heat and to run motors. *The electricity we use in our homes comes from machines called generators.*

elec tro mag net (i lek′trō mag′nət), *n.* a piece of iron surrounded by a coil of wire, which becomes a magnet when an electric current is passed through the wire. *An electromagnet can pick up iron or steel objects as long as there is electricity in the coil.* **elec tro mag nets.**

elec tron (i lek′tron), *n.* one of the tiny particles of negative matter that travel around the nucleus of an atom. *Electrons carry electrical current and have a negative charge of electricity.* **elec trons.**

el e ment (el′ə mənt), *n.* 1. one of the more than one hundred substances in nature that make up all the material in the world. *An element cannot be divided into different substances unless its atoms are split. Some of the more common elements are oxygen, gold, and iron.* 2. a necessary part. *Tubes are elements of television sets. Hard work is an element of success. One of the elements of learning history is remembering the date on which an event happened.* 3. **the elements,** rain, wind, and other forces of nature. *They had to battle the elements to reach the North Pole.* **el e ments.**

el e phant (el′ə fənt), *n.* a large, gray, four-legged animal, having long, white tusks and

a long trunk with which it can grasp or carry objects. *Elephants are found in Africa and in India, where they are used to move heavy logs from the jungle.* **el e phants.**

el e va tion (el′ə vā′shən), *n.* 1. the height or distance above sea level. *Denver's elevation is about one mile.* 2. the height or distance above the ground. *The airliner flew at an elevation of 20,000 feet.* 3. a place higher than the surrounding area. *A camper sets up his tent on a small elevation.* 4. being raised. *Jerry was proud of his elevation to president of the senior council.* **el e va tions.**

el e va tor (el′ə vā′tər), *n.* 1. an enclosed cage that carries people or things up and down in buildings and mines. *Elevators are used in tall buildings.* 2. a building used to store grain. *Elevators have machinery for loading, unloading, cleaning, and mixing the grain.* 3. the flat section of an airplane tail assembly that makes a plane go up or down. *The pilot controls the elevator from his seat in the plane.* **el e va tors.**

elev en (i lev′ən), *n.* 1. the next number after ten; 11. *Seven plus four is equal to eleven.* 2. a football team. *Three of Central High School's eleven will graduate this year.* **elev ens.**

elf (elf), *n.* a tiny imaginary being that appears in some stories, and who is usually playful or mischievous in his dealings with other people in the story. *The elf liked to upset furniture to make people angry, but sometimes he was helpful.* **elves** (elvz).

el i gi ble (el′ə jə bl), *adj.* having the necessary qualities; desirable. *Only high school graduates are eligible for most jobs.* **el i gi bly,** *adv.*

elim i nate (i lim′ə nāt′), *v.* to get rid of in some way; remove. *Doctors have eliminated many diseases. We try to eliminate mosquitoes in the summertime.* **elim i nates, elim i nat ed, elim i nat ing.**

el lipse (i lips′), *n.* an oval with both ends having similar size. *An egg is oval, but since one end is larger than the other, it is not an ellipse.* **el lips es.**

elm (elm), *n.* a tall tree, having a hard wood. *Elm trees give good shade.* **elms.**

elephant

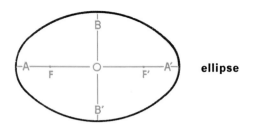

ellipse

else (els), *adj.* 1. other; different. *Have you invited anybody else besides people from school?* 2. in addition; more. *What else may I show you?* *adv.* 3. in a different way or place, or at a different time. *Where else do you think we should look for the lost pup?* 4. otherwise. *Larry needs to finish his book report, or else he won't get his high grade.*

else where (els′hwâr′), *adv.* somewhere else; in, at, or to another place. *The store on the corner was closed, so Alan had to go elsewhere for milk.*

em bar rass (im bar′əs), *v.* to upset or confuse; to make uncomfortable. *You embarrass me when you talk about my mistakes to other people.* **em barrass es, em bar rassed, em bar rass ing.**

em brace (em brās′), *v.* 1. to hold in one's arms to show love or affection; hug. *We all embraced grandma as she stepped off the train.* 2. accept something in a serious way. *Since George was sure he wanted to be a doctor, he eagerly embraced his studies.* 3. surround; enclose. *The tall buildings embraced the little church.* 4. include or contain. *Our school system embraces principals, teachers, clerks, and pupils.* **em bra ces, embraced, em bra cing.**
n. 5. an embracing or holding close; a hug. *Before Ray left on his trip, he held his mother in a warm embrace.* **em bra ces.**

em broi der y (em broi′dər ē), *n.* 1. the art of sewing designs into cloth or other fabrics for decoration. *Embroidery can be done with threads of gold, silver, cotton, silk, or other material.* 2. the sewed designs. *The embroidery consisted of flowers and birds.* **em broi der ies.**

em er ald (em′ər əld, em′rəld), *n.* 1. a precious stone of a clear, deep-green color. *Emeralds are of great value.* **em er alds.**
adj. 2. bright green. *Our school color is emerald.*

emerge (i mėrj′), *v.* 1. to appear in sight; come into view. *The airplane suddenly emerged from behind the clouds.* 2. to realize or know. *After the trial the fact emerged that the man had not told the truth.* **emerg es, emerged, emerg ing.**

emer gen cy (i mėr′jən sē), *n.* a sudden situation that requires something to be done right away. *Fire in a building is an emergency.* **emergen cies.**

emit (ē mit′), *v.* to send out; put forth. *Chimneys*

emit smoke. The angered lion emitted a loud roar. The slightly open door emitted a narrow band of light. **emits, emit ted, emit ting.**

emo tion (i mō′shən), *n.* a strong reaction or feeling. *Love and hate are completely different emotions.* **emo tions.**

emo tion al (i mō′shən l), *adj.* 1. of or having to do with emotions. *The President delivered a very emotional speech.* 2. subject to show feelings or emotions. *She frequently reacts in an emotional manner.* **emo tion al ly,** *adv.*

em per or (em′pər ər), *n.* a man who rules an empire. *An emperor has the same power as a king.* **em per ors.**

em pire (em′pīr), *n.* 1. a number of countries having a single, powerful ruler. *Years ago, the Roman Empire included most of the world then known.* 2. any nation or government ruled by an emperor. *France was once an empire, and Napoleon was the emperor.* **em pires.**

em ploy (em ploi′), *v.* 1. to have in one's business as paid workers; hire. *Railroads employ thousands of people in this country. Mr. Evans decided to employ Anne as his secretary when he saw her good typing.* 2. to use. *During the emergency, private cars were employed as buses.* **em ploys, em ployed, em ploy ing.**

em ploy ee (em ploi′ē or em′ploi ē′), *n.* a person who works for another person or for a business firm. *Firemen are employees of the city or town which they guard against fire.* **em ployees.**

em ploy er (em ploi′ər), *n.* a person or company that hires a person to work for pay. *My employer is such a fine man that I want to do my best for him.* **em ploy ers.**

em ploy ment (em ploi′mənt), *n.* 1. one's work or occupation. *Ed found employment in an accounting firm soon after he moved here.* 2. the hiring of people to do work. *Employment of several hundred people took place before the factory was even completed.*

emp ty (emp′tē), *adj.* 1. having nothing inside. *The milkman picks up empty bottles.* 2. having no people living inside. *The house at the corner is empty, and is for sale or rent.* **emp ti er, emp ti est; emp ti ly,** *adv.*
v. 3. to take out whatever is in something. *After walking along the beach, Ralph emptied the sand from his shoes. His friend Steve emptied his shoes too.* 4. to flow; discharge. *The Hudson River empties into the Atlantic Ocean.* 5. to become empty. *The movie theater emptied quickly after the last show.* **emp ties, emp tied, emp ty ing.**

en a ble (en ā′bl), *v.* to make able; give strength or ability to. *Courage enabled him to overcome disappointments. Good training enabled the troops to survive harsh jungle conditions.* **en a bles, en a bled, en a bling.**

enam el (i nam′l), *n.* 1. a hard, shiny substance used to coat metals, pottery, and glass.

Enamel may be used for protection or for decoration. 2. the hard layer that protects the chewing surface of a tooth. *A dentist can fill a hole if it develops in the enamel.* 3. a shiny kind of paint. *White enamel is often used to paint kitchen walls.* **enam els.**

v. 4. to paint with enamel. *Mother enameled the kitchen cabinets.* **enam els, enam eled, enam- el ing.**

en close (en klōz′), *v.* 1. to close in on every side; surround. *Oklahoma is entirely enclosed by other states.* 2. to put a fence or wall around. *Dad enclosed the garden with chicken wire to keep out animals.* 3. to put in an envelope or pack- age, along with something else. *Phil and Mary wrote their grandparents and enclosed several pictures of the family.* **en clos es, en closed, en clos ing.**

en clo sure (en klō′zhər), *n.* 1. the act of closing in or enclosing. *The enclosure of the garden kept the animals out.* 2. a place or area that is enclosed. *Rabbits lived in the enclosure behind Uncle Stan's house.* 3. something enclosed in a letter. *Uncle Henry's enclosure was a check for ten dollars for me.* 4. a fence or wall that encloses something. *Bob kept his rabbits in a wooden enclosure.* **en clo sures.**

en coun ter (en koun′tər), *v.* 1. to meet unexpectedly. *We encountered bad weather near Alaska.* 2. to meet; have to deal with. *He encountered trouble and illness, but he came out all right.* 3. to meet as enemies in battle. *The settlers going west encountered Indians.* **en coun- ters, en coun tered, en coun ter ing.**

n. 4. a surprise meeting. *On our trip we had several encounters with animals in the woods.* 5. a meeting as enemies; a battle. *The encounter between the tribes was halted by talks between the two chiefs.* **en coun ters.**

en cour age (en kėr′ij), *v.* to give courage to; to urge to greater effort. *The coach encouraged his players to do their best.* 2. to give help or assistance to; aid. *Hot weather encourages the sale of swim suits.* **en cour ag es, en cour- aged, en cour ag ing.**

en cy clo pe dia (en sī′klə pē′dē ə), *n.* 1. a book or group of books that gives general information on many different subjects. *Articles in an encyclopedia are in alphabetical order.* 2. a book or group of books that gives infor- mation on one special subject. *People who like to take good pictures may buy an encyclopedia of photography and learn more about their hobby.* **en cy clo pe di as.**

end (end), *n.* 1. the last or final part of some- thing. *They left the theater before the end of the movie. The buzzer sounded the end of the game.* 2. the point at which something either begins or stops. *A piece of string has two ends. A car has a bumper at either end.* 3. the purpose or goal of something that is done. *To achieve one's ends requires study and hard work.* 4. in football, either

of the players at the ends of the front line of players. *Dan was fast and tall and was a good right end.* **ends.**

v. 5. to come or bring to the end of something. *The story ended with the marriage of the young cowboy. Everyone clapped as the principal ended his speech.* **ends, end ed, end ing.**

en deav or (en dev′ər), *v.* 1. to try hard; make a special effort. *Gary endeavored to move the piano by himself.* **en deav ors, en deav ored, en- deav or ing.**

n. 2. a special effort; a try. *Mary's endeavor to straighten her room and do her homework in three hours was successful.* **en deav ors.**

en dive (en′dīv), *n.* a plant with ragged, green, curly leaves which are used for making salad. *Many people prefer endive to lettuce.*

end point (end′point′), *n.* one of the two points that mark the end of a segment of a line; a point that marks the end of a ray. *This is the end point of the line.* **end points.**

en dure (en dūr′, en dūr′), *v.* 1. to keep on in existence; continue to be. *The teachings of Christ have endured for more than a thousand years.* 2. to bear up under pain or difficulty. *Farmers learn to endure occasional crop failures that are due to heavy frosts.* **en dures, en dured, en dur- ing.**

en e my (en′ə mē), *n.* 1. a person or group that hates or fights another person or group. *Enemies sometimes become friends. In war, whole nations become enemies of each other.* 2. anything that harms something else. *Cats are natural enemies of mice. Rust is an enemy of many metal surfaces.* **en e mies.**

en er gy (en′ər gē), *n.* 1. the power or strength to be busy or to do work. *Jim's energy was so great that he was always doing something.* 2. the power, ability, or capacity to do work. *Electrical energy raises and lowers elevators. The energy in a car battery helps the car to start.* **en er gies.**

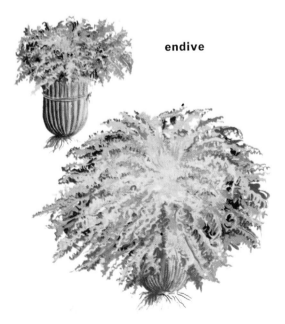

endive

en force (en fôrs´), *v.* to make people obey. *Rules of safety have to be enforced at a beach or swimming pool.* **en forc es, en forced, en forc ing.**

en gage (en gāj´), *v.* 1. to hire; arrange for the use of. *The hunters engaged a guide to lead them through the woods. Will you engage a meeting room at the hotel for us?* 2. to involve attention; to occupy. *Right now I am engaged in making plans for the summer.* 3. to promise to marry. *The happy girl announced that she and Ralph are engaged.* 4. to fight in a battle. *We shall engage the enemy at dawn.* 5. to fit together. *Unless the gears engage properly, your car won't run.* **en gag es, en gaged, en gag ing.**

en gaged (en gājd´), *adj.* 1. pledged to be married. *The engaged couple are making plans for their wedding.* 2. busy; occupied. *He is engaged in a very important project.*

en gage ment (en gāj mənt), *n.* 1. a pledge by a man and a woman to marry. *Their engagement lasted six months, and then they were married.* 2. an appointment. *He always has an engagement for lunch.* 3. a battle. *The enemy was defeated in the first engagement of the war.* **en gage ments.**

en gag ing (en gā´jing), *adj.* charming; pleasing; attractive. *Her engaging manners make you like her at once.* **en gag ing ly,** *adv.*

en gine (en´jən), *n.* 1. a machine that can start other machines working. *An engine in an automobile uses the exploding of gasoline to start motion in the gears and wheels.* 2. the machine that pulls cars on a railroad. *Railroad engines used to get their power from coal, now they use oil.* 3. any machine; any instrument. *A cannon is an engine of war.* **en gines.**

en gi neer (en´jə nir´), *n.* 1. a man whose job is designing and directing the building of bridges, roads, ships, and the like. *An engineer must be trained in science and mathematics.* 2. a man who runs an engine. *The children waved to the engineer as the train went by.* **en gi neers.** *v.* 3. to plan and direct the building of something. *He engineered the tallest dam in the country.* 4. to plan; direct; guide. *George engineered the surprise party we gave for our teacher's birthday.* **en gi neers, en gi neered, en gi neer ing.**

en gi neer ing (en´jə nir´ing), *n.* the science or work of designing and building things useful to man by using the materials and sources of energy found in nature. *The study of mathematics and science is necessary for structural, electrical, chemical, and mechanical engineering.*

Eng lish (ing´glish), *adj.* 1. of or pertaining to England, the largest part of Great Britain. *The English language is spoken all over the world. English literature includes some of the greatest books and authors in the world.* *n.* 2. the people of England. *The English are proud of their history and of their monarchs.* 3. the language spoken in England, Canada, the United States, Australia, South Africa, and

other places. *Many leaders of foreign countries speak English as well as their own languages.*

en joy (en joi´), *v.* 1. to get pleasure from. *Think of all the persons and things there are to enjoy—your friends, games, movies, and so on.* 2. to have the use of; to have. *Famous men enjoy wide popularity. The retired man enjoys the benefits of well-earned leisure.* **en joys, en joyed, en joy ing.**

en joy a ble (en joi´ə bl), *adj.* happy; giving pleasure. *We spent an enjoyable evening at the skating rink.* **en joy a bly,** *adv.*

enor mous (i nôr´məs), *adj.* very large. *The whale is an enormous sea animal, weighing as much as ninety tons.* **enor mous ly,** *adv.*

enough (i nuf´), *adj.* 1. as much or as many as needed. *Doctors say that you should drink enough water—about six glasses a day. We didn't have enough money to go to the movies.* *adv.* 2. as much as needed. *I think they all ate enough.* *n.* 3. a satisfactory amount. *Thank you, I have eaten enough.*

en roll or **en rol** (en rōl´), *v.* 1. to become a member. *Are you going to enroll in the special French classes?* 2. to make a member; put on a list. *The teacher enrolled us in her first class.* **en rolls** or **en rols, en rolled, en rol ling.**

en ter (en´tər), *v.* 1. to go in; come in. *The pupils enter the school through the east doorway. The arrow entered the middle of the target.* 2. to join; become a member of. *Many young men of eighteen enter the army or navy.* 3. to record. *Every day the salesman must enter in a notebook all the money he spent.* 4. to start or begin. *He entered the contest last week. Next week he enters college, and later on he wants to enter the practice of medicine.* 5. to enroll. *Her parents will enter her in our school next semester.* **en ters, en tered, en ter ing.**

en ter tain (en´tər tān´), *v.* 1. to amuse; provide fun for; give pleasure to. *Let's entertain the boy by taking him to the circus. The famous musician has entertained thousands of music lovers.* 2. to have as a guest. *My parents are entertaining six people at dinner.* 3. to have guests. *We are too busy to entertain our friends as much as we would like.* 4. to think about. *The barber is entertaining the idea of owning his own shop.* **en ter tains, en ter tained, en ter tain ing.**

en ter tain ing (en´tər tān´ing), *adj.* giving entertainment; amusing; interesting. *He is an entertaining person, with his jokes and his way of speaking.* **en ter tain ing ly,** *adv.*

en ter tain ment (en´tər tān´mənt), *n.* something that entertains. *People find entertainment in plays, lectures, television, reading, talking, and many other things.* **en ter tain ments.**

en thu si asm (en thü´zē az´əm), *n.* a strong feeling of liking; great interest. *With enthusiasm, he told us of his plans for going on a camping trip with his father.* **en thu si asms.**

en thu si as tic (en thü´zē as´tik), *adj.* filled

sand, āte, bâre, fäther; sent, mē, fėrn; fit, bīke; pot, rōpe, fôrt; run, pùll, rüle, cūte; noise, sound; ch, cheese; ng, long; th, thick; ~~th,~~ those; zh, treasure; ə = a in about, e in waken, i in animal, o in seldom, and u in minus.

with interest and excitement; showing great liking. *Many boys are enthusiastic about baseball and football.* **en thu si as tic al ly,** *adv.*

en tire (en tīr′), *adj.* whole; complete. *We spent the entire day at the zoo.* **en tire ly,** *adv.*

en ti tle (en tī′tl), *v.* 1. to give a right to. *The purchase of a ticket entitles you to go into the theater. All people, rich and poor, are entitled to a fair trial in the courts.* 2. to give a title to. *A famous speedy football player was entitled "The Galloping Ghost."* **en ti tles, en ti tled, en ti tling.**

en trance[1] (en′trəns), *n.* 1. a doorway; place for entering. *The entrance to the bank was guarded by two policemen. Use the back entrance to our apartment building; the front is being painted.* 2. an entering; coming in. *The football fans cheered the entrance of their team on the field.* 3. the right to enter; permission to go in. *A newspaper reporter has entrance to courtrooms, to police stations, and to disaster areas.* **en tranc es.**

en trance[2] (en trans′), *v.* to fill with joy or delight. *A circus entrances children.* **en tranc es, en tranced, en tranc ing.**

en try (en′trē), *n.* 1. the place in a building through which people go in and come out. *The entry to the new theater has paintings hung on its walls.* 2. coming in; entering. *The entry of the President was greeted by cheers.* 3. an item in a list; a note in a diary. *The entry for Tuesday in her diary will be long since it was her birthday. An entry in a dictionary is a word in heavy type, like* **entry** *and, just above it,* **entrance**[2]. 4. a person, animal, or thing entered in a contest. *Our dog was an entry in the dog show and won a prize for obedience.* **en tries.**

en ve lope (en′və lōp′, än′və lōp′), *n.* a paper cover or holder used to hold papers and other materials. *Always put the correct address on the envelope.* **en ve lopes.**

en vy (en′vē), *n.* 1. a feeling of not being content that is caused by wanting something that another person has. *Bill was filled with envy when he found out that Brian was spending the summer on a ranch.* 2. a person or thing that is envied. *Jack was the envy of his friends when he got his new bicycle.* **en vies.**

v. 3. to feel jealousy toward; to want what another person has. *Some people envy rich persons.* **en vies, en vied, en vy ing.**

ep au let (ep′ə let′), *n.* a decoration worn on each shoulder of a uniform. *Epaulets are usually worn by officers in the army and navy.* **ep au lets.**

epis tle (i pis′l), *n.* a formal letter. *The ambassador received an epistle from his government.* **epis tles.**

epaulet

equal (ē′kwəl), *adj.* 1. of the same value, size, rank, amount, etc. *The two boys are of equal weight since they both weigh 140 pounds. A captain in the navy is equal to a colonel in the army.* 2. having enough strength or endurance for. *The captain decided that only two of his men were equal to the job he wanted done.* **equal ly,** *adv.*

n. 3. a person, animal, or thing having the same ability, merit, quality, etc. as another. *The whale has no present-day equal in size among animals.* **equals.**

v. 4. to be of the same value, size, rank, or amount as; to match. *Twelve inches equal one foot, and 5,280 feet equal one mile. Five plus four equals nine.* **equals, equaled, equal ing.**

equal i ty (i kwol′ə tē), *n.* likeness in value, rank, etc. *The equality of all men was proclaimed by the Declaration of Independence.* **equal i ties.**

equal ly (ē′kwə lē), *adv.* in an equal manner. *The two pupils were equally responsible for the Halloween decorations in the room.*

equate (i kwāt′), *v.* to treat or think of as being equal or the same. *You cannot always equate high grades with intelligence.* **equates, equat ed, equat ing.**

equa tion (i kwā′zhən), *n.* a statement showing that two quantities are equal. *This is an equation:* $4 + 4 = 8$. **equa tions.**

equa tor (i kwā′tər), *n.* an imaginary circle around the earth, halfway between the North Pole and the South Pole. *The United States is north of the equator. Australia is south of the equator.*

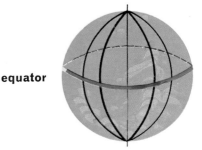

equator

equa to ri al (ē′kwə tôr′ē əl, ek′wə tôr′ē əl), *adj.* 1. of or near the equator of the earth. *Most equatorial regions are hot and moist.* 2. like the conditions at the equator. *The garden of the deserted farm was like an equatorial jungle.* **equa to ri al ly,** *adv.*

equip (i kwip′), *v.* to supply; furnish; fit out with something needed. *The Boy Scouts equipped themselves with food, tents, and sleeping bags for their overnight hike. His house is equipped with air-conditioning.* **equips, equipped, equip ping.**

equip ment (i kwip′mənt), *n.* 1. the things needed for a special purpose; supplies. *Paper, typewriters, desks, and chairs are part of the equipment of an office.* 2. an equipping. *The equipment of the factory took six months.* **equip ments.**

equiv a lence (i kwiv′ə ləns), *n.* being equivalent; equality in force, value, significance, etc. *There is an equivalence between his ability as a musician and the time he spends practicing.*

equiv a lent (i kwiv ə lənt), *adj.* 1. equal or the same. *Twelve inches are equivalent to one foot.* **equiv a lent ly,** *adv.*

n. 2. something that is equal or the same. *The equivalent of* 12×12 *is 144.* **equiv a lents.**

erase (i rās′), *v.* 1. to rub out; scrape away. *After we do a problem on the chalkboard, we erase it.* 2. to remove from the memory. *Erase all those thoughts about last year, and think about today.* **eras es, erased, eras ing.**

eras er (i rās′ər), *n.* anything used for rubbing out. *My pencil has an eraser on one end. We use a soft eraser on the blackboard at school.* **eras ers.**

er rand (er′ənd), *n.* 1. a trip to do something. *The teacher sent John to the principal's office on an errand.* 2. the purpose of such a trip. *My errand is to buy a can of paint for Father.* **er rands.**

er ror (er′ər), *n.* 1. a mistake. *I was happy because my spelling test did not have an error. The right fielder committed an error by dropping the fly ball.* 2. **in error,** being wrong. *You are in error when you say that a whale is a fish.* **er rors.**

es cape (es kāp′), *v.* 1. to get away; get free. *The man escaped from the burning house by jumping safely from a window.* 2. to avoid; keep safe from. *Our family luckily escaped having any colds this winter.* 3. to leak or flow out. *Gasoline escaped from the overturned truck.* **es capes, es caped, es cap ing.**
n. 4. a getting away. *My mother says she wishes she could find an escape from this hot weather.* 5. something used in getting away. *All public buildings have fire escapes. Gardening is my escape from everyday problems.* **es capes.**

Es ki mo (es′kə mō), *n.* a member of a race living on the shores of the Arctic in North America. *Eskimos live in houses called igloos, which may be made of blocks of hard snow. Eskimos use boats called kayaks to travel in the water, and they hunt sea animals with harpoons.* **Es ki mos.**

es pe cial ly (es pesh′əl ē), *adv.* mainly; in particular; unusually. *My brother likes all sports, but he is especially interested in football.*

es sen tial (ə sen′shəl), *adj.* necessary; important; needed. *A good education is essential. The essential requirements of people are food, clothing, and shelter.* **es sen tial ly,** *adv.*

es tab lish (es tab′lish), *v.* 1. to start; set up. *Our country was established in 1776. The police soon established order.* 2. to settle; place in a business. *He wants to establish himself with a different company.* 3. to prove; to show beyond any doubt. *He established the fact that he was the legal owner of the silver mine.* 4. to bring about; to cause to be accepted for good. *Certain customs, like shaking hands, were established a long time ago.* **es tab lish es, es tab lished, es tab lish ing.**

es tab lish ment (es tab′lish mənt), *n.* 1. something that has been established. *A school, a church, and a library are establishments.* 2. a start; a setting up. *The establishment of public schools was an idea of Thomas Jefferson.* **es tab lish-ments.**

es tate (es tāt′), *n.* 1. a large piece of land containing a big home. *The rich man owned an apartment in New York and an estate in the country.*

harpoon

igloo

kayak

Eskimo

2. the property owned by a person. *The man's estate includes a house and furniture, a car, and a bank account.* 3. state; condition. *Young boys look forward to reaching a man's estate.* **es tates.**

es teem (es tēm′), *v.* 1. to have a high regard for. *I will do as he says because I esteem his advice.* 2. to consider. *We esteem it an honor to be invited to the ceremonies.* **es teems, es teemed, es-teem ing.**
n. 3. high regard; good opinion. *The professor is held in esteem for his knowledge.*

es ti mate (es′tə māt′ for 1, es′tə mət for 2), *v.* 1. to guess; to judge what the size, time, etc. will be. *We estimated that the book would contain 606 pages. An experienced carpenter can closely estimate how much his work will cost.* **es ti mates, es ti mat ed, es ti mat ing.**
n. 2. a guess based on experience; a figuring of cost. *The road-building job went to the company that gave the lowest estimate.* 3. an opinion. *I have a high estimate of his ability.* **es ti mates.**

es ti vate also **aes ti vate** (es′tə vāt′), *v.* to pass the summer in an inactive, sluggish condition. *Dry weather causes many snails to estivate. Some toads and frogs estivate, and only become active when it rains.* **es ti vates, es ti vat ed, es ti-vat ing.**

etc. abbreviation of **et cetera.**

et cet era (et set′ərə), and other things of the same kind; and so forth; and so on. *The abbreviation for "et cetera" is etc.*

eter nal (i ter′nl), *adj.* 1. lasting forever; having no beginning and no end. *The universe is eternal.* 2. continuing; not stopping. *The eternal song of the birds is pleasant.* **eter nal ly,** *adv.*

eu ca lyp tus (ū′kə lip′təs), *n.* an evergreen tree that grows in the tropics. *From the eucalyptus we get oil, wood, and gum.* **eu ca lyp-tus es** or **eu ca lyp ti** (ū′kə lip′tī). (See illustration on following page.)

---

sand, āte, bâre, fäther; sent, mē, fėrn; fit, bīke; pot, rōpe, fôrt; run, pull, rüle, cūte; noise, sound; ch, cheese; ng, long; th, thick; ᵗʰ, those; zh, treasure; ə = a in about, e in waken, i in animal, o in seldom, and u in minus.

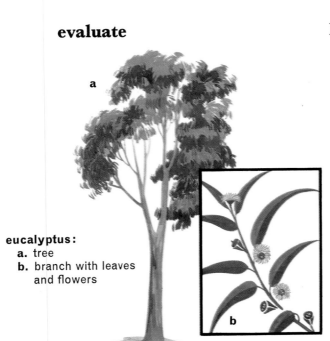

eucalyptus:
a. tree
b. branch with leaves
and flowers

eval u ate (i val′ū āt′), *v.* to find out the value of something; to give an opinion of. *A newspaper usually has a writer who evaluates the new movies as they appear.* **eval u ates, eval u at ed, eval u at ing.**

eval u a tion (i val′ū ā′shən), *n.* an evaluating; the result of evaluating. *Every year a committee of educators presents an evaluation of the schools. A real estate man gave an evaluation of the property before Mr. Hunter bought it.* **eval u a tions.**

evap o rate (i vap′ə rāt′), *v.* 1. to turn into vapor. *Heat evaporates water.* 2. to take moisture from. *Milk is evaporated by removing sixty percent of the water.* 3. to disappear; vanish. *His hopes for a fine day evaporated when dark clouds appeared.* **evap o rates, evap o rat ed, evap o rat ing.**

evap o ra tion (i vap′ə rā′shən), *n.* an evaporating. *After a storm, a wet sidewalk dries by evaporation of the water on it.*

eve (ēv), *n.* 1. the evening or day before certain holidays. *On Christmas Eve we go to Grandmother's apartment.* 2. the time just before. *On the eve of the big game, the coach took the players to the movie.* 3. evening. *Poets often use "eve" for "evening."* **eves.**

even (ē′vən), *adj.* 1. flat; smooth. *The even surface of the road made driving very easy.* 2. regular; steady; not changing. *The even hum of the motor showed it had been repaired properly.* 3. at the same level. *Hang this picture even with the top of the plant.* 4. that can be divided by two without a remainder. *Some even numbers are 2, 4, 6, 8, 10, and 12.* 5. equal. *Divide the money into four even shares.* 6. exact. *It costs an even one dollar.* 7. calm. *Persons with even tempers don't get too excited.* **even ly,** *adv.*
v. 8. to make equal. *Even all these boards by sawing off the ends of the long ones.* **evens, evened, even ing.**

adv. 9. still; yet; by comparison. *This tree is tall, but that one is even taller.* 10. while; at the same time. *Even as I wrote to you, I got your letter.*

eve ning (ēv′ning), *n.* 1. the end of the day and the beginning of the night. *Summer evenings are delightful.* 2. the time between sunset and bedtime. *In winter, evenings are longer because the sun sets earlier.* **eve nings.**

event (i vent′), *n.* 1. anything that happens. *The discovery of nuclear energy was a great event. To a child, a trip to the circus is a great event.* 2. one of the contests in a sports meet. *The next event in the swimming meet is the one-hundred yard backstroke.* 3. **at all events** or **in any event,** whatever happens. *In any event, come home as soon as possible.* **events.**

event ful (i vent′fəl), *adj.* 1. filled with many events or an important happening. *Our most eventful month was May, when we moved.* 2. important; having great meaning. *The next meeting of the United Nations will be eventful.* **eventful ly,** *adv.*

even tu al (i ven′chủ əl), *adj.* finally; at the end; at a later time. *His eventual success was no surprise to his teacher.* **even tu al ly,** *adv.*

ev er (ev′ər), *adv.* 1. at any time. *Have you ever traveled to Europe?* 2. all the time. *The police are ever prepared for serious duty.* 3. in some way. *How did you ever manage to get here early?* 4. **ever so,** very. *I'm ever so glad you came.*

ev er green (ev′ər grēn′), *adj.* 1. staying green all year. *Evergreen trees are used as Christmas trees. n.* 2. a shrub, bush, or tree that stays green all year. *Evergreens need much water.* **ev er greens.**

eve ry (ev′rē), *adj.* 1. each; all of a group. *Every person in the room was asked one question. Joe finished every job around the house before noon.* 2. **every other,** each second person or thing. *Every other pupil was asked to stand.* 3. **every now and then,** once in a while. *Every now and then the sleeping dog opened his eyes.*

eve ry body (ev′rē bud′ē, ev′rē bod′ē), *pron.* all people; each person. *Everybody in our class went to see the parade.*

eve ry day (ev′rē dā′, ev′rē dā′), *adj.* 1. happening on every day; not special. *Making beds and doing dishes are everyday jobs.* 2. ordinary; all right for the usual day or event. *You should wear your everyday clothes to school.*

eve ry one (ev′rē wun′), *pron.* each person; everybody. *Everyone received a notice that the school would be closed on Friday.*

eve ry thing (ev′rē thing′), *pron.* all; each thing. *Everything is going right for me.*

eve ry where (ev′rē hwâr′), *adv.* in all places; in each place. *We looked everywhere for mother's purse, and we finally found it.*

ev i dence (ev′ə dəns), *n.* 1. the facts; something that proves or shows; something that is a good reason for believing. *Mud on his shoes was evidence he had been near the river. The witness gave evidence that the accused man was innocent of* *the crime.* **2. in evidence,** in sight. *In winter not many birds are in evidence.* **ev i denc es.**

v. **3.** to show; prove. *The chewed-up lettuce evidenced that rabbits had been in the garden again.* **ev i denc es, ev i denced, ev i denc ing.**

ev i dent (ev′ə dənt), *adj.* clear; plain; easy to see. *His smile made his happiness evident to us.* **ev i dent ly,** *adv.*

evil (ē′vl), *adj.* **1.** bad; wrong; harmful. *Throwing stones to injure someone or something is an evil thing to do.* **evil ly,** *adv.*

n. **2.** doing wrong; something bad. *Cheating is an evil.* **3.** anything that causes pain and harm. *War is an evil.* **evils.**

evil do er (ē′vl dü′ər), *n.* a person who does wrong. *A person who tries to harm others is an evildoer.* **evil do ers.**

ex act (eg zakt′), *adj.* **1.** correct; right; accurate in every detail. *In building a bridge, every measurement must be exact.* **ex act ly,** *adv.*

v. **2.** to ask for and get; require. *The lawyer exacted a high fee for his advice.* **ex acts, ex act ed, ex act ing.**

ex act ly (eg zakt′lē), *adv.* **1.** precisely; without any change. *Do exactly as the teacher says.* **2.** true; quite so. *"We should get jobs," said Robert. "Exactly!" exclaimed George in agreement.*

ex am in a tion (eg zam′ə nā′shən), *n.* **1.** a test. *Today we had an examination in social studies.* **2.** an inspection; a careful check to get facts. *Every six months you should go to a dentist for an examination of your teeth. Examination showed the car needed a battery.* **ex am in a tions.**

ex am ine (eg zam′ən), *v.* **1.** to look at closely to find out the condition of; inspect. *My mother examined the furniture before she bought it. The cowboy examined the trail for footprints.* **2.** to question; to test. *The class was examined on United States history.* **ex am ines, ex am ined, ex am in ing.**

ex am ple (eg zam′pl), *n.* **1.** one part of something taken to show what the rest is like. *That table is an example of his skill in making things.* **2.** a sample; model; something that may be imitated. *Your cousin is an example of a successful salesman.* **3.** a problem in arithmetic. *Do the first example and the third example in your workbooks.* **4.** something that is a warning to others. *Your injuries from the automobile accident are an example of the results of careless driving.* **ex am ples.**

ex ca vate (eks kə vāt′), *v.* to dig out; to make a hole in. *Tomorrow we will excavate on the north side of the hill.* **ex ca vates, ex ca vat ed, ex ca vat ing.**

ex ca va tion (eks′kə vā′shən), *n.* **1.** a hole or opening made by digging. *There are a number of excavations downtown where they are putting up new buildings.* **2.** the uncovering of something by digging. *The excavation of the ancient temple brought forth many art treasures.* **ex ca va tions.**

excavating
an ancient temple

ex ceed (ek sēd′), *v.* **1.** to go beyond the limit of. *He exceeded all previous speed records in the automobile race.* **2.** to be better than. *John exceeded all other pupils in his class in arithmetic.* **ex ceeds, ex ceed ed, ex ceed ing.**

ex ceed ing ly (ek sēd′ing lē), *adv.* very. *This music is exceedingly difficult to play.*

ex cel (ek′sel), *v.* to do better than others; to outdo. *Of all his subjects, he excels in mathematics.* **ex cels, ex celled, ex cel ling.**

ex cel lent (ek′sl ənt), *adj.* very good. *Their excellent singing received applause from the audience.* **ex cel lent ly,** *adv.*

ex cept (ek sept′), *prep.* **1.** but; not including. *The noon train runs every day except Sunday.*

v. **2.** to omit; to leave out. *All those with high grades were excepted from the final test.* **ex cepts, ex cept ed, ex cept ing.**

conj. **3.** only; but. *I would go with you, except I have to finish the dishes.*

ex cep tion (ek sep′shən), *n.* **1.** a leaving out; omission. *The men worked every day with the exception of Sundays.* **2.** a person or thing that is not like others. *One kind of fish is an exception because it actually can move on land!* **3. take exception,** object to. *I take exception to some of his ideas about books.* **ex cep tions.**

ex cep tion al (ek sep′shən l), *adj.* different; unusual; much better than the ordinary. *She has an exceptional singing voice, and won first place in the fall music festival.* **ex cep′tion al ly,** *adv.*

ex cess (ek ses′ for 1–3, ek′ses, ek ses′ for 4), *n.* **1.** more than the amount needed. *An excess of food can make you fat.* **2.** the amount that is more than needed. *After we had painted the*

house, we used the excess of paint for the garage. 3. **to excess,** too much. *Most of us eat to excess at Thanksgiving.* **ex cess es.**
adj. 4. extra; more than usual. *A special delivery letter requires excess postage.*

ex cess ive (ek ses′iv), *adj.* too much; more than is necessary. *That store's prices are excessive; I won't go there again.* **ex cess ive ly,** *adv.*

ex change (eks chānj′), *v.* 1. to give something in return for another thing. *Jack exchanged his catcher's mitt for a fielder's glove.* 2. to give and get similar things. *The two girls exchanged compliments on their new dresses.* **ex chang es, ex changed, ex chang ing.**
n. 3. a giving of one thing in return for another. *The exchange of books was fair because neither girl had read the other's book.* 4. a giving and receiving. *An exchange of greetings was followed by a long talk. The exchange of students between two countries can build goodwill.* 5. a place where goods and services are traded and sold. *The stock exchange is where stocks are bought and sold.* **ex chang es.**

ex cise (ek sīz′, ek′sīz), *n.* a tax on goods made and sold within a country. *The excise tax on tobacco and liquor is high because they are considered luxuries.* **ex cis es.**

ex cite (ek sīt′), *v.* 1. to stir strong feelings in. *The news that John had won the contest excited him.* 2. to stir to action. *The barking dogs excited the birds into flight.* 3. to bring forth. *Bob's performance in the game excited our admiration.* **ex cites, ex cit ed, ex cit ing.**

ex cit ed (ek sīt′əd), *adj.* aroused; stirred up. *The excited crowd cheered wildly when Barry scored a touchdown.* **ex cit ed ly,** *adv.*

ex cite ment (ek sīt′mənt), *n.* 1. an excited condition; the state of being stirred up or aroused. *Our excitement ended suddenly when we began to lose the game.* 2. anything that excites. *I was exhausted by the excitement of the trip.* **ex cite ments.**

ex claim (eks klām′), *v.* to shout suddenly with strong feeling. *"Look out!" he exclaimed. "The tree is falling!"* **ex claims, ex claimed, ex claim ing.**

ex cla ma tion (eks kle mā′shən), *n.* a sudden, sharp cry showing deep feeling. *Her loud exclamation startled everyone.* **ex cla ma tions.**

ex clude (eks klüd′), *v.* to prevent from entering, joining, etc.; to shut out completely. *Girls are excluded from this club. The thick cover of the trees excluded light from the floor of the forest.* **ex cludes, ex clud ed, ex clud ing.**

ex clu sive (eks klü′siv), *adj.* 1. refusing entrance or membership to all but a select few. *They belong to an exclusive country club.* 2. sole; single; belonging to no other. *He has exclusive ownership of this land.* 3. not letting oneself have any other interests, activities, etc. *He has an exclusive interest in reading.* **ex clu sive ly,** *adv.*

ex cuse (ek skūz′ for 1–3, ek skūs′ for 4 and

5), *v.* 1. to serve as an acceptable reason or proper explanation for. *Ignorance of the law does not excuse your breaking it.* 2. to pardon; forgive; overlook something that is not serious or is not intended. *Please excuse me for bumping into you.* 3. to release from a duty or responsibility. *Since tomorrow is a holiday, you are all excused from your homework.* **ex cus es, ex cused, ex cus ing.**
n. 4. an acceptable reason or proper explanation for something. *What excuse do you have for being tardy to school?* 5. an excusing from a duty. *We were given an excuse from homework tonight.* **ex cus es.**

ex e cute (ek′sə kūt′), *v.* 1. to perform; to carry out. *She executed the difficult dance steps perfectly.* 2. to put into effect; to see that something is carried out completely. *The president of the company executed his plan for making new products.* 3. to construct or make according to a design. *The builder was able to execute the architect's plan of the house.* 4. to put someone to death legally. *Some states have laws which do not allow criminals to be executed.* **ex e cutes, ex e cut ed, ex e cut ing.**

ex ec u tive (eg zek′yə tiv), *n.* 1. a person who organizes and manages the business affairs of a company or organization. *The executives of the bank decided that the bank would lend money for the building project.* 2. a person or group that manages the affairs of a city, state, or country. *A mayor, a governor, and the President are executives of different levels of the government.* **ex ec u tives.**
adj. 3. having to do with an executive or the duties of an executive. *Ralph showed executive ability. The plan for increasing the size of the factory required an executive decision.*

ex er cise (ek′sər sīz′), *v.* 1. to use; to put into action. *You may exercise your knowledge by solving this problem.* 2. to develop or strengthen the body or mind through regular practice or activity. *He exercises his legs by running every day. One way of exercising the mind is by using imagination.* **ex er cis es, ex er cised, ex er cis ing.**
n. 3. an activity that develops or strengthens the body or mind. *He gets all his exercise by walking.* 4. a lesson provided to offer practice in schoolwork. *We do an arithmetic exercise every night for homework.* 5. a program or ceremony for some special purpose. *Hundreds of people attended the graduation exercises.* **ex er cis es.**

ex hale (eks hāl′), *v.* 1. to breathe out. *A swimmer exhales with his face in the water.* 2. to give off as a gas or vapor. *The factory's chimneys exhaled huge clouds of black smoke into the sky.* **ex hales, ex haled, ex hal ing.**

ex haust (eg zôst′), *v.* 1. to use up entirely. *We exhausted our food supply and had to return home.* 2. to empty; to let out the entire contents of something. *The box finally was exhausted.* **ex hausts, ex haust ed, ex haust ing.**

n. 3. the used steam or fuel that is forced out of an engine or other machine. *A black stream of exhaust came from the speeding car.* 4. the forcing out of used steam or fuel from an engine. *Exhaust occurs after the fuel has been burned in the engine.* 5. the pipe or pipes through which used steam or fuel is forced. *Large engines may have a part on the exhaust which reduces the noise of the engine.* **ex hausts.**

ex haus tion (eg zos′chən), *n.* the state of being exhausted; an extremely tired condition. *The rescued soldier was suffering from severe exhaustion.* **ex haus tions.**

ex hib it (eg zib′ət), *v.* 1. to show; to reveal. *The children exhibited excited interest at the circus.* 2. to display; to reveal publicly. *His paintings were exhibited at the art fair.* **ex hib its, ex hib it ed, ex hib it ing.**
n. 3. anything put on display or shown publicly. *Most of the exhibits at the art fair were modern paintings.* 4. a public show or display. *All of the new cars were shown at the automobile exhibit.* **ex hib its.**

ex hi bi tion (ek′sə bish′ən), *n.* 1. a display; a revealing. *He was awarded a medal for his exhibition of courage.* 2. a public display or showing. *We saw an exhibition of paintings at the art museum.* **ex hi bi tions.**

ex ile (eg′zīl, ek′sīl), *v.* 1. to force a person to leave his home or country. *The criminal was exiled to another country.* **ex iles, ex iled, ex il ing.**
n. 2. the state of being forced to leave one's home or country. *The exile of the prisoner was ordered by the government.* 3. a person who is exiled. *The exile was forbidden ever to enter the country again.* **ex iles.**

ex ist (eg zist′), *v.* 1. to be; to be real. *Many animals existed long before man came into being.* 2. to live; to be able to live; to go on living. *Most plants and animals cannot exist without air and water.* 3. to occur. *Very poor living conditions exist in many parts of the world.* **ex ists, ex ist ed, ex ist ing.**

ex ist ence (eg zis′təns), *n.* 1. the fact of existing; the condition of being or of being real. *Dinosaurs passed out of existence many millions of years ago.* 2. life. *Plants depend on water for their existence.* 3. a way of living. *Babies lead a happy and peaceful existence.* **ex ist enc es.**

ex it (eg′zit, ek′sit), *n.* 1. a way of going out of a place. *There was only one exit from the cave.* 2. a going out of a place; a leaving. *The speaker made a quick exit from the hall when he had finished his speech.* **ex its.**

ex pand (ek spand′), *v.* 1. to grow larger by spreading out or opening up. *The balloon expanded as we filled it with air.* 2. to make larger by adding details, more information, etc. *He expanded his talk so that it would last an hour.* **ex pands, ex pand ed, ex pand ing.**

ex pan sion (ek span′shən), *n.* 1. a growing larger by spreading out, opening up, etc. *The expansion of wood in warm weather sometimes causes doors and windows to stick.* 2. anything that has expanded. *The movie was a poor expansion of the play.* **ex pan sions.**

ex pect (ek spekt′), *v.* 1. to look for something to happen; to look forward to. *We expected rain, but the sky was clear.* 2. to require. *You are expected to earn your money by working for it.* **ex pects, ex pect ed, ex pect ing.**

ex pec ta tion (ek′spek tā′shən), *n.* 1. an expecting of something; a looking forward to something. *Our expectations were realized when the snow began to fall.* 2. a hope of something good; good reason to expect something. *We have expectations of taking a long vacation trip next year.* **ex pec ta tions.**

ex pe di tion (eks′pə dish′ən), *n.* 1. a long trip taken for a certain purpose. *The scientists planned an expedition to the South Pole.* 2. the people who go on such a trip. *It took three months for the expedition to arrive at the South Pole.* 3. speed in performing something. *Because of the boy's expedition in turning in the alarm, the fire was put out before it spread.* **ex pe di tions.**

ex pense (ek spens′), *n.* 1. an amount that is

exhibition

spent; the cost of something. *He won a trip to Europe with all expenses paid.* 2. anything that causes spending. *Food is the major expense in our budget.* 3. a spending of something. *Going to school requires an expense of money, time, and energy.* **ex pens es.**

ex pen sive (ek spen′siv), *adj.* costing a great amount; high-priced. *The meals in that restaurant are very expensive.* **ex pen sive ly,** *adv.*

ex pe ri ence (eks pir′ē əns), *n.* 1. a living through an event or series of events; a doing or feeling something. *When you've had some experience as a driver, your ability will improve.* 2. what one learns or gains from doing things. *He doesn't have enough experience to do the job well.* 3. the things that a person has lived through or done. *Did he tell you about his experiences as a sailor?* **ex pe ri enc es.**
v. 4. to feel something; to live through something. *I experienced great pleasure when we won the game.* **ex pe ri enc es, ex pe ri enced, ex pe ri enc ing.**

ex pe ri enced (eks pir′ē ənst), *adj.* skillful because of experience; expert. *After the third performance of the play, we felt like experienced actors.*

ex per i ment (eks per′ə mənt), *n.* 1. a trial or test to learn, discover, or prove something. *The scientist made several experiments before he found the correct chemicals.* **ex per i ments.**
v. 2. to test something to learn, discover, or prove something about it. *The artist experimented with several colors before finding the ones he wanted.* **ex per i ments, ex per i ment ed, ex per i ment ing.**

ex per i men tal (eks per′ə mənt l), *adj.* 1. based on or relating to experiments. *Many studies are experimental sciences.* 2. something that serves as a test or model. *The factory made two experimental engines for their new machine.* **ex per i men tal ly,** *adv.*

ex pert (eks′pėrt for 1, eks pėrt′, eks′pėrt

experiment

for 2), *n.* 1. a person who is very skillful at something or has much knowledge of something. *The police used a fingerprint expert to identify the robber.* **ex perts.**
adj. 2. having a great deal of skill or knowledge about something. *It is obvious that this cabinet was made by an expert carpenter.* **ex pert ly,** *adv.*

ex plain (eks plān′), *v.* 1. to make something clear; to tell what something means. *The teacher explained the difference between nouns and verbs to the class.* 2. to give a reason for something; to tell the cause of something. *Can you explain the fact that you didn't do all of your homework?* **ex plains, ex plained, ex plain ing.**

ex pla na tion (eks plə nā′shən), *n.* 1. a making clear; a telling of the meaning of something. *The teacher's explanation helped us to understand the arithmetic problem.* 2. anything which explains something. *There is no explanation for rude behavior.* **ex pla na tions.**

ex plode (eks plōd′), *v.* 1. to blow up with a sudden, loud noise; to burst. *A firecracker exploded near my window and woke me up.* 2. to cause to blow up with a sudden, loud noise. *Who exploded that firecracker?* 3. to burst forth loudly. *The audience exploded with laughter when the actor's wig fell off.* 4. to prove something to be false. *The belief that the sun moves around the earth was exploded hundreds of years ago.* **ex plodes, ex plod ed, ex plod ing.**

ex plore (eks plôr′), *v.* 1. to travel in unknown lands; to journey in a strange place with hopes of discovery. *Many people explored America before the country was settled.* 2. to examine or go over closely. *Before you decide where to go, explore all the possibilities.* **ex plores, ex plored, ex plor ing.**

ex plor er (eks plôr′ər), *n.* a person who explores. *Our astronauts are explorers of the space frontier.* **ex plor ers.**

ex plo sive (eks plō′siv), *adj.* 1. likely to explode. *Jeff's explosive temper gets him into trouble.* **ex plo sive ly,** *adv.*
n. 2. material that explodes. *Dynamite and other explosives were used to build the mountain tunnels.* **ex plo sives.**

ex port (eks′pôrt, eks pôrt′ for 1, eks′pôrt for 2 and 3), *v.* 1. to send goods from one country to be sold in another. *The United States exports machinery to many countries.* **ex ports, ex port ed, ex port ing.**
n. 2. the act of exporting. *This factory manufactures tractors for export.* 3. any goods which are exported. *Coffee and oil are the major exports of Colombia.* **ex ports.**

ex pose (eks pōz′), *v.* 1. to leave unprotected; to lay open to danger. *We were exposed to the cold wind until we put up our tents.* 2. to display; to put something in a place where it can be seen. *The clerk took the sweaters from the box and exposed them on the counter.* 3. to reveal; to tell

expressway

the details of; to make known. *The alert boy exposed the criminal's plan to the police.* 4. to allow light to reach a photographic film or plate. *Did you expose all the film?* **ex pos es, ex posed, ex pos ing.**

ex press (eks pres′), *v.* 1. to tell in words; to say. *Think for a moment before you try to express your idea.* 2. to make known by actions. *He expressed his lack of interest by shaking his head and walking away.* 3. to send by a rapid means. *The packages were expressed by air mail.* **ex press es, ex pressed, ex press ing.**
adj. 4. definite; clearly intended or stated. *It was his express wish that Tom should receive the award.* 5. rapid; very fast; making few stops. *The freight train pulled to a side track to allow the express train to pass.* **ex press ly,** *adv.*
n. 6. a rapid means of sending goods. *If you have the package sent by express, it will arrive in the city tomorrow morning.* 7. a train, bus, etc. that makes few stops and takes a direct route. *The express to San Francisco leaves the station at eight o'clock.* **ex press es.**

ex pres sion (eks presh′ən), *n.* 1. the act of expressing, especially in words. *At the meeting, the principal gave expression to his hopes for a new auditorium.* 2. a word or phrase used as a common saying. *That television comedian's favorite expression is "How about that!"* 3. a way of saying or doing something that shows feeling. *She read the poem with real expression.* 4. anything that shows feeling, such as a look or an action. *The expression of joy on the child's face made all of us happy.* **ex pres sions.**

ex press way (eks pres′wā′), *n.* a divided highway with a limited number of entrances and exits used for traveling at high speeds by automobiles. *You can travel all the way from Chicago to New York on expressways.* **ex press-ways.**

ex qui site (eks′kwiz ət, eks kwiz′ət), *adj.* 1.

very beautiful and delicate. *She placed the flowers in an exquisite glass vase.* 2. excellent; of the highest quality. *The orchestra played an exquisite symphony at the concert.* 3. sharp; intense. *Winning this award has brought me exquisite happiness. He felt exquisite pain from the toothache.* **ex qui site ly,** *adv.*

ex tend (eks tend′), *v.* 1. to lengthen. *We extended our vacation so that we could visit another national park.* 2. to stretch out. *The river extends for many miles.* 3. to make larger; to increase. *You can extend your knowledge by reading books.* 4. to offer. *He extended an invitation to his party to the entire class.* **ex tends, ex tend ed, ex tend ing.**

ex ten sion (eks ten′shən), *n.* 1. a lengthening; a making larger, longer, greater, etc. *Are you in favor of an extension of the school year?* 2. something added to make a thing larger. *An extension containing a gymnasium and an auditorium has just been added to the school.* **ex ten sions.**

ex ten sive (eks ten′siv), *adj.* far-reaching; widespread. *We made extensive changes in the play after the first performance.* **ex ten sive ly,** *adv.*

ex tent (eks tent′), *n.* 1. the size, amount, distance, degree, etc. to which something extends. *Flood waters covered the extent of his farm. We were amazed at the extent of his knowledge.* 2. degree. *To a certain extent his ideas are valuable.* **ex tents.**

ex te ri or (eks tir′ē ər), *n.* 1. the outside; the outer surface of something. *The exterior of the building needed to be painted.* **ex te ri ors.**
adj. 2. outer; on the outside. *A tree has an exterior layer of bark.* 3. coming from outside. *Most of our decisions are affected to some extent by exterior forces.*

ex ter nal (eks tèrn′l), *adj.* 1. outer; on the outside; exterior. *This medicine is used to treat external skin diseases.* **ex ter nal ly,** *adv.*

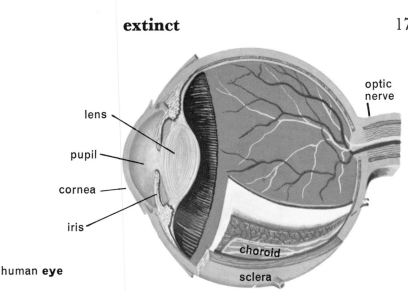

lens

pupil

cornea

iris

human **eye**

optic nerve

choroid

sclera

n. 2. anything seen or felt only on the outside. *Judging by externals, they are a very wealthy family.* **ex ter nals.**

ex tinct (eks tingkt′), *adj.* 1. no longer in existence. *Dinosaurs and mammoths are extinct animals.* 2. inactive; no longer burning. *We saw several extinct volcanoes on our trip to Hawaii.*

ex tin guish (eks ting′gwish), *v.* to put out. *Before he went to bed, he extinguished the fire in the fireplace.* **ex tin guish es, ex tin guished, ex tin guish ing.**

ex tra (eks′trə), *adj.* 1. more than is expected; more than the usual. *I had an extra serving of dessert.*

n. 2. something extra. *He ordered several extras, such as a radio, air conditioning, and whitewall tires on his new car.* 3. a special edition of a newspaper. *The newspapers published extras today that contained the final election results.* 4. a person hired to play a small part in a movie or opera. *He worked as an extra for three years before he got a main role in a movie.* **ex tras.**

ex traor di nary (eks trôr′də ner′ē, eks trə ôr′-də ner′ē), *adj.* out of the ordinary; highly unusual; remarkable. *A snowstorm in July would be an extraordinary occurrence in New York.* **ex traor di nar i ly,** *adv.*

ex treme (eks trēm′), *adj.* 1. of the highest degree; very great. *He deserves extreme praise for his brave act.* 2. far from what is usual or common. *She wears the most extreme clothing she can find.* 3. farthest. *Lanterns hung from the extreme ends of the ship.* **ex treme ly,** *adv.*

n. 4. one of two things that are completely different or opposite. *The explorers experienced the extremes of freezing cold and burning heat on their voyage.* **ex tremes.**

eye (ī), *n.* 1. that part of the body with which man and animals see. *The eye is a delicate organ of the body.* 2. the colored area of the eye. *She has green eyes.* 3. a look. *The teacher cast an angry eye at the noisy students.* 4. a careful watch. *Keep an eye on the crowd for your dad.* 5. the ability to notice and appreciate. *He has a good eye for color.* 6. an opinion. *In his father's eyes, Barry is a great football player.* 7. anything which is like an eye in appearance or use. *The eye of the camera captured his expression perfectly. These potatoes are covered with eyes.* **eyes.**

v. 8. to look at closely; to watch. *The boy eyed the cake and licked his lips.* 9. **catch one's eye,** to attract a person's attention. *We tried to catch the waiter's eye so we could order our dinner.* 10. **see eye to eye,** to agree completely. *The two friends saw eye to eye on everything they talked about.* **eyes, eyed, ey ing** or **eye ing.**

eye brow (ī′brou′), *n.* 1. the ridge of bone that curves above each eye. *The eyebrows protect the eyes from perspiration from the forehead.* 2. the hair that grows on this ridge. *The man had thick white hair and bushy black eyebrows.* **eye brows.**

eye glass (ī′glas′), *n.* 1. a lens used to correct poor vision or to help a person see better. *The eyeglass in the telescope needed to be cleaned.* 2. **eyeglasses,** *n. pl.* a pair of such lenses placed in a frame; glasses. *The old man looked at me through a thick pair of eyeglasses.* **eye glass es.**

eye lash (ī′lash′), *n.* one of the hairs that grow along the edge of the eyelid. *Eyelashes protect the eye by keeping small objects and dirt out of the eyes.* **eye lash es.**

eye lid (ī′lid′), *n.* one of the movable covers of skin that open or close over the eye. *We were so tired that we could hardly lift our eyelids.* **eye lids.**

F or **f** (ef), the sixth letter of the alphabet.

fa ble (fā′bl), *n.* 1. a story that teaches a lesson, especially one in which animals talk and act as men do. *The teacher read us a fable about a proud rooster and a clever fox.* 2. any story that is not true. *He is always trying to fool us with fables about his ability in sports.* **fa bles.**

fab ric (fab′rik), *n.* cloth; a material made by knitting or weaving threads or fibers. *What kind of fabric was used to make that dress?* **fab rics.**

face (fās), *n.* 1. the front part of the head; that part of the head on which the eyes, nose, and mouth are located. *His face was covered by a funny mask.* 2. an expression or look that shows feeling. *You should have seen his face when he saw the puppies. The boys were making faces at the monkeys in the zoo.* 3. the most important or front part of something. *The face of the clock was turned to the wall so that we could not see the time.* 4. the part of an action, idea, etc. that is seen easily. *The plan seemed simple on the face of it, but it turned out to be very difficult.* 5. dignity; reputation; what is thought about a person. *He was afraid to make a mistake because he might lose face with his friends.* 6. boldness; rudeness. *After spending all of his money at the movies, he had the face to ask for more money from his father.* **fac es.**

v. 7. to be turned toward; to have the front toward. *Our school faces the street. The teacher faced the class and began to speak.* 8. to meet with courage. *Firemen must face many dangers in their work.* 9. to cover with a material. *The front of the house was faced with wooden shingles.* **fac es, faced, fac ing.**

fa cil i ty (fə sil′ə tē), *n.* 1. ease in doing something; the ability to do a thing without difficulty. *He has a great facility for writing clearly.* 2. anything which makes doing something easier and more convenient. *The gymnasium has many facilities for indoor sports.* **fa cil i ties.**

fact (fakt), *n.* 1. anything which is known to be true; something that is known to have occurred. *It is a fact that gravity causes objects to fall to the earth.* 2. truth. *The fact of the matter is, we won the game because we tried harder and played better than the other team.* 3. a statement that is supposed to be true or is accepted as true. *He told us as facts many things that he had done.* **facts.**

fac tor (fak′tər), *n.* 1. any of the things that cause or bring about a certain result. *Time is an important factor to consider in cooking.* 2. any of the numbers which are multiplied to obtain a product. *The factors of 27 are 3 and 9, or 3, 3, and 3.* 3. a person who handles business matters for another. *Mr. Smith is my father's factor in England.* **fac tors.**

v. 4. to separate into factors. *If you factor 27, you get 9 and 3, or 3, 3, and 3.* **fac tors, fac tored, fac tor ing.**

fac to ry (fak′tə rē), *n.* a room, building, or group of buildings in which something is manufactured. *He worked all summer in a factory that makes farm machinery.* **fac to ries.**

fac ul ty (fak′əl tē), *n.* 1. the skill or ability to do something. *He has a faculty for making everyone happy.* 2. a natural sense or power of

factory

the mind. *Man has the faculty of speech.* 3. the teachers who teach at a school. *Classes were dismissed so that the faculty could hold a meeting.* **fac ul ties.**

fade (fād), *v.* 1. to become lighter in color; to lose color. *The curtains faded in the sunlight.* 2. to dry up; to grow weak. *Put the flowers in water before they fade.* 3. to become less clear; to grow dim. *The sounds of the parade faded in the distance. The light began to fade as clouds moved in front of the sun.* **fades, fad ed, fad ing.**

Fahr en heit (far′an hīt′), *adj.* of or according to the Fahrenheit scale where the freezing point of water is 32 degrees and the boiling point is 212 degrees. *Temperatures in the United States are measured on the Fahrenheit scale.*

fail (fāl), *v.* 1. to be unsuccessful in doing something; to be unable to do something. *The pirates failed to find the treasure they had hidden. The child failed to stay awake until the company arrived.* 2. to be less than what was expected; to result in nothing. *The crops failed during the dry spell in spite of our efforts to water them.* 3. to neglect. *My father failed to put more fuel in the tank and ran out of gas on the highway.* 4. to be unhelpful to when help is needed; to be absent when called upon. *He has never failed friends when they needed him.* 5. to grow weaker; to become less strong. *As evening comes on, the daylight begins to fail.* 6. to become bankrupt. *Their business failed after the fire destroyed the store.* **fails, failed, fail ing.**

7. **without fail,** for certain; surely. *He promised to meet us downtown without fail.*

fail ing (fā′ling), *n.* fault, weakness. *Her biggest failing is her lack of courage.* **fail ings.**

fail ure (fāl′yər), *n.* 1. a failing to do something; a being unsuccessful. *He was very disappointed at his failure to finish his work on time.* 2. a being short of what was expected or hoped for. *The failure of the crops was due to a lack of rain.* 3. a neglecting to do something. *My failure to carry an umbrella caused me to become wet in the rain.* 4. a growing weaker; a gradual loss of strength. *The failure of the daylight coming through the window reminded me to turn on the lamps.* 5. a becoming bankrupt. *The failure of the bank caused many people to lose their money.* 6. a person, thing, or event that has failed. *The dance was a failure because only a few people came to it.* **fail ures.**

faint (fānt), *adj.* 1. lacking strength; weak and dizzy. *The boys had a faint feeling after playing in the sun.* 2. unclear; dim. *A faint light came from a window in the house.* 3. without courage; cowardly. *The faint-hearted lion ran away.* **faint er, faint est; faint ly,** *adv.*

v. 4. to lose consciousness and lie as if asleep because of illness, weakness, etc. *The man fainted because he was very tired and hungry.* **faints, faint ed, faint ing.**

n. 5. a condition of unconsciousness. *The exhausted runner fell into a faint at the end of the race.* **faints.**

fair[1] (fâr), *adj.* 1. honest; just; not treating one any differently from any other. *The Constitution of the United States guarantees everyone a fair trial. The umpire's decisions in a game should be fair.* 2. in keeping with the rules; according to what is accepted as right. *If you want to play on the team, you must learn fair play. He got a fair price for his bicycle.* 3. average; not a great amount but enough. *They had fair success in raising their garden.* 4. sunny and clear; not stormy or cloudy. *The weatherman said it would be fair today.* 5. very attractive; beautiful. *The fair princess rode through the streets on a white horse.* 6. light in color. *He has fair hair and dark eyes.* 7. in baseball, said of a ball that has been hit onto the playing field, within the foul lines. *The umpire shouted, "Fair ball!" as the ball went into the stands for a home run.* **fair er, fair est; fair ly,** *adv.*

adv. 8. fairly; with honesty. *Some people play fair only when they are winning.*

fair[2] (fâr), *n.* 1. a display of goods and machines where people come to view the exhibits and buy things. *The Junior Achievement Trade Fair was held in a downtown hotel this year.* 2. a gathering of people, especially in a country area, where animals and goods are displayed. *John's prize hog won another prize at this year's fair.* 3. a display of things to be sold to raise money for a particular purpose. *Several hundred dollars were raised at the church fair.* **fairs.**

fair ly (fâr′lē), *adv.* 1. with honesty; in a fair manner; justly. *The judge listened to the evidence and made his decision fairly.* 2. moderately; not extremely good, but not bad. *He plays a fairly good game of golf.*

fairy (fâr′ē), *n.* 1. in stories, old tales, etc., a beautiful, delicate, tiny being who could help

a fair

or hurt people. *The fairy waved her magic wand, and a handsome prince appeared.* **fair ies.**

adj. 2. of, about, or like a fairy. *Mother read a fairy tale to the children.*

faith (fāth), *n.* 1. a belief that does not require proof; trust; confidence. *The trapeze artist has complete faith in his partner.* 2. a belief in God. *His faith remained strong all of his life.* 3. a religion or group of religious beliefs. *People of many different faiths live in our community.* 4. devotion; loyalty. *The people of the nation pledged their faith to the new king.* 5. a promise; a pledge of loyalty. *The mayor kept faith by carrying out the plans he had proposed during the election.* 6. **good faith,** honesty; sincerity. *He sold us the car in good faith, not knowing that it didn't run properly.* **faiths.**

faith ful (fāth′fəl), *adj.* 1. loyal; honest; trustworthy. *He has been a faithful friend to me for many years.* 2. accurate; without mistakes or untrue facts. *He gave a faithful report of what happened at the meeting.* **faith ful ly,** *adv.*

fake (fāk), *v.* 1. to pretend in order to fool or mislead. *He faked sleep until his brother left the room.* **fakes, faked, fak ing.**

adj. 2. pretended; unreal; false. *The man was wearing fake hair until the wind blew it from his head.*

n. 3. something that is false or pretended; someone who pretends to be what he isn't. *The fruit on the table was a fake; it was made of plastic. The blind beggar was a fake; he could see as well as anyone.* **fakes.**

fa kir (fə kir′, fā′kər), *n.* a holy man living in India who tortures himself for religious reasons. *Fakirs believe that the body is not important but that the soul is.* **fa kirs.**

fal con (fôl′kən, fal′kən, fô′kən), *n.* a small, swift hawk that is trained to hunt birds and little animals. *Upon orders from its owner, a falcon flies up, gathers the prey in its claws, and flies back to its owner.* **fal cons.**

fall (fôl), *v.* 1. to drop from a higher place to a lower place; to come down. *Rain fell all during the night. The book fell to the floor with a bang.* 2. to tumble or come down from a vertical position. *Heavy winds caused the tree to fall. I tripped on a stone and fell.* 3. to drop down; to become lower. *The temperature fell below freezing this morning. Their voices fell as I entered the room.* 4. to be killed, especially in battle. *Many brave soldiers fell in the battle.* 5. to be conquered; to be overcome by an enemy. *After a long battle, the fort fell to the enemy.* 6. to become evil; to give in to evil or temptation. *He almost fell into a life of crime because of his companions.* 7. to pass into a certain state or condition. *He fell asleep as soon as he went to bed.* 8. to happen at a certain time; to occur. *Labor Day always falls on a Monday.* 9. to happen; to come to pass. *Night fell as we drove out of the city.* 10. to be separated; to be divided. *Holidays fall into*

fakir

several groups: some are national; some are local; and some are religious.

Fall also has the following special meanings:

fall back, to retreat; to withdraw to the rear. *The attack was so strong that we were required to fall back.*

fall back on or **fall back upon,** to turn to for use or help; to begin to use again. *When we lost our money in the fire, we fell back on our savings account. When the lights failed to work, we fell back on the candles we had stored away.*

fall in, (a) to form a line; to stand in a line. *The captain shouted "Fall in!" just as the parade was about to begin.* (b) to meet or be joined with others. *On his first day in a new city, Larry fell in with a group of boys who were playing football.* (c) to agree. *We fell in with his plan to raise money for uniforms.*

fall on or **fall upon,** to attack, especially by surprise. *The police fell upon the thieves as they returned to their meeting place.*

fall out, (a) to drop out of a place in line. *As soon as the roll had been called, the leader told*

falcon

hand **fan**

the men to fall out. (b) to disagree; to quarrel. *The two friends fell out because of a misunderstanding.*

fall through, to fail. *The plan to buy uniforms fell through because we couldn't raise enough money.* **falls, fell, fall en, fall ing.**

n. 11. a dropping from a higher place to a lower place. *A heavy fall of snow covered the ground.* 12. the amount that drops. *The fall of rain last month amounted to seven inches.* 13. the distance that anything drops. *The fall of the river between those cities is eleven feet. He was injured in a fifteen-foot fall from a tree.* 14. a decrease. *A sudden fall in the temperature forced us to end our picnic and return home.* 15. the destruction or downfall of something, especially a place. *We studied the fall of the Roman Empire in history. Pride goes before a fall.* 16. the season of the year that comes between summer and winter; autumn. *In the fall, the leaves change their colors and drop from the trees.* 17. **falls,** a waterfall. *We visited Niagara Falls on our vacation.* **falls.**

fall en (fôl′ən), *adj.* 1. dropped. *The fallen leaves covered the ground.* 2. no longer upright; on the ground. *We stepped over a fallen tree in the forest.* 3. overthrown; defeated. *The victorious army occupied every building in the fallen city.* 4. dead. *The fallen soldiers were buried with military honors.* *v.* 5. past participle of **fall.** *He had fallen through the ice.*

false (fôls), *adj.* 1. not true. *It is false to say that two plus two is equal to five.* 2. lying. *The robber gave false answers to the policeman who arrested him.* 3. not loyal. *People who only pretend to be friendly are false friends.* 4. not real or genuine. *The man wore a false beard.* 5. not based on true ideas; pretended. *His false pride kept him from accepting help from his friends.* **fals er, fals est; false ly,** *adv.*

false hood (fôls hud), *n.* a lie; a false statement. *The little boy told many falsehoods.* **false hoods.**

fal ter (fôl′tər), *v.* 1. to move in an unsteady way; hesitate. *Tom Brown ran well at the start of the race, but he faltered at the end.* 2. to speak in a broken way; stammer. *Don wasn't used to speaking in public, and his nervousness caused him to falter.* 3. to slow down; to hesitate in action. *The tired explorers faltered and decided to go back.* **fal ters, fal tered, fal ter ing.**

fame (fām), *n.* a state of being well-known and respected. *George Washington was a man of great fame.* **fames.**

fa mil iar (fə mil′yər), *adj.* 1. well-known; seen frequently; common. *Thunderstorms are a familiar sight around here in the summer.* 2. well-acquainted. *A teacher is familiar with many books.* 3. informal; friendly. *The letter was written in a familiar manner.* 4. more friendly than is welcome; bold. *People are offended by his familiar ways.* **fa mil iar ly,** *adv.*

fam i ly (fam′ə lē), *n.* 1. a group that includes a

father, a mother, and their children. *The Stevens family walked to church this morning.* 2. the children of a family. *The father and mother raised a family of three boys and two girls.* 3. a group of people who are related to each other. *The Allen family has lived for years in this town.* 4. a group of plants or animals that are related. *The lion and the cat belong to the same family.* **fam i lies.**

fa mous (fā′məs), *adj.* widely known and talked about. *Some girls dream about becoming famous movie stars.* **fa mous ly,** *adv.*

fan[1] (fan), *n.* 1. anything used to move the air. *Some fans are held in the hand and waved to make a breeze. An electric fan has rotating blades that produce an air current.* 2. anything that looks like an open hand fan. *Turkeys can spread their tails into wide fans.* **fans.**
v. 3. to move or stir up air. *The man fanned himself with a newspaper.* **fans, fanned, fann ing.**

fan[2] (fan), *n.* a person who has great interest or enthusiasm in a sport, activity, or famous person. *Movie fans often collect autographs and pictures of their favorite stars.* **fans.**

fan cy (fan′sē), *adj.* 1. decorated or ornamented; not plain. *A lot of work had gone into the fancy dress that Sue wore to the dance.* 2. better than the usual. *Joan likes fancy pears, which cost more than ordinary fruit.* 3. showing more skill or grace than the usual. *We saw an exhibition of fancy horseback riding.* **fan ci er, fan ci est; fan ci ly,** *adv.*
n. 4. imagination. *Talking animals and fairy-tale creatures are products of fancy.* 5. a liking. *The students took a fancy to the new teacher.* 6. some imagined thing; an idea or notion. *Charles has a fancy that he can't sing, but his voice is actually quite good.* **fan cies.**
v. 7. to imagine; to suppose. *Can you fancy a flying elephant?* 8. to like a great deal. *Ray fancies chocolate candy.* 9. to have an idea without a good reason. *Bill fancies that he wouldn't like pickles, even though he has never tasted any.* **fan cies, fan cied, fan cy ing.**

fang (fang′), *n.* 1. a sharp tooth by which certain animals can grasp and hold their prey. *The wolf held the rabbit in his fangs.* 2. the hollowed or grooved tooth through which a poisonous

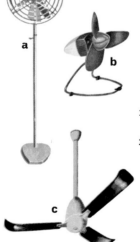

electric ventilating **fans:**
 a. floor fan
 b. desk fan
 c. ceiling fan

sand, āte, bâre, fäther; sent, mē, fèrn; fit, bīke; pot, rōpe, fôrt; run, pull, rüle, cūte; noise, sound; ch, cheese; ng, long; th, thick; t̶h̶, those; zh, treasure; ə = a in about, e in waken, i in animal, o in seldom, and u in minus.

snake sends its venom. *The fangs of the cobra bit through the man's boot.* **fangs.**

fan ta sy (fant′ə sē), *n.* imagination; the result of a fancied idea. *He writes and directs wonderful fantasies for children.* **fan ta sies.**

far (fär), *adj.* 1. a long way off; distant. *The school is far from my house, so I leave early in the morning.* 2. more distant. *You should paint the far side of the house, too.* **far ther** or **fur ther, far thest** or **fur thest.**

adv. 3. very much. *Joe is far faster than Bill.* 4. to a great distance. *The salesman traveled far, from New York to California.*

far a way (fär′ə wā′), *adj.* 1. distant. *Movies show scenes of faraway places.* 2. dreamy. *Helen pretended to be listening, but she had a faraway look on her face.*

fare (fâr), *n.* 1. money charged for a trip. *You pay a fare to ride in a bus, taxi, train, or airplane.* 2. a passenger who has paid to ride. *The taxi driver had seven fares before noon.* 3. food; meals. *The fare in this hotel is almost as good as home cooking.* **fares.**

v. 4. to get along. *How did your parents fare on their trip to Mexico?* **fares, fared, far ing.**

fare well (fâr′wel′), *n.* 1. good-bye. *The boys shouted farewells as we drove away. Their farewell was short because the train was leaving in three minutes.* 2. a leaving or departing. *Our farewells took place early in the morning.* **fare wells.**

adj. 3. parting; final. *At the end of the school year, we have a farewell program in the assembly hall.*

farm (färm), *n.* 1. the land used for growing crops or for raising animals. *My uncle raises wheat on his farm in Kansas.* **farms.**

v. 2. to raise crops or animals. *My uncle has been farming this land for fifty years.* **farms, farmed, farm ing.**

farm er (fär′mər), *n.* a person who works on a farm. *There are not as many farmers on small farms now as there were fifty years ago.* **farm ers.**

far-off (fär′ôf′), *adj.* far away or distant. *The South Pole is a far-off region.*

far sight ed (fär′sīt′id), *adj.* 1. able to see

farm

distant things more clearly than things that are close. *Farsighted people wear glasses when they read.* 2. able to see ahead clearly and to make plans. *A farsighted person tries to save for the future.* **far sight ed ly,** *adv.*

far ther (fär′thər), *adj.* 1. more distant. *Walk over to that farther rock.*

adv. 2. at or to a greater distance. *We drove farther this summer than we did last year.*

fas ci nate (fas′ə nāt), *v.* to attract; to charm. *The new automobile fascinated everyone who stopped to look at it. The new styles in dresses are fascinating.* **fas ci nates, fas ci nat ed, fas ci nat ing.**

fas ci na tion (fas′ə nā′shən), *n.* a great interest, attraction or charm. *Bill had a great fascination for cars.* **fas ci na tions.**

fash ion (fash′ən), *n.* 1. a style of dressing, talking, or behaving. *It was once the fashion for men to wear long wigs. Expensive stores have the latest fashions from New York and Paris.* 2. way or manner. *Edward had a fashion of walking with a cane.* **fash ions.**

v. 3. to shape; to form. *Birds can fashion nests of grass, twigs, and string.* **fash ions, fashioned, fash ion ing.**

fash ion a ble (fash′ən ə bəl), *adj.* in style according to the fashions. *Mary had always been a very fashionable dresser.* **fash ion a bly,** *adv.*

fast[1] (fast), *adj.* 1. quick; able to move, work, read, etc. rapidly. *Bill is a fast runner. Ella is a fast reader. We can make a fast trip home.* 2. ahead of the correct time. *My watch is fast because it shows half-past eleven when the time is only eleven o'clock.* 3. loyal and true. *Henry and Gary have been fast friends since third grade.* 4. not likely to fade. *Blue shirts with fast color will stay blue.* 5. fastened well. *The dog's chain was fast to the tree, so he couldn't run away.* **fast er, fast est.**

adv. 6. with great speed; quickly. *A racing car is built to go fast.* 7. tightly or firmly. *The rowboat was stuck fast in the sand at the river's edge.* 8. completely; soundly. *The baby was fast asleep in spite of the loud noise in the next room.*

farewell

fast² (fast), *v.* 1. to go without food. *Many animals fast when they are sick.* 2. to go without eating certain foods. *Some people fast during certain days in the church calendar.* **fasts, fast ed, fast ing.**
n. 3. a time of going without food. *His fast ended, and he could eat again.* **fasts.**

fas ten (fas′n), *v.* 1. to join; attach. *I fastened the lamp to the wall over my bed.* 2. to lock. *Be sure to fasten the door before you go to bed.* 3. to direct; to fix. *Our attention was fastened on the elephants in the zoo.* **fas tens, fas tened, fas ten ing.**

fat (fat), *n.* 1. a greasy yellow or white substance in animals and plants. *The white part of raw bacon is fat.* 2. the chemical compounds of carbon, hydrogen, and oxygen that are found in these substances. *Fats are just one group of energy foods.* 3. the best part or share. *He lived off the fat of the land.* **fats.**
adj. 4. having much flesh; plump. *The fat man was told by his doctor to go on a diet and lose weight.* 5. having much oil or grease. *Some meat, such as pork, is fat.* 6. well-filled. *The rich man has a fat wallet.* **fat ter, fat test.**

fa tal (fā′tl), *adj.* 1. resulting in death. *Many fatal diseases have been prevented by cleanliness and the proper medicine.* 2. resulting in great loss. *The late frost was fatal to the orange crop.* 3. serious; important; having great effects. *Tomorrow is the fatal day: the day of graduation.* **fa tal ly,** *adv.*

fate (fāt), *n.* 1. a power believed to exist without human control, that influences events or causes things to happen. *He said that they met each other by fate.* 2. what happens to a person. *The jury will determine the fate of the man on trial.* **fates.**

fat ed (fāt′id), *adj.* determined or set by fate. *The politician felt that he was fated to win the election.*

fate ful (fāt fəl), *adj.* having serious results; a fated outcome. *On that fateful morning the man got up early.* **fate ful ly,** *adv.*

fa ther (fä′thər), *n.* 1. the male parent. *Your parents are your father and mother.* 2. a man important to the beginning or making of something. *George Washington is called the father of his country.* 3. a priest. *Reverend Smith and Father Meyer are good friends.* 4. **fathers,** the leaders of a government. *The town fathers agreed to spend the money to rebuild several streets.* 5. **Our Father,** God. *Our Father in Heaven watches over us.* **fa thers.**
v. 6. to become the father of. *Mr. Stevens fathered three handsome sons.* 7. to care for as a father does. *Mr. Armstrong had no children, but he fathered several orphans.* **fa thers, fa thered, fa ther ing.**

fau cet (fô′sit), *n.* a device that limits the flow of a liquid from a pipe, tank, or other container. *The faucet on the sink was broken, and the water dripped constantly.* **fau cets.**

fault (fôlt), *n.* 1. something that is wrong. *His biggest fault is that he won't admit he's ever wrong.* 2. a mistake; an error. *My faults in grammar were corrected by my teacher.* 3. blame; responsibility. *The wet floor was Kent's fault because he forgot to close the window when the rain came.* 4. **at fault,** in the wrong; responsible. *The driver went through a red light and was at fault for the accident.* **faults.**

faun (fôn), *n.* in the stories of ancient Rome, a god with the head and body of a man and the horns, legs, and tail of a goat. *Fauns lived in the country and in the woods.* **fauns.**

fa vor (fā′vər), *n.* 1. a kind or thoughtful act. *We did a favor for our neighbor by carrying her groceries to her apartment.* 2. acceptance; liking. *The audience listened with favor to the well-known singer.* 3. a small, not expensive gift. *The children received favors at the birthday party.* 4. **in favor of,** in support of; approving. *Both our parents were in favor of our taking the trip.* **fa vors.**
v. 5. to approve; like. *The class favored having the party in the gym.* 6. to show kindness or thoughtfulness to. *The pianist favored us by playing our request.* 7. to prefer or help in an unfair way. *He favored the smallest puppy and saw that it got more to eat.* 8. to help. *The warm sunshine favored my cold.* 9. to be careful in using. *Our dog is favoring a sore paw. The doctor told me to favor my eyes for a few months.* 10. to look like. *The Smith children favor their mother.* **fa vors, fa vored, fa vor ing.**

fa vor a ble (fā′vər a bl), *adj.* 1. approving. *I hope I get a favorable answer to my request.* 2. helpful. *Favorable winds helped the sailboat win the race.* **fa vor a bly,** *adv.*

fa vor ite (fā′vər it), *adj.* 1. most liked; preferred. *Vanilla is my favorite flavor for ice cream.* *n.* 2. a person or thing who is liked the most. *John was a favorite among his friends.* 3. the one most likely to win. *Which is the favorite of the World Series teams this year?* **fa vor ites.**

fawn¹ (fôn), *n.* 1. a young deer. *A deer is called a fawn until he is one year old.* 2. a light tan color. *Fawn is an attractive color for a coat.* **fawns.**

fawn² (fôn), *v.* 1. to show fondness or pleasure, usually meaning a dog's friendly actions. *Dogs will fawn on the people they like.* 2. to act humble around someone in order to get something. *He fawned on his brother, hoping that he would be given some candy.* **fawns, fawned, fawn ing.**

fear (fir), *n.* 1. a feeling of fright or worry when danger is near. *The squirrel climbed a tree in fear of the dog. My aunt always shows fear when a storm comes.* **fears.**
v. 2. to be afraid of; have fear of. *My little sister fears thunder and lightning.* 3. to have feelings of concern; worry. *We feared that the river would flood during the rainy season.* **fears, feared, fear ing.**

feathers of different birds:
a. wing feather for flight
b. wing covering
c. body covering
d. down
e. pigeon feather
f. linnet feather
g. turtledove feather
h. peacock feather
i. guinea hen feather

fear ful (fir′fəl), *adj.* 1. frightening. *The lightning was followed by a fearful clap of thunder.* 2. frightened; afraid; showing fear. *Some children are fearful in the dark. The boys heard a noise from the empty room and looked at each other with fearful glances.* **fear ful ly,** *adv.*

fear less (fiər′ləs), *adj.* not afraid; brave. *His fearless rescue saved five lives.* **fear less ly,** *adv.*

feast (fēst), *n.* 1. a big dinner with good food. *When the Indians hunted and killed many buffaloes, they had a feast. We have a feast on Thanksgiving Day.* 2. a religious holiday; celebration. *Christmas is probably the best-known feast of the year.* **feasts.**
v. 3. to eat and enjoy a big dinner. *The family feasted on chicken.* 4. to make a large meal for. *The wealthy man feasted his many friends.* 5. to give great pleasure to. *We feasted our eyes on the changing colors of the autumn landscape.* **feasts, feast ed, feast ing.**

feat (fēt), *n.* an accomplishment showing some special skill or courage. *Diving into the water from a high place is a remarkable feat.* **feats.**

feath er (feth′ər), *n.* 1. a soft, flat part that grows on the body of a bird. *Feathers protect birds from cold and injury.* 2. **feather in one's cap,** anything that a person can be proud of having done. *Winning the scholarship was a feather in Jack's cap.* **feath ers.**
v. 3. to put feathers on something. *The Indians feathered their arrows to make them fly straight.* 4. to turn an oar after a stroke so that the blade is flat and parallel to the surface of the water. *A rower feathers his oars to cut down their resistance to the air.* **feath ers, feath ered, feath er ing.**

fea ture (fē′chər), *n.* 1. a part of the face. *The girl has lovely features; her eyes especially are beautiful.* 2. a part. *One feature was a talk by the Superintendent of Schools.* 3. something that attracts attention; outstanding quality. *Her most important feature is her ability to see mistakes.* **fea tures.**
v. 4. to make prominent. *A singer and a magician are featured at the theater. Most newspapers feature comic strips.* **fea tures, fea tured, fea tur ing.**

Feb ru ary (feb′rù er′ē or feb′ū er′ē), *n.* the second month of the year. *February has twenty-eight days, except in leap years, when it has twenty-nine.*

fed er al (fed′ər əl), *adj.* of or having to do with a nation made up of separate states. *In the United States, fifty individual states are united under a federal government.* **fed er al ly,** *adv.*

fee (fē), *n.* 1. a price charged for admission. *The fee for the concert is two dollars.* 2. a price charged for the professional work done by a doctor, lawyer, or dentist. *The doctor's fee was fifty dollars for a complete physical examination.* **fees.**

fee ble (fē′bl), *adj.* without much strength; weak. *The feeble old man needed help to cross the street. The small baby gave a feeble cry. His feeble excuse for being late made us laugh.* **fee bler, fee blest; fee bly,** *adv.*

feed (fēd), *v.* 1. to give food to. *Mother fed the baby his breakfast. We must feed the horses.* 2. to eat. *The animals in the barn were feeding quietly.* 3. to give or supply with something. *We fed the campfire with logs.* **feeds, fed, feed ing.**
n. 4. the food eaten by farm animals; fodder. *Hay is a common feed for horses and cows.* **feeds.**

feel (fēl), *v.* 1. to touch. *Feel my cold hands. Feel the soft fur of the cat.* 2. to try to find one's way by touching. *He felt his way through the dark room to the light switch.* 3. to have the feeling of being; be conscious of. *You should feel better today now that you have finished that hard job. We felt cold.* 4. to know or discover by the sense of touch. *Feel how soft that fur is.* 5. to hunt for by touch. *She felt in her handbag for a pencil.* 6. to have in one's mind; to experience. *We felt gratitude for all he had done for us.* 7. to be sure; to believe. *I feel that our school will win the football championship this year.* 8. to seem to be. *When you come out of the outdoor swimming pool, the air feels cold even though it may really be warm.* **feels, felt, feel ing.**

n. 9. the way something feels to the touch. *You can tell the difference between an apple and an orange just by the feel of them.* **feels.**

feel er (fēl′ər), *n.* 1. a part of an insect or animal that is used to touch with. *An insect uses its long, delicate feelers for guidance. The whiskers of a cat are its feelers.* 2. a statement or question made to find out the views or opinions of others. *The company sent out feelers to see if public opinion was favorable toward their newest product.* **feel ers.**

feel ing (fēl′ing), *n.* 1. the sense of touch. *Our feeling something helps us to find out whether an object is rough or smooth, cold or hot, or wet or dry.* 2. a sensation; a being aware. *The feeling of dizziness went away as soon as he got out of the hot sun.* 3. an emotion; what is felt in our minds. *On the morning of her birthday, Christine had a feeling of excitement.* 4. pity; sympathy. *Most of us have feeling for the sick and the unfortunate.* 5. a thought or opinion. *My feeling is that the book would have been better if more time had been spent on it.* 6. **to hurt one's feelings,** to make one feel bad. *It is cruel to hurt a person's feelings.* **feel ings.**

feet (fēt), *n. pl.* more than one foot. *A yard is equal to three feet. Animals have four feet.*

feign (fān), *v.* 1. to pretend; to give an appearance of. *Some animals feign death when another animal is after them, and then they are left alone.* 2. to make up something that is not true. *Harry feigned illness, but his mother made him do his homework.* **feigns, feigned, feign ing.**

fe line (fē′lin), *n.* 1. an animal belonging to the cat family. *The ordinary house cat is a feline, but so are lions, tigers, leopards, and lynxes.* **fe lines.**
adj. 2. of or like a cat. *The Indian moved through the forest with feline swiftness and quietness.* (See illustration on page 188.)

fell[1] (fel), past tense of **fall.**

fell[2] (fel), *v.* 1. to knock someone down. *The heavyweight champion felled the other boxer in only two minutes, and the fight was all over.* 2. to chop or saw down a tree. *Lumbermen fell many trees every year to supply the nation's wood.* **fells, felled, fell ing.**

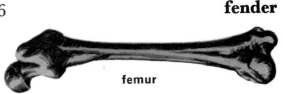

femur

fel low (fel′ō), *n.* 1. a man or boy. *Everyone thinks that Jack is a fine fellow.* 2. an associate; a companion. *The two boys were fellows in misery when they both fell in the mud pond.* 3. one of a pair of something; one that goes with another. *He can't find the fellow to his riding boot.* **fel lows.**
adj. 4. in the same situation; belonging to the same group. *The class president spoke to his fellow students about the need for a big crowd at the game.*

felt[1] (felt), past tense of **feel.**

felt[2] (felt), *n.* 1. a heavy cloth that is made of wool, animal hair, or fur. *Felt is not woven but is pressed together.*
adj. 2. made or formed of felt. *Felt hats are popular.*

fe male (fē′māl), *adj.* 1. belonging to the persons or animals that can produce young. *Female chickens lay eggs and are called hens.* 2. of or for women or girls. *Our school has a female chorus.*
n. 3. a female person or animal. *Girls and women are females.* **fe males.**

fe mur (fē′mər), *n.* the bone in the thigh. *The femur is the largest and longest bone in the body.* **fe murs.**

fence (fens), *n.* 1. a barrier or enclosure of wood, wire, stone, etc. to keep people or animals from going into or out of a certain property. *Some old fences in the country are made of split logs. Barbed-wire fences prevent animals from wandering off and getting lost.* 2. a person who buys and sells stolen goods. *Robbers and burglars dispose of their stolen jewels by selling them to a fence.* 3. **on the fence,** be undecided or unsure about something. *Ann had several friends running for class treasurer, and she was on the fence about whom to vote for.* **fenc es.**
v. 4. to put a fence around. *Dad fenced the backyard.* 5. to fight with swords or foils as a sport. *George enjoyed learning how to fence in college.* **fenc es, fenced, fenc ing.**

fenc ing (fen′sing), *n.* 1. the art or sport of fighting with swords or foils. *Special suits and masks are worn for fencing.* 2. material for making a fence. *The farmer bought fencing that would be used to enclose his property.*

fend (fend), *v.* 1. to ward off a blow or attack. *The army fended off the attack.* 2. to provide oneself with adequate food, shelter, clothing, etc. *The orphaned kitten fended well for itself.* **fends, fend ed, fend ing.**

fend er (fen′dər), *n.* 1. the piece of metal over the wheel of an automobile, truck, or motorcycle which keeps dirt and water from flying

fence

out. *The fender of the car was dented in the accident.* 2. a metal screen in front of a fireplace to stop sparks. *A fender prevents a rug from getting burned.* **fend ers.**

fern (fėrn), *n.* a plant having feathery leaves but no flowers. *Ferns grow best in shady, damp places.* **ferns.**

fer ret (fer′it), *n.* 1. a kind of weasel, sometimes trained to kill rats or to hunt rabbits. *Ferrets are fierce little animals.* **fer rets.**
v. 2. to hunt; to search until someone or something is found. *The detectives spent six months ferreting out the thief.* **fer rets, fer ret ed, fer ret ing.**

fer tile (fėr′tl), *adj.* 1. producing many crops; having good crops. *The fertile soil of the Middle West gives us much corn.* 2. able to bear seeds, fruit, or young. *A chick comes from a fertile egg.* 3. having many ideas. *An inventor has a fertile mind.*

fer til i za tion (fər tl ə zā′shən), *n.* 1. the union of sperm and egg. *The fertilization of eggs will produce chicks.* 2. the act of applying something to soil to make it produce more. *After fertilization, the farm was able to produce more crops.* **fer til i za tions.**

fer ti lize (fėr′tl īz), *v.* 1. to add something to soil to make it richer so that it will produce more. *Lawns are fertilized with a combination of chemicals, such as nitrogen, calcium, and others.* 2. to cause a new animal or plant to develop. *Bees fertilize plants by carrying a powdery substance, called pollen, from one flower to another.* **fer ti liz es, fer ti lized, fer ti liz ing.**

fer ti liz er (fer′tl īz′ər), *n.* something used to put in soil to make it produce more. *Indians*

fern:
  a. spores; **b.** frond; **c.** sprout; **d.** root

fencing

used dead fish as a fertilizer when they planted corn. **fer ti liz ers.**

fes ti val (fes′tə vl), *n.* a time of celebration and feasting to honor a special event. *Thanksgiving is a festival started by the early settlers in New England in 1621.* **fes ti vals.**

fes tive (fes′tiv), *adj.* having to do with a celebration; festival. *My birthday is always a festive occasion.* **fes tive ly,** *adv.*

fetch (fech), *v.* to go and get. *The dog was taught to fetch the newspaper from the porch.* **fetch es, fetched, fetch ing.**

fe ver (fē′vər), *n.* 1. a body temperature that is higher than normal. *A fever usually means an illness has set in.* 2. a disease marked by high fever. *In scarlet fever and other fevers the body temperature is unusually high.* 3. a condition of nervous excitement. *We were in a fever of activity on the night of our school play.* **fe vers.**

few (fū), *adj.* 1. not many. *Few people have read this rare book.* **few er, few est.**
n. 2. a small number. *Only a few came to the meeting on the night of the heavy rain.*

fez (fez), *n.* a cap with no brim that was worn by men in Turkey. *A fez usually has a tassel.* **fez zes.**

fib (fib), *n.* 1. a lie about something that is really not important. *He told a fib so he could leave early.* **fibs.**
v. 2. to tell such a lie. *I told him that I ate the whole pie, but I was only fibbing.* **fibs, fibbed, fib bing.**

fi ber or **fi bre** (fī′bər), *n.* 1. a part that is like a thread. *Muscles are made up of many fibers. The fibers of cotton are made into yarn.* 2. the

fez

ferret

nature of a person. *She is a woman of sensitive fiber.* **fi bers** or **fi bres.**

fib u la (fib′yə lə), *n.* the long, thin outer bone of the human leg. *The fibula is located between the knee and the ankle.* **fib u las.**

fic tion (fik′shən), *n.* 1. writings about imaginary events and people. *Short stories and novels are fiction, although many contain some actions of real people.* 2. something that is made up and does not appear true. *The robber's story to the police was fiction.*

fic ti tious (fik tish′əs), *adj.* not real; imagined. *His story was fictitious.* **fic ti tious ly,** *adv.*

fid dle (fid′l), *n.* 1. a violin. *He plays the fiddle well.* **fid dles.**

v. 2. to play on the violin. *He fiddled an old-time song.* 3. to perform actions that have no meaning; move the hands or fingers nervously.

The embarrassed boy fiddled with his necktie. 4. to spend time in doing useless things. *The day was so hot that we just fiddled it away.* **fid dles, fid dled, fid dling.**

field (fēld), *n.* 1. a piece of open land with no trees, used for grazing by animals or for the planting of crops. *Some fields of wheat are several miles wide.* 2. a piece of land which has a special use. *A football field is one hundred yards long.* 3. an area from which a natural product is obtained. *Some oil fields are under the ocean.* 4. a place where an army fights. *The soldiers marched toward the field of battle.* 5. an area of interest or activity, especially in school or business. *His field is medicine, and hers is cooking. Their son likes the field of politics.* 6. the people in a contest. *At the finish line he led the field in the mile run.* 7. a background on which some-

FELINES

angora cat

lynx

eyes of the common cat

ocelot

tiger

wildcat

Pallas' cat

house cat

lioness and lion

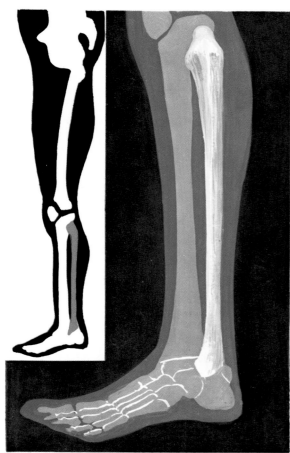

fibula

thing shows. *The American flag has a blue field with fifty white stars on it.* **fields.**

v. 8. to catch a ball; to stop a ball and throw it. *A baseball player is judged by the way he fields a ball, as well as by his batting.* **fields, field ed, field ing.**

field er (fēl′dər), *n.* a player in the outfield in baseball. *He is a poor hitter, but he is one of the best fielders in the league.* **field ers.**

field trip, *n.* a journey to a place that allows people to gather facts by watching and listening. *Today we will go on a field trip to the museum.* **field trips.**

fierce (firs), *adj.* 1. savage; cruel; wild. *The fierce mountain lion attacked a flock of sheep.* 2. violent. *The fierce wind blew at seventy miles an hour.* 3. intense. *You will face fierce competition for the job.* **fierc er, fierc est; fierce ly,** *adv.*

fife (fīf), *n.* a musical instrument somewhat like a flute, having a shrill, high tone. *The fife is often played, together with drums, to make music for marching.* **fifes.**

fif teen (fif′tēn′), *n.* one more than fourteen; ten plus five; 15. *The sum of seven and eight is fifteen.* **fif teens.**

fif teenth (fif′tēnth′), *n.* 1. one of fifteen equal parts. *Each of the fifteen had one fifteenth of the cake.* **fif teenths.**

adj. 2. coming after fourteen others; the fifteenth in order. *I was the fifteenth person to arrive.*

fifth (fifth), *n.* 1. one of five equal parts. *Each of the five people had one fifth of the cake.* **fifths.**
adj. 2. coming after four others; the fifth in order. *Henry was the fifth person in line.*

fif ty (fif′tē), *n.* 1. one more than forty-nine; 50. *I have collected fifty books on space.* 2. **fifties,** the time of life from fifty through fifty-nine. *She was in her fifties, but she looked younger.* **fif ties.**

fig (fig), *n.* a sweet fruit, shaped like a pear and grown in warm climates. *Figs can be eaten fresh, but often they are dried and packaged.* **figs.**

fight (fīt), *n.* 1. a struggle to beat or overcome someone or something by force. *The boys stopped the fight between the two dogs.* 2. any struggle. *The senator put up a fight for the new bill for gun control.* **fights.**
v. 3. to try to overcome someone or something by using force. *Boxers wear padded gloves when they fight. Wild animals fight with their teeth and claws.* 4. to work hard in helping to overcome. *Doctors fight disease.* **fights, fought, fight ing.**

fight er (fīt′ər), *n.* a person who fights. *The two fighters will meet next week for the boxing championship.* **fight ers.**

fig ure (fig′yər), *n.* 1. a shape or outline. *My older sister is on a diet to improve her figure.* 2. a drawing or diagram. *A science book has many figures to illustrate the text.* 3. a pattern; a design. *Do you like the figures in our new curtains?* 4. a symbol for a number. *3, 8, and 96 are figures.* 5. a price. *In fall, you can buy summer clothes at a low figure.* 6. the appearance or character of a person or animal. *The cat was a sad figure as it came in from the rain tired, cold, and wet.* 7. **figures,** arithmetic. *He is good at figures.* 8. **figure of speech,** an unusual way of using words

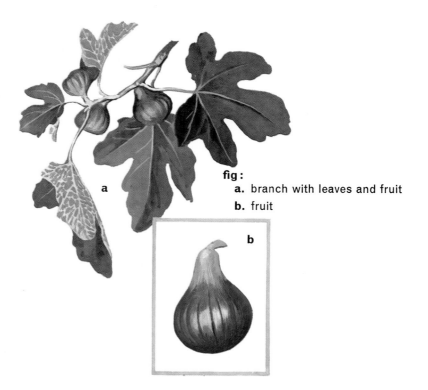

fig:
a. branch with leaves and fruit
b. fruit

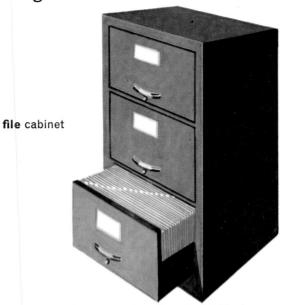

file cabinet

to make a meaning forceful. "*She is a ray of sunshine*" *is a figure of speech that is more effective than* "*she is cheerful.*" **fig ures.**

v. 9. to appear in an important way. *Great scientists figured in developing the use of the atom to produce energy.* 10. **figure in,** to have something to do with. *Hard work figured in his good grades.* 11. **figure out,** (a) to get a result by the use of figures. *He figured out the answer to the arithmetic problem.* (b) to understand. *I can't figure out why the car won't start.* **fig ures, fig ured, fig ur ing.**

fig ured (fig′yərd), *adj.* decorated with figures or designs. *A figured necktie would make a good birthday present.*

file¹ (fīl), *n.* 1. a case or cabinet in which letters and other papers are arranged in order. *We need more files in this office.* 2. the papers, letters, and cards arranged in an orderly way. *In the "A" file you will find a carbon copy of every letter to Mr. Anderson.* 3. a row of people or things one behind the other. *In a fire drill, pupils leave the school in single file.* **files.**

v. 4. to arrange letters and other papers in order. *Miss Jones is accurate in filing.* 5. to move in a line, one behind another. *Let us file out slowly and without any pushing.* **files, filed, fil ing.**

file² (fīl), *n.* 1. a steel bar with a rough surface that is used for smoothing or sharpening hard or uneven surfaces. *Use the file to wear away the rust spots on the bumper of the car.* 2. a flat metal strip used for smoothing the fingernails and toenails. *Use your nail file on that broken nail.* **files.**

v. 3. to use a file for smoothing or sharpening. *File the blades on the lawn mower once a month.* **files, filed, fil ing.**

fil i gree (fil′ə grē), *n.* 1. an ornament made in a delicate, lacy form. *A filigree is usually made of gold or silver wire.* 2. something delicate or fancy. *Filigree designs are used on buildings as part of the decoration.* **fil i grees.**

fill (fil), *v.* 1. to put as much as possible into; make full. *Before crossing the desert, we filled the car's tank with gasoline. We also filled the radiator with water.* 2. to become full. *The swimming pool was slowly filling with water.* 3. to have; hold. *He fills the position of manager of the factory.* 4. to supply what is needed. *The druggist filled the prescription.* 5. to stop up a hole or opening. *The dentist filled my tooth. The workmen filled the break in the street.* **fills, filled, fill ing.**

n. 6. enough to satisfy. *He ate and drank his fill.* 7. anything used to fill a hole or space. *Stones were used as the fill for the country road.* **fills.**

fill ing (fil′ing), *n.* a material used to fill something. *The dentist put two metal fillings in my teeth.* **fill ings.**

film (film), *n.* 1. a thin coating. *After the first cold night the pond had a film of ice on it. A film of dust covered every table in the house.* 2. a thin, flat material coated with a chemical and used for taking photographs. *The roll of film in my little camera will take eight pictures. A longer roll of film is used to take motion pictures.* 3. a motion picture. *Many old films are seen on television.* **films.**

v. 4. to cover with a thin layer. *The window was filmed with ice.* 5. to make a movie. *The movie took seven months to film.* **films, filmed, film ing.**

fil ter (fil′tər), *n.* 1. a device for cleaning a substance like air or water by sending it through sand, cloth, paper, charcoal, etc. *The filter on the furnace is filled with dirt that was prevented*

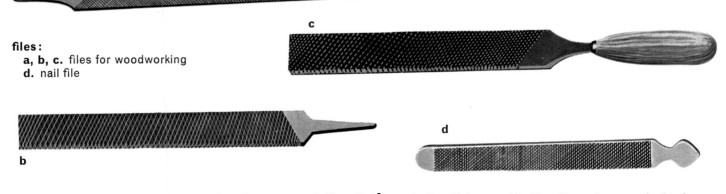

files :
　a, b, c. files for woodworking
　d. nail file

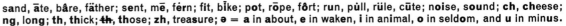

sand, āte, bâre, fäther; sent, mē, fėrn; fit, bīke; pot, rōpe, fôrt; run, pùll, rüle, cūte; noise, sound; ch, cheese; ng, long; th, thick; ᵺ, those; zh, treasure; ə = a in about, e in waken, i in animal, o in seldom, and u in minus.

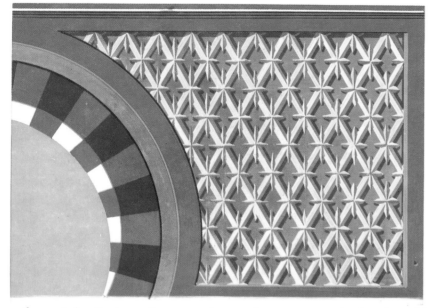

architectural **filigree**

filigree jewelry

from entering the house. 2. an attachment for a camera that prevents certain colors from appearing in a photograph. *A yellow filter partially prevents blue light from reaching the film.* **fil ters.**

v. 3. to pass through a filter. *Drinking water from Lake Michigan is filtered in large buildings near the shore.* 4. to be a filter for. *Charcoal filters water.* **fil ters, fil tered, fil ter ing.**

fin (fin), *n.* 1. one of the movable, winglike parts on the body of a fish. *A fish uses its fins to move and to steer itself in water.* 2. anything like a fin. *Underwater swimmers attach rubber fins to their feet to help them move faster.* **fins.**

fi nal (fī′nl), *adj.* 1. last; closing; coming at the end. *The final examination is given near the end of the semester.* 2. not to be changed. *The umpire's decision is always final.* **fi nal ly,** *adv.*

n. 3. **finals,** the last game or games; the last tests. *The tennis team made the finals and then lost. We have our finals in school this week.*

fi na le (fī nä′lē), *n.* the end of something as the final act of a play or the concluding number of a concert. *After the finale the audience applauded.* **fi na les.**

fi nal ly (fī′nl ē), *adv.* at last. *I finally got the job done.*

fi nance (fə nans′, fī′nans), *n.* 1. the management of large amounts of money. *The banker knows about finance.* 2. **finances,** the amount of money a person has. *Henry mowed lawns to improve his finances.* **fi nan ces.**

v. 3. to pay for. *Dorothy's aunt will finance her trip to New England.* **fi nanc es, fi nanced, fi nanc ing.**

fi nan cial (fə nan′shəl, fī nan′shəl), *adj.* concerning money. *He wants advice on his financial problems.* **fi nan cial ly,** *adv.*

find (fīnd), *v.* 1. to come upon accidentally; locate an object by chance. *You may find my brother at the summer camp.* 2. to look for and

get back a lost object. *We will find my watch.* 3. to learn about; discover. *I find him to be an interesting person. Can you find the dates of the French Revolution?* **finds, found, find ing.**

n. 4. something discovered or found. *The employer told his friends that hardworking Bob was a good find.* **finds.**

fine¹ (fīn), *adj.* 1. good; excellent. *The city has fine parks and beaches. He has a fine record for being on time.* 2. pleasant; clear, with sunshine. *The month of June usually has fine days.* 3. having small grains. *They bought fine sand for the baby's sandbox.* 4. small. *Some of the print in contracts is so fine it is hard to read.* 5. delicate; easily broken. *The rare, expensive, fine dishes from Holland are on display.* 6. **fine arts,** painting, music, sculpture, literature, etc. *The study of the fine arts gives a person an appreciation of beautiful works of art.* **fin er, fin est; fine ly,** *adv.*

fine² (fīn), *n.* 1. money paid as a punishment for breaking a rule or law. *I paid a fine of ten cents because my library book was overdue.* **fines.**

v. 2. to make someone pay money as a punishment. *The judge fined the driver of the speeding car.* **fines, fined, fin ing.**

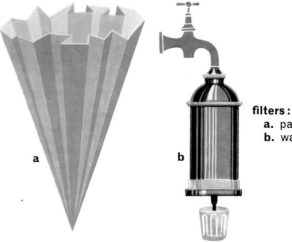

filters:
  a. paper filter
  b. water filter

a

b

fin ger (fing′gər), *n.* 1. one of the five separate parts at the end of the hand. *Sometimes we say that we have four fingers and a thumb.* 2. anything shaped like a finger. *The fingers of the glove were made of leather.* **fin gers.**
v. 3. to touch with the fingers. *He fingered the wood to see if it was smooth.* **fin gers, fin gered, fin ger ing.**

fin ish (fin′ish), *v.* 1. to come to an end; complete or become completed. *He finished his homework and went outside to play. The movie finished at 9:30. Finish your dinner.* 2. to put a certain kind of surface on. *Frank finished the table with paint.* 3. to use up. *I will finish this bottle of milk.* **fin ish es, fin ished, fin ish ing.**
n. 4. an end. *Everyone stayed to the finish of the school play.* 5. a surface. *The boys polished the car so often that its finish was like a mirror.* **fin ish es.**

fin ished (fin′isht), *adj.* completed; final. *The finished painting was very beautiful.*

fi nite (fī′nīt), *adj.* having certain limits; that which can be measured. *The distance from New York to San Francisco is finite.* **fi nite ly,** *adv.*

fiord or **fjord** (fyôrd), *n.* a narrow inlet from the ocean, often between steep cliffs. *Norway has many fiords, which were used as protection for sailing ships years ago.* **fiords** or **fjords.**

fir (fèr), *n.* 1. an evergreen tree with cones and needlelike leaves. *A fir is a popular Christmas tree.* 2. the wood of the evergreen. *Fir has a pleasant smell when burned in the fireplace.* **firs.**

fire (fīr), *n.* 1. a burning material giving off heat and light. *The campers made a fire at night. The fire at the factory luckily started after all the workers had gone home.* 2. strong feeling. *The speech was full of fire.* 3. the shooting of guns. *The soldier's medal was for bravery under fire.* **fires.**

fiord

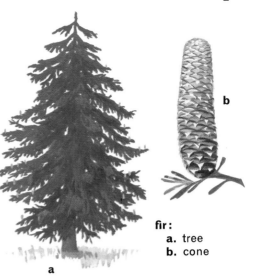

fir:
a. tree
b. cone

v. 4. to set on fire. *The Fire Commissioner said that the building was fired at three o'clock in the morning.* 5. to keep burning; start burning. *The school janitor fires the furnace.* 6. to shoot from a gun. *The rancher fired three shots at the wolf.* 7. to excite; stir up. *The coach fired up his boys during the time out. The story of the early settlers fired my imagination.* 8. to let go; dismiss from a job. *He was fired for a good reason; he didn't work hard enough.* **fires, fired, fir ing.**

fire alarm, *n.* a device that goes off when a fire breaks out. *The fire alarm bell suddenly rang.* **fire alarms.**

fire ball (fīr′bôl′), *n.* 1. something that looks like a ball of fire, such as a ball of lightning. *The fireball appeared in the heavy storm.* 2. a large, bright meteor. *A fireball appeared in the western sky last night.* **fire balls.**

fire crack er (fīr′krak′ər), *n.* a roll of paper containing gunpowder, which explodes with a loud noise when lighted. *Firecrackers are set off on Independence Day (the Fourth of July) as part of a fireworks show.* **fire crack ers.**

fire fly (fīr′flī), *n.* a small flying insect which gives off a light in the dark. *At night during summer the air is filled with little flashing yellow lights from fireflies.* **fire flies.**

fire man (fīr′mən), *n.* 1. a man whose job is to put out fires in buildings. *Firemen rescue people from burning buildings.* 2. a man who tends the fire in a furnace. *The big office building has three firemen.* **fire men.**

fire place (fīr′plās′), *n.* an open place built of brick or stone for holding a fire. *A fireplace in a home is connected to a chimney so that the smoke can escape.* **fire plac es.**

fire proof (fīr′prüf′), *adj.* 1. made of material that cannot burn, or cannot easily burn. *All hotels and schools must be fireproof.*
v. 2. to put something on a material so that it will be fireproof. *Fireproofing the curtains in*

a theater is required by law. **fire proofs, fire-proofed, fire proof ing.**

fire works (fīr′wėrks′), *n. pl.* firecrackers, sky-rockets, sparklers, and other things that make loud explosions or beautiful lights at night. *We celebrate the Fourth of July by going to see the fireworks.*

firm[1] (fėrm), *n.* a business owned by a group of persons. *Butler and Company is the name of the firm owned by Mr. Butler, Mr. McAllister, and Mr. Warner.* **firms.**

firm[2] (fėrm), *adj.* 1. hard; solid. *They left the muddy road and walked on firm ground.* 2. not changing; not moved easily. *The building's foundation is firm. A child has firm faith in his father.* 3. not shaking; steady. *The racing driver keeps a firm hand on the steering wheel.* 4. strong; determined. *The captain of a ship gives firm directions to the crew.* **firm er, firm est; firm ly,** *adv.*

first (fėrst), *adj.* 1. before the others. *Tomorrow we will have the first game of the season. Take the first road to the right.* 2. best. *We eat meat of the first quality.* 3. highest in musical pitch. *He sings first tenor.* **first ly.**
adv. 4. before any others. *She arrived first at the party.* 5. for the first time. *When did you first come to the neighborhood?*
n. 6. someone or something that is first. *He was the first in line.* 7. the beginning. *At first we didn't talk much; now he is my best friend.* **firsts.**

first aid, *n.* emergency help given to a person before a doctor comes. *We are learning first aid at school.* **first aids.**

fish (fish), *n.* 1. an animal that lives in water, has fins, and breathes air through gills. *Most fish have scales covering their bodies. Many fish are good to eat.* **fish** or **fish es.** (See illustration on following page.)
v. 2. to try to catch fish. *Jerry and his father go to the lake each summer to fish.* 3. to search for something. *He fished in the crowded drawer for the ticket.* 4. to try to get something by hinting. *Mary fished for an invitation by saying, "I'd like so much to go!"* **fish es, fished, fish ing.**

fish bowl (fish′bōl′), *n.* a bowl filled with water in which fish are kept. *A fishbowl is a small aquarium.* **fish bowls.**

fish er man (fish′ər mən), *n.* a person who catches fish, either to make a living or just for fun. *The fisherman sold a ton of fish that he caught from his boat in the Atlantic Ocean. Tom and*

fisherman

Harry are good fishermen; they brought home a whole string of fish from the lake. **fish er men.**

fish ery (fish′ər ē), *n.* 1. the business of catching fish. *Fishery is important to the people living near the oceans and the Great Lakes.* 2. a place where the business of catching fish is carried on. *Tuna are caught in the Pacific fisheries.* **fish er ies.**

fish hook (fish′hůk′), *n.* a hook with a sharp end used for catching fish. *Fishhooks are of many sizes, depending on the size of the fish to be caught.* **fish hooks.**

fishing boat, a small ship used in fishing. *Every morning a fleet of fishing boats leaves the harbor.* **fishing boats.**

fist (fist), *n.* the hand, when closed tightly. *A fist is made by bending the fingers inward, the thumb on the outside. Boxers soak their fists in salt water to make them tough.* **fists.**

fit[1] (fit), *v.* 1. to be right and proper for. *Her dignified appearance fits the solemn occasion.* 2. to be the right shape or size. *The dog's new collar*

fishhooks

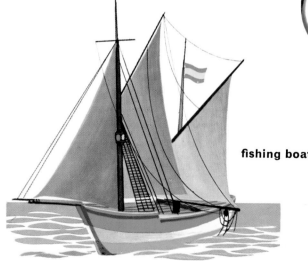

fishbowl

fishing boat

FISH

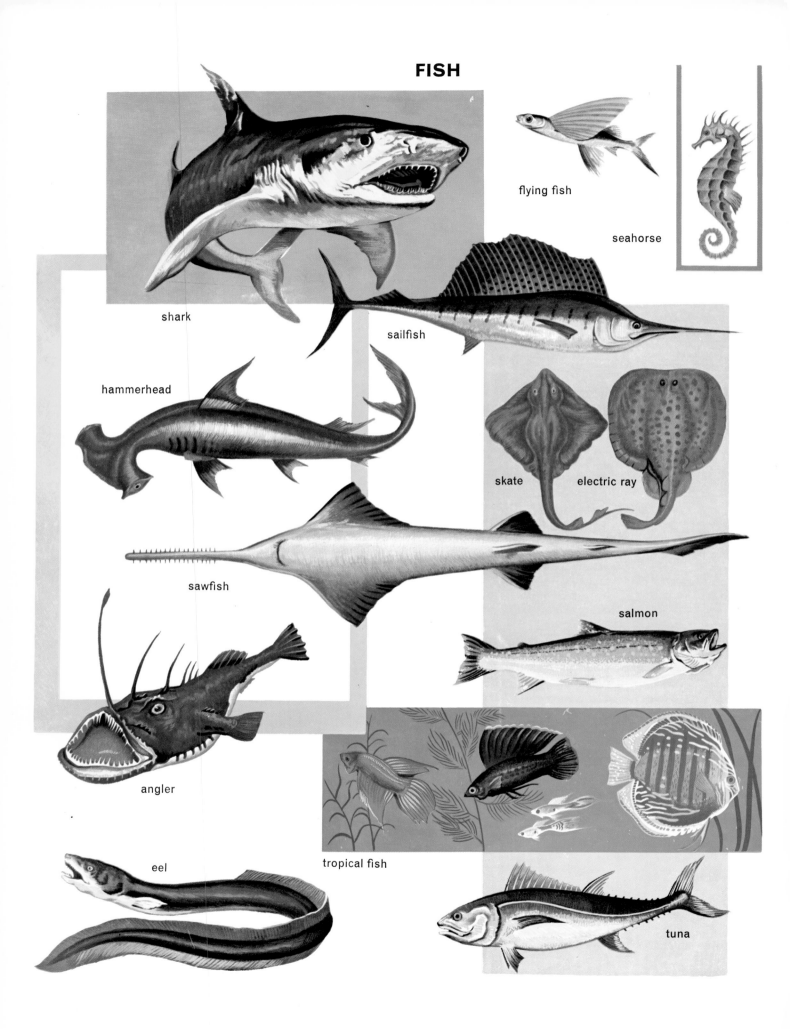

flying fish

seahorse

shark

sailfish

hammerhead

skate   electric ray

sawfish

salmon

angler

tropical fish

eel

tuna

fits. **3.** to make the right size and shape. *The tailor fitted Walter's suit.* **4. fit out,** to get what is needed for some purpose. *The men going to the Arctic were fitted out with warm clothes.* **fits, fit ted** or **fit, fit ting.**

adj. **5.** right and proper; suitable. *This movie is fit for the whole family. It is not fit to interrupt when someone else is talking.* **6.** healthy; in good condition. *The doctor says he is fit.* **fit ter, fit test; fit ly,** *adv.*

n. **7.** the way something fits. *The new shoes are a good fit.* **fits.**

fit² (fit), *n.* **1.** a sudden outburst. *He had a fit of laughter when he saw the comedy.* **2.** an attack, sometimes a disease or emotion that starts suddenly. *Some people have sudden fits of anger.* **3. by fits and starts,** by starting and stopping often; not even. *She cleaned her room by fits and starts.* **fits.**

fit ting (fit′ing), *adj.* **1.** correct; suitable; right. *It is fitting that we honor our fallen soldiers on Memorial Day.* **fit ting ly,** *adv.*

n. **2.** a trying on of a suit, dress, etc. to make sure it will fit. *She went to the tailor for a fitting this afternoon because she is having a coat made.* **3. fittings,** furnishings; fixtures. *The fittings for an office include file cabinets, desks, and chairs.* **fit tings.**

five (fīv), *n.* one more than four; **5.** *The sum of three plus two is equal to five.* **fives.**

fix (fiks), *v.* **1.** to repair or mend. *That broken chair can be fixed by Tim in his workshop.* **2.** to set firmly; make firm. *They fixed the birdhouse in the branches of the tree. Fix important facts in your mind before a test. Fix your attention on the speaker.* **3.** to decide on. *They fixed the date of the spelling contest. The artist fixed a price for his painting.* **4.** to get ready. *I can fix breakfast.* **5.** to put in order. *She is always fixing her hair.* **fix es, fix ed, fix ing.**

n. **6.** a situation that is hard to get out of. *The pup was in a fix when he walked into the mudhole.* **fix es.**

fixed (fikst), *adj.* **1.** fastened or placed securely. *That desk is fixed; don't try to move it.* **2.** settled; final. *Don't try to bargain; it is a fixed price.* **3.** steadily directed. *The ship was on a fixed course.* **fix ed ly,** *adv.*

fix ture (fiks′chər), *n.* anything set in place to stay for a long time. *Fixtures in a house include bathtubs and kitchen sinks.* **fix tures.**

flag¹ (flag), *n.* **1.** a piece of cloth with certain colors and designs. *A flag may stand for a country, a state, a city, or an organization.* **2.** a piece of cloth used as a signal. *A red flag often means "danger."* **flags.**

v. **3.** to signal with a flag. *The fast train was flagged to a stop by the flagman of the freight train.* **flags, flagged, flag ging.**

flag² (flag), *v.* to lose strength; to become weak. *At the end of the hot day, the pupils' energy flagged.* **flags, flagged, flag ging.**

flag³ (flag), *n.* a plant having large flowers and leaves shaped like swords; the iris. *A sweet-smelling flag plant was on the table.* **flags.**

flag man (flag′mən), *n.* a man who signals with a flag. *There are flagmen at busy railroad crossings. A flagman on a freight train has the job of signaling other trains.* **flag men.**

flag pole, *n.* the pole from which a flag is flown. *We have a flagpole in front of our house.* **flag poles.**

flake (flāk), *n.* **1.** a small, thin piece of something. *No two flakes of snow are exactly alike, although every flake has six sides. We use soap flakes to wash clothes.* **flakes.**

v. **2.** to break off in tiny pieces. *The paint on the house is flaking.* **flakes, flaked, flak ing.**

flaky (flāk′ē), *adj.* **1.** of or like flakes. *The flaky white clouds moved rapidly across the sky.* **2.** coming off in layers. *The paint on the old house is flaky.* **flak i ly,** *adv.*

flame (flām), *n.* **1.** the burning gas of a fire that can be seen, usually as yellow, red, or blue. *The flames from the forest fire shot upward.* **2.** anything as hot or as bright as a flame. *Her cheeks looked like flames when we all praised her.* **3.** a very intense feeling. *A flame of eagerness burned within him.* **flames.**

v. **4.** to burn with a flame; blaze. *The campfire flamed.* **5.** to burst out with feeling. *The trapped animal flamed with anger.* **flames, flamed, flam ing.**

fla min go (flə ming′go), *n.* a pink or red bird with long legs and neck. *Flamingos live near the water in warm climates.* **fla min gos** or **fla min goes.**

flamingos

flashlight for a camera

flask

flea

flap (flap), *n.* 1. a part that hangs from one edge only. *The pocket of a coat has a flap over the opening. The flap of an envelope folds over the main part and, when moistened, seals the contents.* 2. a slapping sound or movement from something broad and flat. *The window shade made a flap as it sprang upward. The flap of the bird's wings causes it to fly.* **flaps.**
v. 3. to move up and down or back and forth. *Birds flap their wings to fly.* 4. to move with a slapping sound. *The flag flapped in the wind.* **flaps, flapped, flap ping.**

flash (flash), *n.* 1. a light or something bright that appears suddenly and briefly. *A flash of lightning appeared in the distance.* 2. a sudden outburst. *His flash of humor cheered us all. She felt a flash of joy when she heard the good news.* 3. a very short time. *I'll be there in a flash.* 4. a radio news bulletin. *Here is a flash from the police department.* **flash es.**
v. 5. to shine brightly. *The lights flashed on the electric signs.* 6. to pass or move swiftly. *The cars flashed by on the highway. The results of the election were flashed to Europe.* 7. to show emotion. *Her eyes flashed with anger.* **flash es, flashed, flash ing.**

flash light (flash′līt′), *n.* 1. a small electric light with batteries. *A camper carries a flashlight to find his way in the dark.* 2. a light used to take pictures in darkness or in dim light. *The photographer used his flashlight to take pictures of the graduation.* **flash lights.**

flask (flask), *n.* a bottle that has a small neck. *Flasks are used to hold liquids in laboratories by scientists.* **flasks.**

flat[1] (flat), *adj.* 1. even; level. *The beach is flat. The tabletop is flat.* 2. having very little flavor. *Give me another cola; this one tastes flat.* 3. not very thick. *A dime is flat.* 4. absolute; final. *Tom's mother gave a flat "No" when he asked if he could go out.* 5. having lost air. *He had a flat tire and had to put air into it.* 6. dull. *Use flat paint on your house.* **flat ter, flat test; flat ly,** *adv.*
n. 7. land that is level. *The ground is low and wet along the river flat.* 8. a tone one-half step below the natural tone. *Below G is F, but halfway between G and F is G flat.* 9. the sign in music (♭) which shows that a note is to be played one-half step lower. *Some songs have all notes marked with flats.* 10. a shallow box containing earth in which young plants are sold. *Let's buy three flats of those flowers.* **flats.**
v. 11. to make or become flat. *The player flatted the fourth note.* **flats, flat ted, flat ting.**
adv. 12. in a flat way. *He tripped and fell flat on the ground.* 13. exactly. *He ran the mile in four minutes flat to win the race.*

flat[2] (flat), *n.* an apartment with all rooms on one floor. *You can get tired climbing up the stairs to our third-floor flat.* **flats.**

flat car (flat′kär′), *n.* a railroad freight car with no sides and no top. *A flatcar might carry a load of long logs, which could not fit through the door of a regular freight car.* **flat cars.**

flat ter (flat′ər), *v.* 1. to praise too much without really being honest. *The salesman flattered me because he wanted to sell me something expensive.* 2. to make something or someone seem better or more attractive. *My mother likes this photograph because it flatters her by making her look younger.* 3. to make someone feel honored and pleased. *I was flattered by receiving a personal letter of thanks from the governor.* **flat ters, flat tered, flat ter ing.**

fla vor (flā′vər), *n.* 1. taste. *Most summertime drinks have a sweet flavor.* **fla vors.**
v. 2. to give taste to; to season. *A good cook knows how much salt and pepper to add to flavor the food.* **fla vors, fla vored, fla vor ing.**

fla vor ing (flā′vər ing), *n.* something that gives a certain flavor. *Most children like to drink milk with a chocolate flavoring.* **fla vor ings.**

flaw (flô), *n.* 1. a defect; any crack, scratch, break, etc. *You can see the flaw in this glass.* 2. any fault or mistake. *The flaw in her character is her thoughtlessness.* **flaws.**

flax (flaks), *n.* a plant with thin stems and blue flowers, grown for use of its fibers and seeds. *The fibers of flax stems are spun into thread to make linens. Some oils are made from the seeds of flax.*

flea (flē), *n.* a tiny insect that hops and has no wings. *Fleas bite animals and people to take small amounts of blood.* **fleas.**

fled (fled), past tense and past participle of **flee.**

flee (flē), *v.* to hurry away; run away; escape. *A rabbit will flee from a fox.* **flees, fled, flee ing.**

fleet[1] (flēt), *n.* 1. a number of ships, airplanes, automobiles, etc. moving together. *The fishing fleet sails from the bay every morning.* 2. a group of ships commanded by one officer. *The Sixth Fleet of the United States Navy was ordered to the South Seas.* 3. the navy of a country. *The British fleet has a long history of success.* **fleets.**

fleet[2] (flēt), *adj.* fast; swift. *The fleet horse set a record for the Derby.* **fleet er, fleet est; fleet ly,** *adv.*

flesh (flesh), *n.* 1. the part of the body that is a covering for the bones. *Your body adds flesh when you gain weight.* 2. meat. *We eat the flesh of animals, birds, and fish.* 3. the parts of fruits and vegetables that can be eaten. *The flesh of a plum or orange is sweet.* 4. man's body, but not his spirit. *The pain was almost more than flesh could take.* 5. **flesh and blood,** relative or relatives. *Your cousins are your flesh and blood.*

flew (flü), past tense of **fly.**

flick er[1] (flik′ər), *v.* 1. to shine or burn unsteadily. *The electric lights flickered and then went out. The candles flickered in the breeze.* **flick ers, flick ered, flick er ing.**
n. 2. an unsteady light. *The mountain boy read at night by the flicker of a candle.* **flick ers.**

flick er[2] (flik′ər), *n.* a kind of woodpecker. *The flicker is a brown bird with wings colored yellow or gold on the underside.* **flick ers.**

fli er (flī′ər), *n.* a person or thing that flies. *Aviators are fliers. A fast train making few stops is a flier.* **fli ers.**

flight[1] (flīt), *n.* an escape; a running away. *The animals were put to flight by the sight and sound of the hunters.* **flights.**

flight[2] (flīt), *n.* 1. the act of flying. *The flight of birds has always interested man.* 2. a trip through the air. *The next flight on this airline is at half-past four.* 3. the distance flown. *The flight to Paris by airplane is more than one thousand miles nonstop.* 4. a group of things or beings going through the air together. *A flight of wild geese passed overhead.* 5. a group of stairs between floors. *He lived three flights up.* 6. a going beyond the limits. *He had flights of fancy that carried him away.* **flights.**

fling (fling), *v.* 1. to throw. *Fling this stone into the water.* 2. to move a part of the body rapidly or suddenly. *I saw him fling his arms around his father's neck as he said good-bye.* **flings, flung, fling ing.**
n. 3. a throw or toss. *Bob gave the coin a fling, and it landed on the floor.* 4. a lively dance. *The Highland fling is a well-known Scottish dance.* 5. a time when a person does anything they want. "*Have your fling when you're young,*" *the man said.* **flings.**

flip (flip), *v.* 1. to put in motion with a snap of a finger and thumb; toss. *Tom flipped a coin to see who would go; it came up heads, so Bert went.* 2. to turn rapidly. *That man can do a double flip off the diving board. We flip the pages of a book as we read it.* **flips, flipped, flip ping.**
n. 3. a tossing or throw. *Kenneth won on the first flip of the coin when it came up heads.* **flips.**

flip-flop (flip′flop′), *n.* 1. a backward somersault. *The boys in our gym class learned how to do a flip-flop.* **flip-flops.**
v. 2. to perform a flip-flop or something like it; to make a quick change of opinion or behavior. *The acrobat flip-flopped across the stage.* **flip-flops, flip-flopped, flip-flop ping.**

flirt (flėrt), *v.* 1. to pretend to be in love just for the fun of it. *She liked to flirt with the boys by telling them they were handsome.* 2. to think about, but not to do anything about. *For a while the boy flirted with the idea of running away.* **flirts, flirt ed, flirt ing.**
n. 3. a person who flirts. *Nobody takes Alice seriously because everyone knows she is a flirt.* **flirts.**

flit (flit), *v.* to move quickly and lightly; fly swiftly. *The little bird flitted from branch to branch. Ideas are always flitting through his mind.* **flits, flit ted, flit ting.**

float (flōt), *v.* 1. to stay or move in or on top of air, water, or other liquid. *Ice floats in water. We lay on our backs and watched the clouds floating in the sky.* 2. to make float. *The boy floated his toy boat in the shallow water.* 3. to put into the water. *They made a wooden raft and floated it.* **floats, float ed, float ing.**
n. 4. something that floats. *The float on a fishline bobs up and down when a fish grabs the hook.* 5. a decorated truck or wagon used in a parade. *Some floats made of wood and cloth look like castles, football games, and buildings.* **floats.**

flock (flok), *n.* 1. a group of animals or birds that stay together. *There are fifty sheep in the flock on the grassy hill.* 2. a group of people belonging to a church. *The minister visits each member of his flock.* **flocks.**
v. 3. to gather in large numbers. *People flocked to see the movie star.* **flocks, flocked, flock ing.**

flood (flud), *n.* 1. a great quantity of water produced by rain or by an overflowing river. *During the storm, the river went over its banks, causing a flood in the town.* 2. anything that comes in quantities. *The famous actor received a flood of letters. A flood of sunshine filled the room.* 3. **the Flood,** in the Bible, the water that covered the earth on which Noah's ark floated. **floods.**
v. 4. to flow over its banks. *The river flooded when the heavy snows melted.* 5. to give in large numbers. *They flooded the girl with gifts on her birthday.* **floods, flood ed, flood ing.**

flood gate (flud′gāt′), *n.* a gate that controls

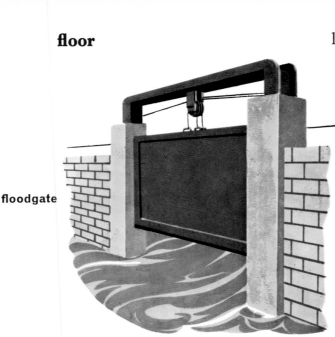

floodgate

the flow of water. *Floodgates are opened and closed in rivers, canals, and streams as the water rises and falls.* **flood gates.**

floor (flôr), *n.* 1. the part of a room or hall on which we walk. *Most rooms have wooden floors, but the entrance floors of office buildings are made of stone or tile.* 2. the bottom of something. *The floor of the ocean contains food plants.* 3. a story of a building. *We live on the third floor of the apartment building.* **floors.**
v. 4. to put a floor in. *They floor their tent on camping trips.* 5. to knock down. *The good boxer floored the other with two punches.* **floors, floored, floor ing.**

flop (flop), *v.* 1. to move; to be blown about. *When our dog sticks his head out of the car, his long ears flop in the wind.* 2. to drop or fall. *We were so tired that we flopped on our cots and went to sleep.* 3. to toss from side to side. *The fish flopped in the net.* **flops, flopped, flop ping.**

Flor i da (flôr′ə də), *n.* a state in the southeastern part of the United States. *Florida is a popular resort state, and the visitors provide about half of the state's income.*

flour (flour), *n.* 1. wheat or any other grain that has been ground to a powder or meal. *Flour is used in making breads and cakes.* **flours.**
v. 2. to sprinkle flour on. *Sometimes meat is floured before it is fried.* **flours, floured, flour ing.**

flour ish (flér′ish), *v.* 1. to grow in a strong and healthy way. *The fruit trees flourished this year.* 2. to be successful; prosper; thrive. *The television industry has flourished rapidly.* 3. to wave something in the air. *The visitor to Texas was handed a cowboy hat, which he flourished.* **flour ish es, flour ished, flour ish ing.**
n. 4. fancy curves and waves sometimes added to handwriting. *The flourishes in his signature made it difficult to read.* 5. a passage of music that is showy. *The flourish of trumpets announced the arrival of the king.* **flour ish es.**

flowerpot

flow (flō), *v.* 1. to move in a stream, as water does. *A river flows to the ocean. The long line of cars flowed to the airport. Blood flows through your body.* 2. to hang loose and waving. *The minister's black robe flowed behind him as he walked.* **flows, flowed, flow ing.**
n. 3. the act of flowing. *A tiny flow of water came from the hose. The flow of people stopped at three o'clock.* 4. a smooth, even, steady movement. *The flow of the sea is restful to watch.* 5. the coming in of the tide. *The flow of the tide is toward the shore at this time.* **flows.**

flower (flou′ər), *n.* 1. the blossom of a plant. *Flowers are usually colorful, and contain the seeds of the plant.* 2. a plant that is grown mainly because it has pretty flowers. *Mother planted flowers to decorate our front yard.* 3. the best part. *The orchestra is made up of the flower of our musicians.* **flow ers.**
v. 4. to produce flowers. *Some plants flower in summer; others flower in fall.* 5. to thrive; to be at its highest point. *The study of science is flowering today.* **flow ers, flow ered, flow er ing.**

flow er pot (flou′ər pot′), *n.* a pot used to hold dirt in which a plant can grow. *Some flowerpots are big and can hold huge plants that will reach to the ceiling.* **flow er pots.**

flow ery (flou′ər ē), *adj.* 1. filled with flowers. *The flowery gardens in the park bring many visitors.* 2. filled with fine language and big words. *If his flowery speech had been simpler, he would have gotten his point across.*

flown (flōn), past participle of **fly.**

flu (flü), *n.* influenza. *Ann caught the flu.*

fluff (fluf), *n.* 1. a soft, light piece of material. *Down and bits of cotton or wool are fluff.* **fluffs.**
v. 2. to make puffy and soft. *The housekeeper fluffed the pillows by shaking them.* **fluffs, fluffed, fluff ing.**

fluffy (fluf′ē), *adj.* like fluff; covered with fluff; soft, loose, and light. *The baby liked the fluffy toy cat.* **fluff i er, fluff i est.**

flume (flüm), *n.* 1. a large, inclined slide built for carrying water downward. *The lumbermen sent logs down the flume to the river.* 2. a deep, narrow valley with a stream at the bottom. *The stream of a flume usually flows fast.* **flumes.**

flung (flung), past tense and past participle of **fling.**

flu o ri da tion (flür′ə dā′shən), *n.* the addition of a small amount of a chemical called fluoride to water. *Scientists have found that fluoridation of drinking water helps prevent tooth decay.*

flute (flüt), *n.* 1. a musical instrument made like a tube, with holes on the side and an opening at one end across which a player blows. *The flute's holes are covered by keys or by the player's fingers to make the different tones of the scale.* **flutes.**
v. 2. to play on a flute. *He fluted an old English song.* **flutes, flut ed, flut ing.**

sand, āte, bâre, fäther; sent, mē, férn; fit, bīke; pot, rōpe, fôrt; run, pùll, rüle, cūte; noise, sound; ch, cheese; ng, long; th, thick; t̶h̶ those; zh, treasure; ə = a in about, e in waken, i in animal, o in seldom, and u in minus.

FLOWERS

corolla

filament

calyx

receptacle

sepal

ovary

PARTS OF A FLOWER

cyclamen iris narcissus geranium dahlia

pansy tulip orchid hyacinth rose

fly

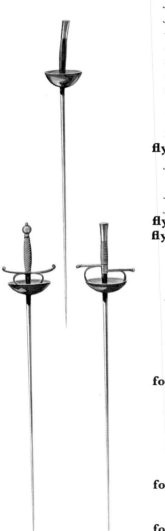

fencing **foils**

flut ter (flut′ər), *v.* 1. to move the wings without flying. *The bird fluttered its wings when it was caught in the bushes.* 2. to move quickly back and forth. *The leaves fluttered in the wind. The sheets fluttered as they hung on the clothesline. The flag is fluttering at the top of the pole.* 3. to hurry in an excited, confused way. *Whenever we go on a vacation, Mother flutters about the house just before we leave.* **flut ters, flut tered, flut tering.**
n. 4. a state of excitement or confusion. *Everyone was in a flutter the day my brother came home from college.* **flut ters.**

fly[1] (flī), *v.* 1. to move through the air by using wings. *Birds are animals that fly.* 2. to move through or in the air. *We will fly to Michigan in the airliner.* 3. to go fast; speed. *The children flew to their Father when he came home.* 4. to float, or cause to float or wave, in the wind. *The flag flies every day in front of our school. The kite flew so high that it appeared only as a speck in the sky.* 5. to hit a fly in baseball. *The batter flied to the left fielder.* **flies, flew, fly ing.**
n. 6. a flap or piece of cloth on clothing which covers up a row of buttons or a zipper. *Mary ripped the fly of her dress by catching the cloth in the zipper.* 7. a baseball hit high in the air in a baseball game. *If the fly is caught, the batter is out.* **flies.**

fly[2] (flī), *n.* 1. an insect with two wings. *A housefly and a mosquito are flies.* 2. a bait used by fishermen and made to look like a fly. *Some flies are bright pieces of feather or silk that attract fish, which bite at them.* **flies.**

fly er (flī′ər), *var. of* **flier.**

fly ing (flī′ing), *adj.* 1. moving with wings. *A mosquito is a flying insect.* 2. floating; waving. *The flying flags on the buildings were taken down at sunset.* 3. moving through the air. *Some people say that they have seen flying saucers.* 4. hurried; hasty. *The salesman made a flying trip that night.* 5. sudden; quick; rapid. *The fox got off to a flying start, and left the hunters behind.*
n. 6. the act of moving through air. *Flying is an enjoyable pastime for many people.*

foam (fōm), *n.* 1. a quantity of small bubbles. *When you pour a glass of cola, foam gathers on top. The big waves of the ocean have foam on top.* **foams.**
v. 2. to produce foam; make tiny bubbles. *The ocean foams during a storm.* **foams, foamed, foam ing.**

fod der (fod′ər), *n.* dry, coarse food for cattle, horses, and sheep. *Hay is a good fodder.* **fod ders.**

foe (fō), *n.* an enemy; opponent. *North High School will be the football foe of South High School next Saturday.* **foes.**

fog (fog), *n.* 1. a cloud near the surface of the land; heavy mist. *Fog, like clouds, is made of tiny drops of water.* 2. a state of confusion. *Tom was in a fog because he received so much advice.* **fogs.**
v. 3. to cover with fog or moisture. *The meadow was fogged. My car windows are fogged.* **fogs, fogged, fog ging.**

fog gy (fog′ē), *adj.* 1. having fog; misty enough to make seeing difficult. *No one wanted to drive on such a foggy night.* 2. confused. *I have only a foggy memory of my vacation.* **fog gi er, fog gi est; fog gi ly,** *adv.*

fog horn (fog′hôrn), *n.* a loud horn used to warn ships of danger, especially during a dense fog. *Ships sound their foghorns to let other ships know they are coming.* **fog horns.**

foil[1] (foil), *n.* 1. a sheet of metal so thin it seems like paper. *Sandwiches are wrapped in aluminum foil.* 2. something that makes another thing look better by contrast. *The black wall was a good foil for the colorful painting.* **foils.**

foil[2] (foil), *n.* a light, thin sword used in fencing. *A foil has a dull point so that no one will get hurt.* **foils.**

foil[3] (foil), *v.* to keep from succeeding. *The bank clerk foiled the robber's plans.* **foils, foiled, foil ing.**

fold[1] (fōld), *v.* 1. to bend something over. *You fold a letter before putting it in an envelope.* 2. to hold together. *The minister folded his hands in prayer.* 3. to wrap. *Fold your lunch in this paper.* **folds, fold ed, fold ing.**
n. 4. a bend made by folding. *The newspaper had a fold in it.* **folds.**

fold[2] (fōld), *n.* a pen for sheep. *The shepherd found the lamb that had gotten out of the fold.* **folds.**

fold er (fōl′dər), *n.* 1. a folded piece of heavy paper or cardboard in which letters and other papers are placed. *The teacher kept a folder of our spelling tests.* 2. a booklet of folded sheets. *An advertising folder is a small book which tells us about a product.* **fold ers.**

fo li age (fō′lē ij), *n.* the leaves of trees and plants. *The foliage in a jungle is thick.*

folk (fōk), *n.* 1. people. *We were treated well by the city folk. It is fun to visit with the folks you meet on a vacation.* 2. **folks,** relatives. *Charles liked to spend the summer with his mother's folks.* **folk** or **folks.**
adj. 3. belonging to the common people. *At the concert we listened to the folk songs of many different countries.*

fol low (fol′ō), *v.* 1. to come after; go after. *Night follows day. The lost puppy followed Scott to his home.* 2. to go on; to travel along. *Follow Howard Street until you get to the school.* 3. to be the result of. *My mother's good cooking follows years of experience. The famous musician's beautiful playing follows twenty years of practicing many hours a day.* 4. to be led by; obey. *Follow my directions. The advice of a doctor should be followed.* 5. to take as one's job; make a living from. *John decided to follow the teaching profession.* 6. to understand; to show interest in. *You didn't seem to follow the lecture.* **fol lows, fol lowed, fol low ing.**

fol low er (fol′ō ər), *n.* a person led by the ideas or beliefs of another; one who follows. *Mary is a follower of the Christian religion.* **fol low ers.**

fol low ing (fol′ō ing), *n.* 1. a number of people who follow or show interest in something. *Baseball has a large following in the United States and Japan.* **fol low ings.**
adj. 2. going or coming after; next. *We met on the following Thursday for lunch.*

fol ly (fol′ē), *n.* 1. the state of being foolish; foolishness. *His folly caused him to put the quarter in the pocket of his coat that had a hole.* 2. any foolish act, idea, etc. *Climbing a mountain without ropes and other safety equipment is utter folly.* **fol lies.**

fond (fond), *adj.* 1. loving; affectionate. *He is very fond of his pet rabbits.* 2. attracted to; liking too much. *He is so fond of baseball that he would rather watch a game than eat his supper.* 3. sincere and warm. *It is my fond wish that you be happy and successful in whatever you do.* **fond er, fond est; fond ly,** *adv.*

food (füd), *n.* 1. anything taken in by people, plants, and animals that maintains life and growth. *No living thing can survive without some form of food.* 2. solid nourishment, rather than liquid. *We enjoyed many kinds of food and drink at the dinner.* 3. anything that promotes growth or development. *Challenging problems are food for the mind.* **foods.**

fool (fül), *n.* 1. a person who is without sense; a person who behaves in a foolish manner. *Only a fool would waste water during a drought.* 2. a person who was formerly kept in a nobleman's court to amuse and entertain people. *The fool performed juggling tricks and danced for the king.* **fools.**
v. 3. to behave in a foolish manner; to act like a fool. *The boys were fooling around, wasting their time, when they should have been working.* 4. to trick or attempt to trick someone. *His costume fooled me into thinking he was someone else.* **fools, fooled, fool ing.**

fool ish (fül′ish), *adj.* senseless; silly; unwise. *Before the invention of the airplane, many foolish attempts to fly were made.* **fool ish ly,** *adv.*

foot (fut), *n.* 1. that part of the body that is at the end of the leg and on which a person or animal stands and walks. *My feet were sore and tired from so much walking.* 2. the bottom part of anything; the lowest part of something. *The dog slept at the foot of the bed. We waited for him at the foot of the stairs. A line was drawn across the foot of the page.* 3. a measure of length that equals twelve inches. *He is over six feet tall.* 4. a unit of rhythm in a line of poetry. *This sentence is marked in feet:* " *There was | an old wo | man who lived | in a shoe |* " *has four feet.* **feet.**
v. 5. to walk. *We footed the entire trip back to the cabin from the lake.* 6. to pay. *Who will foot the bill for this broken window?* **foots, foot ed, foot ing.**

foot ball (fut′bôl′), *n.* 1. a game played on a field by two teams of eleven men each, in which points are scored by carrying a ball over a goal line or by kicking it between two upright posts on the goal line. *Anyone who plays football should wear special pads and a helmet to avoid injury.* 2. the air-filled leather ball used

feet of different animals

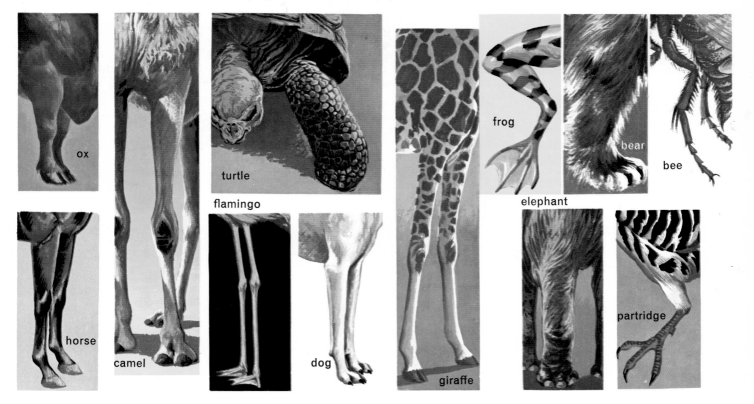

ox

turtle

flamingo

frog

bear

bee

elephant

horse

camel

dog

giraffe

partridge

in this game. *George was given a football and shoulder pads for his birthday.* **foot balls.**

foot print (fùt′print′), *n.* a mark made by a foot. *We followed the footprints of a deer through the woods.* **foot prints.**

foot step (fùt′step′), *n.* 1. a step in walking. *Take one footstep forward, and turn to the right.* 2. the distance covered by such a step. *The tree was twenty footsteps from the cave.* 3. the sound made by a person as he walks. *We heard footsteps coming around the corner of the building.* 4. a footprint. *It was easy to find him by following his footsteps in the sand.* 5. **follow in someone's footsteps,** to do what someone else has done; to be like someone else. *He followed in his father's footsteps by becoming a doctor and taking care of his father's patients.* **foot steps.**

for (fôr), *prep.* 1. with the purpose of; having the object of. *We are going for a ride on our bicycles. I bought a ruler for drawing straight lines.* 2. suited to; to be used by or with. *The movie was for children, so our parents didn't go. The top drawer in the dresser is for shirts.* 3. sent or given to; intended to be received by. *There was a letter for you in the mail today.* 4. during the time of. *He has been sleeping for several hours. For an entire week the weather has been cold.* 5. intending to reach, do, etc. *He left for Europe today. She went to the library for a book.* 6. in place of. *You can use the sofa for a bed if you get tired.* 7. in exchange of. *You can buy this pen for one dollar. I'll give you this bat for your baseball.* 8. in support of. *He voted for Sara in the class election.* 9. with the reason that; because of. *We jumped for joy when the game ended. He was arrested for driving too fast.* 10. as being. *You may accept his story for the truth if you wish.* 11. in the amount of. *The store sent us a bill for eleven dollars.* 12. having feelings toward. *The lost child longed for his parents.*
conj. 13. since; because. *I missed the beginning of the play, for I was late.*

for bid (fər bid′), *v.* to refuse to permit something; to rule against. *Mother forbade us to leave the house. Talking in class is forbidden by the teacher.* **for bids, for bade** or **for bad, for bid den, for bid ding.**

force (fôrs), *n.* 1. strength; power; energy. *The lumberman swung his ax with great force.* 2. strength, power, or energy used against a person or thing. *The window was stuck, but Father got it open by force.* 3. any group of people who are trained to work together. *He is a member of the police force.* 4. anything that causes things to move, stop, or stay where they are. *If you drop something, the force of gravity will pull it to the floor.* **forc es.**
v. 5. to make a person or thing do something. *The robbers forced him to give them his money.* 6. to use strength or power to do something. *He forced his way out of the crowded room.* 7. to break open by using strength or power. *They forced*

the window with an iron bar. 8. to speed the growth of. *The new fertilizer forced the plants to grow quickly.* **forc es, forced, forc ing.**

ford (fôrd), *n.* 1. a place in a river or stream which is shallow enough to allow men and animals to walk or drive across. *The cowboys took the herd along the banks of the river until they found a ford.* **fords.**
v. 2. to cross a river or stream at such a place by walking or driving across. *During the day we forded two streams and swam across another.* **fords, ford ed, ford ing.**

fore cast (fôr′kast′), *v.* 1. to predict something; to tell what will happen in the future. *The weatherman was unable to forecast the weather more than three days in advance.* **fore casts, fore cast** or **fore cast ed, fore cast ing.**
n. 2. a prediction; a telling of what will happen in the future. *The forecast for tomorrow is warm, dry weather and clear skies.* **fore casts.**

fore head (fôr′id, fôr′hed′), *n.* that part of the face which is above the eyes. *His hair was combed down over his forehead.* **fore heads.**

for eign (fôr′ən), *adj.* 1. not in one's own country; outside one's own country or region. *The language spoken in most foreign countries is not English.* 2. having to do with countries other than one's own. *Foreign governments carry on much business with our government.* 3. not natural; not belonging. *Being unhappy is foreign to his usual nature. There is a foreign object floating in the can of oil.*

fore noon (fôr′nün′), *n.* that part of the day that is between sunrise and noon. *We will start our camping trip during the forenoon tomorrow.* **fore noons.**

for est (fôr′ist), *n.* 1. a large number of trees growing closely together over a wide area of land; woods. *Very little light reached the floor of the forest through the thick branches of the trees.* **for ests.**
v. 2. to cover a wide area of land with trees. *Today the high price of lumber makes it profitable for the private landowner to forest his property.* **for ests, for est ed, for est ing.**

for ev er (fər ev′ər), *adv.* 1. for all time; without ending. *Your allowance cannot be expected to last forever.* 2. always. *He is forever stopping work to rest.*

for get (fər get′), *v.* 1. to have no memory of; to be unable to recall. *I forget where I left my books.* 2. to neglect to because of carelessness, lack of interest, etc. *He forgot to bring the present to the birthday party. I forgot to do my arithmetic homework last night.* **for gets, for got, for got ten** or **for got, for get ting.**

for give (fər giv′), *v.* to pardon; to excuse; to stop feeling angry at someone. *He forgave me for taking his book when I explained that it was not done on purpose. Please forgive my error; I thought you were someone else.* **for gives, for gave, for giv en, for giv ing.**

for got (fər got′), past tense and past participle of **forget**.

for got ten (fər got′n), past participle of **forget**.

fork (fôrk), *n.* 1. an instrument having two or more points attached to a handle, used for serving or eating food. *The baby ate her food with a spoon, since she had not yet learned how to use a fork.* 2. a tool with a long handle and two or more long points, used for digging, lifting hay, etc. *The farmer used a fork to pitch hay from the wagon into the loft in the barn.* 3. something shaped like a fork. *The man struck one of the sides of the tuning fork to produce a musical tone.* 4. the place where something divides. *When we came to a fork in the road, we were unable to decide which direction to take.* 5. one of the branches of a thing that is divided. *We took the left fork, and found that it ended at a deserted farm.* **forks.**
v. 6. to use a fork for lifting, digging, etc. *He forked the ground in his garden to loosen it before he planted the seeds.* 7. to divide or be divided into branches. *We will meet in an hour at the place where the road forks.* **forks, forked, fork ing.**

form (fôrm), *n.* 1. the shape of something. *We saw a cloud, having the form of an elephant.* 2. anything that gives shape to something. *The cement was poured into forms to set. Molds, such as those for cakes or cookies, are forms.* 3. a particular kind or variety of something. *Steam is a form of water. Airplanes and helicopters are forms of aircraft.* 4. the way in which something is done. *He is a fast runner, but his form is unusual.* 5. a social custom; an accepted manner of behavior. *It is against form to leave a party without saying good-bye.* 6. a paper containing blank spaces which are to be filled in. *Mark your answers on the answer form, not in the test book.* 7. any of the ways in which a word can be written or said. *The plural form of "child" is "children."* **forms.**
v. 8. to give a shape to something. *The children used snow, buttons, a broom, a carrot, and an old hat to form their snowman.* 9. to take shape; to take a certain shape. *Clouds of steam formed above the boiling water.* 10. to train; develop; instruct. *The patterns of a person's life are formed in his childhood. Education forms the mind.* 11. to make up. *All of the pupils in a school form its student body.* **forms, formed, form ing.**

for mal (fôr′ml), *adj.* 1. according to accepted customs, rules, or practices. *A formal party was held to honor the visiting king.* 2. done officially in an exact, definite manner. *The formal signing of the treaty came several weeks after the war ended.* **for mal ly,** *adv.*

for mer (fôr′mər), *adj.* 1. coming earlier in time or before in position. *A former owner of this house was a vice-president of the United States.* **for mer ly,** *adv.*
n. 2. the first of two things talked about. *Tom was given the choice of visiting Los Angeles or New York, and he chose the former because he had never been to California.*

for mer ly (fôr′mər lē), *adv.* at a previous time; in time past. *The manager had formerly been a member of the baseball team.*

for mu la (fôr′myə lə), *n.* a statement that tells the chemical contents of something or states a rule to be followed in doing something. *The formula "height × width," which means units of height times units of width, is used to find the area of a rectangle. Oxygen is one of the ingredients in the formula for water.* **for mu las** or **for mu lae** (fôr′myə lē).

fort (fôrt), *n.* a building or other place that is built for defense against an attack by enemies. *The fort was located on an open stretch of ground so that no one could approach it without being seen.* **forts.**

forth (fôrth), *adv.* 1. forward in time. *From that day forth the princess lived happily in the castle.* 2. onward in position or place. *The child squared his shoulders and went forth to the school for the first time.* 3. out. *In the spring the trees put forth new buds that will become leaves.*

for ti fi ca tion (fôr′tə fə kā′shən), *n.* 1. a strengthening; a making ready against something. *The fortification of the city was completed moments before the attack began.* 2. anything like a wall, ditch, fort, etc. built for increasing the strength of a place or for protection. *The soldiers were ordered to leave their battlefield fortifications and attack the enemy.* **for ti fi ca tions.**

for ti fy (fôr′tə fī), *v.* 1. to strengthen against attack by building walls, forts, etc. *The soldiers fortified the army post.* 2. to add strength to something. *Some cereals are fortified with vitamins.* **for ti fies, for ti fied, for ti fy ing.**

fort night (fôrt′nīt), *n.* a period of two weeks. *He spent his month's vacation in visiting his grandmother for a week, working on his uncle's farm for a fortnight, and going to the seashore for a week.* **fort nights.**

for tu nate (fôr′chə nit), *adj.* 1. lucky. *You were very fortunate to find the lost bracelet.* 2. bringing good luck; happening by good luck. *Buying those oil stocks was a fortunate investment, since their value has greatly increased.* **for tu nate ly,** *adv.*

for tune (fôr′chən), *n.* 1. a large amount of money, property, etc.; wealth. *He made a fortune by discovering a gold mine.* 2. luck. *It was blind fortune that led me to the place where the treasure map was hidden.* 3. whatever happens to a person, good or bad. *It was his fortune to become a doctor and serve mankind.* 4. what is going to happen to a person; a person's future. *The old woman read my fortune from the lines on my palm.* **for tunes.**

for ty (fôr′tē), *n.* four times ten; one more than thirty-nine; 40. *His father's age is forty.* **for ties.**

for ward (fôr′wərd), *adv.* 1. toward the front.

---

sand, āte, bâre, fäther; sent, mē, fèrn; fit, bīke; pot, rōpe, fôrt; run, pùll, rüle, cūte; noise, sound; ch, cheese; ng, long; th, thick; ~~th~~, those; zh, treasure; ə = a in about, e in waken, i in animal, o in seldom, and u in minus.

The crowd pushed forward to see the magician.
adj. 2. at or near the front. *The forward position in the parade was occupied by two drummers.* 3. to the front; onward. *The forward advance of the team was stopped just short of the goal line.* 4. advanced; better in some way than the ordinary. *A child who can do higher mathematics and read difficult books is forward for his years.* 5. bold; rude. *The forward child interrupted our conversation.*
v. 6. to help; to assist. *Abraham Lincoln forwarded the cause of justice for all people in the United States.* 7. to send on to another place. *Our mail was forwarded to us while we traveled in Europe.* **for wards, for ward ed, for ward-ing.**
n. 8. a player on a team who is stationed near the opponent's goal in position to score. *The center threw the basketball to one of the forwards, who calmly sank the winning basket.* **for wards.**

fos sil (fos′l), *n.* any traces or remains of animals or plants from an earlier age found in earth, ice, coal, or rock. *The boys found several fossils of leaves as they explored the mountain cave. The skeleton in the museum is the fossil of a prehistoric dinosaur.* **fos sils.**

fought (fôt), past tense and past participle of **fight.**

foul (foul), *adj.* 1. dirty; offensive; unpleasant to the senses. *A foul odor filled the air as the rubber tires began to burn.* 2. evil; wicked. *Crimes are foul deeds.* 3. unfair. *When the boy was looking another way, his opponent hit him a foul blow on the back of the head.* 4. stormy. *The boating trip was called off because of foul weather.*
v. 5. to make dirty. *Black smoke from the factory fouled the air of the town.* 6. to tangle or become tangled. *The string on the kite fouled in the tree.* **fouls, fouled, foul ing.**
n. 7. in some sports, a play or action that is against the rules. *A foul was called when someone ran into Ralph just as he was shooting a basket.*

fossil

fountain

8. in baseball, a hit that lands outside the base lines. *The batter had hit four fouls before he struck out.* **fouls.**

found[1] (found), past tense and past participle of **find.**

found[2] (found), *v.* to establish. *This city was founded by a group of settlers from Pennsylvania.* **founds, found ed, found ing.**

foun da tion (foun dā′shən), *n.* 1. the part of a building on which the structure rests. *Ditches were dug and forms were built before the concrete was poured for the foundation of the new building.* 2. an idea or plan on which all other ideas or plans depend. *Your argument is false because its foundation is not correct.* 3. an establishing. *The foundation of the oldest American college was in 1636.* **foun da tions.**

found er[1] (foun′dər), *n.* a person who establishes or founds something. *Thomas Jefferson was one of the founders of the United States.* **found ers.**

foun der[2] (foun′dər), *v.* 1. to take in water and sink. *The boat foundered when it struck a rock in the storm.* 2. to be unable to walk or move properly or easily. *We found the lost cow foundering in the water and pulled her out with a rope.* **foun ders, foun dered, foun der ing.**

foun tain (fount′n), *n.* 1. a natural spring of water. *We were thirsty and exhausted when we found the fountain at the foot of the mountain.* 2. a place where a drink may be obtained. *We went to the soda fountain for a glass of root beer. The drinking fountains in the park are not working.* 3. a stream or spray of water that is forced into the air; the structure through which these streams are forced. *In the center of the park there was a fountain sending water high into the air.* 4. a source; any place where something is obtained. *The library is a fountain of knowledge.* **foun tains.**

foun tain pen, *n.* a writing instrument that contains a refillable supply of ink which is drawn off as the pen is used. *His fountain pen was empty, and he had forgotten to bring a bottle of ink.* **foun tain pens.**

four (fôr), *n.* one more than three; 4. *Those four and Bob formed a basketball team.* **fours.**

four teen (fôr′tēn′), *n.* one more than thirteen; 14. *Fourteen can be subtracted from forty-two three times.* **four teens.**

fourth (fôrth), *adj.* 1. next after the third. *This is the fourth time you have been late to school.* *n.* 2. any of four equal parts. *A quarter is a fourth of a dollar.* **fourths.**

fowl (foul), *n.* 1. any bird. *We saw all kinds of fowl in the bird house at the zoo.* 2. any bird that is raised on a farm to be used for food or to supply eggs. *The farmer had several hundred fowl, including chickens, ducks, and turkeys, on his farm.* **fowls** or **fowl.**

fox (foks), *n.* 1. a wild animal similar to a dog, having a pointed face, pointed ears, and a long, bushy tail. *The fox is a favorite animal in stories and fables because he is supposed to be sly and smart.* 2. this animal's fur. *The collar of this coat is fox, not mink.* 3. a clever or sly person. *That fox fooled me into trading my new kite for a broken baseball bat.* **fox es.**

foxy (fok′sē), *adj.* clever; sly; like a fox. *He tried pretending that he knew something, but we knew he was just being foxy.* **fox i er, fox i est; fox i ly,** *adv.*

frac tion (frak′shən), *n.* 1. one or more of the equal parts into which a thing is divided. *The fraction ¾ represents three of four equal parts.* 2. a small bit; a part of something. *He never does more than a fraction of the work that is assigned.* **frac tions.**

frag ile (fraj′ əl), *adj.* easily broken; delicate. *Glass is more fragile than plastic. Many plants have fragile flowers.* **frag ile ly,** *adv.*

fra grant (frā′grənt), *adj.* having a sweet smell. *Roses are fragrant flowers.* **fra grant ly,** *adv.*

frail (frāl), *adj.* 1. weak; sickly. *She was a little frail after having the flu, but she's much better now.* 2. delicate; easily broken. *A spider spins a frail web across open spaces.* **frail er, frail est; frail ly,** *adv.*

frame (frām), *n.* 1. anything fitted together as the supporting part of a structure. *The frame of the house was built before the roof was put on.* 2. the bones of the body; skeleton. *His frame is larger than his brother's, but he weighs less.* 3. a structure that holds or surrounds something. *Put the picture back in the frame. The window frames on the house need to be painted.* 4. the structure of anything; the way in which something is made or organized. *The frame of our government is described in the Constitution.* 5. mental state; mood. *On their way to the picnic*

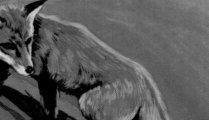

fox

the children were in a happy frame of mind. **frames.**

v. 6. to build; put together; construct; plan. *If you don't understand my question, I'll try to frame it differently.* 7. to put a frame around. *They framed the painting and hung it on a wall.* **frames, framed, fram ing.**

frame work (frām′werk′), *n.* the structure around which a thing is built. *The huge tent was made of canvas on a metal framework.* **frame- works.**

frank (frangk), *adj.* free in speech; openly showing feelings, opinions, etc. *His answers to our questions were frank and honest.* **frank er, frank est; frank ly,** *adv.*

fra ter ni ty (frə tėr′nə tē), *n.* a group of men or boys joined together by common interests or for a common purpose. *My father was a member of a fraternity when he was in college.* **fra ter ni ties.**

free (frē), *adj.* 1. not a slave; not owned or controlled by another person; having liberty. *The citizens of the United States are free people.* 2. not prevented from speaking, acting, or thinking. *The judge was free to discuss the case after the jury had returned its decision.* 3. loose; not tied down or fastened. *We tried to catch the free end of the running dog's leash.* 4. not costing anything; without charge. *Our neighbor gave us free tickets to the baseball game.* 5. **free from** or **free of,** without. *The tickets were given to us free of charge.* **fre er, fre est; free ly,** *adv.*

v. 6. to let go; to set free. *We freed the dog from his leash, and he ran joyfully through the park. The slaves were freed during the Civil War.* 7. to release from something. *He was freed from his debt when he returned the goods to the store.* **frees, freed, free ing.**

free dom (frē′dəm), *n.* 1. the state of having liberty. *The Revolutionary War was fought to gain freedom for our country.* 2. complete and un- limited use. *We gave them the freedom of our house and car while they were visiting us.* 3. open- ness in speaking; frankness. *We were surprised*

by his freedom in asking questions of the speaker.
4. ease in movement. *The desk was so small that he had no freedom when he sat in it.* **free doms.**

freeze (frēz), *v.* 1. to become ice; to turn to ice. *The lake froze during the night.* 2. to chill something until it becomes cold and hard as ice. *Housewives freeze food for use at a later time.* 3. to get very cold. *He froze when he went outside without a sweater.* 4. to be hurt or to die from cold temperatures or frost. *Sometimes the orange trees in Florida freeze and produce no oranges.* 5. to become completely still from fear. *Animals sometimes freeze when they see an enemy.* **freez es, froze, fro zen, freez ing.**
n. 6. a freezing or being frozen. *The berry crop suffered a severe freeze last night.* 7. a time of very cold weather. *A hard freeze lasted almost two weeks last February.* **freez es.**

free zer (frēz′ər), *n.* a cabinet where foods are kept frozen. *A freezer keeps ice cream solid and makes ice cubes.* **free zers.**

freight (frāt), *n.* 1. a load of goods carried from place to place by ship, truck, bus, train, or plane. *Most freight in the United States is carried by rail.* 2. the price or cost of shipping goods. *We paid the freight when the order was delivered.* 3. a railroad train that carries freight and not passengers. *The children counted the cars of the long, slow-moving freight train.* **freights.**

French (french), *adj.* 1. of the country France, the people who live there, or the language they speak. *The French capital is Paris. Joe misplaced his French book.*
n. 2. the people who live in France. *The French are widely known for their excellent food.* 3. the language spoken by the people of France. *French is studied in American schools.*

fre quen cy (frē′kwən sē), *n.* 1. a frequent happening; the fact of happening often. *The*

freezer

frequency of the children's visits gave her great pleasure. 2. the number of times something occurs within a certain time. *The human heart beats with a frequency of about eighty times a minute.* **fre quen cies.**

fre quent (frē′kwənt for 1, fri kwent′ for 2), *adj.* 1. happening often. *Uncle Leo goes on frequent hunting trips, sometimes once a week.* **fre quent ly,** *adv.*
v. 2. to go to often. *Mary frequents several shops, looking for interesting old lamps.* **fre quents, fre quent ed, fre quent ing.**

fresh (fresh), *adj.* 1. newly made, grown, or gathered. *Mother baked fresh bread this morning. This fresh corn was picked from the stalk only a few minutes ago. The sign on the bench says "Fresh Paint," which means that the bench has just been painted and is still wet.* 2. clean. *Breathe this fresh air.* 3. not worn or dirty. *The little girl was wearing fresh clothes.* 4. not tired; lively and wide awake. *A short nap sometimes will make a person feel fresh.* 5. not salty. *Most lakes and rivers are fresh water; the ocean is salt water.* **fresh er, fresh est; fresh ly,** *adv.*

fresh man (fresh′mən), *n.* a student in the first year of high school or college. *Since they are new in the school, freshmen sometimes follow special rules.* **fresh men.**

fret[1] (fret), *v.* 1. to make or become irritated or unhappy. *Kathy is fretting about the test tomorrow. Don't fret about something you cannot do anything about.* **frets, fret ted, fret ting.**
n. 2. a worry; irritation. *Laugh away your frets and cares.* **frets.**

fret[2] (fret), *n.* any of the small ridges beneath the strings of a guitar, banjo, etc. *The right hand plays the strings, and the fingers of the left hand press on the frets.* **frets.**

fret[3] (fret), *n.* a design of short straight lines put together as a decoration. *Frets are often used to ornament chairs, fire screens, benches, and other furniture.* **frets.**

fric tion (frik′shən), *n.* 1. the rubbing of one object against another. *The friction of one cold hand against the other will produce heat.* 2. the force that slows the motion of things that touch. *Walking on ice is difficult because there is not much friction between the shoes and the ice. Eskimos put water on the runners of their sleds, and the water turns to ice, which reduces the friction.* 3. difficulty of any kind caused by disagreement. *The friction between Dave and Larry was caused by their different opinions about football teams.* **fric tions.**

Fri day (frī′dē, frī′dā), *n.* the sixth day of the week. *Friday is the end of the school week.* **Fri days.**

fried (frīd), past tense and past participle of **fry.**

friend (frend), *n.* 1. a person that one likes. *Betty is a good friend who is always ready to cheer me up.* 2. a person who helps out or supports something. *He is a friend of the poor and does his* *best to find jobs for them.* 3. a person who is on the same side. *Friends get together against a common foe.* **friends.**

friend ly (frend′lē), *adj.* 1. in the manner of a friend. *Her friendly manner made everyone relax. The older man gave some friendly advice to the younger man.* 2. showing good feelings; not hostile. *That friendly dog only looks fierce, but he is gentle. Canada is a friendly neighbor of the United States.* **friend li er, friend li est; friend li- ly,** *adv.*

friend ship (frend′ship), *n.* a friendly feeling; friendly association. *The friendship between us has lasted for years.* **friend ships.**

frig ate (frig′it), *n.* a medium-sized warship with sails and three masts. *Frigates, which were in use from about 1750 to 1840, carried from thirty to fifty guns.* **frig ates.**

fright (frīt), *n.* 1. a sudden fear. *The village was filled with fright when the forest fire started.* 2. something that is unpleasant to look at. *After the children played in the mud, their clothes were a fright.* **frights.**

fright en (frīt′n), *v.* 1. to make afraid; to scare. *The Halloween costumes frightened the little girl.* 2. to cause to do something by making afraid. *The campers' fire frightened away the wolves.* **fright ens, fright ened, fright en ing.**

fringe (frinj), *n.* 1. a decorative border on cloth. *A fringe consists of threads hanging loose on the edge of the cloth.* 2. the outside edge. *We stood at the fringe of the crowd, listening to the speaker.* **fring es.**
v. 3. to be placed on the outside edge; to border. *Shrubs fringed the yard.* **fring es, fringed, fring ing.**

frisky (fris′kē), *adj.* lively; wanting to play. *The frisky little dog jumped and ran around the yard.* **frisk i er, frisk i est; frisk i ly,** *adv.*

frog (frog), *n.* 1. a small animal with webbed feet that lives in or around the water. *Frogs have strong legs and are able to jump several times their own length.* 2. **frog in one's throat,** a harsh voice caused by soreness of the throat. *The frog in his throat kept the teacher from talking much today.* **frogs.**

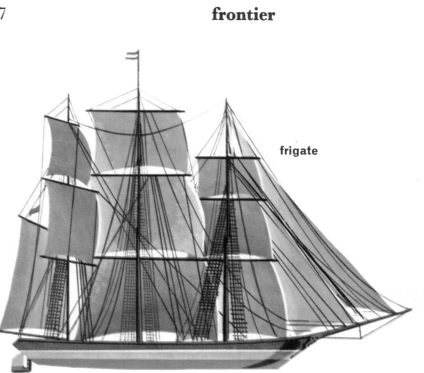

frigate

frol ic (frol′ik), *v.* 1. to play together happily; have fun. *The children ran and frolicked in the park.* **frol ics, frol icked, frol ick ing.**
n. 2. a party where there is a lot of fun; happy play. *On the last day of school, we had a frolic because we all felt we had done well.* **frol ics.**

from (from, frum), *prep.* 1. starting at. *The party will last from two to four in the afternoon. Ten minutes from now we will go. We drove thirty miles from town to get to the picnic area.* 2. out of. *Furniture is made from wood. Take a dollar from the drawer. We live thirty miles from town.* 3. because of; caused by. *He is ill from the cold he got from his sister.* 4. as being unlike. *I can easily tell red from blue.* 5. out of the control of. *Take the magazine from the baby and give her a rubber ball.*

front (frunt), *n.* 1. a part that faces forward. *The pilot sits in the front of the airliner.* 2. the first part. *The front of the house faces the street.* 3. behavior; appearance. *Although the boy was scared, he put up a cheerful front.* 4. the land next to water. *Mr. Bell's cottage is on the lake front.* 5. a place where fighting takes place in a war. *All is quiet on the western front.* 6. **cold front** and **warm front,** masses of cold air or warm air. *A cold front is moving slowly south from Canada.* **fronts.**
v. 7. to face in a certain way. *The old building fronts the river.* **fronts, fronted, front ing.**
adj. 8. located at the first part; of or in the front. *The front lawn needs mowing.*

fron tier (frun tir′), *n.* 1. the farthest edge of the settled part of a country; the begininng of the unknown part. *Our western frontier was the scene of many exciting events in the late 1800's.* 2. boundary; border. *Soldiers are on guard at*

frog

fruit:
a. tomatoes
b. grapes
c. orange

most nations' frontiers. *The United States and Canada have a peaceful frontier.* 3. any new area or idea that is being explored. *We are learning more about the frontiers of space and of medicine.* **fron tiers.**

frost (frôst), *n.* 1. frozen dew or moisture. *Frost forms on the grass in the autumn mornings. In cold weather windows have frost on them.* 2. cold weather. *Frost can hurt a crop of fruit trees.* **frosts.**
v. 3. to cover with icing. *The birthday cake was frosted.* **frosts, frost ed, frost ing.**

frost ing (frôs'ting), *n.* a mixture of sugar, cream, milk or water, eggs, flavoring, etc., used to cover a cake. *Chocolate frosting is my favorite kind.* **frost ings.**

frown (froun), *v.* 1. to wrinkle the forehead and draw the eyebrows together in anger, worry, deep thought, etc. *Mr. Carleton frowned when he heard the boys talking during the program of music. My mother frowns when our old oven doesn't work properly.* **frowns, frowned, frown ing.**
n. 2. a drawing together of the eyebrows,

frying pans

usually in deep thought or in anger. *The girl's frown spoiled her beauty.* **frowns.**

froze (frōz), past tense of **freeze.**

fro zen (frō'zn), 1. past participle of **freeze.** *adj.* 2. covered with ice. *Let's go ice skating on the frozen pond.* 3. killed by a frost or freezing weather. *The frozen blossoms mean we shall have no fruit this year.* 4. kept fresh by a process of freezing. *Frozen foods are used as often as canned foods these days.*

fruit (früt), *n.* 1. the part of certain plants which contains the seeds and is also good to eat. *Oranges, grapes, pears, berries, and peaches are fruits; so is a tomato, although it is used as a vegetable.* 2. the product; the result. *The fruit of his labor is this beautiful drawing.* **fruits.**

fry[1] (frī), *v.* to cook in a pan with fat or grease, over a direct fire. *The odor of bacon frying in the pan is a wonderful smell to a hungry person.* **fries, fried, fry ing.**

fry[2] (frī), *n. pl.* 1. young fishes. *You can't keep the fry; throw them back.* 2. **small fry,** small child or children. *Let's put the small fry to bed.*

fry ing pan, *n.* a long-handled shallow pan used for frying foods. *Mother scrambles eggs in a frying pan.* **fry ing pans.**

fudge (fuj), *n.* 1. a soft candy made of milk, chocolate, sugar, and butter. *Fudge can be made from prepared mixes.* **fudg es.**
interj. 2. nonsense. *Oh fudge, I don't believe it.*
v. 3. gather or put together in a clumsy or untrue way. *Don't fudge your report.* **fudg es, fudged, fudg ing.**

fu el (fū'əl), *n.* 1. anything that is burned to give heat or power. *Coal, oil, wood, and gas are fuels.* 2. anything that makes a strong feeling even stronger. *The unexpected victory added fuel to the crowd's excitement.* **fuels.**
v. 3. to supply with fuel. *The airplane was fueled while in flight.* 4. to get fuel. *The ship had to put into port to fuel.* **fu els, fu eled, fu el ing.**

ful crum (ful'krəm), *n.* the support on which a lever rests when it is lifting an object. *The fulcrum of a seesaw is the bar on which the long board rests.* **ful crums.**

full (fül), *adj.* 1. holding all that is possible. *The full glass of milk almost overflowed. The lake is full of fish.* 2. complete; entire. *We have a full supply of gasoline in the car. Take a full week to rest.* 3. fat and round. *A healthy baby has a full face.* **full er, full est; ful ly,** *adv.*
adv. 4. directly. *He was hit full in the face by the ball.* 5. completely. *The water bucket was filled full of berries.*
n. 6. the greatest amount; the highest degree. *The rich young man lived life to the full.*

ful ly (fül'ē), *adv.* in a way that is complete; wholly. *I am sure that the class fully understands the rule. The bush is fully grown.*

fume (fūm), *n.* 1. a gas; vapor; smoke. *The smell of the fumes from gasoline is strong. The fumes from the burning building lasted for hours.* **fumes.**

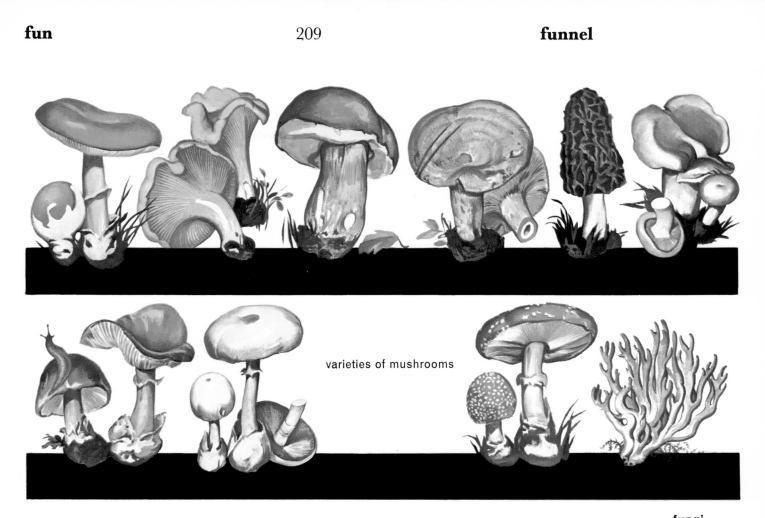

varieties of mushrooms

fungi

v. 2. to give off smoke or vapor. *The wet wood for the campfire fumed but didn't burn.* 3. to show anger and a bad temper by complaining. *The man fumed when the girl at the ticket counter said his plane would leave later than expected.* **fumes, fumed, fum ing.**

fun (fun), *n.* 1. a good time; pleasure; lively and happy play. *We have a lot of fun at the swimming pool on a hot day.* 2. **make fun of,** to make bad jokes about. *The children made fun of the old-fashioned movie.* 3. **in fun,** not seriously; for amusement. *The tricks they played on us were all in fun.*

func tion (fungk/shən), *n.* 1. use; work. *The function of the police is to keep order. Mary has many functions in her new job: she types, files letters, answers the phone, and greets visitors.* 2. a ceremony; an important social gathering. *A function will be held in honor of the famous author. A newspaper reporter goes to many functions, such as weddings, graduations, and parties.* **func tions.** *v.* 3. to do work; run. *Is the New York office functioning well? My watch functions poorly; it seems to be slow all the time.* **func tions, func tioned, func tion ing.**

func tion al (fungk/shən l), *adj.* having a function; working; acting. *There are no useless parts in the functional design of a modern automobile.* **func tion al ly,** *adv.*

fund (fund), *n.* 1. a supply of money. *Albert went to college with expenses paid by a scholarship fund from the school.* 2. a supply; store. *A professor has a fund of knowledge. A storyteller has a fund of stories.* **funds.**

fu ner al (fū/nər əl), *n.* 1. the services held or the things done when the body of a dead person is buried. *The minister spoke and the choir sang at the funeral.* **fu ner als.** *adj.* 2. of a funeral. *The funeral ceremony for the soldier included the firing of rifles as a sign of respect.*

fun gus (fung/gəs), *n.* a plant that has no leaves or flowers or green color. *A mushroom is a fungus. Mold is also a fungus.* **fun gi** (fun/jī) or **fun gus es.**

fu nic u lar (fū nik/yə lər), *adj.* hanging from a rope or cable. *A funicular railway carries people up steep slopes.* (See illustration on following page.)

fun nel (fun/l), *n.* 1. a hollow tube that has a wide cone at one end. *You use a funnel if you want to pour a liquid into a small opening.* 2. the smokestack of a steamship. *Many passenger ships today have fake funnels because the ships burn oil, not coal.* **fun nels.** *v.* 3. to move or pass through a funnel or something like a funnel. *The four expressways funnel traffic into the main highway to the city.* **fun nels, fun neled, fun nel ing.**

sand, āte, bâre, fäther; sent, mē, fėrn; fit, bīke; pot, rōpe, fôrt; run, pull, rūle, cūte; noise, sound; ch, cheese; ng, long; th, thick; ŧ̶h̶, those; zh, treasure; ə = a in about, e in waken, i in animal, o in seldom, and u in minus.

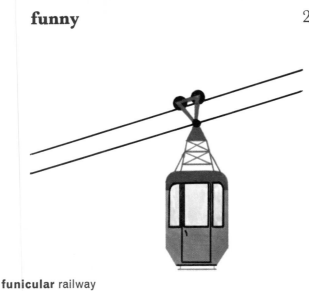

funicular railway

funnels

fun ny (fun′ē), *adj.* 1. comical; that causes laughs; humorous. *Joan and I saw a very funny movie last night; we laughed all the time.* 2. strange; unusual; peculiar. *That is a funny way to act.* **fun ni er, fun ni est; fun ni ly,** *adv.*

fur (fùr), *n.* 1. the thick, soft hair that is on the bodies of many animals. *We brush the cat's fur to keep it shiny.* 2. the skin from a dead animal which has fur. *The Indians presented the white man with many furs.* 3. an article of clothing made of fur. *A fur keeps a person warm.* **furs.** *adj.* 4. made of fur. *Women like to wear fur coats.*

fu ri ous (fyùr′ē əs), *adj.* 1. very angry. *Mother was furious when she found that the puppy had chewed on the furniture.* 2. strong; violent. *The furious storm made the captain of the ship head for a harbor.* **fu ri ous ly,** *adv.*

fur nace (fėr′nis), *n.* an enclosed structure to make a fire in. *Furnaces are used to heat buildings, to melt metal, and to make pottery.* **fur nac es.**

fur nish (fėr′nish), *v.* 1. to supply; to give whatever is necessary. *For the picnic Joan will buy the hot dogs, and I will furnish the potato salad.* 2. to put furniture in. *When are you going to furnish the house?* **fur nish es, fur nished, fur nish ing.**

fur ni ture (fėr′nə chər), *n.* chairs, tables, beds, couches, etc. used in a home. *Styles in furniture change over the years.*

fur row (fėr′ō), *n.* 1. a long, narrow hole made in the ground by a plow. *Seeds are planted in furrows and covered over with earth.* 2. a fold. *When you frown a lot, you sometimes get furrows in your forehead.* **fur rows.**
v. 3. to make furrows in. *The plows furrowed the fields in spring.* **fur rows, fur rowed, fur row ing.**

fur ther (fėr′thər), *adj.* 1. more; extra. *There has been no further news from Buddy.* 2. farther; more distant. *The church is much further away than you think.*
adv. 3. more; to a greater extent. *We will have to think further about going on the trip.* 4. also; besides. *Mother further said she needed some help, so we stayed home.* 5. at or to a greater distance; farther. *You needn't go further.*
v. 6. to help move forward; help to succeed. *The Girl Scouts further their cause by selling cookies.* **fur thers, fur thered, fur ther ing.**

fur ther more (fėr′thər môr′), *adv.* besides; also. *You are late for dinner; furthermore, your hands have not been washed.*

fu ry (fyùr′ē), *n.* 1. great anger. *The peasants were in a fury because the king took all their land.* 2. violence; fierceness. *The old sea captain had been through the fury of many storms.* **fu ries.**

fuse[1] (fūz), *n.* 1. a piece of metal that melts if too much current goes through a wiring

furrows made by a plow

FURNITURE THROUGH THE AGES

Egyptian couch

Etruscan couch

Greek couch

fifteenth century bed

nineteenth century table and chair

eighteenth century table

twentieth century armchair

eighteenth century bed

modern living room furniture

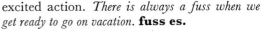

fuse

system. *A fuse is set in a plug that is a part of the electric circuit.* 2. the cord which burns down to a tube filled with gunpowder. *By lighting a fuse, a man has enough time to get out of the way of the explosion.* **fus es.**

fuse² (fūz), *v.* 1. to join metals by melting them together. *Copper and zinc are fused to make brass.* 2. to blend; to unite. *The red and the yellow of the sunset fused to make a beautiful orange.* **fus es, fused, fus ing.**

fuss (fus), *n.* 1. needless bother; unnecessary excited action. *There is always a fuss when we get ready to go on vacation.* **fuss es.**
v. 2. to bother about unimportant matters. *She fussed in the kitchen for three hours before getting dinner.* **fuss es, fussed, fuss ing.**

fus sy (fus′ē), *adj.* 1. very particular. *He is so fussy about his food it's a wonder he eats anything.* 2. heavily decorated. *The fussy dress was decorated with beads, imitation pearls, and flowers. A drawing is fussy when it has too many details in it that are not important.* 3. that cries needlessly. *That fussy baby hasn't been quiet all day—maybe it's the heat.* **fuss i er, fuss i est; fuss i ly, adv.**

fu ture (fū′chər), *n.* 1. the time that is to come. *What are your plans for the future, when you are grown?* **fu tures.**
adj. 2. in the time to come. *The future meetings of the drama club will be announced later.*

fuzz (fuz), *n.* soft hair; down. *A peach has fuzz on its skin.* **fuz zes.**

fuz zy (fuz′ē), *adj.* 1. covered with fuzz. *The kitten is fuzzy.* 2. not clear; blurred. *Some of his snapshots were fuzzy. Carl has a fuzzy memory of the accident.* **fuzz i er, fuzz i est; fuzz i ly, adv.**

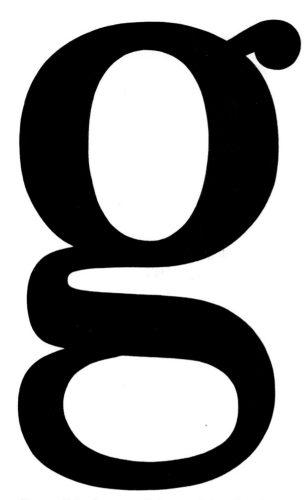

G or **g** (jē), the seventh letter of the alphabet.

gadg et (gaj′ət), *n.* a small, unusual tool with special uses. *Look at this gadget: it's a folding knife, but it also opens to show a fork, spoon, screwdriver, can opener, and four other tools.* **gadg ets.**

gain (gān), *v.* 1. to get; acquire; obtain. *Jimmy gained much baseball experience as bat boy for the Chicago White Sox. I gained ten pounds during summer vacation.* 2. to profit. *He has gained more than one hundred dollars from his investment in stock.* 3. to win. *My mother's cake gained first prize in the baking contest.* 4. to arrive at. *The ship finally gained the harbor.* 5. to make progress; improve. *With much study, he has gained in his speaking of Spanish.* 6. to advance. *The runner in last place slowly gained on the leaders.* **gains, gained, gain ing.**
n. 7. a profit. *This year's gain will be bigger than last year's.* 8. an increase. *The owner of the ball park reported a gain in attendance. His gain in weight, according to the doctor, is good.* **gains.**

gain ful (gān′fəl), *adj.* bringing gain or profits; profitable. *During the summer, many college students need gainful jobs.* **gain ful ly,** *adv.*

gait (gāt), *n.* 1. a measured form of walking. *Bob usually walks with a slow gait.* 2. a pace of a horse. *The fastest gait of a horse is the gallop.* **gaits.**

gal axy (gal′ək sē), *n.* 1. a large group of stars. *No one knows how many galaxies there are in the universe. The Milky Way is the galaxy of which the sun and our solar system are a part.* 2. a brilliant or outstanding group. *The play was performed by a galaxy of famous actors.* **gal ax ies.**

gale (gāl), *n.* 1. a strong wind. *The ship rolled and tossed in the waves made by the gale.* 2. an outburst. *The young man's jokes caused gales of laughter.* **gales.**

gal lant (gal′ənt for 1–3, gə lant′ for 4), *adj.* 1. noble; brave. *The knight was a gallant fighter.* 2. very fine in appearance; stately. *That gallant house was once the home of a nobleman.* 3. very courteous and respectful toward women. *The gallant, young boy offered the woman his seat on the crowded bus.* **gal lant ly,** *adv.*
n. 4. a man who is very fashionable; well dressed. *When he puts on his best clothes he certainly looks like a gallant.* **gal lants.**

gal le on (gal′ē ən), *n.* a sailing ship used by the Spanish between 1400 and 1700. *Galleons were once used to carry treasure, but they were hard to handle and therefore were helpless against pirates.* **gal le ons.**

gal lery (gal′ər i), *n.* 1. an upper floor in a theater, usually the highest. *When we saw the ballet "Swan Lake," we sat in the gallery.* 2. a room or building where art objects are displayed. *The Art Institute of Chicago is a famous art gallery.* **gal ler ies.**

galleon

gal ley (gal′ē), *n.* 1. a long, narrow ship with sails and oars used in ancient times. *Galleys were often manned by slaves or prisoners.* 2. the kitchen of a ship. *Many meals are cooked in the galley.* **gal leys.**

gal lon (gal′ən), *n.* a measurement of liquid. *Four quarts make a gallon. Gasoline is sold by the gallon.* **gal lons.**

gal lop (gal′əp), *n.* 1. the fastest movement of a horse, in which all four feet are off the ground at once at each leap forward. *The horses crossed the finish line at a gallop, with "Blue Boy" far ahead.* 2. a ride on a horse traveling at this pace. *The jockey went for a gallop around the track.* **gal lops.**
v. 3. to ride or run at a gallop. *The horse galloped in the large meadow. She got on her horse and galloped away.* 4. to go fast; hurry. *The orchestra galloped through the music.* **gal lops, gal loped, gal lop ing.**

gal va nize (gal′və nīz′), *v.* 1. to cover iron or steel with a surface of zinc to prevent rusting. *The iron or steel used in making water pipes should be galvanized.* 2. to startle; make someone do something suddenly. *He was galvanized into action by the teacher's command.* **gal va niz es, gal va nized, gal va niz ing.**

gal va nized (gal′və nīzd′), *adj.* covered with a thin coating of zinc to prevent rust. *Galvanized iron is often used for buildings in tropical countries, where damp air rusts metals.*

gam bol (gam′bl), *v.* 1. to run and jump about; to play. *The lambs were gamboling in the meadow.* **gam bols, gam boled, gam bol ing.**
n. 2. a frolic; a playful running and jumping about. *The teachers watched the gambols of the children on the playground.* **gam bols.**

game (gām), *n.* 1. a contest or a playing that follows rules. *The game of baseball is a popular sport. Children play the game of tag. Chess is a game for only two people.* 2. the things needed to play a game. *I got three games for my birthday.* 3. a scheme; a plan. *He tried to fool us, but his game didn't work.* 4. wild animals, fish, or birds that are hunted for sport. *This area of the forest is loaded with game.* 5. the flesh of wild animals used as food. *We had game for dinner.* **games.**
adj. 6. having to do with wild animals that are hunted. *Game birds are hunted for sport. A game warden is a kind of policeman whose job is enforcing game laws.* 7. having courage. *Even though he was afraid of the dark, John was game to camp out.* **gam er, gam est; game ly,** *adv.*

game keep er (gām′kē′pər), *n.* a person whose job is to take care of wild animals and birds on private land. *The gamekeeper keeps watch to see that no animals or birds are trapped or stolen.* **game keep ers.**

gan der (gan′der), *n.* a male goose. *The angry gander chased the puppy.* **gan ders.**

gang (gang), *n.* 1. a group of workmen. *The repair gang is fixing the railroad tracks.* 2. a group

garden

of people who usually are together. *The gang at the office are nice fellows.* 3. a group of criminals. *The gang of bank robbers was led by a well-known man.* **gangs.**

ga rage (gə räzh′), *n.* 1. a building in which cars are kept. *It looked like it was going to rain, so my father put the car in the garage.* 2. a place where automobiles are repaired or are stored. *The workmen in the garage will install new brakes.* **ga rag es.**

gar bage (gär′bij), *n.* spoiled food or waste matter that is thrown away. *We put our garbage in cans in the alley, where it is picked up by trucks.*

gar den (gärd′n), *n.* 1. a piece of ground in which vegetables or flowers are grown. *Rabbits got into our vegetable garden last night and ate some of our lettuce.* 2. a place for exhibiting plants. *A garden like this is called a botanical garden.* 3. a place for exhibiting animals. *Animals are seen in a zoological garden, or "zoo" for short.* **gar dens.**
v. 4. to make and care for a garden. *Mother enjoys having a yard in which to garden.* **gar dens, gar dened, gar den ing.**

gar gle (gär′gl), *v.* 1. to rinse or bathe the throat with a liquid that is kept moving by exhaling through the mouth. *A sore throat can be eased by gargling with salt water.* **gar gles, gar gled, gar gling.**
n. 2. the liquid used for gargling. *Salt water is a good gargle.* **gar gles.**

gar ment (gär′mənt), *n.* an article of clothing. *Pick up your garments and hang them in the closet.* **gar ments.**

gar ter (gär′tər), *n.* a band or strap used for holding up stockings or socks. *I lost a garter yesterday.* **gar ters.**

gas (gas), *n.* 1. a substance that is not solid and not liquid. *Gas is a form of matter that can spread out indefinitely. Oxygen is a gas.* 2. a gas or mixture of gases used for heating and cooking because it burns. *We use gas to heat our house.* 3. a kind of gas that makes a person unconscious, used in medicine and in dentistry so a patient does not feel pain. *My dentist gives his patients gas when he pulls a tooth.* 4. a gaseous

substance that poisons the air. *Mine rescue workers carry masks that are treated to keep out gases.* 5. gasoline. *The car needs gas.* **gas es.**
v. 6. to supply with gasoline. *The racing driver gassed his car in less than two minutes.* 7. to injure or kill with poison gas. *People sometimes get rid of insects by gassing them.* **gas es, gassed, gas sing.**

gas e ous (gas′ē əs), *adj.* of or like gas. *A gaseous odor came from the old stove. Air is gaseous matter.*

gas o line or **gas o lene** (gas′ə lēn′, gas′ə len′), *n.* a liquid used as fuel for certain engines. *Gasoline is made from petroleum and burns fast.* **gas o lines** or **gas o lenes.**

gasp (gasp), *v.* 1. to breathe fast; take in air with difficulty. *After running for half a mile, he was gasping.* 2. to speak while breathing with difficulty. *"Help is on its way," gasped the messenger to the captain of the fort.* **gasps, gasped, gasp ing.**
n. 3. a quick intake of air. *Ben gave a gasp of surprise when he opened his birthday present.* **gasps.**

gate (gāt), *n.* 1. an opening in a fence or wall, usually having a door. *The old garden gate squeaked when it was opened.* 2. a valve or door that stops the flow of water in a canal or pipe when it is shut. *When the crops have enough water, the gate in the irrigation ditch is shut.* 3. the total amount of money paid by people to see a ball game, auto race, etc. *The gate for the football game was $200,000.* **gates.**

gath er (gath′ər), *v.* 1. to bring together; come together. *The teacher gathered the smallest children at the front of the room. When clouds gather like this, it means rain.* 2. to pick up and arrange together; collect. *In spring people gather violets. It is fun to gather different kinds of rocks.* 3. to gain slowly. *The car gathered speed. After Gregory's illness, he gathered his strength by resting.* 4. to understand. *From what I was told, I gather you will come to the meeting.* 5. to sew in folds. *My sister gathered her new dress at the waist.* **gath ers, gath ered, gath er ing.**

gate

gazelle

n. 6. one of the little folds between stitches when cloth is gathered. *The gathers in the sleeve were attractive.* **gath ers.**

gath er ing (gath′ər ing), *n.* 1. a coming together of people; a meeting. *A large gathering attended the play presented by the seventh grade.* 2. a swelling or sore on the body that comes to a head. *A boil is a gathering that can be painful.* **gath er ings.**

gauge (gāj), *n.* 1. an instrument for measuring. *A steam gauge measures the pressure of steam. Gauges are used for finding out the exact thickness of a wire.* 2. an instrument for keeping a record of the amount of rainfall, the force and direction of the wind, etc. *The wind gauge showed that the northeast winds were moving at twenty miles an hour.* 3. a standard of measurement. *On United States railroad tracks the gauge between rails is fifty-six and one-half inches.* **gaug es.**
v. 4. to measure with a gauge. *Gauge the thickness of this wire.* 5. to estimate; judge; guess. *We gauged that the airplane was flying at about six hundred miles an hour. I gauge Bruce to be a fine boy.* **gaug es, gauged, gaug ing.**

gave (gāv), past tense of **give.**

gay (gā), *adj.* 1. merry; happy; full of fun. *The children were gay as they started on the picnic.* 2. bright colored. *The baby was dressed in a gay little suit.* **gay er, gay est; gay ly** or **gai ly,** *adv.*

gaze (gāz), *v.* 1. to look long and steadily. *Ralph gazed out of the train window during the trip to Chicago.* **gaz es, gazed, gaz ing.**
n. 2. a long and steady look. *The child's gaze stayed on the doll that talked.* **gaz es.**

ga zelle (gə zel′), *n.* a small, swift, graceful animal somewhat like a deer. *Gazelles are found in Africa and Asia.* **ga zelles.**

---

sand, āte, bâre, fäther; sent, mē, fėrn; fit, bĭke; pot, rōpe, fôrt; run, pull, rüle, cūte; noise, sound; ch, cheese; ng, long; th, thick; th, those; zh, treasure; ə = a in about, e in waken, i in animal, o in seldom, and u in minus.

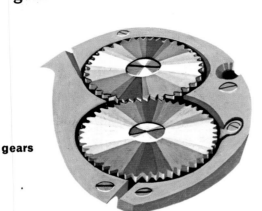

gears

gear (gir), *n.* 1. the equipment, including clothing, supplies, and tools, needed for a certain purpose. *Allen's fishing gear includes two or three fishing rods, a box of fishhooks, boots, and a basket for carrying his catch.* 2. a wheel having teeth that fit into the teeth of another wheel. *When one gear turns, the other gear turns also. Cars and trucks have gears which connect the wheels to the engine.* 3. an arrangement of parts to do a certain thing. *Gears on an automobile may be used either to decrease or increase speed.* 4. **in gear,** with the engine connected to the gear wheels. *When the car is in gear it will move.* 5. **out of gear,** with the gear wheels not connected to the engine. *When a car is out of gear it cannot run.* 6. **high gear,** an arrangement of gears for high speed. *In high gear that car will go over one hundred miles per hour.* 7. **low gear,** an arrangement of gears for less speed but more power. *In heavy traffic cars are run in low gear.* **gears.**
v. 8. to connect by gears. *An automobile moves when the motor is geared to the wheels.* 9. to adjust; ready to handle. *Our shipping room is geared to send out one thousand packages a day.* 10. to supply with gear. *They geared the deep-sea diver with helmet, suit, and air hose.* **gears, geared, gear ing.**

gee[1] (jē), *n., interj.* a command to a horse meaning "go to the right." *"Gee" is the opposite of "haw," which means "go to the left."*

gee[2] (jē), *interj.* an exclamation of surprise. *Bob said "Gee!" when he saw his new bicycle.*

geese (gēs), *n. pl.* more than one goose. *Geese make a kind of honking noise.*

Gei ger count er (gī′gər koun′tər), *n.* an instrument for finding out if the air is radioactive. *A Geiger counter is used to measure the results of the explosion of an atomic bomb. The Geiger counter sends out little clicks that get louder and more frequent when the air is dangerous.* **Gei ger count ers.**

gem (jem), *n.* 1. a precious stone. *Diamonds and emeralds are two kinds of gems.* 2. anything of special value or interest. *The gem of the Museum's collection is the painting by Rembrandt, which cost two million dollars.* **gems.**

gen er al (jen′ər əl), *adj.* 1. having to do with all or almost all. *The general feeling among the students is that the new teacher will be popular. The weather is a subject of general interest.* 2. not given in detail; not definite; rough. *Everyone has a general idea of how an airplane stays in the air. First let's get a general plan worked out.* 3. not special; not limited to a few. *The old house is open for general inspection on Fridays. In that general store, you can buy anything from a soda to a TV set. Today there is general interest in science.* **gen er al ly,** *adv.*
n. 4. a top army officer in command of many men. *A general commands a whole army.* 5. **in general,** usually. *In general, cats dislike being in water.* **gen er als.**

gen er al i za tion (jen′ər əl ə zā′shən), *n.* 1. the act of generalizing; forming a general rule from particular cases. *You shouldn't make a generalization until you have many facts.* 2. a statement made from observing facts and coming to a conclusion. *The teacher's generalization was that certain students learn faster than others.* **gen er al i za tions.**

gen er al ize (jen′ər əl īz′), *v.* 1. to talk or write in a general way without saying anything specific. *It is easy to generalize about the need for better education, but exactly what should be done?* 2. to make a generalization from known facts. *A careful thinker generalizes only after much observation.* **gen er al iz es, gen er al ized, gen er al iz ing.**

gen er al ly (jen′ər ə lē), *adv.* 1. usually; most of the time. *Generally we drive down Western Avenue to go home.* 2. widely; by many people. *The new motion picture was generally liked.*

gen er ate (jen′ər āte), *v.* to bring about; to produce. *Elections generate a lot of interest in government.* **gen er ates, gen er at ed, gener at ing.**

gen er a tion (jen′ər ā′shən), *n.* 1. all the people of about the same age. *All the boys and girls now in grade school belong to the same generation.* 2. the time between one generation and another, about thirty years. *"Two generations ago" means the time your grandfather was your age.* 3. production. *The dam is used for the generation of electricity.* **gen er a tions.**

gen er a tor (jen′ər ā′tər), *n.* a machine that produces electricity, gas, or steam. *The generator was run by a rush of water from the top of the waterfall that turned the machine.* **gen er a tors.**

gen er ous (jen′ər əs), *adj.* 1. willing to share; unselfish; giving happily. *Susan is generous and will let you have some of her candy. The generous Mr. White donated $1000 to the church. The famous athlete was generous with his time in teaching boys how to play football.* 2. large. *We had generous portions of the cake.* 3. good; not having mean feelings. *The generous teacher said she would not give us homework to do over the holidays.* **gen er ous ly,** *adv.*

gen ius (jĕn′yəs), *n.* 1. a person who has outstanding and remarkable ability in science, art, writing, music, etc. *The composer Mozart was a genius; he played the piano beautifully at the age of four and conducted an orchestra at twelve.* 2. any special ability. *Charles has a genius for getting us to do what he wants.* **gen ius es.**

gen tle (jen′tl), *adj.* 1. light; soft. *The gentle breezes rustled through the leaves.* 2. mild; kind; patient. *A good parent is gentle with children.* 3. easy to handle; having a good disposition. *The gentle dog never snaps at anyone.* 4. gradual. *This hill has a gentle slope.* 5. well-born; coming from the upper class. *The lady was of gentle birth.* **gen tler, gen tlest; gen tly,** *adv.*

gen tle man (jen′tl mən), *n.* 1. a man who is thoughtful, polite, educated, and honorable. *The word of a gentleman can be trusted.* 2. a man who comes from a good family. *A gentleman's behavior shows how he was brought up.* **gen tle men.**

gen tly (jen′tlē), *adv.* 1. in a gentle manner; mildly; softly; tenderly. *Handle that pane of glass gently. Snow fell gently from gray clouds.* 2. gradually. *The road curves gently around the mountain.*

gen u ine (jen′yù ən), *adj.* 1. not false; real. *Margaret was given a genuine diamond for her eighteenth birthday.* 2. frank; sincere; not pretending. *We all felt genuine happiness for Phil when he won the prize.* **gen u ine ly,** *adv.*

ge og ra phy (jē og′rə fē), *n.* 1. the study of the earth and its climates, products, people, countries, rivers, oceans, animals, plants, and industries. *In geography we learn that trade and commerce depend upon rivers, mountains, and other natural features.* 2. the landscape of a place. *The geography of Colorado is rugged.* **ge og ra phies.**

ge ol o gy (ji ol′ə ji), *n.* the science that deals with the composition and history of the earth's structure. *In geology rocks are studied.*

Geor gia (jôr′jə), *n.* a state in the southeastern part of the United States. *Georgia is famous for its peaches.*

ge ra ni um (jə rā′nē əm), *n.* a common garden plant having bright flowers. *Geraniums are often grown in flowerpots and window boxes.* **ge ra ni ums.**

germ (jėrm), *n.* 1. a tiny animal or plant that may cause a disease. *Germs are too small to be seen without a microscope.* 2. a seed; a bud. *A germ is the earliest form of a living thing.* **germs.**

Ger man (jėr′mən), *adj.* 1. of or pertaining to Germany, a country in central Europe. *Since 1949, the German nation has been divided into two parts, West Germany and East Germany.* *n.* 2. a person born or living in Germany. *We knew by his speech that he was a German.* 3. the language of Germany. *There are words in English, like kindergarten, that come directly from German.* **Ger mans.**

geyser

get (get), *v.* 1. to obtain; to acquire; to become the owner by receiving or earning. *We will get a new car. He got help from his friend. She will get a fine salary.* 2. to persuade. *See if you can get Mary to go.* 3. to cause to do or be. *Get your work done now. Get ready for dinner. Harry got all his homework done last night.* 4. to become. *You will get cold out here.* **gets, got, got** or **got ten, get ting.**

Get also has the following special meanings:

get along, (a) to move. *We had better get along, we're due there at noon.* (b) to agree. *We get along in almost every situation.*

get away with, to escape punishment for. *He can't get away with this trick!*

get by, to manage. *John gets by on his small allowance.*

get even, to pay back; to take revenge. *John got even with his brother by squirting him with water.*

get on, (a) to succeed. *Mr. Sims is getting on well in his business.* (b) to grow older. *The old man is getting on in years.*

get over, to recover from. *The baby got over the hiccups.*

get through, to finish. *When we get through with this class, we have another.*

gey ser (gī′zər), *n.* a spring that from time to time shoots up hot water or steam. *Some geysers, the most famous being "Old Faithful," spout water at regular times.* **gey sers.**

ghost (gōst), *n.* the spirit of a dead person, which is thought to appear in human form. *The old house is said to be haunted by a ghost that can walk through walls.* **ghosts.**

gi ant (jī′ənt), *n.* 1. an imaginary man of great size and strength. *You can read about giants in fables and fairy tales.* 2. a real man who is much larger and stronger than the average. *The football player was a giant; he was six and one-half*

geranium

feet tall and weighed three hundred pounds. **gi ants.**
adj. 3. very great in size or power. *Look at those giant strawberries!*

gift (gift), *n.* 1. a present; something given. *Walter's favorite gift was his new watch.* 2. talent; natural ability. *Paul has a gift for drawing pictures.* **gifts.**

gill[1] (gil), *n.* the part of a fish, tadpole, or crab used for breathing under water. *Gills in fish are like lungs in man.* **gills.**

gill[2] (jil), *n.* a unit of liquid measurement; one fourth of a pint. *Four gills are equal to one pint.* **gills.**

gin ger (jin′jər), *n.* 1. a spice made from the root of a plant that grows in the tropics. *Ginger is used in cooking.* 2. the root of this plant. *Ginger is made into candy by coating it with sugar or by packing it in syrup.* 3. a liquid made from this root. *Ginger is used in some medicines and in some cookies.*

gin ger bread (jin′jər bred′), *n.* cake or cookies flavored with ginger and molasses. *Mother baked some gingerbread.*

gi raffe (jə raf′), *n.* an African animal with a long neck, long legs, and a spotted skin. *A giraffe eats leaves from trees.* **gi raffes.**

girl (gėrl), *n.* a female child; a young woman. *A little girl likes to play games, but a girl of seventeen would rather go dancing.* **girls.**

give (giv), *v.* 1. to hand over to another as a present. *Let me give you a good pen. Thank you for giving me the watch.* 2. to let have. *Give me your hand and I'll pull you up. Doris gave Ruth*

glasses:
a. eyeglasses; **b.** field glasses

some good advice about hair styles. 3. to provide. *The fan gives a small breeze. Let's give a show for parents' night.* 4. to grant; to allow. *Give me your permission to drive the car.* 5. to pay. *You will have to give Mr. Howard five dollars for his books.* 6. to repeat to another person. *Please give your sister my best wishes.* 7. to move; yield because of push or pull. *We put all our weight against the door to open it, but it didn't give.* 8. **give up,** (a) to stop trying. *I won't give up on this problem.* (b) to do without. *Mr. Kane gave up smoking.* 9. **give in,** to surrender and end a struggle. *Bob gave in when he saw he could not win the checker game.* **gives, gave, giv en, giv ing.**
n. 10. bending under pressure. *An airplane wing should have a certain amount of give.*

giv en (giv′ən), *v.* 1. past participle of **give.**
adj. 2. arranged; agreed upon. *The given time for the meeting was ten o'clock.* 3. inclined; in the habit of. *Charles is given to talking a lot.*

gla cier (glā′shər), *n.* a big mass of ice that slides very slowly down a mountain. *A glacier is formed from snow that has frozen solid. An iceberg is a part of a glacier that has reached the sea.* **gla ciers.**

glad (glad), *adj.* 1. happy; pleased. *We are glad that you could come.* 2. causing a good feeling. *We heard the glad news that your team won the championship.* **glad der, glad dest; glad ly,** *adv.*

glad i a tor (glad′ē ā′tər), *n.* a man who had to fight against other men or against animals to entertain the people of ancient Rome. *Gladiators often used strange weapons, such as fishnets.* **glad i a tors.**

glance (glans), *v.* 1. to look at quickly. *I only glanced at your work, but it seems to be good.* 2. to strike at an angle and bounce off to one side. *The stone he threw glanced off the wall and just missed me.* **glanc es, glanced, glanc ing.**

giraffe

n. 3. a quick look. *It takes only a glance to see that this car cannot be repaired.* **glanc es.**

gland (gland), *n.* an organ of the body that can make and give out some substance. *The saliva gland produces the saliva in our mouths. Sweat is produced by glands.* **glands.**

glare (glâr), *v.* 1. to shine with a strong bright light. *The sun glared down on the snow, almost blinding us.* 2. to stare in an angry way. *The speaker glared at the man who came in late and banged the door.* **glares, glared, glar ing.**
n. 3. a bright, blinding light. *Night driving is sometimes difficult because of the glare from head-lights of other cars.* 4. an angry look. *Miss Martin's glare warned Bill to quit whispering.* **glares.**

glass (glas), *n.* 1. a hard substance that can be seen through. *Glass is used in windows.* 2. something made of glass. *A glass is used for drinking.* 3. a mirror. *Look at yourself in the glass.* 4. **glasses,** *n. pl.* eyeglasses, field glasses, etc. *Glasses correct poor eyesight. Glasses can make distant objects appear closer.* **glass es.**
adj. 5. made of glass. *A greenhouse is a glass house in which plants are grown.*

gleam (glēm), *n.* 1. a beam of light. *Through the darkness we saw a small gleam from the cottage.* **gleams.**
v. 2. to shine. *A light is gleaming in the window. The stars gleam.* **gleams, gleamed, gleam-ing.**

glide (glīd), *v.* 1. to move smoothly and easily. *The skaters glided across the ice.* **glides, glid ed, glid ing.**
n. 2. a smooth, silent movement. *Fred's glide over the ice ended suddenly when he bumped into Ted.* **glides.**

glid er (glīd/ər), *n.* an airplane that has no engine. *A glider, or sailplane, flies on air currents alone. The record distance that a glider has flown is almost seven hundred miles.* **glid ers.**

glim mer (glim/ər), *n.* 1. a faint light that flickers on and off. *The campers went to sleep watching the glimmer of their small fire.* **glim-mers.**
v. 2. to give a faint, flickering light. *Lights glimmered across the water.* **glim mers, glim-mered, glim mer ing.**

glimpse (glimps), *n.* 1. a short look. *We caught a glimpse of the new factory as we drove by.* **glimps es.**
v. 2. to get a quick look at. *Bill stopped whistling when he glimpsed the principal walking through the hall.* **glimps es, glimpsed, glimps ing.**

glit ter (glit/ər), *v.* 1. to shine with flashing light; to sparkle. *The ornaments glittered on the Christmas tree.* **glit ters, glit tered, glit-ter ing.**
n. 2. a bright, sparkling light. *John stopped the car to see the glitter of the snow in the moonlight.* **glit ters.**

globe (glōb), *n.* 1. anything that is round like a

gladiators

drinking **glass**

ball. *This lamp needs a new globe.* 2. the earth. *The first men to sail around the globe took more than two years.* 3. a round model of the earth, with a map on the outside showing mountains, oceans, countries, etc. *The children pointed out on the globe the route by which Columbus reached America.* **globes.**

gloomy (glüm/ē), *adj.* 1. dark and dim. *The heavy clouds have made this a gloomy day.* 2. sad; not cheerful. *He had a gloomy look on his face, so we tried to make him smile.* **gloom i er, gloom-i est; gloom i ly,** *adv.*

glider

glo ri ous (glôr/ē əs), *adj.* 1. producing honor and glory; deserving praise. *The discovery of a way to prevent polio was a glorious triumph in medicine.* 2. beautiful; brilliant. *This is a glorious day.* **glo ri ous ly,** *adv.*

glo ry (glôr/ē), *n.* 1. the honor, praise, and fame that a person receives for doing something great. *The Wright brothers' development of the airplane brought them glory.* 2. a reason for having pride. *The giant redwood trees are among the glories of our West Coast.* 3. great beauty. *The school band, wearing new uniforms, paraded in all its glory.* **glo ries.**
v. 4. **glory in,** to be happy or proud of. *Our school gloried in the honors we won during Good Neighbor Week.* **glo ries, glo ried, glo ry ing.**

glos sa ry (glos/ə rē, glôs/ə rē), *n.* a list of words and their meanings, usually printed at the end of a book. *A glossary is a kind of dictionary.* **glos sa ries.**

glossy (glôs/ē, glôs/i), *adj.* smooth and shiny. *The car looked glossy after it was washed and polished.* **gloss i er, gloss i est; gloss i ly,** *adv.*

glove (gluv), *n.* 1. a covering for the hand, having separate places for each finger. *Gloves keep hands warm in cold weather.* 2. a special covering for the hands. *Doctors wear rubber gloves while performing an operation. Baseball players and boxers wear thick gloves to protect their hands.* **gloves.**

glow (glō), *v.* 1. to give off light because of being very hot; to shine. *After the flames of the campfire died, the hot coals still glowed.* 2. to produce light without any heat. *Fireflies glow in the darkness.* 3. to show a bright color. *Mary's cheeks glowed as she came in from ice skating. The autumn sunset glowed with red and orange.* 4. to brighten; to look eager or happy. *Mike glowed with excitement as he opened his birthday presents.* **glows, glowed, glow ing.**
n. 5. the shine given off from something that is red-hot or white-hot. *You can write a letter by the glow of a fire.* 6. brightness. *The glow of the summer sunrise awakened him at five o'clock.* 7. an eager, happy look. *There was a glow on the boy's face as his father praised his work.* **glows.**

glue (glü), *n.* 1. a sticky liquid that hardens as it dries to hold things together. *Many broken toys can be mended with glue.* **glues.**

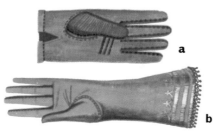

gloves:
 a. man's glove
 b. woman's glove

gnu

v. 2. to fasten with glue; stick together. *When the nose of Betty's doll broke off, Father glued it back on.* **glues, glued, glu ing.**

glum (glum), *adj.* silent and gloomy. *Ellen was glum because she was asked to stay home and watch the baby.* **glum mer, glum mest; glum ly,** *adv.*

gnu (nü, nū), *n.* a large animal with a head like an ox and a long tail. *A gnu is an African antelope with horns like a buffalo.* **gnu** or **gnus.**

go (gō), *v.* 1. to move; travel. *We passed an old car that was going very slowly. They are going to Canada.* 2. to pass. *A year goes by quickly.* 3. to be used up. *Where has my money gone?* 4. to cross. *The road goes over the river.* 5. to pass from one place or person to another. *He goes home from school. First prize goes to George.* 6. to pass from one condition to another. *He goes from bad to worse in his work. He has gone to sleep.* **goes, went, gone, go ing.**
Go also has the following special meanings:
go along with, (a) to accompany. *He always goes along with the boys to the park.* (b) to agree with. *I go along with what he said.*
go beyond, to exceed; do more than. *Please don't go beyond the speed limit.*
go by, to pass. *Time goes by.*
go in with, to join. *Mr. Roberts is going in with Scott and Company.*
go off, to explode. *A firecracker goes off with a bang.*
go on, to continue. *Go on with your work.*

goal (gōl), *n.* 1. a place at either end of a field or court where a score can be made. *The football player was knocked down before he could reach the goal.* 2. a line that marks the place where a race is to end. *The first runner across the goal wins the race.* 3. a purpose; aim; the destination one has chosen in life. *Mark's goal is to play in a great orchestra.* 4. a score in a game. *He made the winning goal.* **goals.**

goat (gōt), *n.* a horned animal about the size of a sheep. *The mountain goat is wild and very quick in climbing rocks. The domestic goat gives milk that is good to drink.* **goats.**

gob ble[1] (gob'l), *n.* 1. the sound that turkeys make. *The hunter heard the gobble of a turkey in the brush and raised his gun.* **gob bles.**
v. 2. to make the sound of a turkey. *The turkeys gobbled louder as the man brought them grain for feed.* **gob bles, gob bled, gob bling.**

gob ble[2] (gob'l), *v.* to eat fast. *Russell gobbled his lunch so that he could hurry outside to play.* **gob bles, gob bled, gob bling.**

gob let (gob'lət), *n.* a drinking glass with a stem and a flat base. *The waiters brought us water in beautiful crystal goblets.* **gob lets.**

goats: a. mountain goat; **b.** domestic goat

a

b

gob lin (gob'lən), *n.* a spirit or elf in the form of a little, ugly man. *In stories goblins are always making trouble for someone.* **gob lins.**

God (god), *n.* the creator and ruler of the universe. *Most religions today are based on a belief in God who is a supreme being.*

god (god), *n.* a being that is worshiped because of the powers his followers think he has. *Early peoples believed in many gods, some of whom represented natural forces they didn't understand, such as sun and rain.* **gods.**

god mother (god'muth'ər), *n.* a woman who promises that she will see that a child has good religious training. *A godmother is usually a close friend of the child's parents.* **god moth ers.**

go ing (gō'ing), *v.* 1. present participle of **go.**
n. 2. a departure; leaving. *The going of the Nelson family to a finer house made us happy for them.* 3. the travel conditions of a road. *The going is a little rough where the highway is being repaired.* **go ings.**
adj. 4. successful. *That business is a going concern.*

gold (gōld), *n.* 1. a heavy, yellow, precious metal, used for making jewelry such as watches, rings, and bracelets. *Some coins of high value used to be made of gold.* 2. money; wealth. *The old man lived a simple life and cared nothing for gold.*
adj. 3. made of gold. *Dick's brother received a gold watch when he finished college.* 4. having a deep, rich yellow color. *The artist used gold paint on his picture of autumn trees.*

gold en (gōld'n), *adj.* 1. made of gold. *She wears small golden earrings.* 2. of the color of gold; bright yellow. *Her golden hair seems to flash in the sun.* 3. very good. *The educated man today has a golden opportunity to make a success of his life.* 4. best; most successful. *The golden days of school will always be remembered.*

gold fish (gōld'fish'), *n.* a small fish, usually having a yellow or orange color. *Pet goldfish should be kept in clean water and fed once a day.* **gold fish** or **gold fish es.**

golf (golf, gôlf), *n.* 1. a game played with a small hard ball and a set of clubs. *The object of golf is to hit the ball into a hole, using the fewest possible strokes.*
v. 2. to play this game. *Our neighbors golf every Saturday.* **golfs, golfed, golf ing.** (See illustration on following page.)

gon do la (gon'də lə), *n.* 1. a long narrow boat with high ends, used in Venice, Italy, much as we use autos or taxis. *Venice is made up of small islands, so part of the city has canals instead of streets and gondolas instead of cars.* 2. a freight car with no top. *Goods that are not hurt by weather are placed in gondolas for transport.* 3. a place for passengers hung beneath a balloon. *A ride in a gondola is noiseless if the balloon has no motor.* **gon do las.**

gone (gôn), *v.* 1. past participle of **go.**
adj. 2. moved away. *The family of robins is gone*

a

b

goblets:
a. wine goblet
b. brandy goblet

sand, āte, bâre, fäther; sent, mē, fèrn; fit, bīke; pot, rōpe, fôrt; run, pùll, rüle, cūte; noise, sound; ch, cheese; ng, long; th, thick; th, those; zh, treasure; ə = a in about, e in waken, i in animal, o in seldom, and u in minus.

golf

gongs:
a. ancient Chinese gong
b. modern gong

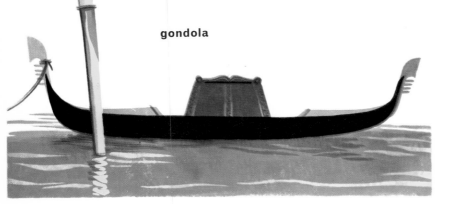

gondola

for the winter. 3. used up; weak. *He's so gone, we had better let him rest here.* 4. dead. *He is gone.* 5. lost. *To try to stop the flood now is a gone cause.*

gong (gông), *n.* a large disk of metal that is hit with a club to make a sound. *Gongs vary in size, tone, and pitch. The large Chinese gong of olden times makes a loud booming sound; the dinner gong is smaller and less loud.* **gongs.**

good (gùd), *adj.* 1. excellent; better than the usual kind. *I saw a very good movie last night. Homemade fudge is good.* 2. suited for its job. *This pill is good for a headache. This is a good meal for a hot day.* 3. honest; just. *He is a good man, doing what he can for others.* 4. well-behaved. *Betty likes to be a baby-sitter when the children are good.* 5. pleasant. *Yesterday it rained, but today is a good day.* 6. kind; helpful. *You are good to carry that heavy load for me.* 7. in sound condition; fresh. *We've had those plums for a week, but they are still good. The baby's health is good.* 8. real; not false or artificial. *The actress wore a good diamond worth thousands of dollars.* 9. thorough; complete. *The doctor gave him a good examination. The team took a good beating, eleven to nothing.* **bet ter, best.**

n. 10. something that is good. *Try to look for the good in people, not the bad.* 11. welfare; benefit. *The donations were used for the good of all the families whose homes were flooded.*

good-by or **good-bye** (gùd′bī′), *interj., n.* farewell. *Before he left, he said, "Good-by."* **good-bys** or **good-byes.**

good-looking (gùd′lùk′ing), *adj.* handsome. *The girls all thought that the new boy in class was good-looking.*

good ness (gùd′nəs), *n.* the condition of being good. *The baby-sitter praised the child's goodness.*

good night, farewell. *We say "Good night" to people at night.* **good nights.**

goods (gùdz), *n. pl.* 1. things that are bought or made to be sold. *Department stores have many goods for sale.* 2. property that can be moved, such as clothes, furniture, etc. *They put all their goods into a truck and left the house.*

goody (gùd′ē), *n.* a piece of candy, cake, or other sweet thing to eat. *Grandma always gives us goodies when we visit her.* **good ies.**

goose (güs), *n.* 1. a swimming bird that looks like a duck, but has a larger body and a longer neck. *The male goose is called a gander.* 2. the flesh of the goose used as food. *We had goose for Thanksgiving dinner.* 3. a silly person. *That girl is really a goose!* **geese.**

goose ber ry (güs′ber′ē), *n.* a small, sour berry that grows on a shrub. *Gooseberries are used in pies.* **goose ber ries.**

go ril la (gə ril′ə), *n.* the largest of all apes. *Gorillas are powerful African animals with long arms, short legs, and huge shoulders.* **go ril las.**

gos ling (goz′ling), *n.* a young goose. *That goose has two goslings.* **gos lings.**

gos sip (gos′əp), *n.* 1. talk, mostly unkind, about the behavior of other people. *Gossip often has no truth to it.* 2. a person who takes part in this kind of talk. *That woman is the town gossip.* **gos sips.**
v. 3. to talk in an idle, unflattering way about the behavior of others. *The ladies in the bridge club gossip a lot.* **gos sips, gos siped, gossip ing.**

got (got), past tense and past participle of **get.**

Goth ic (goth′ik), *adj.* 1. of the style of architecture and art that developed in Europe during the Middle Ages, or roughly from the years 1100 to 1550. *A good example of Gothic architecture is the Notre Dame Cathedral in Paris, France.*
n. 2. Gothic art and architecture. *The Gothic stresses grace and beauty.*

got ten (got′n), past participle of **get.**

gourd (gôrd, gûrd), *n.* a fruit that has a hard covering, many seeds, and grows on a vine.

goose

Dried gourds may be used as bowls, bottles, and rattles. **gourds.**

gov ern (guv′ərn), *v.* to direct; manage; rule. *The mayor and the council govern the city. The teacher governs the conduct of her classes.* **gov erns, gov erned, gov ern ing.**

gov ern ment (guv′ərn mənt), *n.* 1. a system of governing. *Our American government lets the people govern themselves; under some other governments, people have to obey a king or dictator.* 2. the people in charge of a system of governing. *The government has approved the new dam.* **gov ern ments.**

gov er nor (guv′ər nər), *n.* 1. the person elected to be the head of a state of the United States. *A governor is aided by elected representatives*

Gothic art:
a. rose tracery window
b. stained-glass window
c. carved stone gargoyle
d. carved stone capital

from sections of his state. 2. the person who runs or directs a certain kind of organization. *The governor called a special meeting.* 3. a device that controls the speed of an engine. *If a governor is attached to the motor of an automobile and is set for forty miles per hour, the car will not go faster than that speed.* **gov er nors.**

gown (goun), *n.* 1. a woman's dress. *The bride's wedding gown was long and trimmed with lace.* 2. a sleeping garment. *It was a cold night, so she put on her warmest gown.* 3. a loose-fitting dark robe worn by judges, by ministers, and by students during their graduation ceremony. *My brother looked proud in his cap and gown as he received his diploma.* **gowns.**

grab (grab), *v.* 1. to reach for and take hold of suddenly. *I grabbed the hammer from the baby's hand. The boys grabbed their books and coats and hurried to the school bus stop.* **grabs, grabbed, grab bing.**

n. 2. a sudden snatching; a grabbing. *The dog made a grab for the chicken on the table.* **grabs.**

grace (grās), *n.* 1. a beautiful, easy movement or manner. *An expert dancer moves with grace.* 2. a pleasant, attractive way of talking and acting. *The speaker delivered her speech with grace.* 3. mercy; favor. *By Heaven's grace, the pioneers survived the bitter winter.* 4. a short prayer of thanks to God before a meal. *In our family, we take turns in saying grace before meals.* 5. a feeling of what is right and what is wrong. *Joan had the grace to apologize at once for her bad behavior.* 6. **good graces** or **bad graces,** state of being liked or disliked by someone. *That dog is in my bad graces because he barks at me. He is in the good graces of Louise.* **grac es.**

v. 7. to bring honor to. *The coach of a college team graced our school's football dinner.* 8. to add charm to. *Lovely trees graced the lawn.* **grac es, graced, grac ing.**

gra cious (grā'shəs), *adj.* 1. kind; pleasant. *The office clerk was gracious to all visitors to the school.* 2. having comfort and charm. *The Smiths lead a gracious life.* **gra cious ly,** *adv.*

grade (grād), *n.* 1. class or year in school. *The fifth grade is in room 210 this year.* 2. a mark or letter to show how well one has done. *Some pupils get grades that are all A's.* 3. quality. *The good shopper buys only the best grade of meat. All meat has a grade approved by government inspectors stamped on it.* 4. slope. *The road up the mountain has a steep grade.* **grades.**

v. 5. to give a mark or grade to. *A teacher sometimes has to grade a hundred tests.* 6. to place into groups according to size or quality. *Oranges are graded before they are boxed for shipping to the stores.* 7. to make level or flat. *Bulldozers graded the land on which the new house will be built.* **grades, grad ed, grad ing.**

grad er (grād'ər), *n.* a pupil in a certain grade at school. *The first graders will leave early today because of the rain.* **grad ers.**

grad u al (graj'ù əl), *adj.* happening little by little; occurring slowly. *The teacher is happy about the gradual improvement in Carol's handwriting.* **grad u al ly,** *adv.*

grad u ate (graj'ù ət for 1, graj'ù āt' for 2–4), *n.* 1. a person who has finished a course of study and has been given a degree. *The editor-in-chief is a graduate of the University of Chicago, which awarded him a diploma.* **grad u-ates.**

v. 2. to receive a diploma. *It is necessary these days to graduate from high school to get a good job.* 3. to give a diploma to. *The high school will graduate two hundred boys and girls this week.* 4. to mark out in equal spaces. *Thermometers are graduated in degrees for easy reading.* **grad u ates, grad u at ed, grad u at ing.**

grad u a tion (graj'ù ā'shən), *n.* special exercises or ceremony when diplomas from a school are given out. *Sue's graduation is on the night of June 7.* **grad u a tions.**

grain (grān), *n.* 1. the seeds of a cereal plant such as wheat, oats, and corn. *Grain is eaten uncooked by animals. People eat grain in the form of cornflakes, oatmeal, and wheatflakes.* 2. the plants that produce these seeds. *There are many acres of grain in Kansas.* 3. a tiny piece of sand, sugar, or salt. *I spilled a few grains of salt on the table.* 4. any tiny piece. *The lawyer proved that there wasn't a grain of evidence against the man on trial.* 5. smallest unit of weight used by scientist. *A 120-pound boy weighs 840,000 grains.* 6. the markings and lines in wood that show the arrangement and direction of its fibers. *It is more difficult to saw a board against the grain than along the grain, or across the lines.* 7. **go against the grain,** to be unpleasant. *It goes against his grain to see carelessly dressed boys.* **grains.**

gram mar (gram'ər), *n.* 1. the study of the forms and uses of words. *A knowledge of grammar helps us to use words correctly.* 2. using words according to rules of grammar. *"I seen him" is bad grammar; we learn to say "I saw him" or "I have seen him."* 3. a textbook which contains information about correct use of words. *I look in a grammar when I am not certain how a sentence should be written.* **gram mars.**

grand (grand), *adj.* 1. large; beautiful; costing much money. *The king lived in a grand palace.* 2. the most important; main. *The grand prize in the spelling contest was a trip to the state capital.* 3. complete; counting everything. *We collected a grand total of fifty dollars to send to the hospital.* **grand er, grand est; grand ly,** *adv.*

grand child (grand'chīld'), *n.* the child of one's son or daughter. *Arthur's grandmother is very proud of him since he is her only grandchild.* **grand chil dren.**

grand daugh ter (grand'dô'tər), *n.* the daughter of one's son or daughter. *Grandmother loved to have her granddaughter visit her.* **grand daugh ters.**

grape: a. leaf; b. flower;
c. green grapes; d. purple grapes

grand fa ther (grand′fä′thər), *n.* the father of one's mother; the father of one's father. *One of my grandfathers lives here in town; my other grandfather lives in the country.* **grand fa thers.**

grand ma (grand′mä′, gram′ə), *n.* grandmother. *We are going to visit Grandma this Sunday.* **grand mas.**

grand moth er (grand′muth′ər), *n.* the mother of one's father; the mother of one's mother. *Both of my grandmothers are coming to my birthday party.* **grand moth ers.**

grand pa (grand′pä′, gram′pə′), *n.* grandfather. *Grandpa is going to take me fishing.* **grand pas.**

grand son (grand′sun′), *n.* the son of one's son or daughter. *Their grandson reminded them of their son when he was young.* **grand sons.**

grand stand (grand′stand′), *n.* a place where people sit to watch a baseball game, football game, and other events. *We were lucky to get seats in the grandstand to watch the parade.* **grand stands.**

gran ite (gran′it), *n.* a hard, gray rock. *Many buildings and monuments are made of granite because it lasts a long time.*

grant (grant), *v.* 1. to give as a favor; let have. *Will you grant me the loan of your car?* 2. to admit; agree. *Everyone would grant that the United States is powerful.* **grants, grant ed, granting.** *n.* 3. something given. *The college professor has a grant of five thousand dollars to study plant dis-*

ease. *The railroad received grants of land from the government.* **grants.**

grape (grāp), *n.* a sweet fruit that grows in bunches on a vine. *We bought some seedless grapes to eat after lunch.* **grapes.**

grape fruit (grāp′früt′), *n.* a large, yellow fruit somewhat like an orange but with a slightly sour taste. *Grapefruit is often eaten for breakfast.* **grape fruits.**

graph (graf), *n.* a diagram that shows the relationship between one thing and another, especially how one thing changes as the result of change in another. *Last week we made graphs that showed the amount of time we spent studying in relation to the scores we made on our tests.* **graphs.**

graph eme (gra′fēm′), *n.* a group of letters that represents a single sound in speech. *The "f" of "fine," the "ff" of "puff," and "gh" of "cough" are members of one grapheme.* **graph emes.**

graph ic (graf′ik), *adj.* 1. picture-like; strong, clear. *His graphic description of the accident scared us.* 2. of or about diagrams or graphs. *She is studying graphic representations of problems in her math class.* 3. relating to art, printing, or engraving. *All elements of the graphic arts are used in a newspaper.* **graph i cal ly,** *adv.*

graph ite (graf′īt), *n.* a soft, black carbon. *The lead in a pencil is really graphite.*

grasp (grasp), *v.* 1. to hold tightly in the hand. *He grasped the door handle and pulled, but the door would not open.* 2. to understand. *I explained it three times, but he couldn't grasp the meaning.* **grasps, grasped, grasp ing.** *n.* 3. the act of holding tightly. *The dog would not loosen his grasp on the bone.* 4. possession; control. *We had victory in our grasp until the other team scored two quick touchdowns.* 5. the power of holding and controlling; reach. *A wonderful career as an actor was within his grasp before he decided to enter politics.* 6. understanding. *He has a firm grasp of the problems that face the world.* **grasps.**

grass (gras), *n.* 1. green plants that are grown for lawns or that grow wild in pastures, meadows, etc. *He has to cut the grass on Saturday morning.* 2. any of a number of plants that have jointed stems and narrow leaves or blades. *Sugarcane, wheat, and corn are all grasses.* **grass es.**

grass hop per (gras′hop′ər), *n.* a jumping insect with wings and powerful rear legs. *Grasshoppers feed on plants, and large groups of them can destroy crops.* **grass hop pers.** (See illustration on following page.)

grate[1] (grāt), *v.* 1. to break something down into small pieces by rubbing it against a rough surface. *He grated the onions and mixed them in with the hamburger meat.* 2. to produce a harsh, unpleasant sound when rubbed against something. *The cat's claws grated on the screen*

sand, āte, bâre, fäther; sent, mē, fėrn; fit, bīke; pot, rōpe, fôrt; run, pùll, rüle, cūte; noise, sound; ch, cheese; ng, long; th, thick; th, those; zh, treasure; ə = a in about, e in waken, i in animal, o in seldom, and u in minus.

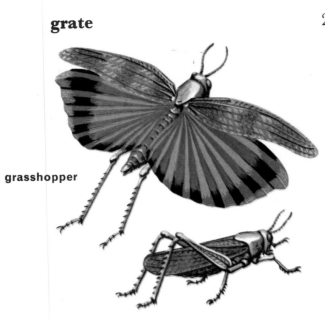

grasshopper

door. 3. to have a harsh effect; to irritate. *Her annoying questions grated on my patience.* **grates, grat ed, grat ing.**

grate[2] (grāt), *n.* 1. a metal framework used to hold fuel as it burns. *I put a fresh log on the grate in the fireplace.* 2. metal bars placed over a window to prevent anyone from entering or leaving. *New grates were ordered for the prison windows to replace the old, rusted ones.* **grates.**
v. 3. to put metal bars on something. *The windows at the bank were grated to prevent robbery.* **grates, grat ed, grat ing.**

grate ful (grāt′fəl), *adj.* 1. thankful. *The workers were grateful for the sandwiches we made for them.* 2. welcome; pleasant. *After a full week of hot weather, a grateful breeze came to cool us.* **grate ful ly,** *adv.*

grat er (grāt′ər), *n.* an instrument or device with a rough surface used to break something down into small pieces by rubbing. *Mother uses a grater to shred cabbage for salads.* **grat ers.**

grat ing[1] (grāt′ing), *n.* a framework of bars set in a window or a door. *Gratings are usually put up so that no one can get in.* **grat ings.**

grat ing[2] (grāt′ing), *adj.* unpleasant; annoying. *The grating sound of the motor bothered us.*

grat i tude (grat′ə tüd, grat′ə tūd), *n.* a being grateful; thanks. *The boy couldn't find words to express his gratitude to the man who returned his lost dog.*

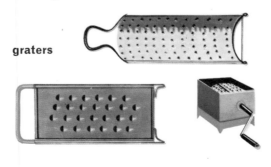

graters

grave[1] (grāv), *adj.* 1. serious; thoughtful. *The judge's expression was grave when he sentenced the prisoner.* 2. requiring serious thought; important. *The President devoted all of his energies to solving the grave problems that faced the country.* **grav er, grav est; grave ly,** *adv.*

grave[2] (grāv), *n.* 1. a hole in the ground in which a dead body is buried. *The boys dug a grave and buried their dead goldfish.* 2. any place used for burying. *The ocean is a grave for many lost ships.* 3. death. *The brave warrior faced the grave but did not fear it.* **graves.**

grav el (grav′l), *n.* 1. small bits of stone and pebbles. *The sides of the highway were covered with gravel.*
v. 2. to cover with gravel. *The driveway was graveled between the street and the garage.* **grav els, grav eled, grav el ing.**

grave yard (grāv′yärd′), *n.* a place where people bury the dead. *At the side of the old church in the country was a small graveyard.* **grave yards.**

grav i ta tion (grav′ə tā′shən), *n.* 1. the force that tends to draw all objects in the universe toward each other. *Gravitation keeps the moon rotating around the earth and the earth rotating around the sun.* 2. the force that tends to draw all objects on earth to the center of the earth. *Gravitation acts the same on all objects, so that light objects fall just as quickly as heavy ones.*

grav i ty (grav′ə tē), *n.* 1. the force that draws all objects toward the center of the earth; gravitation. *A ball that is thrown into the air returns to the ground because of gravity.* 2. the force of gravitation that acts on all objects in the universe. *The moon's gravity causes tides on the earth.* 3. weight. *An object's center of gravity is that point at which it is perfectly balanced.* 4. seriousness. *The gravity of the flood situation caused the governor to close the schools and use them to shelter homeless people.* **grav i ties.**

gra vy (grā′vē), *n.* 1. the juices that flow out of meat while it is being cooked. *The bottom of the roasting pan was filled with gravy from the turkey.* 2. a thickened sauce made from these juices. *Mother made a rich gravy from the beef.* **gra vies.**

gray (grā), *n.* 1. a color obtained by blending black and white. *Gray has always been used to paint battleships.* **grays.**
adj. 2. having this color. *They live in a gray and black house.* 3. dull; gloomy. *It is hard to be cheerful on a gray day like this.* **gray er, gray est; gray ly,** *adv.*
v. 4. to make or become gray. *The actor grayed his hair for his part as an old man in the play.* **grays, grayed, gray ing.**

gray ish (grā′ish), *adj.* somewhat gray. *The children got so dirty while playing that their white suits were still grayish after being washed.*

graze[1] (grāz), *v.* 1. to put cows, sheep, etc., in a field or pasture to eat. *The farmer grazed his cattle in different fields each week.* 2. to eat

grating

grass in a field or pasture. *The cattle grazed in the field along the river.* **graz es, grazed, graz ing.**

graze² (grāz), *v.* 1. to brush against while passing; to rub against and bounce off. *The falling tree grazed the side of the cabin.* 2. to scrape the skin from. *He grazed his elbows when he fell.* **graz es, grazed, graz ing.**
n. 3. a grazing; a rub or scrape. *He wasn't injured by the bullet; it was just a graze.* **graz es.**

grease (grēs), *n.* 1. animal fat that has been melted. *After cooking the bacon, Mother poured the grease out of the pan.* 2. any thick, oily substance. *Spots of grease covered the floor of the garage.* **greas es.**
v. 3. to put grease on. *The swimmer greased his body before diving into the icy water.* 4. to apply oil or grease to. *The man at the service station greased the car.* **greas es, greased, greas ing.**

greasy (grēs′ē), *adj.* 1. covered or smeared with grease. *I won't shake hands with you because my hands are greasy from working on my car.* 2. containing grease. *The hamburgers at that restaurant are always too greasy.* **greas i er, greas i est.**

great (grāt), *adj.* 1. large in size; big. *The farmer showed us a great field of corn that stretched as far as we could see.* 2. large in number. *A great crowd of people was at the carnival.* 3. more than is ordinary or expected. *John did a great job in cutting down the tree.* 4. important; skilled; famous. *There have been many great Presidents in our history.* **great er, great est; great ly,** *adv.*

great ly (grāt′lē), *adv.* very much. *The rescuers were greatly praised for their deed. We were greatly disappointed by the movie.*

greed (grēd), *n.* a selfish desire for more than one needs of a thing. *His greed for money cost him all of his friends.*

greedy (grēd′ē), *adj.* 1. selfishly desiring more than one needs. *The ruler of the country was greedy for more power. The greedy man kept all of his money in a mattress and refused to spend any of it.* 2. very hungry for food or drink. *The greedy dog gulped down his supper and began begging for more food.* **greed i er, greed i est; greed i ly,** *adv.*

Greek (grēk), *n.* 1. a person born in Greece, living in Greece, or descended from parents born in Greece. *The ancient Greeks were the first people to stage plays.* 2. the language of Greece. *Greek is a very hard language to learn.* **Greeks.**
adj. 3. of or from Greece. *The Greek wine was very good.*

green (grēn), *n.* 1. the color of growing grass and many other plants. *In a rainbow, green is between blue and yellow.* 2. a plot of grass. *In the middle of the town square is a green where people may sit or have picnics.* 3. **greens,** (a) a decoration made of green leaves, branches, etc. *We hung greens on our door for the holiday season.* (b) leafy green vegetables used as food. *Mother fixed greens and ham for supper.* **greens.**
adj. 4. having the color green. *We used yellow chalk on the new green chalkboard.* 5. not ripe; not completely grown. *The tomatoes were not good to eat because they were green.* 6. not trained or experienced. *The plumber's green assistant forgot to shut off the water before he disconnected the pipe.* 7. not dried or seasoned. *When they burned green lumber in their fireplace, the entire house was filled with smoke.* **green er, green est.**

green house (grēn′hous′), *n.* a heated building that has a glass roof and glass sides in which plants are grown. *Throughout the winter, flowers bloomed in the greenhouse.* **green hous es.**

greet (grēt), *v.* 1. to address in a friendly manner by saying "Hello," "Good afternoon," etc. *His father always greets me whenever he sees me.* 2. to appear in front of; to present itself to. *When the teacher returned to the room, a strangely quiet scene greeted her eyes.* **greets, greet ed, greet ing.**

greet ing (grēt′ing), *n.* the words or actions used to welcome or address someone. *As I*

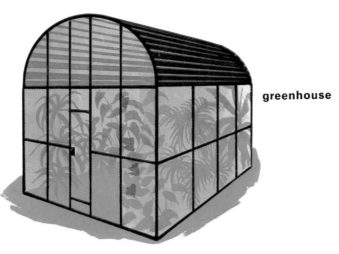

greenhouse

greyhound

n. 3. a wide smile. *His grin caused all of us to smile with him.* **grins.**

grind (grīnd), *v.* 1. to crush or make into small pieces or into powder. *The butcher ground the meat into hamburger. This machine grinds coffee.* 2. to rub or grate against. *He grinds his teeth while he is sleeping. He ground the cigarette out with his shoe.* 3. to smooth or sharpen by rubbing on a rough surface. *He ground the knives on a sharpening stone.* 4. to rule over harshly. *The king ground down any of the people who spoke against him.* 5. to operate by turning a handle. *The old man had taught the monkey to grind a hand organ.* **grinds, ground, grind ing.**
n. 6. long, steady, boring work or activity. *He found that writing such a detailed report was a grind.* **grinds.**

grip (grip), *n.* 1. a tight grasp or hold. *He had a grip on my shoulder to keep me from leaving.* 2. a handle. *She lost one of the grips on her bicycle.* 3. a small handbag or suitcase. *You can send your trunk ahead and carry the small grip with you on the train.* **grips.**
v. 4. to grasp tightly. *He gripped my hand and whispered the message in my ear.* 5. to attract and keep the interest of. *The story gripped our attention.* **grips, gripped, grip ping.**

groan (grōn), *v.* 1. to make a low, moaning sound expressing pain, grief, etc. *The injured man groaned softly as the doctor examined him.* 2. to produce a sound like this, especially as a result of holding a great weight. *The old table squeaked and groaned as we loaded it with food.* **groans, groaned, groan ing.**
n. 3. a deep, moaning sound made in the throat. *The groans of the tired players filled the room after the game.* **groans.**

gro cer (grō′sər), *n.* a person who sells food, household goods, etc. *Our grocer has a nice selection of meats in his store.* **gro cers.**

gro cery (grō′sə rē), *n.* 1. a store that sells food, household goods, etc. *Mother sent me to the grocery for milk and bread.* 2. **groceries,** anything sold by a grocer. *We carried two bags of groceries home from the store.* **gro cer ies.**

gross (grōs), *adj.* 1. total; before anything is taken out. *His gross salary for the week is $125, but his net salary is only $97.* 2. thick; heavy. *The gross vegetation prevented us from moving quickly. The gross body of the elephant crashed against a tree and knocked it over.* 3. very bad; obvious. *She made a gross error in adding the column of numbers.* 4. coarse; not nice. *Even for a child, his manners at the table were gross.* **gross er, gross est; gross ly,** *adv.*

ground[1] (ground), *n.* 1. the surface of the earth. *The model airplane crashed on the ground when it ran out of gas.* 2. soil; earth. *The ground in this field is rich and fertile.* 3. any particular piece of land or region used for a certain purpose. *The forest is his favorite hunting ground.* 4. the

entered the house, he gave me a warm and friendly greeting. **greet ings.**

grew (grü), past tense of **grow.**

grey (grā), var. of **gray.**

grey hound (grā′hound′), *n.* a tall, slender dog famous for its speed. *Greyhounds are used for hunting and for racing.* **grey hounds.**

grief (grēf), *n.* 1. a great sorrow; sadness. *Everyone felt grief when the great leader became ill.* 2. something that causes sadness. *The cancellation of the school picnic was a grief to all the students.* 3. **come to grief,** to result in failure; meet with bad luck. *Our plans for a picnic came to grief when it began to rain.* **griefs.**

grieve (grēv), *v.* 1. to feel sorrow or sadness. *The children grieved until the lost puppy was found.* 2. to cause sadness or sorrow in. *The news of the fire grieved all of us.* **grieves, grieved, grieving.**

grill (gril), *n.* 1. a platform with metal bars used for cooking. *Father cooked the hamburgers on a barbecue grill.* 2. a dish of cooked food, especially meat or fish. *That restaurant serves a delicious mixed grill.* **grills.**
v. 3. to cook on a grill. *Please grill the onions for my hamburger.* 4. to question intensely and without stopping. *The policeman grilled the suspect.* **grills, grilled, grill ing.**

grim (grim), *adj.* 1. fierce; cruel. *They were in a grim battle with the invading soldiers.* 2. unyielding; not giving in. *His grim determination to win the race caused him to practice every day.* 3. fierce or harsh in appearance or manner. *The grim look on his face told us that he was angry.* 4. horrible; frightful. *I read a grim story about ghosts and haunted houses.* **grim mer, grim mest; grim ly,** *adv.*

grin (grin), *v.* 1. to draw the lips back in a broad smile. *When I told him the joke, he grinned and said, "I've heard that joke before, but it is still funny."* 2. to draw the lips back and show the teeth as if in a smile. *The hungry lion grinned and licked his chops as the food was given to him.* **grins, grinned, grin ning.**

land at the bottom of a body of water. *The ship struck ground, and had to wait for high tide before it could move on.* 5. basis; reason for saying or believing something. *There was no ground for his complaint against us.* 6. the background against which something is made or displayed. *The painting showed white houses against a green and blue ground.* 7. **grounds,** (a) land, gardens, and lawns around a building. *The grounds around the hospital are planted with grass and trees.* (b) the small pieces of coffee, tea, etc. that settle to the bottom. *Mary asked for a fresh cup of coffee because hers was full of grounds.* **grounds.**
v. 8. to force to touch the ground; to force to stay on the ground. *The airplane was grounded because of the storm.* 9. to run against the ground; to strike the bottom of a body of water. *We grounded the boat on the beach.* 10. to establish. *That movie was grounded in fact.* 11. to connect an electric circuit or wire with the ground. *A washing machine or an electric stove must be grounded to prevent electric shocks.* **grounds, ground ed, ground ing.**
adj. 12. on the ground; near the ground. *The lobby of the hotel is on the ground floor.*

ground² (ground), *v.* 1. past tense and past participle of **grind.**
adj. 2. anything crushed into small pieces or powder. *Hamburger is ground beef.*

ground hog (ground′hôg′), *n.* an animal like a rabbit or rat with a bushy tail; a woodchuck. *The groundhog nibbles grass, roots, and vegetables all summer, and stays in a hole called a burrow all winter.* **ground hogs.**

ground work (ground′wėrk′), *n.* the foundation for something. *The teacher laid the groundwork of the lesson by reviewing some of the things we had already studied.* **ground works.**

group (grüp), *n.* 1. a number of persons or things gathered together or considered together. *A group of people stood on the corner waiting for a bus.* **groups.**
v. 2. to gather into a group; to form a group. *The hens grouped around the feeding trays in the barnyard.* 3. to arrange in a group. *The trees were grouped in small clumps around the park.* **groups, grouped, group ing.**

grove (grōv), *n.* a group of trees growing together, especially fruit trees. *Last summer we worked in orange groves, picking the fruit.* **groves.**

grow (grō), *v.* 1. to become larger; increase. *The number of customers at the store grows every week.* 2. to live and develop naturally in a certain place. *Willows grow best near water.* 3. to raise by planting seeds and caring for. *This year we are growing tomatoes in the garden.* 4. to become. *The players grew tired at the end of the game.* **grows, grew, grown, grow ing.**

growl (groul), *n.* 1. a deep, threatening sound like that made by a dog. *The robber heard the fierce growl of the watchdog.* **growls.**

v. 2. to make such a sound. *The dog growls whenever he sees a stranger in the house.* 3. to complain about something. *The workers began to growl because they wanted more pay.* **growls, growled, growl ing.**

growth (grōth), *n.* 1. the complete development achieved by growing. *Some plants reach full growth in a single season.* 2. an increase through growing; an amount that is grown. *The company has achieved great growth during the last year.* 3. anything that is growing or that has grown. *When we visited him, his father had two days' growth of beard on his chin.* **growths.**

grub (grub), *v.* 1. to dig, especially to dig something out of the ground. *The wild pigs grubbed for food at the base of the tree.* 2. to work very hard; to labor. *The old man had grubbed all of his life and hadn't been able to save any money.* **grubs, grubbed, grub bing.**
n. 3. an insect in the wormlike larval stage. *Grubs eventually develop into full-grown insects.* 4. food. *The hungry cowboys cooked their grub over the campfire.* **grubs.**

grumpy (grump′ē), *adj.* easily angered; unfriendly and cross. *No one could make friends with the grumpy girl.* **grump i er, grump i est; grump i ly,** *adv.*

guar an tee (gar′ən tē′), *n.* 1. a promise to repair or replace a product if it is not satisfactory to the purchaser or if it is not what it was advertised to be. *All of the repairs needed for the television set were covered by its guarantee.* 2. a promise to pay the debts of another person or meet his responsibilities if he is unable to pay them or meet them. *Since the young man was not old enough to buy the car, his father gave his guarantee that the car would be paid for and driven carefully.* **guar an tees.**
v. 3. to make such a promise; to give a guarantee. *That store guarantees everything that it sells.* 4. to insure. *Going to the baseball park early in the morning does not always guarantee that you will be able to buy a ticket for the game that day.* 5. to say for sure; to promise. *I guarantee that you will enjoy the movie.* **guar an tees, guar an teed, guar an tee ing.**

guard (gärd), *v.* 1. to protect; to keep from harm; to defend. *There were soldiers on duty all night to guard the fort against attack. The doctor put medicine on the cut to guard against infection.* 2. to keep watch over; to prevent from leaving. *The policemen guarded the prisoners as they were taken to jail.* **guards, guard ed, guard ing.**
n. 3. a person or thing that guards against attack, harm, etc. *The guards at the bank watched everyone who entered the building.* 4. a group of soldiers that protect a place or defend it against attack. *The captain ordered that a guard be posted around the edges of the fort.* 5. a close watch. *Stand guard over these men until help arrives.* 6. a defensive position in boxing or

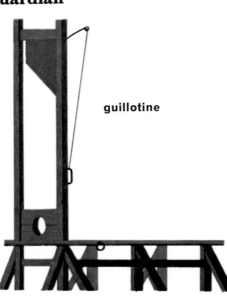

guillotine

classical **guitar**

fencing. *The boxer kept his guard up and used his hands to block the punches of his opponent.* 7. in football, either of the two players alongside the center. *Guards are used to block on running plays and to protect the quarterback on passing plays.* 8. in basketball, either of the two players who play defensive positions near their own basket. *When their opponents have the ball, the guards play near the line at the end of the court under their basket.* 9. **on guard,** ready to defend against attack; prepared for an enemy attack; watchful. *The ship was on guard against pirates as soon as any other ship was sighted.* **guards.**

guard i an (gär′di ən), *n.* 1. a person or thing that takes care of something or protects something. *Every man must act as a guardian of freedom if democracy is to be preserved.* 2. a person who is appointed by a court to care for another person, his property, his business affairs, etc. *The orphan's grandparents were named as his guardians.* **guard i ans.**

guess (ges), *v.* 1. to form an opinion without sure knowledge. *Since I didn't have a watch, I had to guess the time.* 2. to find the correct answer by guessing. *He was very surprised when*

electric **guitar** with amplifier

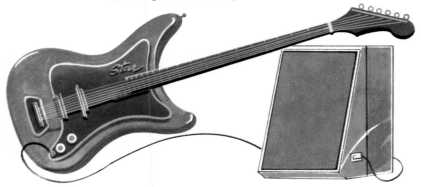

I guessed his weight. 3. to think; to suppose. *I guess he thought that I was someone else when he called to me.* **guess es, guessed, guess ing.** *n.* 4. an opinion decided on by guessing. *It was his guess that the rain would stop in time for the game to be played.* **guess es.**

guest (gest), *n.* 1. a person who visits another's house; a person who has a meal at another's house. *He was our guest for the weekend.* 2. any of the persons who are staying at a hotel. *The manager of the hotel requested that the guests turn in their keys before they left the building.* **guests.**

guide (gīd), *v.* 1. to lead; to point out the way to someone. *The boy guided us through the narrow streets to the house we wanted to see.* 2. to instruct. *My father guided me in my study of the stars and planets.* **guides, guid ed, guid ing.** *n.* 3. a person who is hired to guide. *We needed a guide to take us down the river on our canoe trip.* 4. a book that includes directions and information for travelers. *I arrived in London with nothing but a guide to the city and a little money.* **guides.**

guil lo tine (gil′ə tēn′), *n.* a machine for cutting off condemned people's heads by means of a heavy blade sliding between two posts. *In some countries the guillotine is used for executions.* **guil lo tines.**

guilty (gil′tē), *adj.* 1. having done something wrong and deserving punishment for it; having committed a crime. *The person who is guilty of taking the candy will have chocolate on his fingers. The prisoner was found not guilty and was released.* 2. showing that one has done something wrong. *The boys all had guilty looks on their faces as they gazed at the broken window.* **guilt i er, guilt i est; guilt i ly,** *adv.*

gui tar (gə tär′), *n.* a musical instrument having six strings that are played with the fingers or with a pick. *The entertainer sat in a chair and played her guitar as she sang.* **gui tars.**

gulf (gulf), *n.* a large bay, or part of a sea or ocean, that is partly enclosed by land. *The Gulf of Mexico is a part of the Atlantic Ocean.* **gulfs.**

gull (gul), *n.* a large gray-and-white sea bird with webbed feet that is found near most large bodies of water. *Gulls are graceful fliers and plunge into the water for their food. The gulls eat small fish and foods tossed overboard by ships' cooks.* **gulls.**

gulp (gulp), *v.* 1. to swallow quickly and eagerly. *Don't gulp your food; chew it before you swallow it.* **gulps, gulped, gulp ing.** *n.* 2. the amount swallowed at a single time. *I took a large gulp of water from the drinking fountain.* **gulps.**

gum[1] (gum), *n.* the pink, firm flesh above and below the teeth. *The teeth are partly covered by the gums.* **gums.**

gum[2] (gum), *n.* 1. a sticky substance obtained from certain trees. *Gum is used in paste, glue,*

sand, āte, bâre, fäther; sent, mē, fėrn; fit, bĪke; pot, rōpe, fôrt; run, půll, rüle, cūte; noise, sound; ch, cheese; ng, long; th, thick; th, those; zh, treasure; ə = a in about, e in waken, i in animal, o in seldom, and u in minus.

gulls

drugs, and jellies. 2. chewing gum. *The teacher told me to take the gum out of my mouth.* **gums.**

v. 3. to stick or glue together. *Gum all these envelopes for mailing.* **gums, gummed, gumming.**

gun (gun), *n.* 1. a weapon for shooting; a pistol, rifle, cannon, etc. *Hunters carry guns. Armies use guns.* 2. something like a gun. *Mechanics in garages use grease guns to lubricate cars.* 3. a shooting of a gun as a signal or as a salute. *The starting gun sent the runners racing. A twenty-one-gun salute is fired in honor of the President.* **guns.**

v. 4. to shoot or hunt with a gun. *The farmer went gunning for the wolf that ate his sheep.* **guns, gunned, gun ning.**

gun boat (gun'bōt'), *n.* a small ship used in guarding rivers, harbors, and coastal waters. *Gunboats carry a small cannon and other arms.* **gun boats.**

gun pow der (gun'pou'dər), *n.* an explosive powder used in guns, in fireworks, in blasting, etc. *Gunpowder explodes when it is lighted by a spark or small flame.*

gup py (gup'ē), *n.* a tiny fish that comes from fresh water in the tropics. *Guppies are often kept in aquariums in the home.* **gup pies.**

gur gle (gėr'gl), *v.* 1. to flow with a bubbling sound. *Water gurgles when poured out of a bottle. The little river gurgles over the stones.* 2. to make a bubbling sound. *Babies gurgle when they are happy.* **gur gles, gur gled, gur gling.**

n. 3. a sound of bubbling. *If you blow through a hollow straw into water, you will hear gurgles.* **gur gles.**

gush er (gush'ər), *n.* an oil well from which oil flows freely and forcefully. *The gusher sent a stream of oil high in the air.* **gush ers.**

gust (gust), *n.* 1. a sudden rush of wind or air. *The gust blew dust into my eyes.* 2. a sudden outburst of feeling, such as laughter, anger, etc. *A gust of laughter shook his body.* **gusts.**

gusty (gus'tē), *adj.* stormy; coming in gusts. *The radio warned against sailing in the gusty wind.* **gust i er, gust i est; gust i ly,** *adv.*

gut ter (gut'ər), *n.* 1. an open metal pipe used at the edge of a roof to carry off rain water. *Sometimes gutters get filled with leaves, which must be removed.* 2. a part of a street close to the curb, down which water runs to the opening of a sewer. *The heavy rain made the gutter overflow.* **gut ters.**

v. 3. to wear a channel in. *The floods guttered the farmlands.* 4. to melt quickly and go out. *The candle guttered.* **gut ters, gut tered, gut ter ing.**

guy (gī), *n.* a rope or wire used to hold something in place. *Guys held up the top of the circus tent.* **guys.**

gym (jim), *n.* a gymnasium. *The teams practice in the gym.* **gyms.**

gym na si um (jim nā'zē əm), *n.* a building or large room used for exercising the body and for playing indoor games, such as basketball. *The gymnasiums at some universities can seat ten thousand people for basketball games.* **gym na si ums.**

gym nas tics (jim nas'tiks), *n. pl.* exercises for developing the body. *A well-equipped gymnasium has parallel bars, pulleys, horses, and rings, which are used in gymnastics.*

gyp (jip), *v.* 1. to cheat. *He tried to gyp me out of a quarter.* **gyps, gypped, gyp ping.**

n. 2. a cheat; a thief. *The police will catch that gyp.* **gyps.**

gyp sy (jip'sē), *n.* a person who is one of a wandering people living all over the world. *Gypsies often make a living by telling fortunes and doing odd jobs.* **gyp sies.**

gymnastics

calisthenics

tumbling

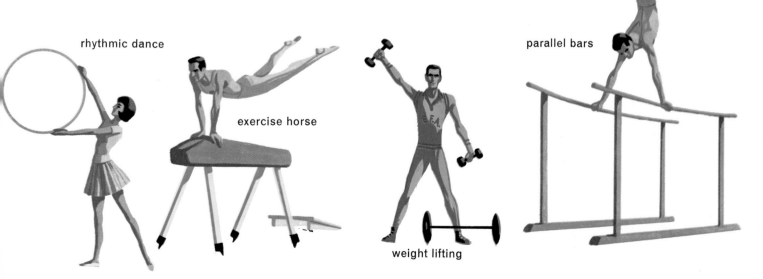

rhythmic dance

exercise horse

weight lifting

parallel bars

h

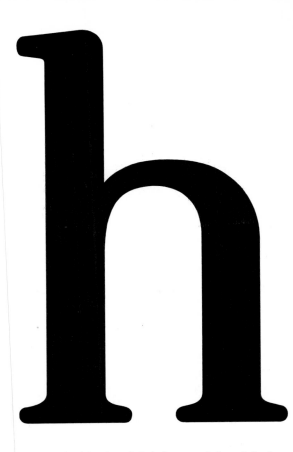

H or **h** (āch), the eighth letter of the alphabet.

ha (hä), *interj.* something said to show joy or surprise. *Ha! The car is fixed.*

hab it (hab′it), *n.* 1. a custom; an action that has been done so often that one does it without thinking. *Some habits are good, like brushing the teeth; others are bad, like biting one's fingernails.* 2. a usual way of doing something. *My dog has a habit of sleeping under my bed.* 3. a kind of clothing worn by members of a religious group; clothing worn for a special activity. *A man or woman going on a hunt on horseback wears a riding habit.* **hab its.**

hab i tat (hab′ə tat′), *n.* a place where an animal or plant lives and grows. *A squirrel's habitat is a tree. The habitat of the giant redwood trees is northern California.* **hab i tats.**

ha bit u al (hə bich′u əl), *adj.* 1. result of custom or habit. *She wore her habitual frown on her face.* 2. doing something by habit or custom. *He is a habitual teller of tales.* **ha bit u al ly,** *adv.*

had (had), past tense and past participle of **have.**

had dock (had′ək), *n.* a food fish that lives in the ocean. *A haddock is somewhat like a cod, but is smaller.* **had dock** or **had docks.**

haddock

hair dryer:
  a. for home use
  b. for use in a beauty shop

hadn't (had′nt), had not. *We hadn't the faintest idea that Bob would come.*

hail¹ (hāl), *v.* 1. to greet; to welcome. *His friends hailed him when he arrived at his birthday party. Crowds hailed the king as he returned from the wars.* 2. to call out to. *From the upstairs window Father hailed the newspaper boy.* 3. **hail from,** come from. *Carl hails from Alabama.* **hails, hailed, hail ing.**
n. 4. a greeting. *From the crowd came a hail of friendship.* **hails.**

hail² (hāl), *n.* 1. small pieces of ice that may fall during a rainstorm. *Hail makes a noise on the top of a car.* 2. anything that falls as hail falls. *A hail of hats, paper cups, and torn paper fell on the football field when the home team won.* **hails.**
v. 3. to pour down hail. *It is raining and hailing at the same time.* 4. to pour down like hail. *The sheriff and his men hailed bullets on the fleeing bank robbers.* **hails, hailed, hail ing.**

hair (hâr), *n.* 1. the mass of thin growths, like threads, that is on a person's or animal's skin. *Elizabeth has a beautiful head of hair; she brushes it often.* 2. any of these thin growths. *Look at the hairs that dog left on the chair!* 3. a growth like thin thread on some plants. *The stem of this flower has hairs on it.* **hairs.**

hair cut (hâr′kut), *n.* a cutting of the hair. *Tom got a very short haircut from the barber.* **hair cuts.**

hair do (hâr′dü), *n.* a way of fashioning one's hair; an arranging of hair. *For the party Mary got a new hairdo.* **hair dos.**

hair dry er (hâr′drī′ər), *n.* an instrument used for drying hair after it has been washed. *A hair dryer sends warm air over the hair.* **hair dry ers.**

hair pin (hâr′pin′), *n.* a metal or plastic wire curved so that it has two ends, like the letter U. *Hairpins hold hair in place.* **hair pins.**

half (haf), *n.* 1. one of two equal parts. *Five is half of ten. Half of a dollar is 100 cents divided by two, or fifty cents.* **halves.**
adj. 2. being one of two equal parts. *A half pound is eight ounces, since sixteen ounces are a pound.* 3. **not half bad,** rather good. *Really, she isn't half bad as a pianist.*
adv. 4. partly. *I half believed he was telling the truth. I could half see him in the darkness.*

half-heart ed (haf′här′ted), *adj.* without courage or interest or concern. *The boy made a half-hearted attempt to catch the ball.* **half-heart ed ly,** *adv.*

hal i but (hal′ə bət), *n.* a fish used as food which is found in northern seas. *Halibut is a very good-tasting fish.* **hal i but** or **hal i buts.**

hall (hôl), *n.* 1. a passageway connecting different rooms in a building. *Pupils are not supposed to be in the halls during classes.* 2. a large room. *The meeting was held in a hall that seats one thousand people.* 3. a college building. *That college has halls for many activities.* 4. a place for doing government business. *The meeting was held in the town hall.* **halls.**

Hal low een or **Hal low e'en** (hal′ō ēn′), *n.* the night of the last day in October. *Halloween is the evening before November 1, which is All Saints' Day.*

ha lo (hā′lō), *n.* 1. a circle of light shown above the pictures of heads of saints and angels. *A halo is used to show holiness.* 2. a circle of light around the sun or moon. *A halo is caused by reflection of light from ice crystals in our sky.* 3. the praise or glamour that surrounds a person or thing. *A halo of love and beauty surrounds Helen of Troy.* **ha los.**

halt[1] (hôlt), *v.* 1. to stop. *The red traffic light halted the cars.* **halts, halt ed, halt ing.** *n.* 2. a stop. *After a short halt for eating, we drove on.* **halts.**

halt[2] (hôlt), *adj.* 1. lame; not able to walk properly. *The halt animals were left behind by the herd.* *v.* 2. to hesitate. *The new boy in class was halting in his speech.* **halts, halt ed, halt ing.**

hal ter (hôl′tər), *n.* a rope for tying a horse. *A halter is also used to lead a horse.* **hal ters.**

halve (hav), *v.* to divide into two equal parts. *If you halve the candy bar, we both will have the same amount.* **halves, halved, halv ing.**

ham (ham), *n.* the upper part of a hog's hind leg, eaten as meat. *Ham comes to us smoked or salted, and many hams are packed in cans.* **hams.**

ham burg er (ham′bėr gər), *n.* 1. ground-up beef. *Joan bought two pounds of hamburger for dinner.* 2. a round, flat piece of ground-up beef, usually fried for eating. *A hamburger is served between the two parts of a roll or bun.* **ham burg ers.**

halter

hammock

ham mer (ham′ər), *n.* 1. a tool for pounding or for driving nails into wood. *A hammer has a metal head and a wooden or metal handle.* **ham mers.** *v.* 2. to pound with a hammer. *Harry made a racket hammering in the basement.* **ham mers, ham mered, ham mer ing.**

ham mock (ham′ək), *n.* a kind of swinging bed or couch made of cloth, canvas, or cords. *A hammock is held up at each end by a cord attached to a wall or post by a metal link.* **hammocks.**

ham ster (ham′stər), *n.* a small animal that looks like a mouse. *Some hamsters are kept as pets.* **ham sters.**

hand (hand), *n.* 1. the part of the arm below the wrist, containing the fingers and thumb. *The hand is used to hold things.* 2. a workman. *How many hands work in this factory?* 3. a pointer on the face of a clock or watch. *When the small hand is at three and the big hand is at twelve, it is three o'clock.* 4. a style of handwriting. *Ethel writes with a clear hand.* 5. a part or share. *All of us took a hand in planting the garden.* 6. ability; skill in doing something. *This old statue shows the hand of a good sculptor.* 7. a person who is used to doing something; a skilled person. *The policeman is an old hand at directing traffic.* 8. control; possession. *Our television is in the hands of a good repairman.* 9. a unit of measurement equal to four inches. *Many horses are fifteen hands high or sixty inches tall.* 10. side. *On the one hand, his mother wanted him to stay home; on the other hand, he felt that it was his duty to go.* 11. one round of a card game. *Surely you can stay for one more hand.* 12. the cards held by a player in a card game. *He knew his hand was too poor to win.* 13. a clapping of hands to show praise. *The actor received a big hand for his excellent performance.* 14. a promise to marry. *A man used to ask a woman for her hand when he wanted to become engaged.* **hands.** *v.* 15. to pass with a hand; give to. *Hand Bill the hammer. He handed her a nice compliment.* 16. to help with the hand. *The conductor handed the lady onto the train.* **hands, hand ed, hand ing.** *adj.* 17. of or for hands; worked by hand.

hammers

Most women use hand cream to keep their skin soft. The men building the house use hand tools, such as a hammer.

Hand also has the following special meanings:

at hand, very near. *An author usually keeps a dictionary at hand.*

by hand, using hands, not machinery. *These dresses were made by hand.*

from hand to mouth, without thinking about the future. *The family that lives from hand to mouth usually has very little money.*

hand down, pass along. *This painting has been handed down from father to son for three generations.*

in hand, under control. *The firemen have the blaze in hand.*

off one's hands, out of one's charge. *The manager hired a clerk to take the job of filing off his hands.*

on hand, nearby; ready for use. *The soldier always slept with his gun on hand.*

out of hand, out of control. *The fire got out of hand, and the factory burned down.*

hand bag (hand'bag'), *n.* a woman's purse. *She had ten dollars in her handbag.* **hand bags.**

hand ball (hand'bôl'), *n.* 1. a game in which a rubber ball is bounced against a wall. *Handball is played with either one or two players on each side.* 2. the rubber ball used in this game. *Handballs are usually very hard.* **hand balls.**

hand cuff (hand'kuf'), *n.* 1. one of a pair of metal bracelets. *Handcuffs are joined together by a chain, and are locked around the wrists of prisoners.* **hand cuffs.**
v. 2. to put handcuffs on. *The policeman handcuffed the bank robber.* **hand cuffs, handcuffed, hand cuff ing.**

hand ful (hand'fůl), *n.* 1. the amount that can be held in one hand. *Paul picked a handful of berries.* 2. very few; a small number. *Only a handful of people came to the meeting.* **hand fuls.**

hand i cap (han'dē kap), *n.* 1. a system of scoring a race or contest that gives either an advantage to the poorer players or a disadvantage to the better players in order to even out their differences and give the poorer players a chance to win. *Our bowling team's handicap is 176 pins.* 2. anything that hinders

a person; something that puts a person at a disadvantage. *The boy's lame leg was a handicap.* **hand i caps.**
v. 3. have a handicap. *His golf game is handicapped at ten.* 4. hinder; put at a disadvantage. *The man was handicapped by his severe cold.* **hand i caps, hand i capped, hand i capping.**

hand ker chief (hang'kər chif), *n.* 1. a small square of soft cloth used for wiping the face or the nose. *I carry more than one handkerchief when I have a cold.* 2. a cloth worn around the neck. *Cowboys and Boy Scouts wear handkerchiefs.* **hand ker chiefs.**

han dle (han'dl), *n.* 1. the part of an object by which it is picked up or held. *Cups, pitchers, hammers, and axes have handles.* **han dles.**
v. 2. to hold or touch with the hands. *Don't handle the fruit in the store.* 3. to deal with; manage. *A businessman knows how to handle the people who work for him. The big store handles hundreds of customers a day.* 4. to get along with. *The teacher handles the children well.* 5. to buy and sell. *A good store handles only good products.* **han dles, han dled, han dling.**

hand some (han'səm), *adj.* 1. very good-looking. *The handsome new church will hold its first services Sunday. We all think that Martin is a handsome boy.* 2. generous; more than enough. *The owners received a handsome amount of money when they sold their property.* **hand som er, hand som est; hand some ly,** *adv.*

hand writ ing (hand'rīt'ing), *n.* 1. writing done by hand with a pen or pencil. *You sometimes add corrections in handwriting after you have typed your homework.* 2. the way in which a person forms his letters when writing by hand. *Dick's handwriting has always been easy to read.* **hand writ ings.**

handy (han'dē), *adj.* 1. skillful. *My brother is handy with tools.* 2. convenient; easily reached. *This handy highway gets us downtown in only twenty minutes.* **hand i er, hand i est; hand i ly,** *adv.*

handy man, *n.* a man who does odd jobs. *You'd better hire a handyman to fix the screen.* **handy men.**

handcuffs

hangars

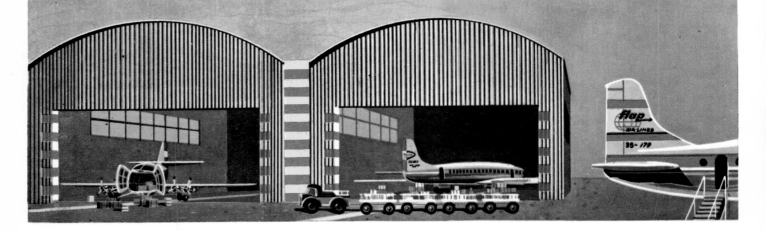

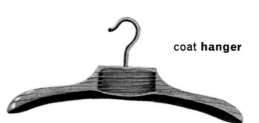

coat **hanger**

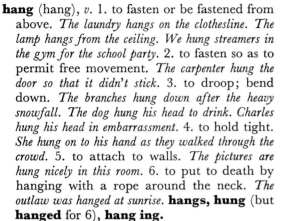

hare

hang (hang), *v.* 1. to fasten or be fastened from above. *The laundry hangs on the clothesline. The lamp hangs from the ceiling. We hung streamers in the gym for the school party.* 2. to fasten so as to permit free movement. *The carpenter hung the door so that it didn't stick.* 3. to droop; bend down. *The branches hung down after the heavy snowfall. The dog hung his head to drink. Charles hung his head in embarrassment.* 4. to hold tight. *She hung on to his hand as they walked through the crowd.* 5. to attach to walls. *The pictures are hung nicely in this room.* 6. to put to death by hanging with a rope around the neck. *The outlaw was hanged at sunrise.* **hangs, hung** (but **hanged** for 6), **hang ing.**

n. 7. the way a thing hangs. *Mother now is satisfied with the hang of her curtains.* 8. the meaning. *I don't get the hang of this problem.*

Hang also has the following special meanings:

hang on, to listen closely to. *The audience hung on every word.*

hang together, to stick together. *No matter what happens, hang together!*

hang up, to put the receiver on the hook of a telephone. *I hung up when our talk was through.*

hang ar (hang′ər), *n.* a building to keep airplanes in. *Airplanes are inspected and repaired in hangars.* **hang ars.**

hang er (hang′ər), *n.* a thing upon which something is hung. *Coat hangers and dress hangers are necessary to keep clothes neat.* **hang ers.**

hank er (hang′kər), *v.* to have a strong wish; to long. *He hankered for fame and money all his life.* **hank ers, hank ered, hank er ing.**

hap pen (hap′ən), *v.* 1. to take place; to occur. *Is anything happening tomorrow afternoon? Something has happened to the train.* 2. to occur by luck. *Charles happened to be first in line, so he was made captain.* 3. **happen on,** to meet without intending to. *We happened on our neighbor at the resort.* **hap pens, hap pened, hap pen ing.**

hap pen ing (hap′ən ing), *n.* something that takes place; an event of some kind. *Sometimes a party can be called a happening.* **hap pen ings.**

hap pi ness (hap′ē nis), *n.* gladness; being happy. *A teacher gets a feeling of happiness when her pupils do well.* **hap pi ness es.**

hap py (hap′ē), *adj.* 1. feeling or showing pleasure; joyful. *The happy man whistled all day.* 2. lucky. *By some happy chance Jim got the job.* **hap pi er, hap pi est; hap pi ly,** *adv.*

har bor (här′bər), *n.* 1. a part of a sea, lake, or river that is protected from storms; a port. *The ship sailed full speed for the harbor.* **har bors.** *v.* 2. to hide; to keep safe. *The hotel harbored several convicts.* 3. to hold; to keep thinking about. *Mrs. Kinzie has harbored a dislike for me for five years.* **har bors, har bored, har bor ing.**

hard (härd), *adj.* 1. not easily cut or broken; solid. *The ice in the lake is hard enough for skating.* 2. harsh; strict; severe. *The boss of the crew was a hard man.* 3. difficult; not simple. *One of the questions on the test was hard to answer.* 4. using energy; determined to do well. *He gets good grades because he is a hard worker.* 5. containing minerals. *Hard water keeps soap from cleaning well.* 6. having much alcohol. *Whiskey is a hard drink.* 7. **hard of hearing,** a little deaf. *Grandma is hard of hearing.* **hard er, hard est.**

adv. 8. with effort. *We worked hard on the house.* 9. with strength. *The Eskimo's dogs pulled hard to get the sled over the hill.* 10. with difficulty. *The girl was breathing hard after jumping rope.* 11. firmly. *Hold on hard!* 12. near; close to. *The building stands hard by the river.*

hard en (härd′n), *v.* 1. to make or become hard. *The ground hardens during cold weather.* 2. to become harsh; unfeeling. *His eyes hardened when he heard the boy's lie.* **hard ens, hard ened, hard en ing.**

hard ly (härd′lē), *adv.* 1. scarcely; barely. *We hardly have time to get there.* 2. probably not. *Doris can hardly get home by Saturday night. His story was hardly true.*

hard ship (härd′ship), *n.* something that is hard to bear; trouble, pain, hunger, etc. *The early settlers went through many hardships.* **hard ships.**

hard ware (härd′wâr′), *n.* articles made from metal. *Tools, pots, pans, nails, bolts, and wire are hardware.*

hard wood (härd′wu̇d′), *n.* 1. wood that is hard. *It is more difficult to saw through hardwood than through softwood.* 2. a tree that has hard

harlequin

harmonica

harp

wood. *Oak, maple, cherry, and mahogany are hardwoods.* **hard woods.**

adj. 3. having hardwood; made of hardwood. *The gymnasium has a hardwood floor.*

har dy (här′dē), *adj.* 1. strong; able to stand bad conditions. *The hardy explorers kept on going in the terrible heat of the jungle. The hardy plants lived through the cold winter.* 2. bold; daring. *Only a hardy man should enter the auto race.* **har di er, har di est; har di ly,** *adv.*

hare (hâr), *n.* an animal like a rabbit, but much larger. *A hare has strong legs and can run fast.* **hares.** (See illustration on preceding page.)

hark (härk), *v.* listen. *Hark! Do you hear that whispering?* **harks, harked, hark ing.**

har le quin (här′lə kwin), *n.* a clown. *Harlequins wear clothes of many colors and a mask.* **har le quins.** (See illustration on preceding page.)

harm (härm), *n.* 1. injury; hurt; damage. *The storm did a lot of harm to the trees, tearing off branches. I am sure Kathy meant no harm by her careless remark to you.* **harms.**

v. 2. to damage; to hurt or injure. *The fire harmed the house. Poor grades will harm your chances of getting into college.* **harms, harmed, harm ing.**

harm ful (härm′fəl), *adj.* causing harm; damaging. *Freezing weather is harmful to orange trees. Leaving school is harmful to your chances of getting a job.* **harm ful ly,** *adv.*

harm less (härm′lis), *adj.* not doing any harm; not wanting to do any harm. *Don't worry about the dog; he looks fierce, but he's harmless.* **harm less ly,** *adv.*

har mon i ca (här mon′ə kə), *n.* a small musical instrument played by blowing air into, or by sucking air out of, a row of holes. *A harmonica is held to the mouth by both hands and is often called a "mouth organ."* **har mon i cas.**

har mo ny (här′mə nē), *n.* 1. a getting on well together; accordance. *The harmony among the workers has helped to make the new store a big success.* 2. a going well together; a pleasant arrangement. *She wears clothes whose colors and designs are in harmony. The harmony of the blue colors in the room was spoiled by the bright red chair.* 3. a pleasing combination of musical sounds. *The choir sang in perfect harmony.* **har mo nies.**

har ness (här′nis), *n.* 1. the straps that attach a horse to something he is to pull forward.

Grandfather remembers how he put a harness on his horse to drive to town in the carriage. **har ness es.**

v. 2. to put a harness on. *The farmer harnessed the horse and hitched him to the sleigh.* 3. to control for a useful purpose. *Water power is harnessed by using dams to make electricity. If you could harness the energy you waste, you could be a better student.* **har ness es, har nessed, harness ing.**

harp (härp), *n.* 1. a musical instrument as tall as a man, having many strings. *The harp is played by a musician seated on a chair who rests the harp's slanting side on his shoulder and pulls the strings with his fingers.* **harps.**

v. 2. to play on a harp. 3. **harp on,** to talk about all the time. *I wish he would quit harping about the income tax.* **harps, harped, harp ing.**

har poon (här pün′), *n.* 1. a spear with a rope attached, and with a hook at the front end, used for catching large fish and whales. *Today most harpoons are fired from powerful guns, although Eskimos still throw them by hand.* **har poons.**

v. 2. to hit with a harpoon. *When a whale is harpooned, it is usually killed instantly.* **harpoons, har pooned, har poon ing.**

harsh (härsh), *adj.* 1. rough; not pleasant; bothering one's hearing or sight or taste or touch. *Father's voice was harsh when he had a cold. The harsh blanket hurt my skin.* 2. unkind; severe; hard. *The manager was so harsh with his workers that they quit the factory.* **harsh er, harsh est; harsh ly,** *adv.*

har vest (här′vist), *n.* 1. a crop. *The harvest of grain will be larger this year than last year.* 2. the gathering in of a crop. *The harvest requires the help of many men.* 3. the time or season of gathering crops. *A farmer needs more workers during the harvest.* 4. result. *A new invention is often the harvest of years of research.* **har vests.**

v. 5. to gather in a crop. *Next week they will harvest the corn.* **har vests, har vest ed, harvest ing.**

has (haz), third person present tense of **have.**

hasn't (haz′nt), has not. *Bill hasn't had lunch yet.*

haste (hāst), *n.* 1. a hurry; a rush. *My uncle in the air force left in haste for Washington.*

v. 2. **make haste,** to hurry. *We must make haste if we want to catch the train.*

has ten (hās′n), *v.* 1. to hurry. *They hastened home for dinner.* 2. to make go faster; to speed up. *The storm clouds hastened the harvesting.* **has tens, has tened, has ten ing.**

hasty (hās′tē), *adj.* 1. quick; hurried. *The mother made a hasty trip to the store to get milk for the baby.* 2. too quick; without really thinking. *He made a hasty decision to go to the city.* 3. easily angered. *Don't walk across the lawn of a hasty neighbor.* **has ti er, has ti est; hast i ly,** *adv.*

hat (hat), *n.* a covering for the head. *Hats can keep your head warm in the winter, and they can keep the sun out of your eyes in the summer.* **hats.**

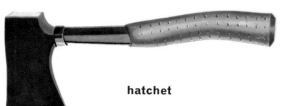

hatchet

hat box (hat′boks′), *n.* a box that can hold a hat. *Most hatboxes are big and round.* **hat box es.**

hatch[1] (hach), *n.* 1. an opening in the deck of a ship. *The cargo of a ship is put in and removed through hatches.* 2. an opening in a floor or roof of a building. *By going up through the hatch, they got to the roof of the apartment house.* 3. a small door in an airplane. *Airliners have escape hatches.* **hatch es.**

hatch[2] (hach), *v.* 1. to cause eggs to produce young. *The hen hatched the eggs by sitting on them to keep them warm.* 2. to keep eggs warm until the young come out. *Turtles lay their eggs in sand or soft ground, where they are hatched by the heat of the sun.* 3. to come out of the egg. *How many chicks hatched today?* 4. to plan secretly. *The boys hatched a surprise for their mother.* **hatch es, hatched, hatch ing.**

hatch et (hach′it), *n.* a small ax. *A hatchet is small enough and light enough to use with one hand.* **hatch ets.**

hatch way (hach′wā′), *n.* an opening in the deck of a ship to the lower part. *The boat's hatchway led down to the sleeping quarters.* **hatch ways.**

hate (hāt), *v.* 1. to dislike very much; to have a deep feeling against. *I hate to see an animal abused.* **hates, hat ed, hat ing.** *n.* 2. a very deep dislike. *Some Indians had a feeling of hate for the white men.* **hates.**

ha tred (hā′trid), *n.* a very strong dislike; hate. *For some reason, there has always been hatred between the two men.* **ha treds.**

hat ter (hat′ər), *n.* a person who makes or sells hats. *My sister spends about an hour at the hatter's when she orders a new hat.* **hat ters.**

haul (hôl), *v.* 1. to pull with force. *The boys hauled their rowboat out of the water onto the shore.* 2. to carry by truck or wagon. *A moving van hauls the furniture when a family goes elsewhere to live.* **hauls, hauled, haul ing.** *n.* 3. the load that is pulled. *Strong trucks are used for heavy hauls.* 4. the distance that something is moved. *From San Francisco to Chicago is a long haul.* 5. the amount taken at one time. *The fishermen made a good haul.* **hauls.**

haunt (hônt), *v.* 1. to visit often; to frequent. *My sister haunts stores looking for sales.* 2. recall often; come frequently to. *Dreams of his accident haunt my father.* **haunts, haunt ed, haunt ing.** *n.* 3. a place frequently visited or recalled. *The special haunt of the kittens was the old barn.* **haunts.**

haunt ed (hôn′tid), *adj.* visited by ghosts. *I read a frightening story which took place in a haunted house.*

have (hav), *v.* 1. own; possess. *They have a new house. The store has many groceries for sale. I have doubts about doing this.* 2. cause to. *Have him play another song. Next time have her telephone you.* 3. accept; take. *Have a piece of candy. Will you have your steak rare?* 4. to be the parents of. *The Smiths have three children.* 5. to be forced; feel obliged. *In the middle of the program they had to leave. All animals and people have to eat.* 6. to put up with; allow. *The teacher won't have any talking during class.* 7. to experience. *Raymond has a cold. I hope she had a pleasant vacation.* 8. **have, has,** and **had** are used as helping words with other verbs. *I have called you twice. Twice he has been late. They had already seen the movie, so we didn't go.* **has, had, hav ing.**

haven't (hav′nt), have not. *We haven't been out of the house today.*

Ha waii (hə wī′ē), *n.* a state of the United States, made up of a group of islands in the North Pacific. *Hawaii was the fiftieth state to be admitted to the Union.*

Hawaiian Islands, the group of islands that make up the state of Hawaii. The largest island of the group is also called Hawaii. *Sugarcane is the largest crop of the Hawaiian Islands.*

hawk[1] (hôk), *n.* a large bird with a strong curved beak, sharp claws, and good eyesight. *A hawk eats smaller birds and animals.* **hawks.**

hawk[2] (hôk), *v.* to sell goods by shouting in the street. *The farmer set up a stand and hawked his fresh vegetables.* **hawks, hawked, hawk ing.**

hawk-eyed (hôk′īd′), *adj.* having keen eyesight, like a hawk. *The hawk-eyed policeman noticed the fire and called the fire department.*

hatchway

haystack

hay (hā), *n.* 1. grass, clover, alfalfa, etc. that is cut and dried for use as food for animals. *In summer the cows ate grass in the meadow, and in winter the farmer gave them hay he had stored in the barn.*
v. 2. to cut alfalfa, etc. and stack it to make hay. *Haying is hard work, but it is fun for a city boy.* **hays, hayed, hay ing.**

hay field (hā′fēld′), *n.* a field in which grass, alfalfa, clover, etc. is grown for hay. *The hay-field was ready for cutting.* **hay fields.**

hay loft (hā′lôft′), *n.* the upper floor of a barn where hay is stored. *The supply of hay in the hayloft will last all winter.* **hay lofts.**

hay stack (hā′stak′), *n.* a large pile of hay stacked in a hayfield. *Children like to play in haystacks.* **hay stacks.**

haz ard (haz′ərd), *n.* 1. a danger; risk. *The tall building near the airport is a hazard to flying. The old wooden house is a fire hazard.* 2. anything placed on a golf course purposely to make the game more difficult. *The pond is a hazard.* **haz ards.**
v. 3. to risk; to take a chance on. *I will hazard a guess that we'll have rain this afternoon.* **haz ards, haz ard ed, haz ard ing.**

haze[1] (hāz), *n.* 1. fog, mist, or smoke. *The haze in the air made it difficult for the pilot to see the airport.* 2. a confused state; unclearness of mind. *The boy walked around in a haze.* **haz es.**

hazelnut:
a. leaves and fruit from the hazel tree
b. shell and seed

a

b

haze[2] (hāz), *v.* to play tricks on; to make someone do unpleasant actions. *In some schools the freshmen are hazed by the older students.* **haz es, hazed, haz ing.**

ha zel nut (hā′zəl nut′), *n.* a small round nut that grows on a bush or small tree. *Hazelnuts are good to eat.* **ha zel nuts.**

he (hē), *pron.* 1. that boy, man, or male animal spoken about. *He works hard in his new job.* 2. pertaining to either sex; anyone. *He who does his homework will pass.* **they,** *pl.*
n. 3. a boy; man; male animal. *The new baby is a he!* **hes.**

head (hed), *n.* 1. the top part of the body in which are the brain, eyes, ears, nose, and mouth. *Put a hat on your head in cold weather.* 2. mind. *Use your head in answering these questions.* 3. the top part of anything. *The head of a pin is small. Put your pillow at the head of the bed.* 4. the front end. *The police cars were at the head of the parade. I was at the head of the line buying tickets.* 5. a person who is a leader, commander, or director. *The head of our company is the president. The head of our state government is the governor.* 6. the beginning; source. *The head of the Mississippi River is in Minnesota.* 7. a topic; title. *The chapter heads of the book tell you what the chapters discuss.* 8. anything rounded like a head. *Buy a head of cabbage and a head of lettuce.* 9. **heads,** the side of a coin having a head stamped on it. *I called heads, but the coin came up tails.* **heads.**
v. 10. to go at the head, top, or front of. *Carl heads the list of honor students. The mayor headed our town's parade.* 11. to move toward. *The little dog headed home when the rain came.* 12. to be the leader of. *The former office boy now heads the company.* **heads, head ed, head ing.**
adj. 13. chief; leading. *The head coach runs the football team. The head man in the race won an award.* 14. coming from in front. *The head winds held down the airplane's speed.*
Head also has the following special meanings:
go to one's head, to make one feel too proud. *His high marks have gone to his head.*
head off, to keep from happening. *Dress warmly in winter to head off a cold.*
over one's head, too difficult to understand. *Some math is over my head.*
put heads together, to plot, plan or think together. *Let's put our heads together and solve our problem.*

head ache (hed′āk′), *n.* a pain in the head. *Too much noise gives some people a headache.* **head aches.**

head ed (hed′əd), *adj.* having a head or heading. *Each chapter in the book is headed, and the titles are listed in the table of contents.*

head ing (hed′ing), *n.* 1. a title at the beginning of a chapter or at the beginning of a part of a chapter. *Under the heading "Uses of Verbs," you will find all the help you need.* 2. a topic. *She*

wrote down four headings to help her in her speech.
head ings.

head line (hed′līn′), *n.* the line or lines in large print at the beginning of a newspaper article. *Headlines give the content of the article in very short form.* **head lines.**

head quar ters (hed′kwôr′tərz), *n. pl.* 1. the place from which orders are sent by a commanding officer of an army or police force. *The soldier was asked to report to headquarters.* 2. the main office from which any organization is directed. *The company has three hundred stores, with headquarters in New York City.* **head quar ters.**

heal (hēl), *v.* to cure; get back to good health. *Doctors heal sick people. His injury healed quickly.* **heals, healed, heal ing.**

health (helth), *n.* 1. a being well; not having any sickness. *The health of our team helped us to win many games.* 2. a condition of the body. *He is still in bad health and can't walk very far.* 3. **drink a health to,** to drink in honor of. *Their friends drank a health to the winners.*

health ful (helth′fəl), *adj.* giving health; good for the health. *All vegetables are healthful foods.* **health ful ly,** *adv.*

healthy (hel′thē), *adj.* 1. having good health. *The doctor said the baby was healthy.* 2. showing good health. *The healthy flowers have large blossoms.* 3. good for the health. *A sea voyage is a healthy way to travel.* **health i er, health i est; health i ly,** *adv.*

heap (hēp), *n.* 1. a pile of things thrown or lying together. *The heap of stones was put into the truck.* **heaps.**
v. 2. to pile; to put or throw together. *The baby's toys were heaped on the floor.* 3. to give in large numbers. *Presents were heaped upon the girl who was getting married.* 4. to fill; load up. *Aunt Betty always heaps our plates with food.* **heaps, heaped, heap ing.**

hear (hir), *v.* 1. to take in sound through the ears. *We could hear every word the speaker said.* 2. to listen to; pay attention to. *The principal said he wanted everyone to hear his announcement about new classes.* 3. to receive news. *I hear that your brother comes home today.* 4. to get a message from. *Have you heard from George in South America?* 5. to listen to in court. *His case will be heard tomorrow.* **hears, heard, hear ing.**

heard (hėrd), past tense and past participle of **hear.**

hear ing (hir′ing), *n.* 1. the ability to take in sounds through the ears. *A dog used in hunting has excellent hearing.* 2. a chance to be listened to in court. *All arrested persons are granted hearings.* 3. the distance that a sound can be heard. *We are within hearing of the children's park.* **hear ings.**

heart (härt), *n.* 1. the large, hollow muscle that pumps blood throughout the body by contracting and expanding. *The heart keeps*

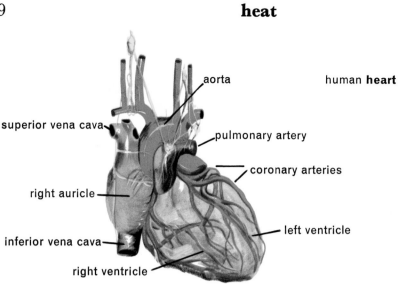

aorta — human **heart**

superior vena cava

pulmonary artery

coronary arteries

right auricle

left ventricle

inferior vena cava

right ventricle

the blood in circulation by receiving it from the veins and sending it out through the arteries. 2. feelings; general nature. *Mothers have generous and tender hearts.* 3. the inner part; middle. *The newspaper's office is in the heart of the city. The heart of the watermelon is the sweetest and juiciest part.* 4. the most important part; main part. *The heart of the teacher's talk was that she is there to help us.* 5. something looking like a heart. *A deck of cards has thirteen cards with hearts on them.* 6. courage. *A race horse has heart. Do you have the heart to tell the boy he can't take the kitten home?* **hearts.**

Heart also has the following special meanings:

after one's own heart, suiting one perfectly. *This is a room after my own heart.*

at heart, in one's real feelings. *At heart he is a kind person, but he doesn't always show it.*

by heart, perfectly; from memory. *I can tell you the poem by heart.*

take heart, to cheer up. *I took heart when my grades went up.*

heart i ly (här′tə lē), *adv.* 1. sincerely; in a friendly way. *Jack greeted his old friend heartily.* 2. with vigor; with a good mood. *His father laughed heartily at Jack's jokes about his camping trip.* 3. with a good appetite. *The dog that followed us home ate the food heartily.* 4. very. *I am heartily sorry that we must go now.*

heart less (härt′lis), *adj.* without kindness; cruel. *John thought that his mother was heartless when she would not allow him to go on the boating trip.* **heart less ly,** *adv.*

hearty (här′tē), *adj.* 1. friendly; sincere. *Al received a hearty welcome when he arrived at the party.* 2. strong; vigorous. *My grandfather is a hearty old man.* 3. big; satisfying. *Hearty meals are served in the school cafeteria.* **heart i er, heart i est; heart i ly,** *adv.*

heat (hēt), *n.* 1. hotness; great warmth. *In summer the heat of the sun is greatest. Fire gives off heat.* 2. hot weather; a hot area. *The heat of summer is pleasant in the woods. The heat of the*

hedge

a

b

heaters:
a. electric heater
b. gas heater

jungle can be bad for the health. 3. a strong feeling; excitement. *The heat of his anger made him say foolish things.* **heats.**

v. 4. to make or become warm. *The furnace heats the house. Water heats on the stove.* 5. to excite. *The coach's talk heated the team members.* **heats, heat ed, heat ing.**

heat ed (hē′tid), *adj.* angry; excited. *The boys had a heated argument about which team would win the championship.* **heat ed ly,** *adv.*

heat er (hēt′ər), *n.* a thing that produces heat. *A furnace is a large heater, which can warm an entire building; a smaller heater can be used to make an individual room warm.* **heat ers.**

heav en (hev′ən), *n.* 1. according to some religions, the place where God and the angels dwell. Browning wrote, "*God's in His heaven, all's right with the world.*" 2. a place or state of happiness. *Pete is in heaven when he is making things in his own little workshop.* 3. **heavens,** the space in which the sun, moon, and stars are seen; the sky. *Our scientists study the heavens through big telescopes.* **heav ens.**

heavy (hev′ē), *adj.* 1. hard to move because of its weight. *This heavy trunk will need two people to lift it.* 2. having much weight for its size. *Gold and lead are heavy metals, weighing more than the same amount of aluminum or tin.* 3. of great force; large; more than usual. *The heavy rain washed away all the dirt from my flower bed. The player's broken ankle was a heavy blow to the team's hopes for a championship. He fell into a heavy sleep.* 4. sorrowful; gloomy. *With heavy hearts the losing team returned to the locker room.* 5. hard to deal with; difficult. *Heavy food cannot be digested easily. The ground is too heavy for a spade. His heavy work wears him out.* 6. weighted down. *The child's eyes were heavy with sleep.* 7. cloudy. *The heavy skies mean rain before noon.* 8. clumsy; slow. *The old man's heavy steps could easily be heard.* 9. dull. *This book is heavy reading, and I don't think you will enjoy it.* 10. loud and deep. *The train announcer uses a heavy voice so that everyone will hear him.* **heav i er, heav i est; heav i ly,** *adv.*

he'd (hēd), 1. he had. *We thought he'd already left.* 2. he would. *I am sure he'd like to help, but he is very busy.*

hedge (hej), *n.* 1. a thick row of bushes planted and used as a fence or boundary line. *A hedge is usually trimmed evenly.* **hedg es.**

v. 2. to put a hedge around. *We hedged the entire backyard.* 3. to avoid giving an answer. *The boy hedged every time he was asked about the broken window.* **hedg es, hedged, hedg ing.**

heel[1] (hēl), *n.* 1. the back part of a person's foot. *When you walk, you put your weight first on your heel.* 2. the part of a sock or stocking that covers the heel. *The heel of a stocking is strongly made because it gets so much wear.* 3. the rear part of a shoe. *You can get new heels put on while you wait.* 4. the end crust of a loaf of bread. **heels.**

v. 5. to put heels on. *The shoemaker heeled her shoes while she waited.* 6. to follow right behind someone. *Dogs are trained to heel.* **heels, heeled, heel ing.**

heel[2] (hēl), *v.* to lean over to one side. *The ship heeled in the wind.* **heels, heeled, heel ing.**

height (hīt), *n.* 1. the distance from the top to the bottom; tallness. *The height of that mountain is 15,000 feet, or nearly three miles. Our gym*

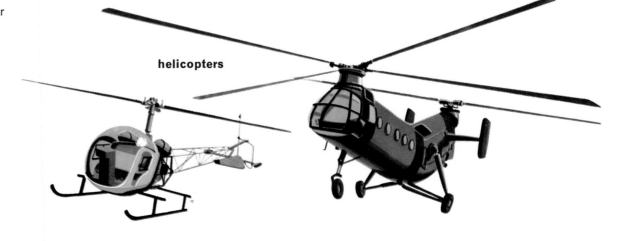

helicopters

helmets:
a. ancient Greek
b. German

a

b

pain that is almost too much to bear. *The pain of breaking his arm was hell.* **hells.**

he'll (hēl), he will; he shall. *He'll be there on time.*

hel lo (he lō′, hə lō′), *interj.* 1. something said to express greeting, to attract attention, or to show surprise. *The policeman at the crossing always says "Hello" as we go by. Hello! What have we here?*

n. 2. a greeting. *Give your family my hellos.* **hel los.**

hel met (hel′mit), *n.* a covering worn to protect the head from injury. *Different helmets are worn by soldiers, by men in construction work, by baseball players at bat, and by football players.* **hel mets.**

helms man (helmz′mən), *n.* a man who steers a ship by using the helm, or wheel. *In today's ships the helmsman is in an enclosed area; in the days of sailing vessels he was in the open at the rear of the ship.* **helms men.**

helmsman

---

heliotrope

teacher is a man six feet in height. 2. the highest point. *The poet was at the height of his fame when we saw him twenty years ago. A professional baseball player usually reaches the height of his abilities at about thirty years of age.* **heights.**

heir (âr), *n.* a person who receives or will receive money or property when the original owner dies. *He is the sole heir to his uncle's house, because he is the only relative. She was one of the heirs of her aunt's estate.* **heirs.**

held (held), past tense and past participle of **hold.**

hel i cop ter (hel′ə kop′tər), *n.* an aircraft that is driven by horizontal rotating blades above it. *Helicopters can go up and come down in a straight line, and can also stay still in the air.* **hel i cop ters.**

he li o trope (hē′li ə trōp′), *n.* 1. a plant with clusters of small flowers varying in color from violet to light purple and even white. *The heliotrope has sweet-smelling flowers, which turn toward the sun.* **he li o tropes.**

adj. 2. reddish-purple. *Mary looks attractive in the heliotrope dress.*

he li um (hē′lē əm), *n.* a chemical element that is one of the lightest gases known. *Helium has no color, no odor, and does not burn or explode. Helium is used to fill balloons.*

hell (hel), *n.* 1. according to some religions, the place where wicked and evil people go for punishment after their deaths. *Hell is the opposite of heaven.* 2. any condition of misery or

---

sand, āte, bâre, fäther; sent, mē, fėrn; fit, bīke; pot, rōpe, fôrt; run, pull, rüle, cūte; noise, sound; ch, cheese; ng, long; th, thick; ~~th,~~ those; zh, treasure; ə = a in about, e in waken, i in animal, o in seldom, and u in minus.

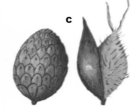

hemp:
a. plant
b. flower
c. seeds

help (help), *v.* 1. to give or do something that is needed or useful; give aid to. *The boys helped their father mow the lawn. Mary helped mother by setting the table. Will you help me with my homework?* 2. to make better. *The doctor's medicine helped my cold.* 3. to stop; keep from. *We couldn't help laughing at our appearance after we fell in the water.* **helps, helped, help ing.** *n.* 4. aid; assistance; something that helps. *The Red Cross gives help to victims of floods, tornadoes, and fires.* 5. a person or thing that aids or assists. *Your help was greatly appreciated by all my family.* 6. a person or persons hired to do jobs around the house. *I know only one family that uses help.* 7. a remedy; relief; a way of making better. *When I had a sore throat, the medicine that the doctor gave me was a big help.* **helps.**

help er (hel′pər), *n.* a person who assists another person. *The truck driver and his helper unloaded the delivery at the factory.* **hel pers.**

help ful (help′fəl), *adj.* giving aid; useful. *Our lazy cat isn't very helpful in catching mice.* **help ful ly,** *adv.*

help ing (hel′ping), *n.* a serving of food. *I am not very hungry, so I only want a small helping.* **help ings.**

help less (help′lis), *adj.* 1. not able to help oneself. *When a person gets ill, he sometimes becomes helpless.* 2. without help or protection. *The cattle were helpless in the blizzard.* **help-less ly,** *adv.*

hem[1] (hem), *n.* 1. a border on a skirt, curtain, etc., made by folding the edge and sewing it to the material. *A hem is a double layer of cloth.* **hems.** *v.* 2. to fold back and sew down the edge of a piece of goods. *She was careful to measure accurately when she hemmed her skirt.* 3. **hem in,** to close in on all sides. *The little house is now hemmed in by huge apartment buildings.* **hems, hemmed, hem ming.**

hem[2] (hem), *interj., n.* 1. a sound that sounds like a clearing of the throat. *"Hem," said Bill as he tried to get our attention.* **hems.** *v.* 2. to make this sound. *He hemmed his disapproval.* 3. to hesitate in speaking. *He hemmed all through his lecture.* **hems, hemmed, hem ming.**

hem i sphere (hem′ə sfir′), *n.* 1. a half of a globe or sphere. *A ball can be cut into two hemispheres.* 2. half of the earth's surface. *The equator divides the earth into hemispheres: the Northern Hemisphere and Southern Hemisphere. A meridian divides the earth into hemispheres: the Eastern Hemisphere and the Western Hemisphere. The United States and Canada are in the Northern and Western Hemispheres.* **hem i spheres.**

hemp (hemp), *n.* a tall plant grown for its tough woody fibers, which are used in making heavy string, rope, or coarse cloth. *Potatoes and grain are shipped in bags made from hemp.*

hen (hen), *n.* 1. a female chicken. *A farmer often sells the eggs that his hens lay.* 2. the female of any bird. *In some states, hunters are not allowed to shoot a pheasant hen.* **hens.**

hence (hens), *adv.* 1. for this reason; as a result. *He ran fast and hence is out of breath.* 2. from this place. *We can be five miles hence in a little over an hour.* 3. from this time. *A year hence we will all laugh at this rainy vacation.*

hen house (hen′hous′), *n.* a house for chickens. *Hens lay their eggs in nests in the hen house.* **hen hous es.**

hep ta gon (hep′tə gon′), *n.* a plane figure with seven sides and seven angles. *That house is built in the shape of a heptagon.* **hep ta gons.**

her (hėr), *adj.* 1. of or belonging to a girl, a woman, or a female animal. *Mary showed us her photographs. Mother can't find her purse. The dog was given her bone for not barking.* *pron.* 2. that girl, woman, or female animal spoken about. *Give the book to her. I went to the movie with her. She's a beautiful bird, and I like her. The cow is hungry, so take her the hay.*

herb (ėrb, hėrb), *n.* 1. a plant whose stems and leaves wither to the ground at the end of summer. The woody stems of other plants live from year to year. *The roots of some herbs remain alive and produce new plants yearly; others have to be replaced by planting new seeds.* 2. such a plant or plant part used for medicines, for seasoning foods, etc. *Mint is an herb that is commonly used for flavoring.* **herbs.**

her bi vore (hėr′bi vōr′), *n.* any animal that eats mostly grass and other plants; an animal that does not eat the flesh of other animals. *A rhinoceros is a herbivore.* **her bi vores.**

her biv or ous (hėr biv′ə rəs), *adj.* feeding on plants. *Cows, horses, deer, and rabbits are herbivorous. A dog is not herbivorous, because it eats meat.*

herd (hėrd), *n.* 1. a number of animals that

hen house

feed together and move about together. *We saw a herd of elephants in a movie about Africa.* 2. a crowd of people; the common people. *A herd of people rushed towards the bus.* **herds.** *v.* 3. to gather together in a group. *A cowboy herds horses into a corral.* 4. to take care of a herd of animals. *Cowboys herd cattle during the winter.* **herds, herd ed, herd ing.**

here (hir), *adv.* 1. in or at this place. *We like living here.* 2. to or into this place. *Please come here.* 3. at this point. *The cars all stop here to get gas before crossing the desert.* *n.* 4. this place. *Let's get out of here before it gets dark.* 5. **neither here nor there,** beside the point. *What you think of him is neither here nor there to me.* *interj.* 6. present. *The children answered "Here!" when the roll was called.*

here af ter (hir af′tər), *adv.* 1. from now on; after this time. *When I fell on the ice, I said that hereafter I would walk carefully.* *n.* 2. the time after death. *The minister urged us to think about the hereafter.*

here to (hir tü′), *adv.* to the thing mentioned. *In his letter he said, "The ticket for the show is attached hereto."*

here to fore (hir′tə fôr′), *adv.* up to this time; until now. *We all found out what had heretofore been known only by a few.*

here with (hir with′), *adv.* along with this. *We are sending the class schedule herewith.*

he ro (hir′ō), *n.* 1. a man or boy who has done a brave thing. *The hero of the fire was Joe Smith, who carried a baby from the burning building.* 2. a man or boy admired for his bravery or for his fine qualities. *George Washington is a national hero.* 3. the important man or boy in a story, book, or movie. *The hero of a story usually is a fine person.* **he roes.**

he ro ic (hi rō′ik), *adj.* 1. brave; courageous; noble. *The heroic boy dived into the cold water to*

heron

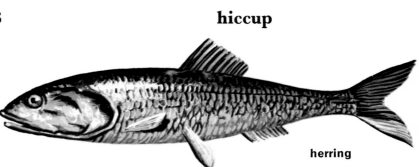

herring

save the puppy. 2. of or like a hero. *It is good to read about the heroic men and women in everyday life.* 3. especially brave or daring action. *His heroic idea saved thousands of lives.* **he ro i cal ly,** *adv.*

her on (her′ən), *n.* a long-legged bird that lives in watery places. *A heron has a long neck, long feet, and a long bill. Herons wade in shallow water in search of food.* **her ons.**

her ring (her′ing), *n.* a small, highly valuable food fish that is abundant in the North Atlantic Ocean. *Many people enjoy eating herring with sour cream.* **her ring** or **her rings.**

hers (herz), *pron.* 1. of her; belonging to her. *The coat on the chair is hers.* 2. the one or ones belonging to her. *Your eyes are brown, and hers are blue.*

her self (her self′), *pron.* 1. her own self. *Edith fell down and hurt herself.* 2. the person or self she usually is. *Betty was not smiling; we guessed she was not herself.* 3. a word used to make a statement stronger. *She herself gave me the recipe. My mother herself said I could go.*

he's (hēz), 1. he is. *He's the best student in the class.* 2. he has. *He told us about some of the schools that he's attended.*

hes i tate (hez′ə tāt′), *v.* 1. to stop or wait because of not being sure of what to say or do. *Since he had forgotten his umbrella, he hesitated before setting out in the rain. The actor hesitated in the middle of his speech because he had forgotten the words.* 2. to feel unwilling. *I hesitate to ask another favor of you, but I have to.* 3. to pause. *We hesitated a moment to look in the store window.* **hes i tates, hes i tat ed, hes i tat ing.**

hex a gon (hek′sə gon′), *n.* a plane figure having six sides and six angles. *All snowflakes have the shape of a hexagon.* **hex a gons.**

hey (hā), *interj.* 1. a word called to get attention. *Hey! You've taken my hat!* 2. a word used to express surprise. *Hey! What have we got here?*

hi ber nate (hī′bər nāt′), *v.* to spend the winter in sleep. *Bears hibernate in deep holes or caves until spring comes.* **hi ber nates, hi ber nat ed, hi ber nat ing.**

hi ber na tion (hī′bər nā′shən), *n.* the act of hibernating. *Most animals that go into hibernation eat vegetables.* **hi ber na tions.**

hic cup (hik′up), *n.* 1. a catching of the breath, with a sharp sound. *Hiccups are caused by a sudden movement of the muscles that control breathing.* **hic cups.** *v.* 2. to have the hiccups. *Sometimes you hiccup*

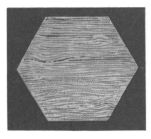

hexagon

sand, āte, bâre, fäther; sent, mē, fėrn; fit, bĭke; pot, rōpe, fôrt; run, pùll, rüle, cūte; noise, sound; ch, cheese; ng, long; th, thick; ~~th~~, those; zh, treasure; ə = a in about, e in waken, i in animal, o in seldom, and u in minus.

after you eat or drink in a hurry. **hic cups, hic cuped, hic cup ing.**

hick o ry (hik′ə rē), *n.* a tree that produces smooth-shelled nuts that are good to eat. *The wood of the hickory is very hard and is used in making canes, baseball bats, and handles for tools.* **hick o ries.**

hid (hid), past tense and past participle of **hide.**

hid den (hid′n), *adj.* 1. concealed; secret. *The explorers searched for the hidden treasure.* *v.* 2. past participle of **hide.**

hide¹ (hīd), *v.* 1. to put or keep out of sight. *Before the guests come, hide all these wrapping papers and gifts in the storeroom.* 2. to keep secret. *He hid the fact that he won the contest.* 3. to keep oneself out of sight. *Little Donald hid behind the fence.* 4. to keep from being seen. *The tall building hides the lake.* **hides, hid, hid den** or **hid, hid ing.**

hide² (hīd), *n.* the skin of an animal. *Indians in the West used the hides of buffaloes to make tepees.* **hides.**

hide-out (hīd′out′), *n.* a secret hiding place used by outlaws. *The robbers' hide-out in the woods was found by the police.* **hide-outs.**

high (hī), *adj.* 1. tall; far above the ground. *Bob is four feet seven inches high. We drove up the high mountain. Walnuts fell from a high branch. My uncle's office is on the thirtieth floor of that high building.* 2. above others; excellent. *Dad has a high position in his company. My grades are very high this month.* 3. main; chief. *The governor holds a high government position.* 4. greater than usual; more than normal. *Prices at this store are high. The ninety degree temperature today is high for this month.* 5. above the usual pitch in music. *Many songs have high notes in them.* 6. joyful; happy. *The class was in high spirits.* **high er, high est; high ly,** *adv.*
n. 7. a high place; a high temperature. *Yesterday's high was ninety-eight degrees.* 8. **high and low,** everywhere. *We searched high and low and finally found the dog in the closet, sound asleep.* 9. **high and dry,** alone and with no help. *When you go away, I'll be left high and dry.* **highs.**

high ly (hī′lē), *adv.* 1. in a high degree; very much. *I thought the book was highly amusing.* 2. at a high price. *The executives of our company are highly paid.* 3. with approval. *Young Richard has always talked highly about you.*

high school, *n.* the school that is above elementary school. *High school includes grades nine through twelve or grades ten through twelve, depending upon local conditions. Junior high schools include grades seven through nine.* **high schools.**

high way (hī′wā′), *n.* a main road. *We drove on highways across the country.* **high ways.**

hike (hīk), *n.* 1. a long walk. *Boy Scouts take hikes through the woods.* 2. an upward movement; an increase. *The hike in the cost of living worries my father.* **hikes.**

v. 3. to take a long walk. *Our class hiked through the woods.* 4. raise; move up. *The store hiked its prices.* **hikes, hiked, hik ing.**

hill (hil), *n.* 1. land that is higher than the land around it, but not so tall as a mountain. *From the top of the hill, we could see for miles.* 2. a small heap of earth. *Ants make hills when they dig tunnels for their underground nest.* **hills.**

hill side (hil′sīd′), *n.* the side of a hill. *In winter we coast down the hillside on our sleds.* **hill sides.**

hill top (hil′top′), *n.* the top of a hill. *From the hilltop we could see Uncle Jerry's farm.* **hill tops.**

hilly (hil′ē), *adj.* having many hills. *The hilly country has a highway that goes up and down.* **hill i er, hill i est.**

him (him), *pron.* the boy, man, or male animal spoken about. *Give the package to him. He's a fine-looking horse, and I like him. We went to school with him.*

him self (him self′), *pron.* 1. his own self. *John fell down and hurt himself.* 2. the person or self he usually is. *Bob is not himself today because he is tired.* 3. a word used to make a statement stronger. *The principal himself gave me permission to leave school early. He himself said I could go.*

hind¹ (hīnd), *adj.* back; rear. *The rabbit's hind legs are longer than its front legs.*

hind² (hīnd), *n.* the female of the deer, especially the red deer, three years or older in age. *The hind is smaller than the male deer and has no horns.* **hinds.**

hin der¹ (hin′dər), *v.* to stop from doing freely; to hold back. *Strong winds hindered the firemen in their efforts to put out the fire.* **hin ders, hin dered, hin der ing.**

hin der² (hīn′dər), *adj.* the back part of something. *The store was in the hinder part of the street.*

hint (hint), *n.* 1. a sign; a slight suggestion. *Mr. Scott's smile gave us a hint of his satisfaction with our job.* **hints.**
v. 2. to suggest something in an indirect way. *By talking about the bargains in suits, Jim was hinting that he wanted a new one.* **hints, hint ed, hint ing.**

hip (hip), *n.* the part of the body on each side just below the waist. *When Mary broke her hip, she also had to have her leg in a cast.* **hips.**

hip po pot a mus (hip′ə pot′ə məs), *n.* a huge, plant-eating, African land and water animal

hippopotamus

with a tough, hairless hide, short legs, and a very large head. *Hippopotamuses are good swimmers and divers and can stay underwater from five to ten minutes at a time.* **hip po pot a mus es** or **hip po pot a mi** (hip′ə pot′ə mī).

hire (hīr), *v.* 1. to employ; pay a person for working. *Because of good business, the store hired three more clerks.* 2. to pay for the use of; to rent. *Father wants to hire a truck to help us in moving.* **hires, hired, hir ing.**
n. 3. the money paid for work. *The boy is worth his hire because he is a hard worker.*

his (hiz), *adj.* 1. of or belonging to a boy, man, or male animal. *You are sitting in his chair. It is all right if the dog plays with that; it is his toy.* *pron.* 2. of or belonging to him. *The chair you are sitting in is his.* 3. the one or ones belonging to him. *His is the small suitcase.*

hiss (his), *v.* 1. to make a sound like s–s–s–s. *A goose hisses. The cocoa boiled over and hissed on the hot stove.* 2. to show dislike by making a sound like s–s–s–s. *The audience didn't like the play, and a few people hissed the actors.* **hiss es, hissed, hiss ing.**
n. 3. a sound like s–s–s. *Hisses came from the angry audience.* **hiss es.**

his tor ic (his tôr′ik), *adj.* famous in history. *We visited historic monuments and buildings on our trip to England.*

his tor i cal (his tôr′ə kl), *adj.* 1. famous in history. *The year 1492 is a historical year.* 2. true; real; that actually happened. *We read a historical account of Benjamin Franklin's life.* 3. based on history. *Some historical movies help us to understand past events.* **his tor i cal ly,** *adv.*

his to ry (his′tə rē), *n.* 1. a written record of man and his achievements. *Some histories are one hundred volumes long.* 2. the study or science of recorded facts of past events. *I am taking a course in the history of the United States.* 3. the things that have happened to a person or thing. *It would take a long time to tell the history of that old car.* **his to ries.**

hit (hit), *v.* 1. to give a blow to; strike. *The boxer hit the punching bag hard.* 2. to strike something aimed at. *Roy's arrow hit the target.* 3. to bump. *John hit his head on the door.* 4. to find; come upon. *He tried and tried, and finally hit upon the answer. Bob hit upon another idea for getting a job. I hoped to hit the right road in the darkness.* 5. to cause unhappiness; to affect badly. *The whole family was hit by the bad news.* 6. to get a hit in baseball. *He hit a long fly the first time up at bat.* 7. **hit it off,** to become friendly. *The two boys hit it off well the first time they met.* 8. **hit the nail on the head,** to say or do something exactly right. *He hit the nail on the head when he told us we would like this place.* **hits, hit, hit ting.**
n. 9. a blow. *The hit on the head made him dizzy for a moment.* 10. a big success. *The song was played for the first time last week, and it's already a hit.* 11. a ball hit in a way that enables the batter to get at least to first base. *A ball player is happy if he gets one hit in three times at bat.* **hits.**

hitch (hich), *v.* 1. to fasten; tie. *The cowboy hitched his horse to the railing. The sailor hitched the small boat to the pier.* 2. to pull or push with short jerks. *The farmer hitched up his overalls. Charley hitched his chair closer to the table.* **hitch es, hitched, hitch ing.**
n. 3. a tug; a pull. *The boy gave his long pants a hitch.* 4. anything that spoils an activity. *The play was presented without a hitch.* 5. a kind of knot. *The sailor put a hitch in the line.* **hitch es.**

hith er (hi t̶h′ər), *adv.* to this place. "*You will come hither after battle and report to me,*" *said the king to his knights.*

hith er to (hi t̶h′ər tü′), *adv.* up to this time. *Hitherto he has been on time.*

hit ter (hit′ər), *n.* a person who hits. *A baseball player should be a good hitter.* **hit ters.**

hive (hīv), *n.* 1. a box or little house used to raise honeybees. *The man kept bees in hives in order to get their honey and sell it.* 2. the bees in a hive. *In the winter the hive feeds on stored honey and pollen.* 3. a place where there are many busy people. *Before Christmas the stores are hives of activity.* **hives.**

hives (hīvz), *n. pl.* a skin disease that causes itching. *Some people get hives from eating strawberries.*

ho (hō), *interj.* a word used to get attention, to show surprise, or to show wonder. "*Ho!*" *said Father, opening his birthday presents, "What have we here?*"

hoard (hôrd), *n.* 1. a secret supply. *The little old lady had a hoard of dollar bills.* **hoards.**
v. 2. to collect and save in a secret hiding place. *Squirrels hoard nuts to eat during the winter.* **hoards, hoard ed, hoard ing.**

hob ble (hob′l), *v.* 1. to limp; to walk clumsily. *My new tight shoes caused me to hobble, so I changed them.* 2. to keep from moving by tying the front legs together loosely. *The cowboys hobbled their horses before putting out the campfire.* **hob bles, hob bled, hob bling.**
n. 3. a clumsy way of walking. *The injured man moved with a hobble.* 4. a rope or strap used to tie up a horse's legs. *Hobbles are used when there is no tree or fence to which to tie a horse.* **hob bles.**

hob by (hob′ē), *n.* something a person does which is not related to his everyday work. *He is a policeman, but his hobby is collecting stamps.* **hob bies.**

hock ey (hok′ē), *n.* a game played on ice or a dry field between two teams, using curved wooden sticks. *The object of hockey is to shoot a disk, called a puck (ice hockey), or a small ball (field hockey), into a goal defended by an opposing player.* (See illustration on following page.)

hoe (hō), *n.* 1. a digging tool with a thin, flat blade and a long handle. *There are many kinds*

ice **hockey**

hoe

of hoes, but all are used for loosening soil and digging up weeds. **hoes.**

v. 2. to dig or loosen soil with a hoe. *Every day, Ellen hoes her small flower garden.* **hoes, hoed, hoe ing.**

hog (hog, hôg), *n.* a pig. *Hogs eat more than half of the corn grown in this country.* **hogs.**

hoist (hoist), *v.* 1. to lift up; pull up; raise. *The heavy bell for the new church was hoisted to the top of the steeple by ropes and pulleys. The players hoisted the coach to their shoulders when they won the game.* **hoists, hoist ed, hoist ing.**

n. 2. a lifting up; a move up. *We gave Gregory a hoist to the top of the fence.* 3. anything used to raise something that is heavy. *One kind of hoist is an elevator built especially to carry bricks and stones to the top floors of a new building.* **hoists.**

hold (hōld), *v.* 1. to take in the hands or arms and not let go. *I was asked to hold the baby. Hold on tight!* 2. to keep in a certain position. *Hold that pose while I take your picture. Hold your head high.* 3. to keep by action against the enemy; defend. *A handful of soldiers held the fort until the new troops arrived.* 4. to control; keep back. *Hold your breath under water. Hold your temper!* 5. to contain. *The big room can hold one thousand people.* 6. to think; believe. *People once held that the sun went around the earth.* 7. to consider; to regard. *The law holds that a person is innocent until he is proved guilty.* 8. to have as one's own; occupy; possess. *He holds an important position in the government.* 9. to stay true; be in force. *He holds to his promises. The manners you were taught at home should also hold in school.* **holds, held, hold ing.**

n. 10. a grasp or grip. *Take a good hold on the rail next to these steps. Your hold on the baby is too tight. The wrestler had a good hold on his opponent.* 11. a place below the deck of a ship where cargo is stored. *The holds were loaded with grain.* **holds.**

Hold also has the following special meanings:

hold forth, to talk for a long time. *The senator held forth for four hours.*

hold in, to keep back. *We should all hold in our stomachs.*

hold on, (a) to keep on. *The pioneers held on in spite of the hardships they encountered.* (b) wait! stop! *Hold on, now; don't go so fast!*

hold out, (a) to keep resisting. *The army held out all winter.* (b) to last. *How long can they hold out?*

hold over, to keep for a longer time. *The play was held over for one month.*

hold up, to rob. *The bank was held up.*

hold with, to agree with. *Older people sometimes don't hold with young people's new ideas.*

hold er (hōl′dər), *n.* 1. something that holds. *We use pencil holders. A pot holder is used in the kitchen for picking up hot dishes.* 2. a person who has or owns something. *That runner is the holder of the world record for the hundred-yard dash.* **hold ers.**

hold ing (hōl′ding), *n.* property owned. *A rich man may have many holdings in stocks and real estate.* **hold ings.**

hold up (hōld′up′), *n.* 1. a robbery committed with a gun. *The holdup of the bank messenger took place on a crowded street.* 2. a delay. *Don't go near the traffic holdup at Montrose Avenue.* **hold ups.**

hole (hōl), *n.* 1. an opening in or through something. *Mother mends the holes in my socks. There was a hole in the sole of Mary's shoe.* 2. a hollow place. *Some animal dug this hole in the ground. The holes in the old road almost caused Henry to fall off his bike.* 3. one of nine or eighteen small sunken cups on a golf course. *The golfer got his ball in the hole using only three strokes.* **holes.**

v. 4. to put into a hole. *The golfer holed the ball.* **holes, holed, hol ing.**

hol i day (hol′ə dā′), *n.* 1. one of the days on which only a few people work. *Thanksgiving Day is the holiday during which we give thanks in the way that the Pilgrims gave thanks for their good crops. Independence Day is the holiday on July 4, to celebrate the signing of the Declaration of Independence.* 2. a vacation. *During the Christmas holiday some people go to Florida.* **hol i days.**

hol low (hol′ō), *adj.* 1. empty; not solid. *The tree trunk is hollow.* 2. shaped like a bowl. *Get one of those hollow dishes.* 3. not real; not worth much. *I never listen to his hollow promises any more.* 4. deep and sunken. *After his illness he had hollow cheeks for several days.* **hol low er, hol low est; hol low ly,** *adv.*

sand, āte, bâre, fäther; sent, mē, fėrn; fit, bīke; pot, rōpe, fôrt; run, pùll, rüle, cūte; noise, sound; ch, cheese; ng, long; th, thick; ~~th~~, those; zh, treasure; ə = a in about, e in waken, i in animal, o in seldom, and u in minus.

n. 5. a hole; a hollow place. *Squirrels often use a hollow in a tree to store nuts.* 6. a small valley. *Spring came early to the quiet hollow.* **hol lows.** *v.* 7. to dig out the inside part. *John bought a pumpkin and hollowed it before cutting a face in it.* **hol lows, hol lowed, hol low ing.**

hol ly (hol′ē), *n.* 1. an evergreen tree or bush with shiny green leaves and red berries. *The holly grows in temperate climates in most parts of the world.* 2. the leaves and berries of the holly. *A wreath made of holly hung on the outside of the door at Christmas.* **hol lies.**

ho ly (hō′lē), *adj.* 1. sacred; set apart for the service of God. *A church is a holy place. Easter is a holy day for Christians.* 2. pure in heart and spirit. *All of us think of him as a holy man.* **ho li er, ho li est.**

home (hōm), *n.* 1. the place where a person lives. *My home is at 1659 Peartree Street.* 2. the city, state, or country where one was born and lived as a child. *New Orleans is my home.* 3. a building or institution for people who need special care. *Every year my family donates money to a home for the aged. Many homes are run by the state.* 4. a place where a certain kind of animal lives. *A polar bear's home is the Arctic. A crocodile's home is warm Africa.* 5. a family; the way a family lives. *A home is kept together by love and understanding.* **homes.** *adv.* 6. to or at home. *Topper, go home!* 7. to the point aimed at. *The speech hit home. The carpenter drove the nails home.*

home ly (hōm′lē), *adj.* 1. fitted to home life; simple; everyday. *Most people enjoy homely pleasures, such as games. Everyone likes homely food.* 2. not good-looking or handsome. *She is a homely girl, but she is very popular.* **home li er, home li est.**

home sick (hōm′sik′), *adj.* unhappy at being away from home; longing for home. *Patricia was homesick when she first went to camp.*

home work (hōm′werk′), *n.* work for school that is done at home. *Our class has ten arithmetic problems for homework.*

hom o nym (hom′ə nim), *n.* a word that is pronounced the same as another word, but has a different meaning and is spelled differently. *"Dear" and "deer" are homonyms; so are "ate" and "eight."* **hom o nyms.**

hon est (on′ist), *adj.* 1. not lying, cheating, or stealing; that can be trusted. *An honest person always tells the truth.* 2. frank and open; not hiding anything. *Brian has an honest face.* 3. obtained by fair and upright methods. *He has always earned an honest living.* **hon est ly,** *adv.*

hon es ty (on′is tē), *n.* fairness; truthfulness; doing what is right. *The witness answered every question with honesty.*

hon ey (hun′ē), *n.* 1. a sweet, sticky, yellow liquid made by honeybees. *Honey tastes good on toast and on bread.* 2. darling; sweet one. *He*

honeycomb

loves her, so he calls her "honey." 3. something superior or very good. *He is a honey of a football player.*

hon ey bee (hun′ē bē′), *n.* a bee that makes honey. *Honeybees buzz around our flowers.* **hon ey bees.**

hon ey comb (hun′ē kōm′), *n.* 1. a group of six-sided little boxes or cells in which honeybees store their honey. *The honeycomb is made of wax, also produced by bees.* 2. anything like a honeycomb. *The apartment building is a giant honeycomb of people.* **hon ey combs.** *v.* 3. to fill with holes. *The hill is honeycombed with caves.* **hon ey combs, hon ey combed, hon ey comb ing.**

hon ey moon (hun′ē mün′), *n.* the time spent by a newly married couple just after their marriage. *My mother and father told me they went to Hawaii on their honeymoon.* **hon ey moons.** *v.* 2. to spend a honeymoon. *My uncle and his bride are honeymooning in Florida.* **hon ey moons, hon ey mooned, hon ey moon ing.**

hon ey suck le (hun′ē suk′l), *n.* a vine with

honeysuckle

flowers that smell sweet. *The flowers of the honeysuckle are yellow, white, pink, purple, or red.* **hon ey suck les.**

honk (hongk, hôngk), *n.* 1. the cry or call of the wild goose. *In the fall we sometimes hear honks as a flock of geese flies south.* 2. the sound of the horn of an automobile. *I did not notice that the green light had come on until I heard a honk behind me.* **honks.**
v. 3. to make this cry or sound. *The geese are honking. The cars in traffic honked.* **honks, honked, honk ing.**

hon or (on′ər), *n.* 1. a good name; credit for doing right. *Robert is a young man of honor, so the company trusts him with important secrets. It is to his honor that he always tells the truth.* 2. fame; glory. *The scientist won great honor for his work.* 3. respect; recognition of ability. *The school held an assembly in honor of the principal.* 4. **your honor** or **his honor,** the way one talks formally to or about a judge, mayor, etc. *May it please your honor, the defense has another witness.* 5. **honors,** schoolwork that gets special mention. *My brother was graduated with honors from the University of California.* **hon ors.**
v. 6. to show respect for. *Men and boys remove their hats to honor the flag.* 7. to do or give something to show admiration for. *We honored the team at a special dinner.* **hon ors, hon ored, hon or ing.**

hon or a ble (on′ər ə bl), *adj.* 1. worthy of being honored and respected. *Mr. Brutus is an honorable man.* 2. showing respect and honor. *The ambassador was given an honorable welcome.* 3. a name given to some officials. *The honorable Mr. Antony, the Secretary of State, will now speak.* **hon or a bly,** *adv.*

hood (hůd), *n.* 1. a covering for the head that leaves only the face showing. *Eskimos wear hoods to keep their heads warm.* 2. the metal cover over an automobile engine. *The man at the gas station opens the hood to add oil.* 3. something like a hood. *Mrs. Murphy's stove has a hood over it.* **hoods.**

hood ed (hůd′id), *adj.* covered with a hood or a hoodlike object. *The fireplace is hooded, so smoke can't enter the room.*

hoof (hůf), *n.* 1. the hard covering on the feet of horses, cows, deer, pigs, etc. *Hoofs provide protection for an animal's feet.* 2. the whole foot of horses, cows, etc. *The horse had a sore hoof.* **hoofs** or **hooves.**

hook (hůk), *n.* 1. a piece of bent metal or other firm material used to catch, to pull, or to hold something. *A hook is used in fishing. Hang your clothes on the hook. She fastens her dress with little hooks. An automobile pulls a trailer by attaching a big hook.* 2. a curve in a road or river. *The mountain road has many hooks.* 3. **by hook or by crook,** in one way or another. *We'll win this game by hook or by crook.* **hooks.**
v. 4. to attach or fasten with a hook. *Help me*

hops

hook the trailer to the car. 5. to catch with a hook. *He hooked a large fish.* 6. to make with a hook. *The women's club hooks rugs every Thursday afternoon.* **hooks, hooked, hook ing.**

hoop (hüp), *n.* 1. a round piece of metal or wood. *A hoop holds the boards in a barrel together.* 2. a round piece of metal or wood used as a plaything by children. *The boys rolled their hoops down the street.* 3. a round piece of wire formerly used in women's dresses. *The wire hoops held the skirt of her gown in a wide circle.* **hoops.**

hoot (hüt), *n.* 1. the cry of an owl. *In the still night the only sounds we could hear were hoots from a distant owl.* 2. a shout that shows dislike or scorn. *The hoots of the crowd didn't bother the baseball player.* **hoots.**
v. 3. to give the cry of an owl. *The owl hooted during the night.* 4. to give a loud shout of disapproval. *The crowd hooted the referee's decision.* **hoots, hoot ed, hoot ing.**

hop[1] (hop), *v.* 1. to move by jumping on one foot. *Children hopped across the playground.* 2. to move by jumping with all feet. *A robin hops. A kangaroo hops.* 3. to jump on, off, across, or over. *The man hopped on the bus. Carl hopped across the little stream.* **hops, hopped, hopping.**
n. 4. a short jump. *It was only a hop to the window.* **hops.**

hop[2] (hop), *n.* 1. a climbing vine with flowers shaped like cones. *Hops are harvested in the early fall.* 2. **hops,** the dried flowers used in making beer and medicine. *Hops add flavor to beer and prevent it from spoiling.* **hops.**

hope (hōp), *n.* 1. a wish that a desired event will happen. *My hope is that someday you will move to this town. Most parents have hopes that their children will be successful.* 2. a person or thing that causes hope. *A home run is our only hope for winning the game. The singer's new record is his hope for success.* 3. the thing wanted. *Her hope is to be elected Miss America.* **hopes.**

v. 4. to expect and desire; to wish. *The class hopes that John will win the contest.* **hopes, hoped, hop ing.**

hope ful (hōp′fəl), *adj.* 1. full of hope; having the idea that everything will work out all right. *The actor is hopeful that the play will be a success.* 2. causing hope; giving hope. *Storm clouds are a hopeful sign when crops need rain.* **hope ful ly,** *adv.*

hope less (hōp′lis), *adj.* 1. having very little chance of working out right. *The boys made a hopeless search in the dark for the lost money.* 2. having no hope. *He is hopeless about his chances of winning the contest.* **hope less ly,** *adv.*

ho ri zon (hə rī′zn), *n.* the line at which the earth and sky appear to come together. *When the sun sets, it drops below the western horizon.* **ho ri zons.**

hor i zon tal (hôr′ə zon′tl), *adj.* going across, not up and down. *The lines of type on this page are horizontal lines. The top of a table is horizontal.* **hor i zon tal ly,** *adv.*

horn (hôrn), *n.* 1. one of the hard, bony growths on the head of cattle, sheep, goats, deer, and other animals. *Horns are usually in pairs, one on each side of the head.* 2. a musical instrument played by blowing, usually made of brass. *An orchestra usually includes some French horns.* 3. a device that makes a loud sound of warning. *All automobiles have horns. The foghorn let the ship's captain know he was too close to shore.* **horns.**

hor net (hôr′nit), *n.* a large flying insect that can give a severe sting. *Hornets resemble bees, but they do not make honey.* **hor nets.**

hor ri ble (hôr′ə bl), *adj.* causing horror; terrible. *We saw a horrible movie about ghosts.* **hor ri bly,** *adv.*

hor ror (hôr′ər), *n.* 1. a feeling of fear or terror. *Mary looks at snakes with horror.* 2. a dislike. *Katherine has a horror of wearing yellow dresses.* 3. a thing that causes fear or terror. *The soldier didn't talk about the horrors he saw in the war.* **hor rors.**

horse (hôrs), *n.* 1. a large, hoofed animal used mainly for riding. *American Indians did not see or use horses until the settlers brought them to this country.* 2. a frame that holds wood as it is being cut. *The wood was placed across the horse*

so it wouldn't slip as it was being sawed.* 3. a frame with legs used as a support or as an obstacle to passage. *The men digging up the street set up horses at night to stop cars from entering the construction area.* 4. a piece of gymnasium equipment used for gymnastic exercises. *The boys lined up and took turns jumping over the horse.* **hors es.**

horse back (hôrs′bak′), *adv.* 1. on the back of a horse. *Some people ride horseback in the park every Sunday.*

n. 2. the back of a horse. *The cowboys rode the range on horseback.*

horse shoe (hôrs′shü′), *n.* 1. a curved piece of metal nailed to the hard hoof of a horse. *Horseshoes protect the hoofs from hard surfaces.* 2. something that is like a horseshoe in shape. *The football stadium was a giant horseshoe, open at one end.* **horse shoes.**

hose (hōz), *n.* 1. stockings; socks. *Aunt Anna always gives me hose for my birthday.* 2. a rubber or plastic tube that attaches to a water faucet. *Every morning John uses a hose to water his garden. The firemen poured water from their big hoses onto the burning building.* **hose** for 1, **hos es** for 2.

v. 3. to wet with a hose. *The sidewalk was hosed every day to keep it clean.* **hos es, hosed, hos ing.**

hos pi tal (hos′pi tl), *n.* a place where sick or injured people are cared for. *Doctors and nurses work in a hospital.* **hos pi tals.**

host (hōst), *n.* a man who has guests in his home or who pays for their entertainment somewhere else. *Jack was a good host, talking briefly with each person as he arrived.* **hosts.**

hos tile (hos′tl), *adj.* 1. unfriendly; showing dislike. *The man we bumped glared at us with a hostile look.* 2. of or like an enemy; warlike. *As soon as the wagon train crossed the western border of Missouri, it was in hostile territory.* **hos tile ly,** *adv.*

hot (hot), *adj.* 1. very warm; having a high temperature. *Summer this year had many hot days. To sleep better, take a hot bath before going to bed.* 2. excitable; violent; full of strong feeling. *Jack's hot temper had to be controlled. There was a hot argument on television last night.* 3. sharp to the taste; causing a burning feeling. *The hot pepper seemed to burn my tongue.* 4. close. *The dogs were hot on the trail of the fox.* **hot ter, hot test; hot ly,** *adv.*

ho tel (hō tel′), *n.* a building used for renting

horseshoes

horses

howitzer

rooms to travelers. *When we were on our vacation, we spent one night at a hotel that was at the edge of a lake.* **ho tels.**

hound (hound), *n.* 1. a dog used for hunting. *Most hounds hunt by scent, but some hunt by sight.* 2. any dog. *This little hound followed me home.* **hounds.**
v. 3. to hunt; chase. *The reporters hounded the man who won the prize in order to get an interview.* **hounds, hound ed, hound ing.**

hour (our), *n.* 1. sixty minutes. *He said he had been waiting half an hour, or thirty minutes.* 2. the time it is. *The hour is six o'clock.* 3. the time in which certain things are done. *The doctor's office hours are from ten to four. Our dinner hour is six o'clock.* **hours.**

hour ly (our′lē), *adv.* 1. every hour. *The bells in our school ring hourly.* 2. very soon. *The school expects the mayor to arrive hourly.* 3. frequently; very often. *The question of who would win the coming election was hourly debated.*
adj. 4. occurring every hour. *The hourly church bell woke me.* 5. for every hour. *My grandfather started work as a boy at an hourly wage of thirty cents.*

house (hous for 1–5, houz for 6), *n.* 1. a building in which to live. *The fine old house is for sale.* 2. a building made for a certain use. *A church is a house of worship. Let's visit the elephant house at the zoo.* 3. an audience. *A full house heard the opera.* 4. the group that makes laws for a country. *Our House of Representatives contains people from all over the country.* 5. a royal family; an important family. *The Queen of England is from the House of Windsor.* **hous es.**
v. 6. to give shelter to. *Grandfather's barn houses hay, horses, and cows.* **hous es, housed, hous ing.**

house hold (hous′hōld′), *n.* 1. all persons living in a house. *Most households consist of one family.* **house holds.**
adj. 2. having to do with a home and a family. *Each child has certain household duties to perform.*

house top (hous′top′), *n.* the top of a house; the roof. *The children liked to hear the poem about Santa Claus landing on the housetop.* **house tops.**

house wife (hous′wīf′), *n.* a woman who takes care of the house for her family. *A housewife* also goes grocery shopping, buys the clothes for the family, and cooks the meals. **house wives.**

house work (hous′wėrk′), *n.* work that has to be done in the house. *Cleaning, ironing, cooking, and shopping are part of housework.*

how (hou), *adv.* 1. in what way. *How can this job be done quickly? I don't remember exactly how the bat broke.* 2. to what degree or amount. *How long can a turtle stay under water? Tell me how far away the moon is. How hot is it outside?* 3. in what condition. *How are you? Tell us how your dog is.* 4. for what reason. *How could you boys play a trick like that?* 5. **how about,** what do you think of. *How about that for a home run? How about his A as a mark in arithmetic?*

how ev er (hou ev′ər), *adv.* 1. to whatever degree; no matter how. *However hot or cold the weather is, the boy delivers our paper.* 2. in what way; in any way. *Read the poem however you think is best.*
conj. 3. nevertheless; yet. *I have never taken that road; however, I'll go that way. Please wait for me; however, you don't have to.*

how itz er (hou′it sər), *n.* a short cannon that fires shells in a high curve. *A howitzer is fired with its barrel pointed upward.* **how itz ers.**

howl (houl), *n.* 1. a long cry or wailing sound made by a dog, a wolf, or a hyena. *The howl of the wolves gave the lonely traveler a feeling of fear.* 2. any cry or wailing like this. *The people in the grandstand gave a howl of disappointment when the team lost.* **howls.**
v. 3. to give a long, sad cry or wail. *Some dogs howl at the moon.* 4. to give a cry of pain or anger. *The child howled when he was told he had to stay home.* 5. to laugh. *The audience howled at the funny movie.* **howls, howled, howl ing.**

hue (hū), *n.* a color or shade of a color. *That dress is a beautiful hue of red.* **hues.**

hug (hug), *v.* 1. to put the arms around and hold tightly. *Nancy hugged her little sister.* 2. to keep close to. *The small boat is hugging the shore because of the rain and wind.* **hugs, hugged, hug ging.**
n. 3. a tight hold with the arms. *His mother gave Paul a hug for being a big help.* **hugs.**

huge (hūj), *adj.* very large. *The elephant is a huge animal. The United States is a huge country.* **hug er, hug est; huge ly,** *adv.*

hulk (hulk), *n.* 1. an old ship that is big and clumsy to manage. *The hulk stayed tied up at the dock for years.* 2. a big, clumsy person; a thing that is hard to handle. *He is such a hulk that he trips over his own feet. The small package was placed next to the hulk that no one could carry.* **hulks.**

hull (hul), *n.* 1. the body or frame of a ship. *The ship's hull was damaged by the iceberg.* 2. frame of an airship or seaplane. *The hole in the airship's hull was fixed immediately.* **hulls.**

hum (hum), *v.* 1. to make a steady buzzing or droning sound, as a bee does. *The automobiles*

sand, āte, bâre, fäther; sent, mē, fėrn; fit, bīke; pot, rōpe, fôrt; run, pull, rüle, cūte; noise, sound; ch, cheese; ng, long; th, thick; ᵺ, those; zh, treasure; ə = a in about, e in waken, i in animal, o in seldom, and u in minus.

HOUSES AROUND THE WORLD

African hut of clay and straw

modern apartment building

Japanese country house with a straw roof

Tunisian house in the desert

house built on log piles in Thailand

Malaysian lake house

Indian tepee made of skins

Canadian log house

Eskimo igloos made from blocks of snow

Mongolian tent made of felt and skins

hummed on the expressway. 2. to sing with the lips closed, not using words. *All day he hummed the songs he heard on the radio.* 3. to be active. *Business is humming.* **hums, hummed, humming.**

n. 4. the act or sound of humming. *The hum of the bees in the afternoon heat put me to sleep. We heard the hum of the car's engine before it came around the corner.* **hums.**

hu man (hū′mən), *adj.* 1. of persons; that persons have. *It is a human weakness to put things off.* 2. having the qualities of man or mankind. *Everybody is a human being. The human body is a wonderful machine.*

n. 3. a man, woman, or child; a person. *A human can think and talk, but an animal cannot.* **hu mans.**

hu man i ty (hū man′ə tē), *n.* 1. people; the human race. *All humanity benefits from the new discoveries about food.* 2. kindness; mercy. *The prisoners were treated with humanity.* 3. **the humanities,** the study of languages, literature, and philosophy. *The author of that book is a professor of humanities.* **hu man i ties.**

hum ble (hum′bl), *adj.* 1. modest; not proud. *He is humble about his many achievements.* 2. not important or grand. *That actor still lives in the humble house in which he grew up.* **hum bler, hum blest; hum bly,** *adv.*

v. 3. to take or bring down; make lower; make to feel unimportant. *The businessman humbled the salesman by keeping him waiting.* **hum bles, hum bled, hum bling.**

hu mid (hū′mid), *adj.* damp; moist. *Humid weather bothers many people. The jungle in South America is humid.*

hu mid i ty (hū mid′ə tē), *n.* 1. dampness; moisture. *The humidity makes a person perspire.* 2. the amount of moisture in the air. *The humidity is high today—about ninety percent.*

hum ming bird (hum′ing bėrd′), *n.* a tiny bird with bright colors that uses its long bill and tongue to get nectar from flowers. *The hummingbird's wings go so fast that they make a faint humming sound.* **hum ming birds.**

hummingbirds

hu mor (hū′mər), *n.* 1. something that makes a person laugh; a funny or amusing quality. *You ought to listen to some of Sam's humor. The humor of the movie is in the acting.* 2. a state of mind; mood. *The cheerful story put me in a good humor.* 3. ability to see the funny side of things. *He has a sense of humor that makes other people feel happy.* **hu mors.**

v. 4. to give in to the wishes of. *She humored the children by reading to them. Many people humor their bosses.* **hu mors, hu mored, hu moring.**

hu mor ous (hū′mər əs), *adj.* funny; comical; amusing. *The audience laughed at the humorous movie.* **hu mor ous ly,** *adv.*

hump (hump), *n.* 1. a round lump that sticks out. *A camel has a big hump on its back.* **humps.**

v. 2. to raise or bend up into a lump. *The cat humped its back when it became angry.* **humps, humped, hump ing.**

hu mus (hū′məs), *n.* the rich, black or brown part of soil made from decaying plants. *All plants grow better if the soil contains humus.*

hunch (hunch), *v.* 1. to bend; to form the back into a hump. *The tall man had to hunch down so he wouldn't hit his head on the low ceiling.* 2. to move forward by jerks. *The woman hunched her way through the crowd of shoppers. You aren't supposed to hunch your hand when playing marbles.* **hunch es, hunched, hunch ing.**

n. 3. a vague feeling that something will happen. *I have a hunch we will all get good marks.* **hunch es.**

hun dred (hun′drəd), *n.* the number 100, which comes after 99 and before 101. *Ten times ten equals one hundred; so does seventy-five plus twenty-five.* **hun dreds.**

hung (hung), past tense and past participle of **hang.**

hun ger (hung′gər), *n.* 1. the need for food. *To satisfy his hunger, he ate a candy bar. Many people in India suffer from hunger.* 2. any strong desire; a need. *The little cat had a hunger for fish.* **hun gers.**

v. 3. to feel hungry. *When he hungered for food, the truck driver stopped at a restaurant.* 4. to long; to desire or want greatly. *The girl at camp hungered to go home because she was lonesome.* **hun gers, hun gered, hun ger ing.**

hun gry (hung′grē), *adj.* 1. wanting food; needing food. *The hungry boys at the picnic ate fifty sandwiches.* 2. having a strong desire or wish; eager. *After five days of being snowed in, the family was hungry for the newspapers.* **hun gri er, hun gri est; hun gri ly,** *adv.*

hunk (hungk), *n.* a large lump; a big piece. *We gave the dog a hunk of meat.* **hunks.**

hunt (hunt), *v.* 1. to go out to kill wild animals or birds. *Some animals are hunted for food, and some are hunted for sport.* 2. to search; to try to find. *The boys hunted for the lost key to the car.* **hunts, hunt ed, hunt ing.**

sand, āte, bâre, fäther; sent, mē, fėrn; fit, bĭke; pot, rōpe, fôrt; run, půll, rüle, cūte; noise, sound; ch, cheese; ng, long; th, thick; ⫽th⫽ those; zh, treasure; ə = a in about, e in waken, i in animal, o in seldom, and u in minus.

HUNTING

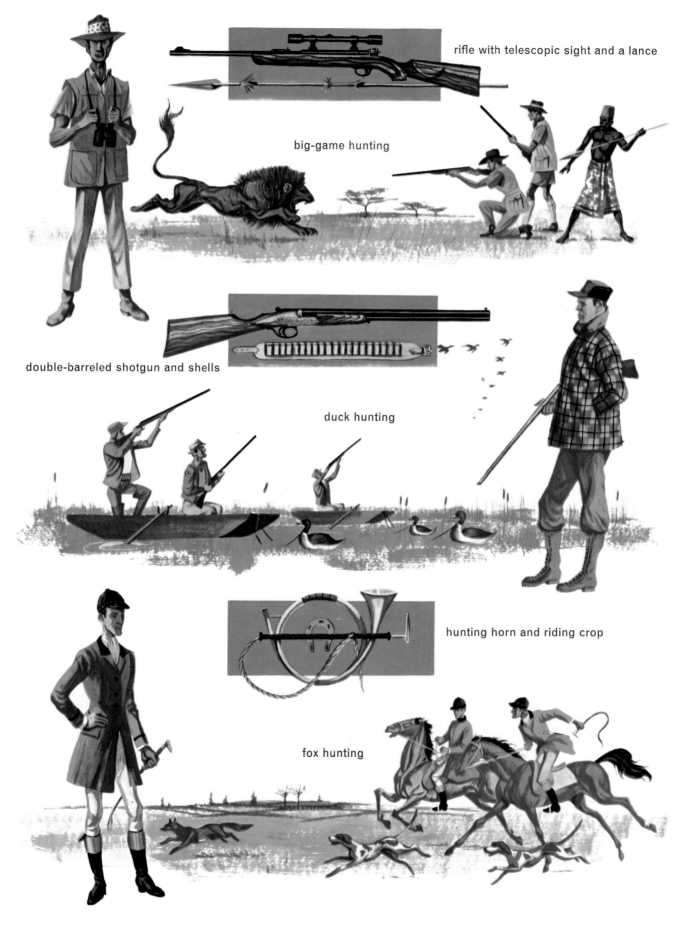

rifle with telescopic sight and a lance

big-game hunting

double-barreled shotgun and shells

duck hunting

hunting horn and riding crop

fox hunting

hydrangea

n. 3. the act of going out to kill wild animals or birds. *Sam left on a deer hunt this morning.* 4. a search; a trying to find something. *The hunt for Mary's glasses lasted one hour.* **hunts.**

hunt er (hun′tər), *n.* a person or animal who hunts. *That man is going to Africa because he is a hunter. This dog is a good hunter.* **hunt ers.**

hunt ing (hun′ting), *n.* 1. the act of a person or animal that hunts. *Many people think hunting is a great sport.*
adj. 2. of or used in hunting. *The hound was trained as a hunting dog.*

hur rah (hə rä′), *interj., n.* 1. a cheer; a shout; a word used to show cheer or success. *"Hurrah! Hurrah! We won the game."* **hur rahs.**
v. 2. to shout hurrah; to cheer. *The crowd*

hydroelectric plant

hurrahed as the team left the field. **hur rahs, hur rahed, hur rah ing.**

hur ri cane (hėr′ə kān), *n.* a very strong storm, often causing great damage. *The hurricane's winds blew down trees and houses.* **hur ri canes.**

hur ried (hėr′ēd), *adj.* done in a hurry; hasty. *The boys ate a hurried breakfast before leaving for school.* **hur ried ly,** *adv.*

hur ry (hėr′ē), *v.* 1. to act quickly; move fast. *I haven't time to talk; I must hurry to school.* 2. to try to make move faster. *I'll do my best to hurry him home.* **hur ries, hur ried, hur ry ing.**
n. 3. haste; a rush; a fast action. *Why are you in such a hurry? We are in a hurry to get to school on time.*

hurt (hėrt), *v.* 1. to cause pain to. *The sting of the bee hurt his arm.* 2. to suffer pain. *If your head hurts, take an aspirin.* 3. to harm or damage. *The expensive tools were hurt by rust. The storm didn't hurt his house.* **hurts, hurt, hurt ing.**
n. 4. an injury; something which causes pain. *The knife can give you a hurt. The hurt to her feelings made her unhappy.* **hurts.**

hus band (huz′bənd), *n.* 1. the man a woman is married to. *He is a kind husband.* **hus bands.**
v. 2. to save; to use carefully; to manage with skill. *If you husband your money, you will be surprised how much further it will go. Husband your strength until the doctor says you are all right.* **hus bands, hus band ed, hus band ing.**

hush (hush), *v.* 1. to make quiet. *The crying baby was hushed by being held in his father's arms.* 2. to be quiet; become quiet. *You have to hush in the library.* **hush es, hushed, hush ing.**
n. 3. a silence; quiet. *A hush came over the crowd as the great musician began to play.* **hush es.**

hut (hut), *n.* a little house or cabin that is plain and simple. *The fishermen lived in huts near the water.* **huts.**

hy dran gea (hī drān′jə, hī drān′ji ə), *n.* a

shrub whose small pink, white, or light blue flowers grow in large bunches. *Hydrangeas need a rich soil and plenty of sun and water.* **hy dran- geas.**

hy dro e lec tric (hī′drō i lek′trik), *adj.* producing electricity by means of waterpower. *Hydroelectric power often comes from the big plants erected near a waterfall or a dam.*

hy dro gen (hī′drə jən), *n.* a very light, colorless gas that catches fire easily and burns quickly. *Hydrogen is the lightest gas that is known. Hydrogen is used in balloons made in Europe; the United States uses helium, which does not burn.*

hy dro plane (hī′drə plān′), *n.* 1. a power boat that travels on the surface of the water. *We rode down the river in a hydroplane.* 2. an airplane that takes off from water and lands on water. *We toured the Great Lakes area in a hydroplane.* **hy dro planes.**

hy dro sphere (hī′drə sfir′), *n.* 1. all the water on the surface of the earth. *The hydrosphere makes up most of the earth's surface.* 2. the moisture in the atmosphere surrounding the earth. *Scientists measure the hydrosphere every day.*

hy e na (hī ē′nə), *n.* a large wild animal somewhat like a big dog. *Hyenas live in Africa and Asia, have a strange howl that sounds like a laugh, and eat the remains of dead animals killed by other animals.* **hy e nas.**

hy giene (hī′jēn), *n.* the science of keeping well; the study of rules of health. *We learn how to avoid the causes of disease in our class in hygiene.*

hy grom e ter (hī grom′ə tər), *n.* an instrument for measuring humidity, or the amount of moisture in the air. *When the hygrometer registers 100, the air is completely filled with moisture.* **hy grom e ters.**

hymn (him), *n.* a song of praise to God. *We sing hymns in church.* **hymns.**

hy phen (hī′fən), *n.* a mark (-) used to divide a word at the end of a line and to join parts of a compound word. *Before you use a hyphen in separating a word, it is best to check with a dictionary.* **hy phens.**

hydroplane

hyena

I or **i** (ī), 1. the ninth letter of the alphabet. 2. the Roman numeral for 1.

I (ī), *n.* a word used to mean oneself. *I am ready to go.*

ibis (ī′bis), *n.* a wading bird with long legs. *The people of ancient Egypt thought that ibises were sacred.* **ibis es.**

ibis

ice (īs), *n.* 1. water that has been frozen solid by cold. *Ice keeps foods and drinks cool. We go skating on the ice in the playground.* 2. a frozen dessert made with flavoring and water. *Orange ice is popular in the summer.* **ic es.**
v. 3. to cover with icing or frosting. *I'll ice the cake.* 4. to make cool by using ice. *Before serving the lemonade, she iced it.* 5. to change into ice. *The pond is icing over now that December is here.* **ic es, iced, ic ing.**

ice berg (īs′bėrg′), *n.* a great big piece of ice that floats in the ocean. *Most of an iceberg is underwater.* **ice bergs.**

ice break er (īs′brāk′ər), *n.* a strong boat used to break openings in the ice. *An icebreaker clears a passage for ships in winter.* **ice break ers.**

ice cream, *n.* a frozen food or dessert, made with milk or cream, sugar, and flavoring. *There are many different flavors of ice cream, including vanilla and chocolate.*

ice-skate (īs′skāt′), *v.* to skate on ice, using ice skates. *He is able to ice-skate backward.* **ice-skates, ice-skat ed, ice-skat ing.**

ice skate, *n.* a shoe with a thin metal runner attached to the sole. *Ice skates are used for skating on ice.* **ice skates.**

ici cle (ī′si kl), *n.* a pointed, hanging piece of ice, formed by the freezing of dripping water. *Icicles hung from the roof of the house.* **ici cles.**

ic ing (īs′ing), *n.* frosting. *The children enjoy helping their mother put icing on the birthday cake.* **ic ings.**

icy (ī′sē), *adj.* 1. covered with ice. *The icy street is slippery.* 2. like ice; cold. *Every morning he takes an icy shower. My hands are icy from going outdoors without mittens.* 3. not friendly; cold. *James greeted me with an icy smile.* **ici er, ici est; ici ly,** *adv.*

I'd (īd), 1. I should; I would. *I'd like to go to the movie, but I have homework.* 2. I had. *I'd a good time last year, so I wanted to go again.*

Ida ho (ī′də hō′), *n.* a western state of the United States. *Idaho is known for its potatoes.*

idea (īdē′ə), *n.* 1. a thought; a belief or understanding. *My idea of a good time is reading books. Anne had no idea of how hard a nurse works.* 2. a plan; a decision or intention. *Bill's idea is to become a doctor. Irene has the sensible idea of staying in school.* 3. a purpose; a reason. *The idea behind the hiring of new people is to get work done faster. In this game, the idea is to win all the cards from the other players.* **ide as.**

ide al (ī dē′əl), *n.* 1. a perfect type; an idea of something that is perfect. *Jack's father is his ideal. Our nation was founded on the ideal that men can govern themselves.* **ide als.**
adj. 2. perfect; exactly as one would wish. *A temperature of eighty degrees and a clear sky are ideal conditions for a picnic.* **ide al ly,** *adv.*

ide al ist (ī dē′əl ist), *n.* 1. a person who has high ideals and tries to live by them. *Tom was an idealist about how a student should study.* 2. a

iceberg :
  a. appearance above water
  b. the part underwater

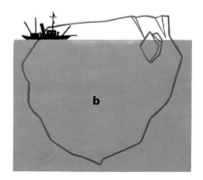

a

b

sand, āte, bâre, fäther; sent, mē, fėrn; fit, bīke; pot, rōpe, fôrt; run, pùll, rüle, cūte; noise, sound; ch, cheese; ng, long; th, thick; <s>th</s>, those; zh, treasure; ə = a in about, e in waken, i in animal, o in seldom, and u in minus.

person who has high ideals but neglects necessities in trying to live by his ideals. *He is such an idealist that he cares nothing for money and, as a result, his family is often hungry.* **ide al ists.**

iden ti fy (ī den′tə fī), *v.* 1. to recognize and tell who a person is; prove a thing to be the same. *The lost boy was identified at the police station by his father. John said he could identify his suitcase by telling what was in it.* 2. to connect; to associate. *Walter identified himself with the heroes he saw in the movies. Is Charles identified with this crazy idea?* **iden ti fies, iden ti fied, iden ti fy ing.**

iden ti ty (ī den′tə tē), *n.* 1. who a person is; what a thing is. *On Halloween we hide our identities by wearing masks. The identity of the automobile was found by checking its license plate and engine number.* 2. sameness. *The identity of the stories led us to believe that the same author wrote them.* **iden ti ties.**

id i ot (id i ət), *n.* 1. a person born with a weak mind who is not able to learn much and who needs constant care. *The idiot could not be taught how to spell.* 2. a stupid or foolish person. *That boy is an idiot.* **id i ots.**

idle (ī′dl), *adj.* 1. not busy; doing nothing. *Our teacher is never idle during school hours.* 2. lazy. *Our idle dog likes to lie in the sun.* 3. having no worth; unimportant; useless. *You hear much idle talk at parties.* **idler, idlest; idly,** *adv.* *v.* 4. to do nothing. *John idled all day Sunday after he went to church.* 5. to run without being in gear. *The engine was not idling properly.* **idles, idled, idling.**

idol (ī′dəl), *n.* 1. an image that is worshipped. *In ancient times people worshiped idols.* 2. a person who is loved or admired. *Jane is the idol of her grandparents.* **idols.**

if (if), *conj.* 1. whether. *No one knows if Jim really likes Joe.* 2. though. *Even if he missed the train, he could still drive here.* 3. in case that; in the event that. *If Christmas comes on Sunday, the store will be closed on Monday.*

ig loo (ig′lü), *n.* an Eskimo house. *Eskimos build igloos from blocks of snow.* **ig loos.**

ig nite (ig nīt′), *v.* 1. to set fire to. *The Boy Scouts had a hard time igniting the wet wood.* 2. to catch fire; burn. *The dry papers ignited quickly.* **ig nites, ig nit ed, ig nit ing.**

ig no rance (ig′nə rəns), *n.* a lack of knowledge; being ignorant. *My ignorance of mathematics is something I can overcome.* **ig no ranc es.**

ig no rant (ig′nə rənt), *adj.* not knowing much; not having education or knowledge. *Jim is not stupid, he is just ignorant of many things.* **ig no rant ly,** *adv.*

ig nore (ig nôr′), *v.* to pay no attention to; not to notice. *Joan ignored the silly remarks made by her small brother. Never ignore the law.* **ig nores, ig nored, ig nor ing.**

ill (il), *adj.* 1. not healthy; sick. *Bob takes care of himself, so he is seldom ill.* 2. harmful; evil; bad.

Smoking cigarettes has an ill effect on the lungs. **worse, worst.**

I'll (īl), I shall; I will. *I'll be home soon.*

il le gal (i lē′gl), *adj.* not legal; against the law. *In many states, it is illegal to litter the highways.* **il le gal ly,** *adv.*

il leg i ble (i lej′ə bəl), *adj.* not able to be read because of poor writing or printing. *Ron's handwriting is illegible.* **il leg i bly,** *adv.*

ill-fat ed (il′fā′təd), *adj.* sure to come to a bad end; unlucky. *The ill-fated ship had been in three wrecks.*

Il li nois (il′ə noi′), *n.* a state in the north central part of the United States. *The capital of Illinois is Springfield, but Chicago is its largest city.*

ill ness (il′nəs), *n.* sickness; a condition of poor health. *Illness kept Craig home from school.* **ill ness es.**

il lus trate (il′əs trāt′, i lus′trat′), *v.* 1. to put in photographs, drawings, pictures, etc. *Three artists will illustrate the book.* 2. to explain; make clear by examples and by comparing. *The population figures illustrate how the country has grown.* **il lus trates, il lus trat ed, il lus trat ing.**

il lus tra tion (il′əs trā′shən), *n.* 1. a picture that explains or makes more attractive. *This dictionary has many colored illustrations.* 2. an example that is used to explain. *The fireman told us some true stories that were illustrations of the bravery of firemen.* **il lus tra tions.**

I'm (īm), I am. *I'm going to the show this Saturday.*

im age (im′ij), *n.* 1. a likeness. *You can see your image in a mirror. A photograph of your father is an image of him. Joan is the image of her mother.* 2. a statue; an object made in the likeness of a person or animal or an imagined thing. *People used to worship images.* 3. a picture in the mind. *The builder had an image of the house he would put up. Tom is very different from the image I once had of him.* **im ag es.** *v.* 4. to tell about; describe. *The tired explorers*

icebreaker

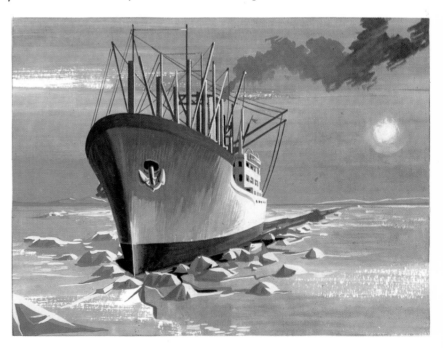

kept going when their leader imaged the successful outcome of their journey. 5. to reflect. *The moon was imaged in the quiet dark water of the little lake.* **im ag es, im aged, im ag ing.**

imag i nary (i maj′ə ner′ē), *adj.* not real; happening only in the mind. *The ghosts in a haunted house are just imaginary.*

imag i na tion (i maj′ə nā′shən), *n.* 1. the power to make up a picture in the mind. *Little children often have big imaginations. A good writer must have a strong imagination to think of a story. Was that my imagination, or did I really hear a robin sing?* 2. the ability to appreciate what others have imagined. *Without imagination you cannot enjoy art, music, and books.* **imag i na tions.**

imag ine (i maj′ən), *v.* 1. to make up an idea or picture in the mind. *I can imagine all the things I would do if I had the time. Nelson imagines that he will be a famous violinist, but he doesn't practice.* 2. to suppose. *I imagine that the play will begin at eight o'clock.* **imag ines, imagined, imag in ing.**

im i tate (im′ə tāt), *v.* 1. to try to be like another person in thought or actions. *Girls often imitate their mothers.* 2. to mimic; to copy. *Emily imitates the chirping of a bird.* 3. to look like something else. *The wooden floor was painted to imitate stone.* **im i tates, im i ta ted, im i tat ing.**

im mac u late (i mak′yə lit), *adj.* free from any mark or stain. *Her white dress was immaculate.* **im mac u late ly,** *adv.*

im me di ate (i mē′dē ət), *adj.* 1. nearest; closest. *Only Dr. Brown's immediate family knew that he was to be the new director of the hospital.* 2. happening right away; without delay. *The immediate effect of the medicine was to stop his coughing.* **im me di ate ly,** *adv.*

im me di ate ly (i mē′dē ət lē), *adv.* right away. *The police came immediately.*

im mense (i mens′), *adj.* very large. *The United States is an immense country. We have an immense amount of work to do if we want to finish on time.* **im mense ly,** *adv.*

im mor tal (i môr′tl), *adj.* 1. living forever. *Most religions teach that man has an immortal soul.* 2. having fame that will last a long time. *Shakespeare's poems and plays are immortal.* **im mor tal ly,** *adv.*

n. 3. a person whose fame will last. *George Washington is one of the immortals of history.* **im mor tals.**

imp (imp), *n.* 1. a child who makes mischief or trouble. *That little imp always gets into the cookie jar when his mother isn't looking.* 2. a trouble-making elf in fairy stories. *The imp changed all the sugar into salt by saying a magic word.* **imps.**

im part (im pärt′), *v.* 1. to tell; pass on to another. *Teachers impart knowledge to pupils. Our neighbor imparts to us the news about people in our block.* 2. to give. *A forest imparts a feeling of peace.* **im parts, im part ed, im part ing.**

im par tial (im pär′shəl), *adj.* fair; not giving one side an advantage over the other. *An umpire in a baseball game must be impartial.* **im par tial ly,** *adv.*

im po lite (im′pə līt′), *adj.* not polite; showing bad manners. *It is impolite to interrupt when another person is speaking.* **im po lite ly,** *adv.*

im port (im pôrt′, im′pôrt for 1, im′pôrt for 2), *v.* 1. to bring goods from one country to another. *Businessmen in the United States import watches from Switzerland and coffee from Brazil.* **im ports, im port ed, im port ing.**

n. 2. something brought into a country. *Bananas are an import.* **im ports.**

im por tance (im pôrt′ns), *n.* being important; value. *That medical book is of no importance to me, but a doctor might find it to be very helpful. Eating the proper foods is of great importance to a person's health.*

im por tant (im pôrt′nt), *adj.* 1. meaning a great deal; serious. *We had important business with the principal. Your birthday is important to you.* 2. having power; seeming to have authority. *We think he is important because he is a judge.* **im por tant ly,** *adv.*

im pose (im pōz′), *v.* 1. to establish as a penalty; to put on as a way of getting money. *The judge imposed a fine on the reckless driver. Our town imposed a tax on all citizens to get funds for a new school.* 2. **impose on,** to put someone to great trouble. *May I impose on you to drive me home?* **im pos es, im posed, im pos ing.**

im pos si ble (im pos′ə bl), *adj.* 1. not possible; not able to happen. *It is impossible for us to live without breathing air, eating food, and drinking water.* 2. not possible to get along with. *That impossible cat has clawed all the new furniture.* **im pos si bly,** *adv.*

im press (im pres′ for 1–4, im′pres for 5), *v.* 1. to mark by pressing; to stamp. *The official paper will be impressed with the government seal.* 2. to affect the opinion of. *His quick mind impressed me favorably.* 3. to get firmly fixed in the mind. *The teacher impressed upon the children the rules of safety.* 4. to seize and force to serve. *Years ago, England impressed men into the navy. Today, a policeman has the right to impress your father's car to chase a robber.* **im press es, im pressed, im press ing.**

n. 5. a mark; a stamping. *The papers carried the impress of the Treasury Department.* **im press es.**

im pres sion (im presh′ən), *n.* 1. a mark made by impressing. *Policemen make an impression of the fingerprints of criminals.* 2. the effect made on the mind. *The book made a great impression on me. If you are loud or impolite, you will give a bad impression of your whole school.* 3. an idea. *I get the impression that he doesn't want to join our club.* **im pres sions.**

im pres sive (im pres′iv), *adj.* having a strong effect on the mind. *The nurse's speech was very impressive.* **im pres sive ly,** *adv.*

im print (im print′ for 1, im′print for 2), v.
1. to mark by pressure; impress. *The envelope
was imprinted with the official government seal.*
im prints, im print ed, im print ing.
n. 2. a mark. *The rabbit left imprints of his feet in
the snow.* **im prints.**

im prove (im prüv′), v. 1. to make better. *You
can improve your dog's appearance by washing and
combing him. We were told today to improve the
looks of our playground by cleaning it.* 2. to become
better. *He improved in health and appearance.*
im proves, im proved, im prov ing.

im prove ment (im prüv′mənt), n. 1. a change
or addition that makes something better. *Very
often an editor makes improvements in an author's
book.* 2. a making better; becoming better.
*The improvement in your appearance will be noticed
by everyone.* **im prove ments.**

im pulse (im′puls), n. 1. a sudden wish or
desire to do something. *The man had an impulse
to speak, but he kept silent.* 2. a push; a driving
force that results in action. *The impulse of the
storm blew our fence down.* **im puls es.**

im pul sive (im pul′siv), adj. 1. acting upon
impulse; doing something without figuring
out the results. *The impulsive child ran into the
street without looking to either side. The kind-
hearted man was too impulsive; he was always giving
his money away.* 2. made on a sudden rush or
impulse. *Her impulsive way of speaking interrupts
the talk of others.* **im pul sive ly,** adv.

im pure (im pyùr′), adj. 1. not pure; not clean.
*Heavy smoke from factories causes impure air. This
water is impure and should not be used.* 2. mixed
with another substance. *Impure gold contains
traces of other minerals.* **im pure ly,** adv.

in (in), prep. 1. inside. *We live in town. My pen is in
my pocket.* 2. during. *It is cold in the morning.*
3. into. *He went in the living room to watch television.* 4. within. *I opened the big box, and a
smaller one was in it.*

in a bil i ty (in′ə bil′ə te), n. a being unable; not
having ability or power. *Old people sometimes
have an inability to sleep well.* **in a bil i ties.**

in ac cu ra cy (in ak′yə rə sē), n. a mistake; an
error; being wrong. *You should correct any
inaccuracies in your homework before handing it in.*
in ac cu ra cies.

in ac tive (in ak′tiv), adj. not active; idle; not
moving around. *Many animals are inactive during
the winter.* **in ac tive ly,** adv.

in ad e quate (in ad′ə kwit), adj. not enough.
His grasp of proper grammar is inadequate.
in ad e quately, adv.

in as much as (in′əz much′), conj. since;
because. *Inasmuch as he wanted to buy some
books, he started a savings account.*

inch (inch), n. 1. a measure of length. *Twelve
inches are one foot.* **inch es.**
v. 2. to move slowly; go ahead little by little.
*Sometimes heavy traffic causes automobiles to inch
along.* **inch es, inched, inch ing.**

in ci dent (in′sə dənt), n. 1. something that
happens. *Life at camp was filled with funny incidents that still make me smile.* **in ci dents.**
adj. 2. **incident to,** likely to happen with.
Cooler weather is incident to a rainstorm.

in ci den tal ly (in′sə den′tl ē), adv. without
much attention; as an incident along with
something else. *Although he is a famous scientist,
he spoke of his work only incidentally during our
conversation.*

in cline (in klīn′ for 1–3, in′klīn′ for 4), v.
1. to lean; slant; slope. *The telephone pole inclines to the south.* 2. to bow; bend forward. *The
speaker inclined his head when the audience
applauded.* 3. to make favorable or willing; to
give a tendency to. *John's performance inclines
me to believe that he is a good actor. Mr. Norman's
promise to be a good mayor inclined us to vote for
him.* **in clines, in clined, in clin ing.**
n. 4. a slope; a slanting surface. *The car easily
went up the incline.* **in clines.**

in clined (in klīnd′), adj. 1. sloping; slanting.
It was hard work walking up the inclined road.
2. having a tendency; willing. *He is inclined
to staying up late.*

in clude (in klüd′), v. 1. to contain; to cover.
*The price of the radio includes the tax. The big
ranch includes more than a thousand acres.* 2. to put
in as part of the total. *Everyone on the team was
there, including the batboy.* **in cludes, in clud-
ed, in clud ing.**

in clu sive (in klü′siv), adj. including; taking
everything into account. *Mother makes an
inclusive grocery list every Saturday.* **in clu sive ly,**
adv.

in come (in′kum), n. money received from
salary, rent, property, business, etc. *Many
people spend their entire income.* **in comes.**

in con ven ience (in′kən vēn′yens), n. 1. a
trouble; a bother. *The inconvenience of many
stops made our trip much longer than usual.* 2. anything that causes trouble or bother. *The street
repairs are an inconvenience to truck drivers.* **in-
con ven ienc es.**
v. 3. to cause trouble or bother. *Driving me
home inconvenienced him, but he was polite.*
**in con ven ienc es, in con ven ienced, in-
con ven ienc ing.**

in crease (in krēs′ for 1, in′krēs for 2–3), v.
1. to make or become greater. *Phillip's salary
increases every year.* **in creas es, in creased,
in creas ing.**
n. 2. an addition; growth. *There was an increase
in the town's population.* 3. the amount by which
something increases. *The boy received an increase
of five dollars in his salary.* **in creas es.**

in debt ed ness (in det′əd nəs), n. 1. the condition of being in debt. *We have an indebtedness
to scientists for making our lives easier.* 2. the
amount owed. *My indebtedness to my parents can
really never be repaid. Frank's indebtedness to the
bank now amounts to five hundred dollars.*

---

sand, āte, bâre, fäther; sent, mē, fẽrn; fit, bīke; pot, rōpe, fôrt; run, pùll, rüle, cūte; noise, sound; ch, cheese;
ng, long; th, thick; ~~th~~, those; zh, treasure; ə = a in about, e in waken, i in animal, o in seldom, and u in minus.

in deed (in dēd/), *adv.* in fact; really. *We are indeed glad that the rain stopped. The food is good at that restaurant; indeed, I have never had better.*

in def i nite (in def/ə nit), *adj.* 1. vague; not clear; not exact. *The directions we were given were so indefinite that we lost our way.* 2. not having an exact limit. *Father will be in Europe for an indefinite length of time.* **in def i nite ly,** *adv.*

in dent[1] (in dent/), *v.* 1. to space or write farther in from the margin. *The first line of a paragraph is usually indented.* 2. to form notches in something. *The waves indented the beach.* **in dents, in dent ed, in dent ing.**

in dent[2] (in dent/), *v.* to make a dent; to press in. *Father indented the front of the car in the accident.* **in dents, in dent ed, in dent ing.**

in de pen dence (in/di pen/dəns), *n.* freedom from the control of others. *The American colonies won their independence from England with the American Revolution.*

in de pen dent (in/di pen/dənt), *adj.* 1. not controlled by anyone else. *He is an independent man, making up his own mind. There are many more independent nations now than there were fifty years ago.* 2. having no connections with another. *The independent grocery is next door to a store owned by a big corporation.* 3. not influenced by others. *Uncle Roscoe is an independent voter.* 4. not supported by another. *Since he got a job, Bill is independent.* **in de pen dent ly,** *adv.*
n. 5. a person who thinks, acts, or votes for himself. *John is an independent in political matters.* **in de pen dents.**

in dex (in/deks), *n.* 1. a list in alphabetical order of the things discussed in a book. *An index gives the page number of each topic in a book, and is used for reference.* 2. something that points out; a sign. *Her ready smile is an index of her good nature.* **in dex es.**
v. 3. to write an index for. *That author usually hires an expert to index his books.* **in dex es, in dexed, in dex ing.**

In di an (in/dē ən), *n.* 1. one of the people who lived in America before the people from Europe came; an American Indian. *Many Indians helped the early settlers, but as they saw their land being taken, they became hostile.* 2. a person who lives in India or the East Indies, or who came from there. *Most Indians live in mud and straw huts in small towns and villages, where they farm small pieces of ground in surrounding fields.* **In di ans.**
adj. 3. of the American Indians. *We bought an Indian blanket out West.* 4. of the Indians in India. *The Indian way of life is hard.*

In di ana (in/dē an/ə), *n.* a middle western state of the United States. *Indiana is a major industrial state, having one of the largest steel mills in the world.*

in di cate (in/də kāt/), *v.* 1. to show; make known. *The sign indicates that we may make a right turn. He indicated his interest by sitting up*
straight and closely watching the speaker in class. 2. to give a sign; to be a sign. *Smoke usually indicates fire.* **in di cates, in di cat ed, in di cat ing.**

in dif fer ent (in dif/ər ənt), *adj.* 1. not having much interest; without caring. *Most people who use public transportation are indifferent to parking problems.* 2. not very good and not very bad. *Most of the scores on the final test were indifferent.* **in dif fer ent ly,** *adv.*

in di go (in/də gō), *n.* 1. a blue dye obtained from certain plants. *Indians used indigo to dye cloth.* 2. a deep violet-blue color. *In a rainbow, indigo is found between blue and violet.* **in di gos** or **in di goes.**

in di rect (in/də rekt/), *adj.* 1. not straight; roundabout. *If you take an indirect way, you will be late.* 2. not straightforward; not to the point. *Say yes or no; your indirect answers confuse me.* 3. having no close connection; not intended. *A new dress was the indirect result of a trip downtown.* **in di rect ly,** *adv.*

in di vid u al (in/də vij/ù əl), *n.* 1. one person; one thing; one animal. *The herd of cattle consisted of fifty individuals. Our Constitution protects the individual and his rights.* **in di vid u als.**
adj. 2. for one; separate. *Please take individual seats. Each person has his own individual record in our files.* 3. different from others; strongly unusual. *The musician has an individual style of playing.* **in di vid u al ly,** *adv.*

in doors (in/dôrz/), *adv.* inside a building. *Children play indoors when rainy weather keeps them from going out.*

in duce (in düs/, in dūs/), *v.* 1. to cause. *Lack of proper food and rest can induce illness.* 2. to influence; get someone to do something. *Bill induced Dave to go swimming. A television commercial may induce people to buy a certain product.* **in duc es, in duced, in duc ing.**

in dulge (in dulj/), *v.* 1. to give in to one's desire for pleasure. *The overweight woman indulged herself by overeating.* 2. to give in to the wishes of another. *The mother indulged her sick child by letting him stay up late.* **in dulg es, in dulged, in dulg ing.**

in dus tri al (in dus/trē əl), *adj.* having to do with industry and the production of goods. *Chicago, Detroit, and Birmingham are industrial cities. Industrial schools teach boys how to work in business and manufacturing.* **in dus tri al ly,** *adv.*

in dus try (in/dus trē), *n.* 1. a part or kind of business or manufacturing. *The automobile industry is concerned with making and selling automobiles.* 2. the production of goods; all businesses thought of as one. *Industry grows partly as the result of new inventions.* 3. hard work. *Jack's industry finally got him a college scholarship, which will pay for his board and room.* **in dus tries.**

in e qual i ty (in/i kwol/ə tē), *n.* 1. being not equal; not having the same size, treatment, value, etc. *Inequality in housing conditions is especially apparent in large cities.* 2. a mathematical expression showing that two quantities are unequal. *An inequality is written like this: 18 is greater than 14, or 18 > 14; 5 is less than 10, or 5 < 10.* **in e qual i ties.**

in ev i ta ble (in ev′ə tə bl), *adj.* sure to happen; not to be avoided or escaped. *My mother's inevitable question is, "Did you clean your room?"* **in ev i ta bly,** *adv.*

in fan cy (in′fən sē), *n.* 1. the time of being a baby; early childhood. *Few people remember their infancy.* 2. an early stage of growing. *Travel in space is still in its infancy.* **in fan cies.**

in fant (in′fənt), *n.* 1. a baby. *She is the loudest infant I've ever heard.* **in fants.** *adj.* 2. having to do with babies. *Some stores sell only infant clothing.* 3. young; in an early stage of growing. *At one time, the automobile business was an infant industry.*

in fect (in fekt′), *v.* 1. to make ill by the introduction of germs. *A wound can become infected if it is not cleaned properly.* 2. to influence. *His enthusiasm infected all of us.* **in fects, in fect ed, in fect ing.**

in fec tion (in fek′shən), *n.* 1. a causing of disease by the spreading of germs. *Impure water is a means of infection.* 2. a disease or sick condition caused by germs. *He got dirt in the cut on his finger, and an infection set in.* 3. a disease that spreads germs from one person to another. *Measles and colds are common infections.* **in fec tions.**

in fe ri or (in fir′ē ər), *adj.* 1. not so good as another. *Inferior material wears out before better material does.* *n.* 2. a person who has a lower rank or position. *A good leader is liked by his inferiors.* **in fe ri ors.**

in fi nite (in′fə nit), *adj.* 1. having no limits; having no end. *Space and time are infinite.* 2. very great. *A mother has infinite love for her children.* **in fi nite ly,** *adv.*

in flate (in flāt′), *v.* 1. to put air into. *The tires of automobiles and bicycles must be inflated regularly.* 2. to make proud or happy. *His high grades inflated him.* 3. to cause to expand beyond the ordinary limits. *New highways and new schools inflate taxes.* **in flates, in flat ed, in flat ing.**

in fla tion (in flā′shən), *n.* 1. an inflating; being expanded. *The inflation of the gas balloon took three hours.* 2. increase of prices due to a country having too much money or credit available. *During inflation the amount of goods a dollar will buy goes down.* **in fla tions.**

in flu ence (in′flü əns), *n.* 1. the power or ability to persuade others. *The teacher has a good influence on his class. Use your influence to get your friends to come to our school fair.* 2. a person who has power. *The editor of the newspaper is an influence in obtaining improvements in the city.* **in flu enc es.** *v.* 3. to have an effect on. *Weather influences the*

growth of plants. **in flu enc es, in flu enced, in flu enc ing.**

in flu en za (in′flü en′zə), *n.* a disease caused by a virus and marked by a fever, a headache, chills, and an aching body. *The informal name for influenza is flu.*

in form (in fôrm′), *v.* to tell. *We informed her that she was on the wrong street.* **in forms, in formed, in form ing.**

in for mal (in fôr′ml), *adj.* not formal; casual. *The party was informal, so we didn't have to dress up. Informal talk is plain, ordinary talk.* **in for mal ly,** *adv.*

in for ma tion (in′fər mā′shən), *n.* 1. an informing or telling. *The bicycle came with a booklet for the information of new riders.* 2. knowledge; facts; something that is told. *We gave the principal the information we had about the broken window. Where can I get more information about raising a dog?*

in gre di ent (in grē′dē ənt), *n.* one of the things that a mixture is made of. *Two of the ingredients of fudge are chocolate and sugar.* **in gre di ents.**

in hab i tant (in hab′ə tənt), *n.* a person or animal living in a certain place. *Our village has twelve thousand inhabitants. Fish are inhabitants of the seas and lakes.* **in hab i tants.**

in hale (in hāl′), *v.* to breathe in; take air into the lungs. *The doctor told me to inhale deeply.* **in hales, in haled, in hal ing.**

in her it (in her′it), *v.* 1. to receive something from a deceased person. *Beth inherited her aunt's ring.* 2. to receive from a parent as a characteristic or trait. *Lisa inherited her father's blue eyes.* **in her its, in her it ed, in her it ing.**

in i tial (i nish′əl), *n.* 1. the first letter of a name. *The initials of the United States of America are U.S.A.* **in i tials.** *adj.* 2. first; beginning. *Classes in school will have their initial meetings on September 6.* **in i tial ly,** *adv.* *v.* 3. to mark with initials. *Mr. Joseph Daniels initials all his letters J. D. to show that he has read them.* **in i tials, in i tialed, in i tial ing.**

in i ti ate (i nish′ē āt′), *v.* 1. to begin; start. *The church initiated a campaign to raise money for missionary work.* 2. to help or teach something new to a person. *The class was initiated into the study of animals by a trip to the zoo.* 3. to admit by special forms and ceremonies. *My brother was initiated into his college club.* **in i ti ates, in i ti ated, in i ti at ing.**

in i ti a tion (i nish′ē ā′shən), *n.* 1. the formal admission into a group or society. *The debate club held the initiation of new members last night.* 2. the ceremonies held to admit a new member. *Only those who belong to an organization know about their initiations.* 3. an introduction; beginning. *The initiation of the new science course took place this year.* **in i ti a tions.**

in jure (in′jər), *v.* to harm; hurt. *No one was*

sand, āte, bâre, fäther; sent, mē, fèrn; fit, bīke; pot, rōpe, fôrt; run, pùll, rüle, cūte; noise, sound; ch, cheese; ng, long; th, thick; th, those; zh, treasure; ə = a in about, e in waken, i in animal, o in seldom, and u in minus.

injured when the chimney fell down. Frost can injure a fruit crop worth thousands of dollars. Careless talk can injure someone's reputation. **in jures, in jured, in jur ing.**

in ju ry (in′jər ē), *n.* harm; damages; hurt. *There were no injuries at camp last summer. The ship came through the terrible storm without injury.* **in ju ries.**

ink (ingk), *n.* 1. a liquid used in a pen for writing or drawing. *Teachers sometimes use red ink to make corrections on a theme.* **inks.**
v. 2. to draw or mark with ink. *The artist quickly inked a picture of the girl.* **inks, inked, ink ing.**

inn (in), *n.* a small country hotel that was popular years ago. *The rider on horseback rode up to the door of the old inn.* **inns.**

in ner (in′ər), *adj.* 1. farther in; interior. *The inner rooms of the big house were not open to the public. I carry my money in an inner pocket.* 2. private; secret. *All of us have inner thoughts that we keep to ourselves.*

in ning (in′ing), *n.* the time in a baseball game in which each team bats until three outs are made. *The visiting team usually bats in the first half of the innings.* **in nings.**

in no cent (in′ə sənt), *adj.* 1. not guilty. *The evidence proved that the man was innocent of the crime.* 2. harmless; having no bad effect. *The brothers played innocent tricks on each other, such as hiding a shoe under the bed.* 3. knowing no evil. *An innocent child fears no one, because he is trusting.* **in no cently,** *adv.*

in oc u la tion (in ok′yə lā′shən), *n.* the introduction of a substance through the skin into the blood to prevent a disease. *Doctors give inoculations to prevent children from getting certain diseases.* **in oc u la tions.**

in quire (in kwīr′), *v.* to ask; to try to find out about. *Let's inquire when the next plane leaves. What did you learn when you inquired about your grades?* **in quires, in quired, in quir ing.**

in quiry (in kwīr′ē, in′kwə rē), *n.* 1. a question. *A policeman answers many inquiries every day.* 2. an investigation; an examination for more facts. *An inquiry into the cause of the fire is being held by the fire chief.* **in quir ies.**

in sect (in′sekt), *n.* a small animal with six legs and a body that has three sections: head, thorax, and abdomen. *Flies, fleas, ants, bees, and grasshoppers are insects. Most insects have wings.* **in sects.**

in side (in′sīd′ for 1–4, in′sīd′ for 5–6), *n.* 1. the part that is within. *The inside of a new car looks clean and even smells good.* **in sides.**
adj. 2. being on the inside. *He has an inside job with an insurance company. My money is in an inside pocket of my jacket.* 3. private; secret. *I have some inside information about when the test will be given.* 4. done by people within a house or building. *Police think the bank robbery was an inside job.*

adv. 5. within; in or to the inside. *Come inside; it is raining.*
prep. 6. in. *The coat is inside the closet.*

in sid er (in′sīd′ər), *n.* a person who knows what the actual conditions or facts are. *The man who makes out the salary checks for a business is an insider.* **in sid ers.**

in sist (in sist′), *v.* to stick to some request or statement; demand. *I insist that you come with us, and I won't go unless you do.* **in sists, in sist ed, in sist ing.**

in spect (in spekt′), *v.* to look at carefully. *The dentist inspected her teeth. The general inspected the soldiers as they marched by.* **in spects, in spect ed, in spect ing.**

in spec tion (in spek′shən), *n.* an inspecting; an examination. *Automobiles are given a careful inspection before they are sold. The inspection of the soldiers will be held when the general arrives.* **in spec tions.**

in spec tor (in spek′tər), *n.* a person who has a job of inspecting. *The fire department sends inspectors to examine buildings for fire hazards.* **in spec tors.**

in spi ra tion (in′spə rā′shən), *n.* 1. a deep, strong feeling that results in action or in thinking. *Seeing the sunset, the poet had an inspiration to write about it.* 2. a person or thing that inspires; an influence for good. *Abraham Lincoln's life has been an inspiration for many Americans. The mountains at twilight were an inspiration to the artist.* 3. any bright idea; an impulse; a sudden thought. *Why don't you get the inspiration to do your homework?* 4. a breathing of air into the lungs. *The doctor listens to your inspiration when you have an examination.* **in spi ra tions.**

in spire (in spīr′), *v.* 1. to cause to have certain thoughts; to arouse good feeling in. *He was so certain we could win that he inspired confidence in all of us. The teacher's praise inspired the class.* 2. to bring about. *The littered playground inspired a school clean-up campaign.* 3. to breathe air in. *A person inspires about sixteen times a minute.* **in spires, in spired, in spir ing.**

in stall (in stôl′), *v.* 1. to put into a place where it can be used. *The new water heater was installed in the basement.* 2. to put into office with ceremony. *The band played when the president of the college was installed.* 3. to put in a place. *In winter the dog installs itself next to the heater and rarely moves.* **in stalls, in stalled, in stall ing.**

in stal la tion (in′stə lā′shən), *n.* an installing; being placed. *The installation of the new furnace took several hours. His installation as mayor was impressive.* **in stal la tions.**

in stance (in′stəns), *n.* 1. an example; a case that proves something. *Your lateness is another instance of your carelessness.* 2. **for instance,** for example. *He is athletic; for instance, he is on the football, basketball, and swimming teams.* **in stanc es.**

in stant (in′stənt), *n.* 1 a short time; a

INSECTS

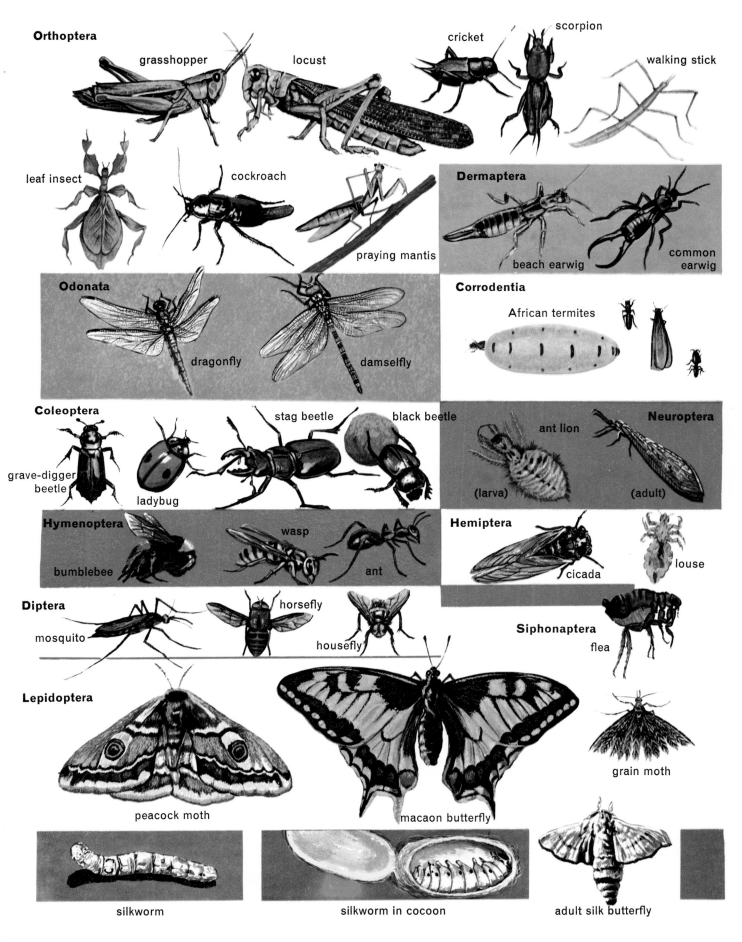

Orthoptera

grasshopper

locust

cricket

scorpion

walking stick

leaf insect

cockroach

praying mantis

Dermaptera

beach earwig

common earwig

Odonata

dragonfly

damselfly

Corrodentia

African termites

Coleoptera

stag beetle

black beetle

grave-digger beetle

ladybug

Neuroptera

ant lion

(larva)

(adult)

Hymenoptera

wasp

bumblebee

ant

Hemiptera

cicada

louse

Diptera

horsefly

mosquito

housefly

Siphonaptera

flea

Lepidoptera

grain moth

peacock moth

macaon butterfly

silkworm

silkworm in cocoon

adult silk butterfly

moment. *The runner paused for an instant to catch his breath.* 2. a certain time. *We heard a clap of thunder, and at that instant the rain started.* **in stants.**

adj. 3. immediate; taking place quickly. *This pill will give instant relief from a headache.* 4. that can be made quickly. *Instant cocoa can be made by pouring hot water over a powdery mixture.* **in stant ly,** *adv.*

in stant ly (in′stənt lē), *adv.* at once. *When I called him, he came instantly.*

in stead (in sted′), *adv.* 1. in place. *I read a book instead of watching television.* 2. in place of something or someone. *Since the manager wasn't in the store, we talked to his assistant instead.*

in step (in′step′), *n.* the upper part of the foot at the arch. *The instep is between the toes and the ankle.* **in steps.**

in stinct (in′stingkt), *n.* 1. the natural way of doing things. *Birds are not taught how to fly; they do it by instinct. The dog's instinct guided him back home.* 2. a talent; the sort of ability that seems to come naturally. *The small child shows an instinct for singing.* **in stincts.**

in sti tute (in′stə tüt′, in′stə tūt′), *n.* 1. a school or organization for a special purpose. *An art institute teaches art and displays paintings. My brother went to an institute to learn engineering.* 2. a building or group of buildings used by such an organization. *My friend and I spent the afternoon in the Chicago Art Institute.* **in sti tutes.**

v. 3. to set up; begin. *Our school instituted a course in French this year.* **in sti tutes, in sti tut ed, in sti tut ing.**

in sti tu tion (in′stə tü′shən, in′stə tū′shən), *n.* 1. an organization or society for the public good. *Hospitals, schools, and churches are institutions.* 2. the building or buildings used by such an organization. *The Institution of Science Research closes at five o'clock.* 3. a custom or law. *Eating turkey on Thanksgiving Day is an American institution.* 4. a setting up; establishing; beginning. *Tomorrow is the day for the institution of one-way streets in this town.* **in sti tu tions.**

in struct (in strukt′), *v.* 1. to teach. *The famous baseball player instructs his neighbors' children in*

the rules of the game. 2. to direct; to order. *The sheriff was instructed to report at his office right away.* **in structs, in struct ed, in struct ing.**

in struc tion (in struk′shən), *n.* 1. teaching; an education. *All children must have instruction. Because he had good instruction, Topper is a well-behaved dog.* 2. **instructions,** directions. *The game came with a booklet of instructions.* **in struc tions.**

in struc tor (in struk′tər), *n.* a teacher. *Our school has fine instructors.* **in struc tors.**

in stru ment (in′strə mənt), *n.* 1. a tool for doing special work. *A dentist's instruments are made for use in the mouth.* 2. a person who acts as a kind of tool; person used by another. *Poor Henry was an innocent instrument of the gang.* 3. a device for making music. *A piano is a musical instrument.* **in stru ments.**

in su late (in′sə lāt′), *v.* to protect from losing electricity or heat. *Electric wires are insulated with rubber or other covering. You can insulate a house by placing a special material within the walls and roof.* **in su lates, in su lat ed, in su lat ing.**

in su la tion (in′sə lā′shən), *n.* material used to keep heat, sound, and electricity from passing through. *The insulation put in the walls of the old house cut the fuel bills.* **in su la tions.**

in su la tor (in′sə lā′tər), *n.* something that insulates. *Electric wires on poles have insulators made of glass.* **in su la tors.**

in sult (in sult′ for 1, in′sult for 2), *v.* 1. to treat with rudeness; to hurt feelings on purpose. *The angry boy insulted the girl by making fun of her new dress.* **in sults, in sult ed, in sult ing.**

n. 2. a remark or act that is rude or that hurts another's feelings. *Slamming the door in someone's face is an insult.* **in sults.**

in sur ance (in shùr′əns), *n.* 1. a payment of money made to a person or his family in case of death, fire, accident, etc. *When his house burned, Mr. Jones received insurance of several thousand dollars.* 2. the money a person must pay to be insured. *The insurance we pay against fire is about sixty dollars a year.* 3. the amount of money for which a person or thing is insured. *Jack's father has fifty thousand dollars of insurance, which will be paid to his family when he dies.*

in sure (in shùr′), *v.* 1. to arrange for a payment of money in case of loss of life, property, health, etc. by paying regularly to an insurance company. *My father insured our house against fire.* 2. to make sure. *Students can insure the correctness of their homework by checking it carefully.* **in sures, in sured, in sur ing.**

in te grate (in′tə grāt′), *v.* 1. to provide schools, housing, transportation, etc. for all people on an equal basis. *In America the government is trying to integrate schools.* 2. to bring together; to unite. *A new course being offered this semester integrates English literature and English*

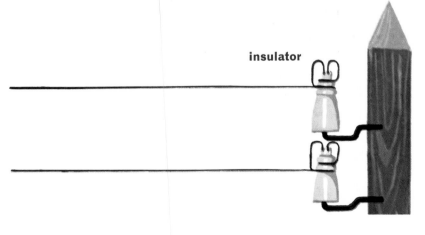

insulator

history. **in te grates, in te grat ed, in te-grat ing.**

in tel lect (in′tə lekt′), *n.* 1. the ability to think, know, and understand. *Solving a problem requires intellect.* 2. intelligence. *The inventor is a man of great intellect.* **in tel lects.**

in tel lec tu al (in′tə lek′chủ əl), *adj.* 1. having to do with intellect or understanding. *Entering college at the age of fifteen shows outstanding intellectual ability.* 2. of the intellect; showing intelligence. *An intellectual person is more interested in ideas than in things.* **in tel lec tu al ly,** *adv.* *n.* 3. person who does intellectual work; a scholar. *The intellectuals of the country were asked to work on its problems.* **in tel lec tu als.**

in tel li gence (in tel′ə jəns), *n.* 1. the ability to learn and know. *His good grades reflect his intelligence.* 2. news; information. *Our army had intelligence of the enemy's plans.*

in tel li gent (in tel′ə jənt), *adj.* 1. able to learn and understand. *Man is an intelligent being.* 2. showing intelligence or understanding. *An intelligent question deserves an intelligent answer.* **in tel li gent ly,** *adv.*

in tend (in tend′), *v.* to plan; to mean. *I intend to spend my summer vacation in Wisconsin. That meat the dog ate was intended for your dinner.* **in tends, in tend ed, in tend ing.**

in tend ed (in ten′dəd), *adj.* 1. planned; proposed. *My intended trip was postponed.* 2. expected or future. *We met his intended wife.*

in tense (in tens′), *adj.* 1. very great; deep; strong. *The excitement of the crowd was intense during the last moments of the ball game.* 2. feeling things very deeply and acting with energy. *Mr. Warren is such an intense worker that he sometimes doesn't stop even for lunch.*

in tense ly (in tens′lē), *adv.* in an intense manner. *We worked intensely all morning, then rested.*

in ten tion (in ten′shən), *n.* a purpose; plan; anything that is intended. *Dorothy went shopping with the intention of buying a new dress.* **in ten-tions.**

in ter est (in′tər əst, in′trəst), *n.* 1. a feeling of wanting to know or take part in something. *He has an interest in music.* 2. the cause of such a feeling. *Music is his main interest. Upholding the law is the interest of a judge and jury. Your troubles have no interest for me.* 3. a share; a part. *A person buying stocks is buying an interest in the company.* 4. an advantage; benefit. *Your parents have always done things for your own best interests.* 5. the money paid for the use of another's money. *You pay about five dollars a year interest if you borrow one hundred dollars.* **in ter ests.** *v.* 6. to get the attention of; to arouse curiosity in. *This book interests me. Let's see if we can interest him in a game of horseshoes.* **in ter ests, in ter est ed, in ter est ing.**

in ter est ed (in′tər əs′təd, in′trəs təd), *adj.*

showing interest. *The interested audience stayed past closing time.* **in ter est ed ly,** *adv.*

in ter est ing (in′tər əs′ting, in′trest ing), *adj.* holding one's attention; arousing interest. *The interesting book kept him reading for two hours.* **in ter est ing ly,** *adv.*

in ter fere (in′tər fir′), *v.* 1. to try to take care of or concern oneself with someone else's affairs. *If my neighbor didn't interfere all the time, I'd get some work done.* 2. to get in the way; to be in opposition. *We had plans to hold our gym class outdoors, but the rain interfered.* **in ter feres, in ter fered, in ter fer ing.**

in te ri or (in tir′ē ər), *n.* 1. the inside. *The outside of the house was ugly, but the interior was beautiful.* 2. the part away from a coast or border. *The interior of Africa contains the jungle. Most of the businesses of the city are located in its interior.* **in te ri ors.** *adj.* 3. on the inside. *The interior walls are painted green.* 4. away from the coast; far from the borders. *The interior cities of the United States include St. Louis, Kansas City, and Chicago.*

in ter nal (in ter′nl), *adj.* 1. on the inside. *The heart is an internal organ. Some medicines are for internal use.* 2. within a country. *Our War Between the States was an internal war.* **in ter-nal ly,** *adv.*

in ter na tion al (in′tər nash′ən l), *adj.* 1. between nations; among nations. *International trade helps all nations.* 2. having to do with the relations between nations. *There are international laws just as there are national laws.* **in ter na tion al ly,** *adv.*

in ter pret (in ter′prət), *v.* 1. to change to a language one can understand; to say in another language. *The visitor from Spain spoke very little English, so Miss Hancock interpreted his speech.* 2. to explain the meaning of. *Poems become more clear if you interpret the thought in your own words.* 3. to show for others the real meaning of something. *An actor interprets an author's work.* **in ter prets, in ter pret ed, in ter-pret ing.**

in ter rupt (in′tə rupt′), *v.* 1. to break in on. *Don't interrupt me while I'm reading!* 2. to interfere with; to get in the way of. *Rain interrupted our picnic. The tall man interrupted my view.* **in ter-rupts, in ter rupt ed, in ter rupt ing.**

in ter sect (in′tər sekt′), *v.* 1. to cross. *I'll meet you where Madison Avenue intersects Michigan Avenue.* 2. to cut or divide by passing through or by crossing. *The little path intersects the big meadow.* **in ter sects, in ter sect ed, in ter-sect ing.**

in ter sec tion (in′tər sek′shən), *n.* 1. an intersecting; a crossing. *At busy intersections, policemen as well as traffic lights are needed.* 2. a point where one thing crosses another. *The letter X has an intersection where the two lines cross.* **in ter-sec tions.**

in ter val (in′tər vl), *n.* 1. the time between;

---

sand, āte, bâre, fäther; sent, mē, fėrn; fit, bīke; pot, rōpe, fôrt; run, pủll, rüle, cūte; noise, sound; ch, cheese; ng, long; th, thick; ~~th,~~ those; zh, treasure; ə = a in about, e in waken, i in animal, o in seldom, and u in minus.

the space between. *There will be an interval of twenty minutes between games. The airplanes fly over at intervals of ten minutes. The shrubs are planted at intervals of three feet.* 2. the difference in pitch between two musical tones. *The band played the song at two different intervals.* **in ter- vals.**

in ter view (in′tər vū′), *n.* 1. a meeting of two people to discuss something. *The college gradu- ate had an interview with the employer about a job.* 2. a meeting with a reporter for a newspaper or news magazine. *The interview revealed that the senator was a candidate.* **in ter views.** *v.* 3. to meet and talk with in the hope of getting information. *The reporter interviewed the delegates to the convention.* **in ter views, in ter- viewed, in ter view ing.**

in ti mate[1] (in′tə mit), *adj.* 1. very well known to one; closely acquainted. *He told only two intimate friends that he was leaving.* 2. private and personal. *Intimate thoughts should be kept to your- self.* 3. complete; close. *A banker has an intimate knowledge of money.* **in ti mate ly,** *adv.*

in ti mate[2] (in′tə māt′), *v.* to suggest in an indirect way; to hint. *The principal intimated that our school would be on a television program soon.* **in ti mates, in ti mat ed, in ti mat- ing.**

in to (in′tù, in′tü), *prep.* 1. to the inside of. *Come into the house. Dick fell into the mud. The employer looked into Craig's past history.* 2. to the condition of; to the form of. *Winter passes into spring. Water turns into ice in cold weather.*

in tox i cate (in tok′sə kāt′), *v.* 1. to make drunk. *Wine can intoxicate some people.* 2. to fill with happiness and excitement. *The little boy was intoxicated with the thought of going to the ball game.* **in tox i cates, in tox i cat ed, in tox- i cat ing.**

in tri cate (in′trə kit), *adj.* difficult to under- stand or figure out. *He solved the intricate problem.* **in tri cate ly,** *adv.*

in tro duce (in′trə düs′, in′trə dūs′), *v.* 1. to present; to bring into contact with. *Mrs. Smith, may I introduce my mother? A boy on a farm is introduced to hard work. The class president intro- duced the speaker at graduation.* 2. to bring in. *Food companies introduce new products to the market. New inventions introduce different ways of doing things.* 3. to begin. *I will introduce my speech with a funny story.* 4. to put in. *The doctor will introduce medicine into the cut on the dog's paw.* **in tro duc es, in tro duced, in tro duc ing.**

in tro duc tion (in′trə duk′shən), *n.* 1. an in- troducing; a being introduced. *The girls have liked each other ever since their introduction. The introduction of television made people wonder how they got along without it.* 2. the first part. *The introduction of the book gave the author's reasons for writing it.* 3. a book for the beginners of a sub- ject. *There are many good introductions to history.* **in tro duc tions.**

in vade (in vād′), *v.* 1. to enter with an army to conquer. *The army invaded the small country.* 2. to crowd. *Thousands of people invaded the beach on the hot day.* **in vades, in vad ed, in vad ing.**

in va lid[1] (in′və lid), *n.* 1. a sick person who needs care. *The nurse took good care of the invalid and made him happy.* **in va lids.** *adj.* 2. ill; not well. *The mother is busy taking care of her invalid child.*

in val id[2] (in val′id), *adj.* having no value or force. *If your pass isn't signed by the teacher or principal, it is invalid.* **in val id ly.**

in vent (in vent′), *v.* 1. to make something that has never been made before. *Thomas A. Edison invented the electric light and the phonograph.* 2. to make up; to imagine. *A writer invents a story. People sometimes invent excuses to get out of work.* **in vents, in vent ed, in vent ing.**

in ven tion (in ven′shən), *n.* 1. an inventing; making something new. *The invention of the airplane changed our methods of travel.* 2. a thing that is invented. *The electric light and the phono- graph are two inventions by Thomas A. Edison.* 3. something that is made up. *His story about being a rich man's son is pure invention.* **in ven- tions.**

in ven to ry (in′vən tôr′ē), *n.* 1. a list of goods, property, or merchandise. *The manager of the store makes an inventory of his merchandise every few months to find out what has been sold.* 2. the stock of goods on hand. *The inventory was low after the sale at the end of the season.* **in ven to- ries.** *v.* 3. to make a list of goods; to prepare an inventory. *The printing company inventoried its books and found that the supply was just right.* **in ven to ries, in ven to ried, in ven to ry- ing.**

in verse (in′vèrs, in vèrs′), *adj.* 1. opposite in position or direction; reversed. *The numerals 3, 2, 1 are in inverse order.* **in verse ly,** *adv.* *n.* 2. the direct opposite. *The inverse of ABC is CBA.* **in vers es.**

in vert (in vèrt′), *v.* to turn upside down. *If you invert a bucket of sand, the sand falls out.* **in verts, in vert ed, in vert ing.**

in ves ti gate (in ves′tə gāt′), *v.* to examine; to look into carefully; to search for reasons. *We investigated the noise on the back stairs. The government investigates a person's background before hiring him for an important job.* **in ves ti gates, in ves ti gat ed, in ves ti gat ing.**

in ves ti ga tion (in ves′tə gā′shən), *n.* an ex- amining; a search; investigating. *The investiga- tion of John's school record showed that he had made good grades.* **in ves ti ga tions.**

in vest ment (in vest′mənt), *n.* 1. a putting of money into a business, property, stocks, etc. to get more money in return. *Buying United States Savings Bonds is a good investment.* 2. the amount of money put in. *The rich man has an*

sand, āte, bâre, fäther; sent, mē, fèrn; fit, bīke; pot, rōpe, fôrt; run, pùll, rüle, cūte; noise, sound; ch, cheese; ng, long; th, thick; ᵺ, those; zh, treasure; ə = a in about, e in waken, i in animal, o in seldom, and u in minus.

iris

investment of ten thousand dollars in the new baseball team. 3. something that money or effort is placed into. *Oil stocks are a good investment. The best investment for the future is a good education.* **in vest ments.**

in vi ta tion (in′və tā′shən), *n.* a request asking a person to come to a dance, party, etc.; inviting. *We sent invitations to all of our parents to attend our school play.* **in vi ta tions.**

in vite (in vīt′), *v.* 1. to ask a person to come to a party, to a dinner, for a visit, etc. *My mother invited my friends to lunch.* 2. to call for; give cause for. *That barking dog is inviting trouble. Good schoolwork invites good grades.* **in vites, in vit ed, in vit ing.**

in vit ing (in vīt′ing), *adj.* attractive. *There are many inviting jobs for students during the summer.* **in vit ing ly,** *adv.*

in voice (in′vois), *n.* 1. a list of the goods sent to a buyer, giving the price of each item. *A buyer compares the invoice with the goods received to prevent mistakes.* **in voic es.**
v. 2. to place in the invoice. *Two tables were invoiced to me by the furniture store.* **in voic es, in voiced, in voic ing.**

in volve (in volv′), *v.* 1. to include; demand; require. *Becoming a doctor involves hard work and constant study.* 2. to be a part of. *Three men were involved in the plans for welcoming Henry.* 3. to occupy oneself; to hold the attention of. *We were so involved in the game that we didn't hear the doorbell.* 4. to mix up. *His stories were so involved they could not be understood.* **in volves, in volved, in volv ing.**

io dine (ī′ə dīn′), *n.* a chemical element used in medicine, in photography, and in some industries. *Iodine is used on cuts and scratches to prevent infection.*

Io wa (ī′ə wə), *n.* a state in the north central part of the United States. *Iowa grows corn.*

iris (ī′ris), *n.* 1. a plant with long, pointed leaves and large, brightly colored flowers. *Irises grow in temperate regions and bloom in spring and summer.* 2. the flower of the iris plant. *Irises are of many different colors and shades.* 3. the circle of color around the pupil of the eye. *Most people have blue irises, brown irises, or gray irises.* **iris es.**

iron (ī′ərn), *n.* 1. a device for taking wrinkles out of clothes. *My mother pressed my shirt with an iron.* 2. a hard and heavy metal from which steel is made. *Iron is used in buildings, automobiles, and big bridges because it is strong.* 3. **irons,** chains to prevent movement. *The captain placed the sailor in irons for not obeying orders.* **irons.**
v. 4. to press clothes, towels, sheets, etc., with an iron. *My older sister irons her clothes every Tuesday.* **irons, ironed, iron ing.**
adj. 5. made of iron. *An iron fence encloses the yard.* 6. like iron; strong. *The player has an iron determination to win.*

iron work er (ī′ərn wėr′kər), *n.* 1. a man whose job is building the metal framework of buildings, bridges, automobiles, etc. *Ironworkers have to be strong.* 2. a man who works in a place where iron is made into iron articles. *An ironworker makes fences of iron.* **iron work ers.**

iron works (ī′ərn wėrks′), *n. pl.* a place where iron is made into iron articles or where it is melted into steel. *The temperature is high in the ironworks because of the huge furnaces.*

ir ri gate (ir′ə gāt′), *v.* 1. to give water to by a system of ditches or pipes. *We must irrigate land that does not get enough rain.* 2. to make clean by a little stream of water. *The doctor may irrigate your ear if it is sore.* **ir ri gates, ir ri gat ed, ir ri gat ing.**

ir ri ga tion (ir′ə gā′shən), *n.* supplying water to dry land by a system of ditches or pipes. *Irrigation is used in the parts of a country that have very little rainfall.*

iron

irrigation:
a. irrigation ditch with floodgate
b. irrigation by spraying
c. irrigation by canal

island

ivy

ir ri tate (ir′ə tāt′), v. 1. to bother; to make angry or upset. *The slowness of the traffic irritates a person in a hurry. Loud noise irritates a person who is reading.* 2. to make sore. *Mosquito bites irritate the skin of most people.* **ir ri tates, ir ri tat ed, ir ri tat ing.**

is (is), v. one form of the verb **be.** *He is here. The weather is nice. Peggy is a helpful girl.*

is land (ī′lənd), n. 1. a piece of land with water all around it. *People who live on an island must take a boat or airplane to go anyplace else.* 2. something like an island. *A library is an island of silence in a noisy city.* **is lands.**

is n't (iz′ənt), is not. *He isn't here; he is over there.*

iso late (ī′sə lāt′, īs′ə lāt), v. to set apart; to separate or keep away from others. *We ought to isolate the sick puppy from the other dogs. Don't isolate yourself; come out and play.* **iso lates, iso lat ed, iso lat ing.**

iso la tion (ī′sə lā′shən, īs′ə lā′shən), n. the act of isolating; separation. *In hospitals people with diseases that are catching are placed in isolation to protect other patients.*

is sue (ish′ü), n. 1. one printing of a magazine, newspaper, etc. *The June issue of the magazine contained two articles about gardening. Newspapers usually have at least three different issues: early, final, and late final.* 2. a subject that must be talked over and thought about. *The big issue in our school is the coming election of officers.* 3. a coming out; flowing out. *The issue of water from the broken water pipe formed a little lake.* **is sues.**
v. 4. to come out; go out; flow out. *Smoke issued from the bonfire. All sorts of rumors issued from the secret meeting.* 5. to send out; pass out. *The report cards will be issued today. The president issued an important statement about the progress of the nation.* 6. to send out something that is printed; publish. *The report on the schools was issued today. About 13,000 new books are issued every year in the United States.* 7. **to take issue,** to disagree. *My father takes issue with many things Uncle Bob says.* **is sues, is sued, is su- ing.**

isthmus

isth mus (is′məs), n. a narrow strip of land that joins two larger bodies of land. *The Isthmus of Panama connects North America with South America.* **isth mus es.**

it (it), pron. 1. the animal or thing spoken about. *I admire your tie; can you get me one like it? We can't take my canary with us; so Mr. Winters will take care of it while we are away.*
n. 2. the player in a children's game who has to look for the others. *Let's play hide-and-seek, and I'll be "it."*

ital ics (i tal′iks), n. pl. letters in slanting type. *This sentence is printed in italics. All example sentences in this dictionary are printed in italics.*

itch (ich), v. 1. to have a tickly irritation on the skin which makes one want to scratch the area. *This poison ivy itches too much!* 2. to feel a desire or longing. *Her brother itches to drive west to California.* **itch es, itched, itch ing.**
n. 3. an area of the skin which tickles. *The itch from this mosquito bite is almost painful.* 4. an uneasy wish or longing. *Cindy has an itch to travel around the world.* **itch es.**

item (ī′təm), n. 1. a separate thing. *Which item shall we buy first?* 2. a piece of news. *There is an item in the newspaper about our school.* **items.**

item ize (ī′tə mīz′), v. to list all the parts or items of. *Ask the grocer to itemize our order.* **item iz es, item ized, item iz ing.**

its (its), adj., pron. of or belonging to it. *The plant lost its flowers because of the frost. The bird left its nest.*

it's (its), 1. it is. *It's too late to go now.* 2. it has. *It's been a long time since we met.*

it self (it self′), pron. 1. its own self. *The bird cleaned itself in the puddle.* 2. a word used to make a statement stronger. *No wonder the house is expensive: the land itself cost thousands of dollars.*

I've (īv), I have. *I've nothing to do.*

ivo ry (ī′və rē), n. 1. the hard, white substance that forms the tusks of elephants. *Ivory is used for ornaments and piano keys.* **ivor ies.**
adj. 2. of or like ivory; creamy-white. *She has a lovely, ivory skin.*

ivy (ī′vē), n. a climbing vine with glossy leaves. *There are many kinds of ivy, including poison ivy. Ivy climbs up the sides of buildings as it grows.* **ivies.**

j

jackal

J or **j** (jā), the tenth letter of the alphabet.

jab (jab), *v.* 1. to poke or make a thrust at, especially with something sharp. *He jabbed me with his finger to see if I was awake.* **jabs, jabbed, jab bing.**

n. 2. a poke. *She gave me a jab on the arm with her pencil.* **jabs.**

jack (jak), *n.* 1. a man; a fellow. *He is a good Jack.* 2. a playing card that ranks next above a ten and next below a queen. *He played his jack, and I took it with my queen.* 3. a device used for lifting heavy objects like a car. *He had to raise the car with a jack before he could change the flat tire.* 4. a small, six-pointed piece of metal used in a child's game. The game of jacks is played by tossing these metal pieces onto the floor and picking them up again during one bounce of a small ball. *She won the game by picking up all of the jacks without dropping any of them.* 5. a small flag used on a ship as a signal or as a sign of the ship's country. *As the ship drew near the other vessel, the sailors raised a jack showing their country's colors.* 6. a male donkey. *Our new donkey is a jack.* 7. an electrical outlet for a plug. *Put the new jack in the bedroom.* 8. **jack-of-all-trades,** a handyman. *We need a jack-of-all-trades to fix all of the broken things in this house.* **jacks.**

v. 9. to lift a heavy object with a jack. *The men jacked up the house to repair its foundation.* **jacks, jacked, jack ing.**

jack al (jak′ôl, jak′l), *n.* a wild dog somewhat like a wolf that lives in Asia and Africa. *Jackals feed upon the remains of animals killed by other animals.* **jack als.**

jack daw (jak′dô′), *n.* a bird somewhat like a crow, living in Europe. *Some jackdaws can be trained to imitate human speech.* **jack daws.**

jack et (jak′it), *n.* 1. a short coat that covers the upper part of the body. *When the weather suddenly became cooler, the children came into the house for their jackets.* 2. any outer covering. *The teacher asked us to put plastic jackets on our school books.* **jack ets.**

jack-in-the-pul pit (jak′in thə pùl′pit), *n.* a plant that bears small, yellow flowers, which have a hood over the upright stalk. *Jack-in-the-pulpits were eaten as food by American Indians.* **jack-in-the-pul pits** or **jacks-in-the-pul pit.**

jack-o'-lan tern (jak′ə lan′tərn), *n.* a pumpkin that has been hollowed out and carved to look like a face, used at Halloween. *We put a candle inside our jack-o'-lantern and set it on the front porch.* **jack-o'-lan terns.**

jacket

jackdaws

jade

jade (jād), *n.* 1. a hard, usually green mineral used in carving and in making jewelry. *Jade is used for necklaces, rings, and ornaments.* **jades.** *adj.* 2. green. *The girl had jade eyes.*

jag uar (jag′wär), *n.* a wild animal of the cat family that looks like a leopard because it has a yellowish color with black spots. *Jaguars live in North and South America, from Mexico to Paraguay.* **jag uars.**

jai alai (hī ä lī′), *n.* a game played on a court with high walls on three sides by using a hard ball and rackets shaped like baskets. *Jai alai is played by two players or by two teams of two or three men each.*

jail (jāl), *n.* 1. a place where persons who have been found guilty of crimes are kept or where persons who are waiting for their court trials are kept. *The guilty person was ordered to pay a fine or spend thirty days in the city jail.* **jails.** *v.* 2. to put a person in jail. *The police jailed several persons who were suspected of the crime.* **jails, jailed, jail ing.**

jam[1] (jam), *v.* 1. to force something into a place by pushing or packing it tightly. *When he became angry, he jammed his hands into his pockets and walked away.* 2. to pack things or people closely together; to crowd. *The ball park was jammed with people who had come to see the game.* 3. to crush, hurt, or break by being squeezed. *He jammed his finger between the two boards.* 4. to force something into a piece of machinery so that it will not operate; to become unable to operate because of being stuck. *Someone had jammed a piece of wood into the wheels of his bicycle.* **jams, jammed, jam ming.** *n.* 5. a large number of persons or things

jar

crowded together and unable to move easily. *We were delayed by a traffic jam on the highway this morning.* **jams.**

jam[2] (jam), *n.* a kind of preserve made by boiling crushed fruit with sugar until the mixture is thick. *His mother makes several jars of strawberry jam every year.* **jams.**

jan i tor (jan′ə tər), *n.* a person who is paid to clean and take care of a building. *When we left the school, the janitor was already at work sweeping the floors.* **jan i tors.**

Jan u ary (jan′yu̇ er′ē), *n.* the first month of the year. *January has thirty-one days.*

Ja pan (jə pän′), *n.* a country made up of islands off the east Asian coast. *The islands of Japan lie in the Pacific Ocean.*

Ja pan ese (jap′ə nēz ′), *adj.* 1. of or belonging to Japan. *The letters of the Japanese alphabet are different from ours.* *n.* 2. a person born in Japan or having ancestors born in Japan. *Many students in our class are Japanese.* 3. the language of Japan. *Japanese is a very difficult language to learn.* **Ja pan ese.**

jar[1] (jär), *n.* 1. a wide-mouthed vessel made of glass, baked clay, etc. *Mother kept the cookies in a jar on the counter.* 2. a vessel like this and what it holds. *We bought two jars of jelly at the store.* 3. as much as a jar will hold. *They ate a whole jar of peanut butter at lunch.* **jars.**

jar[2] (jär), *v.* 1. to shake; to cause to shake. *The force of the earthquake jarred the house.* 2. to make a harsh noise. *The sound of his fingernails against the chalkboard jarred against my ears.* 3. to shock; to have a surprising or unpleasant effect on. *The rude behavior of the audience did not seem to jar the speaker.* 4. to conflict with; to disagree with. *His plans for our vacation jarred with mine.* **jars, jarred, jar ring.** *n.* 5. a sudden shock; a jolt. *Running my bicycle into the tree gave me a severe jar.* **jars.**

jas mine (jas′mən), *n.* a shrub that has sweet-smelling flowers, mostly white, red, or yellow. *Jasmine grows in warm climates.* **jas mines.**

jaw (jô), *n.* 1. the lowest part of the face. *The angry man stuck his jaw out and shouted at us.* 2. the bones that frame the mouth. *Your teeth are rooted in your jaws.* 3. either of two parts of a device used for holding something tightly. *He adjusted the jaws of the pliers to grip the bolt.* **jaws.**

jay (jā), *n.* a noisy, brightly-colored bird with a reputation for stealing and for destroying the eggs and young of other birds. *The most common jay in America is the blue jay.* **jays.**

jay walk (jā′wôk′), *v.* to cross a street without regard for traffic regulations. *He jaywalked by crossing the street against a red light.* **jay walks, jay walked, jay walk ing.**

jeal ous (jel′əs), *adj.* 1. afraid of losing someone's love or afraid that a person loves someone else more than he loves you. *She was very jealous even though her boyfriend never talked with*

jaguar

jasmine:
    a. stem with leaves and
        flowers
    b. flower

other girls. 2. feeling envy because of someone's success. *They didn't even try to be on the team, but they were jealous of him because he played in every game.* 3. watchful; careful lest something be lost. *Everyone should be jealous of his rights as a citizen.* **jeal ous ly,** *adv.*

jean (jēn), *n.* 1. a heavy cotton material used in making trousers. *Mother always buys us trousers made of jean because they wear so long.* 2. **jeans,** trousers made of this material. *His new jeans are dark blue.* **jeans.**

jeep (jēp), *n.* a very firmly built car, usually used by the armed forces. *The jeep was painted a dull shade of green.* **jeeps.**

jel ly (jel′ē), *n.* 1. a food made by boiling fruit juices and sugar or by boiling meat juices. *Jelly is solid and somewhat transparent, but it melts easily when exposed to heat.* 2. anything like jelly in use or appearance. *The doctor smeared an oily jelly on the burned arm.* **jel lies.**
v. 3. to become jelly; to make something become jelly. *The cook jellied the sauce before serving it.* **jel lies, jel lied, jel ly ing.**

jel ly fish (jel′ē fish′), *n.* a bowl-shaped, soft sea animal with an almost transparent body. *Some jellyfish have threadlike parts, hanging below their bodies, which can give a painful sting.* **jel ly fish** or **jel ly fishes.** (See illustration on following page.)

jerk (jėrk), *v.* 1. to move something suddenly by pulling or twisting. *The only way to get him out of bed is to jerk the covers from him.* 2. to move with a jerk. *The trolley car jerked its way up the steep hill.* **jerks, jerked, jerk ing.**
n. 3. a sudden twist or pull. *He gave the rope a jerk and rang the bell.* **jerks.**

jet (jet), *n.* 1. a forceful stream of gas or liquid coming through a small opening. *He stooped to take a drink from the jet of water from the hose.* 2. the opening through which gas or liquid shoots. *The men turned the gas jet off before they installed the new stove.* 3. a plane that is powered by a jet engine. *Jets have greatly reduced the amount of time it takes to fly to other parts of the world.* 4. **jet engine,** an engine that forces heat and burned gases through a small

jai alai

jellyfish

opening at the rear, which produces a forward force. *The airplane has four jet engines.* **jets.**

v. 5. to shoot out in a forceful stream. *A thin stream of water jetted from the hole in the hose.* **jets, jet ted, jet ting.**

Jew (jü), *n.* 1. a member of one of the desert tribes led by Moses who settled in Palestine; any descendants of these people. *Many Jews live in the United States.* 2. one of the followers of the religious belief taught by Moses and other prophets. *Jews worship in synagogues.* **Jews.**

jew el (jü′əl), *n.* 1. a precious stone; a gem. *The movement of this watch contains twenty-one jewels. The jewel was set in a gold pin to be worn by the queen.* 2. a pin, ring, necklace, or other ornament that is set with precious stones. *The woman wore brilliant jewels on her wrists and fingers.* 3. a person or thing that is regarded very highly. *The guide we found to show us around New York City was a jewel.* **jew els.**

jets

v. 4. to decorate or set with jewels or with things like jewels. *The bride's dress was jeweled with diamonds.* **jew els, jew eled, jew el ing.**

jew el ry (jü′əl re), *n.* jewels; precious objects of gold, silver, gems, etc. for wearing. *The famous singer's lawyer advised her to insure all her jewelry.*

Jew ish (jü′ish), *adj.* 1. of or characteristic of the Jews or having to do with their customs and beliefs. *The Jewish religion is one of the oldest religions in the world.*

jig (jig), *n.* 1. a lively dance. *He was so happy at winning the prize that he did a jig when he heard the news.* 2. the music played for such a dance. *The orchestra played a jig, but no one could dance to it because it was too fast.* **jigs.**

v. 3. to dance a jig. *Many people attend dancing schools to learn how to jig.* **jigs, jigged, jig ging.**

jin gle (jing′gl), *n.* 1. a light, ringing sound, as of small bells. *We heard the jingle of coins in his pocket as he walked by.* 2. a simple verse or poem that has repetition of sound. *Many singing commercials are jingles.* **jin gles.**

v. 3. to make a ringing sound. *The bells on the door jingled as we entered the store.* 4. to cause something to make this sound. *He jingled his keys nervously as he talked to us.* **jin gles, jin gled, jin gling.**

job (job), *n.* 1. a piece of work. *He never seems to finish any of the jobs he starts.* 2. a position of employment. *He has a job in the grocery store.* 3. the work that one is hired to do. *His job is to deliver groceries.* 4. the work or an action that one is expected to do; duty; responsibility. *Mother gave her the job of seeing that the cake didn't bake too long.* **jobs.**

job ber (job′ər), *n.* a person who buys large quantities of particular goods and sells them to stores where they are sold to the public. *The storekeeper ordered one hundred pens from his stationery jobber.* **job bers.**

jock ey (jok′ē), *n.* 1. a man or boy who rides

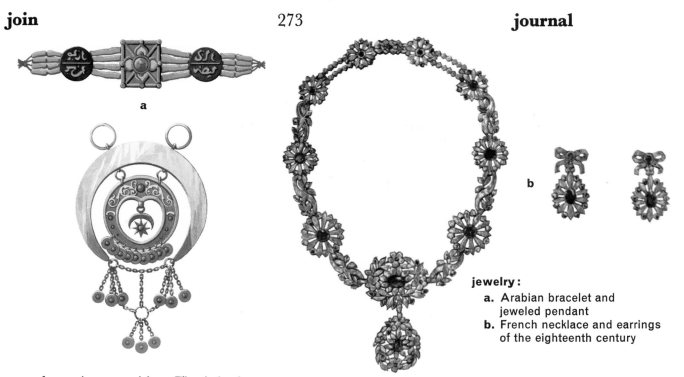

jewelry:
a. Arabian bracelet and jeweled pendant
b. French necklace and earrings of the eighteenth century

racehorses in competition. *That jockey has won eleven races in a row.* **jock eys.**

v. 2. to move or arrange something to a better position. *The man jockeyed his car into the parking place.* **jock eys, jock eyed, jock ey ing.**

join (join), *v.* 1. to put together; to connect. *The caboose was joined to the last car of the train.* 2. to come together; to meet. *A sign indicating directions was placed at the point where the roads joined.* 3. to become a member of. *Next year I will be able to join the Boy Scouts.* 4. to do something with others; to combine with a group in doing something. *Would you like to join us in playing basketball?* **joins, joined, join ing.**

joint (joint), *n.* 1. a part where two bones are connected in an animal, usually allowing motion. *His arm was broken at the elbow joint.* 2. a place where any two things or parts are joined. *There was a leak at one of the joints in the water pipe.* 3. a part which connects two things. *A right-angle joint in the pipe was loosely connected and had to be replaced.* 4. a piece of meat

jockey

cut as a roast. *We had two meals from the joint of beef.* **joints.**

adj. 5. combined; united. *His childhood was molded by the joint influences of school and home.* 6. owned, done, used, or shared by two or more persons. *Raising enough money to build a new school required the joint efforts of everyone in the community.* 7. united, sharing, or joined. *One of the joint owners of the company decided to sell his share of the business.* **joint ly,** *adv.*

v. 7. to connect in a joint or with a joint. *The electric wire was jointed with the main power line at a pole in back of the house.* **joints, joint ed, joint ing.**

joke (jōk), *n.* 1. an action or a statement made to make someone laugh. *He came into the room wearing his father's coat and his mother's hat as a joke.* 2. an object or person laughed at or ridiculed. *The dog was a joke as he tried to catch the leaves falling to the ground.* **jokes.**

v. 3. to make jokes about something. *They joked about being in the play, but they really took it very seriously.* **jokes, joked, jok ing.**

jol ly (jol′ē), *adj.* 1. happy; cheerful; merry. *The jolly old man could always make us laugh.* 2. pleasant; enjoyable. *We had a jolly time at the birthday party.* **jol li er, jol li est; jol li ly,** *adv.*

jolt (jōlt), *v.* 1. to shake suddenly; to jar or jerk. *The bus jolted every passenger when it ran over the curb.* **jolts, jolt ed, jolt ing.**

n. 2. a sudden shake, jar, or jerk. *When our plane landed in the storm, it hit the runway with a jolt.* **jolts.**

jour nal (jėr′nl), *n.* 1. a record kept of daily activities, feelings, etc. *The scientist kept a journal of the results of his experiments.* 2. a daily record of the procedures of a lawmaking body or the transactions of a business. *The treasurer of the company kept a journal of all that had been* bought and sold each day. 3. a newspaper or magazine that appears at regular intervals. *Our town's journal is published twice a week.* **jour nals.**

jour ney (jẽr′nē), *n.* 1. a trip or voyage. *Our journey to England took only a few hours because we traveled by plane.* **jour neys.**
v. 2. to travel to a place. *We journeyed to Japan and the Philippines last year.* **jour neys, journeyed, jour ney ing.**

joy (joi), *n.* 1. a feeling of happiness or pleasure. *Imagine my joy when I received the new bicycle for my birthday.* 2. anything that gives happiness or pleasure. *The performance of a great musician is a joy to hear.* **joys.**

joy ful (joi′fəl), *adj.* full of joy; feeling, showing, or causing joy. *It was a joyful day when my brother returned from the army.* **joy ful ly,** *adv.*

joy ous (joi′əs), *adj.* joyful; glad. *There was a joyous reunion of his classmates from college.* **joy ous ly,** *adv.*

judge (juj), *n.* 1. a government official who presides over a court of law by hearing cases, giving decisions, passing sentences, etc. *A judge must be completely fair while hearing cases in court.* 2. a person selected to settle an argument, determine the winner in a contest, etc. *The judges of the baking contest made a unanimous decision in favor of the chocolate cake.* 3. an expert; a person whose knowledge or experience enables him to determine the value of something. *Their teacher seems to be a good judge of what is important for them to learn.* **judg es.**
v. 4. to preside over a court of law. *He has judged more than one thousand cases during his career.* 5. to decide on the winner in a contest. *Who will judge the debating contest?* 6. to think. *Since he fell asleep during the movie, I judged that he didn't like it.* 7. to criticize; to blame. *Don't judge him harshly just because you didn't make the same mistakes he did.* **judg es, judged, judging.**

judg ment (juj′mənt), *n.* 1. a judging. *The judgment of the case took place shortly after the suspect was arrested.* 2. a decision reached or handed down in a court. *The judgment was in*

his favor, and he was released. 3. any decision reached through careful thought. *The final judgment of the class was in favor of a picnic rather than a trip to the zoo.* 4. opinion. *In my judgment such a plan will never succeed.* 5. the ability to make wise decisions. *He has excellent judgment concerning horses.* **judg ments.**

ju do (jü′dō), *n.* a kind of wrestling used first in Japan. *In judo, skill is more important than strength or weight.*

jug (jug), *n.* a narrow-mouthed vessel for holding liquids. *They brought a jug of vinegar from the farm.* **jugs.**

jug gle (jug′l), *v.* 1. to use the hands in performing stunts, especially by catching and throwing various objects in the air in rapid succession. *He juggled five plates while balancing a broom on his nose.* 2. to deceive by entering incorrect figures in an account book, by changing the facts in a story, etc. *The writer juggled the facts so that no one would recognize the incidents he was writing about.* **jug gles, jug gled, jug gling.**

juice (jüs), *n.* the liquid that can be squeezed out of fruits and vegetables and that comes out of meat as it is cooking. *Mother made a delicious gravy from the meat juices. He has a glass of orange juice with his breakfast every morning.* **juic es.**

juicy (jüs′ē), *adj.* full of juice; containing juices. *I had a sweet, juicy pear after lunch.* **juic i er, juic i est; juic i ly,** *adv.*

Ju ly (jù lī), *n.* the seventh month of the year. *July has thirty-one days.*

jump (jump), *v.* 1. to rise from the ground or another surface by leaping, springing, or bounding. *The running horse jumped over the fence easily. The squirrel jumped from one tree to another.* 2. to cause something to leap. *To escape, he had to jump his horse across a deep stream of water.* 3. to jerk; to make a sudden movement. *The children jumped at the noise of the thunder.* 4. to go up suddenly; to rise. *The price of corn jumped when it was learned that a smaller crop than usual was expected.* **jumps, jumped, jump ing.**
n. 5. a leap from the ground or another surface. *Tom won the high jump in the track meet. He made a jump of six feet and one inch.* 6. a jerk; a sudden movement. *His jump at the sudden noise startled us more than the noise did.* 7. a sudden increase or rise. *No one expected a jump in the price of eggs.* **jumps.**

jumper (jump′ər), *n.* 1. a sleeveless dress worn by women and usually worn over a blouse or sweater. *Sally's new jumper is blue checked and her sweater is dark blue.* 2. a loose jacket worn over the clothes to protect them. *Workmen often wear jumpers to protect their clothes.* **jump ers.**

June (jün), *n.* the sixth month of the year. *June has thirty days.*

jun gle (jung′gl), *n.* an area of land covered by

judo

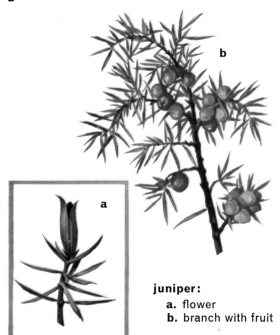

juniper:
a. flower
b. branch with fruit

a dense growth of trees and other plants, especially in a very hot climate. *The guides took the group into the jungle to find animals for zoos.* **jun gles.**

jun ior (jün′yər), *adj.* 1. done for or by younger persons. *The orchestra will present a junior concert this afternoon.* 2. lower in rank or position; less important than others. *He is a junior partner in that business.* 3. of, for, or by students in their third year of high school or college. *The junior class elected its officers in a special election.*
n. 4. a person younger than another. *He is my junior by two years.* 5. a person who is lower in rank or position. *Among the executives of the firm, he is considered a junior.* 6. a person who is in his third year of high school or college. *The juniors will present their class play next week.*
7. **Junior,** the younger; the name used to describe a son who has the same name as his father. *Harry Williams, Junior, gave the award to his father, Harry Williams, Senior.* **jun iors.**

ju ni per (jü′nə pər), *n.* a small evergreen tree or shrub. *The small cones of the juniper look like blueberries.* **jun i pers.**

junk[1] (jungk), *n.* 1. worthless and useless goods; trash; rubbish. *We threw out all of the junk that had been cluttering the garage.*
v. 2. to throw something away because it is useless. *We junked our old washing machine and bought a new one.* **junks, junked, junk ing.**

junk[2] (jungk), *n.* a sailing vessel commonly used in China. *As we neared Hong Kong, we saw that the harbor was crowded with junks.* **junks.**

Ju pi ter (jü′pə tər), *n.* 1. the most important god of the ancient Romans. *Jupiter was supposed to have ruled all of the other gods as well as every aspect of man's life.* 2. the planet in our solar system that is larger than any of the other

planets. *Jupiter is farther from the sun than the planets Mercury, Venus, Earth, and Mars.*

ju ry (jur′ē), *n.* 1. a group of persons who are selected to listen to all of the evidence presented in a court case and who are sworn to make a fair decision from the evidence. *If the jury cannot reach a unanimous decision, they are dismissed and a new trial may be held with a different jury.* 2. any group of persons who are asked to make a judgment, give their opinions, etc. *A jury of the world's finest cooks sampled the dishes prepared for the contest.* **ju ries.**

just (just), *adj.* 1. fair; honest; impartial. *The jury made what they regarded as a just decision.* 2. based on what is known to be true; reasonable. *He felt just anger at the persons who had tricked him.* 3. legal. *He had a just complaint against the people who damaged his property.* 4. deserved. *The criminal received his just reward by being sent to prison.* **just ly,** *adv.*
adv. 5. exactly. *This amount is just enough to make your purchase.* 6. a short time ago; recently. *I just saw him standing at the corner.* 7. barely; with little space or time to spare. *We just made the beginning of the play. The bolt of lightning just missed our house.* 8. only. *We were given just one chance to convince her of our story.*

jus tice (jus′tis), *n.* 1. right and just behavior; honest treatment. *Justice demands that you tell him the horse is lame before you sell it to him.* 2. the administering of the law; the enforcement of the law. *The code of justice maintains the same rights for every person who is being tried for a crime.* 3. rightness; the fact of being just. *The justice of your claim will be decided by the court.* 4. a judge. *He is a Justice of the Supreme Court of the United States.* **jus tic es.**

jus ti fy (jus′tə fī′), *v.* to prove that something is just and right. *Why do you even try to justify things that you know are wrong?* 2. to free from guilt or blame. *The court justified his action because he had acted in self-defense.* **jus ti fies, jus ti fied, jus ti fy ing.**

ju ve nile (ju′və nəl or jü′və nīl), *n.* 1. a young person. *That boy is a juvenile.* 2. an actor who performs in young roles. *He played a juvenile in his last movie.* **ju ve niles.**
adj. 3. of or for young people. *This is a juvenile book.*

junk

kangaroo

K

kettles

K or **k** (kā), the eleventh letter of the alphabet.

ka lei do scope (kə li′də skōp′), *n.* a small tube containing mirrors and many tiny pieces of colored glass. *By looking through the hole at one end of a kaleidoscope and by turning the tube, you can see many designs and patterns formed by the bits of glass.* **ka lei do scopes.**

kan ga roo (kang′gə rü′), *n.* a jumping animal of Australia, having large powerful hind legs, small front legs, and a strong tail. *The female kangaroo carries her young in a pocket-like part on the front of her body.* **kan ga roos.**

Kan sas (kan′zəs), *n.* a state in the central part of the United States. *Kansas is one of the largest wheat-producing states in the United States.*

kay ak (kī′ak), *n.* a kind of canoe made of animal skins fastened tightly around a wooden frame, leaving an opening near the middle in which one person can sit. *The Eskimos were the first to make kayaks.* **kay aks.**

keen (kēn), *adj.* 1. having a sharp cutting edge. *The farmer used a keen saw to cut down the tree.* 2. sharp; biting; cutting. *A keen wind made our faces sting and forced us to seek shelter.* 3. very sensitive. *The keen ears of the dog heard the sound long before we did.* 4. alert; quick; mentally sharp. *He exercised keen judgment when he rescued the drowning child.* 5. eager; intense; enthusiastic. *Terry has a keen interest in animals and has many kinds of pets.* **keen er, keen est; keen ly,** *adv.*

keep (kēp), *v.* 1. to own; to have as one's own. *We are keeping the little puppy we found, since no one knows where it came from.* 2. to hold oneself back from telling. *He can keep a secret.* 3. to hold in one's possession; to maintain possession of. *I decided to keep the fish instead of giving them away.* 4. to watch over and care for; to take care of. *They keep pigs and sheep on their farm.* 5. to hold and guard; to protect. *I will keep your money for you while you are playing.* 6. to go on doing something; to continue. *Keep walking until you come to a covered bridge.* 7. to be in a certain condition or to remain in that condition. *Please keep quiet until I am finished with my speech.* 8. to maintain; cause to continue. *Ice is used to keep things cold. Keep this plant warm and dry during the winter.* 9. to hold back; to restrain. *We failed to keep him from escaping through the window.* 10. to celebrate; to observe. *Christians keep their religious holidays by going to church.* 11. **keep on,** to go on; continue. *We kept on*

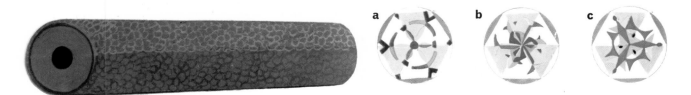

kaleidoscope: a, b, c, show the figures seen through a kaleidoscope

with our work until it became too dark for us to see.
keeps, kept, keep ing.

n. 12. food and shelter. *He doesn't have to work
for his keep because his parents take care of him.*
13. the strongest, most secure part of a castle
or fort. *The enemy was unable to conquer the keep
of the castle.* **keeps.**

keep er (kēp′ər), *n.* a person who holds, protects, or guards something. *The keeper of the
zoo lions feeds them at four o'clock.* **keep ers.**

keep ing (kēp′ing), *n.* 1. care; charge. *The
children were left in their grandmother's keeping
while their mother was at the store.* 2. **in keeping
with,** in agreement with. *His answer was not
in keeping with what he had said before.*

keep sake (kēp′sāk′), *n.* something given as a
remembrance. *That ring was a keepsake from
my grandmother.* **keep sakes.**

Ken tucky (kən tuk′ē), *n.* a state in the central
and southern part of the United States. *One of
the most famous horse races in the world is held in
Kentucky each year.*

kept (kept), past tense and past participle of
keep.

ker nel (kèr′nəl), *n.* 1. the soft, edible part
inside the hard shell of a nut or fruit. *The
kernel of the walnut that Mother gave us was very
good.* 2. a grain or seed, especially wheat or
corn. *We pop kernels of corn. We eat kernels of
wheat in cereals.* 3. the central part of an idea
or plan. *There is a kernel of truth in what you say.*
ker nels.

ketch up (kech′əp), var. of **cat sup.**

ket tle (ket′l), *n.* a pot used for heating liquids.
Put the kettle on the fire. **ket tles.**

key[1] (kē), *n.* 1. a small metal device used to
turn the bolt on a lock. *We couldn't open the
door because I had forgotten my key.* 2. something
that controls the entrance to a place. *A fort
had been built at the narrow gap in the rocks; it was
the key to the large harbor.* 3. anything that provides an explanation or a clue to the solution
of something. *Locating the stolen money was the
key to solving the robbery and capturing the thieves.*
4. the answers to something. *The teacher's hand-
book is the key to all the book's questions.* 5. a list
that explains the symbols used on a map,
in a dictionary, etc. *The key to the map showed
that each inch was equal to thirty miles.* 6. any of
the parts that are pressed down to play a
piano, operate a typewriter, etc. *The keys on a
typewriter are used to produce printed characters on
paper.* 7. in music, a series of notes which are
related to one tone. *The song is written in the
key of C.* 8. a tone of voice or manner of saying
something. *He spoke in a very low key.* **keys.**

v. 9. to adapt to a particular use or occasion.
*The book was keyed to the interests and activities
of teen-agers.* **keys, keyed, key ing.**

key[2] (kē), *n.* a low island; a reef. *Many people
fish among the keys off Florida's coast.* **keys.**

key board (kē′bôrd′), *n.* 1. the row of black

kayak

and white keys on a piano. *There are eighty-
eight keys on the keyboard of a full-size piano.*
2. the rows of keys on a typewriter. *Typewriters of all manufacturers have the letters of the
alphabet in the same positions on the keyboard.*
key boards.

kick (kik), *v.* 1. to strike at with the foot; to hit
with the foot. *The restless horse kicked the boards
in his stall.* 2. to spring back or jump back, as
a gun does when it is fired. *The cannon kicked
so powerfully that it rolled backwards several feet
each time it was fired.* 3. to complain; to find
fault with. *The players kicked when the coach told
them that new uniforms would not be purchased for
them.* **kicks, kicked, kick ing.**

n. 4. a blow made by the foot. *The cow spilled
the bucket of milk with a kick.* 5. the sudden backward push of a gun when it is fired. *The hunter
wore a pad on his shoulder to protect himself from

keys

a

keyboards:
  a. typewriter keyboard
  b. piano keyboard

b

kimonos

the rifle's kick. 6. a feeling of pleasure, excitement, or enjoyment. *The boys got a big kick out of seeing their first baseball game.* **kicks.**

kid (kid), *n.* 1. a young goat. *The kid slept peacefully in the straw beside its mother.* 2. a kind of leather made from the skin of a young goat. *Kid is a very soft leather used in making shoes and gloves.* 3. a child. *All of the kids in the neighborhood are going to the baseball game this Saturday.* **kids.**
v. 4. to joke with; to tease. *Don't take him seriously; he's only kidding you.* **kids, kid ded, kid ding.**

kid nap (kid′nap), *v.* to seize and carry off a person; to capture and hold a person against his will until payment is made for his return. *The son of the rich man was kidnaped, but the boy was soon returned safely.* **kid naps, kid naped, kid nap ing.**

kid ney (kid′nē), *n.* 1. either of two organs in the body that separate and remove waste products from the blood. *The kidneys are located in the lower back at either side of the backbone.* 2. this organ taken from an animal and used for food. *Sometimes we have kidney stew for supper.* **kid neys.**

kill (kil), *v.* 1. to put to death; to take life away from. *They used poisoned food and gas to kill the rats.* 2. to cause the death of something. *Cold weather killed most of the plants in their garden.* 3. to defeat; to cause the failure of. *The lawmakers killed the proposed bill by voting against it.* 4. to use up. *We killed the whole case of root beer in one afternoon. We killed an hour walking around downtown.* **kills, killed, kill ing.**
n. 5. the act of killing. *The hunters circled around*

the bear and closed in for the kill. 6. an animal killed. *Most states limit the number of kills a hunter can make during a season.* **kills.**

kill er (kil′ər), *n.* a person, animal, or thing that kills. *Doctors and scientists are looking for ways to conquer such killers as cancer and heart disease.* **kill ers.**

kilt (kilt), *n.* a knee-length, pleated skirt worn by men in parts of Scotland. *The men who played bagpipes in the parade wore kilts.* **kilts.**

ki mo no (kə mō′nə), *n.* 1. a loose outer garment bound with a sash in the middle. *Kimonos were first used in Japan.* 2. a dressing gown which resembles this. *Put on your kimono over your pajamas and come to breakfast.* **ki mo nos.**

kind[1] (kīnd), *adj.* 1. gentle and caring. *They are always very kind to animals.* 2. friendly; good; thoughtful of others. *She is a very kind person. He always has a kind word to say to everyone.* **kind er, kind est; kind ly,** *adv.*

kind[2] (kīnd), *n.* 1. type; sort; variety. *What kind of ice cream would you like?* 2. group; natural division. *A chimpanzee belongs to the monkey kind.* **kinds.**

in der gar ten (kin′dər gärt′n), *n.* a school or a class for children who will be entering first grade in the next year. *Children in kindergarten learn many things through games, toys, and listening to stories.* **kin der gar tens.**

kin dle (kin′dl), *v.* 1. to start burning; to light. *We can't cook our picnic food until someone kindles the fire.* 2. to start to burn; to catch fire. *Wet newspaper does not kindle easily.* 3. to stir up; to excite. *His bravery kindled courage in all of us.* 4. to become bright. *He kindled with pride and excitement when he shook hands with the President.* **kin dles, kin dled, kin dling.**

kind ly (kīnd′lē), *adj.* 1. kind; gentle; friendly. *The kindly farmer showed us his barn and let us help with the feeding of the animals.* 2. agreeable; pleasing. *A kindly breeze cooled us after our hike.* **kind li er, kind li est.**
adv. 3. in a kind manner. *She smiled kindly at the lost child and helped her to find her mother.*

kind ness (kīnd′nis), *n.* 1. kind manner or behavior. *His kindness to others made him many friends.* 2. a kind or thoughtful act. *Our neighbor did us a kindness by taking care of our dog while we were out of town.* **kind ness es.**

king in chess

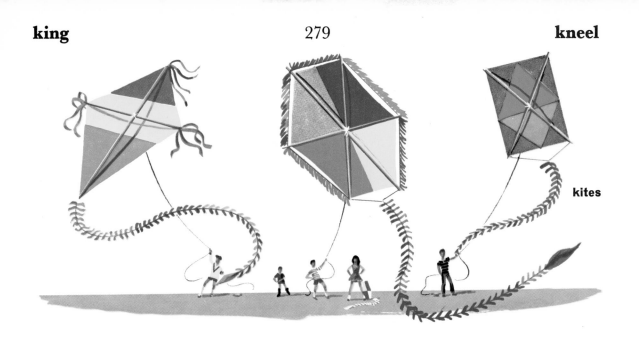

kites

king (king), *n.* 1. the male ruler of a country, especially one who receives his position as an heir and holds it for life. *The kings of most modern countries hold the title of king but do not have strong ruling power.* 2. a person or thing best in its class; one that holds a position above all others. *The lion is the king of the jungle.* 3. a playing card that ranks next above a queen and next below an ace. *He won the hand of cards with two kings and three tens.* 4. in checkers, a piece that has reached the last row of the enemy's line. *The kings are allowed to move backwards and forwards.* 5. in chess, the most important piece in the game. *I lost the game when I was unable to move my king to a safe position on the board.* **kings.**

king dom (king′dəm), *n.* 1. a country, land, or territory ruled by a king or queen. *When the prince was born, the king declared a holiday throughout the entire kingdom.* 2. a sphere within which anything rules or prevails; anything regarded as a kingdom. *That story came from the kingdom of imagination.* 3. one of the major divisions into which all natural things are grouped. *Man belongs to the animal kingdom; roses are in the plant kingdom; sand is part of the mineral kingdom.* **king doms.**

kiss (kis), *v.* 1. to touch with the lips as a sign of love, greeting, etc. *The boys kissed their parents and went to bed.* 2. to touch lightly. *A gentle flow of waves kissed the shore.* **kiss es, kissed, kiss ing.**
n. 3. a touch of the lips as a sign of love, greeting, etc. *His aunt gave him a kiss on the forehead.* 4. a light touch. *The kiss of the breeze stirred the leaves.* **kiss es.**

kit (kit), *n.* 1. a group of tools, materials, etc. to be used for a particular purpose. *She took care of the cut on her hand with iodine and bandages from the first-aid kit.* 2. a bag, box, etc. in which tools or materials are carried. *The doctor packed a supply of medicines in his kit before he visited his patients.* **kits.**

kitch en (kich′ən), *n.* a room in which food is prepared and cooked. *Mother wouldn't allow anyone in the kitchen until everything was ready for dinner.* **kitch ens.**

kite (kīt), *n.* 1. a kind of hawk having long slender wings, noted for its graceful flight. *Kites live near water in many warm parts of the world.* 2. a light frame covered with fabric or paper, floated in the air on the end of a long string. *On the first day of summer, a contest was held to see who could fly his kite the highest.* **kites.**

kit ten (kit′n), *n.* a young cat. *The kitten chased a butterfly around the garden, trying to catch it.* **kit tens.**

kit ty (kit′ē), *n.* a pet name for a kitten or cat. *When we put food out for the cat, we call, "Here, kitty."* **kit ties.**

knap sack (nap′sak′), *n.* a canvas or leather bag worn or carried on the back, and used to hold food, clothing, equipment, etc. *Some of the hikers had so much food in their knapsacks that they couldn't close them.* **knap sacks.** (See illustration on following page.)

knead (nēd), *v.* 1. to work dough with the hands into a round ball. *Mother kneads the bread dough before she bakes it to give it a smooth texture.* 2. to massage with the hands in a squeezing and pressing fashion. *Kneading sore muscles will relax them and make them feel better.* **kneads, kneaded, knead ing.**

knee (nē), *n.* 1. the joint in the middle of a person's leg. *He dropped to his knees and began searching for the lost ring.* 2. the part of clothing that covers this joint. *The farmer wore out the knees of his overalls.* **knees.**

kneel (nēl), *v.* to put one's knees on the ground, floor, etc.; to rest on the knees. *He knelt on the floor and began to pray.* **kneels, knelt** or **kneeled, kneel ing.**

sand, āte, bâre, fäther; sent, mē, fėrn; fit, bīke; pot, rōpe, fôrt; run, pùll, rüle, cūte; noise, sound; ch, cheese; ng, long; th, thick; ᵵħ, those; zh, treasure; ə = a in about, e in waken, i in animal, o in seldom, and u in minus.

knapsack

knew (nū, nū), past tense of **know.**

knife (nīf), *n.* 1. a flat cutting instrument having a sharp-edged blade fastened in a handle. *He sharpened the carving knife before he sliced the meat for dinner.* 2. a blade used for cutting in a machine. *The knives in the machine cut paper into small scraps.* **knives** (nīvz).
v. 3. to cut with a knife. *The hunters knifed their way through the thick growth of the jungle.* **knives, knifed, knif ing.**

knight (nīt), *n.* 1. during the Middle Ages, a warrior or soldier who was honored with a military rank by a king or lord, usually after having served as a page, an armor bearer, or shield bearer. *The king called all of his knights together to plan the battle.* 2. in modern times, a man who has been honored with this rank

pocket knives

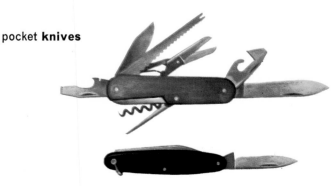

for his achievements or service to his country. *A modern knight has the title "Sir," as in Sir William Brown, but neither the rank nor the title can be passed on to an heir.* 3. one of the pieces in a chess set, usually having the shape of a horse's head. *His knight captured my bishop in a very clever series of moves.* **knights.**
v. 4. to name as a knight; to give the rank of knight to a person as a sign of honor. *The great scientist was knighted by the queen.* **knights, knight ed, knight ing.**

knit (nit), *v.* 1. to make a fabric or garment by weaving yarn in loops with long needles. *My mother knitted a sweater for me.* 2. to become firmly joined together; to grow together. *This broken bone will knit in a few weeks if you are careful of it.* 3. to bring together or join together as friends. *A common interest in sports knits many boys in friendship.* 4. to draw together in ridges or folds. *She knits her forehead when she tries to thread a needle.* **knits, knit ted, knit-ting.**

knives (nīvz), *n. pl.* more than one knife. *The butcher has a large collection of knives.*

knob (nob), *n.* 1. a lump; a rounded bump. *A large knob on his forehead marked the place where he had been hit.* 2. a rounded handle on an umbrella, television set, drawer, etc. *We bought new knobs for the dresser. The knob on the right of the radio controls the volume of the sound.* **knobs.**

knock (nok), *v.* 1. to strike with the fist or with a hard object. *I knocked on their door, but no one answered.* 2. to crash; to come together with force; to bump. *The running boys knocked together as they came to the door.* 3. to make a loud noise because of parts bumping together. *The old engine knocked violently as soon as it was started.* **knocks, knocked, knock ing.**
n. 4. a sharp blow or the sound of a sharp blow. *A sudden knock on the window frightened the children.* 5. a loud noise made by loose parts in an engine. *The regular knock in the engine indicated that repairs were needed.* **knocks.**

knot (not), *n.* 1. a means of fastening rope, string, cord, etc. *The sail was tied down with a slip knot.* 2. a twisted mass of something. *The anchor rope lay in knots in the bottom of the boat.* 3. a problem. *The mayor was unable to solve the knot of getting traffic to move through the city quickly and easily.* 4. a group; a gathering of persons or things. *A knot of people stood waiting for us outside the door.* 5. the hard spot which forms in a tree where a branch grows out; this round spot in a piece of wood. *He knocked the knots out of the wood before he cut the board.* 6. the unit of speed used by ships; a ship mile; 6080 feet per hour. *The top speed of this boat is twenty-four knots.* **knots.**
v. 7. to tie in a knot; to join with a knot. *She knotted the laces on her shoes so that they would not come untied.* **knots, knot ted, knot ting.**

know (nō), *v.* 1. to recognize; to be aware of

what something is or who someone is. *Do you know what kind of fish this is? I know who that person is, but I have never spoken to him.* 2. to be acquainted with. *I have known her for many years.* 3. to understand. *Did he know how to answer the questions on the test?* 4. to be convinced of something; to be sure. *We all know that the earth moves around the sun. I know he went into the room, but I couldn't find him when I looked for him there.* 5. to have information about; to have knowledge of; to have experience with. *Ask him how we are getting there; he knows what arrangements have been made. He knows how to play three musical instruments.* **knows, knew, known, know ing.**

know ing (nō′ing), *adj.* 1. intelligent. *He is a knowing speaker on the subject of space travel.* 2. having or suggesting special knowledge of something. *When the teacher began talking about Halloween pranks, the children exchanged knowing glances.* **know ing ly,** *adv.*

knowl edge (nol′ij), *n.* 1. everything that one knows or understands about something. *His knowledge of the battles of the Civil War is extremely great.* 2. everything that is known to all men;

learning. *There are entire areas of knowledge that I know nothing about. Mathematics is a special field of knowledge.* 3. the fact of knowing something. *The knowledge of his success excited all of us.*

knowl edge a ble (nol′ij ə bl), *adj.* knowing a great deal about something. *He is knowledge-able in the field of chemistry, but he knows very little about music and art.*

known (nōn), past participle of **know.**

knuck le (nuk′l), *n.* 1. any of the joints in the finger, especially the joints that connect the fingers to the hand. *He knocked on the door so hard that he hurt his knuckles.* 2. the knee joint of an animal when eaten as food. *They had pigs' knuckles for supper.* **knuck les.**

Ko rea (kô rē′ə), *n.* a country in eastern Asia that is divided into two countries, North Korea and South Korea. *Korea is located near Japan.*

Ko re an (kô rē′ən), *adj.* 1. of Korea, its people or its language. *Many Korean goods are exported. n.* 2. a person born in Korea or having ancestors born there. *Many Koreans now live in the United States.* 3. the language of Korea. *Korean is similar to Japanese.* **Ko re ans.**

knots:
a. overhand loop
b. running bowline
c. bowline on a bight
d. square
e. carrick bend

L or l (el), 1. the twelfth letter of the alphabet. 2. the Roman numeral for 50.

la bel (lā′bl), *n.* 1. a piece of paper or cloth attached to something and giving information about it. *The label sewn on my new tie says "All Silk." The label on the package said "First Class Mail." The label on many medicine bottles reads "Keep out of reach of children."* **la bels.**

v. 2. to mark with a label; put a label on. *The birthday gift was labeled, "To Tom with best wishes." Mother labeled all my clothes before I went*

labyrinth

to camp. 3. to describe by a name; call. *Don't label Bruce a coward just because he won't fight.* **la bels, la beled, la bel ing.**

la bor (lā′bər), *n.* 1. work. *Cleaning the house is hard labor.* 2. workers. *The former truck driver will get the vote of labor. Labor Day in September is a legal holiday in honor of labor.* 3. a task; a job to be done. *On Sunday people rest from their labors.* **la bors.**

v. 4. to work. *The boys labored to get the car out of the ditch. A housewife labors in the kitchen.* 5. to go slowly and with difficulty. *The heavy truck labored up the hill.* **la bors, la bored, la bor ing.**

lab o ra to ry (lab′ə rə tô′rē), *n.* a room or building where experiments in science are done. *Some medicines are first tried out on mice in a laboratory. High schools have laboratories for work in biology, chemistry, and other science courses.* **lab o ra to ries.**

lab y rinth (lab′ə rinth), *n.* a group of paths that are difficult to follow without confusion. *A labyrinth is often purposely made in the trees and bushes of a park or garden.* **lab y rinths.**

lace (lās), *n.* 1. a string or cord for tying things together. *I broke the lace in my right shoe.* 2. a fabric of thread woven together in a fancy pattern or design. *The wedding gown was trimmed with white lace.* **lac es.**

v. 3. to fasten together with laces. *A child cannot lace his own shoes until he is about five years old.* 4. to trim with lace. *Mother laced the gown with a delicate design.* **lac es, laced, lac ing.**

lack (lak), *v.* 1. to be without; to have not enough. *The meal is good, but the meat lacks salt. The car lacks a headlight.* **lacks, lacked, lack ing.**

n. 2. an absence or shortage of something; being without. *Lack of money kept him from flying to Europe. Lack of food makes you hungry.* **lacks.**

lad (lad), *n.* a boy. *"You're a good lad," said the old man.* **lads.**

lad der (lad′ər), *n.* a series of steps placed between two long sidepieces, used for climbing. *The painter leaned the metal ladder against the wall so that he could reach the top of the wall. The sailor dropped a rope ladder over the side of the ship so that the men in the boat could climb aboard.* **lad ders.**

la dies (lā′dēz), *n. pl.* more than one lady. *The ladies will arrive soon for the club meeting.*

lad ing (lād′ing), *n.* a load; a cargo. *A bill of lading is a receipt in writing from a shipping company that lists the goods they received for shipping.*

la dy (lā′dē), *n.* 1. a woman. *The lady who bakes the best cake will win the prize.* 2. a woman who has fine manners and a sense of honor. *The poor woman proved she was a true lady by her good taste, kindness, and honesty.* 3. a woman who is important in society. *Which lady will be the head of the Charity Ball?* 4. **Lady,** a title given in Great Britain to certain women. *The Fairley*

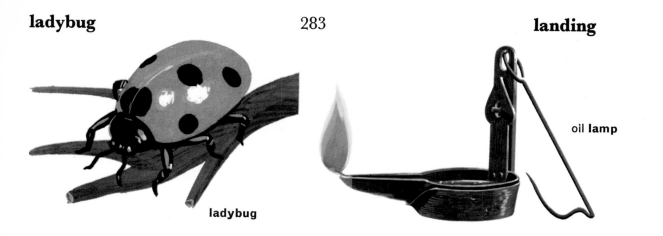

ladybug

oil **lamp**

Castle is closed, and Lady Fairley is in London. **la dies.**

adj. 5. being a lady. *At the wheel of the school bus was a lady driver.*

la dy bug (lā′dē bug′), *n.* a small, round, reddish beetle with black spots on its back. *Ladybugs eat harmful insects.* **la dy bugs.**

la goon (lē gün′), *n.* a shallow body of water near or connected with a larger body of water. *Some lagoons are located at the mouths of rivers.* **la goons.**

laid (lād), past tense of **lay**[1].

lair (lâr), *n.* a den; the home of a wild animal. *The fox makes its lair by burrowing into the ground.* **lairs.**

lake (lāk), *n.* a large body of water entirely surrounded by land. *Lake Michigan is the largest freshwater lake lying entirely within the United States; it is three hundred miles long and seventy-five miles wide.* **lakes.**

lamb (lam), *n.* 1. a young sheep. *The lambs gamboled in the field.* 2. the meat of the young sheep used as food. *Many people like to eat roast lamb.* 3. one who is gentle, innocent, or harmless. *Our dog is such a lamb that he would never hurt anyone.* **lambs.**

lame (lām), *adj.* 1. not able to walk without limping. *Jim was lame for a month after he hurt his leg playing football.* 2. hurt or injured, in a part of the body. *Joe's back is lame from his first day of summer work in the factory.* 3. poor; not easy to believe. *Sue had a lame excuse for not washing the dishes.* **lam er, lam est; lame ly,** *adv.*

v. 4. to make lame. *The dog lamed his leg when he jumped over the fence.* **lames, lamed, lam ing.**

lamp (lamp), *n.* a device for giving light. *Before Edison invented the electric light bulb, people burned oil in their lamps. Early man made lamps by burning animal fat. Modern lamps come in different sizes and shapes; some stand on the floor, and others sit on tables.* **lamps.**

lamp post (lamp′pōst′), *n.* a post that has a lamp on it, used outdoors. *At night we played "hide-and-seek", using the lamppost as the goal.* **lamp posts.**

lance (lans), *n.* 1. a long pole with a sharp point at the end. *Soldiers on horseback once used lances as weapons.* 2. a sharp instrument used by doctors to cut or open. *Doctors use lances to open the skin area where there is an infection.* **lanc es.**

v. 3. to cut open with a sharp instrument. *The doctor lanced the large boil on his patient's arm.* **lanc es, lanced, lanc ing.**

land (land), *n.* 1. the part of the earth that is not water. *The earth contains twice as much water as land.* 2. the ground; the soil. *This rich land is good for planting corn.* 3. a country. *The United States is the land I live in.* **lands.**

v. 4. to arrive. *The ship landed at noon. All day and all night airplanes land at the airport.* 5. to get off. *The passengers landed this morning from the train. Esther's mother was there when she landed from the airplane.* 6. to get someplace. *The careless driver may land in jail. John jumped and landed right in the mud.* 7. to catch. *My little brother landed a tiny fish.* **lands, land ed, land ing.**

land ing (lan′ding), *n.* 1. a platform part of the way up a set of stairs. *Let's pause at the landing till Father gets his breath back.* 2. a coming to the ground. *The airplane made a smooth landing.* 3. place for boats to land; a dock. *The landing was crowded, so three ships waited in the harbor.* **land ings.**

lances

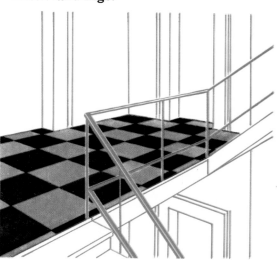

landing

land lord (land′lôrd′), *n.* 1. a man who owns houses or apartments which he rents to other people. *Our landlord is very thoughtful, and sees that we have plenty of heat on cold mornings.* 2. a man who runs a hotel or an inn. *The landlord of the small inn told us to stay for the night.* **land lords.**

land scape (land′skāp), *n.* 1. a view of the land. *From the hilltop the landscape was beautiful.* 2. a picture of a view of the countryside. *Some artists draw or paint landscapes.* **land scapes.** *v.* 3. to increase the beauty of property by planting trees, bushes, grass, and flowers. *Grandfather had an expert landscape his yard.* **land scapes, land scaped, land scap ing.**

lane (lān), *n.* 1. a narrow path. *The boys ran down the lane that led to the pond.* 2. a sort of path that ships and airplanes stay in. *The lane of one airplane may be at fifteen thousand feet; another one may be at seventeen thousand feet.* 3. a part of a highway or street marked off by a line. *Always drive in the right lane.* **lanes.**

lan guage (lang′gwij), *n.* 1. speech; words that are spoken or written. *Language is the way human beings tell others what they think and how they feel.* 2. the speech of a certain nation, tribe, or group of people. *The French language is spoken by the people of France.* 3. the special words and terms used by some groups. *People today have learned a little of the language of science. My father says he can't understand the language of teen-agers.* 4. any way of giving one's own thoughts to others. *Some people use sign language.* **lan guag es.**

lan tern (lan′tərn), *n.* a case, usually made of glass, which surrounds the light of a lamp. *A lantern keeps the light from blowing out in the wind and rain.* **lan terns.**

lap[1] (lap), *n.* 1. the front part of the body from the waist to the knees when a person sits. *The mother held her child on her lap.* 2. a part of a piece of clothing or other material that lies partly over another part. *The lap of my coat has buttonholes.* 3. one complete trip around a racetrack. *Jerry gradually ran ahead of the others in the third lap.* **laps.** *v.* 4. to put something so that it lies partly over something else. *Lap each shingle on the roof six inches over the one beneath it.* 5. in racing, to lead or get ahead of by one lap or more. *The world champion lapped the closest runner.* **laps, lapped, lap ping.**

lap[2] (lap), *v.* 1. to drink by taking up with the tongue. *The cat lapped up the milk.* 2. to hit with a soft splash. *The waves lapped gently against the pier.* **laps, lapped, lap ping.** *n.* 3. the sound of lapping. *When the cat is thirsty, his laps are loud.* **laps.**

la pel (lə pel′), *n.* the front part of a garment which is folded back below the collar. *Most coats have lapels.* **la pels.**

lap ful (lap′fùl′), *n.* as much as the lap can

lark

hold. *The baby has grown, and he is now a lapful.* **lap fuls.**

lapse (laps), *n.* 1. a small mistake; a slight error. *Lack of sleep can cause a lapse in your good work.* 2. the gradual passing of time. *After a lapse of three years, they met each other by accident.* 3. the ending of a right or privilege. *The lapse of an insurance policy can be caused by failure to pay the premiums.* **laps es.** *v.* 4. to go backward into the earlier way of doing things. *After four good years, the dog lapsed into his old habit of running away.* 5. to come to an end. *I let my club membership lapse because I no longer had time to attend.* **laps es, lapsed, laps ing.**

lard (lärd), *n.* 1. the fat of pigs, melted down for use in cooking. *Lard is used in making pie crusts.* *v.* 2. to put lard or other fat on. *Mother larded the chicken before she roasted it.* 3. to add something to. *The principal likes to lard his speeches with jokes.* **lards, lard ed, lard ing.**

large (lärj), *adj.* 1. big. *A whale is large.* 2. **at large,** (a) free. *The lion escaped from the zoo and is at large.* (b) in general. *The public at large approved the President's plan.* **larg er, larg est; large ly,** *adv.*

large ly (lärj′lē), *adv.* mostly; to a great extent. *The teacher is largely responsible for our reading of good books.*

lark[1] (lärk), *n.* a brown songbird with long hind toes that lives in Europe and Asia (the skylark); a similar bird of North America (the meadow lark). *Larks make a high, lovely sound.* **larks.**

lark[2] (lärk), *n.* a good time; fun. *Our class had a lark when we all took the bus to the state capital.* **larks.**

lar va (lär′və), *n.* an insect in its wormlike stage as it comes from an egg. *The larvae of butterflies are caterpillars.* **lar vae** (lär′vē).

lash (lash), *n.* 1. a whip, or the part attached to the handle that is used for hitting. *The lash was used by the rider as a signal for his horse to go faster.* 2. a blow made with a whip. *Years ago criminals were given lashes as a punishment.* 3. one of the little hairs at the edge of the eyelids. *Betty has beautiful, long, dark lashes.* **lash es.**

v. 4. to strike with a whip. *The rider lashed his horse and won the race.* 5. to hit with force; beat. *The heavy wind lashed the trees.* 6. to hit with words; to scold badly. *The team's manager lashed Jack for not remembering the signals.* 7. to tie with a rope. *Sailors lash the cargo to the deck when a storm comes.* **lash es, lashed, lash ing.**

lass (las), *n.* a girl. *She is a pretty lass.* **lass es.**

las so (las′ō), *n.* 1. a long rope with a sliding loop at one end. *The cowboy caught the cattle by throwing his lasso around the neck of each animal.* **las sos** or **las soes.**
v. 2. to catch with a lasso. *You will have to lasso that horse to get him in the barn.* **las sos** or **las soes, las soed, las so ing.**

last¹ (last), *adj.* 1. coming after all others; final. *The last train leaves at six o'clock. The last day of the year is December 31.* 2. before the present time; most recent. *The last party we went to was fun. The last time we met was over three years ago.* 3. remaining. *The last leaf on the tree finally fell.* **last ly,** *adv.*
adv. 4. after everyone else. *I arrived last.* 5. most recently. *You last came to our house on Tuesday.*
n. 6. the person or thing that is last. *This is the last of the candy.* 7. the end. *The soldiers fought to the last.*

last² (last), *v.* 1. to go on; continue. *A football game lasts about two and one half hours.* 2. to continue in existence; stay in good condition. *The United States has lasted almost two hundred years. The stone building will last longer than the wooden building.* **lasts, last ed, last ing.**

last³ (last), *n.* a model of a foot on which shoes are repaired or made. *The shoe-repair man puts shoes on a last to mend them.* **lasts.**

last ing (las′ting), *adj.* going on for a long time. *Their friendship has been a lasting one.* **last ing ly,** *adv.*

late (lāt), *adj.* 1. happening after the usual time; tardy. *Nobody likes to be late for school. We had a late summer this year.* 2. near the end of a certain time. *In late summer our tomatoes ripen.*

lattice

Late last month we had a storm. 3. recent; happening just before now. *The television announcer read the late news.* 4. recently dead. *The late Mr. Dixon was a fine man.* **lat er** or **lat ter, lat est** or **last; late ly,** *adv.*
adv. 5. after the usual time. *The men worked late last night.* 6. toward the end. *He goes to bed late every night.*

late ly (lāt′lē), *adv.* not long ago; recently. *Edna has lately been working harder than ever.*

Lat in (lat′n), *n.* 1. the language of the ancient Romans. *One reason Latin is studied in schools is that it helps us to understand the origin of our own language.* 2. a person from such countries as Italy, Spain, France, and Argentina. *The boat arriving from South America will bring many Latins to our city.* **Lat ins.**
adj. 3. of or pertaining to ancient Rome and its people. *Latin history is the history of the Roman Empire.* 4. having to do with the languages developed from that of ancient Rome. *French is a Latin language.*

lat i tude (lat′ə tüd, lat′ə tūd), *n.* 1. the distance north or south of the equator, measured in degrees. *Lines that show latitude on a map or globe are horizontal lines.* 2. freedom from rules that are strict; freedom of thought and action. *People living in the United States have complete latitude in religious beliefs.* **lat i tudes.**

lat ter (lat′ər), *adj.* 1. the second of two persons or things mentioned. *Spring and fall are pleasant seasons, but I prefer the latter.* 2. later. *During the latter part of August, stores have sales on summer clothes and toys.*

lat tice (lat′is), *n.* a framework of crossed metal or wooden strips that allows air and light to enter. *Lattices are used in windows, gates, and doors. Some lattices are used as supports for roses and other climbing plants.* **lat tic es.**

laugh (laf), *v.* 1. to make quick sounds with the voice to show joy, amusement, or scorn. *Everyone laughed when John entered the room with the little kitten he had found in the rain. Some people in 1910 still laughed at the idea of flying in the air.* 2. to bring to a certain state or condition by laughing. *The movie was so funny that he laughed himself sick. The neighbors laughed him into feeling better.* **laughs, laughed, laugh ing.**
n. 3. the act or sound of laughing. *The happy man has a laugh that makes others smile.* **laughs.**

laugh ter (laf′tər), *n.* laughing; the sound of laughing. *Laughter filled the theater during the funny movie.*

launch¹ (lônch), *n.* 1. an open motorboat used for pleasure. *They bought a launch to use on the lake during weekends.* 2. a large boat carried by a warship. *A launch is used to take the navy crew to shore and back.* **launch es.**

launch² (lônch), *v.* 1. to send upward into space. *The astronauts will be launched toward the moon.* 2. to send into the water. *The new ship was launched while the workmen cheered.* 3. to

launching a ship

start; begin. *Our school launched a cleaning and painting drive in the neighborhood.* **launch es, launched, launch ing.**

laun dry (lôn′drē), *n.* 1. clothes that have been or are ready to be washed. *This week's laundry is in the large basket.* 2. a place to wash clothes. *Our laundry is in the basement.* 3. a company whose business is cleaning clothes. *A truck will pick up your clothes and take them to the laundry.* **laun dries.**

lava (lä′və), *n.* the hot, melted rock that comes from a volcano. *The lava flowed down the side of the mountain and into the deserted town.*

lav en der (lav′ən dər), *n.* 1. a plant with pale purple flowers and narrow leaves. *The oil obtained from the flower of the lavender is used in making perfume.* 2. the dried leaves and flowers of this plant. *Lavender is used to make clothes and closets smell sweet.* 3. a light bluish-purple color; pale violet. *Lavender is a popular spring color.* **lav en ders.**
adj. 4. of the color lavender. *We saw a beautiful lavender outfit at the spring fashion show.*

law (lô), *n.* 1. the set of rules made by the government of a city, state, or nation. *Laws are made for the good of the people and should be obeyed.* 2. a rule. *There is a law against letting a chimney send out heavy smoke. We all should obey the laws of good hygiene.* 3. the study or practice of law. *Charles chose law as his profession.* **laws.**

lawn[1] (lôn), *n.* ground covered with grass that is kept cut short. *The lawn around Mr. Griffin's house is smooth and green.* **lawns.**

lawn[2] (lôn), *n.* a thin, fine cloth. *Lawn is usually made of linen.* **lawns.**

law yer (lô′yər), *n.* a person who makes his living by practicing law; attorney. *The man asked for his lawyer's advice before he signed the document.* **law yers.**

lax (laks), *adj.* 1. not strict; careless. *Jim is lax about doing his homework and often turns his papers in late.* 2. not tight; loose. *The lax rope gave the dog some room to move about.* **lax er, lax est; lax ly,** *adv.*

lay[1] (lā), *v.* to put or place. *You can lay your book on the table. I can't lay my hand on the magazine right away. Lay your work aside now.* 2. to put down in a certain place. *A new gas pipe was laid from Texas to Chicago last year.* 3. to place in fiction or in imagination. *The story is laid in France.* 4. to produce eggs. *Hens lay eggs.* 5. to beat down. *Our little trees were laid low by the wind.* 6. to settle down; to quiet down. *A little rain will lay this dust.* 7. to bet. *I will lay ten pieces of candy that Nancy won't be here.* **lays, laid, lay ing.**
n. 8. the position in which a thing lies. *The Indian scout told the captain about the lay of the land.*
Lay also has the following special meanings:
lay aside, to put down; to put away. *The boy laid aside his magazine and went to lunch.*
lay away, to save; to put away for future.

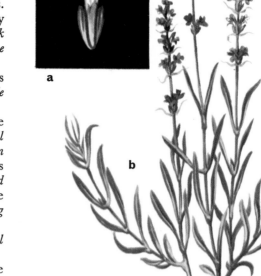

lavender:
a. flower
b. plant

Mr. Jones has laid away money to buy a house.
lay in, to store away; to keep. *The settlers laid in food for the winter.*
lay off, to put out of work. *The factory will lay off one hundred workers next week.*
lay out, to plan or mark out. *The gardener laid out a flower garden.*
lay up, (a) to put aside for future use. *Every Saturday we lay up a supply of groceries.* (b) to cause to be in bed. *The accident laid him up.*

lay[2] (lā), past tense of **lie**[2].

lay[3] (lā), *adj.* referring to ordinary people not members of professional group in religion, law, medicine, etc. *The lay members of the church often teach Sunday school.*

lay er (lā′ər), *n.* 1. a single thickness; a flat piece on top of another. *The fancy cake had three layers.* 2. someone or something that lays. *Some hens are poor egg layers. A man who builds with bricks is a bricklayer.* **lay ers.**

la zy (lā′zē), *adj.* 1. not wanting to work. *He was too lazy to help us move the furniture. The lazy employee was fired from his job.* 2. not very active. *The lazy dog lies in the sun all day.* **la zi er, la zi est; la zi ly,** *adv.*

lead[1] (lēd), *v.* 1. to show the way by going before or with. *The guide led the travelers to a resting place.* 2. to go or be at the head of; to be first in. *The band led the parade. Alice leads the class in spelling.* 3. to be first; to be ahead. *Every year our school leads in the number of scholarships won. Our team led by six points until the fourth quarter.* 4. to be a way. *The narrow road on the right leads to the lake.* 5. to command; to direct. *A conductor leads the band. The general led the army to victory.* 6. in card games, to play first. *Tom led with the king of hearts.* 7. to tend toward a specific result. *Good study habits lead to good grades. Dumping waste in a lake leads to water pollution.* 8. to live; to spend or pass. *Teachers lead a busy life.* **leads, led** (led), **lead ing.**

n. 9. the first place; the position ahead of all others. *The little black horse took the lead in the race. The United States has the lead in the production of automobiles.* 10. influence; example. *We should follow the lead of great men.* 11. the amount that one is ahead. *The Cardinals have a lead of five games over the Cubs. The winning golfer has a lead of two strokes.* 12. a clue; helpful hint. *The police have a lead about the location of the outlaws.* **leads.**

lead[2] (led), *n.* 1. a heavy, soft, gray metal. *Lead is used to make pipes that carry water.* 2. a thin piece of a soft material used in pencils. *The lead in some pencils is softer than in others. Some leads are red, blue, or green.* **leads.**

adj. 3. having lead in it; made of lead. *I often write with a lead pencil. A plumber fixes lead pipes.*

lead en (led′ən), *adj.* 1. made of lead. *The leaden box held the family's valuables.* 2. having the bluish-gray color of lead. *The building had a leaden hue.* 3. a very hard or heavy object or feeling. *It was with a leaden heart that I left my friends.*

lead er (lēd′ər), *n.* a person or thing that leads. *The leader directed the orchestra in playing the opera music. The Boy Scout troop needs a new leader.* **lead ers.**

leaf (lēf), *n.* 1. one of the green, flat parts that grow on bushes, plants, and trees. *We brought home a leaf from each kind of tree that we found during our walk in the woods.* 2. a sheet of paper in a book. *Each leaf has two pages—front and back.* 3. metal that is pounded into a thin sheet. *Gold leaf is used for decorating picture frames.*

4. a flat board used to make a table larger. *When company comes, we put another leaf in the middle of the table.* **leaves** (lēvz).

v. 5. to grow leaves. *The trees begin to leaf in April and May.* 6. to turn the pages without reading carefully. *Phil leafed through the magazines in the dentist's office.* **leafs, leafed, leaf ing.**

league[1] (lēg), *n.* 1. an association or union of persons, groups, or nations formed to maintain and further common interests or to help one another. *The National Football League makes rules for all its teams to follow.* **leagues.**

v. 2. to unite in a league. *The taxpayers thought they would be more powerful if they leagued.* **leagues, leagued, lea guing.**

league[2] (lēg), *n.* an old measure of distance, equal to about three miles. *It was two leagues from the old inn to the castle.* **leagues.**

leak (lēk), *n.* 1. a crack or hole that lets liquid, gas, or powder escape. *Water dripped through the leak in the pipe and flooded the floor. There is a leak in the bag of flour.* 2. the passage of liquid, gas, or powder in or out of a hole. *My front bicycle tire has a slow leak.* **leaks.**

v. 3. to let water, gas, or air in or out. *The pipe is leaking gas. The old rowboat leaks water.* 4. to enter or escape through an opening. *Rain leaked in through a crack in the window. The balloon slowly dropped from the ceiling as the gas leaked out.* 5. **leak out,** to become known by accident or by secret talking. *The story soon leaked out that Mr. Adams would be the new principal.* **leaks, leaked, leak ing.**

lean[1] (lēn), *v.* 1. to bend or slant in order to rest against something. *Don't lean on the newly painted wall. Help me to lean the ladder against the side of the house.* 2. to bend; to slant. *The old tree leans toward the telephone wires.* 3. to depend;

LEAVES

compound leaves

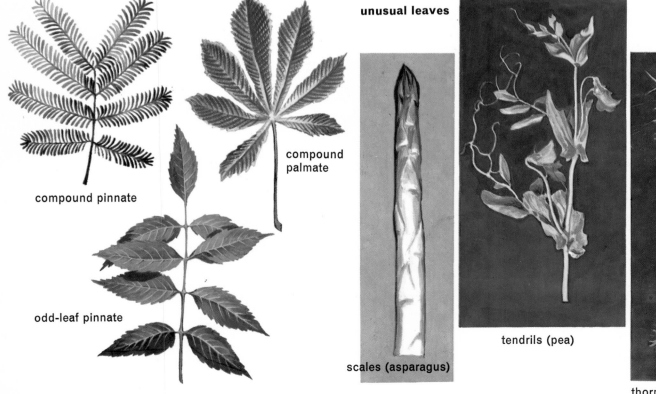

compound pinnate

odd-leaf pinnate

compound palmate

unusual leaves

scales (asparagus)

tendrils (pea)

thorns (barberry)

to rely. *I lean upon your advice.* 4. to tend; to show a liking. *Lately he has been leaning toward poetry as his favorite form of literature.* **leans, leaned** (lēnd) or **leant** (lent), **lean ing.**

lean[2] (lēn), *adj.* 1. thin; without fat. *Most athletes who run the mile are lean. I prefer lean bacon.* 2. not producing much; barely adequate. *Last year was a lean year for men who sell automobiles.* **lean er, lean est; lean ly,** *adv.*

leap (lēp), *v.* 1. to jump. *The horse leaped over the fence. The wild animals are leaping away from the hunters.* 2. to jump across. *The deer leaped the stream to get away.* **leaps, leaped** (lēpt) or **leapt** (lept), **leap ing.**
n. 3. a jump; a bound. *The dog went over the fence in one big leap.* **leaps.**

learn (lėrn), *v.* 1. to get to know; to get some knowledge in. *We go to school to learn reading, arithmetic, history, and geography. A baby learns how to walk and then how to run. Many grown-ups are learning French or Spanish.* 2. to acquire by memory; to get to know by heart. *You can learn a short poem in one hour.* 3. to find out. *We didn't learn about the duties of his new job until a week after he started to work.* **learns, learned** or **learnt** (lərnt), **learn ing.**

learn ed (lėr′nid), *adj.* having knowledge; full of learning. *The learned professor lectured on the new discoveries in science. A library contains many learned books.* **learn ed ly,** *adv.*

learn ing (lėr′ning), *n.* 1. knowledge or skill gained by study. *Men of great learning have written many books about history.* 2. the gaining of knowledge, skill, or ability. *A few tumbles are a part of learning to ice-skate.*

lease (lēs), *n.* 1. a written agreement to use property for a certain length of time by paying rent for it. *The school has a lease on the land it uses as a playground.* 2. the length of time that an agreement lasts. *My father has a ten-year lease on the property.* **leas es.**
v. 3. to get by means of a lease; to rent. *The salesman leased a car for one week.* **leas es, leased, leas ing.**

least (lēst), *n.* 1. the smallest in size, quantity, or degree. *Pam cleaned the floor so well that the least of dirt was gone. The least you can do is hold the door open.*
adv. 2. in the smallest amount. *The singers were good, but I was least impressed by the songs.*
adj. 3. smallest; littlest. *Mother gave the small boy the least portion of cake.*

leath er (leth′ər), *n.* 1. a material made from an animal's skin, which has been cleaned and the hair taken off. *Most shoes are made of leather.* **leath ers.**
adj. 2. made of leather. *We wear leather jackets and leather gloves.*

leave[1] (lēv), *v.* 1. to go away; to go from. *The train left ten minutes ago. I must leave home at half-past seven to be at school by eight o'clock.* 2. to go away from for good; to get out of. *She left home when she was eighteen to become a nurse. Don't leave school before you graduate.* 3. to let stay or be. *Leave your packages here while you shop.* 4. to go without taking something with one. *That careless boy left his book at home again.* 5. to deliver. *The mailman leaves letters at each house.* 6. to give when one dies. *Mr. Mack left all his money to his wife and son.* 7. to have as a remainder. *Six minus four leaves two.* 8. **leave alone,** to stop bothering or disturbing. *Leave*

a

b

leather:
a. boot
b. purse

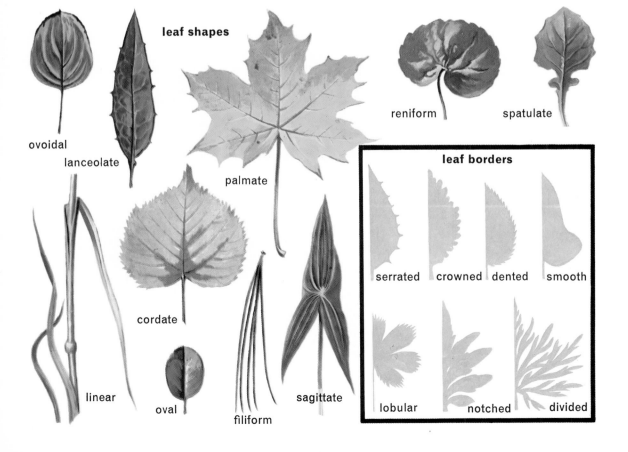

leaf shapes

ovoidal

lanceolate

palmate

reniform   spatulate

cordate

linear

oval

filiform

sagittate

leaf borders

serrated   crowned   dented   smooth

lobular   notched   divided

me alone while I'm reading. 9. **leave out,** to omit. *You can leave out one of the problems in the lesson.* **leaves, left, leav ing.**

leave[2] (lēv), *n.* 1. permission. *The owner gave us leave to use his beach for swimming.* 2. official permission to be away from work, military duty, or school. *The factory gave John a week's leave. Our professor is studying abroad while he is on leave.* 3. **take leave of,** to say good-by to. *The gentlemen took leave of the ladies.* **leaves.**

leave[3] (lēv), *v.* to leaf; to grow leaves. *The apple tree leaved early this year.* **leaves, leaved, leav ing.**

leaves (lēvz), *n. pl.* more than one leaf. *The leaves fell from the trees.*

lec tern (lek′tərn), *n.* a stand with a slanting top from which a book or notes are read. *Ministers often use lecterns when giving sermons. The professor placed his papers on the lectern before the class began.* **lec terns.**

lec ture (lek′chər), *n.* 1. a talk or speech. *The lecture today is about the problems involved in traveling to the moon.* 2. a scolding. *Aunt Joyce gave us a lecture when we banged the door shut.* **lec tures.**
v. 3. to give a lecture. *This summer Dr. Nolan is lecturing about new medical discoveries.* 4. to scold. *The store owner lectured the milkman for being late.* **lec tures, lec tured, lec tur ing.**

lec tur er (lek′chər ər), *n.* a person who gives a lecture. *The lecturer for this evening is the man whose book won a prize last year.* **lec tur ers.**

led (led), past tense and past participle of **lead**[1].

ledg er (lej′ər), *n.* a book in which a business keeps records of all its sales and purchases. *Big businesses have many ledgers.* **ledg ers.**

leech (lēch), *n.* a worm that lives in water or wet soil and often attaches itself to the skin of an animal to suck blood. *Doctors once thought leeches could draw the bad or poisoned blood from a sick person.* **leech es.**

left[1] (left), past tense and past participle of **leave**[1].

left[2] (left), *adj.* 1. referring to or being the hand opposite the right side of the body which is the weaker hand for most people. *Only two people in my class write with their left hand.* 2. located closer to the side opposite the right. *Tom sat on my right side and Sue sat on my left side. We took a left turn at the corner.*
n. 3. the left side. *His house is the one on the left.*

lectern

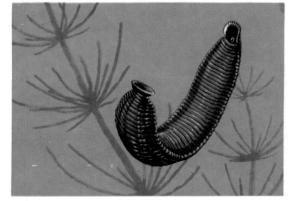

leech

adv. 4. in the direction to the left. *Go left after you reach the stoplight.*

leg (leg), *n.* 1. one of the limbs or members on the lower part of the body, used for supporting the body and for moving about from place to place. *A man has two legs. A dog has four legs.* 2. anything like a leg. *A table usually has four legs. A pair of trousers or slacks has two legs.* 3. a part of a trip. *The boys were on the last leg of their journey across the country.* **legs.**

le gal (lē′gl), *adj.* 1. of the law; based on law. *A judge makes decisions on legal problems.* 2. permitted by law. *A left turn at this corner is not legal.* **le gal ly,** *adv.*

leg end (lej′ənd), *n.* 1. a tale having its beginning in earlier times which has come to be believed as true by many. *The legend of Paul Bunyan is not true, but many people think it is.* 2. a group of stories such as these. *The legends of King Arthur and his court are very interesting.* 3. the writing, imprinting, etc. found on a coin, monument, building, etc. *The legend at the bottom of the Statue of Liberty ends, "I lift my lamp beside the golden door!"* 4. a short written statement below a map, chart, picture, etc. *The legend beneath the map states that one inch equals 400 miles.* **leg ends.**

leg i ble (lej′ə bəl), *adj.* able to be read because of clear printing, writing, or typing. *Mary's handwriting is very legible.* **leg i bly,** *adv.*

le gion (lē′jən), *n.* 1. a division of a large group of soldiers and horsemen in the ancient Roman army. *The Roman legions were composed of up to 6000 men.* 2. any military force made up of many soldiers. *The deeds of the French Foreign Legion are often written about.* 3. a great many people; multitude. *A legion of musicians marched in the parade.* **le gions.**

leg is late (loj′is lat), *v.* to pass laws. *Congress legislates many laws each year.* **leg is lates, leg is lat ed, leg is lat ing.**

leg is la tion (lej′is lā′shən), *n.* 1. the making or passing of laws. *The Constitution gives Congress the power of legislation.* 2. the laws that have been passed. *Legislation concerning new building regulations will be in effect next month.*

leg is la tive (lej′is lā′tiv), *adj.* 1. having the power and duty of making laws. *The Senate and the House of Representatives make up the legislative branch of our government.* 2. having to do with making laws. *The legislative process is very often slow.* **leg is la tive ly,** *adv.*

leg is la ture (lej′is lā′chər), *n.* a group of men and women who make laws. *Each of our fifty states has a legislature elected by the citizens. Our Congress is a legislature.* **leg is la tures.**

le git i mate (lə jit′ə mit), *adj.* 1. that which is right, truthful, or lawful. *She had a legitimate excuse for being late.* 2. that which is reasonable or justifiable. *Sharon has a legitimate fear of water because she once almost drowned.* **le git i mate ly,** *adv.*

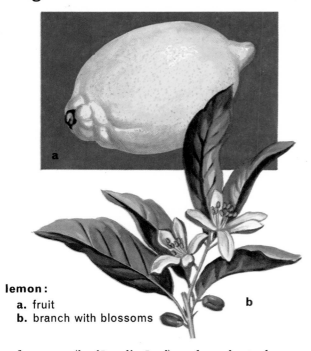

lemon:
a. fruit
b. branch with blossoms

leg ume (leg′ūm, li gūm′), *n.* 1. a plant whose seeds grow in pods. *Peas and beans are legumes.* 2. the seed of this plant used as food. *Legumes such as peas are my favorite vegetable.* **leg umes.**

lei sure (lē′zhər), *adj.* 1. free; not busy. *Our leisure time was spent in reading and listening to the phonograph.* **lei sure ly,** *adv.*
n. 2. the time free from work, when a person does what he chooses. *After an unusually busy season at the store, the manager enjoyed an increase of leisure.*

lem on (lem′ən), *n.* 1. a small, yellow, oval fruit with a sour juice. *The juice of a lemon is used in drinks, in pies, and for flavoring.* 2. the tree that the lemon grows on. *The lemon grows in Florida.* 3. the color of lemons; yellow. *Lemon is a warm color.* **lem ons.**
adj. 4. having the color of lemons. *One of the dresses in the fashion show was red-orange with a small lemon stripe.*

lem on ade (lem′ən ād′), *n.* a drink made of lemons, water, and sugar. *Mike is selling lemonade in front of his house.* **lem on ades.**

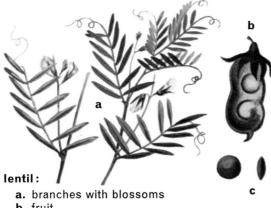

lentil:
a. branches with blossoms
b. fruit
c. seed

lend (lend), *v.* 1. to let someone have or use something for a short time. *She wants me to lend her a book to read.* 2. to provide; to give. *The new paint on the house lends beauty to it. Please lend a little help in lifting this box.* 3. to give temporary use of (money) with the agreement that it will be paid back with interest. *The bank is going to lend five hundred dollars to my father for home improvements.* 4. to make a loan. *He is a generous person who never borrows but always is willing to lend.* 5. **lend itself to**, to be suitable for. *The old furniture lends itself to the new room.* **lends, lent, lend ing.**

length (lengkth, length), *n.* 1. the distance from end to end. *The length of the boat is forty feet.* 2. the amount of time from beginning to end. *The length of the movie is two hours. The length of Uncle John's visit will depend on the weather.* 3. a piece of a certain size. *The plumber fastened together three lengths of pipe. A length of cloth was cut from the big bolt.* 4. **at length,** (a) in great detail. *He spoke at length about his trip.* (b) at last. *At length, the job was finished.* **lengths.**

length en (lengk′thən, leng′thən), *v.* to make or become longer. *This road has been lengthened since I last drove on it.* **length ens, length ened, length en ing.**

lens (lenz), *n.* 1. a piece of clear, curved glass that may bring together or spread apart the rays of light passing through. *Lenses are used in eyeglasses, cameras, telescopes, and microscopes.* 2. a part of the eye that brings light to a point on the back of the eyeball. *The lens of the eye acts like the lens of a camera.* **lens es.**

lent (lent), past tense and past participle of **lend.**

len til (len′tl), *n.* 1. a plant with somewhat flat, small seeds that grow in pods. *Lentils grow in Southern Europe and Asia.* 2. the seeds of this plant, which are used for food. *Mother put lentils in the soup.* **len tils.**

leop ard (lep′ərd), *n.* a large, fierce animal of the cat family, having a yellowish color with black spots. *Leopards live in Africa and Asia.* **leop ards.** (See illustration on following page.)

less (les), *adj.* 1. not so much. *It took less time to do my homework this week than last.* 2. fewer. *I visited the dentist less than two weeks ago.* 3. smaller. *The size of Texas is less than that of Alaska.*
adv. 4. to a smaller extent. *I was less happy than I looked.*
prep. 5. minus. *The paid attendance at the last game was less those who entered on free passes.*
n. 6. a smaller amount. *The store was asking sixty dollars for a new bicycle, but George bought a used one for less.* **less.**

les son (les′n), *n.* 1. something to be taught or learned. *My brother is taking violin lessons.* 2. something to be learned at one time; a unit of teaching. *The arithmetic lesson for today concerns the division of fractions.* 3. something

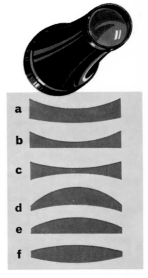

lens: watchmaker's **lens**

lens shapes
a. concavo-convex
b. plano-concave
c. double concave
d. convexo-concave
e. plano-convex
f. double convex

sand, āte, bâre, fäther; sent, mē, férn; fit, bīke; pot, rōpe, fôrt; run, pull, rüle, cüte; noise, sound; ch, cheese;
ng, long; th, thick; th, those; zh, treasure; ə = a in about, e in waken, i in animal, o in seldom, and u in minus.

learned from experience. *Ben learned a lesson in safety when he was almost hit by a train.* 4. a part of the Bible read during a church service. *The lesson for this Sunday is taken from the Old Testament.* **les sons.**

let (let), *v.* 1. to allow; to permit. *He wanted to stay up later, but his parents wouldn't let him. Let me finish that job for you. She let the children have more pie.* 2. to rent. *Ask the man if he has bicycles to let by the day.* **lets, let, let ting.**

Let also has the following special meanings:

let alone, (a) not to mention. *The child can barely walk two blocks, let alone six.* (b) to stop bothering. *Let him alone, or he'll become angry.*

let be, to hold oneself back or keep oneself from bothering. *If the dog is sleeping, let him be.*

let down, to disappoint; to fail. *Donald let us down when he didn't write to us.*

let go of, to release, to give up one's hold on. *She let go of his hand and walked away. He let go of the string, and the balloon sailed away.*

let in, to admit. *Let the dog in; he's shivering from the cold.*

let know, to tell. *Let me know when you are ready.*

let off, to set free; to pardon. *The principal let us off after we promised to behave.*

let on, (a) to pretend. *I will let on that I am ill.* (b) to make (it) known. *I won't let on that I know about the surprise.*

let out, (a) to allow to go out. *Let the cat out.* (b) to make an article of clothing larger. *Betty let out last year's skirt.*

let up, to stop. *Won't this rain ever let up!*

let ter (let′ər), *n.* 1. a symbol for a sound. *There are twenty-six letters in our alphabet.* 2. a

leopard

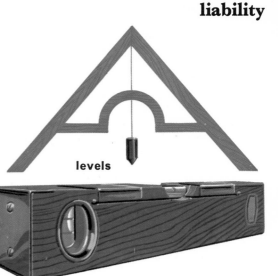

levels

written or typed message sent by mail. *The postman delivers letters.* 3. the exact meaning. *The judge based his decision not only on the letter of the law but on its spirit as well.* 4. the initial of the name of a school, given as a prize. *He won a letter in basketball and wore it on his sweater.* 5. **letters,** literature; the profession of literature. *The professor is a man of letters.* 6. **to the letter,** in all details. *Follow your directions to the letter.* **let ters.**

v. 7. to print by hand. *Letter this information on the chalkboard.* **let ters, let tered, let ter ing.**

let tuce (let′is), *n.* a garden vegetable with green leaves that are used in salads. *Lettuce grows either in large loose leaves or in heads.*

lev el (lev′l), *adj.* 1. flat and even. *The level field stretched for miles without a hill. A bowling lane is level.* 2. having the same height. *The big tree was once level with my head.* 3. sensible; not confused. *This problem needs some level thinking.* **lev el ly,** *adv.*

n. 4. height. *The river rose to a level of sixteen feet.* 5. an instrument used to find out if a surface is horizontal. *The most common level is one that contains a liquid with a bubble that moves to the center when the surface is horizontal. Another kind of level uses a weight hung by a thin rope from the top of a triangle placed on the surface. The carpenter used a level to see if the table top was perfectly straight.* 6. stage; rank. *Mr. Berry has reached the highest level in the fire department.* **lev els.**

v. 7. to make flat. *The gardener leveled the dirt around the flowers. The wreckers leveled all the buildings.* **lev els, lev eled, lev el ing.**

lev er (lev′ər, lē′vər), *n.* 1. a bar used to lift objects. *The lever is rested on a support and pushed at one end to lift the other end.* 2. a part of a machine that is lifted, pushed, or pulled. *To get candy from a machine, you pull down on a lever.* **lev ers.**

lex i cog ra pher (lek′sə kog′rə fer), *n.* a person who writes a dictionary. *It takes many lexicographers to write a good dictionary.* **lex i cog ra phers.**

li a bil i ty (lī′ə bil′ə ti), *n.* a being liable;

responsibility; obligation. *Since he caused the accident, the payment is his liability.* **li a bil i ties.**

li a ble (lī′ə bl), *adj.* 1. responsible; under obligation to pay. *Dick is liable for the damage he caused when he broke the window.* 2. likely; subject to something unpleasant. *People are liable to catch cold in winter. We are liable to be late if we don't hurry. That old car is liable to break down.*

lib er al (lib′ər əl), *adj.* 1. generous. *Mr. Black is liberal with his time in helping me.* 2. plentiful; more than enough. *This restaurant serves liberal portions of meat and potatoes. We received a liberal reward for returning the wallet we found.* 3. broad in covering many topics; not limited to one thing. *Many colleges have stressed liberal education.* 4. willing to allow different opinions and beliefs; not set in an old way of thinking. *The Declaration of Independence was written by liberal men with liberal ideas about human rights.* 5. in favor of new ideas in education, politics, etc. *The candidate is considered to be liberal because he wants to improve the living conditions of the poor.* **lib er al ly,** *adv.*

n. 6. a person who has liberal views about politics and government. *The liberals are outnumbered in the new Congress.* **lib er als.**

lib er ty (lib′ər tē), *n.* 1. freedom. *The African colonies were given their liberty. The jailed man asked for liberty. Speaking one's mind is a liberty some countries do not allow. Children today have more liberty than their parents did.* 2. **at liberty,** allowed. *The workers on the new jet plane were not at liberty to talk about it.* 3. **take liberties,** to be too bold or too free. *Never take liberties with a new employer by calling him by his first name.* **lib er ties.**

li brary (lī′brer′ē), *n.* 1. a room or building containing books and other literary materials that may be read or borrowed. *A library is also used for research and study.* 2. a collection of literary materials. *The professor has a library of more than two thousand books.* **li brar ies.**

lice (līs), *n. pl.* more than one louse. *Lice are small, flat insects. Lice live on the bodies of unclean animals.*

li cense (lī′sns), *n.* 1. permission given by law to do something. *John's uncle has a license to fly passengers in an airplane.* 2. the card or paper that has the permission printed on it. *I saw my parents' marriage license. The 16-year-old boy received his first driver's license today.* 3. too much liberty of action; the wrong use of freedom. *After the football game students took license and crowded into public buses without paying the fare.* **li cens es.**

v. 4. to give legal printed permission to do something. *The state licensed him to practice law.* **li cens es, li censed, li cens ing.**

li chen (lī′kən), *n.* a small plant without flowers or leaves that grows on rocks, trees, and ground. *Lichens can look like dry moss, tiny bushes,*

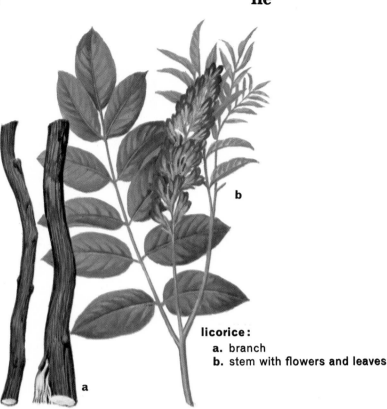

licorice:
a. branch
b. stem with flowers and leaves

leaves, shells, or very thin paper. *Lichens have no roots or stems and do not need soil for growth.* **li chens.**

lick (lik), *v.* 1. to pass the tongue over. *The child licked his lollipop. The cat licks milk from the floor.* 2. to pass over like a tongue. *Huge flames licked the side of the building.* 3. to beat; defeat. *Our team licked theirs, forty-seven to twelve.* **licks, licked, lick ing.**

n. 4. a small amount. *The new boy hasn't done a lick of work today.* 5. a place where animals go to lick salt that comes from the earth. *The salt lick was in the middle of the field.* 6. a moving of the tongue over something. *The cat gave her kitten a lick.* **licks.**

li co rice (lik′ə ris, lik′rish), *n.* a black, sweet flavoring made from the root of a plant that grows in Europe and Asia. *Licorice is used in candy and in some medicines.* **li co ric es.**

lid (lid), *n.* 1. a top or cover for closing the opening of a box, pot, jar, etc. *Put the lid back on the box of candy. Close the lid of the trunk.* 2. an eyelid. *The tired baby's lids slowly closed.* **lids.**

lie[1] (lī), *n.* 1. a false statement made to deceive someone. *Henry told a lie when he said he went to the library.* **lies.**

v. 2. to tell something that is not true on purpose. *Don't lie to me.* **lies, lied, ly ing.**

lie[2] (lī), *v.* 1. to place one's body in a flat position. *Joe was tired, so he decided to lie down. He lay on the couch in the living room.* 2. to be in a flat position. *Your coat has lain on the floor all morning.* 3. to be located or situated. *The school lies one block north of the river.* 4. to be; to exist. *Our chance to win the swimming meet lies with*

George, our best swimmer. 5. to stay in a certain condition. *The ship has lain at the bottom of the harbor for two hundred years.* **lies, lay, lain, lying.**

lieu ten ant (lü ten′ənt), *n.* 1. an army officer ranking next below a captain. *A first lieutenant is above a second lieutenant.* 2. a navy officer ranking next below a lieutenant commander. *A lieutenant is one rank above the lowest officer in the navy.* **lieu ten ants.**

life (līf), *n.* 1. the quality or condition which distinguishes animals and plants from rocks and dead beings. *Something that has life grows, needs food, breathes, and can make more of its own kind.* 2. the time that a person, animal, or plant is alive. *His life covered seventy-three years.* 3. a person. *Doctors work hard to save lives.* 4. a certain way of living. *Life on a farm is different from life in a city. A rich person can live a life of luxury.* 5. the true story of a person's life. *Everyone should read the lives of great men.* 6. a person who has humor and liveliness. *Barbara is always the life of a party with her singing and joke telling.* **lives** (līvz).

life guard (līf′gärd′), *n.* a person who watches over swimmers in a swimming pool or on a beach. *The lifeguard saved the woman from drowning.* **life guards.**

life preserver

life preserver, *n.* a special jacket, belt, or large ring, used to keep a person floating in water. *When the boy fell out of the boat, his companion threw him a life preserver.* **life preservers.**

lift (lift), *v.* 1. to raise from a lower to a higher position. *This box is too heavy for me to lift. John's high grade in the test lifted his spirits. The fog lifted, and we could see the road. Lift the baby into his high chair.* **lifts, lift ed, lift ing.**
n. 2. help. *Karen gave Joan a lift with the house-work.* 3. a free ride. *Mr. Johnson gave us a lift to town in his car. Many states have laws against taking lifts from strangers.* 4. a feeling of sudden cheer. *My father got a lift when his boss praised his good work.* 5. an elevator. *They took the lift to the tenth floor.* **lifts.**

light[1] (līt), *n.* 1. the condition that makes us able to see; the opposite of dark. *The sun gives light.* 2. anything that gives light. *Turn off the light when you leave the room.* 3. brightness. *A*

lighters

candle gives off little light compared with a lamp. 4. a flame to start something burning. *Mr. Cain needs a light for his pipe.* 5. helpful ideas; information. *No one could shed light on the dog's disappearance.* 6. public attention. *The police brought to light some new information about the robbery.* 7. the way in which something appears. *The progress of the class was put in a good light by the teacher. Each of us sees things in his own light.* 8. an outstanding person. *She is one of the shining lights of the school paper.* **lights.**
adj. 9. having a pale color. *His light jacket had dark blue trimming. The baby has light eyes.* **light er, light est; light ly,** *adv.*
v. 10. to give light to. *The new lamps light the whole street.* 11. to set on fire. *They lighted the campfire.* 12. to guide with a light. *The forest ranger lighted our way to the cabin.* 13. to become light; to make bright. *Watch her face light up when she sees this present.* **lights, light ed** or **lit, light ing.**

light[2] (līt), *adj.* 1. not heavy; not having much weight. *In the summer we wear light clothes.* 2. not hard to do; easy to put up with. *The youngest child was given the light work to do.* 3. not violent; not strong. *The birds floated gently in the light breeze.* 4. slight; not serious. *I caught a light cold.* 5. not clumsy; having grace. *A good dancer is light on his feet.* 6. not serious in thought. *To enjoy herself, Betty read light books.* 7. not damp and heavy; well-baked. *Mother baked a nice light cake.* **light er, light est; light ly,** *adv.*
adv. 8. with not much luggage. *The newspaper reporter traveled light.*

light[3] (līt), *v.* 1. to get down. *The jockey lighted from his horse.* 2. to land; to settle. *The bird lighted on the branch. The boy's eyes lighted on the bicycle in the store window.* **lights, light ed** or **lit, light ing.**

light en[1] (līt′n), *v.* 1. to make light; to give light to. *The glow from the fireplace lightened the room.* 2. to make or become brighter. *The storm clouds went away, and the sky lightened. The addition of a red sofa lightened the effect of the room.* 3. to flash with lightning. *It thundered and lightened all night.* **light ens, light ened, light en ing.**

light en[2] (līt′n), *v.* to make or become less heavy. *We lightened his load by carrying some of the heavy packages. His gloomy thoughts were lightened by his daughter's visit. His mood lightened at the sound of her laughter.* **light ens, light-ened, light en ing.**

light er (lī′tər), *n.* a thing that starts something burning. *Cigarette lighters usually use liquid or gas fuel.* **light ers.**

light house (līt′hous′), *n.* a tower built to guide ships at night with a bright light. *Lighthouses are placed near dangerous rocks or at the entrance to a harbor.* **light hous es.**

light ly (līt′lē), *adv.* 1. with not much force.

lighthouse

The wind blew lightly, barely disturbing the water. 2. very little; not much. *People on a diet eat lightly.* 3. with skill and lightness. *She danced lightly through her part in the school musical.* 4. in a cheerful way. *The bus driver lightly greets each passenger.* 5. not seriously. *I am afraid Greg takes his job lightly.*

light ness¹ (līt′nis), *n.* 1. brightness. *The lightness of the morning made every object in the room easy to see.* 2. the amount of light. *The day with the most lightness is the twenty-first or twenty-second of June.*

light ness² (līt′nis), *n.* 1. a being light; not weighing much. *The lightness of the small car made it easy to push when we ran out of gasoline.* 2. a being cheerful. *The lightness of his thoughts was shown by his whistling and smiling.* 3. a lack of force; not being severe. *Everyone was pleased with the lightness of the young man's punishment.*

light ning (līt′ning), *n.* the flashing of light in the sky caused by the passing of electricity from one cloud to another or from a cloud to the ground. *Lightning is usually accompanied by thunder.*

like¹ (līk), *prep.* 1. similar to. *John is like his father, who works hard.* 2. in the same way as. *He can see like a cat in the dark.* 3. characteristic of; typical of. *It is not like Carol to be late.* 4. in the mood for. *I feel like listening to the ball game.* 5. as if there may be. *It looks like rain today.*

lightning

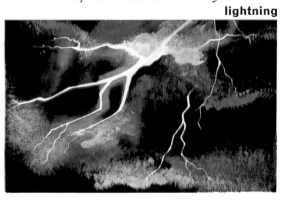

adj. 6. the same or nearly the same. *I'll bring three cans of fruit, so you bring a like amount of vegetables.*
n. 7. a person or thing similar to another; an equal or match. *I'll bet you'll never see his like! I've never seen the like of this lazy dog; all he does is eat and sleep.* 8. **the like,** something similar. *Our teacher told us to eat plenty of apples, oranges, and the like.* **likes.**
conj. 9. as if. *She dances like she had years of experience.* 10. as. *This candy tastes sweet, like candy should.* (Many experts say that *like* is not a conjunction and should not be used as if it were.)

like² (līk), *v.* 1. to be pleased by; to enjoy. *I like listening to music. Harry likes his job as a salesman.* 2. to prefer; to wish. *I'll come to see you whenever you like.* **likes, liked, lik ing.**
n. pl. 3. **likes,** the things enjoyed. *Among my likes are reading and gardening.* **likes.**

like ly (līk′lē), *adj.* 1. liable; probable that something is going to happen. *It isn't likely to snow here in July.* 2. seeming to be just right; suitable. *That restaurant is a likely place to have dinner.* 3. probable; seeming to be true. *Isn't that a likely story!* **like li er, like li est.**
adv. 4. probably. *The stores are likely closed now.*

like ness (līk′nis), *n.* 1. picture; portrait. *This is a good likeness of your mother.* 2. similarity. *The family likeness shows in the faces of all the children.* 3. appearance; form. *The mountain peak had the likeness of a man's face.* **like ness es.**

like wise (līk′wīz′), *adv.* 1. in the same manner. *She made all of her dresses with long sleeves, and I made mine likewise.* 2. also; too. *The senior team won, and the junior team likewise.*

lik ing (līk′ing), *n.* an enjoying; preference; a being fond of something. *Our teacher has a real liking for young people.*

li lac (lī′lək), *n.* 1. a shrub with groups of sweet-smelling white or purple blossoms. *Lilac bushes are a common garden plant.* 2. the blossoms of this shrub. *We picked some lilacs to put on the*

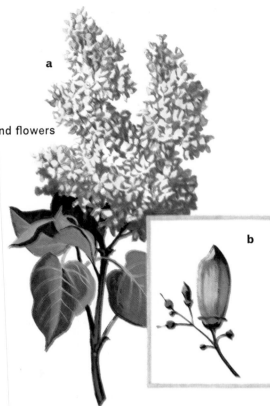

lilac:
a. branch with leaves and flowers
b. fruit

dining-room table. 3. a light pinkish-purple color. *I am going to paint the flowers lilac.* **li lacs.** *adj.* 4. of the color lilac. *Susan has a new lilac dress for the party.*

lily (lil′ē), *n.* 1. a plant that has flowers shaped like a funnel. *Lilies grow from bulbs.* 2. the blossom of the plant. *Lilies are used to decorate many churches at Easter time.* **lili es.**

lily of the valley, *n.* a low plant with tiny white bell-shaped flowers. *Brides often carry lilies of the valley in their bouquets.* **lilies of the valley.**

lily

limb (lim), *n.* 1. an arm, leg, or wing. *The boy mended the limb of the little bird that had fallen from the tree.* 2. the branch of a tree. *You can build a treehouse on the two strong bottom limbs.* **limbs.**

lim ber (lim′bər), *adj.* 1. bending easily; not stiff. *A young tree has limber branches. An athlete has a limber body.* **lim ber ly,** *adv.*
v. 2. to make or become limber. *The players limbered up their muscles by doing exercises.* **lim bers, lim bered, lim ber ing.**

lime[1] (līm), *n.* a white substance made by heating bones, shells, or limestone, which is a kind of rock. *Lime is used in construction, manufacturing, tanning, and farming.*

lime[2] (līm), *n.* a small, sour, light-green fruit that grows on a tree. *Limes look like greenish lemons.* **limes.**

lime stone (līm′stōn′), *n.* a kind of rock used for building, for making roads, etc. *Limestone is used in building.*

lim it (lim′it), *n.* 1. the furthest point; an end. *There is a limit to mother's patience with us.* 2. the greatest amount permitted. *The speed limit here is thirty miles an hour. The limit during the hunting season is eight ducks a day.* 3. **limits,** boundary; boundary lines. *We walked to the city limits and back again.* **lim its.**
v. 4. to set a limit to; keep within a certain amount. *Limit your speeches to ten minutes each.* **lim its, lim it ed, lim it ing.**

lily of the valley

linnet

lim it ed (lim′ə tid), *adj.* 1. making only a few stops. *A limited bus gets to its destination fast.* 2. having a limit; restricted. *The contest is limited to people under eighteen years of age. We have a limited amount of time to finish the job.*

limp¹ (limp), *adj.* drooping; having no strength. *The lack of rain has left all our plants limp and dry. The salesgirl was limp from standing all day.* **limp er, limp est; limp ly,** *adv.*

limp² (limp), *n.* 1. a hobbling, lame walk. *The boy with the sore ankle walks with a limp.* **limps.** *v.* 2. to walk lamely; to move with a limp. *The dog caught a thorn in its paw and limped all the way home.* **limps, limped, limp ing.**

line¹ (līn), *n.* 1. a rope, cord, or wire. *Fishing lines must be strong. Telephone lines extend from one pole to another. Boats are attached to docks by lines.* 2. a long narrow mark. *Draw a line on the paper with your pencil. As a person gets old, he gets lines in his face.* 3. a row of persons or things. *A long line was in front of the ticket office. The line of houses is part of the new section of town.* 4. a system of railroads, buses, or airplanes that carries passengers and freight. *The bus lines use the main highways.* 5. a row of words across a page. *I remember only the first line of the poem.* 6. a boundary; edge. *On the other side of the line is Michigan.* 7. a business; kind of occupation. *What line is your father in? Our neighbor is in the landscaping line.* 8. a short letter. *Write me a line when you're away.* 9. **lines,** (a) the words an actor speaks in a play. *All actors like to get lines that hold the attention of an audience.* (b) a plan for doing something. *The new movie will be written along the lines of a mystery story.* **lines.** *v.* 10. to mark with lines. *The child lined the paper with red crayon. Age lined his face.* 11. to form a line along. *People lined the street for the parade.* **lines, lined, lin ing.**

Line also has the following special meanings: **line of duty,** one's job; a duty that one is supposed to perform. *The sailor showed his courage in the line of duty.*

all along the line, at all points; everywhere. *The mailman was greeted with smiles all along the line.*

bring into line, to cause to agree or to act properly. *Little Joe was brought into line by a talk with his mother.*

read between the lines, to get a hidden meaning from a letter, book, speech, etc. *Jack's letter didn't say he was happy, but I could tell, by reading between the lines, that he was.*

out of line, not in agreement. *The low wages the boy received were out of line with his long hours of work.*

line up, (a) to form a line. *The gym class lined up according to height.* (b) to gather together. *My father lined up three friends for the fishing trip.*

line² (līn), *v.* to cover the inside of. *Mother lined the storage box with heavy paper.* **lines, lined, lin ing.**

lin en (lin′ən), *n.* 1. a thread or cloth made from flax. *Clothes made of linen are strong and attractive.* 2. things made of linen, cotton, etc. *Linens include such articles as sheets, napkins, and tablecloths.* **lin ens.**
adj. 3. of linen. *The girl wore a linen dress.*

lin ger (ling′gər), *v.* to stay on; to be slow in leaving. *Three guests lingered after the party.* **lin gers, lin gered, lin ger ing.**

lin ing (līn′ing), *n.* a material that covers the inner surface of something. *Some overcoats are made with a lining that can be removed.* **lin ings.**

link (lingk), *n.* 1. one of the connecting rings that form a chain. *The links of the dog's chain are small. The links of the chain attached to a ship's anchor are large.* 2. a bond between two people or things; anything that connects. *There is a strong link of friendship between the two boys.* **links.**
v. 3. to join together. *The towns are linked by the new road.* **links, linked, link ing.**

lin net (lin′it), *n.* a small songbird that is found in Europe, Asia, and Africa. *The linnet changes color during its life, sometimes being brown, red, or gray.* **lin nets.**

li on (lī′ən), *n.* 1. a large, powerful, brownish-yellow member of the cat family that lives in Africa and Asia. *The lion is called the king of beasts because of its strength. The male lion has a mane on its neck and shoulders.* 2. a person who is strong and brave. *The knight was a lion in the battle.* 3. **social lion,** a person much in demand at parties. *That movie star is a social lion.* **li ons.** (See illustration on following page.)

li on ess (lī′ən is), *n.* a female lion. *A lioness fiercely protects her cubs from harm.* **li on ess es.**

lip (lip), *n.* 1. either of the two edges of the mouth. *Your lips move when you speak.* 2. anything like a lip, especially the rim or edge of a hollow jar, pitcher, or other vessel. *The lip of this pitcher is cracked.* **lips.**

li que fy (lik′wə fī′), *v.* to make or become

link of a chain

lion

liquid. *Ice cream liquefies in hot weather if it is not kept in a freezer.* **li que fies, li que fied, li que fy ing.**

liq uid (lik′wid), *n.* 1. one of the three main forms of matter, the other two being solid and gas. *A liquid flows easily. Water is a liquid.* **liq uids.**
adj. 2. flowing easily like water. *Gasoline is a liquid fuel.* 3. sweet-sounding. *The liquid song of the bird started at dawn.* **liq uid ly,** *adv.*

liq uor (lik′ər), *n.* a drink that contains alcohol. *There are many laws for the sale and use of liquors.* **liq uors.**

list[1] (list), *n.* 1. a column of names, words, or numbers. *Some housewives take a grocery list to the store. Everyday we have a list of words to spell in class.* **lists.**
v. 2. to write or print in a column or columns. *Our name is listed in the telephone book.* **lists, list ed, list ing.**

Roman **litter**

list[2] (list), *v.* 1. to lean over. *The ship listed dangerously as a result of the storm.* **lists, list ed, list ing.**
n. 2. a leaning over to one side. *The ship with the list will be the first one repaired.* **lists.**

lis ten (lis′n), *v.* to pay attention so that hearing is easier. *The audience listened quietly to the great piano player. Listen carefully to these directions, because they will not be repeated.* **lis tens, lis tened, lis ten ing.**

lit[1] (lit), past tense of **light**[1].

lit[2] (lit), past tense of **light**[3].

lit er ary (lit′ər er′ē), *adj.* having to do with literature, or poetry, novels, and stories. *He is an editor of a literary magazine.*

lit er ate (lit′ər it), *adj.* 1. able to read and write. *The members of this tribe have been taught to be literate.* 2. educated; having a knowledge of literature. *The professor is a literate person.*

lit er a ture (lit′ər ə chər), *n.* 1. writings such as poetry, novels, plays, and short stories, which often have excellent style and present great ideas. *Our library contains much of the famous literature of this century. Courses in literature are given in school and college.* 2. all the writings on a certain subject. *The doctor tried to keep up with medical literature.* **lit er a tures.**

lith o sphere (lith′ə sfir′), *n.* the outer shell of the solid earth. *The lithosphere is about twenty miles thick and is made of solid rock.*

lit ter (lit′ər), *n.* 1. a piece of canvas stretched on a frame for carrying a sick person. *The football player was carried from the field in a litter.* 2. a couch with long horizontal poles at the sides. *Four men carried the Roman king to the palace in his litter.* 3. a number of baby animals born at one time. *The cat had a litter of kittens.* 4. loose paper, empty bottles, rubbish, etc. *Hundreds of men clean up the litter on the grass after Sunday picnics in the city parks.* 5. a bed for animals. *The horse has a comfortable litter of straw and sawdust.* **lit ters.**
v. 6. to make messy with scattered rubbish. *We should not litter our beautiful parks or our schoolyard.* **lit ters, lit tered, lit ter ing.**

lit tle (lit′l), *adj.* 1. small. *An elephant is big and an ant is little.* 2. not much. *There is little food in the house.* 3. a small amount of. *Give me just a little cocoa.* 4. not important. *John made only one little mistake on the test.* 5. short. *We will be there in a little while.* **lit tler** or **less** or **lesser, lit tlest** or **least; less, least,** *adv.*
adv. 6. to a small degree; not much. *It was so late that I little hoped to catch the train.* 7. not at all. *He little knew the dangers he would face.* **less, least.**
n. 8. a small amount. *Patricia showed the teacher a little of her poetry.* 9. a short time. *Please stay a little.*

Little also has the following special meanings: **little by little,** gradually; slowly. *Little by little his work is getting better.*

not a little, very much. *Cleaning the house took not a little work.*

think little of, to think or handle as not important. *Barbara's mother thinks little of Barbara's sewing.*

liv a ble (liv′ə bl), *adj.* suitable for living in. *The house was small but neat and livable.*

live¹ (liv), *v.* 1. to have life. *We live in the twentieth century. Some animals and fishes were living a million years ago.* 2. to continue living; to stay alive. *On television we saw a man who has lived to be one hundred years old. Fish must be in water to live.* 3. to have one's home; to dwell. *My family has lived in this town for sixty years.* 4. to carry on; to support oneself. *My grandfather lives on the small income from his savings.* 5. to feed. *Cows live on grass. Birds live on grain, berries, insects, and worms.* 6. **live down,** to live so that others forget one's past mistakes. *John is still trying to live down the excitement he caused when he broke the window.* 7. **live up to,** to fulfill; to do as well as others expected. *The baseball player lived up to the manager's hopes.* **lives, lived, liv ing.**

live² (līv), *adj.* 1. alive; having life. *Bill kept his live wolf cub until his teacher told him to give it to the zoo.* 2. having much energy. *That live boy is on the football team and has two jobs.* 3. burning; glowing. *Let's cook our hamburgers over the live coals.* 4. carrying an electric current. *Never touch a live wire!* 5. not exploded. *The bullets in the soldier's gun were still live.* 6. of much interest now. *The live issue in our town is the need for new schools.* 7. broadcast while taking place. *Although some television and radio programs are live, most are recorded or filmed.*

live ly (līv′lē), *adj.* 1. full of energy; active. *The lively horse ran full speed across the large meadow.* 2. quick; merry; gay. *The band played lively music as the County Fair opened.* 3. exciting. *The boys had a lively time at camp.* 4. cheerful; bright. *She met us at the door with a lively greeting. We decorated the room in lively colors, like red and orange.* **live li er, live li est.**

liv en (līv′ən), *v.* to make or become full of life; to cheer up; to brighten. *Games, cheerful music, and jokes liven a party. The party livened when she turned on the phonograph.* **liv ens, liv ened, liv en ing.**

liv er (liv′ər), *n.* 1. a large organ of the body, near the stomach. *The work of the liver includes making bile (a yellowish liquid that aids in digestion), storing substances that help the body to function properly, and helping to change food into parts that the body can absorb.* 2. the liver of an animal used as food. *We had beef liver cooked with bacon and onions.* **liv ers.**

lives (līvz), *n. pl.* more than one life. *We study the lives of great men in our history course.*

live stock (līv′stok′), *n.* animals kept on a farm, such as horses, cattle, pigs, and sheep. *The farmer will sell some of his livestock and keep the rest for use on the farm.*

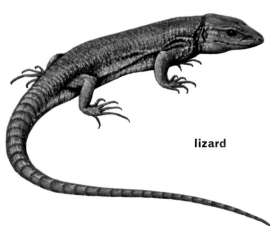

lizard

liv ing (liv′ing), *adj.* 1. alive; not dead. *Biology is the study of living things.* 2. enough to live on. *The boy finally got a job which pays a living wage.* 3. having to do with a way of life. *The living conditions in the little town were better for him than those in the big city.*
n. 4. a way of getting money to support oneself. *What does your father do for a living?* 5. a way of life; the way in which one lives. *Racing drivers enjoy dangerous living.* **liv ings.**

liz ard (liz′ərd), *n.* a kind of reptile found in many shapes and sizes, having dry skin covered with scales. *Lizards can be big with four legs and a long tail or small with a snakelike body and no legs. Many lizards live best in a warm, dry, desert climate.* **liz ards.**

lla ma (lä′mə), *n.* a large, long-haired animal of South America that looks like a small camel without a hump. *Llamas are used to carry heavy loads.* **lla mas.**

load (lōd), *n.* 1. something that is carried. *The load was too heavy for the small car. The camper had a load of equipment on his back.* 2. something that makes one worried or upset. *His father's recovery from illness took a load off Jerry's mind.* 3. the amount of shot or powder in a gun. *The hunter used up his load after only a few hours of hunting.* **loads.**
v. 4. to put a load in or on. *The pioneers loaded their wagons and headed west.* 5. to fill with some-

llama

thing to be carried. *Load the truck with bricks.* 6. to take on as a load. *The bus is loading passengers.* 7. to burden; to weigh down. *The men in the factory were loaded with work.* 8. to put shot or powder in. *The hunter loaded his rifle.* **loads, load ed, load ing.**

load stone (lōd′stōn′), var. of **lodestone.**

loaf[1] (lōf), *n.* 1. a large piece of bread baked in one piece. *Slice the loaf to make sandwiches.* 2. any food baked in the shape of a loaf of bread. *We enjoyed the meat loaf that mother baked.* **loaves** (lōvz).

loaf[2] (lōf), *v.* to do nothing; to pass the time doing as little as possible. *John's boss told him to loaf for a few days because he had worked very hard.* **loafs, loafed, loaf ing.**

loam (lōm), *n.* rich, dark soil. *Loam is made up of sand, clay, and decayed plants.*

loan (lōn), *v.* 1. to lend. *Loan me your book for a minute.* **loans, loaned, loan ing.**
n. 2. a lending; anything that is lent. *The business firm received a government loan. Mother asked for a loan of sugar from the lady next door.* **loans.**

loathe (lōth), *v.* to feel hate or strong dislike for something. *My sister loathes snakes.* **loathes, loathed, loath ing.**

loaves (lōvz), *n. pl.* more than one loaf. *Mother baked two loaves of bread this morning.*

lob by (lob′ē), *n.* 1. an entrance room; an outer hall. *The man took our tickets, and we walked into the lobby of the theater.* 2. a person or group whose job is to get members of a legislature to vote for or against a certain measure. *The sugar lobby was able to prevent the import of more sugar.* **lob bies.**
v. 3. to try to get legislators to vote for or against a certain bill. *Some apartment owners lobbied for the passage of a measure to increase rents.* **lob bies, lob bied, lob by ing.**

lobe (lōb), *n.* a part that is round. *The lobe of the ear is at the bottom of the ear.* **lobes.**

lob ster (lob′stər), *n.* 1. a large sea animal with two big claws and eight legs. *A lobster has a hard shell over its body.* 2. the meat of this animal. *Lobster is a tasty food.* **lob sters.**

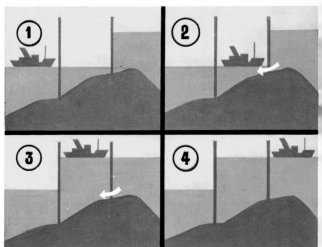

lock: ship enters the lock **(1)**, water flows in **(2)**, water level rises **(3)**, ship leaves the lock **(4)**

lo cal (lō′kl), *adj.* 1. having to do with one certain place. *After the national news, the television shows us local news about our town.* 2. affecting only one part of the body. *The dentist gave me a local pain killer when I had a sore tooth.* 3. stopping at all stations. *A local train is slower than an express train.* **lo cal ly,** *adv.*

lo cal i ty (lō kal′ə tē), *n.* a region or area. *The manager will live in the locality of the new factory.* **lo cal i ties.**

lo cate (lō′kāt), *v.* 1. to find the position or place of. *We located Dad's hat after searching the whole house. Can you locate your state and town on the map?* 2. to place or establish in a certain place. *The store is located in the Jonesville Shopping Center. The school board located the new school near our house.* **lo cates, lo cat ed, lo cat ing.**

lo ca tion (lō kā′shən), *n.* 1. a place or position. *This quiet neighborhood is a good location for a house.* 2. a locating; being located. *The city council is discussing the location of the airport.* **lo ca tions.**

loch (lok), *n.* 1. in Scotland, a word used to mean a lake. *Loch Lomond is the largest lake in Scotland.* 2. a section of the sea partly enclosed by land. *The ships anchored in the loch until the storm passed.* **lochs.**

lock[1] (lok), *n.* 1. a device for fastening a door, drawer, etc. *A lock can be opened by using a special key.* 2. an enclosed part of a canal or river in which water is raised or lowered so that ships can pass to another water level. *Lake Superior is higher than Lake Huron, so ships go through locks to get from one to the other.* **locks.**
v. 3. to fasten with a lock. *Lock the door when you leave home.* 4. to join. *The girls locked arms as they walked to school.* 5. to shut in or out. *The dog was locked in the house. By accident, I was locked out.* **locks, locked, lock ing.**

lock[2] (lok), *n.* a curl of hair. *We cut a lock from the baby's head to keep as a souvenir.* **locks.**

spiny **lobster**

lock er (lok′ər), *n.* 1. a kind of closet that can be locked. *We use lockers at school to hold our books and coats.* 2. a small trunk. *Campers and soldiers keep their belongings in lockers.* **lock ers.**

lock et (lok′it), *n.* a small metal case for carrying a picture or a lock of hair. *A locket is worn around the neck on a chain.* **lock ets.**

lock smith (lok′smith′), *n.* a person who makes or repairs locks for doors, windows, etc. *The locksmith made extra keys for our car.* **lock smiths.**

lo co mo tive (lō′kə mō′tiv), *n.* an engine that pulls railroad trains. *Some locomotives pull freight trains, while others pull passenger trains.* **lo co mo tives.**

lo cust (lō′kəst), *n.* 1. a grasshopper with short feelers. *Locusts travel together in great numbers, destroying crops by eating every bit of greenery.* 2. a thorny tree with thin leaves that look like the leaves of a fern. *The seed cases of a locust look like those of beans.* **lo custs.**

lode stone (lōd′stōn′), *n.* 1. a kind of rocklike substance that can attract iron. *The lodestone was the first kind of magnet.* 2. anything that attracts. *Learning is the lodestone that draws her to books.* **lode stones.**

lodge (loj), *n.* 1. a house used for a special purpose, as a temporary living place. *The men arrived at the hunting lodge ready for a week's shooting. We drove to our lodge on the lake for the summer.* 2. a kind of club. *Father's lodge holds meetings every Friday night.* 3. the den of an otter or beaver. *The beaver was too smart to step into the trap put near his lodge.* **lodg es.**
v. 4. to live in a place for a while. *I will be lodging in a ski resort in Europe during my winter vacation.* 5. to supply with a place to sleep or live in for a while. *The motel lodges about thirty people a night.* 6. to put in a certain place. *The bird lodged his nest near the top of the tree.* **lodg es, lodged, lodg ing.**

loft (lôft), *n.* 1. the top floor of a building. *The loft of the barn holds hay. The factory's loft is used for storing tools and machines.* 2. an upper level in a church where the choir sits. *From the choir loft came the first notes of the hymn.* **lofts.**
v. 3. to hit or throw high. *Howard lofted the ball over my head.* **lofts, loft ed, loft ing.**

lofty lôf′tē), *adj.* 1. high; tall. *The lofty building has one hundred stories. Even in July you can see*

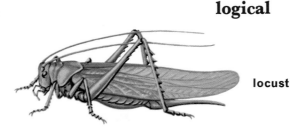

locust

snow at the top of the lofty mountain. 2. grand; noble in thought. *The teacher gave a lofty speech about the value of education.* 3. too proud. *The king's lofty manner made people dislike him.* **loft i er, loft i est; loft i ly,** *adv.*

log (lôg), *n.* 1. a long piece of the trunk or a big branch of a tree that has been cut down. *Logs are cut into smaller pieces for building and for firewood. Many logs are used for telephone and telegraph poles.* 2. the record of what happens on a trip made by a ship or airplane. *The different weather conditions and the number of miles traveled are written in a log.* 3. a device for telling how fast a ship is moving. *The log is made of material that floats and is dragged behind a ship, attached to a line.* **logs.**
v. 4. to cut down trees and make them into logs. *The men logged pine trees for their fireplaces.* 5. to write in a log. *The captain of a ship logs the daily happenings.* **logs, logged, log ging.**
adj. 6. made of logs. *Many early Americans built log cabins to shelter their families.*

log ger (lôg′ər), *n.* a person whose job is to log trees. *Some loggers climb the tall trees to saw off the top branches; other loggers chop or saw down the tree.* **log gers.**

log ger head (lôg′ər hed′), *n.* 1. a stupid person. *Even though I know he is very intelligent, he sometimes acts like a loggerhead.* 2. a large sea turtle. *Loggerheads live in the warm parts of the Atlantic Ocean.* 3. **at loggerheads,** in a quarrel; having a dispute. *The boys were at loggerheads about the day the circus was coming.* **log ger heads.**

log ging (lôg′ing), *n.* the work of cutting down trees and making them into logs. *Logging is a big industry.*

log ic (loj′ik), *n.* good, clear thinking. *Using logic, the lost boy followed the river in the forest until he came to a village.* **log ics.**

log i cal (loj′ə kl), *adj.* using logic; sensible.

locomotives: **a.** steam **b.** diesel

a

b

Being ill is a logical reason for not going to school.
log i cal ly, *adv.*

lone (lōn), *adj.* alone; single. *A lone cloud floated in the blue sky.*

lone ly (lōn′lē), *adj.* 1. unhappy because one is away from family or friends. *When his family moved, Mark was lonely until he made new friends.* 2. not often visited. *My father likes the village on the seacoast because it is lonely.* 3. single. *A lonely airplane flew overhead.* **lone li er, lone li est.**

lone some (lōn′səm), *adj.* 1. lonely; sad from being alone. *The lonesome traveler walked on to the next town.* 2. empty; not having many people. *The lonesome road led to the top of the mountain.* **lone some ly,** *adv.*

long[1] (lông), *adj.* 1. having great distance or length of time. *It's a long walk to the bus stop. That long book has over seven hundred pages. The composer spent a long time writing his song.* 2. having a certain length. *The room is twelve feet long. A year is twelve months long.* **long er, long est.** *adv.* 3. for a considerable time. *My friends have been away long. Legislation on lowering the voting age has long been desired by many college students.* 4. throughout the length of. *The boys exercised all summer long.* 5. **before long,** soon. *Will we see him before long?* **long ing ly,** *adv.*

long[2] (lông), *v.* to want very much; feel a great desire. *The boys longed for their mother and father, who had gone on a trip. She longs to spend a summer traveling around the United States.* **longs, longed, long ing.**

lon gi tude (lon′jə tüd′, lon′jə tūd′), *n.* the distance east or west on the surface of the earth. *Longitude is measured in degrees east or west of a line running north and south through Greenwich, England.* **lon gi tudes.**

look (luk), *v.* 1. to turn or fix one's eyes in order to see. *Look both ways before you cross the street.* 2. to search. *We looked everywhere for the gloves before we found them.* 3. to appear. *Jean looks happy these days.* 4. to face. *The summer cottage looks toward the lake.* 5. to keep the eyes on. *Always look where you're going.* 6. to gaze. *He stood looking out the window.* **looks, looked, look ing.**

n. 7. the act of looking; watching. *The watchman gave us a long look.* 8. an appearance; the way a person or thing seems. *That horse has a healthy look. The girl takes care of her good looks.* **looks.**

Look also has the following special meanings:
look after, to take care of. *We looked after the neighbor's cat while she was away.*

look down on, to think of as bad; despise. *Everyone looks down on a person who cheats.*

look for, (a) to search. *Someone help her look for the key.* (b) to expect. *He is looking for a letter from his son.*

look forward to, to wait eagerly for. *Patsy is looking forward to school.*

look in, to make a quick visit. *The principal looks in on our classroom about once a month.*

look into, to examine. *The repairman looked into the cause of the trouble in the car.*

look on, (a) to consider; think of. *I look on the United States as the greatest country in the world.* (b) to watch. *We played baseball while our parents looked on.*

look out, to be careful. *Look out for the ice on the steps.*

look over, to examine. *The teacher looks over everything we hand in.*

look up, to search for. *Get a timetable and look up the time the train arrives. Look up in the dictionary the words you don't know.*

look up to, to respect. *Little boys look up to their fathers and older brothers.*

look out (luk′out′), *n.* 1. a person who watches. *The lookout high on the ship was the first to see land.* 2. a careful watching. *Keep a lookout for the bus while I buy a newspaper.* 3. a place from which to watch. *This tree is our lookout.* 4. **on the lookout,** in the process of watching. *The police are on the lookout for the bank robbers.* **look outs.**

loom[1] (lüm), *n.* a machine for weaving cloth out of thread. *Years ago many families owned their own looms; today big looms are used in factories.* **looms.**

loom[2] (lüm), *v.* to appear suddenly and not very clearly. *The truck loomed out of the twilight on the lonely road.* **looms, loomed, loom ing.**

loop (lüp), *n.* 1. the shape of a string or wire that turns to go across itself. *A knot in a rope has loops.* 2. a curve in a river, road, etc. that looks like a loop. *The little stream has a wide loop that goes around the camp.* **loops.**
v. 3. to fasten with a loop. *The cowboy looped*

ship's **lookout**

lotus

the rope around the horse's neck. **loops, looped, loop ing.**

loose (lüs), *adj.* 1. not fastened tightly. *The bottom step is loose. I have a loose button on my coat.* 2. not fastened together. *Those loose papers will fly all over.* 3. not tied to something. *The dog is loose again. The rowboat is loose and is drifting across the lake.* 4. not fitting tightly. *The collar of his shirt is too loose.* 5. not put up in a package. *Dad says he used to buy loose coffee and loose sugar which were weighed by the grocer.* 6. lacking or wanting in restraint. *Loose talk about money got him in trouble with his friends. His loose behavior should be corrected.* 7. not exact. *This is the loose meaning of the French poem. Loose planning caused confusion in the scheduling of the meetings.* **loos er, loos est; loose ly,** *adv.*
v. 8. to set free; make loose; untie. *They loosed the horse in the large, fenced-in meadow.* 9. to make less tight. *On a hot day, men loose their collars.* **loos es, loosed, loos ing.**

loos en (lüs′n), *v.* 1. to make loose; make less tight. *Loosen the collar around the dog's neck.* 2. to become loose. *The knot in the rope loosened because it wasn't tied correctly.* **loos ens, loosened, loos en ing.**

loot (lüt), *n.* 1. stolen goods. *The pirates hid their loot from the ship.*
v. 2. to rob. *The thieves planned to loot the train.* **loots, loot ed, loot ing.**

lord (lôrd), *n.* 1. a person who has power to rule others. *The chief was the lord of the Indian tribe.* 2. in England, a nobleman who may sit in the House of Lords. *Years ago, the lords had*

great power. 3. **Lord,** (a) God. *"Bless us oh Lord for these thy gifts."* (b) Jesus Christ. *Christians believe in Christ, the Lord.* **lords.**

lose (lüz), *v.* 1. to put something somewhere or leave it behind so one can no longer find it. *My father has lost his glasses again.* 2. to be unable to find. *It is easy to lose your way in the darkness.* 3. to be deprived of; to have taken away. *The fireman lost his life trying to save the little girl. Unless you come in on time you will lose the privilege of going out in the evening.* 4. to have no longer. *She lost her beauty when she grew older. He was not elected again because he lost the confidence of the people.* 5. to fail to win. *We tried our best, but we lost.* 6. to fail to keep. *Don't lose your temper.* 7. to waste; fail to make use of. *We are losing time just standing here. He lost a good chance for a job when he forgot to see the manager.* 8. to cause the loss of. *His bad temper loses friends.* **los es, lost, los ing.**

los ing (lüz′ing), *adj.* that loses. *The losing team played well.*

loss (lôs), *n.* 1. ruin; destruction. *The forest fire caused the loss of five thousand acres of trees.* 2. a failure to keep or to win. *The loss of the contract cost the company millions of dollars.* 3. a losing. *The doctor approved of the woman's loss of weight. When he moved, Dick felt the loss of his old friends.* **loss es.**

lost (lôst), *v.* 1. past tense and past participle of **lose.**
adj. 2. missing. *The Boy Scouts found the lost boy.* 3. destroyed; ruined. *The lost trees will take years to replace.* 4. not won. *The football team remembers that lost game.* 5. hopeless. *We are fighting for a lost cause.* 6. wasted. *Talking about cleaning up the room is just lost time; let's do something.* 7. **lost in,** absorbed. *He was lost in his book for many hours.*

lot (lot), *n.* 1. one of a group of objects, like slips of paper or sticks, used to decide something by chance. *We drew lots to see who would clean the living room.* 2. the use of lots to decide something. *Five students were chosen by lot to go to the downtown concert.* 3. fate; luck. *It is always my lot to choose rainy days for picnics.* 4. a piece of land. *The house is built on a small lot.* 5. a group. *The new lot of dresses just arrived at the store.* **lots.**

lo tus (lō′təs), *n.* a kind of water lily that grows in Egypt, Asia, and America. *American lotuses are usually yellow, while Egyptian and Asian lotuses may be white, pink, or blue.* **lo tus es.**

loud (loud), *adj.* 1. strong in sound; not soft or quiet. *The alarm clock gives a loud ring.* 2. noisy. *The people in the next apartment have loud parties every Saturday night.* 3. too bright; too colorful, as clothes; not in good taste, as manners. *She wore a loud dress of yellow, red, and green. He was not invited to many parties because of his loud behavior.* **loud er, loud est; loud ly,** *adv.*

Lou i si ana (lù ē′zē an′ə), *n.* a southern state

of the United States along the Mississippi River. *Louisiana has many rich oil fields and fields of natural gas. Some of the crops grown in Louisiana are rice, strawberries, and vegetables.*

louse (lous), *n.* a small, usually flat, insect without wings that lives on the sap of plants and the blood of animals and human beings. *A louse has small, hooked feet for holding on to hairs on the human body.* **lice** (līs).

love (luv), *n.* 1. a deep, fond, affectionate feeling. *A mother's love for her baby is very strong.* 2. a great liking for someone or something. *He has a love of books.* **loves.**
v. 3. to have a deep affection for. *The young couple love each other and will be married.* 4. to like very much. *Football fans love to watch a game.* **loves, loved, lov ing.**

love ly (luv′lē), *adj.* 1. beautiful. *The lovely girl is planning to be a nurse.* 2. pleasing; delightful. *She is a lovely old lady.* **love li er, love li est.**

lov er (luv′ər), *n.* 1. a person who loves another. *The lover of the princess went to fight in the war.* 2. a person having a strong liking. *He is a lover of fine music.* **lov ers.**

lov ing (luv′ing), *adj.* showing or feeling love; affectionate. *Mr. Jenkins is a loving father to his three children.* **lov ing ly,** *adv.*

low[1] (lō), *adj.* 1. not high; not tall. *A skyscraper is tall; an ordinary house is low.* 2. near the ground. *The clouds are low. An airplane flies low near the airport.* 3. soft; not loud. *Speak in a low voice in the library.* 4. not as much as usual. *You get clothes at a low price during the sale.* 5. poor in health; weak. *We sent father on a vacation when he was low.* 6. sad. *The players had low spirits when they lost the game.* 7. almost used up. *The gasoline in the car's tank is low.* 8. not very good; poor. *We have a low opinion of a person who teases a little child.* 9. mean; not kind. *Taking away the puppy's food was a low trick.* 10. below the usual level. *The lake is low this year. Why are your grades low this month?* 11. deep in sound. *The girls will sing the high notes, and the boys will sing the low notes.* **low er, low est; low ly,** *adv.*
n. 12. a low point. *The temperature reached a new low for August.* 13. an arrangement of gears to get the most power. *Put the car into low.* **lows.**

lubricating a car

low[2] (lō), *n.* 1. a moo; the sound a cow makes. *The lows came from the barnyard.* **lows.**
v. 2. to moo; to make this sound. *The cows lowed gently in the field.* **lows, lowed, low ing.**

low er (lō′ər), *adj.* 1. not as high as another; below in place or position. *The office is on one of the lower floors.*
v. 2. to make less; reduce. *The store lowered the price of radios. Lower your voice.* 3. to let down; to take down. *The flag was lowered at sunset.* **low ers, low ered, low er ing.**

loy al (loi′əl), *adj.* faithful. *My parents are loyal Americans. Sam is a loyal friend.* **loy al ly,** *adv.*

loy al ty (loi′əl tē), *n.* a sense of duty; a being loyal. *No one could question our loyalty to our country.* **loy al ties.**

lu bri cate (lü′brə kāt′), *v.* to put on oil or grease to make a machine work more easily. *Father lubricated our car every two thousand miles.* **lu bri cates, lu bri cat ed, lu bri cat ing.**

lu bri ca tion (lü′brə kā′shən), *n.* a lubricating; an application of grease or oil. *The man in the garage is giving the car a lubrication.* **lu bri ca tions.**

luck (luk), *n.* 1. something that seems to happen to a person by chance. *Luck was on my side, and I won the prize.* 2. good fortune. *We had the luck to get the best seats.*

louse

luggage

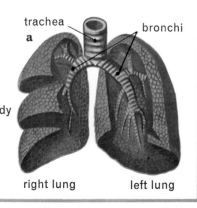

a

trachea

bronchi

right lung   left lung

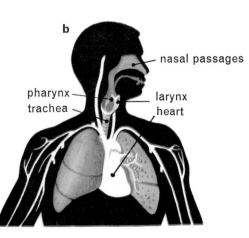

b

nasal passages

pharynx

trachea

larynx

heart

lungs:
 a. parts of the lungs
 b. position of the lungs in the body

lucky (luk′ē), *adj.* 1. having good luck. *Louise is always lucky in card games.* 2. having a good result. *My lucky guess won me the bicycle. It was a lucky day when I met Mrs. Hansen, my teacher.* **luck i er, luck i est; luck i ly,** *adv.*

lug gage (lug′ij), *n.* the baggage; the suitcases, trunks, bags, or boxes that are taken on a trip. *We will have to take a lot of luggage on our trip.*

luke warm (lük′wôrm′), *adj.* 1. neither too hot nor too cold. *The lake water is lukewarm.* 2. lacking enthusiasm. *The teacher was lukewarm toward my idea.*

lum ber[1] (lum′bər), *n.* 1. the planks, boards, etc., cut from logs. *Lumber is used to make furniture and houses.*
v. 2. to cut lumber. *He went to Canada to lumber in the forests.* **lum bers, lum bered, lum ber ing.**

lum ber[2] (lum′bər), *v.* to move in a clumsy, heavy manner. *The bear lumbered along the forest trail.* **lum bers, lum bered, lum ber ing.**

lump (lump), *n.* 1. a small, solid mass with no special shape. *Father broke the candy bar into three lumps.* 2. a bump or swelling. *The mosquito bite caused a lump on my arm.* **lumps.**
v. 3. to put together. *If we lump all the money we have, we will have enough for the gift.* 4. to form into lumps. *Cooked cereal will lump unless it is stirred while heating.* **lumps, lumped, lump ing.**
adj. 5. in one payment. *The plumber asked for a lump sum instead of monthly payments.*

lunch (lunch), *n.* 1. a light meal, usually eaten around the middle of the day. *We have lunch at school at noon.* **lunch es.**
v. 2. to eat a light meal. *We lunched later than usual today.* **lunch es, lunched, lunch ing.**

lunch eon (lun′chən), *n.* 1. a lunch. *We have luncheon at noon.* 2. a formal lunch, with guests. *The mayor gave a luncheon for the new governor.* **lunch eons.**

lung (lung), *n.* One of the two organs in the chest that are used in breathing. *The lungs take in fresh air from which the blood gets oxygen.* **lungs.**

lure (lůr), *v.* 1. to attract by promising something pleasant. *The advertisements in a magazine lure us into buying certain products.* **lures, lured, lur ing.**
n. 2. anything that attracts or lures. *The lure of great riches drove men to look for gold in California.* 3. a fishhook decorated to attract fish. *The fisherman used an artificial fly as a lure.* **lures.**

lute (lüt), *n.* a stringed musical instrument with a flat head, long neck, and tear-shaped body. *Lutes were common in the fourteenth and fifteenth centuries.* **lutes.**

lux u ry (luk′shə rē), *n.* 1. the use of the best things that give comfort and pleasure. *Some people become accustomed to luxury because they have money to buy expensive houses, automobiles, and*

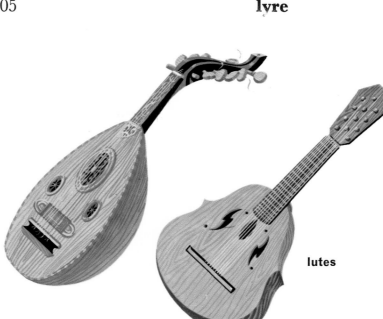

lutes

boats. 2. something that is really not needed, but which gives pleasure or comfort. *My uncle's stamp collection is his only luxury.* **lux u ries.**

lying[1] (lī′ing), *v.* 1. present participle of **lie**[1]. *My brother is not lying; he is telling you what really happened.*
n. 2. an untrue or false statement. *Lying in court is a very serious crime.*
adj. 3. untrue; false. *The lying girl was punished by her mother.*

ly ing[2] (lī′ing), present participle of **lie**[2].

lynx (lingks), *n.* a wild animal of the cat family that has long hair, a short tail, and pointed ears. *Lynxes live in the northern United States and in Canada.* **lynx es** or **lynx.**

lyre (līr), *n.* a stringed, harp-shaped musical instrument that is held in one hand and played with the other. *Lyres were common in ancient Greece and Rome.* **lyres.**

lyre

lynx

m

machete

M or **m** (em), 1. the thirteenth letter of the alphabet. 2. the Roman numeral for 1000.

ma (mä), *n.* an informal term for mother; mama. *Ask your ma to let you go to the game with us.*

ma'am (mam), *n.* madam. *He always answers, "Yes, ma'am," when a lady asks him for help.*

mace (mās), *n.* 1. a heavy club with a metal head, usually with spikes on it. *Maces were used as weapons in the Middle Ages.* 2. a rod used as a sign of authority. *The king held a mace to symbolize his right to rule.* **mac es.**

ma chet e (mə shet′ē), *n.* a big knife. *A machete can be used for cutting sugarcane or for opening a path through the jungle.* **ma chet es.**

ma chine (mə shēn′), *n.* 1. a simple device for doing work or making it easier to do work. *Levers, pulleys, screws, and wheels and axles are simple machines.* 2. a combination of parts, both moving and fixed, for doing work. *The farmer bought a machine that separates the grain or seed from wheat to help him in harvesting his crops.* 3. a vehicle for transportation, as an automobile or airplane. *Grandfather still talks of his surprise when he saw his first flying machine.* **ma chines.**

ma chin ery (mə shēn′ər ē), *n.* 1. machines. *Farm machinery has made it possible to raise larger crops.* 2. the working or moving parts of a machine. *There was something wrong with the machinery of the elevator.* 3. the system, people, and organization which make something work or by which something is done. *The machinery of justice provides a person accused of a crime with many opportunities to prove his innocence.* **ma chin er ies.**

ma cron (mā′kron, mak′ron), *n.* the straight line (-) placed over a vowel to show how it is pronounced. *The macron shows that ā is pro-*
nounced as in ate, ē *as in* me, ī *as in* bike, ō *as in* rope, *and* ū *as in* cute. **ma crons.**

mad (mad), *adj.* 1. crazy; out of one's mind. *The man felt that the constant noise of the power drill would drive him mad.* 2. angry; furious. *Tom was very mad when someone hit him with a snowball.* 3. foolish; not sensible or reasonable. *The criminals had a mad plan for escaping from prison by climbing over the walls.* 4. overly enthusiastic or excited about something. *She is so mad about tennis that she plays for two hours after school every day.* 5. very excited; wild. *The boys made a mad dash for the toy counter as soon as they entered the store.* 6. having rabies. *The police tried to catch the mad dog before he bit anyone.* 7. **like mad**, with all one's energy; very hard and fast. *I ran like mad, but I was still last in the race.* **mad der, mad dest; mad ly,** *adv.*

mad am (mad′əm), *n.* a polite form of address to a woman. *"Is there any way in which I can help you, madam?" asked the clerk.* **mad ams** or **mes dames** (mā däm′).

made (mād), past tense of **make.**

mag a zine (mag′ə zēn′, mag′ə zēn′), *n.* 1. a publication containing articles, stories, poems, etc. that appears regularly. *We receive two weekly and four monthly magazines at our house.* 2. the part of a rifle or pistol in which shells are held. *A bullet became jammed in the magazine, and the gun wouldn't fire.* 3. a room in a fort or ship in which arms, gunpowder, bullets,

mace

sand, āte, bâre, fäther; sent, mē, fėrn; fit, bīke; pot, rōpe, fôrt; run, pùll, rüle, cūte; noise, sound; ch, cheese; ng, long; th, thick; ~~th~~, those; zh, treasure; ə = a in about, e in waken, i in animal, o in seldom, and u in minus.

magician

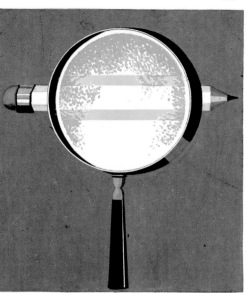

magnifying glass

dynamite, etc. are stored. *The ship sank shortly after the magazine was hit by enemy fire.* 4. a building in which military supplies are stored. *The sergeant ordered more guns, food, and other provisions from the magazine.* **mag a zines.**

mag ic (maj′ik), *n.* 1. the art or skill by which some persons say they can do impossible things or produce effects beyond natural human power. *The evil witch in the story used her magic to change the prince into a frog.* 2. the tricks and skills of a magician. *The magician used magic to make objects disappear.* 3. anything that charms and delights as if by magic. *The magic of the music calmed the animals in the circus.*
adj. 4. done or produced by magic or as if by magic. *The fairy godmother cast a magic spell over the sleeping girl.*

mag i cal (maj′ə kl), *adj.* 1. of magic. *People once thought that witches had magical powers.* 2. very attractive; having an unusual effect. *The magical moonlight and the silence of the forest caused us to walk quietly.* **mag i cal ly,** *adv.*

ma gi cian (mə jish′ən), *n.* a person who entertains by doing tricks that seem impossible to do. *The magician put one handkerchief in his hat and drew out ten.* **ma gi cians.**

mag net (mag′nət), *n.* 1. a piece of iron or steel or a stone containing iron that draws bits of iron and steel to itself. *A huge magnet was used to pick up the scrap iron and put it in trucks.* 2. anything that draws or exercises a pull. *The double feature acted as a magnet in bringing people to the theater.* **mag nets.**

mag net ic (mag net′ik), *adj.* 1. having the properties of a magnet. *You can construct a simple magnetic needle, which will swing around until one end points toward the north and the other toward the south.* 2. having to do with the properties of a magnet displayed by the earth. *The earth's magnetic poles exercise a pull on the needle of a compass, causing the needle to*

move. 3. having great personal charm and an attractive manner. *The singer's magnetic personality completely delighted her audience.*

mag nif i cent (mag nif′ə snt), *adj.* 1. rich in decoration and appearance; splendid; beautiful. *The king lived in a magnificent castle on a huge estate.* 2. noble in character. *He was a magnificent leader of his country.* **mag nif i cent ly,** *adv.*

mag ni fy (mag′nə fī′), *v.* 1. to make something larger or appear larger. *The man magnified the photograph so that we could see all of its details.* 2. to add to; to make something greater or more important than it is. *He magnified the story of his adventure until no one could believe it anymore.* **mag ni fies, mag ni fied, mag ni fy ing.**

magnifying glass, *n.* a lens that makes things seen through it look larger. *If you use a magnifying glass, the small words will appear larger.* **magnifying glasses.**

mag no lia (mag nōl′yə), *n.* 1. a tree or shrub with large blossoms, growing in North America and Asia. *Magnolias have shiny leaves and yellowish-white or pink blossoms.* 2. the blossom of the magnolia. *The magnolia is the state flower of Mississippi and Louisiana.* **mag no lias.** (See illustration on following page.)

mag pie (mag′pī), *n.* 1. a noisy black-and-white bird. *A magpie is somewhat like a crow.* 2. a person who talks a lot. *Virginia is a little magpie, always chattering.* **mag pies.**

magpie

magnolia:
a. flower
b. branch with leaves

maid (mād), *n.* 1. an unmarried woman or girl; maiden. *The young maid was brought to the city by her brother.* 2. a female servant. *The maid in the hotel changed the sheets on our beds every day.* **maids.**

maid en (mād′n), *n.* 1. an unmarried young woman or girl; maid. *The prince took the beautiful maiden to his castle where they were married.* **maid ens.**
adj. 2. not married. *Terry has two married sisters and one maiden sister.* 3. of a maiden; like a maiden. *When the king asked her to dance, a maiden blush colored her cheeks.* 4. made or tried for the first time; first. *The pilot got lost on his maiden flight.* **maid en ly,** *adv.*

mail[1] (māl), *n.* 1. packages, letters, postcards, etc. that are delivered through the post office. *There is always a larger amount of mail during December than at any other time of the year.* 2. the system that carries and delivers mail. *Your order will be shipped to you by mail.* 3. a single delivery of mail. *He received a letter from his brother in the mail today.* **mails.**
v. 4. to send by mail; to place in a mailbox. *Did you mail that letter to your brother today? She walked to the corner to mail a letter.* **mails, mailed, mail ing.**

mail[2] (māl), *n.* an armor covering made of links of metal or of pieces of metal that lap over one another. *Long ago, soldiers wore mail to protect them from the spears and arrows of the enemy.*

mail box (māl′boks′), *n.* 1. a box into which people place letters, parcels, etc. that are to be delivered by mail. *The contents of a mailbox are taken to the post office where they are sorted and* made ready for delivery. 2. a box into which a person's mail is delivered. *There was a letter for me in our mailbox when I got home from school.* **mail box es.**

mail man (māl′man′), *n.* a person who collects, carries, or delivers mail; postman. *The mailman was late with his delivery today because of the heavy snowfall.* **mail men.**

main (mān), *adj.* 1. most important; chief; major. *Roast beef was served as the main course at dinner. The main reason I went to the store was to buy milk.* 2. full; utmost; sheer. *By main strength he lifted the rock and freed the animal from the trap.* **main ly,** *adv.*
n. 3. a pipe that carries gas, water, etc. *The workers had to dig up the street to repair the water main.* 4. the sea. *Pirates once sailed over the main, robbing and destroying ships.* 5. **with might and main,** with great strength and power. *With all his might and main, he forced open the heavy door.* 6. **in the main,** for the most part. *It was a well-played game in the main, but there were a few errors made.* **mains.**

Maine (mān), *n.* a state in the northeastern part of the United States. *Fishing has been one of the major industries of Maine for more than one hundred years.*

main land (mān′land′), *n.* not an island or peninsula; the major part of a land mass. *In Hawaii, continental United States is called "the mainland."* **main lands.**

main ly (mān′lē), *adv.* most importantly; chiefly; for the most part. *The book was about history mainly, but it did include some geography.*

main tain (mān tān′), *v.* 1. to keep up; to hold at a certain level or in a certain condition.

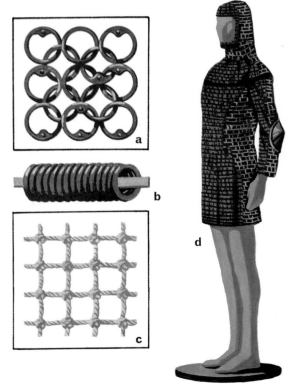

mail: a. interlocked links; **b.** links
c. fishnet; **d.** coat of mail

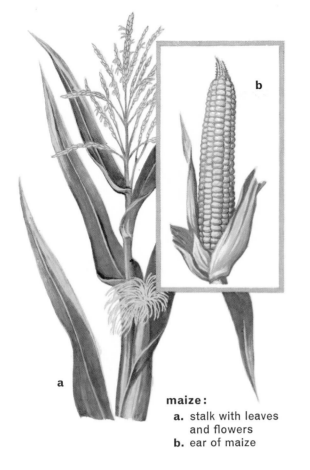

maize:
a. stalk with leaves and flowers
b. ear of maize

It is easy for us to maintain our interest in baseball because we play it often. 2. to support; to take care of. *That man maintains his sister's family as well as his own.* 3. to keep something in good repair and in good condition. *It takes a great deal of time to maintain a house.* 4. to state firmly that something is true. *She maintained that the milk was sour when she bought it.* 5. to defend, often by argument. *The man maintained his innocence even after the court had found him guilty.* **main tains, main tained, main tain ing.**

maize (māz), *n.* a plant whose grain grows on large ears; corn. *Maize is the kind of corn originally grown in America by the Indians.*

ma jes tic (mə jes′tik), *adj.* regal; grand; noble. *That wealthy man lives in a majestic old house in the country.* **ma jes ti cal ly,** *adv.*

maj es ty (maj′is tē), *n.* 1. something that is magnificent in appearance, size, etc. *We stood silently watching the majesty of the stormy sea.* 2. **Majesty,** the title of a king, queen, etc. *His Majesty, the King, entered the room and everyone stood.* **maj es ties.**

ma jor (mā′jər), *adj.* 1. larger; greater. *We spent the major part of the day at the beach.* *n.* 2. an officer in the army, air force, or marines. *A major ranks next below a lieutenant colonel and next above a captain.* 3. an area of study to which a student gives most of his attention. *His major is history.* **ma jors.**

ma jor i ty (mə jôr′ə tē), *n.* 1. a number that is more than half of a total; the larger part. *A majority of the students in our class decided to go to the museum instead of the zoo. The majority of the population lives in cities.* 2. the number of votes by which an election is won. *The vote was thirteen to nine, so he won the election by a majority of four votes.* 3. the age at which one may vote, own property, etc.; legal age. *When he reaches his majority, he will receive the land his father has bought for him.* **ma jor i ties.**

make (māk), *v.* 1. to put together; to build, form, or shape. *Tom enjoys making model airplanes.* 2. to cause; to produce an effect of; to bring about a result of. *The drummer made too much noise. Don't make trouble by starting fights.* 3. to have the abilities, qualities, etc. needed for something. *She will make a fine nurse someday.* 4. to cause something to be or become. *Mother made the dress longer by letting out the hem.* 5. to equal; to add up to. *Seven and three make ten. That makes the fourth time you have asked me that question.* 6. to cause the good fortune of; to cause someone or something to succeed. *His first two books were poor, but the third one made him famous.* 7. to force someone or something to. *The robber made me give him my money.* 8. to do or perform. *He made a face when he tasted the food. I made a mistake when I did the problem.* 9. to reach. *We made the shore just as the storm broke.* 10. to earn. *He made a dollar an hour working in the library.* 11. to judge; to figure. *I make that car to be a 1941 model.* **makes, made, mak ing.**

Make also has the following special meanings:

make away with, to steal; to remove. *Someone made away with my bicycle while I was at the movies.*

make believe, to pretend. *The boys made believe they were cowboys and galloped all around the yard.*

make good, to succeed. *One of my friends made good as a pitcher in the major leagues.*

make off with, to steal. *The thief made off with several thousand dollars of the bank's money.*

make out, (a) to understand. *I couldn't make out what the teacher was saying.* (b) to see; to recognize. *The car was too far away for me to make out the license number.* (c) to perform; to do. *I didn't make out too well on the test.* (d) to fill out. *Make out an application form if you want the job.* (e) to write. *I made out a check for ten dollars to pay the bill.*

make over, to alter; to make again in a different way. *She made over the sweater because the sleeves were too long.*

make up, (a) to invent. *Let's make up a song about her for her birthday.* (b) to put together. *They made up a table from pieces of wood they had found.* (c) to do something later than it should have been done. *If you are absent from school, you will have to make up the work that you missed.*

making up

(d) to become friends again. *After the fight the boys shook hands and made up.* (e) to put eyebrow pencil, powder, etc. on. *She is making up her face and will be ready to go in a moment. Actors make up for a play or circus.*

mak er (mā′kər), *n.* a person who makes or creates. *Who was the maker of this house?* **mak ers.**

male (māl), *n.* 1. a person or animal that belongs to the sex that fathers young. *Men and boys are males; women and girls are females.* **males.**
adj. 2. belonging to this sex; describing this sex; made up of members of this sex. *A rooster is a male chicken. Tom went to an all-male college.*

mal ice (mal′is), *n.* a dislike; a feeling of wanting to harm someone. *The mean old man was filled with malice.*

ma lig nant (mə lig′nənt), *adj.* 1. evil; malicious. *His malignant desire for power led him to become a cruel dictator.* 2. a dangerous, often fatal, infection, growth, or illness. *Malignant tumors can cause death if they are not cared for immediately.* **ma lig nant ly,** *adv.*

mal nu tri tion (mal′nü trish′ən), *n.* lack of enough food, vitamins, etc. *Many poor people suffer from malnutrition.*

ma ma or **mam ma** (mä′mə), *n.* an informal term for mother. *When the baby fell down, he*

mammoth

called "Mama" and began to cry. **ma mas** or **mam mas.**

mam mal (mam′l), *n.* any of a class of animals that are warm-blooded, have a backbone, and the females have milk glands for feeding their young. *Most of the four-footed animals with hair or fur are mammals. Whales, human beings, and bats are also mammals.* **mam mals.**

mam moth (mam′əth), *n.* 1. a kind of elephant that lived thousands of years ago. *Mammoths had hairy skins to protect them from the extreme cold in which they lived.* **mam moths.**
adj. 2. enormous. *The new skyscraper is mammoth. Building the highway was a mammoth job.*

man (man), *n.* 1. an adult male human being. *A boy becomes a man when he is fully grown.* 2. a human being; a person. *All men are created equal.* 3. the human race. *The history of man describes the achievements and adventures of people from very long ago to the present time.* 4. a male servant or employee. *The duke commanded his man to carry the suitcases upstairs. The gas man came today to read our gas meter.* 5. one of the pieces in such games as checkers and chess. *When we were playing checkers, he took one of my men for not jumping one of his.* 6. **man and wife,** husband and wife. *At the end of the wedding service, the minister pronounced the couple "man and wife."* **men.**
v. 7. to provide with men. *There were not enough sailors on the ship to man all of the lifeboats.* **mans, manned, man ning.**

man age (man′ij), *v.* 1. to control; to direct; to take or have charge of, etc. *His father manages the meat department in that store.* 2. to succeed at something, especially to succeed with difficulty. *We finally managed to get the tent set up.* 3. to get along; to get by. *The shipwrecked sailors managed for several weeks on very little water and food.* **man ag es, man aged, man ag ing.**

man age ment (man′ij mənt), *n.* 1. a managing; control. *Through careful management of his money, he was able to save enough to go to college.* 2. the people who manage a store, business, etc. *The management of the company gave all of the employees a two-week vacation.* **man age-ments.**

man ag er (man′ij ər), *n.* a person who manages. *The manager of the baseball team decides who is to play in each game.* **man ag ers.**

man a tee (man′ə tē′), *n.* a large animal that has flat limbs and a flat tail. *Manatees live in warm, shallow water where they eat plants.* **man a tees.** (See illustrations on following page and on page 312.)

man drake (man′drāk), *n.* a plant with a short stem and a thick, carrot-shaped root that is often divided. *The root of the mandrake is used in medicine.* **man drakes.** (See illustration on page 312.)

MAMMALS

tarsier

lions with cubs

porcupine

elephant with young

deer with fawn

hippopotamus with young

tiger with cubs

bat

bear with cub

horse

monkey with young

sea lion

manatee

porpoise

kangaroo with young

armadillo

anteater

cat with kitten

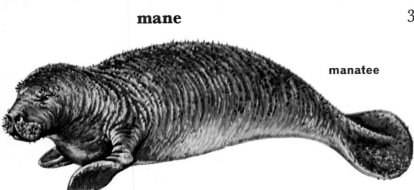

manatee

mane (mān), *n.* the long hair that grows on the back of the neck of a lion, horse, etc. *The frightened boy hung on to the horse's mane to keep from falling out of the saddle.* **manes.**

ma neu ver (mə nü′vər), *n.* 1. an organized movement of military troops and equipment. *Army maneuvers are held regularly.* 2. a clever, well-designed plan. *Her smart maneuvers got her the money she wanted.* **ma neu vers.**
v. 3. move or maneuver. *The troops maneuvered their guns into position.* 4. to plan skillfully; use clever tricks. *Her boss maneuvered her into accepting extra work.* **ma neu vers, ma neu-vered, ma neu ver ing.**

man ger (mān′jər), *n.* a box in a stable or barn from which cows and horses eat. *The farmer lowered the manger so that the younger animals could eat from it.* **man gers.**

man kind (man′kīnd′ for 1, man′kīnd′ for 2), *n.* 1. the human race. *The history of mankind covers tens of thousands of years.* 2. men. *The human race is composed of mankind and womankind.*

man ner (man′ər), *n.* 1. the way in which something is done or the way in which it happens. *The storm hit in a very unusual manner,*

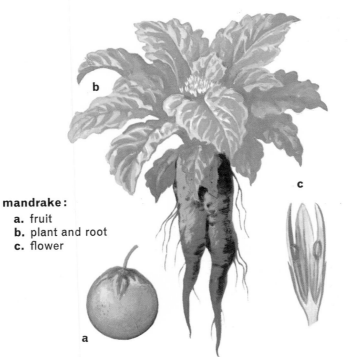

mandrake :
  a. fruit
  b. plant and root
  c. flower

suddenly and without warning. 2. the way in which a person acts or does something. *The teacher's manner was strict and formal.* 3. sort; kind. *Every manner of fish was on display at the aquarium.* 4. **manners,** behavior; ways of acting towards others. *Eating your dinner with your fingers is very bad manners.* **man ners.**

man sion (man′shən), *n.* a distinguished residence; a large, majestic house. *The governor of the state lives in a twenty-room mansion.* **man sions.**

man tel piece (man′tl pēs′), *n.* the shelf above a fireplace. *The pictures of the family were on the mantelpiece.* **man tel piec es.**

man tle (man′tl), *n.* 1. a long, loose garment worn across the shoulders. *The robber hid his face in his mantle and demanded that we give him the gold.* 2. any covering. *A white mantle of snow had fallen on the town during the night.* **man tles.**

man u al (man′yù əl), *n.* 1. a book that contains facts, information, or easy-to-follow directions for doing something. *The manual explained how to use the new typewriter.* 2. a book that tells how another book should be used. *The answers to the problems in the arithmetic book are given in the teacher's manual.* **man u als.**
adj. 3. done or operated by the hands; having to do with the hands. *The antique car had a manual crank instead of an electric starter.* **man-u al ly,** *adv.*

man u fac ture (man′yə fak′chər), *v.* 1. to make by hand or with machines. *This factory manufactures parts that are used in automobiles.* 2. to make into something useful. *Wood pulp and rags are manufactured into paper.* 3. to make up. *The boy manufactured an excuse for not doing his homework.* **man u fac tures, man u fac-tured, man u fac tur ing.**
n. 4. a making of something by hand or with machines. *The manufacture of steel from iron ore takes much time and work.*

man u fac tur er (man′yə fak′chər ər), *n.* a person or a business that manufactures something. *The manufacturer of this chair guarantees that it will last for five years.* **man u fac tur ers.**

man u script (man′yə skript′), *n.* 1. a book, articles, etc. in handwritten or typewritten form. *The author's manuscript was sent to the publisher to be printed as a book.* 2. handwriting, as distinguished from printing. *His manuscript is so bad that I can't read many of the words.* **man u scripts.**

many (men′ē), *adj.* 1. a great number of. *Many people were late to work because of the storm.* **more, most.**
n. 2. a large number. *Many of the stores were closed because it was Sunday.*
pron. 3. a large number of persons or things. *Were there many at the ball game?*

map (map), *n.* 1. a flat picture, drawing, or chart of the surface of the earth or of part of the earth. *Maps show the locations of towns,*

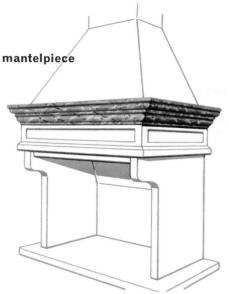

mantelpiece

rivers, mountains, and roads. 2. a diagram of the sky which shows the locations of planets, stars, etc. *We studied maps of the universe before we tried to locate specific stars in the sky.* **maps.** *v.* 3. to show something with a map; to make a map of. *Tom mapped the island and marked the spot where our camp would be set up.* 4. to plan in detail. *The teacher mapped out the work we would do for the semester. The committee mapped the arrangements long before the convention.* **maps, mapped, map ping.** (See illustration on following page.)

ma ple (mā′pl), *n.* 1. a tree with hard wood and a thin sap that is sometimes used in making sugar. *Maples are often grown for beauty as well as for shade.* 2. the wood of this tree. *Maple is used to make strong, light-colored furniture.* **ma ples.**

mar (mär), *v.* to damage; mark; spoil. *A heavy rainfall marred the picnic. Someone had marred the table by carving initials in it.* **mars, marred, mar ring.**

mar ble (mär′bl), *n.* 1. a kind of rock or stone that is made up of a tight mass of crystals and can be polished to a smooth, shiny finish. *Many statues and some floors are made of marble.* 2. a ball of marble, glass, etc. used in certain games. *When Ted stood up to read in school, a marble fell out of his pocket and bounced noisily across the floor.* 3. **marbles,** any of several children's games in which these balls are used. *They played marbles in the playground during recess.* **mar bles.** *adj.* 4. made of marble. *The lobby in the hotel has a marble floor.*

march (märch), *v.* 1. to walk with even, regular steps; to walk as soldiers do. *The high school band marched in the parade today.* 2. to move forward at a regular rate; to go steadily. *Time seems to march faster when you are doing something*

enjoyable. 3. to cause to go. *The prisoner was marched off to his cell.* **march es, marched, march ing.** *n.* 4. a marching. *The army's march to their new camp surprised the enemy who had planned to attack the old camp.* 5. a distance marched or the time spent in marching. *A four-hour march brought us to army headquarters.* 6. a regular, forward movement. *No one can stop the march of time.* 7. the music played for marching. *After the game the band played our victory march.* **march es.**

March (märch), *n.* the third month of the year. *March has thirty-one days.*

mare (mâr), *n.* a female horse, zebra, etc. *Harry wanted to ride the mare because she was gentler than the stallion.* **mares.**

mar gin (mär′jən), *n.* 1. an edge; border. *A number of trees have been planted along the eastern margin of the property.* 2. the border around the writing or printing on a page. *You may use the margin of your test paper to do the problems.* 3. an extra amount. *I have allowed you a margin of two hours to make sure that the work will be done on time.* **mar gins.**

ma rine (mə rēn′), *adj.* 1. of or from the sea. *Marine animals are among the most interesting in the world.* 2. relating to ships or shipping. *Marine equipment is very specialized.* *n.* 3. a branch of the military. *My brother is a marine.* 4. shipping. *The United States Merchant Marine sail the seven seas.* **ma rines.**

mark[1] (märk), *n.* 1. a line, spot, scratch, or stain. *The wet glass left a mark on the surface of the table.* 2. a sign or symbol that is written or printed. *There were two different price marks on the top of the can. When you write the exact words spoken by a person, you should place the statement in quotation marks.* 3. an indication or sign of something. *Men tip their hats to women as a mark of courtesy and respect.* 4. a grade given to show how well one has worked. *He got the highest mark on the spelling test.* 5. a target or goal; something one wants to reach or achieve. *If you set a mark for yourself, don't give up until you*

mare with colt

MAP OF THE WORLD

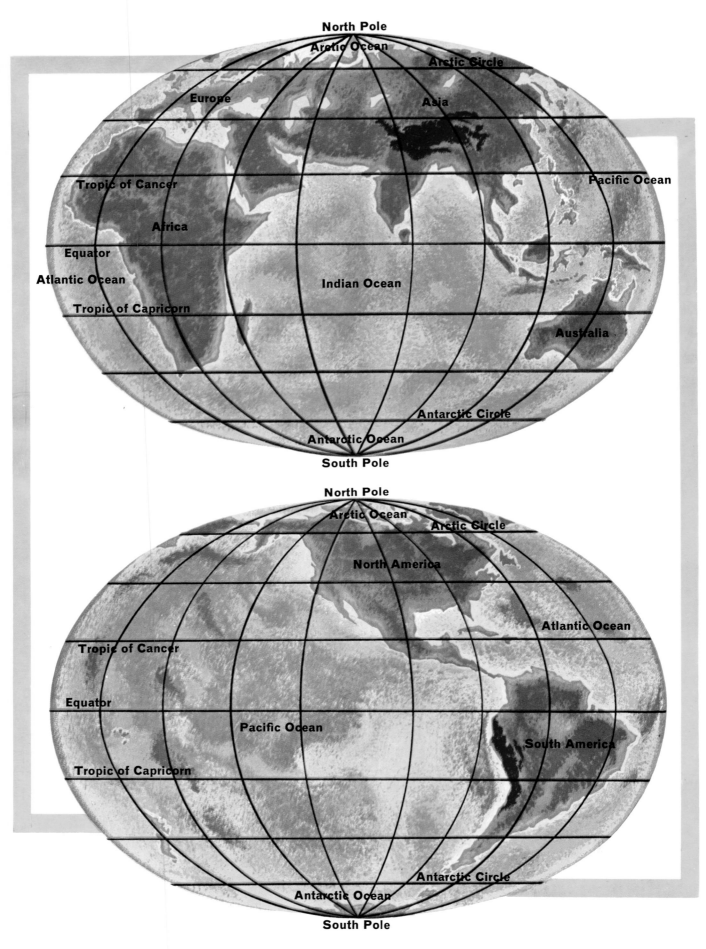

have reached it. *The archer took careful aim at the mark and shot his arrow.* 6. **beside the mark,** not on the target; not on the subject talked about. *The arrow flew far beside the mark. The questions he asked were beside the mark.* 7. **make one's mark,** to become successful. *He made his mark in the scientific world by discovering a new medicine.* **marks.**

v. 8. to make a line, spot, scratch, or stain on a surface. *Someone had marked the walls with a red crayon.* 9. to use or make a sign or symbol in order to show something. *The men marked all of the trees which were to be cut down. The store clerk marked prices on tags and attached them to the merchandise.* 10. to show; to indicate clearly. *The road you should take is marked on this map. The trail is marked by white flags hung on the trees.* 11. to grade; to give a mark for something. *The teacher marked our papers and returned them to us.* 12. to pay attention to; to see or hear. *Did you mark how guilty he looked when the police questioned him?* 13. **mark off** or **mark out,** to show the limits of; to separate. *The teacher marked out a circle in which we were to sit.* 14. **mark time,** to move the feet up and down as if marching, but without moving forward. *The band marked time until the other marchers caught up with them.* **marks, marked, marking.**

mark² (märk), *n.* a unit of money in Germany. *The mark is worth about twenty-five cents.* **marks.**

marked (märkt), *adj.* 1. having marks. *The table was dirty and marked when it was delivered from the store.* 2. easily noticed; plain to see. *There is a marked difference between Indian and African elephants.* **mark ed ly,** (mär′kid lē),*adv.*

mar ket (mär′kit), *n.* 1. a place where things can be bought and sold. *Jack was supposed to take the cow to market and sell it.* 2. a formal gathering of people to buy and sell specific things. *Millions of dollars exchange hands every day in the stock market.* 3. a food store. *Mother sent me to the market for meat and eggs.* 4. the buying and selling of goods or the chance to

marmot

buy or sell. *The umbrella market is always best when it is raining.* 5. a demand for certain goods. *There is not much of a market for raincoats in the desert.* 6. an area, region, country, etc. where goods can be sold. *The United States is a large market for producers of goods from all over the world.* **mar kets.**

v. 7. to buy or sell in a market. *These shirts were marketed in Italy and France before they were sold in America.* **mar kets, mar ket ed, market ing.**

mar mot (mär′mət), *n.* a small, short-legged animal with a thick body and a bushy tail, living in the western part of the United States. *Marmots are somewhat like squirrels.* **mar mots.**

mar quee (mär kē′), *n.* a small roof built over the entrance to a building. *We will wait for you under the marquee of the theater.* **mar quees.** (See illustration on following page.)

mar riage (mar′ij), *n.* 1. married life; life as husband and wife. *The old couple had enjoyed fifty years of happy marriage.* 2. a wedding. *The marriage was held at eleven o'clock in the morning.* **mar riag es.**

mar ried (mar′ēd), *adj.* 1. of marriage; of life as husband and wife. *In their third year of married life, they had a baby son.* 2. joined as

street **market**

sand, āte, bâre, fäther; sent, mē, fėrn; fit, bīke; pot, rōpe, fôrt; run, pùll, rüle, cūte; noise, sound; ch, cheese; ng, long; th, thick; ᵺ, those; zh, treasure; ə = a in about, e in waken, i in animal, o in seldom, and u in minus.

martin

marquee

husband and wife. *Many married couples were guests at the wedding.*

v. 3. past tense of **marry.**

mar row (mar′ō), *n.* a soft substance in the hollow centers of most bones. *Marrow is important in the production of blood in the body.*

mar ry (mar′ē), *v.* 1. to take for a husband or wife. *He wanted to marry Helen, but she married someone else.* 2. to join as husband and wife. *The minister married them at the church.* 3. to become married. *She married when she was twenty years old.* 4. to give in marriage. *He married his only daughter to an architect.* **mar ries, mar ried, mar ry ing.**

Mars (märz), *n.* 1. the fourth planet in order of distance from the sun. *Mercury, Venus, and Earth are nearer to the sun than is Mars.* 2. a Roman god. *Mars was the god of war.*

mar ten (mär′tən), *n.* 1. an animal that looks like an otter and has a bushy tail. *A marten has soft, thick brown hair.* 2. the fur of the marten, which is very valuable. *Marten is used in making coats, stoles, hats, and muffs.* **mar tens.**

mar tin (mär′tən), *n.* a bird having a short beak and a forked or square tail. *A martin is a kind of swallow.* **mar tins.**

mar vel (mär′vl), *n.* 1. a wonderful or marvelous thing. *Space capsules and rocket shots to the moon are modern marvels of science.* **mar vels.**

v. 2. to be struck with wonder; to be astonished. *We marveled at the speed of the cars in the race.* **mar vels, mar veled, mar vel ing.**

mar vel ous (mär′vl əs), *adj.* wonderful; astonishing. *The actors were marvelous in their roles in the play.* **mar vel ous ly,** *adv.*

Mar y land (mer′ə lənd), *n.* a state in the eastern part of the United States. *Maryland is famous for its many farm products.*

mask (mask), *n.* 1. a covering worn to hide or protect the face. *The children bought strange masks to wear on Halloween.* 2. a disguise or anything that is used to hide something. *The thieves entered our house under the mask of being lost travelers.* **masks.**

v. 3. to cover, disguise, or conceal with a mask or as if with a mask. *The robbers masked themselves before they boarded the train. Darkness masked the movement of the enemy troops.* **masks, masked, mask ing.**

ma son (mā′sən), *n.* a person whose work is building with brick, stone, etc. *Masons built the old stone house and the huge brick wall around the garden.* **ma sons.**

mass (mas), *n.* 1. a lump of something that holds together. *The man filled the crack in his sidewalk with a mass of cement.* 2. a large quantity or number. *A mass of people stood watching the fire.* 3. size; weight. *The mass of a buffalo seems small when compared to that of an elephant.* 4. the larger part. *The mass of the people watching*

mason

marten

MASKS AROUND THE WORLD

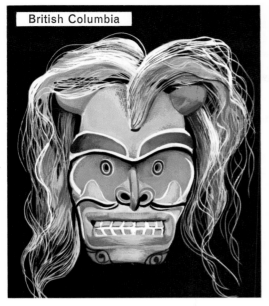
British Columbia

Cameroon

Japan

New Guinea

New Brittany

British Columbia

Central Congo

India

thought the umpire had made a mistake. 5. the quantity of matter contained by a body or object. *The mass of an object does not change when it is broken, melted, or frozen.* 6. **Mass,** the religious service of the Roman Catholic Church and some other churches. *Certain parts of the Mass remain the same, while other parts change from day to day.* **mass es.**
v. 7. to gather together into a group. *The children massed behind the teacher and waited for the bus to arrive.* **mass es, massed, mass ing.**

Mas sa chu setts (mas′ə chü′səts), *n.* a state in the northeastern part of the United States. *Massachusetts was one of the original thirteen colonies that formed the United States.*

mast (mast), *n.* 1. a long, upright pole of wood or metal that supports the sails on a ship. *Large sailing ships sometimes had three masts.* 2. any long, upright pole. *The pole that holds a derrick and the pole on which a flag is hung are masts.* **masts.**

mas ter (mas′tər), *n.* 1. a person who is in charge of another person or thing, especially one who rules a person's actions. *The captain is the master of the ship. The elf did everything his evil master demanded of him.* 2. a person who is an expert or who has great skill. *That carpenter is a master at making cabinets.* 3. a great artist of the past. *The masters painted many magnificent pictures.* 4. a male teacher. *The master of that school teaches all eight grades in a single room.* 5. **Master,** a title used before a boy's name. *The letter was addressed to Master Raymond Watson.* **mas ters.**
v. 6. to control; to be the master of. *No one has been able to master all of the people in the world.* 7. to become skilled in. *She has mastered four foreign languages.* **mas ters, mas tered, mas ter ing.**

mat (mat), *n.* 1. a piece of fabric, woven straw, fiber, etc. *Wipe your feet on the mat near the door before you come in.* 2. a piece of material which is placed under dishes, vases, etc. *The hot dish was placed on a mat so that it wouldn't damage the table top.* 3. anything that grows in a confused mass. *He couldn't even pull a comb through the mat of hair on his head.* **mats.**
v. 4. to twist and weave together like a mat. *Rolling in the grass matted his hair.* **mats, mat ted, mat ting.**

match[1] (mach), *n.* a piece of wood, cardboard, or other material with a chemical substance on one tip that bursts into flame when it is scratched. *Most matches will light only when they are rubbed on a special surface.* **match es.**

match[2] (mach), *n.* 1. a person or thing that is equal or almost equal to another, so that they can compete on even terms. *Our team is no match for their powerful players.* 2. anything that is exactly like another thing. *She tried to find a match for the buttons on her coat.* 3. two persons or things that are similar or go well

with one another. *His tie and suit make an attractive match.* 4. a contest. *He enjoys boxing matches more than fencing.* 5. a marriage. *She and her husband have made a good match for forty years.* 6. a person who is considered as a partner in marriage. *She is a good match for someone because she is kind and likes children.* **match es.**
v. 7. to correspond to; to go together with. *The blue paint on the window frames does not match the brown paint on the rest of the house.* 8. to put things together that are alike or suitable to each other. *I matched the color of my sweater with the color of my skirt.* 9. to face in a contest; to place in opposition or competition. *He matched his strength against Tom's speed in boxing. The old boxer was matched with a young man who had never lost a fight.* 10. to defeat in a contest. *No one could match the boxer, although many tried.* **match es, matched, match ing.**

mate (māt), *n.* 1. one of a pair that matches. *He couldn't find the mate to his glove.* 2. a companion. *The pirate captain and his mates were sentenced to prison.* 3. a husband or wife. *When he was thirty-seven years old, he finally took a mate.* 4. either the male or female of a pair of animals. *The bird guarded the nest until its mate came back with food.* 5. an officer on a ship ranking next below a captain. *The mate took the wheel when the captain went below to sleep.* **mates.**
v. 6. to join as mates. *Many animals mate in the spring.* **mates, mat ed, mat ing.**

ma te ri al (mə tir′ē əl), *n.* 1. the parts or substances of which a thing is made. *Courage is one of the materials of which heroes are made. They delivered the material for the roof in order to finish the house.* 2. fabric; cloth. *Mother bought enough material to make two dresses.* 3. **materials,** the tools and supplies needed to do something. *Be sure you have your writing materials—pencils, pens, and paper—ready for the test.* **ma te ri als.**
adj. 4. made of matter; physical. *Animals and plants are material things.* 5. having to do with the body. *Food and drink are material needs.* 6. important. *Long hours of practice were a material part of the team's success.* **ma te ri al ly,**

ma te ri al ly (mə tir′ē əl ē), *adv.* 1. considerably; to a great extent. *High winds and rain materially affected the firemen's attempts to put out the fire.* 2. in a physical way. *He was successful materially, but he had very few friends.*

math e mat i cal (math′ə mat′ə kl), *adj.* 1. of mathematics; having to do with mathematics. *They used a mathematical formula to solve the problem.* 2. exact; precise. *The carpenter made mathematical measurements of the new house before he began his work.* **math e mat i cal ly,** *adv.*

math e mat ics (math′ə mat′iks), *n.* the study of numbers, measurements, sizes, and their relation to each other. *Arithmetic is a branch of mathematics.*

mat ter (mat′ər), *n.* 1. the substance that a

mast

physical thing is made of; material. *Matter has weight and occupies space.* 2. the ideas or thoughts that are expressed in writing or in speech. *The matter the book dealt with was the author's philosophy of life.* 3. an affair. *That is a matter that does not concern me.* 4. an amount; quantity. *The difference in price was a matter of five dollars.* 5. importance. *Parking problems are of no matter to someone who takes a bus to work.* 6. material that is written or printed. *There is excellent reading matter in the school library.* 7. **as a matter of fact,** actually; to be truthful. *As a matter of fact, it was not I who called you last night.* 8. **for that matter,** as far as that goes. *We played a poor game but, for that matter, so did they.* 9. **matter of course,** anything expected or taken for granted. *Having his work finished on time was a matter of course with him.* **mat ters.** *v.* 10. to be of importance. *He was so interested in his work that nothing else mattered to him.* **mat ters, mat tered, mat ter ing.**

mat tress (mat′ris), *n.* a pad filled with a soft material and often springs, covered with strong cloth and used on a bed. *The mattress was so old that it sagged in the middle.* **mat tress es.**

ma ture (mə tùr′, mə tyùr′), *adj.* 1. fully grown. *When a boy becomes mature, he is a man.* 2. ripe. *Do not pick the fruit until it is mature.* 3. fully developed; completely worked out. *The scientist presented a mature theory from his experiments and observations.* **ma ture ly,** *adv.* *v.* 4. to ripen; to become fully grown. *Because of the warm weather and the rain, the crops matured earlier than we had expected.* 5. to be worked out in detail. *His plan for the new building matured very slowly in his mind.* **ma tures, ma tured, ma tur ing.**

ma tu ri ty (mə tùr′ə tē, mə tyùr′ə tē), *n.* a being mature; a reaching of full growth or development. *Most animals achieve maturity faster than people do.*

max i mum (mak′sə məm), *n.* 1. largest possible number or amount. *Our family saved three hundred dollars for a vacation; this was our maximum.* **max i mums** or **max i ma** (mak′sə mə).
adj. 2. biggest; largest possible. *The maximum speed for cars was eighty miles per hour.*

may (mā), *v.* 1. to have permission to; to be allowed to. *May I be excused? You may bring a friend to the party.* 2. to be likely to. *I may have to miss the game next week. It may snow this morning.* 3. one hopes that. *May you have many more days as happy as this one.* **may, might.**

May (mā), *n.* the fifth month of the year. *May has thirty-one days.*

may be (mā′bē), *adv.* perhaps. *Maybe he hasn't left the train yet, and we can still find him.*

may or (mā′ər), *n.* a person who is elected as the head of a city or town government. *The mayor gave a speech at the opening.* **may ors.**

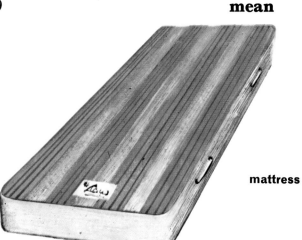

mattress

may pole (mā′pōl′), *n.* a tall, decorated pole around which people dance on May 1. *Flowers and ribbons are hung on the maypole to hail the return of spring.* **may poles.**

me (mē), *pron.* the person who is speaking. *Me is used instead of I when the person who is speaking is the one who receives the action rather than the one who does it. Hand that book to me. She saw me standing at the window.*

mead ow (med′ō), *n.* a field in which grass or hay grows. *The cows grazed in the meadow, eating the grass that grew there.* **mead ows.**

meal[1] (mēl), *n.* 1. breakfast, lunch, dinner, or supper; the time at which food is served. *If you are late for your meals, there will be nothing left for you to eat.* 2. the food eaten or served at one time. *We had a delicious meal at supper last night.* **meals.**

meal[2] (mēl), *n.* 1. ground grain. *Mother made bread from cornmeal.* 2. anything ground very fine. *The medicine was ground into a fine meal and put into capsules.* **meals.**

mean[1] (mēn), *v.* 1. to indicate the idea of. *That word doesn't mean what you say it does.* 2. to intend to state or point out. *By my criticism of your painting, I mean that you should use more color.* 3. to have in mind as a purpose. *He didn't mean to get angry at us.* 4. to intend for a particular purpose. *Fire alarms are meant to be used only when there is a fire.* **means, meant, mean ing.**

mean[2] (mēn), *adj.* 1. unkind; wicked. *The man was very mean to the children who walked on his lawn.* 2. selfish. *He is mean about sharing his toys with other children.* 3. humble; poor. *Abraham Lincoln came from mean surroundings.* 4. inferior. *That store sells many things that are of mean quality.* **mean er, mean est; mean ly,** *adv.*

mean[3] (mēn), *adj.* 1. in the middle; between two extremes or opposites. *The mean temperature is exactly between the high and low temperatures for the day.*
n. 2. anything which is between two opposites or extremes. *A temperature of seventy-five degrees is a happy mean between weather that is too hot and weather that is too cold.* 3. **means,** (a) the way

in which a thing is done. *He used any means to get what he wanted.* (b) wealth. *The banker was a man of means.* 4. **by means of,** by the use of. *He entered the ball park by means of the players' entrance.* 5. **by all means,** at any cost; certainly. *By all means keep looking until you find her.* 6. **by no means,** not at all. *We were by no means happy with the show.* **means.**

mean ing (mēn′ing), *n.* 1. the thing that is meant; the idea intended. *I couldn't understand the meaning of the poem.* 2. purpose. *He doesn't do anything without a particular meaning.* **meanings.**
adj. 3. expressing or having meaning. *The teacher gave me a meaning glance when I spoke out of turn in class.* **mean ing ly,** *adv.*

mean ing ful (mēn′ing fəl), *adj.* full of purpose or significance. *The teacher gave a meaningful talk on the importance of education.* **mean ing ful ly,** *adv.*

meant (ment), past tense of **mean**[1].

mean time (mēn′tīm′), *n.* 1. the time between two times or events. *I'll see you next week, but in the meantime you could give me a call.*
adv. 2. during the time between two times or events. *Class is over at three o'clock, but meantime you can start doing your homework.* 3. at the same time. *Meantime, as the boys hiked on the mountain, their parents were looking for them in the valley.*

mean while (mēn′hwīl′), *n.* 1. meantime. *You have no place to live now, but for the meanwhile you can stay here.*
adv. 2. during the time between now and then. *We will leave at five, meanwhile I will take a nap.*

mea sles (mē′zlz), *n.* a disease marked by a cold, fever, and red spots on the skin. *Most people who had measles as children do not catch the disease as adults.*

meas ure (mezh′ər), *n.* 1. the length, size, amount, etc. of something. *Use the full measure of ingredients called for when making a cake.* 2. something used to find the length, size, amount, etc. of something. *A pint cup and a ruler are common measures.* 3. a unit of weight, area, volume, etc. used in finding the length, size, amount, etc. of something. *A mile, a pound, and a quart are standards of measure.* 4. a system of measurement. *Sixteen ounces liquid measure is not equal to sixteen ounces dry measure.*

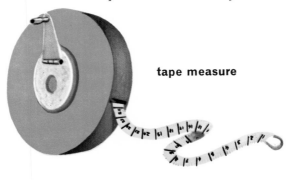

tape measure

5. a quantity or degree. *She enjoyed a measure of success in her acting career.* 6. a means used to do something. *Measures must be taken to make highways safer for drivers.* 7. a proposal of a law in a legislative body. *The measure was accepted by a vote of sixty to eleven.* **meas ures.**
v. 8. to find the length, size, amount, etc. of something. *They measured the floor to determine how large a rug they would need.* 9. to mark off. *We measured fifty yards of rope to use on the boat.* 10. to judge by comparison; to compare. *He measured his experience against his opponent's great strength.* 11. to be of a certain size. *He measures over six feet in height.* **meas ures, meas ured, meas ur ing.**

meas ure ment (mezh′ər mənt), *n.* 1. a measuring; a finding out of the length, size, amount, etc. of something. *A pint, quart, or gallon is used in the measurement of liquid volumes.* 2. the length, size, amount, etc. of something as found by measuring. *The measurements of the box are three feet by two feet by four feet.* 3. a system of measures. *Metric measurement is used in most scientific experiments.* **meas ure ments.**

meat (mēt), *n.* 1. the flesh of an animal used as food. *My favorite meat is roast beef.* 2. anything taken as food. *The boys were hungry for meat and drink at the end of their hike.* 3. the parts of fruits and vegetables that can be eaten. *We took the shells off the nuts and ate the meats.* 4. the important part of something. *The meat of the book was printed in heavy type so that it could be remembered easily.* **meats.**

me chan ic (mə kan′ik), *n.* a person who works with tools to fix machinery. *You should have a mechanic work on the car before our vacation.* **me chan ics.**

me chan i cal (mə kan′ə kl), *adj.* 1. having to do with machines or machinery. *The airplane didn't take off because of mechanical trouble in one of the engines.* 2. made by machinery; operated by machinery. *This washing machine has a mechanical switch which turns it off when the cycle is complete.* 3. done as if by machine; without feeling or expression. *His reading of the poem was dull and mechanical.* **me chan i cal ly,** *adv.*

med al (med′l), *n.* a flat metal badge given to someone as a reward for service. *Soldiers are awarded medals for outstanding bravery.* **med als.**

med i cal (med′ə kl), *adj.* having to do with the study of medicine and the treatment of disease, illness, and injury. *The doctor reads medical magazines every month to learn about new treatments, medicines, and instruments.* **med i cal ly,** *adv.*

med i cine (med′ə sn), *n.* 1. anything used to cure or prevent disease or improve health. *The doctor gave me a bitter medicine to take for my stomachache.* 2. the study of diseases and how to cure, treat, and prevent them. *The new doctor had great knowledge of the field of medicine.* **med i cines.**

me di um (mē′dē əm), *adj.* 1. having, being, or occupying a middle position in quality or condition. *Cook the meat at medium heat. I'll have my steak cooked medium rare.*
n. 2. something which is in the middle; a middle position. *Lower the flame on the stove to medium. This climate offers a happy medium between too much heat and freezing cold.* 3. a means by which something is done or through which something acts. *Newspapers, books, radio, and television are important mediums of communication.* 4. a substance in which anything lives or exists. *Some plants live in a medium of air, others live in a medium of water.* 5. a person who is supposed to be able to receive messages from the dead. *The medium said she was unable to contact the dead man's spirit.* **me di ums** or **me dia** (mē′dē ə).

me dul la (mi dul′ə), *n.* the part of the brain that begins at the base of the skull and forms the lower part of the brain stem. *The medulla controls the actions of breathing and digesting food.* **me dul lae** (mi dul′ē).

meet[1] (mēt), *v.* 1. to come face to face with. *The two friends met each other on the street.* 2. to come together; to join; to connect. *Several roads meet just before you get to the bridge.* 3. to be introduced to. *I met him at a party last week.* 4. to be at a place where a person or thing will arrive. *They will meet me when I get off the train.* 5. to gather as a group or club; to assemble. *The committee will meet again next week.* 6. to satisfy. *He didn't have enough money to meet all of his debts. The company met the demands of the workers for higher pay and longer lunch periods.* **meets, met, meet ing.**
n. 7. a meeting, especially a meeting of teams in competition. *There will be a track meet at the high school on Saturday.* **meets.**

meet[2] (mēt), *adj.* proper; fitting. *It is meet and just that criminals should be punished for their crimes.* **meet ly,** *adv.*

meet ing (mēt′ing), *n.* 1. a coming together of persons. *The accidental meeting of the enemies resulted in their becoming friends.* 2. a coming together of persons for a religious service. *We attended a prayer meeting at the church today.* 3. any gathering of people. *Our meeting with the mayor lasted for several hours.* **meet ings.**

mel o dy (mel′ə dē), *n.* 1. a series of musical tones making up a tune. *He whistled the melody of the song because he didn't know the words.* 2. the main tune in a song. *Everyone could sing the melody, but no one could sing the harmony.* 3. any pleasant sound or arrangement of sounds. *I was awakened by the melody of birds singing at my window.* **mel o dies.**

mel on (mel′ən), *n.* a large, juicy fruit that grows on vines. *The watermelon is one of several kinds of melons.* **mel ons.**

melt (melt), *v.* 1. to change from solid form to liquid form. *Metals can be melted by heating*

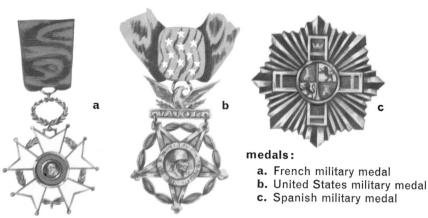

medals:
a. French military medal
b. United States military medal
c. Spanish military medal

them to high temperatures. *Ice becomes water when it melts.* 2. to dissolve; to become liquid or become mixed with a liquid. *Don't chew the candy, let it melt in your mouth.* 3. to cause something to disappear. *The sun melted the heavy layer of fog covering the city.* 4. to become smaller and disappear. *The snowman melted when the sun came out.* 5. to soften. *His angry frown melted into a smile.* **melts, melt ed, melt ing.**

mem ber (mem′bər), *n.* 1. a person or thing that belongs to a group. *Many members of the club voted against having a picnic on Labor Day. Dogs are members of the animal kingdom.* 2. a part of a plant, an animal, or the body, as an arm, leg, branch, etc. *The men tried to save the tree by cutting off its rotting members.* **mem bers.**

mem ber-at-large (mem′bər ət lärj′), *n.* a person at a meeting, convention, etc. who represents a large area rather than a specific group or district. *There is a congressman for each county in the state as well as four congressmen who are members-at-large and represent all of the people in the state.* **mem bers-at-large.**

mem ber ship (mem′bər ship′), *n.* 1. a belonging to a club or group. *His membership was approved by the entire committee.* 2. all members of a club or group. *The membership of the Girls' Athletic Association voted to elect new officers.* **mem ber ships.**

mem brane (mem′brān), *n.* 1. a thin layer of tissue that covers or lines a part of a plant or animal. *A clear membrane covers the pupil of the eye.* 2. any similar layer that covers or lines something. *The membrane on top of the drum had been cut.* **mem branes.**

melon

mem o ran dum (mem'ə ran'dəm), *n.* 1. a short note or statement kept as a reminder of something. *The teacher made a memorandum of the problems that were assigned for homework.* 2. a brief, informal note or report. *Send a memorandum to the electric company informing them that we did not receive a bill this month.* **mem o ran-dums** or **mem o ran da** (mem'ə ran'da).

mem o ry (mem'ə rē), *n.* 1. the power or ability of remembering things. *He has a great memory for telephone numbers and addresses, but he can't remember names.* 2. anything that is remembered. *He has pleasant memories of his high school days.* 3. all that a person can remember. *His memory is filled with funny things that happened to him as a child.* 4. the length of time that one remembers. *That was the most exciting game within memory.* 5. **in memory of,** as a remembrance of; in honor of. *A church service was held in memory of the soldiers who had died in battle.* **mem o ries.**

men (men), *n. pl.* 1. more than one man. *The men helped the lady who had fallen on the ice.* 2. all mankind. *Men are higher beings than animals because of their ability to reason.*

mend (mend), *v.* 1. to repair; to fix. *Mother mended the tear in my shirt. Someone will have to mend the hole in the roof.* 2. to improve; to change for the better. *You are going to have to mend your study habits if you expect to pass.* 3. to regain health; to heal. *That broken bone should mend quickly. With plenty of rest and good food, the sick child soon mended.* **mends, mend ed, mend ing.**
n. 4. a place that has been repaired. *The mend in your coat does not even show. Be careful of your arm until the mend in the bone is stronger.* 5. **on the mend,** improving in health or condition. *After a long, serious illness, the patient was finally on the mend.* **mends.**

men tal (men'tl), *adj.* 1. having to do with the mind. *That scientist has great mental ability.* 2. done in the mind; performed by the mind. *As the car sped away from him, Don made a mental note of its license number.* **men tal ly,** *adv.*

men tion (men'shən), *v.* 1. to talk about briefly; to say something about. *She mentioned meeting the new teacher, but she didn't tell me his name.* **men tions, men tioned, men tion-ing.**
n. 2. a brief statement. *There wasn't even a mention of the fire in the newspaper.* **men tions.**

menu (men'ū), *n.* 1. a list of the foods that are served at a meal, especially such a list in a restaurant. *The waitress gave each of us a menu as soon as we sat down.* 2. the foods served at a meal. *Our dinner menu consisted of soup, roast beef, mashed potatoes, carrots, and pudding.* **men us.**

me ow (mē ou'), *n.* 1. the sound made by a cat or kitten. *We heard a meow at the front door.* **me ows.**

v. 2. to make such a sound. *The cat meows when she wants to go out.* **me ows, me owed, me ow ing.**

mer chan dise (mer'chən dīz', mer'chən dīs'), *n.* goods that may be bought or sold. *A new shipment of merchandise was delivered to the department store.*

mer chant (mer'chənt), *n.* 1. a person who buys and sells goods. *Most of the stores in this area deal with the same merchants.* 2. a person who owns or runs a store. *The owner of this department store is the richest merchant in town.* **mer chants.**
adj. 3. having to do with the buying and selling of goods; having anything to do with trade. *The merchant laws require that a tax be paid on any goods which are brought into the country.*

mer ci less (mer'si lis), *adj.* lack of mercy; without kindness. *The merciless man continued to beat the puppy.* **mer ci less ly,** *adv.*

mer cu ry (mer'kyə rē), *n.* a heavy metal element that is silver in color and that is in liquid form at ordinary temperatures. *Mercury is used in barometers and thermometers.*

Mer cu ry (mer'kyə rē), *n.* 1. the first planet in order of distance from the sun. *Mercury is the smallest planet in the solar system.* 2. the Roman god of trade. *Mercury is also identified as the messenger of the other Roman gods.*

mer cy (mer'sē), *n.* 1. kindness, especially toward an enemy. *The pirates had no mercy for their victims.* 2. a blessing; anything one is thankful for. *After a week of very high temperatures, a cool, rainy day is a mercy.* 3. **at the mercy of,** in the power of; controlled by. *The mountain climbers were at the mercy of the weather until the blizzard ended.* **mer cies.**

mere (mir), *adj.* only; no more than. *There was a mere handful of people at the party.* **mere est; mere ly,** *adv.*

mere ly (mir'lē), *adv.* only; simply. *I wasn't accusing you of anything; I merely asked if you knew anything about the broken window.*

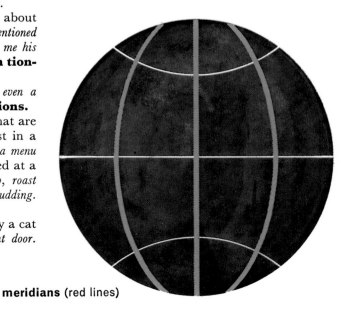

meridians (red lines)

merry-go-round

me rid i an (mə rid′ē ən), *n.* 1. an imaginary line that passes from the North Pole to the South Pole on the surface of the earth. *Toronto, Pittsburgh, and Miami have the same longitude because they are on the same meridian.* 2. the highest position in the sky which the sun or a star appears to reach. *The sun reaches its meridian at noon.* 3. the highest point of success, fame, etc. *Winning an award in science was the meridian of his career.* **me rid i ans.**

mer it (mer′it), *n.* 1. value; worth; anything deserving of praise. *What is the merit of this product as compared with that one? There is great merit in this plan.* 2. the good and bad parts of something considered as a whole. *The jury was asked to make a decision on the merits of the evidence rather than on what they thought of the people involved in the case.* **mer its.**
v. 3. to serve; to earn. *Your suggestion certainly merits further study. Sue merited our praise for her brave actions.* **mer its, mer it ed, mer it ing.**

mer maid (mėr′mād′), *n.* an imaginary sea creature having the tail of a fish and the upper body of a woman. *Mermaids and giant sea horses frequently appear in fairy tales about the sea.* **mer maids.**

mer ry (mer′ē), *adj.* full of happiness and cheer; joyful. *There was a merry crowd of people at the football game. The teacher wished us all a merry Christmas before class was dismissed.* **mer ri er, mer ri est; mer ri ly,** *adv.*

mer ry-go-round (mer′ē gō round′), *n.* a round, rotating platform with seats and animal figures on which people ride. *As the*

merry-go-round turned, happy music was played and the wooden animals went up and down. **mer ry-go-rounds.**

mesh (mesh), *n.* 1. one of the open spaces in a screen, net, sieve, etc. *The meshes of a fishing net are large, and those in a window screen are small.* **mesh es.**
v. 2. to fit together. *The parts of the puzzle meshed when it was solved.* **mesh es, meshed, mesh ing.**

mess (mes), *n.* 1. a dirty or littered condition. *The children's room was in a mess after the pillow fight.* 2. a poor job; a clumsy or bad piece of work. *How did you make such a mess out of cutting the grass? He made a mess out of the class assignment.* 3. a mixed up or difficult situation; confusion. *He got into a mess with the police when his car was stolen.* 4. an amount of food. *They bought a mess of fish to have for dinner.* 5. a group of people who take their meals together. *All of the soldiers in those quarters belong to the same mess.* 6. the meal served to them. *A number of the men missed mess this morning because they had work to do.* **mess es.**
v. 7. **to mess up,** to make dirty or not tidy. *The boys messed up the bathroom by splashing water on the floor.* **mess es, messed, mess ing.**

mes sage (mes′ij), *n.* any news, information, question, etc. sent from one person to another. *We left a message for him to meet us at the swimming pool.* **mes sag es.**

mes sen ger (mes′ən jər), *n.* 1. a person who carries or delivers a message. *The telegram arrived this afternoon by messenger.* 2. anything that tells of the coming of something. *The first robin to be seen is a messenger of spring.* **mes sen gers.**

messy (mes′ē), *adj.* not tidy; dirty; full of litter. *The picnic area was messy after the people had left.* **mess i er, mess i est; mess i ly,** *adv.*

met (met), past tense of **meet**[1].

met al (met′l), *n.* 1. any of a number of substances that are shiny when they are polished and are able to carry electricity. *Most metals are found in solid form, but mercury is a metal that is in liquid form at ordinary temperatures.* 2. substance; composition. *The metal of the troops was tested in a violent battle.* **met als.** *adj.* 3. made of or containing metal. *Many foods are packed in metal cans.*

met a mor pho sis (met′ə môr′fə sis), *n.* 1. a change in form. *Tadpoles become frogs by metamorphosis; they grow legs and lose their tails.* 2. an obvious change in looks, spirit, or character. *Losing weight caused a complete metamorphosis in Mary's attitude.* **met a mor pho ses** (met′ə môr′fə sēz).

me te or (mē′tē ər), *n.* a mass of matter that travels toward the earth at high speeds; a shooting star. *Most meteors do not reach the earth because they burn up as they travel through the earth's atmosphere.* **me te ors.**

me te or ite (mē′tē ər īt′), *n.* a meteor that does not burn up completely in the earth's atmosphere and lands on the surface of the earth. *A meteorite landed in Africa that weighs about 132,000 pounds. It is the largest known meteorite on earth.* **me te or ites.**

me te or ol o gist (mē′tē ər ol′ə jist), *n.* a sci-

meter

entist who studies the earth's atmosphere and the conditions that produce changes in the weather. *Meteorologists from the weather bureau said that a heavy snowfall would reach the city during the day.* **me te or ol o gists.**

me ter (mē′tər), *n.* 1. an instrument which measures and keeps a record of something. *An electric meter tells the amount of electricity being used in a house, apartment, or office.* 2. a unit of length in the metric system. *A meter is about 39.37 inches.* **me ters.**

meth od (meth′əd), *n.* 1. a way of doing something. *Frying is one method of preparing eggs. Do you understand the method used in solving these*

metamorphosis of a frog

one to five days

eight to ten days

twelve to fourteen days

three to seven weeks

two to three years

problems? 2. an orderly system for doing something; an organized way of acting or thinking. *There was no method in his work, and, as a result, he seldom finished anything.* **meth ods.**

met ric (met′rik), *adj.* of or using the metric system. *Metric measurement is used in scientific experiments in every part of the world.*

metric system, *n.* a system of weights and measures which is based on the standard weight of a gram (about $\frac{1}{28}$ ounce) and the standard length of a meter (about 39.37 inches). *The metric system is the measurement system used by scientists in most countries.*

mew (mū), *n.* 1. the sound made by a cat or kitten; meow. *We found the kitten when we heard her mews from under the front porch.* **mews.**
v. 2. to make such a sound; to meow. *The cat mewed softly for her milk.* **mews, mewed, mew ing.**

mice (mīs), *n. pl.* more than one mouse. *He keeps three white mice as pets.*

Mich i gan (mish′ə gən), *n.* a state in the north central part of the United States. *Four of the five Great Lakes touch the borders of Michigan.*

mi crobe (mī′krōb), *n.* an animal or plant so small that it can be seen only with a microscope. *Scientists have found that some diseases are caused by specific microbes.* **mi crobes.**

mi cro phone (mī′krə fōn′), *n.* an instrument used for sending sounds. *Radio and television stations use microphones. A speaker may use a microphone to make his voice heard throughout a large room.* **mi cro phones.**

mi cro scope (mī′krə skōp′), *n.* an instrument having lenses which make very small objects

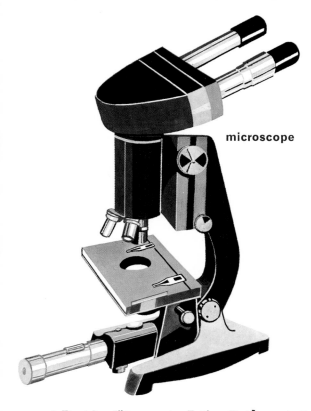

microscope

easily visible to the viewer. *I examined a drop of water under the microscope and was amazed at the number of things I found.* **mi cro scopes.**

mid dle (mid′l), *n.* 1. the point or part which is at the same distance from each side or end. *Your nose is in the middle of your face.* **mid dles.**
adj. 2. being in the middle; occupying a center position. *His middle name is Eugene. The middle person in the first row is my brother.*

mid night (mid′nīt′), *n.* 1. the middle of the night; twelve o'clock at night. *Midnight marks the end of one day and the beginning of another.* **mid nights.**
adj. 2. of midnight; like midnight; happening at midnight. *We watched a midnight movie on television.*

mid point (mid′point′), *n.* the point at the middle of anything. *At the midpoint of the class period, the fire alarm rang.* **mid points.**

midst (midst), *n.* 1. the middle. *The midst of our line of defense fell when the enemy attacked.* 2. **in the midst of,** in the middle of; in the face of. *In the midst of the attack, he stood and fought bravely.* 3. **in our midst,** among us. *There was one in our midst who had betrayed us.*

might[1] (mīt), past tense of **may.**

might[2] (mīt), *n.* power, strength; force. *The might of my opponent was too great for me to overcome.*

mighty (mīt′ē), *adj.* 1. having great power or strength. *The mighty wind blew down trees and houses.* 2. great in size or effect. *The mighty oak stood for more than two hundred years. A mighty crop failure occurred in that country last year.* **might i er, might i est; might i ly,** *adv.*

mi grate (mī′grāt), *v.* 1. to leave one place or region to live in another. *They migrated to California from Colorado.* 2. to travel from place to place as the seasons change. *Many birds migrate south for the winter.* **mi grates, mi grat ed, mi grat ing.**

mi gra tion (mī grā′shən), *n.* 1. the act of migrating. *The migration of people from the East to the West caused a rapid growth in the size of the United States.* 2. the people or animals who migrate. *A huge migration of birds passed overhead.* **mi gra tions.**

mild (mīld), *adj.* 1. kind; gentle. *My father is a mild person who never loses his temper.* 2. not harsh; not severe; warm rather than cold. *We had a mild winter with very little snow last year.* 3. not sharp or biting to the taste. *We ordered mild sausage with our breakfast.* **mild er, mild est; mild ly,** *adv.*

mil dew (mil′dü′, mil′dū′), *n.* 1. a fungus that is found on paper, clothing, leather, etc. during warm and damp weather. *The clothes we had stored in the cellar were spotted with mildew.*
v. 2. to become affected by or covered with mildew. *The blankets we left in the barn mildewed during the summer.* **mil dews, mil dewed, mil dew ing.**

microphones

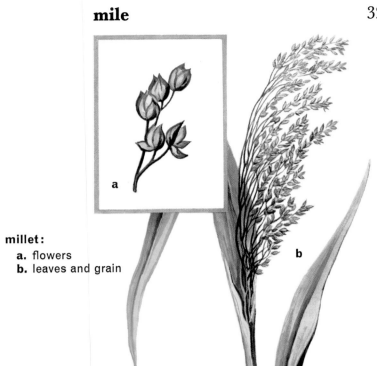

millet:
a. flowers
b. leaves and grain

mile (mīl), *n.* a measure of distance that is equal to 5,280 feet (**statute mile**) or 6,080 feet (**nautical mile**). *We drove four hundred miles on the first day of our trip.* **miles.**

mile age (mīl′ij), *n.* 1. the number of miles covered. *What was the total mileage of the trip?* 2. the money allowed a person for traveling expenses at a fixed rate per mile. *The company gave him twenty dollars a day plus mileage for his trip.* **mile ag es.**

mil i tary (mil′ə ter′ē), *adj.* 1. having to do with soldiers or war. *Many persons receive military training before they enter the army.* 2. fitting and proper for soldiers. *As soon as he arrived at the army camp, he was given a military haircut.* 3. done by soldiers. *Only soldiers were allowed to march because it was a military parade.* **mil i tar i ly,** *adv.*

milk (milk), *n.* 1. a white liquid produced by adult female mammals for feeding their young; this liquid from cows and goats used by people as food. *Milk is pasteurized and treated before people drink it.* 2. a white liquid found in some plants. *He cracked the coconut and drank its milk.* **milks.**

v. 3. to get or draw milk from. *The farmer milks his cows every morning and evening.* **milks, milked, milk ing.**

milk man (milk′man′), *n.* a person who sells or delivers milk. *The milkman makes his deliveries very early in the morning.* **milk men.**

mill (mil), *n.* 1. a building with machinery in which something is manufactured. *Steel is made from iron ore in a steel mill.* 2. a building in which corn, wheat, etc. are ground into flour. *All of the farmers in the area brought their wheat to the same mill.* 3. the machine used to grind grain into powder. *The stone wheel wouldn't turn because the mill was jammed.* **mills.**

v. 4. to grind into powder form. *It took several days to mill the huge shipment of wheat.* 5. to move about restlessly and without purpose. *The crowd milled about waiting for the store to open.* **mills, milled, mill ing.**

mill er (mil′ər), *n.* 1. a person who owns or runs a flour mill. *The miller charged us fifty cents a bushel to mill our corn.* 2. a moth with a fine, powdery covering on its wings. *My fingers were white from holding the miller by the wings.* **mill ers.**

mil let (mil′it), *n.* 1. a small grain used for food in Asia and Africa. *Millet is ground into flour or meal or eaten whole.* 2. the plant the grain grows on. *In the United States, millet is used to feed animals.*

mil lion (mil′yən), *n.* a number equal to one thousand thousands; 1,000,000. *That man has made millions of dollars by buying and selling land.* **mil lions.**

mil lion aire (mil′yən âr′), *n.* a person who has a million dollars or more. *Millionaires can own expensive homes, boats, and cars.* **mil lion aires.**

mim ic (mim′ik), *v.* 1. to copy in appearance or actions. *The baby tried to mimic her brother's way of eating his food.* 2. to poke fun at by imitating. *Bob mimicked the motions of the policeman directing traffic at the corner.* **mim ics, mim icked, mim ick ing.**

n. 3. a person or thing that mimics. *He is a very clever mimic of his teachers.* **mim ics.**

mimosa

adj. 4. not real; pretended. *We held a mimic game to see if everyone knew the plays.*

mi mo sa (mi mō′sə), *n.* a plant that grows in warm climates. *A mimosa has flowers of yellow, white, or pink.* **mi mo sas.**

mind (mīnd), *v.* 1. to object to. *Did you mind not going on the trip with the rest of the class?* 2. to take care of. *Be sure to mind the baby while I am gone.* 3. to obey. *Mind your parents and your teachers.* 4. to pay attention to; to be careful of. *Mind where you are going before a car hits you!* **minds, mind ed, mind ing.**

n. 5. the part of a person that thinks, remembers, judges, etc. *There are many things in your mind that you think you have forgotten.* 6. the ability to think, remember, judge, etc. *He has a fine mind for studying science.* 7. memory. *Keep these answers in mind for our next test.* 8. what a person thinks or believes. *You are free to change your mind whenever you wish.* **minds.**

Mind also has the following special meanings:

be of one mind, to agree completely. *They were of one mind on their plans for their vacation.*

have a mind to, to think about doing; to intend to. *I have a mind to get a perfect score on the test and surprise everyone.*

make up one's mind, to decide. *He made up his mind to get all of his work done on time.*

on one's mind, in one's thoughts. *Our poor showing in the last game has been on my mind ever since.*

put in mind, to remind one of. *That story puts me in mind of another.*

set one's mind on, to want to get; to decide to get. *The boy set his mind on getting a new bicycle for Christmas.*

to one's mind, in one's opinion. *To my mind, summer vacation is the best time of the year.*

mind ful (mīnd′fəl), *adj.* aware of; pay attention to. *You should be mindful of the wishes of your parents.* **mind ful ly,** *adv.*

mine[1] (mīn), *pron.* 1. belonging to me. *This book is mine; that one is yours.* 2. the thing or things that belong to me. *This pen has blue ink in it; mine was filled with black ink.*

mine[2] (mīn), *n.* 1. a large hole, pit, or tunnel in the earth from which minerals can be taken. *We visited a coal mine in West Virginia. The largest diamond mines in the world are in Africa.* 2. a valuable source. *The dictionary is a mine of information about words.* 3. a device that is placed on or below the ground or under-water and explodes when troops or ships make contact with it. *The entrance to the harbor was blocked by mines. Several mines in the field blew up as the troops passed.* **mines.**

v. 4. to dig a mine or mines to locate minerals in the earth. *The men are mining way below the ground for coal.* 5. to dig into to locate minerals. *This entire area has already been mined for coal.* 6. to remove from a mine. *Men mined gold in California during the 1850's.* 7. to lay exploding

detecting a land **mine**

devices on or under. *They mined the bridge after they had crossed it.* **mines, mined, min ing.** (See illustration on following page.)

min er (mīn′ər), *n.* a person who works in a mine. *A coal miner's job is dangerous because of possible cave-ins.* **min ers.**

min er al (min′ər əl), *n.* 1. a substance occurring in nature that is neither animal nor vegetable; especially a substance that is obtained from the earth by mining or drilling. *Oil, coal, and iron ore are minerals.* **min erals.** (See illustration on page 329.)

adj. 2. containing minerals. *Many persons bathe in mineral springs to improve their health.*

min i a ture (min′ē ə chŭr or min′ē ə chər), *n.* 1. a small, complete copy or model of something. *The store sells miniatures of dolls and furniture for dollhouses.* **min i a tures.**

adj. 2. very small; tiny. *I bought a miniature picture at the museum.*

min i mum (min′ə məm), *n.* 1. the least possible or lowest amount, degree, etc. *One hour a night is the minimum you should spend studying.* **min i mums** or **min i ma** (min′ə-mə).

adj. 2. least; lowest. *The minimum amount of rainfall in this area is two inches per month.*

min is ter (min′is tər), *n.* 1. one who performs religious services, especially in a Protestant church. *Our minister spends a great deal of time preparing his weekly sermon.* 2. a person who is sent to a foreign country to represent his government. *Foreign ministers from all over the world met with the President in Washington.* **min is ters.**

v. 3. to give aid or care. *The kind lady ministered to the injured child until a doctor arrived.* **min is-ters, min is tered, min is ter ing.**

mink (mingk), *n.* 1. a small, furry, wild animal that lives near water or in water. *Some people raise mink for their fur.* 2. the fur of the mink.

coal **mine**

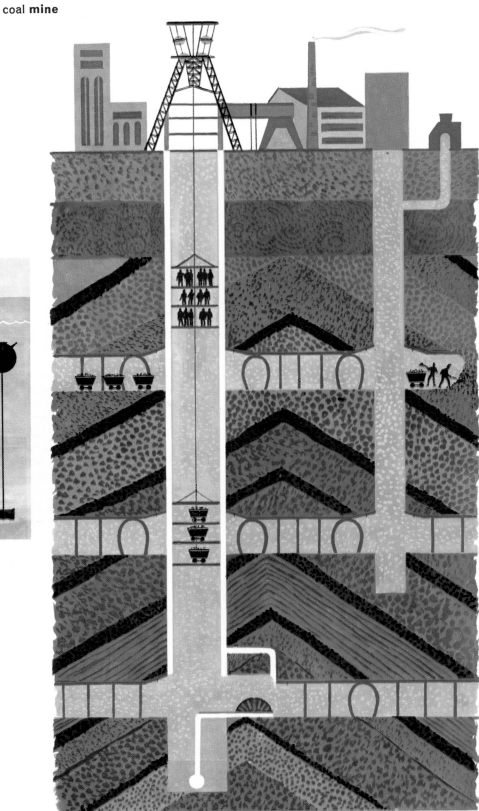

explosive underwater **mines**

MINERALS

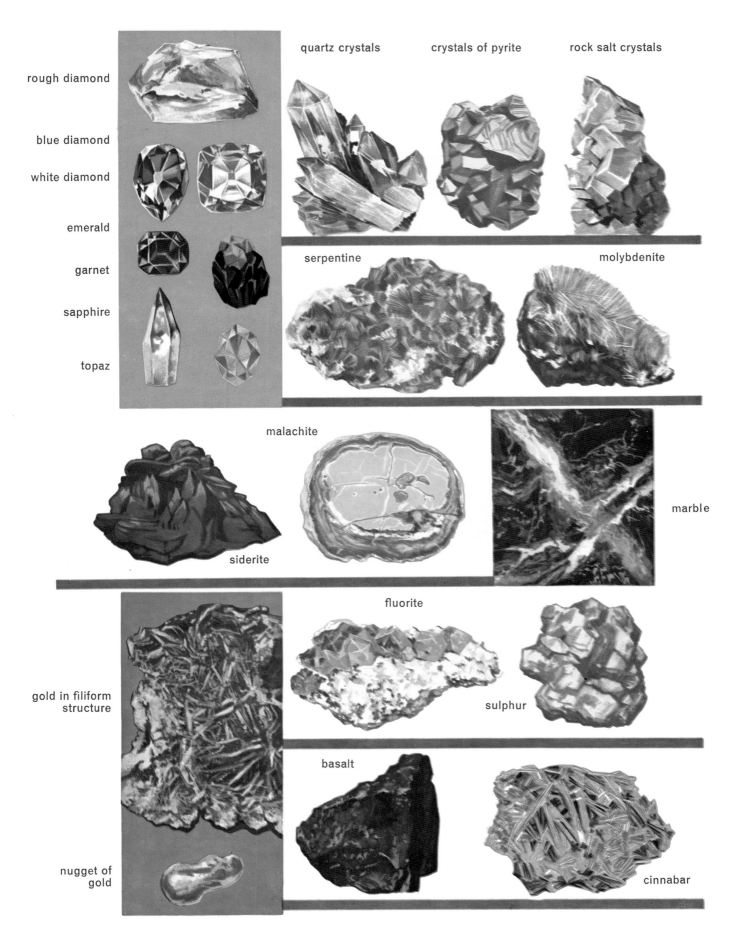

rough diamond

blue diamond

white diamond

emerald

garnet

sapphire

topaz

quartz crystals

crystals of pyrite

rock salt crystals

serpentine

molybdenite

malachite

siderite

marble

gold in filiform structure

fluorite

sulphur

basalt

nugget of gold

cinnabar

mink

Mink is brown or white and is used to make women's coats and jackets. **mink** or **minks.**

Min ne so ta (min′ə sō′tə), *n.* a state in the north central part of the United States. *Minnesota is famous for its dairy products.*

min now (min′ō), *n.* a very small fish found in fresh water. *Minnows are often used as bait to attract larger fish.* **min nows.**

mi nor (mī′nər), *adj.* 1. less in importance, value, etc.; smaller; lesser. *He wasn't the star in the movie since he played only a minor role.*
n. 2. a person who is under the legal age. *You can register to vote while you are still a minor as long as you are of age on or before election day.* **mi nors.**

mint¹ (mint), *n.* 1. any of several plants with sweet-smelling leaves, which are used to flavor foods. *Peppermint is one kind of mint.* 2. a piece of candy flavored with mint. *Mother gave each of us a chocolate-covered mint.* **mints.**

mint² (mint), *n.* 1. a place where coins are made under the authority of the government. *The United States mints are located at Denver and Philadelphia.* 2. a very large amount. *He won a mint of money in the contest.* **mints.**
v. 3. to make coins out of metal. *The government mints pennies from copper.* **mints, mint ed, mint ing.**

min u end (min′yù end′), *n.* the number from which another number is to be subtracted. *In 11 − 9 = 2, the minuend is 11.* **min u ends.**

mi nus (mī′nəs), *prep.* 1. less. *Eleven minus two is nine.* 2. not having; without. *He returned from school minus his jacket.*
n. 3. a sign (−) which shows that the number following it is to be subtracted. *Your answer to the problem is wrong because you didn't see the minus before the second number.* **mi nus es.**

min ute¹ (min′it), *n.* 1. one of the sixty equal parts into which an hour is divided; sixty seconds. *We were given ten minutes to do each part*

minute hand (long hand) of a clock or watch

of the test. 2. a short amount of time. "*I'll be with you in a minute,*" *said the clerk.* 3. the exact moment. *I recognized him the minute I saw him.* 4. **minutes,** the record or account of what happened at a meeting. *The secretary of the club keeps the minutes.* **min utes.**

mi nute² (mī nüt′, mī nūt′), *adj.* 1. tiny; very small. *Minute bits of dust floated through the ray of sunlight.* 2. covering or explaining every small detail. *We heard a minute description of the operation of an engine when we were at the science fair.* **mi nute ly,** *adv.*

mir ror (mir′ər), *n.* 1. a glass or other surface which reflects an image. *She used a mirror to see how her new hair style looked.* 2. anything that gives a true account of something or shows a true picture of something. *Books, magazines, and newspapers are valuable mirrors of the times during which they are written.* **mir rors.**
v. 3. to reflect. *The setting sun was mirrored on the surface of the lake.* **mir rors, mir rored, mir ror ing.**

mis chief (mis′chif), *n.* 1. conduct or actions which cause or could cause harm, injury, or damage. *The children's mischief ended when their parents returned.* 2. harm; injury. *That person did great mischief by spreading false stories.* 3. harmless and merry teasing or pranks. *We were all full of mischief during the holidays.* 4. a person who plays pranks or causes harm or injury to others. *The little mischief knocked over a display of grapefruit in the supermarket.* **mis-chiefs.**

mint

mis chie vous (mis′chə vəs), *adj.* 1. full of mischief; causing mischief. *Some mischievous person had hidden our dry clothes while we were swimming.* 2. causing harm, injury, or damage. *Their mischievous gossip about the grocer made people stay away from his store.* 3. playful; merry and teasing. *The mischievous puppy chewed a hole in my bedroom slippers.* **mis chievous ly,** *adv.*

mis ery (miz′ər ē), *n.* 1. unhappiness, pain, or distress. *He was in great misery from the toothache.* 2. distress caused by very poor living conditions. *After his father lost all his money they lived in misery in an old house by the railroad tracks.* **mis er ies.**

Miss (mis), *n.* 1. the title used before the name of a woman or young girl who is not married. *When Miss Hansen got married, she became Mrs. Moore.* 2. **miss,** a girl or young woman. *A pretty miss waited on us in the store.* **Miss es.**

miss (mis), *v.* 1. to fail to hit, reach, etc. *His arrow missed the target by ten feet.* 2. to fail to get, catch, see, etc. *I missed the train because I arrived at the station late. We were supposed to meet at the game, but we missed each other in the crowd.* 3. to fail to attend. *He missed school yesterday because he was sick.* 4. to fail to understand or hear clearly. *I missed the point of the story until I read it again. I missed what he said because he spoke too softly.* 5. not to accept; to allow to go by. *I missed my chance to go to the game.* 6. to avoid; to escape. *He just missed being hit by the falling rock.* 7. to become aware of the absence of something. *She missed her purse when she got on the bus.* 8. to feel sadness at the absence of someone or something. *The children missed their dog while they were away on vacation.* **miss es, missed, miss ing.**
n. 9. a failure to hit, reach, catch, etc. *In baseball, a miss at bat is called a strike. Your first five shots at the target have been misses.* **miss es.**

mis sile (mis′l), *n.* an object, as a stone, bullet, or spear, that is thrown or shot, especially in a fight. *The missile struck the giant in the head, and he fell to the ground.* **mis siles.**

miss ing (mis′ing), *adj.* lost; absent. *The missing puppy was found after several hours.*

mis sion (mish′ən), *n.* 1. a group of people sent to represent their government or to carry on some particular business. *They are part of a mission to help foreign countries develop better methods of farming.* 2. the business or job of such a group. *Their mission is to rescue the soldiers and bring them back to safety.* 3. a church or other building used or established by religious missionaries. *Many missions built by the Spaniards still stand in California and Mexico.* 4. the work one is best suited for or in which one is most interested; a person's calling. *His mission in life was teaching.* **mis sions.**

mis sion ary (mish′ən er′ē), *n.* 1. a person who tries to convince people of the truth of

his religious beliefs and practices. *The church sends missionaries to all parts of the world.* **mis sion ar ies.**
adj. 2. of or having to do with religious missions or missionaries. *He is doing missionary work in China.*

Mis sis sip pi (mis′ə sip′ē), *n.* 1. a state in the south central part of the United States. *Mississippi produces the largest amount of cotton in the United States.* 2. the largest river in North America. *The Mississippi flows from northern Minnesota to the Gulf of Mexico.*

Mis sou ri (mə zür′ē, mə zür′ə), *n.* 1. a state in the central part of the United States. *Farming and the manufacture of transportation equipment are the major industries of Missouri.* 2. the longest river in North America. *The Missouri begins in the state of Montana and flows into the Mississippi.*

mis spell (mis spel′), *v.* to spell something wrong. *Many people misspell words like niece and neither.* **mis spells, mis spelled** or **mis spelt, mis spell ing.**

mist (mist), *n.* 1. a light cloud of water droplets hanging in the air close to the ground. *From the top of the hill we could see the mist in the valley below.* 2. something that dims or clouds vision. *He didn't recognize me through the mist of tears in his eyes.* **mists.**
v. 3. to come down in mist; to fall in very fine drops. *It was misting when I came to school.* 4. to cover with a mist; to dim or cloud as if with a mist. *The window was misted with spray from the sea.* **mists, mist ed, mist ing.**

mis take (mis tāk′), *n.* 1. an error. *He made a mistake in adding up the numbers.* 2. a misunderstanding. *She wasn't really angry; it was just a mistake.* **mis takes.**
v. 3. to fail to understand. *Did you mistake my question?* 4. to take someone or something for another. *Did you ever mistake me for my sister?* **mis takes, mis took, mis tak en, mis tak ing.**

mis tak en (mis tak′ən), *adj.* 1. having made a mistake; in error. *You are mistaken if you think the earth is flat.* 2. wrong; not correct. *He had a mistaken idea of the problem and subtracted when he should have divided.* **mis tak en ly,** *adv.*
v. 3. past participle of **mistake.**

Mis ter (mis′tər), *n.* a title used before the name of a man; Mr. *A boy or young man is called "Master"; an adult male is called "Mister."* **Mis ters.**

mis tle toe (mis′l tō′), *n.* an evergreen plant with white berries that lives as a parasite on other trees. *Mistletoe is often found growing on apple trees. Mistletoe is used as a Christmas ornament.* **mis tle toes.** (See illustration on following page.)

mis tress (mis′tris), *n.* 1. the woman who is in charge of a household. *The mistress planned the meals to be served each day.* 2. a woman who

mirror

---

sand, āte, bâre, fäther; sent, mē, fėrn; fit, bīke; pot, rōpe, fôrt; run, púll, rüle, cūte; noise, sound; ch, cheese; ng, long; th, thick; <del>th,</del> those; zh, treasure; ə = a in about, e in waken, i in animal, o in seldom, and u in minus.

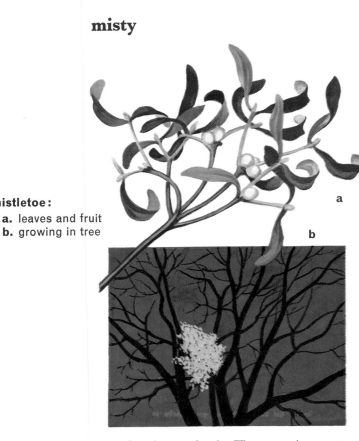

mistletoe:
a. leaves and fruit
b. growing in tree

moccasin

teaches in a school. *The new mistress at our school will be in charge of the third grade.* 3. **Mistress,** a title which was once used before the name of a woman. *Mistress Bowen and Lady Dunne went shopping together.* **mis tress es.**

misty (mis′tē), *adj.* 1. full of or clouded by mist. *The ship sailed slowly through the misty harbor. We saw the defeat of our team through misty eyes.* 2. vague; not distinct; not seen or understood clearly. *The children have only a misty memory of their vacation trip.* **mist i er, mist i est; mist i ly,** *adv.*

mis un der stand (mis′un der stand′), *v.* to fail to understand; to give incorrect meaning to something. *You misunderstand; I didn't mean to take your coat.* **mis un der stands, mis-un der stood, mis un der stand ings.**

mis un der stand ing (mis′un dər stan′ding), *n.* 1. a failure to understand meaning. *His misunderstanding of the directions prevented him from running the machine correctly.* 2. a disagreement. *Because of a misunderstanding, the two boys are no longer friends.* **mis un der stand ings.**

mitt (mit), *n.* 1. a long glove with half fingers or no fingers at all. *The printer wore mitts to keep his cuffs from being stained with ink.* 2. a large, padded glove used in baseball. *The catcher's mitt is the most heavily padded kind of baseball glove.* 3. a mitten. *The child had lost one of his mitts in the snow.* **mitts.**

mit ten (mit′n), *n.* a glove worn in winter with a single covering for the fingers and a separate covering for the thumb. *Mother pinned the baby's mittens to the sleeves of his coat so that he would not lose them.* **mit tens.**

mix (miks), *v.* 1. to put different things together to make one mass. *This paint is made by mixing water and coloring matter.* 2. to become one mass; to blend. *Oil and water do not mix.* 3. to make by putting different things together. *Did anyone mix a pudding for us to have after dinner?* 4. **mix up,** to confuse. *He tried to mix me up with his questions.* **mix es, mixed, mix ing.**
n. 5. a number of things put together in one mass. *We bought a chocolate cake mix.* **mix es.**

mixed (mikst), *v.* 1. past tense of **mix.**
adj. 2. made up of different kinds. *A bowl of mixed fruit was put on the table.* 3. made up of both men and women or of boys and girls. *She and Tom are in the mixed choir at church.*

mixed number, *n.* a whole number and fraction written together. *The number 11 is a whole number, $\frac{3}{4}$ is a fraction, and $11\frac{3}{4}$ is a mixed number.* **mixed numbers.**

mix ture (miks′chər), *n.* 1. anything that is mixed or is being mixed. *When I came into the laboratory, the professor was stirring a thick, blue-green mixture.* 2. a mixing. *The mixture of these chemicals will cause them to explode.* **mix tures.**

moan (mōn), *n.* 1. a low noise sounding like a groan. *The old dog often lets out a sad moan when he lies down. The moan of the winter wind through the trees frightened little Sally.* **moans.**
v. 2. to make a noise like a groan. *The old man moaned in his sleep.* **moans, moaned, moan ing.**

moat (mōt), *n.* a deep ditch, usually filled with water, around a castle, town, etc. *Moats were constructed to make it difficult or impossible to enter or leave a place without crossing a bridge.* **moats.**

mob (mob), *n.* 1. a large, excited, often violent, crowd of people. *The mob calmed down and went home when the sheriff said he would arrest anyone he found on the street.* 2. the common people; the ordinary people. *Do you make your own decisions or are you ruled by the mob?* **mobs.**
v. 3. to attack violently, as a mob does. *The angry crowd mobbed the jail where the prisoner was kept.* 4. to crowd around. *The boys mobbed the baseball star as he left the park.* **mobs, mobbed, mob bing.**

moc ca sin (mok′ə sn), *n.* 1. a soft leather shoe. *American Indians made moccasins from the skins of deer.* 2. a poisonous snake that lives in the southeastern United States. *Water moccasins live near ponds or lakes.* **moc ca sins.**

mock (mok), *v.* 1. to laugh at; to make fun of. *The boys mocked him because he was afraid to jump in the cold water.* 2. to mimic. *The children mocked their classmate's sore foot by pretending to walk with a limp.* **mocks, mocked, mock ing.**
n. 3. an object of laughter or amusement. *They made a mock of the play by forgetting their lines.* **mocks.**
adj. 4. not real. *He fooled us for a moment with his mock injury.*

mode (mōd), *n.* 1. the way in which something

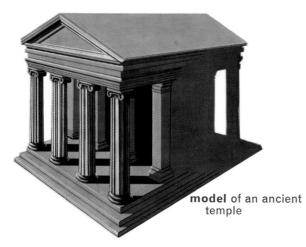

model of an ancient temple

is done. *Riding on a donkey is a very slow mode of transportation.* 2. a fashion or style of dress. *These clothes were the mode a few years ago, but they look very strange today.* **modes.**

mod el (mod′l), *n.* 1. a small, exact copy of something. *He built several models of old automobiles.* 2. a figure, construction, pattern, etc. of something that may be made. *The artist sent a clay model of his sculpture to the king. The mayor approved the models of the new buildings.* 3. a person or thing that is used as an example of something. *These paragraphs are models of good writing. That actress has been Sue's model for many years.* 4. a person who poses for an artist, photographer, etc. *The artist could not afford to pay a model, so he asked his friends to sit for him.* 5. a person who displays clothes that are for sale by wearing them. *The models had to change costumes several times during the fashion show.* **mod els.**
v. 6. to make or shape something. *He modeled a castle out of wet sand.* 7. to form oneself or plan something according to a model. *He modeled himself on a baseball hero. He modeled his life on his older brother's.* 8. to act or serve as a model. *The artist's wife modeled for that painting.* **mod els, mod eled, mod el ing.**
adj. 9. good enough to be copied; being a good example of something. *She has always been a model student who studies hard and behaves herself in school.*

mod er ate (mod′ər it for 1 and 2, mod′ər āt′ for 3), *adj.* 1. not extreme; not too much and not too little. *They paid a moderate price for the house.* 2. limited; medium; not too large or great. *He had moderate success in everything he did.* **mod er ate ly,** *adv.*
v. 3. to calm; to make less extreme. *You'll have to moderate your excitement because you are making too much noise.* 4. to keep within limits; to watch over. *Bill will moderate our panel discussion.* **mod er ates, mod er at ed, mod er at ing.**

mod ern (mod′ərn), *adj.* of the present time; of recent times. *Television, radar, and rocket engines are modern inventions.*

mod est (mod′ist), *adj.* 1. not vain; not full of boasts or too proud of oneself. *The captain was modest about his team's victory.* 2. not extreme in appearance, size, etc. *Even though they are wealthy, they live in a modest house in a quiet section of town.* 3. moderate. *Terry asked for a modest increase in his allowance.* 4. having a sense of what is proper and decent. *The modest girl always wears suitable clothing to school.* **mod est ly,** *adv.*

moist (moist), *adj.* somewhat wet; damp. *The grass was still moist from the rain this morning.* **moist er, moist est; moist ly,** *adv.*

mois ten (moi′sn), *v.* to make or become moist. *Before you clean the spot on the table, moisten the cloth you will use.* **mois tens, mois tened, mois ten ing.**

mois ture (mois′chər), *n.* the very small droplets of water that are in the air or that collect on a surface. *Moisture may affect the weather by remaining in the atmosphere as humidity or by falling to the earth as rain or snow.*

mo lar (mō′lər), *n.* a tooth in the back of a person's jaw that is used for grinding food. *The molars have double roots.* **mo lars.**

mold[1] (mōld), *n.* 1. a hollow shape in which a thing is formed. *Mother poured the ice cream into a mold to harden.* 2. a thing shaped in a mold. *Three chicken-salad molds were prepared for the picnic. The mold of the statue did not harden for several days.* **molds.**
v. 3. to form or shape. *The animal figures had been molded in plaster. He molded his career after that of a great businessman.* **molds, mold ed, mold ing.**

mold[2] (mōld), *n.* 1. a furlike growth of fungi that forms on food, leather, etc. when such material is decaying or has been left too long in a warm, moist place. *The old books in the attic were covered with mold.*
v. 2. to become covered with this fungus. *The bread had molded while we were away on vacation.* **molds, mold ed, mold ing.**

mold[3] (mōld), *n.* loose, rich soil containing much decaying matter. *The plants in the mold grew much faster than those in ordinary soil.*

mole[1] (mōl), *n.* a small, usually brown, spot on the skin. *A small mole on a woman's face is considered to be a sign of beauty.* **moles.**

mole[2] (mōl), *n.* a small, practically blind, animal with smooth fur, and front feet that are suitable for digging. *The mole is a burrowing animal which spends most of its life below the ground.* **moles.**

mole: underside of face and paws are shown at right

MOLLUSKS

octopus

squid

cuttlefish

land snail

marine snail

clam

(closed)

(open)

chambered nautilus

(cross section)

mongoose

mol e cule (mol ə kūl), *n.* 1. the smallest particle into which a thing can be divided and still remain that thing. *If a molecule of water is divided further, it is no longer water. Molecules are made up of atoms.* 2. a small particle. *There isn't a molecule of truth in that story.* **mol e cules.**

mol lusk (mol′əsk), *n.* any of a large group of animals having soft bodies, usually surrounded by a shell. *Mollusks have no bones in their bodies.* **mol lusks.**

mo ment (mō′mənt), *n.* 1. an instant; a very brief period of time. *I saw him for a moment, and then I lost sight of him in the crowd.* 2. a specific instant in time. *I came the moment I heard you were sick.* 3. importance. *The battle is of great moment to the country.* **mo ments.**

mo men tary (mō′mən ter′ē), *adj.* lasting for only an instant. *There was a momentary silence when the lights went out.* **mo men tar i ly,** *adv.*

mon arch (mon′ərk), *n.* a ruler, especially a king or queen. *When the king died, his eldest son became the new monarch.* **mon archs.**

mon as tery (mon′əs ter′ē), *n.* a place where members of a religious society live. *The men who live in a monastery must promise not to own any money and not to marry.* **mon as ter ies.**

Mon day (mun′dē, mun′dā), *n.* the second day of the week, coming after Sunday and before Tuesday. *For most people Monday is the first working day in the week.* **Mon days.**

mon ey (mun′ē), *n.* 1. any metal or paper which has been coined, stamped, minted, or printed by a government and is issued for use in buying and selling. *Do you have any money in your pocket?* 2. wealth. *The president of the company is a man of money.* **mon eys** or **mon ies.**

mon goose (mong′güs), *n.* a small, fierce, fast-moving animal with yellowish-gray or brownish-black hair that lives in Africa, Asia, Hawaii, and southern Spain. *Mongooses kill rats, mice, and poisonous snakes.* **mon goos es.**

mon key (mung′kē), *n.* 1. any of the group of higher animals found mainly in Asia and Africa which is most like man, especially the

MONEY OF DIFFERENT NATIONS

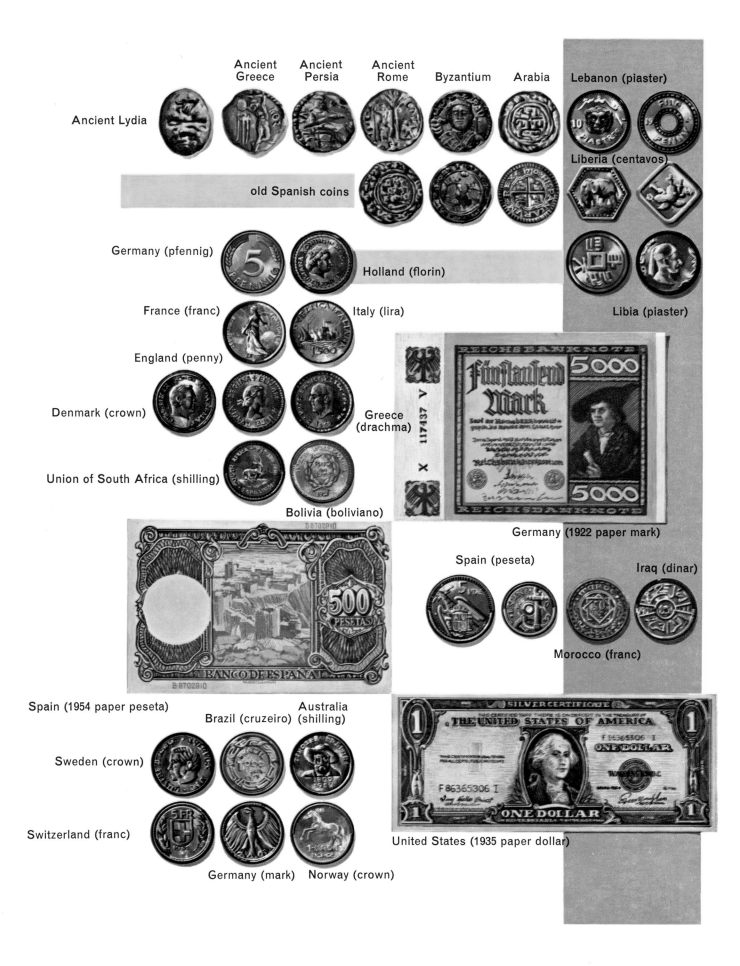

Ancient Lydia

Ancient Greece

Ancient Persia

Ancient Rome

Byzantium

Arabia

Lebanon (piaster)

old Spanish coins

Liberia (centavos)

Germany (pfennig)

Holland (florin)

France (franc)

Italy (lira)

Libia (piaster)

England (penny)

Denmark (crown)

Greece (drachma)

Union of South Africa (shilling)

Bolivia (boliviano)

Germany (1922 paper mark)

Spain (peseta)

Iraq (dinar)

Morocco (franc)

Spain (1954 paper peseta)

Brazil (cruzeiro)

Australia (shilling)

Sweden (crown)

Switzerland (franc)

Germany (mark)

Norway (crown)

United States (1935 paper dollar)

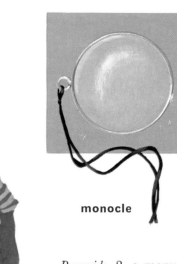

monocle

Pyramids. 2. a monument, statue, pillar, etc. shaped from a large block of stone. *A historical monolith stood at the entrance to the courthouse.* **mon o liths.**

mo not o nous (mə not′n əs), *adj.* having not much change; boring. *The speaker talked in such a monotonous voice that I fell asleep.* **mo not o- nous ly,** *adv.*

mon ster (mon′stər), *n.* 1. an animal or plant that is very different from others of his kind. *A giraffe with a very short neck would be a monster.* 2. an imaginary creature having unusual size or appearance. *The ancient sailors were attacked by an unknown monster from the sea. The "monsters" the boys had seen in the dark turned out to be a couple of lost cows.* 3. any huge thing or animal. *The hotel was a monster with six hundred rooms.* 4. a cruel, wicked, or mean person. *What monster could have tied tin cans to the dog's tail?* **mon sters.**

Mon tana (mon tan′ə), *n.* a state in the north-western part of the United States. *Montana is the fourth largest state in the United States.*

month (munth), *n.* one of the twelve parts into which a year is divided. *The first month of the year is January and the last one is December.* **months.**

month ly (munth′lē), *adj.* 1. for a month; in a month; lasting through a month. *The teacher kept a monthly chart of our progress for our report cards.* 2. happening once a month. *The*

trained **monkeys**

small, long-tailed members of this group. *Monkeys can use their feet like hands to help them climb trees and swing from branch to branch.* 2. a mischievous child. *My brother, the little monkey, tied my shoes together.* **mon keys.**

v. 3. to play; to fool around. *Don't monkey with the radio or you will break it.* **mon keys, mon keyed, mon key ing.**

mon o cle (mon′ə kl), *n.* an eyeglass for only one eye. *Years ago some men wore monocles instead of eyeglasses.* **mon o cles.**

mon o lith (mon′ə lith), *n.* 1. a large block of stone. *The Egyptians used monoliths to build the*

monolith

sand, āte, bâre, fäther; sent, mē, fėrn; fit, bīke; pot, rōpe, fôrt; run, pùll, rüle, cūte; noise, sound; ch, cheese; ng, long; th, thick; t̶h̶, those; zh, treasure; ə = a in about, e in waken, i in animal, o in seldom, and u in minus.

monthly report is due today. Did you pay the monthly bills?

adv. 3. once each month. *This magazine is published monthly.*

n. 4. a magazine published once a month. *Monthlies are usually less expensive per year than weekly magazines.* **month lies.**

mon u ment (mon′yə mənt), *n.* 1. anything built or established in memory of a person or thing or in honor of a person or thing. *The Washington and Lincoln monuments are in our nation's capital.* 2. anything worth remembering or preserving, especially as an example of something. *The Panama Canal is a monument to the skill and hard work of the men who planned and built it.* **mon u ments.**

moo (mü), *n.* 1. the sound made by a cow. *We found the lost cow by listening for her moos.* **moos.**

v. 2. to make this sound. *The cow mooed as she was milked.* **moos, mooed, moo ing.**

mood (müd), *n.* a state of mind; a feeling. *The coach was in an unhappy mood after the team lost the game.* **moods.**

moon (mün), *n.* 1. the body that travels around the earth about once every twenty-eight days. *The moon reflects light from the sun.* 2. the time it takes for the moon to travel around the earth; twenty-eight days. *The Indians used to measure time by moons.* 3. anything shaped like a moon or part of a moon. *The design had a moon and a star on it.* **moons.**

v. 4. to wander around and look dreamily at things. *The boy mooned about all day until his dog was found.* **moons, mooned, moon ing.**

moon light (mün′līt′), *n.* 1. the light of the moon. *The moonlight lighted the road and helped the travelers to find their way in the night.*

adj. 2. happening by or in moonlight. *We went for a moonlight swim last night.*

moon lit (mün′līt′), *adj.* lighted by the moon. *The story began on a moonlit night many years ago.*

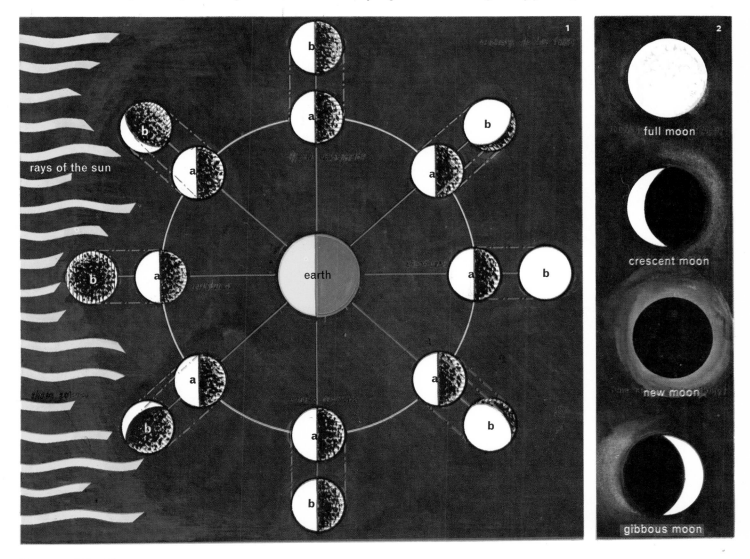

Phases of the Moon

moon: 1. the phases of the moon, for each phase **a** shows how the rays of the sun illuminate the moon and **b** shows how we see the moon from the earth. 2. the progression of the moon's phases as seen from the earth.

moose (müs), *n.* a very large animal related to the deer, found in Canada and the northern part of the United States. *Moose stand about six feet tall and may weigh as much as one thousand pounds.* **moose.**

mop (mop), *n.* 1. a bundle of yarn or fabric, or a sponge, attached to a handle and used for cleaning floors, etc. *Mother uses one mop for washing the floor and another for dusting it.* 2. anything like a mop in appearance. *That boy has a thick mop of red hair on his head.* **mops.**

v. 3. to wipe with a mop or as if with a mop. *Mop the wet floor before someone slips on it. He mopped his brow with a handkerchief.* **mops, mopped, mop ping.**

mor al (môr′əl), *adj.* 1. having to do with what is right and what is wrong. *There is a moral difference between borrowing something with permission and stealing something.* 2. able to determine the difference between right and wrong. *Man is a moral being; animals are not.* 3. acting in an acceptable manner; right; good. *The leader of a country must be a moral man.* 4. teaching a lesson, usually of right and wrong. *The teacher told us a moral story about a boy who thought it was all right to steal.* **mor al ly,** *adv.*

n. 5. the lesson taught by a story. *The moral of the story is that crime does not pay.* 6. **morals,** conduct or behavior. *Criminals are people of very low morals.* **mor als.**

mo rale (mə ral′), *n.* mental feeling or spirit, especially feelings of confidence and hope. *The morale of the soldiers was very high after they saw the special Christmas show.*

mo ral i ty (mə ral′ə tē), *n.* 1. the rightness or wrongness of an act. *Modern morality is not as harsh as it was in the nineteenth century.* 2. a set of rules or principles by which a person acts. *Her morality is a good example to all of us.* **mo ral i ties.**

more (môr), *adj.* 1. greater in number, amount, etc. *There were more people in the park than I had ever seen before. We had more rain this month than we had all last year.* 2. additional. *May I have more money, please?*

n. 3. an additional amount; a greater number. *May I have more of this good cake? The reward was more than I hoped for.*

adv. 4. to a higher extent or greater degree. *I was more tired than I thought and fell asleep immediately.* 5. in addition. *He didn't have to leave right away, so we talked for five minutes more.* 6. more is used to form the comparative form of many adjectives and adverbs. *If you want to be more careful, try to walk more slowly.*

moose

morning-glory

A	.-	M	--	Y	-.--		
B	-...	N	-.	Z	--..		
C	-.-.	O	---	1	.----		
D	-..	P	.--.	2	..---		
E	.	Q	--.-	3	...--		
F	..-.	R	.-.	4	....-		
G	--.	S	...	5	.....		
H	....	T	-	6	-....		
I	..	U	..-	7	--...		
J	.---	V	...-	8	---..		
K	-.-	W	.--	9	----.		
L	.-..	X	-..-	0	-----		

International **Morse Code**

more o ver (môr ō′vər), *adv.* besides; in addition. *I don't want to go swimming today; moreover, the water is too cold.*

morn ing (môr′ning), *n.* the earliest part of the day ending at noon. *We eat breakfast every morning at eight o'clock.* **morn ings.**

morn ing-glo ry (môr′ning glôr′ē), *n.* a climbing vine with flowers shaped like funnels. *The flowers of the morning-glory are blue, purple, pink, or white.* **morn ing-glo ries.**

mor pheme (môr′fēm), *n.* the smallest unit in language which conveys meaning. *A morpheme can be a word, such as "play," or it can be part of a word, such as the "er" of "player," the "ed" of "played," or the "s" of "plays."* **morphemes.**

mor row (môr′ō), *n.* 1. tomorrow; the next day. *"Good night. I'll see you on the morrow."* 2. an old way of saying morning. *"Good morrow, sir," he said when he awoke.* **mor rows.**

Morse code (môrs′ cōd′), *n.* a code or alphabet made up of dots and dashes or long and short sounds. *The Morse code is used in sending telegraph or radio messages.*

mor tal (môr′tl), *adj.* 1. certain to die sometime. *All men are mortal beings.* 2. human; of man. *Even though that man is very great and famous, he has only mortal powers and can sometimes be wrong.* 3. causing death; fatal. *The knight suffered a mortal wound in the battle.* 4. until death. *The two mortal enemies finally met in battle.* 5. great. *We were in mortal fear of the escaped prisoners.* 6. involving death of the spirit. *The priest spoke last Sunday about mortal sin.* **mor tal ly,** *adv.*

n. 7. human being; man. *Mortals should always live up to their goals.* 8. any living thing that will die someday. *Animals are mortal.* **mor tals.**

mort gage (môr′gij), *n.* 1. a legal right to take a property from its owner if a debt is not

paid. *The bank holds a mortgage on our house.*
mort gag es.

v. 2. to give this right to a person or bank that
lends money. *The man mortgaged his house
because he could not pay for it all at once.* **mort-
gag es, mort gaged, mort gag ing.**

mo sa ic (mō zā′ik), *n.* a picture or design
made by putting together small pieces of
colored stone, glass, or tile. *Mosaics are used
on the walls, ceilings, or floors of some fine buildings.*
mo sa ics.

mosque (mosk), *n.* a church for use by believers
of the religion founded by Mohammed.
Mosques are found in countries of the Middle East.
mosques.

mos qui to (məs kē′tō), *n.* a small insect, the
female of which bites people and animals and
sucks their blood. *Mosquitoes are known to carry
disease from one person to another.* **mos qui toes.**

moss (môs), *n.* a small, green plant that grows
in thick patches on damp ground, bark, trees,
etc. *Many mosses help keep the ground damp by
soaking up rain as it falls and holding it.* **moss es.**

mossy (môs′ē), *adj.* 1. covered with moss. *The
frog sat on a mossy stone in the water.* 2. like moss.
*We saw a mossy-colored lizard on the bank of the
pond.* **moss i er, moss i est.**

most (mōst), *adj.* 1. greatest in amount,
number, etc. *This is the most people who have
ever seen a parade in our city. That was the most
money I had ever seen at one time.* 2. practically all.
He enjoys listening to most music.

n. 3. the greatest amount, number, etc. *Get
the most out of your ability and your desire to win.
Is that the most you are willing to pay?*

adv. 4. to the highest extent or greatest degree.
He most deserves our praise for his act of courage,

moth:
  a. larva
  b. adult

though the others also were brave. 5. *most* is used
to form the superlative form of many adjectives and adverbs. *The most beautiful girl in the
class was not the most pleasant girl to be with.*

most ly (mōst′lē), *adv.* mainly; chiefly. *There
were mostly girls in the library.*

mo tel (mō tel′), *n.* a hotel on or near a highway for people who are traveling by car; a
group of cabins or cottages in which travelers
may sleep. *Our motel had a television in every
room and a swimming pool, but we were too tired
to do anything but sleep.* **mo tels.**

moth (môth), *n.* any of a large number of
insects that usually fly at night and resemble
butterflies except for dull-colored wings and
thicker bodies. *The larvae of many moths destroy
food, clothing, and plants.* **moths.**

mosquito

mosaic

mosque

sand, āte, bâre, fäther; sent, mē, fėrn; fit, bīke; pot, rōpe, fôrt; run, pùll, rüle, cūte; noise, sound; ch, cheese;
ng, long; th, thick; ᵺ, those; zh, treasure; ə = a in about, e in waken, i in animal, o in seldom, and u in minus.

moth er (muth'ər), *n.* 1. the female parent. *The teacher wants to see my father and mother.* 2. the cause of something; the source of something. *School is the mother of learning.* 3. a woman who is in charge of a religious group. *The superior of that religious school is called "Mother" or "Mother Superior."* **moth ers.**

v. 4. to care for as a mother does. *We mothered the sick bird until it was healthy again.* **moth ers, moth ered, moth er ing.**

adj. 5. learned from one's mother, or as if from one's mother. *His mother tongue is English, but he understands French and Spanish.* **moth er ly,** *adv.*

mo tion (mō'shən), *n.* 1. the act of moving; movement. *The motion of the train made us sleepy.* 2. a suggestion made at a meeting. *The motion to elect a new president was passed by the members.* **mo tions.**

v. 3. to make a movement or a gesture. *The speaker motioned to us to sit down and be quiet.* **mo tions, mo tioned, mo tion ing.**

mo tion less (mō'shən lis), *adj.* still; unmoving. *When the wind died, the leaves in the trees became motionless.* **mo tion less ly,** *adv.*

mo tive (mō'tiv), *n.* 1. the reason for doing something or for acting in a certain way. *Getting good grades was his motive for studying for his tests.* **mo tives.**

adj. 2. causing motion. *An engine provides the motive power for an automobile.*

mo tor (mō'tər), *n.* 1. an engine that turns power into motion. *The car would not move because the motor wouldn't start.* **mo tors.**

adj. 2. driven by a motor; operated by a motor. *My brother got a new motor scooter for Christmas.* 3. having to do with motion. *A motor center in the brain sends messages to the various muscles in the body to bring about movement.*

v. 4. to travel by automobile. *We motored to Canada on our vacation.* **mo tors, mo tored, mo tor ing.**

mo tor cy cle (mō'tər sī'kl), *n.* 1. a heavy bicycle that is run by a motor. *Some policemen use motorcycles for transportation.* **mo tor cy cles.**

v. 2. to travel by motorcycle. *The men motorcycled to the lake.* **mo tor cy cles, mo tor cy cled, mo tor cy cling.**

mound (mound), *n.* 1. a heap of dirt or stones; a small hill. *A mound marked the place where the pirates had buried their gold.* 2. in baseball, the raised area from which the pitcher throws. *The mound is located in the center of the inner field on a baseball diamond.* **mounds.**

mount[1] (mount), *n.* a word for mountain, usually used in poetry or before a particular name of a mountain. *Mount McKinley is the highest point in the United States.* **mounts.**

mount[2] (mount), *v.* 1. to go up; to climb. *We mounted the steps slowly on the first day of school.* 2. to get up on. *The cowboy mounted his horse and rode away.* 3. to increase; to rise. *The cost of food has mounted during the last few years.* 4. to provide with a horse. *The police department in New York*

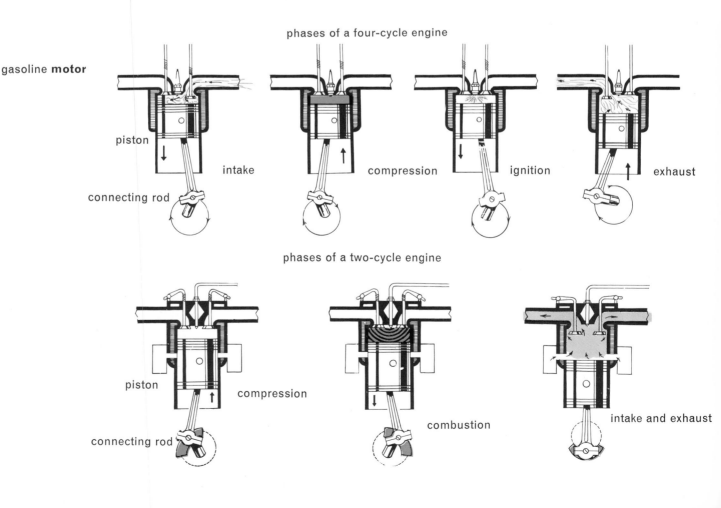

gasoline **motor**

phases of a four-cycle engine

piston   intake   compression   ignition   exhaust

connecting rod

phases of a two-cycle engine

piston   compression   combustion   intake and exhaust

connecting rod

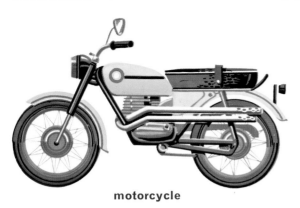

motorcycle

City mounts some of its policemen. 5. to put something in position to be used. *Eighteen cannons were mounted on the ship's deck.* 6. to put in a frame or other setting. *The photographs were mounted and hung on the wall.* **mounts, mounted, mount ing.**

n. 7. a horse used for riding. *The men fed their mounts before they ate anything themselves.* **mounts.**

moun tain (mount′n), *n.* 1. any land that rises like a hill but is much higher than a hill. *We could see the snow on the mountains when we were still very far away.* 2. a great amount, size, etc. *I have a mountain of work to do this evening. A mountain of magazines sat on a table in the dentist's office.* **moun tains.**

adj. 3. anything found on or used on a mountain. *The wild mountain flowers bloomed at the side of the road.*

moun tain ous (mount′n əs), *adj.* 1. having mountains; filled with or covered by mountains. *The western part of the United States contains many mountainous areas.* 2. like mountains; huge. *A mountainous wave momentarily covered the empty boat.* **moun tain ous ly,** *adv.*

mourn (môrn), *v.* to show sorrow for; to grieve; to feel sadness. *The children mourned the death of their pet bird.* **mourns, mourned, mourn ing.**

mourn ful (môrn′fəl), *adj.* sad; full of sorrow. *The unhappy child spoke in a mournful voice.* **mourn ful ly,** *adv.*

mourn ing (môr′ning), *n.* 1. the act of mourning. *Mourning over the loss of the game ruined everyone's fun at the dance afterward.* 2. a period of time during which sadness is expressed and grief demonstrated because of someone's death. *The widow's mourning for her husband lasted for more than a year.* 3. the black clothing worn during this time. *She was dressed in mourning for a long time after his death.*

mouse (mous), *n.* a small animal with white, gray, or brown fur, a long tail and long, sharp front teeth. *White mice are sometimes kept as pets.* **mice** (mīs).

mouth (mouth for 1 and 2, mouŧh for 3), *n.* 1. the opening in the head of a person or animal which contains the tongue and teeth and which is used for taking in food or making sounds. *The boxer wore a special guard in his mouth to protect his teeth.* 2. any opening like a mouth. *The mouth of the river was in a wide, flat place. The boys entered the mouth of the cave.* **mouths.**

v. 3. to speak in a way that is not natural or sincere. *The young man was a poor speaker because he always mouthed his speeches to his audience.* **mouths, mouthed, mouth ing.**

mov a ble or **move a ble** (müv′ə bl), *adj.* that can be moved; not fastened in one place. *Many schoolrooms have movable desks.* **mov a bly** or **move a bly,** *adv.*

move (müv), *v.* 1. to change the place or position of someone or something. *Move your chair so that you will be closer to the light.* 2. to go from one place of living or working to another. *He and his family moved out West last year.* 3. to put in motion; to cause motion in. *The wind moved the sailboat swiftly across the lake. He moved his head when I called him.* 4. to proceed; to progress. *The plans for the new building moved forward rapidly.* 5. to affect the feelings of. *The actor moved the audience with his great performance as Abraham Lincoln.* 6. to act. *The soldiers moved quickly when the attack began.* 7. to suggest or propose in a meeting. *George moved that the meeting be called to order.* 8. to shift the position of a piece in checkers. *Don't move your queen to an unsafe position.* **moves, moved, mov ing.**

n. 9. a moving from one position to another. *A sudden move of his hand startled me.* 10. a change in one's place of living or working. *He was very happy after his move to a larger company.* 11. an action for a certain purpose. *Your first move should be to find some kind of work.* 12. a turn to move a piece in checkers or chess. *It's your move because I just moved my knight.* **moves.**

mouth

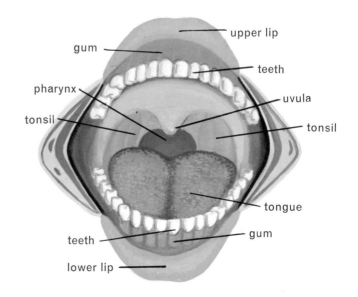

upper lip
gum
teeth
pharynx
uvula
tonsil
tonsil
tongue
teeth
gum
lower lip

move ment (müv/mənt), *n.* 1. a moving. *The children watched the slow but steady movement of the snail across the sidewalk.* 2. a group which acts for a common purpose. *They are part of a movement to get everyone to vote.* 3. the moving parts of a watch, clock, or other machine. *The watch doesn't work because the movement is full of rust.* 4. the rhythm of a piece of music. *The movement of modern music is quite different from that of music written many years ago.* **movements.**

mov ie (müv/ē), *n.* a series of pictures flashed on a screen so rapidly that what is shown appears to be moving. *We saw an old movie without any sound when we were at the museum.* **mov ies.**

mov ing (müv/ing), *adj.* 1. that is in motion. *Don't try to jump onto a moving train.* 2. that causes action. *The general was the moving force in winning the battle.* 3. affecting the feelings and emotions, especially in a sad manner. *The speaker made a moving appeal for the cause of homeless children.* **mov ing ly,** *adv.*

mow[1] (mō), *v.* 1. to cut down with a long blade on a handle or with a machine. *The farmer and his helpers were mowing hay.* 2. to cut the grass or grain in. *The boys mowed the lawn this morning.* **mows, mowed, mowed** or **mown, mowing.**

mow[2] (mow), *n.* the place in a barn where hay, straw, etc., are stored. *During the winter the farmer uses the food in the mow for the cows and horses.* **mows.**

Mr. (mis/tər), the abbreviation for Mister. *Mr. Williams is our new neighbor.*

Mrs. (mis/iz), the abbreviation for Mistress; title put before the name of a married woman. *Our teacher's name is Mrs. Sloane.*

much (much), *adj.* 1. large in amount or degree. *Do you get much rain here? Do you need much food?* **more, most.**

n. 2. a great amount. *I didn't get much at the store. Isn't that too much for you to carry?*

adv. 3. to a great degree; far. *I was much more tired this morning than I am now.* 4. nearly; almost the same as. *They look much the same as other children. He acts much the same as he did ten years ago.*

Much also has the following special meanings:
make much of, to pay a lot of attention to. *Grandparents often make much of their grandchildren.*

not much of a, not very good. *It was not much of a dog, but the boy loved it anyway.*

too much for, more than a match for. *The bear was too much for the hunter to handle and the animal escaped.*

mud (mud), *n.* soft, wet, sticky soil. *The children made pies out of the mud by the river.* **muds.**

mud dy (mud/ē), *adj.* 1. covered with mud; stained with mud. *Take your muddy shoes off before you come into the house.* 2. dull; clouded with mud or as if with mud. *All of the colors in the picture were muddy and mixed together.* 3. vague; not clear. *The speaker suggested several muddy ideas that no one could understand.* **mud di er, mud di est.**

v. 4. to make muddy; to soil with mud. *The children muddied the front stairs with their boots.* **mud dies, mud died, mud dy ing.**

mud guard (mud/gärd/), *n.* a rubber or metal shield placed over or behind a wheel to prevent mud and water from splashing. *The fender on a bicycle serves as a mudguard.* **mud guards.**

mud hole (mud/hōl/), *n.* a pond, river, stream, etc. that contains muddy water or has muddy banks. *The sign said, "No Swimming," but we wouldn't swim in such a mudhole anyway.* **mud holes.**

muff (muf), *n.* 1. a thick, tube-shaped cover, often of fur, in which the hands may be placed to keep them warm. *Muffs are used by women and girls.* 2. in baseball, an error; a failure to catch and hold a ball. *His muff of that fly ball cost us the ball game.* **muffs.**

v. 3. in baseball, to fail to catch and hold a ball; to make an error. *The fielder muffed the play, and the runner was safe.* 4. to handle anything in an awkward and clumsy manner. *He muffed the speech by forgetting what he was going to say.* **muffs, muffed, muff ing.**

mug (mug), *n.* 1. a large, heavy drinking cup made of metal, glass, etc. and having a large handle. *The men drank their coffee out of mugs, while the ladies drank tea from cups.* 2. as much

mulberry: a. branch with fruit; **b.** bare tree

as a mug will hold. *He has a mug of coffee before work each morning.* **mugs.**

mul ber ry (mul′ber′ē), *n.* 1. a tree with wide leaves and purple berries. *One kind of mulberry is grown for its leaves, which silkworms eat.* 2. the purple-red fruit of the mulberry. *Mulberries can be eaten.* **mul ber ries.**

mule (mūl), *n.* 1. a work animal which is part horse and part donkey. *Mules have the size and shape of a horse and the ears and tail of a donkey, but they are stronger than either of those animals.* 2. a machine used for spinning yarn. *A mule makes yarn from cotton or wool and then winds it up in spools.* **mules.**

mul ti ple (mul′tə pl), *adj.* 1. made up of many parts; having many parts; being more than one. *He has multiple interests, including sports, music, and movies.*
n. 2. a number that contains another number a certain number of times without a remainder. *Four is a multiple of two since it contains exactly two twos.* **mul ti ples.**

mul ti pli cand (mul′tə plə kand′), *n.* in arithmetic, a number which is multiplied by another. *In 22 × 97, 97 is the multiplicand.* **mul ti pli cands.**

mul ti pli ca tion (mul′tə plə kā′shən), *n.* 1. a quick way of adding a number to itself several times, the result indicated by another number. *In multiplication, 10 × 9 means that 10 is to be added 9 times.* 2. a multiplying. *The multiplication of the expenses involved forced us to stop building the house.* **mul ti pli ca tions.**

mul ti pli er (mul′tə plī′ər), *n.* in arithmetic, a number by which another number is multiplied. *In 22 × 97, 22 is the multiplier.* **mul ti pli ers.**

mul ti ply (mul′tə plī′), *v.* 1. to add the same number to itself a certain number of times, the result indicated by another number. *When 11 is multiplied by 3, it is the same as adding 11 + 11 + 11.* 2. to increase. *Our fears multiplied as we went deeper and deeper into the cave.* **mul ti plies, mul ti plied, mul ti ply ing.**

mul ti tude (mul′tə tüd′, mul′tə tūd′), *n.* a large number of persons or things. *A multitude of people had come to hear the President speak.* **mul ti tudes.**

mum my (mum′ē), *n.* the preserved, cloth-wrapped bodies of ancient Egyptians. *You can see a mummy in a museum.* **mum mies.**

mumps (mumps), *n.* a disease that causes difficulty in chewing and swallowing and is marked by swelling of the face and neck and high fever. *Mumps is a common childhood disease, but adults are occasionally infected with it.*

mu ral (myu̇r′əl), *adj.* 1. having to do with a wall; on a wall. *The mural decorations in the theater consisted of paintings from many lands.*
n. 2. a picture or design painted on a wall. *The artist painted a mural in the lobby of the auditorium.* **mu rals.**

mule

mur der (mėr′dər), *n.* 1. the killing of another person, especially when it is against the law and planned before it is done. *The man who committed the murder was put in prison for the rest of his life.* **mur ders.**
v. 2. to kill when it is against the law. *The thieves murdered two of the guards at the bank before the police captured them.* 3. to do something very poorly. *Even though the girl had murdered the song, her audience applauded politely.* **mur ders, mur dered, mur der ing.**

mur mur (mėr′mər), *n.* 1. a low sound that cannot be heard clearly. *We couldn't sleep because of the murmur of voices from the next room.* **mur murs.**
v. 2. to make a low sound. *The water in the stream murmured over the rocks.* 3. to speak in a low voice. *We couldn't hear what he was saying because he murmured instead of speaking loudly and clearly.* **mur murs, mur mured, mur mur ing.**

mus cle (mus′l), *n.* 1. a kind of tissue in the body which by stretching or becoming shorter causes the body to move. *When you bend your arm, one set of muscles becomes shorter while another set becomes longer.* 2. all of the tissues which move a certain part of the body. *He has huge muscles in his arms.* 3. strength; power. *It took a lot of muscle to lift that heavy weight.* **mus cles.**

mu se um (mū zē′əm), *n.* a building in which special objects are kept so that they can be seen by people. *In our city there is an art museum, a science museum, and a history museum.* **mu se ums.** (See illustration on following page.)

mu sic (mū′zik), *n.* 1. the art of making beautiful sounds and combining them in a beautiful way. *Music is one of the fine arts.* 2. the sounds made and combined. *We listened to different kinds of music on the radio.* 3. the signs which stand for sounds made in music. *Each of the members of the orchestra read his own music*

musketeers

during the concert. 4. any beautiful sound. *We listened to the music of the rain on the roof.*

mu si cal (mū′zə kl), *adj.* 1. having to do with music. *She can play seven different musical instruments.* 2. pleasing and sweet-sounding to the ear. *She has a musical voice when she speaks.* 3. fond of music; fond of listening to or performing music. *That musical family gives many concerts for their friends and neighbors.* 4. written with music; set to music. *We saw a musical comedy on television.* **mu si cal ly,** *adv.*

musical instrument, *n.* a piano, violin, trumpet, clarinet, etc. used for making music. *There are many musical instruments in an orchestra.* **musical instruments.**

mu si cian (mū zish′ən), *n.* a person who is able to play a musical instrument or to sing. *The musicians in an orchestra are expert players.* **mu si cians.**

museum of natural history

mus ke teer (mus′kə tir′), *n.* in older times, a soldier with a gun or a sword. *Musketeers were employed by French kings as their personal guards.* **mus ke teers.**

must (must), *v.* 1. to be obliged to. *You must obey the laws of the state in which you live.* 2. ought to. *I must try harder to do my work on time.* 3. to be certain to. *He must have gone home when he didn't see us.*

mus tang (mus′tang), *n.* a small, half-wild horse of the western plains of the United States. *Mustangs were used by the Indians and by many of the early cowboys.* **mus tangs.**

mute (mūt), *n.* 1. a human being who cannot talk. *The little girl is a mute.* 2. a device used on musical instruments to soften their sounds. *Today I bought a mute for my trumpet.* **mutes.** *adj.* 3. not able to talk or make noise. *The mute boy smiled at the funny clown.*

mu tu al (mū′chù əl), *adj.* 1. given, received, done, or felt by each one toward the other. *There was a mutual attraction between the two friends. He and I looked at each other with mutual dislike.* 2. known by or held in common by several persons. *I don't know that man, but we have mutual friends.* **mu tu al ly,** *adv.*

my (mī), *pron.* of or belonging to me. *I'll meet you at my house in an hour. Would you like to use my bicycle?*

myr tle (mėr′tl), *n.* 1. a sweet-smelling evergreen shrub with shiny leaves and white flowers. *Myrtle grows in the south of Europe.* 2. a creeping vine with blue flowers. *This myrtle grows in the United States.* **myr tles.** (See illustration on page 346.)

my self (mī self′), *pron.* 1. a word used with *I* or *me* to make a statement stronger. *I myself*

sand, āte, bâre, fäther; sent, mē, fėrn; fit, bīke; pot, rōpe, fôrt; run, pùll, rüle, cūte; noise, sound; ch, cheese; ng, long; th, thick; ᵺ, those; zh, treasure; ə = a in about, e in waken, i in animal, o in seldom, and u in minus.

MUSICAL INSTRUMENTS

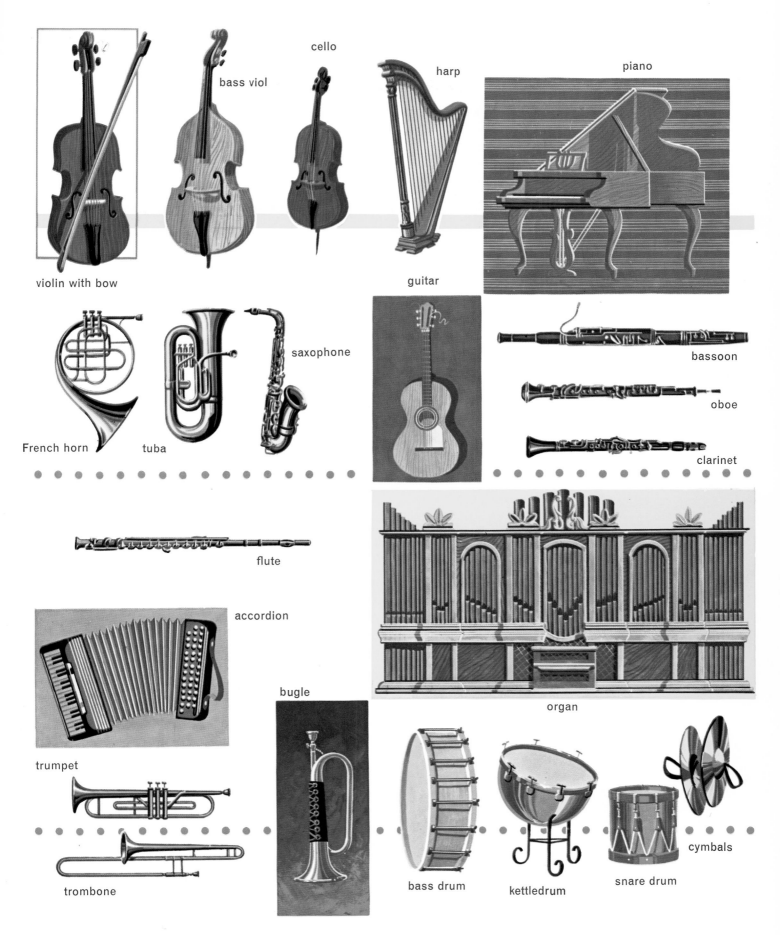

cello

bass viol

harp

piano

violin with bow

guitar

saxophone

bassoon

oboe

French horn

tuba

clarinet

flute

accordion

organ

trumpet

bugle

trombone

bass drum

kettledrum

snare drum

cymbals

myrtle:
a. branches with leaves
b. flower

gods of **mythology:**
a. Ammon (sun god of ancient Egypt)
b. Apollo (sun god of ancient Greece)
c. Odin (Norse god of war and wisdom)

couldn't have done any better. 2. one's own self. *I guessed the answer by myself; no one had to help me.* 3. my normal or usual self. *I was sick for a few days, but I'm beginning to feel like myself again.* **our selves.**

mys te ri ous (mis tir′ē əs), *adj.* full of mystery or the unknown; difficult to understand. *We saw a mysterious light burning in the old, deserted house. A mysterious plane landed in the pasture and frightened the cows.* **mys te ri ous ly,** *adv.*

mys tery (mis′tər ē), *n.* 1. something which is unknown or kept secret. *The name of the stranger was still a mystery to us. His reason for the trip was a mystery until he explained why he went.* 2. something that cannot be known or understood by the human intellect. *No one can explain a religious mystery.* **mys ter ies.**

myth (mith), *n.* an old story or legend about imaginary events and persons. *Some myths attempt to explain the early history of a nation or how certain natural events began.* **myths.**

my thol o gy (mi thol′ə jē), *n.* the myths of a people. *The mythology of the ancient Greeks, Romans, and Egyptians contains stories of their gods.* **my thol o gies.**

n

N or **n** (en), the fourteenth letter of the alphabet.

nail (nāl), *n.* 1. a pointed piece of metal with a flat head. *Pieces of wood can be fastened together by hammering nails into them.* 2. the hard material at the end of each finger and toe. *Father had dirt under his nails after he pulled the weeds in the garden.* **nails.**
v. 3. to fasten with nails. *We couldn't open the window because it was nailed shut.* **nails, nailed, nail ing.**

na ked (nā′kid), *adj.* 1. having no clothes on; bare. *The naked baby ran into the yard.* 2. without usual covering; without natural covering, as plants or trees. *The naked sword was not in its holder. The airplane flew over the naked mountaintops.* 3. **the naked truth,** the plain truth. *Just tell us the naked truth.* 4. **the naked eye,** the bare eye. *No one should look directly at the sun with the naked eye.* **na ked ly,** *adv.*

name (nām), *n.* 1. a word or words by which a person, place, or thing is known. *The dog's name is Topper, and his owner's name is Howard Foster.* 2. reputation. *A good name is more important than great wealth.* **names.**
v. 3. to give a name to; to call. *The parents named their baby boy after his grandfather.* 4. to tell the names of. *Name three past Presidents.* 5. to choose; appoint. *Mr. Lane was named Secretary of the Treasury.* 6. to set; arrange. *We named June 10, as the day for the boat trip.* **names, named, nam ing.**

name ly (nām′lē), *adv.* that is to say. *Only one man has ever been elected president four times—namely, Franklin D. Roosevelt.*

nap[1] (nap), *n.* 1. a short sleep. *Children usually take a nap in the afternoon.* **naps.**
v. 2. to sleep for a short time. *Grandfather napped in his chair.* **naps, napped, nap ping.**

nap[2] (nap), *n.* the fuzzy surface of some cloth. *The nap of the rug tickled my bare feet.* **naps.**

nap kin (nap′kin), *n.* a small piece of cloth or paper used while eating to protect the clothes and to wipe the fingers and lips. *Napkins are often decorated with attractive colors and patterns.* **nap kins.**

nar cot ic (när kot′ik), *n.* a drug that relieves pain or causes sleep. *Narcotics should be used only when directed by a physician.* **nar cot ics.**

nar rate (nar′āt, na rāt′), *v.* to tell about; to tell a story of. *The movie actor narrated his life as an actor.* **nar rates, nar rat ed, nar rat ing.**

nar ra tor (nar′ā tər), *n.* a person who tells a story. *While the narrator spoke, the actors silently acted out the story.* **nar ra tors.**

nar row (nar′ō), *adj.* 1. not wide. *Parking is not allowed on the narrow street.* 2. close. *The child who played in the street had a narrow escape from injury.* 3. not having a broad view; not having sympathy or understanding. *His narrow mind keeps him from listening to others.* 4. small; limited. *The governor was elected by a narrow margin of two hundred votes.* **nar row ly,** *adv.*
v. 5. to become less wide. *The river narrows as it reaches the city.* **nar rows, nar rowed, nar row ing.**

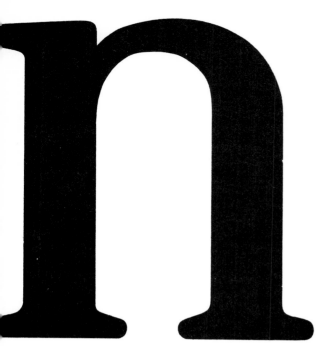

nail:
a. fingernail
b. cross section of the fingertip

sand, āte, bâre, fäther; sent, mē, fėrn; fit, bīke; pot, rōpe, fôrt; run, púll, rüle, cūte; noise, sound; ch, cheese; ng, long; th, thick; ᵺ, those; zh, treasure; ə = a in about, e in waken, i in animal, o in seldom, and u in minus.

n. 6. **narrows,** the narrow part of a river, channel, valley, etc. *They took a canoe trip down the narrows of the river.*

na stur tium (nə stėr′shəm), *n.* a plant, originally from South America, having yellow, red, or orange flowers and leaves that are almost round. *Nasturtiums are common garden flowers.* **na stur tiums.**

nas ty (nas′tē), *adj.* 1. harmful; painful. *Grace received a nasty cut when she fell.* 2. dirty. *The bats built their nests in a nasty old cave at the top of the hill.* 3. not decent; unpleasant. *The nasty weather kept us from going out in the sailboat.* **nas ti er, nas ti est; nas ti ly,** *adv.*

na tion (nā′shən), *n.* a group of people living together under one government, having the same customs and usually speaking the same language. *The United States, Japan, and Sweden are nations. Switzerland also is a nation, although the people speak French, German, or Italian.* **na tions.**

na tion al (nash′ən l), *adj.* 1. belonging to a nation. *The national flag of the United States has stars and stripes.* **na tion al ly,** *adv.*
n. 2. a person who is a citizen of a nation. *Only nationals may vote in a country's elections.* **na tion als.**

na tive (nā′tiv), *adj.* 1. born in a certain place. *She is a native American.* 2. belonging to one because of his place of birth. *Canada is Joe's native land.* 3. natural. *Betty impressed everyone with her native ability to sing.* 4. grown or beginning in a particular place. *Indian corn or maize is a grain native to America.* 5. relating to the first inhabitants, usually not white. *The native tribes welcomed the explorers.* **na tive ly,** *adv.*
n. 6. a person born in a certain country or place. *Dorothy is a native of California.* 7. an animal or plant that was first found in a certain place. *The zebra is a native of Africa.* 8. the people of a less civilized culture, often not white. *The natives believed in evil spirits.* **na tives.**

nat u ral (nach′ə rəl), *adj.* 1. produced by nature; not made by man. *Some natural forests*

nasturtium

are protected by the government. 2. belonging to by nature; happening without teaching. *Eileen has a natural love for art and painting.* 3. normal; usual; to be expected. *It is natural for winters in Florida to be warm.* 4. sincere; not pretending or putting on airs. *The famous author is always natural in talking with people.* 5. of or relating to nature. *The study of animals and plants is called natural science.* 6. that looks like life. *The drawing of you is a natural one.* **nat u ral ly,** *adv.*

nat u ral ly (nach′ə rəl ē), *adv.* 1. in a natural way. *Just speak naturally and the audience will like you.* 2. by nature. *Dora's hair is naturally curly.* 3. of course. *Susan offered me a piece of candy; naturally, I accepted it.*

na ture (nā′chər), *n.* 1. all things in the universe, including the stars, the earth, the moon, the sun, plants, animals, and people. *A storm is one of the forces of nature, because it is not created by man.* 2. natural scenery; trees, lakes, mountains, etc. *The artist painted the beauties of nature.* 3. the instincts or qualities that make a thing or person act in a certain way. *It is the nature of most birds to fly. By nature a cat can climb a tree and a dog can't.* 4. kind; type. *Harry reads books of a business nature.* 5. the character or disposition of a person. *Marjorie has a happy nature.* **na tures.**

naugh ty (nô′tē), *adj.* not behaving properly; refusing to obey; bad. *The naughty boy ate a cookie after his mother said not to.* **naugh ti er, naugh ti est; naugh ti ly,** *adv.*

na val (nā′vl), *adj.* relating to the navy—its people, ships, equipment, or property. *Our naval strength was increased when two new submarines were built.*

nav i gate (nav′ə gāt), *v.* to direct the course of a ship, airplane, etc. *My brother navigates grain ships on the Great Lakes.* **nav i gates, nav i gat ed, nav i gat ing.**

na vy (nā′vē), *n.* 1. the ships, sailors, yards for building and repairing ships, etc. of a nation. *The navy guards its country against attack from the sea and air.* 2. **navy blue,** dark blue. *The color of her dress is navy blue.* **na vies.**

near (nir), *adv.* 1. not far away in time or distance. *My birthday is near. The train drew near.* 2. almost. *Most of us scored near perfect on the test.*
prep. 3. not far from. *The school is near my house, only a block away. I left my bicycle near the school.*
adj. 4. close in association; familiar. *Sylvia and Jane are near friends; they are always together.* 5. close in time. *I will be going to Europe in the near future.* 6. closely related. *Only our near relatives, like Uncle John and Aunt Harriet, will come.* **near er, near est; near ly,** *adv.*
v. 7. to come close to. *The airplane neared the airport and landed.* **nears, neared, near ing.**

near by (nir′bī′ for 1, nir′bī′ for 2), *adj.* 1. not far off. *The nearby ice cream shop gets a lot of business from people in the neighborhood.*

nebula

adv. 2. close at hand. *The dog is sleeping nearby.*

near ly (nir′lē), *adv.* 1. almost. *It is nearly time to go home.* 2. closely. *As nearly as I can tell, the girls are the same age.*

near-sight ed or **near sight ed** (nir′sī′tid), *adj.* able to see clearly only at a short distance. *The near-sighted boy can't see the words on the chalkboard without his glasses.* **near-sight ed ly** or **near sight ed ly,** *adv.*

neat (nēt), *adj.* 1. clean; in order; tidy. *A neat store attracts customers.* 2. pleasant to look at. *The neat colors of the house make it easy to sell.* 3. liking to keep things in order. *A neat person always keeps his clothes tidy.* 4. clever; showing skill. *The trained seals gave a neat performance.* **neat ly,** *adv.*

Ne bras ka (nə bras′kē), *n.* a state in the central United States. *Nebraska is noted for farming, raising hogs and cattle, and meat-packing.*

neb u la (neb′yə lə), *n.* a cloudy mass seen among the stars at night. *A nebula consists of gaseous matter inside the earth's galaxy. Some nebulas outside our own galaxy are actually great groups of stars.* **neb u las** or **neb u lae** (neb′yə lē′).

nec es sar i ly (nes′ə ser′ə lē), *adv.* of necessity. *You don't necessarily have to belong to the country club to have dinner there.*

nec es sary (nes′ə ser′ē), *adj.* 1. needed; required. *A driver's license is necessary to drive a car.* 2. that cannot be avoided; that must happen. *Illness is a necessary result of bad habits in eating and sleeping.* **nec es sar i ly,** *adv.*
n. 3. something that is necessary. *Food, clothing, and shelter are necessaries of life.* **nec es sar ies.**

ne ces si ty (nə ses′ə tē), *n.* 1. something needed; a necessary thing. *Eating is a necessity of life.* 2. a great need of help. *In case of necessity your teacher will go over your work with you.* 3. being poor; being in trouble or in need. *Necessity forced him to borrow money for a few days.* **ne ces si ties.**

neck (nek), *n.* 1. the part of a person or animal that joins the head to the body. *A giraffe has a long neck.* 2. the part of a garment that covers or fits around the neck. *The neck of this dress is too wide.* 3. the most narrow part. *The neck of a vase or bottle is at the top.* 4. **neck and neck,** even. *The horses raced neck and neck and finished in a tie.* **necks.**

neck lace (nek′lis), *n.* an ornament worn around the neck. *A necklace may be made of gems or beads.* **neck lac es.**

neck tie (nek′tī), *n.* a narrow band of cloth worn about the neck, usually under a collar, and tied in front in a knot or bow. *Men's neck-ties have many different patterns or designs.* **neck ties.**

nec tar (nek′tər), *n.* 1. a sweet liquid in flowers. *Bees make honey from the nectars they take from different flowers.* 2. any delicious drink. *We drank the nectar made from the sweet juice of apples.* **nec tars.**

need (nēd), *n.* 1. a want of something; a lack of something that a person or thing must have. *The cities have need of cleaner air and cleaner water. The lonely man is in need of a friend.* 2. poverty; a lack of money or food. *We should help those who are in need.* 3. a time of trouble or sadness. *He was a friend in need, always ready to help others.* 4. **if need be,** if it is necessary. *I will come home early if need be.* **needs.**
v. 5. to require; must have. *Most plants need lots of sunshine to grow. The boy needs new shoes because he grew out of the old ones.* **needs, need ed, need ing.**

nee dle (nē′dl), *n.* 1. a thin, pointed steel tool used in sewing. *A needle has a small hole in one end to hold a thread.* 2. a slender rod used in knitting. *You can hear the needles click together as she knits his socks.* 3. the slender, magnetic part of a compass that indicates direction. *The needle points north.* 4. something that is shaped like a needle used in sewing. *A pine tree has needles instead of leaves. The doctor used a needle to give me the drug.* **nee dles.**
v. 5. to irritate; tease. *The men needled Fred because he caught no fish on the fishing trip.* **nee dles, nee dled, nee dling.**

need less (nēd′lis), *adj.* unnecessary. *It is need-less for you to buy shoes when you already have six pairs.* **need less ly,** *adv.*

need n't (nēd′nt), need not. *You needn't pay for the lunch.*

neg a tive (neg′ə tiv), *adj.* 1. saying no; deny-ing something. *He gave a negative answer to the question.* 2. expressing refusal; lacking a con-structive approach. *His actions clearly showed his negative attitude toward the suggested improvements.* 3. without positive qualities. *The actor was required to portray a very negative character in the play.* 4. less than zero; opposite in sign to a positive number. *The answer to the problem was a negative number.* 5. an electrical charge. *The*

necklace

electrons in an atom have a negative electrical charge.
n. 6. a statement or answer witholding agreement. *The pilot radioed back a negative.* 7. an argument against a proposition. *Even though our school debating team upheld the negative, we won the championship.* 8. a photographic image, in which the lights and shadows are reversed, used for printing positive pictures. *After the negative was developed, he asked the man in the camera store to make six prints.* **neg a tives.**

neg lect (ni glekt′), v. 1. to leave not done; to fail to do. *He went out to play and neglected his homework.* 2. to pay very little attention to. *When we went to the zoo, we were so fascinated by the monkeys that we neglected the other animals. Many people neglect their health.* 3. to forget. *He neglected to close the windows on the night it rained.* **neg lects, neg lect ed, neg lect ing.**
n. 4. a neglecting; lack of care. *The metal toys have all rusted because of neglect.* **neg lects.**

Ne gro (nē′grō), n. a member of one of the races of mankind, having black or brown skin. *African natives are Negro.* **Ne groes.**

neigh bor (nā′bər), n. 1. a person who lives nearby. *I talk with many of our neighbors every day.* 2. a person or thing that is close to another. *Canada is a neighbor of the United States.* **neigh bors.**

neigh bor hood (nā′bər hùd′), n. 1. the part of a town or area where a person lives. *In a big city, some neighborhoods have apartment buildings and others have houses.* 2. the people living near one another. *All the neighborhood welcomed the new family.* 3. **in the neighborhood of,** (a) not far from; about. *The typewriter costs in the neighborhood of seventy dollars.* (b) close to; near. *Toronto is a city in the neighborhood of Lake Ontario.* **neigh bor hoods.**
adj. 4. relating to the neighborhood. *The neighborhood paper comes out every week.*

neigh bor ing (nā′bər ing), adj. 1. nearby. *The hunters heard sounds from a neighboring clump of trees.* 2. next to each other. *The neighboring farms are separated by a fence.*

nei ther (nē′thər, nī′thər), pron. 1. not the one and not the other. *Neither will be asked to go.*
conj. 2. not either. *If you're not going to the movies, neither am I.*
adj. 3. not either. *Neither boy was the correct height for the part in the play.*

ne on (nē′on), n. a gaseous element with no color and no odor. *Colored tubes with neon in them are used for lighting rooms and for advertising.*

neph ew (nef′ū), n. the son of one's brother or sister; the son of one's husband's or wife's brother or sister. *The nephews of your father and mother are your cousins.* **neph ews.**

Nep tune (nep′tūn, nep′tūn), n. the third largest planet. *Neptune can be seen only through a telescope because it is so far from the earth.*

nerve (nèrv), n. 1. one of the fibers or bundles of fibers that carry messages and feelings to

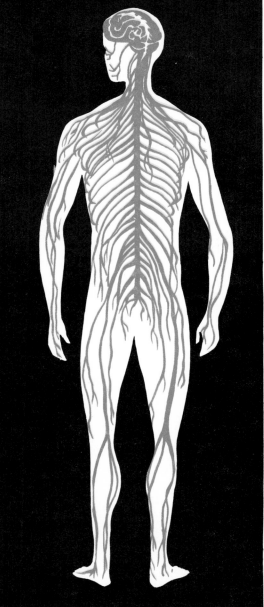

nerves of the human body

and from the brain and all other parts of the body. *Nerves located in the skin of the body help us to feel changes in temperature.* 2. courage; brave spirit. *The early pioneers were men of nerve. Ellen is so shy that it takes nerve for her to make a speech.* **nerves.**
v. 3. to give strength or courage to. *The boys nerved themselves for a visit to the haunted house.* **nerves, nerved, nerv ing.**

ner vous (nèr′vəs), adj. 1. of the nerves. *All the millions of nerves in every part of the body, taken as a whole, are called the nervous system.* 2. fearful; upset; not calm. *The acrobat walking on the tightrope made me nervous.* 3. easily excited or disturbed. *The nervous child wanted the door open while he went to sleep.* **ner vous ly,** adv.

nest (nest), *n.* 1. a place built by a bird for laying eggs. *The robin built its nest outside my window.* 2. a place where some insects or animals live. *Wasps build nests. Mice live in nests. Snakes have nests.* 3. any cozy place to sleep or rest. *The puppy used my old jacket as a nest.* **nests.** *v.* 4. to build and use a nest. *The birds nested in the trees.* 5. to fit into one another. *The boxes were nested to save space.* **nests, nest ed, nest-ing.**

net[1] (net), *adj.* 1. remaining after all expenses have been paid. *If something costs ninety dollars to make and is sold for one hundred dollars, the net profit is ten dollars.* 2. **net weight,** the real weight of goods. *The net weight of a box of candy does not include the weight of the box.* 3. **net price,** the price at which goods are sold. *The net price of an article is the lowest price at which it can be sold and still make a profit.*
v. 4. to get or gain. *The store owner sold ten thousand dollars' worth of goods, but he netted only four hundred dollars after expenses such as rent and salaries were taken out.* **nets, net ted, net ting.**

net[2] (net), *n.* 1. a fabric of cord or thread tied together or woven so that holes of the same size are made. *Nets are sometimes used for catching fish. A hairnet holds a girl's hair in place. A butter-fly net is used to catch butterflies and moths. A mosquito net is used as a protection against mos-quitoes.* 2. a trap. *The guilty person was caught in a net of his own lies.* **nets.**
v. 3. to catch with or as if with a net. *The hobby of the science teacher is netting butterflies. The police netted the man who started the fire in the building.* **nets, net ted, net ting.**

net work (net′wėrk′), *n.* 1. a net. *The fish were caught in the network.* 2. an arrangement of roads, wires, etc. that connect like the ropes in a net. *A network of pipes under the ground carries off the used water from homes and factories.* 3. a combination of radio stations or television stations. *The program was seen not only on one station, but on the network of two hundred stations.* **net works.**

Ne va da (nə vä′də, nə vad′ə), *n.* a state in the western part of the United States. *Nevada's best-known cities are Reno and Las Vegas.*

nev er (nev′ər), *adv.* not ever; not at any time. *Ethel has never been late to school; she is always early. Richard never watches television when he has homework to do.*

nev er the less (nev′ər thə les′), *adv.* in spite of that; however. *The clouds were dark; neverthe-less, the airplane took off and flew above the storm.*

new (nü, nū), *adj.* 1. not known before; invented or found just recently. *Columbus came to a new land. The new song is already very popular.* 2. not the same as the former; different. *We just moved to a new neighborhood. Will we have new teachers this year?* 3. not yet accustomed. *The salesclerk is new to his job.* 4. much better in health. *A short nap made him feel like a new*

nests: a. golden oriole; **b.** wasp; **c.** cliff swallow

man. 5. modern. *We are living in a new age of science.* **new er, new est; new ly,** *adv.*
adv. 6. recently; newly; freshly. *The new-fallen snow sparkled in the moonlight.*

New Hamp shire (nü or nū hamp′shər, nü or nū hamp′shir), *n.* a state in the northeastern part of the United States. *Paper and leather goods are among the important industrial products of New Hampshire.*

New Jers ey (nü jėr′zē, nū jėr′zē), *n.* a state on the northeastern coast of the United States. *New Jersey is important not only for manufacturing but also for its truck farms, dairy farms, and poultry farms.*

New Mex i co (nü mek′si kō′, nū mek′si kō′), *n.* a state in the southwestern part of the United States. *The bright sunshine and dry climate of New Mexico make it popular as a health resort.*

news (nüz, nūz), *n.* 1. information; things that a person has not heard about. *What is the news*

fishing **net**

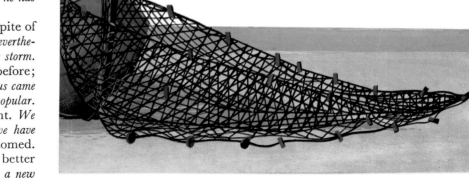

about your brother's new job? 2. recent happenings reported in newspapers and newsmagazines and over television and radio. *We read the news in one of our city's daily newspapers.*

news cast (nüz′kast′, nūz′kast′), *n.* a program of news broadcast over radio or television. *We listen to the six o'clock newscast.* **news casts.**

news pa per (nüz′pā′pər, nūz′pā′pər), *n.* sheets of printed paper, folded together, containing news, advertisements, cartoons, etc. *A newspaper often gives information about motion pictures, books, and concerts, as well as the important events of the day.* **news pa pers.**

New York (nü yôrk′, nū yôrk′), *n.* a state in the eastern part of the United States. *New York City, one of the world's largest cities, is located in southeastern New York. The state of New York has beautiful scenery, with mountains and lakes.*

next (nekst), *adj.* 1. nearest; closest. *The painting is hanging in the next room.* 2. immediately following. *The next number on the program will be a song by the Glee Club.*
adv. 3. in the nearest time, place, or order. *Do your outside reading next. We sit next to each other. Helen talks next, following this speaker.*
prep. 4. beside. *Next to the river is a small house.*

nib ble (nib′l), *v.* 1. to eat with quick, little bites. *The mouse nibbled the cheese. We nibble cookies while watching television.* 2. to bite with caution. *The fish nibbled at our bait.* **nib bles, nib bled, nib bling.**
n. 3. a small bite. *Give the baby a nibble of your cookie. The fish took a nibble of the bait and swam away.* **nib bles.**

nice (nīs), *adj.* 1. agreeable; pleasant. *Did you have a nice time at the picnic? You had nice weather for it. You went with nice girls and boys.* 2. having good manners, good taste, and good language. *He was brought up in a nice family.* 3. having skill and care. *The carvings on the old church show nice workmanship.* 4. showing the ability to know and understand small differences in things. *The artist's nice taste in color makes his work successful.* 5. showing tiny differences; very accurate. *A scale for weighing small articles must have a nice balance.* **nic er, nic est; nice ly,** *adv.*

nick el (nik′l), *n.* 1. a metal that looks somewhat like silver. *Nickel is used in magnets and in mixtures with other metals.* 2. a coin worth five cents. *Coffee used to cost a nickel a cup in restaurants.* **nick els.**

niece (nēs), *n.* the daughter of one's brother or sister; the daughter of one's husband's or wife's brother or sister. *The nieces of your father and mother are your cousins.* **niec es.**

night (nīt), *n.* 1. the time between evening and morning; the time from sunset to sunrise when it is dark. *The stars shine at night.* 2. the darkness of night. *Light a candle to see your way through the night.* **nights.**

night fall (nīt′fôl′), *n.* the ending of the day; the beginning of the night. *Wild birds stop their songs and calls at nightfall.* **night falls.**

night gown (nīt′goun′), *n.* a loose garment worn by some people for sleeping at night. *The little girl in her nightgown kissed her parents goodnight.* **night gowns.**

nine (nīn), *n.* one more than eight; 9. *She said there would be ten people there, but I only counted nine.* **nines.**

nine teen (nīn′tēn′), *n.* one more than eighteen; 19. *Ten plus nine is equal to nineteen.* **nine teens.**

nine ty (nīn′tē), *n.* one more than eighty-nine; 90. *The temperature was over ninety for several very hot days this summer.* **nine ties.**

ninth (nīnth), *adj.* 1. next after the eighth; 9th. *Marty has the ninth seat in the room.*
n. 2. one of nine equal parts. *If you divide the cake into nine parts of the same size, each of us will get one ninth.* **ninths.**

ni tro gen (nī′trə jən), *n.* a gas which forms about four fifths of the air we breathe. *Nitrogen has no color, no taste, and no odor.*

no (nō), *adv.* 1. not at all. *Can you be here no later than noon?* 2. a word used to show that one refuses or does not approve. *No, you can't go to the movies tonight.*
adj. 3. not any. *The dog had no food until we got home. I have no money with me.*
n. 4. the opposite of yes. *My final answer to your question is a definite no.* 5. a vote against. *The noes won.* **noes.**

no ble (nō′bl), *adj.* 1. having great ideals and an excellent character. *The noble doctor has spent his life caring for the poor. George Washington was a noble person.* 2. of a high rank because of family. *In England, a duke is of noble birth.* 3. splendid; majestic. *The Grand Canyon is a noble sight.* **no bler, no blest; no bly,** *adv.*
n. 4. a person of a special privileged family. *The nobles of a country once owned all the land and had all the wealth.* **no bles.**

no ble man (nō′bl mən), *n.* a man who has a noble rank. *A prince is a nobleman.* **no ble men.**

no body (nō′bod′ē), *pron.* 1. no one; no person. *Nobody is here at this time of day.*
n. 2. a person of not much importance. *He was a nobody before he made a fortune.* **no bod ies.**

nod (nod), *v.* 1. to bow the head and raise it quickly to express greeting, acceptance, command, etc. *He nodded to his friend who had said hello. The boy nodded when she asked if he wanted candy, so she gave him some.* 2. to let the head fall forward because of being sleepy. *I started to nod while watching television, so I went to bed.* 3. to move back and forth; bend. *The flowers nodded in the slight wind.* **nods, nod ded, nod ding.**
n. 4. a quick bowing and raising of the head. *A nod from the conductor meant that the orchestra should begin.* **nods.**

noise (noiz), *n.* 1. a sound, especially one that is loud and harsh. *The noise made by the men*

sand, āte, bâre, fäther; sent, mē, fėrn; fit, bīke; pot, rōpe, fôrt; run, pùll, rüle, cūte; noise, sound; ch, cheese; ng, long; th, thick; ~~th,~~ those; zh, treasure; ə = a in about, e in waken, i in animal, o in seldom, and u in minus.

drilling on the street in front of our house woke me up this morning. **nois es.**

v. 2. to tell; to spread by word of mouth. *The story was noised about school that we would have a new principal.* **nois es, noised, nois ing.**

noisy (noiz′ē), *adj.* 1. filled with noise. *The noisy city was a change from the quiet farm.* 2. making noise. *The noisy, old car rattled down the road.* **nois i er, nois i est; nois i ly,** *adv.*

nom i nate (nom′ə nāt), *v.* 1. to choose a candidate for an office; to name. *Mary was nominated for president of the senior class.* 2. to select for a position, job, or office. *The President of the United States nominates his own Cabinet.* **nom i nates, nom i nat ed, nom i nat ing.**

nom i na tion (nom′ə nā′shən), *n.* the selection of a candidate for election. *The senator from New York won the Republican nomination for president; now he will try to beat the man who obtained the Democratic nomination.* **nom i nations.**

none (nun), *pron.* 1. not any; not one. *None of us had the bus fare, so we walked.* 2. no persons or things. *None came to the party, though many were invited.*

adv. 3. not at all. *The car runs none the worse after all that traveling.*

non sense (non′sens), *n.* foolish actions or words; silly talk; an idea or plan that does not make sense. *People once thought that a trip to the moon was nonsense. Babies talk nonsense when they are learning to speak.*

noon (nün), *n.* the middle of the day; twelve o'clock in the daytime. *Our school serves lunch at noon.* **noons.**

nor (nôr), *conj.* and not; and not either. *Neither Paul nor Dick saw the movie, so they want to go. There was neither ice cream nor pop in the refrigerator.*

nor mal (nôr′ml), *adj.* 1. natural; usual; average. *A normal heart beats around seventy-six times a minute. The normal speed here is sixty miles an hour.* **nor mal ly,** *adv.*

n. 2. the usual condition. *His temperature is two degrees above normal.*

Norse (nôrs), *n.* 1. the people of ancient Scandinavia. *The people who lived in Iceland, Sweden, Norway, and Denmark were called the Norse or the Norsemen.*

adj. 2. having to do with the people of ancient Scandinavia. *The Norse expeditions covered thousands of miles over sea and land.*

north (nôrth), *n.* 1. the direction to a person's right when he faces the sunset. *Cold winds blow from the north.* 2. any part of the world or of a country toward the north. *The Eskimo lives in the north.* 3. **the North,** the northern part of the United States. *The North fought the South in the Civil War.* 4. **the North Pole,** the place farthest north on the earth. *Many men tried without success to reach the North Pole, but the first one to do so was Robert Peary in 1909.*

adj. 5. coming from the north. *The north wind blows hard in winter.* 6. to the north; in the direction of north. *The north side of the house faces the highway.*

adv. 7. toward the north. *Birds fly north in the spring.*

North Car o li na (nôrth kar′ə lī′nə), *n.* a

Explorations of the Norsemen

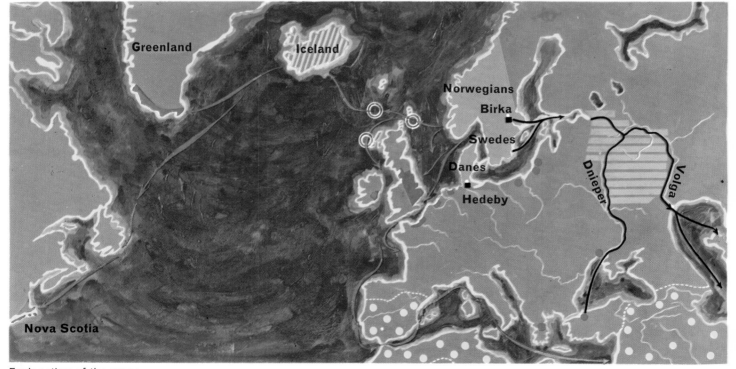

Explanation of the map:

- Norsemen (Scandinavians)
- regions populated by Norsemen
- important cities
- Norse conquests
- Norse settlements
- Norse exploration routes
- regions settled by the Swedes
- Swedish exploration routes
- regions populated by the Moslems

Greenland   Iceland   Norwegians   Birka   Swedes   Danes   Hedeby   Dnieper   Volga   Nova Scotia

state in the southeast United States on the coast of the Atlantic Ocean. *Two important crops of North Carolina are cotton and tobacco.*

North Da ko ta (nôrth də kō′tə), *n.* a state in the north central United States. *North Dakota is a chief producer of wheat and rye.*

north ern (nôr′thərn), *adj.* 1. in or toward the north. *The stars known as the Big Dipper can be seen at night in the northern sky.* 2. from the north. *The northern wind brought snow with it.* 3. of the North. *The Northern army fought the Southern army in the Civil War.*

northern lights, *n. pl.* glowing, moving streaks of light that can be seen at night in regions near the North Pole. *In the United States, the northern lights, or aurora borealis, can often be seen in the states farthest north.*

north west (nôrth′west′), *n.* 1. the direction half the distance between north and west. *Northwest is opposite southeast.* 2. a place or region that lies in this direction from the middle of a country. *Some of the biggest forests in the United States are located in the Northwest.* *adv.* 3. toward the northwest. *The early pioneers traveled northwest to settle the present state of Washington.* *adj.* 4. coming from the northwest. *The northwest wind was bitter cold.*

north west ern (nôrth′wes′tərn), *adj.* 1. in or of the northwest. *A high school principal from the northwestern part of the United States visited our school.* 2. from the northwest. *The northwestern wind is cold.*

nose (nōz), *n.* 1. the part of the face that is just above the mouth of a person or animal. *You breathe air and smell odors through your nose.* 2. ability to smell. *All dogs have good noses, but the noses of hunting dogs are best.* 3. anything that is like a nose because of position or shape. *The nose of an airplane is the part in front.* **nos es.** *v.* 4. to sniff; to smell. *The dog nosed the ground.* 5. to rub with the nose. *The friendly horse nosed my arm.* 6. to search. *The sheriff nosed around town for information about the robbery.* 7. to move carefully. *The ship nosed into the dock.* **nos es, nosed, nos ing.**

nos tril (nos′trəl), *n.* one of the two openings in the nose. *We breathe through the nostrils.* **nos trils.**

not (not), *adv.* a word used to make a sentence mean just the opposite; a word that denies or says no. *He is here. He is not here.*

no ta tion (nō tā′shən), *n.* 1. a note; a short item written down. *The speaker made notations about what he would say.* 2. the signs, symbols, or letters used to stand for numbers, notes, signs, etc. *Music, mathematics, and science have separate systems of notation. The chemistry notation for water is H_2O.* **no ta tions.**

note (nōt), *n.* 1. a very short letter. *Ed's note said he would be home at six o'clock.* 2. a word or sentence written down to help one remember.

The students took notes on the lecture. 3. a short bit of added information. *Some books have notes at the bottom of pages, while others have notes put together at the end of the chapter or book.* 4. a musical tone. *Can you find the note for F sharp on the piano?* 5. the printed sign meaning a certain tone. *Beginning students of the piano start with songs having only a few notes.* 6. greatness and fame. *Abraham Lincoln was a leader of historical note.* **notes.** *v.* 7. to notice; to see. *Mother noted that the window was open.* 8. to write down; to make a note of. *She noted the event in her diary.* **notes, not ed, not ing.**

note book (nōt′buk′), *n.* a book of blank pages for writing notes and comments. *A student uses a notebook to help him remember things.* **note books.**

not ed (nō′tid), *adj.* famous; well-known. *That house is noted for its modern design. The noted scientist spoke to our school assembly.*

noth ing (nuth′ing), *n.* 1. not anything. *Their car is due any minute, but nothing is in sight yet.* 2. something of no importance. *"This cut is nothing," the doctor said.* 3. zero. *Six taken from six leaves nothing.* *adv.* 4. not at all. *The actress looks nothing like her pictures.*

no tice (nō′tis), *n.* 1. an announcement. *The notice on the bulletin board gives the dates of the football games.* 2. an announcement that one will end a contract at a certain time. *We gave notice to the owner of our apartment that we would be leaving in one month.* 3. attention. *Let's get his notice and then talk to him.* 4. a warning. *The driver blew his horn as a notice that he was turning the corner.* 5. a printed comment about something. *The play got very good notices.* **no tic es.** *v.* 6. to see. *Did you notice the new shoes I was wearing yesterday?* 7. to pay attention to; take notice of. *Joan noticed Barbara's new dress right away.* **no tic es, no ticed, no tic ing.**

no ti fy (nō′tə fī′), *v.* to let know; inform. *The teacher notified us that the school would be closed for the holiday.* **no ti fies, no ti fied, no ti fy ing.**

no tion (nō′shən), *n.* 1. an idea. *The girls had no notion of the time, so they were late.* 2. a point of view; opinion. *His notions about foreign people are narrow and not fair.* 3. a sudden thought to do something. *We had a notion to stop at your house, but it was too late.* 4. *pl.* **notions,** small articles such as needles, thread, buttons, etc. *Notions are often sold at a special counter in a big store.* **no tions.**

noun (noun), *n.* a word used to name a person, place, thing, or quality. *Words like girl, Illinois, state, tree, and honor are nouns.* **nouns.**

nour ish (nėr′ish), *v.* 1. to feed; to cause to grow by giving enough of the right food. *Water and sunlight nourished the flowers.* 2. to encourage; hope for; help. *Most actresses nourish the hope*

---

sand, āte, bâre, fäther; sent, mē, fėrn; fit, bīke; pot, rōpe, fôrt; run, pull, rüle, cūte; noise, sound; ch, cheese; ng, long; th, thick; th, those; zh, treasure; ə = a in about, e in waken, i in animal, o in seldom, and u in minus.

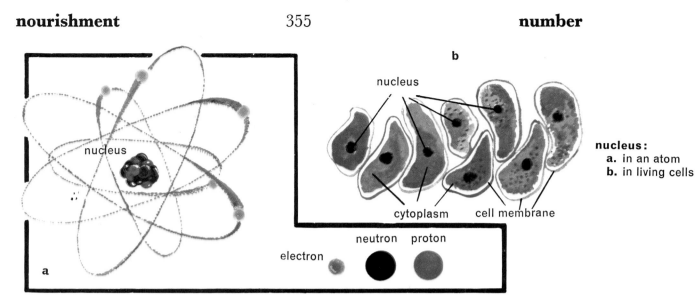

nucleus:
a. in an atom
b. in living cells

that they will become famous. **nour ish es, nour ished, nour ish ing.**

nour ish ment (nėr′ish mənt), *n.* food; anything that nourishes. *That healthy dog gets good nourishment.* **nour ish ments.**

nov el (nov′l), *n.* 1. a long story about imaginary characters and their actions, written to represent real life. *There are many kinds of novels: adventure novels, mystery novels, and romantic novels.* **nov els.**
adj. 2. new; unusual. *Visiting the navy ship was a novel experience for us.*

No vem ber (nō vem′bər), *n.* the eleventh month of the year. *November has thirty days.*

now (nou), *adv.* 1. at the present time. *The television set cannot be delivered now, but it will be here tomorrow. Where are you going to school now?* 2. at the time being talked about; then; next. *The army now began to march in full force against the enemy.* 3. with the way things are. *The car doesn't start; now we will never be on time.* 4. *Now* is used sometimes just to start a sentence. *Now you listen to me. Now, what could have happened?* 5. **just now,** a moment ago. *They left just now.* 6. **now and then,** once in a while. *We see Sam now and then.*
n. 7. the present time. *The baby has been crying until now.*
conj. 8. since. *Now that he is sixteen, he can get a driver's license.*

no where (nō′hwâr), *adv.* not in or at any place; not anywhere. *We looked, but the lost pen was nowhere around the school.*

noz zle (noz′l), *n.* the metal end of a pipe, hose, etc. which serves as an outlet for water or other liquids. *The nozzle of the hose was fixed to send out water in a spray.* **noz zles.**

nu cle ar (nü′klē ər, nū′klē ər), *adj.* having to do with a nucleus. *Nuclear energy is energy released when the nucleus of an atom is split.*

nu cle us (nü′klē əs, nū′klē əs), *n.* 1. the small mass at the center of most living cells. *The nucleus is necessary for cell growth and division.*

2. the central part of an atom. *The nucleus consists of many tiny, tightly packed particles.* 3. the small group which is the center of a larger group. *The nucleus of the club is made up of Kay, Steven, and Elaine, who started it.* **nu cle us es** or **nu clei** (nü′klē ī′, nū′klē ī′).

numb (num), *adj.* 1. lacking in the power to feel. *His toes were numb from the cold.* **numb ly,** *adv.*
v. 2. to make numb. *The cold wind numbs the ears. Fear numbed the rabbit as the fox came close.* **numbs, numbed, numb ing.**

num ber (num′bər), *n.* 1. an amount; the total of persons or things. *The number of students enrolled in our school increased by two hundred this year. Only a small number of people attended the concert on the rainy night.* 2. a word, figure, or numeral that shows exactly how many. *The following are numbers: two, 2, three hundred, and 300.* 3. a large quantity; an indefinite amount. *A number of people saw the parade.* 4. a song, dance, etc. that is performed. *For the next number, the chorus will sing, "This Is My Country."* 5. one issue of a magazine. *Have you seen the latest number of "The Scientists' Journal?"* **num bers.**
v. 6. to give a number to. *Always number the pages of your work.* 7. to include. *Is David numbered among the guests at your party?* 8. to amount to. *Frank's collection of records numbers about two hundred. The states in the United States number fifty.* 9. to limit the number of. *Heavy rains numbered the days we spent at the resort.* **num bers, num bered, num ber ing.**

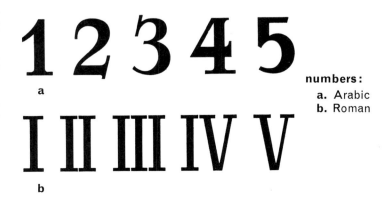

numbers:
a. Arabic
b. Roman

nu mer al (nü′mər l or nū′mər l), *n.* 1. a figure, letter, or word that represents a number. *In class today we learned to write from 1 to 100 in Roman numerals.* **nu mer als.**

adj. 2. representing a number. *Take that paper and write your name on the line after the numeral 1.*

nu mer a tor (nü′mər ā′tər, nū′mər ā′tər), *n.* the term of a fraction that is above the line. *In the fraction ¾, the numerator is 3.* **nu mer a-tors.**

nu mer ous (nü′mər əs, nū′mər əs), *adj.* 1. many. *The children had numerous questions about the arithmetic lesson.* 2. made up of a large number. *The herd of cattle was so numerous that two corrals had to be used to hold them.* **nu mer-ous ly,** *adv.*

nurse (nèrs), *n.* 1. a person who cares for people who are sick. *Nurses in a hospital help the doctors with their patients.* 2. a girl or woman hired to take care of children. *There were many nurses pushing baby carriages in the park last Sunday.* **nurs es.**

v. 3. to care for in sickness. *My older sister nurses the soldiers in the army hospital. My father has been nursing that dying tree for two years.* 4. to give milk to a baby. *The big cat nursed her kittens until they were old enough to find their own food.* **nurs es, nursed, nurs ing.**

nut (nut), *n.* 1. a dry fruit or seed having a hard shell. *We collected a big basket of nuts of different shapes and sizes on our walk through the woods.* 2. the meat of a dry fruit or seed, taken out of the shell. *Nuts are often used on sundaes.* 3. a block of metal having a hole with threads in it. *A nut is screwed onto a bolt having threads to hold the bolt firmly in place.* **nuts.**

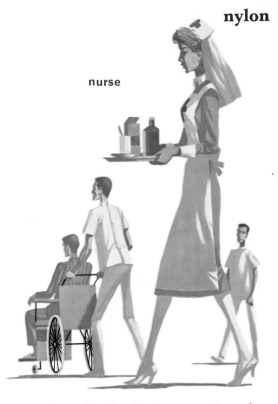

nurse

nut

nut crack er (nut′krak′ər), *n.* a tool used to crack the shells of nuts. *By using a nutcracker, the seed of the nut may be easily removed.* **nut-crack ers.**

nu tri tion (nū trish′ən or nü trish ən), *n.* food. *Proper nutrition is very important to everyone.* **nu tri tions.**

ny lon (nī′lon), *n.* a strong, long-lasting, man-made material. *Nylon is used to make stockings, carpets, clothes, parachutes, and many other things.* **ny lons.**

nutcracker

O

O or **o** (ō), the fifteenth letter of the alphabet.

O (ō), *interj.* oh. *O, why didn't someone tell me?*

oak (ōk), *n.* 1. a large tree having a hard wood and nuts called acorns. *Many kinds of oaks grow in all parts of the world. Three well-known oaks are the black oak, the white oak, and the live oak.* 2. the wood of these trees. *Oak is used for floors and furniture.* **oaks.**
adj. 3. of or from oak. *The oak leaves are beautiful in fall.*

oar (ôr), *n.* 1. a long pole with a flat blade at one end, used to row a boat. *One person usually uses two oars to row a boat.* 2. a person who rows a boat or who is one of those rowing a boat. *The best oar in the race is Sam.* **oars.**

oa sis (ō ā′sis), *n.* a place in the desert where there is water. *Trees, shrubs, and grass grow in an oasis.* (See illustration on following page.)

oat (ōt), *n.* 1. a plant which has seeds that are used as food. *Farmers usually sow oats in the spring and harvest them in the summer.* 2. **oats,** the seeds or grains of the oat plant. *Oats are used to feed farm animals.* **oats.**

oath (ōth), *n.* 1. a formal account or promise calling on God as a witness to the truth of the statement. *Any witness in court must give an oath stating that what he is about to say is true.* 2. the name of God or anything sacred used to show anger or to add force to a statement. *"By heaven," was the oath he used to convince us that he was telling the truth.* 3. a disrespectful word or term as in swearing; a curse. *His oaths were very loud when he hit his finger with the hammer.* 4. **take an oath,** to state solemnly with an oath. *He took an oath stating what he said was true.* 5. **under oath,** to be bound by the taking of an oath. *He gave his testimony under oath.* **oaths.**

oat meal (ōt′mēl′), *n.* oats that are ground into meal. *Oatmeal is a favorite breakfast food.*

ob e lisk (ob′ə lisk), *n.* a tall stone pillar having four sides. *An obelisk comes to a point at the top.* **ob e lisks.**

obey (ō bā′), *v.* 1. to follow the orders of. *Children obey their parents.* 2. to act in agreement with. *Good citizens obey the law.* 3. to submit to. *Teach your dog to obey your commands.* **obeys, obeyed, obey ing.**

ob ject (ob′jikt for 1–3, əb jekt′ for 4 and 5), *n.* 1. a thing that can be seen or touched. *The little shop had many objects made of china. Many historical objects have been found in ancient buried cities.* 2. a purpose; a goal. *The object of this game is to win by getting the highest score. Marian's object is to become a nurse.* 3. a person or thing that causes certain feelings. *The new baby is the object of much love. A teacher often is the object of admiration.* **ob jects.**
v. 4. to make objection; to be opposed. *The fire department objected to our plans for a huge bonfire on school grounds.* 5. to give as a reason for not approving. *The other boys objected that the weather was too cold for playing baseball.* **ob jects, ob ject ed, ob ject ing.**

oar

obelisk

oak tree

a

b

c

oak:
a. acorn
b. branch with leaves and acorns
c. grain of wood

sand, āte, bâre, fäther; sent, mē, fėrn; fit, bīke; pot, rōpe, fôrt; run, pùll, rüle, cūte; noise, sound; **ch, cheese; ng, long; th, thick; th, those; zh, treasure; ə = a** in about, **e** in waken, **i** in animal, **o** in seldom, and **u** in minus.

oasis

ob jec tion (əb jek′shən), *n.* 1. an opposing comment. *John has an objection to make about the work of the committee.* 2. a feeling of not liking. *A quiet person has an objection to noise.* 3. a reason or cause for objecting. *His objection to swimming in the pond is that the water is too deep.* **ob jec tions.**

ob li ga tion (ob′lə gā′shən), *n.* 1. a duty. *You have an obligation to clean up the room after playing in it. I have an obligation to study two hours every night.* 2. something that has to be done because of a debt, promise, etc. *Harold will satisfy his obligation by taking the child to the amusement park.* **ob li ga tions.**

oblige (ə blīj′), *v.* 1. to force; compel; require. *A soldier is obliged to obey anyone of higher rank.*

oboe with carrying case

The man was obliged to drive his car slowly because of the heavy rain. 2. to do a favor for. *Will you oblige Ted by leaving early?* **oblig es, obliged, oblig ing.**

oboe (ō′bō), *n.* a wooden musical instrument that is played by blowing into two thin pieces of reed. *The oboe's smooth and high-pitched sound is an important part of a good orchestra.* **oboes.**

ob ser va tion (ob′zər vā′shən), *n.* 1. the act of seeing, noticing, or watching. *By careful observation doctors can tell the kind of illness a person has.* 2. the act of noting some fact, as in science. *Observations of the height of the river were made every two hours.* 3. a remark; comment. *The superintendent made the observation that a new school is needed.* 4. a being seen; the fact of being noticed. *The famous actor tried to escape observation by wearing dark glasses.* **ob ser va tions.**

ob serv a to ry (əb zėr′və tô′rē), *n.* a building with a telescope and other instruments for studying the stars and planets. *Some observatories are located on high mountains where the air is clearer and there are fewer clouds.* **ob serv a to ries.**

ob serve (əb zėrv′), *v.* 1. to see. *The principal dismissed school early when he observed that a storm was coming.* 2. to follow; obey. *Drivers must observe the speed limits printed on the signs.* 3. to watch carefully; to study. *For two years the scientist observed the behavior of the rare insects through a microscope.* 4. to celebrate. *The Pilgrims first observed Thanksgiving as a day of giving thanks for a good year.* 5. to remark; comment.

sand, āte, bâre, fäther; sent, mē, fėrn; fit, bīke; pot, rōpe, fôrt; run, pùll, rüle, cūte; noise, sound; ch, cheese; ng, long; th, thick; ~~th~~, those; zh, treasure; ə = a in about, e in waken, i in animal, o in seldom, and u in minus.

"It is late," observed John. **ob serves, ob-served, ob serv ing.**

ob serv ing (əb zėr′ving), *adj.* in the habit of noticing. *An observing teacher knows what subjects each of his pupils likes best.* **ob serv ing ly,** *adv.*

ob sta cle (ob′stə kl), *n.* something that stands in the way. *The travelers in the jungle came upon many obstacles that slowed their progress. The fences and ditches were purposely placed as obstacles in the path of the horses in the race.* **ob sta cles.**

ob struct (əb strukt′), *v.* 1. to stop the movement of something; block the way of something. *The fallen tree obstructed the path.* 2. to hinder; to be in the way. *The tall building obstructs our view of the lake.* **ob structs, ob struct ed, ob struct ing.**

ob tain (əb tān′), *v.* to get. *He obtained a ticket to the play.* **ob tains, ob tained, ob tain ing.**

ob tuse (əb tüs′ or əb tūs′), *adj.* 1. not very sharp or pointed; blunt. *These scissors are very obtuse.* 2. very slow in understanding; dull; not bright. *She is a very obtuse student.* **ob tuse ly,** *adv.*

ob vi ous (ob′vē əs), *adj.* easy to see or figure out; clear; plain. *It is obvious that the movie is popular, since the theater is crowded.* **ob vi ous ly,** *adv.*

oc a ri na (ok′ə rē′nə), *n.* a simple, oval-shaped musical wind instrument with holes that produce different notes when covered by the tips of the fingers. *The ocarina has a soft sound like a whistle.* **oc a ri nas.**

oc ca sion (ə kā′zhən), *n.* 1. a particular time; a special event. *On the occasion of the school's anniversary the Governor gave a speech. Going to the carnival was an occasion for the little boy.* 2. an opportunity; a good chance. *Finally we had an occasion to talk with the principal about our plan. I hope you find an occasion to call us while you are traveling.* **oc ca sions.**
v. 3. to cause; bring about. *Her arrival in the city occasioned a party given in her honor.* **oc ca-sions, oc ca sioned, oc ca sion ing.**

oc ca sion al (ə kā′zhən l), *adj.* happening once in awhile. *I get an occasional letter from Anne.*

oc ca sion al ly (ə kā′zhən l ē), *adv.* now and then; once in awhile. *The cat occasionally opens its eyes when it is sleeping.*

oc cu pa tion (ok′yə pā′shən), *n.* 1. business; job. *Mr. Winter's occupation is selling books.* 2. a taking and controlling. *The enemy's occupation of the city lasted for years.* 3. an occupying; being occupied. *The occupation of these houses is set for October first.* **oc cu pa tions.**

oc cu py (ok′yə pī′), *v.* 1. to take up. *The old*

horse jumping over an **obstacle**

magazines occupy a lot of space. Most of his free time is occupied by his hobby. 2. to live in; be in. Who is going to occupy the house next door? 3. to take and control. The army occupied part of the enemy's territory. 4. to hold; to have. He occupies the position of manager in his company.* **oc cu pies, oc cu pied, oc cu py ing.**

oc cur (ə kėr′), *v.* 1. to happen; take place. *Our club's annual picnic occurs every Fourth of July.* 2. to suggest itself in the mind of; to come to the mind of. *It occurred to her that she had enough time to fix her hair. The thought occurred to me that you might prefer the zoo to the museum.* 3. to be found; exist. *Some scholars have counted all the words occurring in Shakespeare's plays.* **oc curs, oc curred, oc cur ring.**

observatory

ocarina

ocean

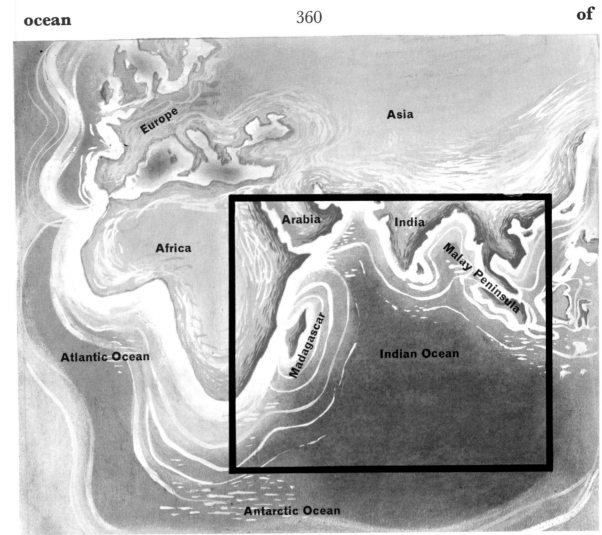

ocher (color)

ocean (ō′shən), *n.* 1. the large body of salt water which covers almost three fourths of the surface of the earth; the sea. *The ocean contains salts and minerals that have washed off the earth's surface.* 2. any of the five main divisions of this body of water—the Atlantic, Pacific, Indian, Arctic, and Antarctic. *The United States is bordered by two oceans.* **oceans.**

ocean og ra phy (ō′shən og′rə fē), *n.* the branch of geography dealing with the ocean. *A student of oceanography learns about the tides, depths, and islands of the oceans.*

oce lot (ō′sə lot′, os′ə lot′), *n.* a wildcat with black spots, living in North America and South America. *An ocelot has short, smooth fur and looks like a small leopard.* **oce lots.**

ocher or **ochre** (ō′kər), *n.* 1. an earth used to give color to paints. *In the paint factory ocher is ground to a powder and mixed with oil.* 2. a brownish-yellow color. *The artist colored his landscape ocher and green.* **ochers** or **ochres.**

o'clock (ə klok′), *adv.* by the clock; according to the clock. *We will meet at eleven o'clock in the morning.*

oc ta gon (ok′tə gon′), *n.* a plane figure having eight sides and eight angles. *A stop sign for traffic is an octagon.* **oc ta gons.**

Oc to ber (ok tō′bər), *n.* the tenth month of the year. *October has thirty-one days.*

oc to pus (ok′tə pəs), *n.* a sea animal having a soft body and eight arms each having two rows of suckers. *An octopus can hold many objects at one time in each of its arms.* **oc to pus es** or **oc to pi** (ok′tə pī).

oc u list (ok′yə list), *n.* a doctor who treats diseases of the eye. *The oculist discovered that John could only see things near to him.* **oc u lists.**

odd (od), *adj.* 1. strange; not usual. *Indian customs seemed odd to the American settlers.* 2. not able to be divided evenly by the number two. *Some odd numbers are 7, 9, and 93.* 3. not matching; not paired. *We found three odd socks which did not go with any of the others that we owned.* 4. not regular; occasional. *The young man is working his way through college by doing odd jobs.* 5. plus a few more. *A thousand-odd letters were written by the candidate before his election.* **odd er, odd est; odd ly,** *adv.*

odor (ō′dər), *n.* a smell. *The girl's perfume has a pleasant odor.* **odors.**

of (ov, uv, əv), *prep.* 1. about; concerning. *We read a story of Robert E. Lee's life. We will think of you when you go.* 2. belonging to. *The news of the day is on at six o'clock. The roof of the house is* brown. *The captain of the ship must be obeyed.* 3. containing. *He bought a box of candy. The family lives in a house of six rooms.* 4. with; having. *That ranch owner is a man of wealth. He is a boy of ability.* 5. made from. *The ancient church had beautiful pillars of stone. The birds live in a nest of twigs and grass.* 6. from. *He lives two miles east of here. Canada is north of the United States.* 7. among. *Some of the dogs were big. He is a leader of men.* 8. by. *The inventions of Edison were many. Have you bought the records of the famous opera singer?* 9. to; before. *Call for me at ten minutes of nine.* 10. that is. *The City of New York is the largest in the United States.*

off (ôf), *adv.* 1. away. *The dog ran off. Christmas is a week off.* 2. away from its present place. *Take your coat off. She took her ring off before washing the dishes.* 3. so that it is not running, working, or going on. *Turn the car's motor off. Everyone preferred to have the radio off.* 4. so as to be less or smaller. *The sales dropped off after Christmas. The pain from his headache passed off after he took some medicine.* 5. completely; in full. *Clean the desk off so that I can use it.* 6. on one's way. *The plane was ready and soon we were off.*

prep. 7. not on; not in place on. *The statue is off its stand. The car is off the road.* 8. from; away from. *The house is two miles off the highway. Let's not get too far off the subject.*

adj. 9. stopped; not connected. *The electricity is off.* 10. not working, taking place, etc. *The trip is off.* 11. not very good; not up to average. *The baseball player had an off day and made three errors.* 12. possible. *There is an off chance he will be here.*

of fend (ə fend′), *v.* to hurt the feelings of; to irritate; make angry. *The remarks about the*

oculist testing vision

ocelot

dress she made offended Eileen. **of fends, of fend- ed, of fend ing.**

of fense (ə fens′ for 1, 2, 4, and 5, ô′fens for 3), *n.* 1. a breaking of a law; crime. *Destroying property is an offense that can be punished by a fine or by a jail term.* 2. an act of offending; hurting someone's feelings. *The child meant no offense in her comment about my large ears.* 3. the group of players in a game whose job it is to score. *The football team has a good defense, but the offense is weak.* 4. **give offense to,** to offend. *Kathy gave offense to her best friend without meaning to.* 5. **take offense,** to feel hurt or offended. *Russell takes offense if you joke about his car.* **of fens es.**

of fen sive (ə fen′siv), *adj.* 1. unpleasant; disagreeable. *There was an offensive odor in the air.* 2. of or used for an attack. *The army has many offensive weapons.* **of fen sive ly,** *adv.*
n. 3. an attack of forces. *The offensive usually begins a battle.*

of fer (ôf′ər), *v.* 1. to say that one is willing. *We offered to help Mr. Eliott start his car.* 2. to present as a suggestion. *The President offered a plan for peace.* 3. to give. *This book offers helpful cooking hints.* **of fers, of fered, of fer ing.**
n. 4. the act of offering. *The Indians accepted the offer of twenty-four dollars in exchange for Manhattan Island.* **of fers.**

of fer ing (ôf′ər ing), *n.* 1. something, usually money, given to the support of a church. *I placed my offering in the collection plate as it was passed among the people in the church.* 2. a giving; a presenting. *An offering of assistance was made to those in need.* 3. a gift. *The girl so loved the artist's work that he made her an offering of one of his paintings.* **of fer ings.**

of fice (ôf′is), *n.* 1. a place or room where business is done or a service is supplied. *The*

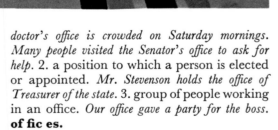

pipeline carrying **oil**
to a refinery

oil can for lubricating
machinery

carafe of salad **oil**

doctor's office is crowded on Saturday mornings.
Many people visited the Senator's office to ask for
help. 2. a position to which a person is elected
or appointed. Mr. Stevenson holds the office of
Treasurer of the state. 3. group of people working
in an office. Our office gave a party for the boss.
of fic es.

of fi cer (ôf′ə sər), n. 1. a person holding some
office. Men and women become officers in a business,
a club, or a government. The National Bank has
twenty-five officers. 2. a policeman. Officer, which
way is Oak Street? 3. a man who commands
in the armed services. Captains and generals
are two kinds of officers. **of fi cers.**

of fi cial (ə fish′əl), n. 1. a person having a
public position; person who is in charge of
some public work. The mayor is the chief official
of the city. The Assistant Secretary of the Army is
an official of the national government. 2. a person
who holds an office. The important officials of a

business are president, secretary, and treasurer.
of fi cials.
adj. 3. having to do with a position of authority. The official duties of the Secretary of Agriculture
take about ten hours a day. 4. coming from someone in authority. The official announcement said
that Mr. Hays had won the election. **of fi cial ly,**
adv.

of ten (ôf′ən, of′ən), adv. many times; frequently. The wind often blows across the lake.

oh (ō), interj. a sound that expresses surprise,
interest, or sorrow. There were laughs, sighs,
and shouts of "Oh! how beautiful" around the tree
on Christmas morning.

Ohio (ō hī′ō), n. 1. a state in north central
United States known for its farm products
and for the manufacture of iron and steel
and rubber tires. Ohio has a number of ports on
Lake Erie. The rich resources of coal, oil, natural
gas, and clay in Ohio help its industries to grow.
2. a river in the United States. The Ohio River
flows into the Mississippi River.

oil (oil), n. 1. a greasy liquid substance obtained
from animals, plants, or minerals. Olive oil
is used for salads. Whale oil is used in perfumes.
2. a petroleum, which is obtained from the
earth. Pipelines carry oil across the country from
oil fields in Texas and Oklahoma. Oil is used to
lubricate machinery. 3. an artist's paint made
with oil. The artist painted with oils. 4. a painting done in oils. There is an exhibit of oils at the
Art Institute. **oils.**
v. 5. to put oil on or in. To keep clocks, automobiles, machinery, and bicycles working smoothly,
you must be sure to oil them regularly. **oils, oiled,
oil ing.**

oka pi (ō kä′pē), n. an animal somewhat like
a short giraffe, which lives in Africa. An okapi
has stripes on its legs. **oka pis.**

Okla ho ma (ō′klə hō′mə), n. a state in south
central United States. Oklahoma's leading
products are oil, cattle, and cotton.

old (ōld), adj. 1. having lived or existed for a
long time. The old man needs a cane to help him
walk, but he still is young at heart. Some old buildings and roads in Italy were built over two thousand
years ago. 2. of age. My dog is six years old. The
trees in one of the forests in California are one
thousand years old. 3. belonging to the past.
Dad likes to visit his old home town. 4. known for
a long time. He is an old friend. 5. coming down
to us from long ago. We all followed the old
custom of having turkey for Thanksgiving. 6. not
new. Wear old clothes when you paint the room.
old er or **eld er, old est** or **eld est.**
n. 7. an old or earlier time. In days of old,
knights wore armor.

old en (ōld′n), adj. ancient; long ago. In olden
days, knights fought in battles with swords and
shields.

old-fash ioned (ōld′fash′ənd), adj. 1. suited to
the past; doing and thinking in the manner

sand, āte, bâre, fäther; sent, mē, fėrn; fit, bīke; pot, rōpe, fôrt; run, pùll, rüle, cūte; noise, sound; ch, cheese;
ng, long; th, thick; ~~th~~, those; zh, treasure; ə = a in about, e in waken, i in animal, o in seldom, and u in minus.

of long ago. *My parents have some old-fashioned ideas about music.* 2. of a previous style; no longer in fashion. *Grandmother wears old-fashioned hats.*

ole an der (ō'li an'dər), *n.* an evergreen shrub with white or pink flowers. *Oleanders are poisonous.* **ole an ders.**

ol ive (ol'iv), *n.* 1. the small, oval fruit of a tree growing in warm climates. *Both black and green olives are good to eat when served alone or when mixed with salads, sauces, and other foods.* 2. the tree on which olives grow. *Olives grow in Spain and California.* 3. the wood of the olive tree. *Olive is used in making fine cabinets.* 4. a yellowish-green, which is the color of olives that are not ripe. *Her dress and hat are olive.* **ol ives.**

Olympic games, *n. pl.* 1. games of physical or mental strength or skill held every four years in ancient Greece in honor of the god Zeus. *Athletes tested their skills at the Olympic games.* 2. modern athletic games held every four years in different countries. *The 1968 Olympic games were held in Mexico City.*

omis sion (ō mish'ən), *n.* 1. a leaving out. *The omission of the principal's name on this pass means it isn't good.* 2. something omitted or not included. *The omissions in the list of states made the list worthless.* **omis sions.**

omit (ō mit'), *v.* 1. to leave out. "*You may omit problems one and five,*" *said the teacher.* 2. to neglect; leave not done. *The boy omitted the sidewalk in shoveling the snow.* **omits, omit ted, omit ting.**

om niv o rous (om niv'ə rəs), *adj.* 1. eating any kind of food, whether animal or vegetable. *Humans are omnivorous beings.* 2. taking in all kinds of things. *Bill is an omnivorous reader.* **om niv o rous ly,** *adv.*

on (on), *prep.* 1. above and held up by. *The lamp is on the table.* 2. upon; against. *Motion pictures are shown on a white screen.* 3. near; close to. *The house is built on the river.* 4. by means of. *I will talk with you on the telephone.* 5. having to do with; about. *The lecture was on the history of our state.* 6. during; at the time of. *The party is on Saturday.* 7. that is a part of. *My uncle on the police force wears a uniform.*

olive:
  a. branch with leaves and fruit
  b. halved olive showing seed

adv. 8. tight to something. *Hold on to the railing.* 9. toward something. *We went on home.* 10. in a forward direction. *Cross the street and go on to the next corner.* 11. without stopping. *She talked on.* 12. into a position of operating. *Now turn the motor on.*

adj. 13. taking place. *The game is on in spite of the rain.* 14. operating. *The light is on.*

once (wuns), *adv.* 1. one time. *We met once and never after that.* 2. formerly. *Horses once were used to plow fields; now we use tractors.* 3. at any time; ever. *If this car once stops, we'll never get it started again.*

n. 4. a single time. *Just this once, I'll stay home.*

Once also has the following special meanings:
at once, (a) immediately. *Tell the doctor to*

okapis

oleander

come at once. (b) at the same time. *Let's all start the song at once.*

once and for all, finally; completely. *We destroyed the weeds once and for all.*

once in awhile, now and then. *Once in awhile I take a nap in the afternoon.*

once upon a time, a long time ago. *Once upon a time there lived a girl named Snow White.*

one (wun), *n.* 1. the number that is written as 1. *One comes before two.* 2. a single person or thing. *He is the one we chose as our leader.* **ones.**

pron. 3. a single person or thing. *I saw one of his drawings.* 4. any person. *The book is short; one can read it in an hour.* 5. **one by one,** one after the other. *The teacher called the children one by one.*

adj. 6. being a single person or thing. *One book fell off the shelf.* 7. some. *One day we'll meet again.* 8. **all one,** of no great meaning; all the same. *It is all one to me if you want to go or stay.* 9. **at one,** united. *The class was at one in their choice of a president.*

one self (wun'self′), *pron.* 1. one's own self, used to show emphasis. *One should take care of oneself.* 2. be oneself; to have control of one's own mind and body; act in a natural way. *To fully enjoy life one must be oneself.*

on ion (un'yən), *n.* a vegetable with a bulb that grows beneath the ground. *Onions have a sharp taste and odor and are eaten either raw or cooked.* **on ions.**

on ly (ōn'lē), *adj.* 1. single; sole; being the only one. *He is the only person who can do the job. This is the only street through the center of town.* 2. best; finest. *This town is the only town for me.* *adv.* 3. no more than; just. *The car has only one gallon of gasoline. The store needs a boy to work*

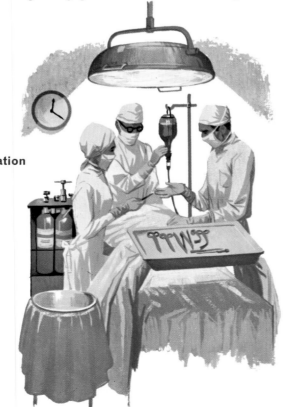

operation

only on Saturdays. 4. without others; solely. *That dog obeys only his owner. Only he came forward to help.*

on to (on'tü), *prep.* to a place on. *George was the first boy to get onto the bus.*

on ward or **on wards** (on'wərd, on'wərdz), *adv.* 1. toward a place ahead; forward. *The football team moved onward to the goal.*

adj. 2. forward; moving ahead. *Darkness prevented the onward march of the explorers.*

ooze (üz), *v.* 1. to flow or leak out slowly. *The honey oozed from the top of the bottle. My courage oozed away the longer I waited.* **ooz es, oozed, ooz ing.**

n. 2. an oozing; something that oozes. *On some tree trunks you can see the ooze of the sap.* 3. soft mud at the bottom of a pond, river, or lake. *The children stirred up the ooze, and the water became dirty.* **ooz es.**

open (ō'pən), *v.* 1. to move from a shut position. *Open the door for Mother. Who opened all the drawers in my bureau?* 2. to begin. *The ceremonies opened with a song.* 3. to begin business. *The new store will open tomorrow.* 4. to remove the outer cover to see what is inside. *Open the envelope and read the letter. Open the packages.* 5. to bring out of a folded state; spread out. *We opened the road map to see where we were. The bud soon opened into a flower.* 6. **open into** or **open onto,** to lead to. *This door opens onto the porch.* 7. **open a person's eyes,** to make aware; awaken. *The exhibition at school opened Father's eyes to my talent.* **opens, opened, open ing.**

adj. 8. not closed or shut. *The dog wandered out of the open door.* 9. not closed in; not blocked; not sealed or tied. *The horses ran around in the open field. Don't look inside the open letter—it isn't yours.* 10. spread out; not folded up. *Don't try to take the open umbrella through the door.* 11. not private; public. *Sometimes newspapers print open letters to mayors or to citizens. The public is invited to the open meeting of the school board.* 12. honest and fair. *We must keep an open mind about many issues.* 13. not decided or settled. *Whether Dad will come with us is still an open question.* 14. **open to,** (a) subject to; liable to. *A man in public office is open to criticism.* (b) ready to listen and consider. *Mother is open to suggestions on how to arrange the furniture.* **open ly,** *adv.*

n. 15. outdoors. *The boys like to sleep and camp in the open.*

open ing (ō'pən ing), *n.* 1. an act of opening. *The managers invited the public to the opening of the new hotel.* 2. an open place; a clear space. *The opening in the woods was a good location for our camp.* 3. the start; the beginning. *We arrived too late for the opening of the football game.* 4. a job or position to be filled. *There are openings for salesmen at Krem's Department Store.* 5. a chance. *We waited for an opening in the discussion to ask our question.* **open ings.**

opium:

a. seed pod of
the opium poppy
b. opium poppy

op era (op′ər ə), *n.* a play in which the actors sing instead of speak. *The soprano played the part of Carmen in the opera.* **op eras.**

op er ate (op′ər āt′), *v.* 1. to be in action; work; run. *The electric fan operates smoothly.* 2. to cause something to run or work. *The engineer operates the engine of a train. The passenger pushed one of the buttons which operated the elevator.* 3. to work on the body, usually with instruments, to restore it to health. *The doctor operated to remove the boy's tonsils.* 4. to be in charge of. *The busy man operates five motion-picture theaters.* **op er ates, op er at ed, op er at ing.**

op er a tion (op′ər ā′shən), *n.* 1. an operating; working. *The operation of our democracy has continued since 1789.* 2. the way in which something works. *Finally I understand the operation of an airplane.* 3. a treatment by a doctor, usually done with instruments, to remedy a disease or other health problem. *An operation was performed on the man's chest.* 4. an action by a military force. *The practice operations will take place in the Pacific Ocean.* **op er a tions.**

op er et ta (op′ər et′ə), *n.* a short opera, usually amusing, with a simple plot and some spoken dialogue. *The music of an operetta is light and pleasant.* **op er et tas.**

opin ion (ə pin′yən), *n.* 1. a belief that is based upon one's own way of thinking. *It was Tom's opinion that the purpose of the club was a good one.* 2. a judgment or impression. *In everyone's opinion, George is a very friendly and pleasant person.* 3. a professional report. *What is the doctor's opinion about your headaches?* **opin ions.**

opi um (ō′pē əm), *n.* a drug obtained from the seed cases of a certain poppy, called an opium poppy. *Doctors use opium to relieve a patient's pain.*

opos sum (ə pos′əm), *n.* a small animal that commonly lives in trees in the southern United States and moves about mostly at night. *An opossum will pretend to be dead when it is scared by an enemy.* **opos sums.**

op po nent (ə pō′nənt), *n.* a person who is against another in a fight, game, business, etc. *Our school's opponent for the game is Deerfield School.* **op po nents.**

op por tu ni ty (op′ər tü′nə tē, op′ər tū′nə tē), *n.* a time or chance that is just right for doing something. *Let's find an opportunity to talk to the principal about the picnic.* **op por tu ni ties.**

op pose (ə pōz′), *v.* 1. to be against; act against. *The mayor opposed the building of a new highway.* 2. to contrast with; to be set against. *Her unhappy expression opposes all the happy faces at the party.* **op pos es, op posed, op pos ing.**

op po site (op′ə zit), *adj.* 1. contrary; completely different; exactly reverse. *Those two men have opposite opinions on how to make a business run. They went together to the corner, then went in opposite directions.* 2. at the other end. *The lake is on the opposite side of the park.* 3. at either end. *We live in opposite parts of the city.* *n.* 4. anything that is the reverse of something else. *Up is the opposite of down. Happiness is the opposite of sadness.* **op po sites.** *prep.* 5. across from. *The candy store is opposite the school.*

op po si tion (op′ə zish′ən), *n.* 1. a being against; resistance; an opposing. *The American colonies clearly stated their opposition to the tax on tea.* 2. a person or persons opposing. *The champion's opposition in the race is a very good runner.* 3. the political party opposed to another. *The opposition was successful when its bill was passed by the city council.*

or (ôr), *conj.* 1. a word used to express a difference or a choice. *Do you want soup or tomato juice?* 2. a word used with *either* to show a choice. *You may either go or stay here.* 3. in other words; namely. *The index, or list of important words used, appears at the end of a book.*

or al (ô′rəl), *adj.* 1. spoken; uttered by mouth. *The teacher gave an oral report on the progress of her pupils.* 2. of the mouth. *The dentist gave me an oral examination.* **oral ly,** *adv.*

or ange (ôr′inj), *n.* 1. a round fruit with a reddish-yellow color. *Oranges are usually peeled before they are eaten.* 2. an evergreen tree, growing in warm climates, on which the fruit grows. *The blossoms of the orange smell sweet.* 3. reddish-yellow; the color of oranges. *Orange is the perfect color for our curtains.* **or ang es.** *adj.* 4. having the color of an orange. *The girl had an orange ribbon in her hair.* (See illustration on following page.)

(See illustration on following page.)

---

sand, āte, bâre, fäther; sent, mē, fèrn; fit, bīke; pot, rōpe, fôrt; run, pùll, rüle, cūte; noise, sound; ch, cheese; ng, long; th, thick; ~~th,~~ those; zh, treasure; ə = a in about, e in waken, i in animal, o in seldom, and u in minus.

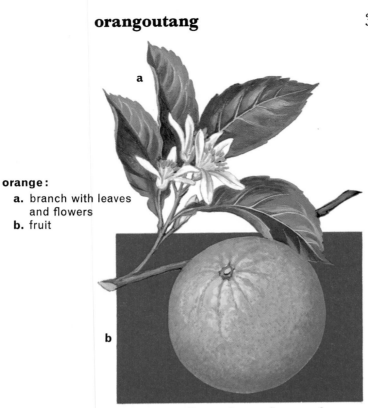

orange:
a. branch with leaves and flowers
b. fruit

orang ou tang (ô rang′ü tang′), var. of **orang-utan.**

orang u tan (ô rang′ü tan′), *n.* a large ape with long arms that lives in trees in Sumatra and Borneo. *The orangutan has reddish-brown hair and may reach a height of four to five feet.* **orang u tans.**

or bit (ôr′bit), *n.* 1. the path of one body going around another. *It takes one year for the earth to travel in its orbit around the sun. Man-made satellites travel in an orbit around the earth.* **or bits.** *v.* 2. to move in an orbit around; to circle. *The moon orbits the earth.* **or bits, or bit ed, or bit ing.**

or chard (ôr′chərd), *n.* 1. a piece of land on which fruit trees are grown. *The apple orchard was two miles long.* 2. the trees that grow in an orchard. *The orchard blooms in the spring.* **or chards.**

or ches tra (ôr′kis trə), *n.* 1. a group of players on various musical instruments. *The orchestra began to play when the conductor gave the signal.* 2. the seats on the main floor of a theater. *We sat in the orchestra at the last play we attended.* **or ches tras.**

or deal (ôr dēl′), *n.* 1. any severe test; an experience that is not pleasant. *Taking an examination is always an ordeal for me.* 2. an old way of finding out a person's guilt by making him go through dangerous tests. *In the ancient ordeal by fire, the person was guilty if the fire burned him and innocent if he wasn't touched by the flames.* **or deals.**

or der (ôr′dər), *n.* 1. a command; an instruction. *He was given an order to appear at the office at nine o'clock.* 2. condition. *Get your room in good order.* 3. the way in which things follow one another. *If our last names are in alphabetical order, Betty Brown will be called after Fred Billings.* 4. a condition of peace and quiet. *The policemen restored law and order to the town.* 5. a request; a statement of things one wishes to purchase. *Father sent in his order for Christmas cards.* 6. the things that have been bought. *Your order from the store has been delivered.* 7. a group of people belonging to a religious or social organization. *That order of priests does much good among the poor. The Order of Sportsmen holds a picnic every year for children.* 8. a group of related plants or animals. *All ants belong to the same order.* **or ders.**

v. 9. to command; to direct. *The Fire Chief ordered his men to leave the burning building.* 10. to request; ask for something one wants to purchase. *Order your tickets early for the concert.* 11. to put in proper arrangement. *I can order my work better now that I have more time.* **or ders, or dered, or der ing.**

Order also has the following special meanings:

in order, in a neat arrangement. *The schoolroom is always kept in order.*

in order to, as a means to. *People must eat in order to live.*

on the order of, somewhat like. *That new hat she bought is on the order of a cap.*

out of order, not working. *The machine is out of order.*

or der ly (ôr dər li), *adj.* 1. in a proper order or arrangement; well-kept. *Mother has an orderly kitchen.* 2. keeping a good order; well-behaved. *We have an orderly class.* 3. having this characteristic. *He has a very orderly mind.*

n. 4. a soldier who assists a military officer. *My brother is an orderly in the army.* 5. a male hospital worker. *The orderly straightened up the room before the new patient was brought in.* **or der lies.**

orangutan

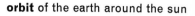

orbit of the earth around the sun
  a. spring equinox
  b. summer solstice
  c. autumn equinox
  d. winter solstice

or din ar i ly (ôrd′n er′ə lē), *adv.* as a rule; usually; normally. *Grandfather ordinarily takes a walk after dinner.*

or din ary (ôrd′n er′ē), *adj.* 1. usual; normal. *The ordinary time it takes to drive downtown is twenty minutes.* 2. not special; average. *His marks show that he is an ordinary student in all subjects but mathematics. The movie we saw was just an ordinary spy story.*

ore (ôr), *n.* a rock or mineral that has metal in it. *Iron ore is dug from the ground in Minnesota and shipped to Chicago for the making of steel.* **ores.**

Or e gon (ôr′ə gon′, ôr′ə gən), *n.* a state on the west coast of the United States. *Oregon is noted for its forests and its fisheries.*

or gan (ôr′gən), *n.* 1. a musical instrument that has a keyboard as well as levers worked by the feet which send streams of air into pipes. *Churches often have pipe organs. Smaller electric organs are used in the home and do not have pipes.* 2. a part of an animal or plant that has a special duty. *The eyes, heart, and stomach are a few of the organs found in men and animals.* 3. a newspaper or other publication. *The radio manufacturer publishes a house organ called "Air Waves."* **or gans.**

or gan i za tion (ôr′gən ə zā′shən), *n.* 1. the act of organizing; a uniting and grouping of people. *The organization of the new club kept its officers busy.* 2. a group of people who work together for a certain purpose. *The Stamp Club is an organization of stamp collectors who meet together to learn about stamps. The Uptown Women's Club is an organization that works for charity.* 3. outlining; planning; the way in which something is put together. *The organization of your thoughts is an important first step in writing a good paper.* **or gan i za tions.**

or gan ize (ôr′gən īz′), *v.* 1. to work out the details for; to plan. *The two girls helped to organize the program for the school assembly.* 2. to form into a group. *The coal miners organized and asked for safer working conditions.* 3. to arrange; to put in order. *Organize the facts in your paper before you start to write it.* **or gan iz es, or gan ized, or gan iz ing.**

ori ent (ôr′ē ənt′), *v.* 1. to get used to a place or a situation. *The new boy in school is orienting himself to his new surroundings.* 2. to put into a certain position concerning north, south, east, and west. *Sailors have oriented themselves by watching the stars.* **ori ents, ori ent ed, ori ent ing.**

n. 3. **the Orient,** the Far East, or eastern Asia. *Chinese people come from the Orient.*

orchestra

piano
string instruments
conductor
woodwind instruments
brass wind instruments
harp
percussion instruments

or i gin (ôr′ə jin), *n.* 1. the persons from whom one is descended. *The boys and girls in the class were of German, Russian, Polish, and Italian origin.* 2. the beginning; the thing from which something comes. *Our custom of shaking hands had its origin in the days when a man held out his right hand to show he carried no weapon.* **or i gins.**

orig i nal (ə rij′ə nl), *adj.* 1. earliest; first. *The original Americans were Indians. Your second speech was better than your original speech.* 2. not copied; new; novel. *She has an original way of using colors in her paintings.* 3. able to present new ideas. *The stories Sam writes show that he has an original mind.* **orig i nal ly,** *adv.*
n. 4. the one from which copies are made. *The original of this drawing is in a museum in Italy.* **orig i nals.**

orig i nal ly (ə rij′ə nl ē), *adv.* 1. at first. *Our land was originally covered with forests.* 2. in a new or different way. *Some originally created works of art seem strange to us.*

or na ment (ôr′nə mənt for 1 and 2, ôr′nə-ment′ for 3), *n.* 1. something pretty used for decoration. *Ornaments are hung on a Christmas tree.* 2. a person who adds honor to a group. *The famous and well-liked professor is an ornament to the profession of teaching.* **or na ments.**
v. 3. to decorate. *The Christmas tree was orna-mented with lights and brightly colored objects.* **or na ments, or na ment ed, or na ment-ing.**

or phan (ôr′fən), *n.* 1. a child whose parents are dead. *Some orphans live in homes run by churches.* **or phans.**
v. 2. to make an orphan of. *Thousands of children were orphaned during the war.* **or phans, or phaned, or phan ing.**

os trich (ôs′trich), *n.* a very large bird of Africa with a long neck, long legs, and large soft tail feathers. *The ostrich cannot fly, but it can run very fast.* **os trich es.**

oth er (u<u>th</u>′ər), *adj.* 1. different. *There are answers to this problem other than the one you gave. I asked the salesman to call some other day.* 2. re-maining. *She held her baby with one arm and clutched her packages with the other one.* 3. addi-tional. *She and two other girls left early.*
pron. 4. the remaining one; the other one. *Raise one hand, and then raise the other.* 5. another person or thing. *You walk with one child, and I'll walk with the other.* **oth ers.**
adv. 6. otherwise. *I cannot do other but leave.*
Other also has the following special mean-ings:
every other, every second. *Read every other page in the book.*
on the other hand, but; opposite to this. *It looks like a beautiful day for a picnic; on the other hand, it might rain.*
the other day, a few days ago. *I saw you in the barbershop the other day.*

oth er wise (u<u>th</u>′ər wīz′), *adv.* 1. differently.

ostrich

You may be right, but I believe otherwise. 2. in other ways. *The boys on the team are tired, but otherwise they are in good shape.* 3. or else. *The doctor told Sylvia to stay home; otherwise she would be here.*
adj. 4. different. *His answer could not be other-wise, because it was the truth.*

ot ter (ot′ər), *n.* 1. an animal that lives in and near water, having feet with webs between the toes for swimming and a long, slightly flat tail. *Otters catch and eat fish.* 2. the fur of this animal. *Otter is thick and soft.* **ot ters.**

ouch (ouch), *interj.* a sound made in showing sudden pain. *George said "Ouch!" when he hurt his finger.*

ought (ôt), *v.* 1. to have a duty. *You ought to allow others to have their rights, too.* 2. to be likely. *He ought to have been here by now.* 3. to be wise. *You ought to wear a coat on a cold day like this.* 4. to be right or suitable. *Running in the halls between classes ought to be stopped.*

ounce (ouns), *n.* 1. a unit of weight. *An ounce is $\frac{1}{16}$ of a pound in ordinary weight. An ounce is $\frac{1}{12}$ of a pound in troy weight, which is used for weighing drugs and precious metals.* 2. a measure of liquids. *An ounce is $\frac{1}{16}$ of a pint.* 3. a small amount. *The coach wondered if his players would have an ounce of strength left during the last quarter of the game.* **ounc es.**

our (our), *adj., pron.* of us; belonging to us. *The dog in that car is our dog.*

ours (ourz), *pron.* the one or ones belonging to us. *That new car is ours.*

our selves (our selvz′), *pron. pl.* our own selves. *We built the little hut by ourselves.*

out (out), *adv.* 1. away from the inside or center. *The air leaked out of the tire. The dancers stepped in and out of the big circle.* 2. away from home or a usual place. *I guess Dad went out for lunch.* 3. into the open; into public knowledge. *The designs for the new automobiles finally came out.* 4. so as to be finished. *The question sheet is filled out.* 5. loudly. *Shout your name out.* 6. so as to be no longer burning or giving light. *The fire went out.* 7. so as to be no longer in fashion. *That hairstyle is going out.* 8. on sale. *That author's new book is coming out next week.* 9. to the end. *The teams fought it out for second place.* 10. seeking to belong; competing openly. *More than two hundred boys tried out for the team.* 11. into activity; so as to be started or begun. *A fire broke out.* 12. in games, so as to be retired from a play. *He was put out at bat by three strikes.*
adj. 13. away from school or work. *He is out because of a cold.* 14. away from the truth. *She is out in her estimate of the cost.* 15. at a loss of money. *John was out five dollars.* 16. in games, retired from play. *The runner was out at first base.*
prep. 17. out of; through. *Walk out that door.*
v. 18. to become known. *The truth will out.*
n. 19. in baseball, failure to reach base safely. *The last out left two men on base.* **outs.**

Out also has the following special meanings:

out and away, by far. *This book is out and away the best in the store.*

out of, (a) from within. *The water came out of the pipe.* (b) from a number of. *Pick your choice out of these pencils.* (c) not having any. *The car is out of gas.* (d) from. *He lives in a house made out of wood.*

out burst (out′bėrst′), *n.* a sudden display of strong feeling or energy. *His outburst of anger when we were late was understandable.* **out bursts.**

out come (out′kum′), *n.* a result; the way something turns out. *What was the outcome of your test?* **out comes.**

out doors (out′dôrz′), *n.* 1. the world outside of buildings; the open air. *Fishermen enjoy the outdoors.*
adv. 2. outside a building; out in the open air. *We played outdoors on the first sunny day of spring.*

out er (out′ər), *adj.* 1. on the outside; external. *The package had an outer cover of paper. Coats and jackets are outer garments.* 2. being beyond the earth's atmosphere; being beyond the sun and planets. *Man makes new discoveries about outer space every day.*

out fit (out′fit′), *n.* 1. the articles necessary for a special purpose. *An outfit for fishing includes bait, rod, line, and the proper clothes. A plumber's outfit consists of tools.* 2. clothes. *What outfit will you wear to church on Sunday?* 3. a group of persons working together. *Several soldiers in that outfit come from the same state.* **out fits.**
v. 4. to equip; supply; furnish. *Mother outfitted the boys with new suits, shoes, and ties.* **out fits, out fit ted, out fit ting.**

out law (out′lô′), *n.* 1. a criminal; a person who runs away from the law. *The police hunted for the outlaw.* **out laws.**
v. 2. to make or declare illegal. *The city outlaws parking on the wrong side of the street.* 3. to take away the protection of the law from someone; to make an outlaw. *The military government outlaws men with different political views.* **out laws, out lawed, out law ing.**

out let (out′let′), *n.* 1. an opening for letting something out. *The river has an outlet into the sea. Plug the iron into the electric outlet.* 2. a way of releasing energy, emotion, etc. *Alan often plays ball after school as an outlet.* **out lets.**

out line (out′līn′), *n.* 1. a drawing that shows only the outer lines, or shape, of an object. *We made an outline of the United States.* 2. a plan; a list of main subjects. *The outline of Martin's speech included all the important items he wanted to talk about.* **out lines.**
v. 3. to draw the outer lines of. *The artist first outlined the figure of a boy; then he drew in the face and clothes.* 4. to make a plan of; to tell about the main ideas of something. *Outline your story before you write it. The teacher outlined the year's work in a short speech.* **out lines, out lined, out lin ing.**

out side (out′sīd′), *n.* 1. the side that is out, not in; the outer side or surface. *Clean the outside of the windows. The house is white on the outside.* 2. any place that is not inside; the area beyond a boundary. *The people in the mountain village listen to the radio to get news from the outside.* 3. **at the outside,** at the most. *The job will cost twenty dollars at the outside.* **out sides.**
adj. 4. on the outside; near the outside. *The outside room has a pretty view of the lake.* 5. coming from somewhere else. *Do we need outside help, or can the two of us do the cleaning?*
adv. 6. outdoors; on or to the outside. *Put the dog outside.*
prep. 7. near, but not in; on the outer side of. *I'll meet you outside the school.*

out stand ing (out stan′ding), *adj.* 1. standing out from all others; well-known. *The old man you talked to was an outstanding football player years ago.* 2. not paid. *The only outstanding debt I have will be paid tomorrow.*

out ward (out′wərd), *adj.* 1. external; that can be seen or observed. *Ruth's outward appearance showed that she was happy.* 2. moving away; going toward the outside. *The car moved into the outward lane to leave the expressway.* **out ward ly,** *adv.*
adv. 3. toward the outside. *Fire laws state that the doors of a public building must open outward.*

oval (ō′vl), *adj.* 1. shaped like an egg or an ellipse. *The athletic field is oval.* **oval ly,** *adv.*
n. 2. anything with an oval shape. *The race was run on an oval.* **ovals.** (See illustration on following page.)

oven (uv′ən), *n.* 1. the enclosed space of a stove used for baking. *The smell of the cake baking in the oven filled the whole house.* 2. a furnace. *Bricks are baked or hardened in an oven.* **ovens.**

otter

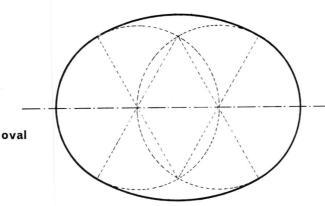

oval

overcoat

over (ō′vər), *prep.* 1. above. *The reading lamp is over the bed. The tall man could see over everyone in the crowd.* 2. on top of; so as to cover. *Put the cover over the basket so the kittens will be warm. Put the scarf over your shoulders.* 3. along; upon. *We always travel over this road.* 4. across. *The boys climbed over the fence to get the ball.* 5. on account of. *Scott's argument with Jean was over a simple difference of opinion.* 6. all through; round about. *The salesman traveled over the Middle West.* 7. during. *You can visit me over the weekend.* 8. about; because of. *The farmers were happy over the rainfall. He is happy over his father's new job as president of the company.* 9. more than. *The flight took over three hours because of the wind.*
adv. 10. above. *The wild ducks flew directly over.* 11. so as to be covered. *My old bicycle has rusted over.* 12. again. *Do this exercise over.* 13. down. *The girl lost her balance and fell over.* 14. so as to bring the bottom side up. *Turn the page over so you can read the rest of his letter.* 15. across the rim or edge. *The soup is boiling over.* 16. more; beyond. *He worked ten hours or over.*
adj. 17. ended. *The children came home when the show was over. The rain is over.*

over all (ō′vər ôl′), *adj.* including everything. *The overall cost of our shopping trip was thirty dollars.*

over alls (ō′vər ôlz′), *n. pl.* loose-fitting pants of strong material worn over other clothes to keep them clean. *Overalls usually have a front piece which extends up over the chest.*

over charge (ō′vər chärj′), *v.* to charge a price that is too much. *The grocer returned some money when he overcharged us by mistake.* **over charg es, over charged, over charg ing.**

over coat (ō′vər kōt′), *n.* a heavy coat worn over regular clothing. *Men and boys wear overcoats in cold weather.* **over coats.**

over come (ō′vər kum′), *v.* 1. to get the better of; defeat. *The brave hunters overcame the roaring rivers, wild animals, and thick forests.* 2. to make weak or helpless. *The miners were overcome by the need to sleep after working all night to rescue the boy.* **over comes, over came, over come, over com ing.**

over due (ō′vər dü′, ō′vər dū′), *adj.* delayed past the time agreed upon for payment, arrival, or return. *This bill is overdue. The airplane is overdue because of the storm. My library book is three days overdue.*

over head (ō′vər hed′ for 1–3, ō′vər hed′ for 4), *n.* 1. the general expenses of running a business. *Overhead includes the cost of rent, heat, light, telephone calls, and office supplies.*
adj. 2. situated above a person's head. *Use an overhead light for reading.*
adv. 3. above the head. *Hold the flashlight overhead.* 4. in the sky; on high. *Birds are flying overhead. We saw the light of a plane overhead.*

over hear (ō′vər hir′), *v.* to hear something said without the speaker's knowing it. *I can overhear you when you speak too loudly.* **over hears, over heard, over hear ing.**

over look (ō′vər lùk′), *v.* 1. to fail to see or notice. *The driver overlooked the stop sign at the corner.* 2. to excuse. *The teacher said that she would overlook my being late this time.* 3. neglect. *Don't overlook the dog at dinner time.* 4. to look down on; have a view over. *The lighthouse overlooks the harbor.* **over looks, over looked, over look ing.**

over night (ō′vər nīt′), *adj.* 1. during the night. *The Boy Scouts made an overnight stop at the river.* 2. staying through the night. *Our overnight guest was Mr. Adams.* 3. used for a short trip. *He carried all he needed in the small overnight bag.*
adv. 4. during the night. *Can you stay overnight?*

over shoe (ō′vər shü′), *n.* a waterproof shoe worn over a regular shoe to keep it dry during wet weather. *Mother put on her overshoes when she saw that it was snowing.* **over shoes.**

over sight (ō′vər sīt′), *n.* a failure to notice or remember something. *Through an oversight, John's name was left off the list.*

over throw (ō′vər thrō′ for 1, ō′vər thrō for 2), *v.* 1. to defeat; bring down. *Many governments have been overthrown by unhappy citizens.* **over throws, over threw, over thrown, over throw ing.**
n. 2. a defeat; ruin. *The overthrow of the government pleased all the people who had opposed it.* **over throws.**

over turn (ō′vər tèrn′), *v.* to turn over; upset. *The dog overturned his empty dish to show that he was hungry.* **over turns, over turned, over turn ing.**

owe (ō), *v.* to have to pay or repay in return for something. *John owes money to the camera store for the film he bought. Sue owes Annette a dime.* **owes, owed, ow ing.**

ow ing (ō′ing), *adj.* 1. not yet paid. *Ten dollars is still owing on your grocery bill.* 2. **owing to,** because of. *Owing to his abilities and neat appearance, Mark got the job he wanted.*

owl (oul), *n.* a bird with a large head, large eyes, and sharp claws. *Owls fly mostly at night.* **owls.**

own (ōn), *v.* 1. to have; possess. *Frank owns a small radio.* 2. to confess; admit. *We owned that we broke the store window by mistake.* **owns, owned, own ing.**
adj. 3. belonging to oneself. *Kate has her own room.*

Own also has the following special meanings:
come into one's own, to get the things one deserves. *The writer worked hard and finally came into his own.*

hold one's own, to take care of oneself. *The good student can hold his own in a discussion.*

of one's own, belonging only to oneself. *Blanche wanted a room of her own.*

own er (ōn′ər), *n.* a person who owns. *The owner of the candy store is a friend to all.* **own ers.**

own er ship (ōn′ər ship′), *n.* the condition of being an owner. *The ownership of a farm means a lot of work for the farmer.*

ox (oks), *n.* 1. a full-grown steer used as a work animal. *An ox is used for plowing and for pulling heavy loads.* 2. any of the group of animals that have hooves divided into two parts and that rechew their food by bringing it up from their stomachs. *Cows and buffalos are oxen because of their hooves and stomachs.* **oxen.**

ox en (ok′sn), *n. pl.* more than one ox. *The oxen moved slowly across the plain pulling the wagons.*

ox i da tion (ok′sə dā′shən), *n.* a combining with oxygen. *Oxidation takes place when paper burns and iron rusts.*

owl

ox y gen (ok′sə jən), *n.* a gas that has no color, taste, or odor. *Oxygen is a chemical element which makes up almost one fifth of the air. All animals and most plants need oxygen to live.*

oys ter (ois′tər), *n.* a mollusk with a soft body surrounded by two rough shells, found in shallow parts of the ocean. *Some kinds of oysters are eaten and others form pearls.* **oys ters.**

P or **p** (pē), the sixteenth letter of the alphabet.

pa (pä), *n.* an informal term for father; papa. *"My pa is the best man in the world," said the little boy.*

pace (pās), *n.* 1. a step. *Beth walked two paces forward to receive her prize.* 2. the length of a step. *A small boy's pace is smaller than a man's pace. Billy came within two paces of walking into the water.* 3. the rate of moving; the speed in walking or running. *The boy ran home to dinner at a fast pace. Most of us try to keep up with the pace of science.* 4. a certain way of walking or running. *They traveled at Boy Scout pace—fifty steps walking followed by fifty steps running.* 5. **keep pace with,** go as fast as; keep up with. *The small dog kept pace with the running boy. I try to keep pace with the news.* **pac es.**

v. 6. to walk. *He paced back and forth while waiting for the bus.* 7. **pace off,** to measure by taking steps and counting them. *We paced off the space for a tennis court.* **pac es, paced, pac ing.**

pack (pak), *n.* 1. a bundle of things wrapped or tied together for carrying. *A camper carried on his back a pack containing food, tools, and a sleeping bag.* 2. a group of animals hunting together. *The pack of wolves was lured by the campfire.* 3. a set of playing cards. *Dad opened a new pack of cards for the bridge game.* **packs.**

v. 4. to put carefully in a box, trunk, etc. *The movers packed our furniture when we left the old house.* 5. to crowd; to fill up. *The theater was packed on the first night of the play.* **packs, packed, pack ing.**

pack age (pak′ij), *n.* 1. a bundle of things that are wrapped together for mailing or sending. *The package of toys arrived in time for the child's birthday.* **pack ag es.**

v. 2. to wrap up; to place in a carton or box. *The store will package all your purchases.* **pack ag es, pack aged, pack ag ing.**

pad (pad), *n.* 1. a flat cushion. *We put a pad under the tablecloth before dinner to protect the top of the table. Norman put the electric heating pad on his sore arm.* 2. a number of blank sheets of paper fastened together on the top or side; a tablet. *Artists use drawing pads. The reporter made notes on a small pad.* 3. the floating leaf of a water plant. *The frog sat on the large lily pad.* 4. the cushion-like part under the feet of some animals. *The cat walks softly on its pads.* **pads.**

v. 5. to stuff with soft material. *A winter jacket is padded with layers of cloth.* 6. to cover with a soft pad. *The wooden chairs were padded.* 7. to add extra, unnecessary words to. *Lawrence padded his speech by telling a long joke.* 8. to walk softly. *The dog padded along beside us.* **pads, pad ded, pad ding.**

pa gan (pā′gən), *n.* a person who does not believe in one God, but instead, who worships many gods. *The ancient Romans were pagans.* **pa gans.**

page[1] (pāj), *n.* one side of a sheet of paper in a book, magazine, newspaper, or letter. *John knew from the first page that he would like the book.* **pag es.**

page[2] (pāj), *n.* 1. a boy or man who carries messages in a hotel. *The page delivered a tele-*

packing a vase

pagoda

gram to a room on the fifth floor. 2. in the Middle Ages, a boy who was being trained to be a knight. *The pages took lessons in riding and in using the sword.* **pag es.**

v. 3. to call by name. *The passengers in the airport are paged over the public announcement system.* **pag es, paged, pag ing.**

pag eant (paj′ənt), *n.* 1. a show. *The water pageant presented boat races, water-skiing, swimming contests, and fireworks.* 2. a play that presents scenes from history. *Donald wore a cowboy costume in the school pageant.* **pag eants.**

pa go da (pə gō′də), *n.* a temple in India, China, Japan, and other Asian countries. *A pagoda has several levels or stories that form a tower.* **pa go das.**

paid (pād), past tense of **pay.**

pail (pāl), *n.* a round vessel or bucket with a handle. *The men filled the pails with water and carried them to the fire.* **pails.**

pain (pān), *n.* 1. an ache, hurt, or sore feeling. *The pain in Elaine's arm soon went away.* 2. **pains,** careful effort. *We took pains to see that everything was ready for the party.* **pains.**

v. 3. to give pain to; hurt. *His toothache pained him.* **pains, pained, pain ing.**

pain ful (pān′fəl), *adj.* causing pain; having pain. *My burned finger is painful. Being away from home for the first time was a painful experience for the little boy.* **pain ful ly,** *adv.*

paint (pānt), *n.* 1. a mixture of liquids and colored powder that can be spread on a surface to color it. *Father is putting some fresh paint on our house.* **paints.**

v. 2. to cover the surface of something with

paint. *The boys painted the fence.* 3. to make a picture of something with paints. *The artist used five shades of blue in painting the sky.* 4. to describe in a lively manner. *That author paints a wonderful picture of his life as a sailor.* **paints, paint ed, paint ing.**

paint er (pān′tər), *n.* 1. a person who paints pictures; an artist. *Some painters like to paint people, while others like to paint scenery.* 2. a person whose job is painting buildings, rooms, and furniture. *The painters are putting new paint on the walls of the gymnasium.* **paint ers.**

paint ing (pān′ting), *n.* a painted picture. *We saw many paintings in the Art Museum.* **paint- ings.**

pair (pâr), *n.* 1. two things of the same kind that go together; a set of two. *Ray was given a pair of ice skates for Christmas. Mother has a new pair of salt and pepper shakers.* 2. something made of two parts that are joined together. *Mother has a pair of scissors. Lawrence thanked his mother for the new pair of pants she gave him.* 3. a couple. *A pair of robins built their nest in a tree. That young pair are newly married.* **pairs.**

v. 4. to arrange in twos. *She paired her socks before putting them away.* 5. **pair off,** to form in twos. *In gym class we paired off for the game.* **pairs, paired, pair ing.**

pa ja mas (pə jä′məz, pə jam′əz), *n. pl.* a suit worn for sleeping. *Pajamas come in two pieces— a jacket and pants.*

pal (pal), *n.* a friend; companion. *Ernie and Roy have been pals since first grade.* **pals.**

pal ace (pal′is), *n.* 1. a large, splendid house in which kings and queens live. *The palace was protected by the royal guard.* 2. any large, fine house. *The rich owner of the oil company lives in a palace.* **pal ac es.**

pale¹ (pāl), *adj.* 1. having not much color; white. *After her illness, Blanche looked pale.* 2. not bright in color; dim. *Ruth wore a pale blue dress. The pale moon was reflected in the water.* **pal er, pal est; pale ly,** *adv.*

v. 3. to turn pale or dim. *The stars paled as the sun came up, and finally could not be seen.* **pales, paled, pal ing.**

pale² (pāl), *n.* 1. a stake of a fence. *Pales are usually pointed at the top.* 2. boundary; limits. *A horse thief was outside the pale of the law in the old West.* **pales.**

Pal es tine (pal′is tīn), *n.* the Biblical home of the Jewish people. It is now divided into Israel and a part of Jordan, and is located in southwestern Asia on the eastern coast of the Mediterranean. *Moses led his people to Palestine.*

pal ette (pal′it), *n.* a small, thin board used by an artist for mixing colors. *A painter holds his palette by means of a thumb hole.* **pal ettes.**

palm¹ (päm), *n.* 1. the inside of a person's hand between the wrist and the fingers. *The child held his nickel tightly in his palm.* **palms.**

v. 2. to hide in the palm. *The man palmed the*

palette

coin before he pretended to take it out of my ear. **palms, palmed, palm ing.**

palm² (päm), *n.* a tree that grows in very warm places. *There are many kinds of palms. Dates grow on date palms, and coconuts grow on coconut palms.* **palms.**

pam phlet (pam′flit), *n.* a small book with a paper cover; booklet. *A pamphlet of instructions came with the camera.* **pam phlets.**

pan (pan), *n.* 1. a dish of metal or glass, used for cooking. *Bacon is cooked in a frying pan.* **pans.** *v.* 2. to wash gravel, sand, earth, etc. in a pan in search of gold or other heavy metal. *The early gold miners in California panned in shallow streams.* 3. **pan out,** to succeed; turn out favorably. *Our idea for a vacation trip didn't pan out.* **pans, panned, pan ning.**

pan cake (pan′kāk′), *n.* a thin cake made of thin dough and fried in a pan. *Our family has pancakes for breakfast every Sunday.* **pan cakes.**

pane (pān), *n.* a sheet of glass with a frame around it. *The glass panes are covered with frost.* **panes.**

pan el (pan′l), *n.* 1. a part of something that is somehow set off from the rest of the wall, as by decoration, positioning, or color. *There is a panel on our living room wall.* 2. a

papering a wall

palm trees and their fruits and fibers

raffia fiber

Raphia ruffia
(raffia palm)

Cocos nucifera
(coconut palm)

coconut

Chamacrops humilis
(fan palm)

Copernicia cerifera
(wax palm)

fruit

picture more long than it is wide. *That panel shows a country scene.* 3. a piece of cloth longer than it is wide that is sewn into the skirt of a dress. *The skirt is blue, but the front panel is green.* 4. a group of persons sitting together and deciding a question, or holding discussions. *The panel met to discuss politics.* 5. a jury. *The panel stayed in debate for four hours.* 6. the front part on the inside of an automobile that holds the steering wheel, dials, etc. *The panel of our car is brown.* **panels.**

v. 7. to put panels on something. *We paneled our living room with walnut panels.* **pan els, pan eled, pan el ing.**

pan ic (pan′ik), *n.* 1. a sudden fear that infects one or many people and often has no real basis. *Panic struck the people when they heard the boat was sinking.* **pan ics.**

v. 2. to act in fear. *Tom panicked when he thought that he had forgotten his homework.* **pan ics, pan icked, pan ick ing.**

pan sy (pan′zē), *n.* a flower with short, broad petals that grows on a low plant. *Some pansies have two or more colors combined in each flower.* **pan sies.**

pant (pant), *v.* to breathe with quick, deep breaths. *The dog panted after he chased the rabbit without catching it.* **pants, pant ed, pant ing.**

pants (pants), *n. pl.* a garment covering the lower half of the body and each leg. *Wear an old pair of pants when you polish the car.*

pa pa (pä′pə), *n.* an informal term for father. *"Here comes Papa," said the little child.* **pa pas.**

pa per (pā′pər), *n.* 1. a material in the form of a thin sheet. *The pages of this book are made of paper. Writing paper is used for letters. Bundles are put together with wrapping paper.* 2. a newspaper. *Get the paper from the newspaper boy.* 3. a written article; a report for class. *The teacher asked us to write a paper about the moon.* 4. a printed legal agreement. *The automobile dealer gave Father the papers which said he had paid for the car.* 5. wallpaper. *Yellow paper will look best in my room.* **pa pers.**

v. 6. to put wallpaper on the walls of; cover with paper. *The paper hanger is papering the baby's room.* **pa pers, pa pered, pa per ing.**

adj. 7. made of paper. *Paper flowers were on each table. Grocery stores use paper bags to hold a customer's goods.*

pa per weight (pā′pər wāt′), *n.* a small, heavy object put on top of papers so they will not blow away. *Paperweights can be made of metal, glass, or stone.* **pa per weights.**

pa poose (pa püs′), *n.* a North American Indian baby. *An Indian mother carries her papoose in a holder on her back.* **pa poos es.**

par (pär), *n.* 1. a standard; middle level;

dates

date seeds

Phenix dactylifers
(date palm)

Arenga saccharifera
(sugar palm)

fruit

part of the leaf

Attalea funifera

fibers

Cariudovica palmata

average. *Tom's grade is on a par with the majority of the class.* 2. a normal amount, quality, or condition. *His work has not been up to par lately.* 3. the value of a stock, bond, etc. that is stated on the face of the paper. *The stocks of that company are selling above par.* 4. the score in a game of golf made by not going over or under the stated amount of strokes. *Ron's last golf game was par.* **pars.**

adj. 5. normal, average or ordinary. *That is a par average on the test.*

par a chute (par′ə shüt′), *n.* 1. a piece of equipment made of fabric that opens up like an umbrella and is used for floating gently down from an airplane. *The men used parachutes to reach the scene of disaster.* **par a chutes.**

v. 2. to jump or drop from an airplane by a parachute. *The men parachuted to the ground.* **par a chutes, par a chut ed, par a chut ing.**

pa rade (pə rād′), *n.* 1. a march or procession. *We watched the circus parade. The Fourth of July parade included soldiers, sailors, school bands, Boy Scouts, and decorated automobiles.* 2. a crowd of people walking for exhibition or display. *The Easter parade gives women a chance to show their new outfits.* 3. a military review of troops by an officer. *The soldiers dressed neatly for the daily parade.* **pa rades.**

v. 4. to march in a procession. *The soldiers paraded to the camp.* 5. to show off. *Allan paraded the medal he won for catching the big fish.* **pa rades, pa rad ed, pa rad ing.**

par a dise (par′ə dīs′), *n.* 1. heaven. *Many people believe in paradise.* 2. a place or condition of happiness or beauty. *His uncle's farm is paradise to young Billy.*

par a graph (par′ə graf′), *n.* a clearly indicated part of a piece of writing; a group of sentences that have something to do with one topic. *The first sentence of a paragraph often is indented from the left margin.* **par a graphs.**

parachuting

par a keet (par′ə kēt′), *n.* a small, slender parrot with a long tail. *Parakeets are kept as pets.* **par a keets.**

par al lel (par′ə lel′), *adj.* 1. going in the same direction but not meeting; being always the same distance apart. *Railroad tracks are parallel not only when they go straight but also when they curve.* 2. similar; alike. *Norman and Joe have parallel thoughts on many things.*

n. 3. a parallel line. *The imaginary lines around the earth that show the degrees of latitude are called parallels.* 4. a comparison that shows how two things are alike. *The movie critic drew a parallel between the two motion pictures.* 5. something like or similar to something else. *Your family is a parallel to mine.* **par al lels.**

v. 6. to be parallel to. *The wall parallels the road.* 7. to equal; to match. *I don't think I can parallel her ability to read.* **par al lels, par al leled, par al lel ing.**

par a site (par′ə sīt′), *n.* 1. a plant or animal that lives on or in another plant or animal, getting food from it. *Fleas are parasites on dogs. Mistletoe is a parasite on trees.* 2. a person who lives at the expense of another person. *A parasite never pays anything back.* **par a sites.**

par cel (pär′sl), *n.* 1. a package; bundle of things wrapped together. *The shopper's arms were filled with parcels.* 2. a piece; section. *The farmer sold a parcel of land.* **par cels.**

v. 3. **parcel out,** to divide into parts for giving away or selling. *Mother parceled out the last piece of cake.* **par cels, par celed, par cel ing.**

parcel post, *n.* the division of the post office which takes care of delivering packages. *My new suit came by parcel post.*

par don (pär′dən), *v.* 1. to forgive or excuse. *Mother pardoned the small boy for his mischief. Pardon me for disturbing your work.* 2. to free from further punishment. *The prisoner will be pardoned because his behavior has been good.* **pardons, par doned, par don ing.**

n. 3. a release from punishment. *The prisoner's pardon was received from the governor.* **par dons.**

par ent (pâr′ənt), *n.* a father or mother. *Either parent may write the reason for an absence.* **parents.**

pa ren tal (pə ren′tl), *adj.* of a parent. *Each person in the class must have parental approval to go on the trip to the museum.* **pa ren tal ly,** *adv.*

pa ren the sis (pə ren′thə sis), *n.* either or both of the curved lines ( ) used as punctuation marks to set off words that explain or limit a word, phrase, or sentence. *Labor Day (the Monday after the first Sunday in September) is a popular holiday.* **pa ren the ses** (pə ren′thə-sēz′).

park (pärk), *n.* 1. a piece of land with trees, lawns, benches, and spaces for games, where people can come to rest or play. *Some cities have parks where boys and girls can play ball.* 2. a large place with beautiful scenery, wild ani-

mals, and lakes that is set aside by the government for the people's enjoyment. *Last year we spent our vacation visiting national parks.* **parks.**
v. 3. to leave an automobile, bus, truck, etc. in a definite spot. *We parked near the movie.* **parks, parked, park ing.**

park way (pärk′wā′), *n.* a wide road that has grass and trees on each side. *Some parkways also have a center strip which is landscaped.* **park ways.**

par lia ment (pär′lə mənt), *n.* the legislative body of a country. *In England, the House of Commons and the House of Lords make up the British Parliament.* **par lia ments.**

par lor (pär′lər), *n.* 1. a room in a house for receiving guests; a living room. *My aunt was talking with the other guests in the parlor.* 2. a room or shop in which a business is carried on. *Many women visit a beauty parlor once a week.* **par lors.**

par rot (par′ət), *n.* 1. a bird found in the tropics, with either green or brightly colored feathers, that is often kept as a pet. *A parrot can learn to repeat the words it hears.* **par rots.**
v. 2. to repeat or copy from memory without understanding. *The girl parroted the answers given in the book.* **par rots, par rot ed, par-rot ing.**

pars ley (pärs′lē), *n.* the curly leaves of a certain garden plant. *Parsley is used for flavoring and for decorating foods.* **pars leys.**

parrots

part (pärt), *n.* 1. a portion of the whole. *He worked in the early part of summer. The boy ate only part of his candy bar.* 2. share. *Each of us will do his part to keep the playground neat.* 3. each of several equal pieces into which a thing may be divided. *A dime is a tenth part of a dollar.* 4. a character in a play; role. *The part of the old grandmother was played by Julia.* 5. the words or lines spoken by a character. *He was chosen to play the hero because he read the part so well.* 6. one side in a dispute. *He always takes his sister's part.* 7. a dividing line. *The girl made a part in the middle of her hair.* 8. one of the voices or instruments in music. *Jane sang the part of soprano in the chorus.* 9. region. *We live in the old part of town. She comes from the western part of the United States.* 10. talent; ability. *He is a man of many parts, who can write poetry, swim well, do wood carving, and play the piano.* **parts.**
v. 11. to divide (the hair) in a line. *Part your hair carefully.* 12. to break or tear. *He parted the rock with a mighty blow of the hammer.* 13. to separate; force apart. *The policeman parted the crowd so the parade could go through.* 14. to go in different directions; to go apart from one another. *We parted at the corner of Montgomery Road and Adams Avenue.* **parts, part ed, part-ing.**

Par the non (pär′thə non′), *n.* the ancient Greek temple on the Acropolis in Athens. *The Parthenon once contained a huge statue of a Greek god.* See **Acropolis.**

par tial (pär′shəl), *adj.* 1. not complete. *We saw a partial eclipse of the moon. My father made a partial payment on a new car.* 2. inclined to favor one side. *An umpire should never be partial when he makes a decision.* 3. **partial to,** fond of. *Julie is partial to ice cream and cake.* **par tial ly,** *adv.*

parsley : **a.** flowers; **b.** seeds; **c.** ripe seed; **d.** leaf

par ti cle (pär/tə kl), *n.* a tiny bit. *Particles of dust floated in the air.* **par ti cles.**

par tic u lar (pər tik/yə lər), *adj.* 1. belonging to one person or thing. *A particular feature of that city is its beautiful buildings.* 2. precise; fussy. *Linda is particular about the appearance of the letters that she types.* 3. special; unusual. *This was a moment of particular joy.* 4. certain; specific. *On this particular test he received a high grade.*
n. 5. a detail; a fact. *Tell me the particulars of your trip to Ohio.* **par tic u lars.**

par tic u lar ly (pər tik/yə lər lē), *adv.* 1. especially. *This ice cream is particularly good.* 2. in a particular way; in detail. *The author examined his writing particularly to see if there were any mistakes.*

part ly (pärt/lē), *adv.* in part; not completely. *My test is only partly finished.*

part ner (pärt/nər), *n.* 1. a person who runs a business with others and shares in the profits. *The camera shop is owned by two young partners.* 2. a person who shares something with another. *The boys were partners on the camping trip.* 3. a person dancing with another. *Lois and Don were partners in the last dance.* 4. a person on one's side in a game. *Mr. Monsen is Father's partner in tennis every week.* **part ners.**

par tridge (pär/trij), *n.* any of several kinds of birds belonging to the same group as the quail and pheasant. *Partridges build their nests on the ground.* **par tridg es** or **par tridge.**

par ty (pär/ti), *n.* 1. a group of people gathered together for a good time; a social gathering. *I had a party at my house last Halloween.* 2. a group of people with similar political views, working together to try to elect certain people to public offices. *The Republican Party and the Democratic Party are the biggest parties in the United States.* 3. a group of people doing some-

partridge

thing together. *The fishing party spent ten days in Canada.* 4. a person who takes part in something. *He was a party to the plan.* **par ties.**

pass (pas), *v.* 1. to go by. *The children pass the fire station on the way to school. The morning passed quickly.* 2. to hand in; hand along. *Pass the books to the front of the room. Pass the butter, please.* 3. to catch up with and go by. *The big car passed the small car.* 4. to go away. *The hot weather passed.* 5. to go successfully through something. *The entire sixth grade passed the test. She took the driver's test and passed it.* 6. to make or approve. *Congress passed the bill which protects wild birds.* 7. to go from one person or thing to another; transfer. *The father's money will pass to his son. Since the small company could not handle a large volume of business, much of its trade passed to a larger company.* 8. to allow to go through or to enter. *The fire chief passed the reporters beyond the ropes that held the crowd back.* 9. to spend. *The lady passes the time sewing.* 10. **pass away,** to die. *The old dog passed away in his sleep.* **pass es, passed, pass ing.**
n. 11. a written note that says one can enter or go. *Were you given a pass to go through the school halls during class?* 12. a narrow road through mountains. *Go slowly through the pass.* 13. a free ticket. *Larry has a pass to the movie.* 14. a condition; situation. *Things have come to a pretty bad pass.* 15. a transfer of a ball from one player to another. *The football player threw a long pass.* **pass es.**

pas sage (pas/ij), *n.* 1. a passing; a moving from one place to another. *We sat on a bench and watched the steady passage of people through the park.* 2. a way that is used for passing; a hall, tunnel, road, etc. *They took the passage through the mountains.* 3. a usually short part of a writing or speech; a sentence, paragraph, verse, etc. *The passage about whales gives much interesting information.* 4. space for a passenger on a ship. *She obtained passage to the other islands.* 5. a voyage. *The passage to the other islands took three weeks.* **pas sag es.**

pas sen ger (pas/ən jer), *n.* a person traveling by plane, train, ship, bus, etc. *Each of the men who was driving to the picnic offered to take three passengers in his car.* **pas sen gers.**

pass ing (pas/ing), *adj.* 1. going by. *Can you hear the passing planes? The passing years affect all persons.* 2. brief; not lasting. *We hurried through the city with only a passing glance at its famous monuments.* 3. showing that one has done the work. *I received a passing grade on my book report.*
n. 4. death. *We mourn his passing.* 5. departure. *I hate to see the passing of summer.*

pas sion (pash/ən), *n.* 1. a very strong feeling, such as love or hate. *In the story we read, everyone hated the wicked witch with passion.* 2. a thing that one is enthusiastic about. *My passion is reading books. Growing flowers is Mrs. Young's passion.* 3. violent anger; rage. *Bert flew into a*

passion when his valuable stamp collection was lost.
4. Passion, the suffering of Jesus from the Last Supper to his death. **pas sions.**

pass port (pas′pôrt), *n.* a special paper given by a government to a citizen, which gives him the right to travel in other countries. *A traveler must be careful not to lose his passport.* **pass ports.**

past (past), *n.* 1. the time that has gone by. *In the past men lived without the convenience of electricity.* 2. the life of a person up to now; the history of a person, group, nation, school, etc. *Tom's past is full of adventure and excitement.* *adj.* 3. gone by. *In past years the graduating class numbered only one hundred; now it is five hundred.* 4. former. *We listened to a speech by our past principal.* *adv.* 5. by and beyond. *The parade marched past.* *prep.* 6. after; later than. *It is ten minutes past nine.* 7. beyond. *She was having such a good time at the party that she was past the point of caring what time it was.*

paste (pāst), *n.* 1. a mixture used for sticking two things together. *We used paste to attach our designs to the poster.* 2. any soft, smooth mixture. *Mother made a sauce from tomato paste.* 3. a dough used in baking. *That apple pie is made from apples, sugar, and paste.* **pastes.** *v.* 4. to fasten with paste. *Eileen pasted pictures of foreign lands in her social-studies notebook.* **pastes, past ed, past ing.**

pas teur ize (pas′tə rīz′, pas′chə rīz′), *v.* to heat at a temperature high enough to kill germs and then to cool quickly. *Laws require dairies to pasteurize the milk they sell.* **pas teur iz es, pas teur ized, pas teur iz ing.**

pas try (pās′trē), *n.* 1. any sweet food made with flour and a lot of shortening and baked. *We had pastry for dessert.* 2. any sweet food like cakes, pies, etc. *We bought some pastries from the bakery.* **pas tries.**

pas ture (pas′chər), *n.* 1. land covered with grass where cattle, sheep, etc. may graze. *The horses were put in the pasture.* 2. the grass eaten by animals. *The farmer's land produced enough pasture to feed all of his livestock.* **pas tures.** *v.* 3. to put animals out to graze. *The cattle were pastured near a brook.* **pas tures, pas tured, pas tur ing.**

pat (pat), *v.* 1. to tap or stroke lightly with the open hand. *We patted the dog's head to show that we liked him.* **pats, pat ted, pat ting.** *n.* 2. a quick, gentle tap. *Albert gave his younger brother a pat on the back.* 3. a tapping sound. *We heard the pat of bare feet on the floor.* 4. a small portion. *The waitress brought us two pats of butter.* **pats.** *adj.* 5. just right; suitable. *We wonder how Frank always has pat answers to questions.* 6. learned. *He read his lesson only once and had it pat.* 7. firm. *The salesman stands pat on his final offer.* **pat ter, pat test.**

patch (pach), *n.* 1. a piece of cloth sewn over a hole or a tear in cloth. *My old pants have patches on them.* 2. any piece of material used to cover a hole. *The workmen put another metal patch on the leaking roof.* 3. a bandage or pad covering an injury. *Mr. Becker wore a patch on his eye for two months.* 4. a small piece of ground. *Father gave me a patch of land to grow tomatoes and lettuce.* **patch es.** *v.* 5. to mend; repair with some material. *The workmen patched the ceiling. Mother patched my pants.* 6. **patch up,** to settle. *The girls patched up their differences.* **patch es, patched, patch ing.**

pat ent (pat′nt for 1–3, pat′nt, pāt′nt for 4), *n.* 1. an official paper from the government which gives to the person who invents something, and to no one else, the right to make and sell his invention. *By law a patent protects an invention from being copied for a certain number of years.* **pat ents.** *v.* 2. to receive a patent for. *The big automobile company patented a new kind of safety lock for doors.* **pat ents, pat ent ed, pat ent ing.** *adj.* 3. protected by a patent. *Patent medicine may mean a medicine that is sold in stores, but is not necessarily recommended by doctors.* 4. clear; easy to see. *After seeing the empty cookie jar, Mother decided it was a patent case of stealing.*

path (path), *n.* 1. a narrow trail or track made by many travelers. *There is an old Indian path through the forest.* 2. the way along which an object moves; a course. *We saw the satellite's path in the sky at night.* 3. a way of life. *He was taught to follow the path of duty.* **paths.**

pa tience (pā′shəns), *n.* the calm acceptance of pain, trouble, delay, etc. without complaining. *Bob's father has great patience with his children.*

pa tient (pā′shənt), *adj.* 1. able to put up with pain, trouble, delay, etc. without saying anything. *The driver was very patient during the half hour he was stalled in traffic.* **pa tient ly** *adv.* *n.* 2. a person under the care of a doctor. *The*

path

three patients in the hospital room gave their nurse a birthday gift. **pa tients.**

pa tri ot (pā′trē ət), *n.* one who loves and loyally defends his country. *George Washington was one of America's greatest patriots.* **pa tri ots.**

pa tri ot ic (pā′trē ot′ik), *adj.* loving one's country and showing loyalty and devotion toward it. *All of us should be patriotic.* **pa tri ot i-cal ly,** *adv.*

pa trol (pə trōl′), *v.* 1. to walk or ride around an area with the purpose of guarding it. *Police patrol our city.* **pa trols, pa troled, pa trol ling.**
n. 2. the men who guard an area. *The patrol guarded the bank.* 3. about eight Boy Scouts or Girl Scouts in a division. *The Boy Scout patrol went to the museum.* 4. a student who helps guard others when they cross the street. *The patrol was on duty even in the rain.* **pa trols.**

pa tron age (pā′trən ij, pat′rən ij), *n.* 1. the financial support and regular attendance given by a customer. *The little restaurant will have my patronage because of its good food.* 2. support and assistance. *The Teen-Age Canteen was under the patronage of the Mothers' Club of the high school.* 3. in politics, the power to appoint certain people to office. *Patronage enabled the political party to put ten of its members in important positions.*

pat ter[1] (pat′ər), *v.* 1. to tap quickly. *The little girl pattered across the floor. The rain is pattering on the window.* **pat ters, pat tered, pat ter ing.**
n. 2. light, quick taps. *We heard the patter of the puppy's feet.*

pat ter[2] (pat′ər), *n.* 1. fast, friendly talk to hold attention. *The magician's patter was so interesting that no one noticed how he had done the trick.*
v. 2. to speak in a fast, easy way, without

peach:
a. branch with leaves and flowers
b. leaves
c. fruit
d. seed

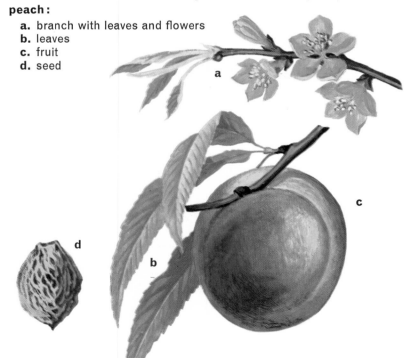

thinking very much; chatter. *Jim patters so much that we often become tired of listening to him.* **pat ters, pat tered, pat ter ing.**

pat tern (pat′ərn), *n.* 1. a plan or guide for cutting out or making something. *Louise cut the material for her new dress according to a pattern.* 2. a model; example; ideal. *Follow John's pattern in being a good student and a good athlete.* 3. a design or figure. *The vase had a flower pattern.* **pat terns.**
v. 4. to make or design according to a model; copy. *Marge patterned her landscape on paintings she had seen in the Art Museum.* **pat terns, pat-terned, pat tern ing.**

pause (pôz), *n.* 1. a short stop or rest. *At ten o'clock the office girls took a pause from work.* **paus es.**
v. 2. to stop for a short time. *He paused in his studying to get a glass of water.* **paus es, paused, paus ing.**

pave (pāv), *v.* to cover a road, street, etc. with a smooth, hard surface. *The dirt road will be paved next week.* **paves, paved, pav ing.**

pave ment (pāv′mənt), *n.* the surface of a road, street, etc. made by paving. *The pavement on some streets is made with crushed rock, clay, and tar.* **pave ments.**

paw (pô), *n.* 1. a foot that has claws. *Dogs, cats, bears, and tigers have paws.* **paws.**
v. 2. to touch and scrape the ground with a front foot. *The nervous horse pawed the ground, ready to go.* 3. to handle clumsily and roughly. *During the sale, women pawed the piles of dresses.* **paws, pawed, paw ing.**

pay (pā), *v.* 1. to give money to someone for goods or for something done. *Jim paid the clerk a dime for the ice-cream bar.* 2. to give what is due. *Did you pay for the goods that were delivered?* 3. to offer; give. *The teacher said to pay attention. We were paid a compliment when the teacher said we were the best class she knew.* 4. to be worth-while; be profitable. *It will pay to do your work well, if you want a better job.* 5. **pay for,** to be punished because of. *A man must pay for breaking the law.* 6. **pay back,** (1) to return borrowed money. *Henry paid back the two dollars.* (2) to get even with. *Walter said that he would pay Art back for playing the trick on him.* **pays, paid, pay ing.**
n. 7. money paid for work done; salary. *Joe's pay is five dollars a day for helping in the store.* 8. anything given or done in return. *Her child's happiness is a mother's pay.*

pay a ble (pā′ə bl), *adj.* due; that must be paid. *The club dues are payable today.*

pay ment (pā′mənt), *n.* an amount of money paid. *Most people who rent a building make a monthly payment to the building owner or his agent.* **pay ments.**

pea (pē), *n.* 1. a small, round seed that is eaten as a vegetable. *Peas grow in long, green seed cases.* 2. the plant it grows on. *My uncle grows peas on his farm.* **peas.**

peace (pēs), *n.* 1. a quiet and calm; stillness. *We like the peace of the country. People try to find peace of mind.* 2. a freedom from war. *Every thinking person wants peace.* 3. law and order. *The policemen told the noisy crowd to go home or they would be arrested for disturbing the peace.* 4. an agreement ending a war. *The two nations that had been at war for nearly three years finally made peace.*

peace ful (pēs′fəl), *adj.* 1. calm; quiet. *The village presented a peaceful appearance.* 2. not liking arguments or quarrels; liking peace. *Although he was a captain in the army, my uncle is a peaceful man who hates war.* **peace ful ly,** *adv.*

peach (pēch), *n.* 1. a sweet, juicy fruit, usually round, having a large, rough stone in the center. *When ripe, a peach has a fuzzy, pinkish-yellow skin.* 2. the tree it grows on. *Peaches take three or four years to bear a large crop.* **peach es.** *adj.* 3. yellowish-pink. *She wore a peach dress.*

peak (pēk), *n.* 1. the pointed top of a mountain. *Some high peaks are covered with snow all year round.* 2. any pointed top. *Many church buildings have peaks.* 3. the highest point. *The peak of traffic comes at about five o'clock in the afternoon. The president of the company is at the peak of his career.* 4. the front part of a cap. *The peak of a baseball player's cap keeps the sun out of his eyes.* **peaks.**

pea nut (pē′nut′), *n.* 1. the seed case or the seed of a plant of the pea family. *The peanut develops below the ground. Peanuts can be eaten whole or made into peanut butter.* 2. the plant which bears peanuts. *The peanut usually has yellow flowers.* **pea nuts.**

pear:
a. branch with leaves and flowers
b. ripe fruit

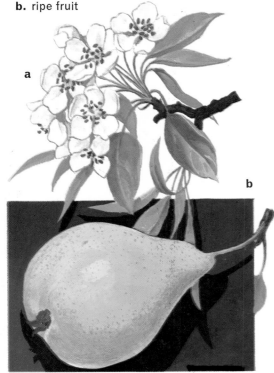

a

b

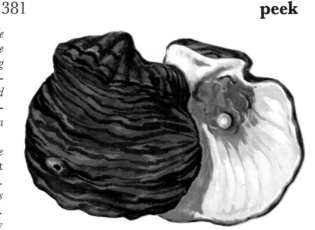

pearl as it is found in an oyster

pear (pâr), *n.* 1. a juicy fruit with a mild flavor. *Pears are yellow, green, or brown. A pear is usually larger at the bottom than at the stem end.* 2. the tree that bears this fruit. *Most pears are very tall, and may grow as high as forty-five feet.* **pears.**

pearl (pėrl), *n.* 1. a smooth, round, hard mass formed inside some oysters. *A pearl is usually creamy-white or blue-gray and is valued as a gem.* 2. something like a pearl. *Pearls of dew covered the ground.* **pearls.**

peas ant (pez′nt), *n.* in Europe, a person who owns a very small farm or who works on a farm. *Peasants were considered to be of low social rank.* **peas ants.**

peb ble (peb′l), *n.* a small stone. *Pebbles are sometimes worn smooth by water running over them.* **peb bles.**

peck[1] (pek), *n.* 1. a measure of volume for dry material. *Grain and vegetables are sold by the peck. Four pecks are the equal of one bushel.* 2. a great deal; a lot. *The kitten was in a peck of trouble when he broke the vase.* **pecks.**

peck[2] (pek), *v.* 1. to strike with the beak. *The pet canary gently pecked Jack's hand.* 2. to pick up by the beak. *The chickens pecked the corn on the ground.* 3. to make by hitting with the beak. *The big hen pecked a hole in the paper box.* 4. to nibble; to eat only a little in small pieces. *Michael just pecked at his food at dinner.* **pecks, pecked, peck ing.**
n. 5. a mark made by pecking. *The angry chicken left a peck on the boy's hand. The tree is filled with pecks made by woodpeckers searching for insects to eat.* 6. a short kiss. *Marvin gave his aunt a peck on the cheek.* **pecks.**

pe cul iar (pi kūl′yər), *adj.* 1. odd; strange. *We were startled by a peculiar noise in the house.* 2. special; particular. *The ancient manuscript was of peculiar interest to the history professor.* 3. **peculiar to,** characteristic of; belonging only to. *Cable cars are peculiar to San Francisco.* **pe cul iar ly,** *adv.*

peek (pēk), *v.* 1. to take a quick, sly look; peep. *Don't peek while I put away your birthday present.* **peeks, peeked, peek ing.**
n. 2. a careful, quick look. *A peek through the fence showed the dog eating his food.* **peeks.**

pelican

pen

peel (pēl), *v.* 1. to take off the outer layer of skin, bark, paint, etc. *We peeled the paper from the wall.* 2. to strip or remove the outer layer from. *We peeled the orange before we ate it.* 3. to come off. *The paint on the old house is peeling.* 4. to lose the outer layer of skin. *My nose peeled from too much sun.* **peels, peeled, peel ing.**
n. 5. the outer skin of some fruits. *The peel of a lemon or orange is made into candy. You can tell if a peach or banana is ripe by the color of its peel.* **peels.**

peep¹ (pēp), *v.* 1. to look through a small opening or from a hiding place. *The child peeped at me from under the covers of his bed.* 2. to begin to come out; to look out, as if peeping from a hiding place. *The first flowers peeped through the ground. The sun peeped from behind the clouds.* **peeps, peeped, peep ing.**
n. 3. a quick look. *I had only a peep at the President as his car drove past.* 4. the first appearance. *Birds sing at the peep of dawn.* **peeps.**

peep² (pēp), *n.* 1. the cry of a young bird. *Peeps came from the nest.* **peeps.**
v. 2. to make such a sound. *The newborn chicks peeped.* **peeps, peeped, peep ing.**

peer¹ (pir), *n.* 1. a person of the same rank or skill; someone who is equal. *A person who is accused of a crime is tried before a jury of his peers. The champion chess player has no peers.* 2. in Britain, a person of noble rank. *A peer has a right to a seat in Parliament.* **peers.**

peer² (pir), *v.* 1. to look at with curiosity; to look long and hard. *The wide-eyed child peered at all the Christmas presents.* 2. to come into sight. *The moon peered over the trees.* **peers, peered, peer ing.**

peg (peg), *n.* 1. a short piece of wood or metal that goes into the ground, fills a hole, or holds things. *A tent peg holds down the sides of a tent. Put a peg in that hole in the barrel to keep the water*

from coming out. *Hang your coat and hat on the clothes pegs in the closet.* 2. a throw. *The pitcher made a quick peg to first base.* 3. **take down a peg,** a humbling. *The criticism took him down a peg, and he is now willing to listen to advice.* **pegs.**
v. 4. to fasten or hold with a peg. *Peg down the tent.* 5. to throw. *Ross pegged the ball back and forth with Pete.* **pegs, pegged, peg ging.**

pel i can (pel′ə kən), *n.* a large water bird with a long bill. *The lower part of the bill of a pelican has a sacklike fold of skin used for catching fish.* **pel i cans.**

pen¹ (pen), *n.* 1. a tool used for writing with ink. *People use fountain pens and pens with a rotating metal ball point.* **pens.**
v. 2. to write with a pen. *Louise penned a letter to her family.* **pens, penned, pen ning.**

pen² (pen), *n.* 1. an enclosed place where animals are kept. *The farmer took food to the pigs in their pen.* **pens.**
v. 2. to shut animals in a pen. *The sheep were penned to keep them from straying.* 3. to surround; to confine. *The sheriff's men penned the outlaw by approaching him from four sides.* **pens, penned,** or **pent, pen ning.**

pen al ty (pen′l tē), *n.* the punishment for breaking a law or rule. *The pentalty for speeding on this street is one hundred dollars.* **pen al ties.**

pen cil (pen′sl), *n.* 1. a long, slender piece of wood with a center of black or colored writing material. *Pencils are used for writing and for drawing.* **pen cils.**
v. 2. to write or draw with a pencil. *He penciled his address on the back of an envelope and gave it to me.* **pen cils, pen ciled, pen cil ing.**

pencil case, a small box or other holder for carrying pencils. *My aunt has always given me a new pencil case at the beginning of each school year.* **pencil cases.**

pend ing (pen′ding), *adj.* 1. not yet decided or settled. *The court case is still pending before the judge.*
prep. 2. while expecting someone or something; until. *Pending the teacher's return, we cleaned the chalkboard and our desks.* 3. during. *The lawyers were active pending the investigation.*

pen du lum (pen′jə ləm, pen′də ləm), *n.* a weight hung so that it swings freely back and forth or around and around. *A pendulum is often used in a tall clock.* **pen du lums.**

pen guin (peng′gwin), *n.* a sea bird with a black back and white breast found near the South Pole. *Penguins can swim but cannot fly.* **pen guins.**

pen in su la (pən in′sə lə), *n.* land that is surrounded on three sides by water. *Our summer house is on a peninsula. The state of Florida is a peninsula.* **pen in su las.**

pen man ship (pen′mən ship′), *n.* handwriting; writing with pen, pencil, or crayon. *We try to improve our penmanship by doing exercises in class.*

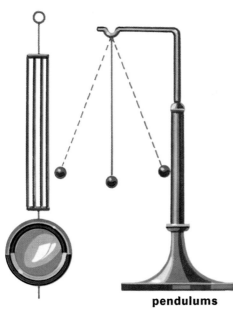

pendulums

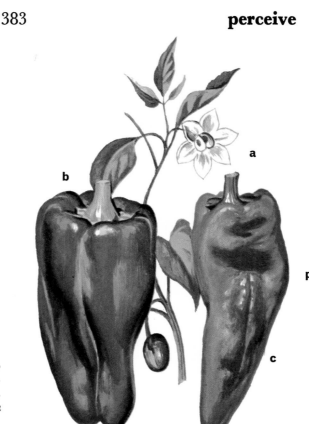

pepper:
a. flower
b. green
c. red

pen nant (pen′ənt), *n.* 1. a long, narrow flag, pointed at one end. *Pennants are flown on ships.* 2. a mark for being champion in baseball. *The Yankees won the pennant in the American League.* **pen nants.**

Penn syl va nia (pen′sl vā′nē ə), *n.* a state in the central part of the eastern United States. *The coal mines of Pennsylvania have produced much of the country's coal. Pennsylvania was one of the original thirteen colonies.*

pen ny (pen′ē), a cent. *One hundred pennies make one dollar.* **pen nies.**

pen ta gon (pen′tə gon′), *n.* 1. a plane figure that has five sides and five angles. *The ornaments were shaped like pentagons.* 2. **Pentagon,** a building near Washington, D.C., that is the military headquarters of the United States. *The Pentagon has five sides.* **pen ta gons.**

peo ple (pē′pl), *n.* 1. human beings; persons; men, women, boys, and girls. *People of all ages attended the fair.* 2. persons belonging to a country, tribe, race, or community. *The people of Italy love the opera. All the peoples of the earth want peace.* 3. a family; relatives. *My people*

penguins

originally came from England. 4. the persons of a certain group; persons living in a certain place. *City people live a crowded life. All the people in this town know each other.* **peo ple** or **peo ples** (for 2).
v. 5. to fill with people. *The western states were peopled by pioneers from the East.* **peo ples, peo pled, peo pling.**

pep per (pep′ər), *n.* 1. a hollow green or red vegetable that is eaten raw, cooked, or pickled. *Some peppers are hot to the taste; others are mild.* 2. a hot-tasting preparation made of the dried black or white berries of an East Indian plant. *Pepper is used to season foods.* **pep pers.**
v. 3. to put pepper on; sprinkle with pepper. *He salts and peppers his vegetables liberally.* 4. to hit with small objects sent at the same time. *The hail peppered the roof of the house.* **pep pers, pep pered, pep per ing.**

pep per mint (pep′ər mint′), *n.* 1. a pleasant-smelling plant of the mint family. *Oil is made from peppermint and is used to give a special taste to food.* 2. candy that is flavored with this oil. *Mother put dishes of peppermints around the room for the party.* **pep per mints.**

per (per), *prep.* 1. for each; for every. *This room is fifteen dollars per day. The race was won by a car that averaged one hundred and sixty miles per hour.* 2. by means of. *The check was sent per special delivery.*

per ceive (pər sēv′), *v.* 1. to be aware of through the senses; see, hear, taste, smell, or feel. *An artist can often perceive changes of color that the*

pennants

ordinary person cannot. 2. to understand. *I perceived what he really wanted to say.* **per ceives, per ceived, per ceiv ing.**

per cent or **per cent** (pər sent′), *n.* out of every hundred; in every hundred. *Ten per cent means ten out of one hundred. Ten per cent of one thousand is one hundred.*

per cent age (pər sen′tij), *n.* a portion of something figured in parts of a hundred; a per cent of the whole. *A large percentage (nearly eighty per cent) of the people voted in the election.* **per cent-ag es.**

per fect (pėr′fikt for 1–5, pər fekt′, pėr′fikt for 6), *adj.* 1. without any defects or flaws. *Once in awhile a perfect diamond is found in a diamond mine.* 2. having no errors; unusually good. *Charlene turned in a perfect paper for her science course.* 3. excellent. *Today is a perfect day for swimming.* 4. absolute. *The man at the door is a perfect stranger to us.* 5. skilled to a high degree. *Al is a perfect carpenter.* **per fect ly,** *adv.*
v. 6. to take away all the faults from; to make perfect. *The company is perfecting a new kind of steel.* 7. to finish; to complete. *The boys perfected the vacation plan.* **per fects, per fect ed, per fect ing.**

per form (pər fôrm′), *v.* 1. to do; carry out. *Elizabeth performs all her jobs well. The driver performed well in the auto race. The minister performs many kinds of duties.* 2. to entertain before an audience; to act out. *The actors performed a new play. The dogs and the clowns performed between acts in a circus.* **per forms, performed, per form ing.**

per form ance (pər fôr′məns), *n.* 1. a doing; carrying out. *The boy's performance of the job showed that he had some training.* 2. a particular action; something done. *Your performance on yesterday's test was very good.* 3. the giving of a public show. *On Wednesday and Saturday there are afternoon performances. This is the old actor's last performance.* **per form anc es.**

per fume (pėr′fūm, pər fūm′ for 1 and 2, pər fūm′ for 3), *n.* 1. a sweet smell. *The perfume of the flowers filled the air.* 2. a sweet-smelling liquid used on the body and clothing. *My sister got a bottle of her favorite perfume for her birthday.* **per fumes.**
v. 3. to give a pleasant odor to. *The blossoms perfumed the orchard.* **per fumes, per fumed, per fum ing.**

per haps (pər haps′), *adv.* maybe; possibly. *Perhaps we will go to the movies tonight.*

per il (per′əl), *n.* 1. a great danger. *The rabbit was in peril when the hunters appeared.* 2. a risk. *Travel this road at your own peril.* 3. something dangerous. *Drugs, alcohol, and tobacco are perils to good health.* **per ils.**
v. 4. to put in danger. *A careless driver perils everyone on the road.* **per ils, per iled, per il-ing.**

per il ous (per′ə ləs), *adj.* dangerous; risky.

The man made the perilous trip across the ocean in a small sailboat. **per il ous ly,** *adv.*

per im e ter (pə rim′ə tər), *n.* 1. the boundary of an area; the line drawn around a figure. *The perimeter of a circle is a round line.* 2. the distance around an area; the sum of the lengths of all sides of a figure. *The square is one inch on each side; its perimeter, therefore, is four inches.* **per im e ters.**

pe ri od (pir′ē əd), *n.* 1. a dot used in printing and in writing. *There should be a period at the end of every sentence.* 2. a length of time. *We had a period of twenty days with no rainfall. During the first period at school, Bert was in the math class.* 3. a portion of time that is a part of history. *We read about the Civil War period.* **pe ri ods.**

per i scope (per′ə skōp′), *n.* a tube made up of mirrors and lenses in such a way that by looking into the lower part, a person can see whatever the top, front part is facing. *Through a periscope a navy captain can see what is on the surface of the water when his submarine is traveling beneath the surface of the water.* **per i scopes.**

per ish (per′ish), *v.* to die. *Plants perish without water.* **per ish es, per ished, per ish ing.**

perk (pėrk), *v.* to raise quickly; to lift in a brisk or saucy way. *The dog perked his ears at the sound of the cat.* **perks, perked, perk ing.**

perky (pėr′kē), *adj.* lively; filled with joy. *The perky, little pup ran around the room.* **perk i er, perk i est.**

per ma nent (pėr′mə nənt), *adj.* lasting for a long time. *Ted has had many summer jobs, but this is his first permanent position. The permanent teeth come in after the baby teeth.* **per ma nent ly,** *adv.*

per mis sion (pər mish′ən), *n.* a permitting; consent. *With the permission of the principal, our class visited the zoo.* **per mis sions.**

per mit (pər mit′ for 1, pėr′mit, pər mit′ for 2), *v.* 1. to let; to allow; to give consent to. *Please permit me to read your magazine.* **per mits, per-mit ted, per mit ting.**
n. 2. a written or printed statement that gives one permission; a license. *Many states require a fishing permit and a hunting permit.* **per mits.**

per pen dic u lar (pėr′pən dik′yə lər), *adj.* 1. straight up and down; standing in a vertical position. *The walls of a building are perpendicular.* 2. at right angles. *A floor is perpendicular to the walls of a room.* **per pen dic u lar ly,** *adv.*
n. 3. a line or surface at right angles to another line or surface. *A square has four perpendiculars.* **per pen dic u lars.**

per se cute (per sə kūt), *v.* 1. to deal with harshly; to harm repeatedly. *Early Christians were persecuted by the Romans.* 2. to irritate; annoy. *Don't persecute the boy by reminding him he failed.* **per se cutes, per se cut ed, per se cut ing.**

per sist (pər sist′), *v.* 1. to keep on; to refuse to change or stop. *Despite objections, Tom persisted in his plan.* 2. to last; to remain. *The fog persisted*

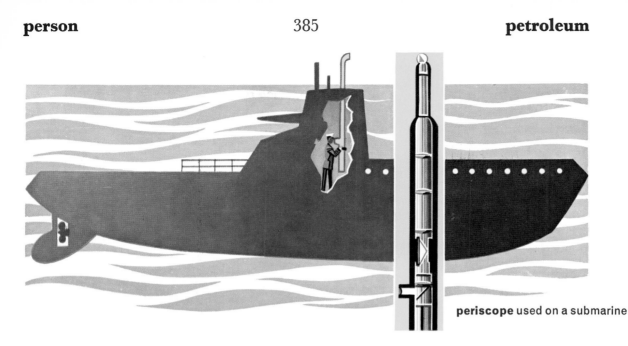

periscope used on a submarine

for three days. **per sists, per sist ed, per-
sist ing.**

per son (pėr′sn), *n.* 1. a human being; a man,
woman, boy, or girl. *No person except the watchman is allowed in the zoo after it closes.* 2. an
appearance. *Keep your person clean and neat.*
3. an actual presence or attendance. *The movie
star appeared in person at the opening of the motion
picture.* **per sons.**

per son al (pėr′sn l), *adj.* 1. private. *Don't read
my personal mail. The actress talked about her
career but not about her personal life.* 2. done or
performed in person. *We held a personal meeting
to settle the question.* 3. of the body. *Personal
health is necessary for this job.* 4. having to do
with a person's appearance, salary, homelife,
etc. *Susan wondered if she could ask Jane a personal
question.* **per son al ly,** *adv.*

per son al i ty (pėr′sn al′ə tē), *n.* 1. the qualities and features of a person which make him
an individual. *Grace has such a strong personality
that it is hard to forget her.* 2. the personal traits
which are considered attractive, such as
charm, humor, and wit. *The guest speaker certainly has personality.* 3. a famous or unusual
person. *The man on the television show interviews
outstanding personalities.* 4. an offensive remark
about a person's looks, his acts toward his
family, or his lack of education. *Let's not get into
personalities in this discussion.* **per son al i ties.**

per son al ly (pėr′sn l ē), *adv.* 1. by oneself; in
person. *A good teacher will talk to each student
personally about any problem. I delivered the message
to him personally.* 2. speaking only for oneself.
I personally think that our idea will work. 3. as a
person. *Everyone disliked the writer personally, but
they admired his novels.* 4. as though it were
directed at oneself alone. *Don't take his remarks
personally.*

per spi ra tion (pėr′spə rā′shən), *n.* sweat. *The
worker in the steel mill was covered with perspiration.*

per spire (pər spīr′), *v.* to sweat. *As he worked
he began to perspire.* **per spires, per spired,
per spir ing.**

per suade (pər swād′), *v.* to get someone to do
or believe something; to convince; to win over.
*The boys persuaded their father to go with them to
the football game.* **per suades, per suad ed,
per suad ing.**

per tain (pər tān′), *v.* to relate; refer. *During the
snowfall most talk pertained to the weather. There
are laws pertaining to speed limits. There is a story
in the newspaper pertaining to the election.* **per-
tains, per tained, per tain ing.**

pest (pest), *n.* someone or something that makes
trouble; an unpleasant thing or person. *Flies
and mosquitoes are pests. Sometimes girls think that
their younger brothers are pests.* **pests.**

pet[1] (pet), *n.* 1. an animal kept as a companion
and treated well. *Dogs, cats, and canaries are
common household pets.* 2. a person who gets
special attention. *Norma has always been Grandfather's pet.* **pets.**
adj. 3. kept as a pet. *Bill has a pet turtle.* 4. favorite. *His pet hope is to be a famous tennis player.*
v. 5. to rub or pat gently. *The dog likes to be
petted on the head.* **pets, pet ted, pet ting.**

pet[2] (pet), *n.* a cross and not happy mood. *She was
in a pet when her photographs were lost.* **pets.**

pe ti tion (pə tish′ən), *n.* 1. a formal request
written to an official or a person in charge.
*The neighbors signed a petition to the mayor, asking
that their street be paved.* **pe ti tions.**
v. 2. to make a formal request to someone or
something. *The men in the club petitioned their
officers for a new club house.* **pe ti tions, pe ti-
tioned, pe ti tion ing.**

pet rel (pet′rəl), *n.* a small sea bird with long
wings. *Petrels fly far out in the ocean.* **pet rels.**
(See illustration on following page.)

pe tro le um (pə trō′lē əm), a dark, natural oil
obtained from the earth by wells which are

sand, āte, bâre, fäther; sent, mē, fėrn; fĭt, bīke; pot, rōpe, fôrt; run, pùll, rüle, cūte; noise, sound; ch, cheese;
ng, long; th, thick; ~~th,~~ those; zh, treasure; ə = a in about, e in waken, i in animal, o in seldom, and u in minus.

sunk deep into the ground. *Gasoline and other fuel-oil products are made from petroleum.*

phar ma cist (fär′mə sist), *n.* a person licensed to give out medicines; druggist. *Our pharmacist is a very friendly man.* **phar ma cists.**

phase (fāz), *n.* 1. a change in the shape of the moon when viewed from earth. *A full moon is one of its phases.* 2. the changing development of a person or thing. *Tom is at a giggling phase.* 3. a view of a subject; aspect. *What phase of reading are you at?* **phas es.**

pheas ant (fez′nt), *n.* a wild bird with a long tail and brightly colored feathers. *Pheasants are hunted for food and sport during certain seasons of the year.* **pheas ants.**

phi los o phy (fə los′ə fē), *n.* 1. the study of the true nature of all knowledge and reality. *Philosophy involves an attempt to understand right and wrong and the other basic principles of living.* 2. a rule or a set of rules which a person follows. *My father's philosophy is to work hard and be kind to others.* 3. wisdom; peace of mind. *Mother's philosophy has helped her through many difficult times.* **phi los o phies.**

phone (fōn), *n.* 1. a telephone. *Answer the phone.* **phones.**
v. 2. to telephone. *Peggy's friends sometimes phone her four or five times a night.* **phones, phoned, phon ing.**

pho neme (fō′nēm), *n.* any of the single sounds that make up words in a language. *Each phoneme is represented by a symbol that tells us how to pronounce the sound. The phonemes in "phrase" are f, r, a, and z.* **pho nemes.**

pho no graph (fō′nə graf′), *n.* a machine that produces sounds from a record by means of vibrations of a needle. *We danced to music from a phonograph at the party.* **pho no graphs.**

pho to graph (fō′tə graf′), *n.* 1. a picture made with a camera. *The photograph of the lake is in color.* **pho to graphs.**
v. 2. to take a picture of someone or something with a camera. *Joan and Laura spent all morning photographing their friends.* **pho to graphs, pho to graphed, pho to graphing.**

petrel

natural gas water
drill petroleum

storage tank

drill

natural gas

petroleum petroleum

water

How **petroleum** is brought up from the ground

pho to graph ic (fō′tə graf′ik), *adj.* 1. of or like photography or a photograph. *He has a photographic mind, and he remembers everything.* 2. having to do with making photographs. *This photographic equipment includes special filters for bright light.* **pho to graph i cal ly,** *adv.*

phrase (frāz), *n.* 1. a group of words that gives a single idea. *In "He swam during the summer," "during the summer" is a phrase.* 2. a short expression. *He used so many scientific phrases that we did not understand him.* **phras es.**
v. 3. to put into words. *Phrase your thoughts carefully.* **phras es, phrased, phras ing.**

phys i cal (fiz′ə kl), *adj.* 1. having to do with the body. *Regular exercise keeps him in good physical condition.* 2. having to do with things that one can see, hear, feel, taste, smell and measure. *Science is the study of physical things.* **phys i cal ly,** *adv.*

phy si cian (fə zish′ən), *n.* a medical doctor. *When you are ill, you should see a physician.* **phy si cians.**

pi ano (pē an′ō), *n.* a large musical instrument played by striking keys arranged in order of sound from lowest to the highest. *The keys of the piano are attached to small hammers which hit wire strings that give out sounds.* **pi anos.**

pick (pik), *v.* 1. to choose. *Arthur picked me to be on his team.* 2. to gather; to pull off. *We picked cherries from the tree.* 3. to start. *There is no need to pick a quarrel with him.* 4. to dig with a tool. *The workmen picked a hole in the ground for the fence post.* 5. to remove something with a sharp instrument, a beak, the teeth, etc. *The dentist picked the pieces of filling from my tooth. The dog picked the meat from the bone. The bird picked the seed from the ground.* 6. to open without a key. *Arnold had an old lock that he could pick with a piece of wire.* 7. **pick up,** (a) to lift. *Two men picked up the heavy chair.* (b) to increase. *The airplane picked up speed on the ground until it finally rose.* (c) to give a ride to. *We will pick you up at nine o'clock.* (d) to learn. *Harry picked up some ideas about business during his summer job.* **picks, picked, pick ing.**

n. 8. a choice. *Take your pick of these books.* 9. a pointed tool with a handle. *The workmen were given picks and shovels to dig the foundation.* **picks.**

pick le (pik′l), *n.* 1. a cucumber which has been preserved in salt, water, and vinegar. *Pickles can be sweet or sour.* 2. the liquid in which a cucumber is soaked. *Meat and vegetables are sometimes preserved in pickle.* 3. a bad situation; trouble; a fix. *Poor Sam is in a pickle.* **pick les.**
v. 4. to preserve in pickle. *Mother pickled onions and beets.* **pick les, pick led, pick ling.**

pic nic (pik′nik), *n.* 1. an outdoor gathering with food, usually away from home. *We had a picnic in the forest preserve.* **pic nics.**
v. 2. to have a picnic. *Last week we picnicked at the beach.* **pic nics, pic nicked, pic nick ing.**

pic to graph (pik′tə graf′), *n.* a drawing that shows statistics by means of pictures. *Pictographs are graphs or charts which are illustrated to make them attractive.* **pic to graphs.**

pic ture (pik′chər), *n.* 1. a painting, drawing, or photograph. *The pictures in the magazine were beautiful.* 2. a likeness; image. *Larry is the picture of his father.* 3. something admired for its beauty. *The well-kept park is a picture.* 4. a description. *His letter gave a good picture of army life.* **pic tures.**

pheasants

v. 5. to make a picture of. *The artist used red and orange to picture the sunset.* 6. to describe or explain. *The boy pictured his day at school to his parents.* 7. to imagine. *I can picture you dropping your purse in the crowd.* **pic tures, pic tured, pic tur ing.**

pie (pī), *n.* a baked food made of fruit, meat, or pudding within a crust. *Apple pie is a favorite in our family.* **pies.**

piece (pēs), *n.* 1. a part; a bit. *The dish fell and broke into pieces.* 2. a small portion. *Would you like a piece of candy? The school board owns a piece of land on Oak Street.* 3. a coin. *A half dollar is a fifty-cent piece.* 4. something written, drawn, or composed. *His sketch is a good piece of art. Will you sing this piece by Stephen Foster?* 5. any one of a set or group of things. *The bride received a set of china consisting of sixty pieces.* 6. a single item; an example. *I have a piece of advice for you. That idea is a piece of nonsense.* **piec es.**
v. 7. to join. *I don't think this broken cup can be pieced together.* 8. to put together from small pieces. *Quilts are pieced using scraps of cloth.* **piec es, pieced, piec ing.**

pier (pir), *n.* a landing place for ships and boats. *Tie your rowboat to the pier.* **piers.** (See illustration on following page.)

pig (pig), *n.* 1. a hog with a thick fat body, raised for its meat. *A pig has a broad head, small*

(See illustration on following page.)

phonograph

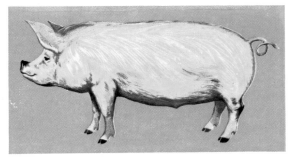
pig

sand, āte, bâre, fäther; sent, mē, fėrn; fit, bīke; pot, rōpe, fôrt; run, pull, rüle, cūte; noise, sound; ch, cheese; ng, long; th, thick; ~~th~~, those; zh, treasure; ə = a in about, e in waken, i in animal, o in seldom, and u in minus.

concrete **pier**

wooden **pier**

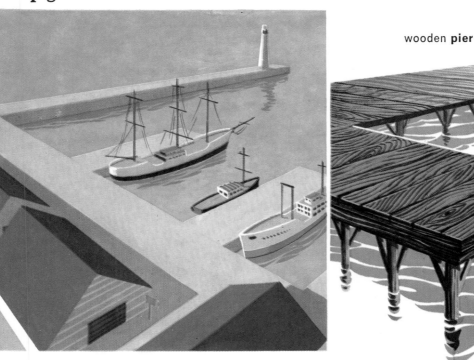

pike

eyes, and a little curly tail. 2. a greedy or dirty person. *Don't be a pig—let us have some of the popcorn.* **pigs.**

pi geon (pij′ən), *n.* a bird with a small head, stout body, and short legs. *Some pigeons are trained to carry messages.* **pi geons.**

pike¹ (pīk), *n.* a long wooden staff with a sharp steel point. *Pikes were used by soldiers long ago.* **pikes.**

pike² (pīk), *n.* a long, slender freshwater fish that lives in cool lakes and streams. *The fishermen caught three pike.* **pike** or **pikes.**

pike³ (pīk), *n.* a road on which a charge is made for traveling; a toll road. *We took the pike all the way across the state.* **pikes.**

pile¹ (pīl), *n.* 1. a heap of things placed on top of each other. *The pile of magazines should be picked up.* 2. a mound or hill. *A pile of dirt was delivered for the garden.* 3. a large amount. *We have a pile of schoolwork to do.* **piles.**
v. 4. to heap; to gather in piles. *The little boy piled all his toys together. The snow piled high in the mountain road.* 5. to fill or load. *They piled the truck with furniture.* **piles, piled, pil ing.**

pile² (pīl), *n.* a long, heavy piece of wood or metal that supports something. *The pier was built on piles.* **piles.**

pile³ (pīl), *n.* the soft surface of carpets, rugs, velvet, etc. *The pile of that expensive rug is about an inch high.* **piles.**

pil grim (pil′grəm), *n.* 1. a person who travels to a holy place. *Pilgrims of all nations journeyed to the Holy Land.* 2. a traveler; a person who wanders about. *The famous author was a pilgrim to distant lands.* 3. **Pilgrim,** one of the people from England who started the colony of Plymouth, Massachusetts, in 1620. *The Pilgrims held the first Thanksgiving Day.* **pil grims.**

pill (pil), *n.* a medicine that is made in the shape of a tiny ball, to be swallowed in one piece. *Take this pill with a glass of water.* **pills.**

pil lar (pil′ər), *n.* 1. a long structure like a post used as a support for a roof or as a monument. *Pillars are usually made of wood, brick, or stone.* 2. a person who is a main support of something. *Mrs. Kahn is a pillar of the Women's Club.* **pil lars.**

pil low (pil′ō), *n.* a support used for the head in resting or sleeping; a cushion. *A pillow is a cloth bag filled with feathers, rubber, or something equally soft.* **pil lows.**

pi lot (pī′lət), *n.* 1. a person who flies an airplane. *Pilots for the large airlines must have years of training.* 2. a person who steers a big ship into

pike

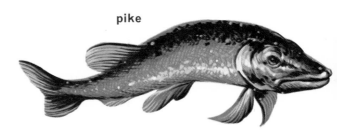

pigeon

or out of a harbor with which he is familiar. *A pilot steered the huge ocean liner out of the busy harbor, and then he returned to land.* **pi lots.**

v. 3. to fly; to steer. *Even though one engine was in trouble, our captain piloted the airplane safely through the storm.* **pi lots, pi lot ed, pi lot ing.**

pin (pin), *n.* 1. a piece of very thin metal with a sharp point and a thick or flat end. *Pins are used to fasten together clothes or pieces of paper. The sharp point of a safety pin is folded into its large head.* 2. any piece of wood or metal that is used for holding things together. *Different pins are used for holding clothes on a line and for keeping a woman's hair in place.* 3. an ornament or badge that is fastened to the clothes. *The girls wear either a class ring or a class pin when they graduate.* **pins.**

v. 4. to fasten with a pin. *Please pin this rip in my coat.* 5. to hold in one position. *The speaker was pinned by the eager crowd.* **pins, pinned, pin-ning.**

pinch (pinch), *v.* 1. to squeeze between the thumb and the first finger. *My grandmother likes to gently pinch the baby's cheek when she greets him.* 2. to squeeze between two surfaces. *The kitten's paw was almost pinched by the closing door.* 3. to press on so that pain is a result. *Phil's new shoes pinched his feet.* 4. to save. *Arthur and I have to pinch every penny for our vacation.* **pinch es, pinched, pinch ing.**

n. 5. a squeeze. *My mother's gentle pinch woke me.* 6. a little bit; the amount taken between the first finger and the thumb. *The soup needs a pinch of salt.* 7. an emergency. *In a pinch I can always telephone Dad.* 8. a hardship. *The lost hunters felt the pinch of cold and hunger.* **pinch es.**

pin cush ion (pin′kůsh′ən), *n.* a small cushion for holding pins when they are not in use. *Stick these pins in the pincushion.* **pin cush ions.**

pine[1] (pīn), *n.* 1. one of several kinds of ever-green trees with leaves like needles and with cones. *Pine cones are of different shapes, depending upon the kind of pine they grow on.* 2. the wood of this tree. *Pine is used often in building houses.* **pines.**

pine[2] (pīn), *v.* 1. to have a strong urge or long-ing. *The old man pined for the days when he was a great athlete.* 2. **pine away,** to get very lonely. *The dog pines away during the family's absence.* **pines, pined, pin ing.**

pine ap ple (pīn′ap′l), *n.* 1. a large, brownish-yellow fruit that has sharp, pointed ridges on its skin and is yellow and juicy inside. *Pine-apples grow in Hawaii and other warm places.* 2. the plant it grows on. *The pineapple has a very short stem and green leaves with sharp points on the edges.* **pine ap ples.** (See illustration on following page.)

pink[1] (pingk), *n.* 1. a pale-red color. *The pink and yellow of the sunset were pleasant to look at.* 2. a plant with flowers having five petals each. *The flowers of the pink are pink, white, or red, and*

pincushion

safety **pins**

have a pleasant, sharp odor. 3. the highest point or degree. *The girl is in the pink of health.* **pinks.**

adj. 4. pale-red. *The pink sky at night meant a clear day would follow.* **pink er, pink est.**

pink[2] (pingk), *v.* to cut into little V-shaped ridges along the edges. *Cloth is pinked so that the threads will not come apart.* **pinks, pinked, pink ing.**

pint (pīnt), *n.* a measure of volume equal to one half of a quart. *We bought a pint of cream and a pint of strawberries.* **pints.**

pi o neer (pī′ə nir′), *n.* 1. a person who goes first and opens the way for others. *The West was settled by pioneers. The ancient Arabs were pioneers in astronomy.* **pi o neers.**

v. 2. to lead the way. *The Wright brothers pioneered in the discovery that man could fly in a machine.* **pi o neers, pi o neered, pi o neer-ing.**

pine cones

a

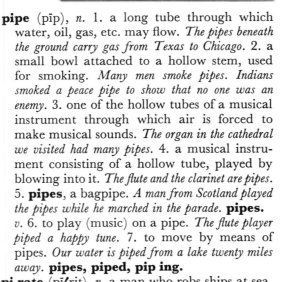

b

pineapple:
a. leaves and fruit
b. cored fruit for eating

pipe

pipe (pīp), *n.* 1. a long tube through which water, oil, gas, etc. may flow. *The pipes beneath the ground carry gas from Texas to Chicago.* 2. a small bowl attached to a hollow stem, used for smoking. *Many men smoke pipes. Indians smoked a peace pipe to show that no one was an enemy.* 3. one of the hollow tubes of a musical instrument through which air is forced to make musical sounds. *The organ in the cathedral we visited had many pipes.* 4. a musical instrument consisting of a hollow tube, played by blowing into it. *The flute and the clarinet are pipes.* 5. **pipes,** a bagpipe. *A man from Scotland played the pipes while he marched in the parade.* **pipes.**
v. 6. to play (music) on a pipe. *The flute player piped a happy tune.* 7. to move by means of pipes. *Our water is piped from a lake twenty miles away.* **pipes, piped, pip ing.**

pi rate (pī′rit), *n.* a man who robs ships at sea. *Pirates once stole money and valuable goods and sometimes hid them on islands.* **pi rates.**

pis tol (pis′tl), *n.* a small gun that is fired by one hand. *Some pistols fire six or more bullets before they need to be loaded again, while others fire only one.* **pis tols.**

pis ton (pis′tən), *n.* a flat or round piece of metal that slides back and forth inside a tube or hollow cylinder. *A piston moves because of pressure, and is connected to a rod which transmits the movement to wheels. In a steam engine steam moves the piston; in a gasoline engine gasoline explodes to move the piston.* **pis tons.**

pit[1] (pit), *n.* 1. a hole in the ground. *A gravel pit is formed by machines taking gravel from the ground.* 2. a tiny hole in the skin caused by chicken pox. *The pits or marks often fade and cannot easily be seen.* 3. the place where the orchestra sits in a theater. *The pit is directly in front of the stage.* **pits.**
v. 4. to make tiny holes in; to mark with pits. *Chicken pox may pit the face.* 5. to match; set to compete. *Our debating team is pitted against Washington School.* **pits, pit ted, pit ting.**

pit[2] (pit), *n.* 1. a seed or stone inside certain fruits. *Cherries, peaches, and plums contain pits.* **pits.**
v. 2. to take the pit from. *Machines pit cherries before they are canned.* **pits, pit ted, pit ting.**

pitch[1] (pich), *v.* 1. to throw; to toss. *The newsboy pitches the paper on our porch.* 2. to put up. *The campers pitched their tent for the night.* 3. to move with the front end rising and falling. *The ship pitched in the big waves.* 4. in baseball, to throw the ball to the person at bat, who tries to hit it. *Tom wants to pitch in this game.* 5. to set at a certain level or degree. *Can you pitch the tone of the song a little lower?* 6. to slope down. *The church steeple pitches sharply.* **pitch es, pitched, pitch ing.**
n. 7. a ball thrown to the batter. *The batter swung and missed the pitch.* 8. a level or point. *His activity was at a high pitch.* 9. the degree of height or depth of a sound. *Dogs can hear notes that are at a pitch too high for human beings to hear.* 10. a sloping down. *The roof has a steep pitch.* **pitch es.**

pirates

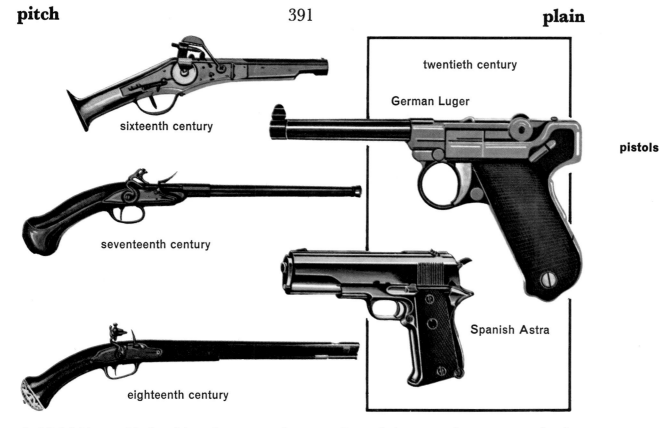

sixteenth century

seventeenth century

eighteenth century

twentieth century

German Luger

Spanish Astra

pistols

pitch[2] (pich), *n.* a black, sticky substance used for filling cracks in pavements, for covering holes in boats and walls, and for other purposes. *Pitch is made from petroleum, coal, or wood.*

pitch er[1] (pich′ər), *n.* a player in a baseball game who pitches the ball to a person at bat. *The pitcher is one of the most important players in the game.* **pitch ers.**

pitch er[2] (pich′ər), *n.* a jar with a large lip used for holding and pouring water, milk, oil, or other liquid. *Pitchers may have one or two handles.* **pitch ers.**

pity (pit′ē), *n.* 1. sympathy; a feeling of sorrow for the suffering of another. *We felt pity for the wet kitten, so we brought her in and fed her.* 2. a cause for feeling sorrow or regret. *It is a pity that you can't come to the party.* **pit ies.**

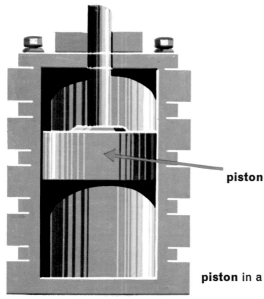

piston

piston in a cylinder

v. 3. to feel sorrow for someone who has trouble. *George pitied the driver whose car wouldn't start.* **pit ies, pit ied, pit y ing.**

pix ie or **pixy** (pik′sē), *n.* a fairy; elf. *Pixies appear in many children's stories.* **pix ies.**

place (plās), *n.* 1. a space where someone or something belongs. *Put the chair back in its place. The place for the automobile is the garage.* 2. a city, town, village, or other area. *Gary goes every year to a place near Alaska.* 3. a house or apartment; residence. *We can go to Mike's place after the game.* 4. a building or space that is used for a special purpose. *When we didn't find him at home, we went to his place of business.* 5. a seat or space for a person. *If you get there early, save me a place.* 6. a certain point; a spot. *The coolest place in town is near the river.* 7. a position or job. *Marie likes her new place in the lawyer's office.* 8. a position in a series. *Our school team finished the season in second place.* 9. a rank; position. *The king's place in history is well known.* 10. the right time or location. *This street corner is not the place to talk about personal matters.* 11. **take place,** to happen; occur. *Our meeting took place yesterday.* **plac es.**

v. 12. to put in a particular position; to set. *Place your pencil on the desk. The child places confidence in his father and mother.* 13. to identify by connecting with some event. *I know I've met her, but I can't place her name.* **plac es, placed, plac ing.**

plain (plān), *adj.* 1. easy to hear or see; distinct. *From the top of the building we had a plain view.* 2. easy to understand; clear. *The directions are plain.* 3. simple; not rich in taste or fancy in

pitchers

appearance. *This restaurant serves plain food, but it is delicious.* 4. with little wealth and simple manners; ordinary. *Abraham Lincoln came from a plain family. My father is a plain workman.* 5. with no decoration. *Ethel wore a plain blue dress.* 6. frank; honest. *The principal gave a plain talk about our duties as citizens.* 7. homely; not good-looking. *This puppy is very plain, but the children love it.* **plain er, plain est; plain ly,** *adv.*

n. 8. a large stretch of flat land. *The plains of the West are used for raising wheat and for grazing cattle.* **plains.**

plan (plan), *n.* 1. a way of doing something that is thought out in advance; a scheme. *Fred is excited about his family's plan for a vacation in California.* 2. a drawing. *Before beginning work on a house, a builder needs a plan showing the location and size of each room, closet, door, and window.* **plans.**

v. 3. to think out in advance. *A good student plans his work before starting it.* 4. to make a plan of. *Engineers from the state highway department are planning a new expressway.* **plans, planned, plan ning.**

plane[1] (plān), *n.* 1. an airplane. *The big planes take off from the airport one minute apart.* 2. a flat, level surface. *The top of your desk is a plane.* **planes.**

adj. 3. having a flat, level surface. *Plane figures have points and lines on a flat surface, including only length and width.*

plane[2] (plān), *n.* 1. a tool used for smoothing wood. *The workman used a plane to make the door fit its frame.* **planes.**

v. 2. to take off a part of something with a plane. *The carpenter planed the side of the door.* 3. to make smooth with a plane. *The boards in the floor were planed.* **planes, planed, plan ing.**

plan et (plan′it), *n.* a large body that rotates around the sun. *There are nine planets that go around the sun and reflect its light: Mercury, Venus, Earth, Mars, Jupiter, Saturn, Uranus, Neptune, and Pluto.* **plan ets.**

platypus

plan e tar i um (plan′ə târ′ē əm), *n.* a kind of theater with a ceiling shaped like a large hemisphere on which are shown pictures of stars and planets. *In a planetarium the movements of the stars, galaxies, and planets can be followed just as if the ceiling were the sky.* **plan e tar i ums.**

plank (plangk), *n.* 1. a long, thick board. *The boys dove from a plank at the side of the pier. The old bridge was made of planks.* 2. one of the ideas or plans of a political platform. *The third plank of the winning party's platform was for better housing.* **planks.**

v. 3. to cover with planks. *The new pier is being planked.* **planks, planked, plank ing.**

plant (plant), *n.* 1. a living thing that is not an animal. *Trees, grass, flowers, vegetables, and fruits are plants.* 2. the buildings and equipment of a factory or business. *The television plant makes hundreds of television tubes a day.* **plants.**

v. 3. to put into the ground so that it will grow. *The farmer planted his corn in the spring.* 4. to set firmly. *John planted his feet and stood there. An idea was planted in my head. Plant the stake in the ground.* 5. to settle or establish. *The new colony was planted by the British.* **plants, plant ed, plant ing.**

plan ta tion (plan tā′shən), *n.* 1. a large farm or estate in warm climates where cotton or sugar is grown. *There are plantations in the South.* 2. a large group of trees that have been planted. *Rubber plantations are found in Brazil in South America.* **plan ta tions.**

plas tic (plas′tik), *n.* 1. any of a large number of substances that are made by chemicals and then are manufactured into various articles. *Plastics are used instead of wood, metal, cloth, or rubber to make things like toys, stockings, tools, raincoats, and ornaments.* **plas tics.**

adj. 2. made of plastic. *Mother has a set of plastic dishes.* 3. that can be molded or shaped. *Soft wax and clay are plastic materials.* 4. concerned with molding or shaping materials. *Carving figures from wood is a plastic art.*

plate (plāt), *n.* 1. a shallow, usually round, dish. *Plates hold food.* 2. the food on a plate. *Finish the plate of vegetables.* 3. the food served to one person at a meal. *The dinner for the retiring manager will cost ten dollars a plate.* 4. dishes and knives, forks, and spoons covered with gold or silver. *The valuable family plate was sold.* 5. a flat piece of metal. *A small plate covers the hole in the wall.* 6. in baseball, the home base. *He was out at the plate.* **plates.**

v. 7. to cover with a thin metal such as gold or silver. *The jeweler plated the dishes with silver.* 8. to cover with metal sheets. *The gunboat was plated with steel.* **plates, plat ed, plat ing.**

plat form (plat′fôrm), *n.* 1. a stage. *Plays are performed on platforms.* 2. any flat surface higher than the area around it. *The train will be at the platform in five minutes.* 3. the statement of ideas and plans set forth by a group. *The candidate for office believes in his party's platform.* **plat forms.**

plat ter (plat⁄ər), *n.* a large, long dish from which food is served at the table. *The vegetables, meat, and potatoes were served from separate platters.* **plat ters.**

plat y pus (plat⁄ə pəs), *n.* a small water animal of Australia that has feet and a beak like a duck's and a tail like a beaver's. *Even though the platypus is not a bird, it lays eggs.* **plat y pus es** or **plat y pi** (plat⁄ə pī).

play (plā), *v.* 1. to take part in a game or activity for fun. *Children like to play tag. Mr. Nelson plays golf every Saturday.* 2. to perform on a musical instrument or instruments. *The orchestra played an opening number before the curtain went up.* 3. to make believe. *The children played that their street was a river.* 4. to amuse oneself. *Please don't play with my glasses.* 5. to move lightly. *The wind played on the still pond.* 6. to act in a certain way. *Scott doesn't play fair.* 7. to compete with in a game. *The basketball team plays Northern tonight.* 8. to act on the stage; perform. *Whom can we get to play the role of the hero?* 9. to cause to act or move. *John played his flashlight on the ground to help find Cora's locket.* 10. **play into the hands of,** to do something that gives an advantage to. *By dropping the ball, I played directly into the hands of the other team.* 11. **play on,** to make use of in order to get something. *He played on his aunt's sympathy to borrow five dollars.* **plays, played, play ing.** *n.* 12. something done for fun. *During the summer we have more time for play.* 13. a quick movement; a light action. *The play of the moonlight on the waves is beautiful.* 14. action; operation. *She brought her imagination into play and wrote a poem.* 15. a certain act or move in a game. *Peggy made a good play, and the game was over.* 16. a story written for or acted on the stage, in the movies, or on television; drama. *The play was about a sheriff and his brother, who was a criminal.* **plays.**

play er (plā⁄ər), *n.* 1. a person who plays in a game. *The best player on the team is big Jim.* 2. a person who plays a musical instrument. *That guitar player is very good.* 3. an actor. *That man is a leading player at the city theater.* **play ers.**

play ground (plā⁄ground′), *n.* a place for playing, used by children. *Swings and slides are in the playground.* **play grounds.**

play house (plā⁄hous′), *n.* 1. a theater. *Every summer the town turns the old barn into a playhouse for visiting actors.* 2. a small house for children to play in. *The little playhouse has two rooms.* **play hous es.**

play mate (plā⁄māt′), *n.* a child who is a good friend of another; a companion in play. *John and Tim have been playmates since the first grade.* **play mates.**

play thing (plā⁄thing′), *n.* a toy. *The baby has many playthings, but she likes her old cloth doll.* **play things.**

plead (plēd), *v.* 1. to ask sincerely; to appeal earnestly. *The boy pleaded for another chance to pass the test.* 2. to argue for or against in a court of law. *Everyone should have a lawyer to plead his case.* 3. to offer as an excuse. *When her boss asked why she was late, Cynthia pleaded illness.* **pleads, pleaded** or **pled** (pled), **plead ing.**

pleas ant (plez⁄ənt), *adj.* 1. delightful; pleasing. *We had a pleasant vacation.* 2. fair and warm. *This is a pleasant day for a swim.* 3. agreeable; friendly. *I have always had pleasant teachers.* **pleas ant ly,** *adv.*

please (plēz), *v.* 1. to give pleasure to; to bring happiness to. *My father's jokes and funny stories please my friends.* 2. to choose; to wish. *Their dog never obeys, but does just as he pleases.* 3. to be so kind as to (a polite way of asking for something). *Please help me. Please pass the bread.* **pleas es, pleased, pleas ing.**

pleas ing (plē⁄zing), *adj.* agreeable; enjoyable. *Joe has a pleasing smile. The children gave a pleasing performance at the class play.* **pleas ing ly,** *adv.*

pleas ure (plezh⁄ər), *n.* 1. a joy; delight; satisfaction. *Her pleasure in meeting the famous actor showed on her face.* 2. something that gives enjoyment or satisfaction. *Going to the zoo was a pleasure for the class.* 3. desire; wish. *Is it the King's pleasure to have food served now?* **pleas ures.**

pledge (plej), *n.* 1. a promise; an agreement. *We made a pledge to be home by ten o'clock.* 2. something that is given or kept as a security or as a guarantee. *The bank is keeping the ownership papers of the man's car as a pledge that he will return the loan.* 3. a toast; a drink to the health of. *Let's have a pledge to the King.* **pledg es.** *v.* 4. to promise to give. *My father pledged one hundred dollars to the welfare fund.* 5. to bind by a promise. *He pledged himself to marry her when he gave her the ring.* 6. to give as a security. *His car was pledged to the bank.* 7. to give a toast to. *The soldiers pledged the King.* **pledg es, pledged, pledg ing.**

Ple ia des (plē⁄ə dēz′, plī⁄ə dēz′), *n. pl.* a group of seven stars in one of the constellations. *In*

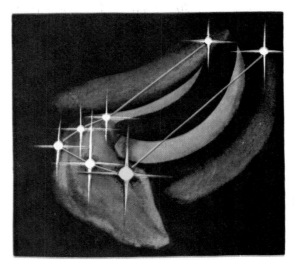

Pleiades

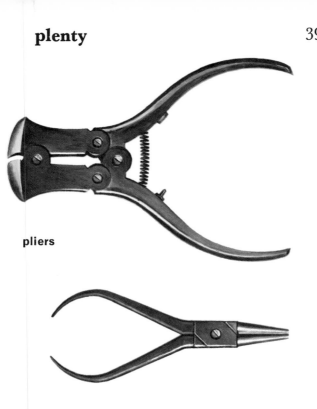

pliers

ancient Greece the Pleiades were thought to be seven sisters in the sky.

plen ty (plen′tē), *n.* a supply that is big enough; an abundant amount. *We have plenty of advice on how to get there. There are plenty of cookies left in the cupboard.*

pli ers (plī′ərz), *n. pl. or sing.* a tool that is used to hold, turn, cut, or bend wire and metal. *A pliers is used to tighten a nut on a bolt.*

plov er (pluv′ər, plō′vər), *n.* a small bird with a long bill that lives on the shore of the oceans. *Plovers have long legs and pointed wings.* **plov ers.**

plow (plou), *n.* 1. a tool used in farming for turning up soil. *Plows have sharp blades and are pulled by horses, oxen, or tractors.* 2. a machine for clearing away snow. *The plows go down our street three times a day during a heavy snow.* **plows.**
v. 3. to work with a plow; to till. *Fields are plowed in the spring for summer crops.* 4. to move or push through. *We plowed our way through the crowd. A ship plows the rough seas.* **plows, plowed, plow ing.**

plug (plug), *n.* 1. a piece of wood, metal, or rubber used to stop up a hole, drain, etc. *Many bathtubs and sinks can be filled with water by using plugs.* 2. an electric connection. *A plug*

plovers

plow

connects a lamp, radio, television, or iron to an electric circuit. **plugs.**
v. 3. to stop up with a plug. *We must plug the hole in the rowboat.* 4. **plug in,** to connect to an electric circuit. *Plug in the iron.* 5. **plug away,** to work steadily. *He plugged away at his work.* **plugs, plugged, plug ging.**

plum (plum), *n.* 1. a small, soft, juicy fruit that is good to eat. *Plums are red, purple, green, or yellow.* 2. the tree the fruit grows on. *Plums are grown in orchards.* 3. something good or desired. *Ted's new job as captain of the football team is a plum for him.* **plums.**

plumb (plum), *n.* 1. a metal weight hung at the end of a line called a plumb line. *A plumb is often used to find out if a wall goes straight up and down.* **plumbs.**
v. 2. to test with a plumb. *The workers plumbed the depth of the well. The builders plumbed the wall.* 3. to search into; examine thoroughly. *The detective in the movie plumbed the motives for the crime.* **plumbs, plumbed, plumb ing.**

plumb er (plum′ər), *n.* a man whose job is putting in and fixing bathroom fixtures, kitchen sinks, water pipes, and gas pipes. *We called a plumber when we found water leaking from the pipes in the basement.* **plumb ers.**

plumb ing (plum′ing), *n.* 1. the pipes and fixtures of the water and gas systems in a building. *This new building has modern plumbing.* 2. the work of a plumber. *Plumbing is an important occupation.*

plunge (plunj), *v.* 1. to dive; to throw oneself. *The swimmer plunged into the pool. The football player plunged over the goal and scored for his team. After his vacation the man plunged into his work.* 2. to force quickly; to make go down. *Mother plunged the boiled egg into the cold water. Jim plunged the shovel into the soft snow and began clearing off the walk. The freezing winds plunged the temperature outside to below zero.* **plung es, plung ed, plung ing.**
n. 3. a dive. *The whale took a plunge into the deep water.* 4. a quick swim. *Let's go for a plunge before breakfast!* 5. a sudden fall. *The plunge of the giant tree disturbed all the birds in the forest.* **plung es.**

plu ral (plur′əl), *n.* 1. the form of a word showing that the writer or speaker means more than one. *The plural of "dog" is "dogs." The plural of "leaf" is "leaves." The plurals of all nouns in this dictionary are shown.* **plu rals.**
adj. 2. showing that more than one is meant. *The plural form of most words is made by adding "s" or "es." Some words have no plural form.*

plus (plus), *prep.* 1. added to; with the addition of; and. *Four plus two equals six $(4+2=6)$. The meal cost eight dollars plus forty cents tax; the total was $8.40.*
adj. 2. showing a greater value than usual. *A grade of B plus means better than B and almost as good as A.*

plum: **a.** Damson plum; **b.** Damson plum seed;
c. green gage plum; **d.** green gage plum seed;
e. branch with blossoms

n. 3. a sign $(+)$ which shows that the number following it is to be added. *Sue carefully noted whether her math problems had pluses or minuses before she began her work.* 4. something added. *His new job as vice-president of the company was a plus in his career.* **plus es.**

Plu to (plü′tō), *n.* 1. the most distant planet in our solar system. *Pluto is ninth in distance from the sun.* 2. the Greek and Roman god of the land of the dead. *Men of ancient times feared Pluto, and did not want to visit his kingdom.*

poach[1] (pōch), *v.* to cook an egg by boiling it in water without its shell. *Mother poached some eggs for breakfast.* **poach es, poached, poaching.**

poach[2] (pōch), *v.* to hunt or fish in an area without permission of the owner. *The hunter was surprised when the gamekeeper told him he was poaching.* **poach es, poached, poach ing.**

pock et (pok′it), *n.* 1. a small bag sewn into clothing to hold small articles. *Men carry money, comb, a handkerchief, and other things in their pockets.* 2. a hole in the ground, usually containing a mineral. *The miner discovered a pocket of silver.* 3. anything like a pocket. *The Boy Scout made pockets in the soft ground for the pegs of his tent. A pool table has six pockets.* 4. **air pocket,** a condition of air which causes an airplane to make a short drop while in flight. *The air pockets over the hills gave us a rough ride.* **pock ets.**

v. 5. to put into a pocket. *He pocketed the money.* 6. to take dishonestly. *The store manager pocketed some of the store's money.* 7. to hide; hold back. *He pocketed his anger and said nothing.* **pock ets, pock et ed, pock et ing.**

pock et book (pok′it bùk′), *n.* 1. a woman's handbag or purse. *Some pocketbooks are large.* 2. a small case for carrying money in a pocket. *His pocketbook fell out as he hung up his coat.* 3. a book usually bound in paper and small enough to carry in a pocket. *He bought a pocketbook to read on the train.* **pock et books.**

pod (pod), *n.* a shell in which grow the seeds of certain plants. *Peas and beans have pods.* **pods.**

po em (pō′əm), *n.* a composition arranged so that it has rhythm and appeals to the imagination. *Often a poem has words that rhyme.* **po ems.**

po et (pō′it), *n.* a person who writes poems. *The famous poet told our English class how he got his ideas.* **po ets.**

po et ry (pō′it rē), *n.* 1. poems. *The poetry of Shakespeare is some of the best that has ever been written.* 2. the act of writing poems. *It is difficult to earn a living by poetry alone.*

point (point), *n.* 1. a sharp end; a narrow tip. *I like a pencil with a fine point. He was stuck by the point of a pin. Let's drive down this point of land to the sea.* 2. a position; a place. *We are at this point on the map. You will have to stop at three points on the road.* 3. a stage; a degree. *The water is at the boiling point. Some boys get to the point of leaving school.* 4. a dot used in writing or in mathematics; a period. *Put your decimal points*

plumb

plumber

in the right places. 5. a purpose; a reason. *What's the point of getting all dressed up?* 6. the meaning. *What's the point of that joke?* 7. a special quality; a trait. *Kindness is one of her good points.* 8. a part; a detail. *Tell us all the points of your plan.* 9. direction. *There are thirty-two points on a compass.* 10. a unit of scoring. *She won the game by two points.* **points.**

v. 11. to aim. *He pointed his arrow at the target. The remarks were pointed at me.* 12. to sharpen. *The pencil was pointed to a thin tip.* 13. to face. *The house points toward the west.* 14. to give extra force to. *His charts and figures pointed his main idea.* 15. **point out,** to call attention to. *A teacher points out mistakes in your work.* **points, point ed, point ing.**

point ed (poin'tid), *adj.* 1. having a point. *John made a spear out of a pointed piece of wood.* 2. sharp; clear and direct. *His pointed remarks about the party were not polite.* **point ed ly,** *adv.*

poi son (poi'zn), *n.* 1. a substance that harms the body. *Some snakes give off a poison when they bite.* 2. anything that is harmful. *Hate is a poison to mankind.* **poi sons.**

v. 3. to injure or kill by poison. *If the tobacco plant is eaten, it can quickly poison a person.* 4. to put poison on. *They poisoned the food that the rats ate.* 5. to have a bad effect on. *Envy of his friend's success poisoned his mind.* **poi sons, poi soned, poi son ing.**

polar bear with cub

poi son ous (poi'zn əs), *adj.* 1. containing poison; dangerous to the body. *Some plants of the buttercup family are poisonous.* 2. having a harmful effect. *Extreme poverty is a poisonous situation.* **poi son ous ly,** *adv.*

poke (pōk), *v.* 1. to push; dig. *The baby poked a finger into the butter.* 2. to thrust forward. *The dog poked his head out of the window.* 3. to move slowly; go forward in a lazy manner. *The boy poked along the country road.* **pokes, poked, pok ing.**

n. 4. a push; a thrust. *Give the ashes a poke to see if the fire will start.* **pokes.**

po lar (pō'lər), *adj.* having to do with the North Pole or the South Pole. *The polar weather is cold.*

polar bear, *n.* a large white bear that lives in the far north. *Polar bears swim in icy waters to catch fish.* **polar bears.**

pole[1] (pōl), *n.* 1. a long, slender piece of wood or metal. *Every morning the flag is raised on its pole. The firemen slid down the pole when they heard the alarm.* **poles.**

v. 2. to move by using a pole. *They poled the boat across the crowded harbor.* **poles, poled, pol ing.**

pole[2] (pōl), *n.* 1. either the north or south end of the earth's axis. *The earth's poles are called the North Pole and the South Pole.* 2. either of the two ends of a magnet or a battery. *The poles of a battery are called positive and negative.* **poles.**

po lice (pə lēs'), *n.* 1. a group of men who enforce law, deal with criminals, and keep peace in a town, city, or state. *Some police keep traffic moving. Some police tour the streets at night watching for signs of danger to citizens. Some police are scientists who work in a laboratory checking criminal evidence.* 2. the department of government to which the police belong. *Call the police in an emergency.* 3. soldiers who keep order. *The military police see that soldiers obey the laws.* **po lice.**

v. 4. to keep the peace in; to enforce the law in. *The officers policed the city.* 5. to clean up. *The soldiers police their camp every day.* **po lic es, po liced, po lic ing.**

po lice man (pə lēs'mən), *n.* a member of the police. *Policemen are on the watch for those who break the law. Policemen also find and return lost pets to their owners.* **po lice men.**

pol i cy[1] (pol'ə sē), *n.* a way of doing things. *That store's policy is to treat customers as if they were always right. Our country's policy has been to lend food and money to nations in need.* **pol i cies.**

pol i cy[2] (pol'ə sē), *n.* the written contract between an insurance company and the person or persons who are insured. *The school has a fire insurance policy.* **pol i cies.**

po lio (pō'lē ō), *n.* a disease of the nervous system that often leaves the persons it attacks unable to move their legs or other parts of the body. *Doctors now have vaccines that can prevent polio.*

pol ish (pol'ish), *n.* 1. a paste, liquid, or wax

polo: a. equipment; b. players

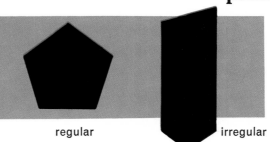

polygons

used to make something clean, shiny, and smooth by rubbing. *Women use one kind of polish on silver and another kind on floors. My father puts a polish on the car every six months.* 2. a smooth, shiny surface. *The table has a fine polish.* **pol ish es.**

v. 3. to make shiny, clean, and smooth by rubbing with a polish. *We polish the car twice a year. How often do you polish your shoes?* 4. to improve; to perfect. *Your short story needs to be polished a little. The teacher said we should polish our talks before giving them in class.* **pol ish es, pol ished, pol ish ing.**

po lite (pə līt′), *adj.* having good manners; courteous; thoughtful. *The polite boy brought in a chair for old Mrs. Perkins.* **po lite ly,** *adv.*

po lit i cal (pə lit′ə kl), *adj.* having to do with politics, the state, or the government. *A political party is a group of people united to elect certain candidates to office.* **po lit i cal ly,** *adv.*

pol i ti cian (pol′ə tish′ən), *n.* a person whose main work is to be active in a political party. *A politician works hard to get his party's candidates elected.* **pol i ti cians.**

pol i tics (pol′ə tiks), *n. pl.* or *sing.* 1. the science and art of government. *Mr. Nelson has studied politics for many years.* 2. the business or profession of governing. *Many men and women enter politics to be more useful citizens.* 2. the activity of a political party. *Mr. Morton has always been interested in politics.*

poll (pōl), *n.* 1. the voting and the counting of votes in an election. *The poll showed that Simpson had more votes than Griffith.* 2. the total number of votes cast. *The poll is small because the snow kept people at home.* 3. **polls,** a place where people vote. *The polls are open from six o'clock in the morning to five o'clock in the evening.* **polls.**

v. 4. to receive votes in an election. *The mayor polled twenty thousand more votes than the other candidate.* 5. to get votes or opinions from. *The magazine polled its readers on the problems of modern youth.* **polls, polled, poll ing.**

pol len (pol′ən), *n.* the yellow powder that is inside a flower. *Flowers use pollen for making seeds that will grow into new plants.*

pol lute (pə lüt′), *v.* to make dirty or impure. *The lake was polluted by the oil dumped into it by the factory.* **pol lutes, pol lut ed, pol lut ing.**

pol lu tion (pə lü′shən), *n.* a polluting; a being impure. *The pollution of the lake caused all the fish to die.* **pol lu tions.**

po lo (pō′lō), *n.* a game played between two teams on horses. *Polo players use long sticks to hit the wooden ball through the other team's goal.*

pol y gon (pol′ē gon′), *n.* a figure having more than four angles and sides. *A pentagon is one kind of polygon.* **pol y gons.**

pond (pond), *n.* a little lake. *Some ponds are formed naturally, and others are made by people.* **ponds.**

pond

pontoon bridge

pony

pon toon (pon tün′), *n.* 1. a boat used as a support for a temporary bridge. *Bridges made with pontoons are often built by soldiers during time of war.* 2. a float on an airplane that allows it to land on water. *A hydroplane will usually have one pontoon on each wing.* **pon toons.**

po ny (pō′nē), *n.* a small horse that grows to less than fifty-eight inches high. *Children ride ponies at an amusement park.* **po nies.**

pool¹ (pül), *n.* 1. any little body of water. *The children sailed boats in the pool in the park.* 2. a tank filled with water and used for swimming. *Pools are built outdoors or indoors.* **pools.**

pool² (pül), *n.* 1. a game played on a special table with six pockets. *In pool the players try to knock balls into the pockets with long sticks.* 2. a common fund; money collected from a group. *How much do we have in the pool?* 3. anything used by a group for the benefit of all. *The company has a car pool for its executives.* **pools.**

poppies

v. 4. to put together into a common fund. *We all pooled our money to buy Mother a present.* **pools, pooled, pool ing.**

poor (pür), *adj.* 1. having little money or no money. *Poor nations need help from rich nations.* 2. not good in quality; not satisfactory; below average. *The crops didn't grow in the poor land. Her grades were poor until she began to spend more time studying. The customer complained about the poor service in the restaurant.* 3. deserving pity; needing sympathy. *The poor child misses his mother.* **poor er, poor est; poor ly,** *adv.*
n. pl. 4. **the poor,** people who have few things or nothing. *The poor need help from those who are more fortunate.*

pop (pop), *v.* 1. to make a sudden, short bursting sound. *The cork popped when George pulled it out of the bottle.* 2. to burst with such a sound. *The balloon popped when I touched it with a pin.* 3. to push suddenly. *The dog popped his head out of the window.* 4. to go or come suddenly. *The children popped out of bed. Our neighbors popped in to say hello.* **pops, popped, pop ping.**
n. 5. a sudden, short, bursting sound. *We heard the pop of the corn as he heated it.* 6. a sweet drink made with soda water; soft drink. *We have orange pop and lime pop.* **pops.**

pop corn (pop′kôrn′), *n.* a kind of corn that bursts open into a white mass when heated. *We like to eat popcorn while watching television.*

pop gun (pop′gun′), *n.* a toy gun that shoots little corks with a popping noise. *Mark wants a popgun for his birthday.* **pop guns.**

pop py (pop′ē), *n.* 1. a plant with beautiful flowers in various shades of red, yellow, or white and leaves that have rough edges. *The seeds of the poppy may be used as bird food or sprinkled on rolls or bread.* 2. the flower of this plant. *Father bought a red poppy to put in his buttonhole.* **pop pies.**

pop u lar (pop′yə lər), *adj.* 1. well-liked. *Arthur's good humor made him the most popular boy in class. That television program is very popular.* 2. of the people; representing the people. *This country has a popular government.* 3. suited to the average

person. *The store sells goods at popular prices.*
4. held by many people; common. *It is a popular belief around school that Jack will be the next class president.* **pop u lar ly,** *adv.*

pop u la tion (pop′yə lā′shən), *n.* 1. the number of people living in a country, state, town, etc. *The population in our town has greatly increased in the past five years.* 2. a group of people having some common characteristic, such as age, location, etc. *The singer is liked by the teen-age population. The farm population would like the price of wheat to be raised.* **pop u la tions.**

por ce lain (pôr′se lin or pôrs′lin), *n.* fine pottery or china, usually very white and durable. *She set the table with her best porcelain.*

porch (pôrch), *n.* a covered entrance to a house or other building. *Our front porch is a favorite place to sit on summer nights.* **porch es.**

por cu pine (pôr′kyə pīn′), *n.* a small, slow-moving animal with stiff, sharp, needle-like hair on its back and tail. *When the porcupine is attacked it lashes its tail and the needles stick in its enemy's body.* **por cu pines.**

pore[1] (pôr), *n.* a tiny opening. *The skin of human beings is covered with pores through which we perspire.* **pores.**

pore[2] (pôr), *v.* to study or think long and intensely. *The professor pored over his books.* **pores, pored, por ing.**

po rous (pô′rəs), *adj.* filled with tiny openings that allow water to go through or to soak in. *A towel is porous.*

pork (pôrk), *n.* the meat of a pig or hog used for food. *The family had roast pork for dinner.*

por poise (pôr′pəs), *n.* a sea animal that is related to the whale. *Porpoises eat fish which they hunt in the ocean.* **por pois es** or **por poise.**

port[1] (pôrt), *n.* a place where ships come to load and remove cargo; a harbor. *Ships usually tie up to a pier in a port.* **ports.** (See illustration on following page.)

port[2] (pôrt), *n.* 1. a small, round window in the side of a ship. *A port lets light and air into the ship's cabins.* 2. an opening in a ship to fire a gun through. *The pirates rolled the cannon up to the port and fired on the cargo ships.* **ports.**

portrait

port[3] (pôrt), *n.* 1. the left-hand side of a ship, boat, or airplane, as one faces forward toward the bow. *Ships show a red light on the port at night.* **ports.**
adj. 2. on the left-hand side of a ship. *A little boat was heading toward the port bow.*

port[4] (pôrt), *n.* a sweet red wine. *Port was originally made in Portugal.* **ports.**

port a ble (pôr′tə bl), *adj.* that can be carried. *Joyce and Harry brought a portable radio to the picnic.*

por tage (pôr′tij), *n.* 1. the carrying of boats and supplies on land from one river, lake, stream, etc. to another. *The portage was easy because the men carried few supplies and their canoe was light.* 2. the place where this carrying is done. *The Indians met at the portage between the two rivers.* **por tag es.**

por tion (pôr′shən), *n.* 1. a part; a share. *A portion of the school day is spent in the study hall. We had small portions of cake at the party.* **portions.**
v. 2. to divide into parts or shares. *Father portioned the food at dinner.* **por tions, por tioned, por tion ing.**

por trait (pôr′trāt, pôr′trit), *n.* a picture of a person. *The portrait of a famous writer hung above the fireplace.* **por traits.**

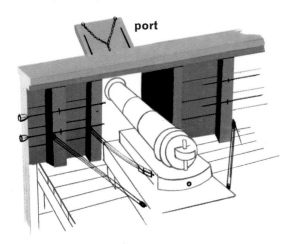

port

porpoise

po si tion (pə zish′ən), *n.* 1. the place where a person or thing is. *The ship radioed its position.* 2. a certain way of holding the body; posture. *The awkward position he was sitting in cramped his muscles.* 3. a job. *My brother has a new position with another company.* 4. rank. *That woman has a high position in the government.* 5. an opinion or attitude; a way of thinking. *What is the new principal's position on school athletics?* 6. the correct place. *We took our positions in line for the parade.* **po si tions.**

pos i tive (poz′ə tiv), *adj.* 1. clearly and definitely stated; definite. *We had positive orders to go home after the game.* 2. without question or doubt. *The hospital tests gave positive proof that he was in good health.* 3. confident; certain. *Gus is positive that his team will win the football game.* 4. helpful; useful. *Ask the teacher for positive suggestions about your idea.* 5. approving; showing agreement. *We received positive answers to all our questions.* **pos i tive ly,** *adv.*
n. 5. a photograph or reel of film showing the

port

lights and darks as they really are. *The camera shop returned his roll of film and two sets of positives.* **pos i tives.**

pos sess (pə zes′), *v.* 1. to have; own. *Some people possess a lot of money and property.* 2. to influence greatly. *John was possessed by the desire to be a great football player, so he practiced every day.* 3. to control. *At one time England possessed India.* **pos sess es, pos sessed, pos sess-ing.**

pos ses sion (pə zesh′ən), *n.* 1. a holding; control. *The teacher has all the test papers in her possession.* 2. something owned. *Mark's most valuable possession is his dog, Topper.* **pos ses-sions.**

pos ses sive (pə zes′iv), *adj.* 1. showing pos-session or ownership. *Words such as "theirs," "yours," "hers," and "mine," are possessive pro-nouns.* 2. showing a strong desire to keep or own. *Children are often possessive about their toys.* **pos ses sive ly,** *adv.*
n. 3. a word that shows possession, such as "Bill's," "its," "ours," etc. *Possessives are formed from nouns and pronouns.* **pos ses sives.**

pos si bil i ty (pos′ə bil′ə tē), *n.* 1. something that can happen or take place. *That he may arrive earlier than we expected is a definite possibility.* 2. a chance. *What are the possibilities of rain for tonight?* **pos si bil i ties.**

pos si ble (pos′ə bl), *adj.* 1. that can be; able to be done. *It is possible to fly an airplane at three thousand miles an hour.* 2. that may happen. *The forecast is for possible showers.* 3. that may be used. *The teacher said that there was only one possible answer to the question.*

pos si bly (pos′ə blē), *adv.* 1. perhaps; maybe. *Possibly my father will take a vacation soon.* 2. by any means. *We can't possibly get the work done by October.*

post[1] (pōst), *n.* 1. a vertical piece of wood, metal, or stone, usually used for support or advertisement. *People often place signs on the post in the town square.* **posts.**
v. 2. to put up on a post or wall for easy view-ing. *Post this notice on the side of the building.* **posts, post ed, post ing.**

post[2] (pōst), *n.* 1. a place where a person is supposed to be. *The soldier's post was the gate at the camp.* 2. an army camp; a place containing soldiers. *The captain must return to the post.* 3. a position; job. *Mr. Compton was appointed to the post of treasurer.* 4. **trading post,** a place or store where trading is done. *The Indians brought furs to the trading post.* **posts.**
v. 5. to place; to station. *They posted a guard at every door.* **posts, post ed, post ing.**

post[3] (pōst), *n.* 1. mail. *The letter came in the morning post.* **posts.**
v. 2. to send by mail. *The letter was posted today.* 3. to inform. *Keep the office posted on your trip.* **posts, post ed, post ing.**

post age (pōs′tij), *n.* 1. the cost of sending a letter or package by mail. *The postage was thirty cents.* 2. **postage stamp,** a government stamp that is put on a piece of mail to show that the cost of sending it has been paid. *A fifty-cent postage stamp was put on the heavy letter.*

post al (pōs′tl), *adj.* having to do with the mail. *The postal service in this city is good.*

post card or **postal card,** *n.* a card used for writing and sending short messages. *Send me a post card while you are away.* **post cards.**

post er (pōs′tər), *n.* a sign. *The poster in the restaurant window showed the school's basketball schedule.* **post ers.**

post man (pōst′mən), *n.* mailman. *The postman comes at nine o'clock in the morning.* **post men.**

post mas ter (pōst′mas′tər), *n.* a person in charge of a post office. *The postmaster told us to write the complete address on our envelopes.* **post-mas ters.**

post office *n.* 1. an office or a building in which people sort mail, sell stamps, and assist in mailing. *Mail these letters at the post office.* 2. the department of the government in charge of the mails. *The post office employs thousands of people.* **post offices.**

post pone (pōst pōn′), *v.* to put off until later; to delay. *The party was postponed until the next Saturday.* **post pones, post poned, post-pon ing.**

post pone ment (pōst pōn′mənt), *n.* the act of postponing. *The postponement of the ball game annoyed many people.* **post pone ments.**

pos ture (pos′chər), *n.* 1. the way a person holds his body. *Stand up straight to improve your posture.* **pos tures.**
v. 2. to put in a certain position. *An actor postures his head and body to show different feelings.* **pos-tures, pos tured, pos tur ing.**

pot (pot), *n.* 1. a vessel made of metal, baked clay, or other material and used for various purposes. *Flowers grow in pots. A pot is used for cooking.* 2. as much as a pot will hold. *We ate a pot of beans for dinner. She made a pot of tea.* **pots.**
v. 3. to put into a pot. *You can pot certain flowers at the end of summer.* **pots, pot ted, pot ting.**

po ta to (pə tā′tō), a thick, solid vegetable that grows beneath the ground. *Potatoes are usually round or oval and have a thin, red or brown skin.* **po ta toes.**

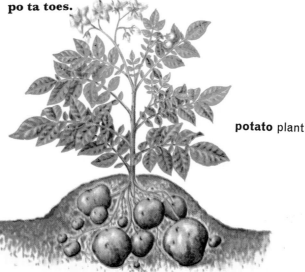

potato plant

pot tery (pot′ə rē), *n.* 1. pots, dishes, and ornaments made of clay which has been hardened by baking. *This shop sells nothing but pottery.* 2. the place where such articles are made. *Our art class is going to visit a pottery on our next field trip.* **pot ter ies.**

poul try (pōl′trē), *n.* birds that are raised for food. *Chickens, ducks, turkeys, and geese are poultry.*

pounce (pouns), *v.* 1. to jump suddenly. *The cat pounced on the ball.* **pounc es, pounced, pounc ing.**
n. 2. a sudden jump. *Whenever Mother begins to knit the cat makes a pounce for her ball of yarn.* **pounc es.**

pound¹ (pound), *n.* 1. a measure of weight equal to sixteen ounces. *Buy a pound of candy for me.* 2. in Great Britain, a sum of money approximately equal to $2.40. *That book costs two pounds.* **pounds.**

pound² (pound), *n.* a place where lost animals are kept and cared for. *Sharon found her dog at the pound.* **pounds.**

pound³ (pound), *v.* 1. to hit heavily and often. *We pounded on John's door to wake him up. After his dinner the baby pounded the table with his spoon.* 2. to crush by beating. *The Indian pounded the herb into a powder and used it for medicine.* 3. to move with loud steps. *The horses pounded down the track.* 4. to beat heavily; throb. *His heart pounded after he ran home from school.* **pounds, pound ed, pound ing.**

pour (pôr), *v.* 1. to let flow in a regular stream. *Should I pour some grape juice for you?* 2. to flow in a steady stream. *The water poured off the roof. The people poured out of the theater.* 3. to rain very hard. *It is pouring outside.* **pours, poured, pour ing.**

pov er ty (pov′ər tē), *n.* 1. the condition of being poor; the lack of money, food, clothing, etc. *Some nations of the world suffer from great poverty.* 2. poor quality; a lack of something desirable. *The poverty of his language makes his talks dull.*

pow der (pou′dər), *n.* 1. a solid that has been made into fine grains like dust. *The Indians ground the corn into a powder.* 2. anything made in powder form for a special purpose. *Girls use face powder. The powder for the guns was wet and useless.* **pow ders.**
v. 3. to make into powder. *In the flour mill, wheat grains are powdered.* 4. to cover lightly. *Snow powdered the ground.* 5. to use powder on. *The barber powdered the man's face after shaving him.* **pow ders, pow dered, pow der ing.**

pow dery (pou′dər ē), *adj.* 1. like powder. *The powdery snow fell softly on the ground.* 2. covered with powder or something like it. *The traveler's hat was powdery with dust.*

pow er (pou′ər), *n.* 1. strength; force; vigor. *The magazine article was written with power. A jet engine is full of power. He used all his power to win the race.* 2. an authority. *Congress has power to make laws. The principal has power to dismiss school early if the weather is bad.* 3. a strong and important nation. *The United States is a world power.* **pow ers.**
adj. 4. supplying power; producing electricity or steam for useful work. *Energy from the waterfall runs the power plant.* 5. run by an engine or motor. *Power boats speed through the water.*
v. 6. to supply with power. *An engine powers an automobile.* **pow ers, pow ered, pow er ing.**

pow er ful (pou′ər fəl), *adj.* having great power; strong. *The king was a powerful ruler. The powerful drug cured him.* **pow er ful ly,** *adv.*

prac ti cal (prak′tə kl), *adj.* 1. doing rather than thinking. *Working is a very practical and important part of life.* 2. a workable manner. *Her practical solution solved the problem.* 3. useful. *Her practical approach to children was a great help.* **prac ti cal ly,** *adv.*

prac ti cal ly (prak′tik lē), *adv.* 1. in a useful way or sensible way. *We have to face this problem practically.* 2. in effect. *That smart boy practically runs the store.* 3. almost. *The movie theater was practically empty last Saturday afternoon.*

prac tice (prak′tis), *n.* 1. actual use. *The Boy Scouts put their study of first aid into practice when Marty cut his hand.* 2. custom; habit. *Our practice is to start school at nine o'clock.* 3. training by doing something over and over. *Daily practice is necessary for a piano player.* 4. the work of a profession. *My father's law practice keeps him very busy.* **prac tic es.**
v. 5. to put into actual use. *She practices what she believes about being kind to others.* 6. to do exercises in something in order to become skilled. *The ball player practices hitting the ball every day.* 7. to work at or follow, such as a profession. *The doctor practices medicine.* **prac tic es, practiced, prac tic ing.**

prai rie (prâr′ē), *n.* a large area of land with much grass but very few trees. *The prairies of the western states were traveled by the pioneers.* **prai ries.**

praise (prāz), *v.* 1. to speak or write good things about. *We like it when the teacher praises our work.* 2. to worship in words or songs. *People go to a church or temple to praise God.* **prais es, praised, prais ing.**
n. 3. a recommendation; a statement that something or someone is good. *Our school received praise for its good scholarship.* **prais es.**

prank (prangk), *n.* a trick. *Children play pranks on Halloween.* **pranks.**

prawn (prôn), *n.* a shellfish that looks like a large shrimp. *The meat of some prawns is good to eat.* **prawns.**

pray (prā), *v.* 1. to speak to God with love and worship. *After the sermon the minister asked everyone to pray.* 2. to ask earnestly. *The lawyer prayed the judge to find the man innocent.* **prays, prayed, pray ing.**

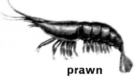

prawn

pray er (prâr), *n.* 1. a request to God that expresses love, gives thanks, and makes an appeal. *He gave a silent prayer for peace.* 2. a thing prayed for. *His prayer was granted.* **pray ers.**

preach (prēch), *v.* 1. to talk on a religious subject; to give a sermon. *The minister preaches every Sunday in church.* 2. to urge; speak earnestly about something. *The teacher preached the need for good study habits.* **preach es, preached, preach ing.**

preach er (prē′chər), *n.* a person who preaches; minister. *The preacher delivered a fine sermon last Sunday.* **preach ers.**

pre cede (prē sēd′), *v.* to go or come before. *January precedes February. The number 8 precedes the number 9 when you count.* **pre cedes, pre ced ed, pre ced ing.**

pre cious (presh′əs), *adj.* 1. having a high price; costing a great deal. *Diamonds are precious jewels.* 2. much loved; dear. *Their precious child brought happiness to the parents.* **pre cious ly,** *adv.*

pre cip i ta tion (pri sip′ə tā′shən), *n.* 1. the sudden bringing on of something. *The precipitation of the applause was caused by the appearance of the famous movie actor.* 2. speed; haste. *An umpire must make a decision with precipitation.* 3. moisture that falls as rain, snow, hail, or sleet. *We have had very little precipitation this summer.* **pre cip i ta tions.**

pre cise (pri sīs′), *adj.* 1. exact. *The man gave me the precise amount of money.* 2. accurate; careful. *The teacher's directions were very precise.* 3. clear; easily understood. *Mother gave precise orders on how we were to behave.* **pre cise ly,** *adv.*

pre fer (pri fėr′), *v.* to like better. *In cold weather the cat prefers to sit by the fire.* **pre fers, pre ferred, pre fer ring.**

pref er ence (pref′ər əns), *n.* 1. a special liking for one person or thing rather than any other. *A polar bear has a preference for cold weather. In books my preference is for stories about the early pioneers.* 2. the thing that is chosen or preferred. *Her preference is the yellow swimming suit.* **pref er enc es.**

pre hen sile (pri hen′sl), *adj.* that is used for grasping, seizing, or holding on. *Some monkeys have prehensile tails. An elephant has a prehensile trunk.*

pre his tor ic (prē′his tôr′ik), *adj.* having to do with the time before written history began. *Prehistoric paintings and tools have been found in many parts of the world.* (See illustration on following page.)

pre lim i nary (pri lim′ə ner′ē), *adj.* 1. coming before the main thing. *The preliminary plans are finished and the builders can begin.* **pre lim i nar i ly,** *adv.*
n. 2. something done first. *A physical examination is a preliminary to joining the team.* **pre lim i nar ies.**

pre mi um (prē′mē əm), *n.* 1. a prize; a reward. *The soap company gave a towel as a premium with each box of soap powder.* 2. a payment to an insurance company. *Fred pays thirty dollars a month premium for hospital insurance.* 3. a sum more than the regular price.

prehensile organs of animals

trunk of an elephant

tail of a monkey

tentacles of an octopus

EVIDENCE OF PREHISTORIC MAN

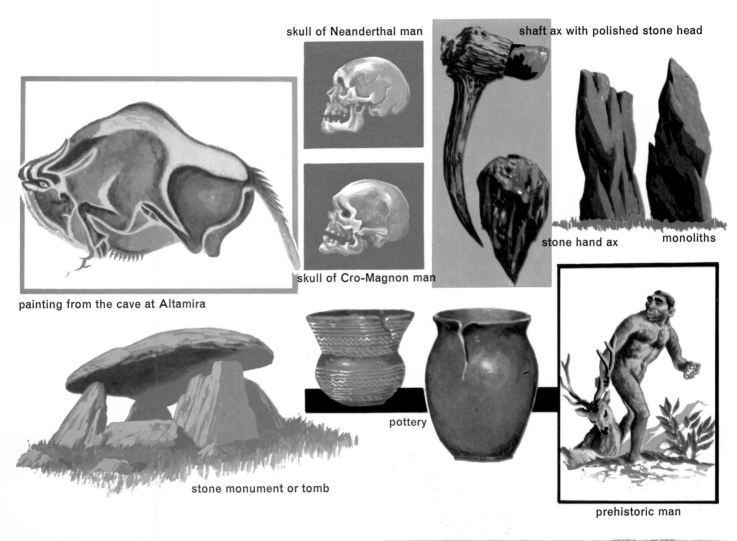

skull of Neanderthal man

shaft ax with polished stone head

painting from the cave at Altamira

skull of Cro-Magnon man

stone hand ax

monoliths

stone monument or tomb

pottery

prehistoric man

prehistoric paintings found on cave walls

Father paid a premium to get good seats at the World Series. **pre mi ums.**

pre paid (prē pād′), *adj.* paid for in advance. *The package was prepaid.*

prep a ra tion (prep′ə rā′shən), *n.* 1. a getting ready; a making ready. *She spent much time in preparation for the test.* 2. something done to get ready; something which prepares. *Education is a preparation for life.* 3. something for a special purpose. *The television commercials told about a new preparation for the hair.* **prep a ra tions.**

pre pare (pri pâr′), *v.* 1. to make ready; get ready. *The school prepared for the Halloween party. The farmer prepares the soil for planting crops.* 2. to make or put together in a certain way. *The chef prepared his special salad.* **pre pares, pre pared, pre par ing.**

pre scribe (pri skrīb′), *v.* 1. to order the use of a certain remedy or medicine. *The doctor prescribed some more cough medicine for me.* 2. to order; to give as a rule. *The law prescribes certain ways in which an automobile may be driven.* **pre scribes, pre scribed, pre scrib ing.**

pres ence (prez′ns), *n.* 1. the fact or condition of being present. *The presence of the flowers made Carol sneeze.* 2. the company; a being near. *Men remove their hats in the presence of women. His name was signed in the presence of witnesses.* 3. behavior; appearance. *He was a man of distinguished presence.*

pre sent[1] (pri zent′ for 1–6, prez′nt for 7), *v.* 1. to give. *The prize was presented to the winner.* 2. to introduce. *On Parents' Night, Julie presented her mother to her teacher.* 3. to send in; to deliver. *The dentist presented his bill for filling my teeth.* 4. to put before the public. *Will the senior class present a play?* 5. to show; to have. *The man presented a neat appearance.* 6. to offer; to bring up for consideration. *May I present a suggestion?* **pre sents, pre sent ed, pre sent ing.**
n. 7. a gift. *You can open your present now.* **pres ents.**

pres ent[2] (prez′nt), *adj.* 1. on hand; here. *On the day of the blizzard, only half the class was present.* 2. existing now. *The present interest in space travel will continue.*

pres ent ly (prez′nt lē), *adv.* 1. soon; in a little while. *The train will arrive presently.* 2. now; at this time. *Mark is presently on a camping trip.*

pre serve (pri zėrv′), *v.* 1. to protect; to keep from harm, ruin, or damage. *The national forests preserve our trees and wildlife. We must preserve our rivers, lakes, and air from pollution by garbage and smoke.* 2. to prepare for later use by canning, pickling, etc. *Some housewives preserve dozens of jars of peaches, beets, and strawberries.* **pre serves, pre served, pre serv ing.**
n. 3. fruit preserved with sugar. *Blueberry preserves taste good on toast.* 4. a place where fish and animals are protected. *The United States*

and the individual states have set up preserves where no one may fish or hunt. **pre serves.**

pre side (pri zīd′), *v.* 1. to have the position of authority. *Mr. Smith presides over this whole business operation.* 2. to have control over a meeting, a company, an area, a group, etc. *Miss Jones will preside at the teachers' meeting tonight.* **pre sides, pre sid ed, pre sid ing.**

pres i dent (prez′ə dənt), *n.* the person who occupies the highest office in a nation, business, company, club, college, etc. *The President of the United States is the head of our government and the Commander-in-Chief of our Army, Navy, and Air Force. My uncle is the president of a big corporation.* **pres i dents.**

press (pres), *v.* 1. to push. *Press the button to make the front doorbell ring.* 2. to iron. *Mother is pressing my shirt.* 3. to hug; to grip. *My aunt pressed the baby close to her. He pressed my hand as we said goodby.* 4. to squeeze out. *Oil is pressed from olives.* 5. to keep on asking; to urge. *The publisher pressed the author for his book.* 6. to crowd; to gather tightly together. *The big audience pressed into the small building.* 7. to worry because of a need for something. *I'm pressed for money this week.* 8. **press on,** to keep going. *They pressed on even though it was getting dark and snow had begun to fall.* **press es, pressed, press ing.**
n. 9. a pressing; pushing. *The press of the crowd kept us apart. The steady press of work made him very tired.* 10. a machine for squeezing, forcing together, stamping, or crushing. *Books and magazines are printed on presses which stamp ink on paper. Grape juice is made by a press which squeezes grapes.* 11. reporters for newspapers and magazines. *The mayor will meet with the press.* **press es.**

pres sure (presh′ər), *n.* 1. a pressing; a use of force. *We applied pressure to the orange to squeeze out the juice.* 2. stress; strain. *Some people work best under pressure.* 3. physical distress. *The pressure of my headache will not let up.* 4. the force against a surface, stated in weight per unit of area. *At sea level, the air pressure is a little over fourteen pounds per square inch. On mountain tops the pressure is much less than at sea level.* **pres sures.**

pre sume (pri zūm′), *v.* 1. to take for granted; suppose. *I presume that Evelyn will be on time.* 2. to dare. *No one would presume to tell the doctor he is wrong.* 3. to suppose to be true without proof. *Susan presumed that the dog had broken the vase just because he was in the room when it fell.* 4. **presume on,** to take advantage of. *Our neighbor presumes on Mother's good nature to borrow most of our tools.* **pre sumes, pre sumed, pre sum ing.**

pre tend (pri tend′), *v.* 1. to make believe. *The little children pretended they were cowboys.* 2. to say or act as if something is true when it isn't; to claim falsely. *They pretend to be poets. You*

cider **press**

can't pretend sickness when you look healthy. **pretends, pre tend ed, pre tend ing.**

pret ty (prit′ē), *adj.* 1. lovely; pleasing; pleasant to look at or to hear. *The baby has a pretty face. The girl has a pretty voice. There are some pretty flowers growing in the garden.* **pret ti er, pret ti est; pret ti ly,** *adv.*

adv. 2. fairly; moderately. *Your painting is pretty good. Carl got one grade that was pretty bad.*

pre vail (pri vāl′), *v.* 1. to win a victory; to triumph. *Jane was about to spend her allowance foolishly, but good sense prevailed. The firemen prevailed over the fire.* 2. to be the general condition; to be common. *Winds from the west prevail during summer.* 3. **prevail upon,** to urge successfully. *The people at the party prevailed upon the famous singer to sing a song.* **pre vails, pre vailed, pre vail ing.**

pre vent (pri vent′), *v.* 1. to keep from happening. *Caution helps to prevent accidents. You can prevent painful tooth problems if you see your dentist often.* 2. to stop. *The heavy fog prevented the planes from taking off or landing.* **pre vents, pre vent ed, pre vent ing.**

pre vi ous (prē′vē əs), *adj.* earlier, prior; former. *The tree has grown since my previous visit here.* **pre vi ous ly,** *adv.*

price (prīs), *n.* 1. the cost in money; the amount of money for which something is sold. *The price of an ice-cream bar is ten cents.* 2. a cost of any kind. *Being tired is the price of working too hard. He saved the boy from the fire at the price of some bad burns to himself.* **pric es.**

v. 3. to ask the price of. *It is best to price several dresses before buying one.* 4. to put a price on. *Ted priced his old bike at fifteen dollars.* **pric es, priced, pric ing.**

prick (prik), *v.* 1. to stick; make a little hole in with a sharp point. *The needle pricked her finger.* 2. to hurt or bother. *Her conscience pricked her after she spoke harshly to her little brother.* 3. to raise. *The dog pricked up his ears when he heard footsteps.* 4. **to prick up one's ears,** to begin to listen closely. *We pricked up our ears when she mentioned the possibility of a beach party.* **pricks, pricked, prick ing.**

n. 5. a small hole made by a sharp point. *The pricks of the pins could be seen in the cloth.* **pricks.**

pride (prīd), *n.* 1. an opinion of oneself that is too high; sense of vanity. *Jack's pride made him feel that he was better than anyone else.* 2. a good opinion of oneself that is just right; respect for one's self or one's achievements. *He had too much pride to admit he had failed, so he tried again.* 3. a feeling of happiness at doing something well. *The artist had pride in his painting.* 4. a thing or person causing happiness or satisfaction. *Don's workshop is his pride. The baby is the family's pride.* **prides.**

v. 5. **pride oneself on,** to be proud of. *She prides herself on having learned how to read faster.* **prides, prid ed, prid ing.**

priest (prēst), *n.* a minister of a Christian church. *The priest spoke to the people.* **priests.**

pri ma ry (prī′mer′ē), *adj.* 1. first in time; first in order. *The primary grades in school are grades one through three.* 2. most important; main. *A doctor's primary interest is the health of his patients.* 3. basic; from which other combinations are made. *The primary colors are red, yellow, and blue.* **pri mar i ly,** *adv.*

n. 4. an election in which members of a political party in a voting district vote for candidates to run in the main state or national elections. *Mr. Smith wants to win the primaries in his state so that he can be his party's candidate for governor.* **pri mar ies.**

prim i tive (prim′ə tiv), *adj.* 1. ancient; of the earliest times. *Primitive men lived in caves because they had no tools for making houses.* 2. simple and crude; of the earliest times. *The museum has an exhibit of primitive tools.* **prim i tive ly,** *adv.*

prince (prins), *n.* 1. the son of a king or queen. *A prince usually becomes the king on the death of his father or mother.* 2. a ruler of a fairly small country; a monarch. *Princes from five countries joined forces in the battle.* **princ es.**

prin cess (prin′sis), *n.* 1. the daughter of a king or queen. *The princess is married to the prince.* 2. a woman ruler with the rank of prince. *The tiny country has been ruled by the princess for many years.* **prin cess es.**

prin ci pal (prin′sə pl), *adj.* 1. most important; chief; main. *Two of the principal ports in the United States are New York City and San Francisco. The principal product of Pittsburgh is steel.* **prin ci pal ly,** *adv.*

n. 2. the head of a school. *The principal announced the winners of the school spelling contest.* 3. an amount of money that earns interest or is owed as a debt. *The principal of the investment is two hundred dollars, and it earns five per cent, or ten dollars, a year.* **prin ci pals.**

prin ci ple (prin′sə pl), *n.* 1. a basic fact; a rule upon which other rules are based. *First we learn the principles of science, and then we see how they work in solving problems and doing experiments.* 2. a rule followed in deciding how to behave. *One of his principles is always to do his job well.* 3. honesty; honor. *Mr. Campbell is a man of principle in business affairs.* **prin ci ples.**

print (print), *n.* 1. a mark made on a surface by pressing, stepping, or touching. *As the wet dog came inside he left little prints on the kitchen floor. His greasy fingers left prints on the glass.* 2. cloth with design that has been stamped on it. *Mother is making a dress out of cotton print.* 3. letters and words stamped on paper by using type which has ink on it. *Some books use large, easy to read print.* 4. a picture or design made by printing. *The colors of the prints in most books and magazines are usually very close to the colors of the original picture.* 5. a photograph. *Here are the prints of the pictures.* **prints.**

---

sand, āte, bâre, fäther; sent, mē, férn; fit, bīke; pot, rōpe, fôrt; run, pùll, rüle, cūte; noise, sound; ch, cheese; ng, long; th, thick; ~~th~~, those; zh, treasure; ə = a in about, e in waken, i in animal, o in seldom, and u in minus.

printed cloth

v. 6. to stamp words, designs, or pictures on. *Huge presses print thousands of pages an hour.* 7. to make into a photograph. *We are having the pictures of our summer vacation printed.* 8. to publish. *The magazine printed the author's first stories.* 9. to form letters the way they appear in print or on most typewriters. *Children usually learn to print in the first grade.* **prints, print ed, print ing.**

pri or (prī′ər), *adj.* 1. previous; earlier. *I could not go to the party because I had a prior appointment.* 2. **prior to,** before. *Prior to coming here, our teacher taught in Illinois.*

prism (priz′əm), *n.* a transparent solid having a base with three or more sides that bends, reflects, or separates light. *By using a prism one can see red, orange, yellow, green, blue, and violet in a single ray of light.* **prisms.**

pris on (priz′n), *n.* a place where people who break the law are placed. *Many prisons have school classes in which prisoners can learn a trade.* **pri sons.** (See illustration on following page.)

pris on er (priz′n ər), *n.* a person who is in a prison. *The prisoners tended the prison garden.* **pris on ers.**

pri vate (prī′vit), *adj.* 1. belonging to a certain person, group of persons, or to one's self; not public. *Your letters are your private property. In the summer we go to my family's private beach in Connecticut.* 2. secret. *The sisters had a private talk about the costumes they would wear for the party.* 3. not having a public office. *When a governor leaves office, he becomes a private citizen again.* **pri vate ly,** *adv.*

n. 4. a soldier who holds the lowest rank. *He is a private in the army.* **pri vates.**

priv i lege (priv′l ij), *n.* 1. a special right; an advantage that not many others have. *The class had the privilege of holding a small party during school hours.* **priv i leg es.**

v. 2. to give a privilege. *Jim was privileged to work in the principal's office.* **priv i leg es, priv i leged, priv i leg ing.**

prize (prīz), *n.* 1. a thing won in a contest. *Joe's prize for spelling the most words correctly was a*

printing presses

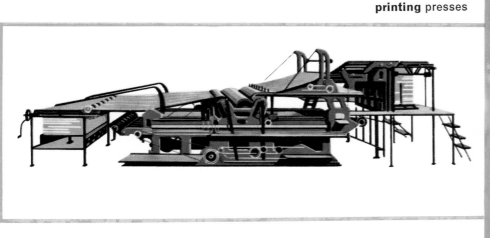

beautiful dictionary. A prize was given to the person who had the winning number. 2. a thing of value. *This beautiful painting is a prize.* 3. an enemy warship captured at sea. *The sailors brought back many prizes.* **priz es.**

adj. 4. worthy of winning some kind of reward or prize. *This young man is our prize second baseman.* 5. having won a prize. *Mr. Collins bought the prize painting at the art show.*

v. 6. to think much of. *I prize my friendship with him.* **priz es, prized, priz ing.**

prob a bil i ty (prob′ə bil′ə tē), *n.* 1. a possibility; a good chance. *There is a probability that our team will win the next football game.* 2. a thing that is probable or likely to happen. *Falling is always a probability when you first learn to ski.* **prob a bil i ties.**

prob a ble (prob′ə bl), *adj.* likely to happen. *The dark clouds and lightning mean that rain is probable.* **prob a bly,** *adv.*

prob lem (prob′ləm), *n.* 1. a question to be worked out and answered. *The arithmetic problems for today will help us to review the week's work.* 2. something for which it is hard to find an answer. *Mrs. Norwood's problem was how to buy clothes for four children on a limited budget.* **prob lems.**

pro ceed (prə sēd′), *v.* to go on; to go forward. *He proceeded with the speech. The men proceeded on their expedition to the North Pole.* **pro ceeds, pro ceed ed, pro ceed ing.**

pro ceed ing (prə sē′ding), *n.* 1. an action; an activity. *The proceedings of the Indians were strange to the Englishman.* 2. **proceedings,** a record of what took place during a meeting. *The secretary reviewed the proceedings of the last meeting for those who had not been present.* **pro ceed ings.**

pro ceeds (prō′sēdz), *n. pl.* the money received from the selling of something. *The proceeds of our candy sale went to the school library fund.*

proc ess (pros′es or prō′ses), *n.* 1. a series of actions which has an expected end; a plan or method. *Most flowers follow a process of growth from bud to bloom. The training of astronauts is a long process.* **proc ess es.**

v. 2. to prepare in a special way. *Grain is processed to make breakfast cereal.* **proc ess es, proc essed, proc ess ing.**

pro ces sion (prə sesh′ən), *n.* a group of persons moving forward in an orderly way. *The graduation procession came down the aisles of the auditorium.* **pro ces sions.**

pro claim (prō klām′), *v.* to announce publicly. *The principal proclaimed a half-day holiday when our school won the champion football game.* **pro claims, pro claimed, pro claim ing.**

pro cure (prə kyùr′), *v.* to get; obtain. *The school procured a famous artist to talk to us.* **pro cures, pro cured, pro cur ing.**

pro duce (prə düs′, prə dūs′ for 1–4, prod′üs, prod′ūs, prō′düs, prō′dūs for 5), *v.* 1. to make or manufacture; to put out. *That big factory produces hundreds of automobiles. Boiling water produces steam.* 2. to show; to exhibit. *The girl's father produced the award he won in college. Produce your ticket at the gate.* 3. to present to the public. *Many towns have groups of people that produce plays.* 4. to grow. *Farmers produce crops. Good soil helps to produce crops.* **pro duc es, pro duced, pro duc ing.**

n. 5. fruits and vegetables. *The produce in this market is always fresh.*

prod uct (prod′əkt), *n.* 1. a thing that is made or grown. *Certain farm products are cheaper in the summer than in the winter. Airplanes are products of a factory.* 2. the outcome; the result. *That shadow you see is a product of your imagination. His success is a product of hard work.* 3. a number that you get by multiplying two or more numbers. *The product of three and five is fifteen.* **prod ucts.**

prison

pro duc tion (prə duk′shən), *n.* 1. the act of making or producing. *Production of automobiles has shown a steady increase in the last five years.* 2. anything that is produced or made. *Some good productions can be seen on television.* **pro duc tions.**

pro fes sion (prə fesh′ən), *n.* 1. a kind of work or occupation that requires special education. *The young man tried to decide whether to enter the legal or the medical profession.* 2. the people in this type of occupation. *The profession praised the lawyer for his fine handling of the case.* 3. an open and free statement or declaration. *In many churches, the faithful members give a profession of faith each Sunday.* **pro fes sions.**

pro fes sion al (prə fesh′ən l), *adj.* 1. having to do with a profession. *A doctor never discusses his professional duties with anyone except another physician.* 2. earning one's living from art, sports, or other activity usually done for pleasure. *Linda is practicing hard to become a professional dancer. Professional baseball players are the best in the country.* 3. having professional players. *The Chicago Bears are a professional football team.* **pro fes sion al ly,** *adv.*
n. 4. a person who makes a living from art, sports, or other activity usually done for pleasure. *Steve has decided to study acting and become a professional.* **pro fes sion als.**

pro fes sor (prə fes′ər), *n.* a college teacher of the highest rank. *Professors are often asked for advice by business and government.* **pro fes sors.**

prof it (prof′it), *n.* 1. the amount of money made from a business after all expenses have been subtracted. *The profits in some businesses are small.* 2. a benefit; an advantage. *John found both profit and enjoyment in taking music lessons.* **prof its.**
v. 3. to gain in money. *Selling his old bicycle profited him fifteen dollars.* 4. to benefit. *I can profit from your experience.* **prof its, prof it ed, prof it ing.**

prof it a ble (prof′ ə tə bl), *adj.* that brings profit or benefit. *The store had a profitable year. Reading good books is a profitable hobby.* **prof it a bly,** *adv.*

pro gram (prō′gram), *n.* 1. a list of events that will take place at a public gathering. *The graduation program prints the order of the speeches and songs. The concert program gave the names of the musical numbers that would be played.* 2. a performance; entertainment. *The program given by the school band was very professional. I like to watch the comedy programs on television.* 3. a plan of action. *What is the town's program for building a new school?* **pro grams.**
v. 4. to place in a program. *Richard's violin solo was programmed third in the concert.* **pro grams, pro grammed** or **pro gramed, pro gram ming** or **pro gram ing.**

prog ress (prog′res for 1 and 2, prə gres′ for 3 and 4), *n.* 1. a movement forward. *The train*

motion picture **projector**

made swift progress toward our destination. 2. an improvement. *The teacher said we all had shown progress in reading.*
v. 3. to move forward; to go ahead. *The game progressed quickly. The building of our new house is progressing right on schedule.* 4. to improve. *She progressed in her work as the year went on.* **pro gress es, pro gressed, pro gress ing.**

pro gres sive (prə gres′iv), *adj.* 1. in favor of new ideas and of changes that will make things better. *Our progressive mayor is planning to build more parks and apartments for the poor people of the city.* 2. moving steadily forward. *Grandfather remembers the progressive development of our town into a city.* **pro gres sive ly,** *adv.*
n. 3. a person who believes in progress and change. *A progressive would like to see social improvements brought about by the government.* **pro gres sives.**

proj ect (proj′ekt for 1, prə jekt′ for 2–5), *n.* 1. a plan; scheme. *The boys' next project is to build a radio.* **proj ects.**
v. 2. to plan; to arrange. *Let's project a way to earn money for some new clothes.* 3. to throw or shoot forward. *An arrow is projected from a bow.* 4. to cause to fall on a surface. *Movies are projected on a white screen.* 5. to stick out. *The posts of the old pier project from the water.* **pro jects, pro ject ed, pro ject ing.**

pro jec tor (prə jek′tər), *n.* a machine for showing movies. *Film is wound on a reel before it is put in the projector.* **pro jec tors.**

prom i nent (prom′ə nənt), *adj.* 1. well-known; important. *Many prominent businessmen were in favor of the new road.* 2. standing out; easy to notice. *The winning score was announced in a prominent headline in the school newspaper.* **prom i nent ly,** *adv.*

prom ise (prom′is), *n.* 1. a statement from a person saying that he will surely do something. *Earl broke his promise to be home early. Jerry always* *keeps his promises.* 2. a cause for hope; a sign of future success. *The girl's singing ability shows promise. Some of the players on the team show promise of becoming champions.* **prom is es.**

v. 3. to give one's word; to make a promise. *Margaret promised to be here at three o'clock.* 4. to agree to give something; to make a promise of. *I promised a new toy to the child.* 5. to give reason to expect. *The blue sky promises a nice day.* **prom is es, prom ised, prom is ing.**

prompt (prompt), *adj.* 1. on time. *We are prompt in arriving at school.* 2. quick; fast. *George got a prompt reply from the company.* **prompt ly,** *adv.*

prompt er (promp′tər), *n.* a person whose job is to remind actors and singers when they forget what to say or do. *During the opera, the prompter helped the singers from a hidden place in the front of the stage.* **prompt ers.**

pro noun (prō′noun), *n.* a word used in place of a noun or name. *The word "she" is a pronoun used in speaking of a girl or woman.* **pronouns.**

pro nounce (prə nouns′), *v.* 1. to make the sounds of; speak. *Pronounce your words clearly so that you can be understood.* 2. to declare officially; to announce with authority. *At the wedding, the minister pronounced the couple man and wife.* **pronounc es, pro nounced, pro nounc ing.**

proof (prüf), *n.* 1. a way of showing the truth of something; anything that shows that something is correct. *Do you have proof of your theory that the dog ate the cake?* 2. a test; a trial. *The scientist put his theory to the proof when he performed the experiment.* 3. a trial sheet or sheets from a book, magazine or newspaper on which corrections can be made. *The editor must approve the proofs of a book before it is printed in final form and sold to the public.* **proofs.**

adj. 4. safe or protected. *The old fortress was proof against attack.*

proof read (prüf′rēd′), *v.* to read proofs of a book, magazine, or newspaper before it is published to see if there are any errors. *Alice marked all of the misspelled words when she proofread the book.* **proof reads, proof read** (prüf′red′), **proof read ing.**

airplane **propeller**

pro pel ler (prə pel′ər), *n.* a device made of blades that whirl around to drive a boat or airplane forward. *The big propeller of a helicopter helps it to fly forward, backward, and straight up and down.* **pro pel lers.**

prop er (prop′ər), *adj.* 1. correct; suitable. *A proper tool for smoothing wood is a plane.* 2. decent; respectable. *Mother expects us to show proper manners at the party.* 3. indicating a particular person; belonging to one or to only a few. *Joan Smith is a proper name.* **prop er ly,** *adv.*

prop er ly (prop′ər lē), *adv.* 1. correctly; suitably. *Marjorie is properly dressed for the hike.* 2. rightly; with reason. *He was properly sorry for what he had done.*

prompter

prop er ty (prop′ər tē), *n.* 1. something that is owned. *That red bicycle is my property. Mr. Warren's property extends a mile into the woods. Sarah's property consists of two hundred dollars in the bank.* 2. a quality belonging to something. *Sweetness is a property of candy.* **prop er ties.**

pro por tion (prə pôr′shən), *n.* 1. a part. *A large proportion of the earth is water.* 2. a proper relation. *This painting is in proportion to the size of the wall it hangs on. The mother's pride in him was out of proportion to the child's real ability at the piano.* 3. the relation of one thing to another in amount, size, or number. *The proportion of boys to girls in our class is two to one; that is, there are twice as many boys as girls.* 4. **proportions,** size. *The United States is a country of vast proportions.* **pro por tions.**

v. 5. to put one thing in the correct relation to another. *He proportions his food purchases to the money he has.* **pro por tions, pro portioned, pro por tion ing.**

pro pose (prə pōz′), *v.* 1. to suggest; to offer as an idea to think about. *The city proposed that the airport be built on the lake.* 2. to name; to present someone's name for office. *Sheila proposed Mark Jones for president of our class.* 3. to intend; to plan. *Dad proposes to buy us all new coats this winter.* 4. to make an offer of marriage. *The young man proposed to the young woman.* **pro pos es, pro posed, pro pos ing.**

prop o si tion (prop′ə zish′ən), *n.* 1. something suggested or proposed; a plan. *We accepted Mr. Peterson's proposition that we shovel snow from his sidewalk.* 2. a statement to be discussed or proved. *The proposition for debate was whether or not we should help poor nations.* **prop o si tions.**

pros pect (pros′pekt), *n.* 1. a broad view. *The prospect from the top of the mountain was thrilling.* 2. something looked forward to; a possibility. *The prospect of getting a better job made him work hard.* 3. a person who may be a possible customer, member, player, etc. in the future. *Salesmen keep a record of prospects. That college* *football player is a prospect for professional football.* **4. prospects,** chances for success. *The coach said his team had excellent prospects.* **pros pects.** *v.* **5.** to search. *The old man prospected for gold and finally found a rich mine.* **pros pects, pros pect ed, pros pect ing.**

pros pect or (pros′pek tər), *n.* a person who searches for valuable minerals or oil. *Some prospectors today use scientific instruments to help them in their work.* **pros pect ors.**

pros per ous (pros′pər əs), *adj.* successful. *The prosperous businessman gave money to the boys' baseball team.* **pros per ous ly,** *adv.*

pro tect (prə tekt′), *v.* to guard; defend; shield; keep from danger. *The police protect citizens from criminals. Some animals will fight fiercely to protect their young. Protect the baby by watching him closely.* **pro tects, pro tect ed, pro tect ing.**

pro tec tion (prə tek′shən), *n.* **1.** care; the keeping from danger. *The job of a gamekeeper is the protection of wildlife. The new animals for the zoo arrived under the protection of a doctor.* **2.** a person or thing that protects or keeps from harm. *A raincoat is a protection in damp weather.*

pro test (prə test′ for 1 and 2, prō′test for 3), *v.* **1.** to object to; to speak out against. *Years ago people protested child labor and made laws to prevent it.* **2.** to declare positively; to insist. *The man protested that he was not guilty.* **pro tests, pro test ed, pro test ing.** *n.* **3.** an objection; a complaint. *We have heard many protests about the election.* **pro tests.**

proud (proud), *adj.* **1.** having a proper regard for oneself. *Mr. Collins is a proud man who likes to do his job well.* **2.** thinking that one is better than others. *The proud boy annoyed his friends by his boasting.* **3.** having satisfaction and pleasure. *The proud mother watched her son graduate.* **4. proud of,** pleased and satisfied with. *We are proud of our school.* **proud ly,** *adv.*

prove (prüv), *v.* **1.** to show to be true. *The doctor's tests proved that Brian was in good health.* **2.** to show, test, or demonstrate by an experiment. *The science class proves scientific theories in the school laboratory.* **3.** to check the answer to (a problem in arithmetic). *You prove a problem in subtraction by adding your answer to the subtrahend and getting the minuend.* **4.** to turn out to be. *The water proved cold.* **proves, proved, proved** or **prov en, prov ing.**

pro vide (prə vīd′), *v.* **1.** to supply; to furnish. *The school provides lunches for students who live far away.* **2.** to prepare; get ready ahead of time. *The theater manager provided for a large crowd.* **3.** to make as a condition. *The rules provide that only residents of the state may enter the contest.* **pro vides, pro vid ed, pro vid ing.**

pro vid ed (prə vīd′id), *conj.* if; on the condition that. *You may go provided you come back early.*

prov ince (prov′əns), *n.* **1.** a division of a country. *Canada is divided into nine provinces.* **2.** the proper activity or interest of a certain field, such as business, government, education, etc. *School studies are the province of education. Enforcing of the law is the province of the police department.* **3. provinces,** the sections of a country away from the large cities. *Many people from the provinces come to the city to work.* **prov inc es.**

pro vi sion (prə vizh′ən), *n.* **1.** a providing; a preparing; a getting ready ahead of time. *The pioneers made provision for hot, wet weather. The school has made provision for any emergency.* **2.** a condition. *One of the provisions for ordering tickets is that you must be a student.* **3. provisions,** a supply of food and water. *The boys took provisions for four days on their camping trip.* **pro vi sions.** *v.* **4.** to supply. *The store provisioned the campers with food.* **pro vi sions, pro vi sioned, pro vi sion ing.**

prune[1] (prün), *n.* a dried plum. *We had cooked prunes for breakfast.* **prunes.**

prune[2] (prün), *v.* **1.** to cut branches from (a tree or bush). *Father is pruning the rose bushes because they are too thick.* **2.** to cut out unnecessary parts from. *You should prune your long letter.* **prunes, pruned, prun ing.**

psy chol o gy (sī kol′ə jē), *n.* the study of the mind. *Psychology attempts to find out the real reasons for the way people think and act.*

pub lic (pub′lik), *n.* **1.** the people. *The library is used by the public.* *adj.* **2.** for the people; used by people. *Public parks are open to all. Public schools give an education to all children.* **3.** of the people. *Public opinion is on the side of the mayor.* **pub lic ly,** *adv.*

pub li ca tion (pub′lə kā′shən), *n.* **1.** a book, magazine, or newspaper. *The library has more than twenty-five thousand publications.* **2.** the printing and selling of books, magazines, and newspapers. *Publication is a large industry with jobs for writers, editors, proofreaders, and salesmen.* **pub li ca tions.**

pub lic i ty (pub lis′ə tē), *n.* the condition of being widely known; public notice. *The movie received publicity through the newspapers, television, radio, and public discussion.*

pub lish (pub′lish), *v.* **1.** to prepare books, magazines, etc. for sale. *That company publishes many of the texts we use in school.* **2.** to make known. *The names of the graduating class were published by the newspaper.* **pub lish es, pub lished, pub lish ing.**

pub lish er (pub′lish ər), *n.* a person or company whose business is to prepare, print, and sell books, magazines, newspapers, or other written matter. *You will find the publisher's name on the first page in this book.* **pub lish ers.**

pud ding (pùd′ing), *n.* a soft, sweet, after-dinner treat. *Mother makes chocolate pudding, bread pudding, and rice pudding.* **pud dings.**

---

sand, āte, bâre, fäther; sent, mē, fèrn; fit, bīke; pot, rōpe, fôrt; run, pùll, rüle, cūte; noise, sound; **ch, cheese;** **ng, long; th, thick; ~~th~~, those; zh, treasure; ə = a in about, e in waken, i in animal, o in seldom, and u in minus.**

pud dle (pud/l), *n.* a small pool of water. *The children played in the mud puddle after the rain.* **pud dles.**

puff (puf), *n.* 1. a short, quick movement of air or smoke. *A puff of wind blew out the candle. Puffs of smoke rose from the campfire.* 2. a shell of sweet, baked dough with a filling. *Bakeries sell cream puffs.* **puffs.**
v. 3. to rise in puffs. *Smoke puffed from the campfire.* 4. to breathe quickly and hard. *The dog puffed after chasing the rabbit.* 5. to move or go with short, hard breaths. *We puffed up the hill.* 6. to blow. *The child puffed out the three candles on her birthday cake.* **puffs, puffed, puff ing.**

pull (pùl), *v.* 1. to draw near or tug at; drag. *Edward pulled the fish into the boat with his reel. Dad pulled the sled with the baby in it.* 2. to get hold of and take out. *Someone ought to pull those big weeds. The dentist pulled one of my teeth.* 3. to move. *The train is pulling in on time. Pull up a chair and sit down.* 4. to tear or to rip. *The strong wind pulled the barn down. The puppy pulled the old sheet to pieces.* **pulls, pulled, pull ing.**
n. 5. a pulling; a tug. *A strong pull will break the rope.* 6. a hard climb. *It was quite a pull to the top of the mountain.* **pulls.**

pul ley (pùl/ē), *n.* a wheel with a furrow in the rim through which a rope moves, used to run a machine or to lift a heavy object. *The rope in a pulley is pulled down at one end to raise an object fastened to the other end. The men used a pulley to lift the big piano onto the truck.* **pul leys.**

pulp (pulp), *n.* 1. the soft, juicy part of a fruit. *We usually peel oranges before eating the pulp.* 2. a material made from rags and wood, and ground into a soft, wet mass. *Pulp is used in making paper.*

pul pit (pùl/pit), *n.* the place in some churches where the minister stands when delivering a sermon. *Some pulpits are above floor level so that the people in the church can see more easily.* **pul pits.**

pu ma (pū/mə), *n.* a large American wildcat. *A puma is also called a mountain lion.* **pu mas.**

pump[1] (pump), *n.* 1. a machine for forcing liquid or gas from one place to another by means of a pipe or hose. *A gasoline pump is used in oil stations. An air pump will fill a tire with air.* **pumps.**
v. 2. to fill by means of a pump. *We pumped the flat tire. Frank pumped a pail of water.* 3. to force from one place to another the way a pump does. *The heart pumps blood to all parts of the body.* 4. to keep on questioning. *The girls pumped Iris about the costume she would wear to the party.* **pumps, pumped, pump ing.**

pump[2] (pump), *n.* a kind of ladies' shoe with low sides. *A pump has no straps or laces.* **pumps.**

pump kin (pump/kin), *n.* a large yellow-orange fruit that grows on a vine, used for making pies and as food for cattle. *On Halloween we carve faces on pumpkins and put lights inside them.* **pump kins.**

pulpit

pulleys

punch[1] (punch), *n.* 1. a tool for making holes in something. *A punch is used on a ticket by a bus driver or a train conductor.* 2. a blow with the fist. *A boxer learns how to avoid a punch.* **punch es.**
v. 3. to hit with the fist. *The two friends punched each other while boxing.* 4. to make holes in by using a punch. *The boy punched holes in the paper so it would fit in his notebook.* **punch es, punched, punch ing.**

punch[2] (punch), *n.* a drink made by mixing fruit juices together. *Carol served punch at her party.* **punch es.**

punc tu a tion (pungk/chù ā/shən), *n.* 1. the use of commas, periods, etc. to make sentences more clear. *In writing, correct punctuation is just as important as correct words.* 2. **punctuation mark,** any of the marks used in writing and printing to make the meaning clear. *Some punctuation marks are the comma, period, question mark, dash, and quotation marks.*

pun ish (pun/ish), *v.* to bring pain, loss, or trouble to a person for doing wrong. *Mother*

puma

punished my little brother by keeping him indoors. **pun ish es, pun ished, pun ish ing.**

pun ish ment (pun'ish mənt), *n.* something that is done to a person because he has done wrong. *Tim's punishment is to stay in his room through dinner. Being kept inside all day is a punishment. Paying a fifty-dollar fine is a punishment for driving too fast.* **pun ish ments.**

pup (pup), *n.* 1. a young dog; puppy. *The pup wagged his long tail in happiness.* 2. name for a young fox, seal, etc. *We saw two fox pups in the zoo.* **pups.**

pu pa (pū'pə), *n.* an insect in the stage between a larva and an adult insect. *The pupa of a moth is inside a cocoon.* **pu pae** (pū'pē) or **pu pas.**

pu pil (pū'pl), *n.* 1. a boy or girl who is in school or who studies under a teacher. *We have thirty pupils in our class.* 2. the dark opening in the center of the eye. *The pupil becomes smaller in bright light and larger in dim light.* **pu pils.**

pup pet (pup'it), *n.* a doll that can be made to move by a person who controls the strings attached to it. *The puppets acted out the story of "Snow White" on a tiny stage.* **pup pets.**

pup py (pup'ē), *n.* a young dog; pup. *The silly puppy tried to chase its own tail.* **pup pies.**

pur chase (pėr'chəs), *v.* 1. to buy. *We purchased the ice cream.* **pur chas es, pur chased, pur chas ing.**
n. 2. a thing that is bought. *Mother's purchases are being delivered by the store.* 3. a firm grip; a secure hold. *Get a purchase on the rope and pull hard.* **pur chas es.**

pure (pyùr), *adj.* 1. not mixed with anything else. *The pure air of the northern woods is good for the health. The locket on that necklace is pure gold.* 2. not bad; good; innocent. *A little child has pure thoughts.* 3. nothing but; mere. *George and Harry met by pure luck.* **pure ly,** *adv.*

pur ple (pėr'pl), *n.* 1. a color that is made by mixing red and blue. *You should use a purple in painting the evening sunset.* **pur ples.**
adj. 2. of the color purple. *Some grapes and plums are purple.*

pur pose (pėr'pəs), *n.* 1. an aim; plan. *Jack's purpose in writing to us was to let us know his new address.* **pur pos es.**
v. 2. to intend. *We purpose to clean the yard today.* **pur pos es, pur posed, pur pos ing.**

purr (pėr), *n.* 1. the low, humming sound made by a cat when it is happy or content. *The cat's purr was heard in the quiet room.* **purrs.**
v. 2. to make this sound. *The cat sat purring in front of the stove.* **purrs, purred, purr ing.**

purse (pėrs), *n.* 1. a small case or bag for holding money. *The old prospector carried a purse filled with pieces of gold.* 2. a handbag carried by a woman. *Mother's purse is large enough to hold keys, face powder, money, handkerchiefs, and letters.* 3. a sum of money. *The pupils collected a purse for the Community Fund.* **purs es.**

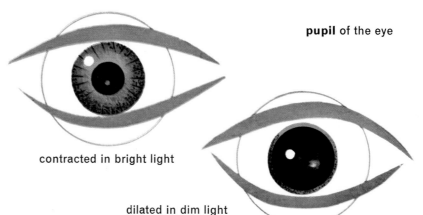

pupil of the eye

contracted in bright light

dilated in dim light

v. 4. to draw together. *You purse your lips in order to whistle.* **purs es, pursed, purs ing.**

pur sue (pər sü'), *v.* 1. to follow in order to catch; to chase. *We pursued his dog down the street.* 2. to keep on with. *She pursued the study of art.* 3. to try to find. *People pursue peace and happiness.* **pur sues, pur sued, pur su ing.**

pur suit (pər süt'), *n.* 1. the act of pursuing; a chase. *The pursuit of the dog ended at the other end of town.* 2. an activity; an occupation. *Our family's favorite pursuit is spending an evening together playing games.* **pur suits.**

push (pùsh), *v.* 1. to press against something in order to move it. *We pushed the car to a garage.* 2. to shove. *The boy standing in line pushed the*

puppet

person in front of him by accident. 3. to thrust. *The plant pushed its roots into the ground.* 4. to move forward by using force. *The hunters pushed through the heavy growth.* 5. to urge; to encourage. *Father quietly pushes us to do our best. The class pushed John to do his magic tricks.* **push es, pushed, push ing.**

n. 6. a shove. *The car needs a push to get started.* **push es.**

puss (puṡ), *n.* a cat. *"Here, puss," called the lady to her pet cat.*

puss y (puṡ′ē), *n.* a pet cat. *Little children often like pussy cats.* **puss ies.**

pussy willow, a willow that bears small, fur-like buds. *Pussy willows start to bloom early in the spring.* **pussy willows.**

put (pu̇t), *v.* 1. to place; set. *Put the books on the desk.* 2. to bring into a certain condition. *He put his room in order before he went out to play.* 3. to state; express; say. *Put your thoughts in writing.* **puts, put, put ting.**

Put also has the following special meanings:

put down, (a) to crush, using force; overcome. *The king put down the revolution.* (b) to write. *He puts down the day's happenings in a diary.*

put off, to delay. *She is putting off her trip until Tuesday.*

put on, (a) to pretend. *They were just putting on that the child surprised them.* (b) to present or act out (a play or show). *We put on an animal show with our dogs.*

put out, (a) to stop from burning or shining. *We put out all the lights.* (b) to irritate; to make angry. *Betty was put out when I forgot to meet her.* (c) to produce. *That company puts out a lot of canned goods.*

put through, to carry out. *Mr. Wilmot put through his new plan.*

put up, (a) to build. *They put up a garage for their car.* (b) to preserve. *Some housewives put up jars of jelly.* (c) to give food and shelter to. *The farmer put us up for the night.*

put up with, to stand for. *Our teacher won't put up with careless work.*

python

puz zle (puz′l), *n.* 1. a game having a problem to be worked out. *Newspapers print word puzzles.* 2. something that is hard to understand. *My little brother's behavior is often a puzzle.* **puz zles.** *v.* 3. to confuse. *The arithmetic problem puzzled me for a few minutes.* 4. **puzzle out,** to solve the meaning of something by careful thinking. *He puzzled out the mystery story before he finished the book.* **puz zles, puz zled, puz zling.**

pyr a mid (pir′ə mid), *n.* 1. a solid figure whose sides are triangles that come together in a point. *A pyramid has a flat base.* 2. **Pyramids,** the three great four-sided stone structures near Cairo, Egypt, that were built in ancient times as tombs for the kings and queens. *One of the Pyramids, the Great Pyramid, is more than four hundred feet high.* **pyr a mids.**

py thon (pī′thon), *n.* a very large snake living in Asia and Africa. *A python is not poisonous, but it can wind around the body of a large animal so tightly that the animal can no longer breathe.* **py thons.**

pyramids

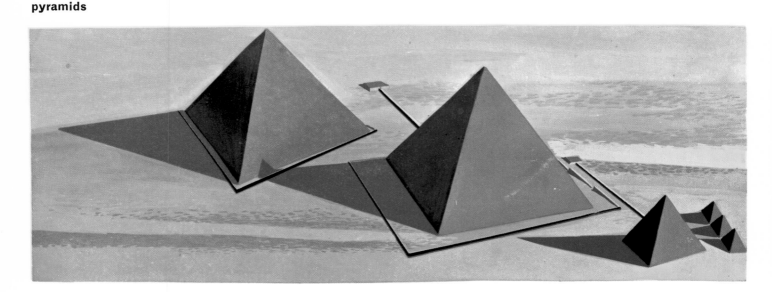

Q or **q** (kū), the seventeenth letter of the alphabet.

quack[1] (kwak), *n.* 1. the sound made by a duck. *We heard the quacks of the wild ducks as they flew overhead.* **quacks.**
v. 2. to make the sound of a duck. *The ducks in the zoo quacked loudly when they saw their food coming.* **quacks, quacked, quack ing.**

quack[2] (kwak), *n.* 1. a person who professionally pretends to be a doctor. *Quacks break the law when they practice medicine or order the use of fake remedies.* **quacks.**
adj. 2. used by quacks; not genuine. *Quack medicines don't do any good.*

quad ri lat er al (kwod′rə lat′ər əl), *n.* a plane figure with four sides and four angles. *Squares and rectangles are quadrilaterals.* **quad ri lat er als.**

quail[1] (kwāl), *n.* a small, game bird that is hunted for food. *Some kinds of quail are called bobwhite or partridge.* **quail or quails.**

quail[2] (kwāl), *v.* to draw back in fear; to be afraid; to lose courage. *The hunter quailed when he heard the lion's roar.* **quails, quailed, quailing.**

qual i fied (kwol′ə fīd′), *adj.* 1. fit; able; having the ability and skills needed. *The football captain is qualified to be a leader.* 2. limited; with reservations. *Paul's plan received only qualified support, since more than half the students in his class voted against it.*

qual i fy (kwol′ə fī), *v.* 1. to be fit or demonstrate ability. *Yesterday I qualified for the school choir.* 2. to make fit or able. *A college degree qualifies you for many different jobs.* 3. to limit; to change. *If you will qualify some of the conditions I will agree to sign this statement.* **qual i fies, qual i fied, qual i fy ing.**

qual i ty (kwol′ə tē), *n.* 1. something which makes a person or thing different from others; characteristics. *A quality I admire is honesty. One of Jim's best qualities is his ability to stay with a hard job until it is finished.* 2. merit; high value. *Some radio stations play only music of quality. Mr. Thorne reads only books of quality.* 3. a grade or standard. *This television set has a picture of poor quality, but it was cheap.* **qual i ties.**

quan ti ty (kwon′tə tē), *n.* 1. amount. *A small quantity of water was added to the mixture.* 2. a large number; a big amount. *Quantities of flowers appear in the park in spring.* **quan ti ties.**

quar rel (kwôr′əl), *n.* 1. an argument; a dispute. *The children had a quarrel about which television program to watch. The quarrel between the two men was over the ownership of the property.* 2. a cause for a dispute. *What is the quarrel this time?* **quar rels.**
v. 3. to fight; to disagree using angry words. *The boys quarreled about whose turn it was to bat.* 4. to find fault. *The woman quarreled with the carpenter's plan for the house.* **quar rels, quar reled, quar rel ing.**

quar ry[1] (kwôr′ē), *n.* an animal that is being hunted. *The hunter's quarry was a fox that disappeared in the thick forest.* **quar ries.**

quar ry[2] (kwôr′ē), *n.* 1. a large hole in the ground where stone is cut, blasted, or dug. *Marble for making statues, ornaments, and fancy floors is dug from a quarry.* **quar ries.**
v. 2. to dig from a quarry. *They are quarrying the gravel to make the new road.* **quar ries, quarried, quar ry ing.**

quart (kwôrt), *n.* 1. a measure of liquids that is

quadrilaterals

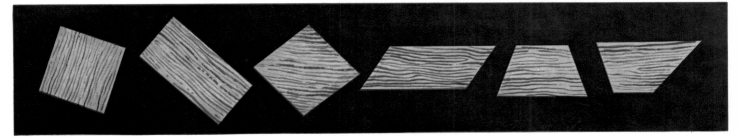

queen used in chess

equal to two pints or one fourth of a gallon. *The milkman delivered two quarts of milk and one quart of orange juice this morning.* 2. a measure for dry things, equal to one eighth of a peck. *I bought a quart of blueberries.* **quarts.**

quar ter (kwôr′tər), *n.* 1. one of four equal parts. *Divide the pie into quarters, so that all four of us have the same amount.* 2. each of the four periods during the monthly revolution of the moon. *The four quarters are called new moon, first quarter, full moon, and last quarter.* 3. one fourth of a year, or three months. *The business firm showed an increase in profit during the first quarter of the year.* 4. one fourth of a dollar; twenty-five cents. *Two dimes and a nickel equal a quarter.* 5. a coin worth twenty-five cents. *The public telephone has openings for depositing nickels, dimes, and quarters.* 6. any one of the four main points of the compass. *The compass showed that the wind was blowing toward the north quarter.* 7. any one of the regions of the four points of the compass. *The famous man's mail came from the four quarters of the globe.* 8. a section; district; area. *The factories are located in the industrial quarter of town.* 9. **quarters,** a resi-

quetzal

dence; a place to stay in. *The captain lives in the officer's quarters.* **quar ters.**

v. 10. to divide into four equal parts. *I quartered the candy bar for the four children.* 11. to provide with a place to live. *The baseball players were quartered in the Palace Hotel.* **quarters, quar tered, quar ter ing.**

queen (kwēn), *n.* 1. the wife of a king. *When the princess married the king, she became queen.* 2. a woman who rules over a country like a king. *If a queen marries, her husband is often called a prince.* 3. a woman who is important in any way. *The college elects a beauty queen each year.* 4. a female ant or bee that lays eggs. *The queen is usually larger than the other insects in a colony.* 5. in chess, the only piece that can move in any direction on the board. *The queen is the most powerful piece in a chess game.* 6. a playing card with the picture of a queen on it. *The queen is just below the king in value.* **queens.**

queen ly (kwēn′lē), *adj.* like a queen; fit for a queen. *The lovely wife of the principal has a queenly manner.* **queen li er, queen li est.**

queer (kwir), *adj.* strange; odd; peculiar. *We have had queer weather this summer.* **queer ly,** *adv.*

ques tion (kwes′chən), *n.* 1. a sentence that asks something. *"What time is it?" is a question.* 2. a doubt. *The doctor said he had no question about her good health.* 3. a problem. *The question of the pollution of our air and water is being discussed tonight.* 4. objection; dispute. *Stanley's honesty is beyond question. Obey the traffic policeman without question.* **ques tions.**

v. 5. to examine by asking questions; to ask questions of. *The lawyer questioned the witness concerning the accident.* 6. to ask; to inquire. *He questioned her whereabouts on the night of July 14.* 7. to have doubts about. *I do not question his ability to do the job well.* **ques tions, questioned, ques tion ing.**

quet zal (ket säl′), *n.* a bird that lives in Central America. *A quetzal has green and red feathers and a long flowing tail.* **quet zals.**

quick (kwik), *adj.* 1. fast; rapid; swift. *The rabbit made a quick leap into the bushes.* 2. lively; active. *Jerry has a quick mind for working puzzles.* 3. happening at once; prompt. *We received a quick reply to our letter.* 4. hasty; too fast. *Marty learned to control his quick temper.* **quick er, quick est; quick ly,** *adv.*

n. 5. the tender flesh under the nails. *The nervous child bit his nails to the quick.* 6. a person's deepest feelings. *The old man was hurt to the quick when strangers laughed at his little dog.* 7. **the quick and the dead,** the living and the dead. *adv.* 8. with speed; rapidly. *Come home quick!*

quick ly (kwik′lē), *adv.* fast; hastily; with speed. *Write your letter quickly to get it in the evening mail.*

qui et (kwī′ət), *adj.* 1. silent; having no noise or very little noise. *The hum of the airplane was the only sound in the quiet night.* 2. still; not moving. *The lake is quiet tonight.* 3. peaceful.

Alice spent a quiet afternoon reading. 4. gentle; mild. *The judge has a quiet way of talking.* 5. not too bright. *At twilight the sky has quiet color.* **qui et er, qui et est; qui et ly,** *adv.*

n. 6. the condition of being quiet; stillness; peace. *Father sometimes likes to leave the city and enjoy the quiet of the country.*

v. 7. to make or become quiet; to calm down. *The mother quieted the crying child. Let's all quiet down.* **qui ets, qui et ed, qui et ing.**

quilt (kwilt), *n.* 1. a bed cover made of two layers of cloth. *A quilt contains a pad of wool or down between the two layers.* **quilts.**

v. 2. to make a quilt; to sew together two layers of cloth, with a soft material inside. *Grandmother sometimes quilts as she listens to the radio.* **quilts, quilt ed, quilt ing.**

quince (kwins), *n.* 1. a hard, yellow fruit shaped like an apple. *Quinces are used in jelly and jam.* 2. the small tree it grows on. *The flowering quince has white or pink flowers.* **quinc es.**

quit (kwit), *v.* 1. to stop. *The men in the factory quit work at five o'clock.* 2. to leave; to give up. *Mr. Walter quit his job to start his own business.* **quits, quit** or **quit ted, quit ting.**

quite (kwīt), *adv.* 1. completely; entirely. *Have you quite finished your dinner?* 2. really; truly. *His drawings are quite good.* 3. very much of; more than slightly. *That boy is quite a worker. Today is quite cool.*

quince:
a. branch with leaves and flower
b. fruit

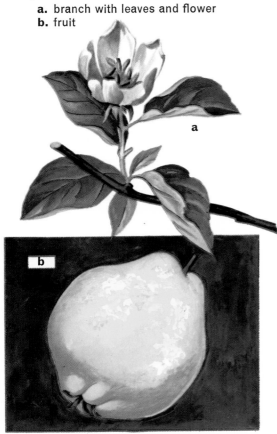

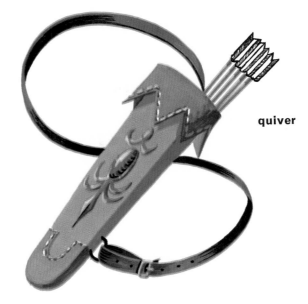

quiver

quiv er[1] (kwiv′ər), *n.* a case for holding arrows. *A quiver may be fastened to a belt or slung on the back.* **quiv ers.**

quiv er[2] (kwiv′ər), *v.* to tremble; to shiver. *The leaves quivered in the breeze. Her shoulders quivered in the sudden cold.* **quiv ers, quiv ered, quiv er ing.**

quiz (kwiz), *n.* 1. a test. *I am sure I did well on the science quiz.* **quiz zes.**

v. 2. to ask questions of; to give a quiz to. *Next week our teacher will quiz us on our social studies lessons.* **quiz zes, quizzed, quiz zing.**

quiz zi cal (kwiz′ə kl), *adj.* questioning. *Mark's quizzical look showed that he didn't understand my explanation.* **quiz zi cal ly,** *adv.*

quo ta (kwō′tə), *n.* part of the total amount due from people, divisions, etc. *Our teacher gave each student their quota of tickets for the graduation ceremony.* **quo tas.**

quo ta tion (kwō tā′shən), *n.* 1. the quoting of someone else's words. *His quotations from the Bible were well done.* 2. a passage repeated from a story, poem, speech, etc. *There are several books of famous quotations that you can buy.* 3. the price of a stock or bond. *Stock quotations appear in newspapers.* **quo ta tions.**

quotation marks, *n. pl.* the marks (" ") that are put at the beginning and end of words and sentences that are quoted. *I forgot to put quotation marks at the end of this quote.*

quote (kwōt), *v.* 1. to repeat exactly the words of another person or a passage from a book. *The speaker quoted Abraham Lincoln in his speech.* **quotes, quot ed, quot ing.**

n. 2. a quotation; a passage repeated from a story or poem. *There are many famous quotes in history books.* **quotes.**

quo tient (kwō′shənt), *n.* a result obtained when one number is divided by another. *If you divide 16 by 2, the quotient is 8.* **quo tients.**

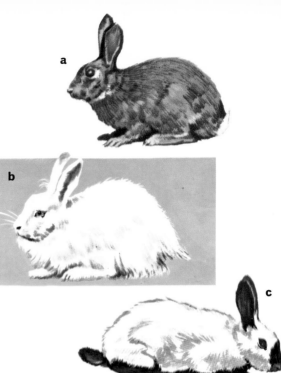

r

rabbits: **a.** Himalayan;
b. Angora; **c.** cottontail

tennis **racket**

R or **r** (är), the eighteenth letter of the alphabet.

rab bit (rab′it), *n.* a small, swift animal with long ears, soft fur, and a short tail. *Rabbits live in holes in the ground.* **rab bits.**

ra bies (rā′bēz), *n.* a disease of dogs and certain other animals that can be communicated to man by a bite. *If a person is bitten by a dog with rabies he will get the disease unless he has immediate medical treatment.*

rac coon (ra kün′), *n.* a small animal having gray fur, a bushy tail, and a mark on its face that looks like a black mask. *Raccoons live in trees and wander around at night hunting for food.* **rac coons.**

race¹ (rās), *n.* 1. a contest of speed. *During the summer we went to the boat races, auto races, and swimming races.* 2. a strong current of water. *The race in this stream turns a water wheel.* **rac es.** *v.* 3. to try to beat in a contest of speed. *I will race you to school.* 4. to run, move, or go fast. *The car raced down the highway.* 5. to cause to run, move, or go fast. *The man raced the motor of his car.* **rac es, raced, rac ing.**

race² (rās), *n.* 1. a group of persons, animals, or plants that have descended from the same parents and have the same characteristics. *The people who come from China or Japan belong to a different race than the people who come from Africa.* 2. any large group of living things. *All of us belong to the human race.* **rac es.**

race track, *n.* a field or course built especially for racing. *Race tracks are used for contests among athletes, among automobiles, and among horses.* **race tracks.**

rack (rak), *n.* 1. a frame or stand with shelves, bars, or hooks used for holding something. *Hang your coat on the clothes rack. Mother arranged the towels neatly on the towel racks.* 2. a device used a long time ago for punishment by stretching a person's arms and legs. *The messenger from the king was put on the rack to force him to tell the truth.* **racks.** *v.* 3. to cause to suffer. *Before the doctor came, pain racked the patient's body.* 4. **rack one's brains,** to think hard. *We racked our brains about a birthday gift for Mother.* **racks, racked, rack ing.**

rack et¹ (rak′it), *n.* a light bat with a frame at one end covered by a net. *In playing tennis, a racket is used for hitting the ball.* **rack ets.**

rack et² (rak′it), *n.* 1. a loud noise. *We knew the children were playing when we heard the racket in the house.* 2. a dishonest, illegal way of making money. *The police heard about the new racket—a man was selling land that he didn't own.* **rack ets.**

finish of a car **race**

ra dar (rā′där), *n.* an instrument that uses radio waves for locating objects in the path of the beam. *Radar is used at airports to find the position of airplanes. Radar locates satellites that have been sent into outer space.*

ra di ant (rā′dē ənt), *adj.* 1. shining; full of brightness. *She looked radiant in a white dress and diamond necklace. Ann has a radiant smile.* 2. sent out in waves from some source. *The earth receives radiant heat from the sun.* **ra di ant ly,** *adv.*

ra di ate (rā′dē āt′), *v.* 1. to give out rays of. *The sun radiates heat and light. The boy's face radiated happiness.* 2. to spread out from a central point. *The streets radiate from the town square. The news radiated through the city.* **ra di ates, ra di at ed, ra di at ing.**

ra di a tion (rā′dē ā′shən), *n.* 1. the giving out of rays of light, heat, or electricity. *The radiation of heat from the sun is necessary for life.* 2. the rays or energy sent out. *A dentist must be sure to protect himself from the radiation from his X-ray machine.* **ra di a tions.**

ra di o (rā′dē ō′), *n.* 1. a way of sending sounds from one place to another by means of electric waves. *Before radio was discovered, messages were sent over wires.* 2. an instrument for receiving such sounds. *Steve heard the results of the election on his radio.* **ra di os.**
adj. 3. used in, sent by, or having to do with radio. *The radio tubes are dead. The radio broadcast of the World Series goes to all parts of the world.*
v. 4. to send by radio. *The ship radioed a message to the shore.* **ra di os, ra di oed, ra di o ing.**

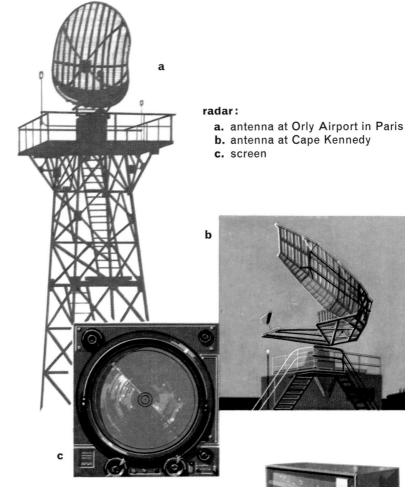

radar :
   a. antenna at Orly Airport in Paris
   b. antenna at Cape Kennedy
   c. screen

radio

race track

500

radish

a man dressed in **rags**

raffia palm

rad ish (rad′ish), *n.* the root of a garden plant, usually red or white. *Radishes have a sharp taste and are often eaten in salads.* **rad ish es.**

ra di us (rā′ dē əs) *n.* 1. a straight line from the center of a circle or sphere to its circumference or surface. *The radius of a circle is half its diameter.* 2. the length of such a line. *The radius is six inches.* **ra dii.**

raf fia (raf′ē ə), *n.* 1. the fiber from the leafstalks of a certain kind of palm tree. *Raffia is used for weaving hats, mats, and baskets.* 2. the tree on which the leafstalks grow. *The raffia grows in the eastern part of India.*

raft (raft), *n.* a platform which floats on water and is made from logs or other material fastened together. *A large raft can carry people and supplies.* **rafts.**

rag (rag), *n.* 1. a waste piece of cloth or a scrap of material torn or cut from a used garment, like a shirt or dress. *Polish the car with this rag.* 2. **rags,** old, torn clothing. *The beggar was dressed in rags.* **rags.**
adj. 3. of or from rags. *Rag rugs are fun to make.*

rage (rāj), *n.* 1. a fit of fury; wild anger. *The lion went into a rage when someone disturbed him during his meal.* 2. the fashion. *Long hair is all the rage this year.* **rag es.**
v. 3. to show great anger. *The tiger raged in its cage.* 4. to be out of control; to continue with fury. *The forest fire raged for three days.* **rag es, raged, rag ing.**

rag ged (rag′id), *adj.* 1. torn; worn out. *This is a ragged coat because it has been worn so often.* 2. wearing torn old clothes. *The ragged old man said he hadn't eaten for three days.* 3. rough; uneven. *Soon we could see the ragged tops of the mountains.* **rag ged ly,** *adv.*

rail[1] (rāl), *n.* 1. a bar of wood or metal. *Rails are used for fences, railroad tracks, porches, and staircases.* 2. the railroad. *Send this package by rail.* **rails.**

rail[2] (rāl), *v.* to scold; to complain loudly. *The angry man railed at the newsboy for being late.* **rails, railed, rail ing.**

rail ing (rāl′ing), *n.* a fence, usually made of posts and rails. *Guard railings are often found on major highways. Porches have railings to keep people from falling off.* **rail ings.**

rail road (rāl′rōd′), *n.* 1. a track made of two steel rails on which trains travel. *The railroad goes through the middle of the town.* 2. a system of tracks, stations, trains, and the people who are in charge of them. *Railroads make more money by shipping freight than by carrying passengers.* **rail roads.**

rail way (rāl′wā′), *n.* a railroad. *Many people travel to work each day by railway.* **rail ways.**

a

b

c

railings:
a. porch
b. along a highway
c. on a bridge

rainbow

rain (rān), *n.* 1. the water which falls from clouds. *Drops of rain fell on the sidewalk.* 2. the falling of such water. *The heavy rains were good for the crops.* 3. a falling of many small or light things. *A rain of leaves fell from the trees.* **rains.** *v.* 4. to fall in drops from the clouds. *It is raining.* 5. to fall like rain. *The ashes from the big fire rained on the campers. Letters and telegrams of praise rained on the singer after his performance.* **rains, rained, rain ing.**

rain bow (rān′bō′), *n.* a curved band of colored light in the sky, caused by the rays of the sun passing through drops of rain, mist, or spray. *We saw a rainbow where the waves broke against the rocks.* **rain bows.**

rain coat (rān′kōt′), *n.* a coat made of water-proof material to keep a person dry during a rainfall. *Wear your raincoat on rainy days.* **rain coats.**

rain fall (rān′fôl′), *n.* 1. a shower of rain. *After the light rainfall the air seemed fresher.* 2. the amount of water from rain, snow, and sleet that falls within a certain time. *The annual rainfall in Washington, D.C., is about forty inches, and in Nevada it is about ten inches.* **rain falls.**

rain gauge, *n.* an instrument for measuring rainfall. *All weather stations have rain gauges that collect the rain and record the amount.* **rain gauges.** (See illustration on following page.)

rainy (rān′ē), *adj.* 1. wet. *Leave your rainy umbrella on the porch.* 2. having much rain. *On rainy afternoons I like to stay inside and read.* **rain i er, rain i est.**

raise (rāz), *v.* 1. to put up; lift. *Raise your arm to get permission to speak. Raise the window for more air.* 2. to build; put up; construct. *The city will raise a monument to its first mayor.* 3. to collect. *Mrs. Collins raised thirty dollars for the hospital fund.* 4. to grow. *Oranges and lemons are raised in Florida and California.* 5. to make higher; increase. *The stores have raised their prices again. Susan raises her voice when she gets angry.* 6. to take care of; to bring up; to provide for. *Mr. and Mrs. Williams raised a family of six fine children.* 7. to bring up for thinking about. *Alice raised the question of how much money was needed.* 8. to promote; to advance in rank or position.

rain

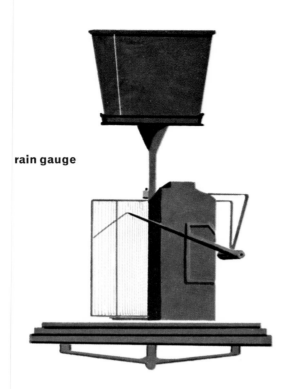

rain gauge

Seven boys were raised to First Class Scout. 9. to cause; bring about. *Her remarks raised laughter.* **rais es, raised, rais ing.**

n. 10. an increase in salary or wages. *The teachers got a raise at the beginning of the school year.* **rais es.**

rai sin (rā′zn), *n.* a sweet grape that has been dried. *The pudding has raisins in it.* **rai sins.**

rake (rāk), *n.* 1. a garden tool with a long handle and a bar with teeth or spikes at one end. *A rake is used on a lawn to collect sticks, leaves, and dead grass. Rakes are also used to smooth soft material like dirt.* **rakes.**

v. 2. to use a rake on. *Rake the lawn today.* 3. to search carefully. *The writer raked the library books for information to use in his book.* 4. to fire guns along the length of. *The soldiers raked the forest in order to bring out the enemy.* **rakes, raked, rak ing.**

ram (ram), *n.* 1. a male sheep. *Some rams have horns.* 2. a heavy wooden pole once used for knocking down gates, doors, and walls. *The king's soldiers forced their way through the castle gate with a ram.* **rams.**

v. 3. to crash into. *The empty car rolled down the hill and rammed the stone wall.* 4. to stuff firmly; to pack tightly. *The workers rammed the pole into the ground.* **rams, rammed, ram ming.**

ran (ran), past tense of **run.**

ranch (ranch), *n.* 1. a large farm where cattle or sheep are raised. *Most American ranches are in the western and southwestern parts of the country.* 2. any large farm. *Greg's ambition is to own a sheep ranch.* **ranch es.**

v. 3. to work on a ranch. *The cowboy has been ranching since he was ten years old.* **ranch es, ranched, ranch ing.**

ran dom (ran′dəm), *adj.* 1. occurring by chance; not planned. *It was by a random choice that I found the article I was looking for.* **ran dom ly,** *adv.*

n. 2. **at random,** not planned beforehand. *She selected a magazine at random from the case.*

rang (rang), past tense of **ring².**

range (rānj), *n.* 1. a series of things or people in a line. *We watched a range of Boy Scouts in the parade.* 2. a connected series or chain of mountains. *The highest mountain range in North America is the Rocky Mountains.* 3. the distance between certain limits. *The prices have a range of one dollar to fifty dollars.* 4. a variety. *This store has a wide range of styles.* 5. an area of land for cattle, horses, etc. *The cattle are grazing on the range.* 6. a large stove for cooking. *Mother couldn't decide whether she wanted a gas range or an electric range.* 7. a place for target practice. *The policeman practices using his pistol every day at the range.* 8. the distance a gun can shoot. *The cannon had a range of ten miles.* **rang es.**

v. 9. to extend or vary within certain limits. *His lecture ranged from music to mathematics. Neckties range in price from one dollar to ten dollars. The weeds ranged from our yard to his.* 10. to travel over; wander through. *Thousands of giraffes range the plains of Africa.* 11. to put in order; to set in rows. *Range those toy animals by size.* 12. to unite. *The knights ranged themselves on the side of the king.* **rang es, ranged, rang ing.**

rang er (rān′jər), *n.* 1. a person whose job is to be in charge of a certain area of a forest. *Rangers guard wildlife and look out for fires.* 2. a member of a police force covering a wide area. *The Texas Rangers are famous for bringing law and order to the West.* **rang ers.**

rank¹ (rangk), *n.* 1. a row of soldiers, side by side. *The troops marched in ranks of four.* 2. a position, grade, or class. *The officer has a rank of captain. The cashier holds a high rank in a bank. Shakespeare has the top rank as an author.* 3. **the ranks,** the ordinary people or workers; the soldiers who are not officers. *The railroad president worked his way up from the ranks. That man was raised from the ranks to become a captain.* **ranks.**

v. 4. to place in a certain rank. *The school board ranked our school high in the "clean schools" contest.* 5. to have a certain position or rank. *Elaine ranks high in the tests. A rabbit ranks as a better runner than a turtle.* **ranks, ranked, rank ing.**

rank² (rangk), *adj.* 1. growing thick and fast. *The rank grass and plants in the jungle make it hard to walk.* 2. bad smelling; bad tasting. *Throw away those rank old fish.* 3. utter; absolute; extreme. *The young boy thought he was a rank* *failure when he lost the swimming contest.* **rank ly,** *adv.*

rap (rap), *n.* 1. a light knock; a quick, sharp blow. *We heard a rap on the door.* **raps.**
v. 2. to hit lightly and quickly. *He rapped on the door to get in.* **raps, rapped, rap ping.**

rap id (rap′id), *adj.* 1. fast; quick. *We made a rapid trip to the college.* **rap id ly,** *adv.*
n. pl. 2. **rapids,** a part of a river where the water rushes swiftly, especially over rocks. *The boys guided their canoe through the rapids.*

rare¹ (râr), *adj.* 1. not often found or seen. *My uncle saves rare postage stamps.* 2. not frequent; very unusual. *A snowfall in the month of May is rare.* 3. extremely good; unusually excellent. *The young man has rare ability as a piano player.* 4. not thick; thin. *The air on a mountain top is rare and breathing is difficult.* **rar er, rar est; rare ly,** *adv.*

rare² (râr), *adj.* lightly cooked. *I like my rare meat.* **rar er, rar est.**

rat (rat), *n.* an animal like a mouse, but much larger, with long, sharp, front teeth. *Rats are black, gray, brown, or white and have a long, thin tail.* **rats.**

rate (rāt), *n.* 1. the amount or degree of something, measured in relation to something else. *The parking rate is fifty cents an hour. Her rate as a baby-sitter is one dollar for the evening.* 2. a speed. *Airplanes travel at a fast rate.* 3. a price. *The artist's rates are expensive.* 4. class; grade. *We saw a movie of the first rate.* 5. **at any rate,** anyhow; in any case. *It's late; at any rate, I must go now.* **rates.**
v. 6. to put a value on. *The jeweler rated the ring as being worth one hundred dollars.* 7. to think of as in a certain rank; to consider. *I rate our neighbors high as friends.* **rates, rat ed, rat ing.**

rath er (rath′ər), *adv.* 1. somewhat. *The baby is rather tired after the long ride.* 2. more readily; more gladly. *The dog would rather stay inside on cold days than go out and play.* 3. more truly; more correctly. *It's raining; rather, it's pouring! His tie is blue, or rather, it is purple.* 4. with better reason. *We should rather pity her than dislike her. We, rather than you, should pay for the lunch.*

rat ing (rāt′ing), *n.* 1. a rank or grade. *He has a rating in the Army of private first class.* 2. an estimate of the ability to pay debts. *All of the stores in town have given my father a good rating.* **rat ings.**

rat tle (rat′l), *v.* 1. to make a number of short, sharp sounds. *The windows rattled when the wind*

raven

blew. 2. to move with short, sharp sounds. *The old car rattled over the bumpy road.* 3. to talk rapidly for a long time. *Aunt Dorothy rattled on about her shopping, her housework, and her diet.* 4. to say quickly. *Bob rattled off his speech and then sat down.* **rat tles, rat tled, rat tling.**
n. 5. a sound of something shaking. *We heard the rattle of the door handle before she walked in.* 6. a toy that makes a noise when shaken. *The baby likes to chew on the rattle.* **rat tles.**

rat tle snake (rat′əl snāk′), *n.* a poisonous snake that gets its name from the rattling sound it makes with its tail. *Rattlesnakes are found throughout the United States.* **rat tle snakes.**

ra ven (rā′vən), *n.* 1. a large bird like a crow. *A raven has shiny black feathers and a sharp beak.* **ra vens.**
adj. 2. black and shiny. *Ann has lovely raven hair.*

raw (rô), *adj.* 1. not cooked. *Strawberries and radishes are eaten raw.* 2. not ready for use; in a natural state. *Raw hides must first be treated with chemicals. Raw milk must be pasteurized.* 3. damp and cold. *We set out on a camping trip one raw morning in November.* 4. sore; with the skin rubbed off. *Our hands became raw from rowing the boat all day. The doctor changed the dressing on the raw wound.* 5. not having any experience. *The manager was once a raw beginner.* **raw er, raw est.**

ray¹ (rā), *n.* 1. a thin beam of light. *We saw the ray of the flashlight in the dark.* 2. one of many lines going from the center in all directions. *A person will usually draw rays around his picture of the sun.* 3. a small amount; a trace. *The dark clouds gave the farmer a ray of hope that there would be rain.* **rays.**

ray² (rā), *n.* a fish having a broad, flat body, with fins on each side, and a tail that is long and thin. *Rays have eyes on top of their heads.* **rays.** (See illustration on following page.)

rat

ray

ra zor (rā´zər), *n.* an instrument having a very sharp blade that is used to cut off hair, especially from the face. *Father shaves with a razor every morning.* **ra zors.**

reach (rēch), *v.* 1. to stretch out one's hand or arm. *He reached to pick the apple from the tree. Will you reach for the book on the top shelf? He reached for my hand when we met.* 2. to extend to. *The old road reaches the river and stops. The population of our school will reach two thousand this month.* 3. to arrive at; to come to. *Columbus reached America. The principal reached a decision about the boy's request.* 4. to get to. *You can reach him at this phone number. The speaker reached the hearts of his audience.* **reach es, reached, reach ing.**
n. 5. a stretching out of a limb or limbs to touch something. *The athlete made a long reach for the basket. The dog made a reach for his bone.* 6. the distance that a person or animal can stretch. *Keep out of reach of the bear. He missed the ball because it was out of his reach.* 7. what the mind is able to grasp; understanding. *That problem in arithmetic is beyond my reach.* **reach es.**

re act (ri akt´), *v.* 1. to act as a result of another happening. *John reacted to the announcement that school would be dismissed early with a shout of "Hurrah!"* 2. to act in response to a person. *John and Bob react with each other, especially in telling jokes.* 3. to act in a chemical way. *Acids react on metals.* 4. to act against something. *Mary reacted to Joan's bad manners with silence.* **re acts, re acted, re act ing.**

re ac tion (ri ak´shen), *n.* 1. the action taken as a result of another happening. *Tom's reaction to the news was unhappiness.* 2. the chemical action occurring when two chemicals react. *The reaction of the chemicals was a burst of smoke.* 3. an action against something. *Her tears were a reaction to the happy news.* **re ac tions.**

read[1] (rēd), *v.* 1. to look at and get the meaning of print or writing. *People read books, magazines, and newspapers.* 2. to show by figures or signs. *The thermometer reads forty degrees.* 3. to understand. *Doctors can read X-rays. Musicians can read written music.* 4. to speak out loud something printed or written. *Please read your story to the class.* 5. to study. *He is reading law.* 6. to tell ahead of time. *I don't believe that anyone can read the future.* 7. **read into,** to interpret in

the wrong way. *You are reading things into my letter that I didn't really mean.* **reads, read** (red), **read ing.**

read[2] (red), *v.* 1. past tense and past participle of **read**[1].
adj. 2. having knowledge obtained by reading a great deal. *She is a well-read woman.*

read er (rēd´ər), *n.* 1. a person who reads. *The fastest reader in our class is Margaret.* 2. a book used to teach reading. *The first-grade reader tells about the adventures of Alice and Jerry.* **read ers.**

read i ly (red´ə lē), *adv.* 1. willingly and quickly. *Father readily loaned me a dollar.* 2. easily. *The dog readily learned how to roll over when told.*

read ing (rēd´ing), *n.* 1. the act of looking at and getting the meaning of something printed or written. *Reading gives Father much pleasure.* 2. a record shown on an instrument. *The reading on a thermometer shows how high the temperature is.* 3. a speaking in public of written or printed words. *The famous actor gave a reading of the poetry of Shakespeare.* **read ings.**

ready (red´ē), *adj.* 1. prepared to do something or to be used at once. *We are ready to go to school. The tailor said your suit is ready.* 2. willing. *My older brother is always ready to help me with my homework.* 3. quick or prompt. *The teacher received ready replies to all her questions.* **read i er, read i est; read i ly,** *adv.*
v. 4. to have ready or prepared. *Jim readied his room for the company.* **read ies, read ied, read y ing.**

real (rē´əl, rēl), *adj.* 1. actual; true; not imagined; not made up. *A dog is a real friend to his owner. My uncle told us a real story about his adventures as a fireman.* 2. genuine. *Her necklace is made of real pearls.* **real ly,** *adv.*

re al i ty (rē al´ə tē), *n.* 1. actual existence. *The reality of "flying saucers" has been discussed for years.* 2. **in reality,** really; in fact. *The two football players seem like enemies on the field but in reality they are good friends.* **re al i ties.**

re al ize (rē´əl īz´), *v.* 1. to understand; to know; to be aware. *Allen suddenly realized that he was late for school.* 2. to make real; to make come true. *David realized his ambition to be president of the class.* 3. to get as profit from the sale of something. *A storekeeper realizes about one penny on each box of cereal.* **re al iz es, re al ized, re al iz ing.**

re al ly (rē´əl ē, rē´lē), *adv.* truly; in fact. *George can really run fast.*

reap (rēp), *v.* 1. to cut down and gather. *The farmer reaps his grain in the summer.* 2. to get or obtain as a reward. *His gift of the toy reaped a happy smile from the child.* **reaps, reaped, reap ing.**

rear[1] (rir), *n.* 1. the back part. *Jim keeps his good suit in the rear of the closet. The Boy Scouts were in the rear of the parade.*
adj. 2. at the back; of the back. *A driver can see*

the road behind him by looking at the rear-view mirror.

rear[2] (rir), *v.* 1. to help grow up; bring up. *The mother reared her children wisely.* 2. to build. *The houses were reared quickly.* 3. to lift; raise up. *The sleeping dog awoke and reared his head.* 4. to rise on the hind legs. *The horse reared suddenly and the cowboy fell off.* **rears, reared, rear ing.**

rea son (rē′zn), *n.* 1. a cause. *Mr. Steele's reason for leaving his job was that he was offered a better one.* 2. an explanation. *Your parents will write the reason for your absence.* 3. the power to think. *You must use your reason in solving these problems. Man has reason; animals do not.* **rea sons.**

v. 4. to think in a sensible way; to decide after studying the facts. *The doctor reasoned that her illness was only a cold. The teacher reasoned that Alice deserved a higher grade because she had worked so hard.* 5. to argue in a careful, sensible way. *Reason with Bill to see if he will change his mind.* 6. **stand to reason,** to be reasonable to believe. *Since he is always here by six o'clock, it stands to reason he will come soon.* **rea sons, rea soned, rea son ing.**

rea son a ble (rē′zn ə bl), *adj.* 1. using reason; showing good sense; just; fair. *He is a reasonable person and will understand your delay. The teacher's decision was reasonable, since it solved the dispute to everyone's satisfaction.* 2. not expensive. *This restaurant charges reasonable prices.* **rea son a bly,** *adv.*

rea son ing (rē′zn ing), *n.* the process of thinking and making conclusions. *Her powers of reasoning are very good.* **rea son ings.**

reb el (reb′əl for 1 and 2, ri bel′ for 3 and 4), *n.* 1. a person who reacts against law or authority. *The rebels fought against the Union in the Civil War.* **reb els.**

adj. 2. a group who reacts against law or authority. *The rebel army fought against the Union in the Civil War.*

v. 3. to react against law or authority. *He rebelled against his parents by not talking.* 4. to be opposed to something. *The students rebelled against the unfair demands of the teacher.* **re bels, re belled, re bel ling.**

re build (rē bild′), *v.* to build again. *They are planning to rebuild the old school.* **re builds, re built, re build ing.**

re call (ri kôl′), *v.* 1. to call back. *Jane's father was recalled to his office on the first day of his vacation.* 2. to remember. *Snapshots help us to recall happy days in our lives.* 3. to take back; cancel. *The store recalled its order for snow shovels when no snow fell in January.* **re calls, re called, re call ing.**

re ceipt (ri sēt′), *n.* 1. a written statement which says that money or goods have been received. *I signed the receipt when the new chair was delivered.* 2. a receiving. *Upon receipt of the good news, we all felt happy.* 3. a recipe. *Grandma gave us a receipt for fudge.* 4. **receipts,** money taken in.

rear-view mirror inside a car **(a)**
and what the driver sees **(b)**

The receipts from the school play will be used to buy better lights for the stage. **re ceipts.**

v. 5. to sign a statement saying that money has been paid or that goods were received. *The milkman receipted our bill by writing "paid" on it and signing his name.* **re ceipts, re ceipt ed, re ceipt ing.**

re ceive (ri sēv′), *v.* 1. to take something that is given or sent. *Tom received a book in the mail. On her birthday she received many gifts.* 2. to take in and hold. *We placed a bucket under the dripping pipe to receive the water.* 3. to support; to hold up; to bear the weight of. *The land at each end of the bridge receives all of the bridge's weight.* 4. to experience. *You will receive an electric shock if you play with those wires.* 5. to allow in one's home or presence; to welcome. *The President received the visiting king and brought him to the White House.* 6. to accept visitors at a certain, regular time. *They receive only on Sunday afternoons.* 7. to change electric waves into sound or pictures, as in a radio or television set. *My radio can receive from stations that are very far away.* **re ceives, re ceived, re ceiv ing.**

re ceiv er (ri sēv′ər), *n.* 1. a person or thing that receives. *The sender of a letter puts the address of the receiver on the envelope. The laundry basket is the receiver for your dirty clothes.* 2. the part of a telephone through which one listens. *The receiver is held to your ear.* 3. the part in a radio or television set that picks up the electric waves which are changed into sounds or pictures. *In a radio, electric waves are sent from the receiver to the speaker, where they become sound.* **re ceiv ers.**

re cent (rē′snt), *adj.* 1. done, made, or happening not long ago. *A recent story in the newspaper told about the progress being made in building safer cars.* 2. of a time not long past. *The successful orbit of the first man-made satellite is a recent event.* **re cent ly,** *adv.*

re cep tion (ri sep′shən), *n.* 1. the act of receiving; the way in which one is accepted or welcomed. *The reception that the host gave us was very warm.* 2. a party, especially a formal party. *After the wedding, a reception was held for the bride and her husband.* 3. the manner in which sound or pictures are seen or heard on a radio or television set. *Our television reception was poor tonight because of the storm.* **re cep tions.**

re cess (ri ses′, rē′ses), *n.* 1. a brief rest from work or the time during which work stops. *During the morning we have a fifteen minute recess* *from our schoolwork.* 2. a small space set back into a wall. *A recess usually has a shelf on which flowers or a statue is set.* **re cess es.**

v. 3. to take a brief rest from work. *The court recessed for two hours so that everyone could have lunch.* **re cess es, re cessed, re cess ing.**

rec i pe (res′ə pē′), *n.* 1. a set of directions which tell how to prepare a certain dish. *A recipe shows what to use, how much of it to use, and how long the food must be cooked.* 2. a set of directions for doing anything. *There is no simple recipe for being successful.* **rec i pes.**

re cite (ri sīt′), *v.* 1. to say something learned or memorized out loud. *The teacher recited the poem to the class.* 2. to say part of a lesson out loud. *Mary recited the answer to the question.* 3. to give a detailed account. *Margaret recited all that she had done in school that day to her mother.* **re cites, re cit ed, re cit ing.**

reck less (rek′lis), *adj.* careless; not thinking of the safety of one's self or others. *His reckless driving led to a terrible accident.* **reck less ly,** *adv.*

reck on (rek′ən), *v.* 1. to count; to add up. *When the salesman reckoned the items on my bill, I discovered that I had forgotten to bring any money with me.* 2. to consider; to judge. *Larry is reckoned the best player on the team.* 3. to think; to suppose. *He reckoned he had studied enough for the test.* **reck ons, reck oned, reck on ing.**

reck on ing (rek′ən ing), *n.* 1. a figuring out of something; a counting. *By the pilot's reckoning, the plane should be directly over the airport.* 2. a settling of an account. *Our time of reckoning came when we were given a test on what we had studied.* **reck on ings.**

rec og ni tion (rek′əg nish′ən), *n.* 1. a knowing again of what one has seen or heard before; a recognizing. *I gave no sign of recognition when I saw him because I had forgotten that I had met him.* 2. favorable attention and approval. *The mayor won recognition because of his honesty and hard work.* 3. acknowledgment of a person's rights or of what he has done. *The student was given recognition for his work.* **rec og ni tions.**

rec og nize (rek′əg nīz′), *v.* 1. to know by association; identify by experience. *He recognized the song after the first few notes. I didn't recognize him because he had put on so much weight.* 2. to admit; to accept the fact. *Tom recognized*

reefs

that he was better in baseball than he was in football. 3. to greet; to show a sign of knowing someone. *She recognized me with a smile.* **rec og niz es, rec og nized, rec og niz ing.**

rec om mend (rek′ə mend′), *v.* 1. to write or speak in favor of. *Who recommended that movie to you? He was recommended for the job by someone for whom he had worked.* 2. to suggest; to advise. *His doctor recommended that he move to a warm, dry climate.* **rec om mends, rec om mend ed, rec om mend ing.**

rec om men da tion (rek′ə men dā′shən), *n.* 1. a statement of favor or approval. *The mayor delivered a recommendation for a new transportation plan for the city.* 2. a letter that expresses approval. *His teacher wrote a recommendation for her student.* 3. a statement of advice. *If you follow the doctor's recommendations you will be well in a few days.* **rec om men da tions.**

re cord (ri kôrd′ for 1–3, rek′ərd for 4–8), *v.* 1. to set something down in writing so that it will be remembered correctly. *The story of our country's beginning is recorded in history.* 2. to register; to show or tell. *A thermometer records temperatures.* 3. to put sounds on a tape or a thin, flat, ridged plate so they can be heard on a tape recorder or phonograph. *The singer recorded two new songs this morning.* **re cords, re cord ed, re cord ing.**

n. 4. an account of facts or events set down in writing so that they can be remembered correctly. *Historical records show that men from northern Europe visited America long before Columbus came here.* 5. a report of achievements. *He had a fine school record in high school.* 6. the best performance in a certain thing. *Who holds the record for the most goals made in a single season?* 7. a thin, flat, ridged plate used on a phonograph to produce sounds. *We listened to a record of the President's speech.* **rec ords.**

adj. 8. outstanding; never reached or done before. *A record crowd was at the last ball game.*

re cord er (ri kôr′dər), *n.* 1. a machine or device that records. *He recorded his voice on a tape recorder. The temperature recorder showed that it was thirty degrees at midnight last night.* 2. a musical instrument that sounds like a flute. *The recorder is held like a clarinet and has eight finger holes.* **re cord ers.**

re cov er (ri kuv′ər), *v.* 1. to get back. *The police recovered the stolen money.* 2. to gain back a healthy condition. *He is recovering at home after his operation. Tom returned to school when he had recovered from the illness.* 3. to make up for. *The factory recovered lost time by remaining open for twenty-four hours.* **re cov ers, re cov ered, re cov er ing.**

rec tan gle (rek′tang′gl), *n.* a figure having four sides and four right angles. *This book has the shape of a rectangle.* **rec tan gles.**

red (red), *n.* 1. the color of blood. *Red is the baby's favorite color.* 2. **Red,** a person who favors revolution, especially a person who favors a Communist revolution. *Just because a person disagrees with some of the things done by the government does not mean he is a Red.* **reds.** *adj.* 3. having the color of blood. *The red fire engine rushed down the street to the fire. They live in a red house.* 4. **Red,** favoring revolution, especially Communist revolution. *The Red revolution was a success.* **red der, red dest.**

red bird (red′bėrd′), *n.* any of several birds which have red feathers. *We saw the redbird's flash of color against the white snow.* **red birds.**

red breast (red′brest′), *n.* a bird having red feathers on its breast. *A robin is a redbreast.* **red breasts.**

re duce (ri düs′, ri dūs′), *v.* 1. to make less. *These pills will reduce the pain you are feeling.* 2. to lose weight by limiting the amount of food that is eaten. *She decided to reduce when her clothes no longer fit her.* 3. to overcome in battle. *The enemy was reduced by a powerful surprise attack.* 4. to change in form. *If you reduce one foot to inches you have twelve inches. Reduce that fraction to its lowest terms.* 5. to lower in rank or condition. *When the war ended, the captain was reduced to a lieutenant.* **re duc es, re duced, re duc ing.**

re duc tion (ri duk′shən), *n.* 1. the act of reducing. *The reduction of prices brought many new customers to the store.* 2. the amount by which something is reduced. *There was a four-dollar reduction in the price of the coat.* **re duc tions.**

reef (rēf), *n.* a group of rocks or a ridge of sand even with the top of water, or slightly under it. *The ship was stuck on the reef.* **reefs.**

reel[1] (rēl), *n.* 1. a spool or a similar device on which thread, a fishing line, rope, or other material can be wound. *Film for a camera comes on a reel. The fisherman bought a new reel for his fishing rod.* 2. the amount wound on a reel. *I need a reel of film for my camera.* **reels.** *v.* 3. to wind on a reel. *This machine reels the yarn as it is spun.* 4. to draw by winding a reel. *The fisherman reeled in a fish.* 5. **reel off,** to speak or write quickly and easily. *Steve reeled off the names of all the past Presidents of our country.* **reels, reeled, reel ing.**

reel[2] (rēl), *v.* 1. to sway about from a blow or shock. *The football player reeled after he was hit by an opposing player.* 2. to walk with a swaying motion. *The stunned fighter reeled back to his corner.* 3. to be in a whirl. *Their heads reeled with happiness as they left for the circus.* **reels, reeled, reel ing.**

reel[3] (rēl), *n.* a lively dance. *Everyone did a reel at the party.* **reels.**

re fer (ri fėr′), *v.* 1. to send to a place, book, or other source for information, help, etc. *The teacher referred him to the encyclopedia for the answer.* 2. to hand over to. *The argument was referred to the music teacher for a decision.* 3. to go to a place, book, or other source for information. *Refer to your dictionary to find the meaning of that word.* 4. to call attention to. *The speaker referred to a statement he had made earlier.* **re fers, re ferred, re fer ring.**

ref er ence (ref′ər əns), *n.* 1. a referring to a place, book, or other source for information. *There was a reference in the magazine article to a book on the subject.* 2. a place, book, or other source where information may be found. *Use the dictionary as a reference when you are unsure of the spelling of a word.* 3. a mention. *There was no reference made in any of the newspapers about the accident.* 4. relation to something. *The children were arranged in groups with reference to their age and size.* 5. a person who can be asked for a statement on another person's character or ability. *He used Judge Harris as a reference when he applied for the job.* 6. a statement on a person's character or ability. *I have several references from people for whom I have worked.* **ref er enc es.**

re fer ral (ri fėr′əl), *n.* an act of referring; a directing to a place for information. *He went to another doctor on the referral of his family doctor.* **re fer rals.**

re fin ery (ri fīn′ər ē), *n.* a building with machinery used to make oil, sugar, or ore more pure. *Oil used in automobiles has been processed in a refinery.* **re fin er ies.**

oil **refinery**

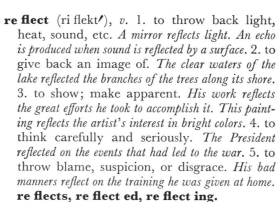

incident ray

how a light ray is
reflected from a surface

reflected ray

re flect (ri flekt′), *v.* 1. to throw back light,
heat, sound, etc. *A mirror reflects light. An echo
is produced when sound is reflected by a surface.* 2. to
give back an image of. *The clear waters of the
lake reflected the branches of the trees along its shore.*
3. to show; make apparent. *His work reflects
the great efforts he took to accomplish it. This painting reflects the artist's interest in bright colors.* 4. to
think carefully and seriously. *The President
reflected on the events that had led to the war.* 5. to
throw blame, suspicion, or disgrace. *His bad
manners reflect on the training he was given at home.*
re flects, re flect ed, re flect ing.

re flec tion (ri flek′shən), *n.* 1. a throwing back
of light, heat, or sound. *We were surprised by the
reflection of our voices in the big canyon.* 2. an
image given back by a smooth surface; likeness. *I looked at my reflection in the mirror.*
3. serious, careful thought. *After much reflection
we decided to abandon our plans.* 4. a statement or
idea that results from serious, careful thought.
*We were all interested in Tom's reflections on the
meaning of the book.* 5. a statement or action
that carries blame, suspicion, or disgrace. *His
charge that I was lying was a reflection on my
honesty.* **re flec tions.**

re flex (rē′fleks), *n.* an automatic action in the
body in response to something. *Blinking the
eyes and sneezing are reflexes.* **re flex es.**

re form (ri fôrm′), *v.* 1. to make better by correcting or removing faults. *Prisons try to reform
criminals rather than punish them.* 2. to improve
one's self; to become better. *If you promise to
reform, I will give you another chance.* **re forms,
re formed, re form ing.**

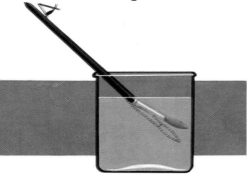

how the eye
sees a **refracted**
image in water

n. 3. an improvement; a correction of a wrong.
*The reforms in the voting laws made it possible for
many more people to elect members of the government.*
re forms.

re frac tion (ri frak′shən), *n.* the bending of a
ray of light as it passes from one medium to
another. *A magnifying glass causes refraction of
light from the air, through the glass, and into the air
again. The refraction of light rays in water makes an
object appear to be in a different place.* **re fractions.**

re fresh ment (ri fresh′mənt), *n.* 1. a making
fresh again. *We felt better after the refreshment of
a good night's sleep.* 2. anything that revives or
makes fresh. *Rain is a welcome refreshment on a
hot day.* 3. **refreshments,** things eaten or
drunk, especially at a meeting or party.
*Coffee and cookies were served as refreshments after
the teachers' meeting.* **re fresh ments.**

re frig er ate (ri frij′ər āt′), *v.* to make or keep
cold. *Milk becomes sour unless it is refrigerated.*
**re frig er ates, re frig er at ed, re frig-
er at ing.**

re frig er at or (ri frij′ər ā′tər), *n.* a box, room,
cabinet, etc. that keeps things cold. *The refrigerator was filled with meat, eggs, milk, fresh vegetables, pop, and cheese.* **re frig er at ors.**

ref uge (ref′ūj), *n.* shelter or protection from
danger. *The soldiers used an old farmhouse for
refuge. Hunting is not permitted on the wildlife
refuge.* **ref ug es.**

ref u gee (ref′ū jē′), *n.* a person who escapes
from danger, especially a person who leaves
his own country to live in another during a
war or other time of hardship. *When the city
was attacked, thousands of refugees fled to the
country.* **ref u gees.**

re fund (ri fund′ for 1, rē′fund for 2), *v.* 1. to
give back something that has been paid. *If
you are not satisfied with your purchase, the store will
refund your money.* **re funds, re fund ed, refund ing.**
n. 2. an amount of money returned. *When you
return the empty bottle you will get a refund of
fifteen cents.* **re funds.**

re fuse[1] (ri fūz′), *v.* 1. to turn down; to decline
to accept. *He refused my offer to help him. I refused
a second helping of pudding.* 2. to deny; to decline
to give. *The teacher refused us permission to leave
the room.* 3. to say no; to decline to consent.
*I asked her to help me with my homework, but she
refused.* **re fus es, re fused, re fus ing.**

ref use[2] (ref′ūs), *n.* useless matter, rubbish;
garbage. *Please place your refuse in the basket
instead of on the floor.*

re gal (rē′gl), *adj.* 1. of a king; belonging to or
used by a king. *The monarch used his regal power
to free the captured soldiers.* 2. fit for a king. *We
ate a regal meal at the banquet.* **re gal ly,** *adv.*

re gard (ri gärd′), *v.* 1. to look at closely; to
examine. *He regarded my face as I spoke to see if
I was telling the truth.* 2. to consider; to think of.

I regard him as one of my best friends. 3. to pay attention to; to listen to and obey. *You must be sure to regard your doctor's advice.* 4. to be concerned with; to relate to. *This problem regards every student in the school.* **re gards, re garded, re gard ing.**

n. 5. consideration; concern. *Mrs. Jones showed her regard for others by giving money to the poor.* 6. a look; a steady gaze. *The cat's regard was fixed on the birds in the grass.* 7. respect; esteem. *The other players have great regard for Dick's batting ability.* 8. **regards,** good wishes; greetings. *Give her my regards when you see her.* **re gards.**

re gard ing (ri gär′ding), *prep.* about; concerning. *I was unable to answer the test questions regarding the Civil War.*

re gard less (ri gärd′lis), *adj.* without regard or consideration. *The boy went swimming in the deep lake regardless of his mother's fears for his safety.* **re gard less ly,** *adv.*

re gent (rē′jənt), *n.* 1. a person who rules a country when the official ruler is unable to rule. *A regent ruled the kingdom until the child king became an adult.* 2. one of the members of the governing board of a university. *The regents voted to build a new library.* **re gents.**

re gion (rē′jən), *n.* 1. a large portion of the surface of the earth. *Cactuses grow in desert regions.* 2. an area; a place on the earth, in a country, in a city, etc. *They live in a farming region in Canada.* 3. a field of thought; sphere. *He is doing research in the region of science.* 4. part of the body. *The infection was in the stomach region.* **re gions.**

reg is ter (rej′is tər), *n.* 1. a list or record of names, facts, etc. *The voting register showed that he had voted in the last election.* 2. a book containing such a list or record. *The teacher had forgotten her register and could not record the attendance of the class.* 3. a device that makes a record. *A cash register adds up prices and shows the total amount of a purchase.* 4. a device which controls the flow of heated air from a furnace. *Close the register in the bedroom before it becomes too hot to sleep in there.* 5. the range of a voice or musical instrument. *He could not sing in the same register when he had a cold.* **reg is ters.**

v. 6. to enter names, facts, or other data in a list. *The visitors to the museum registered their names in the guest book.* 7. to show or record. *The thermometer registered sixty degrees at noon.* 8. to show feelings through expressions of the face or movements of the body. *He registered his anger by frowning at us.* **reg is ters, reg istered, reg is ter ing.**

reg is tra tion (rej′is trā′shən), *n.* 1. the act of registering. *The registration of new students will be done this morning.* 2. an entry in a register. *He checked my birth registration in the official book of records.* 3. the number registered. *Registration at our school reached one thousand this year.* **regis tra tions.**

re gret (ri gret′), *v.* 1. to feel sorry about. *When he failed his test, he regretted his decision not to do his homework.* 2. to mourn. *The children regretted the loss of their dog.* **re grets, re gret ted, re gret ting.**

n. 3. a feeling of sorrow; sadness; disappointment. *Much to my regret, I was unable to see the game.* 4. **regrets,** a polite reply which turns down an invitation. *If you cannot attend the party, you should send your regrets.* **re grets.**

re gret ta ble (ri gret′ə bl), *adj.* that ought to be or is regretted. *It was a regrettable accident that could have been prevented.* **re gret ta bly,** *adv.*

reg u lar (reg′yə lər), *adj.* 1. usual; ordinary. *Our regular practice on Sunday is to have dinner in the afternoon.* 2. frequent; steady. *He is a regular customer at that store.* 3. occurring at fixed intervals of time. *We make regular visits to the dentist.* 4. occurring again and again. *In our house, Monday is a regular cleaning day.* 5. evenly balanced. *The features of the face form a regular pattern.* **reg u lar ly,** *adv.*

n. 6. a member of a team or group who is expected to play or participate all of the time. *Is he a regular or a substitute on the football team? The regulars of the fire department are paid by the city for their work.* **reg u lars.**

reg u la tion (reg′yə lā′shən), *n.* 1. the control or direction of something. *The regulation of speed on the highway is enforced by the police.* 2. a rule, law. *He was arrested for not obeying the traffic regulations.* **reg u la tions.**

adj. 3. required or accepted by rule or custom. *A regulation game in baseball has nine innings.*

reign (rān), *n.* 1. the time during which a king or queen rules. *During his reign the people enjoyed many improvements in the kingdom.* **reigns.** *v.* 2. to rule. *The king reigned for thirty years.* 3. to exist in many places. *Sadness reigned in the city when the team lost the most important game of the season.* **reigns, reigned, reign ing.**

rein (rān), *n.* 1. a long strip of leather attached to the bit in an animal's mouth, by which the animal is controlled and directed. *A horse turns when the reins are pulled to one side or the other.* 2. a means of control; anything that holds something in check. *When the president went on vacation, the vice-president took over the reins of the company.* **reins.**

v. 3. to control. *Rein your temper. Be firm when you rein your horse.* **reins, reined, rein ing.**

rein deer (rān′dir′), *n.* a large kind of deer, with horns on both male and female, found in the Arctic regions. *Reindeer are valuable as work animals, for meat, and for milk.* **rein deer.** (See illustration on following page.)

re ject (ri jekt′), *v.* 1. to refuse to accept an opinion, belief, etc., or to refuse to take a thing. *He rejected the belief that money can buy everything.* 2. to throw something away. *We rejected the old records.* **re jects, re ject ed, re ject ing.**

---

sand, āte, bâre, fäther; sent, mē, fėrn; fit, bīke; pot, rōpe, fôrt; run, pùll, rüle, cūte; noise, sound; ch, cheese; ng, long; th, thick; ~~th,~~ those; zh, treasure; ə = a in about, e in waken, i in animal, o in seldom, and u in minus.

re joice (ri jois′), *v.* 1. to feel joy; to be happy. *We rejoiced at the news that there would be a holiday from school.* 2. to make happy; to make glad. *We were rejoiced by the news of the victory.* **re joic es, re joiced, re joic ing.**

re late (ri lāt′), *v.* 1. to tell about; to give an account of. *He related his experiences as a sailor to the audience.* 2. to show a connection between. *Can you relate the science lesson you read and the experiment you just did?* **re lates, re lat ed, re lat ing.**

re lat ed (ri lā′tid), *adj.* 1. belonging to the same family. *My uncle's children and I are related.* 2. connected in some way. *Oranges and lemons are related fruits.*

re la tion (ri lā′shən), *n.* 1. a telling. *His relation of the incident was not clear because he was so excited about it.* 2. a person who is connected to another by blood or marriage; a relative. *Many of our relations will attend a party celebrating my parents' anniversary.* 3. a connection. *His statement had no relation to the subject of our discussion. There is a great relation between hard work and success.* 4. reference. *You will be pleased with his work if you examine it in relation to what he has done in the past.* 5. **relations,** affairs; dealings. *The President makes the important decisions regarding our foreign relations.* **re la tions.**

rel a tive (rel′ə tiv), *n.* 1. a person who is connected to another by blood or marriage. *All of my relatives, including my aunts and uncles, attended the party.* **rel a tives.**
adj. 2. comparative; compared with another. *The doctor examined the relative weights and heights of the two boys.* 3. meaning something only in connection with something else. *Height is a relative thing because a great height for a man is a poor height for a tree.* 4. **relative to,** concerning;

reindeer

relief on a wooden panel

about. *If you have a question relative to the homework assignment, ask it now.* **rel a tive ly,** *adv.*

rel a tiv i ty (rel′ə tiv′ə tē), *n.* a theory dealing with the relation of matter, energy, space, and time. *The basic principles of relativity were first developed by Albert Einstein in the early 1900's.*

re lay (rē′lā, ri lā′), *n.* 1. a fresh supply. *Relays of horses were provided for the men of the Pony Express so that they would always be riding on a rested horse.* 2. a race between teams in which each member of the team runs only a certain part of the way. *John, Tom, Bill, and Alan teamed up to win the relay.* **re lays.**
v. 3. to take and pass along to another person or place. *Will you relay a message to Joan when you see her?* **re lays, re layed, re lay ing.**

re lease (ri lēs′), *v.* 1. to let go of. *You don't have to push the door closed; release it and it will close by itself.* 2. to let loose. *When he released the brakes, the car began rolling down the hill.* 3. to set free. *We released the bird when its broken wing had healed.* 4. to permit something to be printed, seen, used, etc. *The police released the story to the newspapers as soon as the criminal was caught.* **re leas es, re leased, re leas ing.**
n. 5. the act of letting go or setting free. *The release of the prisoner came as soon as the real robber was caught.* 6. freedom; relief from difficulty, pain, etc. *The operation brought him a release from his pain.* 7. the publication of something. *The release of his latest book came last week.* **re leas es.**

re li a ble (ri lī′ə bl), *adj.* trustworthy; dependable. *Mother baked cookies from a reliable recipe given to her by a friend. Ted is a very reliable worker and always has his assignments finished on time.* **re li a bly,** *adv.*

re lief (ri lēf′), *n.* 1. the removal or ease of worry, pain, etc. *Imagine my relief when someone else was called on to answer the question.* 2. anything that removes or lessens worry, pain, etc. *The cool evening was a relief after the heat of the day.* 3. a release from work or a duty. *There was no chance for relief as we worked through the night to control the forest fire.* 4. a person who takes over the work or duties of another. *I went home from the factory as soon as my relief* *arrived.* 5. money, food, etc., given to people who are in need of them. *Several churches provided relief for the people whose homes had been destroyed by the storm.* 6. a sculpture, ornament, etc. on which figures or a design stand out from a flat background. *The designs on coins are examples of relief. A relief showing a giant buffalo had been carved on the wall of the cave.* **re liefs.**

re lieve (ri lēv′), *v.* 1. to reduce or remove the pain, worry, etc. of something. *These pills will relieve your headaches.* 2. to bring help to. *Workers were sent to relieve the flooded town.* 3. to take the place of a person who is on duty. *He was told to relieve the guard at the main gate at midnight.* 4. to add variety to. *The mountain range helped relieve the dull scenery of the plains.* **re lieves, re lieved, re liev ing.**

re li gion (ri lij′ən), *n.* 1. a belief in or worship of God or gods. *Religion has been an important part of human life from prehistoric times to the present.* 2. a particular form of belief and worship. *He is a member of the Jewish religion.* **re li gions.**

re li gious (ri lij′əs), *adj.* 1. of religion. *He has the same religious beliefs as I do.* 2. devoted to a belief in God. *She is a very religious person who prays and goes to church often.* 3. very careful. *He paid religious attention to the directions as he tried to put the machine together.* **re li gious ly, adv.**

n. 4. a person who has become a member of a religious community, as of priests or sisters. *A large number of religious were among the group attending the meeting.*

re ly (ri lī′), *v.* to trust; to depend. *You can rely on him to do the job.* **re lies, re lied, re ly ing.**

re main (ri mān′), *v.* 1. to stay (in a place). *We remained at home because of the rain. Who will remain after class to clean the chalkboard?* 2. to continue; to last without changing. *Summer weather remained until the last week of October.* 3. to be left after something has been removed, done, etc. *All that remains of my housecleaning is the kitchen floor.* **re mains, re mained, re main ing.**

n. pl. 4. **remains,** (a) that which is left. *The remains of the building still smoked from the fire.* (b) a dead body. *We buried the remains of the dog in a vacant lot.*

re main der (ri mān′dər), *n.* a part, amount, etc.; leftover. *When you have finished your work, you can spend the remainder of the afternoon in the swimming pool. When you take 5 from 11, the remainder is 6. 10 divided by 3 gives 3 and a remainder of 1.* **re main ders.**

re mark (ri märk′), *v.* 1. to say; make a statement; to comment briefly. *The teacher remarked about the high grades the class received on the test. Mother remarked that we had forgotten to brush our teeth.* 2. to notice; to observe. *The*

guide told us to remark the many trees that grew along the forest trail. **re marks, re marked, re mark ing.**

n. 3. a brief comment; a statement. *Several people made flattering remarks about my new suit.* **re marks.**

re mark a ble (ri mär′kə bl), *adj.* unusual; worthy of attention. *He has a remarkable memory for names and dates.* **re mark a bly,** *adv.*

re med i al (ri mē′dē əl), *adj.* designed or planned to correct or improve; providing help. *He took a remedial class in arithmetic because he did poorly in that subject.* **re med i al ly,** *adv.*

rem e dy (rem′ə dē), *n.* 1. anything that removes or lessens pain or sickness. *The only remedy for your cold is to get plenty of rest. Aspirin is a common headache remedy.* 2. anything that removes or lessens an unpleasant or evil condition. *The best remedy when dealing with rude people is to ignore them.* **rem e dies.**

v. 3. to cure; to correct. *He remedied the trouble with the car by putting gasoline in the tank.* **rem e dies, rem e died, rem e dy ing.**

re mem ber (ri mem′bər), *v.* 1. to bring back to the mind; to recall. *I couldn't remember the answer to the question.* 2. to keep in mind. *Remember that you must turn the lights out when you leave the room.* 3. to give a gift to. *Grandmother always remembers us on our birthdays.* 4. to deliver greetings from. *Remember me to your brother when you see him.* **re mem bers, re mem bered, re mem ber ing.**

re mem brance (ri mem′brəns), *n.* 1. the act of remembering. *She was happy with our remembrance of her birthday.* 2. a thing remembered. *We have happy remembrances of our days in school.* 3. a souvenir; anything that helps one to remember something. *She saved a flower as a remembrance of the dance.* 4. length of time that one remembers. *Our remembrances do not include days before television.* **re mem branc es.**

re mind (ri mīnd′), *v.* to cause someone to remember. *Remind me to tell you that story when I have more time. He tied a string on his finger to remind him that he had an appointment.* **re minds, re mind ed, re mind ing.**

re mit (ri mit′), *v.* 1. to send a payment that is due. *Please remit the amount that you still owe on your account.* 2. to forgive; to pardon. *Christians believe that Christ had the power to remit sins.* 3. to cancel. *If you pay half of the amount, we will remit the rest of the debt.* 4. to make less; to reduce. *The rescuers did not remit their efforts until they had freed the men from the mine.* **re mits, re mit ted, re mit ting.**

re mit tance (ri mit′ns), *n.* the money sent as a payment. *I enclosed my remittance when I ordered the goods.* **re mit tanc es.**

rem o ra (rem′ə rə), *n.* a fish with a sucking plate on the top of its head. *Remoras use their plates to attach themselves to sharks.* **rem o ras.** (See illustration on following page.)

---

sand, āte, bâre, fäther; sent, mē, fèrn; fit, bīke; pot, rōpe, fôrt; run, pùll, rüle, cūte; noise, sound; ch, cheese; ng, long; th, thick; ᵺ, those; zh, treasure; ə = a in about, e in waken, i in animal, o in seldom, and u in minus.

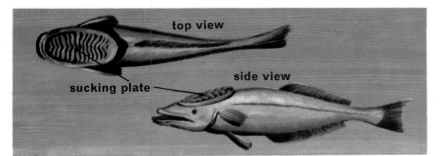

remora

re mote (ri mōt′), *adj.* 1. far off in distance or time. *Their family lived in a remote country before they came to America. In remote ages people lived in caves and used clubs as weapons.* 2. set away from other things; isolated. *The lonely man lived in a remote cabin on top of the mountain.* 3. not closely related; distant. *They are remote relatives of ours.* 4. slight. *We hadn't a remote idea of what he was talking about.* **re mot er, re mot est; re mote ly,** *adv.*

re mov al (ri müv′l), *n.* 1. the taking away of something. *The removal of the street signs confused many visitors to the city.* 2. change of location. *The removal of the criminal to prison came as soon as his trial had ended.* 3. a dismissing from a position. *The removal of the president of the company resulted in the appointment of a new president.* **re mov als.**

re move (ri müv′), *v.* 1. to take away; to take off. *Remove everything from your desk before you leave. Don't remove the covers from these books.* 2. to get rid of. *You can remove this debt by paying the money that you owe.* 3. to dismiss from a position. *The department store will remove fifty employees after the holiday rush.* 4. to leave one house or place and go to another. *Their family is planning to remove to the west coast.* **re moves, re moved, re mov ing.**

n. 5. a distance; an amount of separation. *This job is a far remove from the kind of work you have done before.* **re moves.**

Ren ais sance (ren′ə säns′, ren′ə säns), *n.* the time in Europe in the 1300's, 1400's, and 1500's when there was a new interest in art, literature, and science. *The art of the Renaissance is among the most beautiful in the world.*

ren der (ren′dər), *v.* 1. to cause to be; to make. *I was rendered unconscious by the blow.* 2. to give. *We render thanks for the blessings we have been given. The gardener rendered us a bill for the work he had done.* 3. to perform. *A large number of actors rendered the play. She rendered the song well.* **ren ders, ren dered, ren der ing.**

re new (ri nü′, ri nū′), *v.* 1. to make new again; to make fresh again. *The player's energy was renewed after a few moments of rest.* 2. to start again. *After a brief pause, the boxer renewed his efforts to win the fight.* 3. to restore; fill again. *Mother renews the supply of cookies in the cookie jar once every week.* 4. to cause to continue for a new period of time. *Did you renew your subscription to the magazine?* **re news, re newed, re new ing.**

re new al (ri nü′əl, ri nū′əl), *n.* a renewing; a being renewed. *He has a renewal of interest in school every time he gets his report card. I sent in a request for renewal of my subscription.* **re new als.**

rent[1] (rent), *v.* 1. to pay a sum of money for the use of property or goods. *My parents have rented a small house in the country for their vacation. I rented a canoe when I went to the river.* 2. to allow the use of property or goods in return for a sum of money. *I don't think I will sell my bicycle, but I may rent it.* 3. to be used in return for a sum of money. *This car rents for twelve dollars a day.* **rents, rent ed, rent ing.**

n. 4. a sum of money paid for the use of

Renaissance art and architecture

tomb of Louis XII in the Church of St. Denis in France

Basilica of St. Peter in Rome, Italy

pitcher

jewelry

Pieta by Michaelangelo

property or goods. *The rent for the apartment is eighty dollars a month.* **rents.**

rent[2] (rent), *n.* a tear; a torn place. *There was a huge rent in the knee of his pants after he fell.* **rents.**

re pair (ri pâr´), *v.* 1. to bring back to good condition; to fix; to mend. *When the wheel on my wagon fell off, I had to have the wagon repaired.* 2. to remedy; to make up for. *You must try to repair the injury you have done her.* **re pairs, re paired, re pair ing.**
n. 3. the act of repairing. *The repair of your car will be completed by tomorrow.* 4. the condition of a thing, especially a usable condition. *Several men take care of that truck to keep it in repair. The old house was in very bad repair.* **re pairs.**

re pay (ri pā´), *v.* 1. to pay back. *When will you repay the money that you owe me?* 2. to make return for. *I'll never be able to repay the help you have given to me.* **re pays, re paid, re pay ing.**

re peat (ri pēt´), *v.* 1. to say again. *Will you repeat the question, please?* 2. to do again. *The robber was caught when he tried to repeat his crime.* 3. to tell others. *I asked her not to repeat the news, but she told all of her friends about it.* 4. to say from memory. *Tomorrow each of you will be asked to repeat this poem.* **re peats, re peat ed, re peat ing.**
n. 5. a repeating; a saying or doing again. *The second game was a repeat of the first one and we lost by the same score.* **re peats.**

re peat ed (ri pē´tid), *v.* 1. past tense of **repeat.**
adj. 2. happening more than once. *He was dropped from the team because of his repeated failure to hit the ball.* **re peat ed ly,** *adv.*

re pel (ri pel´), *v.* 1. to drive back. *They repelled the enemy in a fierce battle.* 2. to refuse to take, believe, etc. *The committee repelled his suggestion that a new town hall must be built.* 3. to be very unpleasant to. *The sight of the huge snake repelled me.* **re pels, re pelled, re pell ing.**

re pel lent (ri pel´ənt), *n.* 1. anything used to drive back or keep off insects, water, etc. *The mosquitoes stopped biting me after I sprayed insect repellent on my arms and neck. A special repellent has been put on this fabric to keep it from absorbing water.* **re pel lents.**
adj. 2. displeasing; unpleasant. *His repellent manner made people dislike him.*

rep e ti tion (rep´ə tish´ən), *n.* 1. a saying or doing again; a repeating. *After much repetition of the instructions we were able to understand how to do the problems.* 2. something repeated. *His errors on the test were a repetition of the errors he had made in his homework.* **rep e ti tions.**

re place (ri plās´), *v.* 1. to put back. *When you have finished reading the magazine, kindly replace it on the table.* 2. to take the place of. *No one could replace him in the play when he became sick.* **re plac es, re placed, re plac ing.**

re ply (ri plī´), *n.* 1. an answer. *I did not hear his reply because he spoke too softly.* **re plies.**

reporters interviewing a soccer player

v. 2. to give an answer; to respond. *He refused to reply to any of my questions about the broken window.* **re plies, re plied, re ply ing.**

re port (ri pôrt´), *n.* 1. an account of something; a written or spoken statement. *The newspaper report of the accident did not name any of those who were injured.* 2. a thing that is said by a number of people but is not proved. *We heard a report that there had been a fire at your house.* 3. a loud, sudden noise. *The report of the gun signaling the end of the game could not be heard above the noise of the crowd.* **re ports.**
v. 4. to give an account or statement of. *The president of the company reported the fact that sales had increased during the year.* 5. to make a complaint about someone or something. *Mother reported the clerk's bad manners to the store owner.* 6. to present oneself. *Report for the examination at eleven o'clock tomorrow morning.* **re ports, re port ed, re port ing.**

re port er (ri pôr´tər), *n.* 1. a person who reports. *Who was the reporter of the fire?* 2. a person who gathers news for radio, television, or newspapers. *Several reporters talked to the coach and players after the game.* **re port ers.**

rep re sent (rep´ri zent´), *v.* 1. to show; illustrate; describe. *The painting represents the city as it was fifty years ago.* 2. to be a symbol of; to stand for. *The Statue of Liberty represents the freedom that can be found in the United States.* 3. to speak or act for. *I was chosen to represent our class at the meeting.* 4. to describe or put forth as having a certain quality, value, etc. *The speaker represented himself as a lover of peace.* 5. to be an example of. *The quality of this machine* represents the kind of work we try to do at the factory. **rep re sents, rep re sent ed, rep re-sent ing.**

rep re sent a tive (rep′ri zen′tə tiv), *n.* 1. a person who has the power to speak or act for someone else. *Mike was chosen as our class representative to the student council.* 2. an example. *Tom is a good representative of the type of students we have at our school.* **rep re sent a tives.**

adj. 3. consisting of officials elected by the people to represent them; acting for others. *In the United States we have a representative government.* 4. sample; giving an example; typical. *At the top of the page were representative problems which helped us to understand the work.*

re pro duce (rē′pre dūs′ or rē′prə dūs′), *v.* 1. to make or produce again. *He reproduced the article by hand.* 2. to give birth to. *Rabbits reproduce many offspring.* **re pro duces, re pro-duced, re pro duc ing.**

rep tile (rep′tl, rep′tīl), *n.* any of the creeping or crawling animals whose blood temperature varies according to the temperature of the surrounding medium. *Snakes, lizards, turtles, and alligators are reptiles.* **rep tiles.**

re pub lic (ri pub′lik), *n.* a country or state in which the voters elect the persons who are to run the government. *The United States is a republic.* **re pub lics.**

re pub li can (ri pub′lə kən), *adj.* 1. of or like a republic. *The leaders of the new country favored a republican form of government.* 2. **Republican Party,** one of the two major political parties in the United States. *The Republican Party held a convention at which they selected a candidate to run in the election.*

n. 3. a person who is in favor of a republic. *The men who led the American Revolution against England were republicans.* 4. **Republican,** a member of the Republican Party. *Two*

REPTILES

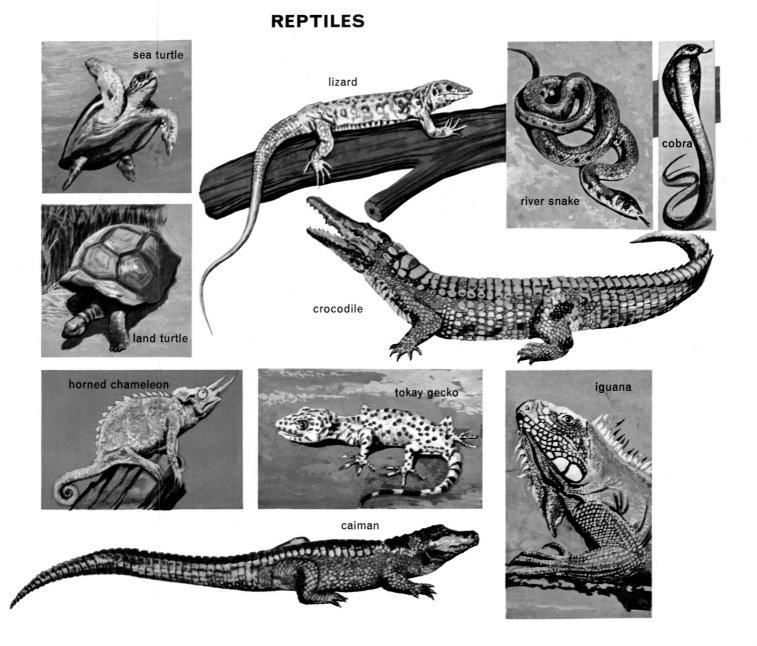

sea turtle

lizard

river snake

cobra

land turtle

crocodile

horned chameleon

tokay gecko

iguana

caiman

Republicans and two Democrats spoke at the meeting. **re pub li cans.**

rep u ta tion (rep′yə tā′shən), *n.* 1. the character, quality, or worth of a person as it is judged by other people. *That store owner is a man of good reputation in this town.* 2. good name. *He ruined his reputation by cheating on the test.* 3. fame. *That baseball player gained a world reputation for his skill as a pitcher.* **rep u ta tions.**

re quest (ri kwest′), *v.* 1. to ask. *The teacher requested me to stay after class.* 2. to ask for. *I requested that book from the library.* **re quests, re quest ed, re quest ing.**

n. 3. an asking; an asking for something. *Please speak louder if you want me to hear your request.* 4. something that is asked for. *Father turned down my request for a larger allowance.* 5. the condition of being asked for; demand. *The library will lend you this book on request.* **re quests.**

re quire (ri kwīr′), *v.* 1. to need. *Man requires food and water to live.* 2. to demand; to command. *Good manners require that you use a knife and a fork when you eat.* **re quires, re quired, re quir ing.**

re quire ment (ri kwīr′mənt), *n.* 1. something needed. *Good food is a requirement for good health.* 2. something demanded; a required condition. *You will graduate if you complete all of the requirements.* **re quire ments.**

req ui si tion (rek′wə zish′ən), *n.* 1. an official demand or request, especially a written demand. *Did you fill out a requisition to get those books?* **req ui si tions.**

v. 2. to demand or request, especially in writing. *The captain requisitioned additional guns and supplies.* **req ui si tions, req ui si tioned, req ui si tion ing.**

res cue (res′kū), *v.* 1. to save from danger; to free from capture or harm. *The soldiers rescued the prisoners of war.* **res cues, res cued, res cu ing.**

n. 2. a saving from danger; a freeing from capture or harm. *The rescue of the men who were trapped in the mine took several hours.* **res cues.**

re search (ri sėrch′, rē′sėrch), *n.* 1. a careful search or investigation to find facts, new information, etc. *The scientist's research helped to prove that his theory was accurate.* **re search es.**

v. 2. to investigate; to research. *Scientists researched the cause of many diseases.* **re searches, re search ed, re search ing.**

re search er (ri sėr′chər, rē′sėr chər), *n.* a person who does research. *The library has several researchers to help you find information.* **re search ers.**

re sem ble (ri zem′bl), *v.* to be like; to look like. *In his appearance and in his voice, that boy resembles his father.* **re sem bles, re sem bled, re sem bling.**

res er va tion (rez′ər vā′shən), *n.* 1. an arrangement to hold something for a person. *The hotel kept a room for us because we had made a reservation.* 2. a reserving; a limiting condition. *Father agreed to let us go to the party with the reservation that we be back by nine.* 3. an area of land set apart for a certain use. *She taught in a school on an Indian reservation.* **res er va tions.**

re serve (ri zėrv′), *v.* 1. to hold back; to keep back. *I reserved my opinion of the speaker until he had finished talking. A certain amount of his weekly salary is reserved to pay his monthly bills.* 2. to arrange to have set aside for one's use. *We reserved a room at the hotel. If I don't have enough money to pay for the tickets now, can you reserve them for me?* 3. to set apart for a certain purpose. *All of her spare time is reserved for her violin practice. Sunday afternoons are reserved for family gatherings at my grandmother's house.* **re serves, re served, re serv ing.**

n. 4. something held for later use; a supply. *Keep a reserve of cash for emergency use.* 5. an area of land set aside for a certain use. *Hunting is not allowed on the wildlife reserve.* 6. a limiting condition or exception. *The members of the club accepted the plan without reserve.* 7. a restraint in speech or action; self-control. *She is a lady of great dignity who always maintains a quiet reserve when we talk to her.* 8. **reserves,** men kept available for battle or other use. *Military reserves are often called upon to help in rescue work when a tornado or flood occurs.* **re serves.**

re served (ri zėrvd′), *adj.* 1. held or set apart for a certain use. *You may not sit in these seats because they are reserved for someone else.* 2. quiet and calm in speech or actions. *The boys were reserved in the classroom but noisy and active on the playground.* **re serv ed ly,** *adv.*

res er voir (rez′ər vwär′, rez′ər vôr′), *n.* 1. a place where water is collected and stored for use. *Rivers are sometimes dammed to make reservoirs so that there will always be a supply of water.* 2. a large or extra supply; a reserve. *The teacher was a reservoir of knowledge.* **res er voirs.** (See illustration on following page.)

re side (ri zīd′), *v.* 1. to live; to make one's home at a place. *Their family has resided in that house for many years.* 2. to be present; to exist. *The right and power to make rules resides in the members of the club, not in its leaders.* **re sides, re sid ed, re sid ing.**

res i dence (rez′ə dens), *n.* 1. a home; the place where one lives; a house. *The wealthy man lived in a huge residence at the edge of the lake.* 2. the act or fact of living in a place. *Residence in the United States is one requirement for voting.* 3. the period of time during which a person lives in a place. *The President's residence in the White House was eight years.* **res i denc es.**

re sign (ri zīn′), *v.* 1. to give up one's position. *The coach of the football team has resigned.* 2. to give up. *He resigned his job when the work became too hard for him.* 3. to give over; to submit without resistance. *He is doing well in school*

reservoir

now because he resigned himself to the fact that he would have to study. **re signs, re signed, re-sign ing.**

re signed (ri zīnd′), *adj.* accepting what is or what comes without complaint or resistance. *He is resigned to the fact that he won't be going to camp this year.* **re sign ed ly,** *adv.*

res in (rez′in), *n.* a sticky substance that comes out of certain trees and plants. *Resins are used in making some kinds of medicine.* **res ins.**

re sist (ri zist′) *v.* 1. to work against; to oppose. *The men resisted their opponents' attempt to push them back.* 2. to be successful against something. *I resisted the desire to laugh at him.* 3. to be able to stand against some action or effect. *That new cloth resists stains.* **re sists, re sist ed, re sist ing.**

re sist ance (ri zis′təns), *n.* 1. a fighting against; an opposing. *Our teacher's resistance caused us to cancel our plans for a trip to the zoo.* 2. the ability to fight against something; power to oppose. *It is difficult to sell anything to a person who has sales resistance. A healthy body has great resistance to germs and disease.* 3. an opposition or force that fights against something or holds it back. *Cars are designed to reduce the resistance of the air.* 4. the opposition of a material to an electric current passing through it. *Electric cords are covered with rubber because rubber has high resist-ance.* **re sist anc es.**

res o lu tion (rez′ə lü′shən), *n.* 1. a decision; something determined. *He made a resolution to finish his lessons before going to bed.* 2. a strength of purpose. *He shows great resolution when he is faced with a problem.* 3. a solution. *The resolution of the mystery came shortly after the crime was committed.* 4. an official statement of the views or opinions of a group. *Congress passed a resolution praising the heroic soldier.* **res o lu tions.**

re solve (ri zolv′), *v.* 1. to make up one's mind; to decide. *He resolved to study harder in the future.* 2. to decide through voting. *The committee resolved to accept the plan to build a new gym.* 3. to dissolve; to clear away. *Mother's fears about our safety were resolved after we called her from the city.* 4. to separate; to break up. *Some substances resolve into a gas and water when heat is applied.* **re solves, re solved, re solv ing.**

n. 5. something resolved; a decision. *He was unable to keep his resolve to work harder.* 6. strength of purpose. *The pioneers showed great resolve when they braved the wilderness to build their homes.* **re solves.**

re solved (ri zolvd′), *adj.* determined; firm in purpose. *Through resolved effort and hard work, he finished the job on time.*

re sort (ri zôrt′), *n.* 1. someone or something toward which one turns for help. *His aunt has always been his first resort when he is in trouble.* 2. a place to which people go for rest and pleasure. *We spent the holiday at a ski resort in the mountains.* 3. the act of turning to someone or something for help. *His resort to swift action in an emergency makes him a valuable fireman.* **re sorts.**

v. 4. to turn for aid or assistance. *Don't resort to force until you have tried everything else.* 5. to go often. *They resort to the beaches in Florida during the winter.* **re sorts, re sort ed, re sort ing.**

re source (ri sôrs′, rē′sôrs), *n.* 1. a supply of something to be used. *They spent all of their resources of money on the new house.* 2. anything used to escape from or to avoid danger or difficulty. *Our only resource during the tornado was to run for shelter.* 3. **resources,** all of the wealth of a person or a nation or the means of producing this wealth. *America is rich in natural resources such as trees, oil, and iron.* **re sourc es.**

re spect (ri spekt′), *n.* 1. honor; esteem; regard. *I have great respect for my father and what he tells me.* 2. detail; feature. *He has mastered the art of hitting a baseball in every respect.* 3. relation. *The punishment is decided with respect to the gravity of the offense.* 4. **respects,** regards; greetings.

We paid our respects to Tom's mother before we left their house after the party. **re spects.**
v. 5. to honor; to show regard for. *Children should respect their parents.* 6. to show consideration for. *They respected the mayor's wishes and voted in favor of his plan.* **re spects, re spect ed, re spect ing.**

re spect a ble (ri spek′tə bl), *adj.* 1. having a good reputation. *The president of the bank is a respectable member of the community.* 2. fairly large; having fair size or quality. *There was a respectable number of people in the auditorium to see the play.* 3. suitable to use or be seen using. *Your playclothes are not respectable enough for school.* **re spect a bly,** *adv.*

re spect ful (ri spekt′fəl), *adj.* showing respect; polite; courteous. *The children were quiet and respectful as the principal spoke to them.* **re spect ful ly,** *adv.*

re spect ful ness (ri spekt′fəl nis), *n.* the quality of being respectful. *The pupil was scolded for his lack of respectfulness towards the teacher.*

re spec tive (ri spek′tiv), *adj.* belonging to or relating to each; individual. *Tom and Bill went to their respective rooms when the bell rang.* **re spec tive ly,** *adv.*

re spec tive ly (ri spek′tiv lē), *adv.* belonging to each in the order named. *Harry, Mark, and Jane won five, ten, and fifteen dollars, respectively.*

res pi ra tion (res′pə rā′shən), *n.* breathing; the inhaling and exhaling of air. *Respiration provides the body with oxygen.*

re spond (ri spond′), *v.* 1. to answer; to reply. *Susan did not respond when I asked her a question.* 2. to act in answer; to show some action or effect as if in answer. *He responded well to the medicine the doctor gave him.* **re sponds, re spond ed, re spond ing.**

re sponse (ri spons′), *n.* 1. an answer. *She made no response to my questions.* 2. the words spoken by the people in answer to the priest or minister in a church service. *The minister waited for the people to complete the response before he began another prayer.* **re spons es.**

re spon si bil i ty (ri spon′sə bil′ə tē), *n.* 1. a being responsible. *John always assumes responsibility for his little sister when his parents are not home.* 2. something for which one is responsible. *The head of that company has many important responsibilities.* **re spon si bil i ties.**

re spon si ble (ri spon′sə bl), *adj.* 1. trustworthy; reliable. *A responsible pupil was chosen to collect the money for the field trip.* 2. liable to be called to account or answer for something. *Who is responsible for turning off the lights when we leave the room?* 3. deserving credit or blame for something. *The cold weather was responsible for the small crowd at the picnic.* 4. requiring a person to assume important duties and obligations. *He holds a responsible job at the factory and is in charge of many workers.* **re spon si bly,** *adv.*

rest[1] (rest), *n.* 1. freedom from activity, work, pain, etc.; quiet. *When the project was finished we took a week's rest.* 2. sleep. *I am tired because I didn't get enough rest last night.* 3. a place of shelter, such as a lodge, cabin, etc. *We spent the night in a hunter's rest in the mountains.* 4. a stopping of motion; a lack of motion. *The car came to rest at the bottom of the hill.* 5. something that serves as a support. *He leaned back on the head rest on the dentist's chair.* 6. in music, a pause or the mark that indicates a pause. *The orchestra came to a rest in the music and was silent for a moment.* **rests.**
v. 7. to stop working; to be still. *Rest a moment before you continue climbing the hill.* 8. to lie down; to sleep. *I can't rest when there is noise all around me.* 9. to be dead. *May they rest in peace.* 10. to give rest to. *Stop and rest your horse when you reach the other side of the river.* 11. to be set on a support; to lean or lie. *The roof rests on the supporting walls. The ladder rested against the side of the house.* 12. to depend. *Our team's success rests on you, so do your best.* **rests, rest ed, rest ing.**

rest[2] (rest), *n.* 1. all that is left; whatever remains. *After you have poured your milk, put the rest back in the refrigerator.* 2. all those that are left; whoever remains. *Bob and I stayed with the rest of the crowd.*

res tau rant (res′tə rənt, res′tə ränt′), *n.* a place where meals are sold and served to people. *We ate dinner in a restaurant downtown.* **res tau rants.**

rest less (rest′lis), *adj.* 1. never still; always in motion. *The restless children twisted around in their seats at every sound.* 2. without rest; giving no rest. *He spent a restless night worrying about his tests in school.* **rest less ly,** *adv.*

res to ra tion (res′tə rā′shən), *n.* 1. the act of restoring to a former state or condition. *The*

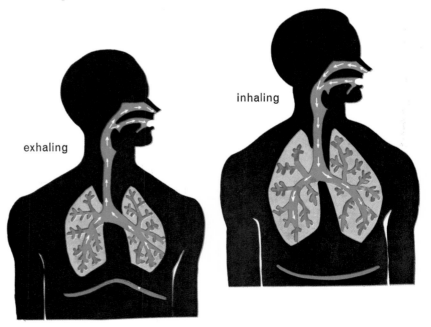

respiration

inhaling

exhaling

restoration of the old building was very expensive.
2. a thing that has been returned to a former
state or condition. *We visited a restoration of an
old theater in London.* **res to ra tions.**

re store (ri stôr′), *v.* 1. to return to a former
state or condition. *They restored the building so
that it looks the way it did two centuries ago.* 2. to
return; to give back. *The police restored the
money to the man from whom it had been stolen.*
re stores, re stored, re stor ing.

re strain (ri strān′), *v.* to hold back; to keep
under control. *He managed to restrain his anger
until the others had gone.* **re strains, re-
strained, re strain ing.**

re straint (ri strānt′), *n.* 1. a holding back; a
restraining. *His imagination showed no restraint.*
2. control of one's emotions, actions, etc.
*That man has great restraint and never seems to
become angry or lose patience.* 3. something that
restrains. *A heavy chain was used as a restraint on
the wild animal.* **re straints.**

re sult (ri zult′), *n.* 1. the outcome; something
which happens as an effect. *He was late to work
as a result of a delay in traffic.* 2. something good
or favorable which happens as an effect. *The
mayor demanded results, not excuses, from his assistants.* 3. an answer to a problem. *If you subtract
fifteen from twenty the result is five.* **re sults.**
v. 4. to happen as an effect. *His injury resulted
from falling down a flight of stairs.* 5. **result in,**
to have as effect. *The automobile accident resulted
in a few minor injuries to the passengers in the car.*
re sults, re sult ed, re sult ing.

re tail (rē′tāl), *n.* 1. the sale of goods, usually in
small amounts, directly to the one who uses
them. *Storekeepers buy large amounts of goods at
wholesale and sell to their customers at retail.*
v. 2. to sell goods in small amounts directly
to the one who uses them. *The clothing store
retails dresses.* 3. to be sold at retail. *This coat
retails for seventeen dollars.* **re tails, re tailed,
re tail ing.**
adj. 4. having to do with selling in small
amounts. *The retail price is higher than the
wholesale price.*

re tain (ri tān′), *v.* 1. to keep; to hold; to continue to have. *Some materials retain heat better
than others.* 2. to hold in place. *A dam was built
to retain the waters of the lake.* 3. to remember.
*Some people find it easy to retain very small details
about history.* **re tains, re tained, re tain ing.**

re tard (ri tärd′), *v.* to delay or slow down the
progress of someone or something. *Too much
water retarded the growth of the plants.* **re tards,
re tard ed, re tard ing.**

ret i na (ret′n ə), *n.* the back part of the eye,
made up of cells that respond to light. *The
retina transfers an image from the lens to the brain.*
ret i nas.

re tire (ri tīr′), *v.* 1. to give up one's work or
position. *He retired after thirty years as owner of a
successful store.* 2. to cause to leave one's work

retort

or position. *Some companies retire their employees
when they reach the age of sixty-five.* 3. to go away.
*He retired to a farm for a few weeks so that he
could rest.* 4. to withdraw; to retreat. *The troops
were forced to retire because of the enemy fire.* 5. to
go to bed. *I retire at eight o'clock every night.*
6. to remove from use. *Worn and torn money is
retired by the government.* **re tires, re tired,
re tir ing.**

re tire ment (ri tīr′mənt), *n.* a retiring; a being
retired. *His retirement surprised us because he was
still young enough to continue working.* **re tire-
ments.**

re tort[1] (ri tôrt′), *v.* 1. to answer back quickly,
cleverly, or angrily. *"No comment," retorted the
mayor when the reporters asked him if he would run
for governor.* **re torts, re tort ed, re tort ing.**
n. 2. a sharp answer. *His retorts stopped people
from asking questions.* **re torts.**

re tort[2] (ri tôrt′), *n.* a glass vessel with a long
neck, in which substances are evaporated,
made pure, or changed by heat. *In the science
laboratory we placed a flame under the retort to heat
the solution.* **re torts.**

re treat (ri trēt′), *v.* 1. to withdraw; to go back.
*The soldiers refused to retreat in spite of the force
of the enemy attack.* **re treats, re treat ed,
re treat ing.**
n. 2. a withdrawing; a going back. *The retreat
of the enemy meant that we had won the battle.* 3. a
signal given to withdraw. *The captain ordered
retreat to be sounded on the drum.* 4. a place where
one can find quiet, peace, and safety. *He built
a retreat at the lake for his summer vacations.*
re treats.

re turn (ri tėrn′), *v.* 1. to come back; to go
back. *We will return after the game is over. Return
to your seat immediately.* 2. to bring back; send
back; give back. *Return that book to me when you
have finished reading it. I forgot to return the scarf
I borrowed from Jean.* 3. to reply; to answer.
"Don't do that again," he returned angrily. 4. to
result in; to yield. *The investment returned a big
profit.* **re turns, re turned, re turn ing.**

n. 5. a coming back; a going back. *The return of warm weather was welcomed by the children. The soldier's return home was a joyous occasion.* 6. a bringing back; a giving back. *His return of the goods was accepted by the store.* 7. a report. *Election returns were heard shortly after the voting was completed.* 8. a profit. *The returns on his investments made him a wealthy man.* **re turns.**
adj. 9. having to do with a return or returning. *We must make a return trip to the Grand Canyon next year.*

re un ion (rē ūn′yən), *n.* a bringing together; a coming together. *Every year we have a family reunion.* **re un ions.**

re veal (ri vēl′), *v.* 1. to show. *The morning sunlight revealed the snow that had fallen during the night.* 2. to tell; to make known. *Don't reveal any family secrets.* **re veals, re vealed, re veal ing.**

re venge (ri venj′), *v.* 1. to harm or attempt to harm the person considered responsible for a wrong, an injury, etc. *The angry man said he would revenge the insult he had suffered.* **re veng es, re venged, re veng ing.**
n. 2. a harm done in return for a wrong, injury, etc. *Jim's revenge for the trick the boys had played on him was to refuse to let them use his football.* 3. a desire for doing harm in return for a wrong, injury, etc. *He satisfied his revenge by turning the criminals who had robbed him over to the police.*

rev e nue (rev′ə nü, rev′ə nū), *n.* income; money, especially tax money. *The President told the nation that the government needed more revenue.* **rev e nues.**

re vere (ri vēr′), *v.* to show great love, respect, etc. for something or someone. *Mary reveres her mother.* **re veres, re vered, re ver ing.**

rev er ence (rev′ər əns), *n.* 1. deep respect, mixed with love, fear, and wonder. *The child looked with reverence on the President of the United States.* **rev er enc es.**
v. 2. to feel deep respect for; to honor greatly. *We reverence great men in history.* **rev er enc es, rev er enced, rev er enc ing.**

re ver sal (ri vėr′sl), *n.* a change to the opposite. *The fox escaped from the hunting dogs through a clever reversal of his direction.* **re ver sals.**

re verse (ri vėrs′), *adj.* 1. turned backward or around in the opposite direction or position. *The answers to the questions were on the reverse side of the paper.* **re verse ly,** *adv.*
n. 2. the opposite. *If I tell her to do one thing she always does the reverse.* 3. a gear or other device in a machine which causes the machine to produce a backward motion. *He put the car in reverse and backed out of the garage.* 4. the back side of a coin or medal. *An eagle is on the reverse of a quarter.* 5. a change to a bad condition; a defeat. *Business reverses caused him to lose all of his money.* **re vers es.**
v. 6. to turn something inside out, backwards,

or upside down. *Reverse your jacket so that the clean side is on the outside.* 7. to change to the opposite. *The court reversed its sentence and freed the prisoner.* **re vers es, re versed, re vers- ing.**

re view (ri vū′), *v.* 1. to study again; go over. *She reviewed the assignments before she took the test.* 2. to inspect formally and officially. *Two generals reviewed all of the soldiers in the camp.* 3. to look back on. *The old man reviewed his life to see what he had accomplished.* 4. to write a criticism of a book, play, etc. *The reporter reviewed the new play in several newspapers.* **re views, re viewed, re view ing.**
n. 5. a studying again of something; going over. *When we finished the review of our lessons we felt sure that we would pass the test.* 6. an inspec- tion. *There will be a review of the troops tomorrow morning.* 7. a criticism of a book, play, etc. *The author was pleased when he read a favorable review of his book.* **re views.**

re vise (ri vīz′), *v.* 1. to read something care- fully in order to change and improve it. *The author revised his manuscript.* 2. to change; alter. *Our plans for the picnic were revised when it began to rain.* **re vis es, re vised, re vis ing.**

re volt (ri vōlt′), *v.* 1. to overthrow something; rebel. *The peasants revolted against the king.* 2. to be disgusted by something. *The rotten apples revolted us.* **re volts, re volt ed, re volt- ing.**
n. 3. an overthrow of something; rebellion. *The peasants planned a revolt against the king.* **re volts.**

rev o lu tion (rev′ə lü′shən), *n.* 1. a great and complete change. *The invention of machinery brought about a revolution in the way people lived and worked.* 2. a complete change in govern- ment. *The forces of the king were defeated in a revolution by the people.* 3. a moving around something in a circle or curve. *The revolution of the earth around the sun produces changes in the weather.* 4. one full turn of a wheel, motor, etc. *This engine can do four thousand revolutions per minute.* **rev o lu tions.**

re volv er (ri vol′vər), *n.* a kind of pistol. *A revolver can be fired several times before it needs to be loaded again.* **re volv ers.**

re ward (ri wôrd′), *n.* 1. something given in return for service, brave conduct, etc. *He received a medal as a reward for his courage.* 2. a sum of money given or offered in return for recovering lost or stolen property, capturing

revolvers

rhinoceros

a criminal, etc. *There was a reward of one thousand dollars for the capture of the bank robber.* **re wards.**

v. 3. to give a reward to or for. *John was rewarded for finding the lost dog. The woman rewarded the boy for returning her watch.* **re wards, re ward ed, re ward ing.**

rhi noc er os (rī nos′ər əs), *n.* a large, clumsy animal with a thick skin and one or two horns above its nose. *The rhinoceros lives in the wet regions of Africa and Asia.* **rhi noc er os es** or **rhi noc er os.**

Rhode Is land (rōd′ ī′lənd), *n.* a state in the northeastern part of the United States. *Rhode Island is the smallest state in the United States.*

rhyme (rīm), *n.* 1. a word that sounds like another; a final sound in a word that sounds like another word or like the final sound in another word. *"Together" is a rhyme for "weather." "Block" is a rhyme for "clock."* 2. a poem with lines that end with the same sound. *Mother read us a rhyme before we went to bed.* **rhymes.**

v. 3. to be or form a rhyme; to sound like another word. *"Feet" rhymes with "meat" and "beat."* 4. to compose in rhyme; to put into rhyme. *She rhymed a song for his birthday party.* **rhymes, rhymed, rhym ing.**

rhythm (rith′əm), *n.* a regular, repeated movement in which a beat, accent, etc. rises and falls or occurs steadily. *The rhythm in music is often provided by the drums.* **rhythms.**

rib (rib), *n.* 1. one of the bones that curve around and enclose the chest. *The ribs protect the lungs and other organs and add support to the upper part of the body.* 2. anything shaped like a rib or that supports like a rib. *After the fire, only the ribs of the giant airplane remained.* **ribs.**

rib bon (rib′ən), *n.* 1. a narrow strip of cloth, especially bright-colored velvet or silk, used as a decoration. *She wore a yellow ribbon in her hair. The first prize for the race was a blue ribbon.* 2. anything like a ribbon. *I need a new ribbon for my typewriter. The flag was torn to ribbons by the high winds.* **rib bons.**

rice (rīs), *n.* 1. the seeds or grain of a plant which is grown in warm parts of the world. *Rice is an important food in India, China, and Japan.* 2. the

plant on which these seeds grow. *Rice is a grass that is grown in very wet ground.*

rich (rich), *adj.* 1. having many possessions, much land, or great wealth; wealthy. *The rich man gave a million dollars to the city to build a new library.* 2. expensive; of great value. *The queen wore a rich gown that was covered with jewels.* 3. fertile. *The land on his farm is very rich.* 4. full; abundant; more than enough. *They enjoyed a rich crop of cotton and tobacco this year.* 5. full of butter, sugar, cream, etc. *The cake was too rich for me to eat but the children enjoyed it very much.* 6. dark and deep in color. *The wine was a rich red.* 7. full and mellow in sound. *The rich tones of the music filled the great hall.* **rich er, rich est; rich ly,** *adv.*

rich es (rich′iz), *n. pl.* wealth. *When his company failed, he lost all of his riches.*

rid (rid), *v.* 1. to free; to clear. *He tried to rid himself of his worries about the final examination.* 2. **get rid of,** to get free from; be relieved of. *I wish I could get rid of this headache.* **rids, rid** or **rid ded, rid ding.**

rid den (rid′n), past participle of **ride.**

rid dle[1] (rid′l), *n.* a puzzling problem; a question to which the answer is unexpected. *The answer to the riddle, "What do you have that other people use more than you do?" is "your name."* **rid dles.**

rid dle[2] (rid′l), *v.* to make many holes in something. *The woodpeckers have riddled that old tree.* **rid dles, rid dled, rid dling.**

ride (rīd), *v.* 1. to sit on an animal, especially a horse, while it is moving. *My cousins live on*

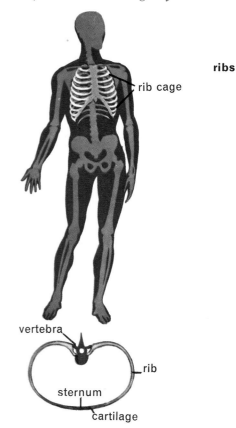

ribs

rib cage

vertebra

rib

sternum

cartilage

rice grains and plant

a farm and learned how to ride when they were very young. 2. to sit on anything that is moving. *Ride your bicycle on the side of the road.* 3. to sit in something and be carried by it. *When we went to the zoo all of us rode in the same bus.* 4. to move or float on; to be carried by. *The gulls rode the wind easily and gracefully. The pirate's ship rode the waves until the wind died down.* **rides, rode, rid den, rid ing.**

n. 5. the act of riding on a horse, bicycle, in a car, etc. *We had an enjoyable ride in the country to pick up a pumpkin for Halloween.* **rides.**

ridge (rij), *n.* 1. a narrow, raised part of something. *Drop the seeds between the ridges of the field.* 2. a long connected group of hills or mountains. *There is a ridge that extends for many miles in the eastern part of Kentucky.* 3. the line made by two sloping sides coming together. *The chimney was built along the ridge of the roof.* **ridg es.**

rig id (rij'id), *adj.* 1. very stiff; not able to be bent. *The branch of the tree was very rigid.* 2. unyielding; not able to be changed. *She followed very rigid rules of behaviour.* **rig id ly,** *adv.*

ri dic u lous (ri dik'yə ləs), *adj.* foolish; silly. *We saw a ridiculous movie about an elephant who could ride a bicycle.* **ri dic u lous ly,** *adv.*

ri fle[1] (rī'fl), *n.* 1. a gun having a long barrel, the inside of which is bored with narrow circular furrows. *A rifle can fire a bullet farther and straighter than a pistol.* **ri fles.**

v. 2. to bore such furrows in. *He rifled the gun barrel so that the bullet would spin and fly straight.* **ri fles, ri fled, ri fling.**

ri fle[2] (rī'fl), *v.* 1. to search through and rob. *Thieves had rifled our apartment while we were out.*

2. to strip bare. *The children rifled the cherry tree, leaving no fruit behind.* **ri fles, ri fled, ri fling.**

right (rīt), *adj.* 1. just; good. *Obeying the law is the right thing to do.* 2. correct; true; accurate. *All the answers Alan gave to the teacher's questions were right.* 3. proper; suitable. *Try to say the right thing to him to cheer him up. Mother taught us the right way to behave at parties.* 4. in good health; well. *The medicine the doctor gave me has made me feel right again.* 5. being the side that is meant to be seen or used. *Turn your shirt right side out.* 6. located on the side opposite to left. *If you face the sun in the morning, the south is on your right side.* **right er, right est; right ly,** *adv.*

adv. 7. correctly; accurately. *Do your work right the first time or you will have to do it over again. I answered right.* 8. properly; in a suitable manner. *Can the baby hold his spoon right? If the children don't act right, we won't take them with us.* 9. straight on; directly. *He looked right at me when he spoke.* 10. exactly; immediately. *He came in right after me.* 11. to the right side. *Turn right at the second stop light.* 12. very. *The right honorable Judge Stevens entered the courthouse.*

n. 13. something good, just, or honorable. *He always tried to do right.* 14. something to which a person has a just claim. *He demanded his right as a citizen to talk to his lawyer.* 15. the side that is opposite to left. *Look to your right as you pass the window.* **rights.**

v. 16. to correct; to set right. *The court righted the wrong that had been done and freed the innocent man.* 17. to bring or return to the proper position. *They righted the boat that had overturned in the rough water.* 18. to put in order. *Mother had to right the entire house after the party.* **rights, right ed, right ing.**

rim (rim), *n.* 1. the outer edge; border. *A rubber tire was placed around the rim of the wheel.* **rims.**

v. 2. to put a rim on or around; to border. *Mother rimmed the garden with low, red flowers.* **rims, rimmed, rim ming.**

ring[1] (ring), *n.* 1. a thin, circular band of metal, wood, ivory, etc., often decorated with precious stones, worn on the finger. *Her wedding ring has five diamonds on it.* 2. a circle. *A ring of fire marked the place where the rocket had blasted off.* 3. any circular band. *He lost his key ring and was unable to open his car.* 4. an enclosed area for exhibitions, contests, etc. *The circus acts*

rings

rifles

were performed in three rings. The boxers shook hands in the center of the ring. 5. a group of individuals united for a wrong purpose. *The ring of robbers were finally captured.* **rings.**

v. 6. to put or form a ring around. *The Indians ringed the fort.* **rings, ringed, ring ing.**

ring² (ring), *v.* 1. to make a clear sound. *The bell rang just as I entered the classroom.* 2. to cause something to make a clear sound. *Ring the bell once and wait for an answer before you enter the house.* 3. to be filled with a ringing sound. *His ears rang from the noise of the traffic.* 4. to echo with sound. *The hall rang with the laughter of the children.* 5. to seem to be. *That explanation rings true.* 6. to call by telephone. *I'll ring you when I find the information you need.* **rings, rang, rung, ring ing.**

n. 7. a clear sound, like that of a bell. *I heard the ring of sleigh bells.* 8. a sound like that of metal striking metal. *We could hear the ring of the blacksmith's hammer.* **rings.**

ring er (ring′ər), *n.* a person or thing that rings or causes something to ring. *The bell ringer at the church slept late this morning and the bells didn't ring until nine o'clock.* **ring ers.**

ri ot (rī′ət) *n.* 1. a violent disorder; a public demonstration without order. *The riots caused a great deal of damage.* 2. an outstanding show or display. *Mother's new dress was a riot of color.* **ri ots.**

v. 3. to act in a disorderly manner; to violently demonstrate in public. *The people rioted against the unfair laws.* **ri ots, ri ot ed, ri ot ing.**

rip (rip), *v.* 1. to tear roughly; to tear apart. *He ripped his pants when he climbed over the fence.* 2. to become torn. *Margaret's dress ripped when she caught her sleeve on a nail.* **rips, ripped, rip ping.**

n. 3. a tear; a place that is torn. *The rip in the sleeve was too great to be repaired.* **rips.**

ripe (rīp), *adj.* 1. ready to be picked and eaten. *The tomatoes will be ripe in another day or two. Harvest the corn as soon as it is ripe.* 2. fully developed. *His ripe knowledge helped him in making his decision.* 3. ready; prepared to act. *The troops were ripe for the attack.* **rip er, rip est; ripe ly,** *adv.*

rise (rīz), *v.* 1. to get up from a lying, sitting, or kneeling position. *He rose and turned to face me.* 2. to get up from bed. *He rose as soon as he heard the alarm clock.* 3. to move to a higher place or position; move upward; ascend. *The balloon slowly rose over the heads of the crowd.* 4. to go higher in price, degree, etc.; to increase. *The price of bacon has risen ten cents a pound. His voice rose as he became more angry.* 5. to advance to a higher rank or position. *After many long years, he rose from a private to a major in the army.* 6. to incline upward. *The smoke rose from the pipe.* 7. to appear to view. *A sail rose on the horizon.* 8. to begin; to have a source in. *The river rises in the mountains and hills of the*

north. 9. to take up arms or weapons. *The people rose against the strict military government.* **ris es, rose, ris en, ris ing.**

n. 10. a going up to a higher position, rank, degree, etc. *His rise to power came rapidly.* 11. a slight incline. *Some of the cattle had gone up a rise to a greener pasture.* 12. the place where a thing begins; source. *We followed the stream to its rise on a snow-covered mountain.* **ris es.**

risk (risk), *n.* 1. a chance of loss or danger. *The risk of fire is very great in an oil refinery.* **risks.**

v. 2. to expose to loss or danger. *He risked his life in order to save the little boy.* 3. to take the risk of; venture. *Would you risk walking across a busy street with no traffic lights or speed limits for the cars?* **risks, risked, risk ing.**

risky (ris′kē), *adj.* dangerous. *It was risky work, but he enjoyed doing it.* **risk i er, risk i est.**

ri val (rī′vl), *n.* 1. one who is trying to do as well or better than another person; one who competes. *The two friends were rivals for the same part in the school play.* **ri vals.**

adj. 2. competing; being rivals. *The rival stores began to lower their prices in order to attract more customers.*

v. 3. to compete with; to try to be better than. *The two schools rivaled each other in baseball and football.* 4. to be the equal of. *His second book rivaled the first in sales.* **ri vals, ri valed, ri val ing.**

riv er (riv′ər), *n.* 1. a large natural stream of water that flows into an ocean, lake, or sea. *The Mississippi is a large river that flows into the Gulf of Mexico.* 2. any large stream or flow. *A river of steel poured out of the red hot furnace.* **riv ers.**

riv et (riv′it), *n.* 1. a metal bolt used to hold steel beams together. *After the rivet is passed through the beam, the end without a head is spread out to form a head.* **riv ets.**

v. 2. to fasten with rivets. *The workman riveted the beams together.* 3. to fix firmly. *The children's eyes were riveted on the clown.* **riv ets, riv et ed, riv et ing.**

road (rōd), *n.* 1. a public passage between places; highway. *New roads have made it possible to travel*

robin

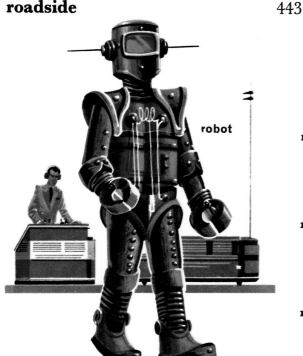

robot

from one section of the country to another very quickly. 2. any way of reaching a place. *The road to success is paved with hard work.* **roads.**

road side (rōd′sīd′), *n.* 1. the land along the side of a road. *Farms and houses lined the roadside.* **road sides.**
adj. 2. built on the side of a road. *We bought tomatoes and corn at a roadside stand.*

roar (rôr), *n.* 1. a loud, deep sound or noise. *The lion's roar could be heard throughout the jungle.* **roars.**
v. 2. to make a loud, deep sound. *The crowd roared when Carl hit a home run.* **roars, roared, roar ing.**

roast (rōst), *v.* 1. to cook over an open fire, in an oven, etc. *Boil the potatoes for a while before you roast them.* 2. to cook or prepare for use by using heat. *Coffee beans are roasted before they are ground.* 3. to make very hot; to become very hot. *We roasted in the warm classroom at school today. The sun was so fierce it roasted us when we went to the beach.* **roasts, roast ed, roast ing.**
n. 4. a large piece of meat that is to be roasted. *Mother bought a beef roast for our dinner.* **roasts.**
adj. 5. roasted. *Have you ever eaten roast duck?*

rob (rob), *v.* 1. to steal from, especially by force. *Two thieves robbed a man on a dark street. An armed man robbed the bank.* 2. to steal. *The police are looking for the men who robbed the jewels.* 3. to take something away from someone; to keep someone from enjoying something. *The rainy weather robbed us of our chance to have a picnic.* **robs, robbed, rob bing.**

rob ber (rob′ər), *n.* a person who robs. *The robber was caught by the police in a very short time.* **rob bers.**

robe (rōb), *n.* 1. a long, loose garment. *After his shower he put on a robe.* 2. a long garment that shows rank or position. *The judge put on his robe*

before he entered the courtroom. 3. a wrap, especially for the lower part of the body. *He drew a robe over his legs before the sleigh ride began.* **robes.**
v. 4. to put a robe on. *The minister robed himself before he went out to give his sermon.* **robes, robed, rob ing.**

rob in (rob′ən), *n.* 1. an American bird with a red breast and a dark back. *In the northern part of the United States, the robin is a sign of spring.* 2. a European bird that is smaller and more brightly colored. *The European robin is called robin redbreast.* **rob ins.**

ro bot (rō′bət), *n.* 1. a piece of machinery that does work like a human being; a machine-made man. *Robots often appear in stories of the future.* 2. a person who works very well but doesn't have to think. *That clerk, writing numbers all day, is a robot.* **ro bots.**

rock[1] (rok), *n.* 1. stone; the mineral that makes up the earth's crust. *After drilling for a while, the men struck rock.* 2. a large piece of stone rising above the surface of the earth. *We climbed onto a rock and dived into the clear water.* 3. anything solid and firm like a rock. *The old man was a rock in his belief that he was right.* **rocks.**

rock[2] (rok), *v.* 1. to move back and forth; to move from side to side. *Mother rocked the cradle until the baby fell asleep.* 2. to shake violently. *The storm rocked the old building. An earthquake rocked the city.* **rocks, rocked, rock ing.**

rock et (rok′it), *n.* 1. a device that shoots into the air and explodes in a shower of sparks, used in fireworks and as a signal for help. *The rockets were the most exciting part of the holiday show.* 2. an engine that is moved through the air in one direction by the combustion of gases that are released in the other direction; jet engine. *The driver used a rocket in his car to enable him to go very fast.* 3. a spacecraft using such an engine. *A rocket is used to lift satellites and space capsules into space.* **rock ets.**
v. 4. to move very quickly; to move like a rocket. *The racing car rocketed towards the finish line.* **rock ets, rock et ed, rock et ing.** (See illustration on following page.)

rocking chair, *n.* a chair that rocks back and forth. *The legs of a rocking chair are set on two pieces of wood that are bent slightly upward at the ends.* **rocking chairs.** (See illustration on following page.)

rocky[1] (rok′ē), *adj.* 1. full of rocks. *He bought a house along a rocky section of the beach.* 2. made of rocks. *The rocky wall had to be rebuilt every year.* 3. like rock; hard. *He maintained a rocky silence until we left the room.* **rock i er, rock i est.**

rocky[2] (rok′ē). *adj.* not solid; likely to rock. *The rocky chair I was sitting in suddenly fell apart beneath me.* **rock i er, rock i est.**

rod (rod), *n.* 1. a thin, straight, metal or wooden bar. *Hang the curtains on the curtain rod above the*

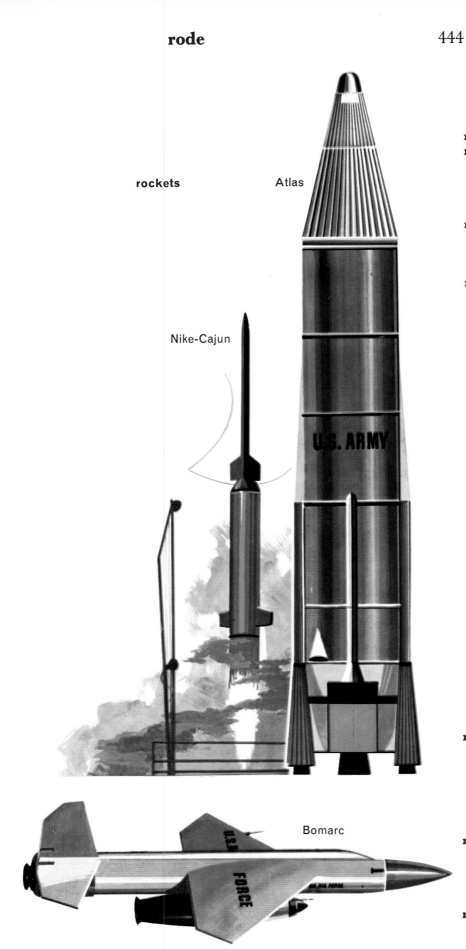

rockets

Atlas

Nike-Cajun

U.S. ARMY

Bomarc

U.S. FORCE

window. 2. a thin stick or twig used to punish. *Spare the rod and spoil the child.* 3. a pole used for fishing. *Dad bought a new rod and reel.* 4. a measure of distance equal to 5½ yards or 16½ feet. *There are 320 rods in a mile.* **rods.**

rode (rōd), past tense of **ride.**

ro deo (rō′dē ō′, rō dā′ō), *n.* 1. a show or contest in which cowboys test their skill in riding and roping. *He rode a wild bull in the rodeo.* 2. a cattle roundup. *The rancher hired four new cowboys to help with the rodeo.* **ro de os.**

role (rōl), *n.* 1. a part in a play; a character in a play. *Who will play the role of George Washington?* 2. a part played in life. *My older sister has taken on the role of wife and mother.* **roles.**

roll (rōl), *v.* 1. to move by turning over and over. *The ball rolled down the hill.* 2. to cause a ball, hoop, etc. to move by turning over and over. *He rolled his hoop on the sidewalk.* 3. to move on wheels. *Roll the wagon over here. We watched the bike roll across the street.* 4. to wrap something around itself. *Roll up that waxed paper, and put it away. She rolled the yarn into a ball and put it in a drawer.* 5. to turn around or from side to side. *Jean rolled her eyes in surprise.* 6. to spread out or make flat and smooth by pushing a heavy cylinder across a surface. *A huge machine rolled the tar on the road until it was even.* 7. to move along smoothly, especially with a rising and falling motion. *The ocean waves rolled into the shore.* 8. to make a long, deep sound. *In the distance we could hear the thunder roll.* 9. to pronounce by vibrating the tongue against the roof of the mouth. *The old man rolled his r's as he spoke.* **rolls, rolled, roll ing.**

n. 10. anything wrapped around itself, forming a tube or a ball. *Give me that roll of string for my kite.* 11. a side-to-side motion; a rolling motion. *The roll of the ship put us to sleep.* 12. a gentle rise and fall. *After the flat plain the roll of the hills was a pleasant change of scenery.* 13. a long, deep sound. *The roll of the drums woke the soldiers.* 14. a list, especially a list of names. *Call the roll of the members of the class to see who is absent.* 15. a small cake or biscuit. *We had sweet rolls and milk for breakfast.* **rolls.**

roll er (rō′lər), *n.* 1. the rod on which something is rolled up. *A window shade winds around a roller.* 2. anything that rolls, or moves by turning over continuously. *The painter sometimes puts paint on a wall by using a roller. The big machine with a roller spread the tar on the street.* **roll ers.**

roller coaster, *n.* a railway with open cars that is made to run up and down steep slopes at great speeds for amusement. *The most exciting event at the carnival was a ride on the roller coaster.* **roller coasters.**

roller skate, *n.* a skate that has small wheels instead of a runner. *Roller skates can be used on sidewalks or floors, but ice skates can only be used on ice.* **roller skates.**

sand, āte, bâre, fäther; sent, mē, fėrn; fit, bīke; pot, rōpe, fôrt; run, pull, rüle, cūte; noise, sound; ch, cheese; ng, long; th, thick; th, those; zh, treasure; ə = a in about, e in waken, i in animal, o in seldom, and u in minus.

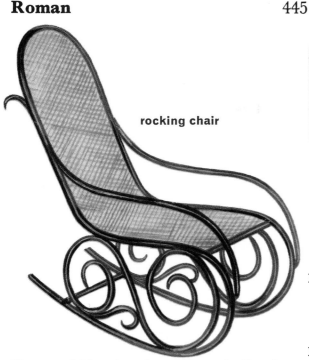

rocking chair

rollers:
a. for painting
b. for inking

v. 6. to make up exciting stories of adventure. *She is always romancing about life several hundred years ago.* **ro manc es, ro manced, ro mancing.**

Ro man esque (rō′mə nesk′), *adj.* having to do with the style of architecture and art in Europe in about the year 1000 to about the year 1200. *Romanesque buildings had round arches.* (See illustration on following page.)

Roman numeral, *n.* one of a group of letters used instead of figures to represent numbers in ancient Rome. *In the system of Roman numerals,* $I = 1$, $V = 5$, $X = 10$, $L = 50$, $C = 100$, $D = 500$, *and* $M = 1000$. **Roman numerals.**

ro man tic (rō man′tik), *adj.* 1. having to do with adventure and excitement. *Robin Hood was a romantic figure.* 2. imaginary; not real. *He told us a strange, romantic tale of a monster in the swamp.* 3. having to do with affection and love. *He discovered that he had a romantic feeling for the girl.* **ro man ti cal ly,** *adv.*

Rome (rōm), *n.* the capital of Italy which was also the capital of the Roman Empire in ancient times. *In ancient times, Rome was the mightiest nation and ruled the world.*

roof (rüf), *n.* 1. the part that covers the top of a house or building. *Many houses have sloping roofs while large buildings have flat roofs.* 2. anything like a roof. *The peanut butter stuck to the roof of his mouth.* **roofs.**

v. 3. to put a roof on or over; to form a roof over. *Father roofed our new house just before a heavy*

Ro man (rō′mən), *n.* 1. a person who lives in Rome, was born there, or whose descendants came from Rome. *The ancient Romans worshipped many gods.* 2. one kind of type in which the letters are not slanted, but upright. *This type is not roman.* **Ro mans.**

adj. 3. of or from Rome. *Roman wines are very good.*

ro mance (rō mans′, rō′mans for 1–5, rō mans′ for 6), *n.* 1. a story of unusual and exciting adventures. *He was reading a romance about pirates and the British Navy.* 2. an adventure story about knights and nobles. *The tales of King Arthur and his knights of the Round Table are romances.* 3. a love story. *That book is a romance about a girl who loves the captain of the football team.* 4. the love, excitement, and adventure that are written about in books. *The lonely man had traveled around the world in his search for romance.* 5. a courting. *A long romance between the prince and the singer led to their marriage.* **ro manc es.**

roller coaster

twelfth century church

chalice

fresco painting

door

capital of a column

Romanesque art and architecture

rosary

rain hit. *The branches of the trees roofed the trail through the forest.* **roofs, roofed, roof ing.**

room (rüm), *n.* 1. a space separated by walls within a house or building. *The guests were invited to wait for the king in a large room. We will eat in the dining room.* 2. space. *Leave plenty of room between these seeds when you plant them. Is there room for one more in the car?* 3. opportunity. *There is room for improvement in your work.* 4. the people in a room. *The entire room laughed when I entered.* **rooms.**
v. 5. to rent a room; to occupy a room. *The stranger decided to room at the hotel for a while.* **rooms, roomed, room ing.**

room mate (rüm/māt'), *n.* a person who shares a room with one or more other persons. *He and his roommate divide the cost of the rent between them.* **room mates.**

roost er (rüs/tər), *n.* a male fowl; a male chicken. *The rooster crows every morning at sunrise.* **roost ers.**

root[1] (rüt), *n.* 1. the part of a plant that grows beneath the ground, supports the plant, holds it in place, and takes in food for it. *Some roots, such as carrots and beets, are eaten as vegetables.* 2. any part of a plant that is beneath the ground. *Potatoes and tulip bulbs can be called roots even though they do not do the things that roots do.* 3. anything like a root in shape, use, position, etc. *She changed the color of her hair right down to the roots.* 4. a part from which something grows; a source; origin. *Lack of ability is at the root of his dislike for sports.* 5. the most important or essential part. *The lawyer immediately got to the root of the matter.* 6. a word from which other words are made. *Tire is the root of tired, tiring, and tireless.* **roots.**
v. 7. to set down roots and begin to grow. *These flowers root very quickly if you give them plenty of water.* 8. to fix firmly in a position. *The frightened boy was rooted to the spot.* 9. **root out,** to dig out and get rid of. *The police tried*

to root out the criminals in the city. **roots, root ed, root ing.**

root[2] (rüt), *v.* 1. to dig up soil. *The pigs rooted in the vegetable garden until they were chased away.* 2. to search thoroughly. *She rooted through all of her clothes before she found her red sweater.* **roots, root ed, root ing.**

root[3] (rüt), *v.* to cheer; give support to an athletic team or an individual. *We rooted for our football team even when they were losing.* **roots, root ed, root ing.**

rope (rōp), *n.* 1. a strong cord made by twisting a number of smaller cords together. *The men climbing the mountain were tied together by rope to prevent any of them from falling.* 2. a number of things tied or twisted together in the form of a cord. *The dancer wore a rope of flowers around her neck.* **ropes.**
v. 3. to tie or fasten with a rope. *The prisoner's*

roses

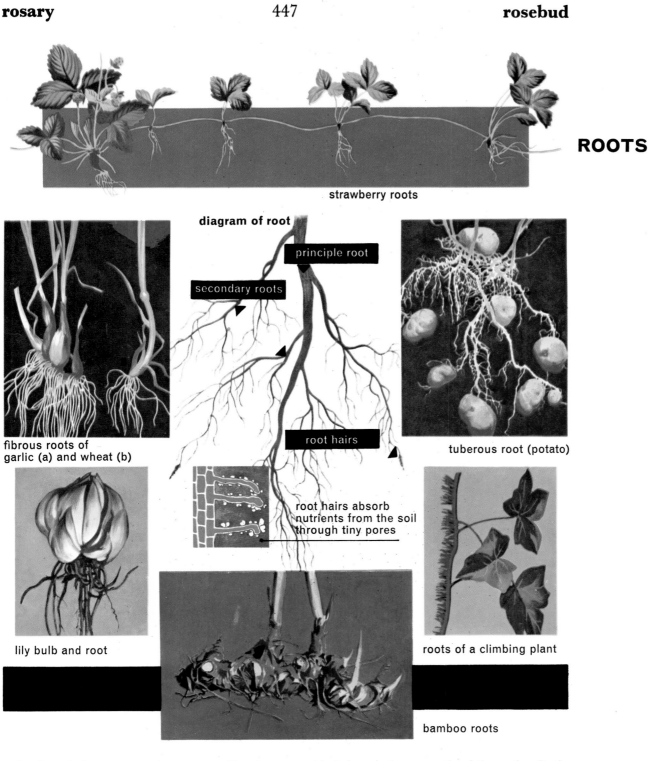

ROOTS

strawberry roots

diagram of root

principle root

secondary roots

root hairs

fibrous roots of
garlic (a) and wheat (b)

tuberous root (potato)

root hairs absorb
nutrients from the soil
through tiny pores

lily bulb and root

roots of a climbing plant

bamboo roots

hands and feet were roped to prevent him from
escaping. 4. to divide or mark by using a rope
as a fence. *The boxing ring was roped off and
raised so that everyone could see it.* 5. to catch with
a lasso. *The cowboy roped the calf and branded it.*
ropes, roped, rop ing.

ro sa ry (rō′zə rē), *n.* a string of beads used for
keeping count when saying a series of prayers.
Rosaries are used by members of the Catholic Church.
ro sa ries.

rose[1] (rōz), *n.* 1. a bush with thorns that bears
red, white, pink or yellow flowers. *Father*

planted roses along one side of the garden. 2. the
flower that grows on this bush. *She was given
a dozen roses at her graduation party.* 3. a pinkish-
red color. *Mother decided to decorate the living
room in rose.* 4. anything shaped like a rose.
*That jewel is called a rose because it is cut in the
shape of a rose.* **ros es.**
adj. of the color rose. *We hung rose curtains in the
bedroom.*

rose[2] (rōz), past tense of **rise.**

rose bud (rōz′bud′), *n.* the bud of a rose. *The
bush was heavy with rosebuds.* **rose buds.**

sand, āte, bâre, fäther; sent, mē, fėrn; fit, bĭke; pot, rōpe, fôrt; run, pu̇ll, rüle, cūte; noise, sound; ch, cheese;
ng, long; th, thick; ~~th,~~ those; zh, treasure; ə = a in about, e in waken, i in animal, o in seldom, and u in minus.

rosemary

rose mary (rōz′mâr′ē), *n.* an evergreen shrub with leaves that smell sweet. *The leaves of the rosemary are used in perfume and as an herb in cooking.* **rose mar ies.**

rose window, a round window used as an ornament. *Most rose windows have a design of lines that radiate from the center. Our new church will have rose windows.* **rose windows.**

rosy (rō′ze), *adj.* 1. like a rose, especially in color. *Those healthy children have bright, rosy cheeks.* 2. bright; full of promise. *The brilliant doctor had a rosy future ahead of him.* **ros i er, ros i est; ros i ly,** *adv.*

rot (rot), *v.* 1. to become rotten; to decay; to spoil. *The crops rotted in the fields because there was no one to pick them.* **rots, rot ted, rot ting.** *n.* 2. the process of rotting. *Rot had ruined most of the old timbers in the house.* 3. a disease of plants and animals. *A strange rot caused the leaves of the plant to turn yellow and then black as the plant died.* **rots.**

ro ta ry (rō′tə rē), *adj.* having a part or parts that rotate. *A rotary press prints on paper by means of rollers that turn.*

ro tate (rō′tāt, rō tāt′), *v.* 1. to turn around a center; to move in a circle. *The wheels on a wagon rotate on their axles.* 2. to take turns. *The members of the team rotated as captain.* 3. to make or cause to take turns. *The players were rotated after each play so that each of them would have a chance to rest.* **ro tates, ro tat ed, ro tat ing.**

ro ta tion (rō tā′shən), *n.* the act of rotating; the process of turning around a center. *The rotation of the earth causes daylight and darkness.* **ro ta tions.**

rot ten (rot′ən), *adj.* 1. decayed; spoiled. *Those eggs were rotten when we bought them.* 2. not safe; in poor condition. *The boards on the old ship were rotten and collapsed when we walked on them.* 3. unpleasant; mean. *That was a rotten trick to play on him.* **rot ten er, rot ten est; rot ten ly,** *adv.*

rough (ruf), *adj.* 1. not smooth or even. *The car bounced and rattled over the rough road.* 2. harsh; violent; not gentle. *Football and hockey are rough sports.* 3. not polished; coarse. *Diamonds are rough when they are mined.* 4. not completed; not exact or full in details. *This sketch should give you a rough idea of how the building will look.* 5. unpleasant; not easy. *The life of a soldier is a rough one.* **rough er, rough est; rough ly,** *adv.*

n. 6. an unpleasant, violent person. *I wish you wouldn't play with those roughs.* **roughs.**

v. 7. to make rough. *Heavy winds roughed the lake.* 8. to treat in a rough way, especially in sports. *He was roughed on the play, but he managed to score anyway.* 9. **rough it,** to live without ordinary comforts. *We had to rough it on our camping trip since we were miles from a house or a store.* **roughs, roughed, rough ing.**

rou lette (rü let′), *n.* a game in which players bet on where a ball rolling on a turning wheel will be when the wheel stops. *Roulette is a game of luck, not skill.*

round (round), *adj.* 1. shaped like a ball. *The earth is round.* 2. shaped like a ring. *Our swimming pool is square, but theirs is round.* 3. forming a circle; moving in a circle. *Some children's games are round dances.* 4. traveling a route that ends at its starting place. *We made a round trip to Europe this summer.* 5. full; complete. *This*

rose window

basket of apples makes a round dozen I've picked today. 6. in whole numbers; in tens or hundreds. *An amount of $152.36 is expressed in round numbers as $150.* 7. large in size or amount. *A round sum of money was given as a reward.* **round er, round est; round ly,** *adv.*

n. 8. anything that is round. *The rungs on a ladder are rounds.* 9. a route or course that ends at its starting place. *A watchman in a building makes rounds.* 10. a number of activities, happenings, etc. that come in a series. *There was a round of parties to celebrate our graduation. The candidate scheduled a round of speeches in the city.* 11. a sudden burst of applause, shouts, cheers, etc. *The audience greeted the actor with a round of applause.* 12. a discharge of guns, each person firing his own weapon once. *The king ordered twenty-one rounds to honor the hero.* 13. the bullets, powder, etc. needed to fire one shot. *Each soldier was supplied with one hundred rounds before the battle began.* 14. one of the periods of time into which a game or sporting event may be divided. *He was knocked out in the first round of the fight.* 15. a dance in which persons move in a circle. *The children danced a round at the end of the play.* 16. a song in which a number of persons sing the same words and tune but start singing one after another. *"Row, Row, Row Your Boat" is a well-known round.* **rounds.**

v. 17. to make round; to cause to become round. *She rounded the lumps of dough and put them in the oven to bake.* 18. to go around. *The car speeded up as it rounded the corner.* 19. **round out,** to complete; to make complete. *The teacher rounded out the day by reading a story to us.* 20. **round up,** to bring together; to collect in one place. *The cowboys rounded up the cattle and branded them.* **rounds, round ed, round-ing.**

adv. 21. in a circle. *The merry-go-round went round and round.* 22. on all sides; about. *We were ordered to gather round for our instructions.* 23. in circumference. *His waist measures twenty-eight inches round.* 24. from one person to another in turn. *Pass this sheet round so that everyone can sign it.* 25. by a longer path or route. *I am late because I came round past the pet shop.* 26. nearby; in the neighborhood. *Everyone round had seen the game.*

prep. 27. so as to circle; around. *A fence was built round the swimming pool.* 28. on all sides of; in all directions from. *There was not a single house for miles round him.*

round up (round′up′), *n.* 1. the bringing together of cattle. *The purpose of the roundup was to mark the cattle with the owner's brand.* 2. the men and horses that round up the cattle. *Several cowboys were hired as part of the roundup.* 3. any gathering of people or things. *The roundup of the members of the gang came just after the bank was robbed.* **round ups.**

route (rüt, rout), *n.* 1. a road, path, etc. to be

rotary printing press

traveled. *The ship takes the northern route across the ocean during the summer.* **routes.**

v. 2. to send in a specified direction. *The airplane was routed to San Francisco through Chicago and Denver.* **routes, rout ed, rout ing.**

row[1] (rō), *n.* a number of persons or things in a line; a line formed by a number of persons or things. *The first row may be dismissed. Who is sitting in the last row?* **rows.**

row[2] (rō), *v.* 1. to move a boat by using oars. *He rowed across the lake and back in less than an hour.* 2. to carry in a boat by using oars. *Row me to the dock.* **rows, rowed, row ing.**

n. 3. a trip in a boat which uses oars. *It was a long row to the island, but it was worth it.* **rows.**

row[3] (rou), *n.* an argument; a quarrel. *We had a row over which school had a better basketball team.* **rows.**

row boat (rō′bōt′), *n.* a small boat that is moved by oars. *A rowboat is flat at the rear end and comes to a point in front.* **row boats.**

roy al (roi′əl), *adj.* 1. having to do with kings and queens. *England has a royal government.* 2. in the manner of a king; like a king. *He has a royal appearance.* 3. fit for or suitable to a king. *We were given a royal welcome when we returned from camp.* **roy al ly,** *adv.*

roy al ty (roi′əl tē), *n.* 1. kings, queens, or other royal persons. *All of the royalty attended the theater.* 2. the position or power of a king or queen. *The throne represents royalty.* 3. regal nature. *The royalty of the lion's appearance has made him king of the animals.* 4. a payment made to the author of a book or to one who invents something. *The author received royalties for each copy of the book that was sold.* **roy al ties.**

roulette

sand, āte, bâre, fäther; sent, mē, férn; fit, bīke; pot, rōpe, fôrt; run, pùll, rüle, cūte; noise, sound; **ch, ch**eese; **ng,** lo**ng; th,** **th**ick; **t̶h̶,** **th**ose; **zh,** trea**s**ure; ə = **a** in about, **e** in waken, **i** in animal, **o** in seldom, and **u** in minus.

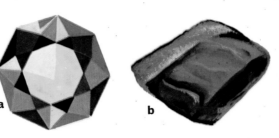

ruby:
a. cut and polished
b. rough and uncut

rub (rub), *v.* 1. to move with friction against the surface of something. *The wheel of my bicycle rubs the fender.* 2. to clean, polish, erase, etc. by using friction or pressure on something. *Ellen rubbed the silver until it gleamed. He rubbed out the last sentence on his paper with his eraser.* **rubs, rubbed, rub bing.**
n. 3. an act of rubbing. *Give the furniture a rub with the dust cloth before the guests arrive.* **rubs.**

rub ber (rub′ər), *n.* 1. a material that is made from the sap of certain trees or from chemicals. *Rubber is used to make balloons, tires, rubber bands, and many other products.* 2. something made of rubber. *Put on your rubbers before you go out in the snow.* **rub bers.**
adj. 3. made of this substance. *Is that a rubber football or a leather one?*

rub bish (rub′ish), *n.* 1. useless material; waste. *The school janitor sweeps up the rubbish at the end of the day.* 2. nonsense; foolish talk, writing, etc. *He told us a lot of rubbish about finding a box full of money.*

ru by (rü′bē), *n.* 1. a red-colored precious stone. *She has a ring set with a ruby.* **ru bies.**
adj. 2. deep-red. *The setting sun was a ruby color.*

rude (rüd), *adj.* 1. impolite; lacking courtesy. *The rude boy stuck out his tongue at his aunt.* 2. roughly made. *The pioneers lived in rude cabins.* 3. harsh; violent. *It was a rude shock to us when we awoke and found the house burning.* 4. without culture. *He comes from a rude country background.* **rud er, rud est; rude ly,** *adv.*

rug (rug), *n.* 1. a thick, heavy floor cover, usually made of fabric. *They have a round rug in their dining room and several small rugs in the living room.* 2. a thick, heavy piece of fabric used as a blanket. *They covered their legs with a rug before the sleigh ride began.* **rugs.**

ru in (rü′ən), *n.* 1. destruction; extreme damage. *The ruin of the house was caused by a violent tornado.* 2. something that has been destroyed or has fallen to pieces. *What was once a beautiful home is now an ugly ruin.* 3. anything that causes destruction, defeat, etc. *The big fire was the ruin of that old building.* 4. **ruins,** the remains of a building or a city, especially the remains of very old buildings or cities. *Among the ancient ruins were found bowls and spoons that had been used thousands of years ago.* **ru ins.**
v. 5. to destroy; to damage; to spoil. *Our garden was ruined by the heavy rain.* **ru ins, ru ined, ru in ing.**

rubber

rule (rül), *n.* 1. a statement that guides behavior and actions. *The rules of sportsmanship require that you congratulate the winner.* 2. usual happening; common practice; custom. *Hard work is not the exception but the rule on the farm.* 3. control; governing. *Under the king's rule many new laws were made.* 4. a straight piece of metal or wood, usually marked to show feet and inches, used for measuring and for drawing straight lines. *Measure the width of your paper with your rule.* 5. **as a rule,** usually. *Baseball games end, as a rule, after nine innings.* **rules.**
v. 6. to control; to govern. *Who will rule the country now that the king is dead?* 7. to decide; to give as a decision. *The mayor ruled that the schools would close for the holiday. The judge ruled that the man should be fined fifty dollars.* 8. to mark into lines with a ruler. *The paper was ruled so that it would be easier to write on.* **rules, ruled, rul ing.**

rul er (rül′ər), *n.* 1. a person who rules. *The king is the ruler of the entire kingdom.* 2. a straight piece of metal or wood, usually marked to show feet and inches, used for measuring and for drawing straight lines. *John used a ruler to mark off the height of the tree house he was building.* **rul ers.**

rum ble (rum′bl), *n.* 1. a low, deep, heavy sound. *We heard the rumble of the thunder just after we saw the flash of lightning.* **rum bles.**
v. 2. to make a low, deep, heavy sound. *The thunder rumbled through the clouds.* 3. to move with a low, deep, heavy sound. *The truck rumbled*

ruins of an ancient city

across the wooden bridge. **rum bles, rum bled, rum bling.**

run (run), *n.* 1. the act of running. *He was extremely tired after his long run.* 2. a distance traveled or the time it takes to travel a distance. *New York is an 850-mile run from Chicago. It's an all-night run to New Orleans by train.* 3. a time during which something is repeated. *We had a run of stormy weather during June.* 4. a series of performances. *The play had a long run in New York, but only a short run in Philadelphia.* 5. a demand, especially a sudden and continuous demand. *During the storm, the store enjoyed a run on umbrellas.* 6. in baseball, the scoring unit. *A run is scored when a player is able to touch the three bases and home plate in order without being tagged out.* 7. freedom of use. *Our guests were given the run of the house for as long as they wished to stay.* 8. a group of fish moving together. *The fishermen saw a run of tuna in the sea.* 9. an enclosed place for animals. *A fox got into the chicken run and killed two hens.* 10. a place where a hole or small tear has developed in some clothing. *She has a run in her stocking.* 11. **in the long run,** eventually; in the end. *You may not wish to study now, but in the long run you will be glad you did.* **runs.**

v. 12. to move faster than one does when walking by making the legs go quickly. *He ran ahead of his friends and won the race. Please don't run in the halls at school.* 13. to go quickly; to hurry. *Run to the medicine cabinet and get me a bandage.* 14. to cause to move quickly. *They ran the horse around the track before the race.* 15. to do as if by running. *Will you run an errand for me?* 16. to go by a certain, usual path or route. *The bus doesn't run along this highway anymore.* 17. to be as much as. *The price of meat runs two dollars a pound.* 18. to climb; to creep in growing. *The vines ran up the side of the house.* 19. to extend; to go on, along, or around. *A private road runs around the house and down to the lake.* 20. to thrust; to drive. *When he grabbed the boards, he ran a nail into his hand.* 21. to flow. *When the pipe burst, water ran across the floor.* 22. to discharge liquid matter. *His nose runs when he gets a cold.* 23. to become. *When the well ran dry, the farmer had to leave his farm.* 24. to spread. *Will this color run if I wash the dress in hot water?* 25. to pass in thought. *It ran through his mind that he would like to buy a new bicycle.* 26. to try to be elected for an office; to be a candidate. *He ran for president of the club three times and was finally elected.* 27. to expose one's self to. *Aren't you running the risk of losing all of your money?* 28. to operate; to keep operating. *He runs a drilling machine in the factory.* 29. to manage. *Does anyone in town run a men's clothing store?* 30. to develop a small tear or hole in. *She ran her stocking when she caught it on a chair.* 31. to go about with no control or governing force. *The soldiers were permitted to run the streets*

until dark. **runs, ran, run, run ning.**

Run also has the following special meanings:

run across, to meet by surprise or by chance. *Last year I ran across a fellow I went to school with.*

run down, (a) to stop working or operating. *My watch has run down.* (b) to speak against; to say evil things about a person. *He spent most of his time running down his boss instead of working.*

run into, to meet by chance. *I ran into my Uncle Bill at a movie this evening.*

run out, to come to an end; to be finished. *His luck finally ran out and he was captured by the enemy.*

run out of, to have no more. *That store ran out of milk so I went to a different one.*

run over, (a) to drive or ride over; to hit. *He was almost run over by the speeding car.* (b) to flow over. *The rain barrel filled up and began to run over.*

run through, to spend quickly. *The foolish man ran through a huge fortune and ended up without a penny.*

rung[1] (rung), past tense and past participle of **ring**[2].

rung[2] (rung), *n.* a round piece used as a step on a ladder or as a support on a chair. *He climbed the ladder slowly, carefully putting each foot on the next rung.* **rungs.**

run ner (run′ər), *n.* 1. a person or animal that runs. *That horse is the fastest runner in the race.* 2. a person who carries and delivers a message. *The Indians sent a runner to the fort to ask the soldiers for help.* 3. one of the long metal pieces on which a sled slides. *He polished his runners so that he could sled faster down the hill.* 4. a long, narrow strip of carpet or other fabric. *Mother used a runner on the stairs that matched the rug in the living room.* 5. a stem that grows along the ground, sending out roots in various places. *Strawberry runners had spread into every part of the garden.* 6. a blade of an ice skate. *One must learn good balance to skate on sharp runners.* **run ners.**

run way (run′wā′), *n.* 1. an open, level strip of ground on which airplanes may take off

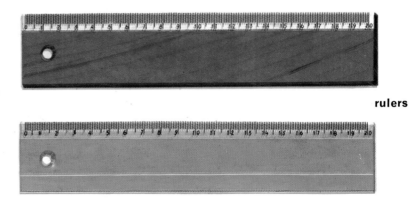

rulers

rush:
  a. flowers
  b. plant

rye:
  a. spike
  b. stalk

and land. *The pilot waited until the runway was clear before he took off.* 2. a path used by animals. *We waited at the side of the runway until the deer passed.* 3. an area, usually fenced, in which animals may run. *The farmer built a new runway for the chickens.* **run ways.**

ru ral (rùr′əl), *adj.* having to do with the country; in the country. *Most people who get* used to rural living do not enjoy city living. **ru ral ly,** *adv.*

rush[1] (rush), *v.* 1. to move quickly and often with force. *The violent winds rushed by our windows.* 2. to carry or take quickly. *The injured boy was rushed to the hospital.* 3. to plunge quickly. *He rushed into the fight without bothering to decide which side was right.* **rush es, rushed, rush ing.**

n. 4. an act of rushing. *The rush of the wave washed the beach clean.* 5. an excited state of activity; hurry. *During the Christmas rush, all of the stores are crowded with shoppers.* 6. a sudden movement of people who are anxious to get to a place. *They went to California during the gold rush.* **rush es.**

adj. 7. requiring haste. *Deliver this rush order first before you deliver the others.*

rush[2] (rush), *n.* a swamp plant having a hollow stem. *Rushes can be used in making baskets and chairs.* **rush es.**

rust (rust), *n.* 1. the coat of red-brown powder that forms on metals when they are exposed to damp air. *Rust covered the rake that had been left outside all winter.* 2. a disease that attacks plants. *The spots on the leaves and stems of the plant showed that it had rust.* **rusts.**

v. 3. to become covered with rust. *Metals will not rust if they are painted with a special paint.* 4. to become weak or spoiled by not being used. *The player's batting arm had rusted during the winter.* **rusts, rust ed, rust ing.**

rut (rut), *n.* 1. a furrow worn in the ground by wheels. *When it rains, the ruts in the road fill up with water.* 2. a fixed way of doing things. *He is in such a rut that he has the same thing for lunch every day.* **ruts.**

v. 3. to make ruts in. *The wagons rutted the dirt roads in the country.* **ruts, rut ted, rut ting.**

rye (rī), *n.* 1. a hardy grass that bears a seed used for food. *Rye is grown in cold regions.* 2. the seed. *Rye is used in making a kind of bread.*

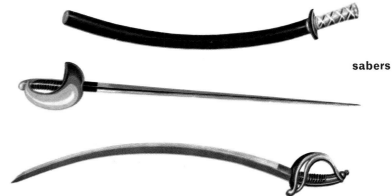

sabers

S or **s** (es), the nineteenth letter of the alphabet.

sa ber (sā′bər), *n.* a heavy sword, usually with a blade that has a slight curve. *Sabers were once used as weapons.* **sa bers.**

sack[1] (sak), *n.* 1. a large bag made of paper or cloth. *Sacks are used to hold potatoes, grain, and flour.* 2. the amount that a sack will hold. *Mother came home from the store with two sacks of groceries.* **sacks.**

v. 3. to put into sacks. *Potatoes are sacked before they are delivered to the stores.* **sacks, sacked, sack ing.**

sack[2] (sak), *v.* 1. to rob after capturing; to loot. *The enemy sacked the city.* **sacks, sacked, sack ing.**

n. 2. the robbing of a city by those who conquered it. *The sack of the town took three days.*

sa cred (sā′krid), *adj.* 1. holy; belonging to God. *A church or temple is a sacred building.* 2. having to do with religion. *A prayer is a sacred act.* 3. worthy of reverence or respect. *This monument is in honor of his sacred memory.* 4. that

cannot be broken. *She gave her mother a sacred promise.* **sa cred ly,** *adv.*

sac ri fice (sak′rə fīs′), *n.* 1. the act of offering something to God or a god. *Sacrifice is an important part of many religions.* 2. the thing that is offered in such an act of worship. *In the Bible, Abraham killed a sheep as a sacrifice to God.* 3. a giving up of something for someone else. *The parents made sacrifices to send their children to college.* 4. a loss. *Ricky sold his bicycle at a sacrifice.* **sac ri fic es.**

v. 5. to make a sacrifice of. *Barbara sacrificed her time for work at the hospital. Ancient people sacrificed oxen and sheep to their gods.* 6. to sell at a loss. *Carl needed some money quickly so he sacrificed his fishing rod.* **sac ri fic es, sac ri ficed, sac ri fic ing.**

sad (sad), *adj.* 1. unhappy. *We were sad when the team lost.* 2. causing or having to do with grief or sorrow. *Many people don't like to read sad books.* **sad der, sad dest; sad ly,** *adv.*

sad dle (sad′l), *n.* 1. a seat fastened to the back of an animal for riding. *Cowboys sit up straight in the saddle.* 2. the seat on a tricycle, bicycle, or motorcycle. *The saddle on the little bike is too small for me.* **sad dles.**

v. 3. to put a saddle on. *They saddled the horse*

saddling a horse

saddles

sand, āte, bâre, fäther; sent, mē, fėrn; fit, bīke; pot, rōpe, fôrt; run, pùll, rüle, cūte; noise, sound; **ch, ch**eese; **ng, long; th, th**ick; **t̶h̶, th**ose; **zh,** treasure; ə = **a** in about, **e** in waken, **i** in animal, **o** in seldom, and **u** in minus.

sails

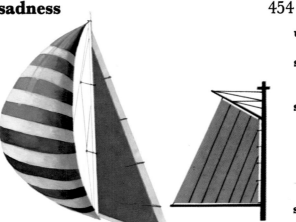

before the race. 4. to load; to burden. *Our teacher was saddled with a hundred test papers.* **sad dles, sad dled, sad dling.**

sad ness (sad′nis), *n.* sorrow; grief. *His sadness made us all unhappy.*

safe (sāf), *adj.* 1. free from harm or danger. *A storm was raging, but we were safe in the house.* 2. capable of being trusted. *Anne is a safe person to leave with the children. The dog is safe with children.* 3. not causing harm or danger. *Only safe toys with no sharp points should be given to children. The ice in the lake is safe to walk on.* 4. careful. *Only safe aviators are allowed to fly passengers. He worked out a safe plan to save money.* 5. in baseball, having reached a base without being put out. *He was safe at second base.* **saf er, saf est; safe ly,** *adv.*

n. 6. a metal box with a lock, for keeping valuable things. *The rich lady keeps her jewelry in a safe.* **safes.**

safe ty (sāf′tē), *n.* 1. freedom from injury or danger. *If you obey the traffic light, you can cross the street in safety.* **safe ties.**

adj. 2. giving freedom from injury or danger. *Father uses a safety razor. The rip in the dress was held together by a safety pin.*

said (sed), past tense of **say.**

sail (sāl), *n.* 1. a large sheet of heavy cloth used to move a boat through water by catching the wind. *The largest ships used to have thirty sails.* 2. a trip in a sailboat. *Let's go for a sail.* 3. something like a sail. *The sailfish gets its name from its sail—a tall fin on its back that can be raised or lowered.* **sails.**

v. 4. to start a trip by water. *We are sailing from New York this Friday, and we will arrive in Europe on Wednesday.* 5. to move along. *The ship sailed down the river. The airplane sailed smoothly overhead. I sailed through the semester with good grades.* 6. to manage and operate a ship or boat. *The captain and crew sailed the ship through the heavy winds.* **sails, sailed, sail ing. Sail** also has the following special meanings:

set sail or **make sail,** (a) to spead the sails and get ready to leave. *We will set sail in an hour.* (b) to begin a trip by water. *The ship made sail and left the port.*

under sail, with the sails spread out. *The ship is under sail and going faster.*

sail boat (sāl′bōt′), *n.* a boat with sails that make it move. *We went for a sail on Joe's little sailboat.* **sail boats.**

sail or (sā′lər), *n.* 1. a man who makes his living by working on ships. *Many sailors have jobs on the big steamships.* 2. a member of the navy who is not an officer. *More than a thousand sailors are needed to operate the large ship.* 3. a straw hat with a flat top. *Sailors were worn in the British Navy.* **sail ors.**

saint (sānt), *n.* 1. in some churches, a holy person, who is declared worthy of reverence. *Statues of saints are seen in many churches.* 2. a person who is humble, patient, and thoughtful of others. *That nurse in the hospital is a saint to my grandmother.* **saints.**

sake (sāk), *n.* 1. purpose; reason. *Some boys act noisy for the sake of getting attention from other people.* 2. benefit; welfare; advantage. *We keep quiet in the hall for the sake of the students who are studying.* **sakes.**

sal ad (sal′əd), *n.* 1. green vegetables, such as lettuce or cabbage, served raw, usually with a dressing. *Many restaurants serve salad before the main course.* 2. a cold mixture of vegetables, fruits, fish, hard boiled eggs, or meats, served with a dressing. *Salads are usually served cold on leaves of lettuce. I had a salad of salmon and eggs for lunch.* **sal ads.**

sal a man der (sal′ə man′dər), *n.* an animal that looks like a lizard, but has no scales and is covered with moist skin. *Salamanders are part of the frog family and live in dark, damp places.* **sal a man ders.**

sal a ry (sal′ə rē), *n.* the money paid to a person at a regular time for work done. *Most workers get their salaries once a week, twice a month, or once a month.* **sal a ries.**

sale (sāl), *n.* 1. the selling of something; an exchanging of something for money. *The sale of his old car brought Mr. Stone two hundred dollars.* 2. a special selling at prices lower than usual. *The store was crowded during the sale of dresses.* 3. *n.* **sales,** the amount sold; gross receipts. *This month's sales are setting a record.* **sales.**

sales man (sālz′mən), *n.* a man whose job is selling things. *Some salesmen work in stores, and others travel to the homes of people.* **sales men.**

sa li va (sə lī′və), *n.* the liquid that is secreted into the mouth by glands. *Saliva helps in the digestion of food.*

salamander

salmon

salm on (sam′ən), *n.* a large fish with silver scales and pink flesh. *Many salmon are canned every year for eating. The ocean salmon lay their eggs far from the ocean in fresh-water streams.* **salm on** or **salm ons.**

salt (sôlt), *n.* 1. a white, grainy mineral found in the earth and in sea water, used especially to flavor and preserve food. *Everyone must have a certain amount of salt in their daily diet.* 2. a chemical compound of a metal and an acid. *Baking soda is a salt.* **salts.**
adj. 3. containing salt. *Salt water is not good to drink.* 4. that is preserved with salt. *We have salt pork for dinner.* 5. tasting or smelling like salt. *The salt breeze comes from the ocean.*
v. 6. to use salt for flavoring, for preserving, or for melting. *He salted his tomato. The pioneer family salted their meat for winter. He salted the icy spot on the sidewalk.* **salts, salt ed, salt ing.**
Salt also has the following special meanings:
salt away, (a) to pack something with salt to preserve it. *The men salted away meat for the long trip ahead.* (b) to save. *Greg salted away one hundred dollars during the summer.*
with a grain of salt, with some doubt. *We knew that he did not always tell the truth, so we took what he said with a grain of salt.*
worth one's salt, worth the money that one is paid. *That new boy is worth his salt.*
salt shaker, *n.* a holder for salt, having holes in the top for shaking out the salt. *Salt shakers are placed on the dinner table.* **salt shakers.**
sal u ta tion (sal′ū ta′ shən), *n.* 1. a greeting; something done to signify recognition. *The boat tooted its whistle in salutation.* 2. a verbal greeting or a written greeting. *The salutation of the letter said, "Dear John."* **sal u ta tions.**
sa lute (sə lüt′), *n.* 1. a formal greeting of respect and honor in the armed forces. *The captain and the general exchanged salutes by raising their right hands to their foreheads.* 2. any greeting. *Brenda waved a salute as she drove past.* 3. a firing of guns as an honor. *The aircraft carrier fired a twenty-one gun salute when the President came on board.* **sa lutes.**
v. 4. to make a salute; to give a formal greeting to. *The soldier saluted his officer as they passed on the street. The audience saluted the singer with applause.* **sa lutes, sa lut ed, sa lut ing.**
sal vage (sal′vij), *n.* 1. money paid for saving a ship or its cargo from the sea. *The men were paid twenty thousand dollars in salvage for bringing up the cargo from the bottom of the river.* 2. the rescue of a ship or its cargo from damage or

danger. *The salvage continued day and night as the wrecked ship pounded on the rocky coast.* **sal vag es.**
v. 3. to save from fire, flood, shipwreck, or other disaster. *The firemen salvaged most of the machinery from the fire in the factory.* **sal vag es, sal vaged, sal vag ing.**
same (sām), *adj.* 1. not another; identical. *The teacher has always taught in the same school.* 2. alike in some way. *Both girls have the same height.* 3. without any change. *The amount of work is the same every day.*
pron. 4. the same person or thing. *Doris wants long hair and I want the same.*
adv. 5. in the same way. *Handle the dog the same as I do, and he won't run away.*
Same also has the following special meanings:
all the same, regardless; nevertheless. *You may not want to go; all the same, you are going.*
just the same, in the same manner. *Feed her cat just the same as you feed your own cat.*
the same, in the same way. *"Sail" and "sale" are pronounced the same.*
sam pan (sam′pan), *n.* a light, flat-bottomed boat with one sail, rowed from the stern. *Sampans are used mainly in China.* **sam pans.** (See illustration on following page.)
sam ple (sam′pl), *n.* 1. a part or one of a number that shows what the rest is like. *The employer would like a sample of your handwriting.* **sam ples.**
adj. 2. that is a sample. *A sample copy of the book is being sent to you.*
v. 3. to test; to try. *We sampled the cookies.* **sam ples, sam pled, sam pling.**
sam u rai (sam′ù rī′), *n.* in ancient times in Japan, a member of the military class. *The samurai were great fighters.* **sam u rai.** (See illustration on following page.)

salt shaker

manufacturing **salt** by the evaporation of sea water

sampan

samurai

sand (sand), *n.* 1. tiny bits of stone in large amounts, found in the deserts and on shores along oceans, lakes, and rivers. *Children like to play in the smooth sand of the beach.* **sands.**
v. 2. to smooth down by rubbing with sand or sandpaper. *Before painting the table, you must sand it.* 3. to cover with sand. *After a heavy snowstorm, the city's traffic department sands the streets.* **sands, sand ed, sand ing.**

san dal (san′dl), *n.* a shoe consisting of a sole held to the foot by cords or bands of leather. *Sandals were much used in ancient times and are still popular in the summer.* **san dals.**

sand blast (sand′blast′), *n.* 1. a strong stream of air which carries sand, used for cleaning buildings made of stone. *The sandblast cuts away dirt and soot.* **sand blasts.**
v. 2. to clean with a sandblast. *The dark and dirty stone was white after it was sandblasted.* **sand blasts, sand blast ed, sand blasting.**

sand stone (sand′stōn′), *n.* a kind of rock made mostly of sand. *Sandstone has a natural cement, like clay, which holds the grains of sand together.* **sand stones.**

sand wich (sand′wich), *n.* 1. two or more slices of bread, with a layer of meat, cheese, jam, lettuce, or other food placed between them. *I like a sandwich made of peanut butter and grape jelly.* **sand wich es.**
v. 2. to squeeze in. *Little Clifford was sandwiched between two huge men at the football game.* **sandwich es, sand wiched, sand wich ing.**

sandy (san′dē), *adj.* 1. made of or filled with sand. *The beach was sandy.* 2. reddish-yellow. *Gordon has sandy hair.* **sand i er, sand i est.**

sane (sān), *adj.* 1. having a healthy mind. *The doctor said the patient was sane.* 2. sensible. *The sane thing to do in an emergency is to call the police.* **san er, san est; sane ly,** *adv.*

sang (sang), past tense of **sing.**

sank (sangk), past tense of **sink.**

San ta Claus (san′tə klôz′), *n.* the fat, jolly man with a white beard and red suit who hands out gifts at Christmas; Saint Nicholas, patron saint of children. *On Christmas Eve, children wait for Santa Claus to come.* **San ta Claus es.**

sap[1] (sap), *n.* a juice that flows through trees and other plants. *The sap in a tree helps it to live and grow.* **saps.**

sap[2] (sap), *v.* 1. to wear down; to dig away at. *The water sapped the wooden supports of the old bridge.* 2. to weaken. *Not getting enough sleep may sap your energy.* **saps, sapped, sap ping.**

sap phire (saf′īr), *n.* 1. a deep-blue, hard jewel that is transparent. *A sapphire is expensive.* 2. deep blue. *The princess chose a gown of sapphire to match her eyes.* **sap phires.**

sar dine (sär dēn′), *n.* a small fish that is caught in nets, preserved in oil, and packed in cans. *Sardines are good to eat.* **sar dines** or **sar dine.**

sash[1] (sash), *n.* a long, broad band of cloth or ribbon worn around the waist or over the shoulder. *The band members in the parade wore sashes as part of their uniforms.* **sash es.**

sash[2] (sash), *n.* the framework which holds the glass in a window. *House windows have sashes which move up and down, move from side to side, or open outward.* **sash es.**

sardine

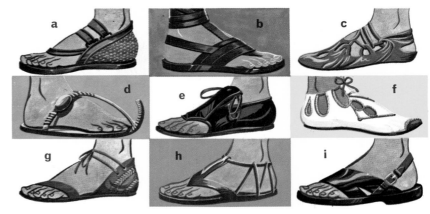

sat (sat), past tense of **sit.**

satch el (sach′əl), *n.* a small bag for carrying personal things, books, and papers. *A satchel is carried by its handle.* **satch els.**

sat el lite (sat′l īt′), *n.* 1. a heavenly body that revolves around a planet or other heavenly body. *The moon is a satellite of the earth.* 2. an object put into space by man to revolve around the earth, the sun, or other heavenly body. *Hundreds of satellites have been sent into space from the earth to gather information about the solar system.* 3. a country that depends upon a larger, more powerful country. *The satellites of the big nation were controlled by it.* 4. a person who always is with another person of more importance. *The powerful noble traveled with his satellites.* **sat el lites.** (See illustration on following page.)

sa tia ble (sā′shə bl), *adj.* capable of being fully satisfied or supplied with too much of anything. *That dog always seems to be hungry, but even he is satiable.*

Saturn

two views of the rings through a telescope

sa ti ate (sā′shē āt), *v.* to be fully satisfied; to have too much of anything. *The boy was satiated with ice cream.* **sa ti ates, sa ti at ed, sa ti at ing.**

sat in (sat′n), *n.* 1. a kind of cloth with a shiny surface. *Satin is a popular material for party dresses.* **sat ins.**
adj. 2. of or like satin; very smooth. *She wore a satin dress.*

sat is fac tion (sat′is fak′shən), *n.* 1. a feeling of being satisfied or contented. *Dan gets satisfaction from his job.* 2. something which causes pleasure or ease of mind. *A winning team is a great satisfaction to the coach and the school.* **sat is fac tions.**

sat is fac to ry (sat′is fak′tə rē), *adj.* good enough to satisfy; enough to please or to meet a need. *Your marks are satisfactory, so you have passed this course.* **sat is fac to ri ly,** *adv.*

sat is fy (sat′is fī′), *v.* 1. to please; to give what is wanted to. *You can satisfy a baby by giving him a toy.* 2. to convince; to make contented. *We satisfied Mother that we would be on time.* 3. to put an end to. *The glass of water satisfied my thirst.* 4. to pay in full. *The business company satisfied all its debts.* **sat is fies, sat is fied, sat is fy ing.**

Sat ur day (sat′ər dē, sat′ər dā), *n.* the seventh day of the week, coming after Friday. *We have no school on Saturday.* **Sat ur days.**

Sat urn (sat′ərn), *n.* 1. the sixth planet away from our sun, and the second largest planet in our solar system. *Saturn has rings around it.* 2. the ancient Roman god of agriculture. *In ancient Rome the people felt that Saturn would give them a good harvest.*

sauce (sôs), *n.* a liquid that is added to food to make it taste better. *We had a delicious chocolate sauce poured on top of our ice cream.* **sauc es.**

sau cer (sô′sər), *n.* a small, shallow dish on which a cup can be placed. *After stirring your cocoa, place the spoon in the saucer.* **sau cers.**

sau sage (sô′sij), *n.* meat that has been ground up and seasoned. *Sausage is usually sold wrapped in skin.* **sau sag es.**

sav age (sav′ij), *adj.* 1. not tamed; wild. *Savage animals live in the jungle.* 2. not affected by

sandals :

  a. ancient Assyrian
  b. ancient Roman
  c. medieval German
  d. ancient Egyptian
  e. ancient Greek
  f. twelfth century bishop
  g. ancient Assyrian
  h. ancient Greek
  i. modern

sapphire

sand, āte, bâre, fäther; sent, mē, fėrn; fit, bīke; pot, rōpe, fôrt; run, pùll, rüle, cūte; noise, sound; ch, cheese; ng, long; th, thick; ᵺ, those; zh, treasure; ə = a in about, e in waken, i in animal, o in seldom, and u in minus.

NATURAL AND ARTIFICIAL SATELLITES

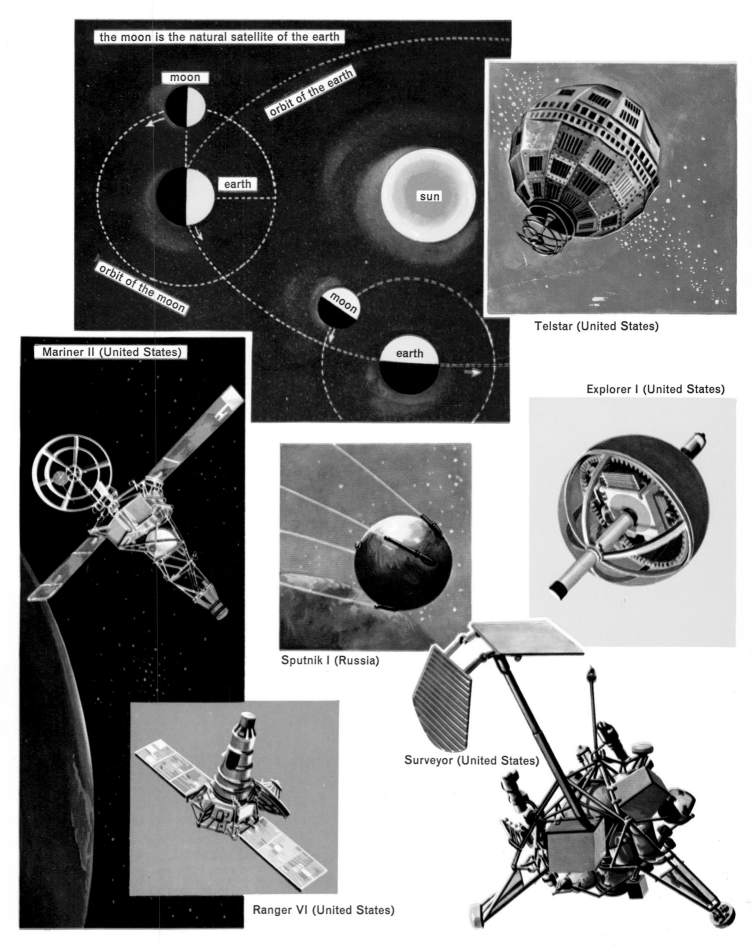

the moon is the natural satellite of the earth

moon

orbit of the earth

earth

sun

orbit of the moon

moon

earth

Telstar (United States)

Mariner II (United States)

Explorer I (United States)

Sputnik I (Russia)

Surveyor (United States)

Ranger VI (United States)

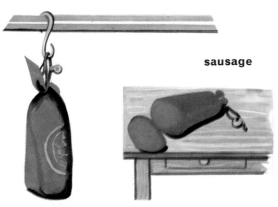

sausage

civilization. *Savage tribes follow religions and laws that seem strange to us.* 3. cruel; fierce. *The savage pirates attacked the ship.* **sav age ly,** *adv.* *n.* 4. a person living in a way not affected by civilization; a person who lives a simple, rough life. *The missionaries were kind and friendly to the jungle savages.* 5. a person who is cruel or fierce. *The savages sacked the city.* **sav ag es.**

save[1] (sāv), *v.* 1. to rescue; to make safe from harm or danger. *The boys saved the cat who was caught between the rocks. The firemen saved the house from burning.* 2. to put away for later use; to keep. *Bert is saving his money to buy a small radio. Many people save stamps.* 3. to keep from wasting. *Save your strength for our big job. We can save time by taking this road.* 4. to treat carefully. *Save your eyes by having good light when you read.* 5. to guard; keep safe. *The crowd outside the palace cried, "God save the King!"* **saves, saved, sav ing.**

save[2] (sāv), *prep.* except; but. *We went to every school game save one.*

sav ing (sāv′ing), *n.* 1. the act of a person who saves. *Buying this chair will be a saving of money.* 2. **savings,** money saved. *I have one hundred dollars in savings.* **sav ings.**

saw[1] (sô), *n.* 1. a cutting tool with metal teeth along the edge of a thin, flat blade. *The carpenter used a saw to cut off part of the board.* **saws.** *v.* 2. to cut with a saw. *The hunter sawed logs into pieces of wood for his fire.* 3. to use a saw. *He sawed like an expert.* 4. to be sawed. *Some wood, like pine, saws easily.* 5. to move the arms through or cut as though using a saw. *The excited boy sawed the air as he argued.* **saws, sawed, sawed** or **sawn, saw ing.**

saw[2] (sô), *n.* a common saying. *An old saw is "It takes all kinds of people to make a world."* **saws.**

saw[3] (sô), past tense of **see**[1].

saw dust (sô′dust′), *n.* the tiny pieces of wood that are made when wood is sawed. *The sawdust gathered on the floor beneath the saw.*

sax o phone (sak′sə fōn′), *n.* a musical wind instrument consisting of a curved brass tube with finger keys. *A saxophone is played by blowing into the mouthpiece and pressing the keys.* **sax o-phones.** (See illustration on following page.)

say (sā), *v.* 1. to speak; utter. *We say "please" when we ask for something.* 2. to report; maintain. *In this book, the author says that camels can go two months without water.* 3. to put into words; to declare; to give as an opinion. *He always says what he believes. I really can't say which flower is the loveliest.* 4. to repeat. *Say your prayers every night.* **says, said, say ing.** *n.* 5. what a person says. *If I had my say, there would not be so many tests.* 6. the power to decide. *Father has the final say in our discussions.* **says.**

say ing (sā′ing), *n.* a short, popular saw; wise words that have come from the past. *An old saying is "A burned child is afraid of fire."* **say ings.**

scale[1] (skāl), *n.* 1. a device or machine for weighing things. *According to the scale in the doctor's office, the boy weighed one hundred pounds.* **scales.** *v.* 2. to weigh. *That big man scales over two hundred pounds.* **scales, scaled, scal ing.** (See illustration on following page.)

sawing

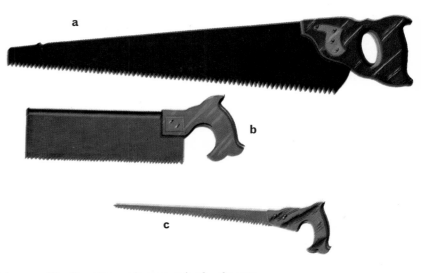

a

b

c

saws:
a. common
b. back
c. keyhole

saxophones:
  a. bass
  b. tenor
  c. alto

scale² (skāl), *n.* 1. one of the thin, flat, hard plates that cover fish, snakes, and lizards. *The scales of the fish shone in the sun as it leaped from the water.* 2. a thin piece or layer. *Dried scales of paint were on the old house.* **scales.**
v. 3. to scrape the scales from. *Scale the fish carefully before cooking it.* 4. to break off in tiny pieces. *The paint is scaling from the front door.* **scales, scaled, scal ing.**

scale³ (skāl), *n.* 1. a series of marks placed on a stick or dial for measuring. *A ruler used in school usually has a scale in inches on it. A thermometer has a scale in degrees of heat.* 2. the distance between places on a map, drawing, or model compared with the real distance. *This map has a*

scale of one inch to every hundred miles. 3. a series of steps or degrees from low to high. *The passing grade on the scale for our history test was 70. The salary scale in that business goes from one dollar to three dollars an hour. The rich man lives on an expensive scale.* 4. a series of tones in music arranged according to pitch from low to high or from high to low. *Every piano player practices scales.* **scales.**
v. 5. to climb. *The painter scaled the ladder. The mountain climber scaled Mount Everest.* 6. to control; to reduce by a certain amount. *Our family decided to scale down our expenses by not buying useless items.* **scales, scaled, scal ing.**

scalp (skalp), *n.* 1. the hair and skin from the top of the head. *When you shampoo your hair you also wash your scalp.* **scalps.**
v. 2. to cut off the hair and skin from the top of the head. *In pioneer days, the Indians often scalped many settlers.* **scalps, scalped, scalp ing.**

scal pel (skal′pl), *n.* a small, very sharp knife used by doctors in operating. *The doctor used a scalpel when he operated.* **scal pels.**

scar (skär), *n.* 1. a mark on the skin from a cut, burn, etc. that has healed but has still left the mark. *She has a scar on her arm from the accident.* 2. an impression. *The leg of the chair left a scar in the rug.* **scars.**
v. 3. to make a mark on the skin. *She scarred herself in the accident.* **scars, scarred, scarring.**

scarce (skârs), *adj.* hard to get; not abundant; rare. *Green grass and trees are scarce in the middle of a big city.* **scarc er, scarc est; scarce ly,** *adv.*

scarce ly (skârs′lē), *adv.* hardly; barely. *There are scarcely any people on the streets at five o'clock in the morning. I scarcely expected such a good grade in science.*

scare (skâr), *v.* 1. to frighten. *The loud noise scared me.* 2. to drive away by a sudden noise or appearance. *The birds were scared off when the dog ran into the yard.* **scarces, scared, scar ing.**

scales:
  a. postage
  b. platform
  c. baby
  d. balance

n. 3. a sudden fear or fright. *Irwin gave us a scare when he appeared in the darkness wearing his Halloween mask.* **scares.**

scarf (skärf), *n.* 1. a long, broad piece of cloth worn over the shoulders, around the neck, or on the head. *Mike wears his wool scarf on cold days. Laura has a beautiful, silk head scarf.* 2. a long strip of cloth used as a cover. *She bought a scarf to place on top of her bureau.* **scarfs** or **scarves** (skärvz).

scar let (skär′lit), *n.* 1. a very bright red color. *Scarlet is a color often used for royal robes.*
adj. 2. very bright red. *The bird had scarlet wings.*

scarlet fever, *n.* a disease that causes a sore throat, fever, and scarlet spots on the body. *Not many children get scarlet fever these days.*

scat (skat), *n.* a word often used to scare away a cat. *The cat ran away from the bird bath when the man said "Scat!"*

scat ter (skat′ər), *v.* 1. to toss in all directions; to throw here and there. *We scattered food for the birds during the winter.* 2. to go in different directions. *The crowd scattered when the rain came.* **scat ters, scat tered, scat ter ing.**

scene (sēn), *n.* 1. the place where a thing happens. *The playground was the scene of the softball game. The police went to the scene of the accident.* 2. the time and place of a story, play, etc. *The scene of the play is laid in a mining town in the old West.* 3. one of the divisions of a play. *I appear in the second scene of the first act of the school play.* 4. the painted background, the furniture, and the other objects on the stage. *The scene is a flower garden.* 5. a view; a landscape. *The scene from the hilltop is lovely.* 6. a show of anger; a display of bad manners before others. *Dennis later said he was sorry for the scene he made when someone bumped him by accident.* **scenes.**

scen ery (sēn′ər ē), *n.* 1. the general view or appearance of a place. *The scenery in the country is lovely.* 2. the painted backgrounds and other items like furniture used on stage. *The scenery for the opera was designed by a famous artist.* 3. the photographed background in a motion picture. *The best thing about the western I saw Saturday was its beautiful scenery.*

sce nic (sē′nik, sen′ik), *adj.* 1. having beautiful scenery. *The United States has many scenic roads and parks.* 2. having to do with the scenery of a play. *The scenic effects included an actual rainfall on the stage.*

scent (sent), *n.* 1. an odor; a smell. *I like the scent of smoke from a campfire.* 2. the odor of an animal that can be smelled only by another animal. *The hunting dogs followed the scent of the wolf.* 3. the sense of smell. *Dogs have a sharp scent.* 4. a trail; a means of trailing or finding. *The police were on the scent of the robbers.* 5. a perfume. *The girl used the scent lightly.* **scents.**
v. 6. to smell. *The dog scented a rat in the rubbish*

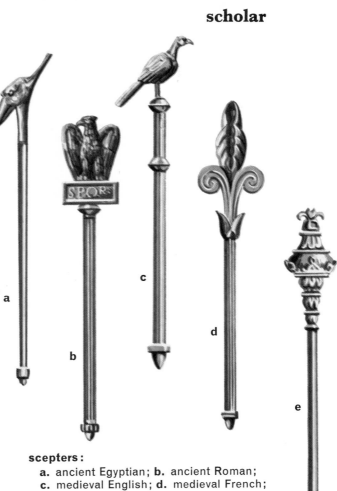

scepters:
a. ancient Egyptian; **b.** ancient Roman;
c. medieval English; **d.** medieval French;
e. medieval Spanish

heap. 7. to get a hint of. *The workers scented changes that would be made in the company.* 8. to fill with an odor. *Roses scented the air.* **scents, scent ed, scent ing.**

scep ter or **scep tre** (sep′tər), *n.* a rod or staff held by a ruler as a sign of his power and authority. *The king greeted the nobles with his scepter by his side.* **scep ters** or **scep tres.**

sched ule (skej′ùl), *n.* 1. a list of things that are to happen in a certain order or at a certain time. *We have our schedule of classes for next semester. According to the time schedule, the next flight leaves at nine o'clock.* **sched ules.**
v. 2. to make a schedule of; to plan. *Schedule your Monday classes so that you can leave early for work. The first concert is scheduled for tomorrow.* **sched ules, sched uled, sched ul ing.**

scheme (skēm), *n.* 1. a plan; a project. *A scheme for using all the school's space was presented to the principal.* 2. a secret plot. *The scheme to give Mother a surprise party failed when she discovered the birthday cake.* 3. a planned arrangement. *The color scheme of the room is blue and orange.* **schemes.**
v. 4. to plan secretly; to plot. *The American soldiers schemed to escape from the enemy's prison camp.* **schemes, schemed, schem ing.**

schol ar (skol′ər), *n.* 1. a person who has

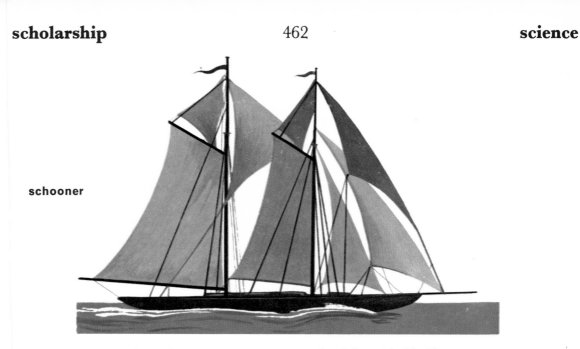

schooner

studied a great deal about one or more subjects. *The famous professor is a great history scholar.* 2. a person who is a student in a school. *This semester there are thirty-two scholars in the science class.* **schol ars.**

schol ar ship (skol′ər ship′), *n.* 1. knowledge that is obtained by study; learning. *The professor of science is a man of scholarship.* 2. a gift of money to a student to help him continue with his education. *Lawrence received a scholarship because of his excellent grades and his work on the school newspaper.* **schol ar ships.**

school[1] (skül), *n.* 1. a place for teaching and learning. *Children learn how to read in school.* 2. the pupils and teachers of a school. *The school will leave early for the game with Northbrook.* 3. the regular time when teaching and learning takes place. *We had no school because of the storm.* 4. a group of people having the same beliefs and opinions. *The new school of artists paints pictures that just seem like a mass of colors.* 5. a part of a university. *Uncle Paul was a student at the medical school.* **schools.**
v. 6. to teach; to train; to educate. *You must school your puppy to obey you.* 7. to control. *School your temper.* **schools, schooled, schooling.**

school[2] (skül), *n.* a large number of one kind of fish that swim and feed together. *A school of minnows was swimming in the warm water near the shore.* **schools.**

school boy (skül′boi′), *n.* a boy who goes to school. *The schoolboys raced around during recess.* **school boys.**

school girl (skül′gėrl), *n.* a girl who goes to school. *The young schoolgirl lost her purse.* **school girls.**

school house (skül′hous′), *n.* the building where school is held. *Our schoolhouse has fifty rooms.* **school hous es.**

school mas ter (skül′mas′tər), *n.* a man who teaches in a school. *The schoolmaster really liked to instruct young people.* **school mas ters.**

school mate (skül′māt′), *n.* a person going to the same school; a companion. *The two boys were schoolmates for nine years.* **school mates.**

school room (skül′rüm′), *n.* the room where students are taught. *Our schoolroom has thirty pupils in it.* **school rooms.**

school yard (skül′yärd′), *n.* the ground around a school. *We play games in the schoolyard.* **school yards.**

schoon er (skün′ər), *n.* a sailing ship with two or more masts. *Schooners are sometimes used as fishing vessels.* **schoon ers.**

sci ence (sī′əns), *n.* 1. knowledge made up of facts learned from research, observation, and experiments and arranged in an ordered system. *The study of science helps us to understand the world we live in.* 2. a branch of this knowledge. *Chemistry is a science which deals with chemical substances.* **sci enc es.**

scimitars

sci en tif ic (sī′ən tif′ik), *adj.* having to do with science. *The scientific method includes conducting experiments and recording and checking the results. Our laboratory at school has scientific instruments.* **sci en tif i cal ly,** *adv.*

sci en tist (sī′ən tist), *n.* a person who is doing scientific work. *The scientist spoke to us about getting fresh water from the oceans.* **sci en tists.**

scim i tar (sim′ə tər), *n.* a sword with a curved blade once used mostly by the soldiers of Turkey and Arabia. *Scimitars are now used mostly as ornaments.* **scim i tars.**

scis sors (siz′ərz), *n. pl.* a tool for cutting consisting of two handles and two sharp blades fastened together. *When the handles are pushed together, the blades of the scissors cut through paper or fabric.*

scle ra (sklir′ə), *n.* the white membrane which covers the ball of the eye. *The cornea, which is transparent, covers the pupil of the eye, while the sclera covers the rest.*

scoff (skôf), *v.* to mock; to make fun. *People scoffed at the Wright brothers when they tried to make a machine that could fly.* **scoffs, scoffed, scoff ing.**

scold (skōld), *v.* 1. to find fault with in an angry way. *The lady next door scolded us for throwing the ball into her flowers.* **scolds, scold ed, scold- ing.** *n.* 2. a woman who often scolds or nags. *Centuries ago a scold was punished by being dumped into a pond.* **scolds.**

scoop (sküp), *n.* 1. a kitchen tool like a small shovel. *Scoops are used to take up flour, sugar, and ice cream.* 2. the bucket of a mechanical shovel which holds and moves coal, grain, sand, etc. *The big steam shovel lowered its scoop into the ship and pulled it up with a load of gravel.* **scoops.** *v.* 3. to take up or out. *Use the shovel to scoop up the sand. Scoop out some ice cream for us, please.* 4. to dig out. *We helped to scoop holes in the ground for the tomato plants.* **scoops, scooped, scoop ing.**

scoot er (süt′ər), *n.* a child's toy for riding on, made of a low board with a wheel at each end and with a handlebar for steering. *You ride a scooter by standing with one foot on the board and pushing against the sidewalk or ground with the other foot.* **scoot ers.**

scorch (skôrch), *v.* 1. to burn slightly. *Whenever I make breakfast, I scorch the toast.* 2. to dry up by heat. *The sun scorched the crops.* **scorch es, scorched, scorch ing.**

score (skôr), *n.* 1. the number of points made in a game. *The final score in the baseball game was 5 to 0.* 2. a group of twenty things. *A score of birds were on the lawn eating the crumbs we set out for them. "Four score and seven years ago" means eighty-seven years ago.* 3. a grade. *Her score on the test was 93.* 4. a debt; account. *Mr. Kean settled his score with the bank.* 5. a printed piece of music showing all the parts for the

scorpion

instruments or voices. *Students of music read the score as they listen to the orchestra play.* 6. a scratch; a mark. *The ice skaters left scores on the ice.* **scores.** *v.* 7. to keep a record of. *You have to give the game complete attention when you are scoring it.* 8. to give a grade to. *The teacher spent all evening reading and scoring the tests.* 9. to make points, runs, or goals in a game. *Bobby scored in the final inning of the baseball game.* 10. to cut; to scratch. *The wooden floor was scored from the spikes on the players' shoes.* **scores, scored, scor ing.**

scorn (skôrn), *n.* 1. a despising; a feeling of shame and disgust. *Most of us had scorn for the student who cheated on the test.* 2. a person who is looked down upon. *He was the scorn of the neighborhood after he broke the grocer's window on purpose.* **scorns.** *v.* 3. to look down upon; to have disgust for. *We scorn a boy who takes pennies from a newspaper stand.* 4. to turn down because it is wrong. *The professor scorned the request to give the star football player a high mark that he had not earned.* **scorns, scorned, scorn ing.**

scor pi on (skôr′pē ən), *n.* a small animal that is related to the spider and has a long, narrow tail with a poisonous sting at its tip. *The scorpion uses its claws to grasp food.* **scor- pi ons.**

scour[1] (skour), *v.* 1. to clean or polish the surface of something or someone by a hard scrubbing action. *The girl had to scour her dirty face.* 2. to make deeper by a continuous scrubbing motion. *The little stream soon scoured a big river.* **scours, scoured, scour ing.**

scour[2] (skour), *v.* move quickly in search or pursuit of something or someone. *We scoured the neighborhood for the lost child.* **scours, scoured, scour ing.**

scout (skout), *n.* 1. a person sent out to get information. *The scout reported that the enemy's camp was twenty miles away. The baseball scout for the White Sox gave a good report on the third baseman at North College.* 2. **Scout,** a member of the Boy Scouts of America; a member of the Girl Scouts of America. *The Boy Scouts go on a camping trip every month.* **scouts.**

scissors

v. 3. to try to get information about. *Our airplane scouted the extent of the forest fire.* 4. to search; hunt. *Scout around the park for your lost sunglasses.* **scouts, scout ed, scout ing.**

scram ble (skram′bl), *v.* 1. to climb, crawl, or walk on hands and knees. *The children scrambled up the side of the hill.* 2. to fight or struggle for something. *The birds scrambled for the food that Mother set out for them.* 3. to mix in a messy way. *I scrambled my books and papers together and ran for the school bus.* 4. to cook eggs while stirring the mixed whites and yolks. *Mother scrambled some eggs for supper.* **scram bles, scram bled, scram bling.**
n. 5. a climb over rough ground. *Mike's jeans were torn in the scramble up the hill.* 6. a confused, hasty struggle or fight. *There was a wild scramble for the dresses on sale.* **scram bles.**

scrap (skrap), *n.* 1. a small piece; a little bit. *The garbage can was filled with scraps of paper. The dog ate the scraps of meat. Do you have even a scrap of information about our grades?* 2. broken, worn out, or useless material; junk. *There are tons of scrap in the yard behind the auto shop.* **scraps.**
v. 3. to throw away as useless. *Scrap these old papers. We scrapped the plan for a swim when the weather turned cold.* 4. to make into scraps; break up. *Old automobiles are scrapped.* **scraps, scrapped, scrap ping.**

scrape (skrāp), *v.* 1. to take off or remove by rubbing with something rough or sharp. *A painter scrapes old paint from the house before he puts on new paint. Scrape the mud from your shoes.* 2. to scratch; to harm the surface of. *The basketball player scraped his knee when he fell. The boy accidentally scraped his bicycle against a brick wall.* 3. to drag; rub with a harsh sound. *Don't scrape your toys on the floor.* 4. to collect with difficulty. *Her older brother scraped together enough money to buy a used car.* 5. **scrape through,** to get through with difficulty. *Michael did little studying and barely scraped through his examinations.* **scrapes, scraped, scrap ing.**
n. 6. a harsh, grating sound. *I dislike the scrape of a nail on a chalkboard.* 7. a difficulty; an unpleasant situation. *Poor George was in a scrape when he could not find his history paper.* 8. a scratch. *You can't see the scrape on the floor now.* **scrapes.**

scratch (skrach), *v.* 1. to mark or cut slightly. *The wooden box scratched the polished floor. The boy scratched his knee by falling on the sidewalk.* 2. to rub or scrape with the fingers or nails. *When a mosquito bite itches, you want to scratch it, but you shouldn't.* 3. to dig with claws or nails. *The dog scratched at the hard ground trying to bury his bone.* 4. to make a harsh, scraping sound. *The shovel scratched against the sidewalk. The cat is scratching at the screen door.* 5. to strike out or draw a line through. *The editor of the school*

screwdrivers

paper scratched two sentences in my news article.* 6. to write carelessly or poorly. *My uncle scratched a few lines on a postcard which I could hardly read.* **scratch es, scratched, scratching.**
n. 7. a mark or cut made in a surface by scratching. *We put a lamp over the scratch on the top of the table.* 8. a small cut on the body. *Let's put a bandage on that scratch to protect it from germs.* 9. the sound of scraping or scratching. *The room was so quiet we could hear the scratch of the chalk on the board.* 10. **from scratch,** from the beginning; from nothing. *She baked the cake from scratch, using no prepared mixture.* **scratch es.**

scream (skrēm), *v.* 1. to cry out loudly. *My mother screamed when she saw the mouse. The children screamed with laughter at the funny movie.* **screams, screamed, scream ing.**
n. 2. a loud cry. *Screams came from the football field when the team won.* **screams.**

screen (skrēn), *n.* 1. wire woven together tightly with tiny openings. *A screen on a door keeps out insects in summer.* 2. a frame that is used to hide or conceal. *The sink is behind the screen.* 3. anything like a screen, used for concealing. *The house is behind a screen of trees. The airplane is behind a screen of clouds.* 4. coarsely woven wire for separating sand, gravel, etc. *If you throw the sand on the screen only the finer grains go through.* 5. a surface on which motion pictures or slides are shown. *We put up the screen to see the movies of our camping trip.* 6. the part of a television set on which the picture appears. *Everyone was excited when the famous singer came on the screen.* **screens.**
v. 7. to hide or shelter. *The thick bushes screen the yard.* 8. to separate coal, sand, or gravel through a screen. *The workmen screened the gravel before using it for the street pavement.* 9. to test and interview. *The company was screening people for jobs.* **screens, screened, screening.**

screw (skrü), *n.* 1. a piece of metal shaped like a nail with a ridge or "thread" twisting around its length, used to fasten things together. *A screw has a slit at the head so that it can be forced into place by turning.* 2. a propeller on a ship or airplane. *The boat's screw would not turn because it was covered with seaweed.* **screws.**
v. 3. to fasten with a screw. *The carpenter screwed the boards together.* 4. to turn as one turns a screw; twist. *The cover of the jar should be screwed on.* **screws, screwed, screw ing.**

screw driv er (skrü′drī′vər), *n.* a tool used for putting in or taking out screws by turning. *The tip of a screwdriver fits into the slit on the head of the screw.* **screw drivers.**

scrib ble (skrib′l), *v.* 1. to write carelessly and in a hurry. *I barely had time to scribble a letter home before the bus left.* **scrib bles, scrib bled, scrib bling.**

n. 2. a careless, hasty piece of writing. *The teacher said she couldn't accept my scribble.* **scrib bles.**

script (skript), *n.* 1. a way of handwriting. *Script is composed of slanted, curved letters.* 2. type set in this style, so it looks like handwriting. *Some typewriters have script letters.* 3. a copy of a play given to actors so they can learn their lines. *The actor memorized the script in three weeks.* **scripts.**

scrub[1] (skrub), *v.* 1. to wash or clean by rubbing hard. *The new soaps make it easier to scrub floors.* **scrubs, scrubbed, scrub bing.**

n. 2. a rubbing. *Give your face a good scrub.* **scrubs.**

scrub[2] (skrub), *n.* 1. a thick group of low trees or bushes. *The dog couldn't find his way out of the scrub.* 2. any person, animal, or plant that is smaller than the normal size. *That scrub of a man is one of the country's famous lawyers.* 3. a player not on the regular team. *The school's football team practiced against the scrubs.* **scrubs.** *adj.* 4. made up of players who are not trained. *For three years Chris played on the scrub team.* 5. inferior; smaller than normal in size. *These scrub oak trees will be replaced.*

sculp tor (skulp′tər), *n.* an artist who makes statues. *Sculptors carve or chisel in wood or stone, model in clay, or cast in metal.* **sculp tors.**

sculp ture (skulp′chər), *n.* 1. the art of cutting, molding, or forming figures from stone, wood, clay, metal, etc. *Sculpture sometimes requires strength as well as talent.* 2. a statue, figure, or other work of art made in this way. *The sculptures in the art museum are here for a special exhibit.* **sculp tures.**

v. 3. to cut, mold, or form wood, stone, clay, metal, etc. into shapes. *He is sculpturing a small boat from a piece of pine.* **sculp tures, sculptured, sculp tur ing.**

scum (skum), *n.* a thin layer that forms on the surface of liquids. *Scum forms on the top of boiling cocoa.*

scur ry (skėr′ē), *v.* 1. to run quickly; to hurry. *The children scurried outside when the rain stopped.* **scur ries, scur ried, scur ry ing.**

n. 2. a hasty running. *After his scurry around the yard, the dog lay down.* **scur ries.**

sea (sē), *n.* 1. the ocean; the large body of salt water that covers most of the earth's surface. *The ship's captain had spent his life sailing the sea.* 2. a large body of salt water smaller than the ocean. *The Caspian is a sea that lies between Europe and Asia in the Caucasus Mountains.* 3. a large, heavy wave; rough water. *The seas nearly turned over the small fishing boat as it tried to escape the storm.* 4. anything like the sea or ocean in size. *He was in a sea of trouble.* **seas.**

Sea also has the following special meanings:

at sea, (a) sailing on the ocean. *The ship was at sea for thirty days.* (b) confused; lost. *On the first day at the new school, Hal felt at sea.*

sea horses

follow the sea, to be a sailor. *Curtis always wanted to follow the sea, so he joined the navy.*

go to sea, (a) to become a sailor. *He went to sea when he was eighteen.* (b) to leave on an ocean voyage. *After many years of planning and saving Uncle Greg has finally gone to sea.*

put to sea, to begin a voyage. *The big pirate ship put to sea after hiding out for several days.*

the Seven Seas, all the oceans in the world. *The Seven Seas are the Arctic, Antarctic, North and South Pacific, North and South Atlantic, and Indian Ocean.*

sea horse, *n.* a kind of small fish with a head that looks somewhat like a horse's head. *The sea horse lives in warm seas around the world.* **sea hors es.**

seal[1] (sēl), *n.* 1. a sea animal with a round head, long body and broad, flat limbs instead of feet. *The seal has a thick layer of fat under its skin to protect it from the cold water in which it swims.* 2. the fur of a seal. *Mrs. Aubrey has an expensive*

sculptor

seal

coat made of seal. 3. a leather made of the skin of a seal. *Eskimos use seal to make tough threads.* **seals.**

v. 4. to hunt seals. *The Eskimos seal in order to provide food and clothing for their families.* **seals, seal ed, seal ing.**

seal² (sēl), *n.* 1. a design that can be stamped on a piece of wax or pressed into a piece of paper to show authority or ownership. *Every country in the world and every state in the United States has an official seal.* 2. a paper stamp with glue on it for putting on letters or packages. *Christmas seals are sold to aid research in major diseases.* 3. a sign; mark. *He put his seal of approval on the document.* **seals.**

v. 4. to close tightly; to fasten as if with a seal. *The envelope was sealed.* 5. to mark with a seal. *The agreement was signed and sealed by both countries.* 6. to settle firmly. *The jury will seal the man's fate.* **seals, sealed, seal ing.**

seam (sēm), *n.* 1. the line or fold made by sewing together two pieces of cloth, canvas, or leather. *The seams in the dress are beginning to come apart.* 2. any mark like a seam; a furrow. *The seam in his forehead is caused by frowning.* 3. a layer of mineral in the earth. *The large seam of coal was removed after twenty years of mining.* **seams.**

v. 4. to join with a seam. *Mother seamed the sides of my dress.* 5. to mark with a line or furrow.

searchlight

The years of thinking and working had seamed the old man's face. **seams, seamed, seam ing.**

sea port (sē′pôrt′), *n.* 1. a port or harbor for ocean ships. *The Navy has many seaports.* 2. a town or city having a port or harbor. *San Francisco is a seaport.* **sea ports.**

sear (sir), *v.* 1. to burn the surface of. *He seared the steak by placing it on the flames.* 2. to dry up. *The hot sun seared the flowers.* 3. to make hard and without feeling. *Years of hardship and suffering have seared that old man.* **sears, seared, sear ing.**

search (sėrch), *v.* 1. to look for something. *Beth searched for her purse all afternoon. All people search for happiness.* 2. to examine; to look through; to go over carefully. *The scientist searched his data for an explanation of the plant's rapid growth.* **search es, searched, searching.**

n. 3. a searching. *After a long search they found the child asleep in a closet.* 4. **in search of,** looking for; trying to find. *The boys went to the fields in search of strawberries.* **search es.**

search light (sėrch′līt′), *n.* 1. a powerful lamp that can be turned to throw a bright light in any direction. *Ships carry searchlights to help with their work at night.* 2. a strong beam of light. *Insects are attracted to a searchlight.* **searchlights.**

sea shore (sē′shôr′), *n.* the land along the ocean or sea. *We go to the seashore in summer.* **sea shores.**

sea son (sē′zn), *n.* 1. one of the four parts into which a year is divided. *Spring is my favorite season.* 2. a special period of time. *Children eagerly wait for the Christmas season. Larry can hardly wait for the football season to begin. The harvest season is in autumn.* **sea sons.**

v. 3. to make more pleasant to the taste. *Season your soup with salt.* 4. to give added interest to. *The speaker seasoned his serious talk with some jokes.* 5. to make ready for use by aging or by drying. *This lumber is seasoned for several years.* **sea sons, sea soned, sea son ing.**

seaweed

seat (sēt), *n.* 1. a thing to sit on; a place in which to sit. *We do not have enough seats for the party. We took our seats in church.* 2. the part of anything that is used for sitting. *We have leather seats on the chairs. Brian tore the seat of his pants while climbing the tree.* 3. a main location; center. *The seat of our government is in Washington, D.C. The seat of the fashion world is Paris, France.* **seats.**
v. 4. to place in a seat. *Jack seated himself in the front row.* 5. to have enough seats for. *The room seats thirty pupils.* **seats, seat ed, seat ing.**

sea weed (sē′wēd′), *n.* any plant or plants that grow in the sea. *The seaweed is too thick here for us to swim.* **sea weeds.**

sec ond[1] (sek′ənd), *n.* 1. one of the sixty equal parts of a minute. *The winner of the race ran a mile in three minutes and fifty-nine seconds.* 2. a very short time. *I'll be ready in a second!* **sec onds.**

sec ond[2] (sek′ənd), *adj.* 1. next after the first. *The first time I spoke he didn't hear me, but the second time he answered. We live in the second house from the corner.* 2. another; one more. *Let me have a second glass of orange juice, please.* **sec ond ly,** *adv.*
n. 3. someone or something that is second. *Mort was the second to finish the test.* 4. a person who gives help or support. *In former times, men who fought duels had seconds to make arrangements. A boxer has a second near the boxing ring.* **sec onds.**
v. 5. to speak in support of. *Tom made a motion to end the meeting, and Ralph seconded it.* **sec onds, sec ond ed, sec ond ing.**

se cret (sē′krit), *adj.* 1. kept from the knowledge of others; hidden; known to just a few. *The members of the club have a secret meeting place by the old pond. The company does secret work for the government.* **se cret ly,** *adv.*
n. 2. something that is hidden or is known to just a few. *The girls in our class share many secrets.* 3. the true cause; explanation. *The secret of his success was hard work.* 4. a mystery. *Science has found out many of nature's secrets.* **se crets.**

sec re tary (sek′rə ter′ē), *n.* 1. a person whose job is to take care of the records and write the letters for a person in business. *The bank president asked his secretary to type a report for him.* 2. a man or woman who is in charge of a department of the government. *The Secretary of Agriculture is the head of all the government people who help farmers and ranch owners.* 3. a kind of desk used for writing. *The secretary has a top part for holding books.* **sec re tar ies.**

se crete (si krēt′), *v.* 1. to hide; to put away carefully in a secret place. *Carol secretes her diary in the back of her closet.* 2. to make and give off a substance. *Glands in the mouth secrete saliva.* **se cretes, se cret ed, se cret ing.**

se cre tion (si krē′shən), *n.* 1. the useful substance that is made and given off by some

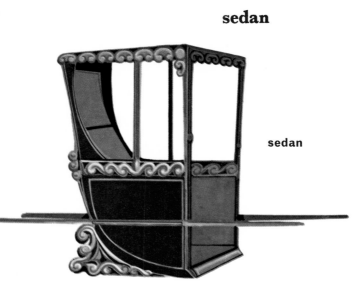

sedan

part of an animal or plant. *Perspiration is a secretion of the skin.* 2. the hiding of something. *Secretion of the truth will not help you, so tell the teacher what really happened.* **se cre tions.**

sec tion (sek′shən), *n.* 1. a part; division; slice. *An orange is divided naturally into sections. Everyone got equal sections of the pie Mother baked.* 2. a division of a book. *The first section in the science book is about energy and its uses.* 3. a region. *The hilly section of Missouri is beautiful. The polar bear lives in cold sections of the world.* 4. a view or drawing of a thing as it would look if cut straight through. *A cross section of an orange shows its slices. A cross section of a building shows its rooms.* **sec tions.**
v. 5. to divide into sections. *Susan sectioned the apple so that each of us could have an equal piece.* **sec tions, sec tioned, sec tion ing.**

se cure (si kyúr′), *adj.* 1. safe from danger or loss; away from harm. *The dog was secure in the shelter that we built for him. During the storm we were secure in the warm house. Your money is secure in a bank.* 2. fastened firmly. *The windows are secure. Is that knot in the rope secure enough to hold the dog?* 3. certain and sure. *The lawyer's success is secure after his fine work on this case.* **se cure ly,** *adv.*
v. 4. to make firm or fasten. *Secure the windows by locking them.* 5. to get; obtain. *We secured the groceries and went home.* 6. to make safe; to protect. *The boat was secured to the dock during the storm.* **se cures, se cured, se cur ing.**

se cu ri ty (si kyúr′ə tē), *n.* 1. a feeling of safety; freedom from danger or fear. *The dog finds security in the corner of the room under the sofa.* 2. protection. *Holding on the rail when walking downstairs is a security against falling.* 3. something or someone that is used to back up an obligation of another. *Our car was the security for my father's bank loan.* **se cu ri ties.**

se dan (si dan′), *n.* 1. a closed automobile with seats for four or more people. *Sedans have two doors or four doors.* 2. a covered chair for one person, carried on poles by two men. *Sedans*

sand, āte, bâre, fäther; sent, mē, fèrn; fit, bīke; pot, rōpe, fôrt; run, pùll, rüle, cūte; noise, sound; ch, cheese; ng, long; th, thick; ᵺ, those; zh, treasure; ə = a in about, e in waken, i in animal, o in seldom, and u in minus.

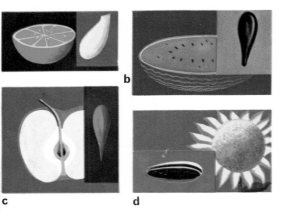

seeds:
   a. orange
   b. watermelon
   c. apple
   d. sunflower

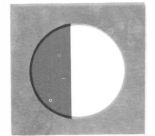

segment of a circle

were used by wealthy people in the 1600's and 1700's. **se dans.**

sed i ment (sed′ə mənt), *n.* the material that settles to the bottom of a liquid. *You can see the sediment form in a large glass bottle of muddy water.*

sed i men ta ry (sed′ə men′tə rē), *adj.* formed from sediment. *Shale and sandstone are sedimentary rocks formed by years of pressure at the bottom of a body of water.*

see[1] (sē), *v.* 1. to look at; to be aware of by using the eyes. *I can see a truck on the road. Linda sees everything better with her glasses.* 2. to have the power of sight. *The old dog barely sees anymore, but he is happy lying in the sun.* 3. to find out. *Let's see if we can help the lady with her packages.* 4. to understand. *Now I see how to work that puzzle.* 5. to make sure. *Will you see that the tickets are in your purse?* 6. to escort; go with. *Mr. Carter will see you home safely.* 7. to visit; call on. *Mother and Dad have been seeing old friends at the hotel.* 8. to know; to have experience with. *The mountain climber has seen danger. The gloves have seen hard wear.* 9. **see through,** (a) to understand the true meaning of. *She saw through the little boy's trick.* (b) to finish; to go through with. *Mike sees every job through.* (c) to help out during a hard time. *The neighbors saw us through the first year in the new town.* 10. **see to,** to take care of. *You see to the sandwiches, and I'll carry the milk and the soft drinks.* **sees, saw, seen, see ing.**

see[2] (sē), *n.* 1. a district in which a bishop has authority. *The bishop's see was the state of Illinois.* 2. the position or authority of a bishop. *The see of New York is very large.* **sees.**

seed (sēd), *n.* 1. the part of a plant from which another plant grows. *I planted carrot seeds and radish seeds. Vegetables, trees, and flowers grow from seeds.* 2. **go to seed,** (a) to come to the time of giving forth seeds. *Flowers go to seed at the end of their blooming.* (b) to become weak, useless, and careless. *My grandfather says if he didn't work he would go to seed.* **seeds.**

v. 3. to plant with seed. *The new lawn was seeded in spring.* 4. to take the seeds from. *Seed the grapefruit before serving it.* 5. to shed seeds. *The tree is seeding.* **seeds, seed ed, seed ing.**

seed ling (sēd′ling), *n.* a young plant or tree that has grown from a seed. *We plant our tomato seedlings in the spring.* **seed lings.**

seek (sēk), *v.* 1. to look for; to try to find. *Some of the early pioneers gave up farming to seek gold in the West. The family is seeking an apartment in Chicago.* 2. to try. *Parents seek to give happiness to their children.* **seeks, sought, seek ing.**

seem (sēm), *v.* to appear to be. *The house seemed empty after the children left for camp. The teacher seems pleased with our behavior. That kitten seems lame.* **seems, seemed, seem ing.**

seem ing ly (sēm ing lē), *adv.* to all appearances; apparently. *That house is, seemingly, the only one open.*

seen (sēn), past participle of **see**[1].

see saw (sē′sô′), *n.* 1. a board balanced on a support at the middle and used by children for playing. *A child at each end of the board can make the seesaw go up and down.* 2. a movement up and down or back and forth. *The seesaw of the boat ride made her somewhat dizzy.* **see saws.**

v. 3. to move like a seesaw. *His thoughts seesawed from one plan to another. The game seesawed with first one team ahead and then the other.* 4. to ride a seesaw. *The youngsters seesawed in the park.* **see saws, see sawed, see saw ing.**

seg ment (seg′mənt), *n.* 1. any one of the parts into which a thing is divided. *An orange is naturally separated into segments. The line segment extended from point A to point B.* 2. a part of a circle cut off by a straight line. *The segment of the circle cuts it in half.* **seg ments.**

seize (sēz), *v.* 1. to take hold of suddenly; to grasp; to grab. *Carl seized the little girl just as she started to fall down the steps. Beth quickly seized the new way of sewing.* 2. to take by force. *The army seized the village. The police seized the thieves.* **seiz es, seized, seiz ing.**

sei zure (sē′zhər), *n.* 1. a seizing or being seized. *The seizure of the town took only one hour.* 2. a sudden attack of illness. *A seizure of coughing kept him in bed for a day.* **sei zures.**

sel dom (sel′dəm), *adv.* hardly ever; rarely. *We seldom see the Jones family since they moved.*

se lect (si lekt′), *v.* 1. to pick out; choose. *We selected green paint for the walls of the room.* **se lects, se lect ed, se lect ing.**

adj. 2. chosen with care; specially picked. *This bakery sells select cakes and cookies.* 3. allowing only certain people to join; not open to all. *That select club chooses its members only from rich or famous families.*

se lec tion (si lek′shən), *n.* 1. the act of selecting; choice. *The selection of the speaker for the assembly was the principal's responsibility.* 2. the thing or things selected. *Have you chosen your selection from the dresses in the store?* 3. an example; a chosen passage. *The textbook contains selections from the writings of famous men.* **se lec tions.**

self (self), *n.* 1. one's own person. *Your self is you. None of us knows the real selves of our friends.* 2. one's own personal interest; one's own welfare. *The doctor put aside all thoughts of self and worked night and day.* **selves** (selvz).

self-con trol (self′kən trōl′), *n.* control of one's self; command over one's actions and feelings. *John kept his self-control during the argument and didn't yell or call names.*

self ish (sel′fish), *adj.* thinking mostly of one-self; not caring much about others. *The selfish man ate all the meat himself and didn't give any to his hungry dog.* **self ish ly,** *adv.*

sell (sel), *v.* 1. to exchange for money or other payment. *Matt sold his old radio for five dollars.* 2. to be on sale; to find buyers. *All books on this table sell for seventy cents. Ice cream sells best in hot weather.* 3. to keep for sale; to deal in. *A bakery sells bread, rolls, cookies, and cakes.* 4. to betray a person or country for money. *The man was so false that he sold his friend for a few pieces of silver.* **sells, sold, sell ing.**

se mes ter (sə mes′tər), *n.* one of the terms of the school year. *Examinations are given at the end of each semester.* **se mes ters.**

sem i an nu al (sem′ē an′yù əl), *adj.* happening or coming twice a year. *The salesman makes a semiannual trip to Europe.* **sem i an nu al ly,** *adv.*

sen ate (sen′it), *n.* 1. a group of persons elected to make laws. *The ancient Romans had a senate. Most of our states have senates.* 2. **Senate,** the upper house of Congress, consisting of two senators from each state. *Congress is composed of the Senate and the House of Representatives, and both make laws for the country.* **sen ates.**

sen a tor (sen′ə tər), *n.* a member of a senate. *A senator in Congress is elected to serve six years.* **sen a tors.**

sen a to ri al (sen′ə tôr′ē əl), *adj.* having to do with a senator or a senate. *The senatorial objection to the new law prevented it from passing Congress.*

send (send), *v.* 1. to cause or order to go. *Let's send a birthday card to Miss Marvin. The principal sent the children home early because of the heavy snowfall.* 2. to drive by force; to make go in a hurry. *The sight of the cat sent the birds flying. The baseball player sent a ball into the stands for a home run.* 3. to make happen. *Cool wind sends relief from the heat.* 4. **send away for,** to order from a distant place. *We sent away for the chair.* 5. **send for,** (a) to summon; to ask someone to come. *The principal sent for Carol.* (b) to place an order for. *We sent for our textbooks six weeks ago.* 6. **send out,** to give forth. *The sun sends out heat and light.* **sends, sent, send ing.**

sen ior (sēn′yər), *adj.* 1. the older. *Leonard Crane's father is Leonard Crane, Senior. The abbreviation of "Senior" is "Sr."* 2. higher in rank; longer in service. *The senior senator from a state is the one who was first elected.* 3. having to

do with the final year at a school or college. *The senior class practiced the graduation march.* *n.* 4. a person in his last year at school or college. *Jim is a senior and his sister is a freshman.* 5. a person of higher rank or longer service. *Mr. Jacobs is the senior of all our teachers.* **sen iors.**

sen ior i ty (sēn yôr′ə tē), *n.* being older; being higher in rank; being longer in service. *Seniority is often a factor in advancing people in business.*

sen sa tion (sen sā′shən), *n.* 1. the ability of one of the five senses: hearing, tasting, seeing, smelling, and feeling. *Because she burned her finger, the sensation of feeling was gone for awhile.* 2. a feeling. *The cool snow gave us the sensation of walking on clouds.* 3. a very excited emotion. *The sensation of landing on the moon swept the country.* **sen sa tions.**

sense (sens), *n.* 1. a power of the body which makes a person aware of things. *The five senses which a human being has are sight, smell, taste, hearing, and touch.* 2. a feeling. *Standing on the corner in winter gives me a sense of cold. When you do your job you have a sense of satisfaction.* 3. judgment; intelligence. *He had the sense to stay out of their silly quarrel.* 4. an understanding; an appreciation. *The comedian on television has a good sense of humor. A good dancer has a sense of rhythm. An artist has a sense of beauty.* 5. the meaning of a word. *The word "senior" has five different senses, according to this dictionary.* 6. **senses,** the ability to think clearly. *If you intend to drive in this storm, you must be out of your senses.* 7. **make sense,** to have a meaning; be sensible. *That speaker made sense.* **sens es.** *v.* 8. to feel; to be aware of. *The king sensed a plot against him.* **sens es, sensed, sens ing.**

sen si ble (sen′sə bl), *adj.* full of good sense; reasonable; wise. *He is too sensible to accept a ride from strangers.* **sen si bly,** *adv.*

sen si bly (sen′sə blē), *adv.* in a sensible way. *He always acts sensibly.*

sen si tive (sen′sə tiv), *adj.* 1. quick to be affected by certain actions, sounds, smells, lights, etc. *A dog's nose is sensitive to the smell of food. Her skin is sensitive to sunlight.* 2. easily hurt. *My aunt is sensitive about remarks relating to her age.* **sen si tive ly,** *adv.*

sent (sent), past tense of **send.**

sen tence (sen′təns), *n.* 1. a group of words that express a complete thought by telling something or asking something. *"Will you come to my party?" is a sentence.* 2. a decision from a judge on the punishment of a person found guilty of breaking the law. *The sentence for the criminal was three years in prison.* **sen tenc es.** *v.* 3. to pass sentence on. *The judge sentenced the speeder to ten days in jail.* **sen tenc es, sen tenced, sen tenc ing.**

sen ti ment (sen′tə mənt), *n.* 1. a feeling in

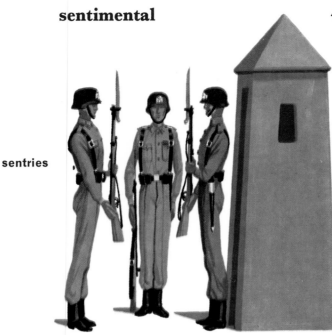

sentries

regard to something; opinion. *His speech about the need for more schools expressed my sentiments exactly.* 2. a thought that is mixed with feeling. *The principal of our school inspires sentiments of loyalty and admiration.* 3. tender feelings, as contrasted with reason and judgment. *Music appeals to sentiment.* 4. an emotion. *Pity and love are sentiments.* 5. a saying that expresses a feeling. *Birthday cards contain serious or clever sentiments.* **sen ti ments.**

sen ti men tal (sen'tə men'tl), *adj.* 1. having tender feelings; full of gentle emotions. *She always becomes sentimental when she listens to romantic music.* 2. of or caused by sentiment. *Ed carries a picture of his family for sentimental reasons.* **sen ti men tal ly,** *adv.*

sen try (sen'trē), *n.* a soldier who guards the entrance to a place to keep away persons who have no right to enter. *Sentries are placed at the entrance to army camps.* **sen tries.**

se pal (sē'pl), *n.* one of the leaflike parts of a flower that are at the bottom of the petals. *The sepals cover the bud until the flower is ready to blossom, and then they spread out.* **se pals.**

sep a rate (sep'ə rāt' for 1–3, sep'ə rit for 4–6), *v.* 1. to divide; to keep apart; to be between. *The new highway separates the two parts of town.* 2. to go apart; to stop being together; to part. *The travelers separated when one went east and the*

sepals (arrows)

other went north. 3. to put or keep apart; to divide into groups. *They separated the pumpkins by size.* **sep a rates, sep a rat ed, sep a rating.**

adj. 4. not connected; set apart. *The men work for the same airplane factory, but in separate buildings.* 5. not shared; for one only. *We have separate desks in school.* 6. single; individual. *The separate parts of an automobile work together to make it move.* **sep a rate ly,** *adv.*

sep a rate ly (sep'ə rit lē), *adv.* in a separate way. *The girls didn't work together; they worked separately.*

Sep tem ber (sep tem'bər), *n.* the ninth month of the year. *September has thirty days.*

se quel (sē'kwəl), *n.* 1. the thing that follows another, earlier happening. *The sequel of her story was that her mother forgave her mistake.* 2. the arrangement of a story in episodes, one following another. *The sequel to that book is just being printed.* **se quels.**

se quence (sē'kwens), *n.* 1. the coming of one thing after another; a succession. *Can you remember the sequence of the acts at the last show we had?* 2. order in which things follow one another. *The children sit at their desks in alphabetical sequence.* 3. the result; something that follows. *The sequence of spending too much is not having any money.* **se quenc es.**

ser e nade (ser'ə nād'), *n.* 1. the music sung or played at night beneath the window of a lady. *She listened to the serenade by the guitar players.* **ser e nades.**

v. 2. to sing or play a serenade to. *The young man serenaded the girl he loved.* **ser e nades, ser e nad ed, ser e nad ing.**

ser ies (sir'ēz), *n.* a number of things placed or happening one after the other. *The newspaper published a series of articles about the town's history. A series of hot days helped the sales of cold drinks. The teams played a series of baseball games.* **ser ies.**

ser i ous (sir'ē əs), *adj.* 1. thoughtful; solemn. *Leonard's face was serious as he did his homework.* 2. in earnest; honest; not joking. *She is serious about becoming a dancer.* 3. needing careful thought; important. *The choice of a job is a serious matter.* 4. dangerous; harmful. *His bump on the head was not serious.* **ser i ous ly,** *adv.*

ser mon (sèr'mən), *n.* 1. a religious talk. *The minister's sermon in church was about thoughtful reading of the Bible.* 2. a serious talk. *Uncle Warren gave us a sermon about dressing neatly and speaking correctly.* **ser mons.**

ser vant (sèr'vənt), *n.* 1. a person whose job is to work in the home of another person. *Cooks, maids, and butlers are servants.* 2. a person who works for a government or the public. *Firemen do a good job as public servants.* **ser vants.**

serve (sèrv), *v.* 1. to work for; to help. *The maid has served them for years. Every citizen should be willing to serve his country.* 2. to perform a term of service or a duty. *The sergeant has served in the army for twenty years. Charlene served as secretary of the club.* 3. to wait on; to bring food to. *The waiter served the guests.* 4. to put food on the table. *Mother served dinner.* 5. to be used; to be of use; to be useful. *A wooden box served as a table in the hut.* 6. to supply; to furnish. *The old car still serves Mr. Keith with transportation.* 7. to treat. *If he has to stay in tonight, it will serve him right for coming home so late last night.* 8. to present. *The landlord served the family with a notice to move by October 1.* 9. in tennis, to put the ball in play by hitting it. *John served the ball to Ted.* **serves, served, serv ing.**

n. 10. in tennis, the act of serving or putting the ball in play. *Whose serve is it now?* **serves.**

serv ice (sėr′vis), *n.* 1. a help; an aid. *The loan of your car was a great service to me. As a service to the passengers, the bus now stops at Oak Street.* 2. the work done for others. *After twenty years his service to the schools has been rewarded. Don't fix the water pipes yourself; you need the services of a plumber.* 3. the way of serving food. *The service in the restaurant was good.* 4. a religious meeting. *Sunday services in the church are held at ten o'clock and four o'clock.* 5. the military. *My cousin is in service.* 6. a set of dishes or other items for serving. *The bride received a service for six people.* **serv ic es.**

v. 7. to put or keep in condition. *The car dealer services the cars he sells for one year.* **serv ic es, serv iced, serv ic ing.**

ses sion (sesh′ən), *n.* 1. a meeting of a class, school, legislative body, court, or club. *During the first session of the Science Club, the students elected Jeff as president.* 2. a large number of meetings coming one after the other. *Congress was in session for six months.* 3. the time when a school, club, etc. meets. *The summer session of school begins in June.* **ses sions.**

set (set), *n.* 1. a group of things that belong together. *We bought a new set of dishes for Mother. A carpenter needs a set of tools. All the odd numbers make up a set.* 2. the way in which a thing is placed. *The set of the boat's sail is good for this wind.* **sets.**

adj. 3. that has been set; fixed, firm, or established. *We follow the set rules of a game. What is the set time for the meeting?* 4. not willing to change; fixed. *That old dog is set in his ways.*

v. 5. to put in a certain place. *Set the television in the corner.* 6. to put in the right position; to put in order; to arrange. *The hunter set a trap for the lion. The doctor set the broken bone in his arm. Set the table for only three people tonight.* 7. to put in some condition. *The rabbit was set free from the trap. The furnace exploded and set the building on fire.* 8. to start. *We set out on the trip at six o'clock in the morning. The teacher's remarks set me thinking about doing better.* 9. to become solid; to make firm. *The new cement in the sidewalk will set in four hours. He set his jaw as he said,*

serenading

"*No.*" 10. to go down; to sink. *The sun was setting in the west.* **sets, set, set ting.**

Set also has the following special meanings:

set about, to begin. *She set about cleaning the room.*

set forth, (a) to start a journey. *He set forth this morning.* (b) to state; make known. *The speaker set forth his ideas about the new rules.*

set in, to begin. *Winter set in early.*

set off, (a) to explode. *The fireworks were set off on the Fourth of July.* (b) to make stand out. *The white dress sets off her tan.* (c) to start. *They set off on their vacation.*

set up, (a) to build. *The city set up an exhibit.* (b) to begin. *He set up a new business.*

set ting (set′ing), *n.* 1. the framework in which a jewel is tightly held. *A diamond was placed in a gold setting to make a ring.* 2. the scenery, costumes, etc. in a play. *The setting of the first act is a living room in a house.* **set tings.**

set tle[1] (set′l), *v.* 1. to agree; decide; to make or come to a decision. *The class settled on Saturday as the day of the picnic.* 2. to establish residence. *The Simpson family has settled in California.* 3. to place in a comfortable position. *The dog settled himself under the table to sleep.* 4. to pay. *John settled his bills on his first payday.* 5. to put or be put in order; arrange. *Mr. Grant has business*

servants

sand, āte, bâre, fäther; sent, mē, fėrn; fit, bīke; pot, rōpe, fôrt; run, pull, rüle, cūte; noise, sound; ch, cheese; ng, long; th, thick; ŧħ, those; zh, treasure; ə = a in about, e in waken, i in animal, o in seldom, and u in minus.

problems to settle before he leaves. 6. to establish colonies in. *The English, Spanish, Dutch, and French settled North America.* 7. to come to rest. *The bird settled on the telephone wire. The cold has settled in my chest. Flakes of snow settled on the ground. The bar of soap settled at the bottom of the tub of water.* 8. to end. *He settled the quarrel between the two children. The two nations settled their differences peacefully.* 9. to quiet. *The medicine settled my stomach.* 10. **settle down,** (a) to become settled. *At last we settled down in our new home.* (b) to act seriously; to become quiet. *The teacher asked the children to settle down and study.* **set tles, set tled, set tling.**

set tle[2] (set′l), *n.* a long wooden bench. *Old-fashioned settles had arms and a high wooden back.* **set tles.**

set tler (set′lər), *n.* one who settles. *The settlers worked together to clear the land.* **set tlers.**

set tle ment (set′l mənt), *n.* 1. a place where a number of people have gone to live; a colony. *There were many English settlements in this land.* 2. a small community or town. *Settlements were formed in great numbers by the pioneers during the expansion of the West.* 3. a settling or being settled. *The settlement of the dispute satisfied both countries.* 4. a payment. *The school received a five-hundred-dollar settlement from the insurance company for damage done by the storm.* 5. a place or building in a crowded neighborhood where families get help and children can play. *Settlements offer classes in English, in cooking, and in music.* **set tle ments.**

sev en (sev′ən), *n.* the next number after six; six plus one; 7. *The sum of seven and seven is fourteen.* **sev ens.**

sev en teen (sev′ən tēn′), *n.* the next number after sixteen; ten plus seven; 17. *The sum of nine and eight is seventeen.* **sev en teens.**

sev enth (sev′ənth), *adj.* 1. coming next after the sixth. *The seventh day of the week is Saturday.* *n.* 2. the one after the sixth. *You are the seventh to call me.* 3. a single one of seven equal parts. *If you divide anything into seven parts of the same size, each part is one seventh.* **sev enths.**

sev en ty (sev′ən tē), *n.* the next number after sixty-nine; seven times ten; 70. *The sum of forty and thirty is seventy.* **sev en ties.**

sev er al (sev′ər əl), *adj.* 1. more than two, but not many. *Several people asked about you today.* 2. separate; different. *The men said good-bye and went their several ways.*

se vere (sə vir′), *adj.* 1. strict; harsh. *It is not easy for a father to be severe with his children.* 2. hard; difficult. *The severe climb up the mountain used up most of his strength. This is a severe examination.* 3. sharp; intense. *The boy suffered severe pain until the doctor came.* 4. simple; plain. *She wore a severe black dress that was more attractive on her than a fancy one would have been.* **se ver er, se ver est; se vere ly,** *adv.*

sew (sō), *v.* 1. to fasten with stitches made by a needle and thread. *She is sewing the buttons on the coat.* 2. to work with a needle and thread. *Her mother taught her how to sew using a machine.* 3. to close by making stitches. *Can you sew up the rip in this coat?* **sews, sewed, sewed** or **sewn, sew ing.**

sew er (sü′ər), *n.* a pipe that is placed under the ground to carry away water and waste matter. *Storm sewers remove rain. Other sewers carry water that has been used in the bathroom or kitchen of a house.* **sew ers.**

sew ing (sō′ing), *n.* 1. the work of someone who sews. *Her sewing won a prize at the school fair.* 2. something to be sewed. *Mother has a basket of sewing to do.*

sex (seks), *n.* the grouping of either male or female into which animals and plants may be divided. *Males are sometimes called the stronger sex, and females the weaker sex.* **sex es.**

shack (shak), *n.* a small house, built very poorly; a hut. *The businessmen built a shack to live in when they went fishing.* **shacks.**

shad (shad), *n.* a large saltwater fish that lives along the Atlantic coast of the United States. *Shad swim into fresh water to lay their eggs.* **shad.**

shade (shād), *n.* 1. a place that is partly dark because it is not in the sun. *We rested in the shade of the trees.* 2. the slight darkness caused by stopping the rays of sunlight. *In the middle of the forest there is always shade.* 3. something that shuts out light. *Window shades keep sunlight out of the house.* 4. the amount of lightness or darkness in a color. *Barry chose a sweater with a dark shade of red.* 5. a small degree or amount. *There was a shade of anger in Joan's voice. Harry is a shade taller than Joe.* 6. a slight difference. *This country allows people to express all shades of opinion about the government.* **shades.** *v.* 7. to cover or protect from strong light or heat. *His dark glasses shaded his eyes from the sun. The big tree shades the house from the heat of the sun.* 8. to make darker in some parts to show shadows or shade. *The artist shaded the ground under the trees in his paintings.* **shades, shad ed, shad ing.**

shad ow (shad′ō), *n.* 1. a dark shape made on a surface by something which cuts off the light. *The big buildings cast their shadows all day on the small building. The shadow of the airplane raced along the ground.* 2. a small amount; a little bit; a trace. *There is not a shadow of a doubt about George's ability to win.* **shad ows.** *v.* 3. to make a shadow upon. *The oak trees shadowed the ground where the cows grazed.* 4. to follow closely and secretly. *The detective*

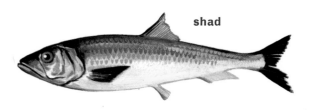

shad

shark

shadowed the man who stole the jewelry. **shad ows, shad owed, shad ow ing.**

shady (shād′ē), *adj.* 1. in the shade. *This shady path is cool and quiet.* 2. giving shade. *Let's sit under the shady trees.* 3. not clearly honest; doubtful. *That business deal sounded shady to the state's attorney.* **shad i er, shad i est; shad i-ly,** *adv.*

shaft (shaft), *n.* 1. the pole or long stick of an arrow, spear, golf club, or rake. *The shaft of the golf club was made of fine steel.* 2. an arrow or spear. *The animal dodged the shafts of the hunters and ran away.* 3. a vertical or inclined passage into a mine. *The miners rode in an elevator down the shaft to their work.* 4. a vertical enclosure in a building. *The elevator shaft is thirty floors high.* 5. a ray or beam. *A shaft of light was seen through the darkness.* 6. a bar which supports the moving parts of an engine or helps make it go. *The drive shaft of an automobile is needed for steering.* 7. a column, or the main part of a column. *Columns in ancient temples consisted of a capital, a shaft, and a base.* **shafts.**

shake (shāk), *v.* 1. to move quickly up and down or from side to side. *After swimming, the dog shook himself to remove most of the water from his body. The wind shook the windows. "Shake well before using" says the label on the medicine bottle.* 2. to tremble. *Sue shook with excitement when her name was announced as the winner. The camper's hand shook from cold as he lighted the fire.* 3. to grasp hands in saying hello or good-bye. *I shook hands with all the guests as they left.* 4. to scatter or throw on or off by short movements. *Shake some salt on your potatoes. Take off your coat and shake the snow from it.* 5. to disturb; to weaken. *My trust in my father has never been shaken.* **shakes, shook, shak en, shak ing.**
n. 6. a shaking. *The shake of his head meant he agreed with us.* **shakes.**

shak er (shāk′ər), *n.* a device used in shaking. *Pass the shaker, please.* **shak ers.**

shall (shal, shəl), *v.* 1. am going to; are going to. *I shall be there tomorrow. We shall see you soon.* 2. to intend to. *I shall study harder this semester.* 3. must; be obliged to. *He shall be there. They shall not beat us.* **shall, should.**

shal low (shal′ō), *adj.* 1. not deep. *The stream is shallow, so we can wade across it.* 2. not having deep feelings or thoughts. *His shallow book report didn't even touch on the main points.* **shallow er, shal low est, shal low ly,** *adv.*

shame (shām), *n.* 1. a guilty feeling caused by doing the wrong thing or a foolish thing. *Shame overcame him when he realized he had been too busy to remember his mother's birthday.* 2. loss of respect; disagree. *Do nothing that will bring shame to your family.* 3. something to be sorry about. *It will be a shame if you aren't able to come to the party.* **shames.**
v. 4. to cause to feel shame; to make ashamed. *The teacher shamed the boy for being late.* 5. to force into something because of a feeling of shame. *Her unhappy looks shamed him into playing the piano, as she wanted.* **shames, shamed, sham ing.**

sham poo (sham pü′), *n.* 1. a liquid or cream used for washing the hair. *The shampoo smelled very good.* **sham poos.**
v. 2. washing the hair with such a mixture. *She shampoos her hair twice a week.* **sham poos, sham pooed, sham poo ing.**

shan't (shant), shall not. *Don't worry; I shan't be late.*

shape (shāp), *n.* 1. form; appearance. *The shape of an apple is round. In the fog, the people were just gray shapes.* 2. condition. *Regular exercise will keep you in good shape.* 3. a condition of being ready; orderly arrangement. *Everything is in shape for the first day in school.* **shapes.**
v. 4. to give shape to; to form. *The children shaped the wet sand.* 5. to develop. *The principal's plans for the new building are shaping up well.* **shapes, shaped, shap ing.**

share (shâr), *n.* 1. a part; a portion. *My share of the pay we received was one dollar. Clarence always does his share of work.* **shares.**
v. 2. to use together. *The brothers share the same room.* 3. to divide into parts. *Let's share the work and finish it faster. Can't you share your candy with me?* 4. to take part in; join in. *If you come, you will share the cost of the trip.* **shares, shared, shar ing.**

shark (shärk), *n.* a large ocean fish that eats other fish. *Some sharks are so fierce that they will attack people in the water.* **sharks.**

sharp (shärp), *adj.* 1. having a fine point or a thin edge for cutting. *The blade of the knife is sharp. The point of a pin is sharp. Cats can climb trees because their sharp claws dig into the wood. A woodpecker has a sharp beak.* 2. pointed; not rounded. *The tin box has sharp edges. The big building rises to a sharp peak.* 3. abrupt; sudden; not gradual. *Slow down the car for the sharp turn just ahead. The lazy boy made a sharp change in his*

---

sand, āte, bâre, fäther; sent, mē, fèrn; fit, bīke; pot, rōpe, fôrt; run, pùll, rüle, cūte; noise, sound; ch, cheese; ng, long; th, thick; ~~th~~, those; zh, treasure; ə = a in about, e in waken, i in animal, o in seldom, and u in minus.

sharpening a knife

sheep

sheepfold

habits and worked hard. 4. very clever; keen. *He understood at once because of his sharp mind. The trainer was sharp in handling the lions.* 5. quickly aware; alert. *A dog has a sharp sense of smell. It takes a sharp eye to see how the magician does his tricks.* 6. harsh; angry. *We were surprised when she made sharp remarks about her friend.* 7. very strong; intense. *The sharp winter winds are blowing. Only once have I had a sharp toothache.* 8. distinct; clear. *They had a sharp difference of opinion. Our television set has a sharp picture.* **sharp er, sharp est; sharp ly,** *adv.*
n. 9. the musical sign (♯) to show that a note is raised by half a tone. *The piano's C sharp was broken.* **sharps.**
adv. 10. exactly. *Please be here at ten o'clock sharp.* 11. keenly; alertly. *Look sharp when crossing streets.*

sharp en (shär′pən), *v.* to put a point on; to give a sharp edge to. *Sharpen your pencil. Knives can be sharpened by grinding them against a rough stone.* **sharp ens, sharp ened, sharp en ing.**

shat ter (shat′ər), *v.* 1. to break into many small pieces. *The baseball shattered the window.* 2. to destroy. *His hopes of seeing the ball game were shattered when his mother asked him to do some errands.* **shat ters, shat tered, shat tering.**

shave (shāv), *v.* 1. to cut hair off closely with a razor. *Most men shave their faces every day.* 2. to cut off in thin slices. *The ham was shaved to the bone.* 3. to come close to; rub lightly against; graze. *The car shaved the garage door.* **shaves, shaved** or **shav en, shav ing.**
n. 4. a cutting off of hair with a razor. *His shave lasts all day.* 5. **close shave,** a narrow escape from danger. *The boy wasn't hurt when the wind blew down the old tree, but it was a close shave.* **shaves.**

shawl (shôl), *n.* a large piece of cloth worn over the shoulders or the head. *Grandmother wears a shawl on cool days.* **shawls.**

she (shē), *pron.* 1. the girl, woman, or female animal spoken about. *She likes to read.* 2. anything thought of as being female, especially a ship or a nation. *The old sailor said, " Yes, she was a good ship."* **they,** *pl.*
n. 3. a girl; woman; female animal. *" Their new dog is a she!" said Sally.* **shes.**

shear (shir), *v.* to cut off. *The rancher hires men to shear the wool from his sheep.* **shears, sheared, sheared** or **shorn, shear ing.**

shears (shirz), *n. pl.* large scissors. *Father uses shears for cutting dead branches from trees. Mother uses shears to cut cloth.*

shed[1] (shed), *n.* a small building used for storing things or animals. *All the farmer's tools are in that shed.* **sheds.**

shed[2] (shed), *v.* 1. to let fall; to drop. *The dog is shedding its hair. My sister always sheds tears at a sad movie.* 2. to throw off. *A raincoat sheds water. Some people shed their worries by working at a hobby.* 3. to give out; to send forth. *The sun sheds light. This book sheds light on the cause of the celebration by explaining exactly what happened.* **sheds, shed, shed ding.**

she'd (shēd), 1. she had. *She'd already sent the message.* 2. she would. *She'd like to go, but she has work to do.*

sheep (shēp), *n.* 1. an animal raised for meat and for the wool that it grows. *Many sheep are raised in the West.* 2. a timid or weak person. *Don't be a sheep, be a man!* **sheep.**

sheep fold (shēp′fōld′), *n.* a place in which sheep are kept. *The sheepfold protects the sheep from wolves.* **sheep folds.**

sheer[1] (shēr), *adj.* 1. thin enough to see partly through. *The sunlight came through the sheer curtains.* 2. complete; absolute. *Sam worked for twelve hours from sheer love of his job. Then he fell asleep from sheer exhaustion.* 3. straight up and down. *The waterfall makes a sheer drop of one thousand feet.* **sheer er, sheer est, sheer ly,** *adv.*

sheer[2] (shēr), *v.* to turn aside; swerve. *The driver of the car sheered to avoid hitting the squirrel.* **sheers, sheered, sheer ing.**

sheet (shēt), *n.* 1. a large piece of cloth used on a bed. *The hotel furnishes clean sheets every day.* 2. a broad, thin piece of anything. *The pond had a sheet of ice on it. The front of the store needs a new sheet of glass.* 3. a single piece of paper. *The teacher handed each of us a sheet of questions.* 4. a surface that is broad and flat. *There wasn't a ripple on the sheet of water.* **sheets.**

shelf (shelf), *n.* a flat piece of wood or metal that is fastened to a wall to hold things. *The clock is on a shelf in the kitchen. Books in a library are kept on shelves.* **shelves** (shelvz).

shell (shel), *n.* 1. the hard outer covering of a fruit, seed, animal, or egg. *We crack the shell of a nut to get to the meat. Crabs, snails, and turtles have shells. The shell of a robin's egg is light blue.*

shepherd

2. anything like a shell. *After the fire, the building was only a shell. The apple pie was baked in a shell of dough.* 3. a light racing boat rowed by a team of men. *Shells are long and narrow and are steered by a man who sits in the stern and directs the crew.* 4. a case holding gunpowder and a bullet to be fired from a gun. *The sailors placed the shell in the ship's gun.* **shells.**

v. 5. to take out of a shell. *Mother asked us to shell the peas.* 6. to separate the kernels or grains of corn from a cob. *The farmer shelled the corn and used it as food for the farm animals.* 7. to fire shells at from large guns. *The enemy's cannons shelled the town.* **shells, shelled, shelling.**

she'll (shēl, shil), she will. *She'll be back by Friday.*

shell fish (shel′fish′), *n.* an animal with a shell that lives in the water. *Lobsters and crabs are shellfish.* **shell fish es** or **shell fish.**

shel ter (shel′tər), *n.* 1. something that covers, protects, or shields. *The old barn was a shelter from the storm.* 2. protection; the condition of being covered or protected. *When the rain started, we found shelter in an old, abandoned house.* **shel ters.**

v. 3. to protect; to give shelter to. *Our house shelters us from the cold weather.* 4. to find shelter. *In winter, the robins sheltered near the house.* **shel ters, shel tered, shel ter ing.**

shelves (shelvz), *n. pl.* more than one shelf. *We need six shelves to hold our books.*

shep herd (shep′ərd), *n.* 1. a man who takes

shells from the sea

racing **shell**

care of sheep. *The shepherds watch their flocks and keep them from danger.* **shep herds.**

v. 2. to lead or to take care of. *The policeman shepherded the little children across the street.* **shep herds, shep herd ed, shep herd ing.**

sher iff (sher′if), *n.* the most important officer to enforce laws in a county. *In large counties a sheriff has a big police force.* **sher iffs.**

shield (shēld), *n.* 1. a piece of armor once carried on the arm by soldiers for protection in battle. *The knight carried his shield.* 2. anything that protects. *There was a shield over the power saw in the woodshop. Dark glasses are a shield against the sun.* **shields.**

v. 3. to protect; to guard. *The raincoat shields you from the rain.* **shields, shield ed, shielding.**

shift (shift), *v.* 1. to move from one person, place, or position to another. *The little boy tried to shift the blame to his brother. The wind shifted from the west to the north.* 2. **shift for oneself,** to make one's own way. *When his parents left town, Bruce shifted for himself for a few days.* **shifts, shift ed, shift ing.**

n. 3. a move from one person, place, or position to another. *The worker made a shift in jobs. Sometimes we have a shift of our ideas.* 4. a group of people working at one time. *The night shift at the factory works from ten o'clock at night until six o'clock in the morning.* 5. a period of time in which work is done. *During the blizzard, the men plowing the snow worked long shifts.* **shifts.**

shin (shin), *n.* 1. the front of the leg below the knee. *Chet was accidentally kicked in the shins during the game.* **shins.**

v. 2. to climb up, using first the hands and then the knees. *We shinned up the tree to get the kite.* **shins, shinned, shin ning.**

shine (shīn), *v.* 1. to give off light. *The sun shines. The searchlight was shining in my eyes.* 2. to make bright; to polish. *I shine my shoes once a week. Mother shined all the knives and forks.* 3. to look bright. *The boys polished the car until it shone.* 4. to be best; to stand out. *Betty shines in spelling.* **shines, shined or shone, shin ing.**

n. 5. a polish. *Give a shine to your shoes.* 6. brightness. *There is a shine on the baby's face.* **shines.**

shin gle (shing′gl), *n.* 1. a small thin piece of material used for covering roofs or walls.

Shingles are placed on roofs so that one laps over another, to keep out rain. **shin gles.**

v. 2. to put shingles on. *The builders shingled the house today.* **shin gles, shin gled, shin gling.**

shin gles (shing′glz), *n. sing.* or *pl.* a disease causing pain and blisters on the skin.

shiny (shīn′ē), *adj.* bright; radiant. *The fresh snow was white and shiny in the morning sun.* **shin i er, shin i est.**

ship (ship), *n.* 1. a large vessel that sails on the oceans. *In former days, ships were moved by sails which caught the wind. The navy has battleships, aircraft carriers, and other kinds of ships.* 2. a rocket for traveling in space. *The ship will take off for the moon in two days.* **ships.**

v. 3. to send. *The family shipped presents early so that they would arrive by Christmas.* 4. to take a job on a ship. *He shipped as a sailor on an ocean liner.* **ships, shipped, ship ping.** (See illustration on following page.)

ship ment (ship′mənt), *n.* the goods sent or delivered to a certain place. *Mr. Jones's dress store receives a shipment from the manufacturer every week.* **ship ments.**

ship wreck (ship′rek′), *n.* 1. the remains of a ship that has been wrecked. *The shipwreck is on the rocks, where the ship was blown during the heavy storm.* 2. the ruin or loss of a ship. *The cargo was lost in a shipwreck.* **ship wrecks.**

v. 3. to destroy; wreck; ruin. *The big ocean vessel was shipwrecked when it hit an iceberg in the fog.* **ship wrecks, ship wrecked, shipwreck ing.**

shirt (shėrt), *n.* a garment for the upper part of the body. *Most shirts have a collar and sleeves, which are either long or short.* **shirts.**

shiv er (shiv′ər), *v.* 1. to shake or tremble from cold, fright, or excitement. *After Mike's walk in the snow, his whole body was shivering. Jan shivered from excitement when she received the prize.* **shiv ers, shiv ered, shiv er ing.**

n. 2. a tremble; a shaking. *A shiver passed through him when the cold wind blew.* **shiv ers.**

shock[1] (shok), *n.* 1. a sudden blow; a violent shake or jar. *Football players wear helmets to lessen the shocks of the hard play.* 2. something that is very disturbing or upsetting. *The news that the old tree would be cut down for the new road was a shock to nature lovers.* 3. the feeling that occurs when an electric current passes through the body. *When Mark touched the two wires on his radio set, he felt a shock.* 4. a weakness of the body caused by severe wounds and pain. *The patient in the hospital was being treated for shock.* **shocks.**

v. 5. to upset; disturb; frighten. *We were shocked when Bill jumped in front of us wearing a mask. The town was shocked at the damage to the crops.* **shocks, shocked, shock ing.**

shock[2] (shok), *n.* 1. stalks of corn or bunches of grain set in a pile. *Shocks of corn and ripe pumpkins are used as decorations on Halloween.* **shocks.**

shoes:
a, b. for women
c, d. for men

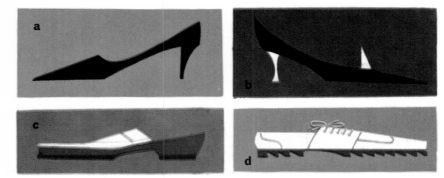

sand, āte, bâre, fäther; sent, mē, fėrn; fit, bīke; pot, rōpe, fôrt; run, pùll, rüle, cūte; noise, sound; ch, cheese; ng, long; th, thick; t̶h̶, those; zh, treasure; ə = a in about, e in waken, i in animal, o in seldom, and u in minus.

SHIELDS

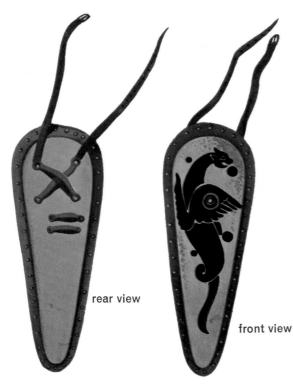

rear view

front view

Norman shield (1066)

shield painted on a tile (sixteenth century)

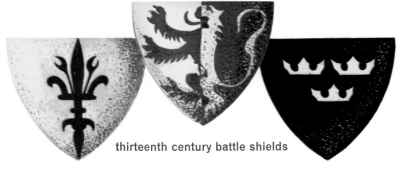

thirteenth century battle shields

shields carved in stone monuments
(fourteenth century)

shields inscribed on coins
(thirteenth and fourteenth century)

SHIPS THROUGH THE AGES

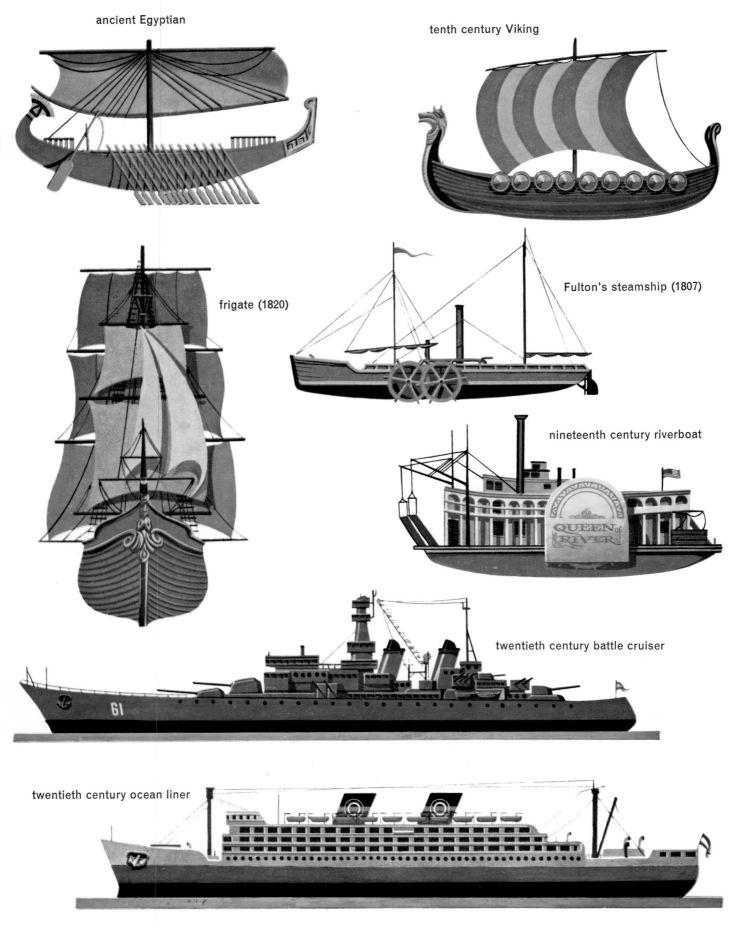

ancient Egyptian

tenth century Viking

frigate (1820)

Fulton's steamship (1807)

nineteenth century riverboat

twentieth century battle cruiser

twentieth century ocean liner

shoeing a horse

v. 2. to put into shocks. *The grain was shocked after it was cut.* **shocks, shocked, shock ing.**

shock³ (shok), *n.* a thick, bushy amount. *The first thing you notice about Al is his shock of hair.* **shocks.**

shoe (shü), *n.* 1. a cover of leather, cloth, or other material for the feet. *Most shoes are made of leather.* 2. a horseshoe. *This shoe on the front hoof is worn.* **shoes.**
v. 3. to make and fit a shoe or shoes. *The blacksmith shoes horses by fastening the metal to their feet.* **shoes, shod, shoe ing.**

shoe mak er (shü′māk′ər), *n.* a person who makes or repairs shoes. *We take our shoes to the shoemaker to be fixed.* **shoe mak ers.**

shone (shōn), past tense and past participle of **shine.**

shook (shŭk), past tense of **shake.**

shoot (shüt), *v.* 1. to hit with a bullet, arrow, etc. *The ranch owner shot the wolf that killed one of his sheep.* 2. to fire a gun. *The policeman shot at a target.* 3. to send out swiftly. *The arrow was shot from the bow. He shot a quick look at me.* 4. to go rapidly; to move fast. *The car shot past us. When the doorbell rings, the dog shoots to the door.* 5. to throw or to play. *The basketball player shoots at a basket. The golf player shoots eighteen holes of golf every Saturday.* 6. to slide a bolt into something that fastens. *When you shoot the bolt on the door, the door is locked.* 7. to go through rapidly. *The men shot the falls in the river.* 8. to put forth buds or branches; to grow. *Warm weather helped the plants to shoot through the ground.* **shoots, shot, shoot ing.**

n. 9. a new part just growing on a plant; a new branch. *In early spring we could see the shoots appearing on the bushes.* 10. a hunting trip. *Some men go on duck shoots in the fall.* **shoots.**

shop (shop), *n.* 1. a small store. *The candy shop is not far from the school. Mother went to the hat shop.* 2. a place where a particular kind of work is done. *The carpenter's shop has many tools. The boy got a haircut in the barber shop.* **shops.**
v. 3. to go to shops and stores to look at things and to buy them. *Mrs. Lee is shopping this afternoon.* **shops, shopped, shop ping.**

shop per (shop′ər), *n.* a person who visits stores to buy things. *On Saturdays the stores are filled with shoppers.* **shop pers.**

shore¹ (shôr), *n.* the land at the edge of a lake, sea, or river. *We like to play in the sand on the shore of the lake.* **shores.**

shore² (shôr), *v.* to support or hold up with long pieces of wood or other material. *The workers shored the beams of the old building.* **shores, shored, shor ing.**

short (shôrt), *adj.* 1. not long. *She wore a short dress. Our short trip lasted only ten minutes.* 2. not tall. *That short boy is liked by everyone.* 3. not having enough. *We are short of gasoline.* 4. brief enough to be thought rude. *He gave a short answer and walked away.* 5. having the sound of *a* as in *add, e* as in *end, i* as in *hit, o* as in *hot,* or *u* as in *pup. Short vowels have no pronunciation mark over them.* **short er, short est; short ly,** *adv.*

n. 6. something short. *The theater has a feature film and two shorts.* 7. **shorts,** short pants. *Men and women wear shorts in hot weather.* **shorts.**
adv. 8. suddenly. *The driver put on the brakes and the car stopped short.* 9. briefly. *Her answer was very short.* 10. not quite reaching the point. *His work fell short of his goal.*

Short also has the following special meanings:
cut short, to end or stop suddenly. *She cut short her talk in order to get home.*

fall short of, to fail to reach. *The arrow fell short of the target.*

for short, as a shorter form. *His name is Benjamin, but we call him Ben for short.*

in short, briefly. *This book is, in short, the best I've read.*

shooting

short age (shôr′tij), *n.* a lack in the amount needed. *The school has a shortage of teachers; it needs three more.* **short ag es.**

short ly (shôrt′lē), *adv.* 1. in a short time; soon. *We will go home shortly.* 2. briefly; in a few words. *I can answer that shortly.*

short wave, *n.* a radio wave sixty meters or less in length. *A special radio set can receive short waves that carry police calls, airplane signals, and foreign broadcasts.* **short waves.**

shot[1] (shot), past tense and past participle of **shoot.**

shot[2] (shot), *n.* 1. the noise of a gun going off. *Two shots were heard in the dark.* 2. small balls of lead for use in a gun. *The hunter removed the shot from the ducks before taking them home.* 3. a person who shoots a gun. *Helen is the best shot in the Gun Club.* 4. a throw. *The basketball player made a good shot at the basket.* 5. a quantity of vaccine or medicine introduced into the body by a needle. *Children get shots which help to prevent them from getting measles and polio.* 6. an attempt; a try. *I'd like to take a shot at being an actor.* **shots; shot** (for 2).

should (shůd, shəd), *v.* 1. have a duty to; ought to. *I should study tonight.* 2. expect to. *We should have this work done tonight.* 3. past tense of **shall.**

should er (shōl′dər), *n.* 1. the part of the human body between the neck and an arm. *The gym teacher said, "Shoulders straight!"* 2. the part of an animal's body between the neck and a front leg. *A horse has powerful shoulders.* 3. the part of a coat or dress that is at the shoulder. *The shoulder of his coat fits closely.* 4. the edge of a road. *The truck driver pulled onto the shoulder*

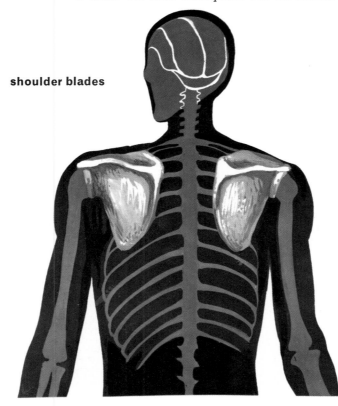

shoulder blades

of the highway to rest for awhile. 5. a cut of meat including the upper part of an animal's front leg and the parts near it. *We had lamb shoulder for dinner.* **should ers.**

v. 6. to push with the shoulders. *We finally shouldered our way through the crowd.* 7. to carry on the shoulders. *The baby likes to be shouldered by her dad.* 8. to take on. *Our room in school shouldered the job of getting the play ready for Thanksgiving.* **should ers, should ered, should er ing.**

shoulder blade, *n.* the flat bone behind each shoulder. *The ball hit me on the shoulder blade.* **shoulder blades.**

shouldn't (shůd′nt), should not. *You shouldn't make noises in class.*

shout (shout), *v.* 1. to call out loudly. *The children shouted with excitement as they played.* **shouts, shout ed, shout ing.**

n. 2. a loud call. *His shouts were heard by everyone in the neighborhood.* **shouts.**

shove (shuv), *v.* 1. to push. *The men shoved the piano across the room.* 2. to push in a rough way. *Passengers in the crowded bus had to shove to get to the exits.* **shoves, shoved, shov ing.**

n. 3. a push. *The big boy accidentally gave the little boy a shove.* **shoves.**

shov el (shuv′l), *n.* 1. a tool with a scoop, used to lift and move dirt, snow, etc. *Get a shovel so we can dig a hole in the sand.* **shov els.**

v. 2. to lift or move with a shovel. *We will have to shovel the snow from the walk.* 3. to make with a shovel. *We shoveled a path in the snow.* 4. to put or throw, as if using a shovel. *The hungry man shoveled his food into his mouth.* **shov els, shov eled, shov el ing.**

show (shō), *v.* 1. to allow to look at; to permit someone to see. *Will you show them the paintings?* 2. to display; exhibit. *The girl's face showed her happiness. The boy showed the new skates to everyone.* 3. to be in sight; appear. *The boy's interest showed when he raised his hand to ask a question. The hole in your sleeve is showing.* 4. to teach; to make clear to; to explain to. *The police captain showed the class how to cross the street.* 5. to point out; to direct; to guide. *I will walk ahead to show the way. I'll show you around the school.* 6. to give. *She always shows kindness to animals.* 7. **show off,** to display in order to make an impression. *Carol likes to show off her pearl ring.* 8. **show up,** (a) to expose. *The rich man was shown up as a selfish person.* (b) to arrive; appear. *Craig didn't show up for work today.* **shows, showed, shown** or **showed, show ing.**

n. 9. a display for the public; a place where things are taken to be looked at. *The automobile show has cars of every kind on exhibition. Mrs. Sills entered her dog in the dog show.* 10. a movie, play, television program, etc. *The Parents' Club of our school put on a show last Friday night.* 11. something that is pretended

dog **show**

or fake. *Gregory's limp is just a show, since he wasn't hurt. His friendship is probably all show.* 12. something that is supposed to attract attention. *The puppy put on a show of being fierce. She wears her jewels for show.* **shows.**

show er (shou′ər), *n.* 1. a short fall of rain. *During the afternoon there were three showers.* 2. a bath in which water comes down on the body in a spray. *Many people take a shower every morning.* 3. anything that falls like rain. *The champions rode down the city street in a shower of bits of paper from office windows. A shower of sparks came from the machinery.* **show ers.**
v. 4. to wet with a spray or drops of water. *Rain showered the crowd at the ball game.* 5. to rain or fall in or as if in a shower. *Telegrams of congratulations showered on the actor after opening night. It showered three times during the night.* 6. to give freely or in abundance. *The relatives showered gifts on the new baby.* 7. to take a shower bath. *The players shower after the game.* **show ers, show ered, show er ing.**

shown (shōn), past participle of **show.**

showy (shō′ē), *adj.* attractive; having much color. *The showy flowers in the park attract many visitors.* **show i er, show i est; show i ly,** *adv.*

shred (shred), *n.* 1. a small piece that has been cut or torn from something; a scrap. *The playful dog left the newspaper in shreds. The bushes tore my shirt into shreds.* 2. a bit; a small amount. *There isn't a shred of evidence that it was Janet who lost the little radio.* **shreds.**
v. 3. to cut or tear into pieces. *The cook shred the cabbage for the salad. That strong wind shredded the flag.* **shreds, shred ded** or **shred, shred ding.**

shrewd (shrüd), *adj.* smart; clever. *The owner of the store was shrewd; he sold it before the big, new store was built across the street.* **shrewd er, shrewd est; shrewd ly,** *adv.*

shriek (shrēk), *n.* 1. a sound that is loud, sharp,

and high-pitched; a scream. *The shriek of the fire siren can be heard for many blocks.* **shrieks.**
v. 2. to make a loud, sharp, high-pitched sound. *The tires shrieked when the car braked suddenly. The children were shrieking with laughter.* **shrieks, shrieked, shriek ing.**

shrill (shril), *adj.* 1. having a high, sharp sound. *When we heard the factory's shrill whistle, we knew it was time to stop work.* **shrill er, shrill est; shrill ly,** *adv.*
v. 2. to make a high, sharp sound. *The whistle shrilled across the football field, starting the game.* **shrills, shrilled, shrill ing.**

shrub (shrub), *n.* a woody plant smaller than a tree; a bush. *A shrub usually has many separate stems starting from the ground. Lilacs and roses grow on shrubs.* **shrubs.**

shrub bery (shrub′ər ē), *n.* a group of low shrubs or bushes. *Shrubbery has been planted at the edge of the park.* **shrub ber ies.**

shud der (shud′ər), *v.* 1. to shake as a result of fear or cold. *I shudder at the thought of going outside in the dark.* **shud ders, shud dered, shud der ing.**
n. 2. this motion. *She gave a shudder when she thought of the frightening story.* **shud ders.**

shuf fle (shuf′l), *v.* 1. to walk with slow, clumsy, dragging steps. *The tired boy shuffled into the room.* 2. to mix up playing cards. *Shuffle the deck of cards and let's start another game.* 3. to move from one place to another. *The teacher shuffled the papers on her desk, trying to find my test.* **shuf fles, shuf fled, shuf fling.**
n. 4. the act of shuffling. *Here are the cards; it's your shuffle.* **shuf fles.**

shut (shut), *v.* 1. to close. *Will you shut the door, please? Shut your eyes and go to sleep.* 2. to fold up; close the parts of. *Shut the folding chairs and put them away.* 3. to enclose; keep from going out. *We shut the dog in the garage so that he wouldn't bother the carpenters.* 4. **shut down,** to stop working; to close for a period of time.

---

sand, āte, bâre, fäther; sent, mē, fèrn; fit, bīke; pot, rōpe, fôrt; run, pùll, rüle, cūte; noise, sound; ch, cheese; ng, long; th, thick; ~~th~~, those; zh, treasure; ə = a in about, e in waken, i in animal, o in seldom, and u in minus.

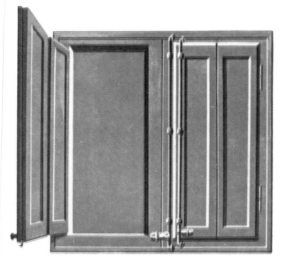

shutters

The factory shuts down during August. 5. **shut off,** to turn off. We shut off all the lights before we left the house. 6. **shut out,** to keep from coming in; to exclude. The curtains shut out most of the sunlight. It isn't nice to shut out the new boy from our games. 7. **shut up,** to close all ways of getting in. We shut up our apartment and went on a vacation. **shuts, shut, shut ting.**

shut ter (shut′ər), n. 1. a cover for a window. The shutters were painted green to match the door. 2. the part of a camera that covers the lens. By opening the shutter, light is allowed to enter the lens and fall on the film. **shut ters.**

shy (shī), adj. 1. uncomfortable in front of strangers. At the party, the shy child didn't say a word all afternoon. 2. easily frightened. A deer is shy. Birds are shy, except for canaries and others kept as pets. **shi er** or **shy er, shi est** or **shy est; shy ly,** adv.

v. 3. to jump back suddenly. The horse shied when the loud noise came. 4. to draw back; to shrink back. The dog shied at going into the cold water for a swim. **shies, shied, shy ing.**

sick (sik), adj. 1. not well; ill; having a disease. Jack stayed home from school yesterday because he was sick. Traveling by boat makes him sick. 2. tired and bored. Don't you get sick of all this cloudy weather? 3. for people who are ill. The man took three days' sick leave from work. 4. troubled by an unhappy feeling. We are sick at the team's defeat, but we'll win next year! **sick er, sick est; sick ly,** adv.

sick le (sik′l), n. a tool with a curved blade and a short handle. A sickle is used for cutting tall grass and grain. **sick les.**

sickles

sick ness (sik′nis), n. illness; poor health. Keith has had only about three days of sickness in his life. **sick ness es.**

side (sīd), n. 1. a surface or a line that bounds something. This box has six sides. There are three sides of a triangle. 2. a surface of an object that is not the front, back, top, or bottom. Use the door at the side to come in the house. 3. either of the two surfaces of a paper, cloth, etc. Write on only one side of the paper. 4. a surface in a certain position. The outer side of the tennis ball feels fuzzy. From the earth we see only one side of the moon. 5. a place or direction. We went to the other side of town. Keep on the right side of the road. 6. the sloping part. The house is on the side of the hill. 7. the right half or left half of the body. I have a pain in my side. 8. any of the groups against each other in a contest or game. Our side won the spelling contest. 9. a part of a family; the relatives of either one's mother or one's father. My family is English on my father's side. 10. a part or quality. She has a happy side that is pleasant. **sides.**

adj. 11. placed on the side. Put this in your side pocket. 12. not so important. The side issues keep us from getting to the big problem. 13. from one side. I had a side view of the building.

v. 14. to take the same position. Most of us sided with Debby in the discussion. **sides, sid ed, sid ing.**

side car (sīd′kär′), n. a small car attached to one side of a motorcycle. A sidecar carries a passenger or packages. **side cars.**

side line (sīd′līn′), n. 1. a line that shows the side of a field used for games. The manager of the football team and the extra players sit behind the sidelines. 2. work that is done that is different from one's main job. As a sideline, the milkman drives a delivery truck. **side lines.**

side walk (sīd′wôk′), n. a path for walking at the side of a street. Sidewalks are usually made of cement, brick, or stone. **side walks.**

side ways (sīd′wāz′), adv. 1. from one side. Seen sideways, the color of the tree was darker. 2. with one side toward the front. He moved his body sideways. Carry this table sideways through the door.

adj. 3. toward one side. John gave the dog a sideways glance. The dog made a sideways movement.

siege (sēg), n. 1. to surround a place for a long time in order to capture it. The army laid siege to the city for three weeks. 2. any persistant attack. Her seige of the flu is over. **sieg es.**

sieve (siv), n. an instrument or device that has holes in it so that liquids and small pieces may pass through, but not the larger pieces. A cook pours flour through a sieve so that there are no lumps. The workman used a sieve to allow only the smaller pebbles through. **sieves.**

sigh (sī), v. 1. to let out a long deep breath. When he finished his homework, he sighed with relief. 2. to make a sound like a person letting out a

sand, āte, bâre, fäther; sent, mē, férn; fit, bīke; pot, rōpe, fôrt; run, pùll, rüle, cūte; noise, sound; ch, cheese; ng, long; th, thick; ~~th,~~ those; zh, treasure; ə = a in about, e in waken, i in animal, o in seldom, and u in minus.

sidecar

deep breath. *The leaves sighed in the wind.* 3. to feel a longing and a sadness. *Some people sigh for the good old days.* **sighs, sighed, sigh ing.**
n. 4. the act or the sound of sighing. *She gave a sigh of sadness because she was leaving her friends.* **sighs.**

sight (sīt), *n.* 1. the power or ability to see. *An aviator's sight must be good. Claire's sight was better when she wore her glasses.* 2. something that is seen. *Father was happy at the sight of the car after we cleaned it.* 3. the distance over which one can see. *The school is in sight. The train passed out of sight down the track.* 4. something that looks strange or odd. *The dog was a sight after he fell into the deep mud puddle.* **sights.**
v. 5. to see. *The sailor sighted land.* 6. to aim. *He sighted the gun at the target.* **sights, sight ed, sight ing.**
Sight also has the following special meanings:
at sight, as soon as seen. *A good player can read music at sight.*
by sight, by having seen, but not by having been friends. *I know Mr. Adams only by sight.*
catch sight of, to see. *I caught sight of the rabbit for just a moment.*
out of sight, where one cannot see. *The car turned the corner and was out of sight.*

sight see ing (sīt′sē′ing), *n.* visiting places that are interesting. *People like to spend vacations by sightseeing in different cities or countries.*

sign (sīn), *n.* 1. a thing or act that stands for something or means something; symbol. *Shaking hands is a sign of friendship. The sign for adding is +. They bowed to the king as a sign of respect.* 2. a board or space used for advertising or for information. *The big sign on the building*

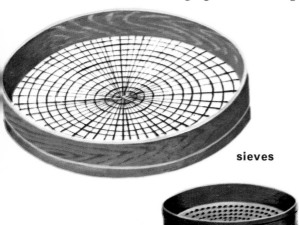

sieves

says, "*Buy Savings Bonds.*" *The traffic sign says,* "*No parking at any time.*" 3. something that indicates or that tells that something is going to happen. *Dark clouds are a sign of rain. Joyce's smile was a sign that she had received a good grade.* **signs.**
v. 4. to write one's name on. *Sign your homework. The officer of the bank signed the check.* **signs, signed, sign ing.**

sig nal (sig′nl), *n.* 1. a sign that gives notice of something. *A red traffic light is a signal for "stop." The ship sent a signal for help by radio. The signal for a fire drill is three rings of the bell.* **sig nals.**
adj. 2. used as a signal. *The signal light was red.* 3. remarkable. *Travel in space is a signal event in science.*
v. 4. to tell by using a signal. *The policeman signaled the driver to stop.* **sig nals, sig naled, sig nal ing.**

sig na ture (sig′nə chər), *n.* 1. a person's name written by himself. *The salesman put his signature on the order.* 2. in music, a sign or set of signs placed at the beginning of a staff to show the key or time in which the music is to be played. *The signature told the musician to play in the key of G.* **sig na tures.**

sig nif i cance (sig nif′ə kəns), *n.* 1. the meaning of something. *Do you know the real significance of the character in the story?* 2. the importance of something. *What the teacher says about the test is of significance to our study for it.* 3. the expressiveness of something. *There was a significance to her quietness.* **sig nif i canc es.**

sig nif i cant (sig nif′ə kənt), *adj.* 1. something full of meaning. *That is a significant story about the discovery of America.* 2. expressive of something. *She has a very significant smile.* 3. something containing a hidden meaning. *Her attitude was significant of the way she felt.* **sig nif i cant ly,** *adv.*

sig ni fy (sig′nə fī), *v.* 1. stand as a symbol or sign of something. *Clouds signify rain.* 2. to make signs, words, or actions to show a feeling. *She signified that she would go by raising her hand.* 3. to be of importance. *What she says always signifies something important.* **sig ni fies, sig ni fied, sig ni fy ing.**

si lence (sī′ləns), *n.* 1. the absence of noise or sound; a stillness. *There was silence in the assembly while the principal spoke.* **si lenc es.**
v. 2. to make quiet; to keep from making noise. *The dog was silenced when he was given a bone. Can't you silence that noisy engine?* **si lenc es, si lenced, si lenc ing.**

si lent (sī′lənt), *adj.* 1. quiet; still; with no sound or noise. *Please be silent in the library so that others may read.* 2. saying nothing; not talking. *He is a silent boy in class, but at recess he talks and shouts when we play.* 3. not said out loud; not spoken. *The businessman's silent wish was to be a fireman. The "e" in "rake" is silent because it is not pronounced.* 4. not active. *A silent*

silkworm and cocoon

partner in a business owns part of it, but does not manage it. **si lent ly,** *adv.*

silk (silk), *n.* 1. a soft, shiny thread that is made by silkworms. *The silkworm spins silk to make its cocoon.* 2. the cloth that is made from this thread. *Some dresses, neckties, stockings, and suits are made of silk.* 3. anything like silk. *Corn silk is found on ears of corn.* **silks.**
adj. 4. made of silk. *I own one silk tie.*

silk grow er (silk′grō′ər), *n.* a person who raises silkworms. *The silkgrower sees that the silkworms live on the right kinds of leaves.* **silk grow ers.**

silk worm (silk′wėrm), *n.* a caterpillar that makes a cocoon of silk threads from which silk is made. *Silkworms live on leaves of a tree called a mulberry.* **silk worms.**

sill (sil), *n.* a board or piece of stone that is the bottom of the frame of a window, door, or house. *The boxes of plants were placed on the window sill to get the sun. The sill of the doorway was worn down by people walking on it.* **sills.**

silly (sil′ē), *adj.* foolish; not sensible. *I was silly to go out in the cold without a coat.* **sill i er, sill i est.**

silt (silt), *n.* 1. fine bits of sand, earth, rock, etc., carried by water and deposited as sediment. *After the flood the land was covered with silt from the river.*
v. 2. to fill up with silt. *The river silted the harbor so that it was too shallow for ships.* **silts, silt ed, silt ing.**

sil ver (sil′vər), *n.* 1. a white precious metal. *Silver is used to make ornaments, spoons, knives, forks, and dishes. Silver is used in making coins, such as the dime, quarter, halfdollar, and dollar.* 2. anything made of silver. *Silver makes a good wedding present.*
adj. 3. made of or looking like silver. *The handsome man had silver hair.* 4. having a clear, pure sound. *We heard the silver song of the church bells on Christmas Eve.*
v. 5. to cover with silver or something resembling its color. *The beauty shop silvered her hair.* **sil vers, sil vered, sil ver ing.**

sim i lar (sim′ə lər), *adj.* almost but not quite the same; alike. *The two boys wore similar*

clothes: dark suits, blue ties, and black shoes. **sim i lar ly,** *adv.*

sim ple (sim′pl), *adj.* 1. easy to understand. *The simple questions did not take long to answer.* 2. plain; bare; with nothing fancy added. *Simple, nourishing breakfasts are served at our house. The teacher told George that she wanted the simple truth.* 3. natural; sincere. *The professor has a simple way of talking.* 4. ordinary. *Most of us will always be simple citizens doing our best.* 5. not having enough experience or intelligence. *A simple man cannot become an astronaut.* **sim pler, sim plest; sim ply,** *adv.*

sim pli fy (sim′plə fī′), *v.* to make something clearer or easier. *The professor simplfiied the science problem by showing me other examples of the same idea.* **sim pli fies, sim pli fied, sim pli fying.**

sim ply (sim′plē), *adv.* 1. plainly; clearly. *Talk to young children simply, in short sentences.* 2. without much ornament; neatly but not fussily. *She is always simply dressed in a light suit.* 3. only; merely. *Don't talk so much; simply answer the question.* 4. really; truly. *The party is simply wonderful!*

sin (sin), *n.* 1. breaking the law of God on purpose; a doing wrong; an offense. *Stealing, lying, and being cruel are sins.* **sins.**
v. 2. to break the law of God; to do wrong. *We sin when we don't help others.* **sins, sinned, sin ning.**

since (sins), *adv.* 1. from a certain time until now. *I bumped my watch two days ago, and it has not worked since.* 2. at some time between a certain time and now. *At first he was not going, but he has since gone.* 3. before now; ago. *Steam engines on railroads have long since disappeared.*
conj. 4. because. *Since I bought a new catcher's mitt, I'd like to give you the old one.* 5. after the time that. *We have not heard from him since he went away.*
prep. 6. ever after. *The school has been on Morton Street since 1958.*

sin cere (sin sir′), *adj.* honest; genuine; really meaning what one says. *Please accept our sincere thanks for this donation to the school.* **sin cer er, sin cer est; sin cere ly,** *adv.*

sing (sing), *v.* 1. to make music with the voice. *The girls were asked to sing on the radio.* 2. to deliver in song. *The glee club will sing, "We're Loyal To You, Benson School," for their first number.* 3. to make pleasant whistling sounds. *Birds sing.* 4. to make a whistling, humming sound. *The kettle of hot water is singing on the stove.* 5. to tell about in song or verse. *The ancient poets sang of the heroes of Greece.* 6. to talk about with excitement. *The teachers sang the praises of one of their pupils who became famous.* 7. to bring into some state or condition by singing. *The mother sang her child to sleep.* **sings, sang** or **sung, sung, sing ing.**

sing er (sing′ər), *n.* a person or bird that sings.

The singers in the church choir practice two nights a week. **sing ers.**

sin gle (sing′gl), *adj.* 1. one and no more; only one. *A single piece of candy is left in the box.* 2. not married. *Two of Mother's friends are single women.* 3. for the use of only one person. *The hotel rents double rooms and single rooms.* 4. having one on each side. *The two knights met in single combat.* **sin gly,** *adv.*

v. 5. to pick out. *Jerry was singled out as the best student and best athlete.* 6. in baseball, to make a one-base hit. *The first man singled, but the next three struck out.* **sin gles, sin gled, sin gling.**

n. 7. in baseball, a one-base hit. *The players got only three singles in the game.* 8. **singles,** in tennis or handball, a game between one person on a side. *My uncle is teaching me how to play singles.* **sin gles.**

sin gu lar (sing′gyə lər), *adj.* 1. exceptional; unusual. *Harry has a singular interest in science.* 2. strange; peculiar. *The old man who lived alone had singular table manners.* 3. in grammar, having to do with only one. *The singular form of "dogs" is "dog."* **sing u lar ly,** *adv.*

sink (singk), *v.* 1. to go down. *The sun sinks in the west. The pebbles sank to the bottom of the goldfish bowl.* 2. to make go under. *The heavy waves sank the little boat.* 3. to dig downward. *The engineers sank a new well.* 4. to fall to a lower level. *The lake has sunk a little because there was no rain. The prices of new cars sank this year.* 5. to make or become weaker; to fail in strength. *Her voice sank to a whisper. The wind is sinking.* **sinks, sank** or **sunk, sunk** or **sunk en, sink ing.**

n. 6. a kitchen or bathroom fixture. *She washed the dishes in the sink.* 7. a sunken place where dirty water stays. *Stay away from the sinks in the prairie.* **sinks.**

sip (sip), *v.* 1. to drink slowly, a little at a time. *Mother sipped her tea.* **sips, sipped, sip ping.**

n. 2. a small drink; a swallow. *Take a sip of this lemonade.* **sips.**

si phon (sī′fən), *n.* 1. a bottle for soda water with a tube inside. *When a valve outside is opened, pressure forces the water out the siphon.* 2. a bent tube or pipe that carries liquid over a higher point. *The siphon must be filled with liquid before the flow will start.* **si phons.**

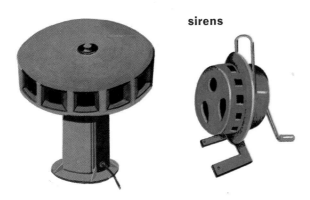

sirens

v. 3. to take out with a siphon. *After the heavy rain the plumber siphoned the water from our basement.* **si phons, si phoned, si phon ing.**

sir (sėr, sər), *n.* 1. a word used to show respect in talking to a man. *Phil said, "I will do it, sir," when he spoke to the principal. The sergeant asked the captain, "May I speak with you, sir?"* 2. **Sir,** a title put before the name of some nobles. *Sir Winston Churchill was a great man.* **sirs.**

sire (sīr), *n.* 1. a title of respect for a king or great noble. *"I will do as you say, Sire," said the servant.* 2. a male parent; male ancestor. *The sire of this colt won sixty races.* **sires.**

v. 3. to be the father of. *This horse sired two champion runners.* **sires, sired, sir ing.**

si ren (sī′rən), *n.* 1. a kind of whistle that makes a loud, high sound. *Fire engines use their sirens on the way to a fire.* 2. in ancient Greek and Roman mythology, a creature like a woman who sang sweetly. *The sailors crashed their ships on the rocks as they came closer to hear the sirens.* **si rens.**

sis (sis), *n.* an informal term for sister. *Is Mother home yet, sis?*

sis sy (sis′ē), *n.* a shy or cowardly man or boy. *The other boys called him a sissy because he never joined in their rough games.* **sis sies.**

sis ter (sis′tər), *n.* 1. a girl or woman having the same parents as another person. *There were three girls and one boy in the family, so the boy had three sisters.* 2. an unusually close friend. *Carol is like a sister to Debby because they know each other so well.* 3. a member of the same club or church. *The minister asked the people to call on their ill sister.* 4. a woman who belongs to a religious society. *The Sisters of the Poor do wonderful work in that neighborhood.* **sis ters.**

sit (sit), *v.* 1. to rest on the lower part of the body. *I will sit in this big chair. The dog sat and looked at us.* 2. to make sit; to seat. *Will you sit your little brother over there? Sit yourself over here.* 3. to settle; to rest. *The bird sat on the branch.* 4. to be located. *The island sat in the middle of the lake. The car is sitting in the garage.* 5. to press or weigh. *The duties and worries of his job sat heavily upon him.* 6. to hold a session. *The Supreme Court will sit next week.* 7. to pose. *The class will sit for a photograph today.* **sits, sat, sit ting.**

Sit also has the following special meanings:

sit down, to be seated. *The teacher asked us to sit down.*

sit in, to take part in. *Mr. Greenleaf sits in Congress. Would you like to sit in the card game?*

sit on, to be a member of a jury. *My father is sitting on a jury that is hearing a case about an auto accident.*

sit out, to remain seated until the end of. *The party was no fun, but I sat it out.*

sit up, (a) to raise the body to a sitting position. *We told our dog to sit up.* (b) to pay attention. *The news made us sit up.*

siphon

skiing:
 a. ski lift
 b. descending a slope
 c. equipment

sit ting (sit′ing), *n.* 1. a meeting or a session of a court or legislature. *At this sitting, the members want to pass a bill giving the state more parks.* 2. a time of being seated. *You can read this book in one sitting.* **sit tings.**
adj. 3. having to do with sitting. *We trained the dog to stay in a sitting position.*

sit u ate (sich′ü āt), *v.* 1. to be located at a site. *Our house is situated on Elm Street.* 2. to settle; place oneself. *I situated myself at the back of the room.* **sit u ates, sit u at ed, sit u at ing.**

sit u at ed (sich′ü ā′tid), *adj.* located; placed. *The store is situated on a busy corner.*

sit u a tion (sich′ü ā′shən), *n.* 1. place; location. *The situation of the new road is convenient to the school.* 2. condition; the way things are. *I faced an uncomfortable situation when I had to explain why I was late.* 3. job; position. *Our teacher has a situation in a library during the summer.* **sit u a- tions.**

six (siks), *n.* the next number after five; five plus one; 6. *The sum of two sixes is twelve.* **six es.**

six teen (siks′tēn′), *n.* the next number after fifteen; ten plus six; 16. *The sum of two eights is sixteen.* **six teens.**

sixth (siksth), *adj.* 1. coming next after the fifth. *The sixth boy in line is my brother.*
n. 2. the one after the fifth. *Thelma was the sixth to arrive.* 3. a single one of six equal parts. *Since there are six kittens, give each one a sixth of the milk.* **sixths.**

six ty (siks′tē), *n.* the next number after fifty-nine; ten times six; 60. *The sum of forty and twenty is sixty.* **six ties.**

size[1] (sīz), *n.* 1. the amount of space that a thing takes up; the proportions or dimensions of anything. *Look at the enormous size of that airplane! The size of the mountain makes the mountain climbers look like ants from here. Books are sold in many sizes.* 2. one of a series of measures. *This store has three sizes of oranges: small, medium, and large.* **siz es.**
v. 3. to sort or arrange according to size. *A machine sizes the peas after they come from the fields.* **siz es, sized, siz ing.**

size[2] (sīz), *n.* 1. a thin paste or glue. *Size is put on cloth and paper to make it stiff.* **siz es.**
v. 2. to put size on. *They sized the paper before putting paint on it.* **siz es, sized, siz ing.**

skate[1] (skāt), *n.* 1. a narrow metal blade fastened onto a shoe for moving over ice. *We had our skates sharpened before we went skating.* 2. a shoe with four wheels used for moving on the ground; a roller skate. *You can rent roller skates at the skating arena.* **skates.**
v. 3. to move along on skates. *Don't skate so fast.* **skates, skat ed, skat ing.**

skate[2] (skāt), *n.* a kind of broad, flat fish that lives in the ocean. *A skate has a long, slender tail.* **skates.**

skat er (skāt′ər), *n.* a person who skates. *The frozen pond was filled with skaters.* **skat ers.**

skel e ton (skel′ə tn), *n.* 1. the framework of a body, supporting or protecting the muscles and organs. *All of the bones of the human body make up the skeleton. The shell of a snail is its skeleton.* 2. a framework. *The steel skeleton of a building is put up first, then the walls and windows and floors.* **skel e tons.**

sketch (skech), *n.* 1. a simple drawing that is made quickly. *The artist drew sketches of the people in the park.* 2. an outline of a story or an article, giving the main points. *The author had a notebook of sketches that might be used in writing a book.* 3. a little play or act. *The school presented a group of sketches instead of a long play.* **sketch es.**
v. 4. to draw sketches of. *The art students sketched the people in the parade as it passed.* 5. to prepare an outline of. *Tonight I will sketch the article; tomorrow I will write it.* **sketch es, sketched, sketch ing.**

ski (skē), *n.* 1. one of two long, slender pieces of wood or metal that can be fastened to a

sand, āte, bâre, fäther; sent, mē, fėrn; fit, bīke; pot, rōpe, fôrt; run, pull, rüle, cūte; noise, sound; ch, cheese; ng, long; th, thick; ~~th,~~ those; zh, treasure; ə = a in about, e in waken, i in animal, o in seldom, and u in minus.

SKELETON

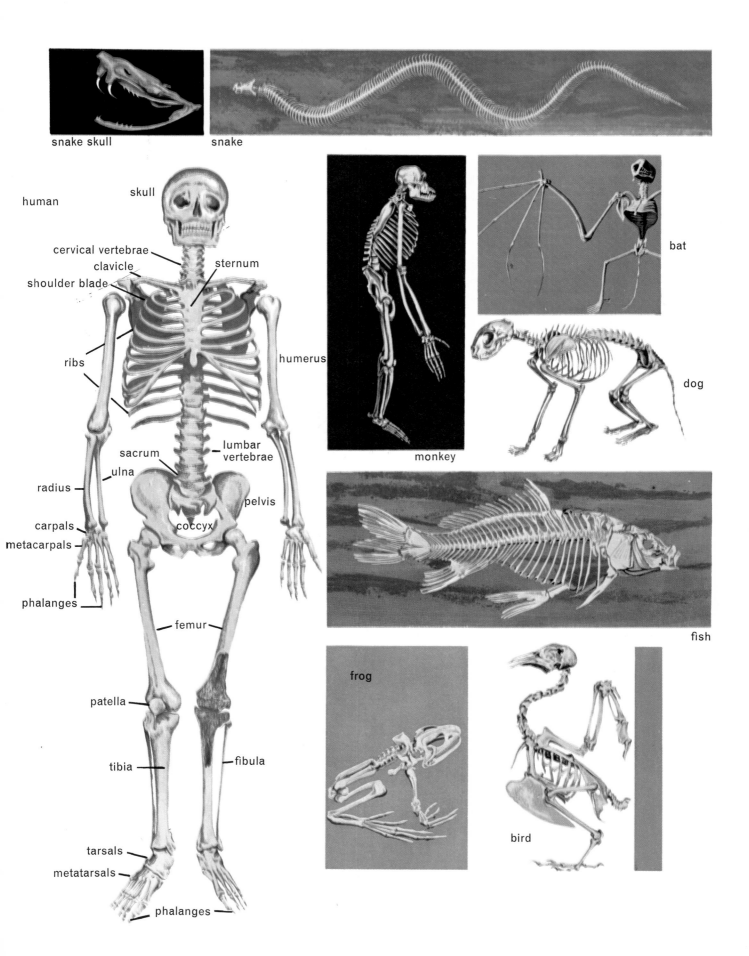

snake skull

snake

human

skull

cervical vertebrae

clavicle

shoulder blade

sternum

ribs

humerus

sacrum

lumbar vertebrae

ulna

radius

pelvis

carpals

coccyx

metacarpals

phalanges

femur

patella

fibula

tibia

tarsals

metatarsals

phalanges

monkey

bat

dog

fish

frog

bird

shoe. *Skis are used for gliding over the snow.* **skis** or **ski.**

v. 2. to glide over the snow on skis. *They skied swiftly down the hill.* **skis, skied, ski ing.**

skill (skil), *n.* 1. the ability to do something well as a result of practice. *The teacher had the skill to manage the children. His skill in playing the violin will some day make him famous.* 2. an art; an ability to use knowledge. *Language skills and arithmetic skills are taught in schools.* **skills.**

skill ful or **skil ful** (skil′fəl), *adj.* having ability; showing the skill to do something well. *She is a skillful piano player because she practices every day.* **skill ful ly** or **skil ful ly,** *adv.*

skin (skin), *n.* 1. the outer layer of an animal body or of a plant. *Alan has a small cut on his skin. The skin of a cow is thick. The apple had a red skin.* 2. the hide of an animal. *That expensive fur coat is made from the skins of beavers.* **skins.**

v. 3. to scrape the skin of. *I skinned my knees on the sidewalk when I fell off the wagon.* 4. to take the skin off. *The hunter skinned the deer.* **skins, skinned, skin ning.**

skip (skip), *v.* 1. to jump or leap lightly off the ground. *The little children skipped on their way to school.* 2. to jump lightly over. *Boxers skip rope to exercise the muscles in their legs.* 3. to bounce or make bounce while crossing a surface. *A small flat stone can be thrown so that it skips across smooth water. The boy skipped the pebble across the pond.* 4. to leave out. *This book is very good, but you can skip the first chapter. "Don't skip your breakfast today," said Mother.* 5. to stay away from. *The teacher said I could skip school on the day my brother came home from the Army.* **skips, skipped, skip ping.**

n. 6. a light leap or jump. *The little boy came home with short skips.* **skips.**

skirt (skėrt), *n.* 1. the part of a dress that hangs below the waist. *She wore a dress with a long skirt.* 2. a garment for a woman or girl that

skunk

hangs from the waist. *Many girls wear a sweater and skirt.* 3. **skirts,** the outer part; the edge. *The fence was built on the skirts of the property.* **skirts.**

v. 4. to pass along the edge of. *We skirted the city to get away from the heavy traffic.* **skirts, skirt ed, shirt ing.**

skull (skul), *n.* the bones of the head; the group of bones that encloses and protects the brain. *The skull can take a hard blow without injury to the brain.* **skulls.**

skunk (skungk), *n.* 1. a small animal with a bushy tail and dark fur that has a white stripe down the middle. *A skunk protects itself by giving off a bad-smelling liquid when it is attacked or frightened.* 2. the fur of this animal. *Skunk is used for coats and jackets.* 3. a person who is mean or bad. *In the movie, the cowboy called the horse thief a skunk.* **skunks.**

sky (skī), *n.* 1. the air high above the world; the upper atmosphere. *On most days the sky in this region is blue with white clouds. Birds and airplanes fly high in the sky.* **skies.**

sky scrap er (skī′skrā′pər), *n.* a very tall building. *New York City and Chicago have many skyscrapers.* **sky scrap ers.**

slam (slam), *v.* 1. to shut hard with a loud noise. *Don't slam the door or you will wake up the baby. The gate slammed shut in the wind.* 2. to hit or throw with force and noise. *The baseball player slammed the ball for a home run. The boys slammed their textbooks on the table and hurried outside to play.* **slams, slammed, slam ming.**

n. 3. a noisy shutting; a loud hitting. *The slam of the car door at night woke up the dog.* **slams.**

slant (slant), *v.* 1. to slope. *That tree slants to one side because of the heavy winds. Most houses are built with roofs that slant downward. The picture hanging on the wall slanted, so Father straightened it.* **slants, slant ed, slant ing.**

n. 2. a slope; a leaning to one side. *The road has an upward slant from here. The flagpole has a slant that the workmen will fix.* **slants.**

slap (slap), *v.* 1. to hit with the open hand. *John slapped his friend on the back and said, "Good work!" To teach the puppy to stay off chairs, we slap him gently every time he jumps on one.* 2. to place noisily or carelessly. *He slapped his books down on the desk. He slapped a sandwich together and hurried back to the television program.* **slaps, slapped, slap ping.**

n. 3. a blow with the open hand or with something flat. *She gave the fly a slap with a folded newspaper.* **slaps.**

slate (slāt), *n.* 1. a gray rock that splits into thin, smooth layers. *Slate is used to cover roofs and for chalkboards or blackboards.* 2. a small blackboard. *Years ago each school child had a slate to write on with chalk.* **slates.**

slave (slāv), *n.* 1. a person who is the property of another person and has no freedom. *A king in ancient times had many slaves to work for him.*

sleigh

slice

2. a person who works long and hard at a job. *The store manager was a slave to his work and never took a vacation.* **slaves.**

v. 3. to work long and hard. *The mother slaved for her children.* **slaves, slaved, slav ing.**

slav ery (slāv′ər ē). *n.* 1. the condition of being a slave. *The people captured by armies in ancient times were often sold into slavery.* 2. the owning of slaves. *Slavery was ended in this country over one hundred years ago.* 3. long, hard work. *Some of the time his job was slavery, and he had no time to rest.*

sled (sled), *n.* 1. a low platform on runners that slides over ice and snow. *It is fun to coast down a hill on a sled. The Eskimos use sleds that are pulled by dogs.* **sleds.**

v. 2. to travel on a sled. *We went sledding after the first snowfall of the winter.* **sleds, sled ded, sled ding.**

sleek (slēk), *adj.* 1. smooth, soft, and shiny. *The black cat had sleek fur. Much brushing made Bea's hair sleek.* 2. smooth in speech and action. *A sleek salesman never argues with a customer.* **sleek er, sleek est; sleek ly,** *adv.*

v. 3. to smooth down. *My mother thinks that boys should sleek their hair.* **sleeks, sleeked, sleek ing.**

sleep (slēp), *n.* 1. the resting of body and mind; not being awake. *Most people need eight hours of sleep at night.* 2. a condition that seems like real sleep. *A hibernating bear spends the winter in sleep.*

v. 3. to be asleep; to rest the body and mind. *A healthy person sleeps about eight hours at night.* 4. to be in a condition like sleep. *The bear will sleep through the winter.* 5. **sleep away,** to waste or spend in sleeping. *I slept away the morning when the alarm didn't go off.* **sleeps, slept, sleep ing.**

sleep er (slēp′ər), *n.* 1. a person who sleeps. *Light sleepers wake up at the smallest noise.* 2. a railroad car that has sleeping accommodations. *You can ride in a sleeper from Chicago to New York.* **sleep ers.**

sleepy (slēp′ē), *adj.* 1. ready to go to sleep. *At ten o'clock at night John feels sleepy. The sleepy dog spends most of his time lying down.* 2. quiet; not active. *The sleepy little town was changed when the big factory opened.* **sleep i er, sleep i est; sleep i ly,** *adv.*

sleet (slēt), *n.* 1. rain that freezes into tiny pieces of ice as it falls. *The sleet stuck to the branches of trees and reflected the light from the street lamps.*

v. 2. to come down as sleet. *It is sleeting and the sidewalks are slippery.* **sleets, sleet ed, sleet ing.**

sleeve (slēv), *n.* the part of a garment that covers an arm. *During summer, boys wear shirts with short sleeves.* **sleeves.**

sleigh (slā), *n.* 1. a carriage with runners instead of wheels, used for traveling on ice or snow. *After the snowfall, we rented a sleigh for a ride in the country.* **sleighs.**

v. 2. to travel in a sleigh. *The senior class went sleighing during Christmas vacation in a large sleigh pulled by two horses.* **sleighs, sleighed, sleigh ing.**

slen der (slen′dər), *adj.* 1. thin; not big around. *This slender tree bends when the wind blows hard.* 2. small; slight; not great or strong. *The team had only a slender chance to win, but the boys tried as hard as they could. There is a slender hope that Janet will not get the mumps.* **slen der ly,** *adv.*

slept (slept), past tense and past participle of **sleep.**

slice (slīs), *n.* 1. a thin, flat piece cut from something. *Give everyone a slice of bread. How many slices of meat do you want on your sandwich?* **slic es.**

v. 2. to cut into slices. *Father sliced the watermelon.* **slic es, sliced, slic ing.**

slid (slid), past tense and past participle of **slide.**

slide (slīd), *v.* 1. to move smoothly and easily. *The man on skis slid swiftly down the snowy mountainside. The window got stuck as she was sliding it open.* 2. to move quietly or without being seen. *The dog slid into the room while we were watching television.* 3. to pass gradually.

slide

slippers

The summer days are sliding by and soon it will be autumn. A person can slide into the habit of putting things off. 4. to slip and fall. *The wet bar of soap slid from my hands.* **slides, slid, slid** or **slid den, slid ing.**

n. 5. a smooth surface on which a person can slide. *Children like to go down the slide in the playground. Ice sometimes makes a good slide.* 6. an act of sliding. *The slide on the toboggan made his cap fly off.* 7. a mass of earth, rocks, or snow that falls down a hill or mountain. *The slide buried the trees in its path.* 8. a small piece of glass to hold things for study under a microscope. *We looked through the microscope at the drop of water on the slide.* 9. a piece of glass or film with a picture on it. *Jean showed all the children in class the slides of her vacation.* **slides.**

slight (slīt), *adj.* 1. not big; small; slender. *The slight athlete fooled all the experts by becoming the star player on the football team.* 2. small in amount, size, etc. *The store will deliver your groceries for a slight charge. Bill has a slight bump on his head from slipping on the ice.* **slight er, slight est; slight ly,** *adv.*

v. 3. to pay little attention to; to neglect or treat rudely. *If you slight your lessons, your grades will not be good. Mrs. Quinn slighted Mrs. Norris by not asking her to the party.* **slights, slight ed, slight ing.**

n. 4. an act showing neglect or lack of consideration. *Margaret paid no attention to the slights of the other girls.* **slights.**

slight ly (slīt′lē), *adv.* 1. to a small degree. *The dog is only slightly ill.* 2. in a slight manner; slenderly. *The child is slightly built.*

sling (sling), *n.* 1. a weapon of ancient times made of a piece of leather with heavy strings attached to both ends. *A stone was held by the leather and the sling was spun overhead by the strings until the stone was flung out.* 2. a stick in the shape of a "Y" with a rubber band stretched across the top. *Slings can shoot small stones.* 3. a cloth which hangs from the neck to support an arm that is hurt. *The doctor put Kay's arm in a sling.* 4. a rope or chain that can be used to lift or hold heavy objects. *The piano was lifted into the apartment by a sling.* **slings.**

v. 5. to carry; to hold; to hang. *The Boy Scout slung his pack over his shoulders.* 6. to throw. *We were slinging stones into the lake to see who could throw the farthest.* **slings, slung, sling ing.**

slip¹ (slip), *v.* 1. to move quietly without being noticed. *The movie star slipped into town before the crowds reached the airport. Time slips by when you are enjoying yourself.* 2. to move or drop by accident. *The wet dish slipped from her hands.* 3. to slide suddenly; to lose one's balance. *The dog slipped on the icy sidewalk.* 4. to put on or take off easily and quickly. *He slipped on his jacket. Helen slipped off her sneakers.* 5. to put, move, pass, slide, etc. smoothly or quietly. *Slip this package in your pocket. Slip the bolt on the door after you come in. Sue slipped a note to Jean during class.* 6. to fall from a certain level. *The baseball player's batting average has slipped this year.* **slips, slipped, slip ping.**

n. 7. a place between piers where a ship stays. *The big vessel moved slowly into the slip.* 8. a fast move; an escape. *The small boy made a slip for the candy counter.* 9. a small mistake. *He doesn't make many slips in adding. By a slip of the tongue, I said "I'm glad you're going" instead of "I'm sorry you're going."* 10. a falling down. *Our neighbor nearly had a slip on the waxed floor.* 11. a fall from a certain level. *There has been a big slip in the cost of electricity.* 12. a garment worn by women beneath their outer clothes. *A slip is the same length as a skirt.* 13. a cover for a pillow. *Mother puts clean slips on every week.* **slips.**

slip² (slip), *n.* 1. a small piece or strip of paper, wood, etc. *Write your name on a slip of paper. Don't lose your sales slip for the dress.* 2. a small branch cut from a plant to grow a new plant. *We planted the slips from the lilac bush.* **slips.**

slip per (slip′ər), *n.* a light, low shoe without laces that can easily be slipped on or off.

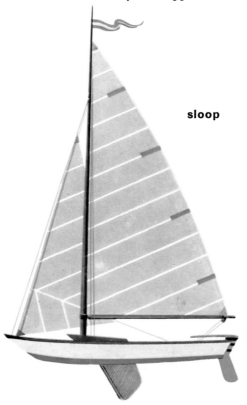

sloop

sloth

Slippers are worn around the house by men and women. **slip pers.**

slip pery (slip′ər ē), *adj.* 1. able to cause slipping. *A sidewalk covered with ice is slippery. Careful drivers go slowly on a street that is slippery from rain.* 2. slipping away easily. *The slippery bar of soap seemed to jump from his hands.* 3. not reliable; not to be depended on. *I liked the way the man talked, but Father said he sounded slippery.* **slip per i er, slip per i est.**

slit (slit), *v.* 1. to make a straight, narrow cut in. *The best way to open an envelope is to slit it at the top.* 2. to cut into strips. *We slit the old sheet to make cloths to polish the car.* **slits, slit, slitting.**
n. 3. a long, straight cut or tear. *There is a slit in the paper bag.* 4. an opening that is narrow. *Light came through the slit between the door and the floor.* **slits.**

slo gan (slō′gən), *n.* a word, phrase, or sentence used in advertising, business, or by individuals to promote something. *The slogan for the toothpaste was, "Gets teeth cleaner."* **slo gans.**

sloop (slüp), *n.* a small sailboat with one mast. *A sloop has two sails.* **sloops.**

slope (slōp), *n.* 1. land that slants up or down. *The children like to roll down the small slope in the park.* 2. the amount of slant. *The mountain rises in a steep slope. This farm has a slight slope that carries the water from rain and snow down to the river.* **slopes.**
v. 3. to slant. *The road slopes upward to the top of the hill. The roof on that house slopes to carry off rainwater.* **slopes, sloped, slop ing.**

sloth (slōth, slôth), *n.* 1. a slow-moving animal that lives in South America. *Sloths hang upside down from the branches of trees, their long, curved claws holding them.* 2. lazy nature. *The boy's sloth made him always late.* **sloths.**

slouch (slouch), *v.* 1. to walk or stand with the head and shoulders bent forward. *The tired man slouched along the street.* **slouch es, slouched, slouch ing.**
n. 2. a person who walks or stands like this.

He doesn't have good posture; he is a slouch. **slouch es.**

slow (slō), *adj.* 1. not fast or quick. *We rode on a slow train that made all stops. He is a slow worker and takes lots of time to complete his lessons.* 2. behind time. *Your watch is ten minutes slow.* 3. not quick to understand. *That slow student needs more help.* 4. not lively or active. *The papers say that business is slow at this time of year.* **slow er, slow est; slow ly,** *adv.*
v. 5. to go slower; to go with less speed. *A driver slows down and stops when he comes to a red light.* **slows, slowed, slow ing.**
adv. 6. in a slow way. *Walk slow in the school halls.*

slum ber (slum′bər), *v.* 1. to sleep. *Frank slumbered all night.* 2. not active. *The ancient city had slumbered in the jungle for years.* **slumbers, slum bered, slum ber ing.**
n. 3. sleep. *Don't wake him from his slumber, because he needs the rest.* **slum bers.**

sly (slī), *adj.* 1. able to do things without letting others know; cunning. *That sly dog grabbed a cookie from the table while no one was in the room.* 2. tricking or teasing in a humorous way. *The boys played a sly joke on their friends by pretending they forgot to bring the food for the picnic.* **sli er** or **sly er, sli est** or **sly est; sly ly,** *adv.*

smack[1] (smak), *n.* 1. a slight taste or flavor. *The ice cream has a smack of chocolate.* 2. a little bit. *There is a smack of truth in his joke.* **smacks.**
v. 3. to have a taste; to have a little. *The sea air smacked of salt.* **smacks, smacked, smack ing.**

smack[2] (smak), *n.* 1. a sharp sound made by opening the lips suddenly. *He gave a smack of pleasure after the first bite of the cake.* 2. a loud kiss. *The little girl gave her uncle a smack on the cheek.* 3. a slap. *I gave the fly a smack with the magazine.* **smacks.**
v. 4. to make a sharp sound by opening the lips suddenly. *We smacked our lips when we smelled the pudding on the stove.* 5. to kiss loudly. *She smacked her father on the cheek and said goodnight.* 6. to slap; to hit with the flat of the hand. *His employer smacked Joe on the back happily and said, "You'll be good at this job."* **smacks, smacked, smack ing.**

smack[3] (smak), *n.* a small sailboat with one mast. *A smack usually has two sails.* **smacks.**

small (smôl), *adj.* 1. little. *A cub is a small bear. People live in small towns and in big cities. He owns a small business.* 2. not important. *Pamela wastes a lot of time worrying about small matters.* 3. mean; not kind. *It was small of Mr. Peterson not to let the shivering dog come into his garage to get warm.* **small er, small est.**
Small also has the following special meanings:

small hours, the early hours after midnight. *The meeting lasted until the small hours.*

small letters, letters of the alphabet that are not capital letters. *This sentence is printed in small letters except for the " T " in the first word.*

small of the back, the narrowest part of a person's back. *After the game, the football player had a pain in the small of his back.*

small talk, light conversation; talk that is not important. *After some small talk, the meeting began.*

small pox (smôl′poks′), *n.* a disease that causes a high fever and sores on the skin. *Children are given vaccine so that they won't get smallpox.*

smart (smärt), *adj.* 1. intelligent; clever; quick in mind. *Don is smart in mathematics.* 2. neat; clean. *The members of the band were smart in their new uniforms.* 3. in the newest style; in the latest fashion. *The magazine showed pictures of this year's smart dresses.* 4. sharp and keen. *I felt a smart pain when the bee stung me.* 5. causing sharp pain. *I banged into the tree and got a smart blow on the head.* 6. active; fast. *The gym teacher said we should walk at a smart pace.* **smart er, smart est; smart ly,** *adv.*
v. 7. to cause a sharp, stinging pain. *The water is so cold that it smarts.* 8. to feel sharp, stinging pain. *My eyes smarted from the smoke of the campfire.* 9. to feel troubled or upset. *The player smarted from the coach's criticism.* **smarts, smart ed, smart ing.**
n. 10. a sharp pain. *The smart of the little cut was gone in a few minutes.* **smarts.**

smash (smash), *v.* 1. to break into pieces. *The ball smashed the window. The plate smashed when Anne dropped it.* 2. to wreck; to destroy. *My uncle's business was smashed by the fire, but he started a new store with the insurance money.* 3. to crash; to move violently. *When the ship smashed into the rocks, the captain and crew escaped safely.* **smash es, smashed, smash ing.**
n. 4. the act or sound of smashing. *The smash of glass woke me.* 5. a crash. *One expressway lane was closed because of a bad smash near the exit.* **smash es.**

smear (smir), *v.* 1. to cover or spread with something sticky or greasy. *The baby smeared jelly on his face. The boy smeared butter on his toast.* 2. to soil; to hurt; to harm unfairly. *The politicians tried to smear the governor's reputation in order to elect the man they chose.* **smears, smeared, smear ing.**
n. 3. a stain; a mark; a spot left by something rubbed on. *The dog had smears of mud all over his body.* 4. a hurting or harming of a person's reputation. *The court of law ruled that the magazine had printed smears about the college president.* **smears.**

smell (smel), *v.* 1. to get the odor or scent of through the nose. *We smelled the pudding that Sue was cooking for dinner.* 2. to sniff at; to breathe in the odor of. *The dog trotted through the house, smelling the carpets and furniture. I like to smell lilacs and roses.* 3. to give out an odor.

snail

Perfume smells sweet. 4. to give out a bad odor. *Garbage smells.* **smells, smelled, smell ing.**
n. 5. an odor; a scent. *The smell of orange blossoms filled the air.* 6. the sense of smelling. *A dog's smell is much sharper than a person's.* 7. the act of smelling; sniffing. *The dog traveled two miles home in the dark by smell.* **smells.**

smile (smīl), *v.* 1. to look happy or amused by turning up the mouth at the corners. *The teachers smiled as we sang our songs at the assembly.* 2. to show with a smile. *He smiled a welcome at the new boy.* 3. to put with a smile. *Smile your troubles away.* **smiles, smiled, smil ing.**
n. 4. the act of smiling; a smiling expression. *There were smiles in the audience when the clowns appeared. A smile can make your day brighter.* **smiles.**

smog (smog), *n.* a mixture of smoke and fog in the air. *Smog hung over the city and made people cough.* **smogs.**

smoke (smōk), *n.* 1. a cloud of gas and tiny solid particles that rise from anything that is burning. *The smoke from the fireplace smells good. It is now against the law for a factory to send heavy smoke from its chimneys.* 2. the act of smoking a pipe, cigar, or cigarette. *Some of the audience went into the lobby for a smoke.* **smokes.**
v. 3. to give out a lot of smoke. *The chimney is smoking. The fireplace smoked, and all of us coughed.* 4. to breathe smoke into the mouth from a pipe, cigar, or cigarette and blow it out again. *Doctors tell us not to smoke.* 5. to preserve or flavor by exposing to smoke. *Our meat market sells ham and fish that have been smoked.* 6. to drive out by smoke. *Bees can be smoked from their hive.* **smokes, smoked, smok ing.**

smooth (smüth), *adj.* 1. having no bumps or rough spots. *The smooth highway made driving a pleasure. A mirror must be smooth to give a good reflection. The lake is smooth tonight because there is no wind.* 2. steady; moving evenly; gentle. *The airplane made a smooth landing. A cat has a smooth way of walking.* 3. too pleasant; too agreeable; too polite. *The smooth salesman sold her an expensive set of books.* **smooth er, smooth est; smooth ly,** *adv.*
v. 4. to make flat or even; to remove bumps from. *The nurse smoothed the sheets for the patient. A carpenter smooths a piece of wood with sandpaper.* 5. to make easier; to free from difficulty. *Father's permission smoothed the way for an overnight trip.* 6. **smooth away,** to get rid of. *The doctor smoothed away the boy's worry about his health.* 7. **smooth down,** to calm. *Little Betty is the only one who can smooth down Uncle Joe's anger.* 8. **smooth over,** to make something unpleasant seem less important. *We smoothed over the girls' quarrel by getting them to laugh at it.* **smooths, smoothed, smooth ing.**

smug (smug), *adj.* showing satisfaction with oneself; too pleased with oneself. *Charlene would* *have more friends if she changed her smug manner.* **smug ger, smug gest; smug ly,** *adv.*

smut (smut), *n.* 1. dirt; dirty marks. *After cleaning the stove, he had smut on his hands and clothes.* 2. a disease that changes the ears of grain into a black dust. *The plants most likely to get smut are wheat, oats, barley, corn, rye, and rice.*

snail (snāl), *n.* a slow-moving mollusk with a soft body and a shell which it can pull into for protection. *The shell of a snail is carried on its back, and its eyes are on long stems. Snails live on land and in water.* **snails.**

snake (snāk), *n.* 1. a long, crawling reptile having scales and no legs. *Snakes usually live on small animals, birds, and insects. Some snakes have a poisonous bite.* **snakes.** *v.* 2. to twist or turn like a snake. *This river snakes its way through the hills.* **snakes, snaked, snak ing.** (See illustration on following page.)

snap (snap), *v.* 1. to grasp eagerly or suddenly. *We snapped at his offer to sell his ice skates.* 2. to make a quick bite. *The fish snapped at the bait and swam away.* 3. to break suddenly. *The string snapped as he was wrapping the package. The little branches of the tree snapped off in the wind.* 4. to make or cause to make a sharp, cracking sound. *The wood in the fire snapped as it burned. The dog comes running when I snap my fingers.* 5. to close with a sharp sound or click. *The door snapped shut. Snap the lock on the drawer. The dog's jaws snapped on the meat I gave him.* 6. to move quickly. *The soldiers snapped to attention when the general walked in.* 7. to speak sharply. *The chief of police snapped orders to his men.* 8. to take a snapshot of. *He snapped their picture.* **snaps, snapped, snap ping.** *n.* 9. a sudden bite or grasp. *The dog made a snap at the bone.* 10. a sudden breaking. *The snap of the television wire took away the picture.* 11. a sharp, cracking sound. *At the snap of my fingers, the dog will lie down. The rubber band broke with a snap.* 12. a fastening; a catch. *The snap on a purse holds it closed.* 13. a snapshot. *Here are the snaps of the parade.* 14. an easy task or job. *Working here is a snap.* 15. a kind of cookie. *Mother makes snaps and flavors them with ginger.* 16. **cold snap,** a spell of cold weather. *The cold snap lasted six days.* **snaps.** *adj.* 17. made quickly without much thinking. *His snap judgments are mostly right because of his experience.* 18. easy. *Some lazy college students take snap courses.*

snap shot (snap′shot′), *n.* a photograph. *My aunt has many snapshots that she took during her last vacation trip.* **snap shots.**

snare (snâr), *n.* 1. a trap made to catch small animals and birds. *A snare is usually made of a rope that pulls tight around the animal's body.* 2. something that traps a person. *Sometimes a man's job turns out to be a snare from which he is unable to escape.* **snares.**

v. 3. to catch with a trap. *The hunter snares animals for the zoos.* **snares, snared, snar ing.**

snatch (snach), *v.* 1. to grab. *The puppy snatched the candy from the girl's hand. Little Henry snatched at the chance to play ball with the big boys.* 2. to take quickly; to act suddenly. *The robber snatched the jewels and ran away.* **snatch es, snatched, snatch ing.** *n.* 3. the act of snatching; a grab. *The player made a snatch at the ball and caught it.* 4. a small part; a little bit. *We heard snatches of the singing as the doors of the auditorium opened and closed.* 5. a short amount of time. *The mother did her housework in snatches while caring for the baby.* **snatch es.**

sneak (snēk), *v.* 1. to move, take, put, bring, etc. quietly, secretly, or slyly. *I sneaked a cookie out of the jar.* 2. to go in a quiet, secret, sly way. *The two men sneaked through the building when no one was in it.* **sneaks, sneaked, sneak ing.** *n.* 3. a person who is dishonest, cowardly, and sly. *The sneak who took our lunch spoiled our picnic.* **sneaks.**

sneak ers (snēk′ərz), *n. pl.* shoes with canvas sides and rubber soles. *Sneakers are used mostly for play and for sports.*

sneer (snēr), *v.* 1. to make a gesture by raising the corners of the mouth to show scorn. *The boy sneered at his brother.* **sneers, sneered, sneer ing.** *n.* 2. to speak or write in this manner. *The article in the paper was a sneer at business.* **sneers.**

sneeze (snēz), *v.* 1. to force out breath suddenly and noisily through the nose and mouth. *He sneezed in class, but he couldn't help it. Getting dust in the nostrils causes a person to sneeze.* **sneez es, sneezed, sneez ing.** *n.* 2. the act of sneezing. *A baby's sneeze is not very loud.* **sneez es.**

sniff (snif), *v.* 1. to take little short breaths through the nose. *When a dog smells food, he usually sniffs. The child's cold caused him to sniff.* 2. to smell by taking short breaths. *Sniff this new perfume to see if you like it. The cat sniffed at her food.* **sniffs, sniffed, sniff ing.** *n.* 3. the act or sound of sniffing. *A sniff of the soup cooking on the stove made me hungry.* **sniffs.**

snipe (snīp), *n.* 1. a shore bird that lives mainly on low, wet land. *A snipe has long legs and a long bill.* **snipes.** (See illustration on following page.) *v.* 2. to shoot from a hidden place. *The enemy soldier sniped at the man who came outside the fort.* **snipes, sniped, snip ing.**

snore (snôr), *v.* 1. to breathe during sleep with a harsh, rough noise. *When my uncle snores, you can hear him in the next room.* **snores, snored, snor ing.** *n.* 2. the sound made by a person who snores. *The snores of the other boys sleeping in the tent kept me awake.* **snores.**

---

sand, āte, bâre, fäther; sent, mē, fèrn; fit, bīke; pot, rōpe, fôrt; run, pùll, rüle, cūte; noise, sound; ch, cheese; ng, long; th, thick; ~~th,~~ those; zh, treasure; ə = a in about, e in waken, i in animal, o in seldom, and u in minus.

SNAKES

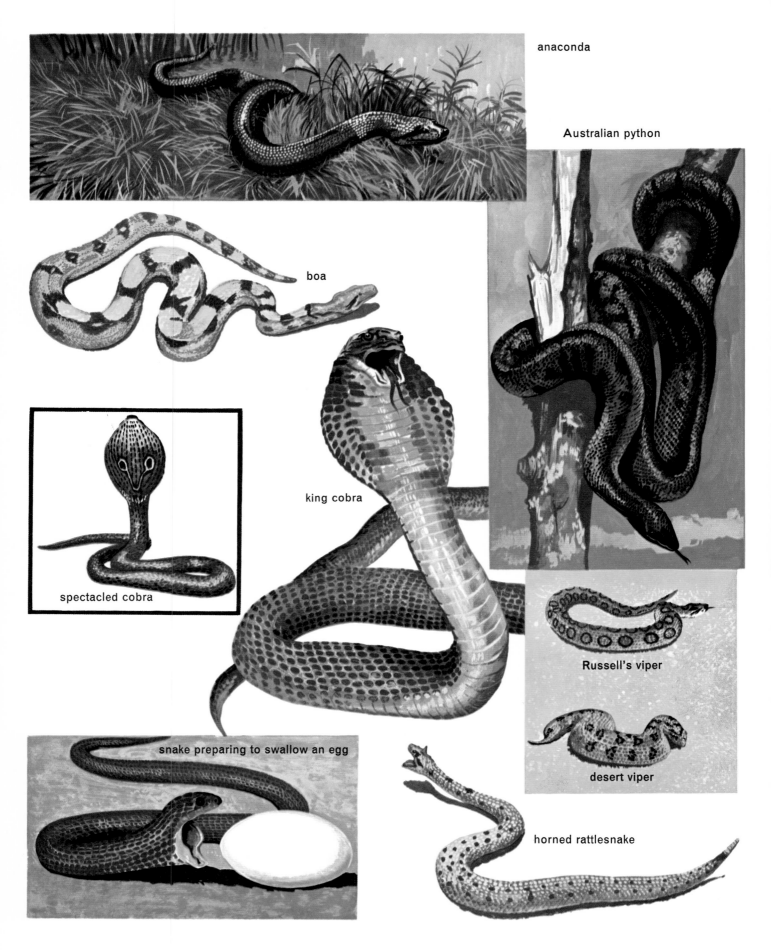

anaconda

Australian python

boa

spectacled cobra

king cobra

Russell's viper

desert viper

snake preparing to swallow an egg

horned rattlesnake

snipe

snort (snôrt), v. 1. to force breath through the nose with a harsh noise. *Horses snort.* 2. to make a sound like this to show disfavor or anger. *When Joe snorted at our idea, we knew he didn't like it.* **snorts, snort ed, snort ing.**
n. 2. a harsh noise made by forcing air through the nose. *The squeals and snorts of the pigs became louder at feeding time.* **snorts.**

snow (snō), n. 1. frozen water crystals that fall to the earth as soft, white flakes. *Snow falls in winter.* 2. a fall of snow. *If the snow is deep, the boys will take out their sleds.* **snows.**
v. 3. to fall as snow. *It has started to snow.* 4. **snow in,** to cover or shut in with snow. *The farmer's family was snowed in until the road was cleared.* **snows, snowed, snow ing.**

snow ball (snō′bôl′), n. 1. snow that is packed together into a ball. *The boys threw snowballs at the trees as they walked.* **snow balls.**
v. 2. to throw snowballs at. *The little children snowballed us as we walked by.* **snow balls, snow balled, snow ball ing.**

snow fall (snō′fôl′), n. 1. a fall of snow. *The snowfall on Christmas Eve excited the children.* 2. the amount of snow at a certain place or at a certain time. *The snowfall in Minnesota was two feet.* **snow falls.**

snow flake (snō′flāk′), n. one of the small, delicate pieces of snow that falls from the sky. *Every snowflake has six sides and an individual design.* **snow flakes.**

snow man (snō′man′), n. snow that has been packed and made into a figure resembling a man. *The children put a hat on their snowman.* **snow men.**

snow plow (snō′plou′), n. a machine used to clear the snow off a street or road. *Shortly after a heavy snowfall, the snowplows move up and down the city streets.* **snow plows.**

snow shoe (snō′shü′), n. a light wooden frame with leather strips stretched across it, which attaches to the shoe and is used for walking on deep snow. *A snowshoe is shaped like a long oval and curves up slightly in front.* **snow shoes.**

snow suit (snō′süt′), n. a warm outer garment with pants and long sleeves, worn by children in cold weather or in snow. *A snowsuit is made to fit tightly around the ankles, wrists, and neck.* **snow suits.**

snowy (snō′ē), adj. 1. having snow. *The little children are sent home from school early on snowy days.* 2. covered with snow. *The snowy tops of the mountains are beautiful.* 3. like snow; white. *The bedsheets were snowy after they were washed.* **snow i er, snow i est; snow i ly,** adv.

snuff[1] (snuf), v. 1. to draw up into the nose. *The doctor said that snuffing steam would help to quiet his cough.* 2. to smell; to sniff. *The dog snuffs the ground as he walks.* **snuffs, snuffed, snuff ing.**
n. 3. a fine powder made from the tobacco plant, which is usually inhaled through the nose. *Snuff was popular in the courts of French kings.*

snuff[2] (snuf), v. 1. to put out the flame of. *The men in the cabin snuffed the candles and went to sleep.* 2. **snuff out,** to end suddenly. *The rain snuffed out our plans for going to the baseball game.* **snuffs, snuffed, snuff ing.**

snug (snug), adj. 1. cozy; comfortable. *The children were snug and warm in their beds. The ship found a snug harbor.* 2. fitting in a tight way. *The coat is too snug for her this year because she has grown so much.* 3. small and neatly arranged. *The little apartment has a snug kitchen.* **snug ger, snug gest; snug ly,** adv.

so (sō), adv. 1. to such a degree or amount. *It was so cold that I wore two sweaters.* 2. as shown; as told. *Hold the golf club just so. He said his mother would help us and she did so.* 3. very; extremely. *The people in this town are so friendly.* 4. very much. *We are sorry that Dee moved, because we liked her so.* 5. in the same way; also. *He is a good friend and so is his brother.* 6. therefore. *I was busy with my studies and so did not take the job.*
conj. 7. in order. *Go to bed early so that you will get a good night's sleep.*
pron. 8. **or so,** more or less. *She worked an hour or so on her spelling lesson.* 9. the same. *I am a good citizen and I will stay so.*
interj. 10. all right! *So! We will do what you want.* 11. well! *So! This is where you live!*

soak (sōk), v. 1. to wet through; to make or become wet. *The heavy rain fell for two days,*

snowflakes

snowplow

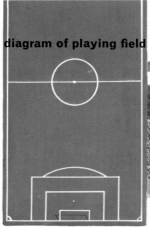

diagram of playing field

soccer

soaking the dry land. I soaked my shoes by walking into the puddle. 2. to let stay in water or other liquid. *The baseball player soaked his sore arm in hot water for an hour.* 3. **soak up,** (a) to take up; to absorb. *The towel soaks up water. We soaked up the sunshine.* (b) to take into the mind. *We soaked up the information in the book.* **soaks, soaked, soak ing.**

n. 4. the act of soaking; a wetting. *The dry field got a good soak last night.* **soaks.**

soap (sōp), *n.* 1. a substance used for washing. *Tom washed his hands with water and a bar of soap. Mother uses liquid soap to wash the dishes.* **soaps.**

v. 2. to rub with soap. *To wash the car, we soaped it and then poured water on it.* **soaps, soaped, soap ing.**

sob (sob), *v.* 1. to cry or weep with short breaths that come in jerks. *The little girl sobbed when she broke her doll.* 2. to make a sound like sobbing. *The night was dark, and the wind sobbed in the trees.* **sobs, sobbed, sob-bing.**

n. 3. a sound of sobbing; a crying or weeping with short breaths. *The boy's mother quieted his sobs.* **sobs.**

so ber (sō′bər), *adj.* 1. serious; solemn. *The teacher's face was sober when she told us about the test. We received sober advice to behave.* 2. plain; not showy. *She looks good in sober colors, like gray and dark blue.* 3. not drunk; not having had too much alcohol to drink. *A person should drive only when he's sober.* **so ber ly,** *adv.*

v. 4. to make or become sober. *The news of their candidate's defeat sobered the happy crowd that wanted him to win the election.* **so bers, so-bered, so ber ing.**

so-called (sō′kôld′), *adj.* named so, but not truly so. *His so-called friend didn't help him when he needed help.*

soc cer (sok′ər), *n.* a game played with a round football that is hit with the feet, legs, body, or head. *In soccer the hands and arms are not used.*

so cial (sō′shəl), *adj.* 1. friendly; liking to be with others. *The new boy in our room is a social person who quickly found many friends.* 2. having to do with human beings in a group. *The social problems of a city include heavy traffic and smog.* 3. living in groups. *Ants and bees are social insects.* 4. of or having to do with people who are rich and who are in polite society. *The big social event this month is the opening night at the opera.* 5. of or for friendship. *We spent a social evening at the home of Father's best friend. Mrs. Ross belongs to a social club that holds a dance every Friday night.* **so cial ly,** *adv.*

n. 6. a friendly party. *The school socials are held every month.* **so cials.**

social studies, *n. pl.* the study of how people live together in different groups and in different regions of the world. *Geography is a part of social studies.*

so ci e ty (sə sī′ə tē), *n.* 1. all people who are living and working together. *Society has been helped by many new medicines. Laws are made for the good of society.* 2. a group of people who work together for some purpose. *Our family joined The Society to Save Our Parks.* 3. company; friendship. *We enjoy Kent's society because he is so thoughtful of others.* 4. the rich, fashionable group of people. *Women like to read the news about society in the newspaper.* **so ci e ties.**

sock (sok), *n.* a short stocking. *Men wear socks. Socks are also worn by children.* **socks.**

sock et (sok′it), *n.* a hollow part into which something fits. *Put a new electric light bulb into the socket of the lamp.* **sock ets.**

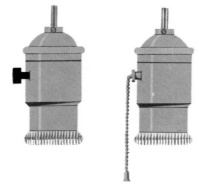

sockets

sod (sod), *n.* 1. grass and the ground it is growing in. *The sod in the park is always kept smooth.*
2. a piece of this grass with the soil containing
its roots. *To make a new lawn, sod is put down
on the prepared ground.* **sods.**
v. 3. to put sod on. *When the new building was
finished, the workmen sodded the ground around it.*
sods, sod ded, sod ding.

so da (sō′də), *n.* 1. water that bubbles because
it has been mixed with a certain gas; soda
water. *Soda is used in making flavored drinks.* 2. a
soft drink; pop. *I bought a carton of orange soda.*
3. a drink made of soda water, ice cream, and
an added flavor. *This time I'll have a strawberry
soda instead of a chocolate soda.* 4. a white powder
used in baking. *Soda is used in making breads and
cakes.* **so das.**

soda water, *n.* water with a certain gas added
to made it bubble. *Soda water is usually sold in
bottles. The man behind the counter put chocolate
in the glass and then added soda water.*

so fa (sō′fə), *n.* a long, soft seat with a back and
two arms, or raised ends. *A sofa usually can
hold three or more people.* **so fas.**

soft (sôft), *adj.* 1. not hard. *The pillow is soft.
We can dig a garden in this soft ground.* 2. smooth;
not rough. *A cat's fur is soft. The baby has soft
skin.* 3. quiet; gentle; mild. *We felt the first soft
wind of spring. She has a soft voice.* 4. weak. *His
muscles were soft because he did not exercise.*
5. kind; tender. *He has a soft heart.* 6. not
bright or sharp. *The drawing had soft colors.
This restaurant has soft lights.* 7. **soft drink,** a
drink that has no alcohol in it. *A cold soft
drink tastes good in summer.* 8. **soft water,**
water that quickly makes bubbles when soap
is added. *Soft water is best for washing clothes.*
soft er, soft est; soft ly, *adv.*
adv. 9. softly, gently. *Speak softly if you do not
wish to disturb others.*

soft ball (sôft′bôl′), *n.* 1. a baseball game played
with a large, soft ball. *Ten men are needed to play
softball.* 2. the ball used in a softball game. *A
softball is hard enough so that the players must
wear gloves as in baseball.*

soft en (sôf′ən), *v.* to make or become soft.
*The rain softened the soil. Ice cream softens in the
heat.* **soft ens, soft ened, soft en ing.**

soft wood (sôft′wùd), *n.* 1. a tree with needles
and with soft wood. *The pine tree is a softwood;
the oak tree is a hardwood.* 2. wood which is easy
to cut. *Father bought softwood for the bookcase
he plans to build.* **soft woods.**
adj. 3. having softwood; made of softwood.
*We made a table of softwood planks because they
are easier to cut.*

soil¹ (soil), *n.* 1. ground; earth; dirt. *Plants grow
in rich, dark soil. Nothing grew in the soil of that
desert until it was irrigated.* 2. land; country.
The traveler wanted to go back to his native soil.
soils.

soil² (soil), *v.* 1. to make dirty. *Pete soiled his new*

sole

suit when he fell in the mud. 2. to bring shame
upon. *Keith soiled his record by cheating on the
examination.* **soils, soiled, soil ing.**

so lar (sō′lər), *adj.* 1. of or having to do with
the sun. *The earth is part of the solar system.*
2. measured by the sun. *A solar day is twenty-
four hours.*

solar system, *n.* the sun and all the planets
etc. that revolve around it. *The earth is one of
the nine planets of the solar system. The other planets
in the solar system are Mercury, Venus, Mars,
Jupiter, Saturn, Uranus, Neptune, and Pluto.*

sold (sōld), past tense and past participle of **sell.**

sol dier (sōl′jər), *n.* 1. a person serving in an
army. *Many men are asked by their government
to become soldiers in time of war.* 2. a person who
works for a cause. *My aunt is a soldier for better
schools.* **sol diers.**

sole¹ (sōl), *n.* a kind of fish that is good to eat.
A sole has two small eyes placed close together.
soles or **sole.**

sole² (sōl), *n.* 1. the bottom of the foot. *The baby
chuckles when his sole is tickled.* 2. the bottom
of a shoe, slipper, or boot. *The soles of Norman's shoes had holes in them.* **soles.**
v. 3. to put a sole on a shoe. *The shoe-repair*

solar system

Pluto

Jupiter

Earth

Venus

Uranus

Sun

Mercury

Mars

asteroid belt

Saturn

Neptune

shop soles shoes while you wait. **soles, soled, sol ing.**

sole³ (sōl), *adj.* 1. one and only; single. *The sole person I want to see is Scott.* 2. only. *The brothers were the sole heirs to their father's money.* **sole ly,** *adv.*

sol emn (sol′əm), *adj.* 1. serious; earnest; grave. *The doctor had a solemn face as he examined the patient. We made a solemn promise to Father that we would do better.* 2. happening in a formal way; done according to strict rules. *The graduation program was solemn.* **sol emn ly,** *adv.*

sol id (sol′id), *adj.* 1. not hollow; having no space inside. *A chimney is hollow, but a brick or a stone is solid.* 2. the same throughout. *She bought a coat of solid red.* 3. firm and strong. *The big building has a solid foundation to hold it up.* 4. hard. *We skated on the solid ice. To become a doctor requires solid work and study.* 5. whole; entire. *The men worked for one solid week to finish the job.* 6. reliable. *Are you giving solid support to your school and its teachers?* **sol id ly,** *adv.*

n. 7. something that is not a liquid or a gas. *Wood, stone, and coal are solids.* 8. something that has length, width, and depth. *A pyramid, cube, and cylinder are solids.* **sol ids.**

so lo (sō′lō), *n.* 1. a piece of music that is played or sung by one person. *Jim played a violin solo at the concert.* **so los.**

adj. 2. done by one person. *After many lessons, the pilot made his first solo flight in the airplane.*

v. 3. to fly an airplane alone. *In 1927, a man named Lindbergh became the first person to solo across the Atlantic Ocean.* **so los, so loed, so lo ing.**

so lu tion (sə lü′shən), *n.* 1. the answer; the explanation. *Let's ask Miss Lynch for the solution to the arithmetic problem. The solution to the puzzle in the magazine is given on page twenty.* 2. a dissolving of something in a liquid. *The solution of sugar in water takes place faster if the water is boiling.* 3. a mixture formed by dissolving something completely in a liquid. *You make a sugar solution when you stir sugar into tea.* **so lu tions.**

solve (solv), *v.* to find the answer to. *I solved the*

puzzle in three minutes. The police solved the crime. **solves, solved, solv ing.**

sol vent (sol′vənt), *n.* 1. a substance that can dissolve another substance. *Water is a solvent of sugar, salt, and alcohol.* 2. to be able to pay all debts. *When you owe more money than you have, you are not solvent.* **sol vents.**

some (sum, səm), *adj.* 1. a certain; not specifically named. *Some girl called while you were out.* 2. a certain amount or number of. *Put some records on the phonograph. Craig wants some work for the summer. Have some peanuts. Some apples are green.* 3. about. *Some fifty students said they will join the new club. Some fifty years ago this big city was just a little town.* 4. any. *Ask some expert for advice.*

pron. 5. a certain number, but not all. *Some think that the test will be difficult, others think it will be easy.*

some body (sum′bod′ē), *pron.* 1. some person who is not named or not known. *Will somebody turn off the television set?*

n. 2. a person who is important. *He thinks he is somebody because his uncle took him to Europe.*

some day (sum′dā), *adv.* at some time in the future. *Someday we will go on a fishing trip.*

some how (sum′hou), *adv.* in one way or another; in some way. *Somehow she managed to get her work done even though she was ill.*

some one (sum′wun, sum′wən), *pron.* somebody; some person. *Someone ought to fix that front door.*

some thing (sum′thing), *pron.* 1. a certain thing that is not specifically named. *Give the dog something to eat. Before we leave, let's see if there is something we forgot to take. There is something about her attitude that is strange.*

n. 2. a person who is important. *The little girl thinks she is something in her pretty new dress.*

adv. 3. somewhat. *She looks something like that new movie star.*

some time (sum′tīm), *adv.* 1. at some time in the future; someday. *Come back to our city sometime.* 2. at a time not specified. *She was ill sometime last July, I think.*

adj. 3. former. *The famous writer visited his sometime sixth-grade teacher to thank her.*

some times (sum′tīmz), *adv.* once in awhile;

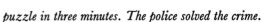
natural **solid** materials

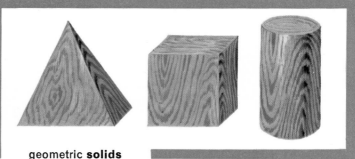
geometric **solids**

now and then. *Sometimes I go out on weekday nights, but mostly I study.*

some what (sum′hwot), *adv.* 1. to some degree; a little. *Little children are somewhat careless, and must be watched. The buildings are somewhat alike.* *n.* 2. some part; a certain amount; more or less. *That boy is somewhat of a stranger because he is so quiet. Our project was somewhat of a success even though it didn't turn out as we had planned.*

some where (sum′hwär), *adv.* 1. in some place; at some place. *The letter is somewhere in the house. They live somewhere in this neighborhood.* 2. at some time. *The house was built somewhere about fifty years ago.*

son (sun), *n.* 1. a boy or man as he is related to his parents; a male child. *The farm belongs to the farmer, his wife, and their two sons.* 2. a man or boy as he is related to a group, country, etc. *The early pioneers were sons of the frontier.* **sons.**

so nar (sō′när), *n.* a device that can locate objects underwater. *Sonar sends out waves of sound and measures the time it takes to get an echo back from the object the sound waves strike.*

song (sông), *n.* 1. a tune; a piece of music to be sung. *The principal asked the chorus to sing another song.* 2. the pleasant, musical sounds of some birds. *The songs of the robins woke me early.* 3. a poem; a verse that can be sung. *The writer wrote songs in praise of his country.* **songs.**

soon (sün), *adv.* 1. before long; before much time has passed. *Spring will soon be here. Dinner will be ready soon.* 2. quickly; not long. *They left here soon after four o'clock.* 3. willingly; gladly. *Wouldn't you as soon get the job done now instead of later?* **soon er, soon est.**

soot (sut or süt), *n.* a black matter that comes from burning materials, such as wood, coal, oil, etc. *Soot makes smoke dark and blackens walls.*

so pra no (sə pran′ō), *n.* 1. the part in music sung by the highest kind of singing voice. *She sings soprano in the choir.* 2. a girl or woman who has a high singing voice. *She is a famous soprano who sings in operas around the world.* **so pra nos.** *adj.* 3. for a soprano. *The soprano part in this operetta is important.*

sore (sôr), *adj.* 1. painful; tender when touched. *Don't step on my sore toe!* 2. filled with grief and sorrow. *A mother's heart feels sore when her children are troubled.* 3. angry; upset. *The man was sore about the delays in delivering his TV set.* 4. causing sadness or misery. *Our team's loss was a sore subject to the coach for a long time.* **sor er, sor est; sore ly,** *adv.* *n.* 5. a painful place on the body; a wound. *The sore on our dog's leg will be all gone in a day or two.* **sores.**

so ror i ty (sə rôr′ə tē), *n.* a club of women or girls. *A sorority in a college usually has its own building in which all the members live.* **so ror i- ties.**

sor row (sor′ō), *n.* 1. grief; sadness; lack of

happiness. *The cowboy felt sorrow when he had to sell his horse.* 2. something which causes grief, sadness, or lack of happiness. *Susan's sickness was a sorrow to her friends.* **sor rows.** *v.* 3. to be sad; to feel or show grief, sadness, or lack of happiness. *The boy sorrowed over the money that he lost.* **sor rows, sor rowed, sor row ing.**

sor ry (sor′ē, sär′ē), *adj.* 1. feeling regret; full of sorrow or sadness. *I'm sorry; I didn't mean to bump you. We were sorry for the little lost dog and let him stay with us until we found his owner.* 2. unpleasant; ridiculous. *The boys were a sorry sight after the walk through mud and rain.* 3. causing feelings of sorrow and pity. *Some poor people live in sorry conditions, with not enough food or heat.* **sor ri er, sor ri est; sor ri ly,** *adv.*

sort (sôrt), *n.* 1. kind; type. *There are all sorts of books in the library. A polar bear likes a cold sort of weather. She is the sort of girl I like, always happy and smiling.* 2. **out of sorts,** not feeling happy; not agreeable. *That child is out of sorts because he needs his nap.* **sorts.** *v.* 3. to separate things and put those that are alike into groups. *The baby sorted the blocks into two piles, one blue and one white. We sorted the snapshots so that she kept the pictures of her family and I kept those of mine.* **sorts, sort ed, sort- ing.**

SOS (es′ō′es′), *n.* a call for help. *The ship's engines stopped, so the Captain sent an SOS by radio.*

sought (sôt), past tense and past participle of **seek.**

soul (sōl), *n.* 1. the part of a person that does the thinking and feeling; the part of a person that is spiritual. *Many religions teach that only the body dies, but the soul lives forever.* 2. deepest feelings. *The writer put his soul into his most famous novel.* 3. a person who is a leader and who gives others the energy to go on. *Christopher Columbus was the soul of the expedition to America.* 4. a person. *Not a soul left until the concert was over.* **souls.**

sound[1] (sound), *n.* 1. anything that is heard; a noise. *The sound of the church bells came softly on the breeze. The sounds in that factory are so loud that you can't hear another person speak. Don't make a sound or you will frighten that deer.* 2. the vibrations producing a sound. *Sound travels through the air.* 3. the distance that the noise of something can be heard. *Although I couldn't see him, he was within sound of my voice.* **sounds.** *v.* 4. to make a sound. *The thunder sounded and the rain fell. His snores sounded all through the house.* 5. to cause to make a noise. *The principal sounded the bell for a fire drill.* 6. to seem; appear. *Your explanation of the lesson sounds confusing. The news about your brother sounds good.* **sounds, sound ed, sound ing.**

sound[2] (sound), *adj.* 1. healthy; normal; free from disease. *The runner has sound legs.* 2. safe;

reliable. *The banks are sound places to keep your money.* 3. strong; firm. *A big building must have a sound foundation.* 4. sensible; wise. *The teacher gave the class some sound information about using good English. The banker has sound ideas about saving money.* 5. deep and peaceful. *The baby is in a sound sleep.* 6. thorough. *The girls' spelling team gave the boys' team a sound defeat.* **sound er, sound est; sound ly,** *adv.*
adv. 7. in a sound way; deeply. *The tired worker was sound asleep.*

sound³ (sound), *v.* 1. to measure how deep water is. *The sailors sounded the river by dropping a line or rope attached to a heavy piece of metal over the side of the ship.* 2. to try to find out the thoughts of. *The reporters sounded the chief of police about traffic problems.* 3. to dive. *The whale sounded deep into the water after coming to the surface for air.* **sounds, sound ed, sound ing.**

sound⁴ (sound), *n.* a long body of water connecting two larger bodies of water or lying between an island and the mainland. *The people went sailing on the sound.* **sounds.**

soup (süp), *n.* a liquid food made by boiling vegetables or meat in water. *Tomato soup is my favorite.* **soups.**

sour (sour), *adj.* 1. not sweet; acid. *A lemon has a sour taste.* 2. spoiled. *The milk is sour because it wasn't in the refrigerator.* 3. unpleasant; disagreeable. *Don't have such a sour attitude toward your work.* **sour er, sour est; sour ly,** *adv.*
v. 4. to become sour. *Milk sours if it is not kept cool.* 5. to make sour. *The hot weather soured the milk.* 6. to make unpleasant or unhappy. *All his troubles soured his view of life.* **sours, soured, sour ing.**

source (sôrs), *n.* 1. the beginning of a stream or river. *The source of the Mississippi River is in Minnesota.* 2. the place from which a thing comes or is obtained; origin. *The wheat fields of Kansas are the sources of much of our wheat. A dictionary is a source for finding the meaning of a word.* **sourc es.**

southwester

south (south), *n.* 1. the direction to the left when a person faces the sunset. *A warm wind blew from the south. South America lies to the south of the United States.* 2. **the South,** the southern states of the United States. *The South fought the North in the Civil War.* 3. **South Pole,** the place farthest south on the earth. *The South Pole is located in the ice and cold and was first reached in 1911.*
adj. 4. coming from the south. *The south wind blows warm air across the country.* 5. to the south; in the direction of south. *The south side of the school contains the parking lot.*
adv. 6. toward the south. *Birds fly south in the autumn.*

South Car o li na (south kâr′ə lī′nə), *n.* a state on the southeastern coast of the United States. *South Carolina raises much cotton and tobacco, and has many factories which make cotton goods.*

South Da ko ta (south də kō′tə), *n.* a state in the north central part of the United States. *South Dakota is a big producer of farm products and cattle.*

south ern (suth′ərn), *adj.* 1. in or toward the south. *The southern climate is warm.* 2. from the south. *The southern wind brought rain.* 3. of the South. *The Southern army fought the Northern army in the Civil War.*

south west (south′west′), *n.* 1. the direction halfway between south and west. *Southwest is opposite to northeast.* 2. a place or region that lies in this direction from the middle of a country. *The Southwest has some of our biggest ranches.*
adv. 3. toward the southwest. *The wagon trains traveled southwest to get to California.*
adj. 4. coming from the southwest. *We often have southwest winds in this latitude.*

south west er (south′wes′tər, sou′wes′tər), *n.* 1. a sailor's waterproof hat, having a wide brim at the back. *The southwester has for years been worn by ocean sailors.* 2. a strong wind or a storm coming from the southwest. *The fishing boats were tossed about by the waves made by the southwester.* **south west ers.**

sou ve nir (sü′və nir′, sü′və nir), *n.* something that is kept as a reminder of a person or an event. *The shop sells souvenirs of the city, like little models of the tall buildings.* **sou ve nirs.**

sow¹ (sou), *n.* a fully grown female pig. *The prize sow at the county fair weighed three hundred pounds.* **sows.**

sow² (sō), *v.* 1. to plant by scattering seeds. *The farmer sows wheat in spring. Every spring the workmen sow the bare spots in the park's grass.* 2. to plant or place in the mind. *The woman we read about in class tried to sow happiness wherever she went.* **sows, sowed, sown** or **sowed, sow ing.**

space (spās), *n.* 1. the area without any limit, in which the planets and stars exist. *The earth travels in space around the sun.* 2. room; a place.

sowing by hand

There is no more space for passengers in the crowded train. Leave some space on your test for the teacher's comments. 3. a distance. *Let's walk the short space to school. There are long spaces between towns in some parts of the country.* 4. a length of time. *You can read this book in the space of one week.* **spac es.**

v. 5. to place with certain distances between. *The buildings are spaced so that they will not be too close together.* **spac es, spaced, spac ing.**

space craft (spās′kraft), *n.* a spaceship. *Moon rockets are one type of spacecraft.* **space crafts.**

space man (spās′man′, spās′mən), *n.* a man who travels in a spaceship. *The spacemen were in their places, ready for taking off.* **space men.**

space ship (spās′ship′), *n.* an aircraft for travel through space. *Powerful rockets send a spaceship above the pull of earth's gravity. Spaceships travel to the planets and the moon.* **space ships.**

spade (spād), *n.* 1. a kind of shovel. *A spade is used for digging into the ground.* **spades.**

v. 2. to dig with a shovel. *In spring, the boys spaded the earth to make a garden.* **spades, spad ed, spad ing.**

span[1] (span), *n.* 1. the part of a bridge or arch between two supports. *The bridge across the river had only one span because its two supports were on each side of the river. Bridges with four supports have three spans.* 2. a certain length of time. *It took a span of three years to build the big church. A dog's span of life is about fifteen years.* 3. the distance between the thumb and the little finger of a man's hand when stretched out. *A span is about nine inches.* **spans.**

v. 4. to stretch across. *The bridge spans the river.* 5. to measure by the stretched-out hand. *Since we have no ruler, we will span the height of the little tree.* **spans, spanned, span ning.**

span[2] (span), *n.* two horses used together. *The*

span strained to pull the carriage out of the mud. **spans.**

Span ish (span′ish), *adj.* 1. of or pertaining to Spain. *Many of the sailors who sailed with Christopher Columbus were Spanish.*

n. 2. the language of the people of Spain, Mexico, Central America, and most of South America. *Spanish is taught in our schools and colleges.* 3. **the Spanish,** the people of Spain. *The Spanish have had many great painters and writers.*

spank (spangk), *v.* to hit with the open hand. *The mother spanked the child because he was naughty.* **spanks, spanked, spank ing.**

spare (spâr), *v.* 1. to keep from hurting or killing; to show mercy to. *The king ordered his soldiers to spare the prisoners. Everyone tried to spare Ann's feelings by not laughing at her error.* 2. to get along without. *We can spare the magazine if you want to read it.* 3. to save or free from something. *I will spare you the trip by going for you.* **spares, spared, spar ing.**

adj. 4. extra. *Every automobile has a spare tire. Have you some spare cash?* 5. free. *You can rest in your spare time.* 6. thin; not fat. *The spare, hungry wolves moved closer to the farm, but were frightened away.* 7. small in amount; just barely enough. *Their spare supply of food was running out.*

n. 8. a spare thing or part, such as a tire. *When the man got a flat tire, he used his spare.* **spares.**

spark (spärk), *n.* 1. a tiny particle of fire. *As the wood burned, it gave off bright sparks.* 2. a flash caused by electricity jumping a gap. *The spark ignited the gasoline to start the motor.* 3. a small amount. *I think that the book is wonderful, but Bob doesn't show even a spark of interest in it.* 4. a little flash of light or fire. *We saw sparks under the wheels of a passing train.* **sparks.**

v. 5. to send out sparks. *The burning wood sparked.* **sparks, sparked, spark ing.**

spar kle (spär′kl), *v.* 1. to give out sparks of light. *The lake sparkled in the moonlight.* 2. to be clever and lively. *His conversation sparkled all evening.* **spar kles, spar kled, spar kling.**

n. 3. a little gleam, flash, or glitter. *From far away, we saw the sparkle of a campfire.* 4. liveliness. *The old lady had a sparkle that made us love her.* **spar kles.**

spark plug, *n.* a piece in the cylinder of a gasoline engine which explodes a mixture of air and gasoline. *Automobiles have six or eight spark plugs, each exploding in turn to make the engine work.* **spark plugs.**

spar row (spar′ō), *n.* a small, gray-brown bird found in all parts of the world except Australia. *The common sparrow seen in American cities is the English sparrow. The white-throated sparrow has a beautiful song.* **spar rows.**

sparrow hawk, *n.* a small reddish-brown bird with black stripes and spots and long pointed

spark plug:
a. outside
b. inside

sparrow hawk

wings. *The sparrow hawk feeds on live sparrows and other small animals.* **sparrow hawks.**

speak (spēk), *v.* 1. to talk; to say words. *Speak clearly so that we can understand you! The baby is just learning how to speak.* 2. to make a speech. *The President will speak tonight on television.* 3. to make known; tell. *You should speak only good things about your friends. If you object to the club's new project, speak your thoughts.* 4. to be able to talk in a certain language. *Our teacher speaks French and Spanish.* 5. **speak of,** to talk about; mention. *Everyone speaks of you with praise.* **speaks, spoke, spok en, speak ing.**

speak er (spēk/ər), *n.* 1. a person who speaks. *The baby is becoming quite a speaker.* 2. a person who makes speeches. *The speaker at the Club told of his adventures in the jungle.* 3. a machine or device that makes sounds louder for easier hearing. *They turned up the speakers so that everyone in the audience could understand the actors.* 4. the person who is in charge of an assembly. *The Speaker of the House of Representatives of our Congress makes decisions about who is to speak next.* **speak ers.**

spear (spir), *n.* 1. a weapon having a long

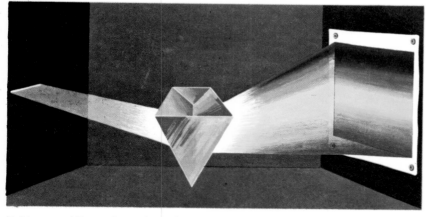

light passed through a prism shows a **spectrum**

handle and a very sharp, pointed head. *Spears are thrown by hand. Years and years ago, spears were used for hunting and for fighting.* **spears.**
v. 2. to put a spear through. *The Eskimos of today spear fish for food.* **spears, speared, spear ing.**

spe cial (spesh/əl), *adj.* 1. unusual; out of the ordinary. *The mayor declared a special holiday when the high school basketball team became the state champions.* 2. great; chief. *John is one of my special friends. My special ambition is to become a doctor.* 3. of a particular kind; different from others. *She has a special kind of plant in her garden that grows only in dry climates. Every snowflake has a special design.* 4. for a particular purpose or function. *A beekeeper wears a special outfit for his work. There are special tires made for driving on snow.* **spe cial ly,** *adv.*

spe cif ic (spi sif/ik), *adj.* particular; definite. *Since you have no specific reason for going out, why not stay inside? Always give specific answers to a question. The child cried for no specific reason that I could figure.* **spe cif i cal ly,** *adv.*

spec i fi ca tion (spes/ə fə kā/shən), *n.* 1. a specifying; a detailed statement. *The teacher gave the class a specification of the books they would read that year.* 2. **specifications,** a description and list of all details, such as materials needed for a job. *The specifications for the new highway were presented to the commissioner by the construction company.* **spec i fi ca tions.**

spec i fy (spes/ə fī), *v.* to mention or name definitely; to state clearly. *Will you specify the time that we should come? The artist specified the exact color he wanted us to use on the cover of this book.* **spec i fies, spec i fied, spec i fy ing.**

speck (spek), *n.* 1. a small spot. *You have a speck of dirt on your cheek.* 2. a tiny particle. *There is a black speck in my glass of milk.* **specks.**
v. 3. to mark with a speck or specks. *The rain specked her white dress.* **specks, specked, speck ing.**

spec trum (spek/trəm), *n.* the group of colors formed by light when it is broken up into its parts by being passed through a prism. *All the colors of the spectrum are in a rainbow, which forms when sunlight passes through the drops of rain. The colors of the spectrum are red, orange, yellow, green, blue, indigo, and violet.* **spec tra** (spek/trə) or **spec trums.**

speech (spēch), *n.* 1. the act of speaking; the use of spoken words. *Courses in speech are given in high schools and colleges.* 2. the power or ability to use words. *Animals do not have speech. Steve lost his speech when he got a severe cold.* 3. something spoken; language. *The speech used by a scientist or doctor contains many words that we never heard of.* 4. a way of speaking. *You can tell that Mr. O'Malley comes from Ireland by his speech.* 5. a talk given in public. *Our*

Superintendent of Schools gives about two speeches a week to clubs and to groups of teachers. **speech es.**

speed (spēd), *n.* 1. swift or quick action. *He finished the job with speed so that he could go to the game.* 2. the rate of movement. *The airplane has a speed of six hundred miles an hour. I walk at a speed of about four miles an hour. The sign says that the top speed on this road is sixty miles an hour.* **speeds.**
v. 3. to go fast. *The train sped past the station.* 4. to cause to go fast. *The children speeded their work by singing a lively song.* 5. to go or drive too fast. *Never speed past a school building when children are going in or coming out.* 6. to wish good luck to. *The family sped him on his way.* **speeds, sped** or **speed ed, speed ing.**

spell[1] (spel), *v.* 1. to say or write the letters of a word or words in the right order. *We taught the child to spell her name. Everyone learns how to spell.* 2. to mean. *Those black clouds spell rain.* **spells, spelled** or **spelt, spell ing.**

spell[2] (spel), *n.* 1. a word or words supposed to have some magic power. *The wizard uttered a spell against the wicked king.* 2. a charm; a strong influence. *The witch cast a spell over the sleeping princess. The beauty of the mountains at sunset cast a spell over us and we didn't feel like talking.* **spells.**

spell[3] (spel), *n.* 1. a period of time. *During the hot spell this summer, Father took us to the lake. My uncle served a spell in the army.* 2. a fit; an attack of something. *He had a coughing spell in church, so he went outside to keep from bothering the others.* 3. a time of work; a shift. *We each took ten-minute spells in sawing apart the big log.* **spells.**
v. 4. to work in place of another for a certain time. *You've been working so hard, I will spell you while you get some rest.* **spells, spelled, spell ing.**

spell er (spel′ər), *n.* 1. a person who spells. *Roberta is a good speller.* 2. a book that teaches how to spell. *The speller has lists of words that we study.* **spell ers.**

spell ing (spel′ing), *n.* 1. the forming of words from letters. *Correct spelling is especially important for girls who become secretaries in a business office.* 2. the way in which a word is spelled. *The spelling of "book" is b, o, o, k. Some words have two spellings that are correct.* **spell ings.**

spelt (spelt), past tense and past participle of **spell**[1].

spend (spend), *v.* 1. to pay out money. *Never spend more than you earn.* 2. to pass time. *We spend Sundays at the airport.* 3. to use up. *Don't spend your energy chasing rainbows.* **spends, spent, spend ing.**

spent (spent), *adj.* 1. tired; worn out. *The football player was spent after the game. The spent old horse could barely move.*
v. 2. past tense and past participle of **spend**.

sperm (sperm), *n.* a fluid substance of a male animal that is used to fertilize the egg of a female. *Sperm is composed of many cells called sperm cells.* **sperms.**

sphere (sfēr), *n.* 1. a round, solid object whose surface is at all points the same distance from the center; a globe. *A ball is a sphere. The earth, moon, stars, and sun are spheres.* 2. a field of activity or knowledge. *In the sphere of chemistry he is a great man.* **spheres.**

sphinx (sfingks), *n.* 1. any ancient Egyptian statue having a lion's body and the head of a man, a ram, or a bird with a sharp beak. *The most famous sphinx is the one that is near the Pyramids of Egypt.* 2. in ancient Greek stories, a figure having a woman's head, a lion's body, and wings. *The sphinx asked a riddle of everyone who passed, and killed those who could not guess the answer.* 3. a person who asks puzzling questions or gives mysterious answers. *People thought him a sphinx because he asked so many puzzling questions.* **sphinx es.**

spice (spīs), *n.* 1. a substance that gives flavor to food. *Pepper is a spice.* 2. something that makes speaking and writing more interesting. *His jokes always give spice to his conversation.* **spic es.**
v. 3. to add flavor or interest to. *Spice the tomatoes. Spice your writing with funny remarks.* **spic es, spiced, spic ing.**

spi der (spī′dər), *n.* a small animal with eight long legs. *A spider spins a web in which it catches insects and bugs for its food.* **spi ders.**

spied (spīd), past tense and past participle of **spy.**

spike[1] (spīk), *n.* 1. a large metal nail. *The men used big hammers to drive spikes into the railroad ties in order to hold the rails in place.* 2. a sharp point on the sole of a shoe. *Baseball players, football players, and runners wear spikes so that*

ancient Greek **sphinx**

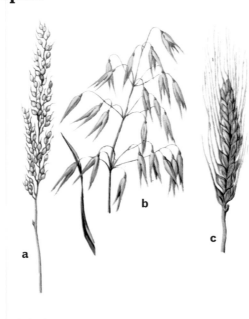

spikes:
 a. rice
 b. oats
 c. wheat

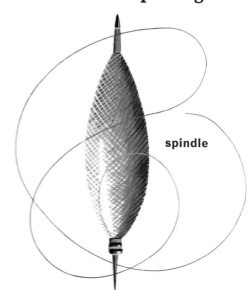

spindle

their feet have a firm grip in the ground. **spikes.**
v. 3. to fasten with spikes. *They spiked the rails
to the ties.* 4. to cut with the spikes on a shoe.
*The player on second base was spiked by the runner
on base.* 5. to stop. *The guards spiked the prisoner's
plan of escape.* **spikes, spiked, spik ing.**

spike² (spīk), *n.* 1. an ear of wheat or other
grain. *A spike of grain comes to a point.* 2. a
number of flowers grouped on a stalk in a
long, pointed arrangement. *Cut off six spikes
for a table decoration.* **spikes.**

spill (spil), *v.* 1. to run out; to flow over. *The
milk spilled on the tablecloth.* 2. to cause to run
out; to let flow over without meaning to. *The
baby spilled his orange juice on the floor.* 3. to
throw off. *The wild horse jumped and spilled the
young cowboy. The boat tipped and the boys were
spilled into the water.* 4. to scatter. *The children
spilled sand over the floor of the car. She spilled all
her quarters, nickels, and dimes on the floor of the
crowded bus!* **spills, spilled** or **spilt, spill ing.**
n. 5. a fall. *He took a spill when he rode the horse.*
spills.

spilt (spilt), past tense and past participle of
spill.

spin (spin), *v.* 1. to go around and around
rapidly. *The wheels were spinning.* 2. to make
turn rapidly; whirl. *The boys were spinning the
bicycle wheel as they fixed it.* 3. to form into
thread. *In former days women spun cotton and other
fibers by hand. Wool is spun to make yarn.* 4. to
make by producing a thread from a liquid
substance in the body. *Spiders spin webs to catch
insects.* 5. to be affected by a feeling of whirling.
When you are ill, your head may spin. 6. to tell.
*The old sailor spun many stories about the days
when he was young.* **spins, spun, spin ning.**
n. 7. a whirling movement; a rapid motion
around and around. *The spin of the wheel made
a humming noise.* 8. a short ride. *They went for a
spin in the new car.* **spins.**

spin dle (spin′dl), *n.* a slender rod, used in
spinning, on which thread is twisted and
held. *The thread winds around a spindle as it is
spun.* **spin dles.**

spine (spīn), *n.* 1. the backbone of an animal
or person. *The football player injured his spine.*
2. a stiff, sharp point. *A porcupine has spines.
Some sea animals have spines.* **spines.**

spinning wheel, *n.* an old-fashioned machine
used for forming thread when it was made by

spines:
 a. on a porcupine
 b. on sea urchins

hand. *A spinning wheel has a large wheel that is turned by hand or by foot. The thread on the spinning wheel winds onto a spindle.* **spinning wheels.**

spi ral (spī′rəl), *adj.* 1. circling about a center; winding. *The lighthouse has spiral stairs leading to the top.* **spi ral ly,** *adv.*

n. 2. something that is spiral in form. *The pilot made a spiral around the airport before landing.* **spi rals.**

v. 3. to move in a spiral. *The bird slowly spiraled upward.* **spi rals, spi raled, spi ral ing.**

spir it (spir′it), *n.* 1. the soul; the part of a person that is not material. *In many religions the spirit is believed to be immortal.* 2. a ghost, elf, or other imaginary being. *People once believed that there were helpful spirits and evil spirits.* 3. energy; vigor. *Our happy little dog has lots of spirit.* 4. a feeling; meaning. *Everyone felt the true spirit of Christmas.* 5. **spirits,** (a) a way of feeling; temper; disposition. *The happy girl was in good spirits.* (b) any liquid containing alcohol. *We have no spirits in our house.* **spir its.**

v. 6. to carry swiftly and secretly. *The singer's friends spirited him away from the crowd.* **spir its, spir it ed, spir it ing.**

spir i tu al (spir′i chù əl), *adj.* 1. having to do with the spirit, not the body. *The minister spoke about the spiritual nature of man.* **spir i tu al ly, adv.**

n. 2. a religious song. *Our chorus sang several spirituals.* **spir i tu als.**

spite (spīt), *n.* 1. an unfriendly feeling; ill will. *They say he destroyed his neighbor's flowers out of spite, but I don't believe it.* 2. **in spite of,** without being prevented by; without regard to the fact of. *In spite of the cold weather, the parade was held.* **spites.**

v. 3. to hurt or bother; to show unfriendly feelings toward. *Bill didn't need the money but he took the job to spite George.* **spites, spit ed, spit ing.**

splash (splash), *v.* 1. to make liquid scatter and fall in drops. *The children were happily splashing water in the swimming pool.* 2. to make wet or dirty. *The car splashed my suit with mud as it sped past. I splashed the bonfire with some water to make sure the fire was out.* **splash es, splashed, splash ing.**

n. 3. a scattering or throwing of a liquid. *The children made a splash as they dove into the water.* 4. the sound made by splashing. *We heard the splash of the oars as he rowed the boat.* 5. a spot made by splashing. *There were splashes of oil on his shirt.* 6. patch. *The new picture makes a lovely splash of color on the gray wall.* **splash es.**

splat ter (splat′ər), *v.* 1. to splash. *Don't splatter water on the tablecloth.* **splat ters, splat tered, splat ter ing.**

n. 2. a splash. *There were splatters of paint on his face.* **splat ters.**

splen did (splen′did), *adj.* 1. bright; brilliant; magnificent. *See that splendid sunset! The king*

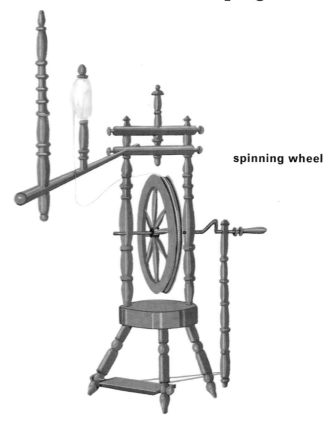

spinning wheel

wore a splendid crown with many jewels for the ceremony. 2. good; excellent. *The team has a splendid chance to win the big game this Saturday.* **splen did ly,** *adv.*

split (split), *v.* 1. to separate or divide from end to end. *The campers split the thick log to make thinner wood for burning.* 2. to divide into parts. *The three boys split the candy bar into three equal pieces.* 3. to share. *We will split the cost of the trip uptown.* **splits, split, split ting.**

n. 4. a break; a crack. *The split in the sidewalk is getting larger.* 5. a division in a group. *There is a split in Mother's club between the members who want to change the meeting time and the members who are against the change.* **splits.**

spoil (spoil), *v.* 1. to ruin; damage; destroy. *The heavy rains spoiled his garden by carrying the dirt away. Don't do anything that may spoil your good record in school.* 2. to become bad or not fit for use. *The meat spoiled when it was left outside in the hot sun.* 3. to cause a person to expect that he will always have his own way. *Some mothers spoil their children by giving in to all their wishes.* **spoils, spoiled** or **spoilt, spoil ing.**

n. pl. 4. **spoils,** things taken by force in time of war. *The armies of ancient times returned home with the spoils of battle.*

spoke (spōk), *v.* 1. past tense of **speak.**

n. 2. one of the bars connecting the middle of a wheel to its rim. *The wheels of the old wagon have three broken spokes.* **spokes.**

spo ken (spō′kən), past participle of **speak.**

sponge (spunj), *n.* 1. a kind of sea animal

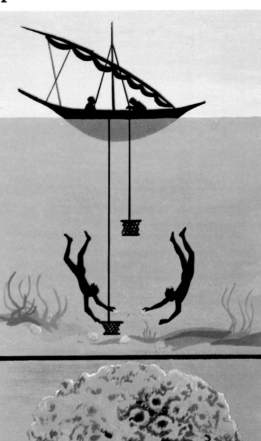

sponge:
a. diving for sponges
b. the animal

spotlight

having a porous framework of tough fibers. *Sponges are found in warm waters of the ocean.* 2. the dried framework of this animal. *We used a sponge to soap the car and to rinse it.* 3. any light substance like a sponge, used for washing. *Some sponges are made of plastic.* **spong es.**
v. 4. to wash with a sponge. *Sponge that dirt off your face.* 5. to get something from someone without paying for it. *That lazy boy often tries to sponge sodas and candy from his friends.* **spong es, sponged, spong ing.**

spon sor (spon′sər), *v.* 1. to approve and to help. *My father is sponsoring Jack's application for a job.* 2. to pay the cost of a television program or radio program. *The automobile company will sponsor the new comedy show.* **spon sors, spon sored, spon sor ing.**
n. 3. one who is responsible for looking after another person. *Mr. Warren is the sponsor of four college boys.* 4. a business firm that pays the cost of a television or radio program in return for the advertising of its product. *The sponsor gave up its television show because so few people watched it.* **spon sors.**

spook (spük), *n.* a ghost. *On Halloween the little*

children dressed in sheets and said they were spooks. **spooks.**

spool (spül), *n.* a short cylinder of wood or metal with a hole in it from end to end. *Thread is wound on spools. Cord and wire are usually sold on spools.* **spools.**

spoon (spün), *n.* 1. a tool with a small bowl and a handle, used in preparing, serving, or eating food. *When setting the table, Mother puts the forks to the left of the plate and the knives and spoons to the right.* **spoons.**
v. 2. to take up in a spoon. *Spoon your soup while it is still warm.* **spoons, spooned, spoon ing.**

spore (spôr), *n.* a tiny cell produced by ferns and other plants, capable of growing into a new plant. *Spores are enclosed in cases which protect them from severe heat, cold, or drought.* **spores.**

sport (spôrt), *n.* 1. any game. *Baseball, football, bowling, swimming, and tennis are sports.* 2. fun; amusement. *It is not nice to make sport of him. Playing with our new kitten is good sport.* 3. a person who plays fair. *A good sport never gets angry when a harmless trick is played on him.* **sports.**
v. 4. to play; to have a good time. *The young horses sported in the field by running and jumping.* 5. to wear. *Did you see that loud tie he is sporting?* **sports, sport ed, sport ing.**

sports man (spôrts′mən), *n.* 1. a man who takes part in sports. *Dale and his father are sportsmen and go fishing almost every weekend.* 2. a person who plays fair and thinks of others. *A good sportsman never boasts if he wins a game or gets angry if he loses.* **sports men.**

sports man ship (spôrts′mən ship), *n.* fair play; decent behavior. *Donna showed good sportsmanship when she congratulated the girl who beat her in the tennis game.*

spot (spot), *n.* 1. a mark; a stain; a speck. *There are ink spots on this paper. The painter has spots of color on his work clothes.* 2. a small part that is different from the parts around it. *The black cat has a white spot on its back. There is a red spot on the child's skin that smarts.* 3. a place. *At last we found a quiet spot to eat our lunch.* **spots.**
v. 4. to make spots on; stain. *In his hurry to finish dinner, Joe spotted his shirt with gravy.* 5. to scatter; to place. *Signs were spotted around the park, reading "Keep off the grass."* 6. to locate; to catch sight of. *How can we spot him in this big crowd?* **spots, spot ted, spot ting.**

spot light (spot′līt), *n.* 1. a strong light that shines on a person or thing. *The spotlight was on the singer.* 2. the lamp used to send out a strong light. *The circus uses many spotlights.* 3. the attention of the public. *Carol was in the spotlight at our school after she won the city's beauty contest.* **spot lights.**

spout (spout), *v.* 1. to send out with force. *The hose suddenly spouted water.* **spouts, spout ed, spout ing.**

SPORTS

cycling

jumping the hurdles

pole vaulting

foot racing

javelin throwing

exercise bar

weight lifting

sidehorse

golf

judo

n. 2. an opening from which a liquid flows. *The broken spout on that teapot should be mended.* **spouts.**

spray[1] (sprā), *n.* a small branch with its flowers and leaves. *A few sprays from the apple tree made a fine decoration in the room.* **sprays.**

spray[2] (sprā), *n.* 1. tiny drops of water or other liquid. *The wind blew the spray from the waves over us. The spray of perfume filled the room with a nice smell.* 2. a stream of tiny drops. *The spray from the garden hose lets water fall gently on the new*

seeds. 3. a device that scatters liquid in tiny drops; a spray gun. *We used the spray to get rid of mosquitoes.* **sprays.**

v. 4. to put on with a spray. *Paint is sprayed on the car. Poison was sprayed on the plants to get rid of the harmful insects.* **sprays, sprayed, spray ing.**

spray gun, *n.* a device that shoots out a spray. *A spray gun is used to apply chemicals to trees and plants.* **spray guns.**

spread (spred), *v.* 1. to open out; unfold.

Spread out the map on the table. They spread a blanket over the sleeping child. 2. to stretch out. *The little bird spread its wings and flew away. Andy's job spread out over the summer, instead of ending in two weeks.* 3. to become known; go from one person to another. *The good news spread quickly in the town. The disease spread among the animals.* 4. to put or apply on a surface. *Spread the paint on this floor. Spread some more butter on my bread.* 5. to set a table for a meal. *Spread the table for dinner.* 6. to extend. *The pretty valley spread beneath them. Fire spread through the building.* **spreads, spread, spreading.**

n. 7. the act of spreading or expanding. *The spread of science courses has been rapid in recent years.* 8. the cover on a bed or table. *The spread on the bed kept him warm.* 9. a stretching out. *The spread of the branches on this tree is ten feet.* 10. a big meal; a feast. *The hungry workers sat down to a spread.* 11. a food for placing on bread or crackers. *I would like some more of the cheese spread.* 12. any distance that something stretches. *The cowboy rode his horse across the entire spread of the ranch.* **spreads.**

spring (spring), *v.* 1. to jump; to leap. *The quiet fox suddenly sprang at the rabbit. The firemen sprang to their places when the alarm rang.* 2. to grow; start up quickly. *Some weeds spring up in only one night. A cool breeze sprang up during the hot afternoon.* 3. to snap back into position. *A stretched rubber band will spring back instantly when it is let go.* 4. to come into being; rise. *He springs from a good family. A town sprang up near the new airplane factory.* 5. to cause to operate suddenly. *The wolf sprang the trap by walking on a hidden stick that released it.* 6. to split or crack; to bend. *This dry weather has sprung the door.* **springs, sprang** or **sprung, sprung, spring ing.**

n. 7. the ability to stretch and then go back to its ordinary size. *There is spring in this new rubber band.* 8. a coil of wire or a strip of metal that goes back into shape after pressure is released. *Automobiles have metal springs that take the shock of bumps, and therefore give a smoother ride. The spring of a watch makes it go. Our new bed has springs that make it comfortable.* 9. a supply of water that comes up out of the ground. *This spring has been used for years by the animals of the forest.* 10. the season of the year which begins about March 21, and ends about June 21. *The weather begins to get warm in spring.* 11. a leap. *The diver took a spring into the water.* 12. bounce; vigor. *The old man walked with the spring of a boy.* **springs.**

spring board (spring'bôrd'), *n.* a board that gives added spring to a dive or a jump. *Swimming pools have springboards.* **springboards.**

spring time (spring'tīm'), *n.* the season of spring. *In springtime the flowers begin to blossom.*

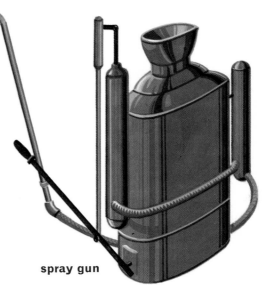

spray gun

sprin kle (spring'kl), *v.* 1. to scatter in small drops or particles. *Sprinkle salt on your egg. The dog sprinkled sand on the floor when he shook himself.* 2. to put water on in small drops. *Don't forget to sprinkle the flowers in the flower box.* 3. to rain a little. *It sprinkled this morning.* **sprinkles, sprin kled, sprin kling.**

n. 4. a light rainfall. *The sprinkle this morning didn't even get the streets wet.* 5. a tiny amount. *The cook put a sprinkle of pepper into the soup.* **sprin kles.**

sprin kling can, *n.* a can used for sprinkling water, usually over house or garden plants. *Someone left the sprinkling can in the rain.* **sprin kling cans.**

spun (spun), past tense and past participle of **spin.**

spur (spûr), *n.* 1. a small spike or piece of metal with sharp points, used to prick the side of a horse to urge it to go faster. *Cowboys wear spurs on their heels.* 2. any point that sticks out like a spur. *A rooster has a sharp spur on each leg.* 3. anything that makes a person do something. *His desire to go to college was a spur to getting good grades.* **spurs.**

spy (spī), *n.* 1. a person whose job is to get secretly the plans of another country. *The spy pretended he was on the enemy's side so that he could get information to send back to his country.* 2. a person who secretly watches the actions of others. *She thought her neighbor was a spy*

sprinkling can

because she seemed to know what everyone was doing. **spies.**

v. 3. to notice; to see. *We spied the airplane while it was only a speck in the sky.* 4. to watch secretly; act as a spy. *Betty's little brother was in the closet spying as she visited with her friends.* **spies, spied, spy ing.**

squab (skwob), *n.* a young pigeon or dove. *When squabs are about a month old, they are sold for food.* **squabs.**

square (skwâr), *n.* 1. a figure having four equal straight sides and a right angle at each corner. *A board for playing checkers is divided into squares.* 2. a tool having two sides that form a right angle. *A carpenter uses a square to check the angles on his work.* 3. an open space in a city or town with streets on all four sides, used as a park, playground, or meeting place. *We used to play in Jefferson Square. The beauty contest will be held in the town square next Tuesday.* 4. a block in a city or town. *The store is only three squares from here.* 5. the number obtained when a number is multiplied by itself. *The square of 3 is 9 because 3 × 3 = 9.* **squares.**

adj. 6. having the shape of a square; having four equal sides and four right angles. *Hand me the square box, not the round box.* 7. forming a right angle. *The corners of a room are square.* 8. fair; honest. *This store is proud of the square way in which it does business.* **squar er, squarest; square ly,** *adv.*

v. 9. to make straight, level, or even. *The gym teacher tells us to square our shoulders.* 10. to settle; to make good or correct. *Jim squared his debt with Debby by paying her the quarter he owed her.* 11. to make square; to make the four sides of something even, with the corners right angles. *The carpenter squared the board.* 12. to fit in with. *Fairy stories do not square with the facts of science.* 13. to multiply by the same number. *If you square 4, the answer is 16, because 4 × 4 = 16.* **squares, squared, squar ing.**

squash[1] (skwosh), *n.* a vegetable that grows on a vine. *There are many kinds of squashes but they all have a hard covering and a soft inside part, which may be eaten.* **squash es.**

squash[2] (skwosh), *v.* 1. to crush. *The soft strawberries were squashed by the heavier groceries in the shopping bag.* 2. to stop. *The other boys squashed Gil's plan for playing on such a hot day.* **squashes, squashed, squash ing.**

n. 3. a game played on a court with four walls using a ball and a light bat consisting of a wood frame with a net stretched across it. *Squash is somewhat like tennis.*

squaw (skwô), *n.* an American Indian woman. *The squaws of a tribe took care of the cooking, gardening, and sewing.* **squaws.**

squeak (skwēk), *n.* 1. a sharp, high-pitched sound. *I could hear the squeak of the old door as John opened it. The squeaks of the little mouse came from the cellar.* **squeaks.**

v. 2. to make a sharp, high-pitched sound. *The old door squeaks. Mice squeak.* **squeaks, squeaked, squeak ing.**

squeal (skwēl), *n.* 1. a sharp, high-pitched cry. *The squeals of the pigs got louder as they saw the farmer bringing their food.* **squeals.**

v. 2. to make this sharp, high-pitched cry. *The pigs squealed. The little baby squealed with happiness.* **squeals, squealed, squeal ing.**

squeeze (skwēz), *v.* 1. to press hard; to force together from several sides. *Squeeze the sponge so that all the water comes out. The baby's little hand squeezed my finger.* 2. to get by pressing hard. *We squeezed juice from the oranges to drink for breakfast.* 3. to push; to force one's way. *He squeezed through the crowded bus to the exit. The dog tried to squeeze through the small opening in the fence, and got stuck.* 4. to force something by pressing. *She squeezed all her clothes into one suitcase.* **squeez es, squeezed, squeez ing.**

n. 5. a squeezing. *Joe gave my hand a long squeeze as we shook hands in saying goodbye.* 6. a hug. *The baby's mother gave the child a squeeze.* **squeez es.**

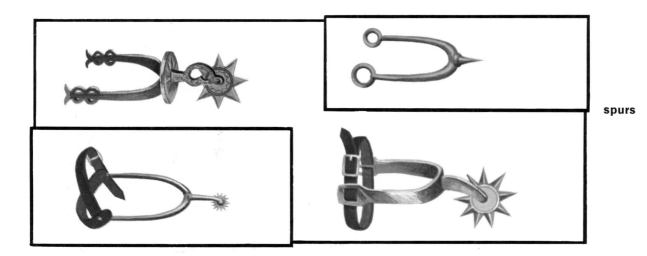

spurs

squirrel

squirm (skwėrm), *v.* to turn and twist the body. *The little boy squirmed in his seat at the concert because he wanted to leave.* **squirms, squirmed, squirm ing.**

squir rel (skwėr′əl), *n.* a small animal with a long bushy tail. *The fur of squirrels is usually red or gray. Squirrels like to eat nuts.* **squir rels.**

squirt (skwėrt), *v.* 1. to send out a liquid in a stream. *The hose squirted water.* 2. to wet with a liquid sent out in a stream. *On a hot day we put on our swimming suits and Father squirts*

us with water from the hose. **squirts, squirt ed, squirt ing.**

n. 3. a small stream of liquid. *Put a squirt of water on this little plant.* **squirts.**

stab (stab), *v.* 1. to wound or kill with something sharp and pointed. *The hunter stabbed the wolf with a knife.* 2. to jab; to stick something pointed into. *Mother stabbed a knife into the meat to see if it was cooked well.* **stabs, stabbed, stab bing.**

n. 3. a jab; a thrust. *The hunter made a stab at the wolf, but missed.* 4. a wound made by something pointed. *Jim got a small stab in his hand when he grabbed a sharp corner of his toy.* **stabs.**

sta ble[1] (stā′bl), *n.* 1. a building in which to keep farm animals. *The horses lived in a comfortable stable.* **sta bles.**

v. 2. to keep in a stable; to put in a stable. *During the heavy snowstorm, the horses were stabled all day.* **sta bles, sta bled, sta bling.**

sta ble[2] (stā′bl), *adj.* 1. firm; steady; solid. *This stable chair won't break.* 2. permanent; likely not to change. *Our country has a stable government. The store has a stable business; it hasn't changed much for thirty years.* **sta bler, sta blest; sta bly,** *adv.*

stack (stak), *n.* 1. a pile of hay or straw. *Stacks of hay were in the field after the harvest.* 2. any neat pile. *Here is a stack of dishes, ready to be placed on the table. This stack of books is yours.* 3. a chimney. *Smoke poured out of the stacks of the factory.* **stacks.**

stadium

v. 4. to place in a stack; to pile up neatly. *Stack the dishes on the table.* **stacks, stacked, stack ing.**

sta di um (stā′dē əm), *n.* a place for outdoor games with rising rows of seats on two or more sides. *The football stadium at the university seats over one hundred thousand people.* **sta di ums** or **sta dia** (stā′dē ə).

staff (staf), *n.* 1. a long cane or pole. *The shepherd used a staff to make the sheep go in the right direction. Long ago, travelers carried staffs to help them in walking and sometimes for defense against wild animals.* 2. a pole that supports something. *The flag waved in the breeze from its place at the top of the staff.* 3. a group of people working together under a leader or manager. *The teaching staff is under the direction of the principal.* 4. the five lines and four spaces between them on which notes are placed. *A song writer puts down the notes of a song on a staff, and a musician can then play the tune.* **staffs** or **staves** (stāvz) for 1 and 2; **staffs** for 3 and 4.

stag (stag), *n.* a male deer that is fully grown. *A stag has large horns.* **stags.**

stage (stāj), *n.* 1. the raised platform on which plays are presented. *The lights dimmed in the theater, the curtain rose, and on the stage the play began.* 2. the profession of acting; the theater. *The stage is John's career.* 3. a step; a period of development or growth. *The doctor can stop a disease in its first stage if the patient goes to him in time.* 4. a scene of action. *The football field was the stage for the big game between the champion Bears and the Rams.* 5. a place where a stop is made during a journey. *The people on the stagecoach got off at the next stage, when the horses were changed.* 6. the distance between stopping places on a journey. *The next stage of the trip is about one hundred miles.* 7. a stagecoach. *They took the stage to Arizona.* **stag es.**

v. 8. to arrange or put on a stage to see. *Our high school stages two plays a year.* **stag es, staged, stag ing.**

stage coach (stāj′kōch′), *n.* a coach or large carriage that carried about eight passengers and several sacks of mail. *In the West, stagecoaches pulled by horses were common before trains were used.* **stage coach es.**

stag

staid (stād), *v.* 1. past tense and past participle of **stay**[1].
adj. 2. serious; calm; quiet. *The two old sisters live a staid life.* **staid ly,** *adv.*

stain (stān), *v.* 1. to make a spot on; to dirty. *If you play in the mud, you will stain your new suit. The juice from the plum stained her new dress.* 2. to color. *The old table was light in color; now it has been stained dark brown and looks like new.* 3. to ruin; to spoil; to dishonor. *His fine reputation was stained by gossip.* **stains, stained, stain- ing.**
n. 4. a spot. *There is a stain on your dress from the gravy that the baby spilled. If you play in the grass, you may get grass stains on your new white suit.* 5. a shame; a disgrace. *The school hasn't any stain on its fine reputation.* 6. a kind of dye that can change the color of wood. *By using a dark stain, the painters made the wooden walls of our house look different.* **stains.**

stained glass, *n.* dyed or painted glass used for windows, especially in churches. *The sun shone through the stained glass.*

stair (stâr), *n.* 1. a single step of a series of

stagecoach

stained glass window

steps going up or down. *When we got to the last stair going up, we were out of breath.* 2. *pl.* **stairs,** steps that go from one story to another in a building. *When the elevator didn't work, the people had to walk up or down the stairs.* **stairs.**

stair case (stâr′kās′), *n.* a set of steps with a rail to hold on to for support. *The staircase in the old apartment building was covered with carpet.* **stair cas es.**

stake (stāk), *n.* 1. a stick or post that can be pounded into the ground because it has a pointed end. *The campers' tent was held in a firm position by ropes which were attached to stakes.* 2. a share. *A big company knows that its employees will work harder if they have a stake in the business.* 3. money or something else of value that is risked. *Some men play golf with each other for high stakes.* 4. a prize. *The stake in the spelling contest was a new, large dictionary.* **stakes.**
v. 5. to mark the limits or ends of by using stakes. *The prospector staked his claim to the mine he discovered.* 6. to hold up with a stake. *We staked the tomato plants.* 7. to bet. *I will stake my*

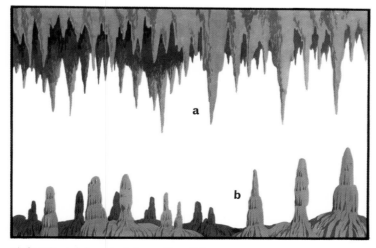

stalactites (a) and **stalagmites (b)**

life on the honesty of that boy. **stakes, staked, stak ing.**

sta lac tite (stə lak′tīt), *n.* a large deposit of stone, shaped like an icicle, that hangs from the roof of a cave. *Stalactites are formed over a long period of time when water carrying tiny pieces of a certain kind of rock drips slowly from the roof.* **sta lac tites.**

sta lag mite (stə lag′mīt), *n.* a large piece of rock, like a stalactite but rising from the floor of a cave. *A stalagmite is formed by water dripping on the floor of the cave. Stalagmites often get the drops that fall from the bottom of the stalactites.* **sta lag mites.**

stalk[1] (stôk), *n.* the stem of a plant. *Flowers have stalks. We eat stalks of celery.* **stalks.**

stalk[2] (stôk), *v.* 1. to hunt quietly; to go after secretly. *The hunter stalked the tiger for an hour.* 2. to walk stiffly and proudly. *When John thought the others were making fun of him, he stalked out of the room.* 3. to spread through. *Years ago, fear stalked the country when smallpox was reported, because there was no way to check the disease.* **stalks, stalked, stalk ing.**

stall[1] (stôl), *v.* 1. to delay; to stop. *The manager of the team stalled the game until his best player arrived. The engine of the car stalled while they were going up the hill.* **stalls, stalled, stall ing.** *n.* 2. a delay. *The teacher wasn't fooled by Henry's stall to keep from reciting, but she said nothing.* **stalls.**

stall[2] (stôl), *n.* 1. a space for one horse or one cow in a stable. *There were twenty horses and twenty stalls. A horse stands in his stall and eats from a kind of tray.* 2. a booth or stand. *At the school's spring fair many of the mothers sold cakes at stalls that had been set up on the lawn.* **stalls.** *v.* 3. to put or keep in a stall. *During the snowfall, the farmer stalled his horses.* 4. to come to a stop. *The engine of the car stalled on the hill.* **stalls, stalled, stall ing.**

stal lion (stal′yən), *n.* a male horse that is fully grown. *A stallion is large and strong.* **stal lions.**

stam mer (stam′ər), *v.* to speak with repetition of certain sounds. *In his fright, the boy stammered " Y-Y-Yes, sir, I w-w-will do-do it right away."* **stam mers, stam mered, stam mer ing.**

stamp (stamp), *n.* 1. a small, printed piece of paper, issued by the government, for sticking on letters and packages to show that the postage has been paid. *When you are at the Post Office, please get me some six-cent stamps and some forty-cent stamps.* 2. a similar piece of paper given by some stores with each purchase; trading stamp. *Stamps are pasted in a little book and when the book is filled, the customer can get a free gift.* 3. anything that makes a mark when pressed on an object. *Rubber stamps are used in offices and stores to save the time of writing words like " Rush" or " Urgent" or " Paid."* 4. a mark pressed on something. *The letters all had the* *stamp of the salesman's name.* 5. a sign; a mark. *Her face always has a stamp of happiness. The little boy's explanation had the stamp of truth.* 6. the act of stamping the foot. *The stamp of the horse's hoof on the wooden floor was loud.* **stamps.** *v.* 7. to put a stamp on. *Stamp the letters and then mail them.* 8. to mark with a stamp. *The clerk stamped the bill "Paid."* 9. to press or print a mark, design, words, etc. *Many people stamp their return addresses on envelopes instead of writing them. Before going back to college this fall, my brother stamped all his clothes with his name or initials.* 10. to mark. *The lady's face was stamped with fear when the baby's carriage rolled into the street.* 11. to beat the ground with the foot. *The donkey stamped to show he was hungry. The child stamped and said "No!"* 12. to put out with the foot. *The fireman stamped out the fire.* 13. to walk heavily and noisily. *The night of the election, the candidate stamped up and down the hall.* **stamps, stamped, stamp ing.**

stand (stand), *v.* 1. to be or place oneself in a vertical position. *The teacher asked those who needed help to stand beside their desks.* 2. to place in a vertical position. *Stand the shovel in a corner; don't let it lie on the floor.* 3. to rest on. *The new one-hundred-story building stands on a solid foundation of rock. A bowl of flowers stood on the top of the piano.* 4. to be placed; to be situated. *The old fort once stood on the land that is now the center of town.* 5. to remain firm; to hold good; to stay without any change. *The principal's rule still stands—no talking in the halls.* 6. to endure; to put up with. *Joanne couldn't stand the sight of the sick puppy, so she took it to an animal hospital to be cured.* 7. to be in a certain state or position. *The poor cat stands accused of killing the bird, but I know he was locked in the basement at the time. In my schoolroom there is a boy who stands high in English but who stands low in arithmetic.* 8. to undergo; to go through. *The prisoner stood trial.* 9. to do the duty of. *A teacher stands guard in the halls.* 10. to pay for. *We can't stand the cost of dinner at that fancy restaurant.* **stands, stood, stand ing.**

Stand also has the following special meanings:

stand by, to be ready to help. *Stand by your friends.*

stand for, (a) to put up with. *Our teacher won't stand for whispering in the class.* (b) to mean. *"Adj." stands for "adjective."* (c) to declare as an ideal; to be in favor of. *My mother stands for the kind treatment of all children. The writers of the United States Constitution stood for equal justice for all citizens.*

stand out, to be easily noticed. *Her beautiful handwriting stands out among all the other test papers.*

stand up for, defend. *Bill always stands up for his brother.*

stand ard (stan′dərd), *n.* 1. a flag; a banner.

standard

The king's standard was carried by a special group of soldiers. The standard of the United States is the American flag. 2. a post or pole that stands up straight to support something. *A flag is carried or flown on a standard.* 3. something that is used as a rule or model. *When food is "below standard," it is not as pure and healthful as most other foods like it. The government sets standards for medicines.* **stand ards.**

adj. 4. made according to a rule that has been agreed upon. *The standard size for typewriter paper is eight and one-half inches wide and eleven inches long.* 5. good; having value that most people recognize. *In literature we study some standard authors, like Mark Twain. The teacher says that the textbook we use in arithmetic is a standard book on the subject.* 6. **standard time,** the system of keeping time in the world or in a large area. *There are four zones of standard time in the United States: Eastern, Central, Mountain, and Pacific.*

stand ing (stan′ding), *n.* 1. position or rank. *Sandra has the highest standing in our class. Mr. Topper has a high standing in our town; he is a banker, the head of the Boy Scouts, and a leader in charity work.* 2. the time that something lasts. *It is hard to change a habit of long standing.* **stand ings.**

adj. 3. going on continuously; permanent. *The family has a standing order for two quarts of milk every day.* 4. done from vertical position. *In some races the runners use a standing start, instead of a kneeling start.* 5. not flowing; still. *The swamp has standing pools of water.*

stand point (stand′point′), *n.* a point of view; an attitude of mind for looking at or judging something. *From my standpoint, winter is the best time of the year.* **stand points.**

star (stär), *n.* 1. any of the large bodies in space

starfish

that we see as small points of light on clear nights. *Our sun is a star which is close to the earth. The brightness of a star depends on its size and temperature.* 2. a figure having five points or six points. *There are fifty stars in the American flag.* 3. a mark (*) that looks somewhat like a star. *A star is used in a textbook to call attention to a word, to refer to a note, etc.* 4. the chief or most important person in an activity. *The star of tonight's play is Muriel, who is an excellent actress.* **stars.**

v. 5. to be an important person in a play or some other activity. *For fifteen years Lou Gehrig starred in baseball, but today other men are starring. Who starred in the movie you saw?* 6. to mark with stars (*). *The names that are starred in the list are those that you should remember.* **stars, starred, star ring.**

starch (stärch), *n.* 1. a white substance, having no taste or smell, that is found in certain plants. *Potatoes, rye, and wheat have starch in them. People who are on a diet are told not to eat much starch.* 2. a powder or liquid made from this substance. *Starch is mixed with water and is used to make some gravies thicker. Some men like to wear collars with starch in them.* **starch es.**

v. 3. to make stiff with starch. *The laundry will starch clothes if asked.* **starch es, starched, starch ing.**

stare (stâr), *v.* 1. to look straight and steadily with the eyes wide open. *Little children will often stare at a person, especially a stranger. The sailor stared at the sea to try to find another ship.* **stares, stared, star ing.**

n. 2. a long, steady look. *Famous people get used to the stares of the crowds.* **stares.**

star fish (stär′fish′), *n.* a small sea animal with a body shaped like a star. *There are several kinds of starfish.* **star fish es** or **star fish.**

star ling (stär′ling), *n.* a bird with black feathers that is about the size of a robin. *Starlings always travel in large flocks.* **star lings.**

start (stärt), *v.* 1. to begin. *Russell starts his new job tomorrow. When does school start in fall? When you press this button, the music starts.* 2. to set in motion; to cause to operate. *Start the car now. Start the phonograph so the party can begin.* 3. to move suddenly; to jump. *The lady started when the doorbell rang loudly.* 4. to cause to move suddenly; startle. *Our appearance started the birds on the grass.* **starts, start ed, starting.**

n. 5. a sudden movement of surprise. *The sleeping dog gives a start when I clap my hands.* 6. a beginning. *The runner was off to a good start in the race. He was ahead at the start, but last at the finish.* **starts.**

star tle (stär′tl), *v.* 1. to surprise; frighten suddenly. *The noise at the window startled the girl.* 2. to cause to move suddenly. *The approach of the car startled the deer and they bounded across the road.* **star tles, star tled, star tling.**

starling

starve (stärv), *v.* to die or suffer from not having enough food. *The men lost in the desert nearly starved before an airplane appeared and dropped some food and water.* **starves, starved, starv ing.**

state (stāt), *n.* 1. the condition of one's mind or body. *The doctor said I was in a good physical state. Frank has changed from his worried state and now is confident he will pass the test. Some people do their best when they are in an anxious state.* 2. a showing of wealth; a display of dignity and formal manners. *The rich man traveled in state, in his own railroad car and his private plane. The king was received in state by the President.* 3. a group of people united under one government; a nation. *The United States was the first state to prove that people can govern themselves without a king.* 4. one of the fifty separate divisions of the United States having its own legislature and governor. *Each state makes its own laws, so long as it does not take away any rights that people have under the government of the United States.* **states.**
v. 5. to say or declare something by writing or speaking. *The writer stated his views in his latest book.* 6. to settle; to set; to fix. *We must state the date of our next meeting before we leave.* **states, stat ed, stat ing.**

stat ed (stāt′id), *adj.* regular; fixed. *The school has stated hours for study periods.*

state ment (stāt′mənt), *n.* 1. something that is said; a report. *The principal made a statement announcing the dates of the Christmas vacation.* 2. a report of how much money one has in a bank. *The bank statement shows I have over fifty dollars in my account.* **state ments.**

stat ic (stat′ik), *n.* 1. noise and fuzzy pictures in radio or television sets. *Static is caused by too great a number of electrical discharges in the air from storms or from electrical equipment nearby.*
adj. 2. at rest; not moving or working. *The water in the pond is static; it never flows. To keep your mind from being static, you should read.* 3. of or having to do with charges of electricity produced by friction. *You can make static electricity by rubbing your feet on a rug on a clear cold day and then touching a radiator with your fingers.*

sta tion (stā′shən), *n.* 1. a regular stopping place for a train or bus, having a building for passengers. *Railroad stations in big cities have many tracks leading into them, and large sheds for loading passengers and freight.* 2. the place where a person is located while on duty. *The waiter's station is at tables one to six at the restaurant. The bell sounded and the sailors rushed to their battle stations.* 3. a building used for a special purpose. *The new fire station is big.* 4. a place with equipment for sending out radio and television programs. *There are seven television stations in the city.* 5. position; standing. *A governor is a man of high station in government.* **sta tions.**
v. 6. to place. *The dog stationed himself at the door.* 7. to assign to a place. *The sailor was stationed at the training center.* **sta tions, sta tioned, sta tion ing.** (See illustration on following page.)

sta tion ary (stā′shən er′ē), *adj.* 1. not moving. *Remain stationary until I count to ten.* 2. fixed in one place. *A stationary engine never moves, but it creates power to move other things.* 3. not changing very much. *Some old towns have a stationary population.*

sta tion ery (stā′shən er′ē), *n.* paper and envelopes used for writing letters. *We bought Mother some good stationery with her name printed on both the paper and the envelopes.*

sta tis tics (stə tis′tiks), *n. pl.* or *sing.* 1. numbers that give information about a subject. *Statistics show that more children are now in school than ever before. According to statistics, prices have gone up in the last year.* 2. the science that deals with collecting, classifying, and using facts and figures. *My brother is taking a course in statistics in college.*

stat ue (stach′ü), *n.* a figure of a person or animal carved in wood, stone, metal, or other material. *Nearly every town has a statue of a famous man.* **stat ues.** (See illustration on following page.)

stat ute (stach′üt), *n.* a law. *Every country has statutes against stealing.* **stat utes.**

stay¹ (stā), *v.* 1. to remain. *The father told his small son to stay in the playground. Let's stay to the end of the movie.* 2. to live for awhile. *The family stayed with friends in California.* 3. to keep on being. *Now that winter has come, we expect the weather to stay cold.* 4. to halt or delay; to put off. *Always stay your final decision until you are sure of all the facts. Marie has a quick temper, so she has learned to stay her anger.* 5. to satisfy for a little while. *Bill stayed his hunger by eating some crackers.* **stays, stayed** or **staid, staying.**

n. 6. a time of staying or remaining. *The gray-haired worker has had a long stay with the company that hired him when he was a young man. Our teacher had an interesting stay in Mexico last year.* **stays.**

stay² (stā), *n.* a rope or wire which helps to hold up the mast of a ship. *The stay stretched from the top of the mast to the deck.* **stays.**

stay³ (stā), *n.* a support; a stake or pole used to hold something up or to hold it steady. *A stay kept the old tree from falling down during the storm.* **stays.**

steady (sted′ē), *adj.* 1. firm. *The table is steady since the carpenter fixed its legs.* 2. regular; not changing. *The cars traveled at a steady speed on the highway.* 3. always the same; usual. *The steady price for the soap is fifteen cents, but it is on* sale this week for eleven cents. 4. trustworthy; reliable. *Kathy has many jobs taking care of children because parents know that she is a steady girl.* 5. not easily excited or upset. *A doctor must have steady nerves and remain calm.* **stead i er, stead i est; stead i ly,** *adv.*

v. 6. to make steady. *Steady the ladder while I climb up.* 7. to become steady. *After he got over being nervous about taking the test, his handwriting steadied.* **stead ies, stead ied, stead y ing.**

steak (stāk), *n.* a slice of meat or fish for cooking. *Steaks mostly are cut from the meat of cattle.* **steaks.**

steal (stēl), *v.* 1. to take without permission. *The burglars stole typewriters from the office. The office worker stole some time from his job to go shopping. The dog stole my steak.* 2. to move quietly and secretly. *We had to leave, so we stole out of the room without disturbing the others.* 3. to take entirely for oneself; to be the best in.

train **station**

statue

All the performers were good, but the girl singer stole the show and got the most applause. 4. to get or win by charm or by being clever. *The little puppy stole the girl's heart when he sat up and shook hands.* **steals, stole, stol en, steal ing.**
n. 5. an act of stealing. 6. a bargain; something bought at an unusually low price. *That record is a steal at seventy-five cents; it originally cost over five dollars.* **steals.**

steam (stēm), *n.* 1. the invisible gas or gaseous state into which water is changed by heating. *Steam cannot be seen.* 2. the kind of cloud or mist formed when the invisible gas is cooled. *The steam from boiling water is wet. Steam forms on windows during cold weather.* 3. steam kept under pressure, to supply heat or power. *Many locomotives were once run by steam.*
v. 4. to give off steam. *The water in the pot is steaming.* 5. to move under the power of an engine run by steam. *The ship steamed out of the harbor.* 6. to cook, soften, or take off by steam. *Mother steamed the hard rolls. You can steam a label from a bottle or can.* **steams, steamed, steam ing.**
adj. 7. using steam. *A steamboat is run by a steam engine.* 8. carrying steam. *Steam pipes are carefully covered to prevent burns.*

steam boat (stēm′bōt′), *n.* a boat that moves by the power of steam. *Steamboats were used on rivers before the days of railroads and airplanes.* **steam boats.**

steam er (stēm′ər), *n.* 1. a boat or ship that is

moved by steam. *The steamer is on time.* 2. an engine driven by steam power. *Some early automobile engines were steamers.* 3. a pan with holes in it. *Food is placed in a steamer which in turn is placed over a pot of boiling water.* **steamers.**

steam roller (stēm′rōl′ər), *n.* a machine with heavy roller, used in building roads. *The steam roller packs down soft surface material.* **steam rollers.**

steam ship (stēm′ship′), *n.* a ship that moves by the power of steam. *We went to Europe on a steamship.* **steam ships.**

steel (stēl), *n.* 1. a strong metal made from iron by mixing it with carbon. *Steel is used for making strong tools. The bodies of automobiles are made of steel.* 2. a sword. *The knight said, " The enemy shall be the victim of my steel!"*
v. 3. to make strong; make tough. *He steeled himself against the possibility of getting a poor mark.* **steels, steeled, steel ing.**
adj. 4. made of steel. *The bank keeps its money in a steel safe.*

steep[1] (stēp), *adj.* 1. slanting sharply up and down. *The steep mountain cannot be climbed.* 2. too high. *The house is for sale at a steep price.* **steep er, steep est; steep ly,** *adv.*

steep[2] (stēp), *v.* to soak. *The hostess steeped the tea leaves in boiling water to make a pot of tea.* **steeps, steeped, steep ing.**

stee ple (stē′pl), *n.* a pointed tower on the roof of a church. *The bells in the steeple ring every Sunday morning.* **stee ples.**

steer[1] (stir), *v.* 1. to direct; to cause to move in the correct direction. *The sailor steered the little boat into a harbor. Turn the wheel of an automobile to the right and you steer the car to the right.* 2. to be guided. *The new car steers easily.* 3. **steer clear of,** to avoid; to stay away from. *Steer clear of that group if you are serious about studying.* **steers, steered, steer ing.**

steer[2] (stir), *n.* a male of the ox family, especially one raised for beef. *Steers are raised on big ranches in the West.* **steers.**

steel razor blade

steel ball bearing

steel bolt and nut

steam roller (1910)

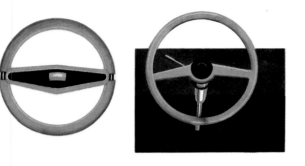

steering wheels

steering wheel, *n.* the wheel that is used to steer a ship, an automobile, etc. *When you drive a car, keep both hands on the steering wheel.* **steering wheels.**

stem (stem), *n.* 1. the main part of a plant that grows up from the ground; a stalk. *Some roses have long stems.* 2. any part that grows from this main part and bears a flower, leaf, etc. *The rose has small stems that have leaves and buds on them.* 3. any slender support like the stem of a plant. *Wine glasses usually have stems. Every night I wind the stem of my watch.* 4. the front part of a ship or boat; the bow. *The ship's stem sliced through the water.* **stems.**
v. 5. to come from; to develop from. *This path stems from the main road. Most of my worries stem from my imagination.* 6. to go against. *The boat had to stem the heavy wind to get to shore.* 7. to stop; to dam up. *The army helped the citizens to stem the flow of water when the river rose. The doctor stemmed the bleeding from the cut on my arm.* **stems, stemmed, stem ming.**

step (step), *n.* 1. a movement made by raising the foot and putting it down in a new position. *People walk by taking one step after another.* 2. the space or distance covered by such a movement. *I was only one step from the house when I remembered the door was still open.* 3. a short distance. *They live just a step from the bus station.* 4. the sound made by putting the foot down. *We heard some steps on the stairs.* 5. a way of walking. *Mr. Carlton is an active man with a fast step.* 6. a footprint. *Steps could be seen in the new snow.* 7. a stair; a rung of a ladder. *The third step of the ladder is broken.* 8. the movement of the feet and body in dancing. *The dancer knows all the latest steps.* 9. an act; an action; a thing to do. *The first step in saving money is to cut down on spending.* 10. a grade in rank. *A principal of a school is one step above an assistant principal.* **steps.**
v. 11. to move by taking steps or a step. *When your name is called, step forward.* 12. to walk a short distance. *Step over here, please.* 13. to place the foot on. *He stepped on the brake to stop the car.* 14. to measure by steps. *Step off ten feet.* 15. **step up,** to speed up; to make go faster. *We will have to step up our work if we want to complete the job on time.* **steps, stepped, step ping.**

ster ile (ster′əl), *adj.* 1. free from living germs. *Doctors and dentists keep their instruments sterile.* 2. not able to produce crops. *This sterile land is impossible to farm.* **ster ile ly,** *adv.*

stern[1] (stėrn), *adj.* 1. severe; strict; not gentle. *Parents sometimes have to be stern with their children.* 2. firm. *The teacher said I should make a stern resolution to do better.* **stern er, stern est; stern ly,** *adv.*

stern[2] (stėrn), *n.* the back part of a ship or boat. *The flag on a small boat usually flies from the stern.* **sterns.**

steth o scope (steth′ə skōp), *n.* an instrument used by doctors for listening to the beat of the heart and to the sounds of breathing in the lungs. *A stethoscope makes these sounds louder and clearer.* **steth o scopes.**

stew (stü, stū), *n.* 1. food cooked by slow boiling. *Most stews contain meat and vegetables.* **stews.**
v. 2. to cook by boiling slowly. *Dried fruits, such as prunes, pears, and peaches, are stewed.* **stews, stewed, stew ing.**

stew ard ess (stü′ər dis, stū′ər dis) *n.* a young woman whose job is to take care of the passengers on an airplane. *On our flight to New York, the stewardesses served us a hot meal.* **stew ard ess es.**

stick (stik), *v.* 1. to stab; to prick with something sharp and pointed. *Don't stick yourself with the needle.* 2. to fasten or attach by pinning

stewardess

or gluing. *Stick a stamp on the envelope. Use pins to stick these two papers together.* 3. to put; to thrust. *We stuck our hands in the air when we had the answer. The dog sticks out his paw to shake hands.* 4. to catch. *The cat is stuck at the top of the tree. Doors sometimes stick in damp weather.* 5. to puzzle; to confuse. *One problem in the arithmetic lesson has me stuck.* 6. to be thrust; extend; project. *The cat's ears stick up.* 7. **stick by,** remain loyal to. *His friends stuck by him through his troubles.* 8. **stick to,** to keep at. *Stick to the job until you finish it.* 9. **stick up for,** defend. *Elaine always sticks up for her little sister.* **sticks, stuck, stick ing.**

n. 10. a long, thin piece of wood; a branch off a tree or shrub. *You can use these dry sticks to start the fire.* 11. a long piece of wood made for a special purpose. *One of the hockey players broke his stick.* 12. something that is like a stick. *Here is a stick of candy for you.* **sticks.**

stick y (stik′ē), *adj.* 1. that sticks. *The sticky candy got caught in the baby's hair.* 2. that makes things stick; hot and humid. *For two weeks the summer air was sticky.* **stick i er, stick i-est; stick i ly,** *adv.*

stiff (stif), *adj.* 1. that does not bend easily. *Some men wear stiff collars.* 2. not able to move easily or smoothly. *The boy's muscles felt stiff the morning after he played ball for the first time this year.* 3. hard to move. *The old rusty lock is stiff and we can't open it.* 4. hard; difficult. *We had a stiff test in English class.* 5. harsh; severe. *The man got a stiff punishment for his crime.* 6. strong. *A stiff wind was blowing papers and dust down the street.* 7. not natural and easy in behavior; too formal. *The woman has a stiff way of speaking and smiling.* 8. thick. *Stir the warm fudge until it is stiff, then set it aside to cool.* **stiff er, stiff est; stiff ly,** *adv.*

still (stil), *adj.* 1. quiet; silent. *His footsteps sounded loud in the still night. The old farmhouse is still.* 2. not moving. *The rabbit remained still so the hunter wouldn't see him.*

n. 3. quiet; silence. *He liked to walk in the still of the night.*

conj. 4. and yet; nevertheless. *The boy works hard; still, he never seems tired.*

adv. 5. even; yet. *Thelma arrived late, but Susan came still later. It was cold last night and it will be still colder tonight.* 6. at the time talked about; up to that time. *The forest fire was still burning the next day.* 7. yet; in spite of that; nevertheless. *He had five pieces of candy and still wanted more.*

v. 8. to make quiet or calm. *Every mother knows how to still her crying child.* 9. to become calm or quiet. *As the violinist prepared to play, the audience stilled.* **stills, stilled, still ing.**

still ness (stil′nis), *n.* 1. quiet; silence. *After the noise of the city, the stillness of the country was a relief.* 2. absence of motion. *The stillness of the air caused the stillness of the water in the pond.*

walking on **stilts**

stilt (stilt), *n.* a long, strong pole with a support for the foot and sometimes for the leg. *Circus clowns are experts at walking and running on stilts.* **stilts.**

stim u late (stim′ū lāt), *v.* to excite; to cause an action. *Nothing will stimulate Bill to do his homework.* **stim u lates, stim u lat ed, stim-u lat ing.**

sting (sting), *v.* 1. to prick or stab with the sharp, pointed organ of some insects and other animals. *The wasp stung the child on the hand and the pain made her cry.* 2. to affect with a sharp pain. *Soap stings the eyes. The temperature was below zero and the wind stung my cheeks.* 3. to hurt by mean remarks. *Any person is stung when his friends make fun of him.* **stings, stung, sting ing.**

n. 4. a stinging. *The sting of some bees is poisonous to some people. The sting of a mosquito irritates the skin and causes a small, red bump.* 5. a wound or pain caused by stinging. *The sting of the bee hurt him for three days. The sting of his friend's unkind comments stayed with him for a long time.* 6. the sharp, pointed organ of some insects and other animals. *The scorpion's tail has a sting on its end.* **stings.**

stin gy (stin′jē), *adj.* not generous; unwilling to spend or give. *The stingy boy wouldn't let his friends play with his new toy train. The stingy man has never sent anyone a present.* **stin gi er, stin gi est; stin gi ly,** *adv.*

stir (stėr), *v.* 1. to move slightly. *The leaves of the tree stirred in the gentle, soft wind. No one was stirring in the darkened house.* 2. to move around

or mix. *Bill stirred his cocoa with a spoon after he put sugar in it. The painter stirred the paint in the can with a short stick.* 3. to affect deeply; to cause strong emotion in. *His wonderful speech stirred the crowd.* 4. to make move; to make active. *Father stirred me to do my homework. Stir the fire with the poker.* **stirs, stirred, stir ring.**
n. 5. movement. *The baby slept through the entire night without a stir.* 6. excitement. *The close election caused a stir among the voters.* 7. a mixing. *Give the pudding a stir so that it won't get burned.* **stirs.**

stir ring (stėr′ing), *adj.* that stirs the feelings; exciting; lively. *The Navy band played a stirring march.* **stir ring ly,** *adv.*

stir rup (stėr′əp, stir′əp), *n.* a ring, loop, or other device that hangs from the side of a saddle and is used to support the foot. *The cowboy put his foot in the stirrup to mount the horse.* **stir rups.**

stitch (stich), *n.* 1. one complete movement of a threaded needle through cloth or other material. *The tailor used ten stitches to repair the rip in Diane's dress.* 2. a sudden, sharp pain. *Clifford got a stitch in his side after he ran all the way home.* **stitch es.**
v. 3. to sew. *Mother is stitching a new dress.* **stitch es, stitched, stitch ing.**

stock (stok), *n.* 1. a supply; an amount of things to sell or to use. *For its big sale, the store ordered a large stock of clothes. The stock of food and water carried by the men lost in the desert was still large.* 2. farm animals; livestock; cattle, horses, pigs, etc. *Some of the farmer's stock won prizes at the state fair.* 3. the family that one

comes from, including those who lived long ago. *My father comes from French stock, and my mother is of English stock.* 4. shares in a business. *If you have stock in a company, you receive a part of the money it makes.* 5. the trunk or stump of a tree; the stem of a plant. *Branches grow from the stock of the tree. That flower has a long stock on which many leaves grow.* 6. the liquid in which meat and vegetables have been cooked. *Cooks use stock for making gravy and soup.* 7. a support or handle. *Hunters hold their rifles by the stock when shooting.* 8. **stocks,** a framework of wood with holes in which a prisoner's feet and hands were locked. *The stocks were used long ago as a punishment.* **stock** (for 2), **stocks** (for all others).
v. 9. to furnish; to supply. *Stock the refrigerator with root beer for the party.* 10. to have a supply of. *The drugstore stocks writing paper and envelopes.* **stocks, stocked, stock ing.**
adj. 11. used very often. *A stock subject of conversation between mothers is the health of their babies.* 12. always kept for sale. *A drugstore keeps a stock supply of medicines.*

stock ing (stok′ing), *n.* a cover of wool, nylon, cotton, etc. for the foot and leg; sock. *Kathy bought a pair of stockings to match her dress.* **stock ings.**

stole[1] (stōl), *n.* a garment of fur or other material that women wear around the neck and shoulders. *My mother is saving to buy a mink stole.* **stoles.**

stole[2] (stōl), past tense of **steal.**

stom ach (stum′ək), *n.* 1. the organ in the body into which food goes after it is swallowed. *The stomach helps to digest the food.* 2. a liking; a desire. *My sister has no stomach for sad movies.* **stom achs.**
v. 3. to put up with. *The people couldn't stomach the king's selfish acts, so they forced him to go away while they set up a fair government.* **stom achs, stom ached, stom ach ing.**

stone (stōn), *n.* 1. rock; a hard mineral matter found in the earth. *Stone is not a metal. Many houses, monuments, statues, office buildings, and schools are built of stone.* 2. a small piece of this material; a bit of rock. *We threw stones in the water. Some roads are made of stones, packed down firmly.* 3. a gem. *Diamonds are precious stones.* 4. a large seed found in certain fruits; pit. *Cherries, peaches, and plums have stones.* **stones.**
v. 5. to throw stones at. *The boys on the ranch stoned the wolf as they saw him coming close to their sheep.* 6. to take out the stones of. *We must stone the cherries so that Mother can make cherry pie for dinner.* **stones, stoned, ston ing.**
adj. 7. made of or having to do with stone. *The Stone Age was the time when people used tools and weapons made only of stone and wood. Some buildings have stone pillars.*

stood (stůd), past tense and past participle of **stand.**

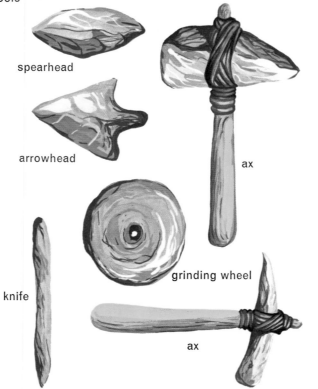

primitive **stone** tools

spearhead

arrowhead

ax

knife

grinding wheel

ax

stool

stool (stül), *n.* 1. a low seat having no back or arms. *The small children sat on stools while Grandfather read them a story.* 2. a seat on long legs, usually with no back or a very short one. *Many restaurants have stools at their counters to seat customers.* **stools.**

stoop[1] (stüp), *v.* 1. to bend forward; bend down. *We stooped to pick up all the coins that Robby dropped on the floor.* 2. to have a bent posture. *The old man stoops when he walks. The trees stooped because of the heavy winds.* 3. to lower oneself. *My mother has never stooped to gossiping about her neighbors.* **stoops, stooped, stooping.**

n. 4. a bent posture. *The old woman walks with a stoop.* **stoops.**

stoop[2] (stüp), *n.* a small porch at the entrance of a house. *The dog likes to sit on the stoop and watch the people walk by.* **stoops.**

stop (stop), *v.* 1. to halt; to prevent from moving, doing, working, etc. *Soldiers stop cars at the entrance to the army camp. The teacher stopped me in the corridor and asked me why I was not in my room.* 2. to come to a halt; to cease moving, acting, doing, etc. *The storm stopped and we could go outside to see the damage it caused. Suddenly the radio stopped; we think it needs a new tube. The car stopped while we were going uphill.* 3. to fill up; to block. *Mud and leaves stopped the entrance to the sewer. She stopped her ears with her fingers when the fireworks exploded.* 4. to stay; to visit. *The salesman stops at a motel every night when he is traveling. At Christmas we stop at Grandmother's house for about three days.* **stops, stopped, stop ping.**

n. 5. a short visit. *We made a stop at the museum on our way home.* 6. a place stopped at. *There is a bus stop at the next corner.* 7. a halt. *The car rolled to a stop at the bottom of the hill. "You boys put a stop to that fighting!" said Mr. Howard firmly.* 8. something that stops. *We put a small, heavy stop made of iron in front of the door and now it doesn't blow shut.* 9. a device for controlling the sounds of certain musical instruments. *An organ has many stops for making certain tones.* **stops.**

stor age (stôr′ij), *n.* 1. keeping things in a safe place. *The best place for storage of money is a bank.* 2. a place where goods are stored or kept safely. *Most of her furniture was put in storage when she moved from the big house into a small apartment.* 3. the money that it costs to store things. *The storage of the piano won't be much, so let's move it out of the house.*

store (stôr), *n.* 1. a place where goods are sold. *A grocery store sells many kinds of food. Mark bought a hammer, a saw, and some nails in the hardware store.* 2. a supply. *We keep a store of light bulbs in the house.* **stores.**

v. 3. to put away for future use; to keep in a safe place. *Store the ornaments for Christmas in the closet. Store your money in a bank.* **stores, stored, stor ing.**

store room (stôr′rüm′), *n.* a room for storing things. *The storeroom in the office has a supply of paper, envelopes, pens, and other writing materials.* **store rooms.**

stork (stôrk), *n.* a bird with long legs, a long neck, and a long bill. *A stork lives near shallow water where it likes to wade.* **storks.**

storm (stôrm), *n.* 1. strong winds often accompanied by heavy amounts of rain, snow, hail, sleet, or flying sand. *In summer a storm usually brings thunder and lightning. The sand from the storm in the desert blinded the travelers.* 2. a sudden, violent expression of one's feelings. *When the driver nearly ran over his bicycle, Charles let loose a storm of angry words. Some great books and paintings met with storms of criticism the first time they were presented.* **storms.**

v. 3. to blow hard and to rain or snow heavily. *It is beginning to storm.* 4. to be angry; to rage. *Mr. Bliss is storming about the high cost of living.* 5. to move quickly and angrily. *Mrs. Taylor stormed into the store and demanded her money back.* 6. to attack with strength. *The soldiers stormed the town where the enemy was.* **storms, stormed, storm ing.**

stormy (stôr′mē), *adj.* 1. of or having to do with storms. *I like stormy weather when I am inside. Last spring was stormy.* 2. angry and excited. *The town council had a stormy discussion about where to locate the park.* **storm i er, storm i est; storm i ly,** *adv.*

sto ry[1] (stô′rē), *n.* 1. a report of something that happened. *The newspaper story gives all the information about the trip we made to Washington, D.C.* 2. a tale or account of an adventure or happening that never really took place. *Stories are made up by authors to interest the readers. The children like to listen to fairy stories. Stories about adventure and sports are written to give pleasure to boys.* 3. a lie. *The boy was caught telling stories about his friends.* **stor ies.**

sto ry[2] (stô′rē), *n.* the space or set of rooms on one level of a building. *My father works on the eighteenth story of an office building.* **stor ies.**

sto ry tel ler (stô′rē tel′ər), *n.* a person who

stork

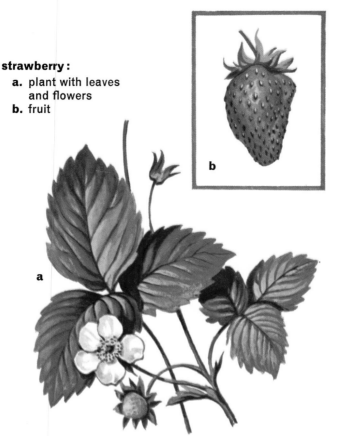

strawberry :
a. plant with leaves and flowers
b. fruit

tells or writes stories. *Grandfather is a good storyteller.* **sto ry tel lers.**

stout (stout), *adj.* 1. fat. *My aunt is going on a diet because she has gotten a little stout.* 2. strong; tough. *The man carried a stout stick to help him in walking.* 3. brave. *A stout crew of sailors fought off the pirates who tried to take their ship.* **stout er, stout est; stout ly,** *adv.*

stove (stōv), *n.* a structure or device used for cooking or heating. *Different stoves use gas, electricity, oil, coal, or wood as a fuel.* **stoves.**

straight (strāt), *adj.* 1. having no curves or bends. *The straight highway goes north all the way to the city. A circle has no straight line. A triangle has three straight lines that meet and form three angles.* 2. neat; in order. *The room is straight. A store or a bank must keep its records straight.* 3. honest; sincere; frank. *You can expect a straight answer from him.* 4. not getting off the main point. *His straight thinking has helped me a great deal.* 5. reliable; not changed. *I've got straight information from the principal about the new school hours.* 6. serious. *It was hard to keep a straight face when the child told about his first day at school.* **straight er, straight est; straight ly,** *adv.*

adv. 7. in a straight line; directly. *The dog trotted straight to his home.* 8. in a way that is straight, direct, honest, sincere, etc. *He treats all people straight. A scholar thinks straight.*

straight en (strāt′n), *v.* 1. to make straight. *Before going into the office, Jack combed his hair and straightened his tie.* 2. to become straight.

After miles of curving, the road straightened. 3. to put in order. *My sister straightens her room in the morning.* **straight ens, straight ened, straight en ing.**

strain[1] (strān), *v.* 1. to stretch; to pull tight. *The heavy church bell strained the cable that was lifting it into place. The dog is straining at his rope.* 2. to weaken; to injure; to hurt. *The pitcher strained a muscle in his arm at baseball practice. Father strained his back while shoveling snow.* 3. to try as hard as possible. *We strained to hear his speech, but his voice was weak.* 4. to stretch beyond the correct limit. *Some people strain the truth to make an adventure sound more thrilling.* 5. to be exerted to the limit. *My muscles strained, but I couldn't pull the heavy box.* 6. to press or pour through a filter. *The cook strained the water from the cooked vegetables.* **strains, strained, strain ing.**

n. 7. a force, pressure, or pull. *The strain on the old rope broke it.* 8. an injury caused by too much stretching. *He had a strain in his ankle and in his shoulder.* 9. extreme or excessive pressure; worry. *He felt no strain during the final examinations because he knew he had done his best.* 10. melody; tune. *The strain of our school song has been going through my mind all day.* **strains.**

strain[2] (strān), *n.* 1. race; stock. *This horse comes from a fine strain of champions.* 2. a quality that may have been passed down from one generation to another. *There is a strain of musical genius in that family.* 3. a trace; a small bit. *There was a strain of humor in the principal's speech.* **strains.**

strange (strānj), *adj.* 1. new; not familiar; not known, heard, or seen before. *There are many parts of our own state that are strange to me.* 2. odd; unusual; different. *The little boy looked strange after his first haircut. The funniest boy in class is always saying strange things.* 3. out of place; shy. *For the first week the new boy felt strange; then he began to make friends. Everybody feels strange when he starts a new job.* **strang er, strang est; strange ly,** *adv.*

strang er (strān′jər), *n.* 1. a person who is not known. *There were many strangers at the party.* 2. someone from another place. *Many strangers came to the town for the big State Fair. A stranger in a city should ask a policeman for directions to get to a place.* 3. a person who is not accustomed to something. *The healthy man is a stranger to illness.* **strang ers.**

strap (strap), *n.* 1. a narrow strip of leather or other such material used to hold things together or in place. *Sometimes we use a strap to hold our schoolbooks together.* **straps.**

v. 2. to fasten with a strap. *The dog was strapped to the pole while we played ball.* **straps, strapped, strap ping.**

strat e gy (strat′ə ji), *n.* 1. a careful, planned way of attack. *The strategy of the boys was to enter the house by the back door and take some* *cookies.* 2. the science of war; the management of a military operation. *The general's strategy was to surround the enemy and attack from all sides at dawn.* **strat e gies.**

straw (strô), *n.* 1. the hollow stalks or stems of grain, such as wheat or oats, after the grain has been removed. *Straw is used as a bed for farm animals. Straw is also used to make hats, baskets, and many other things.* 2. a thin hollow tube of paper. *Straws are served with lemonade for sipping the flavored drinks.* **straws.**
adj. 3. made of straw. *She wears a straw hat in the summer.*

straw ber ry (strô′ber′ē), *n.* 1. a red fruit that has tiny seedlike dots on its surface. *Strawberries are delicious with cream and sugar.* 2. the plant that bears this fruit. *The strawberry has white blossoms.* **straw ber ries.**

straw flow er (strô′flou′ər), *n.* a tall annual herb with red, orange, yellow, or white flowers. *Strawflowers last a long time when they are picked and dried.* **straw flow ers.**

stray (strā), *v.* 1. to lose the way; to wander. *Little children should be taught not to stray from home. Sometimes you can't keep your thoughts from straying even in the classroom.* **strays, strayed, stray ing.**
n. 2. a lost or wandering person or animal. *The little cat seemed to be a stray, so I took him home and fed him milk.* **strays.**
adj. 3. lost. *I kept the stray cat when no one advertised for him.* 4. scattered; here and there. *I saw only a few stray baseball players in the park on the hot afternoon.*

streak (strēk), *n.* 1. a mark or line; a stripe. *He had streaks of grease on his face after he fixed the car.* 2. a narrow band of light. *The streak of light under his door meant that he was still studying. A streak of lightning flashed through the sky.* 3. a certain amount of a good or bad quality. *He has a wonderful streak of humor in him.* 4. a brief time or period. *My father had a streak of bad luck with his business, but he quickly put an end to it.* 5. a layer. *The miners found a streak of gold. Some meat has streaks of fat in it.* **streaks.**
v. 6. to mark with streaks. *The grease streaked his face.* 7. to go fast. *He streaked to school.* **streaks, streaked, streak ing.**

stream (strēm), *n.* 1. a flow of water; a brook or small river. *The stream bubbled over the rocks.* 2. any flow. *A stream of people poured out of the airport. A stream of cars passed on the highway. A stream of cold air flowed into the warm room. A stream of light came from the lighthouse.* **streams.**
v. 3. to move steadily and continuously. *The cars streamed by.* 4. to float; to wave. *The flags streamed from their poles on the holiday.* 5. to flow. *Tears streamed from her eyes when she saw the sad movie.* **streams, streamed, stream ing.**

stream er (strēm′ər), *n.* a long, narrow flag or ribbon. *The children all carried streamers as they marched in the parade.* **stream ers.**

strawflowers

street (strēt), *n.* a road in a city or town. *Houses, apartment buildings, stores, and offices are usually built on each side of a street. It is difficult to find a place to park on this crowded street.* **streets.**

street car (strēt′kär′), *n.* a large car which runs on rails on a street. *A streetcar carries passengers and is run by electricity. Most cities now have buses instead of streetcars.* **street cars.**

strength (strengkth, strength), *n.* the quality of being strong. *He lost some of the strength in his muscles when he stopped exercising. You need strength of resolution to finish some jobs. Let's test the strength of this little bridge by walking on it. Has that rope the strength to hold this big dog?* **strengths.**

strength en (strengk′thən, streng′thən), *v.* to make strong; to become strong. *Exercise strengthens the body.* **strength ens, strength ened, strength en ing.**

stress (stres), *n.* 1. strain; force; pressure. *The stress of heavy traffic made the old wooden bridge weaker every year. His vacation freed him from the stress of his job.* 2. special attention; importance. *Some schools put too much stress on athletics. A doctor puts stress on eating the right foods.* 3. a strong accent given to a part of a word. *In "teacher," the stress is on "teach-"; in "holiday," the stress is on "hol-".* **stress es.**
v. 4. to dwell on; to pay much attention to. *Schools stress the importance of good study habits.* 5. to put a strong accent on a certain part of a word. *Stress the "-lec-" in "electric."* **stress es, stressed, stress ing.**

stretch (strech), *v.* 1. to hold out; to put out;

to extend. *The boy stretched his hand across the table. She stretched her neck to look out the window.* 2. to spread apart. *If you stretch a rubber band too far, it breaks.* 3. to draw out to full length; to extend to full size. *The boy stretched after he woke up. The road stretches for miles. You can stretch the rope between the two posts.* 4. to make seem larger, greater, or more interesting than it really is. *Don't stretch the facts; just tell us what happened.* **stretch es, stretched, stretch ing.**

n. 5. a stretching; a being stretched. *With a quick stretch, the cat got her paw on the ball of yarn.* 6. a continuous length; an extent. *This stretch of the road never has much traffic.* 7. the ability to be stretched. *The rubber band is so old it has lost its stretch.* 8. an effort. *By no stretch of the imagination can I think that I will be rich.* **stretch es.**

strict (strikt), *adj.* 1. keeping closely to the rules; seeing that others follow the rules exactly. *The new teacher is strict, but he is also fair. The army sergeant was strict with the new soldiers.* 2. complete; entire. *She told me in strict confidence that her family was going to move away. The library insists upon strict silence.* 3. perfect; just right. *The men who make the parts of an airplane must use strict measurements.* 4. severe; not gentle. *The judge was very strict in his dealings with criminals.* **strict er, strictest; strict ly,** *adv.*

strike (strīk), *v.* 1. to hit. *The batter struck the ball.* 2. to sound. *The clock strikes every hour.* 3. to light a match. *Little children should never strike matches.* 4. to occur to; to come to the attention of. *A great idea just struck me—let's go swimming!* 5. to impress. *Some of Ben's inventions strike me as being ridiculous.* 6. to stop work as a group in order to get a company, a business, or the public to increase salaries or to give better conditions for working. *The workers felt that they were not being paid enough, so they decided to strike.* 7. to discover; to find or get to. *The company struck oil beneath the ocean near the shore.* 8. to affect by a disease, suffering, etc. *He was stricken by a slight cold, so he stayed in bed until he was well. A sudden attack of sneezing struck the dog, who was breathing the dust from the dry road.* 9. to attack; come suddenly. *The storm struck in the middle of the night.* 10. to go; proceed. *The boys struck through the woods to get to the town.* 11. to make by stamping or printing. *The United States government strikes coins in several mints in the land.* 12. to agree on the details of. *We struck a bargain; I sold him my old bike for five dollars.* 13. to take down. *The ship struck its flag to show it surrendered.* 14. to remove. *Strike his name from the honor roll.* 15. **strike out,** (a) to cross out or erase. *If you misspell a word you can strike out the word and write it again.* (b) to start. *The campers struck out on their hike.* (c) in baseball, to fail to hit or

swing at three good pitches. *Some baseball players strike out when they are up against a good pitcher.* 16. **strike up,** to begin; to start. *Strike up the band. We struck up a friendship the first day we met.* **strikes, struck, struck** or **strick en, strik ing.**

n. 17. a striking; a blow; a hit. *Three strikes of the hammer drove the nail in the wood.* 18. a stopping of work to get better pay or better working conditions. *The truck drivers' union has called a strike.* 19. in baseball, a pitched ball that is thrown just right but which the batter either doesn't swing at or swings at and misses. *Three strikes and you're out.* 20. in bowling, the knocking down of all ten pins on the first roll of the ball. *One of the men on the team got three strikes in a row.* **strikes.**

strik ing (strīk′ing), *adj.* remarkable; unusual; attractive. *The pattern she chose for her new rug was quite striking. Betty wore a striking outfit.* **strik ing ly,** *adv.*

string (string), *n.* 1. a thin cord; a thick thread. *The clerk tied up my packages with string.* 2. a set of things arranged in a row on a cord. *Put a string of lights on the Christmas tree. The child played with a string of beads.* 3. a number of things arranged in a row. *A string of cars filled the road.* 4. the thin cord or wire of some musical instruments. *Violins have strings.* 5. **strings,** the musical instruments with strings that are played by using a bow. *The strings of that orchestra sound beautiful.* **strings.**

v. 6. to put on a cord. *String the pearls. The clothes that had been washed were strung in the back yard.* 7. to put strings on. *Bill has to string his new guitar.* 8. to tie, hang, etc. with a string or cord. *String these packages together. String this notice on the front doorknob.* **strings, strung, string ing.**

strip[1] (strip), *v.* 1. to undress. *When the baby was stripped, the doctor made his examination.* 2. to take off a covering; to remove; to peel. *The painters stripped the old paper from the wall. The Indians used to strip the bark from certain trees to make canoes.* 3. to make bare by taking away; to clear. *The early lumber companies stripped the forests of trees; now trees that are cut down are replaced by young ones.* 4. to rob. *The king stripped some of his people of all their land.* **strips, stripped, strip ping.**

strip[2] (strip), *n.* a long, narrow piece of land or material. *Airplanes land on the strip at the airport. I need one more strip of cloth to finish this decoration.* **strips.**

stripe (strīp), *n.* 1. a narrow band. *The American flag has stripes of red and white. A zebra has stripes of black and white.* **stripes.**

v. 2. to mark with stripes. *A barber's pole is striped with red and white.* **stripes, striped, strip ing.**

stroke (strōk), *n.* 1. the act of hitting; a blow. *With one stroke of the hammer, the nail was driven*

into the soft wood. *A stroke of lightning knocked down the old tree.* 2. a kind of illness that comes on suddenly. *The old man had a stroke which made it difficult for him to move.* 3. a complete movement in an activity, repeated over and over. *That swimmer has a powerful stroke. Watch the stroke of that ice skater. A person rowing a boat should use a long, even stroke.* 4. a single movement made with a pen, pencil, or brush; the mark made by this movement. *An artist uses different kinds of strokes. With a few strokes of the pen, the President approved the new law.* 5. a gentle rubbing. *She gave the cat an affectionate stroke with her hand.* 6. a sound caused by the striking of a clock. *He appeared at the stroke of eight, as we had agreed.* 7. an effort; a bit; an act. *He won't do a stroke of work until he is paid.* **strokes.**
v. 8. to rub gently. *She stroked her cat's head.* **strokes, stroked, strok ing.**

stroll (strōl), *v.* 1. to walk slowly and easily. *We strolled through the park on the beautiful spring day.* **strolls, strolled, stroll ing.**
n. 2. a slow walk for pleasure. *The stroll through the woods was pleasant.* **strolls.**

strong (strông), *adj.* 1. not weak; having much power or force. *We need two strong boys to carry the teacher's desk into the next room. She has a strong desire to get good grades. He may have a weak body, but his mind is strong.* 2. hard to break or knock down; lasting; tough. *That strong wall is a hundred years old. You will need a strong rope to pull all four of us on the sled.* 3. not mild; sharp in taste, sight, sound, or smell. *Some people like strong cheese. The strong smoke from the fire made me choke and cough.* 4. healthy. *Schools help us to have strong minds in strong bodies.* **strong er, strong est; strong ly,** *adv.*

struck (struk), past tense and past participle of **strike.**

struc ture (struk′chər), *n.* 1. something built. *The Pyramids of Egypt are large structures. The new bridge is the longest structure in the world.* 2. the way something is put together; an arrangement of parts. *The structure of a leaf is both beautiful and useful. Careful structure of a sentence is necessary to get your idea across.* **struc tures.**

strug gle (strug′l), *v.* 1. to try hard. *The rabbit struggled to get out of the trap.* **strug gles, strug gled, strug gling.**
n. 2. a strong effort; a hard attempt. *Walking up the hill required a struggle. A wild animal will put up a struggle to get out of its cage when it is first caught.* **strug gles.**

strung (strung), past tense and past participle of **string.**

strut (strut), *v.* 1. to walk in a proud way, mostly to show off. *The winning team strutted around the playground after the game.* **struts, strut ted, strut ting.**
n. 2. a proud walk in order to show off. *The*

rooster's strut made the children laugh. 3. a piece of wood or metal used to support or to make stronger. *A bridge has struts.* **struts.**

stub born (stub′ərn), *adj.* not giving in to anyone; having one's own definite idea. *Charles was stubborn and refused to follow my suggestions.* **stub born ly,** *adv.*

stuck (stuk), past tense and past participle of **stick.**

stu dent (stüd′nt, stūd′nt), *n.* 1. a person who goes to school. *There are two thousand students in our school.* 2. a person who studies. *The Indians were students of nature. This man is a student of Shakespeare.* **stu dents.**

stud ied (stud′ēd), *adj.* carefully thought out or planned; showing effort. *Walter's studied way of telling jokes isn't as good as Pete's more natural manner.*

study (stud′ē), *v.* 1. to try to learn by thinking, reading, and practicing. *In school, we study social studies, English, and mathematics. Brian spends about two hours every night studying his lessons.* 2. to think about; to try to figure out. *You have to study checkers to become an expert player. We studied the directions on how to build the toy castle, but we got all mixed up.* 3. to examine and investigate. *The president appointed five presidents of universities to study the future needs of American education.* **stud ies, stud ied, stud y ing.**
n. 4. the act of reading, thinking, and practicing in order to try to learn something. *Great professors have given much time to study.* 5. a subject that one studies; a part of learning. *Medicine is a difficult study. History is my favorite study.* 6. a written report of the result's of one's efforts in a certain branch of learning. *The doctor published a study of children's diseases.* 7. an investigation; an examination. *Careful study of the economic situation in large cities brought about many suggestions for improvement.* 8. a room used for reading, writing, and learning. *The writer is in his study and cannot be disturbed now.* **stud ies.**

stuff (stuf), *n.* 1. what things are made of. *What is the best stuff for making a dress?* 2. the character or basic part of a person; a quality. *Bruce has the stuff of a great man in him.* 3. things; objects of any kind. *My sister will have to move some of the stuff out of her closet before she puts anything else in it. Don't put any more stuff in the car.* **stuffs.**
v. 4. to fill by packing things into. *The trunk was stuffed with old clothes that we gave to charity.* 5. to fill with a mixture of bread, salt, pepper, herbs, etc. *Mother stuffs the turkey before roasting it.* 6. to fill (one's self) with food. *The food was so good that we stuffed ourselves at dinner.* **stuffs, stuffed, stuff ing.**

stum ble (stum′bəl), *v.* 1. to hit the foot on an object and trip. *John stumbled over his brother's foot.* 2. to walk with a jerky step. *He stumbled into the room.* 3. a clumsy or halting way of

sturgeon

walking or talking. *Mary often stumbles in her speech.* 4. to meet by accident or by chance. *By luck we stumbled on the right answer.* **stumbles, stum bled, stum bling.**

stump (stump), *n.* 1. the part of a tree or plant that is left after the main part has been cut off. *The lumber company cut down the forest and left nothing but stumps.* 2. the part of anything that is left after the main part is gone. *He is writing with the stump of a pencil.* 3. a platform or place used for making speeches. *The candidates for office spoke from the same stump.* **stumps.**
v. 4. to travel around, making speeches at many places. *Before the election, a candidate for governor stumps the state.* 5. to walk heavily or clumsily. *The big bear stumped around in his cage.* 6. to puzzle; to confuse. *That problem stumps me.* **stumps, stumped, stump ing.**

stun (stun), *v.* 1. to knock out; to be unconscious. *The blow stunned the man.* 2. to be in a state of shock; to be dazed. *The news of his death stunned the nation.* **stuns, stunned, stun ning.**

stung (stung), past tense and past participle of **sting.**

stunt[1] (stunt), *v.* to keep from growing or developing. *Poor soil stunts plants.* **stunts, stunt ed, stunt ing.**

stunt[2] (stunt), *n.* something done to show one's ability and skill. *The acrobat performed stunts on a tightrope. Little Kenny learned a stunt; he stands on his head.* **stunts.**

stu pid (stü′pid, stū′pid), *adj.* 1. not smart; very slow to learn. *That boy isn't stupid; he simply hasn't had a chance to go to school or to talk much with people.* 2. foolish; silly. *To make fun of a child is cruel and stupid. That movie had a stupid story.* **stu pid er, stu pid est; stu pid ly,** *adv.*

stur geon (stėr′jən), *n.* a large, slender fish that lives in fresh waters and seas. *Sturgeon is usually smoked before it is eaten.* **stur geon** or **stur geons.**

submarine

style (stīl), *n.* 1. a way of doing something or of making something. *The modern style of building houses is different from the style of fifty years ago. Some authors have a simple style of writing.* 2. fashion. *This year's style in dresses is different from last year's. My father would just as soon wear the same old hat, but Mother asks him to buy the latest style each year.* 3. a particular way of doing something that is not like that of anyone else. *Each person has his own style of walking, talking, laughing, or frowning. This new artist has a fine, original style of using colors.* **styles.**
v. 4. to call; to name. *The American system of public schools is styled the best in the world.* **styles, styled, styl ing.**

sub ject (sub′jikt for 1–6, səb jekt′ for 7 and 8), *n.* 1. a course of study in school. *My favorite subject is English.* 2. a person under the authority of a king. *The knights were loyal subjects of King Arthur.* 3. the person or the topic being talked about or written about. *The subject for today's lesson in history is the invention of the steam engine. The main subject among the students was the final examinations.* 4. in a sentence, the word or group of words about which something is said. *In the sentence "The boy throws the ball," the subject is "boy."* **sub jects.**
adj. 5. being under the control or power of another. *The subject peoples united against the cruel king.* 6. **subject to,** (a) under the control or power of. *He is subject to his big brother's authority when his parents are away.* (b) likely to have or get; disposed or inclined to. *He is subject to fits of laughter.* (c) depending upon. *We will come to your school, subject to the teacher's consent.*
v. 7. to expose. *The travelers were subjected to hardships.* 8. to force to submit (to). *The king subjected his enemies to his rule.* **sub jects, sub ject ed, sub ject ing.**

sub ma rine (sub′mə rēn′ for 1, sub′mə rēn′ for 2), *n.* 1. a boat that can travel under water. *Some submarines carry many men and stay underwater for many weeks.* **sub ma rines.**
adj. 2. growing or living underwater. *A fish is a submarine animal. Seaweed is a submarine plant.*

sub mit (səb mit′), *v.* 1. to give in; yield. *I always submit to my grandfather's wishes. The dog submitted to orders when he heard the voice of his owner.* 2. to offer for someone to look over and to think about. *A new tax bill was submitted in Congress. I submitted my book report today.* **sub mits, sub mit ted, sub mit ting.**

sub scribe (sub skrīb′), *v.* 1. to agree to take and pay for. *My family subscribes to five magazines, which are delivered by mail. If you subscribe to this book club you will be sent one book every month.* 2. to make a promise to give money. *The parents of the boys and girls in the school band subscribed five hundred dollars for new* uniforms. 3. to give approval. *I subscribe to your idea of leaving now.* 4. to contribute. *Mr. and Mrs. Jackson subscribe one hundred dollars a year to their favorite charity.* **sub scribes, subscribed, sub scrib ing.**

sub scrip tion (səb skrip′shən), *n.* 1. a contract to take a certain number of issues of a newspaper or magazine. *The subscription to the magazine costs ten dollars a year. My subscription to "Everyday Science" has two months to go.* 2. the amount promised. *Our subscription to the Charity Fund is ten dollars.* 3. a contribution or payment. *Our charity subscription of twenty dollars included two tickets to the dance.* **sub scrip tions.**

sub stance (sub′stəns), *n.* 1. matter; material; what a thing is made of. *The substance of that building is steel. Iron is a hard substance.* 2. the main point or idea. *The substance of the President's speech was that a great country like ours should help the starving people in the poor countries.* 3. property; wealth. *The owner of the oil wells is a man of substance.* **sub stanc es.**

sub stan tial (səb stan′shəl), *adj.* 1. strong and solid; firm. *A bridge must be substantial.* 2. large; more than usual; more than expected. *When Phil returned the wallet he found, the owner gave him a substantial reward. Aunt Harriet always serves a substantial dinner.* 3. wealthy; prosperous. *Mr. Field owns a small but substantial business.* **sub stan tial ly,** *adv.*

sub sti tute (sub′stə tüt, sub′stə tūt), *n.* 1. a person who takes the place of another person. *The science class had a substitute when the regular teacher had to go out of town. When the basketball player was hurt, the coach sent in a substitute.* 2. a thing used in place of another thing. *If you can't find a ladder, use a strong chair as a substitute.* **sub sti tutes.**
v. 3. to use as a substitute. *They substituted milk for cream.* 4. to be a substitute. *The new teacher substituted for Mr. Hansen.* **sub sti tutes, sub sti tut ed, sub sti tut ing.**

sub tract (səb trakt′), *v.* to take away. *If we subtract 7 from 10, we get 3.* **sub tracts, subtract ed, sub tract ing.**

sub trac tion (sub trak′shən), *n.* the taking away of one number, part, etc. from another. *Many of the problems on our last quiz were solved by the use of subtraction.* **sub trac tions.**

sub tra hend (sub′trə hend), *n.* the number that is subtracted from another number. *In 11 − 9 = 2, the subtrahend is 9.* **sub tra hends.**

sub urb (sub′ėrb), *n.* a district lying outside of the city limits. *We moved from the city to a suburb.* **sub urbs.**

sub way (sub′wā′), *n.* 1. an electric railway that travels beneath the ground. *In some large cities like New York, Chicago, and Philadelphia, subways are a vital part of the transportation system.* 2. any passage that is under the ground. *Use the short subway beneath the highway for walking to the beach.* **sub ways.**

suc ceed (sək sēd′), *v.* 1. to do well. *Linda succeeds in her school work, in sports, and in playing the piano.* 2. to get what one wants; to obtain a hoped for result. *We succeeded in convincing Mr. Brown that he should hire us to work for him during the summer.* 3. to come after. *Daylight succeeds darkness. Mr. Manning succeeded Miss Pearson as the principal of Field School.* **suc ceeds, suc ceed ed, suc ceed ing.**

suc cess (sək ses′), *n.* 1. the getting of what one wants; the result one had hoped for. *The girls had success in getting their favorite singer to autograph their pictures of him. My dad has had success in life, because he is a good husband and father.* 2. the act of becoming rich and famous; fame. *The writer's success didn't change him, and he still visited his old friends.* 3. a person who succeeds. *The movie star is a success. My mother is a success.* 4. a thing that turns out well. *The boat we made was a success.* **suc cess es.**

suc cess ful (sək ses′fəl), *adj.* 1. getting what one wants; having success; turning out well. *Chuck is a successful student and athlete. Read about the hard struggles of some successful businessmen, artists, and writers.* 2. having become rich and famous. *That successful lawyer will often defend a poor person and will not accept payment.* **success ful ly,** *adv.*

suc ces sion (sək sesh′ən), *n.* 1. the coming of one person or thing right after another; a line or order. *In a fire drill, walk slowly in succession until all the students and teachers are outside the building.* 2. the legal right to another person's position or property. *When the king died, three princes quarreled over the succession to the throne.* **suc ces sions.**

such (such), *adj.* 1. so much, so great, so bad, so good, etc. *The girls always had such fun at Sue's house that they went there often. The firemen showed such courage!* 2. of a certain kind. *Such an automobile costs $30,000. Ability such as his is not seen very often.*
pron. 3. such a person or thing. *There may be students who need more time; all such should see Mrs. Perkins.* 4. a person or thing that has been mentioned. *Such is the winter weather here.*

suck (suk), *v.* 1. to draw into the mouth. *Suck the lemonade through a straw. The baby sucked all the milk from his bottle.* 2. to take liquid from. *I cut the orange in half and sucked it.* 3. to take in; to absorb. *Plants suck water from the ground.* 4. to eat by licking with the tongue. *Little children like to suck candies like peppermint sticks.* **sucks, sucked, suck ing.**

sud den (sud′n), *adj.* 1. not expected. *We got caught in the sudden rainfall.* 2. quick; hasty. *Mr. Parker made a sudden decision to visit his brother.* **sud den ly,** *adv.*

suf fer (suf′ər), *v.* 1. to feel pain. *The dog seems to suffer in the hot weather. I suffered when I fell and hurt my knee on the sidewalk.* 2. to endure; to put up with. *The pioneers suffered many hard-*

sand, āte, bâre, fäther; sent, mē, fėrn; fĭt, bīke; pot, rōpe, fôrt; run, pùll, rüle, cūte; noise, sound; ch, cheese; ng, long; th, thick; th, those; zh, treasure; ə = a in about, e in waken, i in animal, o in seldom, and u in minus.

ships on their way West. 3. to be harmed or hurt; to become worse. *Because of his absence from school, his grades suffered. The young trees in the forest suffered when no rain fell.* 4. to permit or allow. *Our teacher will suffer not a whisper in the classroom.* **suf fers, suf fered, suf fer ing.**

suf fer ing (suf′ər ing), *n.* pain; hardship; sorrow. *The doctor quickly relieved the girl's suffering. The nation went through a time of suffering when Abraham Lincoln was shot.* **suf fer ings.**

suf fi cient (sə fish′ənt), *adj.* enough. *We have sufficient toys to give to the children in the hospital.* **suf fi cient ly,** *adv.*

suf fix (suf′iks), *n.* a group of letters added to the end of a word, and changing the meaning of the word. *The suffix "ness" is added to "sad" to make "sadness." The suffix "ful" is added to "hope" to make "hopeful."* **suf fix es.**

sug ar (shug′ər), *n.* 1. a sweet substance in the form of tiny crystals. *I like to put much sugar on my breakfast cereal. Betty should have added more sugar when she made this cocoa.* **sug ars.**
v. 2. to make sweet by adding sugar. *If the lemonade tastes bitter, sugar it. Sugar the dish of fresh strawberries before eating them.* 3. to turn to sugar. *Our chocolate fudge sugared because we boiled it too long.* **sug ars, sug ared, sug ar ing.**

sug gest (səg jest′, sə jest′), *v.* 1. to mention as a possible thing to do; to put into a person's mind. *I suggest that you work harder. Would you suggest that I buy this coat?* 2. to bring to mind. *To me, Christmas suggests snow and Santa Claus. Smoke suggests fire. The baby's nodding head suggested that he was sleepy.* **sug gests, sug gest ed, sug gest ing.**

sug ges tion (səg jes′chən, sə jes′chən), *n.* 1. a suggesting. *Her suggestion that we take an early plane was very sensible. The warm wind was a suggestion of spring.* 2. the thing suggested. *The new traffic sign in the street near our school was the principal's suggestion.* 3. a hint; a small bit. *The suggestion of a smile appeared on the teacher's face when Dick gave his long excuse for being late.* **sug ges tions.**

suit (süt), *n.* 1. a set of clothes worn together. *A boy's suit consists of a coat and pants. A girl's suit has a coat and a skirt.* 2. in a pack of cards, all the cards that have red or black spots of

summerhouse

the same shape. *The four suits are diamonds, hearts, clubs, and spades.* 3. a case in a court of law. *The owner of the damaged car started a suit to collect money from the man whose car hit his.* 4. the courting. *The suit of the knight ended well when the beautiful princess said she would marry him.* **suits.**
v. 5. to please; satisfy. *You can try very hard, but you can't suit everyone.* 6. to look well on. *Your new hat suits you. The color red doesn't suit her, but in blue she looks lovely.* 7. to be suitable for. *Cold weather suits a polar bear. Hot weather suits most plants. What day would suit you for the meeting?* **suits, suit ed, suit ing.**

suit a ble (süt′ə bl, sūt′ə bl), *adj.* proper; fitting; right for the purpose. *Your old shirt is suitable for wearing around the house.* **suit a bly,** *adv.*

suit case (süt′kās′), *n.* a flat bag used for holding clothes when a person travels. *I packed all my suitcases neatly for our trip to California.* **suit cas es.**

sum (sum), *n.* 1. the number made by adding numbers. *The sum of 7 and 3 is 10. The sum of the prices of the things we bought is $9.12.* 2. an amount of money. *After Mr. Blair lost ten dollars on the street, he carried only a small sum with him.* 3. the whole amount. *The sum of the professor's knowledge is in the book he wrote.* **sums.**
v. 4. **sum up,** to tell or review the main points of. *This article in the newspaper sums up the news of the year. The teacher summed up today's lesson at the end of the class.* 5. to get the whole amount. *She summed up the cost of our vacation.* **sums, summed, sum ming.**

sum mer (sum′ər), *n.* 1. one of the four seasons of the year. *In the United States and Canada, summer is the warmest season. Summer is followed by autumn, winter, and spring, which are the other three seasons.* **sum mers.**
v. 2. to spend the summer. *The rich family summered on the big boat.* **sum mers, summered, sum mer ing.**
adj. 3. of summer; for summer. *Some summer days are very hot. She bought a summer dress.*

sum mer house (sum′ər hous′), *n.* a small, open building for use during the summer. *A summerhouse is a cool, shady place to rest.* **sum mer hous es.**

sum mer time (sum′ər tīm′), *n.* summer. *The weather is warm in summertime.* **sum mer times.**

sum mon (sum′ən), *v.* 1. to call together; send for. *The principal summoned all the teachers for a meeting after school.* 2. to order to appear in a court of law. *The boys were summoned as witnesses to the accident.* 3. to call or stir up; make active. *He summoned all his strength to push the car off the road.* **sum mons, sum moned, sum mon ing.**

sun (sun), *n.* 1. the large, hot, bright object in the sky; the star which gives light and heat

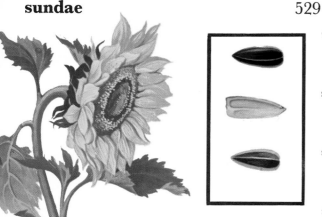

sunflower and seeds

to the earth. *We see the sun during the day and the other stars during the night. The earth and the eight other planets go around the sun.* 2. the light of the sun; the heat of the sun. *The sun hurt her eyes. Don't get too much sun at the beach.* **suns.**

v. 3. to expose to the sun. *We sunned ourselves at the beach.* **suns, sunned, sun ning.**

sun dae (sun′dē, sun′dā′), *n.* ice cream with syrup, nuts, and whipped cream on it. *Many people enjoy a chocolate sundae.* **sun daes.**

Sun day (sun′dē, sun′dā′), *n.* the first day of the week. *Sunday comes before Monday. People go to church on Sunday.* **Sun days.**

sun flow er (sun′flou′ər), *n.* a tall plant with large yellow flowers. *A sunflower looks like a big daisy. The seeds of the sunflower are made into a valuable oil.* **sun flow ers.**

sung (sung), past tense and past participle of **sing.**

sunk (sungk), past tense and past participle of **sink.**

sun light (sun′līt′), *n.* the light of the sun. *The sunlight made us feel warm and sleepy.*

sun ny (sun′ē), *adj.* 1. bright with sunshine. *It's a shame to stay indoors on such a sunny day!* 2. cheerful; bright; happy. *People like to look at the child's sunny face.* **sun ni er, sun ni est; sun ni ly,** *adv.*

sun rise (sun′rīz′), *n.* 1. the coming up of the sun after night; dawn. *Sunrise takes place every morning in the eastern sky.* 2. the time of day when the sun comes up. *Sunrise is earlier in summer than it is in winter.* 3. the light in the sky when the sun rises. *There was a beautiful sunrise this morning.* **sun ris es.**

sun set (sun′set′), *n.* 1. the going down of the sun. *Sunset takes place every day in the western sky.* 2. the time of day when the sun goes down. *Let's meet at sunset.* 3. the light in the sky when the sun sets. *The sunset was orange and gold.* **sun sets.**

sun shade (sun′shād′), *n.* any cover that keeps out the sun, especially a large, gaily colored umbrella. *He was on the beach, lying under a sunshade.* **sun shades.**

sun shine (sun′shīn′), *n.* 1. the light from the sun. *The doctor said that I should sit in the sunshine.* 2. brightness; happiness. *There is sunshine in her smile.*

su per high way (sü′pər hī′wā), *n.* a highway of four lanes or more built especially for high-speed traffic. *A superhighway has few stop signs, and no roads cross it.* **su per high ways.**

su per in tend ent (sü′prin ten′dənt), *n.* a person in charge of something. *The superintendent of schools directs all the activities of all the schools in a district.* **su per in tend ents.**

su pe ri or (sə pir′ē ər), *adj.* 1. higher in position or rank. *A soldier salutes his superior officers.* 2. excellent; better than most. *Bruce's mother is a superior cook. Young Mike has a superior mind.* 3. feeling or showing that one is better than others. *His superior manner and his boasting made him few friends.* 4. **superior to,** (a) higher than; above. *A superintendent of schools is superior to a principal.* (b) better than; greater than. *This television set is superior to our old one.*

n. 5. a person who is better than another in some way. *Edward is my superior in the study of biology, but I am his superior in English.* 6. a person who is higher in position than another. *The vice-president of the company is my father's superior.* **su pe ri ors.**

su per la tive (sə pėr′lə tiv), *adj.* 1. best; greatest; supreme. *My aunt is a superlative cook.* **su per la tive ly,** *adv.*

n. 2. the highest degree of comparison of an adjective or an adverb. *The superlatives of "large," "rosy," and "good" are "largest," "rosiest," and "best."* **su per la tives.**

su per sti tion (sü′pər stish′ən), *n.* a belief resulting from ignorance of what really exists, or a trust in magic or chance. *People*

sunshade

once believed the superstition that walking under a ladder will bring bad luck. **su per sti tions.**

su per vi sion (sü′pər vizh′ən), *n.* direction; management. *Each classroom is under the supervision of a teacher, and all the teachers are under the supervision of the principal.*

sup per (sup′ər), *n.* the last meal of the day. *We eagerly hurried home for supper.* **sup pers.**

sup ple ment (sup′lə mənt for 1, sup′lə ment for 2), *n.* 1. something added to a book or newspaper to bring it up to date or to interest a reader. *The supplement to the Sunday newspaper includes the comics, a magazine, a review of the week's news, and a section for women on dresses and cooking. The science book has a supplement which gives the names of all the atoms.* **sup ple ments.**
v. 2. to add to. *Mr. Field supplements his income by working at the department store evenings.* **sup ple ments, sup ple ment ed, sup ple ment ing.**

sup ply (sə plī′), *v.* 1. to provide; furnish; give. *We supplied food and a sleeping place for the lost puppy. Who will supply the cold soda for our picnic?* 2. to fill. *The store was able to supply our request for a special kind of candy.* **sup plies, sup plied, sup ply ing.**
n. 3. the amount or quantity that is needed; the amount or quantity on hand. *When the snowfall started, the store got a supply of snow shovels. Mother checked the supply of sugar before going to the store.* 4. **supplies,** things that must be bought. *You can get your school supplies at this store.* **sup plies.**

sup port (sə pôrt′), *v.* 1. to hold up; to keep from falling. *The beautiful columns support the roof of the building. This old bridge will not support the big truck.* 2. to take the side of; to help. *My father supported our neighbor in his campaign for cleaner streets.* 3. to provide for; to furnish a home, food, and clothing for. *That man works twelve hours a day to support his large family.* 4. to show the truth of; to help prove. *You must tell us some true examples to support your statement.* 5. to put up with; to bear; to endure. *People can support hardships and sadness if they have hope. We supported the child's crying because we knew he was tired.* **sup ports, sup port ed, support ing.**
n. 6. anything that holds up another thing. *The heavy ropes are supports for the tent.* 7. a person who helps another. *A friend is a support in a time of need.* 8. help. *Parents and teachers give support to a child.* **sup ports.**

sup pose (sə pōz′), *v.* 1. to believe; to think. *I suppose he was invited, but why isn't he here?* 2. to expect; to guess. *I suppose you will go to your friend's house again.* **sup pos es, sup posed, sup pos ing.**

sup posed (sə pōzd′), *adj.* thought of as true, without really being known. *The supposed reason for canceling the performance was a lack of student interest.* **sup pos ed ly,** *adv.*

su preme (sə prēm′), *adj.* 1. most powerful; highest in authority. *In former times kings were the supreme rulers in most countries.* 2. of highest degree. *By a supreme effort, they reached the top of the mountain.* 3. greatest. *This news about the schools is of supreme importance.* **su preme ly,** *adv.*

sure (shur), *adj.* 1. certain; positive. *We are sure that he will be here. Are you sure the clock shows the correct time?* 2. reliable; trustworthy; safe. *The doctor gave me a sure cure for my coughing. Good cooks follow sure recipes that have been used by others. The captain of the airliner is a sure pilot.* 3. firm; steady. *Get a sure hold on the baseball bat and then swing at the ball.* **sur er, sur est; sure ly,** *adv.*

sure ly (shur′lē), *adv.* 1. certainly. *You surely must be joking when you say we came one day early!* 2. with skill; in an expert way. *The experienced carpenter worked surely on the bookcase. Slowly but surely Bob carved a beautiful figure of a horse out of the soft wood.*

sur face (sėr′fis), *n.* 1. the outside. *Put polish on the surface of the furniture. That banana looks brown on the surface but it is not too ripe.* 2. the outside appearance; the way one appears to most people. *On the surface Bob seems shy and reserved, but he is actually a warm and friendly person.* **sur fac es.**
v. 3. to come to the surface. *The submarine surfaced. Whales must surface to breathe air.* 4. to put a new surface on. *The Department of Roads said it will surface this rough highway in summer.* **sur fac es, sur faced, sur fac ing.**
adj. 5. having to do with the surface. *The surface water of a lake is warmer than the lower part because of the sun. A surface scratch on your arm gets well quickly.* 6. not real; not serious. *Our teacher said we were giving surface attention to her question. John and Dick are surface rivals who are actually true friends.*

sur prise (sər prīz′), *v.* 1. to cause to feel wonder or delight; to astonish. *Dick and Jane surprised us by singing the song they had written.* 2. to come upon suddenly. *Uncle Jim surprised us when we were eating dinner.* **sur pris es, sur prised, sur pris ing.**
n. 3. something unexpected. *Little children like surprises, even if they cost only a few cents.* 4. a feeling caused by something unexpected. *To our surprise, Bud's dog stood up and walked on its hind legs.* **sur pris es.**
adj. 5. coming as a surprise. *We will give Joanne a surprise party on her birthday.*

sur pris ing (sər prīz′ing), *adj.* causing surprise. *The boy's increase in height was surprising.* **sur pris ing ly,** *adv.*

sur ren der (sə ren′dər), *v.* 1. to give up oneself or a thing. *The fort would not surrender.* 2. the act of giving up. *We surrendered our ice cream to the hungry boys.* **sur ren ders, sur rendered, sur ren der ing.**

sur round (sə round′), *v.* to shut in on all sides; to enclose. *A high wall surrounds the prison. We were surrounded by people in the concert hall.* **sur rounds, sur round ed, sur round- ing.**

sur vey (sər vā′ for 1 and 2, sėr′vā, sər vā′ for 3 and 4), *v.* 1. to look over; to examine. *The ranger in a high tower surveyed the forest for smoke. The farmer surveyed the sky for a sign of rain.* 2. to measure the size and shape of an area of land so as to know what the exact boundaries are. *A man who surveys uses a special instrument which is a kind of telescope.* **sur veys, sur veyed, sur vey ing.**

n. 3. a study; an examination. *The textbook in American history is a survey of events in this country from 1492 to the present. A survey made by the newspaper shows that most of the people think our schools are excellent.* 4. a surveying of an area of land. *The state asked the owner of the farm to have a survey made.* **sur veys.**

sur vi val (sər vīv′l), *n.* 1. the act of surviving or remaining alive. *The survival of the canary means a lot to Mother.* 2. a custom that has continued for a long time. *The custom of shaking hands is a survival from the days when a knight opened his hand to show he had no weapon.* **sur vi vals.**

sur vive (sər vīv′), *v.* 1. to continue to exist; to remain alive. *The giant trees in that forest in California have survived for a thousand years!* 2. to live longer than. *The healthy old dog survived two of her pups.* 3. to live through. *This oak tree has survived two forest fires and one hurricane.* **sur vives, sur vived, sur viv ing.**

sus pect (səs pekt′ for 1–3, sus′pekt for 4), *v.* 1. to believe to be guilty without proof. *We suspect the dog of taking the small cake.* 2. to guess; to imagine. *I suspect you are tired after this hard day.* 3. to have doubts about; to have no trust in. *Somehow my father suspects the truth about that radio company's advertising.* **sus pects, sus pect ed, sus pect ing.**

n. 4. a person who is suspected, or thought probably to be guilty. *The police arrested three suspects after the bank was robbed.* **sus pects.**

sus pend (səs pend′), *v.* 1. to hang something from above. *The room was bare except for a light bulb suspended from the ceiling.* 2. to appear as if hanging. *The plane seemed suspended in the air.* 3. to rest; stop for a time. *Work was suspended during lunch.* 4. to take a job, activity, or privi- lege away because of misconduct. *The boy was suspended from school because of fighting.* **sus pends, sus pend ed, sus pend ing.**

sus pense (səs pens′), *n.* a state of great fear, worry, uncertainty, etc. about the outcome of an event. *That book kept me in suspense.*

sus pi cion (səs pish′ən), *n.* 1. a suspecting. *Our suspicion that the dog ate the cake was right; he had crumbs of cake on his whiskers!* 2. a feeling or belief. *I have a suspicion that it will rain hard.*

swans

3. a hint; a tiny amount. *In cooking this meat, she used a suspicion of salt.* **sus pi cions.**

swal low[1] (swol′ō), *n.* a small bird with long wings. *Swallows fly swiftly.* **swal lows.**

swal low[2] (swol′ō), *v.* 1. to take something, through the mouth and throat into the stomach. *Chew your meat well before you swallow it. In hot weather he swallowed much water.* 2. to keep from showing. *Donald swallowed his anger when his brother forgot to wake him on time.* 3. to cover. *The airplane was swallowed by the cloud.* 4. to believe without thinking. *Joe will swallow anything I say.* **swal lows, swal lowed, swal low ing.**

n. 5. the act of swallowing. *The boy finished his glass of water with one swallow.* 6. the amount swallowed at one time. *I took a swallow of the medicine.* **swal lows.**

swam (swam), past tense of **swim.**

swamp (swomp), *n.* 1. a soft, very wet piece of land. *It was hard to walk through the swamp.* **swamps.**

v. 2. to fill with water and sink. *The high waves swamped the little boat.* 3. to burden with excess work. *The saleslady was swamped during the sale.* **swamps, swamped, swamp ing.**

swampy (swomp′ē), *adj.* 1. soft and very wet like a swamp. *After the rain the playground was swampy.* 2. consisting of swamps. *The road goes around the swampy land.* **swamp i er, swamp- i est.**

swan (swon), *n.* a large, usually white bird with a long neck, that swims in the water. *The swans swim gracefully in the pond in the park.* **swans.**

swat (swot), *v.* 1. to hit. *Carol swatted the fly when it stood still on the desk.* **swats, swat ted, swat ting.**

n. 2. a hit; a sharp blow. *The baseball player gave the ball a swat and it went over the fence.* **swats.**

sway (swā), *v.* 1. to move slowly back and forth; to swing from side to side. *The tall flowers swayed in the breeze. The boat swayed on the waves of the water. The tall truck swayed as it went around a curve too fast.* 2. to influence. *His wonderful speech swayed the audience to vote for*

him. *The chance to win the gold medal swayed him to enter the race.* **sways, swayed, sway ing.**
n. 3. a swaying; being swayed. *The sway of the branches became faster as the wind increased.* 4. the control or rule; an influence. *Under the sway of hunger, the shy deer appeared in the farmer's yard. The sway of some Presidents has been stronger than the sway of others.* **sways.**

swear (swâr), *v.* 1. to make a serious statement in which one asks God to notice the truth of what will be said. *Every witness in a court trial is asked to swear before giving his evidence.* 2. to declare as true. *The knight swore on his honor that he would obey his king.* 3. to promise seriously. *He swore that he would return.* 4. to use bad language; to use sacred names carelessly. *When the sheriff caught him, the outlaw yelled and swore.* 5. **swear in,** to give an oath of office to. *The Chief Justice of the United States always swears in a new President.* **swears, swore, sworn, swear ing.**

sweat (swet), *n.* 1. perspiration; moisture which comes through the skin. *Sweat appeared on Mike's forehead as he worked hard in the field.* 2. the little drops of water that form on a cold surface. *Sweat collected on the cold glasses of pop.* 3. the act or condition of sweating. *The hot weather and the exercise left him in a sweat. He always was in a sweat from worry before an examination.* **sweats.**
v. 4. to perspire; to give off moisture through the skin. *The worker sweated so much that his whole shirt was wet.* 5. to form little drops of water on a cold surface. *The cold glass of ice water sweats on a warm day.* 6. to cause to perspire. *Buck sweated his horse by racing him for five miles to report a forest fire.* 7. to work hard. *Sometimes we really sweat to get our assignments done.* **sweats, sweat** or **sweat ed, sweat ing.**

sweat er (swet′ər), *n.* a knitted garment worn on the upper part of the body. *Some sweaters button like a coat. Other sweaters have no buttons but are pulled in place over the head.* **sweat ers.**

sweep (swēp), *v.* 1. to clean by brushing away. *Sweep up this dirt with a broom.* 2. to remove; to clear away. *We used a small brush to sweep the*

snow *from the windows of the car.* 3. to remove with great force; to carry away. *The sudden violent flood in the mountain stream swept the bridge away.* 4. to move through quickly with force. *Fire swept the house. A hurricane swept the city. The disease swept through the area, killing many cattle.* 5. to pass over lightly or quickly. *She swept her hand over the paint to see if it was dry.* 6. to move over a wide area. *The traffic policeman's eyes swept over the crowd for any sign of trouble.* 7. to move in a quick and confident way. *The actor swept onto the stage. The fingers of the piano player swept over the keys.* **sweeps, swept, sweep ing.**
n. 8. the act of sweeping; a clearing away. *He made a clean sweep of the toys in the basement.* 9. a moving through quickly with great force. *The sweep of the rushing water tore down the house.* 10. a cleaning by brushing. *The streets get a sweep every week from the new cleaning trucks.* 11. a steady, swift movement. *The sweep of the wind almost blew us to the ground.* 12. a continuous stretch. *From here you see a wide sweep of land.* 13. a swinging steady motion. *The sweep of the oars brought the boat to shore. We could hear the sweep of the broom as she cleaned the porch.* 14. a long curve; a curving line. *The sweep of the roof fits in with the background of mountains.* 15. a person who sweeps chimneys or streets. *Chimney sweeps work mostly in England.* **sweeps.**

sweep ing (swēp′ing), *adj.* 1. moving over a wide area. *The speaker gave his audience a sweeping look and then began.* 2. very broad; large. *The candidate won by a sweeping number of votes, ten thousand to three thousand. There are many sweeping boasts in advertising.* **sweep ing ly,** *adv.*
n. 3. a cleaning and brushing. *The sweeping was finished and the house looked pretty again.* 4. **sweepings,** things that are swept up. *The sweepings from the beach included the usual papers and bottles, but once in awhile a watch was found.* **sweep ings.**

sweet (swēt), *adj.* 1. having the pleasant taste of sugar; containing sugar. *Mother served us sweet rolls for breakfast.* 2. pleasing. *Roses and perfume have a sweet smell. She has a sweet voice. This is a sweet baby. The orchestra played sweet music.* 3. having little or no salt; not sour. *We used sweet butter on our vegetables. Sweet milk is the best drink I can think of.* **sweet er, sweet est; sweet ly,** *adv.*
n. 4. something sweet. *Candy is a sweet.* **sweets.**

sweet heart (swēt′härt′), *n.* a person with whom one is in love. *She is 21 and will marry her sweetheart in June.* **sweet hearts.**

sweet ness (swēt′nis), *n.* the condition of being sweet. *The grocer said we would like the sweetness of these oranges.*

sweet pea, *n.* 1. a flower that grows on a climbing plant. *Sweet peas have a sweet smell and many different colors.* 2. the plant the sweet pea grows on. *It is easy to grow sweet peas.* **sweet peas.**

sweet potatoes

sweet potato, *n.* 1. the yellow root of a certain vine, which is eaten as a vegetable. *Sweet potatoes don't taste at all like ordinary potatoes.* 2. the vine it grows on. *He planted sweet potatoes in the garden.* **sweet potatoes.**

swell (swel), *v.* 1. to make larger; become larger. *Paula swelled her bank account by putting in it the money she got for her birthday. If he really hurt his ankle, it soon will swell.* 2. to extend outward; to fill out. *The wind swelled the sails and the ship plunged through the sea.* 3. to fill or be filled with strong feeling. *A mother swells with pride when someone praises her daughter or son.* 4. to grow louder; to make louder. *The music swelled. Jeff can swell the sound on his new radio set until you can't hear anyone speak.* **swells, swelled, swelled** or **swol len, swell ing.**

n. 5. an increase in size, sound, etc. *The swell of the music told us the marching band was getting closer. The swell of the value of his farm made the farmer rich.* 6. a long, slowly moving wave. *The big whale moved with the swells.* 7. a rising. *In the distance he could see the swell of the hills.* 8. a man who is always dressed in a grand, expensive way. *The movie star looked like a swell to get publicity.* **swells.**

adj. 9. good; excellent. *We had a swell meal at the new hamburger stand on Highway 43.*

swept (swept), past tense and past participle of **sweep.**

swerve (swèrv), *v.* 1. to move suddenly to one side. *Father swerved the car to avoid hitting the cat.* **swerves, swerved, swerv ing.**

n. 2. a turning aside. *The swerve of a car in front made him slow down.* **swerves.**

swift (swift), *adj.* 1. very fast. *The swift runner won the race. We saw the new swift automobile from Italy.* 2. prompt. *The principal always gives us a swift "Yes" or "No" when our committee asks him for his opinion.* **swift er, swift est; swift ly,** *adv.*

n. 3. a small, fast-flying bird that looks like a swallow. *Swifts fly together in groups.* **swifts.**

swim (swim), *v.* 1. to move in water by moving arms, legs, fins, etc. *Fish swim. Many people know how to swim.* 2. to cross by swimming. *We often swim the narrow river. Some men and women have swum the English Channel—twenty miles of rough water!* 3. to glide; to move along smoothly. *White clouds swam in the blue sky.* 4. to be covered. *At supper we had sliced peaches swimming in cream.* 5. to be dizzy. *Her head was swimming from meeting the president when his car stopped at her father's store.* **swims, swam, swum, swim ming.**

n. 6. a period for swimming. *At two o'clock we go for a swim. Did your swim tire you?* **swims.**

swim mer (swim′ər), *n.* a person or animal that swims. *Ricky is a good swimmer and made the swimming team.* **swim mers.**

swim ming (swim′ing), *adj.* 1. capable of swimming. *Three swimming birds are the swan, the duck, and the goose.* 2. used for swimming. *Some swimming pools have a grandstand for people to watch races.*

swimming pool, *n.* a pool, usually man-made, used for swimming. *The two boys dove in and swam the length of the swimming pool.* **swimming pools.** (See illustration on following page.)

swing (swing), *v.* 1. to move back and forth. *The broken branch of the tree is swinging in the wind.* 2. to move in a curve. *Father swings his golf club. The baseball player swung his bat at the ball, and missed it. Slow down, because soon the road swings to the right.* 3. to lift. *The camper swung his pack of supplies on his back and departed.* 4. to move with a loose, free motion. *The*

swimming strokes

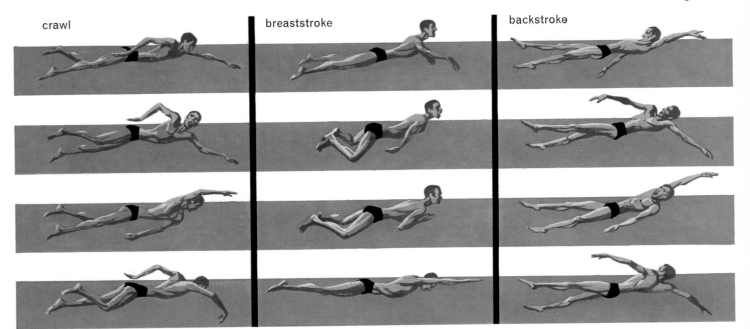

crawl   breaststroke   backstroke

swimming pool

swords

laughing children went swinging down the path. **swings, swung, swing ing.**

n. 5. a swinging movement. *The swing of the dog's long tail knocked a vase from the little table.* 6. a hit, blow, or stroke. *The baseball player took a mighty swing at the ball to get a home run. The swing of a good golf player is smooth and easy, but powerful.* 7. a seat which is used for swinging. *A swing is usually held up by two ropes or chains. Children like to go back and forth on the swings in the park.* **swings.**

swirl (swėrl), *v.* 1. to move with a whirling, twisting motion. *Dust and papers swirled in the street when the wind blew.* **swirls, swirled, swirl ing.**

n. 2. a movement around and around; a swirling. *The water went down the drain with a swirl. The swirl of the falling snow looked beautiful under the streetlight.* 3. a twisted shape; a curl. *Her hair was put up in swirls. A pig's tail has a little swirl at the end.* **swirls.**

swish (swish), *n.* 1. a light, soft, hissing sound. *The little mouse made a swish in the pile of dry leaves as he moved.* **swish es.**

v. 2. to make a light, soft, hissing sound. *The whip swished and cracked loudly as a signal to the horses to move.* 3. to move something back and forth. *Horses swish their tails. The washing machine swishes clothes in the water.* **swish es, swished, swish ing.**

switch (swich), *n.* 1. a thin stick used for whipping. *In the old days teachers kept switches in their classrooms for use in punishing pupils.* 2. a hit given by a switch. *The man gave the dog a harmless switch and the dog stopped his whining.* 3. a change. *We made a switch in our plan to go swimming when it started to rain.* 4. on a railroad, a device for moving a train from one track to another. *Some switches need a man to operate them; other switches are worked by electricity.* 5. in an electrical circuit, a device for making a connection. *When we press a switch, a light goes on.* **switch es.**

v. 6. to hit lightly with a switch. *The boy switched the fence as he walked down the road.* 7. to change. *We switched our party from Friday to*

Tuesday. We switched to the new cereal we saw on television. 8. to move from one track to another. *The long freight was switched to the middle track.* 9. to turn on or off. *Our radio switches off by itself. Switch the light on so I can see.* 10. to swing from side to side. *A horse switches its tail.* **switch es, switched, switch ing.**

swoon (swün), *v.* 1. to faint. *Some people swooned under the hot sun.* **swoons, swooned, swoon-ing.**
n. 2. a fainting spell. *The lady fell in a swoon when she was frightened.* **swoons.**

sword (sôrd), *n.* a weapon that has a long, sharp blade. *Swords were once used to fight wars.* **swords.**

swore (swôr), past tense of **swear.**

swum (swum), past tense and past participle of **swim.**

syl la ble (sil′ə bəl), *n.* a word or part of a word that is pronounced as a unit. Such a unit usually consists of a vowel alone or is composed of vowels and consonants. *There are three syllables in the word "syllable" and they are syl, la, and ble.* **syl la bles.**

sym bol (sim′bl), *n.* a thing that stands for something else. *The sign $ is a symbol for "dollar" or "dollars." A white flag is a symbol for giving up the fight or for trouble. The American flag is a symbol of the United States of America.* **sym bols.**

sym pa thy (sim′pə thē), *n.* 1. the sharing of another person's sorrow; the kind feeling that one person has for another. *My mother's sympathy helped Mrs. Rosemont in her worry about her sick baby.* 2. agreement. *Our likes and dislikes are in sympathy. The teacher is in sympathy with our plans.* **sym pa thies.**

syn a gogue (sin′ə gôg), *n.* a temple used by Jewish people for religious worship. *Friday night is the usual time of services at a synagogue.* **syn a gogues.**

syn o nym (sin′ə nim), *n.* a word that has the same general meaning, or almost the same general meaning, as another word. *The following words are synonyms: buy, purchase; happy, joyful, cheerful; hard, difficult; plain, simple; steal, rob.* **syn o nyms.**

syr inge (sə rinj′, sir′inj), *n.* a small instrument that consists of a narrow tube or nozzle fitted with a bulb or hollow cylinder for drawing in fluids or forcing them out. *Medicines are introduced into the body by means of a syringe attached to a hollow needle. A soft, rubber syringe is used to direct a solution into a wound or cavity.* **syr-ing es.**

syr up or **sir up** (sėr′əp, sir′əp), *n.* a sweet liquid made from certain plants. *Maple syrup is good on pancakes. Corn syrup is used in cooking.* **syr ups** or **sir ups.**

sys tem (sis′təm), *n.* 1 a group of things or parts which go together to make up a whole. *An airline system includes the airplanes, aviators, radio men, stewardesses, office workers, and men on the ground who keep track of the flights. The school system includes the superintendent, the principals, the teachers, the students, the custodians, and the secretaries. The circulation system of the body includes the heart, the blood vessels, and the blood.* 2. an orderly way of doing things. *Debbie has her own system of doing her lessons.* 3. an arrangement; an order. *Our system of government is more like England's than any other country's.* 4. the body as a whole, including the mind. *The lawyer's hard work was bad for his system.* **sys tems.**

syringe

T or **t** (tē), the twentieth letter of the alphabet.

ta ble (tā′bl), *n.* 1. a piece of furniture having legs and a smooth, flat top. *We eat supper at the kitchen table. Put the flowers on the low table in the living room.* 2. the food served at a table. *This restaurant sets the best table in the city.* 3. the people who are sitting at a table. *The entire table applauded after my speech.* 4. brief information arranged in list form. *Does this book have a table of contents? Practice your multiplication tables at home tonight.* 5. a thin, flat piece of wood, stone, metal, etc., on which something may be written; a tablet. *Stone tables with strange writing on them were found in the cave.* 6. **turn the tables,** to change or reverse a situation completely. *The author turned the tables by having the outlaw turn out to be the hero at the end of the book.* **ta bles.**

ta ble cloth (tā′bl klôth′), *n.* a cloth used for covering a table, especially for meals. *Put a tablecloth on the table before you set it.* **ta ble cloths.**

ta ble spoon (tā′bl spün′), *n.* a large spoon used to serve food and to measure ingredients. *A tablespoon holds three teaspoons.* **ta ble spoons.**

ta ble spoon ful (tā′bl spün fůl′), *n.* as much as a tablespoon will hold. *A tablespoonful is equal to three teaspoonfuls.* **ta ble spoon fuls.**

tab let (tab′lit), *n.* 1. a thin sheet of very hard material on which something may be written, drawn, etc. *Before the invention of paper, stone and wooden tablets were used in writing.* 2. a thin sheet of hard material on which something is carved. *The tablet to the right of the main entrance showed the name of the school.* 3. a pad of writing paper fastened together on one side. *You will need one tablet for arithmetic and another tablet for writing.* 4. a thin flat pill or piece of candy. *Did you take your aspirin tablet yet?* **tab lets.**

table tennis, *n.* a game like tennis. *Table tennis is played on a table with a very light, plastic ball and small paddles.*

ta boo (tə bü′), *v.* 1. to forbid the use of something. *Some societies taboo the eating of meat.* **ta boos, ta booed, ta boo ing.**
n. 2. something which is forbidden. *Many people feel that smoking is taboo.* **ta boos.**

tack (tak), *n.* 1. a short nail with a broad, flat head. *The rug was held to the floor with carpet tacks.* 2. the direction in which a ship is moving. *We were sailing on a port tack.* 3. a change of direction. *We had to take several tacks because of the way the wind was blowing.* 4. a direction of action or conduct. *Being honest was a new tack for the criminal.* **tacks.**
v. 5. to attach or fasten with tacks. *Tack this picture up on the bulletin board.* 6. to sew together loosely. *She tacked the hem on the dress to see if it was the right length.* 7. to sail with frequent sharp turns from side to side. *The huge ship tacked its way up the river, against the wind.* **tacks, tacked, tack ing.**

tack le (tak′əl), *n.* 1. equipment used in many sports. *Fishing poles and hooks are examples of fishing tackle.* **tack les.**
v. 2. to lay hold of; grapple with. *Many players get tackled in football.* 3. to try to master something. *Mary tackled the difficult math problem.* **tack les, tack led, tack ling.**

tac tics (tak′tiks), *n. pl.* 1. the planning and arrangement of sending out military forces to fight an enemy; these forces. *The military troops are on tactics.* 2. the plan of operation used to win an argument. *When crying failed, the girl used different tactics.*

tad pole (tad′pōl′), *n.* an early stage in the development of a frog. *Tadpoles grow legs while they live in water.* **tad poles.**

taf fy (taf′ē), *n.* a sticky, soft candy. *We helped Mother make taffy for Christmas.* **taf fies.**

tag¹ (tag), *n.* 1. a small piece of paper, metal,

tables

café table

coffee table

table tennis

etc. tied or attached to something. *There was no price tag on the bicycle in the store.* 2. a metal or plastic piece at the end of a string. *The laces of his sneakers had not broken, but the tags had come off.* **tags.**

v. 3. to attach a tag to; to furnish with a tag. *All of the items in the store are tagged to show how much they cost. The clothing salesmen tagged the suits before hanging them on the racks.* 4. to follow closely. *The puppy tagged after his master.* **tags, tagged, tag ging.**

tag² (tag), *v.* 1. to touch lightly. *The catcher tagged the runner out at home plate.* **tags, tagged, tagging.**

n. 2. a children's game in which one player must chase the others until he catches and touches one of them. *The children played tag in the playground during recess.*

tail (tāl), *n.* 1. the part of an animal's body at the end of its backbone, especially a growth that extends beyond the end of the backbone. *Monkeys can hold on to things with their tails. Pigs have short, curly tails.* 2. anything like an animal's tail in shape or position. *The kite wouldn't fly because we didn't have a tail attached to it.* 3. the rear part of anything. *The cargo was stored in the tail of the airplane.* 4. the side of a coin that is opposite to the head. *The tail of a quarter has an eagle on it.* **tails.**

v. 5. to follow closely behind. *The police tailed the dangerous criminal until they found his hideout.* **tails, tailed, tail ing.**

adj. 6. coming from behind; coming from the rear. *The speed of the airplane was increased because of the tail wind.*

tai lor (tā′lər), *n.* 1. a person who makes or repairs clothes. *The tailor closed his shop early because he had to buy new material.* **tai lors.**

v. 2. to make clothing by fitting, sewing, etc. *I asked him to tailor a suit for me.* **tai lors, tai lored, tai lor ing.**

take (tāk), *v.* 1. to grip; to grasp. *Take my hand while we are crossing the street.* 2. to capture. *The pirates took the castle after a long, hard battle.* 3. to accept or receive. *Take the book because I have already read it. He won't take "no" for an answer.* 4. to catch on. *The fire took as soon as the chimney was opened.* 5. to win. *Who took the prizes in the contest?* 6. to catch. *He takes cold every time he sits in a draft.* 7. to have. *When will you take your vacation?* 8. to receive into the body. *The patient will take certain medicines before the operation. Did you take lunch yet?* 9. to travel on. *We took a plane to Mexico.* 10. to need; to require. *It takes twelve eggs to make a dozen.* 11. to choose. *Take one of the books that you haven't read.* 12. to remove. *Take the dishes from the table.* 13. to subtract. *If you take seven from ten, you have three.* 14. to escort. *Did you take anyone to the ball game or did you go alone?* 15. to carry. *Can anyone take this box of books to the school office?* 16. to make a photograph or picture of someone or something. *My friend took a picture of me with his new camera.* 17. to feel. *The artist takes great pride in his paintings.* 18. to have an effect. *The medicine did not take for a long time.* 19. to assume or suppose as a fact. *I take it that you are not working because you have finished the job.* 20. to consider. *We took her to be a fine actress until we saw her latest movie.* 21. to rent; to accept the use of in return for money. *I will take the apartment if you lower the rent.* 22. to accept and pay for on a regular basis. *We wanted to take the afternoon paper instead of the morning paper.* 23. to please; to attract. *The movie took the public's fancy and became very popular.* 24. to pick up and carry off. *Someone took my pencil.* **takes, took, tak en, tak ing.**

n. 25. the amount received, won, stolen, etc. *The thieves escaped with a take of several thousand dollars.* 26. the process of filming a scene in a motion picture. *When the actors were ready, the director called "take one."* **takes.**

Take also has the following special meanings:

take after, to look or act like. *He doesn't take after anyone in his family.*

take in, (a) to make smaller. *Can you take in the waist of this dress?* (b) to understand; to accept with the mind. *I couldn't take in the importance of what he was saying until he told the whole story.*

take off, to leave the ground in an airplane. *We took off for Los Angeles in a huge jet.*

take to, (a) to like. *The children took to each other immediately.* (b) to go to; to go away to. *The outlaws took to the hills.*

take up, (a) to begin; to start. *He took up swimming when he went to summer camp.* (b) to make shorter or smaller. *She took up the legs of the pants because they were too long.*

tak en (tāk′ən), past participle of **take.**

tale (tāl), *n.* 1. a story. *The teacher told us a tale of a knight and a dragon.* 2. a lie. *The crooks told*

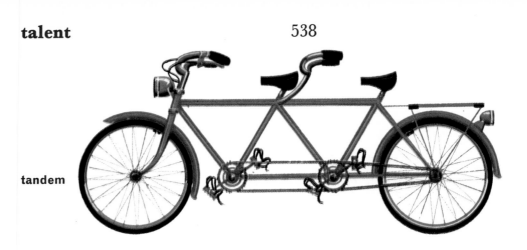

tandem

a tale to the policemen to try to protect themselves. 3. **tell tales,** to spread stories; to gossip. *Don't tell tales about your classmates unless you would like them to tell tales about you.* **tales.**

tal ent (tal′ənt), *n.* 1. special ability; natural skill in something. *She has a great talent for writing, but her brother has a lot of talent in sports.* 2. people who have special abilities and skills. *There is a great deal of talent on the football team this year.* 3. an ancient unit of weight and of money. *In ancient times, a talent of gold was equal to an ox in value.* **tal ents.**

talk (tôk), *v.* 1. to speak; to say words. *Can the baby talk yet?* 2. to discuss. *The men at the party were talking baseball and politics all night.* 3. to speak as a language. *She can talk Spanish and French, as well as English.* 4. to convey information or express ideas in a way other than by speaking. *The boys talked by making signs with their hands.* 5. to influence someone or cause someone to change his mind by talk; to put, drive, bring etc., by talk. *They talked Tom into going to the movies with them. He talks me to sleep every week.* **talks, talked, talk ing.**

n. 6. a conversation. *The two friends had a long talk about the people they used to know.* 7. a short, informal speech. *I gave a talk on the proper care of ski equipment at the last meeting of our ski club.* 8. gossip. *I have heard talk that you are quitting your*

tambourine

lion **tamer**

job. 9. the subject gossiped or talked about. *His new car was the talk of all of his friends.* **talks.**

tall (tôl), *adj.* 1. high; higher than the usual. *There are many tall trees in California forests.* 2. being a stated height; having a height as specified. *That model is almost six feet tall.* 3. hard to believe. *The campers sat around the fire telling tall stories about their adventures.* **tall er, tall est.**

tam bou rine (tam′bərēn′), *n.* a small, thin drum with little metal plates around the rim, played by shaking or by striking with the hand. *The tambourine is an ancient rhythm instrument that jingles when it is shaken.* **tam bou rines.**

tame (tām), *adj.* 1. no longer wild; changed to a domestic state. *There are several tame elephants in that circus.* 2. gentle; not shy. *The animals in the children's zoo are tame and easy for children to handle.* 3. dull; not exciting. *The book was tame because none of the characters ever really did anything.* **tam er, tam est; tame ly,** *adv.*

v. 4. to make tame and gentle; to discipline. *Some animals are very difficult to tame.* 5. to bring under control. *His anger has been tamed by the punishment.* **tames, tamed, tam ing.**

tam er (tām′ər), *n.* a person whose job is to tame animals. *A lion tamer is a popular attraction in a circus.* **tam ers.**

tan (tan), *n.* 1. a yellowish-brown color. *It was difficult to see the tan horse as he walked on the sand.* 2. the condition of having skin of this color as a result of being in the sun. *He had a beautiful tan from working at the beach all summer.* **tans.**

v. 3. to turn a hide into leather by soaking it in a special liquid. *When a hide is tanned, it becomes stronger and less likely to wear out.* 4. to make tan. *The sun had tanned the children's skin.* **tans, tanned, tan ning.**

tan dem (tan′dəm), *n.* a bicycle for two people to ride, one behind the other. *The rider in front steers the tandem.* **tan dems.**

tank (tangk), *n.* 1. something made especially to hold liquids. *The gasoline tank on an automobile is usually in the rear.* 2. a metal-covered vehicle having guns, used in war. *Tanks run on caterpillar treads rather than wheels so that they can be driven over very rough ground.* **tanks.**

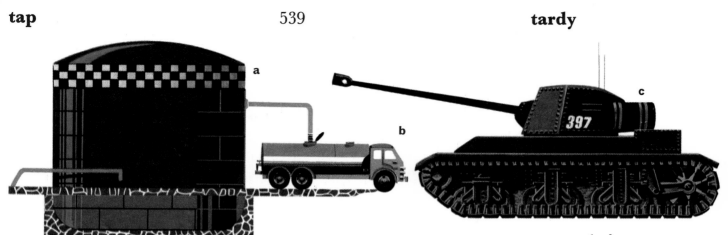

tanks:
a. gasoline storage tank
b. tank truck
c. military armored tank

tap¹ (tap), *v.* 1. to touch or strike lightly. *I turned around when he tapped me on the shoulder.* 2. to do something or make something by striking lightly again and again. *The drummer tapped a beat on his drums. The woodpecker tapped a hole in the trunk of the tree.* **taps, tapped, tap ping.**
n. 3. a light touch or blow. *The boxer was knocked out by a soft tap on the chin. I felt a tap on my shoulder.* **taps.**

tap² (tap), *n.* 1. a long plug or device to stop or control the flow of liquid. *When he removed the tap, the wine ran out of the barrel and onto the floor. Turn the tap off when you have all the water you need.* 2. **on tap,** ready to use; close at hand. *If the first plan of attack fails, we have two other methods on tap. He keeps extra supplies on tap.* **taps.**
v. 3. to make a hole in so as to let out or draw off a liquid; to remove liquid from, by opening or removing a tap. *The men tapped the barrel of beer at the picnic. The farmer tapped his maple trees, and the sap dripped into buckets.* **taps, tapped, tap ping.**

tape (tāp), *n.* 1. a narrow strip or band of metal, cloth, plastic, etc. *His broken ankle was wrapped with tape. Mother used a measuring tape to see how long my arms were.* 2. a ribbon, string, etc., tied across the finish line for a race. *Since Greg was the first to reach the tape, he is the winner.* **tapes.**
v. 3. to tie up, fasten, bind, wrap, etc. with tape. *The broken place on the hose was taped. The doctor taped my wound.* **tapes, taped, tap ing.**

ta per (tā′pər), *v.* 1. to become smaller at one end. *The sword blade tapered to a point.* 2. **taper off,** to become less; to decrease gradually. *The crowd at the fair tapered off as it became dark.* **ta pers, ta pered, ta per ing.**
n. 3. a long, thin candle. *The only light in the castle came from tapers in each room.* **ta pers.**

tape recorder, *n.* a machine for recording sounds and for playing them back on tape. *Tape recorders are used in speech classes to show students what their speech sounds like.* **tape recorders.**

ta pir (tā′pər), *n.* a stout animal that is related to the horse and rhinoceros, but which looks somewhat like a pig. *Tapirs live in the forests of Central America and South America.* **ta pirs.**

taps (taps), *n. pl.* a signal given at night on a drum or horn, at which all lights must be turned off. *Taps was played at nine o'clock every night in the army camp.*

tar¹ (tär), *n.* 1. a thick, black, sticky material obtained from coal or wood. *Tar is used in paving streets and in covering roofs.*
v. 2. to cover with tar. *The wood was tarred to keep it from rotting.* **tars, tarred, tar ring.**

tar² (tär), *n.* a sailor. *An old tar told us exciting stories of his adventures at sea.* **tars.**

ta ran tu la (tə ran′chə lə), *n.* a large, hairy spider. *A tarantula has a bite that is slightly poisonous.* **ta ran tu las.** (See illustration on following page.)

tar dy (tär′dē), *adj.* 1. late; not on time. *You are tardy if you are not at your desk when the bell rings.* 2. slow; moving or happening slowly.

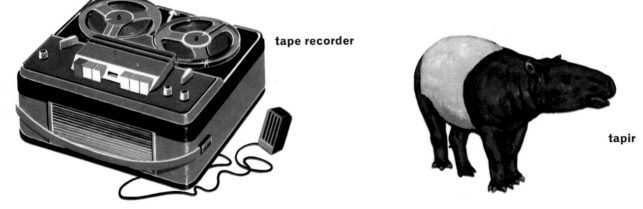

tape recorder

tapir

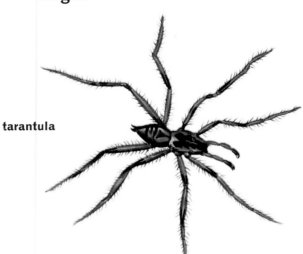

tarantula

All the children were tardy because of the snow. **tar di er, tar di est; tar di ly,** *adv.*

tar get (tär′git), *n.* 1. a mark to aim at; a thing to shoot at. *The arrow landed in the center circle of the target.* 2. anything aimed at; goal. *His target is becoming President of the United States.* 3. anything or anyone who is abused, ridiculed, laughed at, etc. *The artist was a target of insults and jokes until his paintings started to sell.* **tar gets.**

tar tar (tär′tər), *n.* a hard crust that forms on the teeth. *The dentist should remove the tartar from your teeth at least once a year.* **tar tars.**

task (task), *n.* 1. a piece of work to be done. *You may play football after you finish your task of raking the leaves.* 2. **take to task,** to scold; to blame. *He took the workmen to task for using poor materials on the job.* **tasks.**

v. 3. to force to work; to put a burden or pressure on. *The hike tasked my power of endurance.* **tasks, tasked, task ing.**

taste (tāst), *n.* 1. the sense which enables a person to tell the flavor of something he has taken into his mouth. *His sense of taste was dulled by the soap that had gotten into his mouth.* 2. flavor. *This cheese has a funny taste. Lemons have a sharp, bitter taste.* 3. a small bit of something; a sample. *Let me have just a taste of the candy you made. After a taste of life in the city, he was eager to return to the farm.* 4. a liking for something. *He has a strong taste for chocolate.* 5. an appreciation for what is beautiful; the ability to have such appreciation. *Persons of good taste enjoy fine music and art.* 6. a style or pattern of behavior that shows such appreciation. *The movie was done in very good taste.* **tastes.**

v. 7. to determine or test the flavor of something by putting some of it in the mouth. *Taste the gravy to see if it needs more salt.* 8. to have a certain flavor. *Ice cream tastes sweet.* 9. to eat a small bit of something. *Let me taste your piece of cake.* 10. to experience. *Have you ever tasted the thrill of riding in a sleigh?* **tastes, tast ed, tast ing.**

tasty (tās′tē), *adj.* tasting good; pleasing to the taste. *Ice cream is tasty.* **tast i er, tast i est; tast i ly,** *adv.*

tat tle (tat′l), *v.* 1. to tell secrets; to gossip. *Don't tattle to me about what your brother did because I don't want to hear it.* **tat tles, tat tled, tat tling.**

n. 2. foolish talk; gossip. *She always tells me every bit of tattle she hears at school.*

taught (tôt), past tense and past participle of **teach.**

taut (tôt), *adj.* stretched tightly. *Be sure the string is taut before you tie the knot on that package.* **taut er, taut est; taut ly,** *adv.*

tax (taks), *n.* 1. money paid by people to support the government. *Most of the taxes paid in our city are used to improve the schools.* 2. a strain; something that causes a strain. *Lifting the piano put a great tax on my strength.* **tax es.**

v. 3. to put a tax on. *The government taxes property.* 4. to put a strain on. *The hard work taxed the old man's heart.* 5. to take to task; to accuse. *The policemen taxed the robbers for not telling where they hid the stolen money.* **tax es, taxed, tax ing.**

taxi (tak′sē), *n.* 1. an automobile which people hire to carry them for short distances. *A taxi usually has a meter that keeps track of the amount of money that is owed for the ride.* **tax is.**

v. 2. to ride in such an automobile. *We taxied to the theater because we didn't want to wait for a bus.* 3. to move slowly along the ground or on water. *The plane taxied slowly to the end of the runway before it took off.* **tax is, tax ied, tax i ing** or **tax y ing.**

tea (tē), *n.* 1. a low plant with pointed leaves and beautiful pink or white flowers. *Tea grows best in a hot, wet climate.* 2. the dried leaves of this plant. *Tea is used to make a hot drink.* 3. the drink made from these leaves. *Tea is made by pouring boiling water over dried tea leaves and allowing it to stand for a short time.* 4. any similar drink made from other leaves or another substance. *The sick child was given beef tea to give him strength.* 5. a party or gathering in the afternoon at which tea is served. *The women in the club are having a tea on Tuesday afternoon.* **teas.**

teapot

teach (tēch), v. 1. to help to understand; to educate; to instruct. *Did anyone teach you how to read or did you learn by yourself?* 2. to instruct in; to give lessons in. *She taught English at the high school for many years.* 3. to instruct; to give lessons. *She taught at the high school for many years.* **teach es, taught, teach ing.**

teach er (tēch/ər), n. a person who teaches. *Who is your piano teacher?* **teach ers.**

teach ing (tēch/ing), n. 1. the work of a teacher; the profession of a teacher. *Her teaching improved as she gained experience. Robert is preparing for a career in teaching.* 2. something taught. *The boy remembered the teachings of his wise, old grandfather.* **teach ings.**

team (tēm), n. 1. a group of people working, acting, or playing together. *Are you on the school baseball team? A team of experts studied the plans for the new building.* 2. two or more horses, mules, oxen, etc. harnessed together to do work. *The stagecoach was pulled by a team of horses.* **teams.**
v. 3. to join together in a team. *The police teamed with government agents to capture the spies.* **teams, teamed, team ing.**

tea pot (tē/pot′), n. a pot for making and pouring tea. *I chipped the lid of our china teapot.* **teapots.**

tear[1] (târ), v. 1. to rip apart; to pull apart. *Who tore the paper? How did you tear your shirt?* 2. to make by ripping, pulling apart, etc. *The boy tore a hole in his pants when he climbed the fence. I tore a strip of cloth off the sheet and used it as a bandage.* 3. to pull with force. *She tore down the picture from the bulletin board.* 4. to cut deeply. *He tore his foot on a piece of glass.* 5. to make sad or unhappy. *The boy was torn with grief when his dog was stolen.* 6. to become ripped or torn. *How did your shirt tear?* 7. to move quickly; to rush. *The children tore out of the building on the last day of school.* **tears, tore, torn, tear ing.**
n. 8. a hole or cut made by tearing. *He got a tear in the elbow of his jacket when he fell.* **tears.**

tear[2] (tir), n. a drop of clear liquid from the eye. *Tears ran down the cheeks of the lost child.* **tears.**

tease (tēz), v. 1. to bother or irritate by making jokes, asking questions, etc. *The mean boy teased the animals in the zoo by poking them with a stick.* 2. to coax or beg; to ask again and again. *He teased his parents for a new bicycle until they got one for him.* **teas es, teased, teas ing.**
n. 3. a person who teases. *The other children don't like him because he is a tease.* **teas es.**

tea spoon (tē/spün′), n. a spoon that is smaller than a tablespoon. *Teaspoons are used for stirring tea or coffee.* **tea spoons.**

tea spoon ful (tē/spün fúl), n. as much as a teaspoon will hold. *Put one teaspoonful of sugar in my coffee, please.* **tea spoon fuls.**

tech ni cal (tek/nə kəl), adj. 1. of or having to do with science. *That is a technical problem and*

should only be done if you have studied math. *That is a technical word and should be looked up in a science dictionary.* 2. of or having to do with any of the industrial or mechanical arts. *Barbara had the technical problem of deciding what colors she should choose for her painting.* **tech ni cal ly,** adv.

tech nique (tek nēk′), n. the manner in which something is done. *She shows a good technique in playing the piano.* **tech niques.**

tee (tē), n. 1. in golf, the place from which the ball is first hit at each hole. *The seventh tee was located just behind a large pond over which the ball had to be hit.* 2. a small peg of wood, metal, or plastic on which a golf ball is placed. *A tee can only be used for the first shot on each hole; all other shots are made with the ball resting on the ground.* **tees.**
v. 3. **tee off,** to hit a golf ball off a tee. *We teed off on the first hole as dawn was breaking.* **tees, teed, tee ing.**

tee pee (tē/pē), var. of **te pee.**

teeth (tēth), n. pl. more than one tooth. *Did you brush your teeth this morning?*

tel e gram (tel/ə gram′), n. a message sent by telegraph. *He sent us a telegram as soon as he arrived in New York.* **tel e grams.**

tel e graph (tel/ə graf′), n. 1. a system or device for sending and receiving signals over a wire by electrical means. *On a telegraph, dots and dashes represent letters of the alphabet.* **tel e-graphs.**
v. 2. to send a message using this system. *Telegraph the information to me as soon as you can.* **tel e graphs, tel e graphed, tel e graph-ing.**

tel e phone (tel/ə fōn′), n. 1. a system or device for sending and receiving sounds over a wire by electrical means. *Call me on the telephone if you are unable to come.* **tel e phones.**
v. 2. to talk to someone by telephone. *You don't have to write a letter, you can telephone him.* **tel e phones, tel e phoned, tel e phon ing.**

tel e scope (tel/ə skōp′), n. 1. an instrument consisting of lenses in a long tube that makes distant objects appear to be closer. *Scientists use telescopes to study the stars.* **tel e scopes.**
v. 2. to fit or slide the smaller parts or pieces into the larger parts or pieces. *The radio aerial on a car telescopes when it is pushed together.* 3. to force together. *Several railroad cars were telescoped in the crash.* **tel e scopes, tel e scoped, tel e scop ing.** (See illustration on following page.)

tel e vi sion (tel/ə vizh/ən), n. 1. a system of sending pictures through the air or over a wire by electrical means. *Television makes it possible for everyone in the country to see the same thing at the same time.* 2. a device for receiving and showing these pictures. *The television is broken and does not show a clear picture.* **tel e visions.** (See illustration on following page.)

telephones

telescopes

tell (tel), *v.* 1. to relate; narrate. *He told his life history.* 2. to say. *Tell the truth when you are questioned.* 3. to relate to. *Tell us a story.* 4. to make known. *Don't tell the answer to anyone.* 5. to recognize. *How can you tell Tom from Dick?* 6. to order; to command. *He told me to leave the room for a moment.* 7. to have an effect on. *Too much hard work will tell on your health.* 8. to count. *All told there were eighteen people present.* **tells, told, tell ing.**

tell er (tel′ər), *n.* 1. a person who tells something. *The teller of the story stopped to take a drink of water.* 2. a bank employee who receives and distributes money to customers. *When you make a deposit, the teller credits your account.* **tell ers.**

Tel star (tel′stär′), *n.* a small satellite used to relay radio, television, and telephone signals.

television

Messages can be sent from across the ocean by Telstar.

tem per (tem′pər), *n.* 1. the particular mood a person is in; a particular state of mind. *He was in a bad temper when the team lost the game.* 2. a usual disposition or state of mind. *Dorothy has an even temper.* 3. a peaceful or calm state of mind. *When the children broke his window again, he lost his temper.* 4. an angry state of mind. *Don't show your temper so easily. He got into a temper when he learned he had made a mistake.* 5. the degree of hardness or firmness given a substance by tempering. *Steel used in buildings has a softer temper than steel used in knife blades.* **tem pers.**

v. 6. to make softer; to moderate. *A judge should temper justice with mercy.* 7. to change to a desired condition by mixing or preparing in a special way. *Clay is tempered by mixing with water, which makes the clay soft. Steel is tempered by heat, which makes the steel hard.* **tem pers, tem pered, tem per ing.**

tem per ate (tem′pər it), *adj.* 1. neither too hot nor too cold. *The United States has a temperate climate.* 2. not extreme; moderate. *He has a temperate disposition and seldom gets very angry.* 3. moderate in the use of alcoholic drinks. *A temperate man seldom or never drinks alcoholic beverages.* 4. **Temperate Zone,** either of the areas of the earth's surface between the tropics and the polar regions. *The North Temperate Zone contains the United States.* **tem per ate ly,** *adv.*

tem per a ture (tem′pər ə chər), *n.* 1. the degree of heat or cold. *The temperature of the rooms in our home is seventy-two degrees.* 2. the degree of body heat. *His temperature is below normal.* 3. body heat that is greater than the normal body heat of 98.6 degrees. *The sick child had a temperature.* **tem per a tures.**

tem ple[1] (tem′pl), *n.* 1. a building in which a god or gods are worshiped. *The ancient Greeks built many temples to their gods.* 2. any building used for public worship; a church. *Their family attends services at the temple every week.* 3. **The Temple,** any of the three temples built long ago by the Jews. *The Temple was located in the ancient city of Jerusalem.* **tem ples.**

tem ple[2] (tem′pl), *n.* the flat area on either side of the head between the forehead and the top of the ear. *She was rubbing her temples as though she had a headache.* **tem ples.**

tem po rar i ly (tem′pə rer′ə lē, tem′pə rär′ə-lē), *adv.* for a brief time. *Our phone is temporarily out of order.*

tem po rary (tem′pə rer′ē), *adj.* lasting for a brief time; not permanent. *He was the temporary president of the club while the official president was sick.* **tem po rar i ly,** *adv.*

tempt (tempt), *v.* 1. to try to make someone do something by attraction or argument. *The girl was tempted to buy the pretty coat.* 2. to provoke; to test. *Do not tempt fate by walking under a ladder.* **tempts, tempt ed, tempt ing.**

ten (ten), *n.* one more than nine; 10. *The sum of eight and two is ten. Membership in the group grew to ten when Larry joined us.* **tens.**

ten ant (ten′ənt), *n.* 1. a person who pays rent for the use of a house, apartment, or other property. *In that tall building there are seven hundred tenants.* 2. a person or animal who lives in a certain place. *Bears are tenants of the forest.* **ten ants.**

tend[1] (tend), *v.* 1. to be likely or inclined; to have a tendency. *I tend to agree with what he says.* 2. to lead in a certain direction. *The path of the river tends to the south, though it doesn't always flow in that direction.* **tends, tend ed, tend ing.**

tend[2] (tend), *v.* 1. to take care of; to guard and protect. *Shepherds tend their flocks day and night.* 2. to operate; to manage. *Who will tend the*

store while I am gone? He tends a machine in a factory.* **tends, tend ed, tend ing.**

ten den cy (ten′dən sē), *n.* 1. a leaning; tending to move in a certain direction. *Warm air has a tendency to rise above cold air. Taxes have a tendency to increase regularly.* 2. a disposition in thought or actions. *He has a tendency to lose his temper quickly.* **ten den cies.**

ten der[1] (ten′dər), *adj.* 1. soft; not hard or stiff; not tough. *This is a tender piece of meat.* 2. delicate; not strong. *The tender shoots on the plants froze during the cold spell.* 3. fond; loving. *He has a tender feeling for his brothers and sisters.* 4. gentle. *His tender hands quieted the frightened horse.* 5. painful to the touch. *That bruise on his arm is still tender.* 6. kind; feeling sympathy. *His tender heart forgave her for all she had done.* **ten der ly,** *adv.*

ten der[2] (ten′dər), *v.* 1. to offer. *He tendered his application for membership to one of the managers of the club.* **ten ders, ten dered, ten der ing.** *n.* 2. something offered. *They rejected our tender of peace and continued fighting.* 3. **legal tender,** any money that the law approves as acceptable for paying debts. *Silver dollars are still legal tender in the United States, but foreign money is not.* **ten ders.**

ten der[3] (ten′dər), *n.* 1. a person or thing that takes care of something. *He was hired to work as tender of the popcorn machine in the theater.* 2. a small boat that carries supplies, passengers, etc. to a larger ship. *The sailor rode out to his ship in the harbor on the mail tender.* 3. a supply car attached to a steam locomotive. *The tender carried water and coal.* **ten ders.**

Ten nes see (ten′ə sē′), *n.* a state in the southern and central part of the United States. *Farming, mining, and manufacturing are the major industries of Tennessee.*

ten nis (ten′is), *n.* a game played by two or four persons who hit a ball back and forth over a low net. *Points are scored in tennis when a player is unable to hit the ball over the net or when the ball is hit out of bounds.* (See illustration on following page.)

ten or (ten′ər), *n.* 1. a vocal quality that is the highest pitch a male voice can reach. *That man sings tenor.* 2. a course in life. *The tenor of*

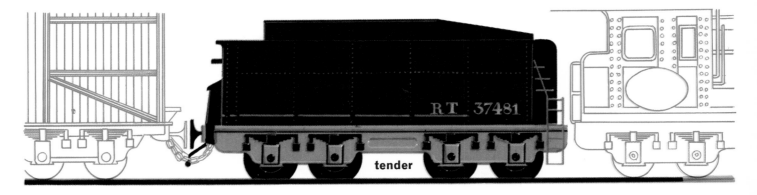

tender

his belief is that he is never wrong. 3. the main idea. *The tenor of her conversation was that blue is a pretty color.* **ten ors.**

tense[1] (tens), *adj.* 1. very uneasy; having a tight, high-strung feeling. *I am always tense before a test.* **tens er, tens est; tense ly,** *adv.*

v. 2. to pull tight; to stiffen. *She tensed herself for the fall.* **tens es, tensed, tens ing.**

tense[2] (tens), *n.* a form of the verb showing whether the action is past, future, or present or any variation of these forms. *The future tense of I am is I will.* **tens es.**

tent (tent), *n.* 1. a portable structure of canvas or other material supported by a pole or poles. *Small tents are used as shelters by campers; large tents are used for circuses.* **tents.**

v. 2. to stay in a tent; to live in a tent. *We tented in the backyard for several nights.* **tents, tent ed, tent ing.**

ten th (tenth), *adj.* 1. next after the ninth; 10th. *I was the tenth person in the line.*

n. 2. one of ten equal parts of a thing. *Since there were ten of us, each person was given a tenth of the pie.* **tenths.**

te pee (tē′pē), *n.* a small cone-shaped tent used by American Indians. *Tepees were made of skins stretched over poles that were fastened together at the top.* **te pees.**

term (tėrm), *n.* 1. a word or group of words that has a special meaning in a particular field or subject. *Can you describe in scientific terms what causes rain?* 2. an established period of time; the fixed period of time during which something may occur. *The school term begins in September and ends in June. The mayor was elected for another term in office.* 3. **terms,** (a) the con-

ditions of an agreement. *You must carry out the terms of your contract if you want to be paid for your work.* (b) relations between people. *Are you on speaking terms with Mary? They have been on good terms with each other for as long as I have known them.* **terms.**

v. 4. to name; to use a term to describe. *The captain termed the soldier's deed heroic.* **terms, termed, term ing.**

ter mite (tėr′mīt), *n.* a small insect that has the ability to eat and digest wood. *Termites are very destructive to all wood products.* **ter mites.**

ter rar i um (tə râr′ē əm), *n.* an enclosure, often made of glass, in which plants are grown or small land animals are kept. *He kept his pet lizards and a small snake in his terrarium.* **ter rar i ums** or **ter rar ia** (tə râr′ē ə).

ter ri ble (ter′ə bl), *adj.* 1. causing terror; horrible. *The monster in the movie was a terrible sight.* 2. causing grief or suffering. *His leg was broken in a terrible automobile accident.* 3. very great in degree; extreme. *The cold at the North Pole is terrible.* 4. bad; poor in quality. *We saw a terrible play at the theater.* **ter ri bly,** *adv.*

ter rif ic (tə rif′ik), *adj.* 1. giving a great amount of fear. *The rainstorm we had last night was terrific.* 2. very well done; excellent. *That was a terrific grade.* **ter rif i cal ly,** *adv.*

ter ri to ry (ter′ə tôr′ē), *n.* 1. an area of land; a region. *Much of the territory in the central part of the United States is used for farming.* 2. land that is ruled by or belongs to a government. *At one time England had territories in many parts of the world.* 3. a district assigned to a person for a certain purpose. *Each of the salesmen has a territory in which he may sell.* **ter ri to ries.**

tennis

tennis court

rackets and balls

shoe

judge

ter ror (ter′ər), *n.* 1. very strong fear. *He has a terror of high places.* 2. something that causes strong fear. *Enemy planes were a terror during the war.* **ter rors.**

test (test), *n.* 1. an examination; a trial. *He had to pass a test before he was given his license to fly.* 2. an examination to determine a student's knowledge in a subject. *There were twenty problems on the arithmetic test.* 3. anything which reveals something through trial. *Going to the dentist should not be a test of your ability to endure pain.* 4. an examination to determine the contents of a material or a substance. *Tests have shown that the soil on the moon is much like the soil on the earth.* **tests.**
v. 5. to try; to examine; to put to a test. *Our teacher tested us in history last week. Steel is tested to determine its ability to support weight.* **tests, test ed, test ing.**

tes ti fy (tes′tə fī), *v.* to give evidence; declare; indicate. *He testified to the truth of her statement in court.* **tes ti fies, tes ti fied, tes ti fy ing.**

tes ti mo ny (tes′tə mō′ni), *n.* evidence; a statement given, especially in court. *His testimony was the deciding factor in the case.* **tes ti mo nies.**

Tex as (tek′səs), *n.* a state in the southwestern part of the United States. *Texas is the second-largest state in the United States.*

text (tekst), *n.* 1. the main body of writing on a page or in a book. *In addition to the text on page 73 there is a map of the state.* 2. the words written by an author. *If you examine the text of his speech you will see that he didn't say what you are telling me.* 3. a brief passage from the Bible. *He always chooses a text as the subject of his sermon.* 4. a subject; a topic. *The text of the article was improvement of education.* 5. a book used to study a subject. *I examined a map of Africa in my geography text.* **texts.**

tex ture (teks′chər), *n.* 1. the appearance of materials or the feel of these materials. *The oil painting appeared smooth, but it had a rough texture.* 2. the arrangement of the different threads in cloth. *That cotton dress has a smooth texture.* **tex tures.**

than (than, thən), *conj.* compared to or with; in comparison to. *She is smarter than Mary. He won the race because he ran faster than the others.*

thank (thangk), *v.* 1. to express gratitude to. *The lady thanked him for giving her directions. Thank you for the bouquet.* 2. **to have oneself to thank,** to be to blame; to be responsible. *She has herself to thank for missing the train.* 3. **thanks to,** because of. *Thanks to Scott's hard work, the party was a success.* **thanks, thanked, thank ing.**

thank ful (thangk′fəl), *adj.* feeling or showing gratitude; grateful. *She was very thankful when I returned her lost purse.* **thank ful ly,** *adv.*

thanks giv ing (thangks′giv′ing), *n.* 1. the act of expressing gratitude. *In thanksgiving for their*

victory, the members of the team praised their coach. 2. an expression of gratitude. *We offer thanksgiving for all of the good things that have been given to us.* 3. **Thanksgiving,** the fourth Thursday in November, a day for thanking God. *Thanksgiving is a legal holiday in the United States.* **thanks giv ings.**

that (that, thət), *pron.* 1. a thing or person pointed out or mentioned. *Did he really tell you that? Whose sweater is that? That is mine.* 2. the person or thing farther away. *Did you wait on this corner or that? This is my house and that is his.* 3. who; whom; which. *The person that called had gone when I arrived. This is the house that I like best.* 4. on which; in which; at which. *It was the first time that I saw him. She does well on her tests because of the way that she studies.* **those.**
adj. 5. being the person or thing pointed out or mentioned. *Do you know that girl? Did you find that information in the newspaper?* 6. being the person or thing farther away. *I like this picture better than that one. He lives in this building now, but he used to live in that building across the street.* **those.**
conj. 7. with the result; having as a result. *It rained so hard that the game was postponed.* 8. with the purpose; having as a purpose. *We study hard so that we will learn more.*
adv. 9. to such a degree or extent. *No one can hit a baseball that far!*

thatch (thach), *n.* 1. a plant material, such as long grass, straw, etc., used as a roof. *Thatch is used on small houses and huts in many parts of Europe.*
v. 2. to cover with long grass, straw, etc. *The native thatches his hut every year.* **thatch es, thatched, thatch ing.**

thaw (thô), *v.* 1. to melt. *The ice on the lake thawed in the spring.* 2. to cause to melt. *The warm weather thawed the snow on the streets.* 3. to become less formal and reserved. *He will thaw and become friendly when he gets to know you better.* **thaws, thawed, thaw ing.**
n. 4. a temperature above freezing; a period of time during which the temperature is above freezing. *A brief thaw melted most of the ice on the skating pond. The rivers and streams are full during the spring thaw.* **thaws.**

the (thē, thə, thi), *adj., definite article.* 1. that or those indicated; a particular. *The book I needed was not on the shelf. Where is the pen I gave to you?* 2. any one of a group; all of a group. *The rose is a beautiful flower. The Romans conquered much of the world.* 3. that which is best. *The world series is the sports event of the fall.*
adv. 4. to what extent; to that extent. *The harder you study, the more you learn.*

the a ter or **the a tre** (thē′ə tər), *n.* 1. a place in which plays or movies are presented. *A theater that presents movies has a large screen; a theater that presents plays has a stage.* 2. any place like a theater in use or in its arrangement of seats. *Medical schools have theaters where students may watch doctors performing operations.* 3. an area where action is going on. *Europe was a major theater of World War II.* 4. the drama; the branch of art that deals with writing or performing in plays. *Bob has worked hard at his career in the theater.* **the a ters** or **the a tres.**

thee (thē), *pron.* an old form of "you." *With this ring, I thee wed.*

theft (theft), *n.* the act of stealing. *The robber was sent to jail for the theft of the money.* **thefts.**

their (thâr), *adj.* 1. of, belonging to, or relating to them. *Is that your cat or their cat?*
pron. 2. **theirs,** (a) of or belonging to them. *We can't take it because it's theirs.* (b) the one or one's belonging to them; their one or ones. *Our car has four doors; theirs has two.*

them (them, them), *pron.* the persons, animals, or things mentioned or referred to. *I knew the children were awake when I heard them talking.*

theme (thēm), *n.* 1. the subject of a speech, article, etc.; topic. *We selected school spirit as the theme of our discussion.* 2. a short composition. *We must write one theme a week in school.* 3. the main tune or melody in a song or other piece of music. *The theme is played many times and in many different ways in a musical composition.* **themes.**

them selves (them selvz′, them selvz′), *pron. pl.* 1. their own selves. *They thought of the plan themselves. The children bathe themselves every night. The boys themselves admitted that they were guilty.* 2. their usual selves. *They were so tired after the circus that they weren't themselves.*

then (then), *adv.* 1. at that time. *I was in school then so I didn't see the program.* 2. soon after; afterward. *We went to the movies and then we came home.* 3. in that case; consequently; therefore. *If you broke the window, then you must*

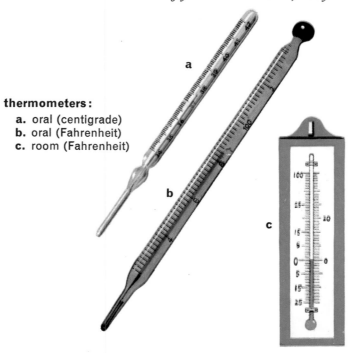

thermometers:
a. oral (centigrade)
b. oral (Fahrenheit)
c. room (Fahrenheit)

fix it. 4. besides. *It was getting too dark to play football, and then we were quite tired.*
n. 5. that time. *I didn't hear the noise because by then I was asleep.*
adj. 6. of the time mentioned; existing at a time mentioned. *When the war began, the then president felt that we could win in a short time.*

the o ry (thē′ə rē, thir′ē), *n.* 1. the principles of a science or art. *You do not have to fly an airplane to understand the theory of flight.* 2. an explanation of how something works or happens that is based on observation and thought. *Scientists have developed many theories about the beginnings of the universe.* 3. a guess; an opinion. *I had a theory that four men were involved in the robbery, although the police said only three men had done it.* **the o ries.**

ther a py (ther′ə pē), *n.* treatment such as exercising, swimming, etc. that a doctor prescribes for the well-being of his patient. *The boy did therapy for his arm after the accident.* **ther a pies.**

there (thâr, ther), *adv.* 1. in or at that place. *Put the flowers over there by the window.* 2. to that place; into that place. *I don't want to go to the city because I went there last week.* 3. in that matter. *I can't agree with you there. You have a point there.*
pron. 4. that place. *I removed the book from there last night.* 5. used to introduce a sentence or clause in which the subject follows the verb. *There is a beach ball on the roof of the school. Is there any chance he will succeed?*

there by (thâr bī′, thâr′bī), *adv.* 1. by that means. *We scored in the last inning and thereby won the game.* 2. nearby. *We stopped in a small town and visited a castle which was built thereby.*

there fore (thâr′fôr), *adv.* for that reason; consequently. *You are late to school; therefore you must stay after class.*

there in (thâr in′), *adv.* 1. in that place, time, or thing. *The building and all therein were destroyed by the fire.* 2. in that matter. *I thought we had too great a lead to lose the game, and therein I made a serious error.*

there of (thâr ov′, thâr uv′), *adv.* 1. of that; of this; or it. *The soldier accepted the peace pipe from the Indian chief and began to smoke thereof.* 2. from that cause. *I took some medicine and became well thereof.*

there on (thâr on′, thâr ôn′), *adv.* on that or it. *We bought one hundred acres of land and all of the buildings thereon.*

there's (thârz), there is. *There's too much traffic on the road today. There's a tree next to my bedroom window.*

ther mom e ter (ther mom′ə ter), *n.* an instrument consisting of a hollow tube and bulb containing mercury or alcohol that measures and indicates temperatures. *The liquid in a thermometer expands and rises in the tube as the temperature becomes warmer.* **ther mom e ters.**

these (thēz), *pron.*, *adj.* plural of **this.** *Give me three of these flowers and three of those. Those are my boots, but who owns these?*

they (thā), *pron. pl.* 1. the persons, animals, or things mentioned or indicated. *The children washed their hands before they ate.* 2. people; some people. *They say it is going to rain tonight.*

they'd (thād), 1. they had. *They'd left by the time we arrived.* 2. they would. *I thought they'd wait for us.*

they'll (thāl), 1. they will. *If you give them a ride to the bus, they'll be able to get to school on time.* 2. they shall. *They'll do better on the next test because they are going to study harder now.*

they're (thâr), they are. *They're going to the game with us.*

they've (thāv), they have. *Do you know where they've gone?*

thick (thik), *adj.* 1. large in size from one side to its opposite; not thin. *The old castle door was very thick. The boat was covered with thick metal plates.* 2. measuring in distance through; in depth. *The geography book is one inch thick.* 3. very heavy and close together. *The soldiers had to cut their way through the thick growth of the jungle.* 4. not watery. *Honey becomes extremely thick when it is cold.* 5. foggy; misty. *During the storm the weather was too thick to permit us to see easily.* 6. not clear in sound; rough and harsh in sound. *They shouted so much at the basketball game that their voices were thick afterwards.* 7. stupid; not bright or clever. *He is so thick that he can't remember the simplest things you tell him.* 8. very friendly; close; intimate. *They have been thick companions for several years.* **thick er, thick est; thick ly,** *adv.*
n. 9. the most active or hardest part. *Whenever there is a fight, you can be sure Pete is in the thick of it.* 10. **through thick and thin,** through the good times and the bad times. *Only your best friends stand by you through thick and thin.*

thick et (thik′it), *n.* a thick growth of shrubs, bushes, trees, etc. *The rabbits had built their nest in a thicket near the garden.* **thick ets.**

thief (thēf), *n.* a person who steals, especially secretly and without force or violence. *A thief has been taking our newspaper from the front porch every morning.* **thieves** (thēvz).

thim ble (thim′bl), *n.* a metal or plastic cap worn on a finger to push the needle in sewing. *The thimble protects the finger that pushes the needle and makes it easier to push the needle through heavy fabrics.* **thim bles.**

thin (thin), *adj.* 1. not thick; having little distance or space from one side to its opposite. *A sheet of paper is thin. This metal may be thin but it has great strength.* 2. slender; lean; not fat or heavy. *Only a very thin man could get into the space between the buildings to rescue the cat.* 3. not set closely together; not growing closely together. *From the road we could see the dry fields with their thin rows of dying plants. He has very*

thin hair. 4. small in number; less than usual in number. *Because of the weather, only a thin crowd came to hear the concert.* 5. like water in substance; weak. *We were served thin soup for lunch.* 6. feeble; not deep. *The crying child spoke in a thin voice.* 7. not firm; easily seen through; easy to doubt. *She had a thin excuse for breaking her appointment with the dentist.* **thin ner, thin nest; thin ly,** *adv.*
v. 8. to make thin or thinner. *Thin the gravy by adding water to it.* 9. to become thin or thinner. *The crowd at the game began to thin when the score reached 47 to 0.* **thins, thinned, thin-ning.**

thing (thing), *n.* 1. any object; anything that exists and can be seen, heard, felt, etc. *He took his clothes, a canteen, a baseball glove, and some other things to summer camp.* 2. an action; a matter; an affair. *What is this thing between you and Tom that makes you so angry with each other?* 3. the person, animal, object, idea, etc. thought of or spoken of. *That's a foolish thing to say! I had a bird, but the poor thing flew away and got lost.* 4. **things,** (a) personal possessions; belongings. *Pack your things and get out!* (b) the state of affairs. *How are things? Things began to improve when we were able to go back to work.* **things.**

think (thingk), *v.* 1. to use the mind to reach decisions, form opinions, etc. *I can't think when there is noise all around me. You don't have to give your decision now; you can think about it for a while.* 2. to have in the mind as an opinion, idea, etc.; to believe. *I think we will win the game. He thought that the show was too long. She thought she knew the answer.* 3. to expect. *I think that I will be home by nine o'clock.* 4. **think of,** (a) to recall; to remember. *I would have introduced you, but I couldn't think of his name.* (b) to imagine; to form in the mind. *Think of a number from one to ten.* **thinks, thought, think ing.**

third (thėrd), *n.* 1. the next after the second. *Who is third in the line?* 2. one of three equal parts. *Maureen answered a third of the questions correctly.* **thirds.**
adj. 3. being a third or the third. *The third person to enter was my father. Tom stood on third base.* **third ly,** *adv.*

thirst (thėrst), *n.* 1. a desire for something to drink caused by a dry feeling in the mouth or throat. *The horses satisfied their thirst by drinking from a stream.* 2. any strong desire. *The ruler of the country had a strong thirst for power.* **thirsts.**
v. 3. to feel thirst. *We thirsted for a drink of water after the football game.* 4. to have a strong desire. *The students thirsted for more information about rockets.* **thirsts, thirst ed, thirst ing.**

thir teen (thėr′tēn′), *n.* one more than twelve; 13. *There were thirteen of us who wanted tickets to the game. Some people think thirteen is an unlucky number.* **thir teens.**

thimbles

sand, āte, bâre, fäther; sent, mē, fėrn; fit, bīke; pot, rōpe, fôrt; run, půll, rüle, cūte; noise, sound; ch, cheese; ng, long; th, thick; th, those; zh, treasure; ə = a in about, e in waken, i in animal, o in seldom, and u in minus.

thir ty (thėr'tē), *n.* one more than twenty-nine; 30. *Three times ten equals thirty.* **thir ties.**

this (this), *pron.* 1. the thing or person indicated or mentioned. *Who wants this?* 2. the closest person, thing, etc. *That is my coat; this is Sally's.* 3. the thing, person, fact, or idea that is being discussed or that is about to be mentioned. *Is this better than the plan we approved last week? The only thing I have to add is this.* **these.**
adj. 4. being the thing or person indicated or mentioned. *This street leads to the shopping center.* 5. being one person or thing as contrasted with another person or thing; the nearer. *This book is newer than that one.* **these.**
adv. 6. to an indicated degree or extent. *I want two boards that are this long.*

this tle (this'l), *n.* a plant having a stem and leaves that are covered with sharp points. *Thistles have attractive, bright purple flowers.* **this tles.**

tho rax (thô'raks), *n.* 1. the middle part of the three parts of an insect's body. *Every insect has a head (top part), thorax (middle part), and abdomen (rear part).* 2. the part of the human body that is enclosed by the ribs; the chest. *The thorax includes the heart and the lungs.* **tho rax es** or **tho ra ces** (thô'rə sēz).

thorn (thôrn), *n.* 1. a sharp point that grows on the stems and branches of some plants. *He cut his finger on a thorn while he was trimming the rose bushes.* 2. a tree, bush, or shrub on which thorns grow. *A rose bush is a thorn.* 3. **a thorn in one's side,** a cause of difficulty or trouble. *That car has been a thorn in my side ever since I bought it.* **thorns.**

thor ough (thėr'ō), *adj.* 1. complete. *He did a thorough job of finding all of the facts.* 2. careful and exact in doing something. *The police were thorough in examining the evidence at the scene of the crime.* **thor ough ly,** *adv.*

those (thōz), *pron., adj.* plural of **that.** *I selected these apples; Tom chose those. Are those boys in your class at school?*

though (thō), *adv.* 1. however. *I didn't really want to win the prize, though.*
conj. 2. in spite of the fact that; although. *Though it was getting late, we decided to play for a while longer.* 3. even if it should happen that. *Though he may be wrong, he has a right to express his opinion.*

thought (thôt), *v.* 1. past tense and past participle of **think.**
n. 2. the act or power of thinking. *He spent many hours in thought about the problem. Thought makes it possible for us to reach decisions and have ideas.* 3. ideas, opinions, beliefs, etc.; what one thinks. *Do you have any thoughts about your new program in school?* 4. care; consideration. *Tom gave no thought to what might happen as a result of his actions. She has a great deal of thought for the feelings of others.* 5. the ideas, beliefs, and way of thinking of a particular group of people or

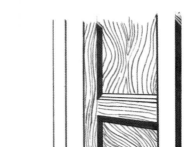
threshold

of a certain time in history; philosophy. *Fifteenth century thought led to many discoveries. Medical thought has brought about great change in the way that we live.* **thoughts.**

thought ful (thôt'fəl), *adj.* 1. concerned with thinking; showing or having thoughts. *He was in a thoughtful mood after he saw the movie.* 2. having consideration for others. *She is thoughtful of her friends and never hurts their feelings.* **thought ful ly,** *adv.*

thought ful ness (thôt'fəl nis), *n.* the act or habit of having consideration for others. *His mother appreciated his thoughtfulness in giving her a present for her birthday.*

thou sand (thou'znd), *n.* one more than 999; 1000. *There were at least a thousand of us at the game. He won one thousand dollars in the contest.* **thou sands.**

thread (thred), *n.* 1. a thin cord or string of spun or twisted fibers. *Thread is used in making fabrics and in sewing cloth together.* 2. anything that looks like a thread. *Broken threads of metal stuck out of the broken clock. A thread of light shone through the window.* 3. the thought that connects the parts of a story, speech, argument, etc. *Your composition is poorly written because you keep losing the thread of your argument.* 4. the metal ridge that winds around a screw, bolt, etc. *The threads on a screw enable it to be firmly attached to something.* **threads.**
v. 5. to put a thread through the opening of. *She was unable to thread the needle because the yarn was too thick.* 6. to move or make one's way carefully among and around obstacles. *She threaded her way through the crowded room.* **threads, thread ed, thread ing.**

threat (thret), *n.* 1. an expression of a desire or intention to hurt or harm someone. *I didn't take his threats seriously because I thought he was joking.* 2. anything that threatens or warns. *We came indoors at the first threat of a storm. The* *threat of danger kept us from playing in the forest.* **threats.**

threat en (thret′n), *v.* 1. to make threats against; to express a desire or intention to harm or hurt someone. *She threatened us with punishment if we did not follow her orders.* 2. to promise as punishment. *The police threatened to arrest anyone who refused to drive carefully.* 3. to warn of; to give warning of. *A red sky in the morning threatens rain later in the day.* 4. to be a source of trouble, harm, or danger to; to hang over. *A water shortage threatened the city because of the lack of rain.* **threat ens, threat ened, threat en ing.**

three (thrē), *n.* one more than two; 3. *Bob had one marble, and Terry had three.* **threes.**

thresh (thresh), *v.* to take grain from a plant, frequently done by a machine. *When it is time to thresh wheat in Nebraska, big machines called threshers are taken into the large fields.* **thresh es, threshed, thresh ing.**

thresh old (tresh′ōld, thresh′hōld), *n.* 1. the piece of wood, metal, or stone at the bottom of a doorway; sill. *The dog sat on the threshold.* 2. the start or beginning place. *He was on the threshold of success.* **thresh olds.**

threw (thrü), past tense of **throw.**

thrift (thrift), *n.* careful management of money; the habit of spending wisely. *By practicing thrift, she saved enough money to take a trip.*

thrill (thril), *n.* 1. a feeling of excitement or pleasure. *I get a great thrill when I go to the circus.* **thrills.**
v. 2. to give a feeling of excitement to. *Flying an airplane for the first time thrilled him.* 3. to have or experience a feeling of excitement. *We thrilled to the beat of the drums. We thrilled at the sight of the huge mountains.* 4. to tremble; to shake. *His voice thrilled with excitement as he described the game.* **thrills, thrilled, thrill ing.**

throat (thrōt), *n.* 1. the passage between the mouth and the stomach and lungs. *He felt a lump in his throat as he spoke. She stayed home from school because she had a sore throat.* 2. the front of the neck. *He grabbed his throat and coughed as he pretended to be hurt.* 3. anything resembling the narrow passage of the throat. *A huge ship blocked the throat of the harbor.* **throats.**

throb (throb), *v.* 1. to beat, especially strongly or quickly. *Our hearts throbbed violently as we neared the end of the race.* **throbs, throbbed, throb bing.**
n. 2. a strong beat. *The throb of the music filled the room.* **throbs.**

throne (thrōn), *n.* 1. the chair used by a king, queen, or other important person on official occasions. *The throne is usually placed on a raised platform.* 2. the power or authority of a king or queen. *The army obeyed the throne and attacked the enemy country.* **thrones.**

through (thrü), *adv.* 1. from one end or side to the other end or side. *The ball struck the window*

and went through. *The board measured two inches through.* 2. from the beginning to the end. *I didn't read the book through because it was too dull.* 3. completely. *He was soaked through from walking in the rain.*
prep. 4. from one end or side to the other end or side of. *A railroad tunnel was dug through the mountains.* 5. as a result of; because of. *He succeeded through hard work.* 6. by means of. *The firemen were able to reach them through the window.*
adj. 7. permitting free or continuous movement. *Traffic moves more quickly on through streets than it does on other streets.* 8. going from one end to another without changing or stopping. *We took a through flight from San Francisco to New York because we didn't want to stop in Chicago.* 9. finished; done. *When you are through with the book give it to me.*

through out (thrü out′), *prep.* 1. during the entire time of. *They have warm weather throughout the year.* 2. in every part of. *We looked for you throughout the building.*
adv. 3. in every part. *The house was decorated with holly throughout.* 4. from beginning to end. *The play held our interest throughout.*

throw (thrō), *v.* 1. to toss or cast through the air. *Throw the ball to Harry.* 2. to project. *The rocket was thrown into space.* 3. to cause to fall off. *The horse jumped suddenly and threw its rider.* 4. to put or bring into a particular state or condition. *The arrival of unexpected guests threw the party into confusion. How many men were thrown out of work when the factory closed?* 5. to put on quickly. *I threw my coat on and came as soon as you called.* 6. **throw cold water on,** to discourage. *They threw cold water on my plan by pointing out how much money it would cost.* 7. **throw in,** to include as an extra or as a gift. *I'll give you my baseball glove for your bicycle, and I'll even throw in my ice skates.* 8. **throw over,** to give up; to abandon. *He threw over his interest in football to be on the track team.* **throws, threw, thrown, throw ing.**
n. 9. an act of throwing; a toss. *His throw to Bob was caught for a touchdown. The player made a bad throw to first base and the runner was safe.* **throws.**

thrown (thrōn), past participle of **throw.**

thrush (thrush), *n.* a bird that has a sweet song. *There are many kinds of thrushes; one kind is the robin.* **thrush es.** (See illustration on following page.)

thrust (thrust), *v.* 1. to push or shove with force. *He thrust his way out of the room. She thrust the money into her purse.* 2. to send forth; to extend. *The old tree thrust its branches across the lane.* 3. to stab; to cause to enter. *He accidentally thrust the needle into his finger.* **thrusts, thrust, thrust ing.**
n. 4. a push. *A sudden thrust from behind knocked me off balance.* 5. a stab or stabbing motion. *He cut through the apple with a thrust of his knife. The*

thrush

tiara

speaker motioned with a thrust of his finger in the air as he spoke. **thrusts.**

thumb (thum), *n.* 1. the short, thick finger on the hand. *Little Jack Horner stuck his thumb into his pie.* 2. something that covers the thumb. *Someone cut the thumbs off my mittens.* **thumbs.**
v. 3. to look through a book, magazine, etc. by turning the pages with the thumb or as if with the thumb. *I haven't read the chapter yet, but I thumbed through it and looked at the pictures.* 4. to wear or make dirty by rubbing with the thumbs. *Most of the pages in the book are badly thumbed.* **thumbs, thumbed, thumb ing.**

thump (thump), *v.* 1. to hit heavily; to pound. *He thumped on the door with his hand.* 2. to beat violently; to throb. *He was so frightened that he could almost hear his heart thumping.* **thumps, thumped, thump ing.**
n. 3. a blow with something heavy. *As I entered the dark room someone gave me a thump on the head.* 4. a dull, heavy sound made by such a blow. *The fighter fell to the floor with a thump.* **thumps.**

thun der (thun′dər), *n.* 1. the loud noise caused by the violent expansion of air heated by lightning. *Thunder always follows lightning.* 2. any loud noise like this. *I couldn't hear what she said because of the thunder of a passing train. The thunder of the explosion woke us.* **thun ders.**
v. 3. to make thunder. *When it began to thunder, we headed for home.* 4. to make a loud noise like thunder. *The train thundered across the old bridge.* 5. to shout; to roar. *The crowd thundered their approval of the team's victory.* **thun ders, thundered, thun der ing.**

thun der head (thun′dər hed′), *n.* a large dark cloud that often appears before an electrical shower or storm. *We called off the hike when we saw several thunderheads forming over the lake.* **thun der heads.**

Thurs day (thėrz′dē, thėrz′dā′), *n.* the fifth day of the week, coming between Wednesday and Friday. *Our Christmas vacation begins on a Thursday this year.* **Thurs days.**

thus (ŧhus), *adv.* 1. in this way or manner. *As you say your lines in the play, you must face the audience thus.* 2. to this degree or extent. *We have won all of our games thus far.* 3. therefore; as a result. *The car ran out of gas, thus we were unable to continue driving.*

thy (ŧhī), *pron.* an old form of "your." *Thy will be done.*

ti ara (tī âr′ə), *n.* an ornament for a woman's head, looking like a small crown. *Tiaras were worn for formal occasions.* **ti ar as.**

tick[1] (tik), *n.* 1. a light tapping sound. *Nothing could be heard except the ticks of the clock.* 2. a small mark, as a check or a dot. *As he mentioned each item he placed a tick beside it on his list.* **ticks.**
v. 3. to make a light tapping sound. *The branches of the tree ticked against the side of the house. That clock has been ticking regularly for forty years.* 4. to mark by making a ticking sound. *The clock ticks off the time slowly and evenly without ever stopping.* 5. to mark with a check or dot. *As he selected each item in the store, he ticked it off on his list.* **ticks, ticked, tick ing.**

tick[2] (tik), *n.* a small insect that attaches itself to animals and sucks their blood. *There were several ticks on the dog when he returned from the farm.* **ticks.**

tick et (tik′it), *n.* 1. a card or paper that gives its holder the right to a certain thing. *Do you have a ticket for the football game? Give your ticket to the conductor on the train.* 2. a card or paper that shows the price, contents, etc. of something to which it is attached. *The ticket on the table showed that the price had been greatly reduced.* 3. a written notice given to a person who has broken a traffic law, telling him to pay a fine or to appear in court. *His father got a ticket for not stopping at a red light.* 4. a list of candidates of one political party who are running for office. *You can vote a split ticket by voting for some candidates from each political party.* **tick ets.**
v. 5. to mark with a ticket; to put a ticket on. *Every item we have for sale is ticketed so that the buyer can see its price and size. The salesman ticketed his merchandise.* **tick ets, tick et ed, tick et ing.**

tick le (tik′l), *v.* 1. to touch lightly to produce a shivering feeling and laughter. *He tickled the baby's feet until she laughed at him.* 2. to have this feeling. *His nose tickles when he has to sneeze.* 3. to amuse. *The clown tickled us with his actions.* **tick les, tick led, tick ling.**
n. 4. a shivering feeling. *I coughed to get rid of the tickle in my throat.* **tick les.**

tide (tīd), *n.* 1. the regular rise and fall of the ocean water that takes place every twelve hours. *Tides are caused by the attraction of the sun and the moon.* 2. the flow of water which accompanies this regular rise and fall. *The place where we had been sitting was covered by the*

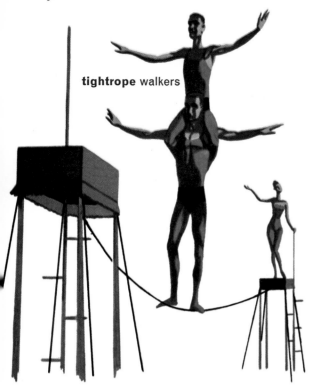

tightrope walkers

tide. 3. anything that changes regularly like the tide. *The tide of interest in the team rises when we win and falls when we lose.* **tides.**

v. 4. **tide over,** to help for a short time, especially during a difficult time. *They gave me some money to tide me over until I found a job.* **tides, tid ed, tid ing.**

ti dy (tī′dē), *adj.* 1. neat and clean; in order. *The treasurer kept the record book tidy. Is your room tidy?* 2. large; considerable in amount. *They offered a tidy reward for the return of their lost dog.* **ti di er, ti di est; ti di ly,** *adv.*

v. 3. to make neat and clean; to put in order. *Tidy your room and make your bed before you go to school.* **ti dies, ti died, ti dy ing.**

tie (tī), *v.* 1. to fasten or bind with a rope, string, etc. *Tie the dog to the fence while you are in the store. Tie up those newspapers and throw them out.* 2. to connect with a knot or a bow; to make a knot or bow in. *Do you know how to tie your necktie?* 3. to form a bow. *The strings of her bonnet tied under her chin.* 4. to fasten or bind by connecting or knotting the ends of. *Tie your shoelaces.* 5. to confine or limit. *He is tied to his job because his family needs to have money.* 6. to make the same score as. *By the end of the game,*

we had tied the other team, fourteen to fourteen. **ties, tied, ty ing.**

n. 7. a necktie. *Sit up, John, your tie is in your soup.* 8. anything that fastens, binds, confines, or limits. *Business ties prevented him from starting a new company.* 9. an equality in points. *The game ended in a tie.* 10. a heavy wooden or metal plank or beam. *Railroad rails are attached to and supported by ties.* **ties.**

ti ger (tī′gər), *n.* a large, fierce cat with yellow fur and black stripes. *Tigers live in Asia and are meat-eating animals.* **ti gers.**

tight (tīt), *adj.* 1. not loose; firm. *The knot was so tight that we couldn't untie it.* 2. fitting very closely. *You can't wear shoes that are too tight for you.* 3. fitting so closely together that water or air cannot pass through. *Is the cap on that bottle tight? Fortunately the boat had tight sides and did not sink in the storm.* 4. stingy. *That tight person wouldn't give a dime to anyone.* **tight er, tight est; tight ly,** *adv.*

adv. 5. firmly. *Keep your mouth shut tight.*

tight rope (tīt′rōp′), *n.* a rope that is stretched tight enough so that acrobats can perform on it. *It takes much practice to walk a tightrope.* **tight ropes.**

tile (tīl), *n.* 1. a thin piece of baked clay, used for covering floors, roofs, etc. *New tiles will be needed to replace the broken ones on the roof.* 2. a thin piece of rubber, plastic, etc., used for covering floors, walls, etc. *He cut the tiles with a scissors and fit them into every corner of the floor.* 3. the tiles used for a particular purpose. *What kind of tile do you have in your kitchen?* 4. a pipe used as a drain. *We had to dig up the ground to find the broken tile.* **tiles.**

v. 5. to cover with tiles; to put tiles on. *Do you plan to tile the kitchen floor this year?* **tiles, tiled, til ing.**

till[1] (til), *prep.* 1. until; up to the time of. *He stayed awake till dawn so that he could see the sunrise.*

conj. 2. up to the time when. *You may read till it is time to go to bed.*

till[2] (til), *v.* to plow and prepare land for planting and growing crops. *The farmer tilled the field and planted corn in the early part of spring.* **tills, tilled, till ing.**

till[3] (til), *n.* a drawer in which money is kept in a store, bank, etc. *Don't forget to close the till before you lock the store for the night.*

tilt (tilt), *v.* 1. to tip; to lean; to incline; to slope or slant. *He tilted forward in his chair as he spoke. The top of the desk tilts.* 2. to cause to tip, slope,

ties

tiger

lean, incline, or slant. *He tilted the lamp so the light shone on his paper. The painter tilted a ladder against the side of the house.* 3. to rush against with spears on horseback. *The knights tilted for a long time before one of them was knocked from his horse.* **tilts, tilt ed, tilt ing.**

n. 4. a slant; the position of being tilted. *The earth is on a tilt which causes the changes in the seasons.* 5. the act of tilting. *She acknowledged his presence with a tilt of her head.* 6. a match or fight with spears on horses. *On some holidays, tilts were held to see which knight was the greatest fighter.* **tilts.**

tim ber (tim′bər), *n.* 1. wood which is used for building things. *Timber is used in building houses and cabinets.* 2. a large, heavy piece of wood used in building, especially to form the framework and support of a structure. *The timbers of the old house were still solid after three hundred years.* 3. living trees or their wood. *Much of Canada is covered with timber.* **tim bers.**

v. 4. to build, furnish, or support with timber. *The house was timbered, but the walk and floors were not yet complete.* **tim bers, tim bered, tim ber ing.**

time (tīm), *n.* 1. the past, the present, and the future; every instant that has been or will be. *Some features of the earth have remained the same since the beginning of time.* 2. any period of time. *You still have time to change your answer. It took a long time for us to reach the airport.* 3. an instant in time when something occurs or has occurred. *The time of their arrival is eight o'clock in the morning. I didn't know what he meant at the time.* 4. the hour, minute, and second as shown on a clock; the day, month, and year as shown on a calendar. *I can't keep track of the time. What time is it?* 5. the usual time for something. *It is past lunch time.* 6. a means of recording or keeping time. *During the summer we use daylight saving time.* 7. one of several repeated acts or occasions. *Henry ran around the school four times. How many times did you call her?* 8. a state or condition in which one lives. *Their family had a hard time until one of them found a job.* 9. an experience at a particular time. *Did you have a good time on your vacation?* 10. rhythm; regular movement in music. *The band played several songs in waltz time.* 11. **in time,** (a) at an early enough time; soon enough. *Will the books be here in time for us to use them?* (b) after a period of time. *I hope to become a doctor in time.* 12. **on time,** not late; prompt. *Our teacher is always on time.* **times.**

v. 13. to measure the time or speed of. *Who will time the runners in the race?* 14. to choose the time for. *The band leader timed the march to begin just as the football players came off the field.* **times, timed, tim ing.**

times (tīmz), *prep.* multiplied by. *Six times four is twenty-four.*

time ta ble (tīm′tā′bl), *n.* a schedule that lists the times of arrival and departure for buses, trains, boats, and airplanes. *The timetable has been changed and says that the train leaves at 3:50 instead of 3:30.* **time ta bles.**

tim id (tim′id), *adj.* feeling afraid; not having much courage or nerve. *That timid woman won't ride in an airplane, a ship, or even a train.* **tim id er, tim id est; tim id ly,** *adv.*

tin (tin), *n.* 1. a soft, white or silver metal. *Tin is used as a part of other metals and to coat other metals.* 2. a thin piece of metal coated with tin. *The roof of the barn was covered with tin.* 3. a box, can, etc. made of tin or coated with tin. *Mother baked the cookies on a cookie tin.* **tins.**

ting-a-ling (ting′ ə ling′), *n.* a soft, ringing sound. *We heard the ting-a-ling of the doorbell.*

tin kle (ting′kl), *n.* 1. a short, high ringing sound. *We heard the tinkle of bells as we walked along the street on Christmas day.* **tin kles.**

v. 2. to make this sound. *A little bell tinkled as we entered the shop.* **tin kles, tin kled, tin kling.**

ti ny (tī′nē), *adj.* very small; wee. *An ant is a tiny animal.* **ti ni er, ti ni est.**

tip[1] (tip), *n.* 1. an end, especially a pointed end of something. *She had ink on the tips of her fingers. A single leaf still clung to the tip of the branch.* 2. a small piece put on an end or serving as the end of something. *He has metal tips on his shoes to keep the rubber from wearing out too quickly.* **tips.**

v. 3. to cover the tip of; to furnish a tip for. *The Indians tipped the darts with poison. Grandfather tipped his cane with a rubber cap.* **tips, tipped, tip ping.**

tip[2] (tip), *v.* 1. to lean or cause to lean; to slant. *Tip your book slightly when you read.* 2. to turn over; to upset. *Be careful or you'll tip the table.* 3. to raise or take off a hat. *Mr. Bailey always tips his hat when he says hello to me.* **tips, tipped, tip ping.**

tip[3] (tip), *n.* 1. a small gift of money for a service performed. *Mother gave a tip to the taxi driver.* 2. a piece of secret or private information; a hint; a suggestion. *Someone gave me a tip on who would win the game, but he was wrong. The coach gave me a tip about how to improve my hitting in baseball.* **tips.**

v. 3. to give a small gift of money to. *Don't forget to tip the waiter before you leave.* 4. to give out a piece of secret or private information. *She wasn't surprised because someone had tipped the news of the party.* 5. **tip off,** to give secret or private information to. *A spy tipped off the enemy troops about the surprise attack.* **tips, tipped, tip ping.**

tip toe (tip′tō′), *adv.* 1. on the ends of one's feet or toes. *She walked tiptoe to avoid making any noise.*

n. 2. the ends of one's feet or toes. *Stand on tiptoe so you can see what is happening.* **tip toes.**

v. 3. to walk on the ends of one's feet or shoes.

He tiptoed into the room so that we wouldn't hear him. **tip toes, tip toed, tip toe ing.**

tire[1] (tīr), *v.* 1. to make weary or exhausted. *Swimming for a long time tires me.* 2. to become weary or exhausted. *The runner tired quickly and had to leave the race.* **tires, tired, tir ing.**

tire[2] (tīr), *n.* 1. a metal band that is fitted around the rim of a wheel. *When the tire came off the wheel of the wagon, the wheel broke in half.* 2. an outer rim of rubber, often filled with air, that is fitted around the rim of a wheel. *The tire on the car is flat because a nail is sticking into it.* **tires.**

tired (tīrd), *adj.* 1. weary; exhausted. *Even though we were tired, we continued to work.* **tired ly,** *adv.*

'tis (tiz), it is. *'Tis the season to be jolly.*

tis sue (tish/ü), *n.* 1. a group of similar cells which carry out a particular function in the body of an animal or plant. *We examined the muscle tissue and skin tissue of a frog in our science class.* 2. a very light, thin cloth. *A tissue of black silk hung across the open door.* 3. a soft, thin paper, often capable of absorbing liquid. *The gifts were wrapped in tissue of many colors. Mother used a tissue to wipe up the water that had spilled.* 4. any thin, easily broken series of things; web. *His story of the accident was a tissue of lies.* **tis sues.**

ti tle (tī/tl), *n.* 1. the name of a book, movie, painting, etc. *When I had finished reading the story, I couldn't remember its title.* 2. a name used to honor a person or to refer to his position or rank. *Mister, lord, king, and queen are titles.* 3. a legal claim of ownership. *We own the title to that land.* 4. the position of being champion. *He held a boxing title when he was in college.* **ti tles.**

to (tü, tù, tə), *prep.* 1. in the direction of; toward. *We are walking to the playground.* 2. as far as. *He gave us a ride to the edge of the city.* 3. for the purpose of. *When the fire started he came to our aid.* 4. for; made or used for. *Do you have a key to this lock?* 5. enough to result in. *The vase was smashed to bits. The animals nearly starved to death during the winter.* 6. on; upon. *You should apply some medicine to that cut. Attach the picture to the wall.* 7. until. *He read right up to the time he fell asleep.* 8. before. *It is a quarter to three.* 9. in harmony with; in rhythm with. *We sang to the music of Nick's accordion. Dance to the music of the band.* 10. as compared with. *We lost the game by the score of eleven to three.* 11. included in. *There are four quarts to a gallon.* 12. per; for each. *The automobile travels fifteen miles to a gallon. His heart beats seventy strokes to a minute.* 13. To is used with verbs to show various states of action. *He expects to learn in school. I like to play baseball.* *adv.* 14. **to and fro,** back and forth. *He walked to and fro across the floor for a long time.*

toad (tōd), *n.* an animal that looks like a frog

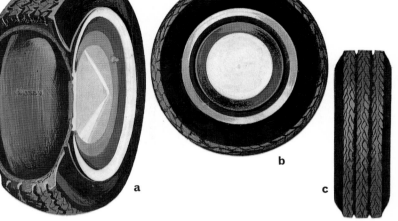

tire:
a. cross section showing inner tube
b. sidewall
c. tread

and has rough, brown skin. *Toads live on land and eat many insects.* **toads.**

toad stool (tōd/stül′), *n.* an umbrella-like fungus that is poisonous. *Animals avoid eating toadstools when they hunt for food in the forest.* **toadstools.**

toast (tōst), *v.* 1. to brown something by heating it. *We toasted hamburger buns over the fire.* 2. to warm; to heat. *We toasted ourselves in the hot sun on the beach.* 3. to drink in honor of a person or thing. *They toasted my health and happiness on my birthday.* **toasts, toast ed, toast ing.** *n.* 4. bread that has been browned by heating it. *We eat toast with our eggs at breakfast.* 5. a drinking in honor of a person or thing. *He proposed a toast to the winner of the election.* **toasts.**

to bac co (tə bak/ō), *n.* 1. a plant with white or pink flowers and broad flat leaves. *Tobacco is grown as a crop in many parts of the southern United States.* 2. the leaves of this plant, especially when dried and used in making cigarettes, pipe tobacco, etc. *Tobacco has been smoked and*

toad

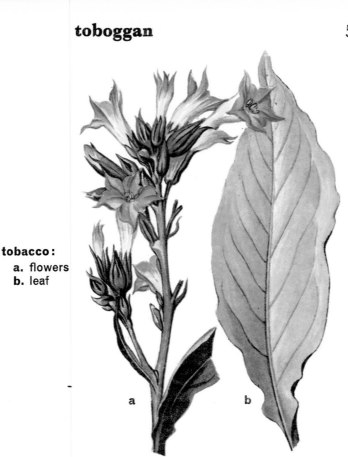

tobacco:
a. flowers
b. leaf

toga

chewed for hundreds of years. **to bac cos** or **to bac coes.**

to bog gan (tə bog′ən), *n.* 1. a long, flat sled without runners that is curved at one end. *A toboggan is steered by leaning to one side or the other.* **to bog gans.**
v. 2. to ride on such a sled. *We spent the day tobagganing down the hills near our house.* **to bog gans, to bog ganed, to bog gan ing.**

to day or **to-day** (tə dā′), *n.* 1. this present day; the present time. *Today is the first day of spring. The children of today will be the leaders of tomorrow.* **to days** or **to-days.**
adv. 2. on this present day. *Are you going to school today?* 3. at the present time. *Schools are quite different today from the schools of the past.*

toe (tō), *n.* 1. one of the separate end parts of the front of the foot. *Man has ten toes and ten fingers.* 2. the part of a boot, sock, shoe, etc. that covers the front part of the foot. *He has a hole in the toe of his boot.* **toes.**
v. 3. to touch with the front part of the foot. *The runners toed the line at the beginning of the race.* **toes, toed, toe ing.**

to ga (tō′gə), *n.* a loose outer garment worn by people of ancient Rome. *Togas often showed the importance of the owner by the colors woven into the border.* **to gas** or **to gae** (tō′jē).

to geth er (tə geth′ər), *adv.* 1. with each other; in one group. *We all walked together on our way to the game.* 2. into one group. *We were called together to vote on a new president.* 3. without

stopping. *I studied for days together to prepare for the test.* 4. at the very same time. *Let us try to sing this song together so that the audience will be able to hear the words.*

toil (toil), *v.* 1. to work hard; to labor. *He toiled for several years before he finished building the house.* **toils, toiled, toil ing.**
n. 2. hard work; difficult labor. *The farmer spent many years of toil in the fields.* **toils.**

toi let (toi′lit), *n.* 1. a bathroom. *While they were rebuilding the house, they added a toilet on the second floor.* 2. a plumbing device used to dispose of body wastes. *The toilet washes waste into a central system where it is carried away and decomposed.* 3. a washing and dressing of one's self. *He made such a hasty toilet that he forgot to comb his hair.* **toi lets.**
adj. 4. used for washing and dressing one's self. *Your toothbrush is a personal toilet article.*

told (tōld), past tense and past participle of **tell.**

tol er ate (tol′ər āt), *v.* 1. to put up with. *We only tolerated his bad humor for a few minutes.* 2. to put up no opposition to. *We tolerate other beliefs even if they conflict with our own.* **tol er ates, tol er at ed, tol er at ing.**

toll[1] (tōl), *v.* 1. to ring a bell, especially with slow and regular strokes. *The people in the town tolled the church bells when the king died.* **tolls, tolled, toll ing.**
n. 2. the sound of a bell when it is struck. *The first toll of the bell woke me up this morning.* **tolls.**

toll[2] (tōl), *n.* 1. a charge made for the use of something or for a certain right or privilege. *We had to pay a toll on each major highway from New York to California.* 2. a charge made for a service, especially for a long-distance telephone call. *The toll for telephone calls to Europe is very high.* 3. something spent, destroyed, lost, etc. *The death toll from automobile accidents reached two hundred.* **tolls.**

toll booth (tōl′büth′), *n.* the place where tolls are paid on a highway, bridge, etc. *On some roads, automatic tollbooths have been installed for drivers who have the exact amount of the toll.* **tollbooths.**

tom a hawk (tom′ə hôk), *n.* 1. a light hatchet used by American Indians as a tool or weapon. *The Indian killed the bear by striking it with his tomahawk.* **tom a hawks.**
v. 2. to strike with a tomahawk. *The bear was tomahawked in the neck.* **tom a hawks, tom a-hawked, tom a hawk ing.**

to ma to (tə mā′tō, tə mä′tō), *n.* 1. a plant with yellow flowers and large red or yellow fruit. *Tomatoes are spreading bushes that grow rapidly in warm weather.* 2. the juicy fruit of this plant, used as food. *Tomatoes are often mixed with lettuce to make a salad.* **to ma toes.**

to mor row (tə môr′ō, tə mor′ō), *n.* the day after today. *Tomorrow is the last day of school.* **to mor rows.**

tomatoes

adv. 2. on the day after today. *We will not be able to go tomorrow.*

ton (tun), *n.* a measure of weight equal to: (a) in the United States, 2000 pounds; a short ton. (b) in England, 2,240 pounds; a long ton. *A truck weighing ten tons caused the wooden bridge to fall.* **tons.**

tone (tōn), *n.* 1. a sound, especially with reference to its quality. *Musical tones from the concert were heard outside the concert hall. The bell rang with a harsh tone.* 2. a musical sound; one of the sounds in a musical scale. *Since the piano key was broken, he couldn't play the tone of C.* 3. a manner of speaking. *He addressed us in an angry tone.* 4. a general spirit or character. *The bright weather set a happy tone for the day of the picnic.* 5. a healthy condition of the body. *We exercise regularly to keep our muscles in tone.* 6. an overall effect of harmony. *Water colors produce a soft, clear tone in a painting.* 7. a particular shade of color. *The artist used tones of green in painting the sea picture.* **tones.**

v. 8. **tone down,** to make softer or quieter. *We can all hear you so tone down your voice.* **tones, toned, ton ing.**

tongue (tung), *n.* 1. a wide, flat organ in the mouth made of flesh and muscle and capable of easy movement. *The tongue is used for tasting, for swallowing, and, in humans, for talking.* 2. this organ taken from an animal, and used as food. *They had boiled beef tongue and cabbage for dinner.* 3. a language. *He spoke in his native tongue, which is French.* 4. the power of speech; the ability to speak. *He was so frightened of speaking before an audience that he lost his tongue for a few moments.* 5. a manner of talking; the way a person speaks. *He had a careless tongue and often used bad grammar.* 6. anything like a tongue in shape or use. *The flap beneath the laces of your shoe is a tongue. The tongue of a wagon is the handle by which it is pulled.* **tongues.**

to night or **to-night** (tə nīt′), *n.* 1. the night of the present day. *Our annual party will be held tonight.* **to nights** or **to-nights.**

adv. 2. on the night of the present day. *I cannot go out tonight because I have too much work to do.*

ton sil (ton′sl), *n.* one of two lumps of tissue on either side of the throat at the back of the mouth. *He had an infection in his tonsils and had to have them removed.* **ton sils.**

too (tü), *adv.* 1. also; in addition. *If you go to the game, we will go too.* 2. more than is needed; more than enough; beyond what is needed or right. *The sheet is too big for the bed. She has been gone too long. He ran too fast for us to keep up with him.* 3. very. *I was only too happy to get a passing grade on the test. I'm not too pleased with the way the scarf I knitted looks.*

took (tùk), past tense of **take.**

tool (tül), *n.* 1. an instrument, device, or machine used in doing work. *Hammers, saws, drills, and planes are tools.* 2. anything used as a tool to bring about a desired result. *Students must use the tools of learning.* 3. a person used as a tool to bring about a desired end. *He was a tool of the pirate and helped him to capture other ships.* **tools.**

v. 4. to do work on something with a tool. *The artist tooled a beautiful design on the wood of the throne.* **tools, tooled, tool ing.**

toot (tüt), *n.* 1. a short, sharp sound made by a horn, whistle, etc. *We couldn't see the boat in the fog, but we heard its toot.* **toots.**

v. 2. to make a short, sharp sound on a horn, whistle, etc. *The engineer tooted the horn as the train entered the tunnel.* **toots, toot ed, toot ing.**

tooth (tüth), *n.* 1. one of the hard structures in the jaw that are used for biting or chewing. *The dentist filled a cavity in my tooth.* 2. anything like a tooth in shape or use. *The points on a saw, rake, or comb are teeth.* 3. one of the projecting parts on a wheel or chain that fits together with the projecting parts of another wheel or chain to transmit or receive motion. *A bicycle has special wheels with teeth to make the bicycle move.* **teeth** (tēth).

teeth

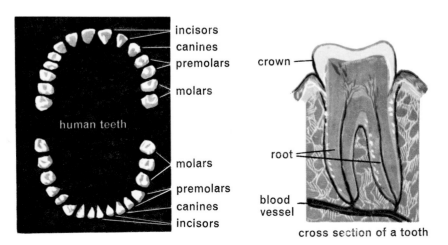

incisors
canines
premolars
molars

human teeth

molars
premolars
canines
incisors

crown
root
blood vessel

cross section of a tooth

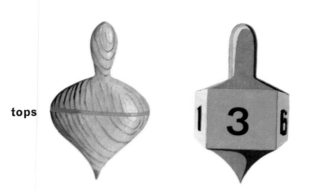

tops

tooth ache (tüth′āk′), *n.* a pain or ache in a tooth. *If you don't take care of your teeth, you may get a toothache.* **tooth aches.**

tooth brush (tüth′brush′), *n.* a brush with a long handle, used to clean the teeth. *When cleaning your teeth, you should move the toothbrush up and down rather than back and forth.* **tooth-brush es.**

tooth pick (tüth′pik′), *n.* a small piece of wood or plastic with a sharp point, used for removing food from between the teeth. *After eating the popcorn, he needed a toothpick.* **tooth picks.**

top[1] (top), *n.* 1. the highest part of something. *A bird sat on the top of the chimney.* 2. the upper side or surface of something. *Did you wash the top of the table? The top of the road was covered with tar.* 3. the part of a plant that is above the ground. *All that could be seen in the field were carrot, beet, and radish tops.* 4. a part that covers a bottle, jar, box, etc. *He lost the top for his fountain pen. Put the top back on the catsup bottle when you have finished making your sandwich.* 5. the highest position; the first place. *He graduated from high school at the top of his class.* **tops.**
adj. 6. highest. *Take the top package so that the others don't fall down.* 7. chief; principal. *The top prize in the contest is a new pair of skates.*
v. 7. to put a top or lid on; to cover with a top or lid. *Top the bottle so that you don't spill the soda while you are carrying it.* 8. to be superior to; to do better than. *She topped everyone in the spelling contest.* 9. to reach or go over the top of something. *A police car topped the hill and came toward us.* 10. to remove the highest part of a plant. *They topped the tree when it grew higher than the telephone wires.* **tops, topped, top-ping.**

top[2] (top), *n.* a child's toy having sides that taper to a point at one end. *A top spins on its point.* **tops.**

top ic (top′ik), *n.* a subject of a conversation, piece of writing, etc. *The topic of his speech was how newspapers are written and printed.* **top ics.**

top soil (top′soil′), *n.* the upper layer of soil. *Flowers and shrubs grow best in rich, black topsoil.* **top soils.**

torch (tôrch), *n.* 1. a brightly burning stick of wood or twisted newspaper or rope that can be carried in the hand. *We used a torch to guide*

us through the dark tunnel. 2. a small device which produces a very hot flame. *The robbers used torches to cut through the metal door of the safe.* **torch es.**

tore (tôr), past tense of **tear**[1].

tor e a dor (tôr′ē ə dôr), *n.* a person, usually Spanish, who fights bulls. *The toreador bowed to the crowd which cheered him.* **tor e a dors.**

torn (tôrn), past participle of **tear**[1].

tor na do (tôr nā′dō), *n.* a violent whirling wind that moves in a narrow path and causes great damage. *A tornado looks like a long, narrow funnel hanging from a black cloud.* **tor na does** or **tor na dos.**

tor toise (tôr′təs), *n.* a turtle that lives on land. *Tortoises are found in very dry places.* **tor tois es.**

toss (tôs), *v.* 1. to throw lightly. *He tossed the basketball through the hoop.* 2. to throw up and down or back and forth. *The wind and waves tossed the small boat.* 3. to move about. *I was so nervous about the trip that I tossed in bed all night.* 4. to lift up suddenly. *The horse tossed his head when I touched him with my spurs.* **toss es, tossed, toss ing.**
n. 5. a tossing; an act of throwing. *I didn't see his toss and the ball hit me on the nose.* **toss es.**

to tal (tō′tl), *adj.* 1. whole; entire. *Is that the total price or will a tax be added to that figure?* 2. complete. *The trip was a total loss since we not only lost the game but two of our players were injured.* **to tal ly,** *adv.*
n. 3. an entire amount; sum. *He won a total of five hundred dollars in the contest. He added the numbers together to find the total.* **to tals.**
v. 4. to add together; to figure the sum of. *I'll have to total my costs before I know how much I*

toreador

spent. 5. to add up to; to amount to. *The cost of our trip totaled three hundred dollars.* **to tals, to tal ed, to tal ing.**

touch (tuch), *v.* 1. to feel with the hand or other part of the body. *He touched the cement to see if it was still soft.* 2. to be next to or against something. *Their farm touches ours. Their bushes touch the back of our fence.* 3. to cause to be next to or against something. *He touched the brush to the canvas.* 4. to strike lightly. *I touched him with a stick to get his attention.* 5. to harm a little. *The edges of the leaves were touched by last night's frost.* 6. to eat a little of. *We were so excited about the picnic that we barely touched breakfast.* 7. to concern; to have an effect on. *Safety is a matter that touches all of us.* 8. to affect the feelings and emotions of. *They deeply touched me by their praise of my work.* 9. **touch on,** to write or speak of briefly; to mention. *I touched on the subject of the new school building, but I didn't say very much about it.* 10. **touch up,** to improve by changing slightly. *Jean's photograph can be touched up.* **touch es, touched, touch ing.**

n. 11. a touching. *The touch of something sharp broke the balloon.* 12. a light tap. *I felt a touch on my shoulder and turned around.* 13. the sense of feeling things or of recognizing things by feeling them. *He lost the sense of touch in his right hand when his fingers were injured.* 14. a small amount. *There was a touch of color on her cheeks when she came into the warm room.* 15. a contact; connection. *Keep in touch with me while you are gone.* 16. a particular manner of playing a musical instrument. *That guitar player has a professional touch.* **touch es.**

touch down (tuch′doun′), *n.* 1. a scoring play in football in which one team moves the ball over its opponent's goal line. *He ran thirty yards and made the winning touchdown.* 2. the score of six points made by this play. *By making three touchdowns, our team had eighteen points.* **touch downs.**

tough (tuf), *adj.* 1. strong but capable of being bent. *The rug is made of very tough materials.* 2. not easy to cut or chew. *The meat we had for dinner was tough.* 3. strong; hardy. *His body was not tough enough for playing football.* 4. rough. *They grew up in a tough part of town.* 5. hard to convince of something. *He has a tough mind and doesn't agree with anything that is said.* 6. difficult. *This is a tough problem and will have to be decided by the police.* **tough er, tough est; tough ly,** *adv.*

n. 7. a rough person who has no regard for the law. *He associated with a gang of toughs until they began to commit crimes.* **toughs.**

tour (tur), *n.* 1. a journey; a trip. *We spent two months on a tour through most of the countries of Europe.* **tours.**

v. 2. to take a tour. *Did you tour by car or by bus?* 3. to travel through. *We toured a different city each day last week.* **tours, toured, tour ing.**

tortoise

tour na ment (tėr′nə mənt, tür′nə mənt), *n.* 1. a contest in which persons or teams compete for the title of champion. *A basketball tournament is held every year to determine the best team in the state.* 2. a contest or fight between knights bearing arms. *Tilts were popular in tournaments during the Middle Ages.* **tour na ments.** (See illustration on following page.)

tow (tō), *v.* 1. to pull by a rope, cable, chain, etc. *The ship was towed into the harbor by a tug.* **tows, towed, tow ing.**

n. 2. an act of towing. *The toboggan was taken up the hill by tow.* 3. the condition of being towed. *A tractor with a car in tow came down the highway.* 4. anything that is towed. *That ship is so large that it takes three tugs to handle it as a tow.* 5. the rope, cable, chain, etc., used in towing. *When the tow broke, the ship crashed into the dock and was seriously damaged.* **tows.**

to ward or **to wards** (tôrd, tə wôrd′; tôrdz, tə wôrdz′), *prep.* 1. in the direction of. *We walked slowly toward the door.* 2. near to; close upon. *The enemy attacked sometime toward dawn.* 3. about; regarding; concerning. *He has a feeling of kindness toward his enemies.* 4. for; with the purpose of. *Many steps have been taken toward ending the war.*

tow el (tou′əl), *n.* a piece of cloth or paper used to dry a wet surface. *Wipe up the spilled milk with this paper towel.* **tow els.**

tow er (tou′ər), *n.* 1. a tall, narrow structure that is higher than the building it is attached to or the buildings around it. *The rich man built a mansion with many towers. The bell tower*

castle **tower**

TOURNAMENT

equipment

sword

spur

helmet

shield

ax

war club

mace

page

knight

shield bearer

combat on foot

jousting on horseback

stands next to the church. 2. a tall structure used for defense against an enemy. *Even though the fort had been captured, we still fired from the gun towers.* **tow ers.**

v. 3. to rise high in the air. *The new building towered above the city.* **tow ers, tow ered, tow er ing.**

town (toun), *n.* 1. a center of population that is larger than a village but smaller than a city. *Life in a town is much more relaxed than life in a large city.* 2. a city. *He decided that Chicago was his favorite town.* 3. the people who live in a town. *The town came out to see the parade.* **towns.**

toy (toi), *n.* 1. a child's plaything. *He was given several toys for his birthday, including a truck and a small guitar.* 2. anything which has little value or importance. *The movie star's boat was just a toy to him.* **toys.**

adj. 3. of, like, or made like a toy. *He has a toy gasoline station.*

v. 4. to play; to amuse oneself. *Don't toy with the pencils on the desk. The cat toyed with a rubber mouse.* **toys, toyed, toy ing.**

trace[1] (trās), *n.* 1. a small mark left by someone or something. *In the morning we saw traces at the brook which showed that deer had been there during the night.* 2. a small bit of evidence. *The thieves disappeared without leaving a trace.* 3. a small amount of anything. *There were traces of sand in his clothes when he returned from the beach.* **trac es.**

v. 4. to follow by means of evidence that has been left behind. *The police traced the robbers to their hiding place.* 5. to mark out; to sketch. *We traced our path through the mountains on a map before starting the trip.* 6. to outline; describe briefly. *The teacher traced the important battles of World War I for us.* 7. to copy by placing transparent paper over a picture and following the lines of the picture with a pencil or pen. *We were told to draw a map, not to trace one.* **trac es, traced, trac ing.**

trace[2] (trās), *n.* either of the two ropes, chains, or lines by which an animal pulls a vehicle. *While they were in the store, the horse slipped out of his traces and ran away.* **trac es.**

trac er (trās**ʹ**ər), *n.* 1. a sheet of paper having questions about what happened to a parcel or package which is missing. *If you think your package may have been lost, the shipping company or the post office will send out a tracer.* 2. a person or thing that traces. *The store's tracer found my package.* **trac ers.**

tra chea (trā**ʹ**kē ə), *n.* the passage that leads from the back of the mouth to the lungs. *Air that is breathed must pass through the trachea.* **tra che ae** (trā**ʹ**kē ē).

track (trak), *n.* 1. a mark or series of marks left by an animal, person, wagon, etc. *We followed the bear's tracks to a nearby cave. We saw the automobile tracks on the snow.* 2. a path, trail, or

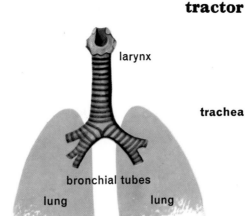

larynx

trachea

bronchial tubes

lung   lung

road. *The only way to get to the cabin is by using this track through the hills.* 3. a special path or course set up for racing. *Have you ever seen the horses at the track? We have a wooden track in the gym.* 4. a number of sporting contests that test skill in running, jumping, etc. *He took part in track in high school and ran in the one-hundred-yard dash.* 5. metal rails on which trains run. *We stopped at the railroad tracks when the red lights began to flash.* 6. **keep track of,** to remain aware of. *I was late because I didn't keep track of the time.* **tracks.**

v. 7. to follow the tracks left by an animal, person, etc. *The hunters used dogs to help them track the fox.* 8. to make marks such as footprints on. *Someone with wet feet had tracked the rug.* **tracks, tracked, track ing.**

trac tor (trak**ʹ**tər), *n.* a large machine on wheels, used for pulling trucks and farm equipment. *The farmer pulled a plow through the fields with his tractor.* **trac tors.** (See illustration on following page.)

tracks: a. human; **b.** deer; **c.** fox; **d.** hare

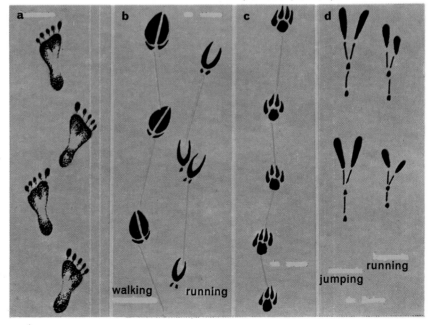

a   b   c   d

walking   running   jumping   running

sand, āte, bâre, fäther; sent, mē, fėrn; fit, bīke; pot, rōpe, fôrt; run, pùll, rüle, cūte; noise, sound; **ch, cheese; ng, long; th, thick; ~~th~~, those; zh, treasure; ə = a in about, e in waken, i in animal, o in seldom, and u in minus.**

tractor

trade (trād), *n.* 1. the business of buying and selling goods. *Our company carries on trade with people all over the world.* 2. an exchange of goods; a bargain. *I made a trade with him, giving him a knife for his yo-yo.* 3. a kind of work that one does for a living; a person's business or occupation. *His father is in the electrical trade.* 4. the people involved in a particular kind of work. *The publishing trade includes writers, editors, and artists.* 5. the number of customers of a store or business. *Our trade increased when we lowered our prices.* **trades.**
v. 6. to buy and sell goods. *Since our business is small, we don't trade with foreign countries.* 7. to exchange. *I'll trade my pen for that book.* **trades, trad ed, trad ing.**

trad er (trād/ər), *n.* 1. a person who trades. *His grandfather was a fur trader to the Indians.* 2. a ship that is used in trade. *It took three days for the trader to take on its cargo of oil.* **trad ers.**

tra di tion (trə dish/ən), *n.* 1. the handing down of customs, habits, and beliefs from one generation to another. *We learn many games, stories, and songs by tradition.* 2. a custom, belief, etc., handed down from one generation to another. *Going to church on Thanksgiving is a tradition in our family.* **tra di tions.**

traffic light

traf fic (traf/ik), *n.* 1. the movement of people, automobiles, etc. along a street, road, etc. *There was very little traffic last night.* 2. the business done by railroad, boat, and airplane companies. *Air traffic includes the passengers and goods that are carried by airplanes.* 3. trade; the buying and selling of goods. *Traffic in umbrellas is always greatest when it is raining.* **traf fics.**
v. 4. to buy and sell goods; to trade. *Several countries in South America traffic with the United States.* **traf fics, traf ficked, traf fick ing.**
adj. 5. of, for, or controlling traffic. *The traffic lights signal cars when to stop and go.*

trag e dy (traj/ə dē), *n.* 1. a serious play that has an unhappy ending. *In a tragedy the hero is unable to do or get what he wants.* 2. a terrible event; a very sad thing. *The death of Jim's dog was a tragedy for him.* **trag e dies.**

trail (trāl), *n.* 1. a path through mountains, a forest, etc. *The old Indian trail ended at the edge of a cliff.* 2. tracks or traces. *The thieves were unable to hide their trail and were captured by the police.* 3. anything that follows behind a moving object. *A trail of smoke came from the rear of the jet plane.* **trails.**
v. 4. to follow or pursue by following tracks or traces left behind. *The policeman trailed the lost boy.* 5. to pull something along. *The baby trailed a toy after her on the floor.* 6. to be pulled along. *Her long skirt trailed behind her.* 7. to fall behind. *He trails all of the other children in his class.* **trails, trailed, trail ing.**

trail er (trāl/ər), *n.* 1. a large vehicle which is pulled by an automobile, truck, etc. *We used a trailer attached to our car to move our furniture.* 2. such a wagon, with a roof and furniture, used as a place to live when it is parked. *We slept in the trailer when we took our automobile trip.* **trail ers.**

train (trān), *n.* 1. a number of connected railroad cars pulled by an engine. *Many people take a train into the center of the city to work every day. He shipped his goods by train.* 2. a line of people or things who are traveling together. *It took seven months for the wagon train to reach California.* 3. a group of people who travel with an important person. *Many lords and dukes were among the king's train.* 4. a connected series of happenings or thoughts. *He finally succeeded after a long train of bad luck. My train of thought was interrupted by the ring of the telephone.* 5. a part of a dress or skirt that trails behind. *You must be careful not to step on her train or you will tear her dress.* **trains.**
v. 6. to bring up; to rear. *You were trained to be kind to the people you meet.* 7. to teach a skill or occupation to. *The carpenter agreed to train Mark if Mark came to work for him.* 8. to get ready by practicing, exercising, etc. *The players trained for the game all week.* 9. to aim. *The guns of the ship were trained on the enemy fort.* 10. to bring into a particular shape or position. *Father*

TRAINS

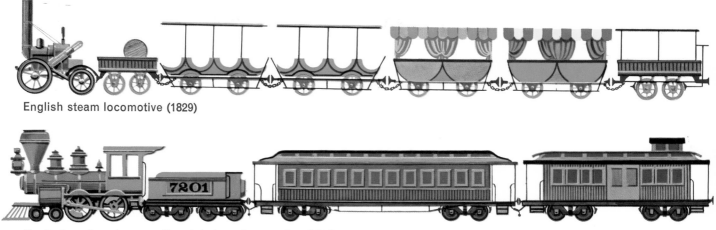

English steam locomotive (1829)

North American transcontinental steam locomotive (1850)

freight train with steam locomotive (1925)

modern passenger and freight train with diesel locomotive

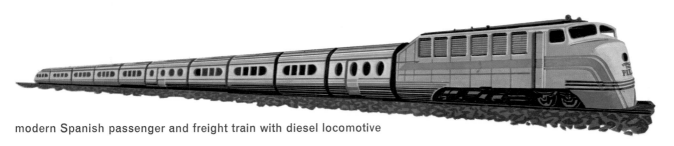

modern Spanish passenger and freight train with diesel locomotive

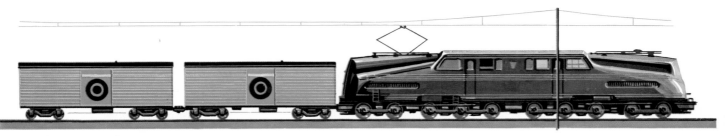

modern electric freight train

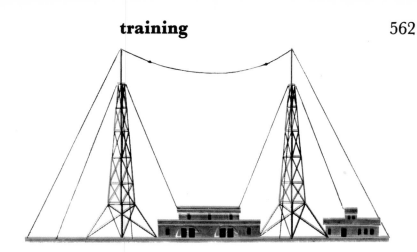

radio **transmitter**

trained the vines to climb and twist around our front gate. He trained his hair to lie flat. **trains, trained, train ing.**

train ing (trān′ing), *n.* 1. the teaching and practical experience given to one who is learning a skill, occupation, etc. *He has had no driver's training before now.* 2. the physical condition reached or maintained by exercise, health habits, etc. *He got in training by running four miles every day.* 3. the exercises, etc. one follows to improve his physical development. *His training consisted of a special diet, plenty of sleep, and regular exercise.* **train ings.**

tramp (tramp), *v.* 1. to walk heavily and slowly. *The hunter tramped through the deep snow.* 2. to step on again and again. *The children tramped on the grass while they were playing.* 3. to walk; to travel by walking. *The soldiers tramped to their new positions because there were no trucks available to carry them.* **tramps, tramped, tramp ing.**

n. 4. the sound of walking or marching feet. *We heard the tramp of the soldiers before we were able to see them.* 5. a long walk; a hike. *We were very tired after our tramp through the desert.* 6. a man who goes from place to place and lives by begging. *We gave some food to a tramp who came to our door.* 7. a freight ship that takes cargo wherever it is hired to and does not have a regular schedule of travel. *Since the regular shipping companies had no room for our cargo, we shipped it on a tramp.* **tramps.**

tram ple (tram′pl), *v.* to walk on and crush. *The big crowd in the park trampled the flowers.* **tram ples, tram pled, tram pling.**

trans act (tran zakt′), *v.* to deal with; manage; carry out a business deal. *In my job I must transact many important matters.* **trans acts, trans act ed, trans act ing.**

trans ac tion (tran zak′shən), *n.* 1. a conducting of a business; a carrying on of business matters. *Mr. Jones is in charge of our transactions with foreign countries.* 2. a deal made in business. *We completed the transaction by paying for the goods we had received.* **trans ac tions.**

trans fer (trans fėr′, trans′fėr for 1–4, trans′fėr

for 5–7), *v.* 1. to take or carry from one person or place to another. *The shipment was transferred from the airport to the railroad station.* 2. to move from one place, position, etc. in business to another. *He transferred from the shipping department to the advertising department.* 3. to change from one bus, train, etc., to another. *I transferred from the 42nd Street bus to the 3rd Avenue bus.* 4. to print a design or pattern from one surface to another. *He transferred the design from the paper to his arm by wetting his arm and pressing the paper to the wet skin.* **trans fers, trans ferred, trans fer ring.**

n. 5. the act of transferring. *The transfer of the troops was slowed when the weather became too bad for flying.* 6. a thing that is transferred. *When the job was completed, we couldn't tell the transfer from the original design.* 7. a ticket which gives a passenger the right to continue traveling on another bus, train, etc. *Since I forgot to get a transfer, I had to pay another fare when I changed buses.* **trans fers.**

trans form (trans fôrm′), *v.* to change the appearance or character. *Dark clouds transformed the sky. In the story the frog was transformed into a prince.* **trans forms, trans formed, trans form ing.**

tran sit (tran′sit), *n.* 1. a passing through, over, or across. *Our transit from one end of the city to the other took two hours.* 2. a carrying from one place to another. *The transit of that cargo from New York to California will take three days.* 3. an instrument used to measure angles. *Men who survey property boundaries use transits.* 4. **in transit,** in passage; on the way. *We couldn't cancel our order because the goods were already in transit.* **tran sits.**

trans late (trans lāt′), *v.* 1. to put one language into another. *Bob can translate Greek into English.* 2. to change from one place or position into another. *The new car translated the man into the world of the motorist.* **trans lates, trans lat ed, trans lat ing.**

trans mit (trans mit′), *v.* 1. to pass along or allow to be passed along; to send. *The captain ordered the lieutenant to transmit his message to the general. Some diseases are easily transmitted from one person to another.* 2. to pass from one generation to another. *In that family, black hair has been transmitted from father to son.* 3. to send out

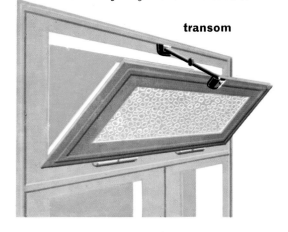

transom

trappings on a horse

by radio or television waves. *The radio station transmits its signal from fifty miles away.* **transmits, trans mit ted, trans mit ting.**

trans mit ter (trans mit′ər), *n.* 1. a person or thing that transmits. *The doctors found out that rats were the transmitters of the disease.* 2. the part of a telephone or telegraph that sends out the sounds. *Speak clearly into the transmitter.* 3. in radio and television, the equipment for sending out the electric waves which carry sound. *Station WMAJ has a powerful transmitter that makes it possible for the station to be heard several thousand miles away.* **trans mit ters.**

tran som (tran′səm), *n.* a window over a door. *Each door in our school has a transom that can be opened to let in fresh air.* **tran soms.**

trans par ent (trans pâr′ənt), *adj.* 1. clear and capable of being seen through: *Many plastics are transparent. We used a transparent cover over our blue chair so that we could still see the color.* 2. easily discovered or found out; obvious. *The fact that his clothes were dry though it was raining outside made his story of having been out for a walk a transparent lie.* **trans par ent ly,** *adv.*

trans por ta tion (trans′pər tā′shən), *n.* 1. the act of carrying or being carried from one place to another. *The cost of the transportation of goods from the factory to the market is included in the price you pay for the goods.* 2. a means of carrying or being carried from one place to another. *When the car wouldn't start, we had to use public transportation to get to work.* 3. the amount paid to go from one place to another. *Transportation on our trip was our largest item of expense.*

trap (trap), *n.* 1. a device used to capture animals. *The tiger fell into a huge trap that had been set in the jungle by the hunter.* 2. a device or trick for catching a person off guard. *He planned a trap to make me tell him our club's secret meeting place.* 3. a special twist or bend in a pipe which prevents gas and small objects from passing through. *The trap provides a sealed*

pipe by maintaining a certain amount of liquid in the pipe at all times. 4. a door in a roof or floor. *The thief escaped through a trap in the roof of the building.* **traps.**
v. 5. to set traps. *The trapper traps animals and sells them for their fur.* 6. to catch in a trap. *The farmer trapped the fox which had been killing his chickens.* **traps, trapped, trap ping.**

tra peze (tra pēz′), *n.* a short bar, held up by a rope on each end, used for stunts in circuses, etc. *The performers in the circus swung from one trapeze to another.* **tra pez es.**

trap per (trap′ər), *n.* a person who traps animals, especially for their furs. *The trapper checked every morning to see if he had caught any animals during the night.* **trap pers.**

trap pings (trap′ingz), *n. pl.* 1. the ornaments sometimes worn by a horse. *The circus horse's trappings included a feather on his head, a colorful blanket, and a silver saddle.* 2. ornaments or fancy decorations worn by a person. *It was impossible to recognize the king without his trappings.*

trash (trash), *n.* something that is no longer valuable; a useless thing; rubbish. *These old toys are trash; throw them out.*

trav el (trav′l), *v.* 1. to go from place to place on a trip or journey. *We traveled from San Diego to New York on our vacation.* 2. to go from place to place as a salesman. *He travels for the biggest steel manufacturer in the world.* 3. to move; go. *How fast does an airplane travel?* **trav els, trav eled, trav el ing.**
n. 4. an act of traveling; the journey taken. *Our travels took us to Japan and China.* **trav els.**

trav el er (trav′l ər), *n.* a person who travels. *Many travelers visit the United States every year.* **trav el ers.**

tray (trā), *n.* a flat holder or platform with a rim, used for holding or carrying something. *Mother put the dishes on a tray before she carried them into the kitchen.* **trays.**

tread (tred), *v.* 1. to walk on. *Our feet were sore from treading the hot sand.* 2. to crush with the feet. *Treading grapes is an old way of making wine.* 3. to make something by the action of walking on it. *By the end of the summer the campers had trod a deep path through the woods.* **treads, trod, trod den** or **trod, tread ing.**
n. 4. a manner of walking. *The athlete moved down the field with a light tread.* 5. the sound

trap for mice

tray

made by walking. *I woke up when I heard his tread on the stairs.* 6. the flat, horizontal part of a stair on which a person steps. *Be careful of the loose tread on the third step from the bottom.* 7. the part (of a wheel or tire) that rolls along the ground. *The tread of this tire is worn and smooth.* **treads.**

trea son (trē′zn), *n.* the act of being not loyal or betraying one's country. *The man was guilty of treason because he sold secrets to the enemy.* **trea sons.**

treas ure (trezh′ər), *n.* 1. money, jewels, and other riches that have been stored up. *We found an old map that showed where treasure was hidden.* 2. anything that has great value. *Several art treasures were destroyed in the fire.* **treas ures.**
v. 3. to save or keep. *The old man treasured all of his money and never spent any of it.* 4. to value greatly. *Grandmother treasured her pictures of the children.* **treas ures, treas ured, treas ur-ing.**

treas ur er (trezh′ər ər), *n.* a person who manages the money of a club, business, etc. *The treasurer reported that we had made a profit of fifty dollars on the club dance.* **treas ur ers.**

treas ury (trezh′ər ē), *n.* 1. a place in which the money of a club, business, etc. is kept. *The city treasury is in the basement of the city hall.* 2. the money owned or held by a club, business, etc. *The members' dues were added to the treasury.* 3. the department of government which has charge of money and spending. *The Treasury of the United States is responsible for collecting taxes.* 4. a collection of something valuable. *We gave our teacher a treasury of poetry at the end of the year.* **treas ur ies.**

treat (trēt), *v.* 1. to take care of; to handle. *Newly planted grass must be treated carefully or it will not grow.* 2. to behave toward. *The angry man treated his dog cruelly.* 3. to try to cure or relieve. *The doctor treated me for the pain in my stomach.* 4. to consider; regard. *Do not treat this assignment lightly.* 5. to deal with something or someone, especially in writing. *This children's story treats animal characters as humans.* 6. to subject to a process or action to bring about an improvement. *The workmen treated the metal with chemicals to make it resist rust. The farmer treated the soil with fertilizer.* 7. to pay food and entertainment expenses for someone. *My uncle treated me when we went to the baseball game.* **treats, treat ed, treat ing.**
n. 8. anything which pleases or gives pleasure. *Seeing a movie at school was a special treat.* 9. a gift of food and entertainment. *When it was his turn for a treat, he gave ice cream to everyone.* **treats.**

treat ment (trēt′mənt), *n.* 1. a way of treating someone or something. *The men objected to the vicious treatment they received from their guards.* 2. anything used to treat something. *We used*

a chemical treatment to make the tree grow faster. *The patient did not respond to medical treatment.* **treat ments.**

trea ty (trē′tē), *n.* an agreement between nations. *The United States has signed many treaties to insure defense against attacks by enemies.* **trea ties.**

tree (trē), *n.* 1. a large plant having a trunk with branches and leaves at its upper part. *Forests are made up of many trees.* 2. a plant that looks like a tree. *We cut these flowers from the rose tree in the back yard.* 3. anything that looks like or has the general form of a tree. *A family tree is a diagram which shows how the branches of a family are related. Hang your hat on the hat tree in the hall.* **trees.**
v. 5. to chase up a tree. *The dogs treed the wildcat and kept it there until the hunters arrived.* **trees, treed, tree ing.**

trem ble (trem′bl), *v.* 1. to shake with fear, cold, etc. *The speaker was so nervous that his hands trembled as he spoke. She trembled with anger.* 2. to move back and forth. *The flag trembled in the light wind.* **trem bles, trem bled, trem bling.**
n. 3. a shaking. *There was a slight tremble of her lip as she began to cry.* **trem bles.**

tre men dous (tri men′dəs), *adj.* 1. terrible; dreadful. *The sudden storm caused tremendous damage to the town.* 2. very great; very large; enormous. *A tremendous wave broke over the boat.* **tre men dous ly,** *adv.*

tres pass (tres′pəs), *v.* 1. to enter another person's property without permission. *The boys trespassed when they went fishing in Mr. Jones' pond without his permission.* 2. to do wrong; sin. *We trespassed when we ate the cake without mother's permission.* **tres pass es, tres passed, tres pas sing.**
n. 3. a wrong; a sin. *The Lord's Prayer says, "Forgive us our trespasses."* **tres pass es.**

tri al (trī′əl), *n.* 1. an act or process of testing. *The trial proved that the motor would fail at high speeds.* 2. a difficulty or hardship; anything that tests a person's faith, strength of character, etc. *The loss of his entire crop was a severe trial to the farmer.* 3. the hearing of a case in court to decide its outcome. *The trial of the bank robber lasted for three weeks. He stood trial for a crime he didn't commit.* **tri als.**
adj. 4. done as a test. *He made a trial run with the car to see how fast it would go on the race track.*

tri an gle (trī′ang′gl), *n.* 1. a closed figure in which three straight lines form three angles. *A triangle has one less side than a square.* 2. anything similar to a triangle in shape. *A triangle of trees outlined the skating pond.* 3. a musical instrument shaped like a triangle with one open end. *The triangle gives forth a clear ringing sound when it is struck with a metal bar.* **tri an gles.**

tri bal (trīb′l), *adj.* of or practiced by a tribe. *The rain dance is a tribal custom.* **tri bal ly,** *adv.*

triangle:
a. equilateral
b. isosceles
c. right
d. scalene

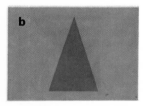

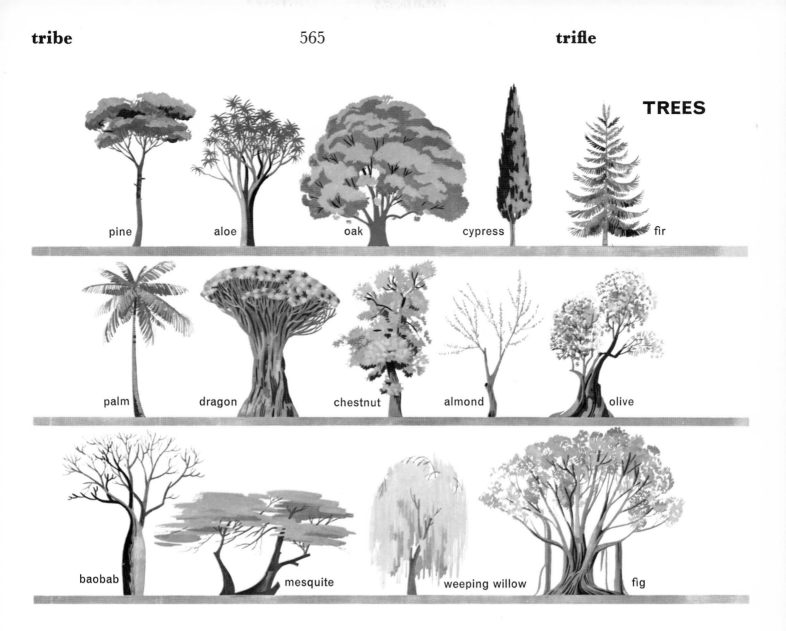

TREES

pine   aloe   oak   cypress   fir

palm   dragon   chestnut   almond   olive

baobab   mesquite   weeping willow   fig

tribe (trīb), *n.* 1. a group of people of the same race who are united in a community with common customs and a common leader. *The tribe of Indians moved west in their search for food.* 2. any group of people. *A tribe of children ran through the playground.* 3. a group of similar plants or animals. *There are many varieties of cats in the cat tribe.* **tribes.**

trick (trik), *n.* 1. something done to deceive. *The phone call was just a trick to get me out of the room while they planned the surprise party.* 2. a prank; an act of mischief. *They played a trick on him by tying his shoes together as he sat.* 3. an act that requires great skill. *We were amazed by the magician's tricks.* 4. a particular way of doing something in order to achieve a result. *Our teacher uses many tricks to hold our attention.* 5. a strange habit or manner. *He has a trick of looking just over your head when he speaks.* 6. the cards played in a single round in a game. *He won the trick with his king.* 7. a time when one has a certain duty to perform; a shift. *Tom*

slept through his trick at the wheel of the boat. **tricks.**

v. 8. to cheat; to deceive. *The fox tricked the hunters by pretending to be injured.* 9. to dress in a fancy manner. *The children tricked themselves up for Halloween.* **tricks, tricked, trick ing.**

tri cy cle (trī′sə kl, trī′sik′l), *n.* a riding device having three wheels that is moved by using the feet to turn a wheel. *Tricycles are usually ridden by small children.* **tri cy cles.**

tried (trīd), *v.* 1. past participle of **try.**
adj. 2. proved through testing or use. *He is a tried actor and always puts on a good show.*

tri fle (trī′fl), *n.* 1. anything which has little value or importance. *I wasn't worried about losing the suitcase because it contained only a few trifles.* 2. a small amount. *This bracelet cost me only a trifle.* **tri fles.**
v. 3. to waste on things that are not important. *He trifles away the evening instead of doing his assignments.* 4. to act or talk without being serious. *The policeman warned the boys not to trifle*

trireme

breakwater

with him when he was on duty. 5. to play with. *She trifled with her hair as she spoke to us.* **tri fles, tri fled, tri fling.**

trim (trim), *v.* 1. to make neat by cutting some away. *I trimmed the grass along the sidewalk. He trims his own hair between haircuts.* 2. to decorate. *We trimmed the Christmas tree with lights and ornaments.* 3. to adjust the sails or cargo in order to maintain the balance of the ship. *We had to trim the sails when a strong wind began to blow.* 4. to defeat. *Our football team trimmed the visiting team by a large score.* **trims, trimmed, trim ming.**
adj. 5. in a neat and tidy condition. *Trim hedges grew on the edge of the garden.* **trim mer, trim mest; trim ly,** *adv.*
n. 6. condition. *At the beginning of the season, the lawn was not in trim. An athlete must keep in trim.*

trip (trip), *n.* 1. a journey; a voyage. *They took a trip around the world last year.* **trips.**
v. 2. to lose one's balance by catching a foot on something. *I tripped on a rake as I reached for the light switch.* 3. to cause to lose one's balance and fall. *A hole in the ground tripped him as he ran for the ball.* 4. to make a mistake. *You tripped on three of the words on the spelling test.* 5. to cause to make a mistake. *The police tripped him by getting him to admit something he had already denied.* 6. to move with quick steps. *The dancers tripped gayly across the floor.* **trips, tripped, trip ping.**

tri ple (trip′əl), *adj.* 1. composed of three parts or sections. *Make triple copies of your work.*
n. 2. three times as much as usual. *We do our work in triple.* 3. a term used in baseball to indicate that a player may advance three bases. *John scored a triple.* **tri ples.**
v. 4. to produce three times. *Triple your answer and you will have the correct amount.* **tri ples, tri pled, tri pling.**

tri reme (trī′rēm), *n.* an ancient ship with three rows of oars, one above the other. *Triremes were used by the Romans as fast ships of war.* **tri remes.**

tri umph (trī′umf), *n.* 1. a great victory; a successful effort. *The soldiers celebrated their triumph in the battle. Finding a cure for a disease is a triumph for science.* 2. the happiness felt because of a great victory. *The team was greeted in triumph as they left the field.* **tri umphs.**
v. 3. to win; to achieve a victory. *The boy triumphed over many hardships by learning to walk again.* 4. to celebrate or feel joy because of a victory. *The scientists triumphed after the rocket was launched successfully.* **tri umphs, tri umphed, tri umph ing.**

troll[1] (trōl), *v.* 1. to sing the parts of a song in succession until everyone is singing. *The campers merrily trolled "Row, Row, Row Your Boat" as they set up camp.* 2. to fish by pulling a hook and line through the water. *We spent the afternoon on the lake trolling from a boat.* **trolls, trolled, troll ing.**
n. 3. a song in which the parts are sung in succession. *It is easy to learn a troll because everyone sings the same words.* 4. the hook and line used to troll for fish. *My troll was broken when it caught on a log beneath the water.* **trolls.**

troll[2] (trōl), *n.* an ugly giant or dwarf written about in children's stories. *Trolls usually lived under the ground or in caves.* **trolls.**

trol ley (trol′ē), *n.* 1. a streetcar or bus that gets its power through an overhead wire. *We waited at the side of the tracks for the trolley to pass.* 2. the wheel on the end of a long pole which carries electric current from an overhead wire to a streetcar or bus. *When the trolley slipped off*

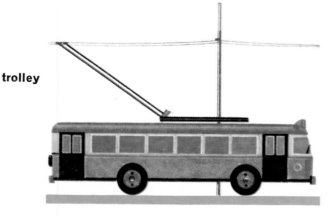

trolley

sand, āte, bâre, fäther; sent, mē, férn; fit, bīke; pot, rōpe, fôrt; run, pùll, rüle, cūte; noise, sound; ch, cheese; ng, long; th, thick; ~~th~~, those; zh, treasure; ə = a in about, e in waken, i in animal, o in seldom, and u in minus.

the wire, the bus stopped and the lights went out.
3. a wheeled basket or wagon that hangs from an overhead track or cable. *The trolley runs from one cliff to another.* **trol leys.**

troop (trüp), *n.* 1. a large group. *A troop of children came to our house for the birthday party.* 2. **troops,** soldiers. *The troops boarded the ships and began their journey home.* **troops.**
v. 3. to move or come together in a large group. *As the game was about to begin, the members of the band trooped off the field.* **troops, trooped, troop ing.**

tro phy (trō′fi), *n.* 1. a prize given for outstanding merit or victory. *Ron won the baseball trophy for best player.* 2. a memento or reminder of past merits. *His only trophy for service was his uniform.* **tro phies.**

trop ic (trop′ik), *n.* 1. one of two imaginary lines around the earth. *Between the tropics lie most of the world's hottest countries.* 2. **the Tropics,** the warmest part of the world. *The jungles are in the Tropics.* **trop ics.**

trop i cal (trop′ə kl), *adj.* of the tropics; associated with the tropics. *When we visited the aquarium, we were delighted by the bright colors of all the tropical fish.* **trop i cal ly,** *adv.*

trop ics or **Trop ics** (trop′iks), *n.* the region of the earth that is between twenty-three and a half degrees north latitude (**the Tropic of Cancer**) and twenty-three and a half degrees south latitude (**the Tropic of Capricorn**). *The weather in the tropics is usually hot and humid.*

trot (trot), *v.* 1. to move at a pace (for horses, etc.) between a walk and a run by lifting a front foot and the opposite hind foot at the same time. *A horse can gallop faster than he can trot.* 2. to cause to trot. *I trotted the horse around the ring until his muscles were exercised enough for him to run.* 3. to run at a quick, steady pace. *In a long race the runners trot for most of the race so that they do not get tired too quickly.* **trots, trot ted, trot ting.**
n. 4. a pace (for horses) between a walk and a run. *Keep the horse down to a trot until his injured leg has healed.* 5. a quick, steady pace. *He came down the street at a trot when I called him.* **trots.**

trou ble (trub′l), *n.* 1. a noisy confusion. *There was plenty of trouble on the street yesterday when the bank was robbed.* 2. something that causes worry or distress; difficulty. *His trouble is that he can't understand the arithmetic lesson. The trouble with our car is that the motor won't run.* 3. a bother; extra effort. *It was no trouble to help her with her packages.* 4. a sickness or a feeling of being sick. *I can't eat certain foods because I have stomach trouble.* **trou bles.**
v. 5. to worry or cause worry. *I am troubled by my failure to get on the team. He troubles his parents by his poor work in school.* 6. to bother; to cause extra work to. *Don't trouble yourself about the*

broken window, I'll fix it. Can I trouble you for a ride to school tomorrow? **trou bles, trou bled, trou bling.**

trou sers (trou′zərz), *n. pl.* pants that reach from the waist to the ankle, usually worn by men and boys. *My father is careful to see that his trousers are always neat and pressed.*

trout (trout), *n.* a fish found in fresh water and used as food. *The fisherman caught three large trout in the lake and cooked them for supper.* **trout** or **trouts.**

trow el (trou′əl), *n.* a tool with a flat blade that is used by men who lay bricks or who put a soft, sticky mixture on walls. *The workmen smoothed the cement with a trowel.* **trow els.**

tru ant (trü′ənt), *n.* 1. a student who stays home from school without his parents' permission; a person who does not carry out his duties. *John was a truant from school for three days. The man was truant from the duties of his job.* **tru ants.**
adj. 2. a person of this type. *The mother was worried about her truant son.*

truck[1] (truk), *n.* 1. a large, heavy, well-built automobile or wagon used to carry heavy loads. *Seventeen refrigerators were loaded on the truck for delivery to customers.* 2. a small frame having two wheels and two long handles used to move small, heavy loads. *Our suitcases were loaded on a truck and pushed to the train.* 3. the frame and wheels on which each end of a railroad car rests. *The truck has heavy springs to prevent the cargo of the car from being damaged by bumps.* **trucks.**
v. 4. to carry on a truck. *Fresh milk is trucked into the city each day.* **trucks, trucked, trucking.**

truck[2] (truk), *n.* 1. dealings. *We have had no truck with that store since they started selling poor quality merchandise.* 2. garden vegetables raised to be sold in the market. *Half of the farm was used to grow truck, while the other half was used as a pasture for the cows.* 3. rubbish. *Get rid of all that truck in your desk.*

trudge (truj), *v.* 1. to walk steadily but with effort. *After working all night, he finally trudged up to bed.* **trudg es, trudged, trudg ing.**
n. 2. a long, hard walk. *What started as a pleasant stroll in the woods ended as a trudge in the rain when we got lost.* **trudg es.**

true (trü), *adj.* 1. in agreement with the facts;

trowel

truck

trunk

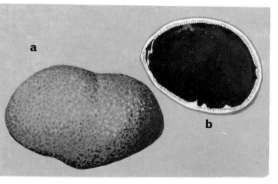

tuft of a peacock

not false. *What she told you is true, but she didn't tell the whole story of what happened.* 2. faithful; loyal. *It is a true friend who helps you when it is not easy for him to help.* 3. real; genuine. *The storm was not a true tornado since there was no black funnel cloud.* 4. accurate; correct; exact. *His model was a true copy of an early airplane.* 5. legal. *The court will decide which of them is the true owner of the property.* **tru er, tru est; tru ly,** *adv.*

adv. 6. in a true manner; accurately. *Tell me true; what has been troubling you?*

truf fle (truf′l), *n.* a kind of black fungus that grows beneath the ground and is used to give flavor to foods. *Truffles are served in very fancy and expensive restaurants.* **truf fles.**

truly (trü′lē), *adv.* 1. honestly; faithfully. *Will you answer me truly if I ask you a question?* 2. in actual fact; really. *Are classes truly dismissed for the rest of the day?*

trunk (trungk), *n.* 1. the main stem of a tree. *The branches and roots of a tree grow out of the trunk.* 2. a large box for holding clothes and other goods for storage or while traveling. *In the spring we packed our winter clothes in two trunks.* 3. the main part of the body, not including the arms, legs, and head. *With the exception of the brain, the most important organs in the body are located in the trunk.* 4. the long nose of an elephant. *The elephant picked up the log with his trunk.* 5. *pl.* **trunks,** the short pants worn by men in some sports. *The boxer in the white trunks won the fight.* **trunks.**

adj. 6. most important; main. *Several railroad lines lead into the trunk line of the railroad.*

trust (trust), *n.* 1. a belief in the honesty, justice, power, or truth of someone or something.

We put no trust in his words since he had not been honest in the past. 2. a feeling of confidence; hope. *I have great trust in his ability to do the job well.* 3. something for which one is responsible. *I believe that keeping a promise is an important trust.* 4. property or money held and used by one person in the interest of another. *The bank managed his trust until he was old enough to manage it himself.* **trusts.**

v. 5. to believe in the honesty, justice, power, or truth of. *You must trust the doctor to do everything possible to cure you.* 6. to hope, or expect. *I trust you have done all of your work.* 7. to give with confidence. *I trusted my car to him since he is a good driver and an honest person.* **trusts, trust ed, trust ing.**

trust ing (trus′ting), *adj.* having trust in others; believing in others. *He was so trusting he would lend money to anyone.* **trust ing ly,** *adv.*

trust wor thy (trust′wėr′thē), *adj.* deserving trust; reliable. *A banker must be a trustworthy person.*

truth (trüth), *n.* 1. a proven fact or principle. *No one doubts the scientific truth that the earth is round.* 2. that which agrees with the facts. *You can trust him because he always tells the truth.* 3. honesty. *We doubted the truth of his report.* **truths.**

truth ful (trüth fəl), *adj.* honest; telling the truth. *The judge asked the woman to be truthful in her answers.* **truth ful ly,** *adv.*

truth ful ness (trüth′fəl nes), *n.* a being truthful. *She admitted breaking the glass, and Sue's mother thanked her for her truthfulness.*

try (trī), *v.* 1. to attempt. *Try to answer all of the questions.* 2. to test. *Try the door to see if it is open.* 3. to conduct a test of something. *They tried the new metal to learn how much weight it would support.* 4. to strain by testing severely. *The noisy child tried his teacher's patience.* 5. to put on trial in a court of law. *The prisoner was tried for stealing jewels from a store.* **tries, tried, try ing.**

n. 6. an attempt; an effort to do something. *He failed to hit the target on his first try.* **tries.**

try ing (trī′ing), *adj.* hard to endure. *He was exhausted from the trying pace of the race.* **try ing ly,** *adv.*

tub (tub), *n.* 1. a wide, open vessel used for bathing or washing. *Soak the clothes in the laundry tub before you put them in the washing machine.* 2. a bathtub. *Mother filled the tub with hot water for*

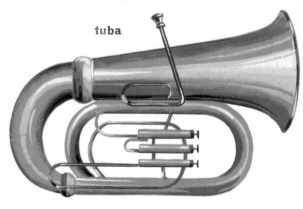

tuba

truffle:
a. outside view
b. cross section

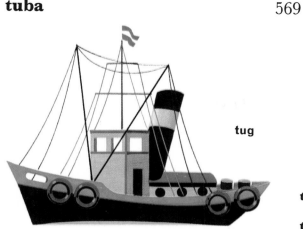

tug

my bath. 3. a bath. *After a hard day of work, I was ready for a hot tub.* 4. a round, wooden vessel used for holding butter, lard, etc. *Take as much butter as you think you will need from the tub.* 5. the amount held by a tub. *The farmer sold fourteen tubs of butter in the market.* **tubs.**

tu ba (tü′bə, tū′bə), *n.* a large brass musical instrument. *A tuba has a very low tone.* **tu bas.**

tube (tüb, tūb), *n.* 1. a long, hollow cylinder made of metal, plastic, glass, etc., used to carry or hold liquids and gases. *A thermometer is a glass tube that is sealed at both ends.* 2. anything like a tube. *The veins are tubes that carry blood in the body.* 3. a cylinder of plastic or soft metal, used to hold toothpaste, etc. *Someone forgot to put the cap on the tube.* 4. a tunnel. *Cars that enter or leave the city travel through tubes that go under the river.* 5. a sealed glass bulb used in a radio, television set, etc. *The picture tube was broken and had to be replaced.* **tubes.**

tub ing (tüb′ing, tūb′ing), *n.* any material in the form of a tube. *This experiment in chemistry requires glass tubing which is curved in the shape of the letter " U."* **tub ings.**

Tues day (tüz′dē, tūz′dē, tüz′dā′, tūz′dā′), *n.* the third day of the week, coming after Monday. *Election day is on a Tuesday.* **Tues days.**

tuft (tuft), *n.* a bunch of feathers, hair, or grass growing close together. *A certain kind of quail has a tuft on its head. The baby has a little tuft on his head.* **tufts.**

tug (tug), *v.* 1. to pull hard. *He tugged on my arm and asked me to follow him.* 2. to pull along with a small, powerful boat. *The huge ship was tugged into the harbor.* **tugs, tugged, tug ging.** *n.* 3. a hard pull. *The rope broke when I gave it a tug.* 4. a small, powerful boat used to pull larger boats. *Every ship that enters or leaves the harbor must be pulled by a tug.* 5. one of the two lines, ropes, etc., by which a horse pulls a wagon. *The load in the wagon was so heavy that the tugs broke when the horses began to move.* **tugs.**

tu lip (tü′lip, tū′lip), *n.* a plant of the lily family that is grown from a bulb and that blooms in the spring. *Tulips have large, many-colored flowers that are shaped like cups.* **tu lips.**

tum ble (tum′bl), *v.* 1. to fall suddenly. *I tripped on a toy and tumbled to the floor.* 2. to cause

to fall suddenly. *The football player was tumbled by a member of the other team.* 3. to roll around. *The boys tumbled on the floor with their dog.* 4. to perform tricks, such as jumping, rolling, and turning. *I learned to stand on my hands when we were taught how to tumble in gym class.* 5. to move in a hurried way. *As soon as the alarm rang, we tumbled out of our seats.* **tum bles, tum bled, tum bling.**

n. 6. a sudden fall. *He took a tumble down the stairs.* **tum bles.**

tu na (tü′nə), *n.* a large fish used for food. *Tuna is very good to eat.* **tu na** or **tu nas.**

tune (tün, tūn), *n.* 1. a melody; the music for a song. *I knew the words to the song, but I didn't know the tune.* 2. the proper pitch of a song. *He is a poor singer because he cannot sing in tune.* 3. harmony; agreement. *We enjoyed the speech because it was in tune with what we had been thinking.* **tunes.**

v. 4. to correct by adjusting to the proper pitch. *The violin player tuned his instrument before the concert began.* 5. to put in good working condition. *The engine was tuned by the man at the garage.* 6. **tune in,** to adjust a radio or television set to receive a particular station or show. *Be sure to tune in next week to hear the rest of the story. Will you please tune in the television set to my favorite program?* **tunes, tuned, tun ing.**

tu nic (tü′nik, tū′nik), *n.* a garment like a loose gown. *Both men and women wore tunics in ancient Greece and Rome.* **tu nics.**

tuning fork, *n.* a piece of steel which gives a certain tone when tapped or struck. *A tuning*

tulips

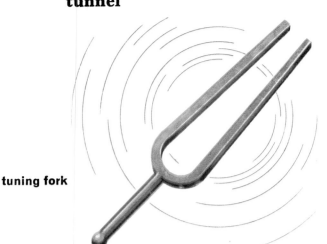

tuning fork

a

b

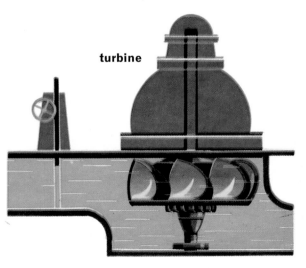

c

fork is used for setting the right note for musical instruments and for singing groups. **tuning forks.**

tun nel (tun′l), *n.* 1. a passage beneath the ground. *The prisoners escaped through a tunnel under the wall.* **tun nels.**
v. 2. to dig a tunnel. *The workers tunneled through the mountain when they built the highway.* **tun nels, tun neled, tun nel ing.**

tur ban (tėr′bən), *n.* a kind of hat for the head made of a scarf wound around and around. *Turbans are worn in countries in the Middle East.* **tur bans.**

tur bine (tėr′bən, tėr′bīn), *n.* an engine operated by the force of water, steam, or air turning a wheel. *Turbines operated by waterfalls are used to produce electric power.* **tur bines.**

tur bot (tėr′bət), *n.* a large, flat fish with a brown color. *Turbots are caught in the ocean around Europe.* **tur bot** or **tur bots.**

tur key (tėr′kē), *n.* 1. a large North American bird covered with thick feathers. *Turkeys can become four feet long and weigh more than thirty pounds.* 2. the meat of this bird, used as food. *We had turkey for Thanksgiving dinner.* **tur keys.**

turn (tėrn), *v.* 1. to move around a center; to rotate. *Wheels turn.* 2. to cause to move around a center. *The door will open if you turn the doorknob.* 3. to do something by rotating. *He jumped up and turned a circle in the air.* 4. to change position by rotating. *He turned to look at me as I spoke.* 5. to change directions. *Turn west when you come to the post office.* 6. to change to. *He turned red when she kissed him.* 7. to spoil; to sour. *The heat of the kitchen turned the milk.* 8. to become sour. *The milk turned because it was not kept cold.* 9. to change into something else. *Their poor playing turned victory into defeat.* 10. to show the reverse side of something. *Turn that page in your book and you will find the answer to my question.* 11. to upset. *The movement of the boat turned his stomach.* 12. to spin; to become dizzy. *I was so sick that my head was turning.* 13. to depend. *The success of the plan turns on each man doing his part.* **turns, turned, turn ing.**
n. 14. a turning; the motion of turning. *Father*

fixed the wheel on my bicycle with a single turn of the screw. 15. a change in direction or condition. *Make a right turn at the next street. The sick man took a turn for the better.* 16. a time to do something. *Whose turn is it to bat?* 17. an act; a deed. *He did a good turn for his friend.* 18. **by turns,** one after another. *We watched over the treasure by turns so that it would always be guarded.* 19. **in turn,** in order. *You will find the right answer if you do each part of the problem in turn.* **turns.**

Turn also has the following special meanings:
turn down, (a) to refuse. *He turned down my offer to help.* (b) to fold over; to fold back. *He turned down a corner of the page to mark his place in the book.*

turn in, (a) to go to bed. *I turned in early last night because I was very tired.* (b) to give in; to hand in. *Turn in your papers when you have finished the test.* (c) to exchange. *I turned in my old ice skates for a new pair.*

turn off, to shut off. *Turn off the light when you go to bed.*

turn out, (a) to shut off. *Turn out the lights and go to sleep.* (b) to send outside. *After the cows were milked in the barn, they were turned out to the pasture.* (c) to come out; to appear. *The entire school turned out for the game.* (d) to make. *The factory turned out three hundred cars last week.* (e) to result. *It turned out that the test was easier than we had expected it to be.*

turn over, (a) to hand over. *He turned over the club records to me when I became the treasurer.* (b) to think over carefully. *Turn the problem over in your mind and try to find a solution.*

tur nip (tėr′nəp), *n.* 1. a plant with large leaves and a thick, round, white or yellow root. *Turnips are grown for food in gardens.* 2. the root of this plant, used as food. *Turnip is usually boiled before it is eaten.* **tur nips.**

tur tle (tėr′tl), *n.* an animal having four legs and a hard shell around its body. *The head and legs of a turtle may be drawn into the shell for protection.* **tur tles.**

tur tle dove (tėr′tl duv′), *n.* a small, dark gray

turbine

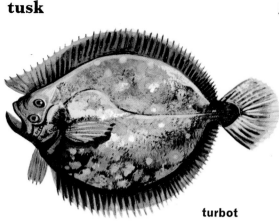

turbot

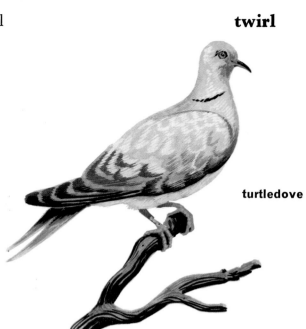

turtledove

bird which has a kind of sad song. *A turtledove has long tail feathers.* **tur tle doves.**

tusk (tusk), *n.* one of the two long teeth of an elephant, walrus, or wild boar. *Hunters kill elephants to get their tusks, which are made of ivory.* **tusks.**

tu tor (tü′tər, tū′tər), *n.* 1. a teacher. *When Joan needed help in her arithmetic, a tutor gave her extra lessons.* **tu tors.**
v. 2. to teach. *Our teacher helps children by tutoring them separately during the summer.* **tu tors, tu tored, tu tor ing.**

tweet (twēt), *n.* the sound made by a bird. *The tweets in the nearby trees woke me up this morning.* **tweets.**

twee zers (twēz′ərz), *n. pl.* a small instrument for grasping or pulling something that is small. *The man in the watch repair shop used tweezers to pick up tiny pieces inside of my watch.*

twelve (twelv), *n.* one more than eleven; 12. *If you bought a dozen pencils, you would receive twelve of them.* **twelves.**

twen ty (twen′tē), *n.* one more than nineteen; 20. *A score contains twenty. We were dismissed at twenty to three.* **twen ties.**

twen ty-five (twen′tē fīv′), *n.* one more than twenty-four; 25. *A quarter is twenty-five cents. There are twenty-five pupils in our room.* **twen ty-fives.**

turkey

twen ty-one (twen′tē wun′), *n.* one more than twenty; 21. *When you are twenty-one, you will be old enough to vote.* **twen ty-ones.**

twice (twīs), *adv.* 1. two times. *He asked me to repeat my answer twice.* 2. doubled. *We need twice as many players if we want to have a game.*

twig (twig), *n.* a very small branch of a tree or other plant. *We stuck hot dogs on twigs, and cooked them over the fire.* **twigs.**

twi light (twī′līt′), *n.* 1. the very dim light in the sky just before sunrise or just after sunset. *The street lights are turned on at twilight.*
adj. 2. of or happening at twilight. *A twilight storm slowed evening traffic in the city.* 3. of or like twilight or the time of twilight. *He spent the twilight years of his life writing about things he had done.*

twin (twin), *n.* 1. either of two persons or animals born to the same mother at the same time. *Most people could not tell which twin was Don and which was Ron.* 2. one of two persons or things that look alike. *Our house is a twin of your house.* **twins.**
adj. 3. being one of two persons or animals born to the same mother at the same time. *My twin brother took my place in the parade because I was sick.* 4. being one of a pair of things that look alike. *There are twin beds in my bedroom.*

twin kle (twing′kl), *v.* 1. to flash or glitter. *The baby's eyes twinkled with happiness. Do you see that star twinkling through the trees?* 2. to move quickly. *The dancer twinkled across the stage with short, quick steps.* **twin kles, twin kled, twin kling.**
n. 3. a flash of light; a glitter of light. *We saw a twinkle from a boat far out to sea.* **twin kles.**

twirl (twėrl), *v.* 1. to spin around; to whirl. *The dancer twirled rapidly on his toes.* 2. to cause to

tweezers

sand, āte, bâre, fäther; sent, mē, fėrn; fit, bīke; pot, rōpe, fôrt; run, pull, rüle, cūte; noise, sound; ch, cheese; ng, long; th, thick; <s>th</s>, those; zh, treasure; ə = a in about, e in waken, i in animal, o in seldom, and u in minus.

spin. *He twirled his yo-yo up and down the string.* **twirls, twirled, twirl ing.**

n. 3. a twirling; a twist or spin. *The teacher gave a twirl to the globe, and stopped it at Australia.* **twirls.**

twist (twist), *v.* 1. to wind. *He twisted his kite string around his fingers.* 2. to wind together. *Threads of metal are twisted to make a cable.* 3. to turn; to bend; to curve. *A narrow road twisted its way around the mountain.* 4. to hurt or injure by turning suddenly. *I twisted my neck as I jumped out of bed at the sound of the alarm.* **twists, twist ed, twist ing.**

n. 5. a turning; the act of twisting or being twisted. *The policeman gave the robber's arm a twist to prevent him from escaping.* 6. anything made by twisting or by being twisted. *A sugar twist is sweet bread that has been twisted and covered with sugar.* 7. a sharp and sudden turn. *A sign warned us of a dangerous twist in the road ahead.* **twists.**

two (tü), *n.* one more than one; *Can you divide eleven by two?* **twos.**

type (tīp), *n.* 1. a particular kind of a thing; a sort; a class. *What type of candy do you like best?* 2. a particular kind of person. *He is the type of fellow who always tries to do his best.* 3. a block of metal with a raised letter at one end, used to produce that letter in printing. *A person who prints a book must set up the type for every letter in the book.* 4. a large quantity of such pieces; all of the pieces required to print a book. *After a book has been written, it is set in type.* **types.**

v. 5. to write with a typewriter. *He signed the letter that he had typed to his friend. Linda typed her book report.* **types, typed, typ ing.**

type writ er (tīp′rīt′ər), *n.* a hand-operated machine for putting letters and figures on paper. *A typewriter makes it possible to write faster and more neatly than can be done with a pencil or a pen.* **type writ ers.**

typ i cal (tip′ə kəl), *adj.* having a quality or appearance that is always the same; being a certain type. *Her appearance is typical. This is a typical rainy day.* **ty pi cal ly,** *adv.*

ty rant (tī′rənt), *n.* 1. a person who rules very harshly or unjustly. *My teacher is a tyrant.* 2. a person who has absolute rule over a country. *Although some tyrants of ancient Rome were harsh, others were kind.* **ty rants.**

U or **u** (ū), the twenty-first letter of the alphabet.

ug ly (ug′lē), *adj.* 1. unpleasant to the sight; not beautiful or handsome. *The story told of an ugly monster who lived under a bridge.* 2. disagreeable; unpleasant. *Cleaning the stables where the horses are kept is ugly work. The angry man had an ugly look on his face.* 3. threatening. *In the morning, ugly black clouds filled the sky.* 4. cross; angry. *The animal became ugly and mean when it was trapped.* **ug li er, ug li est; ug li ly,** *adv.*

ul te ri or (ul tir′ē ər), *adj.* 1. having a meaning beyond what is actually said; a hidden meaning. *She had an ulterior motive in going to the store.* 2. located on the farther side. *The doctor went to the ulterior regions of the jungle.* 3. in the future; following. *We took ulterior care in planning the trip.* **ul te ri or ly,** *adv.*

ul ti mate (ul′tə mit), *adj.* 1. the last or final. *Teaching is my ultimate goal.* 2. the most basic. *The ultimate source of life has not been discovered yet.* 3. the highest possible. *This is the ultimate stress this bridge can bear.* **ul ti mate ly,** *adv.*

um brel la (um brel′ə), *n.* a light metal frame covered with waterproof material, used as a protection against sun or rain. *During the rain, I walked under her umbrella to stay dry.* **um brel-las.**

um pire (um′pīr), *n.* 1. a person who rules on the play of a game, but does not play in the game. *An umpire in baseball calls the balls and strikes, and rules on whether runners are safe or out.* **um pires.**

v. 2. to serve as an umpire in a game. *The principal of the school umpired our baseball game.* **um pires, um pired, um pir ing.**

un a ble (un ā′bl), *adj.* not able. *I was unable to lift the box because it was too heavy.*

un a bridged (un′ə brijd′), *adj.* full length; complete. *An unabridged dictionary contains almost three thousand pages.*

unan i mous (ū nan′ə məs), *adj.* 1. in complete, united agreement. *We were unanimous in our decision to have a picnic.* 2. showing complete, united agreement. *There was unanimous acceptance of the plan.* **unan i mous ly,** *adv.*

un cer tain (un sèr′tn), *adj.* 1. not certain; not sure. *We were uncertain of the outcome of the election until all of the votes were counted.* 2. liable to change; not to be counted on. *The number of people who will attend the game is uncertain because of the weather.* **un cer tain ly,** *adv.*

un cle (ung′kl), *n.* 1. the brother of one's father or mother. *I have seven uncles on my father's side of the family.* 2. the husband of one's aunt. *When Aunt Mary got married, we acquired a new uncle.* **un cles.**

un der (un′dər), *prep.* 1. below; beneath. *I found the money hidden under a rock.* 2. less than. *You can repair the broken window for under two dollars.* 3. because of; as a result of. *I was going to leave, but under the circumstances I'll stay and help you.* 4. during the time of; during the rule of. *No wars were fought under the last king.*

adv. 5. below; beneath. *I dove into the water as soon as I saw him go under.*

adj. 6. lower. *His under lip trembled with fear.*

un der cov er (un′der kuv′ər), *adj.* a job done in secret. *The hero was an undercover agent.*

un der go (un′dər gō′), *v.* to experience; live through. *Every person undergoes happiness and sorrow.* **un der goes, un der went, un der-gone, un der go ing.**

un der ground (un dər ground′ for 1, 2 and 3, un′dər ground for 4 and 5), *adv.* 1. under the surface of the ground. *The tunnel ran underground.* 2. something done secretly. *We went underground to plan the surprise party.* 3. forced into hiding. *Many people had to go underground during the Civil War.*

adj. 4. something done under the surface of the ground. *We rode on an underground train.*

n. 5. a group of people who work against the government. *The French underground saved many lives in World War II.* **un der grounds.**

un der line (un′dər līn′, un′dər līn′), *v.* 1. to draw a line under. *Underline the part of the sentence that contains an error.* 2. to stress the importance of. *The speaker underlined certain parts of his talk by speaking slowly and carefully in a loud tone of voice.* **un der lines, un der-lined, un der lin ing.**

un der stand (un′dər stand′), *v.* 1. to have clearly in the mind. *You can't do the problems unless you understand the directions.* 2. to get the meaning; grasp the idea. *Pay close attention to what I am saying or you will never understand.* 3. to know well; be very familiar with. *He understands motors because he reads about them and works on them. Do you understand German?* 4. to learn; to hear as information. *I understand that you were very sick last week.* 5. to believe as a fact. *We understood you would be coming to the party.* **un der stands, un der stood, un der-stand ing.**

un der stand ing (un′dər stan′ding), *n.* 1. knowledge. *My understanding of the work of the President was greatly increased by the movie.* 2. the ability to know; intelligence. *Our teacher is a person of great understanding.* 3. an agreement. *We finally came to an understanding about how much each of us would pay for the annual party.* **un der stand ings.**

adj. 4. having intelligence or understanding. *Julie is an understanding person who always helps when you are in trouble.* **un der stand ing ly,** *adv.*

un der stood (un′dər stud′), past tense and past participle of **understand.**

un der take (un′dər tāk′), *v.* 1. to try; to attempt. *The runner undertook to run a mile in less than four minutes.* 2. to promise or agree to do something. *She undertook to bring a book to each of us on the next day.* **un der takes, un der took, un der tak en, un der tak ing.**

un der wear (un′dər wâr′), *n.* clothing worn under outer garments. *My father wears heavy underwear during the winter.*

un doubt ed ly (un dout′id lē), *adv.* without question; certainly. *It will undoubtedly rain before we leave school today.*

un dress (un dres′), *v.* 1. to take off one's clothing. *I began to undress and get ready for bed.* 2. to remove the clothing from. *I will get the bath water ready for the baby while you undress her.* **un dress es, un dressed, un dress ing.**

un em ploy ment (un′em ploi′mənt), *n.* out of work; having no job. *My father is now in a state of unemployment.*

un ex pect ed (un′eks pek′tid), *adj.* not expected or planned for. *We did not have enough food to feed our unexpected guests. Being named the player of the year was an unexpected honor.* **un ex pect ed ly,** *adv.*

un fair (un fâr′), *adj.* not fair; not honest or just. *We proved that the election was unfair when we showed that more people voted than were eligible to vote.* **un fair ly,** *adv.*

un fin ished (un fin′isht), *adj.* 1. not finished;

not completed. *Some of the house was still unfinished when we moved into it.* 2. not ready for use; not polished, painted, etc.; rough. *We bought an unfinished dresser and painted it.*

un fold (un fōld′), *v.* 1. to open the folds of. *Unfold the paper before you give it to me.* 2. to become open. *The petals of a flower unfold as the flower blossoms.* 3. to make known. *The general unfolded his plan for attacking the enemy fort.* **un folds, un fold ed, un fold ing.**

un for tu nate (un fôr′chə nit), *adj.* 1. not fortunate; not lucky. *The unfortunate family was helped by neighbors when their house burned down.* 2. not suitable. *That was an unfortunate thing to say to him when he was sick.* **un for tu nate ly,** *adv.*

n. 3. a person without luck. *That poor unfortunate lost all of the money he had saved for his vacation.* **un for tu nates.**

un friend ly (un frend′lē), *adj.* 1. not friendly. *We thought he was unfriendly until we learned that he was shy.* 2. not favorable. *We all looked at the unfriendly sky as we began the hike.* **un friend li er, un friend li est; un friend li ly,** *adv.*

un hap py (un hap′ē), *adj.* 1. not happy; sad; full of sorrow. *He was unhappy until his lost dog was found and returned to him.* 2. unfortunate; not lucky. *He had an unhappy accident when he dropped his books into a mud puddle.* 3. not suitable. *Planning a victory party was an unhappy idea after our team lost the game.* **un hap pi er, un hap pi est; un hap pi ly,** *adv.*

un hurt (un hėrt′), *adj.* not hurt; not injured. *Fortunately, everyone was unhurt after the accident.*

uni corn (ū′nə kôrn), *n.* an imaginary animal similar to a horse, with a long horn in the center of its forehead. *A unicorn was sometimes painted on the shield of a knight because it stood for goodness and honor.* **uni corns.**

uni form (ū′nə fôrm), *adj.* 1. all the same in appearance, form, etc.; alike. *Every window in the building is uniform in size.* 2. not changing; remaining the same; even. *He has a uniform temper, and never gets angry at anything.* **uni form ly,** *adv.*

n. 3. the special clothes worn by persons of a particular order or service when they are on duty. *Policemen wear uniforms so that they will be recognized as policemen.* **uni forms.**

v. 4. to provide with a uniform. *A fund raising drive was begun to uniform the members of the band.* **uni forms, uni formed, uni form ing.**

un ion (ūn′yən), *n.* 1. a joining together of two or more persons or things. *The union of nations for mutual protection is a common type of defense agreement.* 2. a joining together of persons or states under a government. *The United States was formed by the union of the original thirteen states.* 3. **the Union,** the United States of America. *Every effort must be made to protect the Union so that democracy does not die in the world.* 4. a group of workers who are united to

unicorn

protect their interests. *Labor unions deal with companies to improve conditions for the workers in the company.* **un ions.**

unique (ū nēk′), *adj.* 1. unable to be compared; the only one of its kind. *That is a unique lamp.* 2. unusual or rare. *The boy had a unique personality.* **unique ly,** *adv.*

unit (ū′nit), *n.* 1. a single person or thing. *Each of the apartments in this building is a separate unit with its own kitchen and bathroom.* 2. a group of persons or things that operate as a unit or are thought of as a unit. *These ten history lessons form a unit of study.* 3. a standard amount or distance used in measuring. *A second is the smallest whole unit of time.* 4. the lowest whole number; one. *Nineteen divided by five equals three with four units remaining.* **units.**

unite (ū nīt′), *v.* 1. to join together into a unit. *When the competition became too severe, the two newspapers united.* 2. to act as a unit. *The three clubs united in their efforts to raise money for the poor.* **unites, unit ed, unit ing.**

United Nations, *n.* an organization founded in 1945 and made up of most of the nations in the world that works for peace. *The United Nations headquarters is located in New York City.*

United States, *n.* a country in North America that lies between the Atlantic and Pacific oceans, between Canada and the Gulf of Mexico, and includes the island of Hawaii and the region of Alaska. *The United States is made up of fifty states and the District of Columbia.*

uni ty (ū′nə ti), *n.* 1. the state of being together and acting as one. *The people were in unity as to the decision.* 2. harmony. *The couple lived in perfect unity.* 3. the fitting together of parts in art, music, literature, etc., to form a whole. *The book presented a unity of action.* **u ni ties.**

uni ver sal (ū′nə vėr′sl), *adj.* 1. belonging to all; including all; done by all. *The desire to win the most important game of the year was a universal wish of the students.* 2. occurring everywhere. *Having a cold at one time or another is a universal condition among people.* **uni ver sal ly,** *adv.*

uni verse (ū′nə vėrs), *n.* all things that exist, including the earth, planets, and stars. *No one knows how far the universe extends.* **uni vers es.**

uni ver si ty (ū′nə vėr′sə tē), *n.* an institution of learning that is divided into schools and colleges for the study of specific subjects. *He is enrolled in the school of medicine at the university, and will be a doctor when he completes his studies.* **uni ver si ties.**

un kind (un kīnd′), *adj.* not kind; cruel. *Laughing at him when he fell was an unkind thing to do.* **un kind er, un kind est; un kind ly,** *adv.*

un known (un nōn′), *adj.* 1. not known; strange; not familiar. *The answer to your question is unknown to me. I found a heavy box made of an unknown metal.*

n. 2. a person or thing not known or famous.

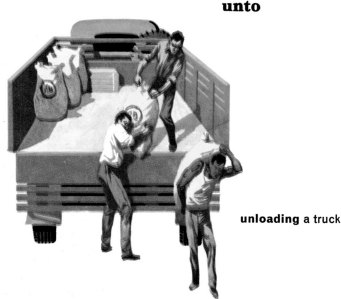

unloading a truck

That movie star was an unknown before she appeared in her first movie. **un knowns.**

un less (ən les′, un les′), *conj.* if the condition does not occur that. *We are leaving now unless you want us to wait for you.*

un like (un līk′), *adj.* 1. different; not equal or alike. *We are not friends because we have unlike interests.* **un like ly,** *adv.*
prep. 2. different from. *This book is unlike anything I have read before.*

un load (un lōd′), *v.* 1. to remove. *The men unloaded sacks of flour from the truck.* 2. to take the load from. *The men unloaded the freight car.* **un loads, un load ed, un load ing.**

un nec es sary (un nes′ə ser′ē), *adj.* not necessary; needless. *Most of the clothes I took on the trip were unnecessary since the weather was warmer than I expected it to be.* **un nec es sar i ly,** *adv.*

un paid (un pād′), *adj.* not paid. *I used all of the money to take care of my unpaid bills.*

un pleas ant (un plez′nt), *adj.* not pleasant; disagreeable. *He made an unpleasant remark about the hat I was wearing. That unpleasant person argues with everything that is said.* **un pleas ant ly,** *adv.*

un sat is fac to ry (un′sat is fak′tə rē), *adj.* not satisfactory; not good enough. *If you find that this product is unsatisfactory, you may return it and get a full refund.* **un sat is fac to ri ly,** *adv.*

un tie (un tī′), *v.* 1. to loosen something that has been tied. *She untied the red ribbon and opened the gift.* 2. to set loose. *Untie the dog and let it run free in the yard.* **un ties, un tied, un ty ing.**

un til (ən til′, un til′), *prep.* 1. up to the time of; till. *I slept until noon today.* 2. before the time of. *He could not stop working until midnight.*
conj. 3. up to the time that. *We waited for you until the show was about to begin.* 4. to the degree, place, or condition that. *She laughed until she cried.* 5. before. *She would not serve dinner until everyone was seated around the table.*

un to (un′tü, un′tu̇, un′tə), *prep.* to. *"Do unto others as you would have them do unto you."*

un u su al (un ū′zhủ əl), *adj.* not usual; not common; not ordinary. *Snowstorms are unusual in July.* **un u su al ly,** *adv.*

un will ing (un wil′ing), *adj.* not willing. *The horse was unwilling to swim in the icy water.* **un will ing ly,** *adv.*

up (up), *adv.* 1. to a higher position; away from the earth. *The rocket went straight up.* 2. in or at a higher place. *Mother keeps the vase up on a high shelf.* 3. to a larger amount or a higher degree. *The price of food continues to go up.* 4. to a position above the line where the sky seems to meet the earth. *The sun came up at five o'clock this morning.* 5. in a standing position. *Get up and show me how tall you are.* 6. out of bed. *I was too sick to get up yesterday.* 7. entirely. *The paint has been used up.* 8. at an end. *A bell will ring when time is up.* 9. in or into action or increased activity. *Someone tried to stir up trouble between the two boys.* 10. to a near position. *I could not keep up with the other runners.* 11. into consideration. *She brought up several problems that none of us had seen before.* 12. aside; away; by. *The old man stored up a supply of fuel for the winter.* 13. **up to,** (a) ready to do; doing. *What are you up to now?* (b) capable of. *Are you up to trying to ski again or are you still too nervous?*
adj. 14. above the ground; above the line where the sky seems to meet the earth. *The sun is up. These flowers will be up in about two weeks.* 15. well-informed. *Try to keep up on what is happening in the world.*
prep. 16. to a higher place on; at a higher position on. *The pirates ran their black flag up the mast.* 17. along; farther along. *We walked up the river for a mile or two.*
n. 18. a period of success. *The team has had its ups and downs this season.* **ups.**

up hill (up′hil′ for 1, up′hil′ for 2 and 3), *adv.* 1. upward toward the top of a hill. *Walk uphill until you come to a tree stump.*
adj. 2. upward; going up. *We became tired quickly on the uphill path.* 3. difficult. *Catching up on the lessons I missed when I broke my leg was uphill work.*

up hold (up hōld′), *v.* 1. to give support to. *Everyone upheld my father's record for honesty. One should always try to uphold the law.* 2. to hold up or support. *The new building will be upheld by four steel columns.* **up holds, up held, up hold ing.**

up on (ə pon′, ə pôn′), *prep.* on. *Place the book upon the table.*

up per (up′ər), *adj.* higher in place, position, rank, etc. *The dentist filled a cavity in one of my upper teeth.*

up right (up′rīt′, up rīt′), *adj.* 1. standing straight. *The upright telephone poles made a pattern across the sky.* 2. honest; trustworthy; good. *Carl will get a better job because he is efficient and upright.* **up right ly,** *adv.*
adv. 3. in a vertical posture; in an erect position. *When your back hurts, it sometimes helps to hold yourself upright.*
n. 4. something standing straight. *Mother does not want a long, wide freezer; she prefers an upright.* **up rights.**

up set (up set′ for 1–4, up set′, up′set′ for 5 and 6, up′set′ for 7), *v.* 1. to turn over; to tip. *The boat was upset by the huge waves.* 2. to disturb. *Bad weather upset our plans for the picnic.* 3. to disturb physically, mentally, etc. *Rich food upsets my stomach.* 4. to defeat, especially by surprise. *A weak team can upset a strong team by trying very hard to win.* **up sets, up set, up-set ting.**
adj. 5. disturbed. *I took some medicine for my upset stomach.* 6. worried. *Mother will be upset if we don't let her know where we are.*
n. 7. an act of upsetting. *The home team suffered a great upset during the last part of the game.* **up sets.**

up side (up′sīd′), *n.* 1. the top side; the upper side. *The upside of a coin usually has a head on it.* **up sides.**
adv. 2. **upside down,** with the upper side on the bottom. *Can you read a book when it is upside down?*

up stairs (up′stârz′), *adv.* 1. up the stairs; to a higher floor. *Go upstairs and go to bed.*
adj. 2. on a higher floor. *Did you clean the upstairs hall?*
n. pl. 3. an upper floor or floors. *Does your new house have an upstairs?*

up town (up′toun′), *adv.* to or in an upper part of a city or town. *We went uptown to see a movie. We were shopping uptown.*

up ward or **up wards** (up′wərd, up′wərdz), *adv.* 1. toward a higher place or position. *The rocket flew upward for one hundred and fifty miles before it went into orbit.*

ushering

2. toward a higher rank, condition, degree, age, etc. *He rose upward from office clerk to president of the company.* 3. above; over; more. *From the age of seven and upward, he has played baseball.* 4. **upward of,** more than. *To pass the test, you must get upward of twenty correct answers.*

ura ni um (yù rā′nē əm), *n.* a heavy chemical element used as a source of energy. *Uranium is very valuable because it is a rare element.*

Ura nus (yùr′ə nəs), *n.* a large planet that is seventh in order of distance from the sun. *Uranus is closer to the sun than Neptune or Pluto.*

ur ban (ėr′bən), *adj.* living in or having to do with a city. *Transportation, housing, and employment are very important urban problems.*

urge (ėrj), *v.* 1. to force or drive. *He urged the dogs to pull the sled forward by cracking a whip above their heads.* 2. to beg earnestly to do something; to plead with to do something. *They urged me to run for president of the class.* 3. to recommend strongly. *The coach urged that all the students attend the game.* **urg es, urged, urg ing.**
n. 4. a strong impulse or force. *I have always had an urge to try to ski, but I never had a chance to do it.* **urg es.**

ur gent (ėr′jənt), *adj.* requiring immediate action or attention. *There was an urgent need to plow the streets after the heavy snowfall.* **ur gent ly,** *adv.*

urine (yùr′ən), *n.* a liquid waste product that is taken out of the blood by the kidneys. *Urine passes from the kidneys to the bladder, and then is carried out of the body.*

us (us, əs), *pron.* the persons speaking when they are receiving the action of the verb. *Throw the ball to us. He told us a story before we went to bed.*

use (ūz for 1–4, ūs for 5–9), *v.* 1. to put into action. *He used a saw to cut down the tree.* 2. to behave toward; to treat. *The coach used his players kindly even though they had lost the game.* 3. to spend or consume by putting to use. *I used the sugar that was left in the bowl. Have you used all of the money you were given?* 4. **used to,** (a) was accustomed or usually found; did in the past. *He used to visit us every week. It used to be warmer in the summer than it is now.* (b) accustomed. *I disliked liver until I became used to it.* **us es, used, us ing.**
n. 5. the act of using. *The use of your books during the test is forbidden.* 6. the act or fact of being used. *That road is no longer in use since the new highway is completed.* 7. value; service; help. *A drink of water is of no use to a person who is drowning.* 8. a way of using something; application. *Doctors study the use of medicines in fighting diseases.* 9. the power, right, or opportunity to use something. *I had the use of a beautiful white horse when I visited the ranch last year.* **us es.**

used (ūzd), *v.* 1. past tense of **use.**
adj. 2. not new; owned by another person in

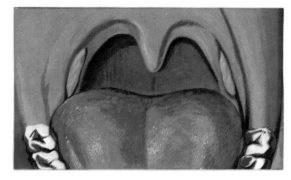

uvula

the past. *He bought a used bicycle from a boy who was too big to ride it anymore.*

use ful (ūs′fəl), *adj.* being of use; that can be used; helpful. *This is a useful tool. She gave me some useful advice about studying for the test.* **use ful ly,** *adv.*

use less (ūs′lis), *adj.* of no use; that cannot be used; having no value; not serving any purpose. *This ax is useless because the edge is too dull. My sled is useless in the summer.* **use less ly,** *adv.*

ush er (ush′ər), *n.* 1. a person who shows people where to sit. *The usher took us to our seats in the seventh row in the theater.* **ush ers.**
v. 2. to show the way to. *He ushered us to our seats.* **ush ers, ush ered, ush er ing.**

usu al (ū′zhù əl), *adj.* common; ordinary. *The usual tool for driving a nail is a hammer.* **usu al ly,** *adv.*

Utah (ū′tô, ū′tä), *n.* a state in the western part of the United States. *Utah includes both mountains and desert regions within its borders.*

util i ty (ū til′ə tē), *n.* 1. something that is useful or satisfying. *The house was equipped with modern utilities.* 2. a company that provides a service necessary for the public. *Gas and electric companies in most areas are public utilities.* **util i ties.**

uti lize (ū′tl īz′), *v.* to put to use; to make use of. *He utilizes his spare time by working around the house.* **uti liz es, uti lized, uti liz ing.**

ut most (ut′mōst′), *adj.* 1. farthest; extreme; greatest. *He finally reached the utmost peak of the mountain.* 2. greatest in degree, value, or amount. *He lost the race even though he put his utmost effort into winning.*
n. 3. the greatest possible amount. *He did his utmost to win the contest.*

ut ter[1] (ut′ər), *adj.* complete; total. *The movie was so dull that it was an utter waste of time.*

ut ter[2] (ut′ər), *v.* 1. to say in words; to speak. *I could barely understand him because he uttered everything so softly.* 2. to give forth as sound. *The crowd uttered a shout of approval when the game ended.* **ut ters, ut tered, ut ter ing.**

ut ter ly (ut′ər lē), *adv.* completely; totally. *He was utterly exhausted after the long hike.*

uvu la (ū′vyə lə), *n.* the small piece of flesh hanging down in the back of the mouth. *The uvula contracts when a person swallows.* **uvu las** or **uvu lae** (ū′vyə lē).

---

sand, āte, bâre, fäther; sent, mē, fėrn; fit, bīke; pot, rōpe, fôrt; run, pùll, rüle, cūte; noise, sound; ch, cheese;
ng, long; th, thick; ~~th,~~ those; zh, treasure; ə = a in about, e in waken, i in animal, o in seldom, and u in minus.

V or **v** (vē), the twenty-second letter of the alphabet.

va can cy (vā′kən sē), *n.* 1. a position or place that is not occupied. *There was only one vacancy at the hotel when I arrived. Who will fill the vacancy when he retires?* 2. an empty space. *We watched a vacancy between the clouds for some sign of the returning airplane.* 3. the state or condition of being vacant. *The vacancy of the store lasted for only a few days.* **va can cies.**

va cant (vā′kənt), *adj.* 1. empty; not occupied. *I found a vacant chair and sat down.* 2. not aware; not thinking; not recognizing or understanding. *He gave me a vacant look when I spoke to him.* **va cant ly,** *adv.*

va ca tion (vā kā′shən), *n.* 1. a period of time during which one is free from work, school, etc. *My father gets a two-week vacation every year. What will you do during summer vacation?* 2. a trip taken for fun and pleasure. *We took a vacation to Hawaii.* **va ca tions.**
v. 3. to take a trip or spend a period of time away from work, school, etc. *We will vacation in the mountains next year.* **va ca tions, va ca tioned, va ca tion ing.**

vac ci nate (vak′sə nāt), *v.* 1. to inject a mild form of smallpox into the body to prevent the disease. *Babies are vaccinated to prevent smallpox.* 2. to inject any form of virus to prevent disease. *We get vaccinated against colds.* **vac ci nates, vac ci nat ed, vac ci nat ing.**

vac cine (vak′sēn), *n.* a mixture containing weak or dead disease germs introduced into the body through inoculation to protect the body against that disease. *Vaccines enable the* body to build up strength against such diseases as measles, polio, and smallpox. **vac cines.**

vac u um (vak′yü əm), *n.* 1. an enclosed space from which all matter has been removed. *A vacuum is called perfect when it has absolutely no air in it.* 2. an empty space. *There was a vacuum in the conversation when everyone stopped talking.* 3. an enclosed space from which almost all the air has been removed. *Bottles having a vacuum between an inner layer of glass and an outer covering are used to keep liquids hot or cold.* **vac u ums.**
v. 4. to clean with a vacuum cleaner. *Vacuum the carpet to pick up that loose dirt.* **vac u ums, vac u umed, vac u um ing.**

vacuum cleaner, *n.* a machine used to clean rugs, curtains, etc. *A vacuum cleaner picks up dirt by sucking in air.* **vacuum cleaners.**

vague (vāg), *adj.* 1. not clearly seen or heard. *A vague figure approached in the darkness.* 2. not clearly expressed. *His speech was vague and hard for me to understand.* 3. not clearly understood. *I have a vague idea of what he wants me to do.* **va guer, va guest; vague ly,** *adv.*

vain (vān), *adj.* 1. too proud of one's appearance, ability, etc. *She is a vain girl who cannot pass a mirror without looking at herself in it.* 2. not successful; not achieving a desired result. *I soon gave up my vain efforts to attract his attention.* 3. empty; useless. *He is full of vain promises to pay us for our work.* 4. **in vain,** without success. *We tried in vain to get the actor's autograph.* **vain er, vain est; vain ly,** *adv.*

val en tine (val′ən tīn), *n.* 1. a greeting or small gift sent as a sign of affection on February 14, St. Valentine's Day. *She sent a valentine to every boy in the class.* 2. a sweetheart, especially one chosen on this day. *Will you be my valentine?* **val en tines.**

Valentine's Day, *n.* February 14, a day on which greetings and gifts of affection are exchanged. *We had a party in school on Valentine's Day.*

val id (val′id), *adj.* 1. truthful or factual. *She had a valid excuse for being late.* 2. being legally sound. *He had a valid court case.* 3. based on facts; a well-reasoned point. *He reached a valid conclusion of the book.* **val id ly,** *adv.*

va lise (və lēs′), *n.* a traveling bag used for carrying clothes or other personal things; a small suitcase. *The salesman carried his work home in a valise.* **va lis es.**

val ley (val′ē), *n.* 1. an area of low land between hills or mountains. *A river flowed through the valley.* 2. a wide, usually flat, region of land drained by a river system. *The Hudson valley extends for many miles on each side of the river.* **val leys.**

val u a ble (val′ū ə bl), *adj.* 1. having great value or worth. *He is a valuable player on the team.* 2. worth a great deal of money; costing a great deal of money. *He owns most of the valuable property in the town.*

vacuum cleaner

valise

n. 3. anything which has great value. *These jewels are the only valuables I own.* **val u a bles.**

val u a tion (val′yu̇ a′shən), *n.* 1. the estimated value of something. *The valuation of the automobile went down sharply when it was damaged.* 2. an estimating of the price or value of something. *The bank's valuation of the house proved that it was being sold at a good price.* **val u a-tions.**

val ue (val′ū), *n.* 1. the proper or fair price; worth in money. *The value of that suit is fifty dollars.* 2. the worth or importance of something. *No one doubts the value of a good education.* **val ues.**

v. 3. to determine the price of something; to fix the worth of. *The diamond dealer valued the jewel at $15,000.* 4. to think of as having great worth. *He values the time that he spends with his children.* **val ues, val ued, val u ing.**

valve (valv), *n.* 1. a device that opens and closes to control the flow of liquids or gases in pipes and other vessels. *The flame on a stove is controlled by a valve.* 2. a part of the body that controls the flow of liquids. *Most of the valves in the heart prevent a backward flow of blood by opening in only one direction.* **valves.**

van (van), *n.* a large, covered truck or wagon. *Our furniture was delivered in a van from the store.* **vans.**

vane (vān), *n.* a device to show which way the wind is blowing. *Many vanes are shaped like an arrow, and point to the direction in which the wind is blowing.* **vanes.**

va nil la (və nil′ə), *n.* 1. a climbing plant that bears seeds which are used to give flavor to food. *Vanilla grows in the tropics.* 2. the seeds of the plant. *A liquid used to flavor food is made from vanilla.* 3. the liquid made from these seeds. *Mix some vanilla into the cake to improve its taste.*

van ish (van′ish), *v.* 1. to disappear from view. *The strange man vanished in the fog. I thought I left my book on the table, but it seems to have vanished.* 2. to cease to exist; to become extinct. *Dinosaurs vanished millions of years ago.* **van ish es, van ished, van ish ing.**

van i ty (van′ə tē), *n.* 1. an excessive pride in one's abilities or appearance. *Because of her vanity she talks of nothing but herself.* 2. something without value, worth, or importance. *The hero in the book turned away from the vanities of the world to serve mankind.* 3. a dressing table, often with a mirror attached. *Mother sits at a little vanity when she puts on her make-up.* **van i-ties.**

va por (vā′pər), *n.* a gas that is formed when a liquid or solid is heated; visible water in the air. *Water vapor appears in the form of steam, fog, or mist.* **va pors.**

va ri e ty (və rī′ə tē), *n.* 1. an assortment of many different kinds. *There was a large variety of foods on the menu from which to choose.* 2. a

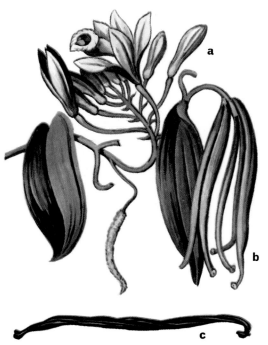

vanilla:
  a. plant with flowers
  b. green fruit (bean)
  c. dried fruit (bean)

kind. *We had a new variety of fruit for breakfast.* 3. a change from the ordinary. *Everyone needs some variety in his life.* **va ri e ties.**

var i ous (vâr′i əs), *adj.* 1. of several different kinds; different. *I have been given various suggestions on how to solve the problem.* 2. several; many. *I saw various people whom I knew at the store today.* **var i ous ly,** *adv.*

vary (vâr′ē), *v.* 1. to change. *His ideas are likely to vary from day to day. The temperature varies with each season of the year.* 2. to cause to change or be different. *People can vary their appearance by*

valley

a   tundra (arctic regions)

b   pine tree forests (cool mountain regions)

c   woods and grassy loam (warm prairies)

d   cactus and brambles (dry desert regions)

e   grassy savanna (regions with periodic rain and heat)

f   jungle (hot and humid regions)

vegetation:
  a. in arctic regions
  b. in the mountains
  c. on the warm prairies; **d.** in the desert
  e. on the plains; **f.** in the jungle

wearing different clothes. 3. to be different. *The movie varied from the story in the book.* **var ies, var ied, var y ing.**

vase (vās), *n.* a jar or other small vessel used to hold flowers. *Most vases are decorated in some way, and are used as ornaments in the home.* **vas es.**

vast (vast), *adj.* great in size or extent; very large. *The traders crossed a vast desert on their way to the sea.* **vast er, vast est; vast ly,** *adv.*

vault[1] (vôlt), *n.* 1. an arched passageway. *The vault at the front of the house is very pretty.* 2. any room with an arched ceiling or roof. *Our front room's roof is a vault.* 3. any underground room, usually made of steel, which is used to store valuables. *Our bank has a vault.* **vaults.**
v. 4. to construct such an arched passageway. *The men vaulted the hall.* **vaults, vault ed, vault ing.**

vault[2] (vôlt), *v.* 1. to jump or leap over something, usually with the use of a pole. *Tim vaulted over the bushes.* **vaults, vault ed, vault ing.**
n. 2. the process of vaulting. *Many boys like to pole vault.* **vaults.**

veal (vēl), *n.* the flesh of a calf, used as meat. *Veal has a milder taste than beef and is often more tender.* **veals.**

veg e ta ble (vej′tə bl, vej′ə tə bl), *n.* 1. a plant or a part of a plant that is used as food. *Potatoes, tomatoes, peas, and beans are vegetables.* **veg e ta bles.**
adj. 2. having to do with plants. *Living things on earth are divided into animal life and vegetable life.* 3. made from plants or parts of plants. *We ate a vegetable salad before dinner. Some kinds of rope are made of vegetable fibers.*

veg e ta tion (vej′ə tā′shən), *n.* plants, trees, and other growing things. *The different parts of the earth have different kinds of vegetation.*

ve hi cle (vē′ə kl), *n.* something that can carry people or goods from place to place. *Cars, trucks, buses, bicycles, sleds, and wagons are vehicles.* **ve hi cles.**

veil (vāl), *n.* 1. a light, thin cloth worn over the face, usually as an ornament. *The bride wore a white dress and a veil.* 2. anything that covers or hides. *The thieves escaped under the veil of darkness.* **veils.**
v. 3. to cover or hide with a veil. *The woman veiled her head before she entered the church.* 4. to cover; to hide. *Darkness veiled the city as night fell.* **veils, veiled, veil ing.**

vein (vān), *n.* 1. one of the many branching tubes through which blood with wastes is carried to the heart from all parts of the body. 2. one of the thin tubes in a leaf or in an insect's wing. *The veins in a leaf carry food and water to the leaf. The veins in an insect's wing help to support the wing.* 3. a layer of ore, gold, etc., between layers of rock. *The old man located a vein of gold in the wall of the cave.* 4. a strip or streak of color running through a material. *The palace walls were made of white marble with* *veins of black.* 5. a way of speaking or writing. *Some of the articles in the newspaper were written in a humorous vein.* **veins.**

vel vet (vel′vit), *n.* 1. a fabric of silk, cotton, etc., that has a short, soft pile. *Red velvet was used to cover the king's throne.* **vel vets.**
adj. 2. made of or covered with velvet. *Velvet curtains covered the windows of the room.* 3. soft, like velvet. *The salesman's velvet words convinced Father to buy the car.*

ven dor (ven′dər), *n.* a person who sells objects; peddler. *The vendor sold balloons.* **ven dors.**

Ve ne tian blind (və nē′shən blīnd), *n.* a kind of window shade made of many thin strips of wood or metal. *The strips of a venetian blind can be set at any angle to control the light or air coming in.* **Ve ne tian blinds.**

venge ance (ven′jəns), *n.* 1. to punish someone because he has mistreated you. *John's vengeance against Bob was to splash him with water.* 2. **with a vengeance,** (a) with great force or power. *The rain beat down on our house with a vengeance.* (b) to a great extent. *With a vengeance the wind tore up the tree.* **venge anc es.**

ven om (ven′əm), *n.* 1. the poison found in snakes, spiders, etc. *The snake's venom killed the man.* 2. a great hate; spite. *The girl hated the man with great venom.* **ven oms.**

ven ture (ven′chər), *n.* 1. a dangerous and risky course of action. *John boasted that he was brave enough for any venture.* 2. a business dealing in which money is risked with the hope of making a profit. *Mr. Jones became rich after his venture in the steel industry.* **ven tures.**
v. 3. to risk; to expose to danger. *The fireman ventured his life in an attempt to save the children in the burning house.* 4. to dare to say or express. *Would you care to venture a guess as to how many people attended the meeting?* **ven tures, ventured, ven tur ing.**

Ve nus (vē′nəs), *n.* 1. the planet that is second in order of distance from the sun. *Venus circles the sun faster than the earth does.* 2. In Roman mythology, the female god of love and beauty. *Venus was the special guardian of lovers.*

verb (vėrb)*n.* a word that expresses action or a state of being. *In the sentences "Go to the store" and "His dog is brown", the verbs are "go" and "is".* **verbs.**

ver be na (vər bē′nə), *n.* a garden plant with red, white, pink, blue, or purple flowers. *Verbenas have a sweet smell.* **ver be nas.**

ver dict (vėr′dikt), *n.* 1. a decision that is reached by a jury or judge. *The verdict of the court was, "Not guilty."* 2. any judgment or decision. *My mother's verdict was that I could go to the show.* **ver dicts.**

Ver mont (vər mont′), *n.* a state in the northern and eastern part of the United States. *Vermont has many mountain ranges, including the Green Mountains and the White Mountains.*

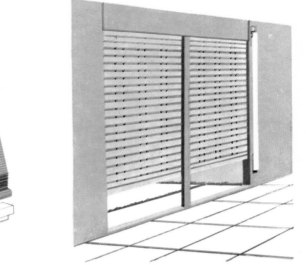

Venetian blinds

ver nac u lar (vər nak′ū lər), *n.* 1. the native language of a country. *The vernacular of the United States is English.* 2. everyday speech patterns and usage. *The vernacular on the east coast is different than the west coast.* 3. special words used in common by members of the same profession. *My brother uses words in the vernacular of doctors.* **ver nac u lars.**

verse (vėrs), *n.* 1. poetry; a poem or a group of poems. *I was given a book of verse for my birthday.* 2. a group of lines in a poem or song. *Everyone knows the first verse of "Jingle Bells," but most people do not know the second verse.* 3. a line in a poem. *The last verse of the poem rhymes with the second line.* 4. a short section of a chapter in the Bible. *Do you know the number of that verse from the Bible?* **vers es.**

ver sion (vėr′zhən), *n.* 1. a translation from another language. *This version of the French*

verbenas

book is very good. 2. a description or account of an event told by one person. *His version of the story was different than Jane's.* **ver sions.**

ver te bra (vėr′tə brə), *n.* one of the bones in the center of the back; a bone in the backbone. *The thick cord of nerves that runs down the back is protected by vertebrae.* **ver te brae** (vėr′tə brē) or **ver te bras.**

ver ti cal (vėr′tə kəl), *adj.* 1. straight up and down. *Draw a vertical line in the middle of your paper to divide it into columns.* **ver ti cal ly,** *adv.* *n.* 2. a line or other object that is straight up and down. *The posts that are used as goals in football are verticals.* **ver ti cals.**

very (ver′ē), *adv.* 1. greatly; extremely. *He was very unhappy when he lost his dog.* 2. absolutely. *I'm very certain that I met him a year ago.* *adj.* 3. same. *This is the very book I used when I was in third grade.* 4. mere. *The very mention of his family made him homesick.*

vest

ves sel (ves′l), *n.* 1. a hollow holder for liquids or other materials. *We washed our hands in a large vessel of water on the table.* 2. a large boat; a ship. *They sailed across the ocean in a huge vessel.* 3. a tube that carries liquids in the body. *Blood vessels are either veins or arteries.* **ves sels.**

vest (vest), *n.* 1. a short jacket without sleeves, sometimes worn under the coat of a suit. *Vests can be worn by both men and women.* **vests.** *v.* 2. to have power or authority. *The President is vested with the right to enforce laws.* **vests.**

vet er an (vet′ər ən), *n.* 1. a person who has served in the armed forces. *He is a veteran of World War II.* 2. one who is experienced in a particular position, trade, etc. *That carpenter is a veteran.* **vet er ans.** *adj.* 3. having many years in a certain profession. *He is a veteran teacher.* 4. having had much experience in the armed services, especially in war. *He is a veteran soldier.*

ve to (vē′tō), *n.* 1. the power or right to stop a plan or action from being put into effect. *Mother had the veto over our plan to go swimming.* 2. the power or right of a president or governor to keep a bill from becoming law. *By not signing the new bill passed by Congress, the President used the veto.* **ve toes.** *v.* 3. to refuse to consent or agree to. *If the President vetoes a bill passed by Congress, it doesn't become a law.* **ve toes, ve toed, ve to-ing.**

vial

vi al (vī′əl), *n.* a small glass or plastic bottle for holding medicine, perfume, or other liquid. *A vial of perfume is a good gift for a girl.* **vi als.**

vi brate (vī′brāt), *v.* 1. to move back and forth quickly. *The strings on a guitar vibrate when they are struck.* 2. to thrill; to tremble. *The children vibrated with joy when the circus began.* **vi brates, vi brat ed, vi brat ing.**

vi bra tion (vī brā′shən), *n.* the act of vibrating; a rapid back and forth movement. *The vibra-*

tion of a guitar string produces a musical sound. **vi bra tions.**

vice (vīs), *n.* 1. an evil habit or moral fault. *Lying is a vice.* 2. evil. *There is a great deal of vice in that section of the city.* **vic es.**

vice-pres i dent (vīs′prez′ə dənt), *n.* a person who ranks next below a president and who takes the place of the president when necessary. *The vice-president helps the president by doing whatever work the president requests him to do.* **vice-pres i dents.**

vi cin i ty (və sin′ə tē), *n.* 1. the area around a place; the neighborhood. *There is only one grocery store in the vicinity of our house.* 2. the being near. *The vicinity of the railroad station makes travel very convenient for us.* **vi cin i ties.**

vi cious (vish′əs), *adj.* 1. very evil or dangerous. *That is a vicious dog.* 2. very mean. *She is a vicious person.* 3. very extreme; painful. *She has a vicious cold.* **vi cious ly,** *adv.*

vic tim (vik′təm), *n.* 1. a person or animal who is injured or killed as a result of a happening. *She was a victim of the flood.* 2. a person who is tricked or fooled. *She was the victim of his joke.* **vic tims.**

vic to ri ous (vik tôr′ē əs), *adj.* having won a victory; conquering. *The victorious team was welcomed by the school.* **vic to ri ous ly,** *adv.*

vic to ry (vik′tə rē), *n.* the act of winning; defeat of the opposite side; triumph in a battle or contest. *The basketball team scored seven victories in a row. The new president of the club had a party to celebrate his victory in the election.* **vic to ries.**

vi cu ña (vi kün′yə, vi kū′nə), *n.* 1. a wild animal that lives in the mountains of South America. *Vicuñas have soft, delicate wool.* 2. the cloth made from the wool of a vicuña. *Coats made of vicuña are very expensive.* **vi cu ñas.**

vid eo (vid′ē o), *n.* 1. television. *A special program was shown on video last night.* **vid e os.** *adj.* 2. of or used in the transmitting and receiving of television images. *The program we saw last night had been recorded the day before on video tape.*

view (vū), *v.* 1. to look at; to see. *We got up early this morning to view the sunrise.* 2. to examine carefully; to inspect. *The policemen viewed the evidence before they searched for the person who had*

vicuñas

Viking

committed the crime. **views, viewed, view ing.**
n. 3. the act of seeing. *We did not recognize the
actor on our first view of him.* 4. anything that is
seen. *From my window I have a beautiful view of
the lake.* 5. a picture of a scene. *A view of
mountains hangs in my room.* 6. the distance one
can see. *Suddenly the fog lifted, and he came into
view.* 7. a way of seeing something; an opinion.
I tried to express my views, but no one would listen.
8. a mental image; an idea. *The book gave me
a good view of life during the Civil War.* **views.**
View also has the following special meanings:
in view, being considered in the mind; under
consideration. *I had another plan in view when
I made my suggestion, but your plan is better.*
in view of, as a result of; because of. *In view
of the bad weather, we will have to put off the picnic
until another day.*
on view, on display. *The paintings will be on
view for one more week.*
with a view to, with the intention of. *He
examined the car carefully with a view to buying it.*

vig or (vig′ər), *n.* strength; energy; force. *The
members of the team played with youthful vigor.
He applied great mental vigor to studying his lessons.*
vig ors.

Vi king *or* **vi king** (vī′king), *n.* one of the
pirates who robbed and looted the ocean
towns of Europe during the eighth to tenth
centuries. *The Vikings lived in the northern part
of Europe.* **Vi kings** *or* **vi kings.**

vil lage (vil′ij), *n.* 1. a number of houses and
buildings in an area that is smaller than a
town. *The children of four villages come to our
town to go to school.* 2. the people who live in a
village. *The entire village agreed that we needed
a new fire truck.* **vil lag es.** (See illustration on
following page.)

vine (vīn), *n.* a plant with a long stem that
grows along the ground or attaches itself to
a support and grows upward. *The castle walls
were covered with a thick growth of vines. Water-
melons, grapes, and pumpkins grow on vines.* **vines.**

vin e gar (vin′ə gər), *n.* a sour liquid used in
flavoring or preserving foods. *Many people use
vinegar and oil as a dressing for salad.* **vin e gars.**

vi o lence (vī′ə ləns), *n.* 1. rough physical force,
especially a force that causes damage or harm.
*The violence of the wind tore the roof off the barn.
He struck the tree with such violence that the handle
of his ax broke.* 2. damage; injury; harm.
Someone did violence to this book by tearing its pages.
vi o lenc es.

vi o lent (vī′ə lənt), *adj.* 1. done with rough
physical force. *The violent storm caused damage
to the house.* 2. caused by rough physical force.
The pirate died a violent death in battle. 3. showing
strong feeling; intense. *We were surprised by his
violent attack against the new tax program.*
vi o lent ly, *adv.*

vi o let (vī′ə lit), *n.* 1. a small plant with sweet-
smelling yellow, white, blue, or purple flowers.
Violets bloom in the spring. 2. the flower that
grows on this plant. *He brought a bunch of
violets home to his mother.* 3. a color made by
mixing red and blue. *Violet is the lowest color
on the rainbow.* **vi o lets.**

vi o lin (vī′ə lin′), *n.* a musical instrument having four strings and played with a bow. *The
violin is held under the chin when played.* **vi o lins.**

vi o lin ist (vī ə lin′ist), *n.* a person who
plays the violin. *Mary hopes to become a great
violinist.* **vi o lin ists.**

vi per (vī′pər), *n.* a poisonous snake, usually
with a thick body and a short tail. *Only one
kind of viper lays eggs; the rest bear living young.*
vi pers. (See illustration on page 585.)

Vir gin ia (vər jin′yə), *n.* a state in the southern
and eastern part of the United States. *Virginia
is one of the thirteen states that originally formed
the United States.*

vir tue (vėr′chü), *n.* 1. moral excellence; goodness. *There is some virtue in everyone.* 2. a particular quality that is morally excellent.

violin

village

Charity and honesty are virtues. 3. a good quality; merit. *One of the virtues of taking part in sports is that exercise keeps you healthy.* 4. the power or ability to produce a good result. *The cough medicine tastes delicious, but it has no virtue in curing a cold.* **vir tues.**

vi rus (vī′rəs), *n.* a tiny substance or agent that causes certain diseases; a disease germ. *A virus attaches itself to a living cell in order to grow and multiply. Mumps and measles are caused by viruses.* **vi rus es.**

vis i bil i ty (viz′ə bil′ə tē), *n.* 1. the state of being able to see. *Fog, rain, and snow affect visibility.* 2. the distance that one can see. *It is dangerous to fly when visibility is less than five miles.* **vis i bil i ties.**

vis i ble (viz′ə bl), *adj.* 1. able to be seen. *Because of the fog, the light from the lighthouse was no longer visible.* 2. clear; apparent. *The table floated in the air with no visible support.* **vis i bly,** *adv.*

vi sion (vizh′ən), *n.* 1. the sense by which one sees; the power or ability of seeing. *He has perfect vision in both eyes. Our vision was dimmed by the fog.* 2. something seen; a sight. *The sunset was a vision of great beauty.* 3. something seen in the mind, in the imagination, or in a dream. *He has visions of becoming a great artist someday.* 4. the power or ability of telling what is going to happen. *A leader with vision plans for the needs of the people of the future.* **vi sions.**

vis it (viz′it), *v.* 1. to go or come to see. *I visited a sick friend in the hospital this afternoon. The principal is coming to visit our class today.* 2. to stay with for a time; to be a guest of. *We visited grandfather's farm for a month during the summer.* 3. to come upon. *As winter began, we were visited by a terrible blizzard.* **vis its, vis it ed, vis it ing.**

vis i tor (viz′ə tər), *n.* a person who visits. *The sick man was not allowed to have any visitors.* **vis i tors.**

vi sor (vī′zər), *n.* 1. the front part of a helmet that protects the face. *The knight raised his visor and showed his face.* 2. the front part of a cap that projects to protect the eyes from too much light. *Some caps have visors.* **vi sors.**

vi tal (vī′tl), *adj.* 1. of life; having to do with life. *The date of your birth is a vital statistic.* 2. necessary for living or remaining alive. *Air and food are vital to most living things.* 3. full of life; having much energy and spirit. *She is such a vital person that she manages to take an active part in the community, hold a job, and care for a home and family.* 4. extremely important; essential. *Plenty of food and rest are vital to you if you hope to get well soon.* 5. producing death, destruction, or great loss. *Fortunately the soldier's wound was not a vital one.* **vi tal ly,** *adv.*

vi tals (vī′təlz), *n. pl.* the parts of the body which are necessary for life. *Your vitals include your brain, heart, and lungs.*

vi ta min or **vi ta mine** (vī′tə min), *n.* a substance found in foods which is necessary for growth and good health. *Lack of certain vitamins may cause disease.* **vi ta mins** or **vi ta mines.**

viv id (viv′id), *adj.* 1. very clear; colorful. *That is a vivid picture.* 2. very lively; clear. *She gave us a vivid account of her accident.* **viv id ly,** *adv.*

vo cab u lary (vō kab′yə ler′ē), *n.* 1. all of the words used by an individual, a group, or all of the persons who use a language. *You can improve your vocabulary by using your dictionary. People who study science, law, or medicine must learn the special vocabularies of those subjects.* 2. an alphabetical list of words and their meanings. *The words in this dictionary are a vocabulary.* **vo cab u lar ies.**

vo cal (vō′kl), *adj.* 1. of the voice. *Without vocal organs, we would not be able to speak.* 2. done or made by the voice. *My favorite type of music is vocal music.* 3. having the ability to speak or make sounds. *Monkeys, lions, and pigs are vocal animals.* 4. inclined to speak freely or without reserve. *Few children are vocal in the presence of*

a

b

visors:
   a. for a medieval helmet
   b. for office work

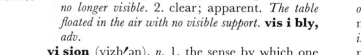

sand, āte, bâre, fäther; sent, mē, fėrn; fit, bīke; pot, rōpe, fôrt; run, pu̇ll, rüle, cūte; noise, sound; ch, cheese; ng, long; th, thick; t̶h̶, those; zh, treasure; ə = a in about, e in waken, i in animal, o in seldom, and u in minus.

strangers. 5. **vocal cords,** membranes in the throat that produce sound by vibrating as air passes through from the lungs. *How loud the tone of your voice is depends upon how hard the air is forced out over the vocal cords.*

voice (vois), *n.* 1. a sound made with the mouth, especially by talking or singing. *We heard his voice above all the others while they were singing.* 2. the power or ability of making sounds with the mouth. *I shouted so much at the football game that I lost my voice.* 3. the type or quality of sound made with the mouth. *He had a very high singing voice as a child. Your voice is too loud; please speak quietly.* 4. an expression of feeling. *He gave voice to the pain that he felt with a loud shout.* 5. an opinion or the right to express an opinion. *The students are given no voice in deciding when school will meet.* 6. anything like human speech or thought of as being like human speech. *I fell asleep with the voice of the sea whispering in my ear.* **voic es.**

v. 7. to say in words; to express. *We voiced our anger.* **voic es, voiced, voic ing.**

vol ca no (vol kā′nō), *n.* a hole, crack, or other opening in the surface of the earth through which lava, steam, and ashes are pushed out, gradually forming a heap or mountain. *The flames from the volcano lighted up the entire sky.* **vol ca noes** or **vol ca nos.**

vol ume (vol′yùm), *n.* 1. the amount of space within an enclosed area. *Find the volume of a tank that is ten feet long, ten feet wide, and three feet deep.* 2. an amount or quantity. *The volume of our business has steadily increased.* 3. tone. *Lower the volume of your voice.* 4. a book. *Please do not remove more than three volumes from the library at a time.* 5. a book that is part of a set of books. *The first volume of the encyclopedia is missing.* **vol umes.**

vol un tary (vol′ən ter′ē), *adj.* 1. an action done by one's own choice. *His trip to the store was a voluntary decision.* 2. done on purpose. *His misconduct was the result of his voluntary actions.* **vol un tar i ly,** *adv.*

vol un teer (vol′ən tēr′), *n.* 1. one who agrees to do something of his own free will, especially one who enters the armed services. *The fighting unit was composed of volunteers.* **vol un teers.**

v. 2. to offer to do something by one's own free will. *Bob volunteered to write the paper.* **vol un teers, vol un teered, vol un teering.**

adj. 3. composed of volunteers. *We have a volunteer police and fire department in our town.*

vote (vōt), *n.* 1. an expression of a person's choice in an election. *A vote may be indicated by writing, speaking, or raising a hand.* 2. the right to indicate a choice in an election. *In most states, a person receives the vote when he is twenty-one years old.* 3. a single expression of choice in an election. *He was elected by four votes. Who*

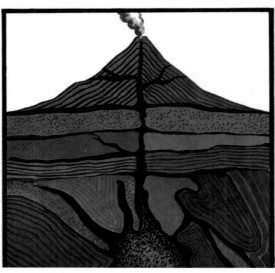

diagram of a **volcano**

counted the votes? 4. all of the expressions of choice made in an election considered together; a number of votes. *Because of rainy weather, the vote was small.* **votes.**

v. 5. to indicate a choice in an election; to cast a vote or votes. *My brother will be old enough to vote next year. Every person should exercise his right to vote.* 6. to choose or decide by vote. *A large sum of money was voted for the library.* **votes, vot ed, vot ing.**

vouch er (vouch′ər), *n.* a receipt that proves that a certain amount of money has been spent or paid. *My bill was canceled when I showed them a voucher that proved I had paid it.* **vouch ers.**

vow (vou), *n.* 1. a solemn promise or pledge. *A man and a woman exchange vows when they get married.* **vows.**

n. 2. to make a solemn promise or pledge. *The prisoner vowed that he would never steal again.* 3. to say strongly and forcefully. *He vowed that he had never seen such an exciting game before.* **vows, vowed, vow ing.**

vow el (vou′əl), *n.* 1. a sound made with the voice when the breath is allowed to pass out of the mouth freely. *The sound of "o" in "go" is a vowel.* 2. any of the letters that stand for such a sound. *The most common vowels are a, e, i, o, and u.* **vow els.**

voy age (voi′ij), *n.* 1. a journey by water. *We visited many small islands on our voyage.* 2. a journey or flight through air or space. *Would you like to take a voyage to the moon?* **voy ag es.**

v. 3. to make such a journey. *We are planning to voyage across all of the seven seas.* **voy ag es, voy aged, voy ag ing.**

vul gar (vul′gər), *adj.* 1. in poor taste; very coarse. *The boy used very vulgar language.* 2. not refined; common. *The ancient language was vulgar.* **vul gar ly,** *adv.*

viper

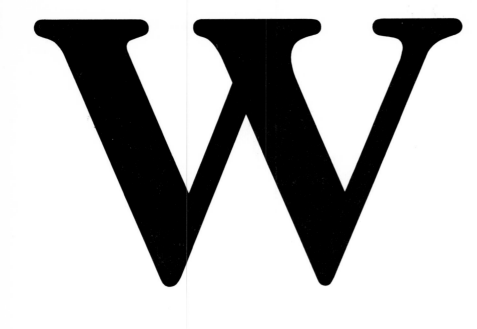

W

W or **w** (dub/l ū), the twenty-third letter of the alphabet.

wad dle (wod/l), *v.* 1. to walk with short, quick steps while rocking from side to side. *He waddled across the room like a duck.* **wad dles, wad dled, wad dling.**
n. 2. the act of walking in this way. *The duck's waddle disappears as soon as it enters water.* **wad dles.**

wade (wād), *v.* 1. to walk through water, mud, snow, or anything else that slows one's movement. *We had to wade through huge drifts of snow to get to the barn after the blizzard.* 2. to get across by wading. *Because of the heavy rains we had to wade through the flooded street.* 3. to go or make one's way slowly and with difficulty. *It took me a long time to wade through the arithmetic assignment.* **wades, wad ed, wad ing.**

wa fer (wā/fər), *n.* a thin, crisp biscuit or cake. *After school I had a glass of milk and some chocolate wafers.* **wa fers.**

waf fle (wof/l), *n.* a kind of pancake cooked between two metal plates with rough surfaces. *The surface of a waffle is marked by a pattern of small squares.* **waf fles.**

wag (wag), *v.* 1. to swing or cause to swing back and forth or up and down. *The puppy wagged his tail as he ate.* **wags, wagged, wagging.**
n. 2. a movement like this. *We saw only the wag of the dog's tail as he hid in the bushes.* 3. a person who enjoys making jokes. *He is such a wag that he always seems to be telling a funny story.* **wags.**

wage (wāj), *v.* 1. to carry on. *The king vowed to wage war against anyone who attacked the kingdom.* **wag es, waged, wag ing.**
n. 2. money paid in return for work. *Do you receive extra wages for working extra hours?* **wag es.**

wa ger (wā/jər), *n.* 1. a bet. *The men made a wager on the outcome of the game.* **wa gers.**
v. 2. to make a bet. *He wagered his team would win.* **wa gers, wa gered, wa ger ing.**

wag on (wag/ən), *n.* 1. an enclosed platform supported by four wheels, used for carrying loads. *An old horse slowly pulled the milk wagon along the street.* 2. a child's cart. *Give your sister a ride in your wagon.* **wag ons.**

wail (wāl), *n.* 1. a loud cry of sadness or pain. *The dog's wail bothered us.* 2. any sad, mournful sound. *In the distance, we could hear the wail of the midnight train.* **wails.**
v. 3. to cry loudly from paid or sadness. *The baby wailed because a pin was sticking her.* 4. to make any sad sound. *The cold, winter wind wails against the windows.* **wails, wailed, wail ing.**

wading birds:
a. white heron
b. crane
c. flamingo

waist (wāst), *n.* 1. the narrow part of the body between the ribs and the hips. *Belts are worn around the waist.* 2. an article of clothing that covers the body from the shoulders to the hips. *A shirt or a blouse may be called a waist.* 3. the middle part of anything, especially an airplane or ship. *The waist of a violin is the narrow part in the main body.* **waists.**

wait (wāt), *v.* 1. to stop doing something or remain in a place until something expected happens or someone expected arrives. *Wait for me at the park. Wait until the light is green before you cross the street.* 2. to delay; to keep ready for a short time. *Don't wait supper for me because I will be very late tonight.* 3. to await. *Wait your turn before you speak.* 4. **wait on,** to serve. *The restaurant was so crowded that it took a long time to get waited on.* **waits, wait ed, wait ing.**
n. 5. the length of time spent waiting for something. *There will be a three-hour wait until the next train leaves.* 6. **lie in wait for,** to hide in order to attack by surprise. *The pirate ship lay in wait for us just outside the harbor.* **waits.**

wake[1] (wāk), *v.* 1. to stop sleeping; to become awake. *I waked at dawn this morning.* 2. to cause to stop sleeping; to awake. *I have to be at school early so please wake me at six o'clock.* 3. to become awake and alert. *We didn't wake to the danger that surrounded us until it was too late.* 4. to become alive. *His interest in football doesn't wake until the fall.* **wakes, waked** or **woke, waked, wak ing.**
n. 5. a watch kept beside a dead person before he is buried. *The funeral follows the wake.* **wakes.**

wake[2] (wāk), *n.* 1. the track left behind a mov-

ing boat or ship. *The violent wake of the ship nearly turned our little boat over.* 2. **in the wake of,** coming soon after; following closely. *In the wake of the storm came very cold weather.* **wakes.**

wak en (wāk′ən), *v.* to awake or cause to awake. *Do not waken me until it is time to leave. He was wakened by the bright sun shining in the window.* **wak ens, wak ened, wak en ing.**

walk (wôk), *v.* 1. to go on foot at a normal rate; to go by steps. *I asked you to walk down the stairs, not to run.* 2. to cross, go, or pass over on foot. *We walked the streets until we found the lost child.* 3. to cause to move at a normal, slow rate. *He gave his horse a rest by walking it for awhile.* **walks, walked, walk ing.**
n. 4. the act of walking. *Would you like to go for a walk with me?* 5. the distance one has to walk. *It is just a short walk to the grocery store.* 6. the way a person or animal walks. *His legs are so long and he moves so quickly that he has a bouncing walk.* 7. a path for walking. *Bicycles are not permitted on the walks in the park.* 8. a way of life or the work one does for a living. *Priests and ministers have chosen a religious walk of life.* **walks.**

wall (wôl), *n.* 1. a structure which divides, encloses, separates, or protects an area or

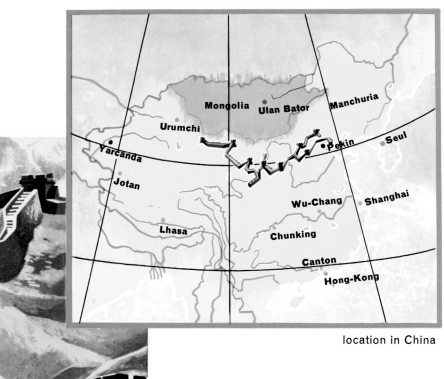

location in China

Great **Wall** of China

which supports a roof over a structure. *Most rooms have four walls. A wall was built around the village to protect the people from attack.* 2. anything like a wall. *A wall of flame kept the firemen from entering the house.* 3. the side or lining of anything. *This medicine coats the walls of your stomach.* **walls.**

v. 4. to build a wall around; to separate with a wall. *Houses in hot climates do not have to be walled on all four sides.* **walls, walled, walling.**

wal let (wol′it), *n.* a small case, usually made of leather, used to carry money or valuables. *We bought our father a wallet for his birthday.* **wal lets.**

wal nut (wôl′nut′, wôl′nət), *n.* 1. a round nut with a hard shell. *Walnuts are often used in cookies and cakes.* 2. the tree on which this nut ·grows. *Walnuts are grown to provide shade as well as for their nuts and valuable wood.* 3. the wood of this tree. *Walnut is often used in making fine furniture.* **wal nuts.**

wal rus (wôl′rəs), *n.* a large sea animal which has two very long white teeth, lives in cold regions, and is related to the seal. *Walruses are valuable for their skin, which is used to make leather.* **wal rus** or **wal rus es.**

waltz (wôlts), *n.* 1. a smooth, graceful dance. *The waltz has three beats to a measure.* **waltz es.** *v.* 2. to dance a waltz. *The couples waltzed around the room.* **waltz es, waltzed, waltz ing.**

wand (wond), *n.* a slender rod that is supposed to have powers of magic. *In the story the beautiful fairy had a magic wand.* **wands.**

wan der (won′dər), *v.* 1. to move about without going to or coming from any place in particular. *I wandered from room to room in the*

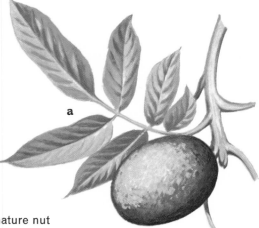

walnut:
  a. leaves and fruit
  b. shell and meat of mature nut

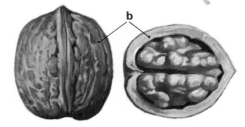

walrus

house looking for something to do. 2. to go without purpose or aim; to stray. *He wandered off into the forest and lost his way.* 3. to talk or think about many things that are not connected. *My mind was wandering when the teacher called me to give the answer to a question.* **wan ders, wan dered, wan der ing.**

want (wont), *v.* 1. to desire; to wish for. *I want a new coat. Do you want to go to the movies?* 2. to need. *The meat wants a little more cooking before it is done.* 3. to lack. *Many people in the world want for vital things as food and clothing.* **wants, want ed, want ing.**

n. 4. a desire for something. *His slightest want is immediately satisfied by his parents.* 5. a need for something. *For want of proper materials and care, the house fell down.* 6. a lack. *There is a serious want of doctors and medicine in that country.* 7. poverty; extreme need. *The old man lived in want for many years.* **wants.**

war (wôr), *n.* 1. a fight or struggle between countries or parts of a country. *There are great losses of life and destruction of property in a war.* 2. any struggle, fight, or contest. *The science of medicine constantly wages war on sickness and disease.* 3. the science or practice of war. *Men are trained in war when they enter the army.* **wars.**
v. 4. to fight; to struggle. *The doctor warred against the disease for many years before he found a cure for it.* **wars, warred, war ring.**

war ble (wôr′bl), *v.* 1. to sing with a vibrating sound. *We could hear a bird warbling far off in the forest.* 2. to make this sound or one like it. *The water warbled as it flowed down the drain.* **war bles, war bled, war bling.**

n. 3. the act or sound of warbling, especially such a sound made by a bird. *The warbles of the birds near my window woke me this morning.* **war bles.**

war bler (wôr′blər), *n.* 1. any person or bird that sings with a vibrating sound. *One of the sopranos in the choir was a warbler.* 2. any of several kinds of small singing birds. *Most warblers have very bright colors.* **war blers.**

ward (wôrd), *n.* 1. an area in a hospital or prison. *I was in the children's ward during my illness.* 2. a person who is under the care of

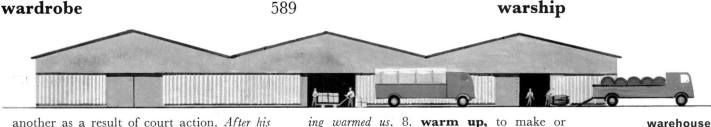

warehouse

another as a result of court action. *After his parents died, the boy was made his uncle's ward.* **wards.**

v. 3. **to ward off,** to keep away from; try to prevent. *By eating and sleeping properly, the boy tried to ward off a cold.* **wards, ward ed, ward ing.**

ward robe (wôrd′rōb′), *n.* 1. all of the clothes owned or worn by a person. *He added three new suits to his wardrobe.* 2. a room or cabinet in which clothes are stored or kept. *Your wardrobe is so full that you don't have space to hang up any more clothes.* **ward robes.**

ware (wâr), *n.* 1. something for sale. *The salesman showed us his wares.* 2. type of goods for sale, usually used with another word. *Stores sell kitchenware, hardware, and silverware.* **wares.**

ware house (wâr′hous′), *n.* a building where goods are kept. *Many goods are stored in warehouses.* **ware hous es.**

warm (wôrm), *adj.* 1. having a small amount of heat; neither hot nor cold. *The popcorn was still warm when we ate it. A blanket kept us warm at the football game.* 2. making or keeping one warm. *We sat before the warm fire and sang songs.* 3. showing excitement or enthusiasm; lively. *The boys had a warm argument over which of them was the better tennis player.* 4. affectionate. *They gave us a warm greeting when we got off the train.* 5. suggesting heat. *Red and yellow are warm colors. The artist used warm oranges and browns in painting the landscape.* **warm er, warm est; warm ly,** *adv.*

v. 6. to make warm; to heat. *Warm the food before you serve it. We warmed ourselves by the fire.* 7. to make or become excited, enthusiastic, happy, or friendly. *The children were warmed by the thought of taking a trip. His friendly greet-*

ing warmed us. 8. **warm up,** to make or become warm. *We were so cold, we thought we'd never warm up.* **warms, warmed, warm ing.**

warn (wôrn), *v.* 1. to inform of a danger or evil that may happen; to put on guard. *We were warned that the bridge was not safe.* 2. to inform; to notify in advance. *The note warned us that all books had to be returned to the library before we left school.* **warns, warned, warning.**

war path (wôr′path′), *n.* 1. a path taken by Indians on their way to a war or fight. *This road was once a warpath that led to a fort.* 2. **on the warpath,** (a) ready for war. *The Indians were on the warpath after they were forced to leave the land that they owned.* (b) ready to fight; angry enough to fight. *The man was on the warpath when he discovered that one of the windows on his car had been broken.* **war paths.**

war rant (wôr′ənt), *n.* 1. anything that gives a right or reason for something. *There was no warrant for the attack; it was completely unfair.* 2. an official document that gives the right and authority to do something. *A warrant was issued for the criminal's arrest.* 3. a guarantee. *The boys on the team were sure that their pitcher's fast ball was a warrant for success.* **war rants.**

v. 4. to give a right or reason for. *Your actions warrant punishment, not praise.* 5. to guarantee. *Will you warrant that this machine will not break in a week?* **war rants, war rant ed, warrant ing.**

war ri or (wôr′ē ər), *n.* a soldier who has fought in battle. *The brave warrior killed the dragon with his sword.* **war ri ors.**

war ship (wôr′ship′), *n.* a ship built for war, used to guard and protect a country. *The United States has many kinds of warships from giant aircraft carriers to small boats.* **war ships.**

warship with three gun decks (eighteenth century)

was (woz, wuz, wəz), past tense of **be.**

wash (wosh, wôsh), *v.* 1. to clean with water or another liquid. *She washed the dishes and the floor while her mother was out.* 2. to clean oneself with water. *Did you wash before coming to supper?* 3. to wash clothes. *Their mother has to wash twice a week because they get their clothes so dirty.* 4. to remove by cleaning with water. *He washed the dirt off his hands. Can you wash that spot out?* 5. to be washed without becoming faded or damaged. *That woolen sweater will not wash; it must be dry-cleaned.* 6. to carry along, away, out, up, down, etc. by water. *The road was washed out by the rain. A strange boat was washed up on the shore.* 7. to flow over; to splash on. *The high waves washed the front of the ship.* 8. to make wet. *The grass was washed by dew this morning.* 9. to cover with a thin coating. *Her bracelet is washed with gold.* **wash es, washed, wash ing.**

n. 10. a washing; the action of washing. *Do you ever give your face a wash?* 11. a number of clothes that are to be washed or have been washed. *It takes all day to do the wash.* 12. material carried and then dropped by flowing water. *The wash from the river built up sand bars wherever the water slowed down.* 13. the motion or sound of moving water. *Can you hear the wash of the waves against the boat?* 14. a liquid used for washing or rinsing. *After brushing my teeth I rinsed my mouth with mouth wash.* 15. a thin covering of metal or color. *The artist used a blue wash to make the painting darker.* 16. the current of water or air left behind a boat or airplane. *The wash from the passing ship splashed against the banks of the river.* **wash es.**

wash er (wosh′ər, wôsh′ər), *n.* 1. a person who washes. *The window washer used a special belt to keep him from falling.* 2. a machine used for washing clothes. *Does your mother have an automatic washer?* 3. a round, flat piece of metal, rubber, or leather used to make a bolt fit tighter. *Rubber washers are used to keep water valves from leaking.* **wash ers.**

Wash ing ton (wosh′ing tən, wôsh′ing tən), *n.* 1. a state in the northwestern part of the United States. *Washington is known for the delicious apples that grow there.* 2. a city in the eastern part of the United States; the capital of the United States. *The President, the Vice-President, and all of the men who make laws for the United States meet and work in Washington.*

wash room (wosh′rüm′, wôsh′rüm′), *n.* a room with washing and toilet facilities; bathroom. *There are several washrooms in the railroad station.* **wash rooms.**

wash tub (wosh′tub′, wôsh′tub′), *n.* a large tub or sink used for washing clothes. *Instead of washing the dog in the bathtub, why don't you use the washtub?* **wash tubs.**

was n't (woz′nt, wuz′nt), was not. *I wasn't ready to leave when you called me.*

wasp (wosp), *n.* a flying insect with a smooth,

wasp

slender body and a very painful sting. *Wasps have strong jaws to grasp their food.* **wasps.**

waste (wāst), *v.* 1. to use up in a poor or foolish manner. *He wasted all of his money on clothes he didn't need and was unable to buy any food.* 2. to destroy; to ruin. *The rich land was wasted by the violence of the flood.* 3. to wear down slowly; to reduce in physical strength. *His strength was wasted by the sickness.* **wastes, wast ed, wast ing.**

n. 4. a poor or foolish use of something. *Watching that program on television was a waste of time.* 5. material that has been or is to be thrown away; garbage; refuse. *Please put your waste in the basket.* 6. a slow wearing down or reduction in physical strength. *It took many months to repair the waste caused by the disease.* 7. a desert or other place where nothing grows. *We decided to rest before crossing the sandy waste that stretched before us.* **wastes.**

adj. 8. lacking worth; useless. *Waste paper is burned at the end of each day.* 9. having nothing living or growing; bare. *There are no farms in the waste regions of the desert.*

watch (woch), *v.* 1. to view carefully; to look closely. *The boys watched while the expert showed them how to hit a golf ball.* 2. to look at. *Did you watch television after school?* 3. to pay attention to; to be careful. *Watch where you are going.* 4. to guard; to take care of. *Will you watch the baby while I go to the store?* **watch es, watched, watch ing.**

n. 5. the act of guarding or protecting. *The sheriff kept watch over the prisoners until help arrived.* 6. a person who guards. *We attacked the pirate's fort as soon as we saw the watch fall asleep.* 7. the period of time during which a person stands guard. *My watch is up at midnight, when someone else will be on guard.* 8. a small clock that is worn on the wrist or carried in a pocket. *I checked my watch before I left the house to be sure I would have the correct time.* **watch es.**

watch ful (woch′fəl), *adj.* wide awake; keeping close watch. *The watchful dog barks at almost any noise during the night.* **watch ful ly,** *adv.*

watch man (woch′mən), *n.* a person who watches and guards a building, especially during the night. *The watchman checks the entire building several times during the night.* **watch men.**

wa ter (wô′tər), *n.* 1. the clear liquid that is found in lakes, rivers, and wells and that falls as rain. *Water becomes ice when it freezes.* 2. any liquid that looks like water. *When he stopped running, beads of water stood on his forehead.* 3. a lake, ocean, river, or stream. *We crossed the water in a huge ship. Pirates sailed the waters looking for ships to capture.* **wa ters.**

v. 4. to put water on. *Did you water the flowers today?* 5. to give water to for drinking. *He watered his horse when he came back from riding.* 6. to make weaker by adding water. *This milk*

waterfall

tastes as if it had been watered. 7. to fill with a liquid like water. *The strong odor made my eyes water. The smell of food makes your mouth water.* **wa ters, wa tered, wa ter ing.**

wa ter fall (wô′tər fôl′), *n.* a flow of water falling from a high place. *In the mountains we saw a waterfall that was more than one hundred feet high.* **wa ter falls.**

water lily, *n.* a plant that grows in the water. *Water lilies have flowers of many colors.* **water lil ies.**

water lilies

wa ter mel on (wô′tər mel′ən), *n.* 1. a large, juicy fruit with sweet red or pink flesh within a hard, green outer cover. *A watermelon must be eaten shortly after it becomes ripe.* 2. the plant this fruit grows on. *The watermelon is a vine that grows along the ground.* **wa ter mel ons.**

water polo (wô′tər pō′lō), a game played in water by two teams using a large leather or rubber ball. *The purpose of water polo is for one team to put the ball into the other team's goal.* (See illustration on following page.)

wa ter proof (wô′tər prüf), *adj.* 1. not allowing water to pass through. *The material in my raincoat is waterproof.*
v. 2. to make waterproof. *You can have this coat waterproofed if you want to use it as a raincoat.* **wa ter proofs, wa ter proofed, wa ter proof ing.**

wave (wāv), *n.* 1. a rising swell of water moving across the surface of a body of water. *The waves splashed against the rocks on the shore.* 2. anything that looks like or moves like a wave. *Light and sound travel in waves.* 3. a curve or several curves. *I have natural waves in my hair.* 4. a sudden rise or increase in feeling or in a particular condition. *A wave of excitement spread through the crowd.* 5. a signal or form of greeting made with the hand. *He gave a wave of his hand as he passed us on the street.* **waves.** (See illustration on following page.)
v. 6. to move up and down or from side to side. *The tree's branches waved in the wind. We waved our flags as the parade passed.* 7. to give a signal or greeting by moving the hand. *We waved good-bye to him as the train left the station.* 8. to arrange in curves or waves. *When did you have your hair waved?* **waves, waved, wav ing.**

wave length (wāv′lengkth′, wāv′length′), *n.* the distance between any point on a wave and the same point of the next wave. *Light has a shorter wavelength than sound.* **wave lengths.**

wa ver (wā′vər), *v.* 1. to be unable to decide; to sway. *Helen wavered between buying the red or the gray dress.* 2. to move from one side to the other. *The car wavered on the road.* 3. to vary in brightness; flicker. *The flame wavered in the wind.* **wa vers, wa vered, wa ver ing.**

watermelon

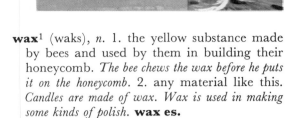

waves (arrows show direction of wind and movement under the surface of the water)

wax[1] (waks), *n.* 1. the yellow substance made by bees and used by them in building their honeycomb. *The bee chews the wax before he puts it on the honeycomb.* 2. any material like this. *Candles are made of wax. Wax is used in making some kinds of polish.* **wax es.**
v. 3. to put wax or polish on. *Did you wash your car before you waxed it?* **wax es, waxed, waxing.**

wax[2] (waks), *v.* 1. to become larger; to increase in size or degree. *The moon waxes until it is full.* 2. to grow or become gradually. *He waxed confident when he saw that we were agreeing with him.* **wax es, waxed, wax ing.**

way (wā), *n.* 1. a path, road, or any course used to go from place to place. *The way was blocked by a tree that had been struck down by lightning. Did you find the way to the new school?* 2. direction. *Come this way.* 3. distance. *It's only a short way from here.* 4. room or space to do something. *I tried to leave the crowded room but no one would make way for me.* 5. motion forward; movement ahead. *The boat lost way as the current became stronger.* 6. a manner. *He has a way of making people comfortable when he talks with them. She has a funny way of talking.* 7. a method of doing something. *I've never tried to swim this way before.* 8. a habit; a custom. *Unless you change your evil ways you will end up in jail.* 9. a wish; a desire. *Why don't you let her have her way?* 10. a detail or feature of something. *In many ways his plan seemed to be working.* 11. a condition. *The house is in a bad way and must be repaired at once.* 12. **by way of,** (a) by taking a route that stops at or passes through a certain place. *Did you come home directly or did you come by way of your friend's house?* (b) as a means of. *She gave me something to eat by way of paying me for shoveling the snow.* 13. **give way,** (a) to fall down; break. *The old bridge suddenly gave way just as the hunters safely reached the other side of the river.* (b) to move back, retreat, or give up. *The enemy began to give way under our fierce attack.* 14. **under way,** moving; going. *After many delays we finally got under way.* **ways.**

way side (wā′sīd′), *n.* 1. the side of a road. *Crowds of people stood along the wayside as the parade passed.* **way sides.**
adj. 2. at, along, or on the side of a road. *We ate our lunch at a wayside picnic table.*

we (wē), *pron.* 1. the persons speaking or writing; the group represented by the person speaking or writing. *We decided not to go. We had a meeting last night.* 2. the person speaking or writing, especially when the person is a king, queen, judge, or author. *"We must not permit the law to be broken without punishing the person who commits the offense," said the judge.*

weak (wēk), *adj.* 1. having little physical strength; feeble; frail. *He was too weak to lift the heavy box. I am still weak from my sickness.* 2. liable to break or fall if pressure is applied. *The weak ladder shook as I stood on it.* 3. having little power or force. *She made up a few weak rules which nobody obeyed.* 4. having little intelli-

water polo

gence or power to think. *He has a weak mind when it comes to doing arithmetic.* 5. having little moral power or strength. *A person who never does the right thing when it is difficult has weak character.* 6. lacking in amount, flavor, volume, etc. *I heard a weak call for help. This coffee is too weak.* 7. lacking ability or strength in something. *He reads very well but he is weak in grammar.* **weak er, weak est; weak ly,** *adv.*

weak en (wē′kən), *v.* to make weak; to become weak. *His legs weakened as he climbed up the mountain.* **weak ens, weak ened, weak en ing.**

weak ness (wēk′nis), *n.* 1. a lack of strength or power. *He could run no longer because of weakness.* 2. a weak point; a fault. *A lack of good pitching is the only weakness of the baseball team.* 3. a special liking. *I have a weakness for chocolate cake.* **weak ness es.**

wealth (welth), *n.* 1. a great deal of money or property. *The old man had spent all of his life seeking wealth.* 2. a large amount. *There is a wealth of information in the encyclopedia.* 3. anything that is valuable. *Our greatest wealth is the knowledge we have.*

wealthy (wel′thē), *adj.* rich; having wealth. *Their family is very wealthy. The United States is a wealthy country.* **wealth i er, wealth i est.**

weap on (wep′ən), *n.* a thing used in fighting. *Guns are dangerous weapons. Birds use their claws as weapons.* **weap ons.**

wear (wâr), *v.* 1. to have on the body. *People wear clothes. She wore a funny costume on Halloween.* 2. to have or use regularly or by habit. *Do you need to wear glasses? My uncle wears a long beard.* 3. to show, display, or have. *He wore a smile because he was happy.* 4. to hold out or last. *This shirt wore very well, lasting for more than a year.* 5. to use up or become used up; to waste. *The rocks on the shore were worn by the waves. Some of the parts on the machine were so worn that they had to be replaced.* 6. to make or produce gradually as a result of rubbing, scraping, etc. *He wore a hole in the sleeve of his sweater. The river wore a deep channel in the rocks.* 7. to pass slowly. *I tried to stay awake as the afternoon wore on.* **wears, wore, worn, wear ing.**

n. 8. a wearing; use. *We needed heavier clothing for winter wear. I got a great deal of wear out of those shoes.* 9. clothing. *They do not sell women's wear in that store.* 10. the damage or change which results from use. *I noticed signs of wear the first time I wore the shoes.*

wea ry (wir′ē), *adj.* 1. tired; exhausted. *The weary travelers spent the night in a hotel. I was weary from the work I had done.* 2. tiring; boring. *I had a weary conversation with a dull man today.* **wea ri er, wea ri est; wea ri ly,** *adv.*

v. 3. to make or become tired. *Cutting down the tree wearied me. I quickly wearied of the long play.* **wea ries, wea ried, wea ry ing.**

wea sel (wē′zl), *n.* a small, wild animal with a long body and short legs. *Weasels eat mice, chickens, and birds.* **wea sels.**

weath er (weth′ər), *n.* 1. outside conditions with regard to temperature, humidity, air pressure, etc. *We have had two weeks of cold weather. The weather is beautiful today.* 2. **under the weather,** feeling sick; ill. *I was under the weather with a bad cold for a few days.*

v. 3. to get through safely or with success. *The ship failed to weather the storm and sank. Were you able to weather the difficulties of your tests last week?* 4. to expose to the weather; to change as a result of being exposed to the weather. *The lumber was weathered before it was used to build the house. The roof was badly weathered and needed repairs.* **weath ers, weath ered, weath er ing.**

adj. 5. in the direction from which the wind is blowing. *No one stood on the weather side of the ship because it was too cold.*

weave (wēv), *v.* 1. to make or form by lacing threads, yarn, strips, etc. under and over each other. *The natives wove wool blankets. Cloth is woven. She is weaving a basket out of straw.* 2. to move in and out among other things. *The police car wove through a group of cars.* 3. to join together into a whole. *He wove an interesting story out of what had happened on his trip.* **weaves, wove, wo ven** or **wove, weav ing.**

n. 4. a pattern of weaving; the way a thing is woven. *The fabric had a tight weave.* **weaves.**

web (web), *n.* 1. a piece of fabric woven at one time. *When you have woven fifty yards of the material, remove the web from the machine and start again.* 2. anything that has been woven. *Spiders catch flies in their webs.* 3. a thing connected like a web. *The clues to the crime formed a web of suspicion around one person.* 4. the skin between

spider in its **web**

the toes of some birds and other animals. *The webs on a water bird's feet enable it to swim.* **webs.**

wed (wed), *v.* 1. to marry. *When did you wed?* 2. to join together; to unite or connect. *A story about knights weds the past with the present because it makes you feel as though you are there.* **weds, wed ded, wed ded** or **wed, wed ding.**

we'd (wēd, wid), 1. we had. *We'd already gone to bed when you called.* 2. we should; we would. *We'd like to talk to you about summer jobs.*

wed ding (wed′ing), *n.* 1. the formal service or series of acts performed when a person marries. *We had our wedding at our church.* 2. an anniversary of a wedding. *A silver wedding is the twenty-fifth anniversary of a marriage.* **wed dings.**

wedge (wej), *n.* 1. a piece of metal or wood that is thick at one end and has a thin edge at the other, used to split a log, hold something in a position, etc. *Put a wedge under the door to hold it open. A wedge was driven into the log to split it.* 2. anything shaped like a wedge. *Would you like a wedge of pie with your coffee?* 3. anything used like a wedge to hold something or force something to change. *We joined arms, formed a wedge, and pushed our way through the crowd.* **wedg es.**

v. 4. to force with or as if with a wedge. *I wedged the books on the shelf apart with my fingers to make room for another volume.* 5. to hold with a wedge. *If the window keeps falling down, wedge it open.* 6. to pack in tightly. *Four more people wedged into the crowded elevator.* **wedg es, wedged, wedg ing.**

Wednes day (wenz′dē, wenz′dā′), *n.* the fourth day of the week. *Wednesday is the day after Tuesday.* **Wednes days.**

wee (wē), *adj.* very small; tiny. *We were surprised to see that the wee baby bird could fly.* **we er, we est.**

weed (wēd), *n.* 1. a useless plant that grows wild. *You'd better get rid of those weeds before you plant the grass.* **weeds.**

v. 2. to dig up these plants and remove them from a place. *Did you weed the lawn yet?* 3. **weed out,** to remove as useless. *Did you weed out the bad fruit before you baked the pie?* **weeds, weed ed, weed ing.**

week (wēk), *n.* 1. a period of seven days, especially between Sunday and Saturday. *This is the third week of the month.* 2. the days during the week when one works. *We go to school all week. He works a forty-hour week.* **weeks.**

week end (wēk′end′), *n.* Saturday and Sunday, as a time for rest, play, visiting, etc. *We are going skiing this weekend.* **week ends.**

week ly (wēk′lē), *adj.* 1. of, for, or lasting for a week. *Do you receive a weekly allowance?* 2. happening each week; done once a week. *I made my weekly trip to the grocery store today.*

n. 3. a newspaper or magazine that appears once a week. *Our town doesn't have a daily newspaper, but we do have a weekly.* **week lies.**

weep (wēp), *v.* 1. to cry; to show feeling by shedding tears. *My leg hurt so much that I wept. He wept with joy when he scored the winning point at the end of the game.* 2. to cry for; to feel sorrow for. *We wept the loss of our dog.* **weeps, wept, weep ing.**

wee vil (wē′vəl), *n.* a small insect whose larvae can damage grain, cotton, and fruit crops. *Weevils are about one-half inch long.* **wee vils.**

weigh (wā), *v.* 1. to determine the weight of by using a scale. *Weigh this package for me so that I'll know how much it will cost to mail it.* 2. to have weight of a certain amount. *She weighs eighty pounds. The truck weighed too much to use the wooden bridge safely.* 3. to measure out by weight. *Please weigh out three pounds of meat for me.* 4. to think over carefully in the mind. *I weighed both sides of the argument before I made a decision.* 5. to have importance. *The price of the ticket doesn't weigh much because I want to see the game.* 6. to bear down on and bend. *The tree was weighed down with ripe fruit.* 7. to be a burden. *The responsibility of taking care of his family weighs on him.* **weighs, weighed, weigh ing.**

weight (wāt), *n.* 1. the amount a thing weighs; how heavy a thing is. *Could you guess the weight of that man?* 2. a piece of metal; having a certain weight, used on a scale or balance in determining how much an object weighs. *Objects are placed on one side of a scale to balance against weights placed on the other side.* 3. a system of units used in determining weight. *Persons who weigh very small objects or quantities often use metric weight.* 4. a heavy object used in athletics. *My brother is strengthening his muscles by lifting weights.* 5. a heavy load or burden. *He fell under the weight of the box he was carrying.* 6. importance. *Do his opinions carry any weight with you?* **weights.**

v. 7. to add weight to. *He weighted his fishing line so that it would sink.* 8. to burden. *I am weighted with sadness because we lost the game.* **weights, weight ed, weight ing.**

wel come (wel′kəm), *interj.* 1. a word of friendly greeting. *Welcome back!*

n. 2. a friendly greeting. *They gave me a warm welcome when I arrived.* **wel comes.**

v. 3. to greet or receive in a friendly way. *As each guest arrived, the host welcomed him.* **wel comes, wel comed, wel com ing.**

adj. 4. gladly accepted or received; pleasant. *There was a welcome change in the hot weather.* 5. gladly permitted. *You are welcome to use any of my tools.* 6. a courteous response to thanks. *When he thanked me I said, "You're welcome."*

wel fare (wel′fâr′), *n.* health, happiness, success, and comfort. *If you were really interested in my welfare, you wouldn't stop me from doing my work.*

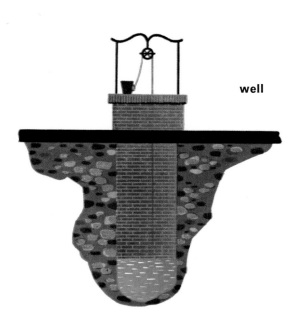

well

well¹ (wel), *n.* 1. a natural spring or other source of water flowing from the ground. *At the foot of the hill was a well with a pool of cool, clear water.* 2. a hole dug in the ground to get water, oil, or gas. *We had to leave the farm when the well went dry.* 3. a supply; a source of anything. *His father is a well of useful information about fixing cars.* 4. a space in a building for an elevator, staircase, or air shaft. *An engineer was in the elevator well repairing a cable.* 5. a space in which something may be stored. *The well of my fountain pen has run dry.* **wells.**
v. 6. to rise; to spring. *Tears welled up in my eyes as I peeled the onions.* **wells, welled, well ing.**

well² (wel), *adv.* 1. in a good or pleasing way; with skill. *He writes well. He did the job well.* 2. comfortably. *I slept well last night.* 3. completely; thoroughly. *You have to shake this salad oil well before you use it.* 4. to a large extent; much. *It was well after midnight before I finally went to sleep.* 5. for sure; in detail. *He knew well what I had asked him to do.* 6. with reason. *You may well doubt that I will keep my promise, but I assure you I will.* **bet ter, best.**
adj. 7. in good health. *Are you still sick or are you finally well?* 8. good; proper. *It is well that you asked for permission.* 9. **well-off,** (a) in a good condition or position. *You are as well-off here as you would be in any other school.* (b) rich; wealthy. *They are very well-off now that their father owns a large business.*
interj. 10. a word used to show surprise, relief, etc. *Well, you have finished at last! Well, I'm certainly glad you could come!*

we'll (wēl, wil), we shall; we will. *If we don't hurry, we'll be late.*

went (went), past tense of **go.**

wept (wept), past tense and past participle of **weep.**

were (wėr, wǝr), past tense of **be.**

we're (wir), we are. *We're going to Hawaii for our vacation.*

weren't (wėrnt), were not. *Weren't you going to bring that book for me today? We weren't interested in the story.*

west (west), *n.* 1. the direction in which the sun sets. *East and west are opposite directions.* 2. the part of a country or region in this direction. *The land in the west of the state is used for farming.* 3. **the West,** (a) the part of the United States that is west of the Mississippi River. *Cowboys live in the West.* (b) the western part of the world, which includes Europe and America. *Population is greater in the East than in the West.* *adj.* 4. in the west; of the west; toward the west. *He lives in the west part of town.* 5. from the west. *A warm west wind blew in the window.* *adv.* 6. toward the west. *We walked west until we came to the edge of a desert.*

west er ly (wes′tǝr lē), *adj.,* 1. toward or from the west. *The ship headed in a westerly direction.* *adv.* 2. coming from the west. *The wind is usually westerly.*

west ern (wes′tǝrn), *adj.* 1. in or toward the west. *The western side of the house was painted in the morning.* 2. from the west. *Western winds brought high winds and heavy rain.* 3. **Western,** of the West. *Nevada and California are Western states.*
n. 4. a movie or story about cowboys living in the western part of the United States. *Many westerns tell about groups of outlaws who robbed banks and trains and were finally caught by the sheriff.* **west erns.**

West Virginia, a state in the eastern part of the United States. *Coal mining is the major industry of West Virginia.*

wet (wet), *adj.* 1. covered or soaked with water or another liquid. *The ground was wet and muddy from the rain.* 2. not yet dry. *Do not touch the paint while it is still wet.* 3. rainy. *You're not having a picnic on a wet day like this, are you?* **wet ter, wet test.**
v. 4. to make wet; to soak with water or another liquid. *If you wet the field before you play, the dust won't be so thick.* **wets, wet or wet ted, wet ting.**
n. 5. rain; water. *That horse is too dumb to come in out of the wet.*

we've (wēv, wiv), we have. *We've started practicing for the school play.*

whack (hwak), *n.* 1. a hard, loud slap. *He gave me a whack on the back to wake me up.* 2. the sound made by such a slap. *There was a loud whack as he struck the table with his hand.* **whacks.**
v. 3. to hit with a hard, loud slap. *He whacked the fly with his newspaper.* **whacks, whacked, whack ing.**

whale (hwāl), *n.* 1. a huge sea animal that looks like a fish and breathes air. *Some whales are one*

wharf

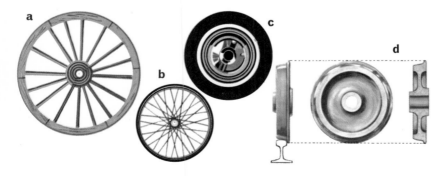

wheels:
a. wagon
b. bicycle
c. automobile
d. railroad

hundred feet long. There are several kinds of whales. **whales.**

v. 2. to hunt for whales. *Men went whaling to get the valuable oil, meat, and bones of whales.* **whales, whaled, whal ing.**

wharf (hwôrf, wôrf), *n.* a long, solid structure built on a shore or out from a shore over the water. *A ship takes on its cargo and passengers at a wharf.* **wharves** or **wharfs.**

what (hwot), *pron.* 1. which thing; which things. *What did you forget?* 2. which kind of thing. *What was that?* 3. that which. *I know what you are thinking.*

adj. 4. which. *What book do you want?* 5. as much; as many. *Send me what money you can spare.*

adv. 6. how much; in what way? *What does it matter that we are late?* 7. **what with,** because of. *What with the bad weather and the heavy traffic we were twenty minutes late for the show.*

interj. 8. a word used to show surprise. *What! Aren't you listening to me? What a game that was!*

what ev er (hwot ev′ər), *pron.* 1. no matter what. *You must be back by noon, whatever the others do.* 2. anything that; everything that. *Ask for whatever you think you may need.* 3. what unexpected or unknown thing. *Whatever are you trying to say?*

adj. 4. any that; any sort of; any. *Use whatever tools you can find.*

what's (hwots), 1. what is. *What's going on here?* 2. what has. *What's been going on here?*

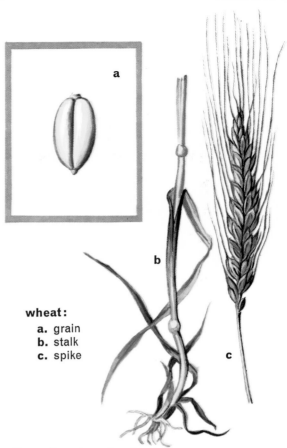

wheat:
a. grain
b. stalk
c. spike

wheat (hwēt), *n.* 1. a kind of grass that bears a grain. *Wheat is widely grown in the United States.* 2. the grain of this grass. *Wheat is used in making flour.* **wheats.**

wheel (hwēl), *n.* 1. a round frame that turns on a central axis. *A bicycle has two wheels. A car is turned by means of a steering wheel.* 2. anything like a wheel. *Yarn is made on a spinning wheel. The captain asked me to take the wheel of the ship for a while.* 3. anything thought of as moving like a wheel. *The wheels of government never stop turning.* **wheels.**

v. 4. to make a turn; to revolve. *The pitcher wheeled and threw the ball to first base.* 5. to move on wheels; to carry on wheels. *We wheeled the baby down the street in her buggy.* **wheels, wheeled, wheel ing.**

wheel bar row (hwēl′bar′ō), *n.* a small cart having one wheel and two handles pushed from behind. *Wheelbarrows are often used by gardeners.* **wheel bar rows.**

when (hwen, hwən), *adv.* 1. at what time. *When will you be ready to leave?*

conj. 2. at the time that. *You may leave when the bell rings.* 3. during a time. *I listened carefully when she explained the directions.* 4. after. *You may go out to play when you have done all of your work.* 5. although. *Why do you continue to sleep when you know that I am trying to talk to you?*

pron. 6. what or which time. *Since when are you an expert?*

whence (hwens), *adv.* 1. from what place. *Whence*

WHALES

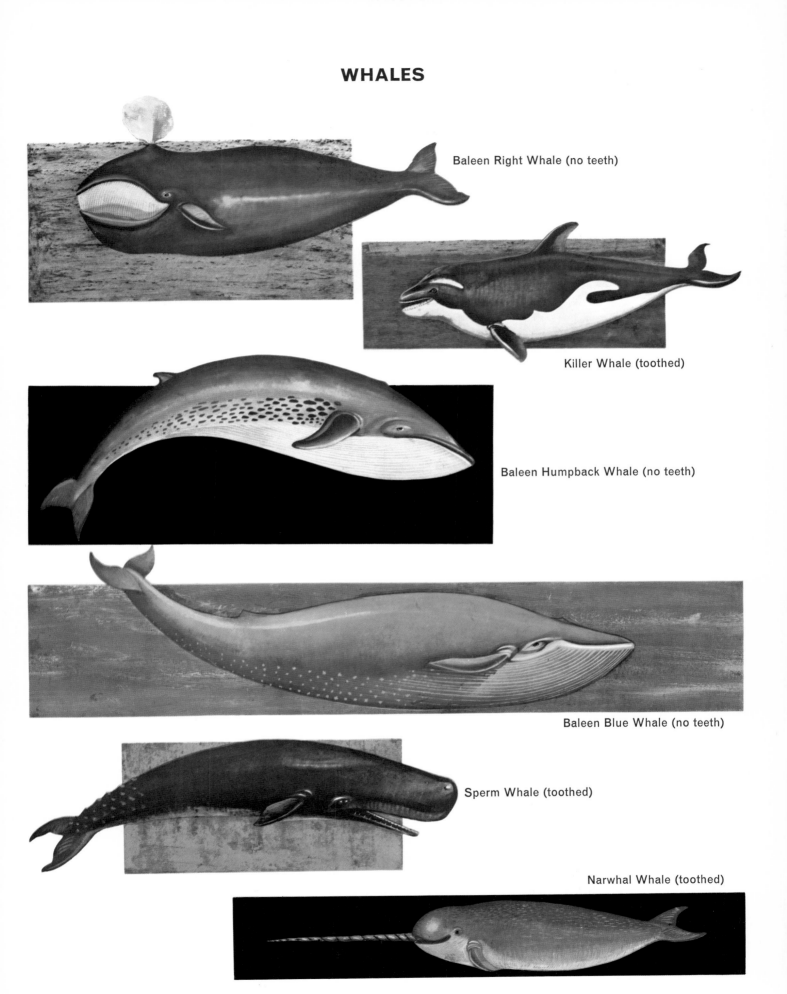

Baleen Right Whale (no teeth)

Killer Whale (toothed)

Baleen Humpback Whale (no teeth)

Baleen Blue Whale (no teeth)

Sperm Whale (toothed)

Narwhal Whale (toothed)

came you to this place? 2. from what person, place, or source. *Whence came this package?*

when ev er (hwen ev′ər), *conj.* at any time that. *I'm ready whenever you are.*

where (hwâr), *adv.* 1. in or at what place. *Where will you be at three o'clock?* 2. to what place. *Where did you send the package?* 3. what place. *Where did this come from?* 4. in what manner; in what way. *Where is the problem in leaving early.*
conj. 5. to the place that; in the place that. *We will go where we are sent. Stay where you are.*
pron. 6. the place at which; the place in which. *Is this where you found the money?*

where a bouts (hwâr′ə bouts′), *adv.* 1. where; at or near what place. *Whereabouts did you leave your jacket?*
n. pl. 2. the place where someone or something is. *No one knew the whereabouts of the lost money.*

where as (hwâr az′), *adv. conj.* 1. considering the fact that. *Whereas he cannot give any reason for his actions, he should be punished.* 2. while on the contrary. *He feels tired when he gets up, whereas most people feel rested.*

where in (hwâr in′), *adv., conj.* 1. how; in what way. *Wherein did I make my mistake?* 2. in which. *We passed the old courthouse wherein history was made.*

where's (hwârz), 1. where is. *Where's the reward you promised to give me?* 2. where has. *Where's everyone gone?*

wher ev er (hwâr ev′ər), *adv., conj.* at, to, in, or from whatever place. *Wherever did you go? I thought of you wherever I went.*

wheth er (hweth′ər), *conj.* 1. if. *He didn't know whether he should laugh or cry.* 2. either. *He will finish the job whether by day or by night.*

which (hwich), *pron.* 1. what one. *Which of the boys is your best friend?* 2. that. *This is not the road which leads to my house.* 3. the one that. *Of the three you may keep which you prefer.*
adj. 4. what. *Which pencil is yours?*

while (hwīl), *n.* 1. a length of time. *Can you wait a while for my answer?* 2. **worth one's while** or **worth-while,** worth the time or effort involved. *Is the book worth-while or should I not read it? It would be worth your while to do more studying.*
conj. 3. during the time that. *Come and see our house while you are here.* 4. although. *While I like the way she sings, I do not like the songs she chooses.*
v. 5. **while away,** to spend in a pleasant way. *He whiled away the entire evening with a book.* **whiles, whiled, whil ing.**

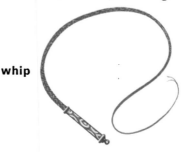

whip

whirlpool

whim per (hwim′pər), *v.* 1. to cry with low, whining, mournful sounds. *The puppy whimpered when we left the house.* **whim pers, whimpered, whim per ing.**
n. 2. a cry like this. *We were awakened by the whimpers of the sick puppy.* **whim pers.**

whine (hwīn), *v.* 1. to make a cry or sound of complaint or distress. *Does your dog whine when he is hungry?* 2. to complain in a childish, unpleasant way. *She whined all during dinner because she didn't like the way the potatoes were cooked.* 3. to say with a whine. *"Can't I watch just one more program on television before I go to bed?" she whined.* **whines, whined, whin ing.**
n. 4. an unpleasant sound of complaint or distress. *We let the dog in when we heard the whine at the door.* **whines.**

whip (hwip), *n.* 1. a heavy cord or a stick with a heavy cord attached, used to strike or beat. *The jockey struck the horse with his whip to make it run faster.* 2. a sweet food made from eggs, cream, etc. *After dinner, everyone had a dish of strawberry whip.* **whips.**
v. 3. to strike with a whip. *The outlaw whipped his horse as he galloped away from the stagecoach.* 4. to move or pull out quickly. *The robber whipped a gun from his pocket.* 5. to beat eggs, cream, etc. until fluffy. *Did you whip some cream to put on the cake?* 6. to blow up and down or from side to side. *The flag whipped in the strong wind.* **whips, whipped, whip ping.**

whir (hwėr), *v.* 1. to spin quickly and make a whistling, whizzing sound. *Some electric fans whir when they are turned on.* **whirs, whirred, whir ring.**
n. 2. the sound made by a spinning object. *There was a sudden whir as the airplane started its engines.* **whirs.**

whirl (hwėrl), *v.* 1. to spin; to move or turn in a

circle. *The dancer whirled from one side of the room to the other.* 2. to move or carry with great speed. *The car whirled around the corner and sped away. We were whirled away in a helicopter.* **whirls, whirled, whirl ing.**

n. 3. a spinning motion. *She made a sudden whirl and began walking in the opposite direction.* 4. a dizzy or confused state. *I'm not sure of anything right now, my mind is in a whirl.* **whirls.**

whirl pool (hwėrl′pül′), n. water that whirls swiftly around in a circle. *Sometimes whirlpools upset rowboats.* **whirl pools.**

whis ker (hwis′kər), n. 1. a hair growing on a man's face. *He has a black beard but there are some white whiskers in it.* 2. one of the long hairs growing near the mouth on some animals. *Cats have whiskers.* 3. **whiskers,** all of the hair growing on a man's face; a beard. *He trims his whiskers once a week.* **whis kers.**

whis key (hwis′kē), n. a strong liquor made from wheat, corn, rye, and other grains. *There is a high percentage of alcohol in whiskey.* **whis keys.**

whis per (hwis′pər), v. 1. to talk very softly. *He whispered while he spoke to the teacher. If you whisper, no one else will hear what you say.* 2. to tell something in a whisper or as a secret. *She whispered the man's name in my ear.* 3. to make a soft, light sound. *The wind whispered through the leaves in the tree.* **whis pers, whis pered, whis per ing.**

n. 4. a very soft sound. *He lowered his voice to a whisper.* 5. something told in a whisper or as a secret. *I heard whispers about school being dismissed for the rest of the day.* 6. a soft, light sound. *Listen to the whisper of the wind in the trees.* **whis pers.**

whis tle (hwis′l), v. 1. to make a high, sharp sound by forcing air through the teeth or lips. *Some people whistle while they work.* 2. to blow a whistle. *The policeman whistled when the traffic light changed to green.* 3. to make or produce by whistling. *Can you whistle that song for me?* 4. to move with a high, sharp sound. *The ball whistled past my ear.* **whis tles, whis tled, whis tling.**

n. 5. a high, sharp sound made by forcing air through the teeth or lips. *When you hear my whistle, you can come out of hiding.* 6. a device used to make a high, sharp sound. *You may stop working when the whistle blows.* **whis tles.**

white (hwīt), n. 1. the color of snow. *Paint the house white.* 2. clothes that are white. *The doctor wore white while he was at the hospital.* 3. the part of a thing which is white. *Hold your fire until you see the whites of their eyes!* **whites.**

adj. 4. having the color of snow. *The bride wore a white dress for the wedding.* 5. pale. *He was white with fear after the accident.* 6. having a light color. *Do you like the white meat or the dark meat on the turkey?* **whit er, whit est.**

whiz (hwiz), n. 1. a buzzing or humming sound.

Can you hear the whiz of the motor on that truck? **whiz zes.**

v. 2. to move with a buzzing or humming sound. *Cars and trucks whizzed past us as we stood on the side of the road.* **whiz zes, whizzed, whiz zing.**

who (hü), *pron.* 1. what person; what persons. *Who gave you that book? Who is it? I already told you who they are.* 2. that. *The person who ordered the book is not here.* 3. a person that. *Who looks for trouble always finds it.*

who'd (hüd), who would. *Who'd like to put this problem on the chalkboard?*

who ev er (hü ev′ər), *pron.* 1. any person that; whatever person. *Whoever figured out this answer did the problem wrong.* 2. no matter what person or persons. *Don't let him in, whoever he is.*

whole (hōl), *adj.* 1. in one piece. *Did you break the dish or is it still whole?* 2. complete; entire. *There are twenty-four volumes in the whole set of books.* 3. not injured or hurt. *Everyone was whole and safe after escaping from the burning building.* **whol ly,** *adv.*

n. 4. the complete amount; the entire extent, body, etc. *The whole of the program was prepared by the students.* 5. a complete thing or system; a unit. *You can't remove a part of a system without affecting the whole.*

whole sale (hōl′sāl′), n. 1. the sale of goods in large quantities to stores or dealers who sell them to individual customers. *Our company deals only in wholesale; if you want to buy our product you can get it at a retail store.*

adj. 2. of or concerned with the sale of goods in large quantities. *Retail stores buy from many different wholesale dealers. The wholesale price is lower than the price you would pay for a single item.* v. 3. to sell in large quantities. *This coat wholesales for less than ten dollars.* **whole sales, whole saled, whole sal ing.**

who'll (hül), who will; who shall. *Do you know anyone who'll help us?*

whol ly (hōl′ē), *adv.* entirely; completely. *The evening was wholly spent in doing my school assignments.*

whom (hüm), *pron.* what person. *To whom did you give the message? Whom do you wish to see?*

whoop (hüp, hwüp), v. 1. to give a loud shout. *He whooped in anger and pain when he struck his thumb with the hammer.* 2. to cough with a gasping sound, especially when one has whooping cough. *The sick child whooped all night long.* **whoops, whooped, whoop ing.**

n. 3. a loud shout. *He gave a whoop of joy when he saw his new bicycle.* 4. a loud, gasping cough. *We were awakened by the whoops of the sick baby.* **whoops.**

whooping cough, n. a disease that causes a person to cough violently and lose his breath. *Whooping cough is a childhood disease.*

who's (hüz), who is. *Who's that coming down the street? I don't know who's going to be at the party.*

whistles

whose (hüz), *pron.* of whom; of which. *Whose jacket did you borrow?*

why (hwī), *adv.* 1. for what reason. *Why did you come to see me?* 2. as a result of which; because of which. *There is only one reason why I have come.*
n. 3. the reason or cause. *I know what he did, but I don't understand the whys of his actions.* **whys.**
interj. 4. a word used to show surprise or other feelings. *Why, here it is! Why, I didn't know you were coming to visit us!*

wick (wik), *n.* the cord or strip in a candle or an oil lamp that burns. *The glass around the oil lamp keeps the wind away from the burning wick.* **wicks.**

wick ed (wik′id), *adj.* 1. bad; evil. *That wicked man stole all of my money.* 2. full of mischief. *He gave me a wicked grin just before we played the prank on my brother.* 3. unpleasant; severe. *I have a wicked pain in my shoulder. That was a wicked storm!* **wick ed ly,** *adv.*

wide (wīd), *adj.* 1. covering or having much space from side to side; broad; not narrow. *Our new car has wide seats.* 2. having a certain distance from side to side. *My room is ten feet wide.* 3. great in extent or range. *A wide selection of dresses was on sale at the store.* 4. opened far; open to a great extent. *Our eyes were wide with excitement.* 5. to one side or another of a point aimed at. *My shot was wide of the target.* **wid er, wid est; wide ly,** *adv.*

wide spread (wīd′spred′), *adj.* 1. spread out; opened wide. *The hawk floats in the air on widespread wings.* 2. covering a large area. *There was widespread damage from the big fire.*

wid ow (wid′ō), *n.* 1. a woman whose husband has died and who has not married again. *My aunt has been a widow for many years.* **wid ows.**
v. 2. to make a widow of. *She was widowed when her children were still very young.* **wid ows, wid owed, wid ow ing.**

wid ow er (wid′ō ər), *n.* a man whose wife has died and who has not married again. *Her father is a widower.* **wid ow ers.**

width (width), *n.* 1. the distance from side to side. *The width of my room is ten feet.* 2. a piece of material having a certain width. *She used six three-foot widths of cloth to make the curtains.* **widths.**

wife (wīf), *n.* the woman a man is married to. *He brought flowers to his wife on her birthday.* **wives** (wīvz).

wig (wig), *n.* a piece of hair or something like hair, worn on the head. *A person who has lost his hair may wear a wig. Some women wear wigs over their own hair.* **wigs.**

wig gle (wig′l), *v.* 1. to move or twist from side to side or up and down with a short, quick motion. *Can you wiggle your ears? Stop wiggling in your chair.* **wig gles, wig gled, wig gling.**
n. 2. a short movement from side to side or up and down. *We watched the wiggles of the fish as they swam in the pond.* **wig gles.**

wig wam (wig′wom, wig′wôm), *n.* a kind of hut or tent made of poles covered with bark or animal skins. *Many Indian tribes used wigwams because they could be built quickly and easily.* **wig wams.**

wild (wīld), *adj.* 1. not tamed; not cultivated; living or growing in a natural condition. *Wild flowers grew along the side of the road. He tried to capture a wild elephant in the jungle.* 2. savage. *The hunters were in danger of being attacked by wild tribes of natives.* 3. having few or no inhabitants. *We drove through the wild desert without seeing another person or car.* 4. not controlled or kept in order. *When the bell rang, there was a wild rush for the door.* 5. violent; stormy. *They were trapped in a cabin in the mountains during a wild blizzard.* 6. reckless; crazy; not sensible. *He has a wild scheme for raising the money we need.* **wild er, wild est; wild ly,** *adv.*
n. 7. **wilds,** a desert or wilderness. *We were lost in the wilds of the northern forests for two days.*

wigs

adv. 8. in a reckless manner. *He threw wild and the ball went over my head.*

wild cat (wīld′kat′), *n.* a wild animal that looks like a large house cat. *The wildcat is about three feet long and is a fierce fighter.* **wild cats.**

wil der ness (wil′dər nis), *n.* any wild area where few or no people live. *Thick forests and empty deserts are wildernesses.* **wil der ness es.**

wild life (wīld′līf′), *n.* wild animals and plants. *Forest fires destroy wildlife.*

will[1] (wil), *n.* 1. the power of the mind to choose, decide, and carry out decisions. *Use your free will in making your choice of careers.* 2. a firm purpose. *He succeeded because he had the will to win.* 3. a wish or desire. *This is not my will but the will of our king.* 4. a feeling or disposition toward another. *A man of good will is interested in the welfare of others.* 5. a legal statement of what a person wants done with his estate after his death. *His will was prepared many years before he died.* **wills.**
v. 6. to wish or desire. *You may do as you will but I am going to do my work.* 7. to decide through the strength of the mind. *I willed that I would not stop until the work was done regardless of how tired and hungry I got.* 8. to give to someone by means of a will. *He willed his money to his son and his house to his daughter.* **wills, willed, will ing.**

will[2] (wil, wəl), *v.* 1. am going to; is going to; are going to. *I will come. He will be here. We will see you next week.* 2. am, is, or are determined to. *He will keep trying until he is successful.* 3. wish to; desire to; want to. *I will have another dish of ice cream, if I may.* 4. am, is, or are able to. *The new airplane will carry over four hundred passengers.* **would.**

will ing (wil′ing), *adj.* 1. ready; consenting. *The boy told the grocer he was willing to work during the summer.* 2. given in a cheerful way. *The teacher offers us willing help on the difficult problems.* **will ing ly,** *adv.*

wil low (wil′ō), *n.* 1. a tree with slender leaves, usually growing in wet ground. *Some willows are called "weeping willows" because their branches and leaves droop.* 2. the wood or branches of this tree. *Furniture is made out of willow. Baskets are woven out of willow.* **wil lows.**

win (win), *v.* 1. to gain a victory. *There were cheers when our team won.* 2. to be the best in; to succeed in. *Nobody could win a race with you. Who won the game today?* **wins, won, win ning.**

wince (wins), *v.* 1. to draw back quickly; pull away. *The boy winced with pain.* **winc es, winced, winc ing.**
n. 2. the act of drawing back. *The girl's wince told me she was in pain.* **winc es.**

wind[1] (wind), *n.* 1. air or a stream of air that is moving. *The wind is from the north. A cool wind feels good on a hot day. A strong wind knocked down the little sign.* 2. breath; the ability to breathe. *The ball hit him in the stomach and knocked*

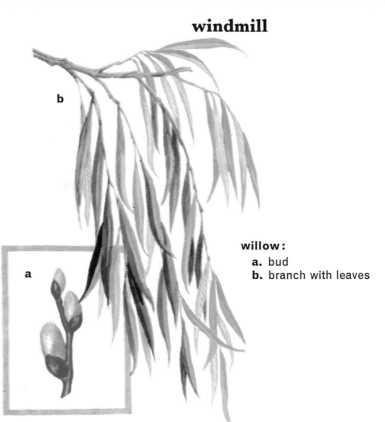

willow:
a. bud
b. branch with leaves

the wind out of him. *The boy was out of wind from running home, so he rested.* 3. a smell in the air. *The dog caught wind of a rabbit in the woods.* 4. a hint; a suggestion. *Don't let the rest of the class get wind of our plans for the party.* **winds.**
v. 5. to make short of breath. *Mr. Walter was winded when he climbed three flights of stairs.* 6. to smell; to follow the odor of. *The hunting dogs winded a wolf and surrounded him until the hunters arrived.* **winds, wind ed, wind ing.**

wind[2] (wīnd), *v.* 1. to wrap; to twist. *The doctor will wind a bandage around the cut on your arm. The boy wound three blankets around himself to keep warm.* 2. to tighten the spring of. *Wind the toy to make it work. Remember to wind your watch every day.* 3. to go in one way and then in another; twist. *The road winds through the hills.* 4. **wind up,** to finish. *"We should wind up this meeting by ten o'clock," said the principal to the teachers.* **winds, wound, wind ing.**
n. 5. a bend or turn. *The farm is near the next wind in the road.* **winds.**

wind[3] (wīnd, wind), *v.* to blow. *The king's hunter winded a horn, as a signal for all to return.* **winds, wound** or **wind ed, wind ing.**

wind ing (wīn′ding), *adj.* 1. that winds or turns or twists. *We followed the winding road for five miles.* **wind ing ly,** *adv.*
n. 2. a bend or turn. *The windings in the old road made it difficult to drive on.* **wind ings.**

wind mill (wind′mil′), *n.* a machine run by wind for pumping water or grinding grain. *The country of Holland has many windmills.* **wind mills.** (See illustration on following page.)

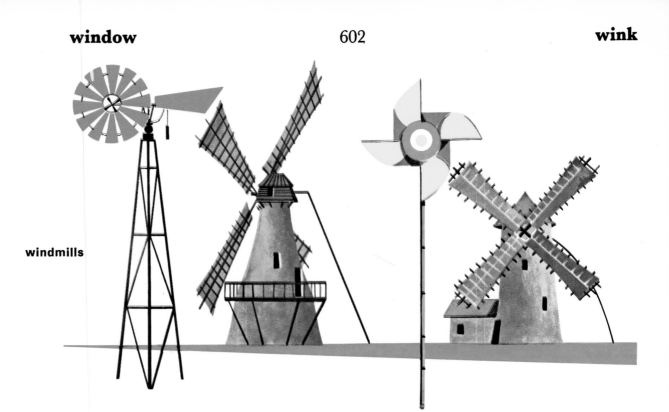

windmills

windows

win dow (win′dō), *n.* an opening in a side of a house, automobile, etc. usually covered with glass. *Windows are used to let in light and air.* **wind ows.**

wind pipe (wind′pīp′), *n.* the tube that carries air from the throat to the lungs. *A person coughs if a bit of food goes into the windpipe; this is the body's way of clearing the windpipe.* **wind pipes.**

windy (win′dē), *adj.* 1. swept by the wind; exposed to the wind. *We felt cool on the windy hilltop, even on a hot day. The corner of Thomas Street and Grant Street is windy.* 2. talking too much; using too many words. *The windy speaker spent two hours making one point.* **wind i er, wind i est; wind i ly,** *adv.*

wine (wīn), *n.* 1. a drink made from the juice of grapes. *Wine contains alcohol.* 2. a drink like this, made from other fruits or plants. *Cherry wine and currant wine are drunk by some people.* **wines.**

wing (wing), *n.* 1. the part of a bird, insect, or bat that keeps it in the air when it is flying. *The large hawk floated in the gentle wind, flapping its wings only a few times. The swallows moved their wings rapidly as they hurried south for the winter.* 2. something like a wing in its looks or use. *Airplanes can fly because they have wings.* 3. in a building, a part that projects from the main part. *They added two wings to the house to have more room.* 4. in the army or navy, soldiers or ships on either side of the main force. *The general said the left wing was not to move forward until the main force had captured the town.* 5. **wings,** in a theater, the spaces on each side of the stage, out of sight of the audience. *The young actor waited nervously in the wings for his time to appear on the stage.* **wings.**

v. 6. to fly. *The birds winged overhead. The airplane winged across the country.* **wings, winged, wing ing.**

wink (wingk), *v.* 1. to close and open one eye quickly as a kind of signal. *Whenever Mr. Paul* scolds us, he winks to show that he is only joking. 2. to close and open one eye or both eyes quickly. *He winked when he came into the bright sunlight.* 3. to twinkle; to send out flashes of light. *The stars winked down over the dark field. The lights of the town winked from the distance.* 4. **wink at,** to pretend not to see or to notice. *Ronald's father winked at his son's little faults, knowing they were not important.* **winks, winked, wink ing.**

n. 5. a quick opening and closing of one or two eyes. *Joe gave Sam a wink as they passed in the hall.* 6. a short period of time. *He will be back in a wink.* 7. a moment of sleep. *Jim hardly slept a wink all night.* **winks.**

win ner (win′ər), *n.* a person, thing, or group that wins. *The team from City School was the winner. Julie's poem was the winner in the writing contest.* **win ners.**

win ning (win′ing), *adj.* 1. that wins; that won. *The winning dog in the dog show belongs to Billy.* 2. attractive. *She has a winning smile.* **win ning ly,** *adv.*

n. 3. the act of winning. *The champion got used to winning.* 4. **winnings,** something won. *The champion in golf had huge winnings for the year.* **win nings.**

win ter (win′tər), *n.* 1. the coldest season of the year. *Winter comes between autumn and spring.* **win ters.**

v. 2. to spend the winter. *Many people winter in Florida, Arizona, or southern California, where the weather is warm.* 3. to keep and feed during the winter. *The farmer winters his livestock in warm barns.* **win ters, win tered, win ter ing.**

adj. 4. of the winter; for the winter. *Ice-skating is a winter sport. The stores carry a supply of winter clothes.*

win ter time (win′tər tīm′), *n.* winter. *Snow falls in the wintertime in most parts of our country.* **win ter times.**

wipe (wīp), *v.* 1. to clean or dry by rubbing. *Wipe your shoes with this cloth.* 2. to remove by rubbing. *Wipe the dust off the table. Wipe the chocolate from your mouth.* 3. **wipe out,** to destroy; to do away with completely. *The farmer's business was wiped out when the frost destroyed all his apple trees.* **wipes, wiped, wip ing.**

n. 4. a wiping. *She gave the top of the table a wipe with the cloth.* **wipes.**

wire (wīr), 1. a thread of metal. *There are many kinds of wire: telephone wires, fence wires, and the thin wires inside an electric light bulb.* 2. a telegram. *Send a wire to Aunt Sylvia on her birthday.* **wires.**

v. 3. to put a wire around. *Some companies wire all their packages and heavy boxes instead of tying them with rope.* 4. to send a message to by telegraph. *Wire us when you get to your destination so we'll know you arrived safely.* 5. to put electric wires in. *The electric company wired the house yesterday.* **wires, wired, wir ing.**

adj. 6. made of wire. *We put up a wire fence.*

Wis con sin (wis kon′sn), *n.* a state in the north central part of the United States. *Wisconsin is famous for its dairy farming and its fruit and vegetable farming. Wisconsin also produces much paper and furniture.*

wis dom (wiz′dəm), *n.* knowledge; good judgment. *Wisdom comes from experience as well as from reading books. A man of wisdom knows how to use it to help himself and others.*

wise[1] (wīz), *adj.* 1. having good sense; showing good judgment. *A wise teacher knows how to treat each pupil as an individual. He made a wise decision.* 2. having much knowledge or information. *Many wise professors teach in that college.* **wis er, wis est; wise ly,** *adv.*

wise[2] (wīz), *n.* way; manner; degree. *The dog is in no wise dangerous, but he barks fiercely.*

wish (wish), *v.* 1. to want; to have a desire for. *You may eat all that you wish. Which of these dresses do you wish? I wish you to do what I ask.* 2. to express to a person; to bid. *I wish you a happy birthday. I wish you a good day.* **wish es, wished, wish ing.**

n. 3. a desire. *She has no wish to see that movie.* 4. something desired. *He finally got his wish—a new radio.* **wish es.**

wit (wit), *n.* 1. the ability to get ideas quickly and to talk about them in an amusing and interesting way. *Because of his wit, others like to listen to him talk.* 2. a person who has this ability. *Two famous wits were Mark Twain and Abraham Lincoln.* 3. **wits,** mind; senses. *The two children were scared out of their wits by the tree*

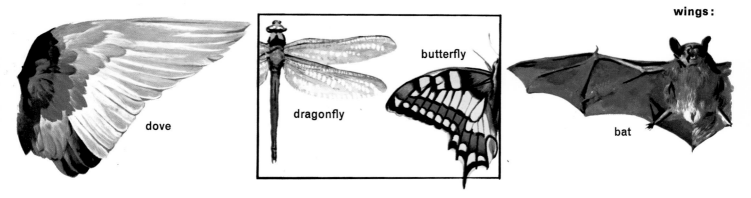

wings:

dove

dragonfly

butterfly

bat

branch tapping at the window. When the lights in the crowded hall went out, Jerry kept his wits and shouted, "Keep to the right! Keep moving!" **wits.**

witch (wich), *n.* 1. a woman that was supposed to have the power of magic. *The wicked witch cast a spell upon the pretty princess.* 2. an ugly old woman. *Although she looks like a witch, she is really very nice.* **witch es.**

with (with, with), *prep.* 1. in the company of. *They went with Uncle Charles. The boy is with his dog.* 2. against. *Why is he always arguing with his own brother?* 3. having. *I like a glass of root beer with much ice in it. He is the boy with the smile.* 4. in regard to. *He gets along well with others. The man was pleased with the doctor's good report.* 5. by means of. *You see with your eyes. Write with a sharp pencil.* 6. because of. *She laughed with happiness. The little kitten is trembling with fear.* 7. at the same time as. *The boy got up with the sun to finish his assignments.* 8. in the care of. *The parents left the young baby with his grandmother while they went to church.* 9. from. *At the end of the school year, I hate to part with my friends.* 10. in spite of. *With all his money, that man has very few friends.* 11. at the time of. *With that remark, he left the house.*

with draw (with drô′, with drô′), *v.* 1. to take away; to remove. *You can withdraw your money from the bank. When the child saw his mother, he withdrew his hand from the cookie jar.* 2. to take back. *The teacher told John to withdraw his remark about the school.* 3. to retire; to leave. *He withdrew from the game in the second quarter to give the other team members a chance to play.* **with draws, with drew, with drawn, with draw ing.**

with er (with′ər), *v.* to dry up; to fade. *Unless flowers and grass get plenty of water, they wither.* **with ers, with ered, with er ing.**

with in (with in′, with in′), *prep.* 1. inside; inside of. *She stayed within her room until all her school assignments were finished.* 2. not beyond. *My best friend lives within six blocks of our home.* *adv.* 3. in or to the inside. *The dog wants to come within because it is cold outside.*

with out (with out′, with out′), *prep.* 1. not having; with no. *The cowboy in the movie was a man without fear. When this five dollars is spent, we will be without money. Without doubt I say he is my friend.* 2. with a lack or neglect of. *He walked right past us without smiling or saying "Hello." Sometimes, I speak without thinking.* 3. on the outside of. *The king's men stood without the castle gates.* *adv.* 4. on the outside. *Without, the house looks old, but within it is very modern.*

wit ness (wit′nis), *n.* 1. a person who saw an event take place. *The witness said that the blue car slid into the red car because of the ice on the street.* 2. a person who, in a court of law, promises to tell the truth. *Each side in the dispute has five witnesses.* 3. a person who is present

wolf

at the signing of a will, a contract, or any other legal document. *The witness signed his name on the sales contract to show he was present.* 4. evidence; proof. *They had a photograph as witness of the meeting. Can you give witness to the truth of your remarks?* **wit ness es.**
v. 5. to see. *We witnessed the accident. We witnessed a good baseball game on television.* 6. to sign as a witness. *Father witnessed Mr. Jones' contract with the automobile company.* 7. to show; to give proof to. *Her smiling face witnessed her happiness in winning the prize.* **wit ness es, wit nessed, wit ness ing.**

wit ty (wit′ē), *adj.* showing wit; clever and amusing. *The witty speaker was able to make the audience laugh.* **wit ti er, wit ti est; wit ti ly, adv.**

wives (wīvz), *n. pl.* more than one wife. *Some ancient kings had several wives.*

wiz ard (wiz′ərd), *n.* 1. a man who is thought to have magic power. *Years ago people believed that a wizard could do impossible things, like changing a frog into a prince.* 2. an expert and clever man. *That workman in the garage is a wizard with automobile engines.* **wiz ards.**

wob ble (wob′l), *v.* 1. to move in a trembling way from side to side. *The little baby's legs wobbled when he tried to walk.* 2. to be unable to decide or make up one's mind. *For days he wobbled between going to the party and staying home.* **wob bles, wob bled, wob bling.**
n. 3. a motion that is not steady. *Can you fix the wobble in this chair?* **wob bles.**

woke (wōk), past tense and past participle of **wake**[1].

wolf (wulf), *n.* 1. a fierce wild animal that looks somewhat like a dog. *Wolves sometimes kill sheep and other farm animals.* **wolves** (wulvz).
v. 2. to eat greedily and fast, as a wolf does. *The hungry man wolfed his dinner.* **wolfs, wolfed, wolf ing.**

wom an (wum′ən), *n.* 1. a grown female

person. *Your mother is a woman.* 2. women in general; women thought of as a group. *The role of the woman has become more important in the business world.* 3. a woman who is a servant. *The woman will clean the room.* **wom en** (wim′ən).

wom en (wim′ən), *n. pl.* more than one woman. *The women meet each Wednesday at the school.*

won (wun), past tense and past participle of **win.**

won der (wun′dər), *n.* 1. an unusual or astonishing thing or event. *One of the seven wonders of the ancient world was the Pyramids. His decision to stay home and clean up the yard was a wonder to all of us.* 2. the feeling caused by seeing something that is strange and marvelous. *You can't help but look with wonder at a beautiful sunset, the stars, or the northern lights.* **won ders.**
v. 3. to be curious to know. *I wonder what I'll get for my birthday. We wondered why he wasn't in class.* 4. to feel surprise. *I wondered that you could read her handwriting.* 5. to feel wonder. *People have always wondered at the beauties of nature and at the inventions of man.* **won ders, won dered, won der ing.**

won der ful (wun′dər fəl), *adj.* 1. causing wonder; remarkable; marvelous. *What a wonderful sight the sunset is today!* 2. very good;

fine. *He is a wonderful actor.* **won der ful ly,** *adv.*

won't (wōnt), will not. *He says he won't go.*

wood (wu̇d), *n.* 1. the hard inside part of a tree, beneath its bark. *Some woods, like oak and walnut, are harder than other woods.* 2. trees cut up for use; lumber. *The workmen used the wood to build the side of the house. Our tree house took longer to build than we expected because we ran out of wood while building it.* 3. **woods** or **wood,** a place where there are many trees; a forest. *The school held a picnic in the woods. The boys like to hike through the wood.* **woods.**
adj. 4. made of wood; wooden. *That wood house is over two hundred years old.*

wood chuck (wu̇d′chuk′), *n.* an animal with a bushy tail and a thick body, about the size of a small dog. *Woodchucks dig holes in the ground to sleep in all winter, safe from storms. A woodchuck is also called a groundhog.* **wood chucks.**

wood cut ter (wu̇d′kut′ər), *n.* a man who cuts down trees; a man who chops up wood into smaller pieces. *A woodcutter uses an ax.* **woodcut ters.** (See illustration on following page.)

wood en (wu̇d′n), *adj.* 1. made of wood. *Some houses are built with stone or bricks; some houses are wooden. In some countries people wear wooden*

The Seven **Wonders** of the Ancient World

a. Pyramids of Egypt
b. Hanging Gardens of Babylon
c. Mausoleum at Halicarnassus
d. Temple of Diana at Ephesus
e. Statue of Zeus on Olympus
f. Colossus at Rhodes
g. Lighthouse at Alexandria

woodcutters

shoes. 2. stiff; clumsy. *When you first learn to play the piano, you often play with wooden fingers.* 3. dull; showing not much life or energy. *That boy never seems to smile; he always has a wooden look.* **wood en ly,** *adv.*

wood peck er (wŭd′pek′ər), *n.* a bird with a beak that is sharp, strong, and pointed. *Woodpeckers poke holes in the bark of trees to get the insects that live under the bark.* **wood peck ers.**

wood wind (wŭd′wind′), *n.* a musical wind instrument. *Once all woodwinds were made of wood.* **wood winds.**

woof (wüf), *n.* the threads that go from side to side in cloth. *In weaving, the woof crosses the threads that go up and down.*

wool (wŭl), *n.* 1. the soft, curly hair of a sheep. *Wool is shaved from the body of a sheep in the spring.* 2. the yarn or cloth made from the hair of a sheep. *In winter he wore a cap of wool.* 3. any material that is light and soft like wool. *Glass wool was put between the two outside walls of the house to keep the heat in.* **wools.**
adj. 4. of wool. *The child is wearing wool mittens.*

wool en or **wool len** (wŭl′ən), *adj.* 1. made of wool. *A woolen sweater keeps you warm.* 2. having

wooden shoe

to do with wool. *The woolen mills make many articles of clothing from wool cloth. There is a woolen sale this week.*
n. 3. **wool ens** or **wool lens,** clothing, blankets, etc. made of wool. *The woolens are stored away during the summer.* **wool ens** or **wool lens.**

word (wėrd), *n.* 1. a group of letters that make sense because they stand for one certain thing. *We use words when we speak and write.* 2. a short remark or expression. *Let me give you a word of caution about playing with matches.* 3. a promise. *He gave his word to keep the secret.* 4. message; news; information. *We received the good word that the airplane had landed safely.* 5. a short talk. *The principal said we could have a word with him this afternoon.* 6. **words,** a quarrel; a dispute. *The two friends had words last week.* **words.**
v. 7. to put into words. *This writer can word the feelings that people have. Word your sentences correctly.* **words, word ed, word ing.**

wore (wôr), past tense of **wear.**

work (wėrk), *n.* 1. the use of strength or skill to make or do something; labor. *Hard work was needed to build the big bridge. Taking a test in school requires hard work.* 2. job; occupation; the thing one does to earn a living. *Her work is modeling clothes. His father's work is being a dentist.* 3. a task; job to be done. *This morning, it is John's work to erase the chalkboard. By doing work for his neighbor, he earned five dollars.* 4. something made, done, written, etc. *This book is the author's most famous work.* 5. **works,** (a) a factory. *My uncle took a job at the iron works.* (b) the moving parts of a device. *Don't try to fix the works of a watch.* (c) deeds; achievements. *The dinner was held to honor the good works of the doctor.* **works.**
v. 6. to have a job for pay in order to make a living. *He works as a clerk in a store. She works in a big office.* 7. to cause to labor or perform. *The football coach worked his players hard in practice. Some people work themselves too hard.* 8. to operate; to do as it should. *"That machine won't work," said people when they saw the first airplane.* 9. to cause to operate. *Can you work this vacuum cleaner?* 10. to make; to shape. *The child worked his clay into the outline of a horse.* 11. to move or cause to move slowly. *My brother wants to work up to manager of the store.* **works, worked** or **wrought, work ing.**

work er (wėr′kər), *n.* a person who works; a person who works for money. *He will pass the test; he is a hard worker. The factory needs more workers.* **work ers.**

work shop (wėrk′shop′), *n.* a room or building in which work is done. *The furniture workshop has workers who make beautiful cabinets.* **work shops.**

work man (wėrk′mən), *n.* a man who works, especially one who works with his hands. *Ten workmen were hired to install the new lights in the theater.* **work men.**

work man ship (wėrk′mən ship′), *n.* 1. the skill of a workman. *His workmanship is getting things done.* 2. something that is made with skill. *All this furniture is his workmanship.*

world (wėrld), *n.* 1. the earth. *There are many different languages spoken in the world.* 2. the entire universe; everything that exists. *There are nine planets in our part of the world.* 3. a planet. *The astronauts are planning to visit another world.* 4. all of the people on earth. *The world rejoiced at the news that a vaccine for polio had been discovered.* 5. a particular part of the earth. *America is in the New World.* 6. a sphere of activity. *He plans to enter the business world after college.* 7. money, success, and social position; society. *He left the world and became a priest.* 8. a great amount. *He got a world of enjoyment out of seeing the circus.* **worlds.**

worm (wėrm), *n.* 1. a small animal with no legs and a soft body. *Worms crawl along the ground.* 2. the larva of some insects. *In a short time the worms had turned into flies.* 3. a person who is despised or looked down upon. *What kind of a worm could be so cruel?* 4. anything that looks like or moves like a worm. *The thread of a screw is a worm.* 5. **worms,** a disease caused by worms in the body. *The doctor treated the dog's worms by giving him medicine.* **worms.**
v. 6. to crawl or creep as a worm does. *We wormed our way across the field and surprised the enemy.* 7. to get or do by slow and clever means. *By asking him many questions, we were finally able to worm the truth out of him.* **worms, wormed, worm ing.**

worn (wôrn), *v.* 1. past participle of **wear.**
adj. 2. damaged by wear; showing signs of use. *The pages of my book are dirty and worn.* 3. very tired. *You look worn; sit down and rest for awhile.*

wor ry (wėr′ē), *v.* 1. to be restless, disturbed, or anxious about something. *I am worried about getting to the airport on time.* 2. to make restless, disturbed, or anxious. *The test worried me, but it turned out to be easy.* 3. to bother or make angry. *They worried the dog by teasing it with a stick.* 4. to bite and shake with the teeth. *Father was angry when he saw the dog worrying his slippers.* **wor ries, wor ried, wor ry ing.**
n. 5. a cause of anxiety or trouble. *Money is a constant worry to him.* **wor ries.**

worse (wėrs), *adj.* 1. more evil, bad, or unpleasant. *The weather is worse today than it was yesterday.* 2. more ill; sicker. *He seemed to be getting better yesterday, but today he is worse.*
adv. 3. in a more unpleasant or bad way. *The orchestra played worse than they ever had before.*
n. 4. a condition that is worse. *His behavior in school has gone from bad to worse.*

wor ship (wėr′ship), *v.* 1. to show or give reverence and respect to. *We worship God in church.* 2. to take part in a religious service. *Many people worship in churches all over the world.*
3. to have great love for. *Parents worship their children.* **wor ships, wor shiped, wor ship-ing.**
n. 4. a religious service or prayer showing reverence and respect for God. *There are as many forms of worship as there are religions.* 5. great love or respect. *Hero worship is a form of admiration for great or famous people.* **wor-ships.**

worst (wėrst), *adj.* 1. most evil, bad, or unpleasant. *This is the worst book I ever read.*
adv. 2. in the most unpleasant or bad way. *He plays worst when he is tired.*
n. 3. that which is worst. *The weather has been bad, but the worst of the winter is yet to come.*
v. 4. to defeat. *We were worsted by a team we should have beaten.* **worsts, worst ed, worst-ing.**

worth (wėrth), *n.* 1. merit. *This book has little real worth, but it's fun to read.* 2. value in money. *What is the worth of these diamonds?* 3. the quantity of something that can be bought for a certain amount. *Can you afford to buy ten dollar's worth of records?* **worths.**
adj. 4. worthy of. *If a thing is worth doing, it's worth doing well.* 5. good enough for. *Was the movie worth the money you spent to see it?* 6. having property and money that amount to. *There is a man worth several million dollars.*

wor thy (wėr′thē), *adj.* 1. having worth; deserving merit. *He gave his money to a worthy charity.* 2. deserving; meriting. *Their perform-ance was worthy of great praise.* **wor thi er, wor thi est; wor thi ly,** *adv.*
n. 3. a great or important person. *The President is one of the worthies of the world.* **wor thies.**

would (wůd, wəd), *v.* 1. past tense of **will**[2].
2. would is also used in the following ways: (a) in expressing a wish. *Would that I had known, I could have helped you!* (b) in expressing what could have happened or been true. *I would have come had I known you were sick.* (c) in making a polite request. *Would you carry this for me?*

would n't (wůd′nt), would not. *I wouldn't do that if I were you.*

wound[1] (wünd), *n.* 1. an injury to the body. *The doctor put a bandage on the wound on my arm.* 2. an injury to the feelings. *Your kindness has helped heal the wounds caused by his angry words.* **wounds.**
v. 3. to hurt or injure. *I was wounded by an arrow. His words wounded me deeply.* **wounds, wound ed, wound ing.**

wound[2] (wound), past tense and past participle of **wind**[2].

wove (wōv), past tense and past participle of **weave.**

wrap (rap), *v.* 1. to enclose in something by winding or folding. *Wrap the baby in warm blankets.* 2. to fold something around. *Wrap a few blankets around the baby.* 3. to cover with paper. *Did you wrap the gift for your mother?* 4. to

sand, āte, bâre, fäther; sent, mē, fėrn; fit, bīke; pot, rōpe, fôrt; run, půll, rüle, cūte; noise, sound; ch, cheese; ng, long; th, thick; th̸, those; zh, treasure; ə = a in about, e in waken, i in animal, o in seldom, and u in minus.

wreck of a ship

hide or enclose completely. *We couldn't see the cabin because it was wrapped in fog.* 5. **wrapped up in,** completely interested in; thinking of little else but. *He was wrapped up in his assignments and didn't realize how late it was.* **wraps, wrapped** or **wrapt, wrap ping.**
n. 6. an outer garment or coat. *It is cold outside so you will need a wrap.* **wraps.**

wrap ping (rap′ing), *n.* material such as paper or cloth used to wrap something. *I'd like to put a red wrapping on this present.* **wrap pings.**

wreath (rēth), *n.* 1. a ring made by twisting branches, leaves, or flowers together. *During the holiday season we hung a wreath of holly on our door.* 2. anything that looks like this. *A wreath of fire surrounded the forest.* **wreaths.**

wreck (rek), *n.* 1. the ruin or destruction of a building, automobile, etc., caused by a storm, accident, etc. *No one was seriously injured in the train wreck.* 2. a thing that has been ruined or damaged. *A truck was sent to remove the wreck from the road.* 3. the ruin or destruction of anything. *Bad weather caused the wreck of our plans for a picnic.* 4. a person without money or good health. *Two old wrecks came to the church to ask for food. All of your questions are making me a nervous wreck.* **wrecks.**
v. 5. to ruin, destroy, or damage. *He wrecked his car in an accident. Lack of rain wrecked the crops.* 6. to tear down. *When was the old school building wrecked?* 7. to severely inure; to cause the loss of health or money. *The heart attack wrecked my plans to become a pilot.* **wrecks, wrecked, wreck ing.**

wren (ren), *n.* a small bird with a long, slender bill and a tail that stands up. *Some wrens built a nest in a tree near our house.* **wrens.**

wres tle (res′l), *v.* 1. to struggle with a person to throw him on the ground, often a school sport. *Next year he will wrestle on the high school team.* 2. to try hard to understand something; to struggle. *He wrestled with Latin for two years.* **wres tles, wres tled, wres tling.**

wretch ed (rech′id), *adj.* 1. very unhappy. *He was wretched when he lost the election.* 2. very poor; unpleasant. *They live in a wretched section of town where the houses are falling apart.* 3. evil; wicked. *The police finally captured the wretched criminal.* **wretch ed ly,** *adv.*

wring (ring), *v.* 1. to twist and squeeze. *Wring that wet cloth before you wipe the table.* 2. to remove by twisting and squeezing. *Wring the water out of the cloth.* 3. to get by force or pressure. *Did they wring the truth out of him?* 4. to cause a feeling of pity or pain in. *The news of the tragedy wrung our hearts.* **wrings, wrung, wring ing.**
n. 5. a twisting and squeezing motion. *Give that wet towel a wring and hang it up to dry.* **wrings.**

wrist (rist), *n.* the joint between the hand and the arm. *The wrist is one of the few joints in the body that allows movement in any direction.* **wrists.**

write (rīt), *v.* 1. to form letters or words with a pen, pencil, or other instrument. *Most people learn to write in school.* 2. to express with written words and letters. *Write your name and address at the top of the paper.* 3. to invent or create; to be the author of. *He wrote a story for the school* *newspaper.* 4. to compose a letter. *You should write to your mother each week while you are away from home.* 5. to show or indicate. *The pain he felt was written all over his face.* 6. **write down,** to put into writing. *Write down your suggestions and give them to me.* 7. **write out,** (a) to put into writing. *He wrote out a description of the event so that he would remember it.* (b) to write in full. *Write out the name of the state; don't use an abbreviation.* 8. **write up,** to describe or tell about in writing. *The team's victory was written up in the newspaper.* **writes, wrote, writ ten, writ ing.**

writ er (rīt′ər), *n.* 1. a person who writes. *She is the best writer in our class.* 2. a person who writes for a living; a person whose profession is writing. *The author of this book has been a writer for twenty years.* **writ ers.**

writ ing (rīt′ing), *n.* 1. the act of forming words or letters. *Writing is taught in school.* 2. anything which is written. *His writings include books, stories, and letters.* 3. written form. *Please submit any questions you might have in writing.* 4. handwriting. *I can't read this messy writing.* 5. the profession or work of a writer. *He wanted to try writing as a career.* **writ ings.**

writ ten (rit′n), past participle of **write.**

wrong (rông), *adj.* 1. not right; bad; wicked. *Stealing and cheating are wrong.* 2. not correct; not true. *Your answer was wrong.* 3. not proper; not suitable. *This is the wrong ball; you were supposed to bring a baseball, not a football.* 4. out of order. *Do you know what's wrong with that telephone?* 5. not meant to be seen. *You are wearing your sweater with the wrong side out.* **wrong ly,** *adv.*

n. 6. anything that is wrong; an evil or harm. *We did him a serious wrong by accusing him of the crime. Two wrongs will never make a right.* 7. **in the wrong,** guilty; at fault. *You were both in the wrong and shouldn't have been fighting.* **wrongs.**

v. 8. to injure or deal unfairly with. *We wronged him by saying that he had lied.* **wrongs, wronged, wrong ing.**

adv. 9. in the wrong way; badly; poorly. *How did you get the right answer when you did the problem wrong?* 10. **go wrong,** (a) to turn out badly. *A wire in the rocket ship came loose and everything went wrong.* (b) to become bad after having been good. *When he was fifteen, he started to go wrong and ended up in jail.*

wrote (rōt), past tense of **write.**

wrought (rôt), *v.* 1. past tense and past participle of **work.**
adj. 2. made; formed. *We opened a heavy door wrought of wood and silver.* 3. shaped by hammering. *They bought wrought iron furniture for the garden.*

wrung (rung), past tense and past participle of **wring.**

Wy o ming (wī ō′ming), *n.* a state in the western part of the United States. *We spent our vacation on a ranch in Wyoming.*

X

X rays

chest

pelvic region

knee joint

foot

X or **x** (eks), the twenty-fourth letter of the alphabet.

xe rog ra phy (zə′räg rə fē), *n.* the art of forming the exact duplicate of an original by use of a machine which reproduces such a picture in a matter of seconds. *By xerography a book can be reproduced in a matter of hours.*

Xmas (kris′məs), *n.* a short, informal way of writing Christmas. *The banner hanging in the store window said, "Merry Xmas."* **Xmas es.**

X ray, *n.* 1. a strong ray that can pass through many solid substances. *An X ray can locate something that is wrong inside a bar of steel or inside the human body.* 2. a photograph made by X rays. *The dentist showed me the X ray of my tooth.* **X rays.**

X-ray (eks′rā′), *adj.* 1. having to do with X rays. *The doctor took an X-ray photograph of the chest of his patient.*

v. 2. to use an X-ray camera on. *A doctor X-rays the broken leg of his patient.* 3. to treat the body with X rays. *The doctors decided to X-ray the patient's blood cells to cure him.* **X-rays, X-rayed, X-ray ing.**

xy lo phone (zī′lə fōn′), *n.* a musical instrument having bars of wood or metal that are hit with little hammers to make music. *The length of the bars of the xylophone determines the different notes of the scale.* **xy lo phones.**

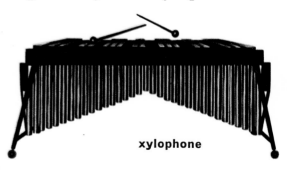

xylophone

Y or **y** (wī), the twenty-fifth letter of the alphabet.

yacht (yot), *n.* a boat used for pleasure cruising. *The yacht in the harbor is very large.* **yachts.**

yam (yam), *n.* 1. the root of a plant that grows in very warm countries. *Yams are used for food. Yams have more sugar and less starch than white potatoes.* 2. a variety of sweet potato. *We eat yams on Thanksgiving.* **yams.**

Yan kee (yang′ki), *n.* 1. the name for a person from the United States. *Foreigners call Americans "Yankees."* 2. a person from any of the northern states. *Southerners often call northerners Yankees.* **Yan kees.**

yard¹ (yärd), *n.* 1. a measure of length equal to three feet or thirty-six inches. *The tailor bought three yards of cloth. The football team had only one yard to go to get the ball over the goal line.* 2. a long pole fastened across the mast of a sailboat. *The yards of a sailboat hold up the sails.* **yards.**

yard² (yärd), *n.* 1. the open ground around a house, school, or any building. *Children were playing in the yard.* 2. a piece of open ground used for a business or other special purpose. *The United States Navy has many yards where ships are painted, repaired, or stored. People can buy automobiles in a used-car yard.* 3. a system of tracks used by a railroad for storing freight cars and passenger cars. *Trains are made up, cleaned, and repaired in the yards.* **yards.**

yard stick (yärd′stik′), *n.* 1. a stick marked in units of measurement up to one yard. *We used a yardstick to measure the length of our house.* 2. any standard of measurement. *The yardstick to good behaviour is given to us by our parents.* **yard sticks.**

yarn (yärn), *n.* 1. a heavy woolen thread used in knitting. *My aunt bought a ball of blue yarn to make a sweater for my birthday.* 2. a story. *The old aviator told us a yarn about the early days of flying.* **yarns.**

yawn (yôn), *v.* 1. to open the mouth wide and take a deep breath. *People yawn when they are sleepy or bored.* 2. to open wide. *The big hole in the ground yawned in front of the child.* **yawns, yawned, yawn ing.**
n. 3. an opening of the mouth and taking a deep breath. *Gayle covered up a yawn in the middle of class.* **yawns.**

year (yir), *n.* 1. a period of 365 days; (every four years 366 days); 12 months. *The calendar year begins on January 1.* 2. any period of twelve months. *From one birthday to another is a year.* 3. the part of a year in which there is a certain activity or work. *Our school year lasts nine months. The sales year for skis depends on the amount of snow on the ground.* **years.**

year book (yir′bук′), *n.* 1. a book published each year, which gives information about the year before. *A yearbook is a kind of history of one year.* 2. a book published each year by a school, telling of the school's clubs and activities, and containing pictures of each person in the class that graduated that year. *Her picture is in the yearbook as president of the class.* **year books.**

yeast (yēst), *n.* a substance that is used in baking bread. *Yeast causes bubbles in the dough and makes it rise. The right amount of yeast makes the bread light.*

yell (yel), *v.* 1. to shout; to cry out; to scream. *You have to yell in that noisy factory to make people hear you. The crowd yelled during the football game.* **yells, yelled, yell ing.**
n. 2. a loud cry; a shout. *The yells of the happy boys could be heard in the next street. The child lost in the woods gave a yell for help, and his father heard him.* 3. a cheer for a team or player. *The crowd gave a yell of "Go, team, go!"* **yells.**

yel low (yel′ō), *adj.* 1. having the color of a lemon or of butter. *Yellow paint was used on the new house.* **yel low er, yel low est.**
n. 2. the color of a lemon or of butter. *Some girls look pretty in a dress of yellow.* 3. the yolk of an egg. *A fried egg has white around the yellow.* **yel lows.**
v. 4. to make or become yellow. *Ten years have yellowed the papers. These newspapers have yellowed with age.* **yel lows, yel lowed, yel low ing.**

yes (yes), *adv.* 1. a word that shows agreement; the opposite of no. *Yes, you are right. Yes, I will be home early.* 2. and in addition to that. *The rough football player was kind, yes, even tender with little babies.*
n. 3. consent; agreement; the act of saying "yes." *The teacher gave his yes to our plan.* **yes es.**

yes ter day (yes′tər dē, yes′tər dā′), *n.* 1. the day before this day. *Today is Saturday and yesterday was Friday.* 2. the past; the time that has gone by. *The older folks like the songs of yesterday.* **yes ter days.**

adv. 3. on the day before this day. *It snowed yesterday.* 4. a short time ago. *It seems only yesterday that he was a child, and now he is six feet tall!*

yet (yet), *adv.* 1. up to now. *The airplane hasn't arrived yet because of bad weather.* 2. still. *There is yet a chance that they will arrive later.* 3. at some time in the future. *My father says he will learn to play the piano yet.* 4. in addition; besides. *Mr. Wilmot caught yet another fish before dark.* 5. even. *The wind blew at a yet higher speed.* 6. but; nevertheless. *He is rich yet unhappy.*

conj. 7. however; but. *Our team was good; yet it lost.*

yield (yēld), *v.* 1. to give in; to give up. *Jim yielded to our wishes and joined the swimming team. The beaten army yielded.* 2. to produce. *The fruit trees yielded a good crop this year.* 3. to render; to give. *The mayor yielded his permission for new stop lights on Greenwood Street.* 4. to give way. *The gate yielded to the touch of a hand.* **yields, yield ed, yield ing.**

n. 5. an amount that is produced. *The farm had a good yield of wheat last year.* **yields.**

yoke (yōk), *n.* 1. a wooden bar or frame placed over the necks of two animals so that they will work together. *The oxen were kept together by a yoke.* 2. two animals that work together. *The farmer had a yoke of oxen to help him plow his field.* **yokes.**

v. 3. to put a yoke on. *He yoked the two animals.* **yokes, yoked, yok ing.**

yolk (yōk), *n.* the yellow part of an egg. *The recipe said to use one egg, separating the yolk from the white.* **yolks.**

yon der (yon′dər), *adj.* 1. being within sight,

yoking oxen

but not near. "*Yonder castle is my home,*" said the knight.

adv. 2. over there; in that place. *The village lies yonder, on the next hill.*

you (ū, yu̇, yə), *pron.* 1. the person or persons spoken or written to. *You may go now. We invite all of you to come.* 2. one; anyone; any person. *If you want to get on an airliner, be on time at the airport.*

you'd (ūd, yu̇d, yəd), 1. you had. *You'd better go now.* 2. you would. *You'd be worn out if you walked that far.*

you'll (ūl, yu̇l, yəl), you will; you shall. *You'll be sorry!*

young (yung), *n.* 1. an animal's babies. *The mother tiger guards her young.*

adj. 2. not old; in the early part of life or growth. *A kitten is a young cat. A baby is a young person.* 3. having the looks of a young person; youthful; full of energy. *Some older people are young for their age.* 4. not so old as another of the same name. *Are you talking about Dr. Bill Wood or young Bill?* **young er, young est.**

young ster (yung′stər), *n.* 1. a child. *She is a smart youngster.* 2. a young person. *My father always does as much work as the youngsters on the job.* **young sters.**

your (yu̇r, yər), *adj.* 1. of or belonging to you. *Is this your coat? Your birthday present to me was perfect!* 2. done by you. *Where is your book report?*

you're (yu̇r, yər), you are. *You're early for class.*

yours (yu̇rz), *pron.* the one or the ones that belong to you. *This coat is yours. Yours is newer than mine.*

your self (yėr self′, yər self′), *pron.* your own self. *Did you hurt yourself when you fell? Do your work by yourself.* **your selves.**

youth (ūth), *n.* 1. young people. *Schools are built for the youth of the country.* 2. a young man. *The youth got his first full-time job after he graduated from high school.* 3. the quality of being young. *Some older people have the energy of youth.* 4. an early stage of anything. *In our country's youth, horses were the only means of transportation.* **youths** (ūths or ūthz).

youth ful (ūth′fəl), *adj.* 1. young. *Mr. Case is almost sixty years old, but he has youthful ideas.* 2. having to do with young people. *This store sells youthful styles in clothes. Baseball is a youthful game.* **youth ful ly,** *adv.*

you've (ūv, yu̇v, yəv), you have. *You've never visited my home.*

Yo yo (yō′yō), *n.* a toy made of a round, flat piece of wood with a slit around the edge, in which a string is wound. *A Yoyo is thrown out and pulled in by the string, which is attached to a finger.* **Yo yos.**

Yule (ūl), *n.* 1. another name for Christmas. *Yule is my favorite time of year.* **Yules.**

adj. 2. of the Christmas season. *On Christmas we burn Yule logs in our fireplace.*

Z

zebu

Z or **z** (zē), the twenty-sixth letter of the alphabet.

ze bra (zē′brə), *n.* a wild animal that looks somewhat like a horse but has stripes of black or dark brown on a light background. *Zebras are difficult to tame.* **ze bras.**

ze bu (zē′bū), *n.* a farm animal somewhat like an ox, which lives in Asia and Africa. *A zebu has long ears, short horns, and a hump on its back.* **ze bus.**

zep pe lin (zep′ə lən), *n.* a large balloon supported by a light metal framework and run by engines. *Zeppelins were once used to carry passengers and freight.* **zep pe lins.**

ze ro (zir′ō), *n.* 1. in mathematics, the figure 0. *In the number 1000, there are three zeros.* 2. the point on a scale or thermometer marked 0. *When there is no weight on a scale, it reads zero. When the temperature is zero or below, the weather is very cold.* 3. nothing. *Two minus two equals zero. A grade of zero on a test means that all answers were wrong.* **ze ros.**

zinc (zingk), *n.* a blue-white metal that is an element. *Zinc is used as a material for roofs because it is not affected by rain or dampness.*

zip (zip), *v.* 1. to fasten with a zipper. *Zip your jacket before you go out.* 2. to move fast; to go with speed and energy. *He zipped through the kitchen and dashed outside.* 3. to travel with a quick, hissing sound. *A snowball zipped past my ear. The bullet zipped through the air into the target.* **zips, zipped, zip ping.**

n. 4. a short hissing sound. *The stone made a zip when thrown.* 5. energy; vigor. *My little brother has lots of zip in the morning, but he's always worn out by bedtime.* **zips.**

zip per (zip′ər), *n.* a device used for fastening, having two rows of teeth that are closed together with a little sliding piece of metal or plastic. *Zippers are used on coats and other clothing in place of buttons.* **zip pers.**

zith er (zith′ər), a musical instrument having thirty or forty strings. *The zither is played with the tips of the fingers.* **zith ers.**

zo di ac (zō′dē ak), *n.* 1. an imaginary band in the sky, which men have divided into twelve parts. *Each part, or "sign," of the zodiac is named after a group of stars.* 2. a round diagram of this band. *The zodiac usually has the names and pictures of persons or animals associated with each sign.*

zither

zebra

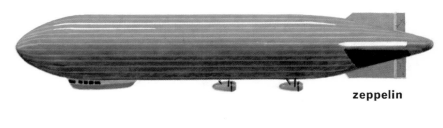

zeppelin

sand, āte, bâre, fäther; sent, mē, férn; fit, bīke; pot, rōpe, fôrt; run, pùll, rüle, cūte; noise, sound; ch, cheese; ng, long; th, thick; t̶h̶, those; zh, treasure; ə = a in about, e in waken, i in animal, o in seldom, and u in minus.

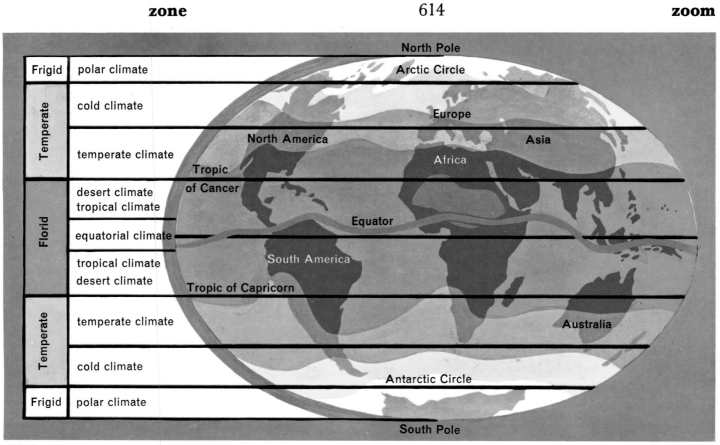

Frigid	polar climate		North Pole / Arctic Circle
Temperate	cold climate		Europe
	temperate climate		North America / Asia / Africa
Florid	desert climate / tropical climate		Tropic of Cancer
	equatorial climate		Equator
	tropical climate / desert climate		South America / Tropic of Capricorn
Temperate	temperate climate		Australia
	cold climate		Antarctic Circle
Frigid	polar climate		South Pole

climatic **zones**

Zodiac

ancient zodiac wheel

Leo (lion)
Gemini (twins)
Sagittarius (archer)
Cancer (crab)
Aries (ram)
Virgo (virgin)
Aquarius (water bearer)
Taurus (bull)
Libra (scales)
Capricorn (goat)
Scorpio (scorpion)
Pisces (fish)

zone (zōn), *n.* 1. any of the five great areas of the earth's surface, named according to the climate in each. *The United States is in the temperate zone.* 2. an area that is set aside for a special purpose. *In a school zone, automobile traffic must slow down.* **zones.**
v. 3. to divide into zones. *The new section of the city will be zoned only for houses and apartments; no factories will be allowed.* **zones, zoned, zon ing.**

zoo (zü), *n.* a place where living animals are kept so that people can see them. *In the zoo the children saw polar bears, lions, monkeys, tigers, and giraffes.* **zoos.**

zo o log i cal (zō′ə loj′ə kl), *adj.* of animals; relating to zoology. *The zoological park, or "zoo," contains many animals.* **zo o log i cal ly,** *adv.*

zo ol o gy (zō ol′ə gē), *n.* the science that deals with animals and animal life. *In zoology classes, college students study all forms of animal life, from the tiny creatures with one cell to the elephant.*

zoom (züm), *v.* 1. to move suddenly upward. *The airplane zoomed over the top of the mountain.* 2. to move with a humming, roaring sound. *The cars zoomed past on the wide highway.* **zooms, zoomed, zoom ing.**
n. 3. a sudden moving upward. *The airplane's zoom carried it above the clouds.* 4. a humming, roaring sound. *We could hear the constant zoom of the trucks on the highway.* **zooms.**

PREFIXES

A *prefix* is a letter or a group of letters added to the beginning of a word to change its meaning. Some of the most common prefixes and their meanings are listed below.

Prefix	Meaning
ab	from, away from
ad	to
anti	opposite, against
auto	self
com	with, together
de	down
dis	apart
en	in
ex	out of, from, off
extra	beyond
in	in, into
in	not
inter	between, within
post	after
pre	before
pro	before, in front of, forward, for
re	over again, back again
semi	half
sub	under
super	above, over
trans	beyond, through, across
un	not, opposite of

These are some examples of the use of prefixes. Each root word, and each new word, is an entry word in the DICTIONARY OF BASIC WORDS.

Prefix	Root Word	New Word
ab	normal	abnormal
ad	venture	adventure
anti	aircraft	anti-aircraft
auto	mobile	automobile
de	scend	descend
dis	honest	dishonest
en	able	enable
extra	ordinary	extraordinary
in	convenience	inconvenience

SUFFIXES

A *suffix* is a letter or a group of letters added to the end of a word to change its meaning.

The most common suffixes and their meanings are listed below.

Suffix	Meaning
able	able, likely
ance	act, condition, fact
dom	state, rank, condition
ed	past tense and past participle
en	made of, like
er	doer, maker
er	comparative adjective
es	(with some verbs ending in a consonant) third person singular
est	superlative adjective
ful	full of, marked by
hood	state, condition
ing	present participle, gerund
ion	action, result, state
ish	suggesting, like
ist	doer, believer
less	lacking, without
like	like, similar
ly	adverb form
ment	means, result, action
ness	quality, state
ous	marked by, given to
s	(with nouns) plural (with some verbs ending in a vowel) third person singular
some	apt to, showing
ward	in the direction of

Other common suffixes are listed below. You can see how adding suffixes to appropriate root words changes the meaning of those words.

Root Word	Suffix	New Word
accept	able	acceptable
perform	ance	performance
light	en	lighten
commission	er	commissioner
cup	ful	cupful
connect	ion	connection
advertise	ment	advertisement
thoughtful	ness	thoughtfulness
prosper	ous	prosperous